Jimmy Swaggart Bible Commentary

Exodus

JIMMY SWAGGART BIBLE COMMENTARY

- Genesis [656 pages 11-201]
- Exodus [656 pages 11-202]
- Leviticus [448 pages 11-203]
- Numbers
  Deuteronomy [512 pages 11-204]
- Joshua
  Judges
  Ruth [336 pages 11-205]
- I Samuel
  II Samuel [528 pages 11-206]
- I Kings
  II Kings [560 pages 11-207]
- I Chronicles
  II Chronicles [528 pages 11-226]
- Ezra
  Nehemiah
  Esther [288 pages 11-208]
- Job [320 pages 11-225]
- Psalms [688 pages 11-216]
- Proverbs [320 pages 11-227]
- Ecclesiastes
  Song Of Solomon [288 pages 11-228]
- Isaiah [688 pages 11-220]
- Jeremiah
  Lamentations [688 pages 11-070]
- Ezekiel [528 pages 11-223]
- Daniel [416 pages 11-224]
- Hosea
  Joel
  Amos [496 Pages 11-229]
- Obadiah
  Jonah
  Micah
  Nahum
  Habakkuk
  Zephaniah [544 pages 11-230]
- Haggai
  Zechariah
  Malachi [448 pages 11-231]
- Matthew [888 pages 11-073]
- Mark [624 pages 11-074]
- Luke [736 pages 11-075]
- John [736 pages 11-076]
- Acts [832 pages 11-077]
- Romans [704 pages 11-078]
- I Corinthians [656 pages 11-079]
- II Corinthians [608 pages 11-080]
- Galatians [496 pages 11-081]
- Ephesians [576 pages 11-082]
- Philippians [496 pages 11-083]
- Colossians [384 pages 11-084]
- I Thessalonians
  II Thessalonians [512 pages 11-085]
- I Timothy
  II Timothy
  Titus
  Philemon [704 pages 11-086]
- Hebrews [848 pages 11-087]
- James
  I Peter
  II Peter [736 pages 11-088]
- I John
  II John
  III John
  Jude [384 pages 11-089]
- Revelation [592 pages 11-090]

For prices and information please call: 1-800-288-8350
Baton Rouge residents please call: (225) 768-7000
Website: www.jsm.org • E-mail: info@jsm.org

Jimmy Swaggart Bible Commentary

Exodus

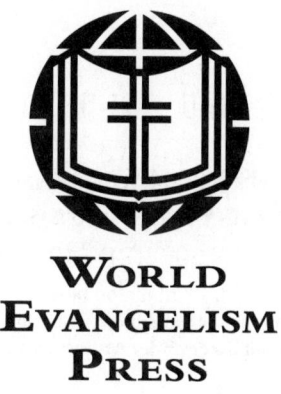

World Evangelism Press

ISBN 978-0-9769530-5-0

11-202 • COPYRIGHT © 2004 World Evangelism Press®
www.jsm.org • email: info@jsm.org
20 21 22 23 24 25 26 27 28 29 / RRD / 13 12 11 10 9 8 7 6 5 4
All rights reserved. Printed and bound in China
No part of this publication may be reproduced in any form or by any means
without the publisher's prior written permission.

TABLE OF CONTENTS

1. Introduction v
2. Exodus 1
3. Index 631

INTRODUCTION

INTRODUCTION TO THE BOOK OF EXODUS

It is February 7, 2002, as I begin the dictation of the notes on the particular work that is sometimes called *"The Second Book of Moses."* I face this task as I have faced every other effort that we have made respecting commentary on the Word of God — with trepidation. Who am I to write anything? But yet the Lord, and for reasons of His Own, has instructed me to make this effort.

As is quickly obvious, I write from the perspective of the Evangelist, for that is my calling. Consequently, perhaps some of the statements are somewhat sharper than would normally be found in a Commentary. A Brother wrote the other day and stated, *"Brother Swaggart, most Commentaries only provide information."* He then went on to say, *"Yours have an added perspective: you constantly challenge my thinking."*

If in fact that is the case, that is what we are attempting to do.

You will find in our Commentaries, the Book of Exodus included, that we address head on what we believe to be false doctrine. No punches are pulled, no quarter is asked, as no quarter is given. Once again we have the Evangelist saying, *"Thus saith the Lord."* Evangelists do not compromise, at least if they are true to their calling. They do not practice diplomacy; they deliver ultimatums. You will find that spirit, the spirit of the Evangelist, in this effort.

I love the Word of God. I have read the Bible completely through at least 50 times. I never tire of its contents, and it never ceases to bless, uplift, and strengthen me. I find that it is alive, and that's about the best way I know how to explain it. That means that it is totally unlike any other book or writing or literature in the world. In fact, the Word of God is the only revealed Truth in the world, and in fact ever has been.

If, by the help of the Lord, we can make this great Book of Exodus a little easier to understand, in some way open up its great truths to you to a greater extent, glean its treasures, then it will have been well worth your while in perusing these contents.

REDEMPTION

George Williams said concerning the great Book of Exodus: *"As the subject of Genesis is man's ruin, so that of Exodus is man's Redemption. The Hebrew title for the Book is 'These are the names.' This accords with the subject of the Book, for Redemption is an individual matter. The Book teaches that this Redemption can only be effected by blood, the blood of the Lamb, the Blood of the Lord Jesus Christ.*

"It opens with Israel as a helpless slave in the power of the enemy, and doomed by him to destruction; it closes with Israel redeemed, enriched, and free. The method of this deliverance was the death of the Paschal Lamb. The Book, therefore, teaches that where there is no blood — the Blood of Christ — there is no Salvation."

EXODUS

The title *"Exodus"* was first applied to the Book by the Greek-speaking Jews, who translated the Hebrew Bible into Greek at Alexandria in the Third and Second Centuries B.C. Exodus means *"departure"* or *"outgoing,"* and was selected as an appropriate name for a work which treats mainly of the departure of the Children of Israel out of the land of Egypt.

While the departure of the Israelites out of Egypt, and the mode in which it was brought about, constitute a great part of the Book, as well, the adoption of Israel as God's peculiar people by the Law given, and the Covenant entered into at Mount Sinai, make up a great part as well.

Prior to this, God's relation to the Israelites was through the Covenant of Abraham, Isaac, and Jacob, one might say. God now brings Israel to Himself in a national way, through Redemption. Because of His redemptive act, the Israelites enter into the Mosaic Covenant, which involves the Tabernacle, Priesthood, and the Shekinah Glory of His Presence.

In fact, the entire Book typifies the Person and Work of Christ. In a very special way, and as we shall see, this is evident in the Tabernacle and the sacrificial ritual, as indicated in I Corinthians, Chapter 10 and the Book of Hebrews.

REDEMPTION BY BLOOD

Concerning the Book of Exodus, Mackintosh said: *"Redemption by blood occupies a prominent place therein — it characterizes the Book. God's many mercies to His redeemed, in the display of His power, the patience of His love, and the riches of His Grace, flow from it. The great question of Israel's relationship to God is settled by the Blood of the Lamb. It changes their condition entirely. Israel within the blood-sprinkled doorposts was God's redeemed, blood-bought people.*

"God being holy, and Israel guilty, no happy relationship could exist between them till judgment had been accomplished. Sin must be judged. A happy friendship once existed between God and man, on the ground of innocence; but sin having entered and snapped the link asunder, there can be no reconciliation but through the full expression of the moral judgment of God against sin. We can only have 'life through death.' God is the God of Holiness, and He must judge sin. In saving the sinner, He condemns his sin. The Cross is the full and perfect expression of this."

THE CROSS

As Genesis portrayed the Cross, Exodus explains the Cross. It takes us into the very heart of what Christ did there, showing it to us by example, type, shadow, and symbolism. In fact, the types and symbolisms are so abundant, that an honest perusal of the Book of Exodus cannot help but see the emphasis.

As the Reader will see, we will take every opportunity to explain the Cross, to portray the Cross, to lift up the Christ of the Cross. In doing so, and of necessity, we will mingle Paul's writings with that which Moses gave us in this great Book called *"Exodus."* In fact, *"Paul"* was the *"Moses"* of the New Covenant.

As Moses gave us the shadows, the types, the symbolisms, etc., Paul in his writings, explained what all of this meant, hence the comingling of the portrayal of Moses and the teaching of Paul. They fit hand in glove.

In 1996, after some five years of seeking the Lord daily, and with tears, He began to open up to me the Message of the Cross, which in effect is not new, but actually the same thing that Paul taught. This portrayed to me, as it portrays to all, God's prescribed order of victory for the Child of God. In other words, without a proper understanding of the Cross, which Paul gave us, and which as well we will see in this great Book of Exodus, we simply cannot live a victorious, overcoming, Christian life. By the help of God, we will endeavor to the fullest extent of our ability, to portray the meaning of the Cross, to where the Reader will have absolutely no misunderstanding as to what the Scripture teaches us as it regards this all-important subject.

MOSAIC AUTHORSHIP

Exodus, and actually the entirety of the Pentateuch (Genesis through Deuteronomy) generally have been assigned to Moses by a unanimous tradition, with which most Jews agree. No other author has ever been put forward as a rival candidate to Moses; and we must either ascribe the work to a wholly unknown and nameless writer, who, with a marvelous humility and self-abnegation, while composing the most important treatise which the world has seen, concealed himself so effectually as to secure his own complete oblivion, or we must admit that the tradition is in the right, and that Moses, the hero of Exodus, and of the three following Books, was also their composer (Rawlinson).

YOUR STUDY

As every Book in the Bible carries its most important place, Exodus must, of necessity, carry a place and position of supreme importance, that is if it's proper to place the relationship of any one of the Books of the Bible above another. One might say, as Genesis showed us the Cross, Exodus brings us to the Cross, and in no uncertain terms. Consequently, to properly understand the Cross, it is absolutely necessary for one to have a grasp of the great Book of Exodus. We would pray that our efforts in this capacity would be of some help to you, the Reader. If so, then this work will not at all have been in vain, and neither will your perusal of these contents.

"On a hill far away stood an old rugged Cross,
"The emblem of suffering and shame;
"And I love that old Cross where the dearest and best
"For a world of lost sinners was slain."

"Oh, that old rugged Cross, so despised by the world,
"Has a wondrous attraction for me;
"For the dear Lamb of God left His glory above
"To bear it to dark Calvary."

"In the old rugged Cross, stained with Blood so Divine,
"A wondrous beauty I see;
"For 'twas on that old Cross Jesus suffered and died
"To pardon and sanctify me."

"To the old rugged Cross I will ever be true,
"Its shame and reproach gladly bear;
"Then He'll call me someday to my home far away,
"Where His glory forever I'll share."

THE BOOK OF EXODUS

(1) "NOW THESE ARE THE NAMES OF THE CHILDREN OF ISRAEL, WHICH CAME INTO EGYPT; EVERY MAN AND HIS HOUSEHOLD CAME WITH JACOB.

(2) "REUBEN, SIMEON, LEVI, AND JUDAH,

(3) "ISSACHAR, ZEBULUN, AND BENJAMIN,

(4) "DAN, AND NAPHTALI, GAD, AND ASHER.

(5) "AND ALL THE SOULS THAT CAME OUT OF THE LOINS OF JACOB WERE SEVENTY SOULS, FOR JOSEPH WAS IN EGYPT ALREADY.

(6) "AND JOSEPH DIED, AND ALL HIS BRETHREN, AND ALL THAT GENERATION.

(7) "AND THE CHILDREN OF ISRAEL WERE FRUITFUL, AND INCREASED ABUNDANTLY, AND MULTIPLIED, AND WAXED EXCEEDING MIGHTY; AND THE LAND WAS FILLED WITH THEM."

The structure is:

1. We look at the 70 souls, Jacob's family, which by the Hand of the Lord were brought from Canaan to Egypt, and brought there for safekeeping, one might say. They were insignificant in the eyes of the world, but if God be in it, we must never despise the day of small things.

2. Joseph and his generation died, which marked the ending of one era and the beginning of another. Even though no principal individuals are recorded during the coming time, still, the Ways of God continued to be taught to the people, at least after a fashion.

3. Because of these being *"God's people,"* they were *"fruitful, and increased abundantly, and multiplied, and waxed exceeding mighty."*

NOTES

The blessings of God are upon that which belongs to God.

THE NAMES

Verses 1 through 5 read: *"Now these are the names of the Children of Israel, which came into Egypt; every man and his household came with Jacob.*

"Reuben, Simeon, Levi, and Judah,

"Issachar, Zebulun, and Benjamin,

"Dan, and Naphtali, Gad, and Asher.

"And all the souls that came out of the loins of Jacob were seventy souls: for Joseph was in Egypt already."

The Book of Genesis is the story of the Fall of man. The Book of Exodus is the story of the Redemption of man. Hence, the work of Redemption by Christ is called His *"Exodus"* (deceased, going out of the world, Lk. 9:31).

As stated, this Book teaches that Redemption can only be effected by blood. It opens with Israel as a helpless slave in the power of the enemy, and doomed by him to destruction. In Exodus, Egypt is a type of the world with all of its evil systems and, as well, ruled by the prince of darkness, Satan. The Book closes with Israel redeemed, enriched, and free. All of this was effected by the death of the Paschal Lamb, which was a Type of the coming Redeemer, Who would suffer for the entirety of the world (Jn. 3:16).

If we are to notice, this Book begins with names, hence Salvation is a personal matter. We must not forget that. It means that Salvation is not corporate, even though the Church may be corporate.

JOSEPH

Joseph died some 140-plus years before

Israel left Egypt, or some 60-plus years before Moses was born. The king who began enslaving Israel reigned during the last part of this 60-odd years, for when Moses was born, his policy was in force.

The conduct of Joseph's brethren against him is what ultimately brought them into Egypt; consequently, we must take two things into account:

1. We see the ugly manner in which the brothers of Joseph conducted themselves toward God.

2. We note the encouraging manner in which God conducted Himself toward the brothers of Joseph.

To be sure, their actions were overly ugly, so ugly in fact, that they could be termed only in the realm of murder. And in a sense, their acting in this manner toward Joseph was the same as them acting toward God, i.e., *"Christ."* Jesus Himself said: *"Verily I say unto you, Inasmuch as you have done it unto one of the least of these My brethren, you have done it unto Me"* (Mat. 25:40).

But then God was in all of this, and He is in it to bring good out of evil. Joseph's brothers might sell him to the Ishmeelites, and they might sell him to Potiphar, and Potiphar might throw him in prison. But God was above all of this, working out His Own Plans.

Concerning all of this, Mackintosh said: *"There are wheels within wheels in the Government of God. He makes use of an endless variety of agencies in the accomplishment of His unsearchable designs. Potiphar's wife, Pharaoh's butler, Pharaoh's dreams, Pharaoh himself, the dungeon, the throne, the fetter, the famine — all are at His sovereign disposal, and all are made instrumental in the development of His stupendous counsels."*

As one studies the Word of God, one quickly finds that with God in the mix, the potentials are endless. And let us understand that exactly as He worked then, He also works now. There is only one requirement that He has, and that is faith. Someone must have Faith, and in the time of the Patriarchs, they were known for their Faith.

THE CHILDREN OF ISRAEL

Verses 6 and 7 read: *"And Joseph died, and all his brethren, and all that generation.*

"And the Children of Israel were fruitful, and increased abundantly, and multiplied, and waxed exceeding mighty; and the land was filled with them."

Joseph died, but God didn't die. He continued to bless the Children of Israel, until they grew into a mighty nation.

From the time that God called Abraham out of Ur of the Chaldees, until the Children of Israel were delivered from Egyptian bondage was 430 years. From the time of Abraham unto the time that Jacob moved into Egypt was a period of some 215 years. So, the Children of Israel actually stayed in Egypt per se for 215 years as well, making a total of 430 years.

Why did God desire that they remain that long in this land? And why did He allow them to be reduced to slavery?

Two reasons:

1. He wanted them to grow into a mighty nation before He brought them into the Promised Land, and that they did. Actually, they would be some three million strong when they left Egypt.

2. He allowed them to be reduced to slavery so they would want to leave. Had they continued as they were during the time of Joseph, actually having the best of the land, and being treated as royal guests, there is no way they would have left Egypt. They had to be reduced to abject slavery, and the worst kind at that, before they were ready to leave.

As someone has well said, man will seldom carry out the Will of God until it's in his own personal interests to do so. That's sad, but true!

(8) "NOW THERE AROSE UP A NEW KING OVER EGYPT, WHICH KNEW NOT JOSEPH.

(9) "AND HE SAID UNTO HIS PEOPLE, BEHOLD, THE PEOPLE OF THE CHILDREN OF ISRAEL ARE MORE AND MIGHTIER THAN WE:

(10) "COME ON, LET US DEAL WISELY WITH THEM; LEST THEY MULTIPLY, AND IT COME TO PASS, THAT, WHEN THERE FALLETH OUT ANY WAR, THEY JOIN ALSO UNTO OUR ENEMIES, AND FIGHT AGAINST US, AND SO GET THEM UP OUT OF THE LAND.

(11) "THEREFORE THEY DID SET OVER THEM TASKMASTERS TO AFFLICT THEM WITH THEIR BURDENS. AND THEY BUILT FOR PHARAOH TREASURE CITIES, PITHOM AND RAAMSES.

(12) "BUT THE MORE THEY AFFLICTED THEM, THE MORE THEY MULTIPLIED AND GREW. AND THEY WERE GRIEVED BECAUSE OF THE CHILDREN OF ISRAEL.

(13) "AND THE EGYPTIANS MADE THE CHILDREN OF ISRAEL TO SERVE WITH RIGOUR:

(14) "AND THEY MADE THEIR LIVES BITTER WITH HARD BONDAGE, IN MORTAR, AND IN BRICK, AND IN ALL MANNER OF SERVICE IN THE FIELD: ALL THEIR SERVICE, WHEREIN THEY MADE THEM SERVE, WAS WITH RIGOUR."

The composition is:

1. The ruins of the great treasure cities, Pithom and Raamses, exist today, and are well known.

2. The Lord evidently gave the Children of Israel excellent health and freedom from disease.

3. The wise planning of the Egyptian Monarch was very clever, so long as he left God out. But the entrance of God into these plans turned their wisdom to folly. All schemes which ignore God illustrate human fallibility (Williams).

THE NEW KING

Verse 8 reads: *"Now there arose up a new king over Egypt, which knew not Joseph."*

According to accounts, the Children of Israel were in Egypt 215 years. This counts from the time that Jacob came into Egypt with 70 souls, until they were delivered some 215 years later.

As well, there is a good possibility that each of the sons of Jacob had a household of a number of people, perhaps even as many as 50. That being the case, it could have been as many as 2,000 people which went into Egypt.

According to some authorities, population tends to double itself, if there be no artificial check restraining it, approximately every 25 years. If, in fact, there were approximately 2,000 people in this entourage, in some 215 years, according to the estimates, they would have multiplied to approximately two million. Considering that they were extremely healthy, and that disease was not carrying them off, as it did many in those days, that number could easily, in the 215 year period, swell to approximately three million people, which is the estimate concerning the number which was delivered. There were six hundred thousand men of war, the Scripture tells us, which wouldn't count all men above 40 years of age, which means there were probably well over one million men. There would have been at least that many adult women, beside all the children.

THE EGYPTIAN RECORDS

It has been stated by some that in the Egyptian records, there is no mention of the Hebrews, as the Bible claims. However, it is known that at about the time of the Hebrew sojourn, there was in Egypt a subject race, often employed in forced labors, called *"Aperu"* or *"Aperiu,"* and it seems impossible to deny that this word is a very fair Egyptian equivalent for the Biblical *"Hebrews."* We are forced, therefore, either to suppose that there were in Egypt, at one and the same time, two subject races with names almost identical, or to admit the identification of the *"Aperu"* with the descendants of Jacob.

The exact numbers of the *"Aperu"* are nowhere mentioned; but it is a calculation by some authorities that under Rameses II, a little before the Exodus, the foreign races in Egypt, of whom the *"Aperu"* were beyond all doubt the chief, amounted certainly to a third, and probably still more, of the whole population. That population was reckoned at approximately eight million, of which a third would be a little over two and one-half million. Without a doubt, it seems obvious that the *"Aperu"* identified in the Egyptian records were indeed the Hebrews.

WHO KNEW NOT JOSEPH

It is believed that the Children of Israel were delivered from Egypt at approximately 1600 B.C.

The *"new king"* mentioned here by Moses was probably either Rameses I, or his son, Seti I. And then some claim it was Rameses IV, surnamed Meiamoun. It is believed that the

Pharaoh who reigned when the Israelites went out of Egypt was Rameses V, named *"Amenophis."*

It seems that the persecution lasted for approximately 100 years. We know that it was in force when Moses was born. He spent 40 years in Egypt, and 40 years, as well, at the backside of the desert. That totals 80 years in which the persecutions continued, with it probably going on some 10 to 20 years before Moses was born.

When Jacob came into Egypt, Joseph was about 38 years old. He died at 110. So it was about 60 years after his death that this *"new king"* began to reign.

When the Scripture says that *"a new king ... which knew not Joseph,"* it means he did not regard him, even though he would certainly have known the name. There is no way that this great thing could have been done in Egypt those years earlier, and instituted by Joseph as it regards the superintending of Egypt during the time of the great harvests and the famine, without this Pharaoh being perfectly aware.

THE CHILDREN OF INRAEL

Verse 9 reads: *"And he said unto his people, Behold, the people of the Children of Israel are more and mightier than we."*

This new king was very well aware of Joseph, and of the Children of Israel, but because of their tremendous population, as well no doubt coupled with their industry, he was fearful of them, and determined to show them no favor whatsoever. In other words, he would make slaves of them.

Most probably, the new Egyptian Pharaoh exaggerated when he spoke of the Children of Israel being more and mightier, even though they were, in fact, very strong, and getting stronger everyday. In fact, he will use this as an excuse to institute his reforms, as he would have called them.

THE PLANS OF PHARAOH

Verse 10 reads: *"Come on, let us deal wisely with them; lest they multiply, and it come to pass, that, when there falleth out any war, they join also unto our enemies, and fight against us, and so get them up out of the land."*

We find in this Verse an evil king (Pharaoh) who sets out to destroy God's people. To be sure, his plans to do so were keen and far-reaching, at least as long as God was left out. But the entrance of God into these plans turned their wisdom to folly. All schemes which ignore God illustrate the same.

The world, not knowing God, little uses its wisdom aright. Only a few times in history record it doing such. The Pharaoh who made Joseph the Prime Minister of Egypt portrays one of the few times of such happening. And to be frank, it would not have happened then, had not God moved upon that particular Monarch. Most of the time, the people of God are opposed more or less, with the world completely misjudging them.

For instance, the Pharaoh of this time passed judgment upon the Israelites, and imagined all sort of evil things. He imagined they would join Egypt's enemies, thereby, fighting against Egypt, etc. The truth was, Israel had no such thing in mind. But as we shall see, the evil plans fomented by Pharaoh were to be used by God, just as the righteous plans were used by God as it regards the Pharaoh of Joseph's day. While man is limited, God is never limited, unless we limit Him through unbelief. He is able to take anything and turn it to good, but He does seek cooperation by Believers.

TREASURE CITIES

Verse 11 reads: *"Therefore they did set over them taskmasters to afflict them with their burdens. And they built for Pharaoh treasure cities, Pithom and Raamses."*

The ruins of Pithom and Raamses exist presently, and in fact, the latter was the residence of the Court. There is a good possibility that the miracles of Moses recorded in Exodus, Chapter 7 took place in this Court (Ps. 78:12, 43). So, the great palaces built by the Children of God, who were used as slaves, would see the mighty Power of God made evident in them.

BLESSED

Verse 12 reads: *"But the more they afflicted them, the more they multiplied and grew. And they were grieved because of the Children of Israel."*

The first phrase of this Verse is interesting indeed, *"But the more they afflicted them, the more they multiplied and grew."*

Concerning this, Mackintosh said: *"In reference to the king of Egypt, it may assuredly be said, he did 'greatly err,' not knowing God or His changeless counsels. He knew not that, hundreds of years back, before even he had breathed the breath of mortal life, God's Word and Oath — 'two immutable things' — had infallibly secured the full and glorious deliverance of that very people, in fact a people which at that time, the time of the Oath of God, didn't even exist, whom he was going, in his earthly wisdom, to crush. All this was unknown to him, and therefore all his thoughts and plans were founded upon ignorance of that grand foundation — truth of all truths, namely, that 'God is.' He vainly imagined that he, by his management, could prevent the increase of those concerning whom God had said, 'They shall be as the stars of Heaven, and as the sand which is upon the seashore.' His wise dealing, therefore, was simply madness and folly."*

THE MORE THEY MULTIPLIED

The idea of this phrase is, the more that Satan engineered, through Pharaoh, the persecution, the more that God increased the Blessings. One must shout *"Hallelujah!"* What God has blessed, nothing can curse.

If man cooperates with God, places his faith aright in Christ and His Cross, and maintains his faith in that Finished Work, it really doesn't matter what Satan does. Admittedly, for awhile it may look very negative, for who would have bought stock in Job when he sat in the midst of an ash heap, with everything gone? Who would have purchased stock in David when he was hiding in caves, running from Saul? Who would have purchased stock in the Early Church, with Caesar vowing its destruction?

But none of that mattered. If believing man will maintain his Faith in Christ and what Christ has done for him at the Cross, and not allow his faith to be moved from that work that is forever finished, ultimately the Blessings will come, and God will pour them on. *"The more that Pharaoh afflicted the People of God, the more that God multiplied them."* *"If God be for us, who can be against us?"* (Rom. 8:31).

What a sad mistake, therefore, for a feeble mortal, no matter how powerful he might be to those around him, to set himself up against the Eternal God, and as one Preacher said, *"To rush against the thick bosses of the shield of the Almighty!"* As well might the Monarch have sought to stem, with his puny hand, the ocean's tide, as to prevent the increase of those who were the subjects of Jehovah's everlasting purpose. Hence, although *"they did set over them taskmasters to afflict them with their burdens,"* yet, *"the more they afflicted them, the more they multiplied and grew."* Thus it must ever be. *"He Who sits in the heavens shall laugh; the LORD shall have them in derision"* (Ps. 2:4). Eternal confusion shall be inscribed upon all the opposition of men and devils.

PERSONAL EXPERIENCE

Personally, I have great reason to be abundantly joyful as it regards this great Truth. I know what it is to have the entirety of the news media all over the world set out to destroy my person. Even worse yet, I know what it is to have most of the Church follow suit. I know what it is to be reduced only to my Faith in God. However, as I have learned, that is a majority, and a great majority at that, in any situation.

I know what it is for the Lord to speak to my heart and say *"I'm not a man that I should lie, neither the son of man that I should repent* (meaning that God won't change His mind about His call on my life), *what I have blessed, nothing can curse."* But of all this, of which I could give many examples, I will relate but one.

In 1985, if I remember the year correctly, Jimmy Swaggart Ministries applied for an educational radio frequency which was available in the city of Baton Rouge, and in fact, the only one that was available. I'm speaking of course of a Radio Station.

When we made our application, a competing group made application at the same time.

They used every means at their disposal, which included telling every type of lie they could think up, to try to get the FCC in Washington to decide in their favor. (The

FCC is the Department of Communications in Washington which makes the decision regarding Radio and Television Stations in this country, plus all other types of communication.) But despite their lies, the FCC decided in our favor. The other side appealed:

Consequently, we had to go through this particular trial all over again, with the FCC once again deciding in our favor. In fact, this happened three times, with the FCC deciding for us each time.

There were two extremely negative situations about all of this. First of all, we had to hire lawyers in Washington to defend our interests, which is not inexpensive to say the least! As well, while all of this was going on, we could not put the Station on the air.

After we had won the third trial, the FCC proceeded to change the rules, which then gave the other side a much better chance to be awarded the Station. In the meantime, we had gotten permission from the FCC to go ahead and erect the Station, which we did, and which serves as our flagship Station presently — WJFM-FM. The competing adversary then made the statement to us that they most definitely were now going to get this Station, and accordingly set out to do so.

SONLIFE RADIO

In the meantime, actually at the beginning of 1999, the Lord by Revelation gave me direction as to what He wanted us to do as it regards Radio. To be frank, before that time, I had absolutely no inkling of such an effort, continuing to promote Television, and continuing to do so very strongly. But the Lord opened up to me what He wanted done, and Radio was to be the key.

First of all, He told me to change the programming on our Mother Station here in Baton Rouge, the Station I've been discussing, plus the other Station then owned by the Ministry, WJYM-AM, in Bowling Green, Ohio, a suburb of Toledo. He told me that all programming must come from Family Worship Center, whether the Ministry of music and singing as it regards worship, plus all Preaching and Teaching.

As well, He told me that we must secure other Stations all over this nation, in effect, covering the nation by Radio.

NOTES

Before the Lord did this thing, I had not heard of any programming such as this, so as far as we knew, we were breaking new ground. When I first mentioned it, most of the people to whom I broached the subject, immediately told me that such wouldn't work. But of course I knew that it would work, simply because the Lord had told me to do it. And to be sure, it most definitely did work, and grandly so!

WHAT THE LORD SPOKE TO MY HEART

But getting back to the FCC changing the rules, and I speak of the manner in which such Stations are awarded, what the Commission did gave our adversaries a much better chance to take over the Station, which would have been catastrophic to what the Lord had called us to do. In fact, something happened on a particular day in 2001 which made the cause of our adversary to seem much more advantageous.

I took the matter to prayer, as I've learned to take all matters to prayer.

I related to the Lord the boasts which the other side had made, and then I asked the Lord to give me a sign concerning this situation.

I remember that I was somewhat ashamed to ask for such, especially considering that the Lord had already given us the Station, and as well, had built and was building a network from that particular Station, a network incidentally, which will ultimately cover almost, if not all, of the United States.

I remember saying to the Lord that I was ashamed to ask for such a sign, but to be honest, fear filled my heart.

After making that petition, I went on praying about other things, and actually forgot about that particular situation. Later on during that time of prayer, the Lord brought to my mind a little chorus which we sing in Family Worship Center constantly. The words are:

> "*We are able to go up and take the country*
> "*And possess the land from Jordan unto the Sea.*
> "*Though the giants may be there our way to hinder,*
> "*The Lord has given us the victory.*"

As I quoted that Verse, not even thinking of the petition I had laid before the Lord, when I came to the last phrase, *"The Lord has given us the victory,"* the Spirit of God came all over me, and I began to weep, as the Lord brought back to my mind the sign for which I had asked.

It didn't matter how many giants were thrown against us, *"The Lord has given us the victory,"* which means that it's already been decided, and nothing can change it.

Instantly, my fear left, and a joy filled my heart as it regards SonLife Radio.

In January of 2002, to make the story short, our competing adversaries, who, incidentally, had opposed us for some 17 years, suddenly bowed out.

Whatever Satan does, if we will continue to believe the Lord, and stay in the center of His Will, the more the affliction comes, the more that the Lord will multiply us and the more that we will grow.

This should give sweet rest to the heart in the midst of a scene where all is apparently so contrary to God and so contrary to Faith. Were it not for the settled assurance that *"the wrath of man shall praise the Lord,"* the spirit would often be cast down while contemplating the circumstances and influences which surround one in the world. Thank God, *"we look not at the things which are seen, but at the things which are not seen: for the things which are seen are temporal; but the things which are not seen are eternal"* (II Cor. 4:18). In the power of this, we may well say, *"Rest in the LORD, and wait patiently for Him: fret not thyself because of him who prospers in his way, because of the man who brings wicked devices to pass"* (Ps. 37:7).

Had Israel *"looked at the things which are seen,"* what were they? Pharaoh's wrath, stern taskmasters, afflictive burdens, rigorous service, hard bondage, mortar, and brick. But, then, *"the things which are not seen,"* what were they?

God's eternal purpose, His unfailing promise, the approaching dawn of a day of Salvation, the *"burning lamp"* of Jehovah's deliverance. Faith alone can enter into such. Faith alone could cause the oppressed Israelite to look from the smoking furnace of Egypt, to the green fields and vine-clad mountains of the land of Canaan. Faith alone could recognize, in those oppressed slaves, toiling in the brickkilns of Egypt, the heirs of Salvation, and the objects of Heaven's peculiar interest and favor (Mackintosh).

The word *"grieved"* insufficiently renders the Hebrew verb, which in fact, *"expresses a mixture of loathing and alarm."* In other words, Pharaoh and his court had a horror of the Children of Israel. They were afraid of them!

THE EGYPTIANS

Verses 13 and 14 read: *"And the Egyptians made the Children of Israel to serve with rigour:*

"And they made their lives bitter with hard bondage, in mortar, and in brick, and in all manner of service in the field: all their service, wherein they made them serve, was with rigour."

According to *"Pulpit,"* the word *"rigour"* is a very rare one. It is derived from a root which means, *"to break in pieces, to crush."*

The tide had now turned completely. From the time that the Children of Israel were looked at as favored guests, and because they were the relatives of Joseph, they now are hated, feared, and are actually made into slaves.

If the *"labor in the field"* included, as Josephus supposed, the cutting of canals, their lives would indeed have been *"made bitter."* There is no such exhausting toil as that of working under the hot Egyptian sun, with the feet in water, in an open cutting, where there can be no shade, and scarcely a breath of air, from sunrise to sunset, as forced laborers are generally required to do. For instance, in the cutting of the Alexandrian Canal, 20,000 laborers out of 150,000 died as a result of the harsh conditions.

In such a social climate, one at this stage would not have given the Children of Israel any chance at all. They were servile slaves, and Egypt was the mightiest nation on Earth, so what could they do?

However, as we look upon this situation, we must take into account three things:

1. Irrespective of the plans that the evil Pharaoh would make, regardless of what he thought, he would not have the final say, that belonging to God.

2. These people belonged to God, and not to Pharaoh. The evil Monarch surely thought they belonged to him, but they didn't. And as well, it should be remembered presently that every single Believer in the world belongs to the Lord Jesus Christ. Irrespective as to where they might live, how totalitarian their government might be, or how bad the situation looks on the surface, these Believers belong to God, and whatever is done to them is done unto God. That should be remembered!

3. Whatever God wants to do with His people, that He will do, and nothing will stop Him. If men get in the way, even the mightiest on the face of the Earth as Pharaoh, they will be subdued, while the slaves gain supremacy.

Pharaoh would have been 10,000 times better off had he treated these people with dignity and kindness. He would have spared the near destruction of his nation.

But then again, had Pharaoh done that, that is made the lives of the Children of Israel easy and profitable, the truth is, they would not have wanted to have left Egypt. So the Lord *"makes even the wrath of man to praise Him"* (Ps. 76:10).

(15) "AND THE KING OF EGYPT SPOKE TO THE HEBREW MIDWIVES, OF WHICH THE NAME OF THE ONE WAS SHIPHRAH, AND THE NAME OF THE OTHER PUAH:

(16) "AND HE SAID, WHEN YOU DO THE OFFICE OF A MIDWIFE TO THE HEBREW WOMEN, AND SEE THEM UPON THE STOOLS; IF IT BE A SON, THEN YOU SHALL KILL HIM: BUT IF IT BE A DAUGHTER, THEN SHE SHALL LIVE.

(17) "BUT THE MIDWIVES FEARED GOD, AND DID NOT AS THE KING OF EGYPT COMMANDED THEM, BUT SAVED THE MEN CHILDREN ALIVE.

(18) "AND THE KING OF EGYPT CALLED FOR THE MIDWIVES, AND SAID UNTO THEM, WHY HAVE YOU DONE THIS THING, AND HAVE SAVED THE MEN CHILDREN ALIVE?

(19) "AND THE MIDWIVES SAID UNTO PHARAOH, BECAUSE THE HEBREW WOMEN ARE NOT AS THE EGYPTIAN WOMEN; FOR THEY ARE LIVELY, AND ARE DELIVERED ERE THE MIDWIVES COME IN UNTO THEM.

NOTES

(20) "THEREFORE GOD DEALT WELL WITH THE MIDWIVES: AND THE PEOPLE MULTIPLIED, AND WAXED VERY MIGHTY.

(21) "AND IT CAME TO PASS, BECAUSE THE MIDWIVES FEARED GOD, THAT HE MADE THEM HOUSES.

(22) "AND PHARAOH CHARGED ALL HIS PEOPLE, SAYING, EVERY SON THAT IS BORN YOU SHALL CAST INTO THE RIVER, AND EVERY DAUGHTER YOU SHALL SAVE ALIVE."

The composition is:

1. Verses 15 through 22 portray the two leading Hebrew midwives, *"Shiphrah"* and *"Puah."* It is ironic that the names of the mighty Pharaohs of that day are all but lost to history, whereas, the names of these two women who obeyed God are recognized by multiple millions in every generation.

2. The faith of these brave women, for they risked their own lives, is recognized by God, and He dealt well with them. It must not be assumed that they were guilty of falsehood. There is no reason to suppose that what they stated was not perfectly true.

3. The statement in Verse 21, coupled with the statements of the prior Verses, means that God protected these midwives from being put to death by Pharaoh; and, that because of their faith, He made them houses; that is, He gave them large families.

KING OF EGYPT

Verse 15 reads: *"And the king of Egypt spoke to the Hebrew midwives, of which the name of the one was Shiphrah, and the name of the other Puah."*

The two named here were evidently in charge of many, if not all, of the midwives among the people of Israel.

To portray the eternal consequences of those who serve the Lord, as stated, the Pharaoh of that particular time is not surely known at present, while the names of these two women, whomever they may have been, are known to millions, and in fact, have been known by millions in every generation.

This tells us that all that is merely human, however solid, however, brilliant, however, attractive, must ultimately fall into the cold grasp of death, and there molder in the dark, silent tomb. The clod of the valley must cover man's highest excellencies and brightest glories; mortality is engraved upon his brow, and all his schemes are transitorial.

On the contrary, that which is connected with, and based upon God, shall endure forever. *"His Name shall endure forever, and His memorial to all generations"* (Mackintosh).

MIDWIVES

Verses 16 through 22 read: *"And he said, When you do the office of a midwife to the Hebrew women, and see them upon the stools; if it be a son, then you shall kill him: but if it be a daughter, then she shall live.*

"But the midwives feared God, and did not as the king of Egypt commanded them, but saved the men children alive.

"And the king of Egypt called for the midwives, and said unto them, Why have you done this thing, and have saved the men children alive?

"And the midwives said unto Pharaoh, Because the Hebrew women are not as the Egyptian women; for they are lively, and are delivered ere the midwives come in unto them.

"Therefore God dealt well with the midwives: and the people multiplied, and waxed very mighty.

"And it came to pass, because the midwives feared God, that He made them houses.

"And Pharaoh charged all his people, saying, Every son that is born you shall cast into the river, and every daughter you shall save alive."

Evidently, these two women, *"Shiphrah"* and *"Puah,"* who were in charge of all the midwives, which no doubt numbered into the thousands, were called before Pharaoh or at least one of his emissaries, and given instructions which they were to give to all the midwives. Every boy baby was to be killed as soon as it was born, with only the little girl babies left alive. This murderous scheme hatched up by Pharaoh or someone in his court was supposed to weaken Israel by denying it further growth. As stated, they were multiplying mightily, with Pharaoh becoming more and more fearful of their size and power. Hence they were reduced to abject slavery, and now this murderous scheme is concocted.

SOWING AND REAPING

In all of this, even though God uses all things, even the wrath of Pharaoh, still, what we sow, we must reap (Gal. 6:7). Whatever the actions of men in wickedness and highhanded rebellion, they are made subservient to the establishment of the Divine counsels of Grace and love . . . even the wrath of man is yoked to the chariot wheel of God's decrees (Dennett).

But why did God allow the descendants of Abraham to suffer such indignities and trials at the hands of the Egyptians?

To which we have already briefly alluded, had Israel not suffered greatly, they certainly would not have wanted to have left Egypt. As well, Israel was not without blame. Great sin was in their camp, as well as in the camp of the Egyptians.

Going some 1,600 years into the future, Israel delivered up Christ into the hands of the Gentiles, and so into their hands they also have been delivered. Christ was shamefully treated by the Romans, but yet, the same people were employed by God to punish the Jews. Christ was *"cut off"* out of the land of the living, and from A.D. 70, Israel, too, was *"cut off"* from the land of their fathers, until 1948. Thus we see again and again how inexorable is the outworking of the law of sowing and reaping.

As it regards Israel and Egypt, in a sense, Israel was paying for what they had done in the past. Remember the terrible sin against Joseph!

THE REAPING OF JUDGMENT CAN BE STOPPED!

In fact, it can only be stopped in one way, and that is by one's acceptance of Christ, which immediately stops all judgment, and of every description. Christ took all the Judgment at the Cross, and for God to continue to visit judgment upon a person who has truly come to Christ would be a mockery. It would in essence say that Christ did not finish His Work, in other words, He did not take all of our judgment. But He did take all of our judgment, and did so in totality.

Even though terrible things are sowed by all unbelievers, and to be sure they will reap the result of what they have sowed, as long as they remain in the unsaved state, the moment they come to Christ, the reaping of evil stops. While there might be a residue that carries over, even that can be greatly ameliorated.

THE FAMILY CURSE

There is a teaching presently referred to as *"the family curse"* which has become very prominent, and has confused many people. Let's look at that particular teaching:

Is there such a thing as a *"family curse"*?

Most definitely there is such a thing as a family curse, a generational curse, the curse of the broken law, in fact, every type of curse possibly that one could think is visited upon the human race.

But that pertains to the unsaved part of the human race. The moment the believing sinner comes to Christ, making Him Lord and Saviour, all curses are completely stopped. What does the Scripture say?

"Christ has redeemed us from the curse of the law, being made a curse for us: for it is written, Cursed is every one who hangs on a tree:

"That the Blessing of Abraham might come on the Gentiles through Jesus Christ; that we might receive the promise of the Spirit through Faith" (Gal. 3:13-14).

Jesus handled every curse at the Cross. None were excluded, which means that no Believer should ever believe the untruth that they are having problems because of a family curse, etc.

Knowing that many Christians do have problems, what then is the cause?

A FAILURE TO UNDERSTAND THE CROSS OF CHRIST

Believers have problems, and problems of every nature, unnecessarily so I might quickly add, because they do not understand the Message of the Cross. They are told by Preachers that their problem is a *"family curse,"* and they need hands laid on them by a Preacher who understands this problem, and then their difficulties will be solved.

Unfortunately, whatever happens to them when hands are laid on them will not stop their problems, with them finding themselves experiencing the same difficulties as they had previously. Jesus said: *"You shall know the Truth, and the Truth shall make you free"* (Jn. 8:32).

While we definitely believe in the laying on of hands, problems of the nature of which we speak will not respond to such, but only to proper faith evidenced in Christ and what Christ has done for us at the Cross.

Every Believer must understand that every single thing that comes to him from God comes exclusively by and through Christ and what Christ has done for us in His Finished Work. Consequently, he is to ever make the Cross the object of his faith, not allowing it to be moved to other things.

When he does this faithfully, which in fact is the very heart of the Gospel, the Holy Spirit will then work mightily on behalf of the Believer, leading him into all truth, and giving him victory over all things (Rom. 6:3-5, 11, 14; 8:1-2, 11; Gal. 6:14; Eph. 2:13-18; Col. 2:14-15).

That and that alone is the answer for the Child of God. This means that the Cross holds the solution to every perplexing problem, the answer to every question, the means by which God gives all good things to His people.

So how is it that certain Preachers proclaim the family curse as the problem?

They're deriving their teaching from an erroneous understanding of Exodus 20:5, and several other similar Passages. That particular Scripture says:

"You shall not bow down yourself to them, nor serve them (idols)*: for I the LORD your God am a Jealous God, visiting the iniquity of the fathers upon the children unto the third and fourth generation of them who hate Me."*

The idea is that your great-great-grandfather, etc., did something terrible, and now you are reaping the results of that, hence the *"family curse."*

However, the Scripture mentions that it only comes upon those *"who hate Me,"* referring to the Lord. In fact, the Sixth Verse of the Twentieth Chapter of Exodus says: *"And showing mercy unto thousands of them who love Me, and keep My Commandments."*

While there is definitely such a thing as a family curse, and it definitely does come down to the third and fourth generation, it is only against those who hate the Lord. The moment that a person comes to Christ, the *"iniquity of the fathers"* is immediately suspended. The mercy of God takes over, which is a part of the Born-Again experience. That's the reason that Paul said:

"Therefore if any man be in Christ, he is a new creature: old things are passed away; behold, all things are become new" (II Cor. 5:17). Now either the *"old things"* have passed away, or else the Apostle Paul didn't tell the truth, and those things are still with us. I choose to believe that he told the truth.

Regrettably, and I think I am correct in my assumption, most at that particular time, among the Children of Israel, were not saved. They were not abiding by the Covenant. While some certainly were, that number would have been few. I think all of this is proven by the difficulties which Moses experienced with them, when the time finally came for them to be delivered. So in a sense, the judgment of God was upon the Israelites, and a little later, would greatly come upon the Egyptians. Let us say it again:

All sin must be addressed and punished. It can either be punished by the judgment of God, and the person ultimately dying eternally lost, and going to Hell, or else the believing sinner can accept Christ, Who has taken our punishment, and suffered for us. Those are the two choices!

THE DESIGN OF SATAN

While Pharaoh desired to weaken the Israelites by demanding that the boy babies be killed at birth, Satan's plan was far more sinister. This is the serpent's enmity against the Seed of the woman. If this could have been carried out concerning the male children being destroyed, there would have been no David, just to name one instance, and if no David, no David's Son.

Even though the midwives possibly feared Pharaoh, they feared God more; consequently, they did not obey this wicked king.

All Believers are to obey government, unless such government violates our conscience and the Word of God. Then we must disobey, but at the same time, be prepared to pay the consequences. But God would protect *"Shiphrah"* and *"Puah,"* and all others who assisted. Not only would the Lord protect them, but He would bless them as well, by giving them large families, i.e., *"houses."*

Not able to have his command obeyed as it regarded the little boy babies being killed at birth, he demanded then that all boy babies be thrown into the river, with the girl babies alone being saved alive. As we shall see, the Lord greatly and wondrously used this to bring about His Divine Will.

"Wounded for me, wounded for me,
"There on the Cross He was wounded for me;
"Gone my transgressions, and now I am free,
"All because Jesus was wounded for me."

"Dying for me, dying for me,
"There on the Cross He was dying for me;
"Now in His death my Redemption I see,
"All because Jesus was dying for me."

"Risen for me, risen for me,
"Up from the grave He was risen for me;
"Now evermore from death's sting I am free,
"All because Jesus has risen for me."

"Living for me, living for me,
"Up in the skies He is living for me;
"Daily He's pleading and praying for me,
"All because Jesus is living for me."

"Coming for me, coming for me,
"One day to Earth He is coming for me;
"Then with what joy His dear Face I shall see,
"Oh, how I praise Him, He's coming for me."

CHAPTER 2

(1) "AND THERE WENT A MAN OF THE HOUSE OF LEVI, AND TOOK TO WIFE A DAUGHTER OF LEVI.

(2) "AND THE WOMAN CONCEIVED, AND BEAR A SON: AND WHEN SHE SAW HIM THAT HE WAS A GOODLY CHILD, SHE HID HIM THREE MONTHS.

(3) "AND WHEN SHE COULD NOT LONGER HIDE HIM, SHE TOOK FOR HIM AN ARK OF BULRUSHES, AND DAUBED IT WITH SLIME AND WITH PITCH, AND PUT THE CHILD THEREIN; AND SHE LAID IT IN THE FLAGS BY THE RIVER'S BRINK.

(4) "AND HIS SISTER STOOD AFAR OFF, TO WIT WHAT WOULD BE DONE TO HIM."

The overview is:

1. Moses was a member of the Tribe of Levi, which was to be the Priestly Tribe. He was a Type of Christ, our Great High Priest.

2. We see that it was great faith that led Moses' mother to do what she did regarding this child. The Lord loaned the child to the mother for three months, and then she was to give him to God, which she did.

3. God is in control of all things, and proper Faith in Him brings about this control to effect our lives in a positive sense.

THE PARENTS OF MOSES

Verse 1 reads: *"And there went out a man of the house of Levi, and took to wife a daughter of Levi."*

Moses was a member of the Tribe of Levi. He was the seventh from Abraham. Abraham was the seventh from Heber and Enoch the seventh from Adam. Miriam and Aaron were already born when Moses was born. Jochebed was his mother, with Amram being his father.

Concerning the birth of Moses, Ellicott said: *"Note the extreme simplicity of this announcement, and compare it with the elaborate legends wherewith Oriental religions commonly surrounded the birth of those who were considered their founders, as Thoth, Zoroaster, Orpheus. Even the name of the father is here omitted as unimportant. It is difficult to conceive anyone but Moses making such an omission."*

The phrase *"daughter of Levi,"* doesn't mean that Jochebed was actually the daughter of Levi, who in fact, had been dead many years, but rather that she was of the Tribe of Levi.

Concerning Moses, Pink said: *"From Adam to Christ there is none greater than Moses. He is one of the few characters of Scripture whose course is sketched from his infancy to his death. The fierce light of criticism has been turned upon him for generations, but he is still the most commanding figure of the ancient world.*

"In character, in faith, in the unique position assigned him as the mediator of the Old Covenant, and in achievements, he stands first among the heroes of the Old Testament.

"All of God's early dealings with Israel were transacted through Moses. He was a Prophet, Priest, and King in one person, and so united all the great and important functions which later were distributed among a plurality of persons. The history of such an one is worthy of the strictest attention, and his remarkable life deserves the closest study."

Haldeman said of this man: *"The life of Moses presents a series of striking antithesis. For instance, he was the child of a slave, and the son of a queen. He was born in a hut, and lived in a palace. He inherited poverty, and enjoyed unlimited wealth. He was the leader of armies, and the keeper of flocks. He was the mightiest of warriors, and the meekest of men. He was educated in the court of Egypt, and yet dwelt in the desert. He had the wisdom of Egypt, and the faith of a child. He was fitted for the city, and wandered in the wilderness. He was tempted with the pleasures of sin, and endured the hardships of virtue. He was backward in speech, and yet talked with God. He had the rod of a shepherd, and the power of the Infinite. He was a fugitive from Pharaoh, and an ambassador from heaven. He was the giver of the Law, and the forerunner of Grace.*

"He died alone on Mount Moab, and appeared with Christ in Judea. No man assisted at his funeral, yet God buried him."

THE FAITH OF JOCHEBED

Verses 2 through 4 read: *"And the woman conceived, and bear a son: and when she saw him that he was a goodly child, she hid him three months.*

"And when she could not longer hide him, she took for him an ark of bulrushes, and daubed it with slime and with pitch, and put the child therein; and she laid it in the flags by the river's brink.

"And his sister stood afar off, to wit what would be done to him."

That which stands out so vividly in this account is the faith of Jochebed, the mother of Moses.

I have no doubt that the Lord moved upon Jochebed from the time of the conception of Moses in her womb, in that she sensed that there was more here than meets the eye. And I believe that feeling not only persisted, but grew in intensity unto the time of her delivery. And when the child was born, she knew beyond the shadow of a doubt that there was something extensively unique about this baby, hence she would go to any length to save its life.

Not being successful in attempting to force the midwives to kill the boy babies when they were born, Pharaoh issued another edict, which demanded that all boy babies be drowned in the Nile River at the time of their birth.

As we follow the narrative throughout the Scriptures, we see that Satan does everything within his power to kill those who are truly called of God. Concerning Christ and Satan, the Scripture says: *"Forasmuch then as the children are partakers of flesh and blood, He* (Christ) *also Himself likewise took part of the same* (became flesh and blood); *that through death* (the Crucifixion) *He might destroy him who had the power of death, that is, the Devil"* (Heb. 2:14).

The death which Pharaoh demanded was typical of the eternal death which Satan brought upon the human race, as a result of the Fall.

THE POWER OF DEATH

What did Paul mean by the term *"the power of death,"* and that the Devil had this power?

Satan's power lies in the realm of sin. The Scripture says, *"the wages of sin is death"* (Rom. 6:23). Sin gives Satan the legal right to hold men in captivity, and which leads to spiritual death, which ultimately means eternal separation from God. In fact, the power of sin and death is so strong that before the Cross, every Saint of God who died, which includes all of the Old Testament Saints, did not go to Heaven, but rather were taken down into Paradise, in the heart of the Earth, and actually held captive there by Satan. While they were not over in the burning side of Hell, with a great gulf separating the Paradise side from the burning side (Lk. 16:26), still, they were held captive by the Evil One. In other words, the sin debt still hung over them, simply because the blood of bulls and goats could not take away sin, which is all that existed before the Cross, and I speak of the sacrificial system, which was a stopgap measure, until Christ would come (Heb. 10:4).

All the Old Testament Saints were waiting for Christ, Who had been promised, to become a partaker of flesh and blood, and we refer to the Incarnation, which perfect human body He would offer up in Sacrifice on the Cross, which would atone for all sin. When that happened, and it most definitely did happen, Jesus Christ then went down into Paradise, and the Scripture says, *"He led captivity captive, and gave gifts unto men"* (Eph. 4:8).

The term *"He led captivity captive"* is a strange term, but yet it holds a wealth of meaning. The word *"captivity"* refers to all the Old Testament Saints held in captivity by Satan, even though he could not put them into the burning side of Hell. But when Jesus died on the Cross, He then went down into Paradise, and liberated every single one of these individuals, thereby making them His captives, and took them with Him to Heaven. This was all because of the Cross, the price paid there, and thereby, all sin being atoned. Now when a Believer dies, and we speak of all time since the Cross, the Saint immediately goes to Heaven to be with Christ because there is no more sin debt hanging over the head of any Child of God (Phil. 1:23).

"Through death," which refers to the Crucifixion, Jesus destroyed Satan's power of death because all sin was atoned. While the wages of sin still is death, because of what Jesus did at the Cross, any person who comes to Christ, expressing faith in Him, can have every single sin washed away, which thereby destroys *"the power of death."*

THROUGH DEATH

And if it is to be noticed, it was *"through death"* that Jesus accomplished this, and not the Resurrection, or going down into the burning side of Hell and suffering there as a sinner, as some teach such foolishness! It was *"through death"* that Christ accomplished this great thing, which refers to the Cross, and the Cross alone.

So, the death that Pharaoh proposed was actually Satan's motif. But through this proposed death, the Lord would turn Pharaoh's edict into victory.

Jochebed hid baby Moses for three months, and incidentally, his name at the time was not Moses. We have no idea as to the name that Jochebed gave him, if any, because the name *"Moses"* was actually given to him by the Egyptian Princess who adopted him.

Led by the Holy Spirit, and evidencing Faith in God, and great Faith at that, she made a little ark for baby Moses, laid him in the ark, and pushed it out into the Nile, and told his sister Miriam to watch from a distance, as to what happened. I think that Jochebed had at least an inkling of knowledge as to what the Lord was going to do. I doubt that she understood it completely, but I believe the Lord told her exactly where to put the ark into the water, which was where the daughter of Pharaoh came to wash herself daily.

(5) "AND THE DAUGHTER OF PHARAOH CAME DOWN TO WASH HERSELF AT THE RIVER; AND HER MAIDENS WALKED ALONG BY THE RIVER'S SIDE; AND WHEN SHE SAW THE ARK AMONG THE FLAGS, SHE SENT HER MAID TO FETCH IT.

(6) "AND WHEN SHE HAD OPENED IT, SHE SAW THE CHILD: AND, BEHOLD, THE BABE WEPT. AND SHE HAD COMPASSION ON HIM, AND SAID, THIS IS ONE OF THE HEBREWS' CHILDREN.

(7) "THEN SAID HIS SISTER TO PHARAOH'S DAUGHTER, SHALL I GO AND CALL TO YOU A NURSE OF THE HEBREW WOMEN, THAT SHE MAY NURSE THE CHILD FOR YOU?

(8) "AND PHARAOH'S DAUGHTER SAID TO HER, GO. AND THE MAID WENT AND CALLED THE CHILD'S MOTHER.

(9) "AND PHARAOH'S DAUGHTER SAID UNTO HER, TAKE THIS CHILD AWAY, AND NURSE IT FOR ME, AND I WILL GIVE YOU YOUR WAGES. AND THE WOMAN TOOK THE CHILD, AND NURSED IT.

NOTES

(10) "AND THE CHILD GREW, AND SHE BROUGHT HIM UNTO PHARAOH'S DAUGHTER, AND HE BECAME HER SON. AND SHE CALLED HIS NAME MOSES: AND SHE SAID, BECAUSE I DREW HIM OUT OF THE WATER."

The exegesis is:

1. God is even in little things, and overrules them as well as great things to help forward His purposes.

2. Little did this Egyptian Princess think that day, as she walked by the river that the God of gods was directing her footsteps.

3. As someone has well said, God floated His Navies on the tears on a baby's cheek.

THE DAUGHTER OF PHARAOH

Verse 5 reads: *"And the daughter of Pharaoh came down to wash herself at the river; and her maidens walked along by the river's side; and when she saw the ark among the flags, she sent her maid to fetch it."*

The Holy Spirit worked all of this out, even down to the minute details. He told Jochebed exactly what to do, and had something in mind that Jochebed could not have possibly dreamed.

As we said in one of the headings, God works in little things, as well as He does in the great things. In fact, He takes little things, such as this before us, and turns it into great things. However, all that God does is by and large done according to the faith of an individual. God seldom works beyond or without our Faith. Jochebed had Faith. She heard the voice of the Lord, and she obeyed the voice of the Lord. All of this requires Faith.

The Holy Spirit had everything timed just right — the place, the person, and the progress. The little ark was floating among the flags where the Princess would bathe, and her eyes fell upon this which would prove to be such a major part in the great Kingdom of God — Moses.

TEARS

Verse 6 reads: *"And when she had opened it, she saw the child: and, behold, the babe wept. And she had compassion on him, and said, This is one of the Hebrews' children."*

The great Power of God that particular day, at least in this instance, was brought down to the tears on a baby's cheeks.

Concerning this moment, George Williams writes: *"Great events have hung upon a tear, but never greater than those which were brought to pass by the tears of this babe! The defeat of Satan, the Salvation of Israel and of the Nations, the trustworthiness of God's Word, and the Salvation of the world through an Incarnate Saviour — all these lay hidden in the tears that wetted that infant cheek upon that day."*

FAITH

Let's once again look at Faith as it regards the entirety of these actions, and especially that of Jochebed and her husband, Amram.

Though Faith vanquished fear as it regards this couple, yet lawful means were used to overcome danger: the mother *"hid"* the child, and later, had recourse to the ark. It is not Faith but fanaticism which deliberately courts danger. Faith never tempts God. Even Christ, though He knew full well of the Father's Will to preserve Him, yet withdrew from those who sought His life (Lk. 4:30; Jn. 8:59). It is not lack of Faith to avoid danger by legitimate precautions. It is no want of trust to employ means, even when assured by God of the event (Acts 27:31). Christ never supplied by a miracle when ordinary means were at hand (Mk. 5:43).

CIVIL AUTHORITIES

Another important truth which here receives illustration and exemplification is that Civil authorities are to be defied when their decrees are contrary to the expressed Word of God. The Word of God requires us to obey the laws of the land in which we live and exhorts us to be *"subject unto the powers that be"* (Rom., Chpt. 13), and this, no matter how wise and just, or how foolish and unjust those laws appear to us.

Yet, our obedience and submission to human authorities is plainly qualified. If a human government enacts a law and compliance with it by a Saint would compel him to disobey some command or precept of God, then the human must be rejected for the Divine. The cases of Moses' parents, of Daniel (Dan. 6:7-11), and of the Apostles (Acts 5:29), establishes this unequivocally. But if such rejection of human authority be necessitated, let it be performed not in the spirit of carnal defiance, but in the fear of God, and then the issue may safely be left with Him. It was *"by Faith"* the parents of Moses *"were not afraid of the king's commandment."* May Divine Grace work in us *"like precious faith"* which overcomes all fear of man.

(The author is indebted to Arthur W. Pink for the statement on *"Faith"* and *"Civil Authorities."*)

A NURSE

Verses 7 through 9 read: *"Then said his sister to Pharaoh's daughter, Shall I go and call to you a nurse of the Hebrew women, that she may nurse the child for you?*

"And Pharaoh's daughter said to her, Go. And the maid went and called the child's mother.

"And Pharaoh's daughter said unto her, Take this child away, and nurse it for me, and I will give you your wages. And the woman took the child, and nursed it."

Evidently the baby was beautiful, because immediately, the daughter of Pharaoh fell in love with the little fellow. Of course, we know the Lord had something to do with this as well.

At about the time that Pharaoh's daughter picked up the child, for she no doubt did so, Moses' sister Miriam, who had been standing nearby, asked those there if she could get one of the Hebrew women to nurse the child. Miriam as well was led by the Lord in this.

Pharaoh's daughter instantly agreed that this would be the thing to do, and told Miriam, with whom she was not acquainted, to go find a nurse. Guess what? Miriam went straight to her mother, who as well was the mother of the child, who immediately came to the river bank.

Pharaoh's daughter told her to take the child and care for it, and she would pay her wages to do so. Of course, she never dreamed that the lady to whom she gave the child was actually the child's mother.

So Jochebed would take care of baby Moses, and be paid by the State for doing so. I wonder what Satan thought of this? His plans to defeat the great Plan of God were foiled, with the Lord even playing a little trick on the Evil One. Getting the Court of Pharaoh, which had given instructions for the boy babies to be killed, to rather pay Jochebed to care for the child, presents itself not only as a defeat for Satan, but also an insult to the Evil One. I think from this we have to come to the conclusion that God also has a sense of humor.

Can you imagine what Satan said to the demon spirits who were supposed to have been attending the funeral of little Moses!

THE ARK

Though Moses was brought to the place of death, he was made secure in the ark. And this speaks to us of Christ, Who went down into death for us. The Righteousness of God made imperative the payment of sin's awful wages, and so his spotless Son *"died the just for the unjust that He might bring us to God"* (I Pet. 3:18).

It was *"faith"* which placed baby Moses in the ark, and it is *"Faith"* which identifies us with Christ. Again, just as Moses was brought out of the place of death, so when Christ rose again, we rose with Him (Rom. 6:3-5; Eph. 2:5-6).

As well, as the Heavenly Father arranged for the tender care of the baby, He as well arranges the same care for us.

All that took place that day were in no way chance happenings. All were designed by the Holy Spirit, as all are always designed by the Holy Spirit, at least as it regards those who follow the Lord. From this we can take a lesson as to how minutely the Lord leads and guides, how He plans every detail, and under Grace, we can be certain that His protection and care are certainly no less.

MOSES

Verse 10 reads: *"And the child grew, and she brought him unto Pharaoh's daughter, and he became her son. And she called his name Moses: and she said, Because I drew him out of the water."*

To show how little the Holy Spirit thought of the palace of Pharaoh, He in effect devotes one Verse to these years of Moses' life.

There are two Passages in the New Testament which throw a little light on Verse 10. In Acts 7:22 we read: *"And Moses was learned in all the wisdom of the Egyptians, and was mighty in words and in deeds."*

Josephus gives the following as it regards this particular time of Moses' life.

He tells us that the daughter of Pharaoh was named Thermuthis, and that she was married, but childless.

Josephus went on to say that when Moses was weaned, which was probably at four or five years old, Thermuthis then took him. At a point in time, she brought the child to her father and said, *"I am bringing up a beautiful, well-behaved child. Since I received him from the bounty of the river, I thought best to adopt him as my son and heir of your kingdom."* It is said that with that, she put the infant into his hands. Pharaoh took the child and kissed him, and playfully put his crown upon the little boy's head. But it is said that Moses threw it down to the ground and trod upon it with his feet in mere childishness.

However, as Josephus continues to relate, an Egyptian Scribe was nearby who saw this. He had earlier prophesied and foretold that a child would be born to the Hebrews who would reduce the dominion of Egypt. Upon seeing the little boy Moses trod upon the crown, the Scribe made a violent attempt to kill him. He cried out, *"This, O King, is that child we must kill to calm our terror! He shows it by treading upon your crown. Kill him, and deliver us from our fear, and thus deprive the Hebrews of the hope he inspires!"*

But Thermuthis stopped him, snatching the child away. Rather giving in to his daughter than the Scribe, Pharaoh passed it off as a joke. Moses was instead, educated with great care.

When grown to be a man, war broke out between the Egyptians and their neighbors, the Ethiopians. They fought a great battle, in which the Ethiopians were victorious, and they determined to conquer all of Egypt. Their armies invaded as far as Memphis and the Sea.

Overtaken by this calamity, the Egyptians turned to oracles and divinations. During this time, someone mentioned Moses and his great ability, and they were urged to seek his assistance, and even make him their general. So Pharaoh commanded his daughter to produce him, which she did.

She made her father swear he would not harm him, and then brought in Moses. But she reproached the priests who had previously advised to kill him, and were now not ashamed to ask his help.

Moses went out leading a great army, and he surprised the enemy before they knew he was coming. They expected that he would attack them by water, since the interior was difficult to traverse due to the vast number of poisonous snakes that infested that area. But Moses devised a marvelous strategy.

Joseph goes on to tell how he took baskets full of ibises, a bird that devours serpents and is their greatest enemy. As soon as he reached the infested region, he released the birds, and drove the serpents away. Moses then achieved his march and defeated the Ethiopians in a surprise attack. They fled Egypt, and were pursued by Moses into their own country and defeated again, to the extent that they were in danger of being reduced to slavery.

There is no Biblical proof of these happenings; however, it is quite possible that it happened as Josephus related.

There is another Passage in Hebrews which throws more light on Verse 10, which we will address momentarily.

THE NAME MOSES

The Egyptian form of the name *"Moses,"* was probably *"Mesu,"* which signifies, *"born, brought forth, child,"* and is derived from a root meaning, *"to produce, draw forth."* The Egyptian language has many roots common to it with Hebrew, whereof this is one.

The Princess' play upon words thus admitted of being literally rendered in the Hebrew — *"She called his name 'Mosheh,' which means, 'drawn forth'; because, she said, I drew him forth from the water."* Incidentally, the name *"Mesu"* is found on the monuments as an Egyptian name under the nineteenth dynasty. It could well be *"Moses."*

(11) "AND IT CAME TO PASS IN THOSE DAYS, WHEN MOSES WAS GROWN, THAT HE WENT OUT UNTO HIS BRETHREN, AND LOOKED ON THEIR BURDENS: AND HE SPIED AN EGYPTIAN SMITING AN HEBREW, ONE OF HIS BRETHREN.

(12) "AND HE LOOKED THIS WAY AND THAT WAY, AND WHEN HE SAW THAT THERE WAS NO MAN, HE SLEW THE EGYPTIAN, AND HID HIM IN THE SAND.

(13) "AND WHEN HE WENT OUT THE SECOND DAY, BEHOLD, TWO MEN OF THE HEBREWS STROVE TOGETHER: AND HE SAID TO HIM THAT DID WRONG, WHEREFORE DID YOU SMITE YOUR FELLOW?

(14) "AND HE SAID, WHO MADE YOU A PRINCE AND A JUDGE OVER US? DO YOU INTEND TO KILL ME, AS YOU KILLED THE EGYPTIAN? AND MOSES FEARED, AND SAID, SURELY THIS THING IS KNOWN.

(15) "NOW WHEN PHARAOH HEARD THIS THING, HE SOUGHT TO SLAY MOSES. BUT MOSES FLED FROM THE FACE OF PHARAOH, AND DWELT IN THE LAND OF MIDIAN: AND HE SAT DOWN BY A WELL."

The synopsis is:

1. From the language of Hebrews 11:24, it is clear that a time came when Moses had the choice of accepting or refusing the throne of Egypt. He refused, and cast in his lot with the hated and oppressed Hebrews.

2. Moved by indignation, compassion, and a consciousness of personal fitness for the enterprise, he resolved to deliver from their cruel bondage. But God cannot give victories to the *"flesh"*; and Moses must spend 40 long years as a shepherd in the deserts of Arabia, in order to fit him to be a shepherd to Israel.

3. An important principle appears in this Chapter. It is that providence and faith must not be confounded. Providence gave Moses (the Palace) what faith taught him to surrender.

4. Earthly wisdom counseled him to use his position in the Egyptian Court as a means for liberating his people. This would have spared him much affliction; but it would have recognized Pharaoh's lordship, and wholly fail to separate Israel from Egypt and

bring her into fellowship with, and dependence upon, God.

THE FLESH

Verses 11 through 13 read: *"And it came to pass in those days, when Moses was grown, that he went out unto his brethren, and looked on their burdens: and he spied an Egyptian smiting an Hebrew, one of his brethren.*

"And he looked this way and that way, and when he saw that there was no man, he slew the Egyptian, and hid him in the sand.

"And when he went out the second day, behold, two men of the Hebrews strove together: and he said to him who did the wrong, Wherefore did you smite your fellow?"

Moses has now come to the place to where he must make a decision. The result of his faith is described in Hebrews 11:24-26: *"By faith Moses, when he was come to years, refused to be called the son of Pharaoh's daughter; choosing rather to suffer affliction with the people of God, than to enjoy the pleasures of sin for a season; esteeming the reproach of Christ greater riches than the treasures in Egypt: for he had respect unto the recompense of the reward."*

Josephus further tells us that Pharaoh had no other children, and that his daughter, Thermuthis, had no children of her own. So most probably Moses would have succeeded to the throne.

Were this scene transported to the present day, I can well imagine what the counsel would be to Moses as it regards the modern Church.

Most, I am certain, would definitely tell Moses that he could do far more for God by remaining in the Palace of Pharaoh, and even becoming Pharaoh, than he could otherwise. The modern Church sells out for far less, so I cannot see the modern Church telling Moses to do what he actually did do. He refused to be called the son of Pharaoh's daughter, which means that he refused the throne of Egypt.

While God was dealing with him about all of this, still, it was Moses who had to ultimately make the decision as to what he would do.

The account of him killing the Egyptian who was smiting the Hebrew is not meant to claim that Moses, at that time, was trying to deliver his people. He was merely trying to address an injustice; however, he was trying to do it in the wrong way, i.e., *"the flesh."*

WHAT DO WE MEAN BY *"THE FLESH"*?

Paul used the term very often. He said: *"So then they who are in the flesh cannot please God"* (Rom. 8:8).

The *"flesh"* pertains to our own personal strength, ability, talent, efforts, etc. Paul described that as *"walking after the flesh"* (Rom. 8:1).

"Walking after the Spirit," pertains to placing our Faith and trust in Christ, and what He did for us at the Cross, within which boundaries the Holy Spirit works (Rom. 8:1-2, 11). In other words, the Holy Spirit charts the course, guides us, shows us, and then we are to be careful to do exactly what He tells us to do.

The *"flesh"* pertains to doing things without being led of the Lord, depending on our own strength and ability, etc. While the motives may be right, the end result of such an effort will never turn out to be right. It is only that which God does, which means that He has planned it, directed it, and carried it out, and done so through us, that He can honor.

THE CROSS OF CHRIST AND THE FLESH

When Believers read Romans 8:1, we definitely do not want to *"walk after the flesh,"* but rather to *"Walk after the Spirit."* But the trouble is, most Believers don't know how to do that. They think that doing spiritual things constitutes *"walking after the Spirit."* It doesn't!

It is impossible for any Believer to *"walk after the Spirit,"* without that Believer properly understanding the Cross. The Holy Spirit works exclusively within the boundaries of the legal work of the Cross of Christ, in other words, what Jesus did at the Cross, all on our behalf. Listen again to Paul:

"For the Law of the Spirit of Life in Christ Jesus, has made me free from the law of sin and death" (Rom. 8:2).

In this one Verse of Scripture, we are told how the Holy Spirit works.

All of this is so ironclad, that it is referred to by the Spirit of God through Paul as a *"Law."* This refers to a Law which was devised in eternity past by the Godhead. It is *"The Law of the Spirit of Life,"* which refers to all the things the Holy Spirit does.

It goes back to the statement made by Christ at the Feast of Tabernacles. He said: *"If any man thirst, let him come unto Me, and drink.*

"He who believes on Me, as the Scripture has said, out of his innermost being shall flow rivers of living water."

John then added: *"But this spake He of the Spirit, which they who believe on Him should receive"* (Jn. 7:37-39).

The idea is this: All that Jesus paid for at the Cross is made available to us by and through the Holy Spirit, which demands our Faith in Christ and what He did for us at the Cross.

However, this *"Law"* is *"in Christ Jesus,"* which means that it is all based on what Christ did for us in His Finished Work. This means that the Holy Spirit will not work outside of these boundaries. The drawn parameters are those which incorporate what Christ did at the Cross regarding His Finished Work. The Cross gives the Holy Spirit the legal right to do all the things He does.

That's the reason that we must exhibit Faith in Christ and the Cross at all times. In fact, the following will help you. It is a short formula that possibly may make it easier to understand.

THE CROSS

The Believer is to understand that everything we receive from the Lord is made possible to us by Christ and what Christ did for us at the Cross. Everything comes to us through that Finished Work.

OUR FAITH

Understanding that everything comes to us through the Cross, it is demanded of the Believer that he evidence Faith in Christ and the Cross at all times. In other words, the Cross of Christ must ever be the object of one's Faith.

THE HOLY SPIRIT

Understanding that the Cross provides the means by which God gives all things to us, and that our Faith must ever be in that Finished Work, the Holy Spirit will then do great and mighty things with us, of us, through us, and in us.

This little short diagram that I've given you is God's prescribed order for a victorious, overcoming, Christian life (Rom. 6:3-5, 11, 14; 8:1-2, 11; I Cor. 1:17-18, 21, 23; 2:2, 5; Gal. 6:14; Eph. 2:13-18; Col. 2:14-15).

So Moses will try to defend the Hebrews by killing an Egyptian. It was a work of the flesh, and as all works of the flesh, it could have nothing but disastrous consequences.

PHARAOH AND MOSES

Verses 14 and 15 read: *"And he said, Who made you a prince and a judge over us? Do you intend to kill me, as you killed the Egyptian? And Moses feared, and said, Surely this thing is known.*

"Now when Pharaoh heard this thing, he sought to kill Moses. But Moses fled from the face of Pharaoh, and dwelt in the land of Midian: and he sat down by a well."

Quoting Josephus again, it seems that the Egyptians, from the throne down, were envious of Moses, and partly afraid of him. They thought, due to his great success in defeating the Ethiopians, that he might take advantage of his good fortune and try to subvert their government. So, when Moses, in defending the Hebrew, killed an Egyptian, this was the proverbial straw that broke the camel's back. Pharaoh then prepared to kill Moses. Learning that there were plots against him, Moses secretly escaped across the desert, since the roads were patrolled.

The next day after killing the Egyptian, he saw two Hebrews fighting among themselves, and proceeded to stop the scuffle. One of the Hebrews said to him, *"Who made you a prince and a judge over us? Do you intend to kill me, as you killed the Egyptian?"*

Realizing that his secret was out, Moses fled Egypt, and not a minute too soon. If Moses had any thoughts of delivering the Children of Israel at this particular time, to be sure, they were now placed on the back burner. He was fleeing for his life.

At any rate, it was not God's time at the present, and for several reasons. Moses wasn't ready, not even close to being ready, and neither were the Israelites ready to be delivered.

MOSES IN THE PALACE

There are some who claim, actually many, that the some 35 years that Moses spent in the palace (probably taken to the palace when he was about five), was a part of his education, which would greatly help him in delivering Israel some 40 years after leaving the palace.

We do know that it was God's Will that Moses spend this amount of time there, but I seriously doubt that all the education he received from the Egyptians did him any stead whatsoever, as it regards the work for which God had called him to do. In the first place, everything that Moses did in delivering these people, and even their 40-year trek through the wilderness, were all designed by God, down to the minute detail. I speak of organization, supply, discipline, etc. In fact, there is no record that Moses ever used any of his Egyptian education in this endeavor. So if in fact that is the case, what purpose was the long stay in the Palace, and all the educational process?

For the task that lay ahead for Moses, at least that which God had called him to do, total and complete consecration would be required. As someone has well said, *"Great Faith must be tested greatly."*

I can well see that the Lord would have Moses go through these many years of education and training, and especially the throne of Egypt his for the taking, which in effect would make him at least one of, if not the most powerful man in the world, in order to test him as to his consecration. We know what his decision was: *"By Faith Moses, when he was come to years, refused to be called the son of Pharaoh's daughter"* (Heb. 11:24). So we know that Moses had to make this decision.

Considering the task that Moses had before him, it would take an unparalleled consecration, with him completely and totally turning his back on the world, even the best the world had to offer. The Lord had to have that type of consecration. So that's the reason, I think, that the Lord allowed all of these years in the Palace of Pharaoh, and even the offer of the throne.

(16) "NOW THE PRIEST OF MIDIAN HAD SEVEN DAUGHTERS: AND THEY CAME AND DREW WATER, AND FILLED THE TROUGHS TO WATER THEIR FATHER'S FLOCK.

(17) "AND THE SHEPHERDS CAME AND DROVE THEM AWAY: BUT MOSES STOOD UP AND HELPED THEM, AND WATERED THEIR FLOCK.

(18) "AND WHEN THEY CAME TO REUEL THEIR FATHER, HE SAID, HOW IS IT THAT YOU ARE COME SO SOON TODAY?

(19) "AND THEY SAID, AN EGYPTIAN DELIVERED US OUT OF THE HAND OF THE SHEPHERDS, AND ALSO DREW WATER ENOUGH FOR US, AND WATERED THE FLOCK.

(20) "AND HE SAID UNTO HIS DAUGHTERS, AND WHERE IS HE? WHY IS IT THAT YOU HAVE LEFT THE MAN? CALL HIM, THAT HE MAY EAT BREAD.

(21) "AND MOSES WAS CONTENT TO DWELL WITH THE MAN: AND HE GAVE MOSES ZIPPORAH HIS DAUGHTER.

(22) "AND SHE BEAR HIM A SON, AND HE CALLED HIS NAME GERSHOM: FOR HE SAID, I HAVE BEEN A STRANGER IN A STRANGE LAND."

The diagram is:

1. Moses, like Joseph, was rejected by his brethren; but, like Joseph, he continued to love them.

2. The priest of Midian had three names, Reuel, Jethro, and Raguel. This latter name means, *"a friend of God."* He was a descendant of Abraham by Keturah. He no doubt, like Job and Melchizedek, was king and priest to his tribe. He was a worshiper of the True God.

3. Moses is about to begin his true education of 40 years duration. Some have said that it took about 40 hours to get Moses out of Egypt, but about 40 years to get Egypt out of Moses.

MIDIAN

Verses 16 through 22 read: *"Now the priest of Midian had seven daughters: and they came and drew water, and filled the troughs to water their father's flock.*

"And the shepherds came and drove them away: but Moses stood up and helped them, and watered their flock.

"And when they came to Reuel their father, he said, How is it that you are come so soon today?

"And they said, An Egyptian delivered us out of the hand of the shepherds, and also drew water enough for us, and watered the flock.

"And he said unto his daughters, And where is he? Why is it that you have left the man? Call him, that he may eat bread.

"And Moses was content to dwell with the man: and he gave Moses Zipporah his daughter.

"And she bear him a son, and he called his name Gershom: for he said, I have been a stranger in a strange land."

For most all of his boyhood, and all of his adult life, Moses had enjoyed the luxury, the splendor, the grandeur, and the greatness of the Egyptian Court. But now, he is reduced to penury, for it seems that he left Egypt with nothing.

Moses is a Type of Christ in many ways. As Moses came from grandeur to nothing, so did Christ. He left the hallowed halls of Heaven, to come down here to this sin-benighted world.

We must assume that the Lord led Moses to Jethro (Reuel), and that Zipporah was destined to be his wife. But yet, Zipporah didn't prove to be as close to Moses as she should have been. There were serious problems there, which will later show up. In fact, the future will show that his son did not turn out too well either, and possibly because of the influence of the boy's mother.

How much grief this caused Moses, we have no way of knowing; however, it is for certain that these situations were not taken lightly, especially considering the heavy load which he had to carry regarding the Call of God on his life.

How blessed a man is, and especially a Preacher, to have a Godly wife, who will stand with him shoulder to shoulder, both pulling together to carry out the great Work of God. But Moses didn't really have that.

(23) "AND IT CAME TO PASS IN PROCESS OF TIME, THAT THE KING OF EGYPT DIED: AND THE CHILDREN OF ISRAEL SIGHED BY REASON OF THE BONDAGE, AND THEY CRIED, AND THEIR CRY CAME UP UNTO GOD BY REASON OF THE BONDAGE.

(24) "AND GOD HEARD THEIR GROANING, AND GOD REMEMBERED HIS COVENANT WITH ABRAHAM, WITH ISAAC, AND WITH JACOB.

(25) "AND GOD LOOKED UPON THE CHILDREN OF ISRAEL AND GOD HAD RESPECT UNTO THEM."

The structure is:

1. The pressure from Egypt is now becoming so hard and so difficult on the Israelites that they are now ready to leave. To be frank, they would in no way have left Egypt had the blessings continued as it was during the time of Joseph. At times, the Lord has to allow difficulties, in order for us to become willing to do His Will.

2. It was now time for the Covenant, which God had made with Abraham, Isaac, and Jacob, regarding the land of Canaan, to be fulfilled. God always keeps His Promises.

3. God looked upon the Children of Israel, exactly as He looks upon all Believers.

4. The glorious Name *"Elohim"* occurs five times in Verses 23-25. As yet, He was not yet known to Israel as *"Jehovah."* Five is the number of Grace. No moral excellence in the Children of Israel attracted God's love; it was their misery that drew out His heart to them.

5. A. He *"heard"* their groaning.
   B. He *"remembered"* His Covenant.
   C. He *"looked"* upon them.
   D. He had *"respect"* unto them.

THE CRY OF THE CHILDREN OF ISRAEL

Verse 23 reads: *"And it came to pass in process of time, that the king of Egypt died: and the Children of Israel sighed by reason of the bondage, and they cried, and their cry came up unto God by reason of the bondage."*

Moses had now been in Midian, and actually the backside of the desert, for some 40 years. Except for the last days in this place, which gives us the account of the burning bush, the Scriptures are silent regarding this time.

Verses 23 through 25 portray the misery and bondage of the Children of Israel. It is not clear here how much the Israelites were conscious of God, or whether they had almost forgotten Him. We do know that it was God Who took the initiative in their deliverance in view of His Covenants and Promises to their fathers.

As well, it is God Who takes the initiative in our Salvation. Many people proclaim, *"I found the Lord,"* when in reality, *"The Lord found them."*

Perhaps a few in Israel knew God, but as a whole, the enslaved nation was in apostasy and rebellion. So, God did not deliver them on the face of their merit, because they had none; He delivered them solely because of His Grace, His Love, and His Promises. Likewise, God does not save us because we merit Salvation, but He does so because He loves us, and because He has promised Redemption.

The Scripture says that the Children of Israel were *"sighing by reason of the bondage,"* and as a result, *"they cried."* But it doesn't say that they were crying to God. They were just crying, *"by reason of the bondage."*

God heard their cries, exactly as He hears our cries. He is never unaware of our situation, irrespective as to what the situation might be. We are His children, bought with a price, the price in fact, which was paid by Christ at the Cross of Calvary.

If He heard their cry, even though they were not necessarily crying to Him, how much more does He hear our cries, when we truly cry to Him!

THE COVENANT

Verses 24 and 25 read: *"And God heard their groaning, and God remembered His Covenant with Abraham, with Isaac, and with Jacob.*

"And God looked upon the Children of Israel, and God had respect unto them."

As we've already stated, all of the initiative is on the part of God. There is no record that any of the Children of Israel at this particular time, truly and sincerely sought the face of the Lord concerning their particular situation. The Faith that Jochebed and Amram evidenced seems to be little in evidence at this particular time. Forty years from their day unto the time in question have taken their deadly toll, spiritually speaking. While the Lord is remembered, and not totally strange to them, there was very little faith. And that's what it always comes down to, faith, or a lack of faith.

However, God had made a Covenant with Abraham, Isaac, and Jacob. He had promised the land of Canaan to their seed, and God always keeps His Promises. And yet, only two of the adults, as it regards this particular generation, and I speak of the ones who came out of Egypt, actually went into the Promised Land. Those two were Joshua and Caleb, and it was because of their Faith.

The Children of Israel became so burdened down with oppression that they were ready to be delivered, but they were not ready to obey God in the wilderness. In fact, their lack of Faith kept them out of the Promised Land.

But as God looked upon the Children of Israel in Egypt, He had respect unto them simply because they were the seed of Abraham, Isaac, and Jacob. In essence, the Faith of these three would deliver this multitude, even though they had long since been dead. But borrowed faith can go just so far. When initiative is needed, it must be the Faith of the individual, and not that borrowed from someone else. Regrettably, Israel lacked such faith, even as we shall see in later study.

"Alas, and did my Saviour bleed?
"And did my Sovereign die?
"Would He devote that sacred head
"For such a worm as I?"

"Was it for sins that I had done
"He groaned upon the tree?
"Amazing pity! Grace unknown!
"And love beyond degree!"

"Well might the sun in darkness hide,
"And shut his glories in,
"When Christ, the mighty Maker died
"For man, the creature's sin."

"Thus might I hide my shamed face
"While His dear Cross appears,
"Dissolve my heart in thankfulness,
"And melt my eyes to tears."

"But drops of grief can never repay
"The debt of love I owe:
"Here, Lord, I give myself to Thee;
"'Tis all that I can do."

CHAPTER 3

(1) "NOW MOSES KEPT THE FLOCK OF JETHRO HIS FATHER IN LAW, THE PRIEST OF MIDIAN: AND HE LED THE FLOCK TO THE BACKSIDE OF THE DESERT, AND CAME TO THE MOUNTAIN OF GOD, EVEN TO HOREB.

(2) "AND THE ANGEL OF THE LORD APPEARED UNTO HIM IN A FLAME OF FIRE OUT OF THE MIDST OF A BUSH: AND HE LOOKED, AND, BEHOLD, THE BUSH BURNED WITH FIRE, AND THE BUSH WAS NOT CONSUMED.

(3) "AND MOSES SAID, I WILL NOW TURN ASIDE, AND SEE THIS GREAT SIGHT, WHY THE BUSH IS NOT BURNT.

(4) "AND WHEN THE LORD SAW THAT HE TURNED ASIDE TO SEE, GOD CALLED UNTO HIM OUT OF THE MIDST OF THE BUSH, AND SAID, MOSES, MOSES. AND HE SAID, HERE AM I."

The composition is:

1. The First Verse tells us so very much about the Ways of God. What God would do with Moses was not learned in the palaces of Egypt, but was learned at *"the backside of the desert."*

2. Forty years of the desert was needed to humble the strength of the *"flesh,"* and to destroy its hope. The possible king of Egypt was now an obscure shepherd.

3. The *"backside of the desert"* is not exactly where most people would aspire to be; however, it was here that the Lord appeared to Moses.

THE BACKSIDE OF THE DESERT

Verse 1 reads: *"Now Moses kept the flock of Jethro his father in law, the priest of Midian: and he led the flock to the backside of the desert, and came to the mountain of God, even to Horeb."*

God not only gave to Moses the faith that led him to identify himself with His people, but also endowed him with the power to deliver them; however, 40 years in the desert was needed to humble the strength of the *"flesh"* and destroy its hope. The latter, and we speak of deliverance, was far more difficult than the former, i.e., *"identification."* It is the same presently.

Identification with Christ is not all that difficult. In fact, untold millions clamor to experience such identification; however, at first they think it's an identification with His miracle-working power, His Person of Deity, His great glory. And that it is; however, for the hope of the flesh to be destroyed, we must as well identify with Him in His Crucifixion, which alone can bring about deliverance. Now read those words carefully, because they are very, very important!

It cost Moses something to identify with his people, but much more to identify with their deliverance.

THE CROSS

That's why the Cross, with which we must identify, is such an offence (Gal. 5:11).

Why is the Cross an offence?

It is an offence because it demands total surrender to Christ, completely trusting in what Christ did at the Cross, all on our behalf. The Cross tells us how evil and wicked that man actually is, and how wonderful and good that God actually is. Man doesn't want to admit either! To admit that he is so bad that he cannot save himself rubs him the wrong way. To admit that God Alone can save us, and that He had to do such by the means of a Cross, and because we were so evil, doesn't set well either.

When Moses identified with Christ, in preference to Egypt, for that's exactly what he did, as stated, there was a price tag attached to that. The Scripture says that he *"esteemed the reproach of Christ greater riches than the treasures in Egypt"* (Heb. 11:26). But what he then experienced was nothing by comparison to what he experienced regarding preparation for deliverance. Even though his identification was proper, he had to be delivered himself, before the Children of Israel could experience deliverance by his hand.

This process was long, slow, hard, and

tedious. And it was not that any of that earned him anything, but simply that the *"flesh"* dies hard. And to be sure, it must totally and completely die, before deliverance can come, and thereby others be delivered as well.

DELIVERANCE FROM WHAT?

The deliverance, whether of Moses or any other Believer, is always in one capacity, *"deliverance from the flesh."* As we've stated, all hope of the flesh must die. *"Self"* is our biggest problem. As someone has well said, Jesus died on the Cross, not only to save us from sin, but as well from self.

When we think of deliverance, almost always, we think of deliverance from particular vices or sins, etc. While that definitely may be the case, and in fact may be necessary, that is never the center of real deliverance. It is the flesh from which we must be delivered, which refers to dependence on self. When that is done, and done completely, then the other problems will melt away.

And how can that be done?

There's only one way, and that is by Faith in Christ, and what Christ has done for us at the Cross. It is to the Cross that we must come in order to be delivered from the work of the flesh. And it is at the Cross that we must remain, after we're delivered from the work of the flesh.

By the term *"the mountain of God,"* Sinai seems to be meant. The phrase, *"even to Horeb,"* should have been translated, *"even toward Horeb."*

MORE ABOUT THE BACKSIDE OF THE DESERT

This position in which Moses now finds himself, and 40 years at that, was a position in which he was placed by the Lord. The manner in which the Lord teaches us is totally different from the ways of the world. Self had to be humbled, and all hope of the flesh had to die.

I believe that Moses sensed the Call of God on his life as it regards the deliverance of the Israelites, and the great part he would play in this process. How much the Lord had related to him up to now, we aren't told. Those 40 years are all but silent; however, as silent as they may have been, much was taking place. Moses was being prepared for the greatest task, at least up to that time, which any man had ever known. Due to interaction with Pharaoh and the nobles of Egypt, it was even more demanding than God had asked of Noah.

One of the great problems with most modern Preachers is they have had no *"backside of the desert"* experience. They've been trained by everyone and everything, except God.

WHAT TYPE OF PREPARATION WAS REQUIRED?

Mere human wisdom and learning, however valuable in themselves, can never constitute anyone a servant of God, nor equip him for any department of Divine service. Such things may qualify unrenewed nature to figure before the world; but the man whom God will use must be endowed with widely-different qualifications — such qualifications as can alone be found in the deep and hallowed retirement of the Lord's Presence.

All God's servants have been made to know and experience the truth of these statements. Moses at Horeb, Elijah at Cherith, Ezekiel at Chebar, Paul in Arabia, and John at Patmos, are all striking examples of the immense practical importance of being alone with God. When we look at the Son of God, we find that the time He spent in private was nearly ten times as long as that which He spent in public. He, though perfect in understanding and in will, spent nearly 30 years in the obscurity of a carpenter's house at Nazareth ere He made His appearance in public. And even when He had entered upon His public service, how oft did He retreat from the gaze of men, to enjoy the sweet and sacred retirement of the Divine Presence! (Mackintosh).

The training that is required is the abnegation of *"self,"* and the laying aside of the *"flesh."* On the surface that seems so simple, but in reality, it is not simple at all. It took 40 years for this thing to be brought about in Moses, over 20 years for David, several years for Paul. . . .

It was much more difficult in Old Testament times for this work of the Spirit to be brought about in these hearts and lives, than it is now. The Cross has made it possible for the Holy Spirit to take up abode permanently within our hearts and lives, which gives all Believers since the Cross a tremendous advantage. But still, it's not something that's done instantly.

Due to the Fall, the lingering affects remain in the hearts and lives of even the most ardent Believers. There is a strong inclination to promote *"self,"* in which climate Christ cannot work.

The only way that such victory can be brought about in any heart and life, whether Old Testament times, or New Testament times, is that the Believer look exclusively to the Cross. It was much more difficult in Old Testament times because the Cross was a prophetical happening, in other words something that would take place in the future. Inasmuch as that great Work had not yet been accomplished, its effectiveness was extremely limited, as would be obvious. But now that we look to a historical Cross, which speaks of a Finished Work, it is a much more simple process.

A proper understanding of the Cross brings about humility within the heart and life, and in fact, it is the Cross alone which can bring about this Work of the Spirit. The Believer is to ever make the Cross the object of his Faith, and then the Holy Spirit can perform His Work, which refers to dealing with the adverse situations in our hearts and lives. Once again, we're speaking of *"self"* and the *"flesh."* In fact, without a proper understanding of the Cross, it is literally impossible for these particular Works of the Spirit to be brought about. The Cross is God's Way, and if we attempt some other way, we automatically abrogate the help of the Holy Spirit; consequently, nothing can really be accomplished in our lives.

But irrespective of the hang-ups, idiosyncrasies, problems, difficulties, hindrances, weaknesses, perversions, or whatever other problem we might think of, the Holy Spirit can deal with that problem, if our Faith is properly placed, and I continue to speak of the Cross. Jesus addressed, at the Cross, every single problem that besets humanity. He excluded none!

THE BURNING BUSH

Verse 2 reads: *"And the Angel of the LORD appeared to him in a flame of fire out of the midst of a bush: and he looked, and, behold, the bush burned with fire, and the bush was not consumed."*

The *"Angel of the Lord"* mentioned here is, in actuality, the Lord Himself.

The flame of fire in the lowly desert bush was an emblem of the Deity and Humanity of Christ. The *"fire"* pertained to the Deity, and the lowly bush pertained to the Humanity of Christ. But yet the *"fire"* did not consume the *"bush."*

As another issue, this is a perfect example of the Holy Spirit functioning in the heart and life of the Believer. While the Spirit is doing what needs to be done, and irrespective as to how hard it might be, there is no danger of the *"bush,"* i.e., *"you and me,"* being consumed. But when we try to do the work by the strength of the flesh, we will soon experience burnout. So how do we come to this place of the fire burning brightly, but not consuming us?

WALKING AFTER THE SPIRIT

In Romans 8:1, Paul mentioned, *"walking after the Spirit,"* which of course refers to the Holy Spirit. This simply means that the Spirit of God is leading and guiding us, and as well, functioning within us, in order that the Work of God may be properly carried out. Once again, we go back to the Cross.

"Walking after the Spirit" is not us doing something which we think is spiritual. No matter how spiritual it might be, whatever is happening in that capacity constitutes the flesh. Let the Reader understand this:

It is never what we do, but rather what we believe. And of course, if we *"believe"* correctly, we will *"do"* correctly. Listen to Paul:

"For in Jesus Christ neither circumcision availeth anything, nor uncircumcision; but faith which worketh by love" (Gal. 5:6).

And then: *"But without faith it is impossible to please Him"* (Heb. 11:6).

And once more: *"Therefore being justified by faith . . ."* (Rom. 5:1).

We keep trying to bring about things by *"doing,"* and because we are *"walking after the flesh"* (Rom. 8:1). We can only bring about the desired result, by believing properly. This means that we must have the correct object of Faith.

THE OBJECT OF OUR FAITH

Every human being in the world has faith. Unfortunately, it's not the type of faith, at least for the far greater majority, which God will recognize; nevertheless, all have faith. Even the atheist who claims he doesn't have any faith, in fact does, because he has faith in his lack of faith, etc.

So the question isn't Faith. The question is, *"the correct object of faith!"*

There is only one correct object of faith, while there are untold millions of incorrect objects. That one correct object is *"Christ and Him Crucified"* (I Cor. 1:17-18, 21, 23; 2:2, 5; Col. 2:14-15; Gal. 5:1-2, 4; 6:14).

In this manner, and this manner alone, will the fire burn within our lives, without consuming the bush.

When Frances and I began in Evangelistic Work in 1956, for years I heard Preachers speaking of *"burnout."* Countless times, Preachers would ask me if I had a hobby. This was supposed to be the answer to burnout.

No, that's no answer at all. It is the *"flesh"* attempting to throttle the *"flesh,"* which of course, will never work. The answer is the Cross, and the answer alone is the Cross.

Serving in Evangelistic Work for many years, and having the opportunity to be around many Preachers, I witnessed many who experienced nervous breakdowns, emotional disturbances, in other words, *"burnout."* It was then said of them as to how they had burned themselves out for Christ, in other words, they had worked so hard for the Lord that they had overdone the situation, etc.

No, that was not their problem. Their problem was functioning in the flesh, which means they were not functioning in the Spirit. And how do I know that?

In the first place, were they functioning in the Spirit, no matter how brightly the fire burned, it would never consume the bush. In fact, it invigorates the man, instead of tearing him down. It's our own efforts of the flesh which bring about emotional disturbances, problems, difficulties, etc. It's trying to do what we cannot do, and which God never intended for us to do because Jesus has already done it.

MOSES, MOSES

Verses 3 and 4 read: *"And Moses said, I will now turn aside, and see this great sight, why the bush is not burnt.*

"And when the LORD saw that he turned aside to see, God called unto him out of the midst of the bush, and said, Moses, Moses. And he said, Here am I."

God Who said *"Moses, Moses,"* is the same One Who said, *"Martha, Martha,"* *"Simon, Simon,"* *"Saul, Saul,"* and also, *"Samuel, Samuel."* It was the same voice that said, *"I have surely seen,"* and *"I have heard,"* and *"I know,"* and *"I am come down to deliver,"* and *"I am come to bring up."*

In a sense, everything that God does is in the form of a miracle. That's the reason faith is required. And that's the reason, or at least one of the reasons, that *"self"* and the *"flesh"* have to be abrogated, or rather properly placed in Christ.

As we see here, God does not function as does anything else. His Ways are not our ways, and it takes faith to comprehend His Ways. So now Moses will turn aside to see the bush that is burning, but yet is not consumed, and now out of the midst of the bush, God will speak to the man.

Nothing can be more interesting or instructive than the mode in which Jehovah was pleased to reveal Himself to Moses. He was about to furnish him with his commission to lead forth His people out of Egypt. And He will reveal Himself as a flame of fire. And as someone has well said, *"Any old bush will do."*

(5) "AND HE SAID, DRAW NOT NIGH HITHER: PUT OFF YOUR SHOES FROM OFF YOUR FEET, FOR THE PLACE WHEREON YOU STAND IS HOLY GROUND.

(6) "MOREOVER HE SAID, I AM THE GOD OF YOUR FATHER, THE GOD OF ABRAHAM, THE GOD OF ISAAC, AND THE GOD OF JACOB. AND MOSES HID HIS FACE; FOR HE WAS AFRAID TO LOOK UPON GOD.

(7) "AND THE LORD SAID, I HAVE SURELY SEEN THE AFFLICTION OF MY PEOPLE WHICH ARE IN EGYPT, AND

HAVE HEARD THEIR CRY BY REASON OF THEIR TASKMASTERS; FOR I KNOW THEIR SORROWS;

(8) "AND I AM COME DOWN TO DELIVER THEM OUT OF THE HAND OF THE EGYPTIANS, AND TO BRING THEM UP OUT OF THAT LAND UNTO A GOOD LAND AND A LARGE, UNTO A LAND FLOWING WITH MILK AND HONEY; UNTO THE PLACE OF THE CANAANITES, AND THE HITTITES, AND THE AMORITES, AND THE PERIZZITES, AND THE HIVITES, AND THE JEBUSITES.

(9) "NOW THEREFORE, BEHOLD, THE CRY OF THE CHILDREN OF ISRAEL HAS COME UNTO ME: AND I HAVE ALSO SEEN THE OPPRESSION WHEREWITH THE EGYPTIANS OPPRESS THEM.

(10) "COME NOW THEREFORE, AND I WILL SEND YOU UNTO PHARAOH, THAT YOU MAY BRING FORTH MY PEOPLE THE CHILDREN OF ISRAEL OUT OF EGYPT."

The construction is:

1. Wherever God is, that place is holy. And it's holy only as long as God is there.

2. Any time the Lord appears, and for any reason, it is always for a purpose. And I think it can be said without fear of exaggeration, that purpose, in one way or the other, is always deliverance. It was time for the Children of Israel to be delivered.

3. And whatever it is that He is to do, God always uses people. Moses will be His instrument at this present time.

4. As well, that which He assigns to His human instrument is always impossible in the natural. In other words, the person must have God and His Power, in order to accomplish the task.

HOLY GROUND

Verse 5 reads: *"And He said, Do not come near: put off your shoes from off your feet, for the place whereon you stand is holy ground."*

The ground was rendered holy by the Presence of God upon it.

Moses was born to be Israel's deliverer, and yet he does not receive his commission until he is 80 years of age. His commission is about to be given. It begins with a *"burning bush,"* which incidentally was not consumed because the fire was of the Presence of God, and then a voice out of that fire.

The very first admonition given to Moses by God is for him to be aware of the Holiness of the place because, as stated, God was there. So his commission starts out with Holiness.

Men oftentimes get the situation backwards. It was not the place that was holy, for there was nothing holy about it. It was God Who made the place holy by His Presence. It is holy only as long as the Lord is there.

Due to the fact that every true Believer is a temple of the Holy Spirit, this means that every true Believer is holy, but only because of the Presence of the Lord. If we do not understand this, and treat this Holiness with contempt, the Scripture says: *"If any man defile the temple of God, him shall God destroy; for the temple of God is holy, which temple you are"* (I Cor. 3:16-17).

This is what makes the New Covenant of such great advantage over the Old Covenant. That which we are reading concerning Moses, and the Lord speaking to him, etc., is in fact a constant thing, with Believers under the new Covenant. Incidentally, the privilege of having the Spirit of God dwell within us on a constant basis, in effect, abiding forever (Jn. 14:16-17), is all made possible by what Jesus did at the Cross. There He paid the terrible sin debt owed by man to God, and did so totally and completely. Concerning Christ, Paul said:

"But now has He (Christ) *obtained a more excellent Ministry, by how much also He is the Mediator of a better Covenant, which was established upon better Promises* (which He did by the Cross)*"* (Heb. 8:6).

The Holiness that is mentioned in Exodus 3:5 could not be translated per se to human beings before the Cross. The blood of animal sacrifices could not cleanse from sin. It served a purpose, which was to point to the One Who was to come. This *"better Covenant"* based on *"better Promises,"* could only come about through a *"better Sacrifice"* (Heb. 9:12-14).

I'm trying to bring out the point that through and by the Cross, we now have much better advantages even than did the great Moses.

WHY WAS MOSES REQUIRED TO PULL OFF HIS SHOES?

Joshua was required to do the same thing (Josh. 5:15).

Once again we come back to the Cross. Before the Cross, man was contaminated. The blood of bulls and goats could not take away sins; therefore, the sin debt still hung over even the greatest among the Prophets, etc.

Now, in a sense, due to the Cross, and the Holy Spirit abiding within Believers permanently, all that is about the Child of God, at least those things which are legitimate, are made holy as well.

In Old Testament times, if a man sold a piece of property, or as a kinsman redeemer he was giving up his right to purchase a certain piece of land, he would pull off his shoe, and give it to the one who bought the land. This meant that he was relinquishing all claims.

When the Lord asked that Moses pull off his shoes, and that He asked the same thing of Joshua, their doing so signified that they were relinquishing all claims, and that they belonged solely to the Lord (Ruth 4:6-9).

THE GOD OF ABRAHAM, THE GOD OF ISAAC, AND THE GOD OF JACOB

Verse 6 reads: *"Moreover He said, I am the God of your father, the God of Abraham, the God of Isaac, and the God of Jacob. And Moses hid his face; for he was afraid to look upon God."*

The word *"father,"* as it is used here, refers to forefathers in general.

Jesus used this Verse (Mat. 22:32) to confirm the Resurrection. He referred to these three and then stated, *"God is not the God of the dead, but of the living."*

He was in essence saying that these men, plus all who have trusted God, were not dead, but alive. In fact, at that moment that the Lord spoke to Moses, and as well, as Christ spoke to the crowd of His day, these three men, plus all other Believers, were in Paradise, in the heart of the Earth. They were there waiting the victory that would be won at the Cross, when in actuality, Jesus would deliver them from this place, and take them to Heaven (Eph. 4:8). Since the Cross, all Believers immediately go to be with Christ in Heaven (Phil. 1:23).

As far as we know, this appearance by God to Moses was the first appearance since Jacob's going down into Egypt about 215 years before.

If it is to be noticed, the Lord didn't say *"I 'was' the God of Abraham, Isaac, and Jacob,"* but *"I 'am,'"* proving that the Patriarchs were still alive, even though they had died physically a long time before. The soul and the spirit of man never die, and will spend eternity, whether with the Lord, or whether in everlasting darkness.

Moses hiding his face was because of the Holiness of God. Each laborer in the vineyard needs to keep constantly before him the fact that the One with Whom he has to do, in Whom he serves, is holy, thrice-Holy. A realization of this will check the lightness and levity of the flesh (Pink).

AFFLICTION

Verse 7 reads: *"And the LORD said, I have surely seen the affliction of My people which are in Egypt, and have heard their cry by reason of their taskmasters; for I know their sorrows."*

The Children of Israel in Egypt were a perfect type of the condition of the natural man who is the bond slave of sin, the captive of Satan. This is true not only of the slave of lust or the helpless victim of drugs, etc., but as well, of the moral and refined. They, too, are in bondage to selfish desire, self-will, pleasure, ambition, greed, unforgiveness, etc. Pink says: *"The 'affliction' which sin has brought is everywhere to be seen, not only in physical suffering, but as well, in mental restlessness and heart discontent."*

The varied *"lusts of the flesh"* are just as merciless as the Egyptian taskmasters of old; and the *"sorrows"* of sins' slaves today just as acute as those of the Israelites midst the iron furnace of Egypt. Pink went on to say:

"What woe there really is behind the fair surface of society! How fearful the misery which has come on the whole race of man through sin! How great the need for the Saviour! How terrible the guilt of despising Him now that He has come!"

However, even though the Seventh Verse of this Third Chapter of Exodus vividly portrays the state of the unredeemed, if the Believer doesn't understand God's prescribed order of victory through the Cross, he can find himself ruled over by the sin nature exactly as he was before conversion.

GOD'S PRESCRIBED ORDER OF VICTORY

In the Sixth Chapter of Romans, the Apostle Paul outlines to us God's method of Sanctification, and we might say, how to have victory over the flesh, or how that we may perpetually keep the sin nature in check.

The Lord only has one way of victory, and that is the way of the Cross.

To explain this which the Lord has done for us, the Holy Spirit through Paul first takes us to the Cross. He said:

"Don't you know, that so many of us as were baptized into Jesus Christ were baptized into His death?

"Therefore we are buried with Him by baptism into death: that like as Christ was raised up from the dead by the glory of the Father, even so we also should walk in newness of life.

"For if we have been planted together in the likeness of His death, we shall be also in the likeness of His Resurrection" (Rom. 6:3-5).

Most Christians brush across these Passages, simply because they think that Paul is speaking here of Water Baptism. Concluding that they have been baptized in water, they do not at all see the tremendous statement which is being made here.

Paul is not speaking of Water Baptism; in fact, he doesn't have Water Baptism in mind, as important as that Ordinance actually is.

He is speaking of the Crucifixion of Christ, how He died, was buried, and then raised from the dead.

As well, we must realize that everything Christ did was done in totality for us, and not at all for Himself. He didn't come down here to die on a Cross for Heaven, for God the Father, for the Holy Spirit, for Angels, or Himself as stated, but altogether for sinners, i.e., *"for us."* Jesus Christ was actually our Substitute, Who Paul referred to as the *"Last Adam"* (I Cor. 15:45). The term *"Last Adam"* is used, because the Work that Jesus would accomplish at the Cross would be so total, so complete, so final, that there would never be the need of another Adam. Where the first man Adam failed, the *"Last Adam"* succeeded in every capacity.

The Fall of the first Adam took everyone down with him, and we speak of all of humanity yet to be born. Due to the Fall, all would be born in original sin, therefore, without God, dead in trespasses and sins.

However, as the first Adam knocked us down, the *"Last Adam,"* the Lord Jesus Christ, picked us up. As we were lost through the first Adam, we were saved through the last Adam.

And how are we saved?

Paul answered that as well: *"For by Grace are you saved through Faith; and that not of yourselves: it is the Gift of God:*

"Not of works, lest any man should boast" (Eph. 2:8-9).

We are all saved through the Goodness of God, which is defined as *"Grace,"* and it is brought about through an exhibition of faith on our part (Jn. 3:16).

In other words, when the believing sinner exhibits Faith in Christ, as far as God is concerned, that believing sinner is actually placed into Christ, in His Death, Burial, and Resurrection. That's what Paul is talking about when he said, *"We are baptized into His Death."* He used the word *"baptized,"* because it's the strongest word that can be used to explain what the Apostle meant. He meant that Christ is in us, and we are in Christ. It's like a ship which has sunk to the bottom of the sea. The water is in the ship, and the ship is in the water, which is an excellent symbol of the word *"baptize"* or *"baptism."* That's what we are in Christ. Jesus said: *"At that day* (after He went to the Cross, and the Holy Spirit was sent back) *you shall know that I am in My Father, and you in Me, and I in you"* (Jn. 14:20).

So when Christ died, we died with Him. In fact, there had to be a death on our part. And as I'm sure the Reader knows, I'm not speaking of physical death. But yet, Jesus definitely did die physically. But our death is that which happens in the spiritual, when we die to the old man, the old way, what we once were.

Man's problem is, he keeps trying to improve the old man. It cannot be done. There is no such thing as moral evolution. In fact, it is the very opposite. Despite all of the thousands of years of education, and technological advancement, still, men are slaughtering each other today even worse than ever.

We were then buried with Christ, which means that all of what we once were, which speaks of sin, iniquity, transgression, etc., were buried with Him.

We were then raised with Him in *"newness of life,"* actually, a new creation, with old things having passed away, and all things having become new (II Cor. 5:17).

All of this which I have described is actually the *"born again"* experience.

THE SIN NATURE

However, even though we are now Born-Again, and even Spirit-filled, the sin nature within us doesn't die. It remains, but dormant! But, the Scripture says that we are *"dead to the sin nature,"* and because of what Christ did at the Cross. Paul said: *"Likewise reckon you also yourselves to be dead indeed unto the sin* (sin nature), *but alive unto God through Jesus Christ our Lord"* (Rom. 6:11).

In this one Verse of Scripture, we find the manner in which we are to believe, i.e., *"to exhibit our Faith,"* in other words, what the correct object of our faith ought to be, which is very, very important.

We are *"dead indeed unto the sin nature,"* because we died with Christ on the Cross. It's as simple as that.

No, we were not there when Christ died, but our Faith in Him, at least in the Mind of God, puts us there.

If you are to notice, I use the term in quoting the Eleventh Verse, *"the sin."* In the original Text as Paul wrote it, he used in front of the word *"sin,"* that which is referred to as *"the definite article."* In other words, he said *"dead indeed unto the sin."* Sin is used here as a noun, which means that he's not referring to particular acts of sin, but rather to the sin nature.

Now once again notice that Paul didn't say that the sin nature was dead, but rather that we are dead unto the sin nature.

HOW DO WE STAY DEAD TO THE SIN NATURE?

That's the great question!

We remain dead to the sin nature, which means that it no longer bothers us, which means that we're living victorious over the world, the flesh, and the Devil, by continuing to exhibit Faith in Christ and what Christ has done for us at the Cross. We must never separate Christ from the Cross, or the Cross from Christ. That is where our victory was won, and that's where our victory remains.

Now this is where Satan will do everything within his power to hinder us. This is what Paul was talking about when he told Timothy: *"Fight the good fight of faith, lay hold on eternal life, whereunto you are also called, and have professed a good profession before many witnesses"* (I Tim. 6:12). The good fight of faith is the fight we are supposed to fight, and it's a fight that we must fight constantly. Satan is ever trying to move our Faith from the Cross to other things. This means we have to fight to keep the Cross as the object of our Faith.

Christians are running around trying to increase their faith, when that's not the problem. The problem is having one's faith in the correct object. That object must always be the Cross of Christ. If it's something else, then we're going to have problems.

The Holy Spirit will function within our hearts and lives only as we stay within the boundaries of the Cross. And that means to maintain our Faith in that Finished Work (Gal. 6:14). Maintaining our Faith in the Cross, the Holy Spirit will then work mightily upon our behalf, which ensures us of victory (Rom. 8:1-2, 11).

Maintaining our Faith in the correct object will guarantee that *"sin shall not have dominion over us"* (Rom. 6:14).

Now this is the way to address the sin nature; however, perhaps the following will provide even more help.

HOW THE CHURCH ADDRESSES THE SIN NATURE

Any time we misunderstand something in the Word of God, it can cause us problems. And there are some things in the Word of God, if misunderstood, can cause us real problems, and the sin nature is definitely one of them.

The following are several ways that the sin nature is addressed by the Church, all of them wrong, with the exception of the last one. They are as follows:

IGNORANCE

Regrettably, most of the Church world, and I think I exaggerate not, knows absolutely nothing about the sin nature. In fact, there are millions of Christians who have never heard one single message on the sin nature, which means they've never had any teaching whatsoever on this subject, despite the fact that Paul addresses it, quite possibly, more so than anything else.

This is tragic, simply because ignorance is no defense. Satan destroys people because of a lack of knowledge. Jesus said: *"Learn of Me . . ."* (Mat. 11:29). About 11 times in Romans, Chapters 6, 7, and 8, Paul uses the word *"know"* or *"knowing,"* or *"known."*

Admittedly, when the believing sinner comes to Christ, he knows virtually nothing about the Lord or God's Word. That is obvious! However, once he has come to the Lord, the Holy Spirit within him pushes him to study the Word of God, that he might know its contents, for that is expected of us.

So again we say, ignorance is no virtue. In fact, it is the cause of untold problems.

DENIAL

There are many Preachers who deny the existence of the sin nature. Most believe that the unsaved have a sin nature, but once the person comes to Christ, they claim that the sin nature no longer exists.

The Scripture does say: *"Knowing this, that our old man is crucified with Him, that the body of sin might be destroyed, that henceforth we should not serve sin"* (Rom. 6:6).

When the Scripture speaks of *"the body of sin,"* it is speaking of the sin nature. However, the word *"Destroyed,"* in the Greek is *"katargeo,"* and means, *"to be rendered useless, to bring to naught, to make void."*

It doesn't mean that it vanishes, or is done away with, but as stated, *"to make useless."* What happens is this:

When the believing sinner comes to Christ, thereby placing his Faith in Christ and what Christ has done in His Finished Work, the guilt of sin is removed, and the power of sin is broken. I'll say it again, *"the sin nature is then rendered useless."* But it doesn't mean, as is obvious, that it is removed. And in fact, it can spring to life very quickly, if we do not function according to God's prescribed order.

So, those who would deny the existence of the sin nature are overlooking all the teaching that Paul gave us on this subject, as recorded in Romans, Chapter 6, and elsewhere. I hardly think the Holy Spirit would have wasted time explaining something that is no longer a problem. The truth is, the sin nature is still a viable force in the heart and life of the Child of God. It can be controlled, and in fact will be controlled, if the Believer functions according to God's prescribed order, which is laid down in Romans, Chapter 6.

LICENSE

Many Christians think that because they have a sin nature, they simply cannot help but sin, meaning they have to sin a little bit everyday, etc. They claim that the only difference in them and the unredeemed is that they trust Christ and the unredeemed don't.

Nothing could be further from the truth. God doesn't save us in sin, but rather from sin. All the teaching that Paul gave in Romans, Chapter 6, is given for the purpose of helping us to overcome the sin nature, and not to live under its rule and reign. So why do these people, who are many in number, believe that?

They believe it, simply because they do not have proper teaching on the Cross of Christ. They try to live for God, at least the few among them who are truly saved, by their own machinations, strength, and ability, which are always woefully insufficient. Consequently they fail, as fail they must.

STRUGGLE

And then there are millions who truly love God, and are truly trying to live for Him, but are engaged in a ferocious struggle, a struggle incidentally which never ends, and actually, which continues to grow in intensity. The more abundant life which Jesus promised escapes these hapless individuals, and it is because they are attempting to live for God in all the wrong ways. Actually, all three of the above headings, ignorance, denial, and license, are all brought into play in their lives.

But let me again emphasize that these people aren't hypocrites. They love the Lord. They are earnestly and honestly seeking to serve Christ, and to be a good Christian. But the truth is, not understanding the Cross, which means they don't understand the Grace of God, they are miserably failing, as fail they must. In fact, the more they struggle, the worse their situation becomes, which proves to be extremely confusing to such Believers. And please understand, the number which falls into this category make up almost all of modern Christendom.

In my study just this morning, in reading behind Charles Haddon Spurgeon, he gave his own account of this *"struggle."*

He spoke of getting up each morning, and resolving to be a better Christian that day than he had been before. But before noon, he went on to say, he would have made a bigger mess of things that day than he had the day before. So he would resolve to pray more and to study the Scriptures more, but as wonderful and helpful as that was, and to be sure, which all good Christians will definitely do, still, he found himself failing more and more.

How do we explain this?

While prayer and the reading and study of the Word are the two great hallmarks of true Believers, it is quite possible to turn these great attributes into works. In other words, if we think that by praying so much and by studying the Scriptures so much we will attain to Holiness, then we are functioning in these blessed realms in all the wrong ways. As stated, we turn our consecration into works, which God can never honor.

That which Spurgeon said, and which has characterized untold millions, I well understand and emphasize. I did the same identical thing. I turned my consecration to the Lord into works. I didn't do it intentionally, but not knowing and understanding the Message of the Cross as it regards our Sanctification experience, I did the only thing I knew to do. And while the Lord greatly blessed me regarding prayer and the study of the Word, still, I found myself failing more and more, which brought about tremendous confusion in my heart and mind. All I knew to do was to resolve to pray more, to study more, which I did, all to no avail! Until I understood the Cross, I did not understand victory. But when I understood the Cross, even as the Holy Spirit revealed it to me from the Word of God, victory was mine.

GRACE

There is only one way that the Believer can successfully live for the Lord, and I speak of walking victorious on a day-by-day basis, with no sin having dominion over such a Believer. That is the way of Grace. Now let's explain that.

Paul said: *"I am crucified with Christ: nevertheless I live; yet not I, but Christ lives in me: and the life which I now live in the flesh I live by the Faith of the Son of God, Who loved me, and gave Himself for me"* (Gal. 2:20).

Paul tells us here how to live a victorious life. By using the term *"I am crucified with Christ,"* he takes us to the Cross. And then when it came to living this life, he said that he did so *"by the Faith of the Son of God."*

One would read that term and think possibly it would be better translated, *"I live by Faith in the Son of God."* But that wouldn't be correct!

"The Faith" refers to what Jesus did for us at the Cross, and our Faith in that Finished Work. When this is brought about, and that in which we engage every single day, the Grace of God can then flow into our hearts and lives.

The Grace of God is simply the Goodness of God extended to undeserving people. It is really the Work of the Holy Spirit within our lives, with the Spirit carrying out the great victories purchased by the Lord Jesus Christ at the Cross of Calvary.

However, if as a Believer we try to live for God by means other than Faith in Christ and what He did for us at the Cross, all we succeed in doing is to *"frustrate the Grace of God"* (Gal. 2:21). By depending on my prayer life and Bible study, I was frustrating the

Grace of God, and so was Spurgeon, and so have millions of others. God operates on one basis, and that is Faith. And when we speak of Faith, we're speaking of Faith in Christ, and what Christ did at the Cross. We must never separate Christ from the Cross, for that is our place of victory.

AFFLICTION

Before we go to the next Verse, let's look at affliction a little more.

Egypt was a type of the world. And to be sure, had the Israelites remained comfortable in Egypt, as they had been under Joseph, they simply would not have wanted to leave. It is the same with the modern Believer.

While we as Believers are definitely in the world, the world definitely is not to be in us. But that's the great problem.

The Lord is fashioning us into the Heavenly Image. First the believing sinner must be Born-Again, which typifies the deliverance of the Children of Israel from Egyptian bondage. Then the training begins. It was the Cross that got the Children of Israel out of Egypt, and it is the Cross which got us out of the domination of the world. As well, it was the Cross which instituted Israel's training, and it is the same with us presently.

But the sadness is, most Christians, knowing little about the Cross, understand it only in the capacity of their initial Salvation experience. Beyond that, they draw a blank. Not understanding the Cross regarding their Sanctification, they proceed to attempt to bring this about by their own ability, strength, and machinations. Then embarks the long road of failure, for there is no victory in self.

God doesn't give victory to man in general or man in particular. He gives all victory to Christ. And the victory that we have, which we can surely have, and in abundance, must come through our association with Christ and Christ Alone. This is done by evidencing Faith in Christ and His Sufferings (Gal. 1:4).

All of this I've stated may seem to be very simple on the surface; however, due to the problems of *"self"* and *"the flesh,"* it can become very complicated. Oftentimes, affliction is necessary, before we will finally cry unto the Lord as we should, thereby, coming to a place of total dependence on Him. The truth is, the Christian will cling to the flesh as long as there is any flesh left. All hope of the flesh must be gone before the Believer will totally look to Christ.

But in the meantime, all Believers think they're looking to Christ, and will proclaim vigorously that they are definitely looking to Christ. But the truth is, and as stated, as long as any part of the flesh remains, and we continue to speak of *"self,"* the Believer will cling to the last shred, and much of the time thinking that he's clinging to Christ.

CHRIST AND HIM CRUCIFIED

Why did Paul use the term in Galatians 2:20: *"I am crucified with Christ"*? He did so for this reason:

The only way that the Believer can truly cling to Christ, truly trust Christ, truly depend on Christ, truly look to Christ for all things is to place his faith and confidence in what Christ has done at the Cross. To try to trust Christ in any other fashion concludes by the person serving *"another Jesus"* (II Cor. 11:4). While the *"other Jesus,"* may look like the real thing, and thereby, make us believe it's the real thing; there will be no positive, Scriptural results from such a union. *"Another Jesus,"* as Paul put it, always, and without exception, refers to Christ apart from the Cross. While Christ is definitely a healing Jesus, we must always understand that the healings come to us strictly through what Christ did at the Cross (I Pet. 2:24). While Christ is definitely a *"blessing Jesus,"* once again, we must always understand that such blessings come, and without exception, through the Cross (Eph. 1:3). While Christ is definitely the Baptizer with the Holy Spirit, He is that simply because of what He has done at the Cross (Mat. 3:11; Jn. 7:37-39). It is the Cross which makes everything possible, and until we understand that, and place our Faith in Christ and what He did for us in His Finished Work, we will never know victory. And so, affliction is often needed to bring us to the place we ought to be.

It's not that the affliction carries within itself any type of power or Grace, for it doesn't. But it does tend to force the issue, by having us look totally to Christ and His Finished Work, thereby forsaking our dependence on the flesh.

DELIVERANCE

Verse 8 reads: *"And I am come down to deliver them out of the hand of the Egyptians, and to bring them up out of that land into a good land and a large, unto a land flowing with milk and honey; unto the place of the Canaanites, and the Hittites, and the Amorites, and the Perizzites, and the Hivites, and the Jebusites."*

Before we look at the delivering aspect, let's look at this land to which the Lord would bring His people. To be sure, it was better, much better, than the land of Egypt. In Egypt, they only had a part of Goshen, whereas the entirety of the land of Canaan was approximately 60,000 square miles. It was truly a *"good land and a large"* (I Ki. 4:20-21).

Eastward of Jordan, the soil is very rich and productive, with vast tracts producing enormous crops of grain, and throughout the year pasturage of every kind in abundance.

The phrase *"flowing with milk and honey,"* first used here, and so common in the later Books (Num. 13:27; Deut. 26:9, 15; 31:20; Jer. 11:5; 32:22; Ezek. 20:6, etc.) was a proverbial expression for *"a land of plenty"* (Pulpit).

The point of all of this is, what they were being given was far greater than what they were leaving. It is the same with the modern Believer and the world. What the Lord brings us out of is far less (much less), than that which He brings us into. In fact, there is no comparison.

As someone has well said, *"The worst day I've ever had in living for the Lord is a thousand times better than the best day I had living for the Devil."*

THE ASPECT OF DELIVERANCE

The phrase, *"And I am come down to deliver them out of the hand of the Egyptians,"* reveals a great fundamental principle regarding the ways of God. It is on the ground of what He is that He ever acts, and not on the ground of what the people are as it regards Righteousness, etc.

Actually, the Children of Israel in Egypt were not paragons of virtue and Righteousness. In fact, they were the very opposite. For them even to exhibit a little faith, they had to be brought to a place of terrible bondage. So the delivering aspect had to do with God's Promises to Abraham, Isaac, and Jacob, which constitutes Who He is, and What He is. If the Lord waited until we were worthy of deliverance, He would never act, simply because no human being has ever reached that place. He only requires faith, and for faith to be had and exhibited, in some way the Word of God must be sent to the people, even as it was under Moses. And then it was affliction that drove them to the place of exhibiting their Faith.

It is the same with us presently. There is no merit in us that triggers deliverance. But yet it's hard for us to come to that place to where we cease to look to ourselves, and thereby look totally to God.

As we will see, even as the Text progresses Chapter by Chapter, that the factor and the principle which ultimately delivered Israel were the shed Blood of the Lamb. All the miracles that God performed only set the stage. They really effected no deliverance. It was totally and completely the Cross of Christ, registered in the symbolism of the slain Lamb, which brought Egypt to her knees, and victory to Israel.

And as we go through this Text, let the Reader understand that as it was with Israel of old, it is presently with Believers, and in fact always has been. There is no saving Grace, no delivering Grace, no healing Grace, outside of the Cross.

If I weary the Reader by my constant, even overbearing attention to the Cross, I do so for a purpose. The Church has been moved so far away from the Cross that it no longer understands its place and position of life and victory. It is so bogged down in legalism, Galatianism, or even the opposite, which is Antinomianism, that it has completely lost sight of victory.

In brief, legalism pertains to Salvation by works, which in reality doesn't exist.

Galatianism, which afflicts most of the modern Church, pertains to Believers who come to Christ by trusting in what He has done for us at the Cross, and then trying to live for God by their own strength and ability, in other words, abandoning the Cross. In that capacity, it is Salvation by Faith, and Sanctification by works, which will never succeed.

Antinomianism is the very opposite, in that it claims that sin no longer matters inasmuch as we are now functioning in Grace. In other words, *"where sin abounded, Grace did much more abound,"* so I don't have to worry anymore about how much I might sin. Of course, that road is a road to disaster. But in one of these three, the majority of the modern Church now resides.

All of it is a failure to understand the Cross, and so that's the reason I address this subject from every angle I know, even to the place of tedious repetition, in order that the Reader will not fail to see what is being said.

ENEMIES IN THE LAND

If it is to be noticed, the Lord mentioned the fact that there would be Canaanites, Hittites, etc., in the land, and of course, we speak of the land to which the Lord would deliver His people.

This refers to the enemies of the soul which seek to drag down the Child of God after having come into the land of Promise, so to speak. Despite the fact that much modern teaching on Faith claims that if we have the proper confession, there will be no difficulties or problems, we find to our dismay that we still have to face the Canaanites, etc. Denying their existence doesn't make them go away, and ignoring them does not provide a place of security and peace. As we shall see, when we come to the Book of Joshua, this great soldier of the Lord had to defeat these enemies, which he did. The Believer must understand that the land of Promise is not necessarily the land of possession. Let's say it in another way:

It's a whole lot easier to receive the Promise, than it is to have the possession. But it definitely can be had, and if we follow that which the Lord has given us, and do so faithfully, we definitely will possess all that Jesus has provided for us.

A GREAT DIFFERENCE

As it regards Joshua, along with the Judges and David, etc., these men served as Types of Christ. The victories they won were types of the victories won for us by Jesus Christ.

But the problem that the modern Saint faces is misunderstanding the possession of the land, he tries to do all over again what Christ has already done. Jesus Christ has totally and completely defeated every single power of darkness. To use the vernacular of Exodus, He has defeated the Canaanites, the Hivites, the Jebusites, etc., which means that we don't have to defeat them. But this is where the Christian slips up. He keeps trying to fight a fight that's already been fought and won, to effect a victory which has already been accomplished. And let me hurriedly say, if we attempt to do that, we will be defeated every single time. There has never been one single winner in this type of conflict. The reasons are many and obvious:

To try to fight a battle which has already been fought and won by Christ is an insult to Christ, and to be sure, a place and position in which the Holy Spirit will not function. But sadly and regrettably, the modern Christian engages in this conflict, simply because he doesn't know or understand God's prescribed order of victory.

Under the New Covenant, which is very, very important, in order to possess all that Christ has done for us, and I speak of this *"more abundant life"* (Jn. 10:10), all we have to do is exhibit Faith in Christ, and yes, you know what I'm about to say next, and what He did for us at the Cross. We place our Faith in that Finished Work, not allowing it to be moved elsewhere, and the Holy Spirit will then guarantee to us all that Christ has done for us (Col. 2:14-15; Rom. 8:1-2, 11).

A PERSONAL EXPERIENCE

When it comes to fighting Canaanites and Jebusites, etc., I am personally, most probably, one of the most experienced in the world. I realize that if every Believer could read this, many would smile, and say, *"Brother Swaggart, you may think you are, but my own experience tops even yours."* Quite possibly that is true, but the further truth is, not a single one of us ever succeeded, as no one will ever succeed in that endeavor.

As we've already stated, to try to do all over again what Christ has already done, and which we cannot do anyway, is an insult of the highest order to the Son of God. When we think about this, we must realize that everything He did, He did solely and completely for you and me. He didn't do it for Himself, for He needed no deliverance. And considering the great price which He paid, and then for us to try to engage this conflict all over again, greatly belittles the Sacrifice which He offered of Himself. While we certainly don't mean to insult Him, that's actually what we are doing. In effect, it is the same as Cain offering up the labor of his own hands in sacrifice to God, which God of course, could never accept (Gen., Chpt. 4).

A DELIVERANCE PREACHER?

Regrettably, most of the modern Church completely misunderstands deliverance. The Denominational Church world little thinks of it at all, and for reasons which I will not now address. Most Pentecostals and Charismatics misunderstand the manner of deliverance, thinking somehow that Preachers can deliver people, etc.

We try to do this by the laying on of hands, which within itself is very Scriptural, but when used in this fashion, becomes unscriptural.

A few nights ago, watching a Preacher for a few moments over television, his entire motif was to bring people before him, and him lay his hands on them, which was supposed to deliver them of their problems. Some of these people were needing healing, in which case the laying on of hands is very Scriptural. Others maybe just wanted to be blessed, which as well is Scriptural; however, with those who were troubled by sins of some nature, bondages of some nature, etc., laying on of hands, at least in that fashion, will not help. Think about it a moment:

If it could have, in other words bring about deliverance for the individual, then Jesus didn't need to come down here and die on the Cross. No! The Preacher, as well as thousands just like him, was drawing attention to himself, instead of Christ. I'm not saying that he meant to do that, and I'm not even questioning his motives, rather believing that those motives were very good; however, the end result will not be good.

Let's say, for the sake of argument, that the Preacher is Godly and sincere, and that the people are sincere. Let's say that the Lord really blesses them, and they even *"fall out in the Spirit,"* etc., or have some other type of like manifestation. Even though all of this is wonderful and good, and will definitely be a blessing to the Child of God, when that Believer gets up from the floor and walks outside, 15 minutes later, or two or three weeks later, whatever, the same problem he had when he went to the Preacher, he will find himself continuing to have. Why?

Did not the Power of God move on him? Yes it did; however, the following is what is wrong:

TRUTH

Jesus said: *"You shall know the Truth, and the Truth shall make you free"* (Jn. 8:32). He didn't say that we would have manifestations, etc., and that would set us free, but rather that we would *"know the Truth."*

The reason these good Christians find that their problem is still with them, despite the fact that God greatly moved upon them, is because they don't know the truth. Listen again to what Jesus said:

"The Spirit of the Lord is upon Me, because He has anointed Me to . . . preach deliverance to the captives" (Lk. 4:18).

If it is to be noticed, He didn't say that we are to *"deliver the captives,"* but rather *"preach deliverance to the captives,"* which is exactly what I'm doing to you in this Commentary.

The term *"preach deliverance"* means to explain what deliverance is, which refers to being delivered from the domain of darkness to the domain of light, and how it is obtained. The latter comes exclusively by our Faith in Christ and what Christ has done for us at the Cross. The Cross is where the Believer's victory is, and it is where the Believer's victory remains. There is only one sacrifice for sin, not ten, not five, not two, only one (Heb. 10:12). That Sacrifice is the Cross. So when we speak of going beyond the Cross, in short, we blaspheme. There is nothing beyond the Cross because there needs to be nothing beyond the Cross, in that the Cross answered all questions and provided all solutions. That's the reason that

Paul referred to the Sacrifice of Christ as *"The Everlasting Covenant"* (Heb. 13:20).

HEBREWS, CHAPTER 6

Many Christians confuse Hebrews 6:1-2, which says: *"Therefore leaving the principles of the Doctrine of Christ, let us go on unto perfection; not laying again the foundation of repentance from dead works, and of Faith toward God,*

"Of the Doctrine of Baptisms, and of laying on of hands, and of Resurrection of the dead, and of eternal judgment."

Many claim that this tells us to leave *"the principles of the Doctrine of Christ,"* and to go on to other things. Well, let me ask this question: what other things are there to which we should go? Christ is everything, and to claim that there is something beyond Christ is, once again, to blaspheme.

Some would claim that this speaks of going on into the Holy Spirit, etc.

We must remember two things about this: A. Christ is the Baptizer with the Holy Spirit (Mat. 3:11); and, as well, B. The business of the Holy Spirit is to glorify Christ and not Himself (Jn. 16:13-14).

No! To go beyond Christ is to completely misunderstand the Word of God, and to thereby, greatly offend the Holy Spirit. There is nothing beyond Christ. So that being the case, what does this Passage in Hebrews mean?

We must understand that the *"Doctrine of Christ"* includes the entirety of the Bible, both Old and New Testaments. So when Paul wrote: *"Therefore, leaving the principles of the Doctrine of Christ,"* he in effect was saying, *"Therefore leaving the first principles of the Doctrine of Christ,"* which refers to the ways of the Old Testament, or the Old Covenant, which Jesus completely fulfilled. In fact, that's what the entirety of the Book of Hebrews is all about.

Some of the Christian Jews, because of discouragement, or whatever, were going back into Judaism, and Paul is telling them here that we must leave those first principles of Old Testament animal sacrifices, etc., and *"go on unto perfection,"* i.e., *"maturity,"* which can only be brought about by trusting in Christ and what He has done for us in His Sufferings.

NOTES

He then says, *"Not laying again the foundation of repentance from dead works, and of Faith toward God,"* which means that our repentance must not be based today on Old Testament principles, because such faith toward God will not be honored by God.

Paul is not telling Believers to go beyond the Cross. He, in effect, is telling these Christian Jews to quit leaving the Cross, in effect, to come back to the Cross. When we leave the Cross, we always go backwards. There is no such thing as going beyond the Cross, for such a place and position simply doesn't exist. So if anyone tries to claim that they've gone beyond the Cross, in effect, they have gone back to Old Testament practices, whether they realize it or not.

In Hebrews 6:2, he mentioned that we must not go back to the *"Doctrine of Baptisms."* What did he mean by that?

The word *"Baptisms"* should have been translated *"washings,"* for that's what he was talking about. There were many *"washings"* associated with the Sacrifices, and the rituals of the Priests, as it regarded the Old Testament system. Paul is saying that we must not place our faith in that, all of it having been fulfilled in Christ.

As well, he said that we must not go back to the *"laying on of hands."* Now what did he mean by that?

He wasn't speaking of the New Testament practice of laying on of hands, but rather how that the believing sinner, when he brought his sacrifice (the little lamb) to the Altar, he would lay his hands on the head of the little animal, and thereby confess all his sins. In Christ, all of that has been done away with.

As it regards *"resurrection of the dead,"* under the Old Testament Covenants, very little knowledge was then known. Until Jesus went to the Cross, and thereby liberated all the righteous souls out of Paradise, which He did at His Resurrection, Resurrection wasn't understood as it is now. The Resurrection of the dead was then just a promise; now it is a fact.

As well, *"eternal judgment,"* referred to the terrible plight in which the entirety of the human race found itself, even Israel of old. As we've stated, the sin debt continued to hang over the heads of all, before the Cross. When Jesus died on the Cross, *"Eternal judgment"* was forever satisfied. And now, I do not face eternal judgment because, as the old song says, *"The old account was settled long ago."*

Let us say it again: If we go beyond the Cross, we in effect do not go further than the Cross, but rather we digress, or go backwards, which, as should be obvious, is disastrous. This means that we go back in some manner to Old Testament practices, which Jesus fulfilled at the Cross, and which is an abomination for us to now engage.

OPPRESSION

Verse 9 reads: *"Now therefore, behold, the cry of the Children of Israel is come unto Me: and I have also seen the oppression wherewith the Egyptians oppress them."*

The Lord knew the *"sorrows"* of His people, He heard their cries, and He saw their oppression. Henry said: *"As the poorest of the oppressed are not below God's cognizance, so the highest and greatest of their oppressors are not above His check, but He will surely visit for these things."*

Oppression comes from Satan. It is lethal, and its deliverance can only be effected by the Power of God. The world of psychology, psychotherapy, psychological counseling, drugs, etc., can only worsen the oppressed. There is no help from these sources. Egypt cannot, and of course will not deliver from Egypt.

GOD'S TIMING

God is now ready to accomplish His Promise made to Abraham, and repeated to Isaac and Jacob. He had not come down to see if, indeed, the subjects of His Promise were in such a condition as to merit His Salvation: it was sufficient for Him that they needed it. Their oppressed state, their sorrows, their tears, their sighs, and their heavy bondage had all come in review before Him; for, blessed be His Name, He counts His people's sighs, and puts their tears into His bottle.

"When" God does a thing is just as important as *"what"* He does. Actually, it wouldn't be in the best interest of all for God to do certain things, until the right time has come.

NOTES

That has to do with the condition of the person. As we've already stated, Israel would not have desired to have left Egypt, if they had continued to be treated in a positive manner as they had been treated under Joseph. Before God's Will can be brought about in our lives, we have to come to the place that we want that will to be brought about. And most often, circumstances have to be brought about for us to come to this frame of mind. *Men do not normally do anything, even obey God, until it is in their best interest to do so.* Consequently, the Lord has to bring circumstances about, until man sees that it is now in his best interest. As long as he is getting by fairly well in the state he's in, no matter how wrong that state might be, he is not apt to change. So the Lord has to allow oppression to come about in order for us to see where we are, and how that we desperately need to change.

THE CROSS

Bringing all of this up to the present time, for that which happened to the Children of Israel is definitely a type of all that happens to us as Believers, there are some things we need to know.

As the Lord would bring Israel to the slain lamb, which in effect was that which would deliver them, which was, of course, a Type of Christ, likewise, most all, if not all of God's dealings with us are to bring us to the foot of the Cross. The Cross is the answer for all depression, oppression, suppression, emotional disturbances, fear, anxiety, worry, etc.

The word *"oppression"* in the Hebrew is *"lachats,"* and means, *"distress, affliction, to crush, force, hold fast, or to press."*

Oppression is one of Satan's greatest hindrances as it relates to the Child of God. Probably a spirit of depression is the culminating result of oppression, etc. As stated, the answer to that, and in fact the only answer, is the Cross.

Now how is the Cross the answer to this dilemma?

Depression is actually a concentrated, overbearing interest in one's self. It is probably the highest form of selfishness, and is an ego gone awry. However, the person so afflicted does not at all see it that way; nevertheless, that is the problem. Now let's look at the solution.

In any case, and in every circumstance, *"self"* is really the major problem with the human being. That's the reason that the foolishness of the *"self-esteem"* theory has made such headway in the last several decades. In that false direction, the idea is, if one's self-esteem can be built up, then their problems will be solved. While it is certainly true that one can have a low self-esteem or a high self-esteem, the problem is still *"self."* The Bible lends no credence whatsoever to this theory of self-esteem, etc.

Whenever a person comes to Christ, they do not cease to be a self. We have Christians trying to eradicate self, and that's something that cannot be done, and neither should it be done.

The correct way is for *"self"* to be placed *"in Christ,"* and to remain *"in Christ,"* which means at the same time that Christ is now in self (Jn. 14:20).

This is exactly what Paul was talking about when he said: *"I am crucified with Christ: nevertheless I live; yet not I, but Christ lives in me: and the life which I now live in the flesh I live by the faith of the Son of God, Who loved me, and gave Himself for me"* (Gal. 2:20).

In fact, whenever the believing sinner comes to Christ, in other words the moment you were saved, whenever that was, you were placed *"in Christ."* So the work was then done, so why is it that many Christians continue to have problems?

THE CAUSE

When the believing sinner comes to Christ, as stated, at that moment he is placed *"in Christ,"* which means that he is beyond oppression, etc. So why is it that many Christians continue to have great difficulties in this capacity?

The cause with this is the same thing as the cause with anything else as it regards the Believer. Not knowing or understanding the Cross as one must understand the Cross, the Believer allows his faith to be moved to other things. In other words, the Cross ceases to be the object of his Faith, with it then being placed in something else.

And please believe me, there are a myriad of Preachers trying to pull your Faith to things and places which will not only be worthless to you, but will actually cause problems, instead of solving problems.

If the Believer places his Faith in the Cross, understanding that it is through the Cross that he receives all benefits from the Lord, and keeps his faith in the Cross, not allowing it to be moved to other things, the Holy Spirit will then guarantee all the benefits of the Cross, in effect, what Jesus did there (Rom. 6:3-5, 11, 14; 8:1-2, 11; I Cor. 1:17-18; 2:2).

That which I have just given you is the only way to walk in victory, and that means victory in every capacity, including oppression, depression, nervous disorders, fear, anxiety, etc. The Lord Alone is the Deliverer, but He always, and without exception, delivers by the means of the Finished Work of Christ.

IS THE CHURCH TAUGHT THIS FOUNDATIONAL TRUTH?

Regrettably, no! The Cross was strongly taught in the 1800's, and perhaps in the early 1900's, but in the last several decades, the Church has been pulled away from the Cross to other things. While there have been many contributing factors toward this, perhaps the worst influence of all has been the so-called Word of Faith doctrine. In fact, that doctrine has been very predominant in the modern Church, especially among Pentecostals and Charismatics, for the last several decades.

In that particular teaching, it was taught that the Believer should have nothing to do with the Cross. In fact, the Cross was, and is referred to in those circles as *"past miseries."* The Cross has been deemed *"as the greatest defeat in human history."* In fact, in many *"Word of Faith"* Churches, no songs are to be sung about the Cross, the Blood, etc.

This doctrine, while it may mention the Blood of Christ in a positive way at times, actually teaches that Salvation comes, not by the Cross, but rather by Jesus going to Hell as a sinner, suffering three days and nights in Hell, and we speak of the burning side of Hell, tormented there by demons, when at the conclusion of the three days and nights, God then said, *"It is enough,"* whereas Jesus was then born again, and raised from the dead. So in effect, they teach that Salvation comes by the means of this fictitious story, because this which I have just stated is not found anywhere in the Bible. It is, as stated, pure fiction!

Some may claim that what we're discussing is nothing more than semantics. In other words, it's the same thing as all other Preachers preach and teach, but worded in a little different way.

No, it's not the same thing. The *"Jesus died spiritually doctrine,"* for that's what it is, is an attack upon the Atonement, and in fact, the greatest attack, more than likely, in human history. Those who practice and proclaim this teaching can only be described as *"enemies of the Cross of Christ."* Of these people, Paul said:

"For many walk, of whom I have told you often, and now tell you even weeping, that they Are the enemies of the Cross of Christ:

"Whose end is destruction, whose god is their belly, and whose glory is in their shame, who mind earthly things" (Phil. 3:18-19).

While there are certainly many other attacks against the Cross, this of which I have mentioned is, I believe, the most lethal and deadly of them all. A sinner cannot be saved by believing the Word of Faith doctrine; hence, very little attempt is even made to get people saved in those circles. And while some few may be saved in those particular meetings, etc., to be sure, they aren't saved by believing that particular doctrine, but by simply trusting Christ. But the truth is, the number of Salvations in that sector is small indeed! In fact, their teachers claim that their business is not to get people saved, but rather to enlighten them after they are saved. As well, there are precious few people baptized with the Holy Spirit in those circles, precious few delivered by the Power of God, and precious few healed. In fact, according to that doctrine, which is totally erroneous, no one, as stated, is saved, delivered, healed, etc. So what is the great attraction to this particular form of doctrine?

The great attraction is greed. The basic thrust of this doctrine is *"money."* In other words, its gurus claim that if one follows their teachings, one will get rich. There seems to be enough greed in all of us to make such a doctrine very enticing.

Let me again quote Paul, when he said, *"Whose god is their belly, and whose glory is in their shame, who mind earthly things."* This describes that doctrine to the proverbial *"T."*

So the Church has been pulled away from the Cross, not only in the realm of which I speak, but also according to the following:

HUMANISTIC PSYCHOLOGY

Almost every major Denomination, and perhaps all major Denominations, promotes humanistic psychology as the answer to the ills of man. And to be sure, these Denominations do not take a neutral position regarding this of which we speak, but rather promote the world of psychology, and do so on an extended basis. While many of these so-called Preachers and religious leaders would claim to believe in the Cross, the truth is, one cannot promote both causes at the same time. As Jesus said: *"No servant can serve two masters: for either he will hate the one, and love the other; or else he will hold to the one, and despise the other. You cannot serve God and mammon"* (Lk. 16:13).

Psychology is not a viable science, and no true scientist will claim that it is. In fact, there is no proof that it's ever helped anyone. The truth is, Psychology is the answer of humanism to the Bible.

We claim that the Bible holds the answer for every spiritual and emotional problem that man might have. We claim there is no other answer except that which is given in the Word of God. Peter said:

"According as His Divine power has given unto us all things that pertain unto life and Godliness, through the knowledge of Him Who has called us to glory and virtue:

"Whereby are given unto us exceeding great and precious promises: that by these you might be partakers of the Divine Nature, having escaped the corruption that is in the world through lust" (II Pet. 1:3-4).

Now either the Lord, as Peter stated, actually did give us *"all things that pertain unto life and Godliness,"* or else Peter lied about the situation. Of course, I know that Peter didn't lie. So the truth is this:

A vote for humanistic psychology is, at the same time, a vote of no confidence as it regards the Cross.

So, through these twin evils of humanistic psychology, and the Word of Faith doctrine, which in reality is no faith at all, at least that which God will honor, Satan has made great inroads in the Church, as it regards a denial of the Cross.

Let me remind the Reader that the only One Who could deliver the children of Israel out of Egyptian bondage was the Lord. At the same time, He is still the only One Who can deliver.

OUT OF EGYPT

Verse 10 reads: *"Come now therefore, and I will send you unto Pharaoh, that you may bring forth My people the Children of Israel out of Egypt."*

As the Lord used Moses as His instrument, He continues to use the fivefold Calling of *"Apostles, Prophets, Evangelists, Pastors, and Teachers"* (Eph. 4:11). Even though man is the instrument, however, it is God Who delivers.

Due to the fivefold Calling functioning under the New Covenant, the manner in which God uses such instruments is a little different now than it was under the Old Covenant. The principle, one might say, is the same, but, the manner is somewhat different.

Under the Old Covenant, things which were carried out by the Prophets were mostly done by that which one would refer to as raw, naked power. Presently, and we should say since the Cross, it is now done by teaching. Jesus said:

"You shall know the Truth, and the Truth shall make you free" (Jn. 8:32). So it's the business of modern Preachers to give truth unto the people, hence Jesus also saying: *"The Spirit of the Lord is upon Me, because He has anointed Me to . . . preach deliverance to the captives"* (Lk. 4:18).

In fact, as I've previously stated, this is exactly what we're doing in this Commentary, *"preaching deliverance to the captives."*

As well, the Lord must bring His people out of Egypt. There is no way they can remain in Egypt and continue to be the people of God. It is the same presently:

The Lord must bring His people presently out of the system of this world. While we're *"in"* the world, we are to never be *"of"* the world. That's the business of the Holy Spirit, as He constantly seeks to separate us from the world.

However, while *"separation"* is definitely that which the Holy Spirit demands, it is not *"isolation."* In fact, as *"lights"* we as Believers are to illuminate this world. And as *"salt"* we are to preserve that which is right and righteous. That's why Jesus also said: *"You are the salt of the Earth . . . you are the light of the world, a city that is set on an hill cannot be hid"* (Mat. 5:13-14).

In fact, the only *"light"* in this world, and we speak of spiritual light, is that provided by the Child of God, who in reality is a reflection of Christ. And the only thing that keeps it from being destroyed, i.e., *"salt,"* is the Righteousness of the Believer.

(11) "AND MOSES SAID UNTO GOD, WHO AM I, THAT I SHOULD GO UNTO PHARAOH, AND THAT I SHOULD BRING FORTH THE CHILDREN OF ISRAEL OUT OF EGYPT?

(12) "AND HE SAID, CERTAINLY I WILL BE WITH YOU; AND THIS SHALL BE A TOKEN UNTO YOU, THAT I HAVE SENT YOU: WHEN YOU HAVE BROUGHT FORTH THE PEOPLE OUT OF EGYPT, YOU SHALL SERVE GOD UPON THIS MOUNTAIN.

(13) "AND MOSES SAID UNTO GOD, BEHOLD, WHEN I COME UNTO THE CHILDREN OF ISRAEL, AND SHALL SAY UNTO THEM, THE GOD OF YOUR FATHERS HAS SENT ME UNTO YOU; AND THEY SHALL SAY TO ME, WHAT IS HIS NAME? WHAT SHALL I SAY UNTO THEM?

(14) "AND GOD SAID UNTO MOSES, I AM THAT I AM: AND HE SAID, THUS SHALL YOU SAY UNTO THE CHILDREN OF ISRAEL, I AM HAS SENT ME UNTO YOU."

The construction is:

1. The carnal mind is not subject to the Law of God, neither indeed can be. The very Moses who in Chapter 2:11-13 stepped forward with energy to champion his people is the very same Moses who in Chapter 3:11-13 steps back and declares himself unequal to the enterprise. True Faith neither steps forward nor backward, but holds His Hand Who says: *"Certainly I will be with you."*

2. The glorious Name *"I AM,"* i.e., *"Jehovah,"* was now first made known to Israel. To Abraham, to Isaac, and to Jacob, He revealed Himself as *"El Shaddai,"* that is, *"God, the Almighty"*; for that was the Revelation they needed. But to Israel, enslaved and helpless, a further Revelation was necessary; and so the glorious Name *"I AM"* was given to her as a blank check, so that she could write after these two words whatever her need demanded.

3. If Israel needed a deliverer, at once she had the answer, *"I AM the Deliverer"*; she needed a comforter and again came the response, *"I AM the Comforter"*; she needed all kinds of provision — needs immeasurably beyond human skill to meet — and at once her faithful God says, *"I AM the Provider"* (Williams).

WHO AM I?

Verse 11 reads: *"And Moses said unto God, Who am I, that I should go unto Pharaoh, and that I should bring forth the Children of Israel out of Egypt?"*

Moses shrinks back at what God proposes. He, just one man, is going to be sent to Pharaoh, the mightiest Monarch, at that time, on the face of the Earth, leader of the most powerful nation on Earth, and the Children of Israel, by this one man, are going to be led out of Egypt. His answer to this monumental task, in fact, the greatest task ever proposed for one man, was *"Who am I?"*

God never asks of us something that we can do. He always asks of us that which is impossible for us to do. In fact, if we can do it, then there's no point in God becoming involved.

This means that every single Calling placed upon an individual, and irrespective of what that Calling might be, is far and away beyond the ability of that person to carry it out. It is designed that way for purpose and reason.

As stated, the Lord uses human instrumentation, but it must be human instrumentation which realizes that it cannot accomplish the task unless the Lord gives the power to do so.

Now while we should know and understand that we within ourselves cannot do this thing, at the same time, we must also understand that with God, we can get the job done. As stated, Faith never moves forward or backwards. It holds the Hand of the One Who is doing the leading, namely the Lord.

In fact, when God began to tell Moses what to do, the die had already been cast. In other words, God had come down to deliver the Children of Israel, and the combined power of Earth and Hell could not hold them in captivity one hour beyond His appointed time.

When Moses went forward in the energy of the flesh (Ex. 2:11), he was full of confidence in the success of his mission. This comes out clearly in Acts 7:25: *"For he supposed his brethren would have understood how that God by His hand would deliver them: but they understood not."* But now that the Call of God has definitely come to him for this work, and as well, that it is God's time, he is very conscious of the difficulties in the way. The discipline of the *"backside of the desert"* had not been in vain. Shepherding had chastened him (Pink).

We Preachers are quick to chasten Moses for his retiring attitude. We label it as a lack of Faith, etc. But I would ask the question, were such a command given by God to any of us presently, would our response be any different, or even as good?

As is obvious, the Lord didn't mince words, but what He is demanding of this man is so absolutely astounding that it defies all description. So in the face of such a task, the question *"Who am I?"* seems to be appropriate. However, as Moses is now to see, *"I AM"* is to be linked to *"I."*

FAITH

Verse 12 reads: *"And He said, Certainly I will be with you; and this shall be a token unto you, that I have sent you: when you have brought forth the people out of Egypt, you shall serve God upon this mountain."*

"Certainly I will be with you," should have been translated, *"Since I will be with you,"* because that's what it actually and literally says in the Hebrew. In other words, there is no doubt about the Presence of God being with Moses, that a guaranteed fact.

Moses is excusing himself on the grounds of insufficiency, but God replies, *"I will supply that which you lack. I will impart all the qualities you need."*

Then He said to Moses that not only would he succeed in leading the Children of Israel out of Egyptian bondage, but that they would then worship on this very mountain, which evidently was Sinai, where the Ten Commandments and the Law would be given.

As well, as the Lord promised to be with Moses, He as well promises to be with every single Believer of whom He calls for a certain task. As Moses had the Promise of God, we as well have the Promise of God. Consequently, we should not look at the task before us, but rather at the God of Glory Who is going to help us to perform the task, always realizing that there is nothing He cannot do. However, we must make certain that God has called us, and we haven't called ourselves, etc.

WHAT SHALL I SAY UNTO THEM?

Verse 13 reads: *"And Moses said unto God, Behold, when I come unto the Children of Israel, and shall say unto them, The God of your fathers has sent me unto you; and they shall say to me, What is His Name? What shall I say unto them?"*

The human heart is full of questions; consequently, it reasons and questions, when unhesitating obedience is that which is due to God; and still more marvelous is the Grace that bears with all the reasonings and answers all the questions. Each question, in fact, seems but to elicit some new feature of Divine Grace.

To the Israelites, God had been known only by titles, such as *"El"* or *"Elohim,"* which means, *"the Lofty One"*; or *"Shaddai,"* which means, *"the Powerful"*; or *"Jahveh"* or *"Jehovah,"* the *"Existent One."*

These titles were used among the Israelites with some perception of their meaning, but yet, these Names were more descriptions than anything else.

As well, the Egyptians used the word *"god"* generically, and had a special name for each particular god — as *"Ammon,"* or *"Phthah,"* or *"Ra,"* or *"Mentu,"* etc. Knowing that the Egyptians set much store by the names of their gods, which in every case had a meaning, Moses reasoned that Israel would want to know the Name of God Who had sent him. As we shall see, Israel came to cherish the Name that God told Moses to use as it regarded the Deity.

Let us not be too quick to condemn Moses here — the Lord did not! This was no small difficulty for Moses. No visible presence would accompany him. He was to go alone to the enslaved Hebrews and present himself as the Divinely-sent deliverer. He was to tell them that the God of their fathers had promised to free them. But, as we shall see later, this was not likely to make much impression upon a people who were, at least for the most part, sunk in the idolatries of the Egyptians. So, the great Law-Giver to be, felt that they would quickly want to know, Who is this God? What is His Character? Prove to us that He is worthy of our confidence.

Concerning this, Pink says: *"And does not a similar difficulty arise before us! We go forth to tell lost sinners of a God they have never seen. In His Name we bid them trust. But cannot we anticipate the response — 'Show us the Father, and it sufficeth us' is still, in substance, the demand of the doubting heart. Moses felt this difficulty; and so do we."*

I AM THAT I AM

Verse 14 reads: *"And God said unto Moses, I AM THAT I AM: and He said, Thus shall you say unto the Children of Israel, I AM has sent me unto you."*

It is said that the quotation, *"I AM THAT I AM,"* is the best translation that can be given of the Hebrew words. Some have translated it, *"I will be that I will be,"* and others, *"I am because I am"*; however, *"I AM THAT I AM"* says it better.

This Name was cherished by the Jews as a sacred treasure, and recognized as the proper appellation of the One and only God Whom the Israelites worshiped. It is found in this sense on the Moabite stone, and in the fragments of Philo-Byblius, and elsewhere (Pulpit).

The idea expressed by the Name, *"I AM THAT I AM,"* is that expressed of a *"real, perfect, unconditioned, independent existence."*

Dr. Pentecost translated the Name, if we would call it that, *"I AM THAT I AM,"* as,

"I was, I am, and I shall always continue to be."

Pink says, *"The principle contained in this word of Jehovah to Moses contains timely instruction for us. We are to go forth declaring the Name and nature of God as He has been revealed. No attempts are to be made to prove His existence; no time should be wasted with men in efforts to reason about God. Our business is to proclaim the Being of God as He has revealed Himself in and through Jesus Christ. The 'I AM' of the burning bush now stands fully declared in the blessed Person of our Saviour Who said, 'I am the Bread of Life', 'I am the Good Shepherd', 'I am the Door', 'I am the Light of the world', 'I am the Way, the Truth, and the Life', 'I am the Resurrection and the Life', 'I am the True Vine'. He is the eternal 'I AM' — 'the same yesterday, and today, and forever.'"*

In the Name or appellative, *"I AM THAT I AM,"* we have a depth which no finite mind can fathom. It means that God is Self-existent, beside Whom there is none else. He is without beginning, and without ending, *"from everlasting to everlasting"* He is God. None but He can say, *"I AM THAT I AM"* — always the same, eternally changeless.

THE TITLE

The title which God gives Himself here is one of great significance. When we look at the various Names which God has given Himself, we see that these Names are connected with the particular needs of the people. For instance:

"Jehovah-Jireh" means, *"The Lord will provide."*

"Jehovah-Nissi" means, *"The Lord my banner."*

"Jehovah-Shalom" means, *"The Lord is my peace."*

"Jehovah-Tsidkenu" means, *"The Lord our Righteousness."* And of course, there are many other titles such like that we could give.

But all these titles are unfolded to meet the necessities of His people; when He calls Himself *"I AM,"* it comprehends every title. In effect, the Lord, in taking this title, was furnishing his people with a blank check, to be filled up to any amount. He calls Himself, *"I AM,"* and Faith has but to write over

NOTES

against that precious Name whatever we want. God is the only significant figure, and human need may add the ciphers. If we want life, Christ says, *"I AM the Life"*; if we want Righteousness, He is *"The Lord Our Righteousness"*; if we want peace, *"He is our Peace,"* etc. (Mackintosh).

THE PRESENT MEANING

As we've already stated, the Revelation of God to man has taken on many appearances; however, all of these Revelations have led up to the great Revelation, in fact, the greatest of them all, and in actuality, the final Revelation, and we speak of God revealing Himself in Jesus Christ. When Philip asked our Lord to show him and the other Disciples the Father, Jesus answered: *"Have I been so long time with you, and yet have you not known Me, Philip? He who has seen Me has seen the Father"* (Jn. 14:8-9).

When Jesus gave all of His followers the right to use His Name (Mk. 16:17), He was, in effect, saying the same thing that God said to Moses, *"I AM THAT I AM."*

The blank check holds true as much presently as it did then. But it must be looked at in the following way:

The Lord will never allow His Name or His Word to be used against Himself, in other words, to bring about that which is not His Will. Such a disposition would be none other than catastrophic.

It is the business of the Believer to ascertain the Will of God, which can definitely be done if the person will consecrate to the Lord, and then, in the context of the Will of God, the blank check holds, but only in that context.

But in that context, and incidentally that is the context which is correct and right, great and mighty things can be done, and in fact, great and might things have been done. My Grandmother used to tell me, and in fact, told me many times and in many and varied ways, *"Jimmy,"* she would say, *"God is a big God, so ask big."* I have never forgotten that advice, and it has helped me to touch this world for the Lord Jesus Christ. God is big, so we should ask big.

Moses was to tell the Children of Israel, *"I AM has sent me unto you."* There could be no higher authority than that. And to be sure, it would be proven by the miracles which would follow.

At this present time, we have all type of Preachers claiming all type of things, and doing so in the Name of the Lord, when in reality, the Lord has not sent them. How do we know that?

When precious few people are saved, precious few baptized with the Holy Spirit, precious few who are delivered, and precious few who are truly healed, that is a telltale sign that something is wrong. And that is the state of most of the modern Church.

As it regards most Evangelists, while the crowds may be large, and the accolades may flow thickly and freely, when the dust settles and the smoke clears, one finds very little that's truly being done for Christ. It's mostly all fluff.

Just last night, a dear lady was in our Service at Family Worship Center, and related to me how a particular Evangelist, who is well known, claimed to be speaking prophetically, and told her that she would live to be 100 years of age.

To cut straight through to the bottom line, this man is a false prophet. And I'm not so sure that the dear lady didn't shorten her life by seeking the help of this false prophet. Great and glowing statements made by these individuals, who claim to be of God and from God, most of the time turn out to be the opposite. In other words, the patient who is declared to be healed suddenly dies.

The point I'm making is, I'm concerned that in many of these cases, these false pronouncements by these false prophets actually put a curse upon the people instead of a blessing.

But yet, the far greater majority of the modern Church goes on its merry way, and few question these false pronouncements, irrespective as to how off base they actually are, and how much they prove to be empty, hollow, and worthless. Satan is a master at getting people to believe that what is of God isn't, and what isn't of God is!

(15) "AND GOD SAID MOREOVER UNTO MOSES, THUS SHALL YOU SAY UNTO THE CHILDREN OF ISRAEL, THE LORD GOD OF YOUR FATHERS, THE GOD OF ABRAHAM, THE GOD OF ISAAC, AND THE GOD OF JACOB, HAS SENT ME UNTO YOU: THIS IS MY NAME FOREVER, AND THIS IS MY MEMORIAL UNTO ALL GENERATIONS.

(16) "GO, AND GATHER THE ELDERS OF ISRAEL TOGETHER, AND SAY UNTO THEM, THE LORD GOD OF YOUR FATHERS, THE GOD OF ABRAHAM, OF ISAAC, AND OF JACOB, APPEARED UNTO ME, SAYING, I HAVE SURELY VISITED YOU, AND SEEN THAT WHICH IS DONE TO YOU IN EGYPT:

(17) "AND I HAVE SAID, I WILL BRING YOU UP OUT OF THE AFFLICTION OF EGYPT UNTO THE LAND OF THE CANAANITES, AND THE HITTITES, AND THE AMORITES, AND THE PERIZZITES, AND THE HIVITES, AND THE JEBUSITES, UNTO A LAND FLOWING WITH MILK AND HONEY.

(18) "AND THEY SHALL HEARKEN TO YOUR VOICE: AND YOU SHALL COME, YOU AND THE ELDERS OF ISRAEL, UNTO THE KING OF EGYPT, AND YOU SHALL SAY UNTO HIM, THE LORD GOD OF THE HEBREWS HAS MET WITH US: AND NOW LET US GO, WE BESEECH YOU, THREE DAYS' JOURNEY INTO THE WILDERNESS, THAT WE MAY SACRIFICE TO THE LORD OUR GOD."

The composition is:

1. Moses was commanded to tell the Children of Israel that this mighty God, Jehovah, was the God of Abraham, the God of Isaac, and the God of Jacob. This was His Name forever and His memorial to all generations.

2. He changes not; He is the same yesterday, today, and forever. His Name is Jesus; and that is God's greatest Name!

3. The glad tidings of great joy that Moses was to carry to Israel were these: *"I will bring you up out of the affliction of Egypt into a land flowing with milk and honey."* This was the Message; and Moses' faith in delivering it was strengthened beforehand by the Divine assurance that it would be believed.

4. The three days' journey of Verse 18 was not deceitfully proposed by God, but furnished as a test for Pharaoh.

THE GOD OF ABRAHAM, THE GOD OF ISAAC, AND THE GOD OF JACOB

Verses 15 and 16 read: *"And God said*

moreover unto Moses, Thus shall you say unto the Children of Israel, The LORD God of your fathers, the God of Abraham, the God of Isaac, and the God of Jacob, has sent me unto you: this is My Name forever, this is My memorial unto all generations.

"Go, and gather the Elders of Israel together, and say unto them, The LORD God of your fathers, the God of Abraham, of Isaac, and of Jacob, appeared unto me, saying, I have surely visited you, and seen that which is done to you in Egypt."

As is understood, the Lord is telling Moses these things, while he's still at the backside of the desert. In essence, the Lord tells him several things which will happen:

1. Upon arriving in Egypt, Moses was to gather the Elders of Israel before him, which pertained to the leaders of the enslaved Tribes. Perhaps, these were the heads of the Tribes.

2. He was to tell them that *"The Lord God of your fathers, the God of Abraham, the God of Isaac, and the God of Jacob, has sent me unto you."*

3. The Name of God was to be *"I AM THAT I AM,"* which was a new Revelation to Israel.

4. Moses was to tell the Israelites that God had seen, and in fact, continued to see, all the evil that was being done to them in Egypt.

5. God has said that He would bring them out of the affliction of Egypt unto the land of the Canaanites, etc.

6. It was a land flowing with milk and honey.

7. Whereas some 40 years before the leaders of Israel had not hearkened unto Moses, this time, the Lord remonstrated, they definitely would hearken to the voice of Moses, for evidently, the Lord would prepare the way.

8. Moses and the Elders of Israel, along with Aaron, the brother of Moses, it would later prove, were to appear before Pharaoh.

9. They were to demand of Pharaoh that he let Israel go for a three days' journey into the wilderness, that they may sacrifice there to the Lord their God.

10. The Lord foretold that Pharaoh would not heed their demand, and then God said that He would smite Egypt with all miracles and wonders.

11. After that, Pharaoh would definitely let the people go.

NOTES

12. But when the Israelites would leave Egypt, they would not leave empty, but would be loaded down with silver, gold, and raiment, which the Egyptians would give them.

So in a few words, the Lord told Moses exactly what was to happen, therefore, what he could expect.

A WITNESS

The phrase, *"I have surely visited you, and seen that which is done to you in Egypt,"* proclaims the fact that the Lord is not unmindful of anything that happens to His children. Sometimes it may seem as if He is not observing that which is happening, but most definitely He is. And to be sure, exactly as we see what happened to Egypt, the Lord is going to require of the offender every iota of that which has been practiced on the offended. That's the reason He told us not to avenge ourselves, *"but rather give place unto wrath: for it is written, Vengeance is Mine; I will repay, saith the Lord"* (Rom. 12:19).

We are to place all wrongs, all injustices, all hurts tendered toward us and upon us, into the hand of the Lord. We are to forgive the people, whomever they might be, ask the Lord to help us forget about the situation, and proceed on with our lives and living for the Lord, leaving all in His hands.

To be sure, God never forgets, unless it's sins of which we repent.

BEFORE PHARAOH

Verses 17 and 18 read: *"And I have said, I will bring you up out of the affliction of Egypt unto the land of the Canaanites, and the Hittites, and the Amorites, and the Perizzites, and the Hivites, and the Jebusites, unto a land flowing with milk and honey.*

"And they shall hearken to your voice: and you shall come, you and the Elders of Israel, unto the king of Egypt, and you shall say unto him, The LORD God of the Hebrews has met with us: and now let us go, we beseech you, three days' journey into the wilderness, that we may sacrifice to the LORD our God."

The glad tidings of great joy that Moses was to carry to Israel were these: *"I will bring you up out of the affliction of Egypt into a land flowing with milk and honey."* This was the Message; and Moses' faith in delivering it was strengthened beforehand by the Divine assurance that it would be believed.

By the Lord telling Moses that the Elders of Israel would definitely believe his Message tells us that Moses had expressed fear that they wouldn't.

The idea is, the hearts of men are in God's hands, and He is able to bring about that which He desires, without infringing upon the free moral agency of anyone.

This is at least one of the reasons that we should look to the Lord for leading in all things. We as Believers should never trust in our own personal wisdom, acumen, ability, or strength. Our knowledge of situations is very limited, while God's knowledge is unlimited. Our ability as well is very limited, while the ability of God is unlimited. We should trust Him, ardently seeking His face about everything we do, whether it be small or great.

It is easy to see here that God already had things planned out, and through foreknowledge knew exactly what would happen. All Moses had to do was to follow the leading of the Lord, which he definitely did. It is the same with us presently because God cannot change, and He doesn't need to change.

He has things on our behalf, already planned out, and that which He has planned will definitely be accomplished, that is, if we cooperate with Him, thereby, walking in Faith. But remember, there must be cooperation on our part, and that cooperation is summed up in one word, *"Faith."*

WHAT DO WE MEAN BY FAITH?

God is not looking for perfection in people, because sadly and regrettably, there isn't any perfection. But He definitely is looking for Faith. He wants us to believe Him. If we will believe Him, thereby having our Faith in the correct object, despite our shortcomings, He can see us through.

As we shall see, the Children of Israel were to place their Faith in God, which would ultimately carry out to Faith in the slain lamb, which in effect, would bring about their deliverance from Egypt. It was the Cross then, of which the slain lamb was a Type (the Passover Lamb), and it is the Cross now. If our Faith is placed there, understanding that the great Plan of God in its totality is centered up in the Cross, making the Cross the centrality of the Gospel, victory will most definitely be ours.

It was a part of God's design that Sacrifice, interrupted during the sojourn in Egypt for various reasons, should be resumed beyond the bounds of Egypt by His people. Consequently, it was *"Sacrifice"* which was first mentioned to Pharaoh, regarding the first visit by Moses to that Monarch.

Demanding that the Israelites be allowed to go three days' journey into the wilderness, in order that they may sacrifice unto the Lord, was not meant to deceive Pharaoh, but rather, to test him.

Going back to Verse 15, the Lord told Moses to tell the Children of Israel that *"The Lord God of your fathers, the God of Abraham, the God of Isaac, and the God of Jacob, has sent me unto you: this is My Name forever, and this is My memorial to all generations."*

This statement contains a very important truth — a truth which many professing Christians seem to forget, namely, that God's relationship with Israel is an eternal one. He is just as much Israel's God now as when He visited them in the land of Egypt. Only, because of rejecting their Messiah, they are, in His governmental dealings, set aside for a time. But His Word is clear and emphatic: *"This is My Name forever."* He does not say, *"This is My Name for a time, so long as they continue what they ought to be."* No; *"This is My Name forever, and this is My memorial unto all generations."*

When Paul said, *"God has not cast away His people which He foreknew"* (Rom. 11:2), this meant they were His people still, whether obedient or disobedient, united together or scattered abroad, manifested to the nations, or hidden from their view. Whether they like it or not, they are His people, and He is their God.

This doesn't mean that all of them are saved. In fact, precious few of them presently are saved; consequently, those in that state, however many there are, have died, and will die, eternally lost. But it does mean that the Promises of God as it regards the nation and these people as a whole, will definitely be realized. Exodus 3:15 is unanswerable.

God means what He says; and He will, ere long, make manifest to all the nations of the Earth that His connection with Israel is one which shall outlive all the revolutions of time. *"The gifts and calling of God are without repentance."* When He said, *"This is My Name forever,"* He spoke absolutely. *"I AM"* declared Himself to be Israel's God forever; and all the Gentiles shall be made to bow to this; and to know, moreover, that all God's providential dealings with them in all their destinies, are connected, in some way or other, with that favored and honored, though now judged and scattered, people.

"When the Most High divided to the nations their inheritance, when He separated the sons of Adam, He set the bounds of the people according to the number of the Children of Israel. For the LORD's portion is His people; Jacob is the lot of His inheritance" (Deut. 32:8-9).

Mackintosh asked this question: *"Has this ceased to be true? Has Jehovah given up His 'portion,' and surrendered 'the lot of His inheritance'?"*

To reply to these questions would be to quote a large portion of the Old Testament, and not a little of the New Testament. In answer we must say, let not Christendom be ignorant of this mystery, that blindness in part has happened to Israel, until the fullness of the Gentiles be come in. *"And so all Israel shall be saved"* (Rom. 11:25-26) (Mackintosh).

THE SACRIFICE

To which we've already briefly alluded, the first thing that Moses was to mention to Pharaoh was the fact of the Sacrifice, and its necessity.

The Sacrifice of an innocent victim, which was either a lamb, a goat, a heifer, an ox, or a ram, was instituted upon the Fall of the First Family. Every evidence is that God told Adam and Eve as to how fellowship could be restored and sins forgiven, which would be by virtue of the Sacrifice, and more particularly, what it represented, namely the coming Christ. A perfect description of this is given in Genesis, Chapter 4, as it regards Cain and Abel. Abel offered up the sacrifice that was pleasing to God, which was an innocent victim, which typified Christ, and the sacrifice being accepted, the sacrificer was accepted as well. God didn't really look at the sacrificer, but rather the sacrifice. He continues to do the same presently. Likewise, if the sacrifice was rejected, even as it was with Cain, then the sacrificer was rejected also.

Thereafter until Moses, a period of about 2,400 years, the Patriarch of each family was to serve as the Priest of that family, and superintend the offering up of Sacrifices, which in fact were continued throughout that period of time.

After the deliverance of the Children of Israel from Egyptian bondage, which we are now in the process of studying, the Lord gave to Moses and the Children of Israel His Law, which covered every aspect of their daily lives and living. The center or core of the Law was the sacrificial system. It was carried out in elaborate detail, and was meant to symbolize Christ, as in fact all sacrifices were meant to symbolize Christ.

In fact, the blood of bulls and goats was merely a stopgap measure, which was to be used until Christ would come, and would ever point to Him. Animal blood could never take away sin, but the spotless, pure, unsullied Blood of the Lord Jesus Christ definitely could take away sin, and in fact, did atone for all sin, in it being shed (Eph. 2:13-18; I Pet. 1:18-20).

When Christ came, animal sacrifices were no more needed, as would be obvious because Christ had fulfilled that symbol. Unfortunately, the Christian Jews, and we especially speak of those in Jerusalem, continued to try to meld the Sacrifice of Christ with the ancient sacrificial system, as carried out at the temple. As I think the historical narrative records, this was not pleasing to the Lord. So, in A.D. 70, the Lord used, as His instrument, the Roman General Titus, who headed up the mighty Tenth Legion, to destroy Jerusalem, and above all, the Temple. It was so completely destroyed that there was nothing left, with even a harrow being dragged over the spot where it had once stood.

In effect, the Lord was saying that Christ

must no longer be insulted by animal sacrifices continuing to be offered, so He removed the means and the manner of those Sacrifices.

THE GOVERNMENT OF GRACE

While the modern Church doesn't engage itself in the ancient Jewish rituals, still, it functions mostly under the government of law instead of the government of Grace.

The only way that one can function under the government of Grace is by and through Faith, and we speak of Faith in Christ and His Finished Work (I Cor. 1:17-18, 21, 23; 2:2, 5).

Some Christians erroneously believe that because this is the Dispensation of Grace, and it definitely is that, then automatically we're functioning in Grace. No we aren't!

Paul said: *"I do not frustrate the Grace of God: for if Righteousness come by the Law, then Christ is dead in vain"* (Gal. 2:21).

This Passage proves to us that it is possible to frustrate the Grace of God. *"Frustrate"* in the Greek is *"atheteo,"* and means, *"to set aside, to neutralize or violate, bring to naught."*

So we know from this statement that it definitely is possible to stop the flow of the Grace of God into our lives, which brings on untold problems. The only way we can function as Christians is by a steady, uninterrupted flow of the Grace of God, which simply means that the Goodness of God is extended to undeserving Believers.

The Grace of God, which constitutes the government of Grace, functions on the principle of the Cross of Christ, and through no other means. In fact, God has no more Grace today than He had thousands of years ago. Due to the fact that the blood of bulls and goats couldn't take away sin, this hindered the full flow of the Grace of God from coming to Believers.

Upon the advent of the Cross, which removed the terrible sin debt (Jn. 1:29), the Grace of God could now flow copiously to all Believers. In order to have this uninterrupted flow, this abundant supply, the only thing that is required of the Child of God is that we have Faith in Christ, and what Christ has done for us in His Finished Work of the Cross (I Cor. 1:17-18). Continued Faith in the Sufferings of Christ guarantees a continued and uninterrupted flow of the Grace of God. So what did Paul mean by frustrating the Grace of God?

THE FRUSTRATION OF THE GRACE OF GOD

Whenever the Believer pulls his Faith from Christ and the Cross, thereby placing it in something else, in the mind of God, that Believer has then gone from Grace to Law. And Paul plainly says that if we can gain Righteousness by the Law or by keeping certain laws, then Christ died in vain. That's a pretty strong statement!

Whenever the Christian does this, and I speak of our Faith being anchored in something other than the Cross, we are in effect saying, whether we realize it or not, that the Work of Christ on the Cross was insufficient, and we need to add something to that particular Work. Or else, we are saying that it was not the Cross which effected our Redemption, but something else altogether. Either way, we are on the road to spiritual disaster.

When Paul mentions *"Law,"* he is either talking about the Law of Moses, or law which we have devised ourselves, or rather is man-devised in some fashion. And actually, these laws, most of the time, are very good within themselves. And because they are very good, this fools us. It makes us believe that by the doing of such, such is the means of victory, overcoming power and strength, Righteousness, Holiness, Christlikeness, etc. But the only thing we actually succeed in doing is to develop self-righteousness in our lives, which can cause us untold problems.

Our victory is solely in Christ and Christ Alone. It is in Christ solely by virtue of what He did for us in the giving of Himself on the Cross. That's why the Apostle said: *"But God forbid that I should glory* (boast), *save in the Cross of our Lord Jesus Christ, by Whom the world is crucified unto me, and I unto the world"* (Gal. 6:14).

(19) "AND I AM SURE THAT THE KING OF EGYPT WILL NOT LET YOU GO, NO, NOT BY A MIGHTY HAND.

(20) "AND I WILL STRETCH OUT MY HAND, AND SMITE EGYPT WITH ALL MY

WONDERS WHICH I WILL DO IN THE MIDST THEREOF: AND AFTER THAT HE WILL LET YOU GO.

(21) "AND I WILL GIVE THIS PEOPLE FAVOR IN THE SIGHT OF THE EGYPTIANS: AND IT SHALL COME TO PASS, THAT, WHEN YOU GO, YOU SHALL NOT GO EMPTY.

(22) "BUT EVERY WOMAN SHALL BORROW OF HER NEIGHBOR, AND OF HER THAT SOJOURNETH IN HER HOUSE, JEWELS OF SILVER, AND JEWELS OF GOLD, AND RAIMENT: AND YOU SHALL PUT THEM UPON YOUR SONS, AND UPON YOUR DAUGHTERS; AND YOU SHALL SPOIL THE EGYPTIANS."

The overview is:

1. Through foreknowledge, as recorded in Verse 19, God knew that Pharaoh would not allow the Children of Israel to leave.

2. Consequently, as is portrayed in Verse 20, He would use Pharaoh's obstinate heart to serve as a warning of the Power and Glory of God to all the surrounding nations.

3. God can take whatever is done and turn it to His good if His people will only believe Him.

4. Verses 20 through 22 tell us that God planned that His people should receive proper wages for all their hard labor before leaving Egypt.

5. The word *"borrow"* in Verse 22 does not mean to borrow in the sense that we use the term. It means, *"to ask"* or even to *"demand."* The implication is that the Egyptians had stripped from the Israelites their valuables. Now, Israel would not only receive back what had been taken from them, but also what they had earned by their hard labor.

FOREKNOWLEDGE

Verse 19 reads: *"And I am sure that the king of Egypt will not let you go, no, not by a mighty hand."*

Through foreknowledge, the Lord knew exactly what Pharaoh would do. In other words, through foreknowledge, God knows the future, which of course is beyond the comprehension of mere mortals.

However, when we speak of foreknowledge, we are not meaning that God predestines all things. While He definitely does predestine some things, all of these things which He does predestine are beyond the pale of man's free moral agency. In other words, God never tampers with the free moral agency of man, always respecting our free wills.

As we survey the Scripture, we also find that everything which God predestines is in the realm of *"what"* will happen, instead of to *"whom"* it will happen. For instance, Paul said:

"For whom He did foreknow (God knows who will accept Him as Lord and Saviour, even before we are born), *He also did predestinate to be conformed to the Image of His Son, that He might be the firstborn among many brethren"* (Rom. 8:29).

The Scripture doesn't state here that a person is predestinated to be saved, while it definitely does say that God foreknew who would be saved. But that is far different than someone being predestinated to be saved or lost.

But He did say that once that person accepts Christ, making Him one's Lord and Saviour, that person is *"predestinated to be conformed to the Image of God's Son."*

Even then, this does not always happen; however, if the person cooperates with the Lord as it regards their Faith, they most definitely will be conformed to the Image of the Son.

As well, all other Scriptures which have to do with predestination always refer to *"what"* is predestinated, instead of *"whom."*

The great theme of the Gospel is always *"whosoever will"* (Rev. 22:17; Jn. 3:16). The idea that God has predestinated some people to go to Heaven and some people to go to Hell, and there is nothing they have to say in the decision is not taught in the Word of God.

THE POWER OF GOD

Verse 20 reads: *"And I will stretch out My hand, and smite Egypt with all My wonders which I will do in the midst thereof: and after that he will let you go."*

The idea of this Verse is, God is Almighty, and thereby, He has the power to do whatever it is that He desires to do. So in effect, Moses is saying that even though the mighty Hand of God is stretched out over Egypt to perform signs and wonders, Pharaoh will continue to be obstinate, refusing to let the Children of Israel go. Therefore, the Lord will keep increasing the pressure, even with greater and greater acts of demonstration of power, which will ultimately break down the stubborn heart of the Egyptian Monarch. In fact, the greatest miracle of all would be that of the Passover Lamb, which would bring about the death of all the firstborn in the land of Egypt. This caused the knees of Pharaoh to buckle, so to speak.

RICHES

Verses 21 and 22 read: *"And I will give this people favor in the sight of the Egyptians: and it shall come to pass, that when you go, you shall not go empty:*

"But every woman shall borrow of her neighbor, and of her that sojourneth in her house, jewels of silver, and jewels of gold, and raiment: and you shall put them upon your sons, and upon your daughters; and you shall spoil the Egyptians."

I'm certain that when this word was given by Moses to the Elders of Israel concerning the great riches which would be heaped upon the Israelites when they left Egypt, these Elders must have done a double-take. They couldn't imagine Pharaoh letting them go, much less, loading them down with jewels and raiment, etc. However, whatever God says that He will do, irrespective as to how preposterous it might seem at the beginning, how unlikely, how virtually impossible, to be sure, His Word will come to pass, and will do so exactly as He has said. God cannot lie!

In this, we see the Egyptians willingly paying the Israelites for their hard work, and in effect, paying for what they had stolen from them as well.

One might say that God keeps books on everything. Nothing escapes His notice or attention. And to be sure, the bottom line will always come out as it ought to, whenever God is overseeing the situation.

"My sins laid open to the rod
"The back which from the law was free;
"And the Eternal Son of God
"Received the stripes once due to me."

"No beam was in His eye, nor mote,
"Nor laid to Him was angry blame;
"And yet His cheeks for me were smote
"The cheeks that never blushed for shame."

"I pierced those sacred hands and feet
"That never touched or walked in sin;
"I broke the heart that only beat
"The souls of sinful men to win."

"That sponge of vinegar and gall
"Was placed by me upon His tongue;
"And when derision mocked His call,
"I stood that mocking crowd among."

"And yet His Blood was shed for me,
"To be of sin the double cure;
"And balm there flows from Calvary's tree
"That heals my guilt and makes me pure."

CHAPTER 4

(1) "AND MOSES ANSWERED AND SAID, BUT, BEHOLD, THEY WILL NOT BELIEVE ME, NOR HEARKEN UNTO MY VOICE: FOR THEY WILL SAY, THE LORD HAS NOT APPEARED UNTO YOU.

(2) "AND THE LORD SAID UNTO HIM, WHAT IS THAT IN YOUR HAND? AND HE SAID, A ROD.

(3) "AND HE SAID, CAST IT ON THE GROUND. AND HE CAST IT ON THE GROUND, AND IT BECAME A SERPENT; AND MOSES FLED FROM BEFORE IT.

(4) "AND THE LORD SAID UNTO MOSES, PUT FORTH YOUR HAND, AND TAKE IT BY THE TAIL. AND HE PUT FORTH HIS HAND, AND CAUGHT IT, AND IT BECAME A ROD IN HIS HAND:

(5) "THAT THEY MAY BELIEVE THAT THE LORD GOD OF THEIR FATHERS, THE GOD OF ABRAHAM, THE GOD OF ISAAC, AND THE GOD OF JACOB, HAS APPEARED UNTO YOU.

(6) "AND THE LORD SAID FURTHERMORE UNTO HIM, PUT NOW YOUR HAND INTO YOUR BOSOM. AND HE PUT HIS HAND INTO HIS BOSOM: AND WHEN HE TOOK IT OUT, BEHOLD, HIS HAND WAS LEPROUS AS SNOW.

(7) "AND HE SAID, PUT YOUR HAND NOW INTO YOUR BOSOM AGAIN. AND HE PUT HIS HAND INTO HIS BOSOM AGAIN;

AND PLUCKED IT OUT OF HIS BOSOM, AND, BEHOLD, IT WAS TURNED AGAIN AS HIS OTHER FLESH.

(8) "AND IT SHALL COME TO PASS, IF THEY WILL NOT BELIEVE YOU, NEITHER HEARKEN TO THE VOICE OF THE FIRST SIGN, THAT THEY WILL BELIEVE THE VOICE OF THE LATTER SIGN.

(9) "AND IT SHALL COME TO PASS, IF THEY WILL NOT BELIEVE ALSO THESE TWO SIGNS, NEITHER HEARKEN UNTO YOUR VOICE, THAT YOU SHALL TAKE OF THE WATER OF THE RIVER, AND POUR IT UPON THE DRY LAND: AND THE WATER WHICH YOU TAKE OUT OF THE RIVER SHALL BECOME BLOOD UPON THE DRY LAND."

The exegesis is:

1. The hesitating and timid Moses of Mount Horeb was the same courageous and self-reliant Moses who smote the Egyptian dead! His strength then unfitted him as a Divine instrument, and now his weakness unfitted him.

2. God can use neither one nor the other, if the strength is trusted, or if the weakness is sheltered behind as an excuse.

3. Weakness, as in the case of Moses budded into unbelief, and blossomed into rebellion. But how tenderly God dealt with him!

UNBELIEF

Verse 1 reads: *"And Moses answered and said, But, behold, they will not believe me, nor hearken unto my voice: for they will say, The LORD has not appeared unto you."*

How hard it is to overcome the unbelief of the human heart. How slow we are to believe the Promises of God; how slow we are to have Faith in Him. Concerning this, Mackintosh says: *"The most slender reed that the human eye can see is counted more substantial, by far, as a basis for nature's confidence, than the unseen 'Rock of Ages.'"*

Men will rush to any broken cistern, and do so rapidly, rather than abide by the unseen *"Fountain of Living Waters."*

We watch the Church presently, as it opts for the broken reed of humanistic psychology, rather than trust the Cross of Christ. And that's what it is: a lack of Faith in that which Christ has done, so we spring for the pitiful prattle of unredeemed man.

NOTES

THE CROSS

I believe I can say without fear of contradiction, at least as it regards the modern Church, that all erroneous directions lead away from the Cross. That which is Biblical, therefore, true and right, always, and without exception, leads to the Cross. So it's a matter of the Cross, and more particularly, it's a matter of Faith.

I maintain that without a proper understanding of the Cross, which in reality is a proper understanding of the Word, that one cannot really have Faith, at least the proper Faith that God will honor. Whatever failure we behold in our own personal lives, or the lives of others, whatever wrong directions are taken, we will find, that is if we dig enough, that the problem is a lack of Faith in Christ and Him Crucified (I Cor. 2:2).

Moses raises questions, and still God answers them; and, as we have remarked, each successive question brings out fresh Grace.

THE ROD

Verses 2 through 5 read: *"And the LORD said unto him, What is that in your hand? And he said, A rod.*

"And He said, Cast it on the ground. And he cast it on the ground, and it became a serpent; and Moses fled from before it.

"And the LORD said unto Moses, Put forth your hand, and take it by the tail. And he put forth his hand, and caught it, and it became a rod in his hand:

"That they may believe that the LORD God of their fathers, the God of Abraham, the God of Isaac, and the God of Jacob, has appeared unto you."

Concerning this, Williams says: *"To assure Moses, God gave him two promises and three signs. The promises were: 'I will be with you'; and 'You shall serve God upon this mountain' (Horeb). The three signs were: the serpent, leprosy, and blood. The serpent, Satan and his power; leprosy, sin introduced by him; blood poured out, the Wrath of God.*

"These three signs taught Moses that the Divine Power, which was to fit him for his mission, could make Satan as helpless as the rod in his hand, and use him in the accomplishment of God's counsels. Further,

that Divine Power could cleanse away sin — a malady as loathsome and incurable as leprosy; and, lastly, that that same Almighty Power would judge with death those who despised that Grace."

THE SERPENT

By the rod turning to a serpent, a venomous one at that, Moses in essence was being told that he was going to come up against the powers of darkness. Egypt was actually ruled by demon spirits, which worked through Pharaoh and the magicians, etc. It was a nation wholly taken over by demon spirits, and ruled thereby.

In fact, most of the nations of the world presently fall into the same state. Every religion in the world was instituted by demon spirits. Christianity is not a religion, but rather a relationship, and with Christ.

So, the Lord was showing Moses that which he was coming up against.

The Lord then told Moses to take the snake by the tail, and when he obeyed, it instantly became a rod, the same rod which would be used by God to bring about miracles. This told Moses that he had power over Satan.

He was to catch this serpent by the tail, simply because the time for its head to be bruised, as was predicted in the Garden of Eden, had not yet come about. That would take place at the Cross (Gen. 3:15).

Therefore, we find here that Moses was going into Egypt with great power, the Power of God behind him, which was greater than all the demon forces of Egypt, even as Egypt was to belatedly see.

Moses was to perform these three signs in the sight of the Elders of Israel, and possibly many of the people as well, which he did.

By the use of the appellative, *"The God of Abraham, The God of Isaac, and The God of Jacob,"* Moses was letting the people know that he was functioning within the boundaries of the same Promises which God had given to the Patriarchs. God, Who is Jehovah, Who had appeared unto these three, appeared as well to Moses.

LEPROSY

Verses 6 and 7 read: *"And the LORD said furthermore unto him, Put now your hand into your bosom. And he put his hand into his bosom: and when he took it out, behold, his hand was leprous as snow.*

"And he said, Put your hand into your bosom again. And he put his hand into his bosom again; and plucked it out of his bosom, and, behold, it was turned again as his other flesh."

Leprosy is a type of sin, which is the cause of all the problems in the world. The idea is, the Lord was delivering the Children of Israel from Egyptian bondage, and as well, would give them a land flowing with milk and honey, all for the purpose of bringing the Redeemer into the world, Who would address this terrible problem of sin, which He would do at the Cross.

Putting his hand into his bosom and bringing it out, and seeing it leprous, portrayed to him the terrible horror of the plague of sin which gripped the human race in totality.

He was instructed once again to put the leprous hand in his bosom, and then take it out, and would find that it had now been made perfectly whole, without any sign of leprosy. Thus we see here in this particular *"sign,"* that which Jesus Christ can perform as it regards the Salvation of the soul. He can cleanse from all sin, and He Alone can cleanse from all sin. There is no other solution to this terrible problem. It is Christ and Christ Alone, and more particularly, it is *"Christ and Him Crucified"* (I Cor. 1:23).

Who Jesus is, and What Jesus did at the Cross is the answer to man's dilemma, and in fact, the only answer to man's dilemma. Man is a moral leper, and anything and everything he might try to do outside of Christ to alleviate the situation leaves him a moral leper. Changing the clothes on a leper in no way changes the leprosy. But that's what man seeks to do.

By having Moses put his hand in his bosom, the Lord was showing Moses that sin is more than an external problem, but rather a problem that begins in the very heart of man, i.e., *"the bosom."* Consequently, external remedies will not suffice. And to be sure, man has no remedy, at least within himself, that can go to the heart of the matter. That could only be accomplished by Christ, and it could only be accomplished at the Cross (Gal. 3:13-14).

THE BLOOD

Verses 8 and 9 read: *"And it shall come to pass, if they will not believe you, neither hearken to the voice of the first sign, that they will believe the voice of the latter sign.*

"And it shall come to pass, if they will not believe also these two signs, neither hearken unto your voice, that you shall take of the water of the river, and pour it upon the dry land: and the water which you take out of the river shall become blood upon the dry land."

The idea of this last sign is, the only answer to the serpent, i.e., *"Satan,"* and the sin which he causes, which is so hideous it can only be symbolized by the dread disease of *"leprosy,"* is the Blood, the Precious Blood, of the Lord Jesus Christ. As the serpent was a symbol of Satan, and leprosy a symbol of sin, the blood here is a symbol of what Christ would do in order to deliver humanity, and I speak of the shedding of His Precious Blood on the Cross of Calvary.

I'm afraid the Church doesn't understand the hideousness and the power of sin, that is, if it believes in sin at all. In fact, if the modern Church understood what it was facing, and I continue to speak of Satan and sin, then to be sure, the modern Church would preach the Cross, for there is no other solution.

Ineffably holy in Himself, Jesus had no sin (Heb. 4:15), did no sin (I Pet. 2:22), and knew no sin (II Cor. 5:21). But in infinite Grace, He took our place — all praise to His peerless Name — and *"was made sin for us"* (II Cor. 5:21). *"He bear our sins in His Own Body on the Tree"* (I Pet. 2:24). Because of this, He was, at that time, in the sight of God what the leper was — defiled, unclean; not inherently so, but by imputation. In other words, God imputed the defilement to Him, exactly as He imputes (gives) Righteousness to us.

The leper's place was *"outside"* the camp (Lev. 13:46), away from where God dwelt between the Mercy Seat and the Cherubim in the Tabernacle. And on the Cross Christ was separated for three terrible hours from the thrice-Holy God. But after the awful penalty of sin had been endured, and the Work of Atonement was finished, the Forsaken One is seen again in communion with God — *"Father into Your hands I commit My Spirit"* evidences that. And it was as *"the Holy One"* (Ps. 16:10) He was laid in the sepulcher, not a defiled sinner as some teach.

Thus, after Moses thrust his leprous hand into his bosom, he drew it forth again perfectly whole — every trace of defilement gone. In their foreshadowings of Christ, then, the first sign intimated that the great Deliverer would *"destroy the works of the Devil"* (I Jn. 3:8), which He would do by His death on the Cross, while the second sign of the leper signified that He would *"take away our sins"* (I Jn. 3:5), which he also accomplished on the Cross.

While the third sign *"the Blood"* also represents the Cross, we must understand that it is in the form of judgment as much as it is the form of Salvation.

If it is to be noticed, the third sign was to be wrought only if the testimony of the first two was refused. It, therefore, tells of the consequences of refusing to believe what the other signs so plainly bore witness to. If man rejects the testimony of God's Word that he is under the dominion of Satan and is depraved by nature, and thereby refuses the One Who Alone can deliver from the one and cleanse from the other, which can only be done by the shed Blood, which speaks of life, nothing but Divine judgment awaits him. Accepted, the Blood speaks of life; rejected, the Blood speaks of death!

(10) "AND MOSES SAID UNTO THE LORD, O MY LORD, I AM NOT ELOQUENT, AND NEITHER HERETOFORE, NOR SINCE YOU HAVE SPOKEN UNTO YOUR SERVANT: BUT I AM SLOW OF SPEECH, AND OF A SLOW TONGUE.

(11) "AND THE LORD SAID UNTO HIM, WHO HAS MADE MAN'S MOUTH? OR WHO MAKES THE DUMB, OR DEAF, OR THE SEEING, OR THE BLIND? HAVE NOT I THE LORD?

(12) "NOW THEREFORE GO, AND I WILL BE WITH YOUR MOUTH, AND TEACH YOU WHAT YOU SHALL SAY.

(13) "AND HE SAID, O MY LORD, SEND, I PRAY YOU, BY THE HAND OF HIM WHOM YOU WILL SEND.

(14) "AND THE ANGER OF THE LORD WAS KINDLED AGAINST MOSES, AND HE SAID, IS NOT AARON THE LEVITE YOUR BROTHER? I KNOW THAT HE CAN SPEAK WELL. AND ALSO, BEHOLD, HE COMES FORTH TO MEET YOU: AND WHEN HE SEES YOU, HE WILL BE GLAD IN HIS HEART.

(15) "AND YOU SHALL SPEAK UNTO HIM, AND PUT WORDS IN HIS MOUTH: AND I WILL BE WITH YOUR MOUTH, AND WITH HIS MOUTH, AND WILL TEACH YOU WHAT YOU SHALL DO.

(16) "AND HE SHALL BE YOUR SPOKESMAN UNTO THE PEOPLE: AND HE SHALL BE, EVEN HE SHALL BE TO YOU INSTEAD OF A MOUTH, AND YOU SHALL BE TO HIM INSTEAD OF GOD.

(17) "AND YOU SHALL TAKE THIS ROD IN YOUR HAND, WHEREWITH YOU SHALL DO SIGNS."

The synopsis is:

1. Verses 10, 11, and 12 portray the Call of God upon man. *"I am not eloquent."* And even if we were, it would not save anyone.

2. In Verse 12, the Lord says, *"I will be with your mouth."* These are the Preachers we need!

3. Verse 13, in effect, says that Moses registered unbelief. The Fourteenth Verse says, *"And the anger of the Lord was kindled against Moses."* Unbelief angers God.

EXCUSES

Verse 10 reads: *"And Moses said unto the LORD, O my Lord, I am not eloquent, neither heretofore, nor since You have spoken unto Your servant: but I am slow of speech, and of a slow tongue."*

God has never called anyone yet who had it all together. In fact, no such human exists. We can prepare ourselves to a certain extent, and should do all that we can, but the final analysis must find the Lord preparing the man, as He Alone can do.

Furthermore, even as we see here, the Lord doesn't enjoy at all us bringing up our deficiencies, except in the sense of knowing that we have them, and we must depend totally and completely on the Lord to see us through. Otherwise, it is unbelief, which God cannot tolerate.

According to Jewish tradition, Moses had a difficulty in pronouncing some of the letters, which in effect, would make him seem to be somewhat stupid. So if in fact this was true, it was an embarrassment to the great Law-Giver to be.

What was the answer of the Lord concerning the unbelief of Moses? That we will see momentarily.

Any complaint of this nature always registers unbelief, so we should take that into consideration the next time we try to make excuses regarding that which the Lord has told us to do.

THE POWER OF GOD

Verses 11 and 12 read: *"And the LORD said unto him, Who has made man's mouth? Or who makes the dumb, or deaf, or the seeing, or the blind? Have not I the LORD?*

"Now therefore go, and I will be with your mouth, and teach you what you shall say."

In answering the complaint of Moses in this fashion, the Lord in essence is telling him that whatever his problem might be, it can be easily handled by the Power of God. Regarding this, Pulpit says: *"God could and would have cured the defect in Moses' speech, whatever it was; could and would have added eloquence to his other gifts, if he had even at this point yielded himself unreservedly to His guidance and heartily accepted his mission. Nothing is too hard for the Lord."*

The Lord in essence is telling Moses that He would teach him what to say, would supply the thought and the language by which to express it. But the reply in Verse 13 stopped the hand of the Lord.

UNBELIEF

Verse 13 reads: *"And he said, O my Lord, send, I pray You, by the hand of him whom You will send."*

The answer given by Moses may be concluded by some to be that of humility; however, it cannot be called humility to refuse to take the place which God assigns, or to tread the path which His hand marks out for us. That it was not true humility in Moses is obvious from the fact that *"the anger of the Lord was kindled against him."* Actually, it was unbelief!

Concerning this, Mackintosh says: *"Nothing is more dishonoring to God, or more dangerous for us, than a mock humility. When we refuse to occupy a position which the Grace of God assigns us, because of our not possessing certain virtues and qualifications, this is not humility, inasmuch as if we could but satisfy our own consciences in reference to such virtues and qualifications, we should then deem ourselves entitled to assume the position."*

The question may be asked, how much eloquence would Moses have needed to furnish him for his mission? The answer is, without God, no amount of human eloquence would have availed in any case; but with God, the most pitiful stammerer would have proved an efficient Minister.

Unbelief is not humility, but thorough pride. It refuses to believe God because it does not find in *"self"* a reason for believing. This is the very height of presumption. If, when God speaks, I refuse to believe, on the ground of something in myself, I make Him a liar (I Jn. 5:10). For instance, when God declares His love, and I refuse to believe because I do not deem myself a sufficiently worthy object, I make Him a liar, and exhibit the inherent pride of my heart (Mackintosh).

Christ took the sinner's place on the Cross, that the sinner might take His place in the glory. Christ got what the sinner deserved, that the sinner might get What and Who Christ is. Thus *"self"* is totally set aside, and this is true humility.

THE CROSS

No one can be truly humble until he has reached Heaven's side of the Cross; and there he finds Divine life, Divine Righteousness, and Divine favor. He is done with himself forever, as regards any expectation of goodness or Righteousness, and he feeds upon the princely wealth of another, namely Christ.

As we look at this situation regarding Moses, we must not for a moment think that we would have done any better. The truth is, we probably would not have done nearly as well. So, the way we should look at it is that we learn from the situation here tendered toward us by the Holy Spirit. As a result, we should learn to judge ourselves and to place more implicit confidence in God, to set self aside, that He might act in us, through us, and for us. This is the true secret of power.

THE ANGER OF THE LORD

Verse 14 reads: *"And the anger of the LORD was kindled against Moses, and He said, Is not Aaron the Levite your brother? I know that he can speak well. And also, behold, he comes forth to meet you: and when he sees you, he will be glad in his heart."*

We are reading here God's reaction to unbelief. Consequently, we must not allow this lesson to be lost on us.

Concerning this, Williams says: *"Despite the promises and signs, the unbelief of Moses' heart ripened into rebellion, and he refused to go; but he immediately consented on being promised the companionship of his brother Aaron. Such is man's heart! Promised the companionship of God, Moses refuses to go, but willingly volunteers if accompanied by a feeble fellow-creature. He would feel safer leaning on the arm of Aaron than leaning on the arm of Jehovah! And yet Aaron was no real help to him, but the contrary; for he made the golden calf. But how full of tender pity was God! He provided this companion, and bade Moses take 'this rod' in his hand wherewith he was to do 'the signs.'"*

I think one can say without any fear of contradiction that all sin, in some way, can be traced back to the foundational sin of *"unbelief."* Whatever direction it takes, whatever is done, whatever the problem, in one way or the other, if inspected closely, one will find *"unbelief"* as the real problem.

Also, unbelief can be traced, in one way or the other, to an improper understanding of the Cross. The Scripture plainly says that *"faith comes by hearing, and hearing by the Word of God"* (Rom. 10:17). However, the Word of God is the story of the Cross, while the Cross is the meaning of the Word of God. To properly understand the Word, we must first of all understand the Cross. The believing sinner is saved as he expresses Faith in

Christ and what Christ has done for us at the Cross, even though he may understand precious little, if anything, about Christ. But once he is saved, with his faith firmly anchored in Christ, which always includes what Christ has done at the Cross, that is if properly believed, the Holy Spirit then begins to give understanding as it regards the Word. But the Cross, in a most simplistic way, comes first.

But at the same time, there is actually no difference in the Cross and the Word. To believe the one, that is to believe properly, is to believe the other.

AARON

Verses 15 through 17 read: *"And you shall speak unto him, and put words in his mouth: and I will be with your mouth, and with his mouth, and will teach you what you shall do.*

"And he shall be your spokesman unto the people: and he shall be, even he shall be to you instead of a mouth, and you shall be to him instead of God.

"And you shall take this rod in your hand, wherewith you shall do signs."

It is believed that Aaron was going to see Moses in order to bring him the message that the Pharaoh who had tried to kill him those years before was now dead; however, Verse 27 proclaims the fact that he did not start on the journey, till God gave him a special direction.

The Lord would give Moses the words to say, and it would be the duty of Aaron to accept what Moses said as Divine.

Possibly to chide Moses, the Lord called attention to the wooden rod in the hand of Moses. He then said to him, *"Wherewith you shall do signs."*

In effect, He was telling Moses that He could use anything, even a wooden stick. This shows up greatly the foolishness of Moses in questioning God.

(18) "AND MOSES WENT AND RETURNED TO JETHRO HIS FATHER IN LAW, AND SAID UNTO HIM, LET ME GO, I PRAY YOU, AND RETURN UNTO MY BRETHREN WHICH ARE IN EGYPT, AND SEE WHETHER THEY BE YET ALIVE. AND JETHRO SAID TO MOSES, GO IN PEACE.

NOTES

(19) "AND THE LORD SAID UNTO MOSES IN MIDIAN, GO, RETURN INTO EGYPT: FOR ALL THE MEN ARE DEAD WHICH SOUGHT YOUR LIFE.

(20) "AND MOSES TOOK HIS WIFE AND HIS SONS, AND SET THEM UPON AN ANIMAL, AND HE RETURNED TO THE LAND OF EGYPT: AND MOSES TOOK THE ROD OF GOD IN HIS HAND.

(21) "AND THE LORD SAID UNTO MOSES, WHEN YOU GO TO RETURN INTO EGYPT, SEE THAT YOU DO ALL THESE WONDERS BEFORE PHARAOH, WHICH I HAVE PUT IN YOUR HAND: BUT I WILL HARDEN HIS HEART, THAT HE SHALL NOT LET THE PEOPLE GO.

(22) "AND YOU SHALL SAY UNTO PHARAOH, THUS SAITH THE LORD, ISRAEL IS MY SON, EVEN MY FIRSTBORN:

(23) "AND I SAY UNTO YOU, LET MY SON GO, THAT HE MAY SERVE ME: AND IF YOU REFUSE TO LET HIM GO, BEHOLD, I WILL SLAY YOUR SON, EVEN YOUR FIRSTBORN.

(24) "AND IT CAME TO PASS BY THE WAY IN THE INN, THAT THE LORD MET HIM, AND SOUGHT TO KILL HIM.

(25) "THEN ZIPPORAH TOOK A SHARP STONE, AND CUT OFF THE FORESKIN OF HER SON, AND CAST IT AT HIS FEET, AND SAID, SURELY A BLOODY HUSBAND ARE YOU TO ME.

(26) "SO HE LET HIM GO: THEN SHE SAID, A BLOODY HUSBAND YOU ARE, BECAUSE OF THE CIRCUMCISION."

The diagram is:

1. The hardening of Pharaoh's heart doesn't mean that God tampered with Pharaoh's will, but rather by foreknowledge, looked at the heart of the Monarch, knowing what Pharaoh would do. God would simply supply the opportunity.

2. The sun hardens clay and softens wax; so it is with Truth. The result is not in the sun (or in God), but in the materials.

3. In Verse 23, God calls the nation of Israel His son and firstborn, as contrasted with the firstborn of Egypt. Pharaoh would understand this terminology fully, for he, himself, was called *"Son of Ra,"* or *"Beloved of his god."*

4. At the very beginning, Moses was to tell Pharaoh that if he didn't let the children of

Israel go, God would kill his firstborn. So the Monarch was not without warning. At any point he could have repented, and his firstborn would have been spared, as well as the destruction of Egypt.

5. Verses 24 through 26 portray the fact of the justness of a just God. Moses would learn that God would judge him before He judged Pharaoh, and that rebellion in the one was the same as rebellion in the other.

JETHRO

Verse 18 reads: *"And Moses went and returned to Jethro his father in law, and said unto him, Let me go, I pray you, and return unto my brethren which are in Egypt, and see whether they be yet alive. And Jethro said to Moses, Go in peace."*

Moses courteously asked leave of Jethro to return to Egypt, for, in a sense, he was Jethro's servant.

Concerning this, Williams says: *"The Midian in which Jethro lived was not the Midian of the Dead Sea region, but of the eastern shore of the Gulf of Akaba. The town of Madyan stands there today; and the Moslems of the town welcome pilgrims on the way to Mecca shouting, 'Come into the city of the brother-in-law of Moses.'"*

Had Moses left for Egypt without first notifying his father-in-law, it would have been grossly discourteous and even the height of ingratitude. This act of Moses manifested his thoughtfulness of others, and his appreciation of favors received.

Let writer and Reader take this to heart. Spiritual activities, as important as they may be, and nothing could have been more important than this which God had called Moses to do, never absolves us from the common amenities and responsibilities of life. To be a good Christian is to practice Christliness, and Christ ever thought of *"others."*

EGYPT

Verse 19 reads: *"And the LORD said unto Moses in Midian, Go, return into Egypt: for all the men are dead which sought your life."*

From the way the Lord commands Moses here, it would seem that he was still reluctant to go. The Lord would reassure him by telling him that *"all"* the men who sought to kill him from 40 years back were now dead. So, there need be no fear from this source.

As we've already stated, we should not read of the reluctance of Moses, and think of him as less than ourselves. We must remember that what God was telling him to do was of such magnitude as to defy all description. One can well understand the fear and the trepidation, even though it was wrong.

THE ROD OF GOD

Verse 20 reads: *"And Moses took his wife and his sons, and set them upon an animal, and he returned to the land of Egypt: and Moses took the Rod of God in his hand."*

His sons were Gershom (Ex. 2:22), and Eliezer, who was probably an infant (Ex. 18:4).

This *"Rod"* is the same one of Verse 2, which had now become *"the Rod of God"* and because of the miracle of Verses 3 and 4. The Lord commands him to take this Rod to Egypt.

I think it would be good for us to carefully observe this scene. We have here a man and his older son, most likely walking, while his wife and infant son are riding on the back of a donkey. The man has a *"Rod"* in his hand, which of course is a wooden stick. What other goods they had with them, we aren't told, but they seemed to have been traveling very lightly.

The irony of all of this is, this which we see and observe is the instrumentation that God will use, namely Moses, to deliver between two million and three million people from Egyptian bondage, which the Monarch of that country in no way desires to let them go. To the natural man, this at the most would be laughable, and at the least would be ludicrous. But yet, that's exactly what would happen. Nearly three million people, despite the opposition of the mightiest Monarch on the face of the Earth, would come out of Egypt. Furthermore, Egypt would be little more than a wreck when those people departed, and this the most powerful nation on the face of the Earth.

If it is God's Will that something be, and God can get a man to believe Him, there is nothing that cannot be done. As the song says, *"What a mighty God we serve!"*

THE HARDENED HEART

Verse 21 reads: *"And the LORD said unto Moses, When you go to return into Egypt, see that you do all those wonders before Pharaoh, which I have put in your hand: but I will harden his heart, that he shall not let the people go."*

This particular Passage, plus several others similar regarding Pharaoh, has been a source of contention, I suppose, from the very beginning. However, it should not be a problem.

The meaning is, God provided the means which occasioned Pharaoh hardening his own heart.

Among the natural punishments which God has attached to sin, would seem to be the hardening of the entire nature of the man who sins. If men *"do not like to retain God in their knowledge, God gives them up to a reprobate mind"* (Rom. 1:28); if they resist the Spirit, He *"takes His Holy Spirit from them"* (Ps. 51:11); if they sin against light, He withdraws the light; if they stifle their natural affections of kindness, compassion, and the like, it is a law of His providence that those affections shall wither and decay.

Pulpit says: *"This seems to be the 'hardening of the heart' here intended — not an abnormal and miraculous interference with the soul of Pharaoh, but the natural effect upon his soul under God's moral governments of those acts which he willfully and wrongfully committed."*

THE FIRSTBORN

Verses 22 and 23 read: *"And you shall say unto Pharaoh, Thus saith the LORD, Israel is My son, even My firstborn:*

"And I say unto you, Let My son go, that he may serve Me: and if you refuse to let him go, behold, I will slay your son, even your firstborn."

What did the Lord mean by referring to Israel as His firstborn?

Israel was the only people and nation that He had adopted because He had taken them into Covenant. As a result, they were to be unto Him, *"a peculiar people above all the nations that are upon the Earth"* (Deut. 14:2). In fact, Israel's sonship is mentioned here for the first time.

In fact, the whole of the Plan of God for the human race was ensconced in these people called *"Israelites."* They were raised up for three purposes:

1. To give the world the Word of God, which they did. Every correct standard of righteous law or righteousness in any capacity is based squarely on the Bible.

2. To serve as the womb of the Messiah, which means they would bring the Redeemer into the world, which was predicted even from the Fall in the Garden of Eden (Gen. 3:15). This they did as well, even though they did not recognize Him when He came.

3. They were, as well, to evangelize the world, but regrettably, in which they failed.

The Eleventh Chapter of Romans is the most striking Chapter in the entirety of the New Testament, even the Bible for that matter, as it regards the Fall of Israel, and their coming Restoration, which will most definitely take place. All the great Promises made to the Patriarchs and Prophets of old will be kept in totality. In other words, Israel is going to ultimately accept Christ as their Messiah, their Lord, and their Saviour. Zechariah, plus many other Prophets, prophesied that this would take place at the Second Coming (Zech., Chpts. 12-13).

Up front, Moses was to tell Pharaoh that the firstborn of God, namely Israel, must be set free. Refusing that, the next statement, to be sure, is drastic. The Lord, without mincing words, says, *"I will kill your son, even your firstborn."* This meant that the heir to the throne of Egypt would be killed, which the future proved to be the case.

Pharaoh was not without warning. At any time along the way, he could have repented, and his firstborn would have been spared, as well as the destruction of Egypt. So, it was the Mercy of God in speaking to Pharaoh thusly. The choice of what happened was Pharaoh's and not God's. The Israelites belonged to God. They were His Personal property. They were His people, and He had the right to take them out.

The religion of Egypt looked at their firstborn as carrying on their name for each family, guaranteeing its success in this life, and even in the afterlife, and more particularly, the afterlife. If the firstborn was cut off before maturity, or before the father died, all of this would be interrupted. So, the idea that the God of the Hebrews was to kill every firstborn in the land of Egypt, even that of the cattle, etc., was about the worst thing that Pharaoh could hear. But yet, his stubborn, obstinate, hardened heart refused to believe the announcement of Moses because he reasoned that the gods of Egypt were greater than the God of the Hebrews. He was to have a rude awakening!

THE LESSON THAT MOSES WAS TO LEARN

Verses 24 through 26 read: *"And it came to pass by the way in the inn, that the LORD met him, and sought to kill him.*

"Then Zipporah took a sharp stone, and cut off the foreskin of her son, and cast it at his feet, and said, Surely a bloody husband are you to me.

"So He let him go: then she said, A bloody husband you are, because of the circumcision."

The rite of Circumcision was the seal of the Covenant which God had given to Abraham, some 400 years before (Gen. 17:10-14).

The rite of Circumcision included the separation of flesh and the shedding of blood, both which typified Christ and the Cross, in other words, what He would do in order to redeem fallen humanity. Consequently, it was very important that this particular commandment be obeyed to the letter because of its symbolism.

It seems that the son of which they are speaking here is not Gershom, who was the oldest, and who had, no doubt, been circumcised, but rather Eliezer, who was an infant, and probably several months old.

Evidently Zipporah was opposed to the rite of Circumcision, seemingly thinking that it was a barbarous act. So we find here that the wife of Moses was not too very much in sympathy with the things of God. So Moses, not desiring to create a family problem, had evidently acquiesced to his wife, and had neglected to circumcise the baby boy.

Abruptly, the Scripture says that the Lord suddenly appeared to Moses, and because of his neglect in circumcising the little boy, the Lord threatened to kill the child. It is a strong statement, and must not be dismissed hastily.

NOTES

Why was the matter this serious?

Concerning this, Williams says: *"Moses was commanded to announce to Pharaoh that Jehovah, the God of Israel, was about to slay his son. But Moses had to learn that disobedience and rebellion in him was just as hateful as in Pharaoh; and that God, because of His nature, must judge with death, sin wherever found.*

"On approaching Egypt, therefore, this Holy God sought to judge his little boy, Eliezer, because of Moses' disobedience in not having had him circumcised, as God had commanded. The Passage throws a great light upon the inner life of Moses. It may be assumed, from what is related, that he yielded to the wishes of his wife in this matter, though he knew he was disobeying God. The particulars are not fully given because the Holy Spirit did not think this necessary, but evidently in order to save the child's life, and urged to it by Moses, she circumcised him herself, and then with anger and passion declared that her husband's religion was a religion of blood, i.e., 'of blood-stained rites.'

"Thus Moses had to learn that God would judge him before He judged Pharaoh, and that rebellion in the one was the same as rebellion in the other; and this lesson must have enabled Moses to proclaim this dreadful truth with the force of a personal experience."

THE CROSS

Williams continues to say, and I continue to quote: *"This is a moral principle which Romans 6, Colossians 2, and many other Scriptures teach. Christians, under the New Covenant, are circumcised in the death of Jesus Christ; that is, we 'die' as to our old nature. We then go forth with a message of death and of life; but we must have a personal experience of the bitterness, to the natural will, of that spiritual circumcision. We must consent to 'die' if we would be effective messengers of the Cross."*

This is all very dear to me personally.

Until I understood the part the Cross plays in our Sanctification experience, in other words, our daily living before the Lord, I could not live a victorious life, and neither can anyone else. And the sadness is, very few in the modern Church understand that of which I've just mentioned, so that means that almost all of the modern Church are living far less than God intends, which means they do not have nearly all the *"firstfruits"* they can have, according to what Jesus did at the Cross.

God has one prescribed order of victory, not five, not three, not two, just one. If we follow that prescribed order, we will reap the results, which is victory on a perpetual basis. If we ignore what the Lord has said, even as Moses did regarding the circumcision of his little son, or if we function in unbelief as it regards the Cross, because the Cross is the prescribed order, the results will be disastrous. It can be no other way.

This which the Lord has shown me, even though it incorporates the entirety of the New Covenant, I believe can be reduced down to the following three points. Of course, such an abbreviation leaves much to be desired; still, it will give the Reader a working knowledge of God's prescribed way.

GOD'S PRESCRIBED ORDER OF VICTORY

Before I give that prescribed order, I want the Reader to understand that the Cross of Christ is not a mere Doctrine. In fact, it is the foundation of all Doctrine. Every Doctrine in the Bible is built squarely on the Cross of Christ. And if any doctrine is proposed by men and it doesn't have the Cross as its foundation, that doctrine, pure and simple, is wrong.

I think that Jesus looked at what He did on the Cross, the great price that He paid, in fact, that which was planned from before the foundation of the world, as far more than mere Doctrine. No, and as stated, the Cross of Christ is the foundation of all Doctrine. That must be understood up front.

THE CROSS

The first thing the Believer must understand is, everything that we receive from God, and I mean everything, comes to us exclusively by and through the Cross of Christ. In other words, the Cross is what made everything possible. I speak of Salvation, the Baptism with the Holy Spirit, victorious Christian living, deliverance, Divine Healing, financial prosperity, emotional well-being, in fact, victory in every capacity.

Let us look at the Cross in this fashion: If all of this had stopped at the Deity of Christ, and to be sure, Christ is God, the great Salvation Plan would be incomplete. As God, Jesus had no beginning, has always been, will always be, is unformed, unmade, and uncreated. Even though His Deity was an absolute necessity, had it stopped there, not a single sinner would have ever been saved.

As well, His Virgin Birth was an absolute necessity; nevertheless, had it stopped there, not one single person would have ever been saved.

His Perfect Life falls into the same category, but that alone would have saved no one.

His miracles were a necessity, but even though they were grand and glorious, they could save no one.

It remained for Jesus to go to the Cross, which in reality was the reason that He came (Jn. 1:29), in order that the terrible debt of sin might be paid, which was paid with the shedding of His Precious Blood, actually, the giving of Himself in Sacrifice.

So it is the Cross that has made and does make everything possible, as it regards God's relationship with man (Gen. 3:15; 15:6; Rom. 6:3-5, 11, 14; Eph. 2:13-18; Col. 2:14-15).

YOUR FAITH

It is not the quantity of Faith that is so important, but rather the object in which our Faith is placed, which must be the Cross, and that being the case, is quality Faith. Inasmuch as the Cross is the instrument used whereby all things are given to us by God, that is where we must place our Faith, and not allow it to be moved to other things. That's the reason we keep saying, even to the degree of being overly repetitious, that we must make certain that the object of our Faith is always the Cross. Satan will fight harder here than he does anywhere else, in order to move our Faith from the Finished Work of Christ to other things. And to be sure, he really doesn't care too very much what those other things might be, or even how holy they might be in their own right. Just as long as the Believer doesn't have his Faith in the Cross of Christ, Satan knows that such a Believer will live a life of spiritual defeat, and more than likely, defeat in every other manner as well.

If we ask most Christians to explain Faith, most really would not understand as to how to do that. They would answer with the statement, *"I have Faith in God,"* or *"I have Faith in His Word,"* etc. They might even say, *"Jesus died for me, and I believe that."* All of these things are right as far as they go; however, they really don't say very much.

The Believer must understand that to properly comprehend Faith, he must ever have the Cross as its object. Always and without exception, when Paul speaks of Faith, he is speaking of having Faith in Christ and what Christ did at the Cross. In fact, the word *"faith,"* carries such a power that the Christian experience is oftentimes referred to as *"the faith"* (Gal. 2:20; 5:6).

The truth is, everyone in the world has faith. While it's not Faith in God and His Word, still, it is faith. But it's not faith that God will recognize. In fact, He doesn't even recognize most of the faith held by those who are a part of the Church, or who claim Salvation. Their faith is in things other than the Cross; consequently, such faith is that which God cannot recognize. Unfortunately, the faith that's been taught and practiced in the last few decades, at least for the most part, has been faith in things other than the Cross. As a result, it is *"useless faith"* or *"worthless faith."* It is only Faith in the Cross that is true, Biblical Faith, therefore, the Faith that God will recognize (I Cor. 1:17-18, 21, 23; 2:2, 5).

THE HOLY SPIRIT

Anything and everything that we receive from the Lord, not only comes through the Cross, but is always superintended by the Holy Spirit. He, Alone, can develop fruit within our lives; hence it is called *"the Fruit of the Spirit"* (Gal. 5:22-23). In fact, if it's from God, it is the Holy Spirit Who makes it real to us, thereby, guaranteeing the fruit of that which Jesus paid for at the Cross. Actually, Jesus lives in us by and through the Holy Spirit, Who lives constantly within our hearts and lives (I Cor. 3:16; Gal. 2:20; Jn. 16:13-15).

NOTES

Concerning this, Paul said: *"For the preaching of the Cross is to them that perish foolishness; but unto us which are saved it is the Power of God"* (I Cor. 1:18).

The *"Power of God,"* is always ensconced in the Holy Spirit (Acts 1:8). Now many Believers think if they are baptized with the Holy Spirit with the evidence of speaking with other tongues, which definitely is Scriptural (Acts 2:4), this means that the Holy Spirit will do all type of things for them.

While that is definitely a giant step forward, and as well an absolute necessity for every Believer, still, have you noticed that Spirit-filled people suffer failure, just about a much as the non-Spirit-baptized variety? So what's wrong?

When the Holy Spirit comes into our hearts and lives in a baptism of power, which He definitely does when we are baptized with the Spirit, He in fact can do many things. But all of these things are potential, and not necessarily factual. To be sure, He is no respecter of persons, and will do for one what He has done for the other. But just because one is baptized with the Spirit does not mean that one is home free, so to speak. The potential is there, but at that stage, the potential only.

The Holy Spirit doesn't demand much of us, but He does demand that we exhibit Faith in the Cross of Christ, and keep our Faith in that Finished Work. He said:

"There is therefore now no condemnation to them which are in Christ Jesus, who walk not after the flesh, but after the Spirit."

He then said: *"For the Law of the Spirit of Life in Christ Jesus has made me free from the law of sin and death"* (Rom. 8:1-2).

Romans 8:2 tells us that the Holy Spirit works exclusively within the parameters of the Finished Work of Christ. That's what is meant by the term *"in Christ Jesus."* As well, the Holy Spirit will not work outside of those parameters.

In the first four Verses of the Seventh Chapter of Romans, and I'll be brief, Paul in effect tells us that Believers, who are married to Christ, must receive everything we need from Him and Him Alone! This is done by having Faith exclusively in Christ and what Christ has done for us at the Cross. If we veer outside of those parameters, thereby beginning to have faith in law, which speaks of *"works,"* we are then being unfaithful to our Lord, and God then looks at us as a *"spiritual adulterer"* (Rom. 7:3).

I should think that it would be understood by all that it's a very serious thing for God to conclude us as a *"spiritual adulterer."* This simply means that we are being unfaithful to our Lord. He has all that we need, which He furnishes to us through the Cross, but if we attempt to live this life by placing our faith in other things, then we place ourselves in a very precarious position indeed. Now let me ask this question:

If the Lord considers such a person a *"spiritual adulterer,"* which He definitely does, do you honestly think that the Holy Spirit is going to help such a person in their endeavors which are going wrong? I don't think so! And to be sure, if we are to live the life we must live, we must have the help of the Holy Spirit. And He will help us only in the realm of the Cross of Christ, and our Faith in that Finished Work.

So that's the reason that many Spirit-filled people fail the Lord. To be sure, the Holy Spirit doesn't leave them, but at the same time, He doesn't help them because He cannot be involved in that which God clearly labels as *"adulterous"* (Rom. 7:1-4). To have His help, which we must have, and because He is God, and He can do anything, we simply have to express Faith in Christ and Christ exclusively, which refers to what he did at the Cross for us. Doing that, the Holy Spirit will bring about total victory within our hearts and lives because that is *"walking after the Spirit,"* and then *"sin will not have dominion over us"* (Rom. 6:14).

It seems that the rite of Circumcision was an offense to the wife of Moses, just as the Cross is an offense to many today (Gal. 5:11).

So there you have it, even though it is in abbreviated form. It is *"The Cross, our Faith, and the Holy Spirit."*

(27) "AND THE LORD SAID TO AARON, GO INTO THE WILDERNESS TO MEET MOSES. AND HE WENT, AND MET HIM IN THE MOUNT OF GOD, AND KISSED HIM.

(28) "AND MOSES TOLD AARON ALL THE WORDS OF THE LORD WHO HAD SENT HIM, AND ALL THE SIGNS WHICH HE HAD COMMANDED HIM.

(29) "AND MOSES AND AARON WENT AND GATHERED TOGETHER ALL THE ELDERS OF THE CHILDREN OF ISRAEL:

(30) "AND AARON SPAKE ALL THE WORDS WHICH THE LORD HAD SPOKEN UNTO MOSES, AND DID THE SIGNS IN THE SIGHT OF THE PEOPLE.

(31) "AND THE PEOPLE BELIEVED: AND WHEN THEY HEARD THAT THE LORD HAD VISITED THE CHILDREN OF ISRAEL, AND THAT HE HAD LOOKED UPON THEIR AFFLICTION, THEN THEY BOWED THEIR HEADS AND WORSHIPPED."

The structure is:

1. Verses 27 and 28 record the Lord telling Aaron, *"Go into the wilderness to meet Moses."* Aaron met Moses at Mount Sinai, perhaps very shortly after he received the Revelation of the burning bush, etc. The brothers had been separated for some 40 years.

2. Verses 29 through 31 record the first spiritual revival of the Children of Israel since they had been in Egyptian bondage.

3. The Scripture says, *"They bowed their heads and worshipped."* This is a perfect description of every moving of the Holy Spirit. God will *"do signs,"* and then, if the people believe, the Spirit of God will fall and result in the worship of the Lord.

AARON

Verses 27 and 28 read: *"And the LORD said to Aaron, Go into the wilderness to meet Moses. And he went, and met him in the Mount of God, and kissed him.*

"And Moses told Aaron all the words of the LORD Who had sent him, and all the signs which he had commanded him."

Aaron evidently had come from Egypt, and had not seen his brother in 40 years. So this meeting would be one of great joy. It would be a scene of sweet, brotherly love and union.

The two men conversed, with Moses telling his older brother of the great things the Lord had shown him and told him. And now Aaron was to find out that he was to be the spokesman for Moses as it regarded the tremendous confrontation which would take place quite a number of times, between Moses and the Monarch of Egypt.

Aaron, like Moses, was barred from entering Canaan at the end of the wilderness wanderings; he died and was buried on Mount Hor, on the Edomite border, and his functions and vestments as the High Priest of Israel passed to his son, Eleazar (Num. 20:22). Actually, the Priesthood in Israel came to be known comprehensively as *"the sons of Aaron."*

THE ARRIVAL IN EGYPT

Verse 29 reads: *"And Moses and Aaron went and gathered together all the Elders of the Children of Israel."*

The Scripture is silent regarding the trip to Egypt. The Scripture seems to indicate that Moses sent his wife and children back to Jethro (Ex. 18:2). To be frank, considering what he had to do, that was the prudent thing to have done.

The journey from Horeb, for that's where Aaron met Moses, to Goshen probably occupied some weeks. It seems that immediately upon arriving in Goshen, the two brothers, in obedience to the Divine command, proceeded at once to *"gather together all the Elders of Israel."* This would have included the heads of the Tribes, plus other important men, which no doubt numbered several hundreds.

THE SIGNS

Verse 30 reads: *"And Aaron spoke all the words which the LORD had spoken unto Moses, and did the signs in the sight of the people."*

It seems that Moses performed all the signs, concerning the serpent, the leprous hand, and the blood, all observed by the Elders, who then went and gathered together a tremendous large group of people, with Moses once again doing the signs *"in the sight of the people."*

This was God's time, with the people in an entirely different frame of mind than they had been those years before. Beside that, Moses was an entirely different man now than he had been then.

FAITH

Verse 31 reads: *"And the people believed: and when they heard that the LORD had visited the Children of Israel, and that He had*

NOTES

looked upon their affliction, then they bowed their heads and worshipped."

All of this shows that during the time between the death of Joseph and the arrival of Moses for the purpose of deliverance, the people had at least been taught some things about God. Even though their situation in the wilderness would prove to be extremely negative, with none of the adults going into the Promised Land, with the exception of Joshua and Caleb; still, there seems to be some semblance of instruction given during the time in question. Their *"worshipping"* even as they did, proves this.

When God works, every barrier must give way. Moses had said, *"The people will not believe me."* But the question was not as to whether they would believe him, but whether they would believe God. Their faith reached out at this time, and in fact, they did believe.

"O sacred Head, now wounded, with
　grief and shame weighed down;
"Now scornfully surrounded with thorns,
　Thine only crown;
"How are You pale with anguish, with
　sore abuse and scorn;
"How does that visage languish, which
　once was bright as morn!"

"O Lord of life and glory, what bliss till
　now was Thine!
"I read the wondrous story; I joy to call
　Thee mine.
"What Thou, my Lord, has suffered was
　all for sinners gain;
"Mine, mine was the transgression, but
　Thine the deadly pain."

"What language shall I borrow to thank
　Thee, dearest Friend,
"For this Thy dying sorrow, Thy pity
　without end?
"Oh, make me Thine forever; and,
　should I fainting be,
"Lord, let me never, never outlive my
　love to Thee."

"Be near when I am dying, Oh, show
　Thy Cross to me;
"And for my succor flying, Come, Lord,
　to set me free:
"These eyes, new faith receiving, from
　Thee shall not remove,

"For he who dies believing, dies safely through Thy love."

CHAPTER 5

(1) "AND AFTERWARD MOSES AND AARON WENT IN, AND TOLD PHARAOH, THUS SAITH THE LORD GOD OF ISRAEL, LET MY PEOPLE GO, THAT THEY MAY HOLD A FEAST UNTO ME IN THE WILDERNESS.

(2) "AND PHARAOH SAID, WHO IS THE LORD, THAT I SHOULD OBEY HIS VOICE TO LET ISRAEL GO? I KNOW NOT THE LORD, NEITHER WILL I LET ISRAEL GO.

(3) "AND THEY SAID, THE GOD OF THE HEBREWS HAS MET WITH US: LET US GO, WE PRAY YOU, THREE DAYS' JOURNEY INTO THE DESERT, AND SACRIFICE UNTO THE LORD OUR GOD; LEST HE FALL UPON US WITH PESTILENCE, OR WITH THE SWORD.

(4) "AND THE KING OF EGYPT SAID UNTO THEM, WHEREFORE DO YE, MOSES AND AARON, LET THE PEOPLE FROM THEIR WORKS? GET YOU UNTO YOUR BURDENS.

(5) "AND PHARAOH SAID, BEHOLD, THE PEOPLE OF THE LAND NOW ARE MANY, AND YOU MAKE THEM REST FROM THEIR BURDENS."

The construction is:

1. The close of Chapter 4 presents the people worshipping in believing joy. The close of Chapter 5 sets before the Reader the same people filled with unbelieving bitterness. The glad tidings of Salvation is one thing; the struggle against the power that tries to keep the soul in bondage is quite another.

2. Satan will not easily let his captive go free; and God permits the bitter experience of his power in order to exercise and strengthen Faith.

3. It is good for a man to learn painfully the nature of sin's dominion, and his absolute helplessness in the grip of that Monarch (Williams).

PHARAOH

Verse 1 reads: *"And afterward Moses and Aaron went in, and told Pharaoh, Thus saith the LORD God of Israel, Let My people go, that they may hold a feast unto Me in the wilderness."*

According to many authorities, the Pharaoh at that time was Meneptah, the son, and successor of Rameses II. History records that he was a weak individual, but because of certain events, had an exalted opinion of himself.

Egypt had been invaded recently, actually at the beginning of his reign, which had been met and completely repulsed; however, it was not by his skill at the head of his army, but rather by the skill of his generals. Nevertheless, Menephthah claimed to be in direct communication with the Egyptian gods, who revealed themselves to him in visions, which he used as an excuse not to lead his army. Still, he counted the successes gained by his generals as his own, and conducted himself as the leader. Such was the man before whom Moses and Aaron appeared.

THE HOLY SPIRIT

If it is to be noticed, the Holy Spirit in giving Moses direction regarding the Sacred Text, in no way recognizes the splendor of Egypt, even though the trappings of grandeur were no doubt copiously obvious, with the throne a dazzling object of magnificence. This was the throne of Pharaoh, the mightiest nation on the face of the Earth at that time, therefore, the mightiest Monarch.

For a few moments, I want the Reader to imagine the scene that must have presented itself to Moses and Aaron as they stood before Pharaoh. These two Prophets of God stood there in their simple shepherd's garb, standing before a man graced by every bauble of jewelry and the finest of garments, which would feed his ego.

There is a possibility that Moses was very familiar with this palace, and even that he may have been raised in this domain. In fact, the throne on which Pharaoh is now seated could have been his. But if so, what a step down it would have been.

When he looked at Pharaoh, the scene that met his eyes must have been graphic. On Pharaoh's head very probably would have been the replica of a coiled cobra made of gold. The cobra's head, with two rubies for its eyes, would have protruded like a hood over the head of the Monarch. The cobra was one of the gods of Egypt.

They would now confront Pharaoh in person. His temper toward the Hebrews was well-known; his heartless cruelty had been frequently displayed. Pink says: *"It was, therefore, no small trial of their faith and courage to beard the lion in his den."* Pink goes on to say: *"The character of the Message they were to deliver to him was not calculated to compromise or pacify. They were to tell him in no uncertain terms that the Lord God required him to let that people go whom he held in slavery, and hold a feast unto Jehovah in the wilderness."*

As well, they went before this Monarch knowing that the Lord had told them that He would harden Pharaoh's heart, which meant they would be met with no favorable response.

While the Lord had used the term to Moses that he was to speak to Pharaoh, when in fact he would stand in his presence, *"Thus saith the Lord,"* as it is now uttered in the presence of the Monarch, the words *"Thus saith the Lord God,"* are used here for the first time. It will be used untold numbers of times in the coming years and centuries. But this is the first.

In this statement, God identifies Himself with this beleaguered band of slaves, by saying, *"Thus saith the Lord God of Israel. . . ."* As a result, the might and power of Heaven are now registered on the side of Israel. Irrespective of whom they might be, or where they might be, or whom their captors might be, the opposing party cannot win. *"Thus saith the Lord,"* presents itself as the death knell to all who would stand in the way of the Will of God. In fact, a short time later, when Israel would leave Egypt, this mighty nation, possibly at that time the most powerful on the face of the Earth, would be left a wreck. If God has spoken, only fools would dare oppose Him or the one or ones whom He sponsors.

A FEAST

Careful attention should be paid to the terms of their request. The Lord had already promised Moses that he and the Children of Israel would worship God on Mount Sinai (Ex. 3:12), and to be sure, that was far more than a three days' journey from Egypt.

So why did not Moses plainly tell Pharaoh that he must relinquish all claims on the Hebrews, thereby giving them permission to leave his land for good?

Even though it is not mentioned in the First Verse, in Verse 3, the Lord had told Moses to ask for a three days' journey into the desert, where they would there sacrifice unto the Lord. Urquhart answers this question:

"God is entering upon a controversy with Pharaoh and with Egypt. He is about to judge them; and, in order that they may be judged, they must first be revealed to themselves and to all men. Had they been asked to suffer the Israelites to depart from Egypt, so large a demand might have seemed to others, and certainly would have appeared to the Egyptians themselves, as so unreasonable as to justify their refusal.

"A request is made, therefore, against which no charge of the kind can be brought. A three days' journey into the wilderness need not have taken the Israelites much beyond the Egyptian frontier. It was also a perfectly reasonable request, even to heathen nations, that they should be permitted to worship their God after the accepted manner. Consequently, the heart of Pharaoh and of his people was, therefore, revealed in their scornful refusal of a perfectly reasonable request. In this way they committed themselves to what was manifestly unjust; and in proceeding against them, God was consequently justified even in their own eyes."

THE JUDGMENT OF GOD

I think it can be said that God has never judged a people, whom He has not first dealt with in this very way, or at least in a similar way. For instance, Carlyle traces the fearful blow which fell upon the clergy and the aristocracy in the French Revolution to the murder of St. Bartholomew. France had sought to crush the Reformation as Egypt had sought to crush Israel.

Spain is another case in point: she dug the grave for her greatness and her fame in the establishment of her Inquisition, which saw untold thousands slaughtered because of their stand for Christ, or refusal to recognize the Pope.

Frances and I stood in Toledo, Spain, and observed the torture racks that were used to take the lives of untold numbers of people, and that they died in a most horrible fashion. But as I looked at these instruments of torture, all perpetrated in the name of religion, the words drummed upon my mind and my soul: *"Be not deceived; God is not mocked: for whatsoever a man soweth, that shall he also reap"* (Gal. 6:7).

But yet, we have to go even further to find the full reason and explanation for this request as offered by God to Pharaoh.

Do we not see in all of this the Mercy, the Grace, and the Love of God?! God is all-powerful, meaning that He can do anything. Pharaoh was no more to God than a flea on a dog, so to speak, that is if we are to compare power. He didn't have to ask Pharaoh anything. Above all, he didn't have to ask him time and time again. He could have done what He desired to do, what He wanted to do, and could have done so instantly, and there would have been absolutely nothing that Pharaoh could have done about it.

But God never uses His Power capriciously. He always seeks the best for men. If they will not yield to His Ways and Will, He will then take stronger measures. But He always deals with Patience, Mercy, and Grace.

He had every right to do what He did. He was not demanding anything even remotely unreasonable. These were His people. He had nurtured them and brought them to this present place and position. Beside that, Pharaoh had almost worked them to death as slaves, had used them unmercifully, and had abused them to a great degree, which in effect, added insult to injury.

Let it ever be known that when we touch those who belong to God, we have in effect touched God. This entire scenario of God's dealings with Pharaoh should be a prime example of this of which I speak.

THE PURPOSE OF GOD

All of this battle that we see played out before us was definitely to deliver Israel from their bitter bondage; however, it was definitely not merely for that. And neither was it fought and won solely that Israel might be able to go forth and possess the land promised to her fathers. That was important, but there were reasons which were greater.

The great reason was that Israel was redeemed to be God's people. Her one mission was and is to serve Jehovah. The conflict was being waged over the destiny of a race, its place in history, and in the service of humanity. Was Israel to be slave, or priest? Egypt's beast of burden, or the anointed of Jehovah? That was the great question; and was it possible that God could have done other than put that question, written large and clear, in the forefront of this great controversy?

So we find God acting here, not in wrath, but in mercy. This is ever His way. Before He would drown the world by water, He would send forth Enoch as a herald of this coming storm, long before the Flood descended upon the antediluvians. He sent forth Noah as a Preacher of Righteousness years before the first drop of rain began to fall, at least as it regards the Flood.

Even regarding Israel centuries later, He sent forth one Prophet after another, before He banished them into captivity. And later, He sent forth His Own Son, followed by the Apostles, before He used the Roman Tenth Legion to destroy Jerusalem in A.D. 70.

So it is presently. God is now dealing in Grace and longsuffering, sending forth His servants far and wide, bidding men flee from the wrath to come. But this Day of Salvation is rapidly drawing to a close, and once the Lord rises from His place at God's Right Hand, the door of Mercy will be shut, and the storm of God's Righteous anger will burst upon this world.

We are not without warning, the Book of Revelation, plus even the stentorian tones of the Master Himself in Matthew, Chapter 24, proclaim to us in no uncertain terms that judgment is just ahead. So the world is without excuse. Preachers can deny the validity of the Book of Revelation, but its Message throbs a little louder with each passing day, and only a fool will ignore its warnings.

WHO IS THE LORD?

Verse 2 reads: *"And Pharaoh said, Who is the LORD, that I should obey His voice to let Israel go? I know not the LORD, neither will I let Israel go."*

Let it be known that nothing can ever satisfy God in reference to His elect, but their entire emancipation from the yoke of bondage. *"Loose him and let him go"* is really the grand motto in God's gracious dealings with those who, though held in bondage by Satan, are nevertheless the objects of His eternal love.

Mackintosh said: *"When we contemplate Israel amid the brickkilns of Egypt, we behold a graphic figure of the condition of every child of Adam's fallen race by nature. There they were, crushed beneath the enemies galling yoke, and having no power to deliver themselves. The mere mention of the word 'liberty' only caused the oppressor to bind his captives with a stronger fetter, and to lade them with a still more grievous burden. Consequently, it was absolutely necessary that deliverance should come from without."*

Even the smallest thing that we allow in our lives that is not under the control of the Holy Spirit is completely sufficient to account for spiritual confusion. The business of the Holy Spirit is to make us free from every binding force as it regards the world, the flesh, and the Devil. That's the reason that the Holy Spirit had Paul to write: *"For the flesh lusteth against the Spirit, and the Spirit against the flesh: and these are contrary the one to the other: so that you cannot do the things that you would"* (Gal. 5:17).

The Holy Spirit cannot tolerate the supremacy of the flesh in anything, simply because He knows the terrible destructive force that such possession will bring about. Forever, the Holy Spirit is pitted against the flesh, and there will never be quarter asked or given.

The manner in which Paul used the word *"flesh,"* refers to our own ability, strength, and way, which of course speaks of man going his way without the Spirit, and attempting to do by his own strength and ability that which the Spirit Alone can do.

It does not lie within man to make himself holy or righteous. It simply cannot be done. The holdovers from the Fall guarantee the failure of such an effort. Not even the Believer, to whom Paul writes, even though a new creation, even though baptized with the Holy Spirit, can effect this work within his life.

Oh! How many of us have had to learn this the hard way. How many times have we beaten upon this anvil with our hammers of strength and power! But alas, sooner or later, the hammers break, but the anvil remains. To be sure, the anvil will not move by our strength, but it will move and in fact, must move, as the Power of the Holy Spirit is registered against it. Irrespective as to how great Pharaoh must be, he is doomed to fail, and God will not tolerate a partial deliverance, only that which is total.

THE PRESENCE OF GOD

As I dictate these notes, I sense greatly the Presence of God. I sense the Holy Spirit saying through me that all who read these words, if they will only follow the great Word of God, put their Faith and trust in Christ and what He did at the Cross, victory can be yours.

How many times have the tears blanketed your cheeks! How many times has despair filled your heart! How many times have you failed, and then have said, *"I will try again!"*

But you can be free. There is no doubt about it! What Jesus did at the Cross addressed every single problem that man might have. He left nothing undone, hence that which He did is referred to as the *"Finished Work."* He is the *"Last Adam,"* which means there will never again be the need for another one.

Your victory is in the Cross. More particularly, it's in what Jesus did there because He did it for you. God means for you to be completely free. Jesus didn't die on that Cross in order that you might have a partial victory. But He died on that Cross that you might have victory in every capacity and perpetually.

"Who is the Lord?" Pharaoh will soon find out Who the Lord is. He is the One Who is going to set Israel free, totally defeating her conquerors, and the same God with all His miracle-working power, Who rescued Israel, and did so with a high and mighty hand, is the same God you are serving today. He has not changed. And to be

sure, He has revealed Himself even in a greater way in the presentation of His only Son, and our Saviour, the Lord Jesus Christ.

Pharaoh's response to the overtures of God's Grace is recorded in this Verse. Unacquainted with God for himself, he defiantly refuses to bow to His mandate. Consequently, the character of Egypt's king stands fully revealed: *"I know not the Lord, neither will I let Israel go."*

THE GOSPEL

In a sense, untold millions answer God presently in the same manner as did Pharaoh. The mandate from Heaven is, *"Repent! Believe!"*

Oftentimes we speak of the Gospel as an invitation. In a sense it is, but it is more than that. It is rather a *"declaration"* of what God demands from the sinner — yes, I said demands — *"God now commandeth all men everywhere to repent"* (Acts 17:30). It should be obvious, true Prophets and true Evangelists do not deliver a diplomatic word, but rather an ultimatum. But the response of the natural man all too often is, *"Who is the Lord that I should obey His voice?"* Thus speaks the pride of the man who hardens his neck against the Blessed God.

Pharaoh bluntly thunders, *"I know Him not,"* and those same words express the heart of much of the world presently. And what makes it even worse, ignorant man seems to have no desire to correct this ignorance. They do not know, and if they did know, they would not believe, that one day soon, God will be revealed *"in flaming fire taking vengeance on them who know not God, and who obey not the Gospel of our Lord Jesus Christ"* (II Thess. 1:8).

SACRIFICE

Verse 3 reads: *"And they said, The God of the Hebrews has met with us: let us go, we pray you, three days' journey into the desert, and sacrifice unto the LORD our God; lest He fall upon us with pestilence, or with the sword."*

If attention is called to the practice, we find that *"Sacrifice"* had been practiced from the time of the Fall in the Garden of Eden, and was never to be set aside. The sacrifice of a clean animal, such as a lamb, a goat, a heifer, an ox, or a ram, typified the coming Redeemer Who would give Himself, in order to pay the terrible sin debt owed by man to God. This was God's Way of restored fellowship, which brought about forgiveness of sin, and was done through the shed blood of the innocent animal.

More than likely, the Children of Israel had little kept up this practice during their years of sojourn in the land of Egypt. And the very first thing that God demands is that this practice would be reinstituted. In a sense, one might say that God was demanding that Israel once again preach the Cross. Of course, that would have been terminology that they would not at all have understood, but in reality, that's exactly what it meant.

THE MODERN CHURCH

For all practical purposes, the Church presently has ceased to preach the Cross. It is preaching everything else that one can imagine, supposedly to address itself to the ills of man, but not the Cross. Let the Reader understand that every Preacher which preaches something else other than the Cross is in effect, preaching *"another gospel."* Paul said:

"I marvel that you are so soon removed from Him Who called you into the Grace of Christ (the Holy Spirit) *unto another Gospel* (a so-called gospel which is not the Cross).*"*

He then said: *"Which is not another . . ."* (Gal. 1:6-7), meaning that this other Gospel will not set any captive free, will not bless anyone, and in fact, will not save anyone.

The Apostle was so strong as it regards this of which I say, that he also said: *"But though we, or an Angel from Heaven, preach any other Gospel unto you than that which we have preached unto you, let him be accursed"* (Gal. 1:8). You will find that in Galatians 1:9, he in essence said the same thing again. That's how critical, how significant, how weighty, how important all of this is.

Every once and a while, I will turn for a few moments to that which proposes itself to be *"Christian Television."* I'll be frank; I cannot watch most of that which goes under the guise of the Gospel. The reason I cannot view such presentation, or hear what is being said, is simply because most of these

Preachers aren't preaching the Cross. And I know that what they are preaching might be good in some respect, but in effect, due to the fact that they're not preaching the Cross, the Holy Spirit labels it as *"another gospel."* As such, it will change no lives; break no bondages of sin, set no captives free, etc.

What we're speaking of here is not a side issue, but actually the main theme of the presentation of Jesus Christ to this world. This is of such moment, and I continue to speak of the Cross, that the Holy Spirit through Peter said:

"Forasmuch as you know that you were not redeemed with corruptible things, as silver and gold... But with the Precious Blood of Christ, as of a lamb without blemish and without spot:

"Who verily was foreordained before the foundation of the world, but was manifest in these last times for you" (I Pet. 1:18-20).

As should be obvious, from these Passages we gather the fact that the Cross of Christ was decided upon by the Godhead as it regards the Redemption of Adam's fallen race, even before the foundation of the world. This means that God knew that man would fall, even before He made man, even before the world was brought back to a habitable state. At that time, it was the Cross which was decided upon, as to be the instrument and vehicle of Redemption, and that means before anything else was addressed.

JUDGMENT

On that first meeting of Moses with Pharaoh, he said to the Monarch that all of Israel must go three days' journey into the desert, *"And sacrifice unto the Lord our God: lest He fall upon us with pestilence, or with the sword."*

Even though Moses didn't explain this to Pharaoh, this simple statement tells us, even as given to Moses by the Lord, that it is the Cross only which holds back the Judgment of God. In other words, the only thing standing between the lost sinner and the burning fires of Hell is the Cross of Christ. That's the reason we are to *"preach the Cross,"* and do so in every capacity.

That doesn't mean that every single Message has to be about the Cross, but it does

NOTES

mean that our understanding must be that the Cross is the foundation of the entirety of every Doctrine, and if it's not the foundation of all Doctrine, then whatever doctrine is being espoused is, pure and simple, wrong doctrine.

This demand for sacrifice as proclaimed by Moses to Pharaoh proclaimed the fact of what God's heart sought, and what man's sin needed.

Back up in the First Verse, it was said that they would hold a *"feast unto the Lord in the wilderness."* The *"feast"* points to rejoicing; the *"Sacrifice"* to what makes rejoicing possible.

As well, Israel was confessedly guilty and, therefore, deserving of punishment, and the only way of escape was through an Atonement being made for them. God must be placated: blood must be shed: the Divine justice must be propitiated. Only thus could God be reconciled to Israel.

And to be sure, the only manner in which God can be reconciled to man today is through man's Faith in Christ, and what Christ did for us at the Cross. As we have said over and over in this Volume, we must never separate Christ from the Cross, or the Cross from Christ. It was for this very cause that Jesus Christ came into this world. Of Christ, John the Baptist said of Him in the introduction of the Son of God: *"Behold the Lamb of God, which taketh away the sin of the world"* (Jn. 1:29).

If it is to be noticed, he first of all, did not introduce Christ as the Healer, as the Miracle-Worker, as the Prophet, or King, etc., but rather as the *"Saviour,"* meaning that He would be the Sacrifice for sin.

THREE DAYS

The *"three days' journey into the desert,"* as demanded by Moses, speaks of the interval between Death and Resurrection. Of course Israel would not have understood that then, and possibly Moses didn't either: but that's exactly what it meant. It is only on a resurrection-ground, as made alive from the dead, that we can hold a feast unto the Lord! This goes forward to Romans, Chapter 6. There Paul said: *"Do you not know, that so many of us as were baptized into Jesus Christ were baptized into His death?*

"Therefore we are buried with Him by Baptism into death: that like as Christ was raised up from the dead by the Glory of the Father, even so we also should walk in newness of life.

"For if we have been planted together in the likeness of His death, we shall be also in the likeness of His Resurrection" (Rom. 6:3-5).

Let it be understood that Paul is not speaking of Water Baptism in these Passages, but rather of the Death of Christ on the Cross, and of believing sinners literally being in Christ at His death, at least in the Mind of God, which is all brought about by Faith. In other words, when the believing sinner expresses Faith in Christ, this performs the work. As well, it is the same with the Christians, even veteran Christians who have been living for the Lord for many, many years. We must continue, and I emphasize the point, to manifest Faith in Christ and what He has done for us at the Cross, which alone is the means by which victory comes to the Child of God, and is maintained by the Child of God. That's why Paul also said:

"For in Jesus Christ neither circumcision availeth anything, nor uncircumcision; but Faith which works by love" (Gal. 5:6).

In this one Passage in Galatians, Paul is telling Believers that it's not *"works,"* which we perform that gives us victory, but rather *"Faith."* And every time Paul speaks of Faith, always and without exception he is speaking of Faith in Christ, and what Christ did at the Cross (I Cor. 1:17).

THE MESSAGE

Such was Jehovah's message to Pharaoh. He claimed full deliverance for the people in the ground of their being His, and thereby, their right and obligation to offer Sacrifice unto Him. This means that nothing could ever satisfy God in reference to His elect, but their entire emancipation from the yoke of bondage.

When we contemplate Israel amid the brickkilns of Egypt, we behold a graphic condition of every child of Adam by nature, and even regrettably, many Christians who do not know their place and position in Christ. There they were, crushed beneath the enemy's galling yoke, and having no power to deliver themselves.

As we read between the lines, we find that the mere mention of the word *"liberty"* only caused the oppressor to bind his captives with a stronger fetter, and to laden them with a still more grievous burden. Consequently, it was absolutely necessary that deliverance should come from without.

But from where could such deliverance come? Where were the resources to pay such a ransom? Or where was the power to break their chains? And even were there both the one and other, where was the *"will"*? Who would take the trouble of delivering them?

The answer to that dilemma, which holds just as true presently as it did then, is God! Their refuge was in God then, just as it is in God now! God has both the Power and the Will. He can accomplish a Redemption both by price and by power. In Jehovah, and in Him Alone, was there Salvation for ruined and oppressed Israel. Thus it is in every case.

"Neither is there Salvation in any other: for there is none other name under Heaven given among men, whereby we must be saved" (Acts 4:12).

The sinner is in the hands of one who rules him with despotic power. He is *"sold under sin"* — *"led captive by Satan at his will,"* fast bound in the fetters of lust, passion, and temper, *"without strength," "without hope," "without God."*

THE VERY NATURE OF THE UNREDEEMED

Nor is it merely a question of the sinner's condition; his very *"nature"* is radically corrupt — wholly under the power of Satan. Hence he not only needs to be introduced into a new condition, but also to be endowed with a new nature. In fact, the nature and the condition go together. If it were possible for the sinner to better his condition, what would it avail so long as his nature was irrecoverably bad? There must be a nature to suit the condition; and there must be a condition to suit the capacity, the desires, the affections, and the tendencies of the new nature.

THE GOSPEL OF THE GRACE OF GOD

In this great and glorious Gospel, this Gospel of the Grace of God, we are taught that the Believer is introduced into an entirely new condition; which is brought about by the *"born again"* experience. His condition is so new that he is no longer viewed as in his former state of guilt and condemnation, but as in a state of perfect and everlasting Justification. It is a state of full pardon, and so full in fact that infinite Holiness cannot so much as find a single stain, which is brought about solely by the Blood of Jesus Christ (Eph. 2:13-18), and in fact, can be brought about in no other way or manner. That sinner is placed into an absolutely and eternal state of a new condition of unspotted Righteousness. Now please note the following, and note it carefully:

NO SUCH THING AS MORAL EVOLUTION

It is not, by any means, that his old condition is improved, for that's exactly what the world attempts to do. This is utterly impossible. *"That which is crooked cannot be made straight." "Can the Ethiopian change his skin, or the leopard his spots?"* Jeremiah would ask (Jer. 13:23).

Nothing can be more opposed to the fundamental truth of the Gospel than the theory of a gradual improvement in the sinner's condition, which, as should be obvious, completely blows to pieces the hypothesis of humanistic psychology. The sinner is born in a certain condition, and until he is *"born again,"* he cannot be in any other condition. He may try to improve, he may resolve to be better for the future — to *"turn over a new leaf"* — to live a different sort of life; but, all the while, he has not moved a single hair's breadth out of his real condition as a sinner. He may become *"religious,"* as it is called; he may try to pray, he may diligently attend to some ordinances, and exhibit an appearance of moral reform; but none of these things can, in the smallest degree, affect his positive condition before God. Think about this for a moment:

NATURE

How can a man alter his nature? He may make it undergo a process, he may try to subdue it — to place it under discipline, which is the way of psychology, but it is a nature still. *"That which is born of the flesh is flesh."*

For there to be a change in the human being, there must be the insertion of a new nature, as well as a new condition. And how is this to be had?

It is to be had only by believing God's testimony concerning His Son. *"As many as received Him, to them gave He power to become the sons of God, even to them who believe on His Name: Which were born, not of blood, nor of the will of the flesh, nor of the will of man, but of God"* (Jn. 1:12-13).

Here we learn that those who believe on the Name of the Only Begotten Son of God have the right and privilege of being sons of God. They are made partakers of a new nature: they have received eternal life. *"He who believes on the Son has everlasting life"* (Jn. 3:36).

Jesus said: *"Verily, verily, I say unto you, he who 'hears' My Word, and 'believes' on Him Who sent Me, 'has' everlasting life, and shall not come into condemnation; but is passed from death unto life"* (Jn. 5:24).

Such is the plain Doctrine of the Word in reference to the momentous questions of condition and nature. But on what is all this founded? How is the Believer introduced into a condition of Divine Righteousness and made partaker of the Divine nature?

It all rests on the great truth that *"Jesus died and rose again."* He died on the Cross, under the full weight of the transgressions of all of mankind. By so doing, He Divinely met all that was or could be against us. He magnified the law by keeping it perfectly, and, thereby, made it honorable; and, having done so, He was made a curse as well, by being placed on the tree. There, every claim was met; there, every enemy was silenced; there, every obstacle was removed; there, *"Mercy and Truth are met together; Righteousness and Peace have kissed each other."*

There, infinite justice was satisfied; there, infinite love could once again flow, in all its soothing and refreshing virtues, even into the broken heart of the sinner; there, the cleansing and atoning stream that flowed from the pierced side of a Crucified Christ, perfectly met all the cravings of a guilty and convicted conscience. There, the Lord Jesus, on the Cross, stood in our place; there, He was our

Representative; there, He died, *"the Just for the unjust."* There, *"He was made sin for us"* (II Cor. 5:21; I Pet. 3:18). There, He died the sinner's death, was buried, and rose again, having accomplished all. Hence, there is absolutely nothing now against the Believer. He is linked with Christ, and stands now in the same condition of Righteousness. *"As He is, so are we in this world"* (I Jn. 4:17).

This is so important, let us say it again: There, and we continue to speak of the Cross, the Blood of the Lamb has canceled all the Believer's guilt; there, Jesus blotted out the sinner's heavy debt; there, Christ gave to all who will believe a perfectly blank page, meaning that all the sins have been washed away.

THE CROSS

In all of this, we find that the Cross must be viewed in two ways:
1. As satisfying God's claims.
2. As expressing God's affections.

If I look at my sins in connection with the claims of God as a Judge, I find, in the Cross, a perfect settlement of those claims. God, as a Judge, has been Divinely satisfied — yes, glorified, in the Cross. But there is more than this.

God has affections as well as claims; and, in the Cross of the Lord Jesus Christ, all those affections are sweetly and touchingly told out into the sinner's ear; while, at the same time, he is made partaker of a new nature which is capable of enjoying those affections and having fellowship with a heart from which they flow. *"For Christ also has once suffered for sins, the Just for the unjust, that He might bring us to God"* (I Pet. 3:18).

Thus, we are not only brought into a *"condition,"* but unto a *"Person,"* even God Himself, and we are endowed with a *"nature"* which can delight in Him. The Scripture says, *"We also joy in God, through our Lord Jesus Christ, by Whom we now have received the reconciliation"* (Rom. 5:11).

THE BELIEVER AND THE CROSS

Everything we have said thus far speaks of the sinner coming to Christ, and the tremendous change which takes place in his life, a change which is so drastic in fact, that he is now referred to as a *"new creation,"* all in Christ Jesus (II Cor. 5:17). But unfortunately, unless the Believer is taught how to *"live"* for God, the new life that has been imparted to him can be hindered and weakened, causing failure, consternation, and acute difficulty in such a Believer. Unfortunately, most Believers fall into this situation, simply because they are taught incorrectly once they come to Christ.

The Believer must understand that this which brought him eternal life, and we continue to speak of Christ and the Cross, is that as well, which maintains eternal life. In other words, the way the Believer is to live a victorious, overcoming, Christian life, which as Peter said, is *"joy unspeakable and full of glory,"* is to continue to look to the Cross, understanding that it is through the Cross that the Grace of God continues to flow to the Believer.

Each and every Believer is meant to live under the Government of Grace. But unfortunately, many have fallen back to the Government of Law. Let us explain:

THE GOVERNMENT OF GRACE

Paul said: *"For you are not under the law* (the Government of Law) *but under Grace* (the Government of Grace)*"* (Rom. 6:14).

This refers not only to the Dispensation under which we now live, which began at the Cross of Christ, but as well, it refers to the *"way"* and *"manner"* in which we live and conduct ourselves. What do we mean by that?

Many Christians erroneously think that because this is the Dispensation of Grace, and to be sure it definitely is, this means that we are no longer troubled by law. They consider that due to the fact that this is the Dispensation of Grace, this Grace just automatically comes to them. It doesn't!

It is possible to frustrate the Grace of God, and to do so to the extent that we stop or hinder its flow, irrespective of the fact that we are living in the Dispensation of Grace (Gal. 2:21).

The Believer must understand that the Dispensation or Government of Grace simply refers to the manner in which God deals with the human race. He deals with it in Grace, simply because the Cross has made this possible.

Now Grace doesn't mean that we have a license to sin, as some think, but rather that the Goodness of God, which is actually what Grace actually is, will flow to us in an uninterrupted stream, so to speak, because of what Jesus did for us at the Cross.

It troubles me greatly when I hear Christians refer to *"greasy Grace,"* or *"easy Grace."* These individuals, pure and simple, whomever they might be, are functioning under the Government of Law. In fact, they are despising Grace, because it sets aside the Government of Law.

There is no such thing as *"greasy Grace,"* or *"easy Grace."* Such people who say these things are, in effect, despising Grace, claiming that it gives people a license to sin. In fact, the exact opposite is the truth.

It is by the Grace of God, which is the Goodness of God, all brought about by what Jesus did at the Cross, and which gives the Holy Spirit the latitude to work within our lives, that gives us total and complete victory over sin. This of which Paul taught, and which we are teaching, is the way to have victory over sin, and in fact, the only way to have victory over sin. If anyone tries to do it any other way, that person, whether they realize it or not, is repudiating the Cross of Christ, which can only play out to a disastrous conclusion.

So what do we mean by the term *"Government of Grace"*?

In simple explanation, we are referring to the fact that the Believer understands that everything comes to him through Christ and what Christ did for us at the Cross. He is to continue to believe in that Finished Work, which then enables the Grace of God to come to him in an uninterrupted flow. That's all it takes is *"Faith,"* and when we speak of Faith, as always, we're speaking of Christ and His Finished Work. That's why Paul said: *"For in Jesus Christ neither circumcision availeth anything, nor uncircumcision; but Faith which worketh by love"* (Gal. 5:6).

This, the Government of Grace, is God's prescribed order for victorious, Christian living. As long as the Believer continues to manifest Faith in Christ and the Cross, Grace will always come to him in an uninterrupted flow, which actually refers to the Holy Spirit working unhindered within his heart and life.

THE GOVERNMENT OF LAW

This particular type of Government rested on Israel for a period of about 1,600 years. It was given to Moses, and was concluded by Jesus Christ. John said: *"For the Law was given by Moses, but Grace and Truth came by Jesus Christ"* (Jn. 1:17).

The Cross of Christ introduced a completely new manner of living. Even though the following has recently been said in this Volume, it is so important that I think it's necessary to say it again:

The Deity of Christ was absolutely necessary; however, not a single soul has ever been saved because Christ was and is God. In other words, the fact of Jesus being Deity, this fact alone could not save anyone. As well, the Virgin Birth was absolutely necessary; however, the Virgin Birth within itself could not save one single soul. Jesus' Perfect Life was absolutely necessary; but had it stopped there, not one soul would have been saved. His miracles were necessary, but the miracles alone could not save anyone.

It was the Cross Alone, which is the Atonement, which is where Christ shed His Precious Life's Blood, which satisfied the demands of a thrice-Holy God, and thereby atoned for all sin, which effected Salvation. Jesus' Perfect Life means that He kept the Law in every respect, but as well, His Perfect Death, which refers to Him offering up His Perfect Body, as a Perfect Sacrifice, atoned for all sin, and was an absolute necessity, if the terrible sin debt was to be paid, and man could be saved. So the Law was satisfied by Christ in two ways:

1. It was perfectly kept, which Jesus did as our Substitute, and as well,

2. Its penalty was perfectly met, which also was demanded, and which took place at the Cross.

All the precepts of the Law were perfectly kept by Christ; all the conditions of the Law were perfectly met by Christ. Concerning this, Paul also said:

"Blotting out the handwriting of ordinances that was against us (the Law), *which was contrary to us, and took it out of the*

way, nailing it to His Cross." This means that Jesus met every condition of the Law, and did so, all on our behalf (Col. 2:14).

Sin is what breaks the law, and sin is the legal means by which Satan holds man in bondage. But when Jesus died on the Cross, He atoned for all sin. When He did this, which means that all sin was removed, this *"spoiled principalities and powers, making a show of them openly, and triumphed over them in it"* (Col. 2:15).

This means that Satan was totally defeated, along with every fallen angel and demon spirit. This also means that Satan can no longer hold man in bondage, at least those who will believe in Christ and what Christ has done at the Cross.

Because this is the Dispensation of Grace, many Christians think it's impossible for one to revert to Law. In fact, most Christians have little knowledge of what the Law is all about. But the tragedy is, most Christians who think this way are in fact, whether they realize it or not, living under the Government of Law. This is proven by the constant failure within their hearts and lives.

Why do you think that Paul talked so much about law in his Epistles? If it was not possible for a Christian to revert to Law, then the Apostle was wasting his breath. Listen to what he said:

"Stand fast therefore in the liberty (Government of Grace) *wherewith Christ has made us free, and be not entangled again with the yoke of bondage* (he's speaking here of the Law)" (Gal. 5:1).

He then said: *"Behold, I Paul say unto you, that if you be circumcised* (fall back to Law) *Christ shall profit you nothing.*

"For I testify again to every man who is circumcised, that he is a debtor to do the whole Law."

And then: *"Christ is become of no effect unto you, whosoever of you are justified by the Law* (who seek to be justified by the Law); *you are fallen from Grace"* (Gal. 5:2-4).

Let us say it again: If it's not possible for the Believer to revert back to Law, then Paul used a lot of ink for nothing.

No! This of which we speak, Christians living under the Government of Law, is the greatest problem in the Church, and in fact,

NOTES

proven by what Paul said, the greatest problem for all time, at least since the Government of Grace began.

If you will notice carefully what Paul said, he used terms like, *"Christ shall profit you nothing,"* and *"Christ is become of no effect unto you,"* which presents a chilling prospect. And this is the problem in countless hearts and lives of modern Christians, and in fact, almost all.

How? Why?

If the Believer doesn't understand the Cross, and how it affects his everyday living before God, and how he must maintain Faith in the Finished Work of Christ at all times (Rom. 6:3-5, 11, 14), then without fail, he will revert to the Government of Law. There are only two governments under which a person can function, and that is under Law, or under Grace. So if the Cross is not understood, which means that we stop the Grace of God, there is no place else to go but Law. Let's look a little closer at the modern scene:

MODERN PRACTICES

Everything I'm about to say proves that such Christians, as sincere as they might be, are living under the Government of Law, and not under Grace. And because it is so important, let us say it again:

If the Believer doesn't understand the Cross as it refers to his Sanctification, this means that he doesn't understand Grace, and whether he realizes it or not, he is functioning, or trying to do so, under Law. As such, he will live a life of failure, simply because the Holy Spirit will not help such a Christian, and this means that such a Believer is left to his own strength, which is hopelessly inadequate. As I explained to you some pages back, such a Christian in the eyes of God is actually looked at as a *"spiritual adulterer."* It means that while they are married to Christ, they are being unfaithful to Him, by being married to the Law as well (Rom. 7:1-4).

This is a miserable existence for a Christian. That's why Paul said: *"O wretched man that I am! Who shall deliver me from the body of this death?"* (Rom. 7:24).

After Paul was saved and baptized with the Holy Spirit, at that time, not knowing and understanding the Cross, or Grace for that matter, the great Apostle, for a period of time, attempted to live for God under the Government of Law, which is all he knew. In his defense, no one else at that time knew and understood the Government of Grace. In fact, it was to Paul that the meaning of this great Government was given, and which he gave to us in his 14 Epistles. Regrettably, most Christians presently are living in the Seventh Chapter of Romans, simply because they don't know any better. Now let's look at the practices:

ERRONEOUS PRACTICES

Millions of Christians, who are having problems and troubles within their Christian experience, are running all over the world, trying to find a Preacher who will lay hands on them, and solve their problem. While the laying on of hands is definitely Scriptural, the manner in which it is usually performed will, in fact, bring no relief whatsoever.

Despite the fact that the Spirit of God definitely moves in such cases, with at times great manifestations taking place, which are of God as well; but still, when that Christian leaves that place of blessing, and goes back out to his regular and normal living, he will find himself in the same condition as he was before the blessing. Why?

Jesus said, *"You shall know the Truth, and Truth shall make you free"* (Jn. 8:32). This means that it's not a touch which is so much needed, but rather the *"Truth."*

The reason that such a Believer continues to have problems, even after the Lord has manifested Himself to that Believer, is because the Believer doesn't know in the first place as to why he's having problems, and doesn't know the cure for those problems. As a result, there is no way that he can overcome that which He seeks to overcome.

His need is not for a Preacher to lay hands on him, because that's not God's Way. His need is to know and understand the Truth, and apply it thereby, to his heart and life. And what is that Truth?

Notice again what Paul said:

"For Christ sent me not to baptize, but to preach the Gospel: not with wisdom of words, lest the Cross of Christ should be made of none effect.

NOTES

"For the preaching of the Cross is to them who perish foolishness; but unto us which are saved it is the Power of God" (I Cor. 1:17-18).

Notice again: *"But God forbid that I should glory, save in the Cross of our Lord Jesus Christ, by Whom the world is crucified unto me, and I unto the world"* (Gal. 6:14).

Every Christian in the world who is having problems can have those problems solved by understanding what we are teaching here, and I speak of an understanding of the Cross, and what Christ there did for us as our Substitute. Our Salvation was brought about by what Christ did at the Cross, and our continued victory in this Salvation, which refers to living an overcoming, victorious life, is maintained by continuing to have Faith in Christ and His Finished Work. Notice as to what John the Beloved said: *"For whatsoever is born of God overcomes the world, and this is the victory that overcometh the world, even our Faith"* (I Jn. 5:4).

And when John speaks here of *"Faith,"* even as Paul, he is speaking of Christ, and what Christ did at the Cross. Notice again what he said:

"This is He Who came by water and blood, even Jesus Christ; not by water only, but by water and blood" (I Jn. 5:6).

The *"water"* refers to the Incarnation. In other words, it refers to Jesus being born as a human being by and through the Virgin Mary.

"Blood" refers to what He did to redeem the human race, which is the reason He came. He died on the Cross, thereby shedding His Life's Blood, which atoned for all sin, past, present, and future, at least for those who will believe (Jn. 3:16).

I have preached the Gospel now not much short of a half century. During these many years, I have seen many things in the realm of Christendom, and I speak of ways that Christians engage in order to live an overcoming life.

When Frances and I first began in the Ministry, the great craze then was *"casting demons out of Christians,"* etc. This referred to Christians who had problems, with these problems being diagnosed as a demon of lust, or a demon of greed, or whatever it might be. They were encouraged to go to

Preachers who believed this, where hands would be laid on them, and this particular demon cast out of them, and their problem would then be solved. Pure and simple, all of that is unscriptural.

I then watched the *"confession craze"* as it began in the Church. The way to overcome was to simply confess and to do so over and over again, whatever the need was, and whatever the Believer hoped to be. That swept the Church like wildfire, and is unscriptural as well.

Now as we go down through these things, if the Believer will think a moment, he will realize that there is some truth in all of these situations. But of course, that is one of Satan's chief ploys. He puts a little truth into the situation, in order to serve as bait.

For instance, demon spirits definitely do get involved wherever sin occasions itself. But the proposed solution is definitely not the answer. Also, a good and proper confession is definitely right and Scriptural, but not in the manner in which it was taught.

I then watched the *"buddy system"* take hold, which is really a take off on humanistic psychology. In other words, certain Preachers were advocating that every Believer should have a confidant. To this other person, we would confess all of our problems, with the idea being that the strength of two is far greater than the strength of one. Again, there is a small measure of truth in this, but neither is that the answer.

I then watched the *"falling out"* craze take effect, which seems to be with us constantly. In other words, if hands could be laid on the individual, as we mentioned some paragraphs back, with the person *"falling out under the power,"* this person's problems are then solved. While we definitely believe in the laying on of hands, and while *"falling out under the power"* is definitely of the Lord, that is if He is the One truly doing such, still, this is not an answer for the ills of man.

In the early 1990's, *"the laughing phenomenon"* took hold in the Church. It was advised that if every one could have the Spirit of God move on them, thereby engaging in peals of laughter for a given period of time, this would bring about victory, etc. Again, this is not Scriptural.

NOTES

And then we have the *"family curse,"* which claims that certain Preachers can lay hands on people, rebuking the family curse, and victory will then join itself to that particular Believer.

These things, and scores we haven't named, have no validity, Scripturally speaking. The reason is, the Lord doesn't deliver people by and through manifestations, or particular works. People are delivered by Faith, and by that, we are speaking of Faith in Christ and what Christ has done at the Cross. That and that alone is the answer. Again I emphasize, that's why Jesus said, *"You shall know the Truth, and the Truth shall make you free"* (Jn. 8:32).

All of this is what I mean by Christians abandoning the Cross, resorting to other things, which automatically places them under the *"Government of Law."* When this happens, even as Paul said, *"Christ then profits them nothing,"* which means that what He did at the Cross has become of no effect (Gal. 5:2, 4).

People who live under the Government of Law have placed their faith in *"works,"* which then has to do with their *"performance,"* which is always lacking. And let the Reader understand this as well:

One cannot trust in Christ and what Christ has done for us in His Finished Work, and at the same time, trust in works. Such proclaims a *"double-minded man,"* which the Holy Spirit through James told us *"is unstable in all his ways."* He also said of such a man: *"For let not that man think that he shall receive anything of the Lord"* (James 1:7-8).

THE MESSAGE OF THE CROSS

Any time the Christian answers the Message of the Cross by saying, *"I believe that, but . . ."* the truth is, that Christian doesn't believe that. In other words, he is paying lip service to the Cross, if that, with his faith actually being anchored in his own concoction, whatever that might be.

Sometime back, one of my very close associates was speaking with a Preacher about this very thing. The man pastored a quite large Church in a major American city.

To the Message of the Cross, the Preacher answered, *"That's alright for some people, but not necessarily for all."*

What in the world type of answer is that? What in the world could a man mean by such an answer?

Whether he realized it or not, he was saying that the Cross of Christ was needed for some, but not for all. What is that man preaching to his congregation?

The tragedy is, this very Preacher was found out just a little later to be suffering a tremendous problem within his life, which was threatening to destroy him. And yet, as he answered my associate, despite his problem, which he had been struggling to try to overcome for years, he was in effect putting himself in the position as not needing the Cross.

We are speaking here of pride, which seems to affect all of us, and which is a fallout from the problem in the Garden.

Pride is very bad, and religious pride is the worst pride of all. It refuses to admit its need or its condition. Why?

Such a person is trying to live for God under the Government of Law. As such, they have engaged themselves in certain works and practices, and it's hard for them to admit that all of these things are to no avail. That's why Paul said: *"For in Jesus Christ neither circumcision availeth anything, nor uncircumcision"* (Gal. 5:6).

In effect, these Galatians were saying, *"I believe in the Cross, but I also believe that Christian men have to be circumcised."* To such a belief, the Apostle said, *"Christ is become of no effect unto you, whosoever of you are justified by the Law."* He then offered a chilling statement, *"You are fallen from Grace"* (Gal. 5:4).

In other words, such a Christian is not functioning under the Government of Grace, but rather the Government of Law.

A little later, the problem of the Preacher mentioned some paragraphs back surfaced, causing tremendous embarrassment, as well as great hurt and harm to himself, his family, and his Church. Unfortunately, this is not an isolated incident, but rather a common occurrence.

The only answer for the Child of God, in fact for the entirety of the world, is *"Jesus Christ and Him Crucified."* To look elsewhere is to look in vain.

NOTES

THE BURDENS

Verses 4 and 5 read: *"And the king of Egypt said unto them, Wherefore do you, Moses and Aaron, let the people from their works? Get you unto your burdens.*

"And Pharaoh said, Behold, the people of the land now are many, and you make them rest from their burdens."

With the words registered in these Fourth and Fifth Verses, the first confrontation between the Israelite leaders and the Egyptian Monarch ends.

The word *"burdens"* is apropos as it regards the condition of the Children of Israel at this time. As we shall see, their lot was difficult to say the least.

As should be obvious, and which the Holy Spirit intends for us to understand, their plight is a type of the sinner in the world loaded down with *"burdens."* The Scripture plainly says: *"The way of transgressors is hard"* (Prov. 13:15).

But yet, as the Children of Israel, it seems that they did not too very much mind being slaves in Egypt, until the burdens became so heavy that they could not be borne. Oftentimes, it's the same way with the unsaved soul. Until the situation becomes intolerable, with the proverbial back to the wall, that person will not say, *"yes"* to Christ. Why?

SPIRITUAL BLINDNESS

Every unsaved person in the world is spiritually blind, and they are spiritually blind because they are spiritually dead. At the Fall in the Garden of Eden, man died. This means that he spiritually died, which means that all access to God was cut off because of sin. This means that the unredeemed man is totally depraved, and has no idea or correct knowledge of God whatsoever. In fact, it is impossible for him to have any knowledge of God or God's Word. Dead is dead, and means exactly what it says (Gen. 3:3).

So, being spiritually dead the individual doesn't really understand the state that he's in. If he looks at Christians at all, which he oftentimes does, it is a mystery to him, as to how they could reap any enjoyment out of going to Church and reading the Bible, etc. In fact, he really cannot think of anything that's more boring than that which we've just stated.

Consequently, being spiritually dead, he has absolutely no knowledge of the joy of the Lord, of the peace which passes all understanding, of the joy unspeakable and full of glory. If a Christian tries to explain these things to the unredeemed, at best he will only draw a blank stare. Again let us emphasize it:

Being spiritually dead, man is totally depraved, which means that not only does he have no knowledge of God, neither does he have any knowledge of sin. Sin is natural to him, actually being his very nature, i.e., *"the sin nature."*

So, Satan piles the burdens on such an individual, but he thinks that such are natural. As stated, until those burdens become insurmountable, he is not prone to turn to Christ.

THE WORD OF GOD AND THE HOLY SPIRIT

There is only one way that the unredeemed can be brought out of their unsaved state, out of their spiritual vacuum, our of their spiritual blindness. In some way, the Word of God has to be ministered to them. And along with that, the Holy Spirit has to anoint that Word, thereby bringing conviction to the soul of the unredeemed. And what do we mean by conviction?

This the Holy Spirit convicting the lost sinner of his condition, making him for a moment see his lost condition, and at the same time, to see the Lord Jesus Christ as the Saviour (Jn. 16:7-14).

The sinner then Has to make a choice as to whether he will accept Christ or reject Christ. The Scripture says, *"whosoever will"* (Rev. 22:17).

At the very moment of Holy Spirit conviction, some accept immediately, while others try to run from this convicting power, but will ultimately accept Christ. Others reject the call of the Spirit, and in fact continue to reject, until they finally grow hardened, which means they will go deeper and deeper into sin, and be eternally lost.

As the Holy Spirit moves upon the Word of God, boring deep into the heart of the convicted sinner, at the same time, the Divine Spirit gives Faith to that believing sinner, in order that they may have the power to believe, that is if they so desire. Again let us understand that the unsaved person is spiritually dead, and has no faith whatsoever, at least the type of Faith that God will recognize. So, the Holy Spirit has to impart to that individual a measure of Faith, which He definitely does, in order that the person might believe (Rom. 12:3).

FREE WILL

God never tampers with the free moral agency of a person. He will deal with that person, speak to that person, move upon that person, even convict that person by the Power of the Holy Spirit, but He will not force the issue. God always respects the free will of an individual. As stated, it is *"whosoever will"* (Rev. 22:17; Jn. 3:16).

Of course, God through foreknowledge knows who will accept and who will reject, but foreknowledge doesn't at all mean that God tampers with the will. It just simply means that He foreknows through His omniscience what is going to happen in the future. However, let me explain something about the *"will of man"* that most people do not know or realize.

The will of an individual, as it regards spiritual things, is limited to the *"will"* to follow the Lord, or to reject the Lord. For instance:

If the worst alcoholic in the world desires to do so, that is as the Holy Spirit moves upon his heart, he can accept the Lord, and all the powers of darkness cannot stop him. He doesn't have the will to quit drinking, or to committing a myriad of other sins, but Satan is not allowed to stop his will as it regards accepting Christ, that is, if he *"wills"* to do so. It is still *"whosoever will."* And of course, after turning to Christ, as millions have in this state, the Holy Spirit then rids that person of the demon spirits which are controlling him, and gives him as well, victory over sin, etc.

Strangely enough, many, if not most, Christians have an erroneous viewpoint of the *"will"* of the Believer. Most think that once they come to Christ, their willpower is greatly strengthened, and now they have the power to do what they didn't have the power to do before being saved, and that is to say *"no"* to sin. Nothing could be further from the truth.

In effect, the will of man as it regards the Lord is the same in the Believer as it is the unbeliever. By that I mean, the Believer has the will to say, *"yes"* to Christ, and at the same time, if he so desires, he can also say *"no,"* exactly as the unredeemed. The Lord doesn't strengthen the willpower of the Believer, as many think. In fact, even though the *"will"* is always very much involved in what the Believer does, and he definitely has to *"will"* to have all that Christ has afforded him, but that's as far as it goes. No Christian has any super willpower, or anything like that.

I had a dear Brother to say to me not long ago, *"Before I was saved,"* he went on to say, *"I couldn't say 'no' to drugs. But now that I'm saved, I can say 'no' to that terrible scourge."*

The dear Brother has been taught wrong, and following that particular course, he will find himself in trouble very shortly, if in fact that trouble hasn't already come by now.

SO HOW DOES THE CHRISTIAN WALK IN VICTORY?

Exactly as the unsaved has the capacity to use his will to accept Christ, the Believer has the same identical capacity. He is to *"will"* to go God's Way, which means the way of the Cross, thereby placing his faith in that Finished Work, which then gives the Holy Spirit the latitude to work mightily in that Believer's life. There is no place in the Scripture that it says that it is by the *"will"* of the Believer, but rather by *"Faith."*

Paul said: *"For we through the Spirit wait for the hope of Righteousness by Faith."*

He then said, *"For in Jesus Christ neither circumcision availeth anything, nor uncircumcision; but faith which worketh by love"* (Gal. 5:5-6).

The great Apostle also said: *"Therefore being justified by faith . . ."* (Rom. 5:1). He then said: *"For by Grace are you saved through faith"* (Eph. 2:8). Let us say it again:

The *"will"* is important only as a means of desiring that which is of the Lord. That's as far as it can go. Having done that, we are to will to register Faith in Christ and what Christ has done for us at the Cross. That and that alone brings victory. Listen again to Paul:

"For I know that in me (that is, in my flesh,) dwells no good thing: for to will is present with me; but how to perform that which is good I find not" (Rom. 7:18).

Paul plainly says here that he had the *"will,"* but simply that wasn't enough. He was to later find out that it was Faith in Christ and what Christ has done for us at the Cross, which brings about victory in one's life.

But unfortunately, most Christians think that it is *"willpower"* which is the source of the Christian's strength.

SIN AND THE CHRISTIAN

Before coming to Christ, every unredeemed person has a *"human nature,"* and as well, a *"sin nature."* The *"sin nature"* came about at the Fall, and actually is the cause of all the suffering and heartache in the world today, and in fact, ever has been. But when that person comes to Christ, they now add a third nature, which Peter calls the *"Divine nature"* (II Pet. 1:4). The *"sin nature"* has had its power destroyed, and its guilt removed (Rom. 6:6). However, it does not leave the Believer, as Paul explains in Romans, Chapter 6, but is rather dormant in the Believer's life. In fact, the Scripture plainly tells us that we as Believers are to be *"dead"* to the sin nature, but it doesn't say that the sin nature itself is dead (Rom. 6:11).

At any rate, due to the *"Divine nature"* now being a part of the Child of God, the Christian hates sin. This means that he doesn't want to sin, doesn't desire to sin, and will struggle against sin, etc. So that being the case, why is it that Christians, at times, sin?

In fact, all Christians, at times, sin, and when it happens, the true Believer cannot rest until he makes it right with God, with fellowship then being restored, which means that all is forgiven (I Jn. 1:9).

Christians sin, because they do not understand their rightful place and position in Christ, as a result of what Christ did at the Cross. Not understanding the Message of the

Cross, which is the only Message of Victory, most Christians put their faith in something other than the Cross, which denies that person the help of the Holy Spirit, which guarantees failure on the part of the Child of God. In fact, even as we've already explained in this volume, if the Christian doesn't understand the Cross, he can find himself being ruled by the sin nature, exactly as he was before conversion. Paul said so:

"Let not sin (the sin, which is the sin nature) *therefore reign in your mortal body, that you should obey it in the lusts thereof"* (Rom. 6:12).

Now if it wasn't possible for the sin nature to once again rule and reign in the Believer's life, then the Apostle would not have mentioned it in this fashion. If such is not possible, there's no point in even bringing up the subject. But the truth is, if the Believer doesn't understand Christ and the Cross, which Paul is teaching in Romans, Chapter 6, that Believer is going to ultimately be ruled by the sin nature in one way or the other.

In fact, such a Believer will fight against these ungodly impulses with all of his strength and power, but conclude by doing exactly what Paul also said: *"For that which I do I allow* (understand) *not: for what I would, that do I not; but what I hate, that do I"* (Rom. 7:15).

This means that no matter how hard the person struggles against sin, and the true Believer will definitely struggle against sin, in such a state, and we're speaking of having no knowledge of the Cross, that person is going to fail.

Now what should be done with such a person?

GRACE OR LAW

The Church, little understanding the Cross, operates on the principle of *"willpower,"* and, therefore, concludes that if a Christian sins, it's simply because they have willed to sin. In other words, in the thinking of most in the Church, all that Christian has to do is simply say *"no"* to sin. They don't seem to realize that such a Christian has said *"no"* to sin untold numbers of time, but to no avail, exactly as Paul said.

NOTES

So, thinking that the matter of *"sin"* is just a matter of saying *"yes"* or *"no,"* most of the time the Church operates from the position of *"Law."* In other words, the person has broken the rules, so that person must be punished.

However, there is nothing in the Word of God that speaks of one Christian punishing another. And in fact, the Church Leaders who are doing the punishing are probably in worse shape spiritually than the one they are punishing.

The truth is, Jesus took our punishment on the tree (Gal. 3:13). And for us to think that we can punish a fellow Christian, in effect is saying that Christ wasn't punished enough, and we have to add some punishment to that which He has already suffered. If you think about it a little bit, such an attitude borders on blasphemy! Let me ask this question!

What good does punishment do? How does that help a Christian get victory over his problem, whatever the problem is?

The truth is, punishment only makes a bad matter worse. It does not help at all, and in fact, is a form of penance, which God can never accept.

SO WHAT SHOULD BE DONE TO THE CHRISTIAN WHO SINS?

Paul told us what should be done. He said: *"Brethren, if a man be overtaken in a fault* (the word *'fault'* here refers to a moral failure)*, you which are spiritual, restore such an one in the spirit of meekness; considering yourself, lest you also be tempted"* (Gal. 6:1).

The word *"spiritual"* carries the connotation of someone who understands God's prescribed order of victory, which is the Message of the Cross (I Cor. 1:17-18; 2:2, 5).

Such a Believer is to tell the one who has failed the Lord, and irrespective as to what the failure might be, that they have failed, simply because their faith was in something other than Christ and the Cross. In other words, the person is to be brought back to the Cross, and made to understand that what Jesus did there is the source of his victory, and in fact, the only source of his victory. He is to get his Faith once again in the right place, which is the Cross.

The reason for failure, and this speaks of any Believer, is because our Faith has been pulled from Christ and the Cross to other things. In fact, this is something that Satan relentlessly tries to do. This is why Paul also told us to *"fight the good fight of faith"* (I Tim. 6:12).

So why is it that most so-called Christian Leaders don't relay this to failing Believers, Preachers, or otherwise?

They do not relate this great Truth to Believers, simply because they do not know and understand the Truth themselves, or else they do not believe the Truth.

Have you noticed that in the last several decades, more and more, the Church is directing failure to humanistic psychology? The great statement is, *"He (or she) needs professional help."* Regrettably, there is no help from that source. And not only is there no help from that source, there is actually harm from that source, simply because it pulls one away from the true victory that one can have in Christ, and as well, as in all error, demon spirits are involved, with the latter state of that individual being worse than at the beginning.

Sin, and sin of any stripe, is to be taken to the Cross. The Cross was brought about because of sin, and is the only answer to this dread malady. For any Believer, Church Leader, or otherwise, to think that there is another solution can only be described as *"blasphemy!"* That's exactly why Paul said:

"But though we, or an Angel from Heaven, preach any other Gospel unto you than that which we have preached unto you, let him be accursed" (Gal. 1:8).

This means that those who preach *"humanistic psychology"* are cursed by God, and all who come under such preaching and teaching are cursed as well.

It also means that all who subscribe to the so-called *"Word of Faith doctrine,"* which repudiates the Cross of Christ, are cursed as well.

It also means that all *"modernism"* is cursed by God, and simply because it denies Christ and the Cross.

THE LAST DAY PLOY OF SATAN

When I was a young man just getting started in Evangelistic work, it was the Modernists who denied Christ and the Cross, and it was obvious as to what they were. But Satan has been successful at making his terrible error much more palatable. It falls in again with what Paul said:

"Now the Spirit speaks expressly that in the latter times (the times in which we now live) *some shall depart from the faith* (the Message of the Cross) *giving heed to seducing spirits, and doctrines of devils"* (I Tim. 4:1).

Today, the ones denying the Cross fall into the category of those who claim to be Spirit-filled, and claim to believe all the Bible, etc. Consequently, it is much more subtle than it was under the Modernists. In fact, this present thrust claims to perform great miracles, and above all, claims to be able to make all followers rich. The latter is a heady doctrine, appealing to greed, of which all of us seem to have to some measure. I once again speak of the *"Word of Faith"* doctrine, which in reality is no faith at all.

I realize that my words may seem hard and harsh; however, we are speaking here of the souls of men; consequently, I would much rather be too clear and too plain, than not clear and plain enough. As stated, the souls of men are at stake.

This doctrine denies the Cross, actually claiming that a person is saved by trusting in a Christ (another Jesus) who died spiritually on the Cross, which means that he died a sinner, and then suffered the Wrath of God in the burning side of Hell for three days and nights, and was then born again, and raised from the dead. In other words, as is clearly obvious, they deny that the Atonement is ensconced in the Cross, rather placing it in the depths of the burning side of Hell. While it is true that Jesus did go down into Hell after His death, there is no record that He went into the burning side, but only into Paradise, to lead captive those who had been there since their deaths, in fact, awaiting the Cross, which would guarantee their deliverance. I speak of all the Old Testament Saints (Lk. 16:19-31; Eph. 4:8).

These people, who incidentally talk out of both sides of their mouths, in effect, say that the Blood does not cleanse. While they might mouth the words that the Blood cleanses, they will, at the same time, claim that the shedding of the Blood of Christ wasn't enough. They then claim that the actual work was carried out in the burning side of Hell, even as we've already explained.

These same people claim that the Cross is *"past miseries,"* and *"the greatest defeat in human history."* They deny all songs about the Blood, about the Cross, about the Sufferings of Christ on the Cross, etc., claiming that these are defeatist songs. They can be labeled as none other than *"enemies of the Cross of Christ."*

Paul then said: *"Whose end is destruction, whose god is their belly, and whose glory is in their shame, who mind earthly things"* (Phil. 3:18-19).

It is my belief that this particular doctrine is the greatest thrust that Satan has ever made against the Church. He has saved his greatest blow for the *"latter times,"* even as Paul said that he would. It is all carried out by *"seducing spirits and doctrines of devils."*

Again, I personally believe that this *"Word of Faith"* doctrine is even worse than the doctrine of law under the Judaizers in Paul's day. Those were more clear-cut than these presently.

These presently speak in tongues constantly, claim to perform miracles, claim to believe the entire Bible, and of course, claim to be Spirit-filled and, therefore, Spirit-led.

When we began to point out over our daily Radio Program, plus the Telecast, this erroneous doctrine, that's dragging untold numbers to perdition, many Christians who believed in this particular message, hardly knew what they actually believed. Most of them had never even heard of the *"Jesus died spiritually doctrine,"* which refers to Him dying as a sinner on the Cross. And if they had heard it, they didn't really understand what they were hearing, and let it pass.

The great lure to this doctrine is, pure and simple, *"money."* As previously stated, the leaders of this doctrine claim that if their teaching is followed, the Christian will get rich. Consequently, they appeal to greed, which is a powerful factor.

All of this sounds right, and even looks right; however, what the people are hearing is *"an angel of light."* And the Ministers who propagate this false doctrine can be labeled as none other, even as Paul said, than *"Satan's Ministers"* (II Cor. 11:13-15).

As a result of that doctrine, no one is saved, no one is baptized with the Holy Spirit, no one is delivered, no one is healed, and no one is set free. While great claims are made, the truth is, they are empty claims.

While some precious few people might be truly saved in these Meetings, the truth is, they were not saved as a result of this doctrine, but despite that doctrine.

IS IT THE LORD?

A lady wrote me just the other day, asking the question, *"If this doctrine is wrong, why does the Spirit of the Lord move greatly in these meetings?"*

I answered her according to the following:

There is no Spirit of the Lord in these meetings. There is that which claims to be the Spirit of God, and such will deceive many; however, what is purported to be the Spirit of God actually isn't.

This is the tragedy of these last days. Many, if not most Christians don't know what is of God and what isn't of God.

What is truly of God is not determined, in fact, is never determined by manifestations alone. It must always be determined by the Word of God. Does it match up totally and completely with the Scripture? And by that, I don't mean taking one Scripture out of context, bending that Scripture to try to make it mean something it doesn't mean, and using that as a proof text.

I mean that what is being taught, preached, and practiced does not line up with the general tenor of the Word of God. And to be sure, people who are enemies of the Cross definitely do not line up with the Word of God. And please believe me, the Word of Faith doctrine, propagated by the Word of Faith people, definitely falls into that category. So do those who propagate humanistic psychology as the answer to the ills of man. So do the Modernists, etc.

Once again I remind the Reader that we aren't speaking here of natural preferences, but rather the eternal souls of men. God has one prescribed way of Salvation, and one prescribed way of victory. Both are summed up in the Cross of Christ. That's why Paul said: *"We preach Christ Crucified"* (I Cor. 1:23).

(6) "AND PHARAOH COMMANDED THE SAME DAY THE TASKMASTERS OF THE PEOPLE, AND THEIR OFFICERS, SAYING,

(7) "YOU SHALL NO MORE GIVE THE PEOPLE STRAW TO MAKE BRICK, AS HERETOFORE: LET THEM GO AND GATHER STRAW FOR THEMSELVES.

(8) "AND THE TALE OF THE BRICKS, WHICH THEY DID MAKE HERETOFORE, YOU SHALL LAY UPON THEM; YOU SHALL NOT DIMINISH OUGHT THEREOF: FOR THEY BE IDLE; THEREFORE THEY CRY, SAYING, LET US GO AND SACRIFICE TO OUR GOD.

(9) "LET THERE MORE WORK BE LAID UPON THE MEN, THAT THEY MAY LABOR THEREIN; AND LET THEM NOT REGARD VAIN WORDS.

(10) "AND THE TASKMASTERS OF THE PEOPLE WENT OUT, AND THEIR OFFICERS, AND THEY SPOKE TO THE PEOPLE, SAYING, THUS SAITH PHARAOH, I WILL NOT GIVE YOU STRAW.

(11) "YOU GO, GET YOU STRAW WHERE YOU CAN FIND IT: YET NOT OUGHT OF YOUR WORK SHALL BE DIMINISHED."

The structure is:

1. Oftentimes, the setting to carry out the Will of God will result in Satan's anger, with opposition being increased.

2. Foolishly, some Christians believe that if it's the Will of God, and I speak of whatever it is that we are doing, there will be no difficulties. Actually, the reverse is true. The carrying out of the Will of God can bring great opposition from Satan.

3. It is good for a man to learn painfully the nature of sin's dominion, and his absolute helplessness in the grip of that Monarch.

OPPOSITION TO THE SACRIFICE

Verses 6 through 8 read: *"And Pharaoh commanded the same day the taskmasters of the people, and their officers, saying,*

"You shall no more give the people straw to make brick, as heretofore: let them go and gather straw for themselves.

"And the tale of the bricks which they did make heretofore, you shall lay upon them; you shall not diminish ought thereof: for they be idle; therefore they cry, saying, Let us go and sacrifice to our God."

The sacrifice of an innocent animal was meant to typify the coming Son of God, Who would give Himself on the Cross, which alone could break the bondage of darkness, exampled here by Pharaoh. Let the Believer take a lesson from this:

At the mention of Sacrifice, Pharaoh increased the pressure and the work load, almost to a killing pace. This is the lesson we must learn:

When the Christian first hears the Message of the Cross, which should be the very first thing he hears after coming to Christ, but tragically, most of the time isn't, upon embarking upon this course, which is the only course of victory, he will find Satan greatly opposing him. The opposition will be intensified, which is meant to throw such a Believer off course, and actually, to deny the Cross.

Many Christians are confused at this point. Many get it in their minds that the Cross means that there will never be any more opposition from Satan. And when they face that opposition, even intensified, possibly above anything they have heretofore experienced, many are left without understanding. This example of the Children of Israel should be a lesson to us.

Satan wants you to get discouraged and to quit. He wants you to deny the Cross, which means to deny all that Christ has done for you. And to do this, he will usually not lead you to deny Christ, but rather to turn your faith to something else, and if he can get you to do so, he has succeeded. He will be now even tighter in his grip of bondage, with no victory on the horizon, and works of the flesh running havoc in your life.

BUT WHAT IF I FAIL?

I don't mean to be negative, but more than likely, there will be failure of some sort. In such a situation, the Believer is to understand that he is the one who has failed, and not the Cross. What Christ did at the Cross cannot fail. So if there is failure, then it simply means that we have failed.

But why have we failed?

It's always a question of faith. In other words, failure, which speaks of sinning in some way, is always a failure of faith. Our faith is not as strong as we think it is, not as strong as it ought to be, and as well, it is because we are just beginning to learn about the Cross. In fact, the Cross is sectionalized, one might say, into a *"daily"* effort.

Jesus said: *"If any man will come after Me, let him deny himself, and take up his cross daily, and follow Me"* (Lk. 9:23).

"Denying one's self" is not asceticism, as many believe. This particular word refers to a denial of all pleasure, etc. That's not what Jesus is speaking about.

He is meaning that we are to deny ourselves regarding our own strength and ability, totally and completely, placing our trust and faith in Christ and what Christ has done at the Cross. *"Taking up the Cross,"* refers to subscribing to its benefits, understanding that what Jesus did there is the answer to our problems.

When he spoke of this being done on a *"daily"* basis, he was meaning that in essence, we should begin all over again each and every day, resolving that our faith will be placed in the Cross, believing that what Jesus did there is sufficient for all things.

To say it a better way, one should forget about what happened yesterday, and I especially speak of failure, etc. Today is a brand-new day, and I'm going to trust God totally and completely, by denying my own strength and ability, and taking up the Cross, which means that I will trust totally and exclusively in what Christ did there for me. This will be my source of victory; this will be the object of my faith.

Such a Believer will find himself, little by little, growing stronger and stronger, even as he begins to understand the Cross and the great Work accomplished there, more and more. No, the Bible doesn't teach sinless perfection, but it does teach that *"sin shall not have dominion over you"* (Rom. 6:14).

In effect, this means that the sin nature will not dominate you, will not rule over you, will not reign in your life, but instead, you will rule and reign over it, by and through the Lord Jesus Christ, trusting in what He has done for you at the Cross (Gal. 2:20-21).

INTENSIFIED OPPOSITION

Verses 9 through 11 read: *"Let there more work be laid upon the men, that they may labor therein; and let them not regard vain words.*

"And the taskmasters of the people went out, and their officers, and they spoke to the people, saying, Thus says Pharaoh, I will not give you straw.

"Go ye, get you straw where you can find it: yet not ought of your work shall be diminished."

Pharaoh regarded as *"vain words"* the idea of going some three days into the wilderness in order to *"hold a feast unto God,"* and to offer *"Sacrifices."* Such meant nothing to him; therefore, he would ignore the request.

Not only that, he would make the lot of the people much harder than they had previously experienced.

The unbelief of Pharaoh comes out plainly here: where God Himself is unknown, and He definitely was unknown in Egypt, His words are, as well, but idle tales. To talk of the Cross of Christ is meaningless to the man of the world.

The Bible tells man that he is a fallen creature, unprepared to die, unfit for the Presence of a Holy God. The Bible also tells him of the wondrous provision of God's Grace, and presents a Saviour all-sufficient for his acceptance. The Bible warns him faithfully of the solemn issues at stake, and asks him how he shall escape if he neglects so great Salvation. The Bible plainly tells him that he who will not believe shall be damned, and that whosoever's name is not found written in the Book of Life shall be cast into the Lake of Fire.

But these solemn statements are but *"vain words"* to the skeptical heart of the natural man. He refuses to receive them as a message from the Living God addressed to his own soul.

But let him beware. Let him be warned by the awful case of Pharaoh. If he continues in his unbelief and obstinacy, Pharaoh's fate shall be his — God most certainly will bring him into judgment.

Once again we emphasize the severe measures which Pharaoh ordered to be taken upon the Hebrews, illustrate the malignant efforts of Satan against the soul that God's Grace is dealing with. When the Devil recognizes the first advances of the Holy Spirit toward a poor sinner, he at once puts forth every effort to retain his victims. That goes for Christians as well!

Satan never gives up his prey without a fierce struggle. This is why so many convicted souls find that their case gets worse before it is bettered. So it was here with the Hebrews.

Just as hope was awakened, the opposition against them became stronger: just when deliverance seemed nigh, their oppression was increased.

(12) "SO THE PEOPLE WERE SCATTERED ABROAD THROUGHOUT ALL THE LAND OF EGYPT TO GATHER STUBBLE INSTEAD OF STRAW.

(13) "AND THE TASKMASTERS HASTED THEM, SAYING, FULFILL YOUR WORKS, YOUR DAILY TASKS, AS WHEN THERE WAS STRAW.

(14) "AND THE OFFICERS OF THE CHILDREN OF ISRAEL, WHICH PHARAOH'S TASKMASTERS HAD SET OVER THEM, WERE BEATEN, AND DEMANDED, WHEREFORE HAVE YOU NOT FULFILLED YOUR TASK IN MAKING BRICK BOTH YESTERDAY AND TODAY, AS HERETOFORE?

(15) "THEN THE OFFICERS OF THE CHILDREN OF ISRAEL CAME AND CRIED UNTO PHARAOH, SAYING, WHEREFORE DEAL YOU THUS WITH YOUR SERVANTS?

(16) "THERE IS NO STRAW GIVEN UNTO YOUR SERVANTS, AND THEY SAY TO US, MAKE BRICK: AND, BEHOLD, YOUR SERVANTS ARE BEATEN; BUT THE FAULT IS IN YOUR OWN PEOPLE.

(17) "BUT HE SAID, YOU ARE IDLE, YOU ARE IDLE: THEREFORE YOU SAY, LET US GO AND DO SACRIFICE TO THE LORD.

(18) "GO THEREFORE NOW, AND WORK; FOR THERE SHALL NO STRAW BE GIVEN YOU, YET SHALL YOU DELIVER THE TALE OF BRICKS."

The composition is:

1. The first move of Israel toward deliverance plunged her into deeper misery so that the people would have preferred being left quiet in their slavery. This is oftentimes the spiritual experience of awakened sinners.

2. Instead of crying unto the Lord, these leaders of the Israelites turned unto Pharaoh for relief. So often we as modern Believers follow suit. We appeal to man instead of God.

3. The natural man ever prefers to lean upon an arm of flesh than be supported by Him Who is invisible.

THE TASKMASTERS

Verses 12 through 14 read: *"So the people were scattered abroad throughout all the land of Egypt to gather stubble instead of straw.*

"And the taskmasters hasted them, saying, Fulfill your works, your daily tasks, as when there was straw.

"And the officers of the Children of Israel, which Pharaoh's taskmasters had set over them, were beaten, and demanded, Wherefore have you not fulfilled your task in making brick both yesterday and today, as heretofore?"

Satan's plan is to make the hardships of the Children of Israel harder yet, and to do so to such an extent that they will want to drop all ideas of leaving Egypt, if Pharaoh will only lessen the pressure, and allow them to again be as they once were. In other words, Satan wanted them to be willing to remain as slaves in Egypt. He almost succeeded!

Let me say it again: The moment you as the Believer hear the great Message of the Cross, and what it can do in your heart and life, if you truly love the Lord, you will realize that what you are hearing is truth, and your spirit will immediately tell you so. But then Satan begins to come against you in full force, perhaps even stronger than ever before. He doesn't want you to know and have the deliverance which the Cross alone can bring. So he opposes with all the strength of Hell.

Many times, his *"taskmasters,"* will be so-called fellow Believers. They will try to dissuade you, discourage you, try to make you believe something other than the truth, and then they will load you down with guilt because the Government of Law is being abandoned, with the *"Government of Grace"* being accepted.

TOTAL COMMITMENT

When one accepts the Message of the

Cross, one soon begins to find that this involves every aspect of his faith and believing. He will find, much to his dismay, that most of the Church world is operating in another direction. In other words, what is being done is not Scriptural. Consequently, that person might even have to leave his Church because they are not preaching the Cross. As well, family and friends may have to be laid aside, simply because this Message pertains itself to a complete lifestyle. Everything comes under the scrutiny of the Cross, and as a result, many feel that it's too difficult, too hard.

As stated, the *"taskmasters"* will more than likely be that which is of one's own rank. But the truth is, they are *"Egyptians!"*

THE SACRIFICE TO THE LORD

Verses 15 through 18 read: *"Then the officers of the Children of Israel came and cried unto Pharaoh, saying, Wherefore deal you thus with your servants?*

"There is no straw given unto your servants, and they say to us, Make brick: and, behold, your servants are beaten; but the fault is in your own people.

"But he said, You are idle, you are idle: therefore you say, Let us go and do sacrifice to the Lord.

"Go therefore now, and work; for there shall no straw be given you, yet shall you deliver the tale of bricks."

It is the *"Sacrifice"* which rankled Pharaoh, even though he would not have been totally aware as to exactly what it all meant.

The Scripture says, regarding this grave problem, that the officers of the Children of Israel came and cried unto Pharaoh.

Why didn't they go to the Lord? Tragically, God is generally our last resource! Deeply humbling is this! And amazing is the Grace which bears with such waywardness. Grace not only has to begin the work of Salvation, but it also has to continue and complete it. It is all of Grace from first to last, or else we wouldn't be here.

Little good it did for Israel's *"officers"* in appealing to Pharaoh. And little good it will do to appeal to man in any case.

Our dependence, our trust, our faith must always and without exception be in the Lord.

NOTES

We must take everything to the Lord in prayer, realizing that He Alone can bring about what is needed. He has the power to do so, and He is willing and able to do so.

So why is it that we go to Pharaoh, instead of the Lord?

The greatest problem, more than likely, is unbelief. In fact, most modern Christians have very little relationship with the Lord. As such, there is very little faith and confidence in Him. And as well, I firmly believe that the major reason for this is a lack of understanding of the Cross of Christ. Not understanding the Finished Work, one really doesn't understand Christ. As a result, faith is placed elsewhere, and I might quickly add, gets the same results as the Children of Israel did with Pharaoh.

This is not meant to say that we are to eliminate all human contact. That's not the idea. In fact, we have to work with individuals, and at times ask help from individuals; however, everything must be soaked in prayer, knowing that God is able to maneuver the situation to where we will receive the help we need, however it comes.

In Denominations, the truth is, these organizations are at least as political, and perhaps even more political than politics itself. It's the old, *"I'll scratch your back, if you'll scratch mine,"* syndrome. It's people pulling wires, manipulating other people, all to try to get them to do what one wants done.

Once you're out of such, and you look back at the situation, it becomes sickening. It portrays people who claim the Lord, but in reality, have precious little confidence in the Lord, if any at all. They are trusting in themselves or other men, and while they claim trust in the Lord, their actions prove otherwise.

We should learn that it's not Scriptural for us to make plans, and then ask God to bless those plans. If God makes the plans, they are assured of blessing. So, leave Pharaoh alone, and depend exclusively on the Lord for all that is done.

(19) "AND THE OFFICERS OF THE CHILDREN OF ISRAEL DID SEE THAT THEY WERE IN EVIL CASE, AFTER IT WAS SAID, YOU SHALL NOT MINISH OUGHT FROM YOUR BRICKS OF YOUR DAILY TASK.

(20) "AND THEY MET MOSES AND AARON, WHO STOOD IN THE WAY, AS THEY CAME FORTH FROM PHARAOH:

(21) "AND THEY SAID UNTO THEM, THE LORD LOOK UPON YOU, AND JUDGE; BECAUSE YOU HAVE MADE OUR SAVOUR TO BE ABHORRED IN THE EYES OF PHARAOH, AND IN THE EYES OF HIS SERVANTS, TO PUT A SWORD IN THEIR HAND TO SLAY US.

(22) "AND MOSES RETURNED UNTO THE LORD, AND SAID, LORD, WHEREFORE HAVE YOU SO EVIL ENTREATED THIS PEOPLE? WHY IS IT THAT YOU HAVE SENT ME?

(23) "FOR SINCE I CAME TO PHARAOH TO SPEAK IN YOUR NAME, HE HAS DONE EVIL TO THIS PEOPLE; NEITHER HAVE YOU DELIVERED YOUR PEOPLE AT ALL."

The construction is:

1. The second part of the first sentence in Verse 22 should read thus: *"Lord, wherefore have You suffered Your people to be so evil entreated?"*

2. The opposition of Pharaoh, and the unbelief and anger of Israel were a double discouragement for Moses.

3. The first effort of a Christian to do good is often chilled by similar unbelief on the part of the Church, and by opposition on the part of the world.

THE COMPLAINT OF THE PEOPLE

Verses 19 through 21 read: *"And the officers of the Children of Israel did see that they were in evil case, after it was said, You shall not minish ought from your bricks of your daily task.*

"And they met Moses and Aaron, who stood in the way, as they came forth from Pharaoh:

"And they said unto them, The LORD look upon you, and judge; because you have made our savour to be abhorred in the eyes of Pharaoh, and in the eyes of his servants, to put a sword in their hand to slay us."

The people now criticize Moses, and in essence, through Moses, criticize the Lord.

Moses was no doubt prepared for the rebuff which he had himself received from Pharaoh, for the Lord had plainly said that He would harden the king's heart. But, so

NOTES

far as the inspired record informs us, nothing had been told him that he would meet with discouragement and opposition from his own brethren. A real testing was this for God's servant, for it is far more trying to be criticized by our own Brethren, by those whom we are anxious to help, than it is to be persecuted by the world.

But sufficient for the servant to be as his master. The Lord Himself was hated by His Own Brethren according to the flesh, and the very ones to whom He had ministered in ceaseless Grace unanimously cried, *"Crucify Him"* (Pink).

THE LORD

Verses 22 and 23 read: *"And Moses returned unto the LORD, and said, LORD, wherefore have You so evil entreated this people? Why is it that You have sent me?*

"For since I came to Pharaoh to speak in Your Name, He has done evil to this people; neither have You delivered Your people at all."

We may well question how far genuine faith, or a mortified will, dictated the *"wherefore"* and the *"why"* of Moses, in the above quotation? Still, the Lord does not rebuke a remonstrance drawn forth by the intense pressure of the moment. By contrast, the Lord, as we shall see in the next Chapter, graciously replies to Moses.

To Moses' credit, he did take his problem to the Lord, even though his words were not exactly Faith-filled.

We erroneously tend to think that when the Lord is about to do something for us, everything will suddenly smooth out. All the pieces expertly fall into place, and everything seems to function exactly as it ought to function.

It is seldom that way, however! It should be understood that Satan doesn't desire the Lord to do anything for anyone. And whenever a Saint of God begins to believe God for something, the Evil One then seeks to hinder, and to hinder greatly, this which the Lord is about to do. He tries to get the Believer to grow discouraged, to complain, hopefully, to quit.

A PERSONAL EXPERIENCE

Just this morning, one of my associates called me and informed me that one of our

Radio Stations was once again off the air. We have had more trouble with that particular Station, than all the other Stations we have put together. It seems like something breaks down every single week, or even more often.

Even though it's disconcerting, discouraging, and exasperating, I believe that the Lord is mightily going to use that particular Station, which is our largest incidentally, to touch a tremendous number of people for the cause of Christ; consequently, Satan is doing everything he can to hinder and to hurt. But he will not succeed!

"O Christ, what burdens bowed Your head:
"Our load was laid on Thee;
"You stood in the sinner's stead
"To bear all ill for me.
"A victim led, Your Blood was shed!
"Now there's no load for me."

"Death and the curse were in our cup;
"O Christ 'twas full for Thee!
"But You have drained the last dark drop,
"'Tis empty now for me;
"That bitter cup, love drank it up,
"Now blessings draught for me."

"Jehovah lifted up His rod:
"O Christ it fell on Thee!
"You were sore stricken of Thy God;
"There's not one stroke for me."
"Your tears, Your Blood, beneath it flowed;
"Your bruising healed me."

"The tempest's awful voice was heard;
"O Christ it broke on Thee!
"Your open bosom was my ward,
"It braved the storm for me.
"Your form was scarred, Your visage marr'd,
"Now cloudless peace for me."

"Jehovah bade His sword awake:
"O Christ, it woke 'gainst Thee;
"Your Blood the flaming blade must slake,
"Your heart its sheath must be.
"All for my sake, my peace to make:
"Now sleeps that sword for me."

"For me, Lord Jesus, You have died,
"And I have died in Thee:
"You are risen my bands are untied;
"And now You live in me;
"When purified, made white, and tried,
"Your Glory then for me."

CHAPTER 6

(1) "THEN THE LORD SAID UNTO MOSES, NOW SHALL YOU SEE WHAT I WILL DO TO PHARAOH: FOR WITH A STRONG HAND SHALL HE LET THEM GO, AND WITH A STRONG HAND SHALL HE DRIVE THEM OUT OF HIS LAND.

(2) "AND GOD SPOKE UNTO MOSES, AND SAID UNTO HIM, I AM THE LORD:

(3) "AND I APPEARED UNTO ABRAHAM, UNTO ISAAC, AND UNTO JACOB, BY THE NAME OF GOD ALMIGHTY, AND BY MY NAME JEHOVAH WAS I NOT KNOWN TO THEM.

(4) "AND I HAVE ALSO ESTABLISHED MY COVENANT WITH THEM, TO GIVE THEM THE LAND OF CANAAN, THE LAND OF THEIR PILGRIMAGE, WHEREIN THEY WERE STRANGERS.

(5) "AND I HAVE ALSO HEARD THE GROANING OF THE CHILDREN OF ISRAEL, WHOM THE EGYPTIANS KEEP IN BONDAGE; AND I HAVE REMEMBERED MY COVENANT.

(6) "WHEREFORE SAY UNTO THE CHILDREN OF ISRAEL, I AM THE LORD, AND I WILL BRING YOU OUT FROM UNDER THE BURDENS OF THE EGYPTIANS, I WILL RID YOU OUT OF THEIR BONDAGE, AND I WILL REDEEM YOU WITH A STRETCHED OUT ARM, AND WITH GREAT JUDGMENTS:

(7) "AND I WILL TAKE YOU TO ME FOR A PEOPLE, AND I WILL BE TO YOU A GOD: YOU SHALL KNOW THAT I AM THE LORD YOUR GOD, WHICH BRINGS YOU OUT FROM UNDER THE BURDENS OF THE EGYPTIANS.

(8) "AND I WILL BRING YOU IN UNTO THE LAND, CONCERNING THE WHICH I DID SWEAR TO GIVE IT TO ABRAHAM, TO ISAAC, AND TO JACOB; I WILL GIVE IT TO YOU FOR AN HERITAGE: I AM THE LORD."

The overview is:

1. Instead of turning away from so unbelieving and petulant a people, God in His love, pity, and Grace encourages them and Moses by telling them Who He was, What He was, and What He would do.

2. In His Message to them, through Moses, He bids them look at the strength of the Divine hand that would surely deliver them.

3. Five times He declares that He is *"Jehovah"* (Vss. 2-3, 6-8); and seven times He utters the great words *"I will"* (Vss. 6-8); and three times He declares, *"I have"* (Vss. 4-5).

Three speaks of Resurrection, five speaks of Grace, and seven speaks of perfection.

So, the Lord would *"Resurrect"* Israel, do so by *"Grace,"* and give them a *"perfect"* deliverance.

A STRONG HAND

Verse 1 reads: *"Then the LORD said unto Moses, Now shall you see what I will do to Pharaoh: for with a strong hand shall he let them go, and with a strong hand shall he drive them out of his land."*

The *"Strong hand"* is not Pharaoh's, but God's. In essence the Lord is saying, *"By means of My strong hand"* (or *"overpowering might"*) *"laid upon him shall he be induced to let them go,"* etc. (Pulpit).

The words *"drive them out,"* expresses the final anxiety of Pharaoh to be rid of the Israelites, which most surely would come.

The defiant Pharaoh had emphatically stated that he would not let Israel go, but the Most High declares that he will let them go because of the strong hand of God.

This should be a note of great encouragement for every Believer. No matter how much the enemy may roar and rage against us, he is quite unable to thwart the Almighty — *"There is no wisdom, nor understanding, nor counsel against the Lord"* (Prov. 21:30).

Concerning all of this, Pink says: *"There is much for us to learn in this. We defeat ourselves by being occupied with the difficulties of the way. God has made known to us the triumphant outcome of good over evil, and instead of being harassed by the fiery darts which the Evil One now hurls against us, we ought to rest on the assuring Promise that*

NOTES

'The God of peace shall bruise Satan under your feet shortly'" (Rom. 16:20).

JEHOVAH

Verses 2 and 3 read: *"And God spoke unto Moses, and said unto him, I am the LORD:*

"And I appeared unto Abraham, unto Isaac, and unto Jacob, by the name of God Almighty, but by My Name JEHOVAH was I not known to them."

The Lord reminds Moses that He had spoken, and even Personally appeared to Abraham, Isaac, and Jacob, and did so by the Name of *"God Almighty"* (El Shaddai), *"The All-Sufficient One."* So as God reveals Himself to the Patriarchs, He begins immediately by assuring them that whatever He tells them, He is able also to perform.

In dealing with them, He used the Name *"God Almighty"* instead of *"Jehovah,"* which means, *"The Self-Existing"* or *"Eternal One"* Who keeps Covenants and fulfills Promises.

In fact, the Name *"Jehovah"* was used from the very beginning; however, the full meaning of it was not made known unto man, until it was time to fulfill the Promises and Covenants with Israel as a nation.

So the Lord is actually saying the following:

The Lord proved to the Patriarchs Himself as *"El Shaddai,"* or *"All-Sufficient One,"* and did so by His continual provision and protection of them. But now, He would make known the full meaning of *"Jehovah"* to their descendants in the deliverance from Egypt and the settlement in Canaan as promised Abraham and Jacob.

As we should by now know, the Name which God used to reveal Himself to His people was always of utmost significance. In effect, the Name chosen refers to the manner in which God will work with them, and the degree of power which will be evidenced on their behalf. Now they will know the full meaning of the Name *"Jehovah,"* the One Who keeps Covenants and fulfills Promises.

COVENANT

Verses 4 and 5 read: *"And I have also established My Covenant with them, to give them the land of Canaan, the land of their pilgrimage, wherein they were strangers.*

"And I have also heard the groaning of

the Children of Israel, whom the Egyptians keep in bondage; and I have remembered My Covenant."

To calm the fears of Moses, and let us not criticize him, for had we been in the same place, would we have done any better, or even as well? The Lord reminds Moses how He established His Covenant with the Patriarchs. This Covenant consisted of the Promise that the land of Canaan was to be given to them. So, in light of that Covenant, it was impossible for the Egyptians to continue to hold the Children of Israel as slaves. Pharaoh wasn't coming up against mere people, but rather the God of these people, Who in fact was and is the only God in existence. The idea is, if Jehovah had established a Covenant, and He most definitely had, then of necessity, it must be fulfilled, for that Covenant was actually unconditional.

There are many who claim that modern Saints under the Dispensation of Grace are not related to God by Covenant bonds; however, this is erroneous.

In Hebrews 13:20, we read of *"the Blood of the Everlasting Covenant."* Before the foundation of the world was ever laid (I Pet. 1:18-20), the Father entered into a Covenant with His Son, the Lord Jesus Christ (Titus 1:2). That Covenant was sealed by the Blood shed at Calvary's Cross, by our Saviour, Who is the Head of the Church.

Oh yes, we definitely do presently live under a Covenant. It's called the *"New Covenant"* (Heb. 8:6-8, 13; 12:24).

THE NEW COVENANT

The beautiful and wonderful thing about the *"New Covenant,"* is the manner in which it is brought about. It is a Covenant that's absolutely unbreakable, hence, being referred to as *"The Everlasting Covenant"* (Heb. 13:20).

For a Covenant to be in force, there must be at least two parties or more who enter into such a Covenant. Whatever the conditions of the Covenant actually are, it is binding on all parties concerned.

The Old Covenant, given to Moses, was established between God and man, which man consistently broke. The New Covenant is also established between God and man, but it is all in Christ, inasmuch as Christ is both God and man. That's the reason that we say that the Covenant is unbreakable. It is not based upon the weaknesses and the foibles of mere man, but rather on the foundation of *"The Man, Christ Jesus."*

Consequently, Jesus Christ being both God and Man, actually referred to as the *"Last Adam"* and the *"Second Man"* (I Cor. 15:45-50), whatever mere mortals do, the Covenant holds true. As stated, it is all in its entirety based upon Christ.

Men enter into this Covenant by Faith (Eph. 2:8-9). If man so foolishly desires, he can get out of the Covenant by a lack of Faith, which sadly, some have. However, the Covenant is not altered at all by such action and attitude, only the individual involved. The Covenant remains true and unsullied, and actually, unbreakable. Let us say again, it is all in Christ.

The Lord heard the groaning of His people, and He remembered His Covenant, which in fact, He couldn't forget.

ADVERSITY

While God does permit situations and events to come to pass, which on the surface seem to be very negative, and which brings about the *"groanings,"* still, we do know that God *"hears them."* Now why does He permit events which bring about such, considering that we are His children, and He is our God, and He is able to do anything?

The Scripture tells us that He is *"touched with the feeling of our infirmities"* (Heb. 4:15). So why allow the infirmities at all?

God doesn't bother to explain everything to us. He desires that we believe Him for great and mighty things, and if He in fact permits us to be thrown into prison, as was Joseph, or to be hunted like a common criminal, as was David, or to suffer unimaginably so as did Paul, we are to understand that everything He causes or allows is all for our good. It may not seem that way at the beginning, but to be sure, it will definitely play out in that fashion, that is, if we continue to trust Christ.

Even though we are redeemed, which means that we are new creations in Christ Jesus, still, there are many clinging vines of the flesh attached to us. Even the best of us, whomever that might be, are not nearly as holy as we think we are, not nearly as righteous as we think we are! Many times, it takes the *"furnace of affliction"* to burn out the dross in our lives.

A PERSONAL EXPERIENCE

When Frances and I first married, I obtained employment for a few weeks with a plumber. He was an ungodly man, but the Lord ultimately helped me to bring him to Christ. But that's another story.

I watched him as he melted lead in order to pour into the calking joints, in order to put the pipe together. The fire from a gas burner would heat the receptacle, with the lead bars melting. When those bars melted, all the impurities in the bars would rise to the top, be skimmed off, leaving nothing but pure lead.

Every time I saw this done, or even did it myself, it would always teach me a spiritual lesson. Whenever I would look at the bar of lead, it didn't seem to have any impurities. But the *"furnace of the fire"* always brought out the impurities, and to be sure, I never saw a single bar of lead, but that there were impurities, which would be shown up when the lead was melted by the heat.

How so apropos of us presently. Sometimes, it is not observable that of which the Lord knows. Only the *"furnace of affliction"* will show exactly what is there, hence the Lord allowing such.

I'm sure there might be many other reasons as well, but I think that which we have attempted to explain is at least one of those reasons, and perhaps the most important reason.

Pressure is a very necessary thing, if the worth of a thing is to be realized. It has to be put to the test. And pressure is the only thing that will provide the type of test to let one know just how strong the object is.

Pressure brings out either good or bad in an individual. It tells what we are made of. To be sure, the Lord already knows, the point is that we know as well!

THE PROMISE OF GOD

Verses 6 through 8 read: *"Wherefore say unto the Children of Israel, I am the LORD,*

NOTES

and I will bring you out from under the burdens of the Egyptians, and I will rid you out of their bondage, and I will redeem you with a stretched out arm, and with great judgments:

"And I will take you to Me for a people, and I will be to you a God: and you shall know that I am the LORD your God, which brings you out from under the burdens of the Egyptians.

"And I will bring you in unto the land, concerning the which I did swear to give it to Abraham, to Isaac, and to Jacob; I will give it to you for an heritage: I am the LORD."

The following are the things that the Lord said He would do:

1. I am the Lord.
2. I will bring you out from under the burdens of the Egyptians.
3. I will rid you out of their bondage.
4. I will redeem you with a stretched out arm, and with great judgments.
5. I will take you to Me for a people, and I will be to you a God.
6. You shall know that I am the Lord your God, which brings you out from under the burdens of the Egyptians.
7. And I will bring you unto the land concerning the which I did swear to give it to Abraham, to Isaac, and to Jacob.
8. And I will give it to you for an heritage: I am the Lord.

If it is to be noticed, the Promises begin with the statement, *"I am the LORD,"* and ends with the statement, *"I am the LORD."*

All of these great Promises can be broken down into three divisions. They are as follows:

A. The Lord will deliver.
B. You will be My people and I will be your God.
C. I will give you the inheritance.

In effect, this is a compendium of the Salvation process. The Lord delivers the sinner out of the bondage and imprisonment of Satan. This is the first thing that must be done. Satan's hold upon the individual must be broken, and as well, it is only Christ, and what Christ has done at the Cross, which can affect such a deliverance. Man only fools himself, if he thinks it can be done any other way. Humanistic psychology has no answer;

social spectrums have no answer; government has no answer; money has no answer; education has no answer.

The sinner is being held captive by an intelligent force, namely Satan and his demon spirits. Consequently, they do not yield to the Band-Aids of man. They will only yield to a superior force, and the only superior force in the universe is the Lord Jesus Christ.

Paul tells us how that deliverance is effected. He said:

"Blotting out the handwriting of ordinances that was against us, which was contrary to us, and took it out of the way, nailing it to His Cross;

"And having spoiled principalities and powers, He made a show of them openly, triumphing over them in it" (Col. 2:14-15).

Satan's legal hold upon humanity is *"sin."* But when Jesus satisfied the demands of the broken law by what He did on the Cross of Calvary, He in effect removed all sin because He, by His death, atoned for all sin. Paul used the term, which we will explain momentarily, *"nailing to His Cross."*

With all sin taken away, this destroyed Satan's legal right to hold man in captivity. So through what happened at the Cross, all principalities and powers were spoiled, meaning their legal hold was condemned. In fact, they were so defeated that Jesus made a show of them openly in the spirit world, meaning that every single demon knows that Satan, as well as themselves, have been totally defeated. By what Christ did at the Cross, Jesus has triumphed over all their claims, and did so by removing all sin, past, present, and future, at least for all who will believe (Jn. 3:16).

NAILING IT TO HIS CROSS

This statement as used by Paul was more than likely taken from an old Jewish custom called *"possessing the double."* Isaiah mentioned it by saying:

"For your shame you shall have double; and for confusion they shall rejoice in their portion: therefore in their land they shall possess the double: everlasting joy shall be unto them" (Isa. 61:7).

Now what did Isaiah mean by that?

In ancient Israel, when someone was unfortunate enough to fall on hard times, and have to declare bankruptcy, a certain procedure must take place.

The individual in question must take an animal skin, and on that skin, write every debt he owed, and to whom it was owed. It was to be posted at the city gate, where all business was transacted, in effect, where everyone could see what had happened. In other words, the account of the bankruptcy was put on display for all to see. And to be sure, inquisitive eyes and gossiping tongues would be certain to see the account, and spread the news. All of this, of course, would bring shame to the one who had been forced to submit to such indignity.

Every once and a while, whether a relation or even a rank stranger, such a person who was financially able, would go to the particular account nailed to the wall. He would take down the account, double it over, hence the term, *"possessing the double,"* and then write his name on the backside of the skin. It means that all to whom money was owed by this particular individual could come to this man, whomever he might be, and collect their money to the full.

The doubling over of the skin now meant that no one could any more look at the amounts owed and to whom it was owed, for the simple reason that due to it being paid, it no longer existed.

The benefactor would then nail the doubled over skin back to the wall. Whenever anyone came to look and to observe, instead of seeing the indebtedness which occasioned the bankruptcy, they would see this particular man's name, and would know that he now stood good for all the debt.

That is what is called *"possessing the double."* That's what Paul as well was referring to when he spoke of *"nailing it to His Cross."*

Man owed a terrible debt to God, a debt incidentally he could not pay. Morally and spiritually, he was totally bankrupt, and bankrupt for all the spirit world to see.

But when Jesus died on the Cross, shedding His Life's Blood, He in effect paid all the debt, which means the record was cleared and cleansed, and in effect, the ledger on which it was written was doubled over, with Jesus figuratively nailing it to His Cross. In other words, He was saying, if anyone doubts that it's been paid, come and see Me.

Now Satan had no more claim. The Name *"Jesus Christ"* is scrawled in Blood on the doubled over account, meaning that every debt has been satisfied. And the beautiful thing about this is:

It was satisfied not for just one poor, bankrupt soul, but for every human being who walks this Earth, at least for those who will believe (Jn. 3:16).

RELATIONSHIP

But it doesn't stop there. Not only does the Lord totally and completely deliver us from the clutches of Satan to where he has no more hold on us, but as well, the Lord now takes us into the great family of God, makes us His children, and makes Himself our God. It is the same thing as a beggar becoming a joint heir with the richest king who has ever lived. In effect, that's exactly what Paul said:

"For you have not received the spirit of bondage again to fear; but you have received the Spirit of adoption (we have been adopted into the family) *whereby we cry, Abba, Father.*

"The Spirit Himself beareth witness with our spirit, that we are the Children of God.

"And if children, then heirs; heirs of God, and joint-heirs with Christ; if so be that we suffer with Him, that we may be also glorified together" (Rom. 8:15-17).

This rich benefactor called the Lord Jesus Christ, Who has paid our debt, didn't stop there. He, as well, has adopted us, beggars though we be, into His royal family. And now, everything that is His, as well, is ours, in that we are *"joint-heirs with Christ."* What a privilege! What a wonder! What a joy! I who deserved nothing have received everything.

As the song says:
"I traded my sins for Salvation.
"I traded my load for relief.
"What I got was so much more than what He received;
"I sure got the best of the trade."

THE INHERITANCE

Not only does He deliver us; not only does He make us a part of the family; but as well, He brings us into a land that is of such magnitude that it defies all description. He referred to it as *"the land flowing with milk and honey."*

Spiritually speaking, it is truly *"joy unspeakable and full of glory."* Spiritually speaking, *"the half has never yet been told."* This is the *"more abundant life,"* of which Jesus spoke, and promised to provide, and provide He did (Jn. 10:10).

He not only delivers us from something, but as well, He delivers us to something.

Living for God is the greatest life there is, in fact there is nothing that can remotely compare with it, that is if it's lived the right way. And by that, I speak of evidencing constant Faith in Christ, and what Christ has done for us in His Finished Work.

"And I will give it to you for an heritage: I am the Lord."

(9) "AND MOSES SPOKE SO UNTO THE CHILDREN OF ISRAEL: BUT THEY HEARKENED NOT UNTO MOSES FOR ANGUISH OF SPIRIT, AND FOR CRUEL BONDAGE.

(10) "AND THE LORD SPOKE UNTO MOSES SAYING,

(11) "GO IN, SPEAK UNTO PHARAOH KING OF EGYPT, THAT HE LET THE CHILDREN OF ISRAEL GO OUT OF HIS LAND.

(12) "AND MOSES SPOKE BEFORE THE LORD, SAYING, BEHOLD, THE CHILDREN OF ISRAEL HAVE NOT HEARKENED UNTO ME; HOW THEN SHALL PHARAOH HEAR ME, WHO AM OF UNCIRCUMCISED LIPS?

(13) "AND THE LORD SPOKE UNTO MOSES AND UNTO AARON, AND GAVE THEM A CHARGE CONCERNING THE CHILDREN OF ISRAEL, AND UNTO PHARAOH KING OF EGYPT, TO BRING THE CHILDREN OF ISRAEL OUT OF THE LAND OF EGYPT."

The exegesis is:

1. Verse 9 says: *"But they hearkened not."* Such is the unbelief of the natural heart once pressure is applied. Lest we criticize them, how many of us have done any better?

2. Verse 12 portrays a discouraged Moses. There is an answer to this problem.

3. Verse 13 declares that God answered

the complaints of Israel and the discouragement of Moses with *"a charge."* In other words, *"God drew a line."* Egypt would let Israel go, or Egypt would be destroyed. What God says He will do, God will do!

THE UNBELIEF OF THE PEOPLE

Verse 9 reads: *"And Moses spoke so unto the Children of Israel: but they hearkened not unto Moses for anguish of spirit, and for cruel bondage."*

Concerning this moment, Pulpit Commentary says: *"Hope deferred makes the heart sick. The Israelites, who had expected a speedy deliverance, and found themselves the more downtrodden for Moses' interference, were too much dispirited to be cheered even by the gracious promises and assurances which Moses was commissioned to give.*

"They had no longer any trust in one who they thought had deceived them. He was a dreamer, a visionary, if not worse. They did not intend hearkening to him any more. 'Anguish of spirit' possessed their souls, and 'cruel bondage' claimed their bodies, day after day. They had not even the time, had they had the will, to hearken."

The Samaritan version of this account says: *"And they said to Moses, Let us alone, and let us serve the Egyptians; for it is better for us to serve the Egyptians than die in a wilderness."*

THE BATTLE IN THE SPIRIT WORLD

Let's once again go back to the Cross. The Believer, for the first time in his life, hears this great Message, realizes in his spirit that what he is hearing is definitely Scriptural, of God, and in fact, the Way of the Lord. It cheers him to no end, even as it should.

In a moment's time, he transfers his faith from whatever else in which it had been, and anchors it firmly in the Finished Work of Christ. Joy fills his heart and soul, with every fiber of his being and soul telling him that this is the right way.

However, Satan, he now finds, doesn't give up that easily. A battle begins to ensue in the spirit world. If Satan cannot get the person to reject God altogether, he'll try to get the Christian to reject God's Way altogether, knowing that such a Christian is then doomed to continuous failure.

NOTES

Meeting with opposition, and not quite understanding why the opposition is there, many simply quit. They will state, *"I tried it and it didn't work,"* or *"Quite possibly this is good for others, but not for me,"* etc.

No, as we said some pages back, you may have failed, but the Cross for sure did not fail.

The struggle that such a Christian now undergoes is the same struggle, in a sense, which the Children of Israel faced in Egypt. Instead of their situation getting better, for a short while it would get even worse. And I think I can say without any fear of contradiction, that is the way it always is.

Satan does everything he can to discourage the Believer, to apply added pressure, to bring added hardships upon the individual, and it's at that time that our Faith is tried by the most severe test.

I am standing here today in the place of Moses, and so is any other Preacher who preaches the Cross, in effect, telling you to hold on, victory is coming, and a victory of such unimagined proportions that it defies all description. But at the moment, it is an *"anguish of spirit,"* and even *"cruel bondage."*

By the latter, I'm referring to the fact, exactly as the Israelites did, that this bondage which the Cross is supposed to break, is not only not broken, it seems to be worse than ever.

True! But the process has only begun. If you will keep believing, keep your Faith in Christ and what Christ did for you at the Cross, not allowing it to be moved elsewhere, to be sure, that *"cruel bondage"* most definitely will be broken, and the *"anguish of spirit"* will be replaced, by a joy of spirit, even joy unspeakable and full of glory.

PHARAOH

Verses 10 and 11 read: *"And the LORD spoke unto Moses saying,*

"Go in, speak unto Pharaoh king of Egypt, that he let the Children of Israel go out of his land."

So what does the Lord tell Moses to do?

Moses is to continue to demand of Pharaoh that he let Israel go. And that's the same thing that you must do as a Believer.

Because the demon forces of darkness did not yield at the beginning, doesn't mean they aren't going to yield. You are to stand your ground, keep believing that what Jesus did at the Cross is sufficient, which it most definitely is, and keep commanding the Evil One to go.

Exactly as we observe this contest between Moses and Pharaoh, exactly is the conflict which we presently are facing. Jesus Christ is our Heavenly Moses. Pharaoh is a type of Satan, and to be sure, he has no choice but to obey what Moses demands, even though he will not give up without a fight.

We must always understand that whatever Christ has done at the Cross, the great victory He won there, to that victory Satan most definitely will yield. But I'm afraid, just as Moses had problems with the Children of Israel, as well, Christ has problems with us.

UNCIRCUMCISED LIPS

Verse 12 reads: *"And Moses spoke before the LORD, saying, Behold, the Children of Israel have not hearkened unto me; how then shall Pharaoh hear me, who am of uncircumcised lips?"*

Exactly why Moses referred to himself as a man of *"uncircumcised lips,"* we have no clue.

More than likely, he is referring to his impediment of speech, which is the same complaint he laid before the Lord when first called to this task (Ex. 4:10).

The Lord had told Moses to go in once again to Pharaoh and to demand the release of the Children of Israel.

The implication seems to be that the Lord was telling him personally to do this thing, instead of allowing Aaron to be his mouthpiece. If in fact that is the case, Moses complains about his impediment, and that possibly he will be a laughingstock before the Monarch.

Concerning this, Matthew Henry says: *"Though our infirmities ought to humble us, yet they ought not to discourage us from doing our very best in any service we have to do for God. His strength is made perfect in our weakness."*

If it is to be noticed, the next Verse tells us that God completely ignored the complaint of Moses.

A CHARGE

Verse 13 reads: *"And the LORD spoke unto Moses and unto Aaron, and gave them a charge unto the Children of Israel, and unto Pharaoh king of Egypt, to bring the Children of Israel out of the land of Egypt."*

As stated, the Lord ignored the complaint of Moses, rather giving a *"charge"* to both Moses and Aaron. The *"charge"* would involve both Pharaoh and the Children of Israel.

They were to tell the Children of Israel that for sure they were going to be delivered, and they were to tell Pharaoh that for certain he was going to allow them to be delivered. Perhaps we can say it better another way.

Irrespective as to how rebellious or doubting the Children of Israel became, they were going to quit Egypt. As well, irrespective as to how much Pharaoh fought against this deliverance, he was going to fail, and as of that, there was no doubt.

THE PRESENT CHARGE

The *"charge"* addressed here as it regards Moses, Aaron, Pharaoh, and the Children of Israel, is still just as appropriate now as it was then, and even more so.

The Lord has charged every true Preacher of the Gospel to proclaim the Scriptural fact that every single Believer who in fact will believe, who will trust the Lord, is going to be delivered from every single, solitary problem or power that may seek to hold them in check. I want every Reader who looks at these words to understand that this promise is to him. It doesn't matter how bad the situation may now look; it doesn't matter how difficult that things may seem to be; it doesn't matter how many failures you have had; as a Minister of the Gospel, I am charged by the Lord to tell you that if you will put your eyes on Christ and the Cross, not allow your eyes and your Faith to be diverted elsewhere, victory most certain is yours. And when I say *"victory,"* I'm speaking of victory in every single capacity. The Lord has told us to *"preach deliverance to the captives,"* and if He had not intended to deliver them, He would not have told us to preach an empty message (Lk. 4:18). That is the *"charge"* that I have, and as Paul said, *"I must not be disobedient to the Heavenly Vision"* (Acts 26:19).

The Lord has told me to tell you, *"Sin shall not have dominion over you"* (Rom. 6:14).

He has told me to *"preach Jesus Christ and Him Crucified"* (I Cor. 1:23). He has told me to say unto you: *"If I boast, I will boast in the Cross of our Lord Jesus Christ, to Whom I died unto the world, and the world unto me"* (Gal. 6:14). That's why I *"determined to know nothing among you save Christ and Him Crucified"* (I Cor. 2:2).

God has given me this *"charge"* to *"preach the Cross,"* and by His help and Grace, that's exactly what I have done, what I am presently doing, and what I plan to do.

THE CHARGE TO PHARAOH

The charge I've just mentioned pertains to what Moses was to tell the Children of Israel. They were going out, and of that there was no doubt. But a part of that charge was to be directed toward Pharaoh, who is a type of Satan.

He was to be told by Moses and Aaron that irrespective as to what he did, no matter how obstinate he proved to be, no matter how much power he exerted, the Children of Israel were going out. They would not remain in Egypt. That was the *"charge"* that God told Moses to address to that Monarch.

We're speaking here of drawing a line in the sand, of throwing down the gauntlet, so to speak. In other words, it's high noon in Dodge City.

Let the Believer understand as well that whenever we say *"yes"* to the Promises of God, at the same time, we are saying *"no"* to Satan.

There is a difference now in the powers of darkness than during the time of Moses. At the time of the great Lawgiver, the Cross was yet to be, which means that Satan, at that time, still had the power of death (Heb. 2:14).

But when Jesus went to the Cross, He *"through death, destroyed him who had the power of death, that is, the Devil"* (Heb. 2:14).

Old Testament Saints looked forward to a victory that was to be won in the future, while we today look backward to a victory that has already been won, and will never have to be fought again. So what am I saying?

I'm saying that the charge we give to Satan to let God's people go carries much more weight than the charges given in Old Testament times. Our *"charge"* is based upon a Finished Work. In other words, it's not something to be accomplished, but something rather already accomplished.

THE MANNER OF THE CHARGE

However, the charge given to Satan by most, and I speak of the present time, is not based on the victory won by Christ at the Cross, but other things entirely. To such a charge, Satan will not yield. He yields alone to Christ, and what Christ has done for us at the Cross. If we appeal to him on any other basis, we are in effect appealing to him, whether we realize it or not, on the basis of *"self."* Such faith God will not stand behind or guarantee. He guarantees alone the Faith of the Believer, which is anchored in Christ and Christ Crucified. That's why Paul said:

"For the preaching of the Cross is to them who perish foolishness; but unto us which are saved it is the Power of God" (I Cor. 1:18).

The death of Christ on the Cross was meant to save our souls, and at the same time, give us victory in every capacity as it regards our everyday lives and living. It is all in the Cross and is in nothing else but the Cross. And that's where the Believer must anchor his faith, that is, if he wants the help of the Holy Spirit (Rom. 8:1-2, 11).

(14) "THESE BE THE HEADS OF THEIR FATHER'S HOUSES: THE SONS OF REUBEN THE FIRSTBORN OF ISRAEL; HANOCH, AND PALLU, HEZRON, AND CARMI: THESE BE THE FAMILIES OF REUBEN.

(15) "AND THE SONS OF SIMEON; JEMUEL, AND JAMIN, AND OHAD, AND JACHIN, AND ZOHAR, AND SHAUL THE SON OF A CANAANITISH WOMAN: THESE ARE THE FAMILIES OF SIMEON.

(16) "AND THESE ARE THE NAMES OF THE SONS OF LEVI ACCORDING TO THEIR GENERATIONS; GERSHON, AND KOHATH, AND MERARI: AND THE YEARS OF THE LIFE OF LEVI WERE AN HUNDRED THIRTY AND SEVEN YEARS.

(17) "THE SONS OF GERSHON; LIBNI, AND SHIMI, ACCORDING TO THEIR FAMILIES.

(18) "AND THE SONS OF KOHATH; AMRAM, AND IZHAR, AND HEBRON, AND UZZIEL: AND THE YEARS OF THE LIFE

OF KOHATH WERE AN HUNDRED THIRTY AND THREE YEARS.

(19) "AND THE SONS OF MERARI; MAHALI AND MUSHI: THESE ARE THE FAMILIES OF LEVI ACCORDING TO THEIR GENERATIONS.

(20) "AND AMRAM TOOK HIM JOCHEBED HIS FATHER'S SISTER TO WIFE; AND SHE BEAR HIM AARON AND MOSES: AND THE YEARS OF THE LIFE OF AMRAM WERE AN HUNDRED AND THIRTY AND SEVEN YEARS.

(21) "AND THE SONS OF IZHAR; KORAH, AND NEPHEG, AND ZICHRI.

(22) "AND THE SONS OF UZZIEL; MISHAEL, AND ELZAPHAN, AND ZITHRI.

(23) "AND AARON TOOK HIM ELISHEBA, DAUGHTER OF AMMINADAB, SISTER OF NAASHON, TO WIFE; AND SHE BEAR HIM NADAB, AND ABIHU, ELEAZAR, AND ITHAMAR.

(24) "AND THE SONS OF KORAH; ASSIR, AND ELKANAH, AND ABIASAPH: THESE ARE THE FAMILIES OF THE KORHITES.

(25) "AND ELEAZAR AARON'S SON TOOK HIM ONE OF THE DAUGHTERS OF PUTIEL TO WIFE; AND SHE BEAR HIM PHINEHAS: THESE ARE THE HEADS OF THE FATHERS OF THE LEVITES ACCORDING TO THEIR FAMILIES.

(26) "THESE ARE THAT AARON AND MOSES, TO WHOM THE LORD SAID, BRING OUT THE CHILDREN OF ISRAEL FROM THE LAND OF EGYPT ACCORDING TO THEIR ARMIES.

(27) "THESE ARE THEY WHICH SPAKE TO PHARAOH KING OF EGYPT, TO BRING OUT THE CHILDREN OF ISRAEL FROM EGYPT: THESE ARE THAT MOSES AND AARON.

(28) "AND IT CAME TO PASS ON THE DAY WHEN THE LORD SPOKE UNTO MOSES IN THE LAND OF EGYPT,

(29) "THAT THE LORD SPOKE UNTO MOSES, SAYING, I AM THE LORD: SPEAK THOU UNTO PHARAOH KING OF EGYPT ALL THAT I SAY UNTO YOU.

(30) "AND MOSES SAID BEFORE THE LORD, BEHOLD, I AM OF UNCIRCUMCISED LIPS, AND HOW SHALL PHARAOH HEARKEN UNTO ME?"

The synopsis is:

NOTES

1. The Grace that gave the Promises of the First Chapter records the names of those whom Pharaoh declared to be his slaves.

2. God numbers those who belong to Himself, and He calls them *"My people"* though they still were in the power of the enemy.

3. To make this Grace more amazing, the three Tribes of Reuben, Simeon, and Levi are chosen as representing the whole nation.

THE GRACE OF GOD

Due to the nature of these 17 Verses, which concludes the Sixth Chapter of Exodus, we will dispense with our usual procedure.

It is the genealogy of both Moses and Aaron that is given here, even though Reuben and Simeon are mentioned. Both Moses and Aaron, being Levites, would come under the genealogy of Levi. We will deal with that in a moment.

But why is it that the Tribes of Reuben and Simeon are mentioned as well? Why not all the other Tribes such as *"Gad," "Issachar,"* or *"Judah,"* etc.?

Reuben is given because he was the firstborn of Jacob.

Simeon was given because he was included in the curse that was leveled at both he and Levi (Gen. 49:5-7). But in a sense, the curse for both Tribes was turned into a Blessing. Simeon was allowed to be a part of the inheritance of Judah, which was the Kingly Tribe, which ultimately produced the Messiah; consequently, nothing could be more grand and glorious than that, in which Simeon had the privilege to participate.

Levi became the Priestly Tribe, even though included in the curse. As such, it turned into a great blessing. And this is the Tribe which produced both Moses and Aaron, for they were both Levites. To these two, God would give the charge, and to these two would come the victory, despite the fact that Moses was a man of *"uncircumcised lips."*

"Have you read the story of the Cross,
"Where Jesus bled and died;
"Where your debt was paid by the Precious Blood,
"That gushed from His wounded side?"

"Have you read how they placed the crown of thorns

"Upon His lowly brow,
"When He prayed, Forgive them, Oh! Forgive;
"They know not what they do?"

"Have you read that He saved the dying thief,
"When hanging on the tree,
"Who looked with pleading eyes and said,
"Dear Lord, remember me?"

"Have you read that He looked to Heaven and said,
"'Tis finished, 'twas for thee?
"Have you ever said, I thank You Lord,
"For giving Your life for me?"

CHAPTER 7

(1) "AND THE LORD SAID UNTO MOSES, SEE, I HAVE MADE YOU A GOD TO PHARAOH: AND AARON YOUR BROTHER SHALL BE YOUR PROPHET.

(2) "YOU SHALL SPEAK ALL THAT I COMMAND YOU: AND AARON YOUR BROTHER SHALL SPEAK UNTO PHARAOH, THAT HE SEND THE CHILDREN OF ISRAEL OUT OF HIS LAND.

(3) "AND I WILL HARDEN PHARAOH'S HEART, AND MULTIPLY MY SIGNS AND MY WONDERS IN THE LAND OF EGYPT.

(4) "BUT PHARAOH SHALL NOT HEARKEN UNTO YOU, THAT I MAY LAY MY HAND UPON EGYPT, AND BRING FORTH MY ARMIES, AND MY PEOPLE THE CHILDREN OF ISRAEL, OUT OF THE LAND OF EGYPT BY GREAT JUDGMENTS.

(5) "AND THE EGYPTIANS SHALL KNOW THAT I AM THE LORD, WHEN I STRETCH FORTH MY HAND UPON EGYPT, AND BRING OUT THE CHILDREN OF ISRAEL FROM AMONG THEM.

(6) "AND MOSES AND AARON DID AS THE LORD COMMANDED THEM, SO DID THEY."

The diagram is:

1. Moses having declared that he was of *"uncircumcised lips,"* that is, that he was wanting in eloquence, Grace once more pities his fears, and Aaron is appointed to be his prophet, i.e., *"his spokesman."*

2. Verses 1 through 5 speak of *"great judgments"* that would come upon Egypt. God's Will is not always carried out, but God's Plan, to the contrary, is always carried out. Nations that defy Him are *"judged."* Egypt, at this time, was the mightiest nation on the face of the Earth. In about six weeks time it will be totally destroyed.

3. The process of deliverance, God assures Moses, is just about to begin.

SUPERIORITY

Verse 1 reads: *"And the LORD said unto Moses, See, I have made you a god to Pharaoh: and Aaron your brother shall be your Prophet."*

The first six Chapters of this great Book of Exodus concern themselves more so with the *"Person of the Deliverer,"* with the next six Chapters taking into account the *"Work of Redemption."*

The Sixth Chapter closes with Moses deeply dejected, and bemoaning the seeming hopelessness of his task. Concerning this, Pink says: *"Thus the 'weakness' of the instrument was fully manifested that it might the better be seen that the 'power' was in Jehovah Alone, and of Jehovah acting not so much in response to Faith, as in Covenant faithfulness and in sovereign Grace."*

However, this First Verse of the Seventh Chapter portrays the fact that the Lord will place a particular aura about Moses. He is no more, as we shall find, timid, hesitant, and discouraged. The omnipotence of the Lord is displayed in every scene. This means that the conflict from here forward is not in the form of mere words, but rather of mighty deeds. The gauntlet has been thrown down, and now it is open war between the Almighty and the Egyptians.

What is taking place before us here is far more than a mere episode of ancient history, but rather a conflict played out on the world stage; and incidentally, it is a conflict that continues to be played out in exactly the same manner.

Even as we see here, which is given to us in microcosm, the forces of evil may seem for a while to win. But ultimately, Righteousness will prevail. God chooses His men, anoints them with power from on high, and great victories are then won.

As someone has well said, had it not been for the preaching of John Wesley, England could very well have faced the same type of revolution as did France. The same could be said for the United States, but in a different way.

It was the preaching of great men of God back in the 1600's and the 1700's, which helped shape this nation, until it embraces the greatest freedoms and privileges the world has every known.

The Moses whom Pharaoh will face now is not the same man he faced some days earlier. As stated, the words will change to action.

THE COMMAND

Verse 2 reads: *"You shall speak all that I command you: and Aaron your brother shall speak unto Pharaoh, that he send the Children of Israel out of his land."*

The idea was, God was to speak to Moses, and Moses was to speak to Aaron, and Aaron was to speak to Pharaoh. This, in effect, was what the Lord meant by Aaron being the Prophet of Moses.

In essence, we find here a definition of the office of the Prophet. God's Prophet then is God's spokesman: he acts as God's mouthpiece, the Lord putting into his lips the very words he would utter. While Moses would be a *"god to Pharaoh,"* Aaron would act as his (Moses') Prophet.

All of this meant that Moses was not free to make a selection from Jehovah's words, and, thereby, communicate these to Aaron, those which he deemed most advisable to say unto Pharaoh, but he was to speak *"all"* that had been commanded him.

To be frank, a similar charge is laid upon God's servants presently: we are to *"preach the Word"* (II Tim. 4:2) and to *"hold fast the form of sound words"* (II Tim. 1:13), and are warned that *"If any man teach otherwise, and consent not to wholesome words, even the words of our Lord Jesus Christ, and to the Doctrine which is according to Godliness; he is a fool, knowing nothing"* (I Tim. 6:3-4). But we find how few there actually are who faithfully shun not to declare *"the whole counsel of God."*

A COMMAND FROM THE LORD

Beginning approximately at the turn of the new Millennium, the Lord has begun to lay it on the hearts of the Preachers in this particular Ministry to take an open, vocal stand against false doctrine. I speak of the Satanic music that goes under the heading of *"Christian Contemporary,"* whatever that means, I also speak of humanistic psychology, and most of all, against the so-called Word of Faith doctrine. To be frank, these three particular directions cover almost the entirety of the Pentecostal and Charismatic Church worlds.

Whenever the Lord says to do something of this nature, it is seldom met with approval by hardly anyone. Even those who know what you're preaching is right will seldom stand with you, but will rather fade into the shadows. In other words, they don't want to take the criticism and persecution that goes along with such a stand. Concerning these things, Paul had much to say. His words were:

"For many walk, of whom I have told you often, and now tell you even weeping, that they are the enemies of the Cross of Christ:

"Whose end is destruction, whose god is their belly, and whose glory is in their shame, who mind earthly things" (Phil. 3:18-19).

"But God forbid that I should glory, save in the Cross of our Lord Jesus Christ, by Whom the world is crucified unto me, and I unto the world" (Gal. 6:14).

"But we preach Christ crucified" (I Cor. 1:23).

"For I determined not to know anything among you, save Jesus Christ, and Him Crucified" (I Cor. 2:2).

That, plus many other Passages we could quote, lays to rest the Word of Faith doctrine, which repudiates the Cross.

Regarding humanistic psychology, Paul also said: *"For the preaching of the Cross is to them who perish foolishness; but unto us which are saved it is the Power of God"* (I Cor. 1:18).

He then said: *"That your faith should not stand in the wisdom of men, but in the Power of God"* (I Cor. 2:5).

Peter said: *"According as His Divine Power has given unto us all things that pertain unto life and Godliness, through the knowledge of Him Who has called us to glory and virtue:*

"Whereby are given unto us exceeding great and precious promises: that by these

you might be partakers of the Divine Nature, having escaped the corruption that is in the world through lust" (II Pet. 1:3-4).

When it comes to so-called Contemporary Christian music, Paul said:

"Now the Spirit (Holy Spirit) *speaks expressly, that in the latter times* (the times in which we now live) *some shall depart from the Faith* (Christ and Him Crucified), *giving heed to seducing spirits, and doctrines of Devils"* (I Tim. 4:1).

"Be not unequally yoked together with unbelievers: for what fellowship has Righteousness with unrighteousness? And what communion has light with darkness?

"Wherefore come out from among them, and be ye separate, saith the Lord, and touch not the unclean thing; and I will receive you" (II Cor. 6:14, 17).

John said: *"Love not the world, neither the things that are in the world. If any man love the world, the love of the Father is not in him.*

"For all that is in the world, the lust of the flesh, and the lust of the eyes, and the pride of life, is not of the Father, but is of the world" (I Jn. 2:15-16).

When the Children of Israel came out of Egypt, to be sure, they didn't bring the music of Egypt with them, but rather, the Lord gave His people music that would glorify His Name. The Psalms constitute the very first music, as far as we know, which God gave to man. Actually, Moses wrote the first Psalm, and perhaps two Psalms. For sure he wrote Psalm 90, and more than likely, Psalm 91 as well.

At any rate, considering that the Church has, for the most part, bought into all three of these false directions, to come against these doctrines of devils, and that's exactly what they are, does not exactly win friends. However, the true Preacher of the Gospel has only one thing in mind, and that is to hear from Heaven, and then to faithfully deliver what he has heard — irrespective as to what the Message might be.

THE HARDENED HEART

Verse 3 reads: *"And I will harden Pharaoh's heart, and multiply My signs and My wonders in the land of Egypt."*

NOTES

Some argue that God hardened the heart of Pharaoh, which, therefore, makes Him the author of Pharaoh's sins; and as such, God was unrighteous in punishing him for them.

The truth is, God brought about the means by which Pharaoh hardened his own heart. It is the same as the sun melting wax but hardening clay. The sun is the same for both ingredients, but yet one melts while the other hardens. So the fault in not in the sun, but rather in the ingredients upon which it shines.

It is the same with men the world over. The Spirit of God moves, and some melt under that moving, thereby accepting Christ, while others harden, and reject Christ, even though the Moving and Operation of the Holy Spirit has been the same on both. So, the Scripture can then say that the Holy Spirit melted one, and at the same time, hardened the other.

We do not find in Scripture where God ever tampers with a person's free moral agency. The Scripture plainly says, *"Whosoever will"* (Jn. 3:16; Rev. 22:17).

To properly understand the Scriptures, we must join together all the Scriptures as it regards a particular subject, and if we do so, which means that we quit pulling Scriptures out of context, we will find that they all agree. In other words, Scripture interprets Scripture, and is meant to do so.

As it regards Pharaoh, the haughty Monarch, which attitude and spirit shows in all that he does, had set himself to resist the sovereign will and course of the Most High God; and, as a just consequence, he was given over to judicial blindness and hardness of heart.

In contemplating Pharaoh and his actions, the mind is carried forward to the stirring scenes of the Book of Revelation, in which we find the last proud oppressor of the people of God bringing down upon his kingdom and upon himself the seven vials of the Wrath of the Almighty.

It is God's purpose that Israel shall be preeminent in the Earth; and, therefore, everyone who presumes to stand in the way of that preeminence must be set aside. Divine Grace must find its object; and everyone who would act as a barrier in the way of that Grace must be taken out of the way, whether it be Egypt, Babylon, or *"the beast that was, is not, and yet is"*; it matters not. Divine power will clear the channel for Divine Grace to flow, and eternal woe be to all who stand in the way. They shall taste, throughout the everlasting course of ages, the bitter fruit of having exalted themselves against *"the Lord God of the Hebrews"* (Mackintosh).

EGYPT

Verses 4 through 6 read: *"But Pharaoh shall not hearken unto you, that I may lay My hand upon Egypt, and bring forth My armies, and My people the Children of Israel, out of the land of Egypt by great judgments.*

"And the Egyptians shall know that I am the LORD, when I stretch forth My hand upon Egypt, and bring out the Children of Israel from among them.

"And Moses and Aaron did as the LORD commanded them, so did they."

The idea is, Pharaoh would not yield, would not give in, would not heed the voice of God as given him through Moses and Aaron, so the Lord turns the tables on him, using his obstinacy to further the Work of God.

He will allow Egypt to do her worst, to put forth her best, to use all the power that she possessed to keep the Children of Israel as slaves, but despite this power, the Lord would prevail. Not only would He prevail, but the word would be heard all over the world of that day, as to the prevailing situation, that Moses, by the Hand of God, had been able to effect the release of nearly three million subjects of Egypt, and there was nothing the might and power of Egypt could do about it.

(7) "AND MOSES WAS FOURSCORE YEARS OLD, AND AARON FOURSCORE AND THREE YEARS OLD, WHEN THEY SPOKE UNTO PHARAOH.

(8) "AND THE LORD SPOKE UNTO MOSES AND UNTO AARON, SAYING,

(9) "WHEN PHARAOH SHALL SPEAK UNTO YOU, SAYING, SHOW A MIRACLE FOR YOU: THEN SHALL YOU SAY UNTO AARON, TAKE YOUR ROD, AND CAST IT BEFORE PHARAOH, AND IT SHALL BECOME A SERPENT.

NOTES

(10) "AND MOSES AND AARON WENT IN UNTO PHARAOH, AND THEY DID SO AS THE LORD HAD COMMANDED: AND AARON CAST DOWN HIS ROD BEFORE PHARAOH, AND BEFORE HIS SERVANTS, AND IT BECAME A SERPENT.

(11) "THEN PHARAOH ALSO CALLED THE WISE MEN AND THE SORCERERS: NOW THE MAGICIANS OF EGYPT, THEY ALSO DID IN LIKE MANNER WITH THEIR ENCHANTMENTS.

(12) "FOR THEY CAST DOWN EVERY MAN HIS ROD, AND THEY BECAME SERPENTS: BUT AARON'S ROD SWALLOWED UP THEIR RODS.

(13) "AND HE HARDENED PHARAOH'S HEART, THAT HE HEARKENED NOT UNTO THEM; AS THE LORD HAD SAID."

The structure is:

1. Verses 8 and 9 portray the beginning of miracles, at least as it regards Egypt. Each miracle was designed by God to embarrass and show the utter helplessness of Egypt's gods against the God of Israel.

2. The magicians, Jannes and Jambres (II Tim. 3:8), by the power of Satan, seek to imitate the Power of God; imitation is the best that Satan can do.

3. It is Satan's desire, in all ages, and on all possible occasions, to set up counterfeits of things Divine, in order to confuse men's minds, and make them mistake the false for the true.

THE MIRACLE

Verses 7 through 10 read: *"And Moses was fourscore years old, and Aaron fourscore and three years old, when they spoke unto Pharaoh.*

"And the LORD spoke unto Moses and unto Aaron, saying,

"When Pharaoh shall speak unto you, saying, Show a miracle for you: then you shall say unto Aaron, Take your rod, and cast it before Pharaoh, and it shall become a serpent.

"And Moses and Aaron went in unto Pharaoh, and they did so as the LORD had commanded, and Aaron cast down his rod before Pharaoh, and before his servants, and it became a serpent."

Now begins the miracles, but yet this first miracle is not counted among the ten which would affect Egypt. The first miracle that would affect Egypt, which would be the first of the ten, would be the turning of all water to blood, including the mighty Nile River.

This haughty Monarch had set himself to resist the sovereign will and course of the Most High God; and, as a just consequence, he was given over to a judicial blindness and hardness of heart.

Moses and Aaron now stand before Pharaoh, the mightiest Monarch on the face of the Earth. Moses was 80 years old, and his brother Aaron was 83.

They professed to come in the Name of the Lord, the Lord of Glory incidentally, of Whom Pharaoh didn't recognize. In fact, Egypt worshipped many gods, with Pharaoh himself thought of as a *"god."* So at a point in time, the Lord knew that Pharaoh would demand some *"sign"* from this God the Hebrews professed to worship. When the sign was commanded, which it ultimately was, the Lord had told Moses what to do. He was to tell Aaron to throw his rod down before Pharaoh, and it would become a serpent.

As to why the Lord wanted this, perhaps the following will be of some small help:

1. The serpent is a type of Satan. Even though Pharaoh would not have agreed to such, the Lord was saying by this rod turning to a serpent that the kingdom of Egypt was Satanic.

2. By Moses' rod, which had turned into a snake, consuming the others, this portrayed the fact to Pharaoh that Jehovah was stronger than all the gods of Egypt. It also portrayed the fact that Calvary would ultimately defect sin and Satan.

3. In fact, the serpent represented one of the gods of Egypt, and in the process which followed, Pharaoh was made to know and understand that this *"god"* would not help him.

THE MAGICIANS

Verses 11 through 13 read: *"Then Pharaoh also called the wise men and the sorcerers: now the magicians of Egypt, they also did in like manner with their enchantments.*

"For they cast down every man his rod, and they became serpents: but Aaron's rod swallowed up their rods.

"And he hardened Pharaoh's heart, that he hearkened not unto them; as the LORD had said."

When the rod of Aaron became a serpent after being thrown down on the floor, Pharaoh called together his wise men, sorcerers, and magicians. The words *"they also did in like manner with their enchantments"* proclaim the fact that these magicians did actually bring about this miracle, in which Satan himself helped them.

In fact, Pharaoh acts throughout as the representative of Satan, and the fact that he was able to summon magicians who could work such miracles only serves to illustrate and exemplify the mighty powers which the Devil has at his disposal. It is both foolish and mischievous to underestimate the strength of our great enemy.

The one who was permitted to transport our Saviour from the wilderness to the temple at Jerusalem, and the one who was able to show Him *"all the kingdoms of the world in a moment of time"* (Lk. 4:5), would have no difficulty in empowering his emissaries to transform their rods into serpents.

Make no mistake about it, Satan has power. But yet, the Power of God, of course, is far greater than the power of Satan. But here is one thing we must know and understand:

The only power in this world that is greater than the powers of darkness is the Power of God. That's the reason there is no remedy against sin, no remedy against the world of spiritual darkness, except that of Jesus Christ and what He did for us at the Cross.

In fact, Satan's power over the human race came about through the Fall of man in the Garden of Eden. That power was defeated only by what Jesus did at the Cross. Of course, God's power has always been far greater than Satan. Satan is a created being, while God is the Creator. God is Almighty, while Satan cannot even remotely approach such degree of power. Nevertheless, he still has great power. But the Cross removed his power, because there Jesus atoned for all sin, and sin, being the legal means by which Satan can hold man captive, has now been taken away (Col. 2:14-15).

(14) "AND THE LORD SAID UNTO MOSES, PHARAOH'S HEART IS HARDENED, HE REFUSES TO LET THE PEOPLE GO.

(15) "GET THEE UNTO PHARAOH IN THE MORNING: LO, HE GOES OUT UNTO THE WATER; AND YOU SHALL STAND BY THE RIVER'S BRINK AGAINST HE COME; AND THE ROD WHICH WAS TURNED TO A SERPENT SHALL YOU TAKE IN YOUR HAND.

(16) "AND YOU SHALL SAY UNTO HIM, THE LORD GOD OF THE HEBREWS HAS SENT ME UNTO YOU, SAYING, LET MY PEOPLE GO, THAT THEY MAY SERVE ME IN THE WILDERNESS: AND, BEHOLD, HITHERTO YOU WOULD NOT HEAR.

(17) "THUS SAITH THE LORD, IN THIS YOU SHALL KNOW THAT I AM THE LORD: BEHOLD, I WILL SMITE WITH THE ROD THAT IS IN MY HAND UPON THE WATERS WHICH ARE IN THE RIVER, AND THEY SHALL BE TURNED TO BLOOD.

(18) "AND THE FISH THAT IS IN THE RIVER SHALL DIE, AND THE RIVER SHALL STINK; AND THE EGYPTIANS SHALL LOATHE TO DRINK OF THE WATER OF THE RIVER."

The structure is:

1. The Nile — like the serpent — was one of the great gods of the Egyptians. It was turned into blood, as well as all the streams and rivers and ponds fed by it. It was by the shed Blood of Christ that Satan was defeated.

2. Verse 15 suggests that this plague took place at the moment that Pharaoh arrived upon the bank of the river in order to worship it. Men *"worship and serve the creature more than the Creator, Who is blessed forever"* (Rom. 1:25).

3. Egypt would find out, to her dismay, just exactly Who the Lord actually was.

THE WORD OF THE LORD

Verses 14 through 16 read: *"And the LORD said unto Moses, Pharaoh's heart is hardened, he refuses to let the people go.*

"Get thee unto Pharaoh in the morning; lo, he goes out unto the water; and you shall stand by the river's brink against he come; and the rod which was turned to a serpent shall you take in your hand.

"And you shall say unto him, The LORD God of the Hebrews has sent me unto you, saying, Let My people go, that they may serve Me in the wilderness, and, behold, hitherto you would not hear."

Verse 14 portrays the fact that the Lord did not purposely harden the heart of Pharaoh, but that he hardened his own heart by his obstinate refusal to obey what the Lord demanded. Of course, the Lord knew that he would do that, and judged everything accordingly.

Moses and Aaron were to meet Pharaoh by the riverbank, where he no doubt had come to worship, and was to give him a message that would be startling to say the least. The Lord reminds Pharaoh through Moses and Aaron that the reason for these plagues coming upon Egypt was because he refused to let Israel go. So in essence, the fault was not that of God, but rather that of the Monarch's.

Men are prone to blame God for the difficulties and problems that come to them; however, it is never God's fault; we are always the ones to blame.

BLOOD

Verses 17 and 18 read: *"Thus saith the LORD, In this you shall know that I am the LORD: behold, I will smite with the rod that is in my hand upon the waters which are in the river, and they shall be turned to blood.*

"And the fish that is in the river shall die, and the river shall stink: and the Egyptians shall loathe to drink of the water of the river."

The miracle proposed by Moses must have seemed preposterous to Pharaoh. The rod smiting the water of the mighty Nile, and it turning to blood?

This which the Lord proposed to do was a far greater blow than would at first meet the eye. It was not only a severe punishment to the Egyptians to be deprived of their fish supply, it was also implied contempt in regard of their religious worship, since at least three species of the Nile fish were sacred — the *"oxyrhineus,"* the *"lepidotus,"* and the *"phagrus."*

The Nile, at this particular juncture, is a quite large river. I've been there a number of times, and for all of this water to turn to blood, which it definitely did, and adding to that the stink of the untold thousands of dead and dying fish, would not have presented a very pleasant picture.

(19) "AND THE LORD SPOKE UNTO MOSES, SAY UNTO AARON, TAKE YOUR ROD, AND STRETCH OUT YOUR HAND UPON THE WATERS OF EGYPT, UPON THEIR STREAMS, UPON THEIR RIVERS, AND UPON THEIR PONDS, AND UPON ALL THEIR POOLS OF WATER, THAT THEY MAY BECOME BLOOD; AND THAT THERE MAY BE BLOOD THROUGHOUT ALL THE LAND OF EGYPT, BOTH IN VESSELS OF WOOD, AND IN VESSELS OF STONE.

(20) "AND MOSES AND AARON DID SO, AS THE LORD COMMANDED; AND HE LIFTED UP THE ROD, AND SMOTE THE WATERS THAT WERE IN THE RIVER, IN THE SIGHT OF PHARAOH, AND IN THE SIGHT OF HIS SERVANTS; AND ALL THE WATERS THAT WERE IN THE RIVER WERE TURNED TO BLOOD.

(21) "AND THE FISH THAT WERE IN THE RIVER DIED; AND THE RIVER STANK, AND THE EGYPTIANS COULD NOT DRINK OF THE WATER OF THE RIVER; AND THERE WAS BLOOD THROUGHOUT ALL THE LAND OF EGYPT.

(22) "AND THE MAGICIANS OF EGYPT DID SO WITH THEIR ENCHANTMENTS: AND PHARAOH'S HEART WAS HARDENED, NEITHER DID HE HEARKEN UNTO THEM; AS THE LORD HAD SAID.

(23) "AND PHARAOH TURNED AND WENT INTO HIS HOUSE, NEITHER DID HE SET HIS HEART TO THIS ALSO.

(24) "AND ALL THE EGYPTIANS DIGGED ROUND ABOUT THE RIVER FOR WATER TO DRINK; FOR THEY COULD NOT DRINK OF THE WATER OF THE RIVER.

(25) "AND SEVEN DAYS WERE FULFILLED, AFTER THAT THE LORD HAD SMITTEN THE RIVER."

The construction is:

1. We find that the effect on Pharaoh's heart was to harden it. Such is the incurable hatred of the natural heart that Divine judgments harden instead of subduing it.

2. Man is not saved or lost through intellect; he is saved or lost either through the acceptance or rejection by his heart. Preachers make a mistake when they appeal to the intellect. The Holy Spirit appeals to the heart.

3. The River Nile was worshipped by the Egyptians under various names and symbols. It was called the *"father of life"* and the *"father of the gods."* Thus, this miracle was a blow to the gods of Egypt. The Egyptians abhorred blood, and their horror must have been extreme when they see their sacred river, and all other water in their country, turned to blood.

THE FIRST PLAGUE

Verses 19 and 20 read: *"And the LORD spoke unto Moses, Say unto Aaron, Take your rod, and stretch out your hand upon the waters of Egypt, upon their streams, upon their rivers, and upon their ponds, and upon all their pools of water, that they may become blood; and that there may be blood throughout all the land of Egypt, both in vessels of wood, and in vessels of stone.*

"And Moses and Aaron did so, as the LORD commanded; and he lifted up the rod, and smote the waters that were in the river, in the sight of Pharaoh, and in the sight of his servants; and all the waters that were in the river were turned to blood."

The first sign had been exhibited, which was the rod turning into the serpent, then eating the other serpents, and then turning back into a rod. It had failed to open the eyes of Pharaoh. Now the *"judgments"* were to begin.

When Moses told the Monarch what he was to do, evidently Pharaoh did not believe him. The Nile turning to blood? All the tributaries, ponds, and lakes doing likewise? And above all of that, all the fish dying?

Furthermore, it was not merely that the water would turn to the color of blood, but for all intents and purposes, it was to turn to blood.

No doubt, a large retinue of servants and aides accompanied Pharaoh. One can well imagine this scene of Moses and Aaron standing before the might and majesty of Pharaoh.

After Aaron tells Pharaoh what he is about to do, with Moses giving him instructions, Pharaoh stands there surveying the scene, no doubt with a smirk on his face.

What a preposterous claim, he must have thought! How utterly ridiculous!

But then it grows very quiet, and Moses nods his head at Aaron, and Aaron lifts up his rod over the river, and then smites it sharply, and all of a sudden, *"the waters that were in the river were turned to blood."*

This miracle completely laid waste the claims of the Egyptians that the River Nile was a god. Whatever it was, they would have to admit, it was not as great as the God of the Hebrews.

Nothing could have seemed more revolting to Pharaoh, more terrible and shocking, than the conversion of his pure, clean, refreshing, life-giving, god-like stream, into a mass of revolting putridity.

ENCHANTMENTS

Verses 21 through 25 read: *"And the fish that were in the river died; and the river stank, and the Egyptians could not drink of the water of the river; and there was blood throughout all the land of Egypt.*

"And the magicians of Egypt did so with their enchantments: and Pharaoh's heart was hardened, neither did he hearken unto them; as the LORD had said.

"And Pharaoh turned and went into his house, neither did he set his heart to this also.

"And all the Egyptians digged round about the river for water to drink; for they could not drink of the water of the river.

"And seven days were fulfilled, after that the LORD had smitten the river."

The Scripture says, *"And there was blood throughout all the land of Egypt."* This means that every drop of water in the land of Egypt had turned to blood, even that which was in *"vessels of wood, and in vessels of stone."* So in effect, there was no water for the people to drink for a period of some seven days.

What the magicians did with their enchantments we aren't told. But whatever it was made Pharaoh believe that they could do the same. But how could they? Every drop of water in the nation had turned to blood.

The first miracle that Moses performed, at least as it regards the judgment of Egypt, was the turning of the water to blood. The first miracle performed by our Lord Jesus was turning the water into wine. The Law was given by Moses, and it was a dispensation of death and terror; but Grace and Truth, of which wine was a type (actually, grape juice), make glad the heart, which comes by Jesus Christ.

To slake the thirst, it seems like the Egyptians found water by digging not so far from the river, at least water they could drink. The Lord allowed this in order that thirst wouldn't kill the entirety of the people of the nation.

"Christ our Redeemer died on the Cross,
"Died for the sinner, paid all his due;
"Sprinkle your soul with the Blood of the Lamb,
"And I will pass, will pass over you."

"Chiefest of sinners, Jesus will save;
"All He has promised, that He will do;
"Wash in the fountain opened for sin,
"And I will pass, will pass over you."

"Judgment is coming, all will be there,
"Each one receiving justly his due;
"Hide in the saving sin-cleansing Blood,
"And I will pass, will pass over you."

"O great compassion! O boundless love!
"O loving kindness, faithful and true!
"Find peace and shelter under the Blood,
"And I will pass, will pass over you."

CHAPTER 8

(1) "AND THE LORD SPOKE UNTO MOSES, GO UNTO PHARAOH, AND SAY UNTO HIM, THUS SAITH THE LORD, LET MY PEOPLE GO, THAT THEY MAY SERVE ME.

(2) "AND IF YOU REFUSE TO LET THEM GO, BEHOLD, I WILL SMITE ALL YOUR BORDERS WITH FROGS:

(3) "AND THE RIVER SHALL BRING FORTH FROGS ABUNDANTLY, WHICH SHALL GO UP AND COME INTO YOUR HOUSE, AND INTO YOUR BEDCHAMBER, AND UPON YOUR BED, AND INTO THE HOUSE OF YOUR SERVANTS, AND UPON YOUR PEOPLE, AND INTO YOUR OVENS, AND INTO YOUR KNEADINGTROUGHS:

(4) "AND THE FROGS SHALL COME UP BOTH ON YOU, AND UPON YOUR PEOPLE, AND UPON ALL YOUR SERVANTS.

(5) "AND THE LORD SPOKE UNTO MOSES, SAY UNTO AARON, STRETCH FORTH YOUR HAND WITH YOUR ROD OVER THE STREAMS, OVER THE RIVERS, AND OVER THE PONDS, AND CAUSE FROGS TO COME UPON THE LAND OF EGYPT.

(6) "AND AARON STRETCHED OUT HIS HAND OVER THE WATERS OF EGYPT; AND THE FROGS CAME UP, AND COVERED THE LAND OF EGYPT.

(7) "AND THE MAGICIANS DID SO WITH THEIR ENCHANTMENTS, AND BROUGHT UP FROGS UPON THE LAND OF EGYPT.

(8) "THEN PHARAOH CALLED FOR MOSES AND AARON, AND SAID, ENTREAT THE LORD, THAT HE MAY TAKE AWAY THE FROGS FROM ME, AND FROM MY PEOPLE; I WILL LET THE PEOPLE GO, THAT THEY MAY DO SACRIFICE UNTO THE LORD.

(9) "AND MOSES SAID UNTO PHARAOH, GLORY OVER ME: WHEN SHALL I ENTREAT FOR YOU, AND FOR YOUR SERVANTS, AND FOR YOUR PEOPLE, TO DESTROY THE FROGS FROM YOU AND YOUR HOUSES, THAT THEY MAY REMAIN IN THE RIVER ONLY?

(10) "AND HE SAID, TOMORROW. AND HE SAID, BE IT ACCORDING TO YOUR WORD: THAT YOU MAY KNOW THAT THERE IS NONE LIKE UNTO THE LORD OUR GOD.

(11) "AND THE FROGS SHALL DEPART FROM YOU, AND FROM YOUR HOUSES, AND FROM YOUR SERVANTS, AND FROM YOUR PEOPLE; THEY SHALL REMAIN IN THE RIVER ONLY."

The composition is:

1. Verse 1 portrays the demand by God to Satan, *"Let My people go, that they may serve Me."* This is the only power that Satan recognizes. The Church flounders helplessly when it uses the *"ways of Egypt"* to attempt to deliver men from Egypt. It simply cannot be done. Only God can deliver.

2. Verse 2 proclaims the judgment of *"frogs."* This plague was directed against the frog-god that was an object of worship in Egypt. It was worshipped as the symbol of fruitfulness.

3. When Moses asked Pharaoh as to when he wanted the frogs removed, the Monarch stupidly replied, *"Tomorrow."* *"One more night with the frogs."*

THE PLAGUE OF FROGS

Verses 1 through 4 read: *"And the LORD spoke unto Moses, Go unto Pharaoh, and say unto him, Thus saith the LORD, Let My people go, that they may serve Me.*

"And if you refuse to let them go, behold, I will smite all your borders with frogs:

"And the river shall bring forth frogs abundantly, which shall go up and come into your house, and into your bedchamber, and upon your bed, and into the house of your servants, and upon your people, and into your ovens, and into your kneadingtroughs:

"And the frogs shall come up both on you, and upon your people, and upon all your servants."

Through Moses, the Lord tells Pharaoh, *"Let My people go, that they may serve Me."* It is not a request, but rather a demand. And if the demand is not met, a plague of frogs will come upon the land.

Frogs were, among the Egyptians, sacred animals. One of their deities, *"Heka,"* was a frog-headed goddess; and they seem to have regarded the frog as a sacred emblem of creative power and fruitfulness.

Consequently, the multiplication of frogs, and especially to the extent to which they were multiplied, presented itself as a curse of unimagined proportions. Due to the fact that the frog was a god to the Egyptians, they could not kill them, but yet the frogs drove them to the point of insanity. Their animal-worship was thus proved absurd and ridiculous.

The type of frog that invaded Egypt at that time has the scientific name of *"Rana Mosaica,"* and resembles our toad, and is a disgusting object, which crawls rather than leaps, and croaks perpetually.

To have the whole country filled with these disgusting reptiles, to be unable to walk in the streets without treading on them, to find them not only occupying one's doorstep, but also in possession of one's house, and even one's bedchamber, and even upon one's bed, to hear their dismal croak perpetually, like a throated roar that never stopped, to see nothing but their loathsome forms wherever one looked, to be in perpetual contact with them and to feel the repulsion of their cold, rough, clammy skin, would quickly prove to be unbearable.

INCREASED JUDGMENT

As we observe these plagues, we find that they become increasingly more severe. In other words, little by little, the Lord increases the pressure. At any time, Pharaoh could have acquiesced. To be sure, he definitely was going to ultimately give in. There was no question about that, but he would not do so until he had no other choice.

Unfortunately, the obstinacy of Pharaoh presents a picture of the majority of the human race. Things happen to people, cities, even entire nations, which ought to turn one to repentance; however, men do not repent quickly or easily.

It is a sober thing to observe individuals to whom God has been so gracious and merciful, turn away from God, with the Lord then applying pressure, and doing so in one form or the other, but to no avail. They do not seem to see what the problem actually is, so they continue going toward the wrong direction, seemingly not realizing that no man can outdo God. Pharaoh found that out the hard way, and so have untold numbers of others.

The Egyptian gods were utterly powerless to aid their worshippers. There was not the shadow of help to be derived from them.

THE MAGICIANS

Verses 5 through 7 read: *"And the LORD spoke unto Moses, say unto Aaron, Stretch forth your hand with your rod over the streams, over the rivers, and over the ponds, and cause frogs to come upon the land of Egypt.*

"And Aaron stretched out his hand over the waters of Egypt; and the frogs came up, and covered the land of Egypt.

"And the magicians did so with their enchantments, and brought up frogs upon the land of Egypt."

Considering that the land was literally inundated with frogs, with even the houses of the people being filled with the things, I'm sure the people really appreciated the Egyptian magicians bringing even more frogs on the scene.

As stated, the people were not supposed to kill the frogs, actually thinking of them as a *"god"*; however, it was very difficult, if not impossible, to put down one's foot without putting it on frogs. The things were in the people's beds, in their kitchens, on their tables, even in the bowls where the dough was mixed in order to make bread. It had to be a stinking, loathsome, putrid situation! But yet the evidence is that none of these plagues had any effect on the area of Goshen, where the Israelites resided.

To be plagued with a multitude of reptiles, which might not be put to death, yet on which it was scarcely possible not to tread, and which, whenever a door was opened were crushed, was a severe trial to the religious feelings of the people, and tended to bring the religion itself into contempt. The visitation was horrible to the senses — nauseous, disgusting. The frogs were hideous to the eyes, grating to the ear, and repulsive to the touch.

Their constant presence everywhere rendered them a continual torment. Perhaps other plagues were more injurious, but the plague of frogs was perhaps of all the most loathsome.

Whatever it is the magicians of Egypt did, it cannot be concluded that they had the power to create frogs. What seems to be expressed here is that it seemed to Pharaoh and to his Court that they were able to do on a small scale what Moses and Aaron had done on the largest possible scale. To be frank, whatever it is they did was probably sleight-of-hand.

It has been well observed that they would have shown their own power and the power of their gods far more satisfactorily had they succeeded in taking the frogs away. But this, of course, they couldn't do.

ONE MORE NIGHT WITH THE FROGS

Verses 8 through 11 read: *"Then Pharaoh called for Moses and Aaron, and said, Entreat the LORD, that He may take away the frogs from me, and from my people; and*

I will let the people go, that they may do sacrifice unto the LORD.

"And Moses said unto Pharaoh, Glory over me: when shall I entreat for you, and for your servants, and for your people, to destroy the frogs from you and your houses, that they may remain in the river only?

"And he said, Tomorrow. And he said, Be it according to your word: that you may know that there is none like unto the LORD our God.

"And the frogs shall depart from you, and from your houses, and from your servants, and from your people; they shall remain in the river only."

It's amazing that the magicians did not try to take away the frogs, but rather added to the misery by producing more, that is, if that's what they actually did.

So Pharaoh calls for Moses and Aaron, which is the first time this has been done. As well, he asked of them to entreat the Lord, that He (the Lord) may take away the frogs. This was an admission that the Lord was greater than all the gods of Egypt.

Even though the Scripture is silent regarding this, it is more than likely possible that his magicians tried to take away the frogs, but could not succeed in doing so. He then promised that he would allow the people to leave Egypt for a period of time, and to *"do sacrifice unto the LORD,"* a promise, incidentally, which he did not keep.

Moses then asked of Pharaoh a peculiar question. In essence he said, *"When do you want the frogs removed?"* Pharaoh gave the most startling and ridiculous answer that one could ever contemplate. He said, *"Tomorrow."*

"One more night with the frogs."

He could have had the frogs removed instantly, but for some ridiculous reason, he said, *"Tomorrow."* So he and all the people of Egypt would put up with these loathsome reptiles for another 12 to 20 hours, and unnecessarily we might quickly add. But isn't that so much like the world!

The Spirit of God deals with a human being, and so often their answer to His appeal is, *"Tomorrow!"* As Pharaoh, they want to continue on in their misery, suffering, bondage, and heartache — *"Tomorrow."*

Satan is a master at getting people to delay their soul's Salvation. Being a liar, he can tell them anything he so desires, anything he can get them to believe. So if he cannot get them to deny the Lord altogether, he'll try to get people to put off to a later date, i.e., *"tomorrow,"* that they then will obey, and serve the Lord. During the intervening time, Satan tightens his noose ever tighter, makes certain the prison doors are locked even to a greater extent, in other words, it's *"one more night with the frogs."*

TODAY

The Holy Spirit says: *"Today if you will hear His voice, harden not your hearts, as in the provocation, in the day of temptation in the wilderness"* (Heb. 3:7-8).

With the Lord, it is always *"today."* It is never *"tomorrow,"* as it regards living for Him, and being what we ought to be in Him.

So Pharaoh got exactly what he wanted; the frogs remained one more day, with Moses saying to him, *"Be it according to your word."*

If there is a Believer reading these words, who in some way is bound by the powers of darkness, and please believe me, many Believers are, you can be totally and completely free, and free today, if you will only believe. So what does it mean to *"only believe"*?

If you will place your Faith entirely and completely in Christ and what He has done for us at the Cross, victory is yours today. If you try to obtain victory in any other manner, it will always be *"tomorrow,"* and in essence, you will be saying, *"One more night with the frogs."*

As a Believer, you must be desirous of removing anything in your heart and life that causes you spiritual difficulties. In fact, the Holy Spirit is jealous over you with a Godly jealousy, that any hindrance in your life be removed. And as stated, if you will put your Faith in Christ and His Finished Work, you can be free today, in essence, this very moment. In fact, you were actually set free 2,000 years ago. It is only a matter of you believing, and believing correctly, which speaks of Christ and His Finished Work.

You don't have to live in defeat any longer! You don't have to live in failure from today forward. You can be totally free because you are totally free. It just remains for you to believe correctly. Now remember this:

It's not what you do, but rather what you believe. Believe in Christ and His Cross, and instant victory is yours.

(12) "AND MOSES AND AARON WENT OUT FROM PHARAOH: AND MOSES CRIED UNTO THE LORD BECAUSE OF THE FROGS WHICH HE HAD BROUGHT AGAINST PHARAOH.

(13) "AND THE LORD DID ACCORDING TO THE WORD OF MOSES; AND THE FROGS DIED OUT OF THE HOUSES, OUT OF THE VILLAGES, AND OUT OF THE FIELDS.

(14) "AND THEY GATHERED THEM TOGETHER UPON HEAPS: AND THE LAND STANK.

(15) "BUT WHEN PHARAOH SAW THAT THERE WAS RESPITE, HE HARDENED HIS HEART, AND HEARKENED NOT UNTO THEM; AS THE LORD HAD SAID.

(16) "AND THE LORD SAID UNTO MOSES, SAY UNTO AARON, STRETCH OUT YOUR ROD, AND SMITE THE DUST OF THE LAND, THAT IT MAY BECOME LICE THROUGHOUT ALL THE LAND OF EGYPT.

(17) "AND THEY DID SO; FOR AARON STRETCHED OUT HIS HAND WITH HIS ROD, AND SMOTE THE DUST OF THE EARTH, AND IT BECAME LICE IN MAN, AND IN BEAST; ALL THE DUST OF THE LAND BECAME LICE THROUGHOUT ALL THE LAND OF EGYPT.

(18) "AND THE MAGICIANS DID SO WITH THEIR ENCHANTMENTS TO BRING FORTH LICE, BUT THEY COULD NOT: SO THERE WERE LICE UPON MAN, AND UPON BEAST.

(19) "THEN THE MAGICIANS SAID UNTO PHARAOH, THIS IS THE FINGER OF GOD: AND PHARAOH'S HEART WAS HARDENED, AND HE HEARKENED NOT UNTO THEM; AS THE LORD HAD SAID."

The construction is:

1. With the plague of frogs lifted, Pharaoh reneges on his promise to let the people go, which is indicative of most of humanity. God is quickly forgotten when the judgment lifts.

2. The unannounced plague of lice compelled Jannes and Jambres to say, *"This is the finger of God."* They could, perhaps by Satanic power, imitate God, at least to a certain degree, but they could not create life (Williams).

3. In short, the servant of Christ and the witness for the truth is surrounded, on all sides, by the spirit of *"Jannes and Jambres."* They imitate God, but that is all that it is, an imitation.

DEAD FROGS

Verses 12 through 14 read: *"And Moses and Aaron went out from Pharaoh: and Moses cried unto the LORD because of the frogs which He had brought against Pharaoh.*

"And the LORD did according to the word of Moses; and the frogs died out of the houses, out of the villages, and out of the fields.

"And they gathered them together upon heaps: and the land stank."

Hundreds of millions of frogs died at once, and one can well imagine the stench that filled the land. The people attempted to push the millions of dead bodies into piles or heaps, but such did not alleviate the smell.

When Pharaoh persisted in holding, with an iron grasp, the Israel of God, the vials of Divine wrath were poured forth upon him, and the land of Egypt was covered, throughout its entire length and breadth with darkness, disease, and desolation. So will it be by and by, when the last great oppressor, a fallen angel who will inspire the Antichrist, shall emerge from the Bottomless Pit, armed with Satanic power, to crush beneath his *"foot of pride"* the favored objects of Jehovah's choice, the Jewish people.

But his throne shall be overturned, his kingdom devastated by the seven last plagues, and, finally, he himself plunged, not into the Red Sea as Pharaoh, but *"in the lake that burneth with fire and brimstone"* (Rev. 17:8; 20:10).

Not one jot or one tittle of what God has promised to Abraham, Isaac, and Jacob shall fail. He will accomplish all. Notwithstanding all that has been said or done to the contrary, God remembers His Promises, and He will fulfill them. They are all *"yes and amen in Christ"* (Mackintosh).

THE PLAGUE OF LICE

Verses 15 through 19 read: *"But when*

Pharaoh saw that there was respite, he hardened his heart, and hearkened not unto them; as the LORD had said.

"And the LORD said unto Moses, Say unto Aaron, Stretch out your rod, and smite the dust of the land, that it may become lice throughout all the land of Egypt.

"And they did so; for Aaron stretched out his hand with his rod, and smote the dust of the Earth, and it became lice in man, and in beast; all the dust of the land became lice throughout all the land of Egypt.

"And the magicians did so with their enchantments to bring forth lice, but they could not: so there was lice upon man, and upon beast.

"Then the magicians said unto Pharaoh, This is the finger of God: and Pharaoh's heart was hardened, and he hearkened not unto them; as the LORD had said."

The hardened heart of the Monarch was answered by a plague of lice. The literal dust of the land turned into lice, which spoke of great creative power on the part of God, and of course, we're speaking of billions of the little insects.

This blow was aimed more directly at the person of the Egyptians. Their bodies covered with lice were a sore rebuke to their pride. Herodotus refers to the cleanliness of the Egyptians: *"So scrupulous were the priests on this point that they used to shave their heads and bodies every third day, for fear of harboring vermin while occupied in their sacred duties."*

Pink says in regard to this third plague: *"The key to the moral significance of this plague lies in the source from which the lice proceeded. Aaron smote the dust of the land 'and it became lice in man and beast.' In the judgment which God pronounced upon disobedient Adam, we read that He said, 'Cursed is the ground for your sake' (Gen. 3:17), and again, 'For dust you are, and unto dust shall you return' (Gen. 3:19).*

"When Aaron smote the 'ground,' and its 'dust' became lice, and the lice came upon the Egyptians, it was a graphic showing-forth of the awful fact that man by nature is under the curse of a holy God."

When the magicians tried to imitate this miracle, their admission is noteworthy: *"This is the finger of God,"* they said!

It is not probable that the magicians believed in a single God, or intended in what they said to express any such idea. The term actually reads, *"of a God."* All that they meant to say was, *"This is beyond the power of man — it is supernatural — some god must be helping the Israelites."*

SATAN'S METHODS

In marking the forms of Satan's opposition to the truth of God, we find that his method has ever been, first, to oppose it by violence; and then, if that does not succeed, to corrupt it by producing a counterfeit (Mackintosh).

If it is to be noticed, the Devil first sought to kill Moses (Ex. 2:15), and having failed to accomplish his purpose by that method, he sought to imitate his works. To be frank, this is Satan's method at the present time.

The Church world falls readily for manifestations. Never mind that some have no Scriptural foundation. If it looks like God, and acts like God, and above all, claims to be of God, it is automatically accepted as the Lord. The truth is, the far greater majority of the time, it is Satan posing as an *"angel of light"* (II Cor. 11:13-15). Paul said: *"Therefore it is no great thing if his ministers also be transformed as the ministers of Righteousness; whose end shall be according to their works."*

Almost without exception, those who oppose the Cross fall into the category of our discussion. They claim all type of miracles, and as well, give forth all types of prophecies, which to my knowledge never come true. But regrettably, very few Christians, if any, question these claims, even after they have proven to be bogus. Yes, the spirit of Jannes and Jambres is still alive and well, and the truth is, this situation will get worse as we get nearer to the Rapture of the Church, coming into full flower immediately after the Rapture. Paul said:

"Now the Spirit (Holy Spirit) *speaks expressly, that in the latter times some shall depart from the Faith, giving heed to seducing spirits, and doctrines of devils"* (I Tim. 4:1).

(20) "AND THE LORD SAID UNTO MOSES, RISE UP EARLY IN THE MORNING, AND STAND BEFORE PHARAOH; LO,

HE COMES FORTH TO THE WATER; AND SAY UNTO HIM, THUS SAITH THE LORD, LET MY PEOPLE GO, THAT THEY MAY SERVE ME.

(21) "ELSE, IF YOU WILL NOT LET MY PEOPLE GO, BEHOLD, I WILL SEND SWARMS OF FLIES UPON YOU, AND UPON YOUR SERVANTS, AND UPON YOUR PEOPLE, AND UPON YOUR HOUSES: AND THE HOUSES OF THE EGYPTIANS SHALL BE FULL OF SWARMS OF FLIES, AND ALSO THE GROUND WHEREON THEY ARE.

(22) "AND I WILL SEVER IN THAT DAY THE LAND OF GOSHEN, IN WHICH MY PEOPLE DWELL, THAT NO SWARMS OF FLIES SHALL BE THERE; TO THE END YOU MAY KNOW THAT I AM THE LORD IN THE MIDST OF THE EARTH.

(23) "AND I WILL PUT A DIVISION BETWEEN MY PEOPLE AND YOUR PEOPLE: TOMORROW SHALL THIS SIGN BE.

(24) "AND THE LORD DID SO; AND THERE CAME A GRIEVOUS SWARM OF FLIES INTO THE HOUSE OF PHARAOH, AND INTO HIS SERVANTS' HOUSES, AND INTO ALL THE LAND OF EGYPT: THE LAND WAS CORRUPTED BY REASON OF THE SWARM OF FLIES."

The overview is:

1. Verses 20 through 24 portray the fourth plague, which is *"flies."* This plague was a severe blow to the idolatrous worship of Egypt and designed to manifest the helplessness of Beelzebub, the god of flies, who was supposed to have power to prevent flies.

2. Cleanliness was necessary in such worship, and the putrid conditions brought about by unclean flies would be a great hindrance to the idolaters.

3. All of this proved that the God of Israel was more powerful than any other supposed god.

THE PLAGUE OF FLIES

Verses 20 and 21 read: *"And the LORD said unto Moses, Rise up early in the morning, and stand before Pharaoh; lo, he comes forth to the water; and say unto him, Thus saith the LORD, Let My people go, that they may serve Me.*

"Else, if you will not let My people go, behold, I will send swarms of flies upon you, and upon your servants, and upon your people, and into your houses: and the houses of the Egyptians shall be full of swarms of flies, and also the ground whereon they are."

The type of fly mentioned here is said to have been the *"Blatta Orientalis."* It was a kind of beetle, which inflicts very painful bites with their jaws. They also gnaw and destroy clothes, household furniture, leather, and articles of every kind, and either consume or render unavailable all eatables. It is said they can even drive people out of their houses, and at the same time, devastate the fields.

What madness in the king to keep up this foolish, this suicidal contest! But the conflict of every sinner with Jehovah is of the same infatuated character. Stroke after stroke descends; yet impenitence continues.

More than likely, when Pharaoh arrived at the Nile for his early morning time of worship, Moses and Aaron are waiting for him. The command is the same, *"Let My people go, that they may serve Me."*

And then, if it is refused, swarms of flies will come upon the entirety of the nation of Egypt. It will be upon Pharaoh, upon his servants, in fact, upon every single person in the country, with the exception of the Israelites.

The Scripture is silent as to exactly what Pharaoh said, but we do know that he rejected that demanded by Moses.

GOSHEN

Verses 22 through 24 read: *"And I will sever in that day the land of Goshen, in which My people dwell, that no swarms of flies shall be there; to the end you may know that I am the LORD in the midst of the Earth.*

"And I will put a division between My people and your people: tomorrow shall this sign be.

"And the LORD did so; and there came a grievous swarm of flies into the house of Pharaoh, and into his servants' houses, and into all the land of Egypt: the land was corrupted by reason of the swarm of flies."

Most Commentators claim that the plague of flies presents the first time that the Lord spared Goshen, where the Israelites dwelt. Even though it is not mentioned previously, I cannot really see that the Lord was just now drawing the line, so to speak. Otherwise, all the water in Goshen would have been blood, exactly as it was elsewhere in Egypt; frogs would have filled Goshen the same as they did elsewhere; and lice would have infected the Israelites, even Moses and Aaron, exactly as it did all Egyptians. There doesn't seem to be any evidence whatsoever that this was the case.

"Flies" are a little different than the other plagues, in that they can fly some distances.

For the Lord to stop these billions of insects from crossing into Goshen would have been a miracle within itself. So what am I saying?

I'm saying that none of the plagues affected the Children of Israel, and neither were they meant to affect the Children of Israel. Why would the Lord have brought judgment upon His Own people?!

There is evidence that these things, as stated, bit the people, plus the animals, and even devastated the crops. With the exception of Goshen, exactly as the Scripture says, *"The land was corrupted by reason of the swarm of flies."*

(25) "AND PHARAOH CALLED FOR MOSES AND FOR AARON, AND SAID, GO YE, SACRIFICE TO YOUR GOD IN THE LAND.

(26) "AND MOSES SAID, IT IS NOT MEET SO TO DO; FOR WE SHALL SACRIFICE THE ABOMINATION OF THE EGYPTIANS TO THE LORD OUR GOD: LO, SHALL WE SACRIFICE THE ABOMINATION OF THE EGYPTIANS BEFORE THEIR EYES, AND WILL THEY NOT STONE US?

(27) "WE WILL GO THREE DAYS' JOURNEY INTO THE WILDERNESS, AND SACRIFICE TO THE LORD OUR GOD, AS HE SHALL COMMAND US.

(28) "AND PHARAOH SAID, I WILL LET YOU GO, THAT YOU MAY SACRIFICE TO THE LORD YOUR GOD IN THE WILDERNESS; ONLY YOU SHALL NOT GO VERY FAR AWAY: ENTREAT FOR ME.

(29) "AND MOSES SAID, BEHOLD, I GO OUT FROM THEE, AND I WILL ENTREAT THE LORD THAT THE SWARMS OF FLIES MAY DEPART FROM PHARAOH, FROM HIS SERVANTS, AND FROM HIS PEOPLE, TOMORROW: BUT LET NOT PHARAOH DEAL DECEITFULLY ANY MORE IN NOT LETTING THE PEOPLE GO TO SACRIFICE TO THE LORD.

(30) "AND MOSES WENT OUT FROM PHARAOH, AND ENTREATED THE LORD.

(31) "AND THE LORD DID ACCORDING TO THE WORD OF MOSES; AND HE REMOVED THE SWARMS OF FLIES FROM PHARAOH, FROM HIS SERVANTS, AND FROM HIS PEOPLE, THERE REMAINED NOT ONE.

(32) "AND PHARAOH HARDENED HIS HEART AT THIS TIME ALSO, NEITHER WOULD HE LET THE PEOPLE GO."

The exegesis is:

1. The first compromise is made by Pharaoh: *"Sacrifice to your God in the land."* It is Satan's trick that the Believer be not only in the world, but as well, of the world.

2. The Monarch makes a second concession: *"Only shall you not go very far away."* Satan doesn't mind a little religion; just don't go all the way.

3. As we will see later on, Pharaoh will make two more concessions, making four in all concerning Israel sacrificing to the Lord. These are Satan's tactics, which he continues unto this very hour.

COMPROMISE

Verses 25 through 28 read: *"And Pharaoh called for Moses and for Aaron, and said, Go ye, sacrifice to your God in the land.*

"And Moses said, It is not meet so to do; for we shall sacrifice the abomination of the Egyptians to the LORD our God: lo, shall we sacrifice the abomination of the Egyptians before their eyes, and will they not stone us?

"We will go three days' journey into the wilderness, and sacrifice to the LORD our God, as He shall command us.

"And Pharaoh said, I will let you go, that you may sacrifice to the LORD your God in the wilderness; only you shall not go very far away: entreat for me."

Satan's efforts always are directed to prevent a definite breach between the Church and the world. In other words, he wants the Church to be a part of the world, and the world to be a part of the Church. Compromise is the means by which he would seek to do this. He used this tactic some four times with Moses, and it is still the bane of the Church.

The Word says, *"Come out from among them"*; however, Satan says, *"You can be of the world and still worship God."* If that does not succeed, he will say, *"Don't go very far away."* In other words, *"Don't be fanatical about it."*

Even though two of the compromises are ahead, we will list all four here.

1. *"Sacrifice in the land"* (Vs. 25).

As stated, be of the world as well as in the world.

2. *"Only you shall not go very far away"* (Vs. 28).

Don't get too taken up with serving the Lord. Bend a little; don't be fanatical.

3. *"Let your men go only"* (Ex. 10:11).

If the entirety of the family didn't go, the Monarch knew that the men would not stay. And he was right. The entirety of the family must serve the Lord.

4. *"Go, but leave your flocks behind"* (Ex. 10:24).

Moses' answer to this compromise is extremely colorful, *"Not one hoof shall be left behind."*

THE HARDENED HEART

Verses 29 through 32 read: *"And Moses said, Behold, I go out from you, and I will entreat the LORD that the swarms of flies may depart from Pharaoh, from his servants, and from his people, tomorrow: but let not Pharaoh deal deceitfully any more in not letting the people go to sacrifice to the LORD.*

"And Moses went out from Pharaoh, and entreated the LORD.

"And the LORD did according to the word of Moses; and He removed the swarms of flies from Pharaoh, from his servants, and from his people; there remained not one.

"And Pharaoh hardened his heart at this time also, neither would he let the people go."

Even though the compromise offered by Pharaoh was unacceptable, Moses entreated the Lord anyway, that the swarms of flies would be lifted.

The Lord heard Moses, and did as was requested. But the Scripture again says, *"And Pharaoh hardened his heart at this time also, neither would he let the people go."*

"Beneath the Cross of Jesus I fain would take my stand,
"The shadow of a mighty rock within a weary land;
"A home within the wilderness, a rest upon the way,
"From the burning of the noontide heat, and the burden of the day."

"Upon that Cross of Jesus my eye at times can see
"The very dying form of One Who suffered there for me;
"And from my smitten heart with tears two wonders I confess
"The wonders of redeeming love, and my unworthiness."

"I take, O Cross, your shadow for my abiding place;
"I ask no other sunshine than the sunshine of His Face;
"Content to let the world go by, to know no gain nor loss
"My sinful self my only shame, my glory all the Cross."

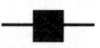

CHAPTER 9

(1) "THEN THE LORD SAID UNTO MOSES, GO IN UNTO PHARAOH, AND TELL HIM, THUS SAITH THE LORD GOD OF THE HEBREWS, LET MY PEOPLE GO, THAT THEY MAY SERVE ME.

(2) "FOR IF YOU REFUSE TO LET THEM GO, AND WILL HOLD THEM STILL,

(3) "BEHOLD, THE HAND OF THE LORD IS UPON YOUR CATTLE WHICH IS IN THE FIELD, UPON THE HORSES, UPON THE ASSES, UPON THE CAMELS, UPON THE OXEN, AND UPON THE SHEEP: THERE SHALL BE A VERY GRIEVOUS MURRAIN.

(4) "AND THE LORD SHALL SEVER BETWEEN THE CATTLE OF ISRAEL AND THE CATTLE OF EGYPT: AND THERE SHALL NOTHING DIE OF ALL THAT IS THE CHILDREN'S OF ISRAEL.

(5) "AND THE LORD APPOINTED A SET TIME, SAYING, TOMORROW THE LORD SHALL DO THIS THING IN THE LAND.

(6) "AND THE LORD DID THAT THING ON THE MORROW, AND ALL THE CATTLE OF EGYPT DIED: BUT OF THE CATTLE OF THE CHILDREN OF ISRAEL DIED NOT ONE.

(7) "AND PHARAOH SENT, AND, BEHOLD, THERE WAS NOT ONE OF THE CATTLE OF THE ISRAELITES DEAD. AND THE HEART OF PHARAOH WAS HARDENED, AND HE DID NOT LET THE PEOPLE GO."

The structure is:

1. The Ninth Chapter of Exodus portrays the plagues of God deepening in their intensity. When they are concluded, mighty Egypt will be seriously affected.

2. Verse 1 says that the Lord God of Heaven was not ashamed to call Himself *"the Lord God of the Hebrews,"* individuals who were slaves. He calls them *"My people."*

3. The plague of *"murrain,"* which was directed against the gods of Egypt, who were supposed to be manifested in the various animal forms, all of which were considered sacred, proved once again that the God of Israel was greater than the gods of Egypt who were powerless to protect themselves.

4. God would even differentiate between the *"cattle of Israel"* and the *"cattle of Egypt."* That which belongs to God's people is special in God's eyes.

LET MY PEOPLE GO

Verse 1 reads: *"Then the LORD said unto Moses, Go in unto Pharaoh, and tell him, Thus saith the LORD God of the Hebrews, Let My people go, that they may serve Me."*

For the first time, the property of Egypt, which constituted its prosperity, would be greatly affected. While it had experienced some suffering previously, it was minor by comparison to what would now happen.

Jehovah refers to Himself as the *"Lord God of the Hebrews,"* in order to distinguish Himself from the Egyptian gods. His command is as ever, *"Let My people go, that they may serve Me."* This specifies in its short statement that the Israelites were under no consideration to serve any of the gods of Egypt.

NOTES

There was to be a distinct separation.

If one goes through the entire catalog of the genuine fruits of Christianity, it will be deeply interesting to observe, wherever we look in the Bible, we will find that separation from the world is put forward as an indispensable quality in the true service of God. Nothing could be acceptable before God — nothing could receive from His hand the stamp of *"pure and undefiled,"* which was polluted by contact with an *"evil world." "Come out from among them, and be ye separate, saith the Lord, and touch not the unclean thing; and I will receive you, and will be a Father unto you, and you shall be My sons and daughters, saith the Lord Almighty,"* proclaims in no uncertain terms that which God demands (II Cor. 6:17-18).

There was no meeting-place for Jehovah and His redeemed in Egypt. As far as God is concerned, Redemption and separation from Egypt were one and the same thing. God had said, *"I am come down to deliver them,"* and nothing short of this could either satisfy or glorify Him. A Salvation that would have left them still in Egypt could not possibly be God's Salvation.

The record is clear; it is essentially necessary now, in order to have a clear and unequivocal testimony for the Son of God, that all who are really His should be separated from this present world. Such is the Will of God; and for this end, Christ gave Himself. Paul bluntly said: *"Grace unto you and peace from God the Father, and our Lord Jesus Christ, Who gave Himself for our sins, that He might deliver us from this present evil world, according to the Will of God and our Father; to Whom be glory forever and ever. Amen"* (Gal. 1:3-5).

THE GALATIANS

The Galatians were beginning to accredit a carnal and worldly religion — a religion of ordinances — a religion of *"days, and months, and times, and years"*; and the Apostle commences his Epistle by telling them that the Lord Jesus Christ gave Himself for the purpose of delivering His people from that very thing. God's people must be separate, not, by any means, on the grounds of our superior personal sanctity, but because we are His people, and in order that we may rightly and intelligently answer His gracious end in taking us into connection with Himself, and attaching His Name to ours.

A people still amid the defilements and abominations of Egypt could not have been a witness for the Holy One; nor can anyone now, while mixed up with the defilements of a corrupt, worldly religion, possibly be a bright and steady witness for a crucified and risen Christ.

(The above material on separation from the world is credited to the scholarship of C. H. Mackintosh.)

THE WORLD AND GOD'S PEOPLE

The spirit of the world attacks the Child of God long before the acts of the world become prominent in the life of the Believer. The far greater majority of the time, and possibly all of the time, that we see the Christian succumbing to the lures of this present world, it is because the Child of God has attempted, and is attempting, to live for God in all the wrong ways. The Christian can make his attempt to live for God in one of two ways. He can place himself under the *"government of law,"* or the *"government of Grace."* In fact, he has no other alternatives, that being the only two, and to be sure, he will be in one or the other. And if he doesn't understand the government of Grace, by default he will automatically be in the government of law.

THE GOVERNMENT OF LAW

Paul said: *"For sin shall not have dominion over you: for you are not under the law, but under Grace"* (Rom. 6:14). And that is where the Child of God, under the New Covenant, is to be, under the government of Grace; however, if the Christian doesn't understand the government of Grace, as stated, by default, he will automatically find himself under the government of law. And what is that government?

It is the efforts of the flesh to attempt to live for God, which means to do so in one's own energy, power, strength, efforts, ability, etc.

While none of these things are wrong within themselves, they constitute wrong simply because it's not God's Way. And let's see why it's not God's Way.

When the Christian sets out to live this life by keeping rules and regulations, by subscribing to particular laws, which unfortunately make up most of modern Christendom, the Holy Spirit simply will not help the Believer do these things, which leaves the Believer on his own, which means he is guaranteed to fail.

It is not that there is something wrong with law, in fact, there is nothing wrong with law. With some exceptions, law is very good. Of course, all the Laws devised by God are holy and righteous, etc. So the problem is not with law; the problem is with us. And let me explain.

Due to the Fall, man cannot keep the Laws of God. No matter how holy those laws are, no matter how hard man may try, and no matter how dedicated he might be, he still cannot keep those laws. If he tries to keep them, every single time he will fail.

Now the question may be asked as to why the Holy Spirit will not help Christians keep the law? Every one of us recognizes the fact that these laws are good. And of course, we're speaking of laws such as *"Thou shalt not steal," "Thou shalt not commit adultery,"* etc. The Holy Spirit refuses to help us in this capacity for two reasons:

1. First of all, due to the fact that we do not have the strength to keep the laws by our own ability, the Lord Jesus Christ has kept them for us, and did so in totality. He was the perfect Law-Keeper, even going so far as to satisfy the penalty of the broken law by dying on the Cross of Calvary. To understand the price that He paid to do this thing, we then should be made to realize just how helpless we are to try to carry it out by our own strength.

So for us to set about to live this Christian life by keeping laws, etc., is an insult to Christ of the highest proportions. He has already done this for us, and has already done it perfectly.

2. If the Holy Spirit gave us power to keep the laws, it would not fall out to righteousness, but rather to unrighteousness. Again, let me explain:

Man's problem is pride. That's what caused

the Fall in the Garden of Eden, and is probably the foundation sin of all sin. And if the Holy Spirit gave us power to keep the law, it would only tend to build self-righteousness in our hearts and lives, which is the problem we have anyway. Man wants to think he can get along without God, and even Believers have the problem of thinking they can live this life without the benefits of Christ and what He did at the Cross.

So if the Christian attempts to live this life by trying to subscribe to rules, regulations, laws, etc., he will find nothing but failure in his life, simply because the Holy Spirit will not be a party to such action. He will not help the Believer commit spiritual adultery. And when we call ourselves *"Christians,"* which means we are to serve Christ and depend totally on Him, and at the same time try to serve the law, this means we are being unfaithful to Christ, which God deems as *"spiritual adultery,"* and which should be understandable, to which the Holy Spirit will not be a party (Rom. 7:1-4).

THE GOVERNMENT OF GRACE

Due to the fact that we are now living under the New Covenant, the Holy Spirit intends for us to live under the *"government of Grace."* In fact, it is only under this government that we can walk victorious over the world, the flesh, and the Devil. As we've already said many times in this Volume, God doesn't have several means of victory, but only one prescribed order, and that is the order of the Cross.

Paul said: *"For by Grace are you saved through faith; and that not of yourselves: it is the Gift of God:*

"Not of works, lest any man should boast."

He then went on to say: *"But now in Christ Jesus you who sometimes were far off are made nigh by the Blood of Christ."*

Then: *"And that He might reconcile both* (Jews and Gentiles) *unto God in one body* (the Church) *by the Cross, having slain the enmity* (hatred) *thereby"* (Eph. 2:8-9, 13, 16).

Living under the Government of Grace is the simplest thing in the world, and at the same time, the most complicated. We will address the latter first:

The Cross is not an addendum, which refers to something added. The Cross, and by that, we refer to what Jesus did there, is the complete means by which we live this Christian experience, actually, the very meaning of the New Covenant (I Cor. 11:24-30). It cuts across every strata of life. Actually, it is not possible for one to live the Cross experience, which in effect is to live the New Covenant by half-measures. It is either all or nothing. And one of the great sins of the modern Church is for it to try to include the Cross in its erroneous direction, of which the Lord will not sanction at all.

That's the reason that entire Denominations go astray. Little by little, they formulate their rules and regulations, basing them on the Word of God less and less, until the Word has no bearing whatsoever on what they do; consequently, the Cross is just simply thrown into the mix, if at all, with their spiritual experience now becoming little more than a hollow shell.

The Believer lives under the government of Grace by simply looking to Christ in a total manner, and what He did at the Cross on our behalf, as providing everything we need to live this Christian life. In other words, it is all by faith — but faith in Christ and His Finished Work. As we've said over and over in this Volume, the object of faith must always be *"Jesus Christ and Him Crucified."*

This means that man does not place dependence on himself, but all in Christ. The Old Testament sacrifices served as excellent examples.

For instance, God did not look at the one offering the sacrifice, but rather at the sacrifice. If the sacrifice was accepted, then the one offering the sacrifice was accepted as well. If the sacrifice was rejected, then the one offering the sacrifice was also rejected. Now think about that for a moment, and it becomes very, very significant.

Our problem presently is we have inverted that order. We have offered up to God ourselves, and Christ and the Cross become merely an addendum. Let's say it again:

God doesn't look so much at the sacrificer, as He does the sacrifice. If the sacrifice is acceptable, then whoever and whatever the sacrificer might be, he is acceptable as well. In this case, the Sacrifice is the Lord Jesus

Christ. If we present Him, irrespective as to who we are, due to the fact that we have placed our faith, trust, and confidence in the Sacrifice of Christ, which God has readily accepted, this means that we are accepted also. That is the government of Grace.

1. We understand that everything we receive from God comes by and through Christ and what He did at the Cross.

2. That being the case, the object of our faith must always be the Finished Work of Christ.

3. The Holy Spirit can then work mightily within our hearts and lives, for this is the ground on which He works, the Sacrifice of Christ (Rom. 6:3-14; 8:1-2, 11; I Cor. 1:17-18, 21, 23; 2:2; Gal. 6:14; Eph. 2:13-18; Col. 2:14-15).

FRUSTRATING THE GRACE OF GOD

Paul said: *"I do not frustrate the Grace of God: for if righteousness come by the law, then Christ is dead in vain"* (Gal. 2:21).

The great Apostle tells us here, and in no uncertain terms, that if man could live for God by means of the government of law, then Jesus didn't need to come down here and die on a Cross. And if we as Believers attempt to live for God by the government of law, we will conclude by *"frustrating the Grace of God,"* which means to make the Grace of God void within our lives. Now we've got a problem!

If the Believer doesn't understand the Cross as Paul taught the Cross, then the Believer is going to attempt to live for God by means of the government of law, whether he understands that or not, which will only fall out to a frustration of Grace. And due to the fact that the modern Church understands almost nothing about the Cross, at least as it refers to our Sanctification, this means that most of the modern Church is functioning in law, which means that the modern Church is failing on every hand. In fact, it simply cannot be otherwise.

The only way the Christian can live this life, and live it as it ought to be lived, is by the Grace of God. Now almost every Believer would agree with that statement; however, understanding how to do that, and I refer to living under the government of Grace, most

NOTES

Christians regrettably because of what we've just said regarding the Church not understanding the Cross, have no idea as to how this life is to be lived.

FADS

Now this becomes quickly obvious, by the ridiculous fads that seem to plague the Church, one after the other. Christians fail in every capacity, and nobody seems to know the reason why.

In one particular series of meetings, which lasted for a long period of time, which took place in the late 1990's, many who had come to the meetings were heard to say, *"If I don't find help here, I don't know what I'm going to do,"* or words to that effect. What were they talking about?

For the most part, even though most would not have admitted it, they were speaking of sin in their lives. It was something they were struggling to overcome, had not been able to do so, with in fact, the problem becoming worse and worse instead of better, and that despite their struggle.

They had heard that God was moving in this place, and in their mind, if they could get this Preacher to lay hands on them, whomever the Preacher might have been, and especially if they experienced some type of manifestation, they thought that this would solve their problem, and they would go home victorious.

Now while God definitely does use Preachers, and while the laying on of hands is definitely Scriptural, not one single solitary person found victory, despite the many thousands who came, in this particular manner. Not one! Why?

While a *"touch"* is greatly desirable, and something that we all want; still, it's not a *"touch"* which the Church needs, but rather the *"Truth."* Jesus said:

"You shall know the Truth, and the Truth shall make you free" (Jn. 8:32). The problem is, the modern Church little knows the truth.

What is the truth of which Jesus spoke?

Paul answered that question by saying: *"We preach Christ Crucified"* (I Cor. 1:23). He also said:

"I determined not to know anything

among you, save Jesus Christ, and Him Crucified" (I Cor. 2:2).

He then said: *"That your faith should not stand in the wisdom of men, but in the Power of God"* (I Cor. 2:5).

The Church desperately needs to be brought back to the Cross, and then the fads would be over, simply because the Church would then know the truth, and would be able to live a victorious life.

Through nearly a half century of Ministry, I have watched the Church go through fad after fad. It seeks to cast demons out of Christians, claiming that is the problem. It then went into the *"confession"* mode, claiming that is the answer. Then the *"laughing phenomenon"* became the craze. And then the *"family curse"* which was big for awhile, and I suppose still is. In all of this, the laying on of hands and the *"falling out"* played a big part.

Some of this is very real, at least in its own perspective; but most of it isn't, and none of it is the answer. Let me ask the Reader a question:

First of all, I want it understood that anything the Lord does is that which I want and desire. I don't care what it is, if it's of the Lord, that's exactly what I want to do, and where I want to be. So as it regards my own personal likes or dislikes, I don't really have any. If the Holy Spirit wants something, and of course anything the Holy Spirit wants will always and without exception be based directly on the Word of God. That's what I want. Let's look at it a little further.

FRUIT

In the Seventh Chapter of Matthew, the Lord explicitly warned us of *"false prophets."* He went on to tell us *"You shall know them by their fruits."* Now that's a very simple statement, very easy to understand, and something we must take to heart (Mat. 7:15-27).

The Message of the Cross falls out to changed lives. People are saved, baptized with the Holy Spirit, healed, delivered from the terrible vices of darkness, and are given eternal life. That's the fruit of the Ministry of the Cross. As well, that coincides perfectly with the Book of Acts, which the Holy Spirit gave us as a description of what the Church ought to be.

NOTES

If a Ministry doesn't have the type of *"fruit"* mentioned, then pure and simple, even though it may sound like God, may claim to be of God, the truth is, it is not of God. It is Satan masquerading under the aura of *"an angel of light"* (II Cor. 11:13-15). Once again let us look at the fruit:

Are people being saved? Are people being baptized with the Holy Spirit? Are people being healed? Are people being delivered? Are lives being changed?

Now when I ask these questions, I'm not talking about wild claims being made of every type of thing that one could think, which happens constantly. But rather, I'm speaking of that which is genuine, in other words, fruit which can be found.

All type of claims are made by many of miracles and great healings, etc., and I speak of those which oppose the Cross, but the truth is, when these miracles and healings are put to the test, they cannot be found.

To be sure, God still performs miracles, and still heals the sick. But let the Reader understand that every single thing He does in this capacity, always comes by and through what Jesus did at the Cross, and no other way. Every miracle performed before the Cross was performed on the basis of that work which definitely was to come. In other words, it was borrowed faith. Every miracle now performed is performed on the basis of a work that is finished, and will never need to be duplicated again. That's why Paul called it the *"Everlasting Covenant"* (Heb. 13:20). I can sense the Presence of God even as I dictate these words.

The Cross stands at the center of history. Not only does it stand at the center of history, it is also the centrality of the Gospel. The Cross, as we have repeatedly stated, is not a mere doctrine, but rather the foundation on which every form of Doctrine must be built. Paul stated: *"But God be thanked, that you were the servants of sin* (the sin nature), *but you have obeyed from the heart that form of Doctrine which was delivered you"* (Rom. 6:17).

Let me ask you, the Reader, this question: Are you obeying that form of Doctrine which was delivered you in the Word of God?

Paul is speaking of what Jesus did at the

Cross. Actually, he is referring back to Verses 3 through 5 of Romans, Chapter 6. That is where he spoke of believing sinners being *"baptized into Jesus Christ,"* which refers to His death. We were then *"buried with Him by baptism into death,"* and then, *"As Christ was raised up from the dead by the glory of the Father, even so we also should walk in newness of life."* In other words, we were baptized into His death, buried with Him, and raised with Him in newness of life (Rom. 6:3-5).

No, he's not speaking there of Water Baptism, but rather the Crucifixion, burial, and Resurrection of Christ. That is where our Faith is to be anchored, and where our Faith is to ever be anchored.

THE PLAGUE ON THE POSSESSIONS

Verses 2 through 4 read: *"For if you refuse to let them go, and will hold them still,*

"Behold, the hand of the LORD is upon your cattle which is in the field, upon the horses, upon the asses, upon the camels, upon the oxen, and upon the sheep: there shall be a very grievous murrain.

"And the LORD shall sever between the cattle of Israel and the cattle of Egypt: and there shall nothing die of all that is the Children's of Israel."

All of this affords a striking demonstration of the absolute rulership of God. He completely controls every creature He has made. The herds of the Egyptians might be dying all around them, but the cattle of Israel were as secure as though there had been no epidemic at all.

There is a spiritual meaning and application to all of this. And it is that meaning that we here, as Believers under the New Covenant, must derive.

This world and all its works will yet be burned up — destroyed as completely as were the beasts of Egypt. By contrast, the sparing of the cattle of the Israelites intimates that the works of the new nature in the Believer will *"abide"* (I Cor. 3:14).

Does the Reader understand what we are saying?

Of course, the description given to us in these Verses is exactly what happened, and presents a literal experience. But we as modern Believers are meant to see beyond the literal, physical happenings, and to thereby ascertain as how it applies to us presently.

Looking at all of this in the spiritual sense, the idea is, and that which I believe the Holy Spirit desires that we know and understand, pertains to our *"works."*

Concerning these works, Paul said: *"For other foundation can no man lay than that is laid, which is Jesus Christ"* (I Cor. 3:11).

As Paul speaks here of Jesus Christ, he is speaking of Christ and what He did at the Cross, in other words, the great benefits there derived. Our foundation must be based on that and that alone. That is why I constantly say that the Cross is not a mere doctrine, but rather the foundation of all Doctrine. To help us understand it easier, perhaps the following would be of some service:

Whatever we purport to produce for Christ, and if it is done by the means of the flesh, which speaks of our own strength and ability, this is a work which God cannot accept. It is the same as Abraham and Sarah producing Ishmael. While their motives may have been good, and while they may have thought they were doing God a great service, the facts were, it was the very opposite. By their own strength and ingenuity, they had brought a child into this world, but it was all by the flesh. Sarah being barren had told Abraham to go in to Hagar, the Egyptian maid, and the child that would be born as a result of this union would be looked at by the culture of that time as belonging to Sarah. But as far as God was concerned, it belonged to Hagar and not Sarah, and was, therefore, unacceptable.

In fact, Isaac could not be born, and was not born, until all hope of the flesh had died. When that took place, then God performed a miracle, and the miracle child was born, which would be in the lineage of Christ, all for the purpose of bringing the Redeemer into this world.

The modern Church is too much guilty of borrowing the methods of the world. Preachers attend Broadway-type plays, to try to get ideas as to how to put on productions in their own Churches, which are supposed to draw the crowds. To be sure, such will draw crowds, but it will serve no spiritual purpose.

We send those in need to humanistic Psychologists, claiming they need *"professional help,"* which at the same time says that the Lord cannot really do them any good. Oh yes, we try to justify all of this by claiming that the Lord is the One Who has given this great wisdom to these atheistic thinkers, but that holds no water at all. In the first place, the soul of man is strictly in the domain of the Lord, and He Alone can meet the need. The world of humanistic psychology holds no answer for itself, much less those who claim to belong to the Lord.

At the least, I must say *"shame"* on those who claim Christ, but thereby reject Him as the answer for humanity, thereby recommending humanistic philosophies. At the worst, it is blasphemy!

Why was Paul stating the fact to the Corinthians that the foundation must be laid squarely on *"Jesus Christ"*?

First of all, he was speaking of the Finished Work of Christ, which must be the foundation of all things. Interlopers were coming into the Churches, actually the Judaizers, and were claiming that the Law had to be added to the Gospel of Grace, that is, if men were to be saved. Pure and simple, this was *"another Jesus"* (II Cor. 11:4). And regrettably, this *"other Jesus"* didn't die with the Early Church. He is alive and well with us today, and what do I mean by that?

If the Preacher is not preaching *"Jesus Christ and Him Crucified"* as the answer to the ills of man, then pure and simple, he is preaching *"another Jesus."* As I've already said any number of times in this Volume, this locks the door on all of the Word of Faith doctrine, and as well, it applies to those who recommend humanistic psychology. With that done, the number left is very small.

It is better for the *"foundation"* to be right if small, than to be wrong and large.

All the cattle that were in the field, which belonged to the Egyptians, were killed by this disease, while all the cattle of the Israelites were spared. That which was of *"gods"* died, while that which was of *"God"* lived.

Let all know and understand that the Lord shall sever between that which is of the flesh, and that which is of the Spirit. And by now, if you have even halfway followed this Text, I think you can understand what the *"flesh"* actually is, and as well, what the *"Spirit"* actually is.

A SET TIME

Verses 5 through 7 read: *"And the LORD appointed a set time, saying, Tomorrow the LORD shall do this thing in the land.*

"And the LORD did that thing on the morrow, and all the cattle of Egypt died: but of the cattle of the Children of Israel died not one.

"And Pharaoh sent, and, behold, there was not one of the cattle of the Israelites dead. And the heart of Pharaoh was hardened, and he did not let the people go."

If it is to be noticed, the Lord gave time to Pharaoh to repent, in other words to obey in allowing Israel to leave, before He brought this other plague on the land. But all was to no avail. When the following day arrived, the heart of the Monarch was just as hard, or even harder, than it had been the day before.

It would seem, would it not, that what the Lord had already done was enough to open the blindest of eyes, or to melt the hardest of hearts, but miracles, as wonderful as they are, have never really brought men to Christ. It is the Cross and the Cross alone of which we are given here glaring examples, which can accomplish this task.

The Cross of Christ has not only put away the Believer's sins, but also dissolved forever our connection with the world; and, on the ground of this, we are privileged to regard the world as a crucified thing, and to be regarded by it as a crucified one. Thus it stands with the Believer and the world — it is crucified to him and he to it. This is the real, dignified position of every true Christian.

The world's judgment about Christ was expressed in the position in which it deliberately placed him. It got its choice as to whether it would have a murderer or Christ. It allowed the murderer to go free, but nailed Christ to the Cross, between two thieves.

Now, if the Believer walks in the footprints of Christ — if he drinks into and manifests His spirit, he will occupy the very same place in the world's estimation; and, in this way, he will not merely know that, as to standing before God, he is Crucified with Christ, but be led to realize it in his walk and experience every day.

But while the Cross has thus effectually cut the connection between the Believer and the world, the Resurrection has brought him into the power of new ties and associations. If in the Cross we see the world's judgment about Christ, in Resurrection we see God's judgment. The world crucified Him, but *"God has highly exalted Him."* Man gave Him the very lowest, God the very highest place; and, inasmuch as the Believer is called into full fellowship with God in his thoughts about Christ, he is enabled to turn the tables upon the world, and look upon it as a crucified thing.

If, therefore, the Believer is on one Cross and the world on another, the moral distance between the two is vast indeed. And if it is vast in principle, so should it be in practice. The world and the Christian should have absolutely nothing in common; nor will we, except so far as we deny our Lord and Master. The Believer proves himself false to Christ to the very same degree that he has fellowship with the world.

All this is plain enough; but where does it put us as regards this world? Truly, it puts us outside, and that completely. We are dead to the world and alive with Christ, or at least that's the way we should be.

(The above material regarding the Cross and the world is that of C. H. Mackintosh. Living in the 1800's, this man influenced Christianity greatly, which influence continues even unto this hour.)

(8) "AND THE LORD SAID UNTO MOSES AND UNTO AARON, TAKE TO YOU HANDFULS OF ASHES OF THE FURNACE, AND LET MOSES SPRINKLE IT TOWARD THE HEAVEN IN THE SIGHT OF PHARAOH.

(9) "AND IT SHALL BECOME SMALL DUST IN ALL THE LAND OF EGYPT, AND SHALL BE A BOIL BREAKING FORTH WITH BLAINS UPON MAN, AND UPON BEAST, THROUGHOUT ALL THE LAND OF EGYPT.

(10) "AND THEY TOOK ASHES OF THE FURNACE, AND STOOD BEFORE PHARAOH; AND MOSES SPRINKLED IT UP TOWARD HEAVEN; AND IT BECAME A BOIL BREAKING FORTH WITH BLAINS UPON MAN, AND UPON BEAST.

(11) "AND THE MAGICIANS COULD NOT STAND BEFORE MOSES BECAUSE OF THE BOILS; FOR THE BOIL WAS UPON THE MAGICIANS, AND UPON ALL THE EGYPTIANS.

(12) "AND THE LORD HARDENED THE HEART OF PHARAOH, AND HE HEARKENED NOT UNTO THEM; AS THE LORD HAD SPOKEN UNTO MOSES."

The composition is:

1. The *"furnace"* mentioned here was probably the furnace where human victims to the god Typhon were offered in sacrifice.

2. These victims were offered in order to avert plagues.

3. If the sacrifices of human victims among the Egyptians were offered to avert plagues, the ashes which Moses was ordered by the Lord to scatter, instead of doing so, brought a fresh one.

THE SIXTH PLAGUE

Verse 8 reads: *"And the LORD said unto Moses and unto Aaron, Take to you handfuls of ashes of the furnace, and let Moses sprinkle it toward the heaven in the sight of Pharaoh."*

The *"furnace"* mentioned here was probably where human victims were offered in sacrifice to the Egyptian god Typhon. Pharaoh was probably standing before this furnace. Moses, in the sight of Pharaoh, cast the ashes up toward Heaven, which he was told to do by the Lord. This means that whatever was done was decided by Heaven, and not by idol gods, or demon gods, etc.

This was the sixth plague, and was brought about without any notice. It was also, like the third, a plague which inflicted direct injury upon the person.

The offering up of human sacrifices here was believed to be done in order to avert plagues. So Pharaoh evidently was there, thinking that this demon god Typhon could help him in his contest with Moses, i.e., *"God."* Whether he had offered a human sacrifice at this time we aren't told. However, Moses took some of the ashes, held them up before Heaven, and let them drift from his hands, which brought about a very serious plague, proving, of course, that these things Egypt worshiped were of no benefit for anything.

While the world presently is far more sophisticated, at least in some places, superstition still runs riot in the thinking of many, if not most, of the individuals of this world. So they resort to foolish practices, exactly as did the Egyptians and others of old.

And then, those who consider themselves to be intellectual and educated, they resort to humanistic psychology, which in effect, is no better than the ignorance of superstition.

THE CROSS ALONE

The Cross Alone is the answer to the ills of man, and that refers to every problem that man might have in the spiritual sense. It is understandable as to the world not knowing that, or even caring about that, but not so understandable as it regards the Church. Regrettably, virtually all of the Church world places no confidence at all in Christ and what He did at the Cross, but rather place their confidence in the wisdom of men. Paul said:

"That your faith should not stand in the wisdom of men, but in the Power of God" (I Cor. 2:5).

I watch Christians undergo terrible oppression from the powers of darkness, and I speak of depression, even to the point of nervous breakdowns. I watch others with difficulties and problems which are, at the least, taking away their joy and happiness, and at the worst, wrecking their lives, when in reality, help is so near at hand, but they do not seem to know or understand.

If the Message of the Cross is not available, and regrettably, it's not available in most places, that's one thing. But when it is available, and that is becoming more and more the case, and it is still ignored, such an attitude and spirit presents a blueprint for total disaster. And regrettably, such disasters are happening constantly, causing tremendous pain and suffering, simply because trust and faith are placed in things other than the Cross of Christ.

Some of the saddest words ever spoken were uttered by Christ. He said: *"And you will not come to Me, that you might have life"* (Jn. 5:40).

I remind the Reader that Jesus was speaking to those who claim to be Believers. But they would not heed Him. Is it any different presently?

NOTES

The Holy Spirit is going to make, and in fact is already making, the Cross of Christ so obvious as to its power, that no one will misunderstand. In other words, the Church is quickly being brought to the place to where they will have to either reject the Cross or accept the Cross. There will be no middle ground. In fact, and as I've already said many times, the Cross of Christ is the dividing line between the True Church and the apostate Church.

Every single thing that man lost at the Fall, and every nuance and problem which the Fall has brought about since that dark day in the Garden of Eden, were addressed by Christ at the Cross. While it is true that we do not now have all the benefits of what He did there, now having only the *"firstfruits,"* still, there is enough victory in the *"firstfruits"* to answer every particular problem we may presently have (Rom. 8:23).

BOILS

Verses 9 and 10 read: *"And it shall become small dust in all the land of Egypt, and shall be a boil breaking forth with blains upon man, and upon beast, throughout all the land of Egypt.*

"And they took ashes of the furnace, and stood before Pharaoh; and Moses sprinkled it up toward Heaven; and it became a boil breaking forth with blains upon man, and upon beast."

As Moses held up the ashes in his hand and let it go, it began to waft like dust in the breeze, and was spread by the air evidently, throughout all Egypt, even as any dust is wont to be spread. Of course, all of this was done by the miracle-working Power of God.

As that dust settled upon man and beast, ulcerous sores, i.e., *"boils,"* no doubt extremely painful, and as well, probably running puss and corruption, broke out on the physical bodies, sparing none.

Of all the things we should learn from this, one very important thing is that God has total and complete control over health and sickness. In the last few decades, many have tried to claim that God never sends sickness on anyone, etc. I think that these Passages, plus many more in the Word of God, prove such thinking to be erroneous.

While of course, sickness originated with the Devil because of the Fall in the Garden of Eden, still, Satan doesn't have latitude to do anything unless he first has permission from the Lord. As well, even though all of the ills, sicknesses, and problems of humanity which were brought about by the Fall definitely did not originate with God, still, the Lord is still in charge, and can use these things as He so desires, in which He often does.

Even though the Scriptures do not plainly say, I think it is obvious that these boils did not come upon the Children of Israel, but only those and that which pertain to the Egyptians.

THE MAGICIANS

Verses 11 and 12 read: *"And the magicians could not stand before Moses because of the boils: for the boil was upon the magicians, and upon all the Egyptians.*

"And the LORD hardened the heart of Pharaoh, and he hearkened not unto them; as the LORD had spoken unto Moses."

The *"magicians,"* who were supposed to be the so-called prophets of the gods of Egypt, were placed in a very serious situation as it regards appearance, position, and their own personal power, which up beside that of God, was nothing.

The phrase, *"And the magicians could not stand before Moses because of the boils,"* refers to them making no attempt to exert their so-called magical powers. In fact, the evidence is that they had to leave the presence of Moses, and Pharaoh as well, to try to attend to the pestilence upon themselves.

The boils were upon Pharaoh as well. But instead of it causing him to humble himself before God, it seemed to have the very opposite effect.

We have discussed this previously, but as the Holy Spirit saw fit to mention it again, such is not done without purpose and reason.

As we've already stated, these statements about the heart of Pharaoh being hardened are not meant to insinuate that the Lord overrode this man's will, forcing him into a position which he possibly did not want to entertain. There is no record in the Word of God that the Lord has ever done such a thing

NOTES

regarding spiritual matters. The will of man is sacred in the eyes of God, with the Scripture constantly stating, *"whosoever will,"* proving the validity of this of which we say (Mat. 11:28-30; Jn. 3:16; 7:37-38; Rom. 10:13; Rev. 22:17). The idea is, God provided the means by which Pharaoh could go in the direction of the hardened heart, if he so desired, which evidently he did so desire. As stated some pages back, the sun softens wax and hardens clay. The process is not in the sun, but in the materials. And thus it was and is with Pharaoh and those like him. Men respond to the Call of God in various ways. Some accept; most refuse.

THE HEART

The heart of man, and by that we do not speak of the physical organ referred to as such, but rather the very being and spirit of man, which includes the free moral agency, presents itself as very difficult to understand. Why will the heart of Esau rebel against God, when the heart of his brother, Jacob, actually his twin, will accept the Lord? Concerning the heart, the Prophet Jeremiah said: *"The heart is deceitful above all things, and desperately wicked: who can know it?"*

And then the Lord through the Prophet continued to say: *"I the Lord search the heart, I try the reins* (the mind), *even to give every man according to his ways, and according to the fruit of his doings"* (Jer. 17:9-10).

So the Holy Spirit through the Prophet tells us that the heart is first of all *"deceitful,"* and that *"above all things,"* and second, is *"wicked,"* and *"desperately so."* Furthermore He tells us that only the Lord can truly know the heart.

However, this of which we speak can be changed by the Power of the Holy Spirit, Who Alone can change such things. But for such to be changed, the individual has to desire such a change. As repeatedly stated, the Lord will never force the will. And also, there is not a single heart that doesn't need changing. All fall under the category, at least at the beginning, of being deceitful and wicked. So, for man to attempt to change himself by changing his environment, his intellect, his wealth or position, presents itself as futile. If man is to be changed, the change must begin at the heart, and it is the Lord Alone Who can do such, and it is called the *"born again"* experience.

(13) "AND THE LORD SAID UNTO MOSES, RISE UP EARLY IN THE MORNING, AND STAND BEFORE PHARAOH, AND SAY UNTO HIM, THUS SAITH THE LORD GOD OF THE HEBREWS, LET MY PEOPLE GO, THAT THEY MAY SERVE ME.

(14) "FOR I WILL AT THIS TIME SEND ALL MY PLAGUES UPON YOUR HEART, AND UPON YOUR SERVANTS, AND UPON YOUR PEOPLE; THAT YOU MAY KNOW THAT THERE IS NONE LIKE ME IN ALL THE EARTH.

(15) "FOR NOW I WILL STRETCH OUT MY HAND, THAT I MAY SMITE YOU AND YOUR PEOPLE WITH PESTILENCE; AND YOU SHALL BE CUT OFF FROM THE EARTH.

(16) "AND IN VERY DEED FOR THIS CAUSE HAVE I RAISED YOU UP, FOR TO SHOW IN YOU MY POWER; AND THAT MY NAME MAY BE DECLARED THROUGHOUT ALL THE EARTH.

(17) "AS YET EXALT YOU YOURSELF AGAINST MY PEOPLE, THAT YOU WILL NOT LET THEM GO?"

The overview is:

1. God will further show Pharaoh that He is the Supreme One over the elements, and that they, under His will and command, can be either instruments of blessing or destruction.

2. Verse 15 proclaims Grace, for it gave Pharaoh warning.

3. Verse 14 proclaims the fact, and gives warning to Pharaoh, that the hour of mildness, if one could refer to these plagues as such, is now gone by. Now he is to expect something far more terrible.

LET MY PEOPLE GO

Verse 13 reads: *"And the LORD said unto Moses, Rise up early in the morning, and stand before Pharaoh, and say unto him, Thus saith the LORD God of the Hebrews, Let My people go, that they may serve Me."*

As should be obvious, all of this is happening in repetitive order. In other words, there aren't weeks or even days, at least for the most part, between plagues. They follow one after the other, with some few exceptions.

The same message, *"Let My people go,"* is constantly repeated, even using the same words, and done so as a token of God's unchangingness (Ex. 8:1, 20; 9:1; 10:3; etc.).

The phrase, *"The LORD God of the Hebrews,"* is meant to portray the separation of Jehovah from the Egyptian gods, which in fact were no gods at all.

The Holy Spirit is jealous over any hold that Satan might have in the heart and life of a Child of God; consequently, He works tirelessly in order to rid the Believer of any such intrusion. And as well, He has a way of doing this, and in fact only one way. Unfortunately, the Church is not too well versed on this, which in fact, is the single most important aspect of the Christian experience. I again speak of the Cross. Egypt must have no part in the Child of God, and the Child of God must have no part in Egypt.

The avenue of victory for the Believer is always and without exception, the avenue of Faith; however, the Faith of which Paul constantly speaks, as well as the other writers, is always and without exception, Faith in Christ and what Christ did at the Cross.

The Believer is to anchor his faith exclusively in the Finished Work of Christ, keep his faith there, which in fact is all that the Holy Spirit demands of us (Rom. 6:3-14; 8:1-2, 11). Then the Holy Spirit will work mightily on our behalf, ridding us of the works of the flesh, and developing in us the *"Fruit of the Spirit"* (Gal. 5:22-23).

PLAGUES

Verses 14 through 17 read: *"For I will at this time send all my plagues upon your heart, and upon your servants, and upon your people; that you may know that there is none like Me in all the Earth.*

"For now I will stretch out My hand, that I may smite you and your people with pestilence; and you shall be cut off from the Earth.

"And in very deed for this cause have I raised you up, for to show in you My power; and that My Name may be declared throughout all the Earth.

"As yet you exalt yourself against My people, that you will not let them go?"

As should be overly obvious, there was a purpose for all that the Lord was doing, as it regards the plagues, as there is always a purpose for anything and everything that the Lord does.

Failing to respond to Mercy and Grace, the Lord resorts to judgment, i.e., *"plagues,"* and first of all for the purpose that Egypt, and all the other surrounding nations, might know that their gods, whatever they were, were nothing but fanciful objects, and in reality, there was only one God, i.e., *"Jehovah."*

He would prove that by sending plagues and pestilence, and He would do it in this fashion, simply because He was left no alternative.

Considering that Pharaoh was going to be extremely obstinate, the Lord would use him in order to show the world the Power of God. And when He was through with Egypt, He would be the talk of all the people in all the nations of the world at that time, at least those nations that had business with Egypt.

The idea is, the Lord has already sent enough judgments in order for any people to humble themselves and repent, but Pharaoh, in his obstinacy, has exalted himself against God's people, and flatly refuses to let them go. So the Lord asked the question of Verse 17, and does so in the form of a threat. In other words, God is saying:

"You are saying that you will not let them go; we will see as to whether you will let them go or not."

(18) "BEHOLD, TOMORROW ABOUT THIS TIME I WILL CAUSE IT TO RAIN A VERY GRIEVOUS HAIL, SUCH AS HAS NOT BEEN IN EGYPT SINCE THE FOUNDATION THEREOF EVEN UNTIL NOW.

(19) "SEND THEREFORE NOW, AND GATHER YOUR CATTLE, AND ALL THAT YOU HAVE IN THE FIELD; FOR UPON EVERY MAN AND BEAST WHICH SHALL BE FOUND IN THE FIELD, AND SHALL NOT BE BROUGHT HOME, THE HAIL SHALL COME DOWN UPON THEM, AND THEY SHALL DIE.

(20) "HE WHO FEARED THE WORD OF THE LORD AMONG THE SERVANTS OF PHARAOH MADE HIS SERVANTS AND HIS CATTLE FLEE INTO THE HOUSES:

(21) "AND HE WHO REGARDED NOT THE WORD OF THE LORD LEFT HIS SERVANTS AND HIS CATTLE IN THE FIELD.

(22) "AND THE LORD SAID UNTO MOSES, STRETCH FORTH YOUR HAND TOWARD HEAVEN THAT THERE MAY BE HAIL IN ALL THE LAND OF EGYPT, UPON MAN, AND UPON BEAST, AND UPON EVERY HERB OF THE FIELD, THROUGHOUT THE LAND OF EGYPT.

(23) "AND MOSES STRETCHED FORTH HIS ROD TOWARD HEAVEN: AND THE LORD SENT THUNDER AND HAIL, AND THE FIRE RAN ALONG UPON THE GROUND; AND THE LORD RAINED HAIL UPON THE LAND OF EGYPT.

(24) "SO THERE WAS HAIL, AND FIRE MINGLED WITH THE HAIL, VERY GRIEVOUS, SUCH AS THERE WAS NONE LIKE IT IN ALL THE LAND OF EGYPT SINCE IT BECAME A NATION.

(25) "AND THE HAIL SMOTE THROUGHOUT ALL THE LAND OF EGYPT ALL THAT WAS IN THE FIELD, BOTH MAN AND BEAST; AND THE HAIL SMOTE EVERY HERB OF THE FIELD, AND BREAK EVERY TREE OF THE FIELD.

(26) "ONLY IN THE LAND OF GOSHEN, WHERE THE CHILDREN OF ISRAEL WERE, WAS THERE NO HAIL."

The exegesis is:

1. The Lord gave warning as to when the next plague was going to come — tomorrow.

2. The ones who believed the Word of the Lord, and feared it, would get under shelter. He who did not regard the Word of the Lord would ignore the shelter — but to their peril.

3. This plague was *"hail,"* mingled with fire, such as Egypt, and no doubt the world, had never seen.

4. In the land of Goshen, where the Children of Israel were, *"there was no hail."*

HAIL

Verses 18 through 21 read: *"Behold, tomorrow about this time I will cause it to rain a very grievous hail, such as has not been in Egypt since the foundation thereof even until now.*

"Send therefore now, and gather your cattle, and all that you have in the field; for upon every man and beast which shall be

found in the field, and shall not be brought home, the hail shall come down upon them, and they shall die.

"He who feared the Word of the LORD among the servants of Pharaoh made his servants and his cattle flee into the houses:

"And he who regarded not the Word of the LORD left his servants and his cattle in the field."

The severity of this plague is marked by several particulars. They are:

1. It was *"a very grievous hail."*
2. It was *"such as had not been in Egypt since the foundation thereof even until now."*
3. The hail was accompanied by an electric storm of fierce intensity, so that *"the fire ran along upon the ground."*
4. *"The hail smote throughout all the land of Egypt all that was in the field, both man and beast; and the hail smote every herb of the field and broke every tree of the field."*

As the *"boils"* were physical portrayals of the spiritual morality of unredeemed man, likewise, this judgment was expressive of the wrath of a holy and sin-hating God.

As the only answer for sin is the Cross of Christ, likewise, the only thing that will stop the Judgment of God is, as well, the Cross of Christ.

Does the Reader think I extol the virtues of the Cross too much? If in fact I do err, I would rather err on the side of caution, rather than the opposite. I would rather say too much about the Cross, than too little. I would rather hold that Blood-stained banner too high, rather than not high enough.

We must ever remember that we are speaking here of the only solution for the terrible sin-scar of the human race. The Cross alone holds that distinction.

GRACE

The Lord would plainly tell the Egyptians that this plague would be held off until tomorrow. But strangely enough, still there was no repentance, even though what was coming was to be of such magnitude that the nation had never seen such before.

In a sense, a challenge was thrown out: if the people feared the Word of the Lord, they would find shelter; otherwise, they would ignore what was being said, and, thereby, suffer the consequences.

THUNDER, HAIL, AND FIRE

Verses 22 through 26 read: *"And the LORD said unto Moses, Stretch forth your hand toward Heaven, that there may be hail in all the land of Egypt, upon man, and upon beast, and upon every herb of the field, throughout the land of Egypt.*

"And Moses stretched forth his rod toward Heaven: and the LORD sent thunder and hail, and the fire ran along upon the ground; and the LORD rained hail upon the land of Egypt.

"So there was hail, and fire mingled with the hail, very grievous, such as there was none like it in all the land of Egypt since it became a nation.

"And the hail smote throughout all the land of Egypt all that was in the field, both man and beast; and the hail smote every herb of the field, and broke every tree of the field.

"Only in the land of Goshen, where the Children of Israel were, was there no hail."

This plague of *"thunder, hail, and fire,"* was directed against Isis and Osiris, the gods of light, health, fertility, arts, and agriculture. Water, fire, earth, and air were all objects of Egyptian idolatry. God showed Pharaoh and his people that He was the Supreme One over these elements, and that instead of helping the Egyptians, they, under His Will and Command, were instruments of destruction.

The plague consisted of a series of thunder peels, which evidently covered the entirety of Egypt, with large hailstones falling, and continuous fire that ran along the ground devouring everything in its path, but which did not touch the land of Goshen, the part of Egypt where the Children of Egypt dwelt.

THE LORD JESUS CHRIST

Since the Advent of Christ, the knowledge of God has vastly increased in the world, and has had some 2,000 years to do so; consequently, all advancement in the world, and in whatever capacity, can be ascribed to the Advent of Christ.

And it must be understood that the only way that men can have knowledge of God is through Christ, and as well, through the Word of God; however, it is impossible for man to understand the Word, unless man has first accepted the Lord Jesus Christ as his Lord and Saviour. And further still, the Christ Who is accepted must be the Crucified One, or else, the Christ being worshiped will be, in the words of Paul, *"another Christ,"* i.e., *"another Jesus"* (II Cor. 11:4).

So the god that most of the world speaks of is not the God of the Bible, and even the Christ spoken of by many, if not most, is not the Christ of the Bible, but a Christ of one's own invention.

THE MODERN CHURCH WORLD

Most of the Denominational Church world, and I think I exaggerate not when I use the word *"most,"* is shot through with humanism and modernism; consequently, with some few exceptions, there is no faith or confidence in the Word of God, with much of the Word being disbelieved. As well, the Message of Jesus Christ and Him Crucified has long since been discarded. At best, it is a humanistic, religious sociality, which denies the power thereof (II Tim. 3:1-5).

The Pentecostal and Charismatic parts of the Church world, which make up about half of the entirety, are as well shot through with unbelief. There are some exceptions, and thank God for those exceptions, but they are, I fear, few and far between.

Both groups are shot through with humanistic psychology. In other words, the Cross of Christ has been abandoned, or else ignored, in favor of the psychological way. While many, if not most, of these would claim to still believe in the Cross, the truth is, one cannot have it both ways. As Jesus bluntly said: *"No man can serve two masters: for either he will hate the one, and love the other; or else he will hold to the one, and despise the other. You cannot serve God and mammon"* (Mat. 6:24).

THE JESUS DIED SPIRITUALLY DOCTRINE

Most Christians who are followers of the Word of Faith message, little know or understand the *"Jesus died spiritually doctrine."* Many simply don't know what you're talking about when these words are expressed.

Why?

NOTES

The major theme of the Word of Faith message is money. It's not Righteousness, Holiness, Christlikeness, or anything of that nature. Pure and simple, it is money. So, anything that's said other than directions as to how to amass more money is given little attention. In fact, the head gurus of this particular message, which is false from A to Z, claim that they have been raised up by God to tell the Church how to amass wealth. And they are not talking about spiritual wealth either, but rather material things.

Of course, there's absolutely nothing in the Word of God that even remotely gives evidence to such teaching, but that seems to matter little. In fact, Scriptures are repeatedly pulled out of context, perverted, and then dished up as the Scriptural proof of these particular, nefarious doctrines. But there seems to be enough greed in the hearts of all of us to make this message very palatable.

The truth is, the only ones getting rich in this *"get rich quick scheme,"* and that's exactly what it is, are the Preachers. They are amassing millions of dollars, given by gullible Christians, who think that by doing such they are going to hit the jackpot as well. As stated, there is enough greed to keep all of this going.

In this particular genre, great claims are made of astounding miracles and healings, with prophecies constantly uttered, but with no proof of any of these things actually happening. Once again, the greed is so heavy that all of these false claims are overlooked or ignored, because the next pull of the handle is surely going to bring about the jackpot. At least that's what these Preachers keep saying, and the people keep believing.

There's not an iota of difference in this particular *"lust"* and lust it is, than those who were hooked on gambling at the casinos, who just know that they are going to get rich with the next throw of the card. It is the same spirit propelling both.

Now as stated, even though the Jesus died spiritually doctrine is taught in these circles, most of the adherents little know what you're talking about when you use these words because, as again stated, their interest does not lie in this direction. They have about as much concern for the Atonement as I have for the next presentation of the Academy Awards. And I can assure you, that I have no interest in that whatsoever.

Irrespective, it is a deadly doctrine because it strikes at the very heart of the Atonement, and is, consequently, blasphemous.

What does this doctrine mean? In simple, abbreviated terms, it means that Jesus, while taking the sin penalty on the Cross, actually became a sinner, and because He became a sinner, died and went to Hell, and we speak of the burning side of Hell. They claim that He suffered horribly so in the burning side of Hell for some three days and nights, while demons danced in hellish glee, and Satan gloated.

But at the end of the three days and nights of suffering in Hell as a lost sinner, actually burning in the flames, God then said, according to this perverted doctrine, *"It is enough."* At that moment, Jesus was *"born again,"* and then resurrected from the dead.

Now of course, there's not a shred of any of this in the Bible, with this concoction being just that, a concoction made up out of proverbial whole cloth. In other words, it is bogus.

So they teach that if a person is saved, the Cross has nothing to do with it, even with the shedding of the Blood of Christ being an incidental matter. They actually teach that the shedding of His Blood within itself was not enough. So, their so-called Salvation consists of believing in a lost Jesus, a Jesus Who has become a sinner, and Who went to Hell. And the actual Atonement, they say, is the suffering of Christ in Hell, once again, repudiating the Cross.

In fact, they refer to the Cross as *"past miseries,"* even saying that it was the *"greatest defeat in human history."*

Those who participate in this particular teaching, which means to adhere to the Word of Faith doctrine, will not come away unsullied.

Some may feel that I'm a little too hard on these particular false doctrines; however, I must remind the Reader that we're speaking here of the single most serious thing on the face of the Earth — your eternal soul. If you miss it here, you've missed it, and missed it completely.

To be wrong about anything in the Bible will always bring about negative results, but may not be lethal; however, to be wrong about the Atonement is to be wrong about the very heart of the Gospel, which can cause your soul to be lost.

The judgment poured out upon Egypt at this juncture did not reach to the *"land of Goshen,"* where the Children of Israel were because their trust was in the Lord. Let the Reader know and understand that judgment is coming. The only means by which that judgment can be escaped is by Faith in Christ, and what Christ did at the Cross.

(27) "AND PHARAOH SENT, AND CALLED FOR MOSES AND AARON, AND SAID UNTO THEM, I HAVE SINNED THIS TIME: THE LORD IS RIGHTEOUS, AND I AND MY PEOPLE ARE WICKED.

(28) "ENTREAT THE LORD (FOR IT IS ENOUGH) THAT THERE BE NO MORE MIGHTY THUNDERINGS AND HAIL; AND I WILL LET YOU GO, AND YOU SHALL STAY NO LONGER.

(29) "AND MOSES SAID UNTO HIM, AS SOON AS I AM GONE OUT OF THE CITY, I WILL SPREAD ABROAD MY HANDS UNTO THE LORD; AND THE THUNDER SHALL CEASE, NEITHER SHALL THERE BE ANY MORE HAIL; THAT YOU MAY KNOW HOW THAT THE EARTH IS THE LORD'S.

(30) "BUT AS FOR YOU AND YOUR SERVANTS, I KNOW THAT YOU WILL NOT YET FEAR THE LORD GOD.

(31) "AND THE FLAX AND THE BARLEY WAS SMITTEN: FOR THE BARLEY WAS IN THE EAR, AND THE FLAX WAS BOLLED.

(32) "BUT THE WHEAT AND THE RYE WERE NOT SMITTEN: FOR THEY WERE NOT GROWN UP.

(33) "AND MOSES WENT OUT OF THE CITY FROM PHARAOH, AND SPREAD ABROAD HIS HANDS UNTO THE LORD: AND THE THUNDERS AND HAIL CEASED, AND THE RAIN WAS NOT POURED UPON THE EARTH.

(34) "AND WHEN PHARAOH SAW THAT THE RAIN AND THE HAIL AND THE THUNDERS WERE CEASED, HE SINNED YET MORE, AND HARDENED HIS HEART, HE AND HIS SERVANTS.

(35) "AND THE HEART OF PHARAOH WAS HARDENED, NEITHER WOULD HE

LET THE CHILDREN OF ISRAEL GO; AS THE LORD HAD SPOKEN BY MOSES."

The diagram is:

1. Verse 31 is important in helping to show that the ten plagues, it seems, occupied from three to four months in duration.

2. The resistance of Pharaoh to the Grace of God is astounding to say the least. But is it any different now?

3. With each resistance of the Holy Spirit, the heart, as that of Pharaoh, grows harder.

INSINCERE REPENTANCE

Verses 27 and 28 read: *"And Pharaoh sent, and called for Moses and Aaron, and said unto them, I have sinned this time: the LORD is righteous, and I and my people are wicked.*

"Entreat the LORD (for it is enough) that there be no more mighty thunderings and hail; and I will let you go, and you shall stay no longer."

Everything that needed to be said as it regards repentance was said here. Pharaoh admitted that he had sinned. He proclaimed the Lord as Righteous and his people as wicked, which was certainly the truth. He then asked that the Lord would lift the plague, as no doubt, many cattle had been killed, and as well, the crops were ruined.

But even though he said the right things, which means that in his heart, he knew the right things, in other words, he knew what he should do; still, his words were hollow.

This tells us that even the most rank heathen, even as Pharaoh, when exposed to the Word of the Lord, will soon come to realize What the Lord actually is, Righteous, and what they actually are, wicked.

But man is still loath to go God's way. Oftentimes he will continue to resist, which only makes a bad matter worse, and will fall out to the loss of the soul, if continued in that direction.

MOSES

Verses 29 and 30 read: *"And Moses said unto him, As soon as I am gone out of the city, I will spread abroad my hands unto the LORD; and the thunder shall cease, and neither shall there be any more hail; that you may know how that the Earth is the LORD's.*

"But as for you and your servants, I know that you will not yet fear the LORD God."

Moses preaches, warns, and then announces.

He proclaims the fact that the Earth belongs to the Lord and, consequently, He may do with it whatsoever He desires.

Either the Lord spoke to Moses, or else he detected in the demeanor of Pharaoh the insincerity that would surface probably the next day.

THE TIME FRAME

Verses 31 and 32 read: *"And the flax and the barley was smitten: for the barley was in the ear, and the flax was bolled.*

"But the wheat and the rye were not smitten: for they were not grown up."

These two Verses tell us that the entirety of the time frame of the ten plagues probably was about three to four months in duration. There are some who think the time was even shorter than that, and it may very well have been.

THE HARDENED HEART

Verses 33 through 35 read: *"And Moses went out of the city from Pharaoh, and spread abroad his hands unto the LORD: and the thunders and hail ceased, and the rain was not poured upon the Earth.*

"And when Pharaoh saw that the rain and the hail and the thunders were ceased, he sinned yet more, and hardened his heart, he and his servants.

"And the heart of Pharaoh was hardened, neither would he let the Children of Israel go; as the LORD had spoken by Moses."

The plague was stopped, and when it was stopped, Pharaoh reneged on his promise, and hardened his heart even more.

The Scripture says, *"He and his servants,"* meaning that they either went along with him because they feared not to do so, or else they were not yet convinced of the Power of God, and the uselessness of resistance.

*"There is a green hill far away,
"Outside a city wall,
"Where the dear Lord was crucified,
"Who died to save us all."*

*"We may not know, we cannot tell
"What pains He had to bear;*

"But we believe it was for us
"He hung and suffered there."

"He died that we might be forgiven,
"He died to make us good,
"That we might go at last to Heaven,
"Saved by His Precious Blood."

"There was no other good enough
"To pay the price of sin;
"He only could unlock the gate of Heaven,
"And let us in."

CHAPTER 10

(1) "AND THE LORD SAID UNTO MOSES, GO IN UNTO PHARAOH: FOR I HAVE HARDENED HIS HEART, AND THE HEART OF HIS SERVANTS, THAT I MIGHT SHOW THESE MY SIGNS BEFORE HIM:

(2) "AND THAT YOU MAY TELL IN THE EARS OF YOUR SON, AND OF YOUR SON'S SON, WHAT THINGS I HAVE WROUGHT IN EGYPT, AND MY SIGNS WHICH I HAVE DONE AMONG THEM; THAT YOU MAY KNOW THAT I AM THE LORD.

(3) "AND MOSES AND AARON CAME IN UNTO PHARAOH, AND SAID UNTO HIM, THUS SAITH THE LORD GOD OF THE HEBREWS, HOW LONG WILL YOU REFUSE TO HUMBLE YOURSELF BEFORE ME? LET MY PEOPLE GO, THAT THEY MAY SERVE ME.

(4) "ELSE, IF YOU REFUSE TO LET MY PEOPLE GO, BEHOLD, TOMORROW WILL I BRING THE LOCUSTS INTO YOUR COAST:

(5) "AND THEY SHALL COVER THE FACE OF THE EARTH, THAT ONE CANNOT BE ABLE TO SEE THE EARTH: AND THEY SHALL EAT THE RESIDUE OF THAT WHICH IS ESCAPED, WHICH REMAINS UNTO YOU FROM THE HAIL, AND SHALL EAT EVERY TREE WHICH GROWS FOR YOU OUT OF THE FIELD:

(6) "AND THEY SHALL FILL YOUR HOUSES, AND THE HOUSES OF ALL YOUR SERVANTS, AND THE HOUSES OF ALL THE EGYPTIANS; WHICH NEITHER YOUR FATHERS, NOR YOUR FATHERS' FATHERS HAVE SEEN, SINCE THE DAY THAT THEY WERE UPON THE EARTH UNTO THIS DAY. AND HE TURNED HIMSELF, AND WENT OUT FROM PHARAOH."

The overview is:

1. The god Serapis was believed by the Egyptians to protect them from the locusts. This eighth plague struck at that belief (Williams).

2. Verse 3 presents the great question that God ever asks the human family, *"How long will you refuse to humble yourself before Me?"*

3. Pride, the capital sin of mankind, is the opposite of humility, and in fact, the foundation of all sin.

4. The statement, *"The Lord God of the Hebrews,"* literally means, *"The Eternal, Self-existing, Covenant-keeping One, the Supporter, Defender, Protector, and Creator of the Hebrews."*

HARDENED

Verse 1 reads: *"And the LORD said unto Moses, go in unto Pharaoh: for I have hardened his heart, and the heart of his servants, that I might show these My signs before him."*

There are three different Hebrew verbs that can be translated or rendered *"harden,"* or *"hardened."* They are, *"kabad," "qashah,"* and *"khazaq."*

The first of these, which occurs in Exodus 7:14; 8:15, 32; 9:7, 34 is the weakest of the three, and means to be *"dull"* or *"heavy"* rather than *"to be hard."*

The second, which appears in Exodus 7:3, and 13:15 is a stronger term, and means, *"to be hard,"* or *"to make hard."*

The third word has the most intensive sense, implying fixed and stubborn resolution. It occurs in Exodus 4:21; 7:22; 8:19; 9:35; and elsewhere.

"Hardened" in the last Verse of the previous Chapter speaks of the hardest of hard, i.e., *"khazaq."*

"Hardened" in Verse 1 of Chapter 10 is the weakest of the three, i.e., *"kabad."* It refers, as stated, to *"dull"* or *"heavy."*

Pharaoh had already hardened his heart as much as he humanly could. The Lord added to that hardness, but did so only lightly. He both willfully hardened his own heart, and God, by the unfailing operation of His moral laws, further blunted or hardened it.

The word *"I"* is expressed in the original and is emphatic. If a person willfully sets themselves to rebel against God, and despite all the Mercy and Grace shown to that person, God will not only allow such to take place, but as well, will add to the direction so desired.

THE HOLY SPIRIT

No human being can resist the Holy Spirit, and do so successfully. Without exception, the person, the city, the nation, even a continent, is left harder, more wicked, more sinful, than it had been when the offer of Mercy was extended.

God will use the situation either way. Had Pharaoh yielded, well and good! Inasmuch as he rebels, God will use that to *"show these My signs before him."*

I AM THE LORD

Verse 2 reads: *"And that you may tell in the ears of your son, and of your son's son, what things I have wrought in Egypt, and My signs which I have done among them; that you may know that I am the LORD."*

God would do such great things that even the Holy Spirit would constantly speak of this particular time in the centuries that followed. The Psalms proclaim this fact (Ps. 68:6-7; 77:14-20; 78; 81:5-6; 105; 106; 124:1-3; 135:8-9; 136:10-15).

HUMBLE YOURSELF

Verse 3 reads: *"And Moses and Aaron came in unto Pharaoh, and said unto him, Thus saith the LORD God of the Hebrews, How long will you refuse to humble yourself before Me? Let My people go, that they may serve Me."*

In this Verse, as stated, we have the question that the Lord not only asked Pharaoh, but has asked most every individual in the world; *"How long will you refuse to humble yourself before Me?"*

Concerning this, Pulpit Commentary says: *"The confession recorded in 9:27 had been a distinct act of self-humiliation; but it had been cancelled by subsequent self-assertion. And, moreover, humility of speech was not what God had been for months requiring of Pharaoh, but submission in act. He would not really 'humble himself' until he gave the oft-demanded permission to the Israelites that they might depart from Egypt."* In fact, he would never honestly give this permission, as we shall see.

Why is it so hard for the human being to humble himself before his Maker?

In fact, this is the hardest thing for man to do. A lot of reasons enter into the situation. Most unsaved people don't want to give up their sins. As well, they like to brag that they bow to no man, and that spirit carries over to God.

Humbling one's self before God admits that one is wrong and that God is right. This seems simple, but it's very difficult for man to admit. And not only is man wrong, but he has been wrong all along, and not only is God right, but He has been right all along.

Pride is the opposite of humility, and in fact, that which stands in the way of humility. A person cannot be both prideful and humble at the same time. One or the other must go. In this context, man likes for others to see him as *"macho,"* and to humble one's self before God is the very opposite of the macho image.

It becomes even more difficult when the individual is rich, or in a place of power, or both, such as Pharaoh. That's why Jesus said: *"It is easier for a camel to go through the eye of a needle, than for a rich man to enter into the Kingdom of God"* (Mat. 19:24).

He didn't say it was impossible, but rather very difficult. The reason being, the rich man depends on his riches, and furthermore, he's not normally accustomed to taking orders from anyone, and that goes for God as well! But the fact is, everyone, both rich and poor, must come the same way, and that's by humbling one's self before God. So the rich don't like the idea of having to come to the Lord the same way as the poor individual stricken by poverty.

LET MY PEOPLE GO

The words are the same that had been used previously, *"Let My people go, that they may serve Me."* The Holy Spirit is jealous of any involvement that the Evil One has in the heart and life of the Believer. The price that Jesus paid at the Cross addressed itself to every single problem which humanity faces. Consequently, and as we've already stated several times, this means that no single Believer need ever be overcome by the powers of darkness in any capacity. Tragically, all have, but it is because of not knowing and understanding what the Lord has done for us at the Cross of Calvary, and our part in that Finished Work.

Even though I have already given the following in this Volume, and will probably give it several more times before its conclusion, due to its vast significance, I would urge the Reader to peruse the following again very carefully. What I'm going to give will be very abbreviated, and will leave much to be desired. However, all the other things in this Volume that we have said or will say about the Cross will hopefully fill in the blanks.

FOCUS

Every Believer must without fail put his focus on *"Jesus Christ and Him Crucified"* (I Cor. 2:2). Jesus Christ is the answer to every single problem, and more particularly, what He did for us at the Cross. That's why Paul also said: *"If I boast, I will boast in the Lord Jesus Christ, to Whom I died unto the world and the world unto me"* (Gal. 6:14).

The Believer must never separate Christ from the Cross, or the Cross from Christ. Please note the following:

When John was given his great vision of Heaven, and more particularly, the Throne of God, the following is what he saw:

"And I beheld, and, lo, in the midst of the Throne and of the four Living Creatures, and in the midst of the Elders, stood a Lamb as it had been slain, having seven horns and seven eyes, which are the Seven Spirits of God sent forth into all the Earth" (Rev. 5:6).

If it is to be noticed, as John is given this Vision, he sees Christ, but in the crucified form. This refers to the fact that before the Throne of God, which is the highest tribunal in the universe, it is the Cross which has made everything possible. That being the case in Heaven, it certainly should be the case in the Church, don't you think?!

So the focus must always be on *"Jesus Christ and Him Crucified."*

THE OBJECT OF FAITH

With the Cross as our focus, and that which remains our focus, this means that the Finished Work of Christ must always be the object of our Faith. This is critically important.

It is not so much how much faith that you have as a Believer, but rather the correct object of your faith.

Paul said: *"Stand fast therefore in the liberty wherewith Christ has made us free* (what He did at the Cross, and our faith in that Finished Work) *and be not entangled again with the yoke of bondage* (do not go back into the government of law)."

He then said, *"Behold, I Paul say unto you, that if you be circumcised* (depend on such for your Salvation or a part thereof), *Christ shall profit you nothing* (what Jesus did at the Cross would be of no avail to you)."

He then said: *"Christ is become of no effect unto you, whosoever of you are justified by the law* (seek to be justified by the law); *you are fallen from Grace"* (Gal. 5:1-4).

All of this tells us that the Cross of Christ must ever be the object of our faith, and not works that we might carry out, etc.

POWER SOURCE

If our focus is on the Cross, and the Finished Work of Christ is the object of our Faith, and remains such, the Holy Spirit will then grandly and gloriously help us to be what we ought to be (Rom. 8:1-2, 11).

Without the Holy Spirit, no Believer is going to get anything done. In fact, every single work carried out in the Believer's life is carried out by the Holy Spirit.

And then we must realize that He works exclusively within the parameters of the Finished Work of Christ. Notice again what Paul said:

"For we through the Spirit (Holy Spirit) *wait for the hope of Righteousness by Faith"* (Gal. 5:5).

So it's the Holy Spirit Who brings about the hope of Righteousness in our hearts and lives, which comes by faith in what Christ did at the Cross on our behalf.

By the Spirit, anything can be done, that is, anything which is the Will of God. Without the Spirit, which means we are relying on our own strength, nothing can be done, at least that which pertains to the Lord.

RESULTS

If our focus is correct, and our object of faith correct, with then the Holy Spirit being our power source, we can be guaranteed of results which are constantly victorious. In other words, we have now learned how to live for God, exactly as the Holy Spirit related all of this to Paul, and then Paul gave it to us (Rom. 6:14; 8:2).

WRONG WAY

Let's look at this same abbreviated formula, turn it around in the manner in which most Christians attempt to live this life, and see what happens:

Focus: Most Christians try to live this life by performing certain particular *"works."* The great question is, how many works are enough? The sad fact is, no amount of works will suffice. While works are important, they are important only as a result of our Faith, and never as the cause of our faith.

Object of Faith: If our focus is on works, regrettably as it is with most Christians, then the object of our faith becomes our *"performance."* While performance is definitely required as it regards the Child of God, it is never to be the object of our Faith. If it is, this means the Holy Spirit will back off, and we're left holding the proverbial bag, and for the simple reason that our performance is actually never good enough, that is if we're going to try to use it to pay a debt, which in fact we can never pay, and which in fact we no longer owe, because Jesus has paid it all.

Power Source: With our focus on works, and the object of faith becoming our performance, then our power source is *"self,"* which leaves us with a big problem. But tragically, that again is where most Christians presently are.

When we do such a thing, we are then being unfaithful to Christ, in effect, committing *"spiritual adultery,"* with which the Holy Spirit will have no part (Rom. 7:1-4).

Every Believer is married to Christ; however, if we as well try to function under the government of law, we are, in a sense, then married to law as well, which makes us married to both Christ and the law, which makes us *"spiritual adulterers,"* which is a serious charge indeed. But that's exactly what the Holy Spirit through Paul said. I would invite you to read very carefully the first four Verses of Romans, Chapter 7.

Results: Living out this scenario as we have portrayed it guarantees failure on the part of the Believer. The sin nature will begin to rule and reign in such a life, and regrettably because most of the modern Church knows little about the Cross as it regards Sanctification, this which we have given is the way that most Christians are presently living (Rom. 6:12-13).

LOCUSTS

Verses 4 through 6 read: *"Else, if you refuse to let My people go, behold, tomorrow will I bring the locusts into your coast:*

"And they shall cover the face of the Earth, that one cannot be able to see the Earth: and they shall eat the residue of that which is escaped, which remains unto you from the hail, and shall eat every tree which grows for you out of the field:

"And they shall fill your houses, and the houses of all your servants, and the houses of all the Egyptians; which neither your fathers, nor your fathers' fathers have seen, since the day that they were upon the Earth unto this day. And he turned himself, and went out from Pharaoh."

This plague was to be most extreme. And yet, the Lord through Moses had said that it would come *"tomorrow,"* which means that Pharaoh had time to repent, and to avoid this terrible thing which was coming. But regrettably, he would not repent.

Concerning this, the Lord said several things:

1. He said that this plague of locusts would be so powerful that there would be no one in Egypt who had ever seen such a thing. The Earth would literally be covered by these insects.

2. He said that every single thing which was left of the crops, the plant life, plus the leaves from all trees, were to be eaten, and eaten in totality, with nothing left.

3. And along with all of this, these insects were to fill the houses, which means they would be in every room, and covering the floor, plus all furniture, etc.

Upon making this announcement, and without awaiting any reply, Moses abruptly, "turns himself, and goes out from Pharaoh." This would be the eighth plague.

(7) "AND PHARAOH'S SERVANTS SAID UNTO HIM, HOW LONG SHALL THIS MAN BE A SNARE UNTO US? LET THE MEN GO, THAT THEY MAY SERVE THE LORD THEIR GOD: DO YOU NOT KNOW THAT EGYPT IS DESTROYED?

(8) "AND MOSES AND AARON WERE BROUGHT AGAIN UNTO PHARAOH: AND HE SAID UNTO THEM, GO, SERVE THE LORD YOUR GOD: BUT WHO ARE THEY WHO SHALL GO?

(9) "AND MOSES SAID, WE WILL GO WITH OUR YOUNG AND WITH OUR OLD, WITH OUR SONS AND WITH OUR DAUGHTERS, WITH OUR FLOCKS AND WITH OUR HERDS WILL WE GO; FOR WE MUST HOLD A FEAST UNTO THE LORD.

(10) "AND HE SAID UNTO THEM, LET THE LORD BE SO WITH YOU, AS I WILL LET YOU GO, AND YOUR LITTLE ONES: LOOK TO IT; FOR EVIL IS BEFORE YOU.

(11) "NOT SO: GO NOW YOU THAT ARE MEN, AND SERVE THE LORD; FOR THAT YOU DID DESIRE, AND THEY WERE DRIVEN OUT FROM PHARAOH'S PRESENCE."

The exegesis is:

1. The Seventh Verse proclaims for the first time that Pharaoh's Officers intervened and requested Pharaoh to yield. Their question is, *"Do you not know that Egypt is destroyed?"* Great is the Power of God.

2. The god Serapis was believed by the Egyptians to protect from locusts. This eighth plague struck at that belief.

3. The third compromise is proposed by Pharaoh. He will let the men go and offer sacrifice unto the Lord, but not the wives and children. Of course he knew that this being the case, the men would return.

EGYPT

Verse 7 reads: *"And Pharaoh's servants said unto him, How long shall this man be a snare unto us? Let the men go, that they may serve the LORD their God: do you not know that Egypt is destroyed?"*

The Officers of Pharaoh were very wealthy men, but most of their wealth was in land, cattle, crops, etc. How much had already been destroyed must be ascertained as considerable. But now they are facing the destruction of everything they have, which will financially ruin them. So they implore Pharaoh to let the people go.

Heretofore they had said little or nothing, and at one particular time, it was even said that they *"hardened their hearts"* like Pharaoh (Ex. 9:34). But now, facing impoverishment and ruin, and realizing that whatever Moses has said is going to happen, definitely will happen, they implore the Monarch to cease and desist, but regrettably, to no avail!

COMPROMISE

Verses 8 through 11 read: *"And Moses and Aaron were brought again unto Pharaoh: and he said unto them, Go, serve the LORD your God: but who are they who shall go?*

"And Moses said, We will go with our young and with our old, and with our sons and with our daughters, with our flocks and with our herds will we go; for we must hold a feast unto the LORD.

"And he said unto them, Let the LORD be so with you, as I will let you go, and your little ones: look to it; for evil is before you.

"Not so: go now you who are men, and serve the LORD; for that you did desire. And they were driven out from Pharaoh's presence."

At the insistence of the Officers of Pharaoh's court, Moses and Aaron are brought again unto Pharaoh, which evidently means that some of the Officers asked for them to come back.

As Moses and Aaron stand before the Monarch, he asked them, *"But who are they who shall go?"*

There was no reason for this question, considering that the demand had been very clear in the past, that everyone that pertained to Israel would go; however, so that there would be no mistake, Moses plainly and clearly stated that not only would the men go, but as well the wives would go, along with all the children, and even all the flocks and herds.

So for sure, Pharaoh now had no doubt as to what was demanded.

He now accuses Moses and Aaron of evil. So he makes his third proposal, which is another compromise.

The men could go, but not the women and children. He knew, this being the case, that the men would then return to Egypt. Of course, his proposal was turned down flat. At this, they were driven from the presence of the Monarch, meaning that they were somewhat manhandled. To be sure, Pharaoh made a big mistake.

Here, again, we have the enemy aiming a deadly blow at the testimony to the name of the God of Israel. Men in the wilderness, and their wives and children in Egypt! This would only have been a half deliverance, at once useless to Israel, and dishonoring to Israel's God. This could not be. If the wives and children remained in Egypt, the men could not possibly be said to have left it, inasmuch as the entirety of the family presented itself as a unit or a whole.

The most that could be said in such a case was that in part they were serving Jehovah, and in part Pharaoh. But Jehovah could have no part with Pharaoh. He would either have all or nothing (Mackintosh).

This tells us in no uncertain terms that the entire family is meant to serve God, not just a part thereof. This means the father and the mother and all the children, however many there are. As Christian parents, we must not be satisfied with only a part of the family living for God; we must claim every member.

Naturally, it's not possible to force people to live for God; however, there are many things we can do, not the least of them being intercession before the Lord. I firmly believe if Godly parents, or even one Godly parent, will earnestly intercede before the Lord, and continue to believe God, not giving up hope or faith, ultimately and eventually, every single member of the family will come in. Listen to what Paul said as he spoke to the jailor:

"Believe on the Lord Jesus Christ, and you shall be saved, and your house" (Acts 16:31).

I am not saying here that God has promised that every single time, every single member of every single family will come to Christ, that is, if there is one person in that family who is a Believer. We are still free moral agents; however, this I do know:

Even if only one member of the family is truly saved, and that person truly seeks God, and will not give in to doubt or unbelief, more than likely, every single member of that family is going to come to Christ. The Holy Spirit will put so much pressure on each member, irrespective as to what type of life they may be living, that most will say *"yes."* The deliverance, as implied here, is meant to include the entirety of the family, with nothing left behind, even the material possessions.

When a person comes to God, as we shall see, everything that person has is to be included.

(12) "AND THE LORD SAID UNTO MOSES, STRETCH OUT YOUR HAND OVER THE LAND OF EGYPT FOR THE LOCUSTS, THAT THEY MAY COME UP UPON THE LAND OF EGYPT, AND EAT EVERY HERB OF THE LAND, EVEN ALL THAT THE HAIL HAS LEFT.

(13) "AND MOSES STRETCHED FORTH HIS ROD OVER THE LAND OF EGYPT, AND THE LORD BROUGHT AN EAST WIND UPON THE LAND ALL THAT DAY, AND ALL THAT NIGHT; AND WHEN IT WAS MORNING, THE EAST WIND BROUGHT THE LOCUSTS.

(14) "AND THE LOCUSTS WENT UP OVER ALL THE LAND OF EGYPT, AND RESTED IN ALL THE COASTS OF EGYPT: VERY GRIEVOUS WERE THEY; BEFORE THEM THERE WERE NO SUCH LOCUSTS AS THEY, NEITHER AFTER THEM SHALL BE SUCH.

(15) "FOR THEY COVERED THE FACE OF THE WHOLE EARTH, SO THAT THE LAND WAS DARKENED; AND THEY DID EAT EVERY HERB OF THE LAND, AND ALL THE FRUIT OF THE TREES WHICH THE HAIL HAD LEFT: AND THERE REMAINED NOT ANY GREEN THING IN THE TREES, OR IN THE HERBS OF THE FIELD, THROUGH ALL THE LAND OF EGYPT."

The synopsis is:

1. The Power of God was once again to be made evident in Egypt, but not in Mercy, that having been rejected, but rather in Judgment.

2. Mercy rejected always, and without exception, brings on Judgment. This means that the United States is possibly in worse spiritual condition than it's ever been in its history.

3. The Judgment of God came in the form of locusts, but it could come in any form.

THE MIRACLE

Verse 12 reads: *"And the LORD said unto Moses, Stretch out your hand over the land of Egypt for the locusts, that they may come up upon the land of Egypt, and eat every herb of the land, even all that the hail has left."*

If Egypt by now wasn't totally destroyed, it was about to be.

This was an agricultural country, depending on its crops, and in fact, the areas around the Nile were extremely fertile. Egypt not only had the ability to feed its own population, but as well, could sell much grain to surrounding countries, etc. But to be sure because of the obstinacy of Pharaoh, Egypt was to be totally destroyed, with all crops lost, and most all cattle killed.

Having rejected the Mercy of God, the Lord now tells Moses to bring forth the plague of the locusts, and to do so by *"stretching out his hand over the land of Egypt."*

As we have seen, each plague grew more intense in ferocity and destruction. And yet, none of this was necessary. Pharaoh could have yielded to the demands of the Lord because they were just demands. But he set his heart to rebel against God, and God gave him the means to do so, and did so in triplicate, one might say.

THE LOCUSTS AND THE LAND OF EGYPT

Verses 13 through 15 read: *"And Moses stretched forth his rod over the land of Egypt, and the LORD brought an east wind upon the land all that day, and all that night; and when it was morning, the east wind brought the locusts.*

"And the locusts went up over all the land of Egypt, and rested in all the coasts of Egypt: very grievous were they; before them there were no such locusts as they, neither after them shall be such.

"For they covered the face of the whole Earth, so that the land was darkened; and they did eat every herb of the land, and all the fruit of the trees which the hail had left: and there remained not any green thing in the trees, or in the herbs of the field, through all the land of Egypt."

I can well imagine that Pharaoh and his Officers slept very little that night. Did he not realize that the plagues which had already been sent by God proved that the plague of the locust would come about as well?

All night the east wind blew, and it gathered all the locusts from the countries surrounding Egypt in that direction. It would be a greater infestation than anyone had ever seen, in fact, completing denuding the land, until there was not a single green thing left. The crops were all gone, the plant life was all gone, and every single leaf on every single tree was eaten.

An awful illustration of this pertains to Israel having rejected the Lord Jesus Christ, and not only rejected Him, but as well, crucified Him. The end result of that was not to be a pretty picture to behold, in fact, the most horrifying spectacle the world has ever known. I think that can be said without any fear of contradiction.

In A.D. 70, Titus, the son of Vespatian, the Roman Emperor, commanding the mighty Tenth Legion, totally and completely destroyed Jerusalem, leveling the Temple until there was absolutely nothing left, with Roman soldiers even running a harrow over the place where the Temple had stood.

Over one million, one hundred thousand Jews were killed in that carnage. There were so many of them hung on crosses, that there was no more place to put crosses.

As well, the slave markets of the world were glutted with hundreds of thousands, if not millions of Jews, until the price of a slave was only a pittance as to what it normally had been. No wonder Jesus said: *"O Jerusalem, Jerusalem, you who kill the Prophets, and stone them which are sent unto you, how often would I have gathered your children together, even as a hen gathereth her chickens under her wings, and you would not!*

"Behold, your house is left unto you desolate" (Mat. 23:37-38).

He also said: *"Verily I say unto you, there shall not be left here one stone upon another, that shall not be thrown down"* (Mat. 24:2).

Mercy rejected was judgment imposed!

(16) "THEN PHARAOH CALLED FOR MOSES AND AARON IN HASTE: AND HE SAID, I HAVE SINNED AGAINST THE LORD YOUR GOD, AND AGAINST YOU.

(17) "NOW THEREFORE FORGIVE, I PRAY YOU, MY SIN ONLY THIS ONCE, AND ENTREAT THE LORD YOUR GOD, THAT HE MAY TAKE AWAY FROM ME THIS DEATH ONLY.

(18) "AND HE WENT OUT FROM PHARAOH, AND ENTREATED THE LORD.

(19) "AND THE LORD TURNED A MIGHTY STRONG WEST WIND, WHICH TOOK AWAY THE LOCUSTS, AND CAST THEM INTO THE RED SEA; THERE REMAINED NOT ONE LOCUST IN ALL THE COASTS OF EGYPT.

(20) "BUT THE LORD HARDENED PHARAOH'S HEART, SO THAT HE WOULD NOT LET THE CHILDREN OF ISRAEL GO."

The exegesis is:

1. This scenario presents the first time Pharaoh asked forgiveness for his stubbornness and sin against the Children of Israel.

2. However, it was not the kind of repentance that brings about Salvation, but rather, as one Preacher said, *"A shallow-mouth-confession,"* which acknowledged that he was in the wrong, but without a real change of heart, which would cause him to forsake sin (Prov. 28:13).

3. Pharaoh wanted relief, but he didn't want to do that which would bring about the relief. So is the response of millions of others.

I HAVE SINNED

Verse 16 reads: *"Then Pharaoh called for Moses and Aaron in haste; and he said, I have sinned against the LORD your God, and against you."*

How many hours or days the locusts stayed in Egypt before Pharaoh sent for Moses and Aaron, we aren't told; however, it was probably only a few hours, when Moses and Aaron were hastily called back.

It seems that Pharaoh went straight to the point. He said, *"I have sinned against the Lord your God, and against you."*

This was not the problem with Pharaoh only, but in fact, is the problem with every human being on the face of the Earth. The Scripture plainly says: *"All have sinned and come short of the Glory of God"* (Rom. 3:23).

All sin, either directly or indirectly, is directed against God. It is an affront to His Holiness, His Righteousness, and to His very Being. It is the ruination of all that is good!

There is only one answer to sin, and that is the Cross of Christ. Every other proposed solution falls down; only the Cross can break the power of sin, and remove its guilt (Rom. 6:6).

Millions try to better themselves by *"turning over a new leaf,"* or making *"New Year's resolutions,"* or by a hundred and one other means and ways; however, the problems caused by sin are never alleviated, because it is only the exterior which is being addressed, when in fact, sin has its source in the evil hearts of men. So if sin is to be properly addressed, the heart of man, which constitutes his innermost being, even his spirit, must be addressed. Only God can do such, which He does by and through His Word. The Holy Spirit anoints the Word, brings conviction to the soul of the lost individual, and then makes him aware of his problem, which is sin, and of the solution, Who is Christ.

Nevertheless, for a confession of sin to be real, and we speak of true repentance, the person must be willing to forsake the sin. As stated, the solution to all of this is the Cross. The part the individual must play is to evidence faith. When we speak of *"Faith,"* we're speaking of having Faith in Christ and what Christ did at the Cross, which must ever be the object of Faith (Rom. 5:1; 10:9-10, 13).

FORGIVE

Verses 17 through 20 read: *"Now therefore forgive, I pray you, my sin only this once, and entreat the LORD your God, that He may take away from me this death only.*

"And he went out from Pharaoh, and entreated the LORD.

"And the LORD turned a mighty strong west wind, which took away the locusts, and cast them into the Red Sea; there remained not one locust in all the coasts of Egypt.

"But the LORD hardened Pharaoh's heart, so that he would not let the Children of Israel go."

Pharaoh asked for forgiveness, thereby admitting his sin, and asked that Moses would plead with the Lord that the locusts would be removed.

Moses did not argue with Pharaoh, nor did he seem to answer him at all, rather doing what he was requested to do, which was to entreat the Lord.

True to His Word, the Lord turned the wind from the west, which took away the locusts, and cast them into the Red Sea. He did so to such an extent that there was not one single locust, the Scripture says, left in all of Egypt.

But then, the Word tells us that the Lord hardened Pharaoh's heart, so that even now, he wouldn't let the Children of Israel go. The following may help us to understand a little more as to what is actually happening here as it regards the Lord hardening Pharaoh's heart.

If Mercy is sought by the individual, Mercy is always granted, and always without reservation, that is, if the individual attempts to go God's Way. If Mercy is extended, and the individual hardens himself against God, in effect putting himself into a state of rebellion, Mercy will probably be extended even further; however, there will come a time that Mercy will be withdrawn, and the Lord will place events in the path of the individual in question, to actually speed up the process of the hardened heart. In other words, if that's what the person wants, God will see to it that's what the person has.

Incidentally, the Hebrew word used here for *"hardened"* is *"khazoq,"* and is the strongest word that can be used. To buttress what we've just said, Pharaoh's prolonged obstinacy and impenitence was receiving aggravation by the working of the just Laws of God (Pulpit).

The Lord will extend Mercy to a far greater degree than any human would ever think of doing such, but there can come an end to that Mercy, even as it did here with Pharaoh.

(21) "AND THE LORD SAID UNTO MOSES, STRETCH OUT YOUR HAND TOWARD HEAVEN, THAT THERE MAY BE DARKNESS OVER THE LAND OF EGYPT, EVEN DARKNESS WHICH MAY BE FELT.

(22) "AND MOSES STRETCHED FORTH HIS HAND TOWARD HEAVEN; AND THERE WAS A THICK DARKNESS IN ALL THE LAND OF EGYPT THREE DAYS:

(23) "THEY SAW NOT ONE ANOTHER, NEITHER ROSE ANY FROM HIS PLACE FOR THREE DAYS: BUT ALL THE CHILDREN OF ISRAEL HAD LIGHT IN THEIR DWELLINGS.

(24) "AND PHARAOH CALLED UNTO MOSES, AND SAID, GO YE, SERVE THE LORD; ONLY LET YOUR FLOCKS AND YOUR HERDS BE STAYED: LET YOUR LITTLE ONES ALSO GO WITH YOU.

(25) "AND MOSES SAID, YOU MUST GIVE US ALSO SACRIFICES AND BURNT OFFERINGS, THAT WE MAY SACRIFICE UNTO THE LORD OUR GOD.

(26) "OUR CATTLE ALSO SHALL GO WITH US; THERE SHALL NOT AN HOOF BE LEFT BEHIND; FOR THEREOF MUST WE TAKE TO SERVE THE LORD OUR GOD; AND WE KNOW NOT WITH WHAT WE MUST SERVE THE LORD, UNTIL WE COME THITHER.

(27) "BUT THE LORD HARDENED PHARAOH'S HEART, AND HE WOULD NOT LET THEM GO.

(28) "AND PHARAOH SAID UNTO HIM, GET YOU FROM ME, TAKE HEED TO YOURSELF, SEE MY FACE NO MORE; FOR IN THAT DAY YOU SEE MY FACE YOU SHALL DIE.

(29) "AND MOSES SAID, YOU HAVE SPOKEN WELL, I WILL SEE YOUR FACE AGAIN NO MORE."

The structure is:

1. This is the ninth plague, and it robs the Egyptians of their supreme god, the Sun, and proved Jehovah Alone to be God.

2. In reply to Pharaoh's proposal that Israel should leave their flocks and herds in Egypt, Moses replied that not only would they take every beast with them, but that also Pharaoh himself must provide them with cattle for the Burnt-Offerings (Williams).

3. The statement at the close of Verse 26 points a lesson true at all times. The second step in the spiritual life is not revealed until the first is taken (Jn. 7:17). *"Egypt"* must be left, that is the first step, before the nature of spiritual worship, which is the second step, can be learned.

DARKNESS

Verses 21 and 22 read: *"And the LORD*

said unto Moses, Stretch out your hand toward Heaven, that there may be darkness over the land of Egypt, even darkness which may be felt.

"And Moses stretched forth his hand toward Heaven; and there was a thick darkness in all the land of Egypt three days."

As we've already stated, Egypt served and worshiped many gods. In fact, even Pharaoh considered himself as god, even as the Caesars would, as well, consider themselves.

In fact, little has changed from then until now, at least as it regards those who do not have at least some knowledge of the God of the Bible. And as well, this strikes hard at the First Commandment, which would shortly be given to Moses: *"You shall have no other gods before Me"* (Ex. 20:3).

In fact, there are no other gods; but Satan imposes himself very much as such. In addressing this, Paul said: *"In whom the god of this world* (Satan) *has blinded the minds of them which believe not, lest the light of the Glorious Gospel of Christ, Who is the Image of God, should shine unto them"* (II Cor. 4:4).

It is said that there are seven major religions in the world. Christianity is included, even though in fact, it is actually not a religion, but rather a relationship, and with a Person, the Man, the Lord Jesus Christ. Christ is Christianity and Christianity is Christ.

"Religion" consists of rules, ways, and means, devised by man, in order to reach God, or to better one's self in some way. Being devised by man, it is not of God, and in essence, is of Satan. Regarding spiritual things, nothing can come from the depraved heart of man, and it truly be of God.

To those who truly know the Lord, it is quickly obvious as to the falseness of the religions of this world, which in effect is *"another god."* And as well, even parts of Christianity are the result of *"seducing spirits, which produce doctrines of devils"* (I Tim. 4:1). I speak of Catholicism, and Mormonism, along with Jehovah's Witnesses, and in fact, any particular part of Christianity, or doctrine, which proclaims a gospel, that is in fact, *"another gospel"* (Gal. 1:6).

In a sense, these *"other gospels"* are very little different than the false gods worshiped by Egypt, and other heathenistic people.

In Egypt, the Sun was worshiped under the title of *"Ra."* In fact, the name *"Ra"* came conspicuously forward in the title of the kings, Pharaoh, or rather *"Phra,"* meaning, *"the Sun."*

So when Moses, under the direct orders of the Lord, stretched forth his hand toward Heaven, and the thick darkness covered all the land of Egypt for some three days, with the exception of Goshen, where the Children of Israel were, this was a direct strike at one of the major gods of Egypt. This portrayed the fact that the god they worshiped was now obscured and his powerlessness demonstrated — a proof, had they but eyes to see, that a mightier than the Sun, yes, the Creator of the Sun, was dealing with them in judgment.

LIGHT

God is light: darkness is the withdrawal of light. Therefore, this judgment of darkness gave plain intimation that Egypt was now abandoned by God. Nothing remained, as we shall see, but death itself. The darkness continued for three days, which was a full manifestation of God's withdrawal (Pink).

In fact, this *"darkness"* was of such degree that it literally could be *"Felt."* In the Hebrew, the word *"felt"* is *"mashash,"* and means *"to feel of, to grope, to search."* Consequently, the meaning of the statement is not so much that the darkness itself could be felt, but rather that the people could not see anything, and had to grope about, in order to go from one place to the other, however short the distance.

Being lost without God is spoken of as *"outer darkness."* Jesus said: *"But the children of the kingdom* (the Jews, who were meant to be in the Kingdom of God, but were thrust out because of their rejection of Christ) *shall be cast out into outer darkness: there shall be weeping and gnashing of teeth"* (Mat. 8:12).

The *"darkness"* of which Jesus mentions here is spiritual darkness, which means to be without God, of which the darkness of Egypt was but a type. In fact, every single person in the world who doesn't know God, which means they've never accepted Christ as their Saviour, walks and lives in spiritual darkness (Acts 26:18; Rom. 2:19; 13:12; I Cor. 4:5; II Cor. 6:14; Eph. 5:8, 11).

As the opposite of this, Revelation, Chapters 21 and 22 constantly speak of *"light,"* even the Light of the Lord, which will characterize the New Jerusalem. Even though the light mentioned in those Passages is literal, its literalness is anchored in the spiritual.

THE WORD OF GOD

The Word of God is our light, and in fact always has been. As I've said many times, I'll say again, *"The Word of God is the only revealed Truth in the world, and in fact ever has been."* The Psalmist said: *"Your Word is a lamp unto my feet, and a light unto my path"* (Ps. 119:105). Jesus said of Himself: *"I am the Light of the world: he who follows Me shall not walk in darkness, but shall have the light of life"* (Jn. 8:12).

It was also said of Him: *"In the beginning was the Word, and the Word was with God, and the Word was God . . . In Him was life; and the life was the light of men"* (Jn. 1:1, 4). In essence, Jesus and the Word are one and the same. It is impossible to know the Word, without knowing Christ. And it is impossible to properly know Christ, unless one understands Christ in the realm of *"Jesus Christ and Him Crucified"* (I Cor. 1:23; 2:2).

The Holy Spirit is the One Who portrays the Light of the Word and of Christ, as symbolized by the Old Testament *"Golden Lampstand."* While the lamp was a Type of Christ, and even His Church (Rev. 1:20), the *"oil"* in the lamps typify the Holy Spirit, without which, the lamp gives no light (Ex. 25:31-37).

If it is to be noticed, Moses did exactly what the Lord told him to do, in essence, obeying His Word to the full. This should be a lesson to us that we follow the Word of God implicitly. We must not take from it, or add to it. We must not pervert it, twist it, or misinterpret it. To understand it properly, which the Holy Spirit will help us to do, is to have the *"Light"* in order to find the *"Way."*

HEAVEN

Verse 22 says that *"Moses stretched forth*

NOTES

his hand toward Heaven," signifying that God was in complete and full charge, and not man. Whatever man may say or do, Heaven will always have the final word. This we must understand.

When we pray, Jesus taught us to say, *"Our Father Who is in Heaven . . ."* (Mat. 6:9). Our help comes from above, and this we must ever understand.

But yet, far too many Christians seek help from men, instead of God. And how do I know that?

I know that, because there is so little prayer among modern Christians. The prayer rooms are empty, which tells us that there is little faith, which means that man is looking elsewhere for help.

Let all know and understand that there is no help except from Heaven, i.e., *"God."* The Christian should take everything to the Lord in prayer. He should seek God's help as it regards leading and guidance, and above all, the Will of God. And it really doesn't matter who the Christian is, or whatever his occupation might be. He belongs to the Lord, bought with a price, and should seek the Face of the Lord about all things.

Solomon said many wonderful things, but one thing he said, which most Christians little understand, is absolutely fascinating. He said: *"If the tree fall toward the south, or toward the north, in the place where the tree falls, there it shall be"* (Eccl. 11:3).

At first glance, this Passage seems to be a mere statement with little meaning; however, if we put all the Verses together of this particular Eleventh Chapter, we will find that the Holy Spirit through him is actually saying that it really doesn't matter what our circumstances are, or whatever the problems might be, the Lord is able to turn any negative situation around.

Millions of Christians bemoan the idea that circumstances are against them. They always consider themselves to be in the wrong place at the wrong time, or whatever. But the Spirit of God is telling us that it really doesn't matter where we are, who we are, or what the circumstances; God is not limited to any circumstances. It doesn't matter if the tree falls toward the north, the south, or even the east or the west; if the Believer will truly believe

God, fully obey the Word of the Lord, at least to the best of his ability, look to Christ and what He has done for us at the Cross, the Lord can make that particular person and place a blessing of unprecedented proportions.

But if you *"observe the wind, you shall not sow; and if you regard the clouds, you shall not reap"* (Eccl. 11:4). In other words, forget about circumstances, put your Faith in God, and believe Him for great and mighty things. Take everything to Him in prayer. Look to Heaven, because your help comes from the Lord and nowhere else.

THE CHILDREN OF ISRAEL AND LIGHT

Verse 23 reads: *"They saw not one another, neither rose any from his place for three days: but all the Children of Israel had light in their dwellings."*

The light, as portrayed here, of course, was literal; however, it was as well, I believe, meant by the Holy Spirit to symbolize the spiritual light which the Children of Israel did have, and which the Egyptians did not have. As we've already stated, it has not changed from then until now. It is only those who follow the Lord, who have true illumination as far as light is concerned.

Look at the nations of the world which do not espouse Jesus Christ, but are rather subservient to another so-called deity. These nations, wherever they might be, and however large they might be, are controlled by demon spirits. As a result, poverty, ignorance, and superstition are the general rule.

Now this doesn't mean that the nations which espouse Christ do so as they should. In fact, all of these nations, wherever they might be, including the United States, leave much to be desired. But yet, with what little knowledge of Christ is held in these countries, which is a knowledge of the Word, has given these nations the greatest freedoms and prosperity the world has ever known. As someone has well said, *"No Bible, no freedom; little Bible, little freedom; much Bible, much freedom."* In fact, it is the Word of God, and the acceptance of Christ as Lord and Saviour, which have made Western Civilization what it is presently. In other words, the Word of God and the acceptance of Christ is the key to all blessings.

WESTERN CIVILIZATION

Some years ago, a billionaire from Texas donated several millions of dollars to Yale University, with the understanding that it would establish a *"chair"* on Western Civilization. In other words, it was to offer the meaning of Western Civilization, and how it began, as one of its regular courses.

Several years passed with no action taken, and the billionaire ultimately inquired as to what might be the problem. Their answer was somewhat revealing:

"We do not know how to teach such a course, and simply because we do not really know and understand the origin of Western Civilization," they said!

To properly understand Western Civilization, one must understand the Bible, and as well, Christ, as to Who and What He actually was and is. Sadly, it is probably true that no one at prestigious Yale University had that type of knowledge.

As to the establishment of Western Civilization, which incidentally, and as stated, has given the world the greatest prosperity and freedoms it has ever known, that honor must go primarily to the Apostle Paul. While of course the Word of God and Christ are its foundation, the establishment of that foundation, which speaks of the beginning stages and spread of Christianity, must be laid at the feet of the little Jew from Tarsus. He, as no other man, established the Church, and in doing so made possible for this *"Light"* to continue. That is the reason for the *"light in our dwellings."* If we lose the Word of God, and, thereby, lose Christ, we will have lost the *"light,"* for there is light in no other. Regrettably and sadly, the so-called western world is losing that light.

It loses it first of all in the Church, and then it is lost to the balance of society. That's why Jesus said, *"You* (Believers) *are the light of the world"* (Mat. 5:14). However, in a sense, we are light only by the fact that we are a reflection of His Light, Who is the True Light (Jn. 8:12; 9:5).

COMPROMISE

Verse 24 reads: *"And Pharaoh called unto Moses, and said, You go, serve the LORD; only let your flocks and your herds remain:*

let your little ones also go with you."

The demand all along to Pharaoh had been, *"Thus saith the LORD, Israel is My son, even My firstborn: and I say unto you, Let My son go, that he may serve Me"* (Ex. 4:21-23).

Two truths are proclaimed here:

1. To Israel, in the words of Paul, pertained *"the adoption"* (Rom. 9:4). This first point has a twofold meaning:

A. This adoption was meant to portray individual adoption, as all Believers are adopted into the Family of God (Rom. 8:15).

B. It is meant to portray the fact that Israel as a nation has been singled out as the object of God's special favors. He said, *"I am a Father to Israel, and Ephraim is My firstborn"* (Jer. 31:9). The title of *"firstborn"* speaks of dignity and excellency (Gen. 49:3; Ps. 89:27). This means that Israel will yet occupy the chief place among the nations, and be no more the *"tail"*, but the *"head"*. The place of the *"firstborn"*, then, is that of honor and privilege. To the firstborn belonged a double portion.

2. While the first truth pertained to Israel, the second truth pertains to the order of that which God demanded of His people. It affects us even unto this present hour, and in fact, was meant to be a symbol of what we now have in Christ.

THE ORDER

A. The Sacrifice: The thought of *"Sacrifice"* comes first! This is required to avert God's Judgment. Only as the sinner places *"blood"* between himself and the thrice-Holy God, can he stand in His august Presence. Nothing but simple Faith in an accomplished Atonement enables the heart to be quiet before Him. *"Without shedding of blood is no remission of sins"* (Heb. 9:22).

In this order, we of course see the Cross, which in fact, the sacrifice was meant to symbolize. That's the reason we preach the Cross, and preach it constantly. That's the reason that we proclaim the fact that the Cross alone stands between mankind and the wrath of Almighty God (Jn. 3:16; Eph. 2:13-18; Rom. 8:1).

Paul said: *"Christ sent me not to baptize, but to preach the Gospel: not with wisdom of words, lest the Cross of Christ should be made of none effect"* (I Cor. 1:17).

That's why he also said: *"Christ is become of no effect unto you, whosoever of you are* (seek to be) *justified by the law; you are fallen from Grace"* (Gal. 5:4).

It is only by the shed Blood of Christ that all sins are washed away, and man is allowed to gain entrance to the very Presence of God (Heb. 9:14-15, 20-28).

We are saved and justified by Faith in that shed Blood of Christ, and by no other means or ways (Eph. 2:13; Ex. 12:13; Rom. 5:1-2).

B. Service: None can serve God acceptably until they are properly reconciled to Him. Paul said: *"Whose I am, and Whom I serve,"* which presents the Divine Order (Acts 27:23).

Let it be clearly stated, if we are confused about the Sacrifice, i.e., *"The Atonement,"* then our service to God will be flawed as well. The Children of Israel were to sacrifice to the Lord their God, that they, in the words of the Lord, *"may serve Me"* (Ex. 4:23).

The implication is, and in fact, far greater than an implication, but rather a statement of fact, for service to be accepted, Sacrifice must be enjoined. Let us say it again:

Only as the sinner places *"blood"* between himself and the thrice-Holy God, can he stand in His august Presence.

The major problem of the modern Church is, it is trying to offer service to the Lord, but rather service based upon an improper understanding of the Atonement. The Holy Spirit will have no part of such; and for the simple reason that such a person is looked at by God as a *"spiritual adulterer"* (Rom. 7:1-4).

C. Fellowship: Following this comes *"the feast,"* which speaks of *"fellowship"* and *"gladness."* But this cannot be until the *"will"* is broken and the *"yoke"* has been received — for this is what true *"service"* implies (Mat. 11:28-30).

But all, *"service"* and *"fellowship"* are predicated on the proper Sacrifice. As previously stated, the Sacrifice being accepted, the sacrificer is accepted as well. And it is only the Sacrifice of Christ that is accepted before God.

To all of this, Pharaoh proposed to Moses that he could go and serve the Lord, and with all of Israel, *"only let your flocks and your herds be stayed."*

With what perseverance did Satan dispute every inch of Israel's way out of the land of Egypt! He first sought to keep them *"in"* the land, then to keep them *"near"* the land, next to keep *"part"* of themselves in the land, and finally, when he could not succeed in any of these three, he sought to send them forth without any ability to serve the Lord. If he could not keep the servants, he would seek to keep their ability to serve, which would answer much the same end. If he could not induce them to sacrifice in the land, he would send them out of the land without sacrifices!

This would be Pharaoh's last compromise.

NOT ONE HOOF WILL BE LEFT BEHIND

Verses 25 and 26 read: *"And Moses said, You must give us also sacrifices and burnt offerings, that we may sacrifice unto the LORD our God.*

"Our cattle also shall go with us; there shall not an hoof be left behind; for thereof must we take to serve the LORD our God; and we know not with what we must serve the LORD, until we come thither."

Moses' answer is revealing indeed: *"Not an hoof will be left behind,"* meaning that every single cow, every single lamb, in other words, every single possession held by the Children of Israel would leave with them out of Egypt.

It is as though one is saying that when one comes to Christ, everything that one has as well comes to Christ. To be somewhat facetious, one's bank account gets saved as well; one's pets, such as dogs and cats, get saved as well; one's automobile gets saved; as stated, every possession one has gets saved.

Of course, we know that material things do not get saved, but at the same time, there is a sense in which they do, as it regards the Believer. *"There shall not an hoof be left behind."*

Moses further said, *"And we know not with what we must serve the LORD, until we come thither."*

While in Egypt, it was not known strictly as to what God required. And it is the same presently.

The Believer cannot have the world and God at the same time. The admonition is crystal clear, *"Wherefore come out from among them, and be ye separate, saith the Lord, and touch not the unclean thing; and I will receive you"* (II Cor. 6:17).

While all of us are *"in the world,"* we must never be *"of the world."* The latter being the case, we cannot properly serve the Lord.

As long as the ship is on the water, it can be of great service; however, the moment the water begins to get into the ship, we then have a catastrophe, with all service being ended.

God must have full and undisputed possession of us. And only when that is accomplished can we have full and undisputed possession of Him. This is the wealthy place into which the precious Blood of Christ introduces us. While the Lord does not require *"isolation,"* and in fact strictly forbids it, He very well demands *"separation"* (Mat. 5:13-16).

THE HARDENED HEART

Verses 27 through 29 read: *"But the LORD hardened Pharaoh's heart, and he would not let them go.*

"And Pharaoh said unto him, Get you from me, take heed to yourself, see my face no more; for in that day you see my face you shall die.

"And Moses said, You have spoken well, I will see your face again no more."

The reply of Pharaoh indicates violent anger. Greatly enraged, he gives vent to his rage, with a want of self-control, telling Moses that under the penalty of instant death, he will not be allowed to come into the presence of the Monarch again.

The answer of Moses was blunt and to the point, *"I will see your face no more."*

It is generally believed that Moses did not leave out of the presence of Pharaoh with these particular words, but continued to address the Monarch for some little time, actually his parting words being those which are given in Verses 4 through 8 of the next Chapter.

As we've already stated, God provided the means by which Pharaoh's heart could be hardened. This was done, as should be obvious, for a particular reason.

That reason was to show Israel, and in fact, all of mankind, even unto this present hour, that it is the shed Blood which delivers, and the shed Blood alone which delivers. And of course, we're speaking of the shed Blood of Christ, of which all of this would be but a type.

Pharaoh would not, and in fact, did not succumb to any of the miracles performed, as great and grandiose as they may have been. But he most definitely would respond to the shed blood of the Paschal Lamb, which was a Type of Christ. As that shed Blood meant the Redemption of Israel, which was God's firstborn (Jer. 31:9), it would also mean the destruction of the firstborn of Pharaoh, even as we shall see.

So, when the Lord saves us, He not only redeems us from wrath, but as well, that wrath is poured out upon Satan, and all of his cohorts of darkness (Col. 2:14-15).

"Up Calvary's mountain one dreadful morn,
"Walked Christ my Saviour weary and worn;
"Facing for sinners death on the Cross,
"That He might save them from endless loss."

"'Father, forgive them!' Thus did He pray,
"Even while His life-blood flowed fast away;
"Praying for sinners while in such woe,
"No one but Jesus ever loved so."

"O how I love Him, Saviour and Friend,
"How can my praises ever find end!
"Through years unnumbered on Heaven's shore,
"My tongue shall praise Him forevermore."

CHAPTER 11

(1) "AND THE LORD SAID UNTO MOSES, YET WILL I BRING ONE PLAGUE MORE UPON PHARAOH, AND UPON EGYPT; AFTERWARDS HE WILL LET YOU GO HENCE: WHEN HE SHALL LET YOU GO, HE SHALL SURELY THRUST YOU OUT HENCE ALTOGETHER.

(2) "SPEAK NOW IN THE EARS OF THE PEOPLE, AND LET EVERY MAN BORROW OF HIS NEIGHBOR, AND EVERY WOMAN OF HER NEIGHBOR, JEWELS OF SILVER AND JEWELS OF GOLD.

(3) "AND THE LORD GAVE THE PEOPLE FAVOR IN THE SIGHT OF THE EGYPTIANS. MOREOVER THE MAN MOSES WAS VERY GREAT IN THE LAND OF EGYPT, IN THE SIGHT OF PHARAOH'S SERVANTS, AND IN THE SIGHT OF THE PEOPLE."

The overview is:

1. The tenth and last plague, *"one plague more,"* would touch the dearest of all in Egypt, the firstborn, and that from Pharaoh down. Sin touches all!

2. Egypt, by now, was wreckage. What had formerly been the most powerful nation on the face of the Earth was now virtually destroyed. Anyone or anything who and which sets themselves against God, no matter how strong, or rich, or powerful, will face certain doom.

3. To understand God is to know that the plagues were not the vengeful wrath of a despotic ruler, but were actually the Mercy of God.

ONE MORE PLAGUE

Verse 1 reads: *"And the LORD said unto Moses, Yet will I bring one plague more upon Pharaoh, and upon Egypt; afterwards he will let you go hence: when he shall let you go, he shall surely thrust you out hence altogether."*

This plague, the last, would be the worst of all. But let the Reader understand that what we are seeing carried out in these first Chapters of Exodus is not, as stated, the vengeful wrath of a despotic ruler, but if properly evaluated, will prove to be the Mercy of God. The Children of Israel belonged to God; they did not belong to Pharaoh. They had been treated like slaves and, in fact, were slaves for well over a century. God had the right to demand their release. At any time Pharaoh could have relented and repented; however, his stubborn, obstinate heart would not allow such to be done.

In fact, God deals the same way presently, in that He speaks with Mercy; however, if the individual, or nation, will not heed the

Mercy, He then speaks with judgment. If the obstinacy continues, He increases the pressure. Some relent and are saved; some reject and are eternally lost.

How many people had died as a result of the previous plagues, we have no way to know; however, all of those particular plagues were designed to increase pressure, and not to kill. So probably the number were few who succumbed.

However, this last plague, a plague of death, even as sin always is, would touch every single family in Egypt, with the exception of the Children of Israel. Let the Reader understand that sooner or later, sin always brings death, for the *"wages of sin is death"* (Rom. 6:23).

And as this *"death,"* the death of the firstborn would touch every house in Egypt, from the most elaborate and luxurious, down to the least hovel, likewise, sin does the same presently. It ultimately brings death, and we speak more so of spiritual death than anything else.

Even though this was physical as it regards this last plague, still, it as well was spiritual. First, second, and third opportunities are on this side of the grave. After death, there remains nothing but the judgment. Let the Reader understand that there is no such thing as Purgatory. That is a fiction, which was fabricated by the Catholic Church (Heb. 9:27).

HE WILL LET YOU GO

The Word of the Lord to Moses was emphatic. For the last several months, concerning the duration of the previous plagues, Pharaoh had reneged on every promise. But the word is now emphatic, after this next and last plague, the death of the firstborn, *"He will let you go."*

As we study the remainder of this Chapter, and especially Chapter 12, we will find that the Cross, of which the Paschal Lamb was a Type, is twofold in its application. While it brings life to the Believer, it brings death to the unbeliever. To accept what Jesus did there, all on our behalf, guarantees eternal life (Jn. 3:16). To reject what He did there guarantees eternal death (Rev. 20:11-15).

DELIVERANCE

Unfortunately, there are millions of Christians presently who are held in the clutches of the Evil One, in fact, *"entangled again with the yoke of bondage"* (Gal. 5:1).

How could this be as it regards a Child of God?

Let the Reader understand that the only means of Salvation in Egypt, regarding the time of our study, were faith and trust in the Paschal Lamb, and its blood applied to the doorposts of the houses of the Children of Israel, and them safely ensconced in these particular houses. In fact, had anyone of the Children of Israel attempted to save themselves in any other manner, they would have been eternally lost. The Holy Spirit states in I Corinthians 5:7 that the Passover pictured Christ's sacrifice of Himself in order to save sinners sentenced to die.

Two great facts appear in the Passover, even as we shall study when we arrive at the Twelfth Chapter. Those two facts are: the certain doom of the firstborn, and his certain Salvation. He was doomed to death by God, not because of his conduct, but because of his birth. This latter fact he could not alter; and he was, therefore, hopelessly lost.

He was, however, absolutely saved, because of the value of the life sacrificed for him. He knew he was saved because God had pledged Himself to most certainly save all who sprinkled the shed blood upon their doorposts.

All sinners are justly doomed by God to death. But He loves them as He loved the firstborn and, therefore, the Lamb of God has suffered that death. His precious Blood, that is, His priceless Life, poured out, attests the fact. The Word of God promises eternal safety to whoever will seek Salvation in that atoning Saviour. The Believer in Christ knows, therefore, that he shall never perish; and this knowledge is based on two facts outside of himself: these are the preciousness of Christ's Blood to God; and, the faithfulness of God to His Own promise (Williams).

So what am I saying?

I am saying, as the Cross is the only means of Salvation for the sinner, likewise, it is the only means of Sanctification for the Saint. Millions of Christians, after trusting Christ and what He has done at the Cross as it regards their Salvation, have regrettably now shifted their faith from the Cross to other things. Consequently, when this is done, and sadly, it is done by most, the sin nature once again gains control over the Believer, and he finds himself now being controlled by passions and lusts, which he, within himself, is powerless to stop. And let the Reader understand the following:

If the Believer doesn't understand the Cross as it refers to his Sanctification, then without fail, and irrespective as to how hard he might try otherwise, he is again to be *"entangled with the yoke of bondage."* The Holy Spirit plainly said through Paul that in such a case, *"Christ is become of no effect unto you, whosoever of you are justified by the law* (seek to be justified by the law); *you are fallen from Grace"* (Gal. 5:4).

Let me make the statement again: Due to the fact that the Cross has been so little preached in the last several decades, and in fact, has been preached almost none at all as it regards Sanctification, almost the entirety of the Church falls into the category of *"bondage entanglement."* This refers to Preachers as well as to the Laity. Without a proper understanding of the Cross, which means that our Faith is properly placed in the Sacrifice of Christ, the works of the flesh will most definitely manifest themselves in our lives in some way. Now those are not my words, but rather the words of the Holy Spirit through Paul (Gal. 5:19-21).

The only answer to this problem is the Cross, and Paul labeled it as *"walking in the Spirit."* What did he mean by that?

WALKING IN THE SPIRIT

Unless one walks in the Spirit, Satan will hold that Believer in bondage, Just as Pharaoh held the Children of Israel in bondage. Before we deal with the erroneous conclusions drawn by many Christians, let us first of all give the answer as to what Paul is addressing here.

Pure and simple, *"walking in the Spirit,"* is the result of *"walking after the Spirit"* (Rom. 8:1).

This is done by the Believer understanding that everything he has in the Lord has come to him, and continues to come to him, through and by the great Sacrifice of Christ.

NOTES

The manner and the way in which these things are received, and continue to be received, are by simple Faith in that which the Lord has done at the Cross. Paul said:

"For we through the Spirit (this is the way the Holy Spirit works) *wait for the hope of Righteousness by Faith.*

"For in Jesus Christ neither circumcision availeth anything, nor uncircumcision (works); *but faith which works by love"* (Gal. 5:5-6).

Now how do we know this?

As we've already explained several times in this one Volume, Paul also said, which proves the point: *"For the Law* (a Law devised by the Godhead from before the foundation of the world) *of the Spirit* (Holy Spirit) *of life* (that which guarantees us all for which Christ has paid such a price) *in Christ Jesus* (this *'Law'* is based on what Jesus did at the Cross) *has made me free from the law of sin and death"* (Rom. 8:2).

In fact, the only *"law"* in the universe that is greater and more powerful than the *"law of sin and death,"* is the *"Law of the Spirit of Life in Christ Jesus."* Notice that it's *"in Christ Jesus,"* which refers to what He did at the Cross, and that exclusively.

So, if the Believer understands that the Cross is the means by which he receives all things from God, and that the Cross is to ever be the object of our Faith, Satan will never gain victory over him (Rom. 6:14). This is the means and the ways of *"walking in the Spirit."*

ERROR

The problem with most Christians because they do not understand the Cross, is that *"Christ profits them nothing"* (Gal. 5:2). This means that because of their erroneous objects of Faith, whatever that might be, all that Christ did on the Cross on their behalf is wasted, at least as far as they are concerned.

Now what do most Christians think that walking in the Spirit actually is?

Were that question to be asked point blank to most, they would automatically begin to list any number of *"works"* which would bring this to pass. They would tell you that *"walking in the Spirit"* is being more faithful to Church, reading more of the Word of

God, having a stronger prayer life, witnessing to souls, giving more money to the Work of the Lord, etc.

While all of these things are good, and in fact things which every good Christian will definitely do, still, by the Believer making such things the object of his faith, instead of Christ, he has just transferred his Faith to *"works,"* which God can never accept. He accepts alone the Work of Christ on the Cross, and not at all our works. Now to be sure, if we properly understand Christ, and properly make the Cross the object of our Faith, most definitely, there will be good works which will follow, in fact, in even a much greater way than the Christian who is depending on works. But the difference will be this:

Whereas the Believer heading in the wrong direction will be doing these things in order to try to bring about faith, the one who properly understands the Cross will do these things because of his Faith. To be sure, the difference is great!

In fact, almost the whole of the Christian world presently is bogged down in *"works,"* which constitutes *"law."* It is the same thing that Paul addressed in his Epistle to the Galatians. In fact, he bluntly said:

"Behold, I Paul say unto you, that if you be circumcised, Christ shall profit you nothing" (Gal. 5:2).

Paul wasn't speaking here of circumcision as it regards a health practice. He was speaking of Believers who were being told by false teachers that in order to please the Lord, they not only had to accept Christ, but as well, the men had to be circumcised, and the little boy babies at eight days old. He was speaking of Believers making those things the object of their faith, and to be frank, it could be circumcision, or a thousand and one other things. Irrespective as to what it might be, if our faith is anchored in those things, *"Christ shall profit you nothing."* And the tragedy is, the modern Church little understanding the Cross because it's been little taught and preached these last several decades, falls under the category of a profitless Christ. In other words, all that He did on the Cross is to no avail for much of the modern Church, and simply because their faith is not in His Finished Work, but rather in other things.

If the Word of God is not faithfully preached, then there is no way that faith can grow in the hearts and lives of Believers (Rom. 10:17).

Humanistic psychology has made such inroads into the Church in modern times that any more the Word of God is little preached, but rather psychological jargon. And as well, and perhaps even to a greater extent, the *"Word of Faith"* doctrine, which in fact is no faith at all, at least that which God will recognize, has perhaps made greater inroads than even humanistic psychology. In fact, it has almost destroyed the faith, and I speak of true faith, of the modern Church. The purveyors of this particular error, and error it is, have so denigrated the Cross, until without a doubt, this must be Satan's trump card, so to speak, for these last days. Paul plainly said:

"Now the Spirit (Holy Spirit) *speaks expressly, that in the latter times* (the times in which we now live) *some shall depart from the faith, giving heed to seducing spirits, and doctrines of devils"* (I Tim. 4:1).

SPIRITUAL ADULTERY

When the Believer who is married to Christ, at the same time embraces the Law, he is looked at by God as a spiritual adulterer. Paul said so (Rom. 7:1-4). He likened this problem to a woman who is married to one man, and then marries another man as well. She in fact has two husbands, which is the very state of most modern Christians. We are married to Christ, but at the same time, we are flirting with the law, or even have embraced the law. Let me explain that:

When we speak of *"Law,"* most Christians don't really know that of which is being addressed. They automatically think of the Law of Moses, thereby dismissing it as not applying to them.

In a sense that is true; however, the problem with the modern Believer is not so much the Law of Moses, as it is laws that we make up ourselves, or laws devised by our Church or Denomination, or Preachers, etc. In fact, we turn many good things into laws, but irrespective as to what it is, in the eyes of

God, it is constituted as *"law."* Our faith is to be exclusively in Christ, and what Christ has done for us at the Cross. If it is shifted to other things, we are looked at by God as a *"spiritual adulterer."*

Does that mean that such a Christian is lost?

No it doesn't. Paul himself functioned in such a state, and we speak of a period of time after his initial Salvation and being baptized with the Holy Spirit. In fact, the Seventh Chapter of Romans records this particular time in the life of the Apostle. He was trying to serve Christ by adhering to law, and the Lord revealed to him that in fact, he was committing *"spiritual adultery."* The Apostle cried to the Lord, and out of this desperation, the Lord gave him the great Revelation of the meaning of the New Covenant, which in effect, was and is the meaning of the Cross, which he gave to us in all of his Epistles, but especially the Sixth and Eighth Chapter of Romans.

But this one thing is for sure: if the Believer has placed himself in the position of *"spiritual adultery,"* his life will be a far cry from that which is intended by the Lord. In other words, even though he has more abundant life, he definitely will not be enjoying more abundant life (Jn. 10:10).

And as well, and as stated, the works of the flesh will manifest themselves in his life, and the facts are, such a person, if remaining in that state, can definitely lose his soul (Gal. 5:21).

THE CROSS

All of this which I am attempting to teach you, I have lived. And to be sure, I think for one to properly understand the Gospel, in one way or the other, one has to live the Gospel.

If the Reader thinks that I press the issue too much regarding the Cross, then let the Reader understand the following:

The pendulum has swung so far the other way, and I speak of the opposite direction of the Cross, that greater pressure than usual must be applied, in order to bring things back to a proper equilibrium. In other words, the Cross has been so little taught and preached in the last several decades that any more, the modern Church is all but Cross illiterate. To be ignorant on many things constitutes whatever it constitutes; however, to be ignorant on the Cross is to be ignorant of the very Gospel itself, with such ignorance bringing unmitigated disaster.

And as well, at times, and especially spiritual things, things have to be said over and over again, approaching them from every way possible, in order for the Believer to finally hear what is actually being said. As it regards the Cross, I have found that in order for the Believer to have a proper understanding of what the Bible teaches concerning this all-important factor, first of all, one has to break through the shell of false doctrine and even unbelief. Most Christians think as one man wrote me the other day: *"Why do you keep talking about the Cross? Every Christian already understands all about the Cross,"* he asked! The truth is, very few Christians know anything about the Cross, beyond the initial Salvation experience; and the truth is, they actually know precious little about even that.

I believe the Holy Spirit is going to make the truth of the Cross of Christ so plain in these last days that the Believer is going to have to come down on one side or the other. In fact, I believe that the great foundation message of the Cross of Christ is going to be, and in fact is, the dividing line between the True Church and the apostate church. This line is not Denominations, particular Churches, or even particular doctrines, but is rather the Cross of Christ.

THE CROSS IS NOT A DOCTRINE, BUT RATHER THE FOUNDATION OF ALL DOCTRINE

While the Message of the Cross definitely contains doctrine, in fact, within itself it is not doctrine, but rather the foundation of all Doctrine. Any and every doctrine which is not based squarely on the foundation of the Cross of Christ will, without fail, go into error.

I'm sure that Jesus looked at what He did on the Cross, considering the great price that He paid, as far more than a mere doctrine. In fact, it is the New Covenant, proven to us by the description of the Lord's Supper (I Cor. 11:24-31).

Actually, if one doesn't understand the Message of the Cross, then one really doesn't understand the Bible. Paul said:

"For the preaching of the Cross is to them who perish foolishness; but unto us who are saved it is the Power of God" (I Cor. 1:18).

The Greek word translated here *"preaching,"* is *"Logos,"* and should rather have been translated *"word"* or *"message,"* for that's actually what it means. Paul was really saying: *"For the Message of the Cross is to them who perish foolishness. . . ."* In other words, he was saying that if one doesn't understand the Message of the Cross, they will ultimately *"perish."* That's blunt, but oh so true!

That's the reason I take every opportunity given to me in writing commentary on this great Book of Exodus to portray to you, the Reader, the great Message of the Cross. In fact, I cannot do less!

PREPARATION

Verses 2 and 3 read: *"Speak now in the ears of the people, and let every man borrow of his neighbor, and every woman of her neighbor, jewels of silver and jewels of gold.*

"And the LORD gave the people favor in the sight of the Egyptians. Moreover the man Moses was very great in the land of Egypt, in the sight of Pharaoh's servants, and in the sight of the people."

The words in Verse 2, *"Speak now in the ears of the people,"* were the signal that it was time now to go; consequently, all preparations are now to be made.

I want to say the same thing to those who are reading this Commentary. I am speaking the Word of the Lord into your ears, and I'm telling you that you have been bound by the Evil One long enough, if in fact that is the case. It's time for you to go on to victory, and total victory. There must not be any weight or sin left within your heart and life. The Holy Spirit is telling you that now you know the right way, the Way of the Cross. Place your faith in that Finished Work is what the Spirit is speaking into your ears, and victory will be yours (Rom. 6:3-5, 11, 14).

I'm not saying that there won't be difficulty. If we are to look at this situation as given to us in these first Chapters of Exodus, we find that Pharaoh did not let Israel go easily; and neither will the Evil One let you go easily. He will put up a fight. But if your faith will anchor into the Cross, and you will not allow it to be moved, irrespective of the initial failures that may come your way, ultimately, total and complete victory will be yours. The Scripture tells us, and in no uncertain terms: *"For sin shall not have dominion over you: for you are not under the law, but under Grace"* (Rom. 6:14).

Again I say it; the Holy Spirit is speaking these words into your ears. Act upon them. Jesus said: *"You shall know the Truth, and the Truth shall make you free"* (Jn. 8:32).

A PREDICTION

Continuing to deal with the phrase, *"Speak now in the ears of the people,"* I am speaking to you what I believe the Lord has spoken to me.

It is March 18, 2002, as I dictate these notes. I believe the Lord has spoken to my heart, and I'm speaking these words to you, that He is about to do great and mighty things.

I have just returned from Prayer Meeting. There was a great moving of the Holy Spirit upon my heart, as I began to seek the Lord, and concerning these very words. I believe the Lord has told me to *"speak now in the ears of the people,"* that what He is now about to do is going to be greater than anything He has ever done. The Lord never subtracts, but always multiplies. He takes what has been done in the past, and builds on that, and enlarges it.

I believe we're going to see more people saved, more people baptized with the Holy Spirit, and more people delivered by the Power of God, than we've ever seen before. I believe what is going to be done is even going to eclipse what was recorded in the Book of Acts. The Lord has said: *"And it shall come to pass in the last days, saith God, I will pour out of My Spirit upon all flesh"* (Acts 2:17). This is what I'm speaking into your ears, and this is what I believe is going to shortly come to pass, and in fact, has already begun.

BORROW

The Hebrew word *"Shaal,"* translated, *"borrow,"* actually should have been translated *"ask."* *"Borrow"* carries the connotation that the object obtained will be returned; however, Israel wasn't coming back into

Egypt, so there was no thought of returning these items.

As the Scripture says that the *"Lord gave the people favor in the sight of the Egyptians,"* it means that the Egyptians gladly gave these items to the Children of Israel, and furthermore, the terminology can be made to read, *"Press them to take."*

Concerning this, Pulpit Commentary says: *"It is worthy of notice that gold and silver ornaments, earrings, collars, armlets, bracelets, and anklets, were worn almost as much by the Egyptian men of that particular period as by the women."*

The word *"jewels"* carries a very wide meaning, and might even include drinking-cups and other vessels, etc.

With Egypt virtually destroyed, and the general populace knowing that Moses was the man who had brought about these plagues, the entirety of Egypt now looked at him almost like a *"God."* Even the Court of Pharaoh looked at him in this manner, and no wonder!

In all of this, we deduce that Christ will have all that He has died to purchase; all that He has bought with blood He will have; not a fraction of the purchased possession will He lose. Every Believer should by all means lay claim to the great Promises of God. We must have all for which Jesus died. Whatever the Lord has planned for us, and He definitely has planned something even an inheritance, for every single Believer, we must resolve that we shall have it. To be sure, the Evil One will do all within his power to hinder, but if we keep believing, he must deliver up all that belongs to us, for he dare not cross the line regarding that for which Jesus died, and for which we believe.

(4) "AND MOSES SAID, THUS SAITH THE LORD, ABOUT MIDNIGHT WILL I GO OUT INTO THE MIDST OF EGYPT:

(5) "AND ALL THE FIRSTBORN IN THE LAND OF EGYPT SHALL DIE, FROM THE FIRSTBORN OF PHARAOH WHO SITS UPON HIS THRONE, EVEN UNTO THE FIRSTBORN OF THE MAIDSERVANT THAT IS BEHIND THE MILL; AND ALL THE FIRSTBORN OF BEASTS.

(6) "AND THERE SHALL BE A GREAT CRY THROUGHOUT ALL THE LAND OF EGYPT, SUCH AS THERE WAS NONE LIKE IT, NOR SHALL IT BE LIKE IT ANY MORE.

(7) "BUT AGAINST ANY OF THE CHILDREN OF ISRAEL SHALL NOT A DOG MOVE HIS TONGUE, AGAINST MAN OR BEAST: THAT YOU MAY KNOW HOW THAT THE LORD DOES PUT A DIFFERENCE BETWEEN THE EGYPTIANS AND ISRAEL.

(8) "AND ALL THESE YOUR SERVANTS SHALL COME DOWN UNTO ME, AND BOW DOWN THEMSELVES UNTO ME, SAYING, GET THEE OUT, AND ALL THE PEOPLE WHO FOLLOW YOU: AND AFTER THAT I WILL GO OUT. AND HE WENT OUT FROM PHARAOH IN A GREAT ANGER.

(9) "AND THE LORD SAID UNTO MOSES, PHARAOH SHALL NOT HEARKEN UNTO YOU; THAT MY WONDERS MAY BE MULTIPLIED IN THE LAND OF EGYPT.

(10) "AND MOSES AND AARON DID ALL THESE WONDERS BEFORE PHARAOH: AND THE LORD HARDENED PHARAOH'S HEART, SO THAT HE WOULD NOT LET THE CHILDREN OF ISRAEL GO OUT OF HIS LAND."

MIDNIGHT

Verse 4 reads: *"And Moses said, Thus saith the LORD, About midnight will I go out into the midst of Egypt."*

It seems that Verse 4 picks up where Verse 29 of Chapter 10 left off, and continues through the conclusion of Chapter 11. Moses gives Pharaoh the final word from the Lord, and to be sure, it was a chilling assessment.

The *"midnight"* of which the Lord spoke was specified to be on the twenty-first day of the month, the month *"Abib,"* which was to be *"the beginning of months"* (Ex. 12:2, 18).

Even though the Lord would definitely give Israel explicit instructions as it regards what was to be done, even as we will study regarding the next Chapter, it is not known if the information concerning the exact time was to be given to Pharaoh or not. But yet, concerning what Moses had said to Pharaoh as it concerned the death of the firstborn, and the preparations being made by the Children of Israel, most definitely, Egypt would have been well aware of these happenings.

Truly it was *"midnight"* for Egypt. The day of Grace was over, and judgment was about to begin.

As well, I think one can say without any fear of Scriptural contradiction that it is *"midnight"* for the world. This dispensation has about run its course. The dark clouds of world tribulation loom over the horizon, and the great prophecies of the Book of Revelation are about to be fulfilled; consequently, the Rapture of the Church must be very, very close (I Thess. 4:13-18).

THE FIRSTBORN

Verse 5 reads: *"And all the firstborn in the land of Egypt shall die, from the firstborn of Pharaoh who sits upon his throne, even unto the firstborn of the maidservant who is behind the mill; and all the firstborn of beasts."*

The death of all the *"firstborn"* in Egypt constituted a severe blow. The monarchy was hereditary, and the oldest son was known as the *"hereditary Crowned Prince."* Estates descended to the oldest son and in many cases high dignities also. No severer blow could have been sent on the nation, if it were not to be annihilated, than the loss in each house of the hope of the family.

And to consider that even Pharaoh, who was looked at as a god in Egypt, was not to be excluded as well, with this terrible darkness running to the poorest of the poor also, even including the animals, one can see the severity of this plague.

(If there were no males in the family, the oldest daughter would serve in that capacity.) However, in most families, it was a male which was the firstborn, for the simple reason that the family name could not continue unless there was a male born into the family. Therefore, most families continued having children until a boy was born.

In the 1700's, massive graves were opened in Egypt by archaeological excavations. These contained the bodies of multiple thousands of males. The ages were from little infants up to adults.

Tests showed they all died and were embalmed at approximately the same time period. Even though there is no concrete proof that the burial of all these males at the same time pertained to the tenth and last plague, still, it was ascertained that they were buried at approximately the same time of the Exodus from Egypt, and could very well have been the bodies of those, the firstborn, stricken by the death angel.

SORROW

Verse 6 reads: *"And there shall be a great cry throughout all the land of Egypt, such as there was none like it, nor shall be like it any more."*

The *"cry"* that was registered in Egypt must not be blamed on a loving and compassionate God, but on the stubbornness of Pharaoh, and as well, of a hard-hearted people.

THE DIFFERENCE

Verse 7 reads: *"But against any of the Children of Israel shall not a dog move his tongue, against man or beast: that you may know how that the LORD does put a difference between the Egyptians and Israel."*

The idea is, the Children of Israel will suffer no hurt whatsoever. Not even so much as a dog will bark at them.

From this one statement, concerning the Lord putting a difference between the Egyptians and Israel, we learn as to the love that the Lord has for His people. It certainly has changed no less now with the Church.

DOES GOD SEND JUDGMENT UPON HIS CHILDREN?

In a word, no!

He will certainly send judgment on those who have once been His children, but have turned their backs on Him, and are now living in a state of rebellion. But the sad fact of that matter is, they are no longer His Children.

All the judgment was placed upon Christ, just as the death of the Paschal Lamb will illustrate here. So, the idea that God would continue to send judgment upon His Children, in effect states that Jesus didn't suffer enough, and we need to add something to His suffering. To be frank, such is an insult to Christ and the tremendous price that He paid at the Cross, all on our behalf.

But while the Lord does not send judgment on His Children, He definitely does chastise all Believers. In fact, if there is no chastisement, then the Scripture plainly tells us that we are *"bastards and not sons"* (Heb. 12:8).

There is, however, a vast difference between chastisement and judgment. The case of judgment is meant to punish, while chastisement is meant to correct.

ANGER

Verse 8 reads: *"And all these your servants shall come down unto me, and bow down themselves unto me, saying, You get out, and all the people who follow you: and after that I will go out. And he went out from Pharaoh in a great anger."*

This Passage portrays Moses delivering the last Message to Pharaoh. It is straight and to the point.

Moses informed the Monarch that the high Officers of the Court, who were even then standing about Pharaoh, would come to Moses when the blow fell, and prostrate themselves before him as if he were their king, and beseech him to take his departure with all his people. With their firstborn dead, and the whole nation in mourning, they would now beg Israel to leave.

Moses went out from the presence of Pharaoh with great anger, because he knew that all of this was so unnecessary. Hundreds of thousands would die, and the truth is, not one single person needed to die. Moses was angry at the stubbornness and obstinacy of the Monarch, who had watched Egypt little by little as it was destroyed, but still refused to acquiesce to the demands of Almighty God.

Let the Reader know and understand that it is useless to fight against God. And whenever men fight against God's people, they are fighting against God. Another thought as well, needs to be inserted here.

Believers should be very, very careful that they do not oppose the one who is of God. To oppose one who is of God is to oppose God. And even Christians can find themselves in perilous straits, because of such opposition.

Do you think the Lord blandly overlooked the Believers during Paul's day, who sought to hinder the great Apostle, especially considering the Call of God on his life? I don't think so.

NOTES

While it's bad enough for unbelievers to oppose God, it is even worse for Believers to oppose God. Believers should know better; but regrettably, far too often Believers are led by men instead of by the Lord.

WONDERS

Verse 9 reads: *"And the LORD said unto Moses, Pharaoh shall not hearken unto you; that My wonders may be multiplied in the land of Egypt."*

There is no doubt that all the surrounding nations knew minutely of all that had gone on, and was going on in Egypt. It had to be the talk of that part of the world. Never before in history had such a thing taken place in any nation. And when one considers that Egypt was at least one of, if not the most powerful nation on the face of the Earth, this made everything of even greater significance.

Two men, shepherds, without an army, without prancing steeds of war, had brought the mightiest nation on Earth to its knees. But of course, it was the Lord Who did this, and not Moses and Aaron. They were merely instruments, but the heathen did not really know or understand this. As stated, in the eyes of the people of Egypt, Moses was to them, a God!

THE HARDENED HEART

Verse 10 reads: *"And Moses and Aaron did all these wonders before Pharaoh: and the LORD hardened Pharaoh's heart, so that he would not let the Children of Israel go out of his land."*

What was Pharaoh thinking?

While the other plagues had been terrifying, this last plague was of such horror as to defy all description. The firstborn in every home would die, even beginning with Pharaoh. And yet, Pharaoh continues to rebel and resist.

Once again we state the fact that God did not force the will of the Monarch, but that He definitely took advantage of the direction that Pharaoh was going — the direction of rebellion. As previously stated, the Sun which hardens clay, softens wax. The fault or the difference is not in the Sun or its rays, but in the material upon which it acts.

God did not force Pharaoh to take the position he took, but He definitely did supply the means by which Pharaoh could travel this road of rebellion, if he so desired, and most definitely God would take advantage of the situation, which He did!

Nations that place themselves in the path of God, with obstinate desire to circumvent His Plan, are always destroyed.

I looked at the gas ovens of Auswitz, to my knowledge the first concentration camp to be built by the Germans, as it regarded the destruction of the Jewish people. It is said that in Munich, about 30 miles away, when the wind was blowing in that direction, those in the city could smell the bodies being burned. Germany was going to rule the world, or so they thought! Along the way, they would exterminate the Jewish people, and in fact did slaughter some six million.

Germany is no more; her cities pulverized by American and British bombers. Despite Germany's hideous actions, Israel is today a State because that is what the Lord wanted.

Men thought it would take a hundred years for the Berlin Wall to come down; it came down in hours. Others thought the Iron Curtain would never crumble; it crumbled in days. At this moment, the nations of the world are being jockeyed into position for the Great Tribulation Period and the rise of the Antichrist. The Bible is God's Word. As He spoke to Pharaoh through Moses and carried out exactly what He said He would do, as well, He will do exactly what He says He will do in these last days. God's Word is true!

"The strife is over, the battle done;
"The victory of life is won;
"The song of triumph has begun;
"Hallelujah!"

"The powers of death have done their worst,
"But Christ their legions has dispersed;
"Let shouts of holy joy outburst:
"Hallelujah!"

"The three sad days have quickly sped,
"He rises glorious from the dead;
"All glory to our risen Head:
"Hallelujah!"

"Lord, by the stripes which wounded Thee,
"From death's dread sting Your servants free,
"That we may live and sing to Thee:
"Hallelujah!"

CHAPTER 12

(1) "AND THE LORD SPOKE UNTO MOSES AND AARON IN THE LAND OF EGYPT SAYING,

(2) "THIS MONTH SHALL BE UNTO YOU THE BEGINNING OF MONTHS: IT SHALL BE THE FIRST MONTH OF THE YEAR TO YOU.

(3) "YOU SHALL SPEAK UNTO ALL THE CONGREGATION OF ISRAEL, SAYING, IN THE TENTH DAY OF THIS MONTH THEY SHALL TAKE TO THEM EVERY MAN A LAMB, ACCORDING TO THE HOUSE OF THEIR FATHERS, A LAMB FOR AN HOUSE:

(4) "AND IF THE HOUSEHOLD BE TOO LITTLE FOR THE LAMB, LET HIM AND HIS NEIGHBOR NEXT UNTO HIS HOUSE TAKE IT ACCORDING TO THE NUMBER OF THE SOULS; EVERY MAN ACCORDING TO HIS EATING SHALL MAKE YOUR COUNT FOR THE LAMB.

(5) "YOUR LAMB SHALL BE WITHOUT BLEMISH, A MALE OF THE FIRST YEAR: YOU SHALL TAKE IT OUT FROM THE SHEEP, OR FROM THE GOATS:

(6) "AND YOU SHALL KEEP IT UP UNTIL THE FOURTEENTH DAY OF THE SAME MONTH: AND THE WHOLE ASSEMBLY OF THE CONGREGATION OF ISRAEL SHALL KILL IT IN THE EVENING."

The structure is:

1. The Twelfth Chapter of Exodus is a perfect picture of Christ, the True Paschal Lamb.

2. The Passover was to forever serve as the *"type"* of Christ, and it had been kept for nearly 1,600 years, when He died on the Cross. Actually, Christ died at 3:00 p.m. at the exact time the Passover Lamb was being offered.

3. Considering that the blood of bulls and goats could never take away sins, it was not by such a sacrifice that people were saved, but by having Faith in the One which the

Sacrifice represented, namely, the Lord Jesus Christ. Salvation has always been by Faith.

THE BEGINNING

Verses 1 and 2 read: *"And the LORD spoke unto Moses and Aaron in the land of Egypt saying,*

"This month shall be unto you the beginning of months: it shall be the first month of the year to you."

The Twelfth Chapter of Exodus is, without a doubt, one of the singular most important Chapters in the entirety of the Bible. It ranks with the Fourth Chapter of Genesis, and other similar Chapters.

Its vast significance covers much theological area. Not only was the means of deliverance effected for the Children of Israel, which extricated them from the clutches of Pharaoh, a type of Satan himself, but as well, the pattern was drawn as it regards the coming Redeemer, and what He would do as it regards the Salvation of the entirety of mankind. I speak of the Cross, and most of all, of the price that Jesus would pay on that wooden gibbet.

Another great lesson learned here is the fact that neither Moses nor Aaron introduced any legislation of their own, either at this time or later. The whole system, spiritual, political, and ecclesiastical was received by Divine Revelation, commanded by God, and merely established by the agency of the two brothers (Pulpit). This proclaims the fact that Salvation is all of God and none of man. The problem presents itself when man attempts to insert his means and ways, into that which God has devised.

Verse 2 proclaims the fact that the month of *"Abib,"* became the first month of the year, which corresponds with our April. (Abib would later be called *"Nisan."*)

In effect, this tells us that a person doesn't begin to live, until he comes to Christ. From that particular time everything ends, and everything begins. It is actually *"the beginning."*

I can sense the Presence of the Lord even as I dictate these words. How wonderful it is to know the Lord, to have this new life, this eternal life!

I was saved, i.e., *"born again,"* at the age of eight. The year was 1943, and I regret very much that I do not remember the month or the day.

It must as well be remembered that the Children of Israel were condemned to death, just as much as were the Egyptians. The difference was, the Children of Israel availed themselves of God's deliverance and Redemption Plan.

Exodus, Chapter 12 records the last of the ten plagues. This was the death of the firstborn, and inasmuch as death is *"the wages of sin,"* we have no difficulty in perceiving that it is the question of *"sin"* which is raised here and dealt with by God. This being the case, both the Egyptians and the Israelites alike were obnoxious to His righteous judgment, for both were sinners before Him. In this respect, the Egyptians and the Israelites were alike: both in nature and in practice they were sinners. There is no difference: for all have sinned and come short of the Glory of God (Rom. 3:22-23).

While it is true that God had purposed to redeem Israel out of Egypt, He would do so only on a righteous basis. Holiness can never ignore sin, and neither can Covenants, no matter where it is found. When the angels sinned, God *"spared them not"* (II Pet. 2:4). The elect are *"children of wrath even as others"* (Eph. 2:3). In fact, God made no exception, even as it regarded His Own Blessed Son: when He was *"made sin for us"* (II Cor. 5:21) — He spared Him not (Rom. 8:32).

A SUBSTITUTE

The further we go into the business of sin, and the more we realize that all fall under its dread yoke, this only seems to make the problem more impossible of solution. The Israelites were sinners: their guilt was irrefutably established: a just God can *"by no means clear the guilty"* (Ex. 34:7): sentence of death was passed upon them (Ex. 11:5). Nothing remained but the carrying out of the sentence.

And why would we go into such detail here, as it regards this fact?

A reprieve was out of the question. Justice must be satisfied; sin must be paid its wages. Human wisdom has no solution. And yet, infinite wisdom says, *"Where sin abounded, Grace did much more abound"* (Rom. 5:20).

But yet, Grace is never extended at the expense of Righteousness. We must always remember that. Every demand of justice must be satisfied; every claim of holiness must be fully met. So how could it be done?

It can only be done by the means of a *"substitute."* Sentence of death was executed, but it fell upon an innocent victim. That which was *"without blemish"* died in the stead of those who had *"no soundness"* (Isa. 1:6) in them.

The *"difference"* between the Egyptians and Israel was not a moral one, but was made solely by the blood of the Paschal Lamb! It was in the Blood of the Lamb that *"Mercy and Truth met together, and Righteousness and Peace kissed each other"* (Ps. 85:10).

SACRIFICE

Yesterday morning at Family Worship Center, actually preaching on the subject of the deliverance of the Children of Israel from Egyptian bondage, the Holy Spirit helped me to bring out the point that it was always the sacrifice which was inspected, and not the bringer of the sacrifice. It was a foregone conclusion that the offerer of the sacrifice was sinful and wicked. In fact, that was the very purpose and reason for the sacrifice. There was no doubt about that!

Therefore, forgiveness and pardon could never be based upon the Righteousness of the sinner, so it was the Sacrifice which was inspected closely. If it met the criteria, if in fact it was accepted, this instantly meant that the offerer of the sacrifice was accepted as well.

When I said these words, the Spirit of God flowed like a river over the congregation, as they caught the meaning of what was being said to them.

We are saved and we are kept, not because we are good, but because our Faith is in One Who was and is good, and I speak of the Lord Jesus Christ. But it was not His goodness that saved us, not by a long shot, but rather the Sacrifice of Himself, in the giving and shedding of His Own Precious Blood. Paul said: *"Who gave Himself for our sins, that He might deliver us from this present evil world, according to the Will of God and our Father"* (Gal. 1:4).

Because of its great significance, let me say it again: *"If the sacrifice is accepted, the sacrificer is accepted as well. If the sacrifice is rejected, the one offering the sacrifice is also rejected."*

There is only one Sacrifice that's acceptable to God, and that is the Sacrifice of His Son and our Saviour, the Lord Jesus Christ. Faith in Him guarantees acceptance by God of our person. The rejection of Him and the price that He paid at the Cross as our Substitute, guarantees our rejection. That's the reason I preach the Cross so strongly! That's the reason I proclaim the veracity of the shed Blood of the Lamb! That's the reason that Paul also said:

"But though we, or an Angel from Heaven, preach any other Gospel unto you than that which we have preached unto you, let him be accursed" (Gal. 1:8).

A LAMB FOR AN HOUSE

Verse 3 reads: *"Speak ye unto all the congregation of Israel, saying, In the tenth day of this month, they shall take to them every man a lamb, according to the house of their fathers, a lamb for an house."*

In the Fourth Chapter of Genesis, it is a lamb for each person, one might say. Now it is a lamb for each house. Upon the giving of the Law, it would be a lamb for the entirety of the nation. But when Jesus came, He would be the Lamb for the entirety of the world.

John said of Him: *"Behold the Lamb of God, which taketh away the sin of the world"* (Jn. 1:29).

Why a lamb?

Actually the Hebrew word used for lamb *"seh,"* could be applied equally to sheep or goats. But history records that almost without exception, it was lambs which were offered. The Lord is the One Who demanded that this type of animal be offered. Under the Law, goats, bullocks, heifers, and rams could also be offered, but for the most part it was lambs.

The lamb represented innocence and gentleness. The Prophets represented the tender compassion of God for His people under the figure of the shepherd and the lamb (Isa. 40:11), and ultimately the intention of

God for His people used the lamb as an important symbol.

David, in writing Psalm 23, carried the imagery of the shepherd and the lamb to its most beautiful expression. Likewise the lamb was the climax of prophetic symbolism of the suffering of God's people, the servant nation, which the New Testament found to be a prefiguring of Jesus (Isa. 53:7; Acts 8:32). The lamb was a worthy symbol of Jesus Who, in innocence, patiently endured suffering as our Substitute (I Pet. 1:19).

Of special interest is the use of the term *"lamb"* in the Book of Revelation where it occurs 28 times, all in symbolic reference to Christ.

The introductory reference in Revelation 5:1-14 is to the Lamb triumphant. This description of the Lamb and the works attributed to Him clearly identify Him as the Christ.

The use of the title or the name *"Lamb"* in the Book of Revelation is somewhat different than its use elsewhere in the New Testament; however, it is most likely that it really has the same meaning, a symbolic representation of the Redemptive Work of Christ, with the added representation of that Redemptive Work viewed in connection with its triumphant victory over all things (Drumwright).

SOULS

Verse 4 reads: *"If the household be too little for the lamb, let him and his neighbor next unto his house take it according to the number of the souls; every man according to his eating shall make your count for the lamb."*

Several things are said here:

1. Every person had to partake. This was mandatory. Due to the fact of all the miracles which had been performed, I can hardly think that there would have been even one Israelite who would have been reticent in this.

2. As we shall later see, the entirety of the lamb had to be consumed, which has a tremendous spiritual meaning, which we will deal with more fully, when we come to Verse 10.

3. The whole family was to participate, men, women, and children.

A TYPE OF CHRIST

Verse 5 reads: *"Your lamb shall be without blemish, a male of the first year: you shall take it out from the sheep, or from the goats."*

It was fitting that the Paschal Lamb should be without defect of any kind, as especially typifying *"the Lamb of God,"* who is *"holy, harmless, undefiled"* — a *"lamb without spot."*

It is said that in later years, after the Law was given, that each lamb at the morning and evening sacrifices was minutely inspected. In fact, after it was killed, the flesh would be laid open at the backbone and inspected minutely for even a slight discoloration. If so, it would be laid aside, and another lamb selected. As stated, this represented Christ, and had to be *"without blemish."*

In fact, these particular sacrifices were referred to as *"most holy"* (Lev. 6:17, 25, 29; 7:1, 6; 10:12, 17; 14:13).

This debunks the erroneous idea, as proclaimed by some, that Jesus died spiritually on the Cross. They teach that not only did He die physically, but as well He died spiritually, which refers to the fact that He, they claim, died as a sinner. They extend His bearing the sin penalty, which He definitely did, to Him actually becoming a sinner.

However, several things must be noted:

First of all, one cannot be said to be a sinner, unless one has sinned, and Jesus Christ never sinned. As stated, He definitely did bear the penalty of sin, and that for the entirety of the world, and for all time; however, there is a world of difference in bearing the penalty for something, which incidentally was death, than actually being that for which the penalty must be borne. In fact, had He been a sinner, which means to have sinned even one time, He would have been totally unfit to serve as a sacrifice. He had to be, both physically and spiritually, *"without blemish,"* which He most definitely was.

They claim that He died as a sinner, went to Hell, and we speak of the burning side of Hell, where He suffered there for three days and three nights, with Satan believing that he had won this conflict. At the end of the three days and nights, they claim, God said, *"It is enough,"* and Jesus was then *"born again,"* exactly as any sinner is born again.

Now you will look in vain in the Bible for this foolishness, because it simply doesn't exist, because it never happened.

The death of Christ on the Cross, planned from before the foundation of the world (I Pet. 1:18-20), was meant to pay the penalty of sin, which it did. In that, the shedding of His Life's Blood, for the life of the flesh is in the blood, guaranteed our Salvation, at least for those who will believe (Jn. 3:16). While His death definitely included punishment, it was not punishment which effected our Salvation, but rather the paying of the penalty.

"A male of the first year," was meant to portray the virulent manhood of Christ. In other words, He didn't die in the throes of old age, but rather the prime of manhood.

THE EVENING SACRIFICE

Verse 6 reads: *"And you shall keep it up until the fourteenth day of the same month: and the whole assembly of the congregation of Israel shall kill it in the evening."*

On the tenth day (Vs. 3) they were to select the lamb, and then on the fourteenth day it was to be killed. During the intervening four days, they could inspect the animal minutely, making certain that it was *"without blemish."*

Each house was to kill the little animal *"in the evening,"* which corresponds with the time of the evening sacrifice, which was at 3:00 p.m., which would later be enacted. This was the time that Jesus died on the Cross — 3:00 p.m.

However, the *"evening"* mentioned here probably referred to any time before sunset.

(7) "AND THEY SHALL TAKE OF THE BLOOD, AND STRIKE IT ON THE TWO SIDE POSTS AND ON THE UPPER DOOR POST OF THE HOUSES, WHEREIN THEY SHALL EAT IT.

(8) "AND THEY SHALL EAT THE FLESH IN THAT NIGHT, ROAST WITH FIRE, AND UNLEAVENED BREAD; AND WITH BITTER HERBS THEY SHALL EAT IT.

(9) "EAT NOT OF IT RAW, NOR SODDEN AT ALL WITH WATER, BUT ROAST WITH FIRE; HIS HEAD WITH HIS LEGS, AND WITH THE PURTENANCE THEREOF.

(10) "AND YOU SHALL LET NOTHING OF IT REMAIN UNTIL THE MORNING; AND THAT WHICH REMAINS OF IT UNTIL THE MORNING YOU SHALL BURN WITH FIRE.

NOTES

(11) "AND THUS SHALL YOU EAT IT; WITH YOUR LOINS GIRDED, YOUR SHOES ON YOUR FEET, AND YOUR STAFF IN YOUR HAND; AND YOU SHALL EAT IT IN HASTE: IT IS THE LORD'S PASSOVER."

The composition is:

1. The blood represented the shed Blood of the Lord Jesus Christ.
2. The *"fire"* spoke of the Judgment of God that should have come upon us, but came upon Christ instead.
3. The *"unleavened bread"* spoke of His sinless Body. Leaven is a form of rot or sin. Christ *"knew no sin."*
4. They were to eat all of the lamb, referring to the fact that we must accept all of Christ.

THE BLOOD

Verse 7 reads: *"And they shall take of the blood, and strike it on the two side posts and on the upper door post of the houses, wherein they shall eat it."*

The whole value of the blood of the Paschal Lamb lay in its being a Type of the Lord Jesus — *"Christ our Passover is sacrificed for us: Therefore let us keep the feast"* (I Cor. 5:7-8). Here is Divine authority for our regarding the contents of Exodus, Chapter 12 as typical of the Cross-Work of our Blessed Saviour. And it is this which invests every detail of our Chapter with such deep interest.

May our eyes be anointed so that we shall be able to perceive some, at least, of the precious unfoldings of the Truth which are typically set forth in this great Chapter (Pink).

At this time, the blood, which represented the shed Blood of Christ, was to be put on the side posts and the upper posts of the house. Later, it would be applied to the Mercy Seat on the Great Day of Atonement. Now, by Faith, it is applied to our hearts (Jn. 3:16).

The blood applied to the doorway is probably to be connected with the idea that the secondary agency producing death, whatever it was, would enter by the door — and if the door showed the house to have been atoned for, would not enter.

Concerning all of this, Mackintosh said: *"Now, the lamb taken on the tenth day,* and kept up until the fourteenth day, shows us Christ foreordained of God from eternity, but manifest for us in time. God's eternal purpose in Christ becomes the foundation of the Believer's peace. Nothing short of this would do.

"We are carried back far beyond creation, beyond the bounds of time, beyond the entrance in of sin and everything that could possibly affect the groundwork of our peace. The expression, 'foreordained before the foundation of the world,' as Peter used the term, conducts us back into the unfathomed depths of eternity, and shows us God forming His Own councils of redeeming love, and basing them all upon the atoning Blood of His Own precious, spotless lamb. Christ was ever the primary thought in the Divine mind; and hence, the moment He began to speak or act, He took occasion to shadow forth that One Who occupied the highest place in His counsels and affections; and, as we pass along the current of inspiration, we find that every ceremony, every rite, every ordinance, and every sacrifice pointed forward to 'the Lamb of God that taketh away the sin of the world,' and not one more strikingly than the Passover. The Paschal Lamb, with all the attendant circumstances, forms one of the most profoundly interesting and deeply instructive types of Scripture."

The family gathered round the lamb, even as we will see in the following Verses, and partaking of this particular feast, i.e., *"the Passover,"* presents the picture of the Church, gathered by the Holy Spirit, all in the Name of Jesus. The entirety of the Bible is about Christ, and more particularly, what Christ did in order to redeem lost humanity, and as well, to satisfy the Righteousness and Justice of a thrice-Holy God. For the Cross, as we will later see, had a twofold effect. It was both manward and Godward.

BITTER HERBS

Verse 8 reads: *"And they shall eat the flesh in that night, roast with fire, and unleavened bread; and with bitter herbs they shall eat it."*

The *"eating the flesh"* pertains to the Words of Christ, when He said: *"I am the living bread which came down from Heaven: if any man eat of this bread, he shall live forever: and the bread that I will give is my flesh, which I will give for the life of the world."*

He then said: *"Except you eat the flesh of the Son of Man, and drink His Blood, you have no life in you.*

"Whoso eats My flesh, and drinks My Blood, has eternal life" (Jn. 6:51, 53-54).

What did Jesus mean by all of this?

He would momentarily ask the question, *"Does this offend you?"*

He then said: *"It is the Spirit Who quickens; the flesh profits nothing: the words that I speak unto you, they are spirit, and they are life"* (Jn. 6:61, 63).

By using this terminology, Jesus was speaking of the death He would die on the Cross, by the giving of Himself, i.e., *"the flesh,"* and the Blood that He would shed.

In essence, *"we eat His flesh, and drink His Blood,"* when we evidence Faith in what He did at the Cross. When such Faith is evidenced, in the Mind of God, the Believer is literally baptized into the Death of Christ, buried with Him, and raised with Him in newness of life (Rom. 6:3-5).

It is far more than a mere mental acceptance or even a philosophical acceptance of something. Faith puts us into Christ, and what He did for us, which the eating of the lamb at the Passover represented.

The Passover represented Salvation, in that we were delivered from the powers of darkness to the Lord of Glory. But if it is to be noticed, the Sacrificial System did not begin and end with the Passover. In fact, there were five different Sacrificial Offerings instituted in the Law of Moses, with all of them, with the exception of one (the meat or food Offering), pertaining to the shedding of blood. So what are we saying?

We are saying that exactly as the sinner is to look to Christ and the Cross for Salvation, likewise, the Believer is to continue to look to Christ and the Cross, as it regards his Sanctification.

HOW TO LIVE FOR GOD

Just this morning on our daily Radio program, *"A Study In The Word"*, I made the statement, which I realize is controversial, *"Most Christians in the modern*

Church simply do not know how to live for God." Now that's quite a statement, but it is true.

The way to properly live for God according to the Word of God can perhaps be described in the following brief formula:

1. Focus: Christ and Him Crucified.
2. Object of Faith: The Finished Work of Christ.
3. Power Source: The Holy Spirit.
4. Results: perpetual victory.

But regrettably, that which we have given is little taught and understood in most Churches, with the following rather being the manner in which most Believers try to live for God.

1. Focus: Works.
2. Object of Faith: Performance.
3. Power Source: Self.
4. Results: perpetual defeat.

Paul addressed this by saying: *"But now we are delivered from the law* (from its penalty by and through the Death of Christ), *that being dead wherein we were held; that we should serve in newness of spirit, and not in the oldness of the letter"* (Rom. 7:6).

The first diagram I gave pertained to the *"newness of spirit."* The second pertains to the *"oldness of the letter."*

God has one way of Salvation, which is Jesus Christ and Him Crucified (I Cor. 1:23). He also has one way of victory for the Saint, and that is *"Jesus Christ and Him Crucified"* (I Cor. 2:2).

As is obvious, it is the same for both Salvation and Sanctification.

DO YOU UNDERSTAND THE CROSS?

In fact, the Cross of Christ is the simplest system in the world. Concerning this, Paul said:

"But I fear, lest by any means, as the serpent beguiled Eve through his subtilty, so your minds should be corrupted from the simplicity that is in Christ" (II Cor. 11:3).

The Cross is not simple to some, simply because their minds are cluttered with all type of unbelief. And please understand, all false ways are connected with unbelief.

The truth is, most Christians are functioning in *"law,"* even though they do not really understand that to be the case. In fact, there are only two places that a Believer

NOTES

can position himself spiritually. It is either *"Grace"* or *"Law."*

Regrettably, many Christians have the idea that because this is the Dispensation of Grace, and it definitely is, this means that we are automatically under Grace. It doesn't!

Paul also said: *"I do not frustrate the Grace of God: for if Righteousness come by the Law, then Christ is dead in vain"* (Gal. 2:21).

The Apostle said several things in this one Passage.

First of all, he informs us that it is definitely possible to *"frustrate the Grace of God,"* which means to stop the Grace of God from coming to us.

So if it is possible to frustrate the Grace of God, and it definitely is, how is it done?

Whenever we seek to bring about Righteousness by law-keeping of some nature, we frustrate the Grace of God.

To make it simpler, this refers to Christians doing certain good things, or not doing certain bad things, which they think makes them righteous. Paul here bluntly tells us that such activity can never bring about Righteousness. In fact, as he goes on to say, if it could, *"then Christ is dead in vain,"* meaning that Jesus needlessly came down here to die on a Cross.

But the truth is, He did not needlessly die on a Cross. He did so, simply because there was no way that man could make himself righteous. In fact, Righteousness can come only in one manner and one way. That is by the Believer evidencing Faith totally and completely in Christ and what Christ has done for us at the Cross. When this is done, Righteousness is automatically imputed to the individual. Paul said:

"For by Grace are you saved through faith; and that not of yourselves (not by keeping laws, etc.); *it is the Gift of God:*

"Not of works, lest any man should boast" (Eph. 2:8-9).

To know how to be saved is one thing. To know how to live for God after one is saved is something else altogether. If it is to be noticed, there is very little information given in the Word of God as it regards the sinner being saved. To be sure, there are plenty of Passages that inform us of this great truth (Rom. 10:9-10, 13; Rev. 22:17; Jn. 3:16). But the greater bulk of the Word of God (far greater) is given over to telling the Believer how to live for God.

JUDGMENT

The lamb was to be roasted with fire, which typified the Judgment of God, which would come upon Christ, instead of coming upon us. That is the Godward part, which Calvary produced.

The manward part pertains to what the Cross made possible, and I speak of the Advent of the Holy Spirit. In other words, due to Christ atoning for all sin, which means the sin debt in its totality is paid, the Holy Spirit can now take up permanent residence within the heart and life of any Believer (Jn. 14:16-17). The Holy Spirit is also represented by fire, which symbolizes that which Calvary effects, the cleansing and purification of the Saint. The Cross satisfied the Righteousness and Justice of God, and at the same time, makes the Believer a fit subject for the Kingdom of God.

UNLEAVENED BREAD

This made typical the fact that Christ was and is Perfect. He was Perfect in His humanity in every respect, hence being worthy as a Perfect Sacrifice. *"Leaven"* is used in the Bible as representing sin and imperfection. The bread that was to be used in the Passover contained no leaven, proclaiming the fact that Jesus would have no sin. As we've already stated, had there been sin in Him in any capacity, He would not have been an acceptable Sacrifice. Only a perfect sacrifice could satisfy the Righteousness of God.

To the manward side, this portrays the fact that the Believer can as well live such a life, that sin will not have dominion over him (Rom. 6:14).

BITTER HERBS

The *"bitter herbs"* were to remind the Children of Israel of the slavery which they experienced in Egypt (Ex. 1:14).

THE PURTENANCE

Verse 9 reads: *"Eat not of it raw, nor sodden at all with water, but roast with fire; his head with his legs, and with the purtenance thereof."*

The purtenance pertained to the intestines, which were removed and washed, and then placed back in the animal and as obvious here, to be eaten when the lamb was consumed.

(Some claim that the intestines were not included here, but rather the heart, liver, and kidneys; however, it probably did include the intestines.)

"Eat not of it raw," has two meanings:

1. The Egyptians ate raw flesh in honor of one of their gods, Osiris. Thus, God was seeking to impress upon Israel that Egyptian practices must not be included in the instructions given concerning this all-important feast.

2. The *"roast with fire,"* as we've already stated, spoke of the Finished Work of Christ in taking the judgment intended for us upon Himself.

It speaks of the fact that Christ accepted, minus the Cross, affords no Salvation. Regrettably, this is the condition in which much of the modern Church world now finds itself. Calvary has been placed in a subservient position, if any position at all. In fact, the Word of Faith doctrine, which has made such inroads into Pentecostal and Charismatic Churches, openly repudiates the Cross, referring to it as *"the greatest defeat in human history."* Consequently, in many of their Churches, songs about the Blood, the Cross, the Sacrifice, and the price that Jesus paid, are not allowed to be sung. So, the error of these Churches and these Preachers is the worst error of all. To misunderstand anything as it regards the Word of God, always has a negative affect; however, to misunderstand the Atonement is to misunderstand the very heart of the Gospel. One can be saved and still at the same time believe many erroneous things; however, one cannot be saved and have a misunderstanding of the Atonement, and we speak of disallowing the Cross.

So, the lamb had to be *"roasted with fire,"* typifying the death that Christ would die on the Cross, of which the Altar was ever a type.

ALL OF CHRIST IS TO BE ACCEPTED

Verse 10 reads: *"And you shall let nothing of it remain until the morning; and that which remains of it until the morning you shall burn with fire."*

Two things are said here:

1. All of the lamb must be eaten;
2. Whatever was left concerning bones and fragments were to be burned with fire.

All of this tells us several things:

A. Christ would give His all for us, and we are to give our all for Him.

B. One must accept all of Christ, or one cannot have any of Christ. There are millions of Christians who want the prosperity Christ, but they don't want the Christ of the Cross. There are others who want the Salvation Christ, but not Christ the Baptizer with the Holy Spirit.

But the Scripture is emphatic. Christ is to be accepted in totality, and this means, and above all it means, that it is *"Jesus Christ and Him Crucified."* To accept Christ as merely a great Teacher, a great Miracle Worker, a great Provider regarding material things, or even a great Healer, and refuse to accept Christ and the Cross, are plainly forbidden here. It's all or nothing!

In fact, the only way that one can have Christ the Healer, the Provider, the Miracle Worker, etc., is to have Christ the Saviour, which speaks of the Cross.

To vividly portray Calvary, not only must the animal be roasted with fire, but as well, and as stated, even the scraps were to be burned and consumed with fire.

C. Last of all, it had to be eaten at one setting. Nothing was to be allowed to *"remain until the morning,"* meaning that a second meal would not be prepared, etc.

This tells us that Christ cannot be received in stages. He can only be received in totality.

To use a crude example, it's not possible for a woman to be partially pregnant. Neither can one partially accept Christ. Once again, it's all or nothing.

THE LORD'S PASSOVER

Verse 11 reads: *"And thus shall you eat it; with your loins girded, your shoes on your feet, and your staff in your hand; and you shall eat it in haste: it is the LORD's Passover."*

The *"loins girded,"* and the *"shoes on the feet,"* and the *"staff in the hand,"* proclaim the fact that they were leaving. Egypt was to be put behind them, and Canaan-land was to beckon.

NOTES

The same admonition holds true for the modern Believer, and in fact all Believers who have ever lived. Even though we have been saved out of this world, we are still in the world. We eagerly await the moment when the Trump of God shall sound, and, thereby, rapture us away (I Thess. 4:13-18).

After the Law was given, and Israel was safely ensconced in the Promised Land, they were to eat the Passover resting, and for all the obvious reasons. But the *"type"* still holds as it regards modern Believers, and our awaiting the Rapture of the Church.

Jesus said: *"Watch therefore, for you know neither the day nor the hour wherein the Son of Man cometh"* (Mat. 25:13).

If it is to be noticed, it is referred to as *"the Lord's Passover."* This emphasizes a side of the Truth which is much neglected today in Evangelical preaching.

What little is presently preached about the Cross is, for the most part, one-sided. It has much to say about what Christ's death accomplished for those who believe in Him, and rightly so; however, very little is said about what that death accomplished *"Godwards."*

Concerning this, Pink says: *"The Death of Christ glorified God if never a single sinner had been saved by the virtue of it."*

He then went on to say: *"The more we study the teaching of Scripture on this subject, and the more we lay hold by simple Faith of what the Cross meant to God, the more stable will be our peace, and the deeper our joy and praise."*

As we survey the first time in Scripture that there is a direct reference to the word *"lamb,"* we read that Abraham said to Isaac, *"God will provide Himself a lamb for a Burnt Offering"* (Gen. 22:8). It was not simply that God would *"provide"* a lamb, but that He would *"provide Himself a lamb."* The Lamb was *"provided"* to glorify God's Character, to vindicate His Throne, to satisfy His Justice, and to magnify His Holiness.

And then on the Great Day of Atonement, which came about once a year, we read of two goats. Why two?

One was to portray justice satisfied, with the other goat portraying Redemption completed. The latter was the *"scapegoat."*

It is this aspect of truth which is before us in Romans 3:24-26, *"Being justified freely by His Grace through the Redemption that is in Christ Jesus. Whom God has set forth to be a 'propitiation' through Faith in His Blood to declare His 'Righteousness'... that He might be 'just,' and the 'Justifier' of him who believes in Jesus."* In I Corinthians 5:7 we read: *"Christ our Passover."* He is now *"our"* Passover, because He was first *"the LORD's Passover"* (Ex. 12:11) (Pink).

THE CROSS AND SATAN

As we have stated, the Cross was meant to address itself to both man and God. It would satisfy the justice of God, and it would redeem man.

The Cross had absolutely nothing to do with Satan, even though the Cross, or at least what was accomplished there, totally and completely defeated him, as well as all of his minions of darkness. Paul said:

"Blotting out the handwriting of ordinances that was against us (satisfied the demands of the broken Law), *which was contrary to us* (man could not keep the Law), *and took it out of the way* (satisfied its demands by paying its debt), *nailing it to His Cross* (Atonement was totally and completely effected at the Cross);

"And having spoiled principalities and powers (by Jesus atoning for all sin, and sin being the legal claim which Satan had over humanity, with that removed, he has no more claim, at least for all who will believe) *He made a show of them openly* (all of the spirit world knows that Christ is Victor), *triumphing over them in it* (by what Christ did at the Cross, Satan and his demons were totally defeated)*" (Col. 2:14-15).

This is the reason that Satan hates the Cross. It spelled his doom, wrote *"finished"* over his efforts, took away his claims, and left him nothing. Let me say it again, all was accomplished at the Cross.

That's the reason that Paul said: *"For Christ sent me not to baptize, but to preach the Gospel: not with wisdom of words, lest the Cross of Christ should be made of none effect"* (I Cor. 1:17).

This tells us here several things:

1. The emphasis must always be on the Cross. If it's on anything else, and as important as those other things might be, then it becomes unscriptural.

2. We are told in this one Verse that the *"Gospel"* is *"Jesus Christ and Him Crucified."*

We are also told that men are not saved by appealing to the intellect, i.e., *"wisdom of words,"* but rather by God dealing with their hearts, as the Cross of Christ is preached.

3. And last of all, the Cross can be *"made of none effect,"* simply because emphasis is placed elsewhere, which then destroys the effectiveness of the Gospel.

As well, the Jew from Tarsus said: *"But we preach Christ Crucified,"* meaning that we must not just preach Christ, but we must preach Christ Crucified (I Cor. 1:23).

We are to preach the Cross, despite the fact that it is *"unto the Jews a stumblingblock, and unto the Greeks foolishness."* None of this must deter us!

The reason?

The Cross of Christ makes possible the *"Power of God, and the Wisdom of God"* (I Cor. 1:24).

(12) "FOR I WILL PASS THROUGH THE LAND OF EGYPT THIS NIGHT, AND WILL SMITE ALL THE FIRSTBORN IN THE LAND OF EGYPT, BOTH MAN AND BEAST; AND AGAINST ALL THE GODS OF EGYPT I WILL EXECUTE JUDGMENT: I AM THE LORD.

(13) "AND THE BLOOD SHALL BE TO YOU FOR A TOKEN UPON THE HOUSES WHERE YOU ARE: AND WHEN I SEE THE BLOOD, I WILL PASS OVER YOU, AND THE PLAGUE SHALL NOT BE UPON YOU TO DESTROY YOU, WHEN I SMITE THE LAND OF EGYPT.

(14) "AND THIS DAY SHALL BE UNTO YOU FOR A MEMORIAL; AND YOU SHALL KEEP IT A FEAST TO THE LORD THROUGHOUT YOUR GENERATIONS; YOU SHALL KEEP IT A FEAST BY AN ORDINANCE FOREVER.

(15) "SEVEN DAYS SHALL YOU EAT UNLEAVENED BREAD; EVEN THE FIRST DAY YOU SHALL PUT AWAY LEAVEN OUT OF YOUR HOUSES: FOR WHOSOEVER EATS LEAVENED BREAD FROM THE FIRST DAY UNTIL THE SEVENTH DAY, THAT SOUL SHALL BE CUT OFF FROM ISRAEL.

(16) "AND IN THE FIRST DAY THERE SHALL BE AN HOLY CONVOCATION, AND IN THE SEVENTH DAY THERE SHALL BE AN HOLY CONVOCATION TO YOU; NO MANNER OF WORK SHALL BE DONE IN THEM, SAVE THAT WHICH EVERY MAN MUST EAT, THAT ONLY MAY BE DONE OF YOU.

(17) "AND YOU SHALL OBSERVE THE FEAST OF UNLEAVENED BREAD; FOR IN THIS SELFSAME DAY HAVE I BROUGHT YOUR ARMIES OUT OF THE LAND OF EGYPT: THEREFORE SHALL YOU OBSERVE THIS DAY IN YOUR GENERATIONS BY AN ORDINANCE FOREVER.

(18) "IN THE FIRST MONTH, ON THE FOURTEENTH DAY OF THE MONTH AT EVENING, YOU SHALL EAT UNLEAVENED BREAD, UNTIL THE ONE AND TWENTIETH DAY OF THE MONTH AT EVENING.

(19) "SEVEN DAYS SHALL THERE BE NO LEAVEN FOUND IN YOUR HOUSES: FOR WHOSOEVER EATS THAT WHICH IS LEAVENED, EVEN THAT SOUL SHALL BE CUT OFF FROM THE CONGREGATION OF ISRAEL, WHETHER HE BE A STRANGER, OR BORN IN THE LAND.

(20) "YOU SHALL EAT NOTHING LEAVENED; IN ALL YOUR HABITATION SHALL YOU EAT UNLEAVENED BREAD."

The construction is:

1. It must be understood that the Children of Israel, in respect to personal holiness, were no different than the Egyptians. The difference would be *"the Blood."*

2. *"When I see the blood, I will pass over you,"* are, no doubt, the greatest words that were ever uttered.

3. The shed Blood of Jesus Christ is the only panacea for the *"plague"* of sin which destroys the human race.

4. Blood applied gave security to the home. Doubt by the occupants might destroy the peace but not the security, because the security was founded on God's Word.

5. The Passover is to be *"for a memorial,"* and is to be kept forever. The *"Lord's Supper"* of Christianity is an outgrowth of *"the Passover,"* and, thereby, fulfills the command. There is some indication that the Passover and other memorials will be kept forever, or at least through the Kingdom Age (Ezek. 45:17; 46:14).

NOTES

I AM THE LORD

Verse 12 reads: *"For I will pass through the land of Egypt this night, and will smite all the firstborn in the land of Egypt, both man and beast; and against all the gods of Egypt I will execute judgment: I am the LORD."*

The words *"pass through"* could be translated *"go through,"* since the word used is entirely unconnected with the *"Passover."* Egypt by now has come to recognize Jehovah, and to recognize fully that His Power was Almighty.

Whether Jehovah went Personally through the land of Egypt that particular night, or whether He sent the death Angel, we aren't told; however, it is almost certain that He worked through an Angel (Ex. 12:23).

We may wonder why the *"beasts"* would be included.

Animal worship was an important part of the religion of the Egyptians. At four great cities, Memphis, Heliopolis, Hermonthis, a sort of suburb of Thebes, and Momemphis in the Western Delta, animals were maintained, which were viewed as actual incarnations of Deity — the Apis Bull at Memphis, a bull called Mnevis at Heliopolis, one termed Bacis, or Pacis at Hermonthis, and at Momemphis a White Cow.

In other parts of Egypt, sheep were worshiped, as well as goats, and even dogs and cats. Crocodiles and hippopotami were included as well, along with frogs.

A sudden mortality among the sacred animals would be felt by the Egyptians as a blow struck against the gods to whom they belonged, and as a judgment upon *"them."* In fact, many of the gods of Egypt were represented by some beast.

But even above all of that, the *"firstborn"* of each family in Egypt, even including the family of Pharaoh, being smitten, struck a blow at Egypt of unprecedented proportions.

As previously stated, the religion of Egypt included the firstborn taking on the name and the ability even into eternity, or the *"afterlife,"* as it was called. So when the *"firstborn"* prematurely died, this affected the eternal consequences of that particular family.

So the Lord would *"execute judgment against all the gods of Egypt,"* and simply because He Alone was *"the Lord,"* and not these supposed deities.

THE BLOOD

Verse 13 reads: *"And the blood shall be to you for a token upon the houses where you are: and when I see the blood, I will pass over you, and the plague shall not be upon you to destroy you, when I smite the land of Egypt."*

In this Chapter, which is one of the greatest in the Bible, we now come to the particular Verse which is the most important in this Chapter. And in this Verse, the one phrase, *"When I see the Blood, I will pass over you,"* in effect constitutes one of the most important statements in the entirety of the Bible. In fact, it sums up the entirety of the Word of God.

It didn't matter if the house was beautiful, expensive, ornate, or the poorest of poor structures. None of that counted. The only thing that counted was the blood that was applied to the doorposts. That's what the Lord saw, and that only.

Again, as it regards the individuals in these respective houses, it didn't matter that they could trace their lineage back to Abraham, that their genealogy was perfect, or that they observed all the ceremonies, that which secured their deliverance was not these things, but rather their personal application of the shed blood, and of that alone.

The blood applied to the doorposts meant that their faith and trust were in the Paschal Lamb. They may not have understood very much about what was taking place, but this one thing they did know: if they were to be safe on this memorable night, the blood had to be applied to the doorposts, and that was all that mattered.

PERSONAL APPLICATION

No doubt, there were some in these houses who had not lived as proper as they should have lived. Perhaps fear filled their hearts because they knew that they deserved the death penalty.

But they had heard the Word of the Lord from Moses, and that Word had been, *"When I see the Blood, I will pass over you."* The lamb had taken the fatal blow, and because it had taken the blow, the one in the house would be spared. It was not a question of personal worthiness. Self had nothing whatever to do in the matter. It was a matter of faith. And all under the cover of the blood were safe, just as all presently under the cover of the Blood are safe.

This means they were not merely in a savable state, but rather that they were *"saved."* They were not hoping or praying to be saved; they knew it as an assured fact, on the authority of that Word which shall endure throughout all generations. As well, they were not partly saved and partly exposed to judgment; they were wholly saved because there is no such thing as a partial justification. The Blood of the Lamb and the Word of the Lord formed the foundation of Israel's peace on that terrible night in which Egypt's firstborn were laid low.

THE VERY HEART OF CHRISTIANITY

Even though the words *"Christians,"* or *"Christianity,"* were at that time no way known; still, what we are studying here is the very heart of Christianity. It's what true Christianity is all about. It's the story of the Bible, because in effect, it's the story of the Cross.

Satan does everything within his power to obscure this foundational truth from humanity, and even the Church. Religious men are so very bad, awful in fact, about adding things to the Finished Work of Christ. They seem to not realize that when this is done, they are insulting Christ, and with the most awful of insults. They are in effect saying that what He did at the Cross is insufficient, and to be sure, such thinking, if not outright blasphemy, borders very close.

If we do not see the absolutely settled character of Redemption through the Blood of Christ, and in its application to ourselves, then we are not aware of full forgiveness, Grace, and Mercy, simply because full forgiveness rests upon the simple fact that a full and complete Atonement has been offered. We either trust it or we don't trust it!

FAITH IN THE SHED BLOOD OF THE LORD JESUS CHRIST

When we claim to trust Christ, but at the

same time add our particular Church, or a particular doctrine, or good works, etc., to that Finished Work, we have only succeeded in abrogating the great Plan of God for our lives. And nothing could be more serious than that. But I'm afraid this is the state of the majority of the modern Church. And how do I know that?

I know that because of the attitude and position taken by many, if not most, Church leaders, which are followed by most of the laity. And what attitude is that?

Simple repentance for sin is not enough for most Church leaders, i.e., *"so-called leaders!"* In fact, most of the modern Church believes in, and practices penance, although most would probably deny such a position.

A PERSONAL EXPERIENCE

A friend of mine, who is an attorney, was discussing these things with the leader of one of the largest Pentecostal Denominations in the world.

He told me later that after he left and was thinking about their conversation, he realized that what this man was advocating, he went on to say, was penance.

The Catholic Church openly advocates penance, and even though the Protestant world would blanch at the word, still, for the most part, it practices the same thing. And let the Reader understand that *"penance,"* which in effect is punishment, is an insult of unprecedented proportions to Christ. In effect it states that the terrible price that He paid at the Cross was not enough, and needs more punishment added. Let me ask this question:

What if it had been prescribed by some, that Israelites also stand on their heads in their homes, and I speak of the night that the death Angel would pass through? Would them performing this particular acrobatic feat have made them any safer? Let's also say that it was recommended that they stay on their knees all night long. Would this have made them any safer?

I think we all know the answer to that. None of that, and irrespective as to what it might have been, would have been looked at by the Lord. He was looking for one thing, and that was the blood applied to the doorposts. Anything else which was proposed would have been ignored.

It is the same presently. The Word that He gave some 3,500 years ago, *"When I see the Blood, I will pass over you,"* holds true at this present hour, as much as it did then. Why can't we see that? Why don't we believe that? Why don't we preach that? Why would we try to add other things to that great Promise?

If your faith and trust is in Christ and Him Crucified, you are saved. And there's nothing you can do to make yourself more saved.

SELF

There are millions of Christians, and I think I exaggerate not, who claim to believe totally in the shed Blood of Christ, but yet they have no peace. In fact, the great blessing of Faith in the shed Blood of Christ is the Peace of God which floods one's soul. So what's wrong?

While these individuals claim to be looking to the Blood, the truth is, they are looking to themselves. They are occupied with their interests and their faith, instead of with Christ's Blood and God's Word. In other words, they are looking *"in"* at self, instead of *"out"* at Christ. This is not Faith, and, as a consequence, they have no peace.

For the most part, the ways of God are totally opposite to the ways of this world. With God, the way up is down. With God, we keep what we give. With God, if we save our lives, we will lose them, etc. I think you get the point.

ONE OF THE GREAT KEYS TO VICTORY

What I'm about to say to you, that is if the Lord will help me to say it properly, is in fact a great truth, which can bring you victory. It is the key to victory.

We have a tendency to measure our victory by looking at ourselves. When we do this, it's going to cause us problems. We are to always look to Christ and what Christ has done for us at the Cross. I am saved and my name is written in the Lamb's Book of Life, not because of my excellent performance, but because of Christ and what He has done for me at the Cross.

But after we are saved, we realize that our

performance should shape up, and that is correct; however, the way to worsen the condition is to keep looking at yourself, and thereby devising means and ways to be an overcomer, etc. That is the sure road to disaster, simply because it's not Faith. Please note the following very carefully:

If you will forget about yourself, and look exclusively to Christ, and measure your victory according to what Christ has done for you, you will find something beginning to take place in your life.

As you begin this great quest, your faith being imperfect, you will probably in some way fail. If that happens, as despicable as it is, ask the Lord to forgive you, and then get your faith anchored once again in Christ and the Cross. In fact, this might happen several times, even many times. But irrespective of that, don't look at yourself, and above all, don't look at your poor performance; rather look to Christ and His Cross. Why do you think that Paul said:

"God forbid that I should glory (boast), *save in the Cross of our Lord Jesus Christ, by Whom the world is crucified unto me, and I unto the world"* (Gal. 6:14)?

Instead of boasting in yourself, or doing the very opposite, which means to chastise yourself because of your failures, rather look to the Cross, and boast about that great Finished Work performed there by Christ. You will find yourself little by little getting stronger and stronger, and the time will definitely come that the problems causing you great difficulty will no longer be there.

To fail the Lord in any capacity is a hurtful thing; but the way to overcome what is causing the failure is not through self, but exclusively through Christ. Unfortunately, most Christians, not understanding the Cross, which means they do not properly understand Justification, if they fail, will automatically concoct particular laws of their own making, or the making of someone else, which they think will bring them victory. And please understand, we can just about make a law out of anything. But they find to their chagrin that these things they are practicing do not bring victory; in fact, if the truth be known, their situation is rather getting worse. And that's the way it always is. If we are trying to live under the government of law, failure, and continued failure, is going to be our lot. It is because the Holy Spirit will not help us in such capacities, and simply because, whether we realize it or not, as previously stated, we are committing spiritual adultery. We are married to Christ, but at the same time, we are flirting with the law, or else have embraced the law. So in effect, and to use street terminology, we have two husbands, Christ and the Law, which makes us a spiritual adulterer, which the Holy Spirit cannot tolerate (Rom. 7:1-4).

AN OVERCOMER

To the seven Churches of Asia, Jesus addressed seven Messages (Rev., Chpts. 2-3). In each of these seven Messages, He made a statement concerning Believers being overcomers. While each statement was different, He strongly implies that we must be an overcomer.

When reading these statements, what do you think as it regards yourself and your position as an overcomer? Do you think of yourself as an overcomer? Or do you think in your mind that this is something you are working on?

Better yet, were I to ask you as to how the Believer can be an overcomer, what would your answer be?

The Scripture says: *"And they overcame him* (Satan) *by the Blood of the Lamb, and by the word of their testimony; and they loved not their lives unto the death"* (Rev. 12:11).

When most Believers think of overcoming, they think of themselves as doing something, or ceasing to do something, etc. No! The Scripture says that we overcome by the *"Blood of the Lamb."* What does that mean?

It refers to Faith. Paul said:

"For in Jesus Christ neither circumcision availeth anything, nor uncircumcision; but faith which worketh by love" (Gal. 5:6).

We overcome simply by placing our Faith and trust in Christ, and what Christ has done for us at the Cross, knowing that He shed His Life's Blood there, which atoned for all sin, and thereby, as well, defeated Satan and all of his cohorts. When Faith is properly registered in Christ, and it can't be properly registered in Him, unless it is also registered in what He did for us at the Cross, we will then have the help of the Holy Spirit, and victory will be ours (Rom. 8:1-2, 11).

Our being an overcomer is not in what we do, but rather what He has done, and our Faith in Him. Of course I speak of Christ. That's the reason the loud voice from Heaven cried that we overcome Satan by the *"Blood of the Lamb."*

THE WORD OF OUR TESTIMONY

The loud voice from Heaven also stated that we overcome not only by the *"Blood of the Lamb,"* but also *"by the word of our testimony."* What is meant by that?

It simply means that our testimony is to the effect of the very things I've been saying here. We are to testify that our Faith is exclusively in Christ and what He has done for us in His great sacrifice. That is our testimony, and must ever be our testimony. If it changes, and I speak of it changing from the Blood of Christ to other things, then it's a testimony that God will not honor or recognize.

Our *"Testimony"* is tied to the *"Blood of the Lamb."* That's where our Faith is registered, and whenever we speak of victory, without exception, we must speak of Christ and Him Crucified. That is the *"word of our testimony."*

TOKEN

"Token" in the Hebrew is *"owth,"* and means, *"a flag, beacon, monument, evidence."* Probably the word *"evidence"* would explain this more than anything else.

The blood on the doorposts was evidence of their faith in that which was commanded of them.

To the mind of the natural man, this was consummate folly. What difference will it make, proud reason might ask, if *"blood"* be smeared upon the door? That's the reason that Paul said:

"For the preaching (Message) *of the Cross is to them who perish foolishness; but unto us which are saved it is the Power of God."* He also stated: *"But we preach Christ Crucified, unto the Jews a stumblingblock, and unto the Greeks foolishness"* (I Cor. 1:18, 23).

It is faith, not reasoning, which God requires; and it was faith which rendered the Passover-sacrifice effective; *"Through Faith he kept the Passover, and the sprinkling of the blood lest He who destroyed the firstborn should touch them"* (Heb. 11:28).

Some nine miracles or plagues had come and gone, and the Children of Israel were still held captive by Pharaoh. So how could this last plague be any different?

It was different because the Power of God struck at the very heart of the Egyptian Empire, by bringing about the deaths of all the firstborn, both man and beasts. When this took place, and take place it did, Pharaoh relented — but just long enough for the Children of Israel to leave. He would come after them, which would prove to be his undoing.

How does all of this tie in with our present Salvation?

Presently, our Salvation, as then, is centered up in the Blood of the Lamb. When Jesus died on the Cross, thereby shedding His Life's Blood, which atoned for all sin, this took away Satan's legal right to hold man in bondage. Sin is what gave him that legal right, but all sin now atoned, left him with nothing. That's why Paul said:

"Blotting out the handwriting of ordinances that was against us, which was contrary to us, and took it out of the way, nailing it to His Cross;

"And having spoiled principalities and powers, He made a show of them openly, triumphing over them in it" (Col. 2:14-15).

So the question might be asked, if Satan has lost his legal right to keep mankind in bondage, at least regarding those who believe, how is that he's still causing so much trouble for many Christians?

SATAN'S PSEUDO-AUTHORITY

Satan exercises control over Christians through a pseudo-authority. And what do we mean by that?

It means that he really doesn't have any authority, except that which we give him.

Now that may come as a shock, and I speak of us giving him authority, which he then turns and uses against us. Again I state, he has no authority of his own, that having been addressed at Calvary. So if he exercises authority now, it has to be a pseudo-authority.

When it comes to the unsaved, of course he exercises authority over them constantly, but once again, that is a pseudo-authority as well. They don't trust Christ, so that gives Satan an opening in their lives, which he uses to the full extent.

When it comes to Christians, it's the same thing. If the Christian doesn't understand what Christ has done at the Cross, and how His great Finished Work brings about our Sanctification, and thereby tries to bring victory some other way, this falls right into Satan's hands. In other words, we have left the gate open.

He then takes the authority we aren't using, whether through ignorance or otherwise, and uses it against us to cause us all kinds of problems. But if the Believer will exercise authority in the sense of evidencing Faith in Christ, and what Christ has done for us in the great Sacrifice of Himself, realizing that this alone brings us total and complete victory, then Satan has no authority whatsoever, and is a defeated foe. Never forget that the triumph of Jesus over Satan and all his cohorts was final, total, and complete.

The Scripture plainly says that Jesus *"made a show of them openly, triumphing over them in it,"* which He did by His accomplishment at the Cross. Satan knows he's defeated, but the sadness is, most Christians don't!

Oh yes! Almost every Christian will talk about how Satan is defeated, but most of the time their thinking is in themselves, and not in the Cross. In other words, they're boasting of themselves, and not boasting of Christ (Gal. 6:14).

Exactly as the Children of Israel of old, *"The blood is a token where we are,"* referring to the fact of the Cross, and what Jesus accomplished there. That's why Paul also said:

"But now in Christ Jesus you who sometimes were far off are made nigh by the Blood of Christ" (Eph. 2:13).

"Much more then, being now justified by His Blood, we shall be saved from wrath through Him" (Rom. 5:9).

Jesus said, that the New Testament or New Covenant is *"in My Blood"* (I Cor. 11:25).

The Blood alone is the token. And if anyone tries to put anything else as a token, they have just abrogated God's Plan of Salvation, and will bring upon themselves utter, spiritual ruin.

THE PLAGUE

Whatever the *"plague"* was, it would take the lives of the firstborn of both man and beast. It was a type of *"sin,"* which destroys.

The only remedy for sin is the *"shed Blood of the Lamb,"* i.e., *"the Cross."* It is the Blood of Christ which gives peace, imparts perfect Justification — Divine Righteousness, purges the conscience, brings us into the holiest of all, justifies God in receiving the believing sinner, and constitutes our title to all the joys, the dignities, and the glories of Heaven (Rom. 3:24-26; 5:9; Eph. 2:13-18; Col. 1:20-22; Heb. 9:14; 10:19; I Pet. 1:19; 2:24; I Jn. 1:7; Rev. 7:14-17; 12:11).

One Preacher in the Word of Faith doctrine made the statement that the Blood of Jesus alone would not effect Redemption. His reasoning was that scores of other people died on Crosses that day, and their blood did not effect any Redemption.

Such thinking proves a serious lack of knowledge of the Word of God. Of course the shed blood of the other individuals who died on crosses that day did not effect Redemption because it could not effect Redemption. The Blood of Jesus effected Redemption, bringing about the possibility of the changed life, i.e., *"the born again experience,"* simply because of Who Jesus was. All others who died that day were sinners; therefore, their blood was polluted, tainted, ill-affected, etc. Consequently, God could not accept any of them, as He could not accept any man. In fact, God would have to become Man, which He did, keep the Law perfectly, and then pay its penalty on the Cross, which He did by the Sacrifice of Himself (Gal. 1:4).

Only God could do this great thing, and He could do it only in the form of a Man. It had to be this way, because it was not Angels who were being redeemed, and it certainly wasn't members of the Godhead being redeemed, but rather man. So God would have to become a Man, which He did.

Jesus Christ was Perfect in every respect; therefore, God could accept His poured out life, of which the Blood was a token, as payment for the terrible sin question.

WHY BLOOD?

We have addressed this already, but suffice to say, the life of the flesh is in the blood. So when the blood is poured out, this means the life is given, which is what Christ did.

It was not so much that the blood within itself had some magical effect, neither did it mean that it being shed had some magical effect; rather, it refers to the life of Christ being given, which paid the price.

But at the same time, His Life had to be given in the form of the shedding of His Blood. That's the reason that He could not be stoned to death, or killed in any other manner. It had to be on a Cross, and for two reasons:

WHY THE CROSS?

1. When Jesus paid the price, it was a price that included every single sin, and irrespective as to how bad it was. In other words, He atoned for all sin (I Jn. 1:7).

In the Old Testament economy, when a person committed a dastardly crime, he was first stoned to death, and then his body was placed on a tree for several hours, to show that he was cursed by God. It was not to remain on the tree *"all night,"* but was to be taken down before the dawn of the next day, and then buried (Deut. 21:22-23).

Paul would refer to this by saying: *"Christ has redeemed us from the curse of the law, being made a curse for us: for it is written, Cursed is everyone who hangs on a tree"* (Gal. 3:13).

In fact, Jesus had to die on a Cross; however, it should be understood that He really wasn't cursed by God, but was rather *"made a curse,"* which is far different than being cursed. Sin causes one to be cursed by God. Jesus had never sinned, so He could not be cursed by God, but He could be made a curse, which simply refers to the fact of bearing the penalty of sin, which is death.

2. While on the Cross, He poured out His Life's Blood, through the many wounds on His Body, which in effect, poured out His Life, which atoned for all sin. *"Without the shedding of blood there is no remission of sin"* (Heb. 9:22).

But once again, we emphasize the fact that it had to be the Blood of Christ; it could be no other. His Blood alone would suffice because it was untouched by the Fall in the Garden of Eden. In fact, that's the reason that Jesus had to be born of a virgin. To have been born otherwise, that is, as man is normally born, would have inculcated upon Himself the results of the Fall, which would have meant that He would have been born in sin, as all other men. But due to the fact that He was born of the Virgin Mary, which means that He was not procreated by man, means that He was born without original sin.

THE PLAGUE OF SIN

As we have repeatedly stated, it was only Christ in His sacrificial, atoning death that could address the terrible problem of sin. It cannot be addressed by education, money, power, or in fact, anything that man does. Its power is beyond the ability of man. That's what makes it so foolish as it regards the Church stooping to man's ways, and we refer to humanistic psychology, to address this terrible monster. It can be addressed only by the Cross, and the Cross alone!

This which I have just stated could not be any clearer, and in fact crystal clear, than portrayed here in this Twelfth Chapter of Exodus, and in fact, the entirety of the Bible. Sin will destroy you. And the only answer for sin is the Cross, i.e., *"the shed Blood of Christ."*

That's the reason that Satan will do everything within his power to push the Church away from the Cross, He really doesn't care too very much about whatever direction the Church takes, just as long as it's away from the Cross.

That's why Paul preached the Cross so strongly. When the Lord explained to him the meaning of the New Covenant, which was the meaning of the Cross (Gal. 1:11-12), he then knew that the only answer for man's dilemma was the Cross of Christ (Gal. 6:14).

That's the reason the Judaizers were so wrong in Paul's day; they were pulling people away from the Cross. That's the reason the modern Word of Faith doctrine is so wrong; it pulls people away from the Cross. That's the reason humanistic psychology and its devotees are so wrong; it pulls people away from the Cross.

A FEAST TO THE LORD

Verse 14 reads: *"And this day shall be unto you for a memorial; and you shall keep it a feast to the LORD throughout your generations; you shall keep it a feast by an ordinance forever."*

The Passover is continued in the Lord's Supper (I Cor. 5:7-8). In this way the Passover may be regarded as still continuing under Christianity, and as intended to continue, at least throughout the Kingdom Age, which is yet to come.

The Passover per se is not continued, simply because it represented the *"type,"* which was carried out through the offering of animals, i.e., *"lambs, goats, etc."* Now that Christ has come, and fulfilled the type, it would not be proper to eat the Passover as it once was celebrated, because what the Passover symbolized or represented was fulfilled in Christ.

A MEMORIAL

This event, the Passover, was required to be kept on the Fourteenth of Abib, each and every year, *"throughout your generations."* The Scripture says in this Verse that it is to be done *"forever."*

As already stated, it actually continues in the participation by Christians of the *"Lord's Supper,"* which in a sense is an outgrowth of the Passover. In fact, God doesn't recognize the Old Testament Passover anymore, and in fact, hasn't recognized it since Jesus died on the Cross, and rose from the dead.

It was not God's Will after this great event for men to continue to look to the *"type,"* when in fact, the *"antitype"* had come, and had fulfilled all the type. Why does one want to offer up sacrifices of animals, when *"The Sacrifice"* has been offered!

In fact, this was a terrible problem for the Christian Jews in the early Church. They kept trying to keep the Law as well as serve Christ. It caused the Apostle Paul great problems, with these individuals attempting to continue the Old Testament practices, when in fact, Christ and what He did for us at the Cross is our Passover (I Cor. 5:7).

FOREVER

The question might well be asked as to the meaning, as it is used here, of the word *"forever."* In the Perfect Age to come, which is graphically outlined in Revelation, Chapters 21 and 22, seven times in this account the word *"Lamb"* as it refers to Christ, is used. Now please understand, in this Perfect Age to come, Satan and all his minions of darkness, plus every unsaved soul, will be in the Lake of Fire. And to be sure, they will be there forever. There will be no more sin or transgression of any nature, but yet, the Holy Spirit refers seven times, as stated, to the *"Lamb."* So I think that this tells us that in some fashion, this *"memorial"* will be kept forever. The word *"Lamb"* referring to Christ, is used in this fashion, I think, in order that all Believers might know and understand that the great and glorious privileges that we will have forever and forever, even with the New Jerusalem coming down from God out of Heaven, with God literally transferring His Headquarters from Heaven to Earth, are all brought about as a result of what Jesus did at the Cross.

That's at least one of the reasons that the Cross must be the central theme of the Gospel. In fact, there is no Salvation, no victory, no Grace of God outside of the Cross. If we preach anything else, we're preaching a false Gospel, and the Apostle Paul said, *"Let him be accursed"* (Gal. 1:8-9).

AN ILLUSTRATION

Why is it that the Church ignores the Cross, when in reality, its theme is so abundantly presented in the entirety of the Word of God? Why do we insist upon promoting other means of life and victory, when in fact, there are no other means? That's why Paul was so adamant as it regards this Gospel Message. The truth is, and the facts are, the Gospel is the Cross, and the Cross is the Gospel (I Cor. 1:17-18, 21, 23; 2:2, 5).

A short time ago, a Charismatic Leader had a severe spiritual problem, in other words, a bondage of a severe nature. It was found out, and the Church regrettably and sadly took its usual course.

The following is the solution they presented for his problem, which pretty well mirrors the so-called solution of most of the modern Church presently.

It consisted of the following:

1. He was not to preach for three months.
2. He was to place himself under the authority of two particular Preachers, one, if I remember correctly, who lived in Europe, and another who lived at least 1,000 miles from him.
3. He was to undergo an extensive period of counseling from a Psychologist.

Now that was the solution that the Church presented, which completely ignores, and in fact, repudiates the Cross.

In the first place, how in the world does preaching or not preaching affect the bondage that grips this man? What in the world does not preaching for three months have to do with his deliverance?

Second, what in the world can those two Preachers do for him as it regards his bondage? Him calling them everyday and talking to them over the phone will effect no answer for his dilemma.

And then the crowning insult of all is the turning to Egypt for relief, i.e., *"the Psychologists."*

What do you the Reader think that a Psychologist actually does? I can tell you very easily what they do.

They just talk to the individual. They don't have a miracle drug they can give him or her, in order that the problem might be solved. They can only talk. Now let me ask you another question:

If this terrible problem of sin could be *"talked away,"* then Jesus needlessly came down here and died on a Cross (Gal. 2:20-21).

The truth is, this Brother can engage in these particular pursuits as long as he desires, and with great dedication, and he'll be the same man when he comes out as when he went in. This means that if he doesn't come to the Cross, his life and Ministry are wrecked and ruined. There is no way that victory can be his in such a capacity.

In the first place, sin is so awful, so terrible, and so powerful that there is no way that it can be addressed, at least properly, other than faith exercised in Christ and what He has done for us at the Cross. When this is done, the Holy Spirit comes in, and performs His great and glorious work, which guarantees victory.

BIBLICAL RESTORATION

It's a shame, but the far greater majority of the modern Church doesn't have the slightest idea as to the meaning of Biblical restoration; consequently, there is precious little Scriptural restoration in its ranks. What does the Bible teach as it regards this subject?

Paul said:

"Brethren, if a man be overtaken in a fault (a moral failure), *you which are spiritual, restore such an one in the spirit of meekness; considering yourself, lest you also be tempted"* (Gal. 6:1).

The key to this is the word *"spiritual."* It refers to one who *"walks after the spirit"* (Rom. 8:1-2).

A *"spiritual"* man or woman is one who understands that everything we have in Christ comes to us due to what He did for us at the Cross. They place their Faith in that *"Finished Work,"* and maintain their Faith in that Finished Work; consequently, the Holy Spirit works grandly within their hearts and lives (Jn. 7:37-39; 16:7-14).

If a person fails the Lord, irrespective as to what the failure might be, the one who is *"spiritual,"* is to tell such a person why they failed. And why did they fail?

All failure can be attributed to faith that is taken from the Cross of Christ, and in fact, placed in something else. Such a position guarantees failure. There is only one victory over sin. Paul graphically explained it to us. He said:

"For the Law of the Spirit of Life in Christ Jesus, has made me free from the law of sin and death" (Rom. 8:2).

This *"Law of the Spirit of Life in Christ Jesus,"* refers to the manner and the way in which the Holy Spirit works. The short phrase *"in Christ Jesus,"* proclaims the basis on which He works.

It refers to what Jesus did at the Cross, which demands faith on our part.

So the *"spiritual"* one is to explain to the one who has failed the Lord that he failed simply because his faith was placed in things other than Christ and the Cross, which in effect, at least in the eyes of God, makes him (or her) a *"spiritual adulterer"* (Rom. 7:1-4). And of course, the Holy Spirit, as we have repeatedly stated, is not going to have anything to do with such a position. He honors Faith in the Cross, and Faith in the Cross alone.

The *"spiritual"* one is to get the person's faith back in the Cross, which means it is now exclusively in Christ and what He has done for us, and that person will once again begin to walk in victory. That is Biblical restoration. Anything else is outside of the scope of the Word of God, and is guaranteed to bring no positive results.

That's the reason that Paul also said in this same Sixth Chapter of Galatians: *"But God forbid that I should glory* (boast), *save in the Cross of our Lord Jesus Christ, by Whom the world is crucified unto me, and I unto the world"* (Gal. 6:14).

IGNORANCE OR UNBELIEF?

When the Lord began to open this great Truth of the Cross to me in 1996, which by no means is new, but which is that which was preached and taught by the Apostle Paul, I at first thought that the reason the Church has so gone astray is because of Scriptural ignorance as it regards this subject. Of course, that is true in many cases; however, I have come to see, I think, that the majority of the cases don't fall into the category of ignorance, but rather of *"unbelief."*

In other words, most of the modern Church, Preachers included, simply don't believe that what Jesus did at the Cross is the answer to hurting, sick, ailing humanity. They rather resort to the wisdom of men, which in effect, is no wisdom at all.

Unbelief is a deadly thing. It is, perhaps, the basis of all sin, and the result of all sin.

In fact, this is the first work of the Holy Spirit. Jesus said:

"Nevertheless I tell you the truth; it is expedient for you that I go away: for if I go not away, the Comforter will not come unto you; but if I depart, I will send Him unto you.

"And when He is come, He will reprove (convict) *the world of sin, and of righteousness, and of judgment:*

"Of sin, because they believe not on Me" (Jn. 16:7-9).

The only answer for sin in any form is the Cross of Christ. We must remember that, never forget that, and ever understand that. If anything else is promoted, we sin, and we sin greatly.

So, the Preachers who are promoting these other ridiculous methods as it regards the Brother we have just mentioned, who has suffered a problem, are sinning, and sinning greatly. If he adheres to that foolishness, he will be sinning as well. In fact, there could be no greater insult to Christ than to ignore the price that He has paid on the Cross of Calvary, rather resorting to other measures. Such presents rebellion against the Plan of God, and nothing could be worse than that.

THE FEAST OF UNLEAVENED BREAD

Verses 15 through 20 read: *"Seven days shall you eat unleavened bread; even the first day you shall put away leaven out of your houses: for whosoever eateth leavened bread from the first day until the seventh day, that soul shall be cut off from Israel.*

"And in the first day there shall be an holy convocation, and in the seventh day there shall be an holy convocation to you; no manner of work shall be done in them, save that which every man must eat, that only may be done of you.

"And you shall observe the feast of unleavened bread; for in this selfsame day have I brought your armies out of the land of Egypt: therefore shall you observe this day in your generations by an ordinance forever.

"In the first month, on the fourteenth day of the month at evening, you shall eat unleavened bread, until the one and twentieth day of the month at evening.

"Seven days shall there be no leaven found in your houses: for whosoever eateth that which is leavened, even that soul shall be cut off from the congregation of Israel, whether he be a stranger, or born in the land.

"You shall eat nothing leavened; in all your habitations shall you eat unleavened bread."

This Feast was to be kept in conjunction with the Passover Feast. Of course, Jesus fulfilled this which is given here, just as He did the Passover; however, the great truths contained therein are minutely significant for us presently. What did it all mean?

1. The unleavened bread, first of all,

typified Christ as it regards His Perfect Life, free from all sin and contamination. *"Leaven"* is yeast, which brings about rot and fermentation.

In the Old Testament, even as here, it is used as a type of sin and evil.

Jesus would have no sin, no evil, and was the fulfillment of the Feast of Unleavened Bread.

2. The Believer is to live accordingly as his Master. There is to be no sin within our lives. This doesn't refer to sinless perfection, because the Bible doesn't teach such. But it does refer to the fact that sin must not have dominion over us in any way (Rom. 6:14). As long as we live in this physical body, which is not yet redeemed, there will be, at times, evil thoughts, or even evil acts, which constitute sin. We don't like to admit it, but it is the truth. But that is a far cry from sin dominating the person in some way. The *"Feast of Unleavened Bread"* proclaims the fact that such is not to be. As stated, the Scripture plainly states, *"Sin shall not have dominion over you"* (Rom. 6:14). The only way this type of life can be lived, and I mean the only way, is by the Believer understanding, as we have repeatedly stated, that all things come to him from God, due to what Christ did at the Cross. His faith is to be anchored completely in the Cross and the Cross alone, which in effect, refers to what Jesus did there, and then the Holy Spirit will work mightily on his behalf (Rom. 6:3-5, 11).

3. The *"Feast of Unleavened Bread"* was to last for seven days. The number *"seven"* denotes God's number of perfection, completion, and totality. So in essence, the meaning of the number *"seven"* as it is given here, refers to the fact that the entirety of our lives in totality is to be a *"Feast of Unleavened Bread."* In other words, victorious living is to be ours seven days a week, 52 weeks of the year, for the entirety of our existence on this Earth.

4. The Believer was to *"put away out of their houses."* This corresponds with the words of Paul: *"I beseech you therefore, Brethren, by the Mercies of God, that you present your bodies a living sacrifice, holy, acceptable unto God, which is your reasonable service"* (Rom. 12:1).

NOTES

He then said: *"Wherefore seeing we also are compassed about with so great a cloud of witnesses, let us lay aside every weight, and the sin which does so easily beset us, and let us run with patience the race that is set before us"* (Heb. 12:1).

Now the great question is, how is the Believer to do this?

The amazing thing about the Message of the Cross is that it applies itself to every facet of our lives and living. In fact, the Believer can do this, only in one way:

As stated over and over, the Believer is to place his Faith in the Sacrifice of Christ, realizing this is the only manner in which we can overcome the world (Gal. 6:14). In fact, the Holy Spirit is the One Who must do these things for us, and through the Holy Spirit Alone can it be done. He works exclusively within the parameters of the Finished Work of Christ (Jn. 14:16-18; 16:7-14). He demands only that our Faith ever be in that Finished Work.

5. The Scripture plainly tells us, if the Believer in Old Testament times ignored this Feast, his *"soul would be cut off from Israel,"* meaning that he would be eternally lost.

Paul said this same thing as well, when he listed the *"works of the flesh"* and then said, *"Of the which I tell you before, as I have also told you in time past, that they which do such things shall not inherit the Kingdom of God"* (Gal. 5:19-21).

The Lord saves us from sin, not in sin. The idea that we can continue to allow sin to dominate us in any fashion, considering the price that Christ paid on the Cross, is a perversion of the Word of God.

Domination of sin will harden the heart. Such will always ultimately bring on unbelief. While the Lord will never throw over a Believer because of sin, even the vilest of sin, the Believer can definitely cease to believe, thereby becoming an unbeliever, and thereby be eternally lost. The key to accepting Christ and serving Christ is faith. If Faith in Christ be lost, the soul will be lost as well. And to be sure, sin domination definitely can bring on unbelief, and in fact, will bring on unbelief, if allowed to continue.

But it doesn't have to continue, victory can be ours, and in every capacity, if we will only make the Finished Work of Christ the object of our Faith.

6. Verse 16 tells us *"no manner of work shall be done in them,"* referring to these particular seven days. This foreshadows the fact that Salvation and victory are not of works, but rather of Faith. Listen again to Paul:

"For in Jesus Christ neither circumcision availeth anything, nor uncircumcision, but faith which works by love" (Gal. 5:6).

It is all by Faith, and not at all by works (Eph. 2:8-9).

When we say *"Faith,"* without exception, we are always speaking of Faith in Christ and what Christ has done for us at the Cross. Christ and His Work must never be divided or separated in any manner. It is always, even as Paul said: *"We preach Christ Crucified"* (I Cor. 1:23).

7. The Feast of Unleavened Bread was to be a *"holy convocation,"* which referred to a gathering together, and all participating. While later on, when safely ensconced in the land of Israel, this would be carried out literally, with a male from each household attending the Feast at Jerusalem, it could only be carried out symbolically in Egypt, which would be obvious.

It corresponds to the fact that all of this was very important in the eyes of God, and must be subscribed to without fail.

It is typified under the New Covenant by the *"assembling of ourselves together . . . exhorting one another: and so much the more, as you see the day approaching"* (Heb. 10:25).

Our Church Services should be the express purpose of *"preaching the Cross."* It must be preached in order for sinner's to be saved; it must be preached in order for Christians to live victoriously. There is no other way!

8. This Feast of Unleavened Bread was meant to celebrate the deliverance of the Children of Israel from Egyptian bondage. We are to *"boast in the Cross"* because it has delivered us through Christ from the world, the flesh, and the Devil (Gal. 6:14).

9. It is to be observed *"in your generations by an ordinance forever."*

Paul referred to what Jesus did as *"an Everlasting Covenant"* (Heb. 13:20). The Cross, which is the fulfillment of why Christ came, Who was Perfect in every respect, and, thereby, the Perfect Sacrifice, is to be celebrated forever.

10. The phrase *"in the first month"* as it regards Verse 18, refers to the fact that Christ and His Cross is to be first and foremost. In fact, and as stated, the Cross is not within itself a Doctrine, but rather the foundation of all Doctrine.

11. The phrase, *"whether he be a stranger, or born in the land,"* of Verse 19 proclaims the fact that Jesus and Him Crucified is the answer for the entirety of the world.

12. Verse 20 says, *"You shall eat nothing leavened,"* meaning that God cannot accept sin in any form. Christ is to never be associated with sin, except in the respect of *"Taking it away"* (Jn. 1:29).

(21) "THEN MOSES CALLED FOR ALL THE ELDERS OF ISRAEL, AND SAID UNTO THEM, DRAW OUT AND TAKE YOU A LAMB ACCORDING TO YOUR FAMILIES, AND KILL THE PASSOVER.

(22) "AND YOU SHALL TAKE A BUNCH OF HYSSOP, AND DIP IT IN THE BLOOD THAT IS IN THE BASON, AND STRIKE THE LINTEL AND THE TWO SIDE POSTS WITH THE BLOOD THAT IS IN THE BASON; AND NONE OF YOU SHALL GO OUT AT THE DOOR OF HIS HOUSE UNTIL THE MORNING.

(23) "FOR THE LORD WILL PASS THROUGH TO SMITE THE EGYPTIANS; AND WHEN HE SEES THE BLOOD UPON THE LINTEL, AND ON THE TWO SIDE POSTS, THE LORD WILL PASS OVER THE DOOR, AND WILL NOT SUFFER THE DESTROYER TO COME IN UNTO YOUR HOUSES TO SMITE YOU.

(24) "AND YOU SHALL OBSERVE THIS THING FOR AN ORDINANCE TO YOU AND TO YOUR SONS FOREVER.

(25) "AND IT SHALL COME TO PASS, WHEN YOU BE COME TO THE LAND WHICH THE LORD WILL GIVE YOU, ACCORDING AS HE HAS PROMISED, THAT YOU SHALL KEEP THIS SERVICE.

(26) "AND IT SHALL COME TO PASS, WHEN YOUR CHILDREN SHALL SAY UNTO YOU, WHAT MEAN YOU BY THIS SERVICE?

(27) "THAT YOU SHALL SAY, IT IS THE SACRIFICE OF THE LORD'S PASSOVER, WHO PASSED OVER THE HOUSES OF THE

CHILDREN OF ISRAEL IN EGYPT WHEN HE SMOTE THE EGYPTIANS, AND DELIVERED OUR HOUSES. AND THE PEOPLE BOWED THE HEAD AND WORSHIPPED.

(28) "AND THE CHILDREN OF ISRAEL WENT AWAY, AND DID AS THE LORD HAD COMMANDED MOSES AND AARON, SO DID THEY."

The structure is:

1. The Passover and the Feast of Unleavened Bread began at the same time, the fifteenth day of Abib, or as it was later called, Nisan, which would be sometime after sundown on the fourteenth.

2. The blood was to be applied to the doorposts of the houses with *"hyssop."* It speaks, not of Christ, but of the sinner's appropriation of His Sacrifice.

3. *"And when He sees the blood,"* not our good works, our Church membership, our social contacts, our wealth, but *"the Blood,"* and the Blood of Christ at that, He will keep back *"the destroyer."*

THE COMMAND

Verse 21 reads: *"Then Moses called for all the Elders of Israel, and said unto them, Draw out and take you a lamb according to your families, and kill the Passover."*

Concerning the Passover, Pink says: *"The institution and ritual of the Passover supply us with one of the most striking and blessed foreshadowments of the Cross-work of Christ to be found anywhere in the Old Testament. Its importance may be gathered from the frequency with which the title of 'Lamb' is afterwards applied to the Saviour, a title which looks back to what is before us in Exodus, Chapter 12.*

"Messianic prediction contemplated the suffering Messiah 'brought as a Lamb to the slaughter' (Isa. 53:7).

"John the Baptist hailed Him as 'Behold the Lamb of God which taketh away the sin of the world' (Jn. 1:29).

"The Apostle speaks of Him as 'a Lamb without blemish and without spot' (I Pet. 1:19).

"While the one who leaned on the Master's bosom employs this title no less than 28 times in the closing Book of Scripture. Thus, an Old Testament Prophet, the Lord's forerunner, an Apostle, and the Apocalyptic Seer unite in employing this term 'Lamb' of the Redeemer."

Throughout the entirety of the Old Testament, we find pictures and portrayals of the Sacrificial Work of Christ. But this Twelfth Chapter of Exodus, I think, supplies the grandest picture of all in the prefiguring account.

The Passover portrays to us, and in fact sets before us, the *"Godward"* and the *"manward"* aspects of the Atonement. It portrays Christ satisfying the demands of Deity, as it regards the Righteousness, Holiness, and Justice of God, while at the same time, it views Christ as a Substitute for believing sinners. There is hardly any picture of the Cross which is not supplied in this Twelfth Chapter account.

As stated, the *"Passover"* and the *"Feast of Unleavened Bread"* were to begin at the same time, which was the fourteenth day of Abib, which somewhat corresponded with our April. The blood was to then be applied to the doorposts, with the Feast of Unleavened Bread then beginning, and concluding on the twenty-first day of the month. More than likely, the deliverance was effected the night of the twenty-first, or at the latest, the twenty-second.

Each family was to kill a *"Lamb,"* unless the family was too small to do such, and then they would join with the family next door. But the fact was, all were to slay the *"Lamb."* Not that every particular individual, man, woman, and child, shared in the act itself, but that they did so representatively. The head of the household stood for, and acted on behalf of, each member of his family.

All are guilty of sin, and worthy of judgment; consequently, all who respect Christ as the true Paschal Lamb can have absolute and conscious Redemption from all sin. As a result, there will be a consequent separation from, and deliverance out of, this present evil world.

The *"Lamb"* was to be *"killed,"* typifying Christ, and the death He would suffer on the Cross, which was necessary in order for man to be redeemed. That's why Paul said, *"We preach Christ Crucified"* (I Cor. 1:23).

The Church presently, at least for the most part, is serving *"another Jesus"* (II Cor. 11:4).

By that I refer to a Jesus other than the Jesus of the Cross. And let it ever be understood, if the Cross ever ceases to be the center of emphasis, then pure and simple, it is *"another Jesus"* whom man is serving.

Paul is the man to whom the meaning of the New Covenant was given, which in effect, is the meaning of the Cross. That's the reason that he so solemnly *"preached the Cross"* (I Cor. 1:21). He knew that if anything else was preached, it would bring destruction to the ones who heeded the false message. And regrettably, at the present time, almost all that comes from behind modern pulpits can be deduced as none other than *"false."* There is one thing for certain: the message presently being preached is not *"Jesus Christ and Him Crucified."* So where does that leave the people?

That leaves the people without the blood applied to the doorposts, i.e., *"the heart."* You can draw your own conclusions thereafter.

Again I state, this is the reason that Paul wrote his Epistle to the Galatians in the manner in which he did. In fact, he was angry when this Epistle was written. And by that, I speak of a righteous indignation.

The Galatians had been brought to Christ under his Ministry, or else those who were associated with him. Consequently, they were brought in right.

But after Paul left and went to other fields of endeavor, false teachers came in, and attempted to promote the doctrine of works, by linking such with Grace. In other words, they were saying that while Jesus must be accepted, as well, the Law of Moses must be kept. Paul called that *"another gospel,"* which in effect was no gospel at all (Gal. 1:6-7).

He knew this false Message would save no sinners, and give no victory to Christians. Therefore, he would further say:

"But though we, or an Angel from Heaven, preach any other gospel unto you than that which we have preached unto you (Jesus Christ and Him Crucified), *let him be accursed"* (Gal. 1:8).

I think it should go without saying that these are strong words. In fact, what the Apostle says here places every single Preacher in the world on one side or the other. In other words, they are preaching the Cross, or they aren't preaching the Cross. So let me ask the Reader, how many Preachers presently are preaching the Cross?

HYSSOP

Verse 22 reads: *"And you shall take a bunch of hyssop, and dip it in the blood that is in the bason, and strike the lintel and the two side posts with the blood that is in the bason; and none of you shall go out at the door of his house until the morning."*

The *"hyssop"* was not connected with the *"Lamb,"* but with the application of its blood. It speaks, then, not of Christ, but of the sinner's appropriation of the Sacrifice of Christ.

The *"hyssop"* is never found in connection with any of the Offerings which foreshadowed the Lord Jesus Himself. It is beheld, uniformly, in the hands of the sinner. Thus, in connection with the cleansing of the leper (Lev., Chpt. 14); and the restoration of the unclean (Num., Chpt. 19), we find the application as well of the word *"hyssop."*

From Psalms 51:7, we may learn that *"hyssop"* speaks of *"humiliation of soul, contrition, and repentance."*

Note that in I Kings 4:33, *"hyssop"* is contrasted with *"the cedars,"* showing that *"hyssop"* speaks of *"lowliness."*

Incidentally, *"hyssop"* was a type of grass which grew in crevices between the rocks.

The word *"bason"* is not exactly the best translation. It should read, *"with the blood that is on the threshold."*

The idea is, the lamb was killed in front of each house, or at least somewhere close to the house, which, in effect, served as the *"threshold"* or the place where the house was entered, i.e., *"the door."* But when the actual blood was applied, it was to be applied only on the side posts and the header.

Whenever the people went into their houses at night, and this was after the blood was applied, they were to remain in the house all night, not coming out until the next morning.

This tells us that the death Angel was to come through at night, and beyond the protection of the Blood of the Lamb, there was no assurance of safety. In fact, there was no safety outside of this application, just as there is no safety presently outside of this application.

THE CROSS

We are to never regard the Cross of Christ as a mere circumstance in the life of Christ referring to His sin-bearing. It was the grand and only scene of sin-bearing. Peter said: *"His Own Self bear our sins in His Own Body on the Tree"* (I Pet. 2:24).

He did not bear them anywhere else. He did not bear them in the manger, nor in the wilderness, nor in the garden; but *"only on the Tree."* In fact, He never had aught to say to sin, save on the Cross; and there He bowed His head, and yielded up His precious life, under the accumulated weight of His people's sins. Neither did He ever suffer at the Hand of God, save on the Cross; and there Jehovah hid His face from Him because He was *"made to be sin"* (II Cor. 5:21) (Mackintosh).

In contemplating the Cross, we find in it that which cancels all our guilt. This imparts sweet peace and joy. But we find in it also the complete setting aside of nature — the crucifixion of *"the flesh"* — the death of *"the old man"* (Rom. 6:6; Gal. 2:20; 6:14; Col. 2:11).

THE DESTROYER

Verse 23 reads: *"For the LORD will pass through to smite the Egyptians; and when He sees the blood upon the lintel* (header)*, and upon the two side posts, the LORD will pass over the door, and will not suffer the destroyer to come in unto your houses to smite you."*

The Hebrew word for *"destroyer"* is *"shachath,"* and means, *"to decay, ruin, cast off, perish, waste, destroy."*

It has been debated as to whether the Lord is referring to Himself as a *"Destroyer,"* or rather a destroying Angel, or even the death Angel.

I think it can be safely said that the Lord is speaking here of a destroying Angel. When the Lord speaks of doing things, and puts Himself in the position as the actual participant, such doesn't necessarily mean that He Personally carried out whatever it is that's being done. He is said to have done certain things, when in fact, He will use agents to carry out that which he desires. But the fact is, they, whether Angels, or men, or even Satan, can only do what He bids be done.

There is another lesson here, even of far greater significance than that which we have just addressed. It concerns the fact that anyone who stands in the way of the Plan of God, or the people of God, will ultimately face the *"destroyer."* With the Children of Israel serving as slaves in Egypt, and that nation being possibly the most powerful on Earth, serves as a perfect example. It doesn't really matter how seemingly weak God's Way may seem to be, or how strong the opposing forces seem to be, the actual truth is the opposite. The Scripture says: *"If God be for us, who can be against us?"* (Rom. 8:31). Nothing is stronger than God, which should be obvious. So all who oppose Him will ultimately face the *"destroyer,"* and all should heed carefully those words.

THE BLOOD

Again let it be emphasized, the only thing, and we mean the only thing, which stood between the Children of Israel and the destroyer was the *"blood."* It is no less the same at the present. It is the Blood alone which protects the individual. That's why He said: *"When I see the blood, I will pass over you, and the plague shall not be upon you to destroy you"* (Vs. 13).

Of course, when we speak of *"the Blood,"* we are at the same time speaking of *"the Cross."* In fact, *"the Cross"* is a synonym for the Death, Burial, Resurrection, Ascension, and Exaltation of the Lord Jesus Christ. In other words, it incorporates all that He did for lost humanity in regard to the price that He paid; however, of these things we have just named, it is the Cross where the price was actually paid. All the other things, the Resurrection, the Ascension, and Exaltation are predicated solely on the fact of the Cross. It was on the Cross where Jesus shed His Blood, pouring out His life as a sacrifice, which atoned for all sin, past, present, and future, at least for those who will believe (Jn. 3:16).

This means that as important as was His Virgin Birth, His Perfect Life, His miracles, etc., none of that redeemed lost humanity. Had His life and mission stopped there, not one single soul would have been saved. It took the Cross to bring about Heaven's Redemption Plan. That's why Paul, under the inspiration of the Holy Spirit, said: *"But God forbid that I should glory* (boast), *save in the Cross of our Lord Jesus Christ..."* (Gal. 6:14).

That's why he also said: *"For Christ sent me not to baptize, but to preach the Gospel: not with wisdom of words, lest the Cross of Christ should be made of none effect"* (I Cor. 1:17).

It grieves me to no end, when I see Christians, even Preachers, who are in deep trouble, and yet they place their faith in the silly rules made up by men, or else they have concocted themselves, which means that they are throwing over the Cross. They may deny this; however, one cannot have it both ways. One is either trusting Christ and what He did for us at the Cross, or else, one is trusting other things, and the two can never mix.

In the first place, the Work of Christ on the Cross was and is a *"Finished Work"* (Heb. 1:2-3).

FOREVER

Verse 24 reads: *"And you shall observe this thing for an ordinance to you and to your sons forever."*

Some three times the Lord ordered Israel to *"keep the Feast of the Passover forever"* (Ex. 12:14, 17, 24), and implied it in Exodus 13:10.

In essence, this tells us that the Work of Christ on the Cross was and is a *"Finished Work,"* which means that it will never have to be repeated, and there will never have to be anything added.

In fact, under the Old Covenant, which Moses will receive from the Lord very shortly, the duties of the Priests were never finished; consequently, while there were many other items of sacred vessels, utensils, and furniture in the Tabernacle and Temple, there was no chair. The work had to keep going constantly, simply because the blood of bulls and goats could not take away sins (Heb. 10:4). Actually, the very meaning of the Crucifixion is that it was a work that was accomplished in time past, will never have to be repeated, with its blessings continuing forever, and in fact will never be discontinued.

This is why we sin greatly, when we ignore the Cross, or else we try to add to the Cross. Such constitutes grievous sins, with Paul even referring to such people as *"enemies of the Cross"* (Phil. 3:18-19).

The Cross was the Plan of God formed before the foundation of the world (I Pet. 1:18-20), it is the Plan of God now, and it will continue to be the Plan of God forever. There is nothing else coming, because there is nothing else needed.

THE PROMISE

Verse 25 reads: *"And it shall come to pass, when you have come to the land which the LORD will give you, according as He has promised, that you shall keep this service."*

Every *"Promise"* of God is based without exception on the great Sacrifice of Christ. Now that's quite a statement, and needs to be enlarged upon.

The central core of the Plan of God is the Sacrifice of Christ. The central core of that Sacrifice is the Blood.

But it's not just any Blood, rather *"the blood of a Divinely appointed victim."* That *"Victim"* is the Lord Jesus Christ. As well, this Divinely appointed Victim was *"spotless,"* as it refers to His Life, which means that He was *"holy, harmless, undefiled, separate from sinners"* (Heb. 7:26).

Furthermore, His Blood atoned for all sin, past, present, and future; however, it is only for those who will believe (Jn. 3:16).

And the most important of all, Faith in the shed Blood of Christ can save the soul, and it alone can save the soul (I Pet. 1:18-20).

And let us once again say, even as we've already said many times in this Volume, the Cross of Christ is not only the center of circumference, so to speak, for the Salvation of the soul, but as well, for the Sanctification of the Saint (Rom. 6:3-5, 11, 14; 8:1-2, 11).

God had promised the Children of Israel the *"Promised Land."* It was based entirely upon the Sacrifice of Christ. And how was this so?

THE SACRIFICE OF CHRIST

Despite the Children of Israel being a chosen people, even raised up specifically by the Lord for an expressed purpose, still, they were a sinful people. Due to that sin, God could not deal with them directly, but had to do so through intermediaries, and I speak of the Priests, but most of all, the sacrificial system. It was the duty of the Priests to faithfully carry out the commands of the Lord, as it regarded this particular system. Through the sacrificial system, God could have a modicum of fellowship and rapport with His people. While animal blood could not take away sin, it did serve as a temporary atonement, until Christ would come, to which every animal sacrifice always pointed.

So, for dealings to be carried on by God with His people, it could be done by no other means than the Sacrifice. Otherwise, the Children of Israel would have been destroyed along with the Egyptians, etc.

Even though we presently have a much better contract, so to speak, and due to Christ having gone to the Cross, still, God deals with us on the same basis as He did the Children of Israel. It was Faith then in the coming One, represented by the animal sacrifices, and it is Faith now in the One Who has come, and Faith alone (Gal. 5:5-6).

If we believe in the Promises of God, and in whatever capacity those Promises might be, we must ever understand that they are based on the Sacrifice of Christ, and the Sacrifice of Christ alone! Our Faith in the Finished Work of Christ presents itself as the key ingredient. Whatever the Word of God says that I can have, that is what I want. And I will obtain it by Faith in the Cross. Everything He has Personally guaranteed me, I will receive on the same basis, and that basis alone.

YOUR CHILDREN

Verse 26 reads: *"And it shall come to pass, when your children shall say unto you, What mean you by this service?"*

In this Passage, we are plainly told that it is our responsibility to properly relate and explain the great Sacrifice of Christ to our children. This we must not fail to do.

Verse 26 plainly tells us that it is God's intention that we relate to the children this simple, yet grand, and glorious story. They can well understand the Doctrine of the expiatory Sacrifice. In fact, it was meant to be a Gospel, not only for the elder, but as well for the youngest.

I was saved and baptized with the Holy Spirit when I was eight years old. While I did not remotely know and understand what I know and understand presently, still, I knew enough at that tender age about the Atonement, i.e., *"Jesus died for me,"* in order to respond favorably to Christ, when He spoke to my heart through the Person and Agency of the Holy Spirit.

I grieve when I see the Church trying to reach young people by using the things of the world. By that I speak of the efforts to copy the rock shows, thinking this will draw youth to Christ. How foolish can we be?

It is the Holy Spirit Who convicts of sin, and the Holy Spirit Alone. He does so on the Gospel being given, and by the Gospel, we speak of the preaching of the Cross (I Cor. 1:23; 2:2).

Over the SonLife Radio Network, which covers a great part of this nation, and even goes all over the world by and through the Internet, we never use the music to try to reach a certain segment of people. Rather, we try our best to be led by the Spirit, and to play the music that we feel the Lord would want. We'll then have to let Him take care of the rest, for He Alone can do such.

No, using the ways of the world definitely doesn't bring young people to Christ, or anyone else for that matter!

DELIVERANCE

Verses 27 and 28 read: *"That you shall say, It is the Sacrifice of the LORD's Passover, Who passed over the houses of the Children of Israel in Egypt, when He smote the Egyptians, and delivered our houses. And the people bowed the head and worshipped.*

"And the Children of Israel went away, and did as the LORD had commanded Moses and Aaron, so did they."

As is obvious, the Scripture plainly states here that *"It is the LORD's Passover,"* meaning that all, as it pertains to Salvation, is of the Lord, and of the Lord Alone!

The application of the Blood spelled Salvation for the Children of Israel, but destruction for the Egyptians. It is no less presently!

The Cross either saves or condemns, depending upon acceptance or rejection. If one rejects the Cross, then they face the Wrath of God.

God poured out His wrath upon His Only Son, the Lord Jesus Christ, Who was meant to be a Substitute for the human race. But if men refuse to accept Him, they must expect the Wrath of God, simply because, *"The Wrath of God is revealed from Heaven against all ungodliness and unrighteousness of men, who hold the truth in unrighteousness"* (Rom. 1:18).

WORSHIP

When the people heard the instructions as given by Moses concerning the Paschal Lamb, and how they would be delivered, the Scriptures say that they *"bowed the head and worshipped."*

This should ever be the response, even of modern Believers, when the story of the Cross is related to us. It must never grow old, and must ever elicit worship from our hearts, and for all the obvious reasons.

One of the major problems in the modern Church is worship based on something other than the Cross, which in fact, God will not accept. Now let the Reader study these words very carefully.

It doesn't matter how much we run, jump, leap, or what type of demonstration we may refer to as *"worship"*; if it's not based strictly on the Cross of Christ, as Verse 27 proclaims, it's not acceptable to the Lord. And regrettably, that means that most of the worship in the modern Church is unacceptable.

What does it mean for our worship to be based on the fundamentals of the Cross?

It means simply that our Faith ever be anchored in the Cross of Christ, that it ever be our object, which means that we understand that everything we receive from the Lord comes to us exclusively through the Finished Work of Christ, and by no other means. This is the means by which the Holy Spirit works, and that type of understanding makes us acceptable to God, Who then accepts our worship (Rom. 8:1-2).

OBEDIENCE

Upon hearing the instructions, as somber as they must have been, after they had worshipped the Lord, they then went away to do what the Lord had commanded that should be done.

This had to be one of the solemn moments in history. It was taking these people to a place and position they had not heretofore been, and in fact, a place and position where no one had ever been. In essence the Cross was being presented to them, and in essence, it would affect their deliverance, as well as the defeat of the Egyptians.

(29) "AND IT CAME TO PASS, THAT AT MIDNIGHT THE LORD SMOTE ALL THE FIRSTBORN IN THE LAND OF EGYPT, FROM THE FIRSTBORN OF PHARAOH WHO SAT ON HIS THRONE UNTO THE FIRSTBORN OF THE CAPTIVE WHO WAS IN THE DUNGEON; AND ALL THE FIRSTBORN OF CATTLE.

(30) "AND PHARAOH ROSE UP IN THE NIGHT, HE, AND ALL HIS SERVANTS, AND ALL THE EGYPTIANS; AND THERE WAS A GREAT CRY IN EGYPT; FOR THERE WAS NOT A HOUSE WHERE THERE WAS NOT ONE DEAD.

(31) "AND HE CALLED FOR MOSES AND AARON BY NIGHT, AND SAID, RISE UP, AND GET YOU FORTH FROM AMONG MY PEOPLE, BOTH YOU AND THE CHILDREN OF ISRAEL; AND GO, SERVE THE LORD, AS YOU HAVE SAID.

(32) "ALSO TAKE YOUR FLOCKS AND YOUR HERDS, AS YOU HAVE SAID, AND BE GONE; AND BLESS ME ALSO.

(33) "AND THE EGYPTIANS WERE URGENT UPON THE PEOPLE, THAT THEY MIGHT SEND THEM OUT OF THE LAND IN HASTE; FOR THEY SAID, WE BE ALL DEAD MEN.

(34) "AND THE PEOPLE TOOK THEIR DOUGH BEFORE IT WAS LEAVENED, THEIR KNEADINGTROUGHS BEING BOUND UP IN THEIR CLOTHES UPON THEIR SHOULDERS.

(35) "AND THE CHILDREN OF ISRAEL DID ACCORDING TO THE WORD OF MOSES: AND THEY BORROWED OF THE EGYPTIANS JEWELS OF SILVER, AND JEWELS OF GOLD, AND RAIMENT:

(36) "AND THE LORD GAVE THE PEOPLE FAVOR IN THE SIGHT OF THE EGYPTIANS, SO THAT THEY LENT UNTO THEM SUCH THINGS AS THEY REQUIRED. AND THEY SPOILED THE EGYPTIANS."

The overview is:

1. Mercy refused is always followed by judgment.

2. The blame for all the deaths of the firstborn in Egypt had to be laid at the feet of Pharaoh, and not God.

3. Whatever God says He is going to do, that He will do. The quicker that man falls in line with God's Plan, the better it is for everyone.

MIDNIGHT

Verse 29 reads: *"And it came to pass, that at midnight the LORD smote all the firstborn in the land of Egypt, from the firstborn of Pharaoh who sat on his throne unto the firstborn of the captive who was in the dungeon; and all the firstborn of cattle."*

It is obvious that the day of this visitation had not been fixed. More than likely, it took place on the twenty-first day of the month, or possibly on the twenty-second day. The exact time was *"midnight."*

All were affected, from the highest to the lowest. It even affected the *"firstborn of cattle,"* and probably all other animals as well.

Over and over again, Pharaoh had been warned, but to no avail. And now, not only would he have to pay for his obstinacy, but the entire nation of Egypt also.

That night, when the firstborn were to be destroyed, no Israelite must stir out of doors till toward morning, when they would be called to march out of Egypt.

Man must learn that God says what He means, and means what He says. But the trouble is, man is loath to take God at His Word.

Despite some nine astounding miracles, in fact, miracles of unprecedented proportions, it seems that Pharaoh simply did not believe that all the firstborn would die. It would seem to me that it would be impossible for him not to have acquiesced, if he actually believed that God was going to do this which Moses said.

Did he doubt the Power of God? Did he doubt that God could do such a thing? It would seem that he had seen enough, as it regards the miracles which had been performed, that he ought to know exactly what God could do.

The tenderest time for Pharaoh was after the first miracle was performed. But with each succeeding rejection, his heart becomes harder and harder, for that's what sin does to those who rebel against God. Each negative answer carries with it a penalty of hardness that makes it more difficult the next time to yield. I think it's possible that a person can become so hard because of rebellion, that even though they may want to yield to the Lord, they simply do not have the capacity to do so anymore.

CHRISTIANS?

It is very possible for Christians to fall into the same trap. Little by little they cool off, until they no longer sense or feel the Presence of God. They can sit through service after service, even with God moving mightily, and it never seems to touch them. That's a very, very dangerous position for a Christian to find himself.

Such a position has little to do with what is actually happening. In other words, Judas lost his way, right in the midst of the greatest Move of God the world had ever known. And I speak of the Ministry of the Master. And in that type of atmosphere, if Judas could lose his way, which he did, we should well understand that it could very easily be done in present circumstances.

Why and how do Christians fall into such a trap?

I think the reason is twofold:

1. Such a Christian ceases to look to the Cross, but rather to other things.

2. He ceases to be diligent. Peter said: *"Wherefore, beloved, seeing that you look for such things, be diligent that you may be found of Him in peace, without spot, and blameless"* (II Pet. 3:14).

Living for the Lord is like a marriage. It has to be diligently attended, and one has to work at being what one ought to be. It's not that we earn something. That's not the idea at all! But the simple fact is, if we want to be the Christian we ought to be, we have to be diligent about that which is so very, very precious to us, or at least it certainly should be.

JUDGMENT

Verse 30 reads: *"And Pharaoh rose up in the night, he, and all his servants, and all the Egyptians; and there was a great cry in Egypt; for there was not a house where there was not one dead."*

In the religion of the Egyptians, which was not true, nevertheless they believed it anyway, the entirety of their being, past, present, and future, had just been decimated. Believing that the afterlife consisted of the prosperity of the firstborn, what had happened to them was tantamount to a Christian being consigned to eternal darkness, the loss of the soul. Understanding it in that fashion, we can see how the death of the firstborn affected the entirety of the nation of Egypt.

Exactly how these deaths came about, we aren't told; however, it should be obvious that the Lord could have brought about this tragedy in any number of ways. Again, let us emphasize the fact that none of this had to be. The Lord had the right to demand the release of His people, who in fact had been worked as slaves for over 100 years. All Pharaoh had to do was to obey, and all of this tragedy would have been avoided. But we find that he wouldn't obey, until he had no choice but to obey.

The *"great cry"* that filled Egypt that early morning hour was not only registered toward the tremendous loss that every house had experienced, but as well, it was a demand that Pharaoh would let the Children of Israel go.

At the very beginning, weeks earlier, before even the first miracle had been performed, the very first message which the Lord commanded Moses to deliver to Egypt's ruler was, *"Thus saith the LORD, Israel is My son, even My firstborn: And I say unto you, Let My son go, that he may serve Me: and if you refuse to let him go, behold, I will kill your son, even your firstborn"* (Ex. 4:22-23). So, as is overly obvious, Pharaoh was without excuse.

EXCEPT YOU REPENT

In reality, the message delivered and carried out then is the same presently. All through this Christian Dispensation the solemn word has been going forth, *"Except you repent, you shall all likewise perish"* (Lk. 13:3): *"He who believes not shall be damned"* (Mk. 16:16). But, even as with Pharaoh, for the most part, the Divine warning has fallen on deaf ears. The vast majority does not believe that God means what He says.

While it is true that God is *"slow to anger,"* and long does He leave open the door of mercy, but even His longsuffering has its limits. It was thus with Pharaoh and his people. Pharaoh received plain and faithful warning, and this was followed by many appeals and preliminary judgments. But this haughty king and his no less defiant subjects only hardened their hearts. And now the threatened judgments from Heaven fell upon them, and neither wealth nor poverty provided any exemption — *"There was not a house where there was not one dead."*

Let those, even in this day of Grace, take solemn warning. The message is no less now than then, and in fact, even more so. In Old Testament times, it says that God winked at ignorance; *"but now commands all men everywhere to repent"* (Acts 17:30).

JUDGMENT AND THE CROSS

God must judge sin, and in fact, He has judged sin. He judged it by the smiting of His Own Son (Isa. 53:4). In other words, the blow that we should have taken, He took in our place. The difference is, judgment upon us would not have effected Salvation, while judgment upon Him paid the price for our sins, and Faith expressed in Christ and what He did for us at the Cross, guarantees Redemption, and exemption from the Judgment of God. But let the Reader understand the following:

Humanity accepts Christ and what He has done for us, and thereby escapes judgment, because in fact, Jesus has already taken our judgment, or else, judgment will come upon the Christ rejecter, just as surely as it came upon Egypt of so long ago. And let me say the following, and let me say it clearly:

The only thing that stands between humanity and the judgment of Almighty God is the Cross of Christ. Think about that statement; allow it to penetrate your heart; understand the truthfulness of what is being said. If the Cross is rejected, then Christ is rejected. And let that be made abundantly clear. It is impossible to accept Christ, to know Christ, to have Christ, to have and afford His Salvation, without accepting what He has done for us in the Sacrifice of Himself on the Cross.

Mackintosh said: *"True Christianity is but the manifestation of the Life of Christ,* implanted in us by the operation of the Holy Spirit, in pursuance of God's eternal counsels of sovereign Grace; and all our doings previous to the implantation of this life are but 'dead works,' from which we need to have our consciences purged just as much as from 'wicked works'" (Heb. 9:14).

And let me say in following that statement, the only way that we can have the Life of Christ implanted in us is by Faith in Christ and the substitutionary Offering of Himself on our behalf. Paul explained this graphically, which leaves no room for misunderstanding. He said:

"Don't you know, that as many of us as were baptized into Jesus Christ were baptized into His death?

"Therefore we are buried with Him by baptism into death: that like as Christ was raised up from the dead by the Glory of the Father, even so we also should walk in newness of life.

"For if we have been planted together in the likeness of His death, we shall be also in the likeness of His Resurrection" (Rom. 6:3-5).

First of all, let the Reader understand that even though Paul used the word *"baptized,"* he is not at all speaking of Water Baptism. In fact, Water Baptism has absolutely nothing to do with this particular statement. He is speaking of the Crucifixion, Burial, and Resurrection of Christ, and our part in that great work, which comes to us by Faith. Let me explain:

Jesus Christ was and is our Substitute. In other words, He did for us what we could not do for ourselves.

When He died on the Cross, God, in a sense, looked at Him as being us.

Even though He definitely was punished on the Cross, punishment was not really the primary purpose of the Crucifixion. The paying of the price, i.e., *"the paying of the ransom,"* is what the Cross was all about. Jesus said of Himself:

"Even as the Son of Man came not to be ministered unto, but to minister, and to give His life a ransom for many" (Mat. 20:28).

Paul said: *"For there is one God, and one Mediator between God and men, the Man Christ Jesus;*

"Who gave Himself a ransom for all, to be testified in due time" (I Tim. 2:5-6).

Whenever the believing sinner expresses Faith in Christ and what Christ did at the Cross, in the Mind of God, the believing sinner is literally placed in Christ, in His Death, Burial, and Resurrection.

To explain this, the strongest word that could be used is the word *"baptize."* The word literally means that the person is literally placed into that into which he is baptized, and that into which he is baptized is placed into him. It's like a ship that is sunk, and goes to the bottom of the sea. The ship is in the sea and the sea is in the ship, which is an apt description of Baptism.

RESURRECTION PEOPLE?

Many presently are fond of claiming themselves to be Resurrection people. That is true after a fashion, but only if it is properly understood as to its correct meaning.

Unfortunately, most of the time, when people use such a term concerning the Resurrection, they are belittling the Cross. Concerning the Resurrection, the Believer must know and understand the following:

Paul plainly told us that while it is true that we are *"in the likeness of His Resurrection,"* which definitely makes us Resurrection people, we have this great privilege, this great glory and honor, which gives us power to live a resurrected life, simply because, *"We have been planted together in the likeness of His death"* (Rom. 6:5). In other words, the Cross is what made possible His Resurrection, and as well, made possible our Resurrection life.

It is the understanding of His death, which speaks of the Crucifixion, and what He accomplished there, and our part in that great work, which we gained by Faith, that makes this Resurrection life possible. If we understand it in that fashion, then we have a proper understanding of the term *"Resurrection people,"* etc. He atoned for every sin on the Cross, which guaranteed His Resurrection, and our Resurrection Life.

The destroying Angel passed through the land of Egypt to destroy all the firstborn; but Israel's firstborn escaped through the death of a Divinely-provided substitute. Saved by the blood of the lamb, they are privileged to consecrate their ransomed life to Him Who had ransomed it. Thus it was only as redeemed that they possessed life. The Grace of God alone had made them to differ, and had given them the place of living men in His presence.

In their case, assuredly, there was no room for boasting, for, as to any personal merit or worthiness, we learn from the following Chapter that they were put on a level with an unclean and worthless thing, as we shall see upon arriving at that study.

PHARAOH, MOSES, AND AARON

Verses 31 and 32 read: *"And he called for Moses and Aaron by night, and said, Rise up, and get you forth from among my people, both you and the Children of Israel; and go, serve the LORD, as you have said.*

"Also take your flocks and your herds, as you have said, and be gone; and bless me also."

Before daylight, in fact, very probably not long after midnight, whatever actually happened brought forth the realization that the firstborn in each house had suddenly died. So, before dawn, Pharaoh, having suffered the loss of his own son, evidently sends a delegation to Moses and Aaron. The message is to the point:

The Children of Israel can leave, and also they can take their flocks and their herds. Trembling with fear, the Monarch requests of Moses and Aaron that they would *"bless him also."* Exactly what he meant by that is anyone's guess.

As we have said repeatedly, the Passover, which was a type of the Offering of Christ, spelled either Redemption or Judgment, according to acceptance or rejection. For all who accept Christ and His Cross, there is Redemption. For all who reject Christ and His Cross, there is Judgment.

In a sense, Pharaoh is a type of Satan, holding men in bondage, and refusing to let them go. So how is it that the Cross of Christ forces him to lift the bondage?

SATAN AND THE CROSS

While the Cross of Christ had everything to do with Satan, in a sense, it had nothing to do with him. No, that's not a contradiction. Hear me out:

Jesus didn't go to the Cross to appease Satan, or to pay some type of ransom to Satan, as some teach. While He definitely paid a ransom, it was not to Satan, but rather to God. In other words, the Cross was totally and completely of God and for God. The price that was paid was paid to God; and what was that price?

The price was death, but not just any death. It had to be the death of the Son of God, Who was unsullied, untainted, unspoiled, in other words, the perfect Sacrifice.

Jesus in totality was our Substitute (I Cor. 15:45-50). When He died, He did so in a sense, in our place — but yet, a place that we never could have filled or fulfilled because we were sinful and, therefore, unacceptable.

In fact, His death was contrived. He did not die as ordinary mortals. Actually, no one really killed Him as far as the act was concerned, even though murder was in their hearts. The truth is, He literally laid down His Life, and literally took it up again. He said:

"No man takes it from Me, but I lay it down of Myself. I have power to lay it down, and I have power to take it again. This Commandment have I received of My Father" (Jn. 10:17-18). There is every evidence that the Holy Spirit hovered over Christ at the Crucifixion, and literally told Him when He could die. The Scripture says:

"How much more shall the Blood of Christ, Who through the Eternal Spirit (Holy Spirit) *offered Himself without spot to God"* (Heb. 9:14).

When He died, even as the perfect Sacrifice, which is what He was and intended to be, His death atoned for all sin, i.e., *"paid for all sin,"* which addressed not only *"sins"* in the plural, but *"sin"* in principle (Jn. 1:29). In other words, Jesus did not merely address the symptom, which would have been the case had He only dealt with *"sins,"* but He rather went to the heart of the matter, the cause of all sin, who is Satan.

Satan has a legal right to hold man in captivity as a result of sin, which he gained at the Fall. When I say *"legal right,"* I mean that God gave him that right. But when Jesus atoned for all sin, Satan lost that legal right. So, due to what Christ did at the Cross, Satan has no choice but to let the Believer go free. The bondage is broken. Isaiah described it in this manner:

"I the LORD have called You (Christ) *in*

Righteousness ... To open the blind eyes, to bring out the prisoners from the prison, and them who sit in darkness out of the prison house" (Isa. 42:6-7).

Continuing to prophesy concerning Christ, the Prophet said: *"The Spirit of the Lord GOD is upon Me; because the LORD has anointed Me ... to proclaim liberty to the captives, and the opening of the prison to them who are bound"* (Isa. 61:1).

Does the Reader fully understand what is being said here? Do you fully know what the Lord has actually done?

This means, and I speak of what Jesus did at the Cross, that in fact, every single human being on the face of this Earth has been set free from every single bondage of darkness, no matter how bad or horrible it might be. This means that every homosexual and lesbian can be set free from that terrible bondage; every drunkard can be set free; every gambler can be set free; every drug addict can be set free; the bondage of nicotine is broken; jealousy, envy, malice, hatred, racism, unforgiveness, etc., all and without exception have had their chains splintered, and the door is thrown open to those who were bound, and the person once a captive, can now go free.

All that has to be done is for Christ and His Cross to be accepted. And along with the *"freedom,"* eternal life will be granted, which, as Peter said, is *"joy unspeakable and full of glory."*

With every sin atoned, Satan has lost his legal right to hold man captive. To obtain this benefit, Faith alone is required, and in fact, Faith alone is accepted. But it must be Faith in Christ and the Cross.

QUITTING EGYPT

Verses 33 through 36 read: *"And the Egyptians were urgent upon the people, that they might send them out of the land in haste; for they said, We be all dead men.*

"And the people took their dough before it was leavened, their kneadingtroughs being bound up in their clothes upon their shoulders.

"And the Children of Israel did according to the Word of Moses; and they borrowed of the Egyptians jewels of silver, and jewels of gold, and raiment:

NOTES

"And the LORD gave the people favor in the sight of the Egyptians, so that they lent unto them such things as they required. And they spoiled the Egyptians."

Several things are said here:

1. The Egyptians were begging the Children of Israel to leave. With the firstborn now dead, they no doubt feared that all the men of Egypt might die next. At this stage, they were not comfortable in taking any chances.

2. The Children of Israel were prepared and ready to go. They even had their bowls ready, in which they mixed up the dough in order to make bread.

3. Last of all, the Egyptians thrust upon the Israelites gold and silver, along with beautiful clothing.

The word *"borrowed"* is an unfortunate translation. These items were not given with any thought that they would be returned, nor were they taken with any thought of returning them.

It was the Lord Who put it in the hearts of the Egyptians to give freely to the Israelites, and for all the obvious reasons. By now, the Egyptians were so fearful of all Israelites, that they did not want to do anything that would seem to be contrary, but rather that which was favorable.

Hitherto, the Israelites were not permitted to depart; now they are commanded to depart. Such terror Pharaoh was in, that he gave orders by night for their discharge, fearing lest, if he delayed any longer, he himself should fall. He sent them out not as men hated, as some pagan historians have represented this matter, but as men feared, as plainly discovered by his humble request, *"Bless me also."*

As well, the Lord took care that the hard-earned wages of the Israelites should at last be paid, and that the people should be provided for their journey; consequently, they departed laden with the wealth of Egypt. Even though He may tarry long, God, to be sure, will take care of His people.

(37) "AND THE CHILDREN OF ISRAEL JOURNEYED FROM RAMESES TO SUCCOTH, ABOUT SIX HUNDRED THOUSAND ON FOOT THAT WERE MEN, BESIDE CHILDREN.

(38) "AND A MIXED MULTITUDE WENT UP ALSO WITH THEM; AND FLOCKS,

HERDS, EVEN VERY MUCH CATTLE.

(39) "AND THEY BAKED UNLEAVENED CAKES OF THE DOUGH WHICH THEY BROUGHT FORTH OUT OF EGYPT, FOR IT WAS NOT LEAVENED; BECAUSE THEY WERE THRUST OUT OF EGYPT, AND COULD NOT TARRY, NEITHER HAD THEY PREPARED FOR THEMSELVES ANY VICTUAL.

(40) "NOW THE SOJOURNING OF THE CHILDREN OF ISRAEL, WHO DWELT IN EGYPT, WAS FOUR HUNDRED AND THIRTY YEARS.

(41) "AND IT CAME TO PASS AT THE END OF THE FOUR HUNDRED AND THIRTY YEARS, EVEN THE SELFSAME DAY IT CAME TO PASS, THAT ALL THE HOSTS OF THE LORD WENT OUT FROM THE LAND OF EGYPT.

(42) "IT IS A NIGHT TO BE MUCH OBSERVED UNTO THE LORD FOR BRINGING THEM OUT FROM THE LAND OF EGYPT: THIS IS THAT NIGHT OF THE LORD TO BE OBSERVED OF ALL THE CHILDREN OF ISRAEL IN THEIR GENERATIONS."

The exegesis is:

1. There were between two and three million Israelites who made the exodus at this time from Egypt.

2. Verse 40 doesn't say that the Children of Israel dwelt in Egypt for 430 years, but that the entirety of the time of their sojourning was that long. The whole of the sojourn was from the seventy-fifth year of Abraham's life when he entered Canaan, to this day of exodus. The entire sojourn took place in Mesopotamia, Syria, Canaan, Philistia, and Egypt. The actual time in Egypt was only 215 years, one-half of the 430 of the whole period.

3. The 430 years presents the whole link of the Dispensation of Promise — from Abraham to Moses.

THE EXODUS

Verses 37 and 38 read: *"And the Children of Israel journeyed from Rameses to Succoth, about six hundred thousand on foot who were men, beside children.*

"And a mixed multitude went up also with them; and flocks, and herds, even very much cattle."

NOTES

This is no doubt the Rameses of Exodus 1:11. It was a new town built in the reign of Rameses II. It was actually now used as the capital.

"Succoth" seems to be a town about 15 miles due south of Rameses.

Considering there were upwards of three million Israelites, and that they were scattered all over Egypt, we are probably to suppose the main body with Moses and Aaron to have started from Rameses, while the others, obeying orders previously given, started from all parts of Egypt, and more specifically, Goshen, with them converging upon Succoth, which was the first rendezvous.

Each body of travelers would have been accompanied by its flocks and herds, as well as Egyptian sympathizers.

There was probably no marching along roads, with few then existing. Each company could spread itself out at its pleasure, and go at its own pace. All knew the point of meeting, and marched towards it, in converging lines, there being little or no obstacle to hinder them (Pulpit).

The *"six hundred thousand men"* mentioned here would have been men of war, between 20 and 50 years of age. You could add six hundred thousand women to that, along with all the children, and those above 50 years of age, and including the *"mixed multitude,"* there could well have been three or more million people involved.

PREPARATION

Verse 39 reads: *"And they baked unleavened cakes of the dough which they brought forth out of Egypt, for it was not leavened; because they were thrust out of Egypt, and could not tarry, neither had they prepared for themselves any victual."*

The idea of this Verse is to proclaim the fact that they had been told to prepare to leave on very short notice. It takes a while, several hours, for leaven to set up in dough. So we learn from this that they didn't even have that much time. In fact, they were ordered to leave the very night of the Passover. The notice was probably given about daylight, and the great march would begin.

As we look back on this, we should realize that the account of these happenings, while definitely historical, is much more. In fact, every single thing that took place as recorded in the Word of God is a step closer to the Redemption which we now enjoy. It didn't come easy, and neither was it simple. So, when we read these accounts, we should always read them with the idea in mind that this is the story of Redemption — a Redemption which ultimately came to me, and which is the greatest thing that ever happened to me. And of course, I speak of every Believer.

THE CONCLUSION OF THE DISPENSATION OF PROMISE

Verses 40 through 42 read: *"Now the sojourning of the Children of Israel, who dwelt in Egypt, was four hundred and thirty years.*

"And it came to pass at the end of the four hundred and thirty years, even the selfsame day it came to pass, that all the hosts of the LORD went out from the land of Egypt.

"It is a night to be much observed unto the LORD for bringing them out from the land of Egypt: this is that night of the LORD to be observed of all the Children of Israel in their generations."

The 430 years mentioned here began with Abraham, when he was 75 years old, and called of God to leave Ur of the Chaldees, and to go *"unto a land that God would show him"* (Gen. 12:1-3). This was the Dispensation of Promise.

The actual fulfillment of the Promise was Christ; however, for this *"Promise"* to be realized, a people had to be prepared, and this is the account of that preparation. To these people, the Law would be given, which would institute the Dispensation of Law, which would last until Christ would come. John said: *"For the Law was given by Moses, but Grace and Truth came by Jesus Christ"* (Jn. 1:17).

Verse 41 refers to the Israelites as *"the hosts of the LORD,"* meaning that they belonged to Him.

Verse 42 proclaims the fact that this night, the night of the first Passover, presented itself as an astounding happening. It was to be celebrated in all generations. In fact, it was commanded that the Passover was to be kept yearly, forever.

Concerning this, Matthew Henry said: *"The great things God does for His people are not to be only a few days' wonder, but the remembrance of them is to be perpetuated throughout all ages, especially the work of our Redemption by Christ."*

He went on to say: *"This first Passover-night was a night of the Lord, much to be observed; but the last Passover-night, in which Christ was betrayed, and in which the first Passover, with the rest of the ceremonial institutions, was superseded and abolished, was a night of the Lord, much more to be observed; when a yoke, heavier than that of Egypt, was broken from off our necks, and a land, better than that of Canaan, set before us. That first Passover was a temporal deliverance to be celebrated in their generations; this an eternal Redemption to be celebrated in the praises of glorious Saints, world without end."*

TEMPORAL BLESSINGS

While the Blessing of our Redemption must ever be set before us, and must ever be talked about, preached about, and celebrated in our songs and worship, as well, we should not forget the temporal blessings. The Lord is constantly doing good things for us, of which we should constantly remind ourselves, and constantly thank Him, Who is the Fount of all Blessings.

In prayer, even on a daily basis, I will notice that the Holy Spirit will bring to my mind, even over and over again, the beautiful and wonderful things which the Lord has done for me, which elicits praise on my part, as well it should. I sometimes think that future blessings are hindered by a failure to properly thank the Lord for past and present blessings. We must never forget what He has done, and to be sure, and as stated, the Holy Spirit will constantly bring it to our attention, and He does that for a purpose.

(43) "AND THE LORD SAID UNTO MOSES AND AARON, THIS IS THE ORDINANCE OF THE PASSOVER: THERE SHALL NO STRANGER EAT THEREOF:

(44) "BUT EVERY MAN'S SERVANT WHO IS BOUGHT FOR MONEY, WHEN YOU HAVE CIRCUMCISED HIM, THEN SHALL HE EAT THEREOF.

(45) "A FOREIGNER AND AN HIRED SERVANT SHALL NOT EAT THEREOF.

(46) "IN ONE HOUSE SHALL IT BE EATEN; YOU SHALL NOT CARRY FORTH OUGHT OF THE FLESH ABROAD OUT OF THE HOUSE; NEITHER SHALL YOU BREAK A BONE THEREOF.

(47) "ALL THE CONGREGATION OF ISRAEL SHALL KEEP IT.

(48) "AND WHEN A STRANGER SHALL SOJOURN WITH YOU, AND WILL KEEP THE PASSOVER TO THE LORD, LET ALL HIS MALES BE CIRCUMCISED, AND THEN LET HIM COME NEAR AND KEEP IT; AND HE SHALL BE AS ONE WHO IS BORN IN THE LAND: FOR NO UNCIRCUMCISED PERSON SHALL EAT THEREOF.

(49) "ONE LAW SHALL BE TO HIM WHO IS HOMEBORN, AND UNTO THE STRANGER WHO SOJOURNS AMONG YOU.

(50) "THUS DID ALL THE CHILDREN OF ISRAEL; AS THE LORD COMMANDED MOSES AND AARON, SO DID THEY.

(51) "AND IT CAME TO PASS THE SELFSAME DAY, THAT THE LORD DID BRING THE CHILDREN OF ISRAEL OUT OF THE LAND OF EGYPT BY THEIR ARMIES."

The construction is:

1. The *"Passover,"* i.e., *"the Crucifixion of our Lord,"* provides the foundation for this amazing deliverance.

2. Circumcision has its antitype in the Cross. The male alone was circumcised; the female was represented in the male. So, in the Cross, Christ represented His Church, and hence the Church is crucified with Christ; nevertheless she lives by the life of Christ, known and exhibited on Earth, through the Power of the Holy Spirit.

3. The ordinance of circumcision formed the grand boundary line between the Israel of God, and all the nations that were upon the face of the Earth; the Cross of our Lord Jesus Christ forms the boundary between the Church, and the world.

THE PASSOVER

Verse 43 reads: *"And the LORD said unto Moses and Aaron, This is the Ordinance of the Passover: There shall no stranger eat thereof."*

The idea is, they were the Lord's by purchase — *"bought with a price,"* and that price *"not corruptible things as silver and gold, but with the precious Blood of the Lamb!"*

This *"ordinance of the Passover,"* was for Israel's guidance in the future.

We may wonder as to why the Lord gave these instructions here, instead of giving them at the time He gave the Law, which would be some weeks later. There is a reason for that.

I think these instructions were given at this particular time, which may have seemed to have been inopportune and even premature, simply because the Lord wanted the Children of Israel to know and realize that their deliverance had come about, simply because of and through the Passover. He wanted them to realize its vast significance, which I think should be obvious as it regards all the instructions given.

The *"stranger"* was not to partake of the Passover, unless they came under the auspices of the Covenant, which entails circumcision for the males, etc. In other words, it was available to all, but only under certain conditions.

The Gospel of Jesus Christ presently is available to all, but again, only under certain conditions. There must be Faith, and we speak of Faith in Christ and His Cross. And when there is proper Faith, it will be obvious as to the Work of the Lord that's carried out in such an individual's life.

CIRCUMCISION

Verses 44 and 45 read: *"But every man's servant who is bought for money, when you have circumcised him, then shall he eat thereof.*

"A foreigner and an hired servant shall not eat thereof."

While the rite of circumcision didn't save anyone, the idea was that faith had been enjoined, in the acceptance of the Covenant, with circumcision then applied.

It involved the cutting of the flesh, which of necessity occasioned the shedding of blood. It typified the separation of the individual from the world and its system, with the shedding of blood typifying the price that would be paid by Christ for the Redemption of mankind.

In fact, circumcision was not something new, being practiced by several heathen nations; however, these nations were not a part of the Covenant of the Lord, which pertained only to Israel.

This Feast of the Passover was for Israel alone, therefore, no stranger must participate. The reason is obvious. It was only the children of Abraham, the family of Faith, who had participated in God's gracious deliverance, and they alone could commemorate it.

Second, no hired servant should eat the Passover. A *"hired"* servant is an outsider; he is actuated by self-interests. He works for pay. But no such principle can find a place in that which speaks of Redemption: *"To him who worketh not but believeth on Him Who justifieth the ungodly, his faith is counted for Righteousness"* (Rom. 4:5).

Third, no uncircumcised person could eat the Passover. This applied to Israel equally as much as to Gentiles. *"Circumcision"* at that time was the sign of the Covenant, and only those now who belong to the Covenant of Grace can feed upon Christ. Circumcision was God's sentence of death written upon nature. Circumcision has its antitype in the Cross (Col. 2:11-12).

A wall, one might say, was erected to shut out enemies, but the door was open to receive friends. No hired servant, and it speaks again of strangers, could participate in the Feast, but a bond-servant who had been purchased and circumcised, and who was now one of the household, could. So, too, the foreigner who sojourned with Israel, providing he would submit to the rite of circumcision. In this we have a blessed foreshadowing of Grace reaching out to the Gentiles, who though by nature were *"aliens from the commonwealth of Israel and strangers to the Covenants of Promise,"* are now, by Grace, *"no more strangers and foreigners, but fellowcitizens with the Saints and of the household of God"* (Eph. 2:12, 19) — a statement which manifestly looks back to Exodus, Chapter 12 (Pink).

NO BROKEN BONES

Verses 46 and 47 read: *"In one house shall it be eaten; you shall not carry forth ought of the flesh abroad out of the house; neither shall you break a bone thereof.*

"All the congregation of Israel shall keep it."

The flesh of the Passover (the Lamb) was not to be taken out of the house, but rather eaten in the house, typifying the fact that none are saved outside of the family of God. Paul said:

"For every house is built by some man; but He Who built all things is God.

"And Moses verily was faithful in all his house, as a servant, for a testimony of those things which were to be spoken after;

"But Christ as a Son over His Own house; Whose house are we, if we hold fast the confidence and the rejoicing of the hope firm unto the end" (Heb. 3:4-6).

The *"house"* of course, is Christ. And let it be known, there is no Salvation out of this *"house."* This means that all who subscribe to Islam, Buddhism, Shintoism, Confucianism, Hinduism, Catholicism, Mormonism, or any form of Christianity that is corrupt, cannot be saved. As stated, outside of this *"house"* there is no Salvation, as there can be no Salvation. It is *"Christ and Him Crucified,"* or else it is spiritual ruin and wreckage.

ANOTHER JESUS

The greatest problem in Christianity, which has existed from the days of the Early Church, is the problem of the Church worshipping and serving *"another Jesus."* Concerning this, Paul said:

"For if he who comes preaches another Jesus, whom we have not preached, or if you receive another spirit, which you have not received, or another gospel which you have not accepted, you might well bear with him" (II Cor. 11:4).

To the Galatians, he basically said the same thing: *"I marvel that you are so soon removed from Him Who called you into the Grace of Christ unto another gospel:*

"Which is not another; but there be some who trouble you, and would pervert the Gospel of Christ" (Gal. 1:6-7).

What was Paul talking about as it regards these statements?

To Paul was given by Christ the meaning of the New Covenant, which in effect, is the meaning of the Cross (Gal. 1:11-12). That's why he so adamantly said, *"We preach Christ Crucified"* (I Cor. 1:23).

Very adamantly he also said: *"For Christ sent me not to baptize, but to preach the Gospel: not with wisdom of words, lest the*

Cross of Christ should be made of none effect" (I Cor. 1:17).

In fact, to Paul was given the responsibility by Christ of being the founder of the Church, so to speak. He referred to himself as the *"Masterbuilder"* (I Cor. 3:10).

Concerning that responsibility, he also said: *"For other foundation can no man lay than that is laid, which is Jesus Christ"* (I Cor. 3:11). In essence, this also says, *"Jesus Christ and Him Crucified."*

Paul established the Churches on the foundation of the Cross. But regrettably, so-called Christian Jews came out of Jerusalem and Judea and ministered in these Churches established by Paul, or those in association with Paul. Of course, they did this after Paul had gone on to other fields of labor.

These interlopers claimed to believe in Christ, claimed to accept Christ, and claimed Christ as the Messiah; however, they also claimed that in order for one to be saved, one had as well to keep the Law of Moses. That's why Paul strongly stated: *"For in Jesus Christ neither circumcision availeth anything, nor uncircumcision; but faith which works by love"* (Gal. 5:6). In fact, he wrote the entirety of the Epistle to the Galatians to counteract this false teaching.

So in essence, what these people were preaching was *"another Jesus,"* which refers to Jesus being held up in any manner other than *"Jesus Christ and Him Crucified."* In fact, that was not only the great sin of the Early Church, but it is also the great sin presently. In most Churches, and I think I exaggerate not, the Jesus Who is preached is not the Jesus of the Cross, but rather *"another Jesus."* If *"another Jesus"* is preached, the people will not receive the Moving and Operation of the Holy Spirit, but rather *"another spirit."* All of this will constitute *"another gospel."*

Let me ask a question which I've already asked several times in this Volume:

How many Churches are presently preaching the Cross?

Including both Catholics and Protestants, the Catholic Church actually preaches the Church, which means it is not preaching Christ. So whatever Jesus they do preach is *"another Jesus."*

NOTES

The Protestant world is divided basically into three classes:

1. The Modernists: These people do not believe the Bible to be the Word of God, nor do they believe that Jesus Christ is the Son of God. In Fact, they don't believe much of anything. Regrettably and sadly, they probably make up about 50 percent of that which refers to itself as *"Christianity."*

2. Those who preach the Cross for Salvation: There are many Protestant Churches which fall into this category. They somewhat understand the Cross as it refers to Salvation, but understand it not at all as it refers to Sanctification. Consequently, the people who attend these Churches, for the most part, live defeated Christian lives.

3. Those who preach the Cross for both Salvation and Sanctification: Actually, this is the Message that Paul preached, which means that it is the correct Message. There aren't many Preachers preaching this Message, but thankfully, this number is increasing steadily.

LEGALISM, ANTINOMIANISM, AND GALATIANISM

It probably can be said without any fear of contradiction that the entirety of the world, in one way or the other, falls into one of these three categories. To be frank, most Christians have probably never even heard of Antinomianism or Galatianism. Whether the words are familiar or not isn't that important. But what they mean is very, very important.

Let's break them down, and perhaps their meanings might be of help to you the Reader, as it refers to understanding the Word of God, and how Satan seeks to pervert the Gospel.

LEGALISM

In fact, most of the world falls under the category of legalism, in one way or the other. I refer not only to professed Christianity, but as well, to the other major religions, or to one's own private religion, which he has devised out of his own mind, which applies to many in the world.

To make it simple and easy to understand, I have often referred to *"Legalism"* as the *"Brownie point system."* In other words, individuals think they are saved, or have attained some type of religious position, according to good things they do, or bad things they don't do. In one way or the other, almost the entirety of the world functions on this particular basis.

Even those who do not know anything at all about the Bible, and are not even certain if there is a God, much less a Heaven or a Hell, will often say, *"I think I'm alright, whatever there is out there after death,"* or words to that effect. As stated, they are basing their thoughts on good things they claim to do, or bad things they claim to not have done.

These people do not trust Christ at all, and in fact, don't even believe in Christ.

Going 180 degrees from Christianity, we look for a moment at the world of Islam. This particular religion is strictly a form of legalism. When Muslims attempt to kill others who oppose their religion, they are taught that this is a good deed, and they will guarantee themselves a place in Heaven, etc. Most other religions, although not this militant, function at least somewhat in the same manner, at least as far as *"works"* are concerned, etc.

Christians have to be very careful as well, that their faith is not placed in *"works,"* but rather in Christ. In fact, this is probably the great battle in Christianity. Simply because the doing of good things constitutes that which is *"good,"* at least good in our sight, we tend to think of it as earning us something with God. It doesn't! The sadness is, most Christians will agree with what I've just said, and then turn right around and place their faith in *"works."* All of this is Legalism.

For instance, some pages back, we discussed the restoration process of the modern Church, which is mostly unscriptural. It is unscriptural because it is anchored in *"works,"* and not at all in *"faith."* Pure and simple, it is *"Legalism."* In other words, you are righteous if you do these particular things, and I speak of works devised by men, and if you don't do those particular things, you are unrighteous.

ANTINOMIANISM

"Anti" in the Greek means, *"to be against."* The word *"nomi"* in the Greek means, *"law."* So the word *"Antinomianism"* means, *"against law."*

At first glance, that might seem to be correct; however, what such people who practice Antinomianism are actually doing is to take liberty into license.

Paul faced this same problem in the Early Church, exactly as he did the problems of Legalism and Galatianism. He had stated: *"But where sin abounded, Grace did much more abound"* (Rom. 5:20).

Some of the Christians of that particular time took his statement to excess. In other words, they surmised that due to the fact that Grace was so abundant and so powerful that it didn't really matter about sin. In other words, they could do whatever it is they wanted to do, and without any fear of any repercussions. The Apostle answered that by saying:

"What shall we say then? Shall we continue in sin, that Grace may abound?

"God forbid. How shall we, who are dead to sin, live any longer therein?" (Rom. 6:1-2).

In fact, the Church is full of these type of people presently. They have the erroneous conclusion that sin doesn't matter, and that Grace automatically covers their sin the moment it is committed, and so it's no big deal. In other words, they are *"lawless."*

Paul further answered that by saying: *"All things are lawful unto me, but all things are not expedient: all things are lawful for me, but I will not be brought under the power of any"* (I Cor. 6:12).

The true Christian must always understand that *"liberty,"* as it is given to him by Christ, refers to liberty to live a holy life, and not liberty to sin. In fact, the Cross of Christ is God's answer to sin, which means that the Cross not only atoned for sin, but as well, Faith in that Finished Work of Christ gives us victory over all sin, which refers to the Sanctification of the Saint.

As a Believer, I am definitely subject to the moral law, which should be obvious. But I'm not subject to that moral law as it refers to Commandments. Jesus has answered all of that, and if my Faith is properly in Him, and what He has done for me at the Cross, the Holy Spirit will then work powerfully within my heart and life, thereby keeping the moral law in every respect, and without difficulty.

There are many things as a Christian that I won't do, even as Paul said, because it's not expedient; in other words, it doesn't bring Glory to God. But I never think about these things, only my Faith in Christ and His Finished Work. It then becomes easy to live this Christian life. But if we try to do so by means of keeping commandments, etc., we will quickly find ourselves in a perilous situation.

Concerning this, Paul also said: *"I am crucified with Christ* (trusting in what Christ did at the Crucifixion)*: nevertheless I live* (am able to live this Christian life)*; yet not I, but Christ lives in me: and the life which I now live in the flesh* (my everyday walk) *I live by the faith of the Son of God* (Faith in Christ and what He has done for me at the Cross), *Who loved me, and gave Himself for me."*

He then said: *"I do not frustrate the Grace of God* (by trying to live a *'works'* religion)*: for if Righteousness come by the law* (the Believer trying to earn Righteousness by keeping laws), *then Christ is dead in vain* (if one can attain to Righteousness by keeping laws, then Christ died on the Cross needlessly)" (Gal. 2:20-21).

As a Christian, I'm definitely not against the Laws of God, but I address those Laws through Christ, and not at all by my own strength, etc.

GALATIANISM

Galatianism refers to the teaching that Paul gave us in his Epistle to the Galatians. These people had been saved by *"Faith,"* but now were trying to sanctify themselves by *"works."* They were doing this because of false teachers who had come in, claiming that they had to also keep the Law, etc.

I think that one could say without fear of contradiction that *"Galatianism"* is the greatest problem for the true Child of God. And why is it such a great problem?

Almost every true Christian understands the Cross, at least up to a point, as it regards Salvation; however, most know absolutely nothing about the Cross as it regards Sanctification. There, they draw a blank.

The major problem is, most Christians are loath to admit that they lack understanding as it regards the Cross. They look at the Cross as something that's elementary, thereby, having learned all about that, when they first got saved.

Just yesterday, a dear Brother was in my office, and mentioned to me that it was very hard for him to admit, when he first began to hear us teach about the Cross, that he was bereft of this great knowledge. He, as most Christians, had been living for God for many, many years. In fact, he definitely was and is a very dedicated Christian. So the idea that he didn't understand all about the Cross, at least at first, was very difficult for him to admit. Regrettably, it is the same with most Christians.

But the truth is, very few Christians, including Preachers, understand the Cross as it regards Sanctification. In other words, they simply don't know what Romans, Chapters 6, 7, and 8 actually mean.

In fact, most Preachers interpret Romans, Chapter 7 in one of two ways:

1. The group that subscribes to Antinomianism uses Romans, Chapter 7 as their foundation text, claiming that one cannot help but sin, etc. Romans 7:15 is their oft used text: *"For that which I do I allow not* (understand not)*: but what I would, that do I not; but what I hate, that do I."*

2. Another group relegates the Seventh Chapter of Romans to Paul's experience before conversion; so they just pass it off in that fashion, thereby, little understanding what the Apostle is saying there.

No, Paul in Romans, Chapter 7 is not teaching that Christians have to sin a little bit everyday, and neither is he giving his experience before conversion. In fact, Paul is dealing with his experience after conversion, and after being Baptized with the Holy Spirit. Not understanding the Cross, at least at that particular time, he tried to live for God the way most Christians do, which refers to keeping rules and regulations, etc. He found that he couldn't carry out the task as he should, which left him in a very perilous situation: *"O wretched man that I am! Who shall deliver me from the body of this death?"* (Rom. 7:24).

Out of that desperation, the Lord gave to Paul the Revelation of the Cross, which in effect, is the meaning of the New Covenant, in which he then gave it to us in his 14 Epistles.

But getting back to our original thought, not understanding the Cross as it refers to Sanctification, because most don't understand what Paul taught about this all-important subject, most Christians seek to sanctify themselves, and to do so, by a regimen of *"works."* God can never sanction such, and simply because, when we do this, we are in fact, practicing *"spiritual adultery"* (Rom. 7:1-4). But regrettably, this is the position of most modern Christians.

GRACE

Grace is simply the goodness of God extended to undeserving people. More than all, it is the Holy Spirit carrying out all the benefits of the Cross within our hearts and lives, at least if we allow Him to do so.

The Grace of God is made possible by the Cross. In fact, God has always had Grace, and has always functioned in Grace. In truth, the Lord doesn't have any more Grace presently, even though this is the Dispensation of Grace, than He did in Old Testament times. The problem in Old Testament times was, due to the fact that the blood of bulls and goats couldn't take away sins, God was limited as to the Grace He could extend to individuals.

Since the Cross, which paid the terrible sin debt, which is the key to the great Plan of Salvation, the Grace of God can now be extended to Believers in an uninterrupted flow.

For that flow to continue uninterrupted, it only requires that we have Faith in Christ and what Christ has done for us at the Cross, ever making that the object of our Faith. Then the Holy Spirit works mightily within us, continuing to extend to us the Grace of God. In fact, the *"Cross"* and *"Grace"* are forever interlocked. The Believer cannot have one without the other. And one of the reasons that there is very little Grace which is evident, is because of a lack of understanding of the Cross.

Not understanding the Cross, most have a confused idea of Grace, even referring to such as *"greasy Grace,"* or *"easy Grace,"* etc. Were it not for ignorance, such would border on blasphemy!

It is impossible for the Believer to live a victorious life without a constant flow of the Grace of God. This means that the Holy Spirit has to constantly help us. In fact, without Him and His Work, we can do nothing. This is what Jesus was speaking of when He said: *"I am the Vine, you are the branches: he who abides in Me, and I in Him, the same brings forth much fruit: for without Me you can do nothing"* (Jn. 15:5).

When He used the phrase, *"For without Me you can do nothing,"* He was referring to what He carries out within our lives through the Person, Work, Agency, and Power of the Holy Spirit.

He also said: *"If any man thirst, let him come unto Me, and drink.*

"He who believes on Me, as the Scripture has said, out of his innermost being shall flow rivers of living water.

"But this spake He of the Spirit" (Jn. 7:37-39).

When Jesus speaks in this manner, referring to Himself as the Fountain and Source of all life, which He definitely is, He is referring to what He did at the Cross, which makes it all possible. The Holy Spirit works very closely with Him, constantly glorifying Christ, always working within the parameters of the Finished Work of Christ. That's what Paul was talking about when he said: *"For the Law of the Spirit of Life in Christ Jesus, has made me free from the law of sin and death"* (Rom. 8:2). This *"Law of the Spirit of Life"* of course refers to the Holy Spirit, but the phrase, *"in Christ Jesus,"* refers to Christ and what Christ did at the Cross, as proven by the little word *"in."*

FRUSTRATING THE GRACE OF GOD

Paul said: *"I do not frustrate the Grace of God: for if Righteousness come by the Law, then Christ is dead in vain"* (Gal. 2:21).

We are plainly told here, and as we've already addressed in this Volume, that it is possible to frustrate the Grace of God. When this is done, the Grace of God is greatly hindered in its coming to us, or even stopped. We are then left on our own, which means that we do not have the help of the Holy Spirit, which guarantees failure.

So how can a Christian frustrate the Grace of God?

We frustrate the Grace of God when we attempt to live for God by means of keeping laws, etc. In other words, if we're trying to live for the Lord by any method other than simple Faith in Christ and what Christ has done for us at the Cross, all we will succeed in doing is to frustrate the Grace of God.

As we've already stated, to have an uninterrupted flow of Grace, all we have to do is to have Faith in Christ and His great Sacrifice of Himself, and continue to have Faith in that respect, ever making the Cross of Christ the object of our Faith. Then the Grace of God will flow to us like a river, and we will find that living for the Lord then becomes a joy instead of a chore. We will also find ourselves overcoming every sin, transgression, and iniquity, with which in the past, we have had great problems. In fact, this is the only way that the Believer can live a victorious, overcoming, Christian life.

NO BROKEN BONE

Concerning the Passover, the Scripture plainly said that the Children of Israel, in the partaking of this Feast, was not to break a single bone thereof. What did that represent?

It refers to Christ. The Spirit of Prophecy, concerning Christ, had David to write: *"He keeps all His bones: not one of them is broken"* (Ps. 34:20).

When Jesus was crucified, *"The Jews therefore, because it was the preparation that the body should not remain upon the Cross on the Sabbath day (for that Sabbath was an high day), besought Pilate that their legs might be broken, and that they might be taken away"* (Jn. 19:31). Here was Satan, in his malignant enmity attempting to falsify and nullify the Written Word. Vain effort was it.

"Then came the soldiers and broke the legs of the first, and of the other which was crucified with Him" (Jn. 19:32).

Concerning this, Pink said: *"Thus far might the agents of the Roman Empire go, but no farther — 'But when they came to Jesus and saw that He was dead already, they break not His legs' (Jn. 19:33). Here we are given to see the Father 'keeping' all the bones of His Blessed Son.*

"Pierce His side with a spear a soldier might, and this, only that prophecy might be fulfilled, for it was written, 'They shall look on Him Whom they pierced' (Zech. 12:10). *But break His legs they could not, for 'a bone of Him shall not be broken', and it was not!"* (Pink).

The bones not being broken carried the idea of the wholeness of Christ. While they might do all type of other things to Him, the initial frame of His sinless, Perfect Body, was not broken. This signified that He would carry out all that He had come to do, which He, in fact, did. Consequently, when we accept Christ, we do not accept a broken Christ, but rather, the whole Christ, Who gave Himself for us (Gal. 1:4).

As His Personal body is one (unbroken), likewise, His Church is one as well. It is to be unbroken, referring to the fact that the True Church, and irrespective as to what name it has, is one with Christ by one simple method, and that is Faith in Christ and His Cross.

CIRCUMCISION

Verse 48 reads: *"And when a stranger shall sojourn with you, and will keep the Passover to the LORD, let all his males be circumcised, and then let him come near and keep it; and he shall be as one who is born in the land: for no uncircumcised person shall eat thereof."*

Several things are said in this Verse:

1. The word *"stranger"* refers to Gentiles, meaning that Gentiles could definitely come into the Covenant, that is, if they came God's Way.

2. If they entered the Covenant, all the males in that particular family would have to engage in the rite of circumcision. This, as previously stated, concerned itself with separation of the flesh and the shedding of blood.

The *"separation,"* which circumcision entailed, pertains, in the spiritual sense, to the Believer separating himself from the efforts of the flesh, depending totally on the Spirit. Once again, we go back to the Cross.

The *"shedding of blood,"* which always accompanied circumcision, pertained to the price that would be paid by the coming Redeemer, the Lord Jesus Christ, in His death on the Cross.

3. Having done this, the *"stranger"* is in fact, no more a stranger, but is to be treated as *"one who is born in the land."* In other words, in the eyes of God, he had now become a Jew.

4. If one refused to do this which was commanded by the Lord, he was not to be allowed to partake of the Passover, which means that he wasn't saved.

ONE LAW

Verse 49 reads: *"One law shall be to him who is homeborn, and unto the stranger who sojourns among you."*

The Lord doesn't have two ways of Salvation, only *"one."* That is Christ, even as it has always been Christ.

In fact, when Paul asked the question and made the statement: *"What then? Are we better than they* (are Jews better than Gentiles)*? No, in no wise: for we have before proved both Jews and Gentiles, that they are all under sin"* (Rom. 3:9).

Under the old Law (the Law of Moses), the Holy Spirit said that Gentiles had to come in the same way as the Jews. Under Grace, the Holy Spirit says that Jews have to come the same way as Gentiles. There is only *"one way,"* and that is Christ, irrespective as to the person or their nationality.

DELIVERANCE

Verses 50 and 51 read: *"Thus did all the Children of Israel; as the LORD commanded Moses and Aaron, so did they.*

"And it came to pass the selfsame day, that the LORD did bring the Children of Israel out of the Land of Egypt by their armies."

The words in Verse 51, *"Even the selfsame day,"* indicate that Abraham began his sojourn on the fifteenth day of Nisan or April, exactly 430 years before the Exodus.

The word *"armies"* refers to the fact that the people were organized as they came out of Egypt, which means they did not come out as a rabble. As well, God looked at them as *"Armies,"* simply because He was their Captain, and through Him, they possessed great power.

The leaders of Egypt, at least at the beginning, had probably laughed at the demands of Moses, maybe even asking the question as to where the army of Israel was, that would free them from the land of Egypt. Well, the Lord would show Egypt just exactly who this army was, and the source of their power.

NOTES

"Days are filled with sorrow and care,
"Hearts are lonely and drear;
"Burdens are lifted at Calvary,
"Jesus is very near."

"Cast your care on Jesus today,
"Leave your worry and fear;
"Burdens are lifted at Calvary,
"Jesus is very near."

"Troubled soul, the Saviour can see
"Every heartache and tear;
"Burdens are lifted at Calvary,
"Jesus is very near."

CHAPTER 13

(1) "AND THE LORD SPOKE UNTO MOSES, SAYING,

(2) "SANCTIFY UNTO ME ALL THE FIRSTBORN, WHOSOEVER OPENS THE WOMB AMONG THE CHILDREN OF ISRAEL, BOTH OF MAN AND OF BEAST: IT IS MINE.

(3) "AND MOSES SAID UNTO THE PEOPLE, REMEMBER THIS DAY, IN WHICH YOU CAME OUT FROM EGYPT, OUT OF THE HOUSE OF BONDAGE; FOR BY STRENGTH OF HAND THE LORD BROUGHT YOU OUT FROM THIS PLACE: THERE SHALL NO LEAVENED BREAD BE EATEN.

(4) "THIS DAY CAME YOU OUT IN THE MONTH ABIB.

(5) "AND IT SHALL BE WHEN THE LORD SHALL BRING YOU INTO THE LAND OF THE CANAANITES, AND THE HITTITES, AND THE AMORITES, AND THE HIVITES, AND THE JEBUSITES, WHICH HE SWORE UNTO YOUR FATHERS TO GIVE YOU, A LAND FLOWING WITH MILK AND HONEY, THAT YOU SHALL KEEP THIS SERVICE IN THIS MONTH.

(6) "SEVEN DAYS YOU SHALL EAT UNLEAVENED BREAD, AND IN THE SEVENTH DAY SHALL BE A FEAST TO THE LORD.

(7) "UNLEAVENED BREAD SHALL BE EATEN SEVEN DAYS; AND THERE SHALL NO LEAVENED BREAD BE SEEN WITH YOU, NEITHER SHALL THERE BE LEAVEN SEEN WITH YOU IN ALL YOUR QUARTERS.

(8) "AND YOU SHALL SHOW YOUR

SON IN THAT DAY, SAYING, THIS IS DONE BECAUSE OF THAT WHICH THE LORD DID UNTO ME WHEN I CAME FORTH OUT OF EGYPT.

(9) "AND IT SHALL BE FOR A SIGN UNTO YOU UPON YOUR HAND, AND FOR A MEMORIAL BETWEEN YOUR EYES, THAT THE LORD'S LAW MAY BE IN YOUR MOUTH: FOR WITH A STRONG HAND HAS THE LORD BROUGHT YOU OUT OF EGYPT.

(10) "YOU SHALL THEREFORE KEEP THIS ORDINANCE IN HIS SEASON FROM YEAR TO YEAR."

The composition is:

1. The *"firstborn"* who were to be sanctified to the Lord, which means set apart unto the Lord, were meant to typify Christ.

2. Immediately after Israel was redeemed out of Egypt, instructions were given respecting the annual observance of the Passover. That is to say, Israel was to perpetually confess to the world that her Salvation out of Egypt, and her settlement in Canaan, was wholly due to the preciousness of the Blood of the Paschal Lamb.

3. The *"sign"* of Verse 9, and the *"token"* of Verse 16 figuratively mean that what is done by the hand, desired by the eye, and spoken by the mouth, is all to be subject to the Word of God.

THE FIRSTBORN

Verses 1 and 2 read: *"And the LORD spoke unto Moses, saying,*

"Sanctify unto Me all the firstborn, whatsoever opens the womb among the Children of Israel, both of man and of beast: it is Mine."

The *"firstborn"* were to be sanctified unto the Lord, which means set apart unto the Lord, because they were to be a representation or a Type of Christ. They were to be a picture of the Salvation Plan. Jesus is referred to as *"The Firstborn among many brethren"* (Rom. 8:29).

This doesn't mean that Jesus was *"born again"* after the Crucifixion, as some teach, but rather that He was the Originator or the Father, one might say, of the Salvation experience, which means that through the Cross, He made Salvation possible.

The whole of Israel was to be a Type of Christ, with the *"firstborn"* being even a greater type. This extended, as is obvious here, even to the firstborn of animals. If it belonged to Israel, the type was to carry all the way through, even to that which they possessed, at least as far as the animals were concerned.

I want the Reader to notice that even before the Children of Israel were delivered from Egyptian bondage, instructions were being given to them, and instructions which were very detailed regarding character and scope. These people had been raised up for a particular purpose, and that was in effect to serve as the womb of the Messiah. They were to also give the world the Word of God, which they did do.

But as Israel was in the world, the Church is to be as well. The difference is, the Word of God has already been given, and the Church is to exemplify that Word. As well, Christ has already come, so the Church is to portray Christ. But whether Israel or the Church, all are to portray Christ, and above all, what He did at the Cross on behalf of lost humanity.

As we've already stated, true Christianity is but the manifestation of the Life of Christ, implanted in us by the Operation of the Holy Spirit (Mackintosh).

DELIVERANCE FROM THE HOUSE OF BONDAGE

Verses 3 and 4 read: *"And Moses said unto the people, Remember this day in which you came out from Egypt, out of the house of bondage; for by strength of hand the LORD brought you out from this place: there shall no leavened bread be eaten.*

"This day came you out in the month Abib."

Israel was to understand, and to understand fully, that they had been delivered out of this *"house of bondage,"* not by their own ingenuity, strength, ability, or talent, but by *"the strength of the hand of the Lord."* There was no way they could have extricated themselves from this bondage, and even with God, it took His miracle-working Power.

In essence, the Lord was telling the Israelites that they were now His people, for He had bought them; and that they were, therefore, to be holy. They had been slaves to Pharaoh; now they were to be slaves to Jehovah. However, as the Master would say: *"Take My yoke upon you, and learn of Me; for I* am meek and lowly in heart: and you shall find rest unto your souls.

"For My yoke is easy, and My burden is light" (Mat. 11:29-30).

Due to that *"yoke"* being easy, and that *"burden"* being light, many, if not most, Christians little function as they should. They take the Blessings of the Lord for granted, actually demanding much, and give Him precious little in return. Perhaps, that is the case with all of us.

At the least, I think one can say without any fear of contradiction that the best among us, whomever that might be, little serve as we should.

A redeemed people become the property of the Redeemer, which should be obvious. Consequently, the first exhortation in Romans, which follows the doctrinal exposition in Chapters 1 through 11 is, *"I beseech you therefore, Brethren, by the Mercies of God, that you present your bodies a living sacrifice, holy, acceptable unto God, which is your reasonable service"* (Rom. 12:1). Personal devotion is the first thing which God has a right to expect from His Blood-bought people.

THIS DAY

Verse 4 specifies that on a certain day, even in a certain month, that the Children of Israel were brought out of Egyptian bondage. This tells us, and in no uncertain terms, that Salvation is not merely a philosophical quest, but rather, a genuine, know so Salvation. In other words, the believing sinner knows the exact moment that Christ comes into his heart. At that moment, in the portals of Glory, the Lord writes down the name of that individual in the Lamb's Book of Life. Forever, that date, time, and place are written down in Glory, so that it can be forever said, *"This day came you out. . . ."* Oh how I sense the Presence of God, even as I dictate these words. How so much the Lord has done for us; how so great is His Salvation; how so glorious the moment we passed from death to life, from darkness to light, from sin to Salvation!

UNLEAVENED BREAD

As the following Verses explain, the instruction given here pertaining to *"Unleavened Bread,"* concerns itself with that Feast which is to take place every year, at the time of the Passover. During this time, no leavened bread was to be eaten because this bread represented Christ, Who is Perfect, sinless, Holy, undefiled, etc.

Christ was the Deliverer of the Children of Israel, as He is the Saviour of all who trust in His Name. As well, He delivered them by and through the type of the shed Blood of the Lamb. In effect, one might say they were delivered on credit, awaiting the day when He would come to this world, and die on a Cross, thereby *"taking away all sin"* (Jn. 1:29). In fact, all the great Feasts of Israel, totaling seven, and conducted at three different times of the year, which required a male of every house to attend, all and without exception proclaimed Christ and His expiatory, substitutionary Work.

A LAND FLOWING WITH MILK AND HONEY

Verse 5 reads: *"And it shall be when the LORD shall bring you into the land of the Canaanites, and the Hittites, and the Amorites, and the Hivites, and the Jebusites, which He sware unto your fathers to give you, a land flowing with milk and honey, that you shall keep this service in this month."*

Several things are said in this Passage:

1. Without fail, the Lord would bring them into the Land of Promise. Regrettably, because of unbelief, Israel would take some 40 years to arrive there, when they should have taken only about two years or less. In fact, the only thing that hinders the Lord is unbelief.

2. While it was true that the land was filled with enemies, He specifically stated that He would give it to them, which means that He would defeat all of these enemies. The difference now is, He has already defeated all of these enemies; therefore, we make a sad mistake when we try to fight this battle all over again, as many of us have done. The victory is not ours to obtain, for the simple reason that it is victory already possessed. We have it and we maintain it, by simply trusting in Christ and what Christ has done for us at the Cross.

3. The Word of God had been given,

"which He swore unto your fathers to give you," and it was, therefore, guaranteed of fulfillment.

4. Furthermore, it was a land *"flowing with milk and honey."* Everything that God gives is glorious, wonderful, and good. In fact, He has absolutely nothing that is bad in any respect. While He definitely does demand that we give up some things, what He gives us to take their place is so far more than what we lose, that there is no comparison. Regrettably, at times we sully His great and glorious gifts, but the fault is ours and not His.

5. During the month of Abib (Nisan), each and every year, this great deliverance was to be celebrated by three particular Feasts celebrated at this particular time. It was to be the Feast of Passover, the Feast of Unleavened Bread, and the Feast of Firstfruits.

The first Feast pictured Christ as the Deliverer of His people, and the price He would pay on the Cross for that deliverance. The second Feast portrayed the perfection of Christ, which made the Sacrifice of Himself acceptable. The third Feast pictured His Resurrection. So we have *"Death, Perfection, and Resurrection."*

A FEAST TO THE LORD

Verses 6 and 7 read: *"Seven days you shall eat unleavened bread, and in the seventh day shall be a Feast to the LORD.*

"Unleavened bread shall be eaten seven days; and there shall no leavened bread be seen with you, neither shall there be leaven seen with you in all your quarters."

In fact, this Feast lasted throughout the entirety of the seven days, but the first day and the last were to be kept especially holy (Lev. 23:6-8).

These injunctions have in fact already been given in Chapter 12 (Vss. 15, 19). It was repeated, no doubt, in order to deepen the impression that the lesson the Holy Spirit desired to be taught would be amply learned.

The number *"seven"* here is not without significance. As used in the Word of God, it portrays in its final analysis the glory, totality, and perfection of the Lord Jesus Christ. In fact, all of these Feasts, as given by God to Israel, were meant to portray the Ministry of Christ in some fashion, which we will more fully explain when we come to the installation of the Feasts in the giving of the Law (Ex., Chpt. 23; Lev., Chpt. 23).

The seventh day of the seven days, deemed as a special day, refers to the Finished Work of Christ, in that His Mission would be a completed Mission.

The *"Unleavened Bread"* as stated, signified the perfection of Christ, as it regards His Perfect Body, Perfect Mind, Perfect Actions, in other words, that there was no sin in Him. The Scripture says of Him that He was and is *"holy, harmless, undefiled, separate from sinners, and made higher than the heavens"* (Heb. 7:26).

"Leaven" is used in the Old Testament, and as well by Paul, as a type of sin (Gal. 5:9). So during these seven days, unleavened bread only was to be eaten, which typified that the coming Messiah would have no sin.

CHRIST IN US

Even though all of this typifies Christ, even as it is meant to do, at the same time, it typifies the Sanctification of the Believer for all of us; at least all who are Born-Again, who are in Christ.

To eat *"Unleavened Bread"* signifies separation from all evil, in order that we may feed upon Christ. That this Feast lasted *"seven days,"* which is a complete period, tells us that this is to last throughout our whole sojourn on Earth. It is to this that Paul refers: *"Purge out therefore the old leaven, that you may be a new lump, as you are unleavened. For even Christ our Passover is sacrificed for us; therefore let us keep the Feast not with old leaven, neither with the leaven of malice and wickedness; but with the unleavened bread of sincerity and truth"* (I Cor. 5:7-8).

All of this was a *"type"* as it regarded Old Testament means and methods; however, it was meant to portray that which Christ would do within our hearts and lives.

Every Christian knows that all sin must be purged out of our lives; however, the great question is, how is this done? If we miss it here, then we miss it altogether.

THE CROSS

Once again, we go back to the Cross.

Remember that Paul said, *"For even Christ our Passover is sacrificed for us."*

While the Scripture doesn't teach sinless perfection, it definitely does teach that sin shall not have dominion over us, and this basically speaks of the sin nature (Rom. 6:14).

There is only one way that the Child of God can walk in victory, not five ways, three ways, or even two ways, only one way.

We go back to the original meaning of this Text in Exodus, Chapter 13 as it speaks of Christ. The Church has run aground in ten thousand different ways, attempting to carry out this of which we speak, and I refer to living an overcoming, Christian life. It can only be done in Christ, but how is it done in Christ?

The clue is in what Paul said concerning Christ's Sacrifice of Himself (I Cor. 5:7). As the Second Man, i.e., *"the Representative Man"* (I Cor. 15:45-50), which refers to Christ being our Substitute, He has done all things for us, simply because it was impossible for us to do it ourselves. In other words, if man was to be saved, Salvation would wholly have to come from outside of man, which it did in the realm of Christ.

While everything Christ did played a great part in the Redemption process, the Believer must first of all, that is if he is to understand Redemption, zero in on the Sacrifice of Christ, even as Paul stated. As is obvious, this refers to the Cross.

You must understand as a Believer that every single thing you have from the Lord, and irrespective as to what it might be, has been made possible by what Christ did at the Cross. That must be the foundation of believing, the foundation of our Faith.

Having anchored our Faith in the Sacrifice of Christ, which means we have made the Cross of Christ the object of our Faith, the Holy Spirit, who is the key to all of our victory, can then function and work unhindered within our hearts and lives (Rom. 6:3-5, 10-14; 8:1-2, 11).

But far too often, we attempt to rid ourselves of sin, by man-devised rules and regulations, which in fact, the Holy Spirit will never honor. In other words, unless the Holy Spirit works within us, which He of course desires to do, we will be left functioning within the capacity of our own personal strength, which we will quickly find to be woefully insufficient.

To get you started, and which I've already stated any number of times in this Volume, always understand that Christ gives us all things through what He did at the Cross; consequently, our Faith must rest in that Finished Work, which then gives the Holy Spirit latitude to work within our lives. As stated, I have said this over and over, and will continue to say it throughout this Volume, because it's so very, very important.

The Holy Spirit works entirely within the parameters of the Sacrifice of Christ (Jn. 14:16-17; 16:8-14).

A SIGN

Verses 8 through 10 read: *"And you shall show your son in that day, saying, This is done because of that which the LORD did unto me when I came forth out of Egypt.*

"And it shall be for a sign unto you upon your hand, and for a memorial between your eyes, that the LORD's Law may be in your mouth: for with a strong hand has the LORD brought you out of Egypt.

"You shall therefore keep this Ordinance in his season from year to year."

The great things which the Lord has done for us, and He to be sure has done many, must never be forgotten. They must be related over and over, and for a number of reasons:

1. We must ever be mindful that it is the Lord Who has done these things, and not we ourselves.

2. The relating of great events as done by the Lord to our children builds Faith in them that they might expect great and mighty things as well.

3. All of this relates to an accomplished fact. The basis of this Feast was what the Lord had done for Israel in delivering them from the land of bondage. In other words, its foundation was Redemption accomplished, entered into, known, and enjoyed. It speaks of a work already accomplished. Until this joy of assurance is ours, there cannot be any feasting upon Christ.

PHYLACTERIES

There can be little doubt that the Jewish

system of *"phylacteries,"* grew mainly out of this Passage, and was intended as a fulfillment of the commands contained in it (Pulpit).

These *"phylacteries"* of which Jesus mentioned were strips of parchment with Passages of Scripture written upon them and deposited in small boxes, which were fastened by a strap either to the left arm, or across the forehead.

The original intention by the Holy Spirit was according to the following:

It was to be a *"sign"* upon the hand that signified that all service was consecrated to God. It was also to be a *"memorial between the eyes,"* that is, upon the forehead, where all could see; which being interpreted, signifies an open manifestation of separation unto God.

Finally, it was to be accompanied with *"The Lord's Law in their mouth,"* which means that the Law was ever to be the basis of all action taken.

Used in the right manner, it would be a great blessing to the people. As a front for *"self-righteousness,"* which happened with some, Jesus replied:

"But all their works they do for to be seen of men: they make broad their phylacteries, and enlarge the borders of their garments" (Mat. 23:5).

The idea was, as is obvious, some in Jesus' day wore large phylacteries to make themselves seem spiritual to others. Our Lord condemned this, and did so strongly.

From its original purpose, the Jews had come to believe, and we continue to speak of the time of Christ, that the wearing of these things warded off demon spirits; however, this was reducing the Word of God to mere superstition and some type of magic incantation.

CONFESSION OF SCRIPTURE

The modern confession of Scripture as enjoined by the Word of Faith practitioners comes perilously close to this condemned by Christ.

They teach that if a problem is encountered, one should find particular Scriptures which address that problem, whatever it might be, memorize them, and then quote them over and over, etc. This is supposed to stir the Holy Spirit into action, in order for the problem to be addressed.

The memorizing and quoting of Scriptures are something that every Believer ought to do, and which will always be a great blessing if used in this manner, however, if not used in this manner it comes out to the same result as the Jews of old — superstition.

The quoting of Scriptures over and over doesn't force God into action. Neither does it manipulate some type of force in the spirit world that brings forth positive results. Again we state that all of that is superstition, which God can never honor.

The Word of God, in its true form, is always linked to the Sacrifice of Christ. Unfortunately, the Word of Faith people have divorced the Word from its Author, and the price that He paid (Jn. 1:1).

Everything we receive from the Lord comes to us through Christ and what He has done for us at the Cross. If we try to impose another way or method, we insult Christ, and, therefore, do violence to the Word of God.

(11) "AND IT SHALL BE WHEN THE LORD SHALL BRING YOU INTO THE LAND OF THE CANAANITES, AS HE SWORE UNTO YOU AND TO YOUR FATHERS, AND SHALL GIVE IT TO YOU,

(12) "THAT YOU SHALL SET APART UNTO THE LORD ALL THAT OPENS THE MATRIX, AND EVERY FIRSTLING THAT COMES OF A BEAST WHICH YOU HAVE; THE MALES SHALL BE THE LORD'S.

(13) "AND EVERY FIRSTLING OF AN ASS YOU SHALL REDEEM IT WITH A LAMB; AND IF YOU WILL NOT REDEEM IT, THEN YOU SHALL BREAK HIS NECK: AND ALL THE FIRSTBORN OF MAN AMONG YOUR CHILDREN SHALL YOU REDEEM.

(14) "AND IT SHALL BE WHEN YOUR SON ASKS YOU IN TIME TO COME, SAYING, WHAT IS THIS? THAT YOU SHALL SAY UNTO HIM, BY STRENGTH OF HAND THE LORD BROUGHT US OUT FROM EGYPT, FROM THE HOUSE OF BONDAGE:

(15) "AND IT CAME TO PASS, WHEN PHARAOH WOULD HARDLY LET US GO, THAT THE LORD SLEW ALL THE FIRSTBORN IN THE LAND OF EGYPT, BOTH THE FIRSTBORN OF MAN, AND THE

FIRSTBORN OF BEAST: THEREFORE I SACRIFICE TO THE LORD ALL THAT OPENS THE MATRIX, BEING MALES; BUT ALL THE FIRSTBORN OF MY CHILDREN I REDEEM.

(16) "AND IT SHALL BE FOR A TOKEN UPON YOUR HAND, FOR FRONTLETS BETWEEN YOUR EYES: FOR BY STRENGTH OF HAND THE LORD BROUGHT US FORTH OUT OF EGYPT."

The structure is:

1. Verse 13 legislated for the Redemption of a man and of an ass by the death of a lamb. This is humbling to human pride. The ass was an unclean animal; and with its broken neck fitly pictured the true moral condition of the most highly cultivated man. But the death of the lamb obtained redemption. Only thus can sinners be saved (Williams).

2. This animal is a most stupid and senseless creature. So also is the natural man. Proudly as he may boast of his powers of reason, conceited as he may be over his intellectual achievements, the truth is, he is utterly devoid of any spiritual intelligence.

3. Again, the *"ass"* is stubborn and intractable, often as hard to move as a mule. So also is the natural man. The sinner is rebellious and defiant. He will not come to Christ that he might have life (Jn. 5:40). It is in view of these things that Scripture declares, *"For vain men would be wise, though man be born like a wild ass's colt"* (Job 11:12) (Pink).

REDEMPTION

Verses 11 through 14 read: *"And it shall be when the LORD shall bring you into the land of the Canaanites, as He swore unto you and to your fathers and shall give it to you,*

"That you shall set apart unto the LORD all that opens the matrix, and every firstling that comes of a beast which you have; the males shall be the LORD's.

"And every firstling of an ass you shall redeem with a lamb; and if you will not redeem it, then you shall break his neck: and all the firstborn of man among your children shall you redeem.

"And it shall be when your son asks you in time to come, saying, What is this? that you shall say unto him, By strength of hand the LORD brought us out from Egypt, from the house of bondage:"

Unredeemed man thinks very highly of himself; however, as we can see from these Passages, the Lord puts him in the same category as a dumb mule or donkey.

In Verse 13, we find two classes — the clean and the unclean. Man is classed with the latter. The lamb was to answer for the unclean; and if the ass was not redeemed, his neck was to be broken; so that an unredeemed man was put upon the same level with an unclean animal, and, that, moreover, in a condition in which nothing could be more worthless and unsightly. What a humiliating picture of man in his natural condition!

The lamb is pictured as a clean animal because it typifies Christ. In essence, Christ was the Lamb — the clean, the spotless Lamb: we were unclean; but He took our position, and, *"on the Cross"* was made sin, and treated as such. That which we should have endured throughout the countless ages of eternity, He endured for us on the tree. He bore all that was due to us, there and then, in order that we might enjoy what is due to Him, forever. He got our deserts that we might get His. The clean took, for a time, the place of the unclean, in order that the unclean might take forever the place of the clean. Thus, whereas by nature we are represented by the loathsome figure of an ass with its neck broken, by Grace we are represented by a risen and glorified Christ in Heaven. Amazing contrast! It lays man's glory in the dust, and magnifies the riches of redeeming love. It silences man's empty boasting, and puts into his mouth a hymn of praise to God and the Lamb, which shall swell throughout the courts of Heaven during the everlasting ages.

GRACE

It is interesting to see that by nature we are ranked with an unclean animal; by Grace we are associated with Christ the spotless Lamb. There can be nothing lower than the place which belongs to us by nature: nothing higher than that which belongs to us by Grace. Look, for example, at an ass with its neck broken; there is what an unredeemed man is worth. Look at *"the Precious Blood of Christ"*; there is what a redeemed man is worth. *"Unto you who believe is the preciousness."* That is, all who are washed in the Blood partake of Christ's preciousness. As He is *"a living stone,"* we are *"living stones"*; as He is *"a precious Stone,"* we are *"precious stones."* We get life and preciousness all from Him and in Him. We are as He is. Every stone in the edifice is precious, because purchased at no less a price than *"the Blood of the Lamb."* May the people of God know more fully our place and privileges in Christ!

(This writer is indebted to C. H. Mackintosh for the above material on man redeemed and man unredeemed.)

ALIVE WITH CHRIST

Paul said: *"Now if we be dead with Christ, we believe that we shall also live with Him"* (Rom. 6:8). What did Paul mean by this wonderful statement?

First of all, we can only *"live with Him,"* if we are in Christ. Otherwise, we are *"dead in trespasses and sins"* (Eph. 2:1). Outside of Christ is no life; in Christ is all life.

However, if we are to truly live with Christ, which means to enjoy all that He is, all that He has, and all that He has done, which speaks of a victorious, overcoming, Christian experience, we must first of all *"be dead with Christ."* What does that mean?

In this statement as given by the Apostle, he is referring back to Romans 6:3-5. This speaks of Christ being crucified, buried, and then rising from the dead, all on our behalf.

When the believing sinner evidences Faith in Christ, even though he understands very little about what is happening, God likens that particular individual as literally being in Christ when the Saviour died, was buried, and rose from the dead. In other words, Christ died as our Substitute, becoming, in a sense, what we were (bearing the penalty of our sin), that we might become what He is — Righteousness (II Cor. 5:21).

The Apostle plainly told us: *"For if we have been planted together in the likeness of His death, we shall be also in the likeness in His Resurrection"* (Rom. 6:5). That, in essence, says the same thing as Verse 8: *"Now if we be dead with Christ, we believe that we shall also live with Him."*

As is obvious here, everything hinges on the Cross. This is how man is redeemed, which means that he is redeemed in no other way. The *"lamb"* in Verse 13 is a Type of Christ, and what He would do to redeem humanity, by dying on the Cross.

So we find in Verses 11 through 13 of Exodus, Chapter 13 that several things are said:

1. When the Children of Israel finally arrived in Canaan, which was the Promised Land, they were to conduct themselves in a specific manner. Unfortunately, because of unbelief, it would take them approximately 40 years to get there.

2. All the firstborn of both man and beast were to be dedicated to the Lord, and we speak of boy babies, and male animals. The *"firstborn"* were to represent Christ.

3. Whenever the first of a boy baby was born, and as well, the firstborn of an ass, both were to be redeemed at birth by the parents offering up a *"lamb"* in sacrifice. As we've already stated, this portrays the fact that unredeemed man is worth no more than a dumb mule.

4. If the animal was not redeemed by a lamb, or in other words, the owner had no lamb to offer, then by law, he was to break the neck of the newborn animal, thereby killing it. This proclaims the fact that unredeemed man is destined to die without God.

THE COMPARISON OF UNREDEEMED MAN AND THE DUMB ANIMAL

It is instructive to trace the various references to the *"ass"* in Scripture. The first mention of this animal is found in Genesis, Chapter 22; from it we learn two things:

1. The Scripture says: *"Abraham rose up early in the morning and 'saddled' his 'ass.'"* This, as is obvious, means that this animal is not free. It is a beast of burden, *"saddled."* So, too, is the sinner — *"serving diverse lusts."*

2. Abraham said to the young men with him and Isaac, *"Abide you here with the ass;"* I and the lad will go yonder and worship (Gen. 22:5). This tells us that the animal could not accompany Abraham and Isaac to the place of worship. Nor can the sinner worship God.

In Genesis 49:14, we read, *"Issachar is a strong ass, couching down between two burdens."* The sinner is heavily laden as well (Mat. 11:28).

We also find that God forbade His people to plow with an ox and an ass together (Deut. 22:10). This means that the sinner is shut out from the service of God.

In I Samuel 9:3, we are told: *"And the asses of Kish Saul's father were lost,"* and though Saul and his servants sought long for them they recovered them not. The sinner, too, is lost, away from God, and no human power can restore him.

In Jeremiah 22:19, we read, *"He shall be buried with the burial of an ass, drawn and cast forth beyond the gates of Jerusalem."* Pink says: *"Fearfully solemn is this."* The carcass of the ass was cast forth outside the gates of the Holy City. So shall it be with every sinner who dies outside of Christ; he shall not enter the New Jerusalem, but be *"cast into the Lake of Fire."*

The final reference to the *"ass"* is found in Zechariah 9:9: *"Rejoice greatly O daughter of Zion; shout, O daughter of Jerusalem, behold, your King comes unto you, He is just, and having salvation; lowly, and 'riding upon an ass.'"* Most blessed contrast is this. Here we see the *"ass"* entering Jerusalem, but only so as it was beneath the controlling hand of the Lord Jesus! Here is the sinner's only hope — to submit to Christ!

In Genesis 16:12, we have a statement which is very pertinent in this connection, though its particular force is lost in most translations.

The Revised Version says, and correctly so, *"And he shall be a wild-ass man among men; his hand shall be against every man, and every man's hand against him."*

Those were the words of the Lord to Hagar. They were a prophecy concerning Ishmael. From Galatians, Chapter 4, we learn that Ishmael stands for the natural man, as Isaac stands for the Believer, the seed of Promise. In full accord, then, with all that we have said above is this striking description of Sarah's *"firstborn."* Of course, we're speaking of Ishmael. He was a *"wild-ass"* man.

The Bedouin Arabs are his descendants, and fully do they witness to the truth of this ancient prophecy. We find it in the religion of Islam.

But solemn is it to find that here we have God's description of the natural man. And more solemn still is what we read of Ishmael in Galatians, Chapter 4; he *"persecuted him who was born after the Spirit,"* and in consequence had to be *"cast out"* (Gal. 4:29-30).

So in effect, God classifies the religion of Islam as bogus, a religion of the flesh, and is held by *"wild-ass"* men. Biblically, that's a very apt description.

(The writer is indebted to Arthur W. Pink for the above material regarding the *"ass"* as found in Scripture.)

DELIVERANCE

Verses 15 and 16 read: *"And it came to pass, when Pharaoh would hardly let us go, that the LORD slew all the firstborn in the land of Egypt, both the firstborn of man, and the firstborn of beast: therefore I sacrifice to the LORD all that opens the matrix, being males; but all the firstborn of my children I redeem.*

"And it shall be for a token upon your hand, and for frontlets between your eyes: for by strength of hand the LORD brought us forth out of Egypt."

These admonitions are given in order that the Children of Israel would never forget the manner of their Redemption in the days of their prosperity. What do we mean by that statement?

Prosperity has a subtle influence in leading away the heart from God. This danger is one to be jealously watched against.

Man's firstborn is a type of the firstborn of God, in His authority and Priestly function among His brethren, and as the object of the Father's love and trust. In both Egypt's and Israel's firstborn we find the twofold type of Christ and His people. Egypt's die; Israel's are saved. The death of Egypt's firstborn bursts the bonds of Israel; the death of God's firstborn, the bonds of His people.

So the Cross has a double effect: it condemns the Christ-rejecter, and it brings to Salvation the Christ-acceptor.

This was to ever be kept before the Children of Israel by the sacrifice of a lamb offered up at the time of the firstborn child, a male.

The phrase, *"But all the firstborn of my children I redeem,"* could be translated, *"But all the firstborn of My children I redeem by My Firstborn, Who is Christ."*

None of this means that the firstborn were automatically saved by virtue of their being born first. They were merely to serve as a Type of Christ.

The *"token"* was the *"phylacteries"* of which we have already mentioned, which were to be prominent on the left wrist and on the head between the eyes.

As we've already stated, the whole idea of all of this is that Israel not forget how she was delivered. We should let that be a lesson to us, that we not forget the Cross. It must ever be paramount in our *"doing,"* and in our *"seeing."*

Israel celebrated her deliverance by the keeping of the Passover: we celebrate our deliverance by the keeping of the Lord's Supper, which is an outgrowth of the Passover. The difference is, the first was a Type of the One Who was to come, while the latter is a celebration of the One Who has come, namely Christ.

(17) "AND IT CAME TO PASS, WHEN PHARAOH HAD LET THE PEOPLE GO, THAT GOD LED THEM NOT THROUGH THE WAY OF THE LAND OF THE PHILISTINES, ALTHOUGH THAT WAS NEAR; FOR GOD SAID, LEST PERADVENTURE THE PEOPLE REPENT WHEN THEY SEE WAR, AND THEY RETURN TO EGYPT:

(18) "BUT GOD LED THE PEOPLE ABOUT, THROUGH THE WAY OF THE WILDERNESS OF THE RED SEA: AND THE CHILDREN OF ISRAEL WENT UP HARNESSED OUT OF THE LAND OF EGYPT.

(19) "AND MOSES TOOK THE BONES OF JOSEPH WITH HIM: FOR HE HAD STRAITLY SWORN THE CHILDREN OF ISRAEL, SAYING, GOD WILL SURELY VISIT YOU; AND YOU SHALL CARRY UP MY BONES AWAY HENCE WITH YOU.

(20) "AND THEY TOOK THEIR JOURNEY FROM SUCCOTH, AND ENCAMPED IN ETHAM, IN THE EDGE OF THE WILDERNESS.

(21) "AND THE LORD WENT BEFORE THEM BY DAY IN A PILLAR OF A CLOUD, TO LEAD THEM THE WAY; AND BY NIGHT IN A PILLAR OF FIRE, TO GIVE THEM LIGHT; TO GO BY DAY AND NIGHT:

(22) "HE TOOK NOT AWAY THE PILLAR OF THE CLOUD BY DAY, NOR THE PILLAR OF FIRE BY NIGHT, FROM BEFORE THE PEOPLE."

The composition is:

1. We see that God was leading Israel regarding the route they would take, and in like manner He will lead every Believer.

2. At times, God leads us into a *"wilderness,"* but which is always for our good.

3. Verse 19 tells us that Moses *"took the bones of Joseph with him."* The Passage suggests as well that the bodies of *"the fathers"* were also taken from Egypt.

THE LEADING OF THE LORD

Verse 17 reads: *"And it came to pass, when Pharaoh had let the people go, that God led them not through the way of the land of the Philistines, although that was near; for God said, Lest peradventure the people repent when they see war, and they return to Egypt."*

We learn from this Passage that God was leading Israel, exactly as He desires to lead us presently. They were His people, so He would lead them.

How much does the average Christian seek the Lord as it concerns His leading and guidance? We know from the Word of God that the Lord desires to lead us; but we have to seek such leading, and not take it for granted (Jer. 33:3). In fact, we should pray about everything, asking the Lord for His Will in all things, and to be sure, the Lord will definitely answer that type of prayer (Mat. 21:22; Mk. 11:24-25; Jn. 14:14; 15:7).

As well, the Lord would lead Israel in a way that they would not normally go. If one looks at a map, one can see that the nearest route between Egypt and the land of Israel, then known as Canaan, is by the Mediterranean Sea. But going this route, before long, they would have run into the Philistines, who were a war-like people, and which the Lord knew would be disconcerting to the Children of Israel. In other words, their faith wasn't yet up to this level, and the Lord does not take us beyond our Faith. He said: *"Lest peradventure the people repent when they see war, and they return to Egypt."*

As a new convert, the Lord is very jealous over us, and leads and directs us minutely; however, He expects us to grow in Grace and the knowledge of the Lord. But please understand, the Lord is developing us, and as well, Satan is ever present to hinder that development. But if we follow the Lord as we should follow Him, which means that we understand that all we have from Him comes to us through Christ and what Christ did at the Cross, and place our Faith there, ever making the Cross the object of our Faith, the Holy Spirit, to be sure, will see us through.

ORDER

Verse 18 reads: *"But God led the people about, through the way of the wilderness of the Red Sea: and the Children of Israel went up harnessed out of the land of Egypt."*

This tells us that Israel's departure from Egypt was not a disorderly rout, but rather an orderly departure. God is never the author of confusion.

The word *"harnessed"* could be translated, *"The Children of Israel went up by five in a rank out of the land of Egypt."* The fact that Israel went forth by *"five in a rank"* exemplified and expressed God's Grace, for five in Scripture ever speaks of Grace or favor. This probably refers to five large groups.

As well, when they went out of Egypt, even though it is not given in this account, the Psalmist said: *"There was not one feeble person among their Tribes"* (Ps. 105:37).

If there was ever a miracle, this was a miracle! Not a single one in all that vast host was sickly or infirmed, irrespective of their age. In fact, the entirety of that Verse says: *"He brought them forth also with silver and gold: and there was not one feeble person among their Tribes."*

What does this mean to us presently? Does it mean that every Believer ought to be wealthy and healthy?

In a sense, I definitely believe that it can mean that. The deliverance of the Children of Israel out of Egyptian bondage is a type of our Salvation experience. And in some way, their experience is our experience, and our experience is their experience. Granted, their experience was literal and material as well as spiritual, but still, I believe that the type holds.

WEALTH AND HEALTH

While *"wealth and health"* certainly was not the purpose of the Children of Israel, but rather their being brought out from under the iron yoke of Pharaoh, who was a type of the Devil, and to whom they actually belonged as slaves; still, health and wealth were given to the Children of Israel, even though it was not the prime purpose of their deliverance. It is the same presently:

Our Salvation in being brought from unrighteousness to Righteousness, from darkness to light, from Satan to Christ, is of course, the central purpose and theme of Redemption. And we must never forget that, and must ever place the preeminence in Christ and the Cross, even as Israel was to do as it regards the yearly keeping of the Passover.

Making certain that we keep our priorities right, it is perfectly proper, and even Scriptural, and rightly so, that we believe God for finances as well as health, etc. We have a whole Salvation. This means that we are saved spiritually, physically, financially, and mentally. But it doesn't mean that the Believer will never sin again, or that we will never be sick, or at times that we won't have financial difficulties. Sometimes we erroneously attempt to push the Kingdom Age into the present, which of course, is unscriptural. But having said that, the Lord will do great and mighty things for anyone who will dare to believe Him.

When it comes to finances, we had best check our motives. Why do we want to be blessed? I realize that all of us instantly retort by saying that we want blessings for the Work of God.

Just today at noon, I was speaking with Roy Chacon, who incidentally, along with his wife, Beulah, is one of our Board Members, concerning this very thing. I made mention to him that not many Christians, even when the Lord does abundantly bless them as He does some, really help the Work of God as they actually can. Some few do, while most don't.

SONLIFE RADIO

Along with Television, the Lord has given me a mandate regarding Radio.

First of all, the Lord told me to change the programming on the two Radio Stations the Ministry owned, which was in the first part of

1999, if I remember correctly. All programming was to come from Family Worship Center, whether the music and worship, or the preaching and teaching. This we immediately set out to do, and thankfully, the Lord has given us some excellent Engineers, Musicians, and Singers, along with the congregation of Family Worship Center, which helped make all of this possible.

The Lord then instructed me to begin buying Radio Stations all over this nation, which we began to do in the year 2000. We began with two, as stated, and at the time of this writing (April, 2002), we have 56 Stations on the air.

However, to completely cover this nation, which I believe the Lord has called us to do, it's going to take at least one billion dollars. We do not have any of these funds, and in fact, we'll have to believe God for these needs to be met in their entirety.

The impact that SonLife Radio is having on the nation at large, and the Church in general, is phenomenal, to say the least. Of course, we give the Lord all the praise and all the glory. But the point is, we need help to get this thing done; and most specifically, the Lord definitely blesses certain people in order that they might help. The problem is in getting Believers to fulfill, after the Lord has opened up the windows of Heaven for them.

As Believers, we belong to Christ. This means, as well, that everything we have belongs to Him. The Lord is always very generous with us; however, He definitely will hold us accountable at the Judgment Seat of Christ, and that we must always remember.

THE WILDERNESS

There were many reasons that the Lord led the Children of Israel by the way of the wilderness.

1. The Egyptians would be drowned in their attempt to cross the Red Sea, in which the Israelites had just crossed on dry ground. So the Lord would rid Israel of her primary enemy, and do so in one fell swoop.

2. The Lord would teach Israel faith and trust in the wilderness. In fact, the wilderness was such that whatever it was that was supplied to Israel, as it regards their sustenance and maintenance, would have to be provided by the Lord. It was a most inhospitable place. But the Lord would show them that He was able to set a table, even in the wilderness, and for some three million souls at that!

WHAT WE LEARN FROM THE WILDERNESS EXPERIENCE

All of us want Blessings, and rightly so; however, while we learn great things about God from blessings, the truth is, we learn next to nothing about ourselves. It is through adversity, and I continue to speak of the *"wilderness experience"* that we learn about ourselves. How do we react? What does it take to reduce us to grumbling and complaining?

While the Lord is the great Blesser, the truth is, He tempers His Blessings with adversity. He is training the whole man, and I speak of how we should act toward God during times of Blessings, and how we should react as it regards adversity.

So the Lord would teach Israel much in the wilderness; however, the sadness is, they didn't come out too well.

JOSEPH

Verse 19 reads: *"And Moses took the bones of Joseph with him: for he had straitly sworn the Children of Israel, saying, God will surely visit you; and you shall carry up my bones away hence with you."*

Joseph was 110 years old when he died. He had been the Vice-Regent of Egypt for a number of years, actually saving that nation from starvation, plus surrounding nations as well. In effect, he had possibly been the second-most powerful man in the world. But even though he had the glory of Egypt, given to him by God, his heart never was in Egypt, but in Canaanland, for that was the land promised to Abraham by God, where a mighty nation would rise up, a nation totally different than any other nation in the world, a people who belonged exclusively to Jehovah.

Joseph knew by Revelation that a day was coming that God would deliver the Children of Israel out of the land of Egypt. In fact, they were few when Joseph died, possibly several thousands at the most. As well, up until the time of his death, and even some time afterward, they were treated royally by Pharaoh. But another Pharaoh arose, who did not recognize Joseph, and made slaves of the Children of Israel. But irrespective of all of this, Joseph knew, by Revelation from the Lord, that God was going to deliver the Children of Israel out of this land, and take them to Canaan. Consequently, he gave explicit instructions that when this time would come, as most surely it would, his embalmed body, which no doubt was deposited in a mummy case, would be taken to Canaan as well.

All of this was evidently known among the Israelites, because Moses was very careful to carry out this request. So when they did quit Egypt, somewhere in that possession was the embalmed body of a man of Faith, a man who had been one of the most beautiful Types of Christ found in the entirety of the Old Testament.

His body had probably been deposited at Tanis, which was the capital of the Shepherd kings, and from which it was now retrieved.

As well, there is some small evidence in the Text that not only was the body of Joseph brought out, but also the bodies of all the sons of Jacob. There is no reason why they would not have given the same instructions, and if in fact that did happen, to be sure, they would have been brought out as well.

Joseph had said: *"God will surely visit you: and you shall carry up my bones away hence with you,"* which they did!

RESURRECTION

Not so very long from now, there's going to be another exodus. Jesus referred to it as *"the Resurrection of the Just"* (Lk. 14:14). Paul called it *"a better Resurrection"* (Heb. 11:35). John called it *"the first Resurrection"* (Rev. 20:5).

At that coming time, which could happen at any hour, the sacred dust of those sacred bones, as well as every other Saint of God who has ever lived and died, will be raised, for God knows where every speck is, and which will be made into a glorified body, which will join with the soul and the spirit, which is now with Christ. Paul said: *"But God giveth it a body as it has pleased Him, and to every seed his own body"* (I Cor. 15:38).

NOTES

In this *"First Resurrection,"* which Jesus guaranteed by His Resurrection from the dead, every Saint of God who has ever lived will take part. As well, all on Earth who are alive at that moment, and who are in Christ, shall experience this glorious Resurrection. Paul said: *"For this we say unto you by the Word of the Lord, that we which are alive and remain unto the coming of the Lord* (the Resurrection) *shall not prevent them which are asleep* (the Saints of God who have died in the past, which includes all).

"For the Lord Himself shall descend from Heaven with a shout, with the voice of the Archangel, and with the Trump of God: and the dead in Christ shall rise first:

"Then we which are alive and remain shall be caught up together with them in the clouds, to meet the Lord in the air: and so shall we ever be with the Lord" (I Thess. 4:15-17).

Paul also said: *"Behold, I show you a mystery; we shall not all sleep* (some Saints will be alive at that time), *but we shall all be changed,*

"In a moment, in the twinkling of an eye, at the last trump: for the trumpet shall sound, and the dead shall be raised incorruptible, and we shall be changed" (I Cor. 15:51-52).

THE GLORY

As well, the *"glory"* of the Saints will be different. In other words, as should be obvious, some Saints live Godlier lives than others. In fact, many gave their lives for the Cause of Christ. Concerning this *"glory"* which will be forever and forever, Paul also said:

"There is one glory of the Sun, and another glory of the Moon, and another glory of the Stars: for one star differeth from another star in glory.

"So also is the resurrection of the dead" (I Cor. 15:41-42).

Here he plainly tells us that some will have more glory than others, with the measurement no doubt being *"faithfulness"* (Mat. 25:21).

THE EDGE OF THE WILDERNESS

Verse 20 reads: *"And they took their journey from Succoth, and encamped in Etham, in the edge of the wilderness."*

"Succoth" means, *"booths"* or *"tents."*

This spoke plainly of the *"pilgrim"* character of the journey which lay before them. This was one of the great lessons learned by the first pilgrims: *"Here we have no continuing city"* (Heb. 13:14); for *"by Faith he sojourned in the land of Promise, as in a strange country, dwelling in tents with Isaac and Jacob, the heirs with him of the same promise"* (Heb. 11:9). In fact, *"booths"* are all that we have down here, for *"our citizenship is in Heaven"* (Phil. 3:20). But as just stated, the day is now near at hand when we shall exchange our temporary *"tents"* for the eternal *"mansions"* of the Father's House. For, *"As we have borne the image of the earthy, we shall also bear the image of the Heavenly"* (I Cor. 15:49).

A MIXED MULTITUDE

Back in Exodus 12:38, it says that *"a mixed multitude went up also with them."*

Concerning this, Pink said: *"It has been well said that when a movement of God takes place, men are wrought upon by other motives than those by which the Holy Spirit stirs the renewed heart, and a mass of such attach themselves to those who are led forth.*

"Witness the fact that when God called Abraham alone (Isa. 51:2), Terah (his father) and Lot (his nephew) accompanied him (Gen. 11:31). Witness the Gibeonites making a league with Joshua (Josh., Chpt. 9). So, too, we find that after the Jewish remnant returned from the captivity 'a mixed multitude' joined themselves to Israel (Neh. 5:17), though later 'they separated from Israel all the mixed multitudes' (Neh. 13:3).

"So, too, we read of the Pharisees and Sadducees coming to John the Baptist" (Mat. 3:7)!

Pink went on to say: *"The ungodly among the congregation of the Lord has been the great bane of God's Saints in every age, the source of our weakness, and the occasion of much of our failure. It is because of this the Spirit of God says, 'Wherefore come out from among them and be ye separate'"* (II Cor. 6:17).

The Children of Israel are about to go into the wilderness; however, something will now happen, which will be grand and glorious. The Lord never asks us to do anything, but that He always goes with us, and for the express purpose of teaching and leading us, and as well, to guarantee our success.

THE PILLAR

Verses 21 and 22 read: *"And the LORD went before them by day in a pillar of a cloud, to lead them the way; and by night in a pillar of fire, to give them light; to go by day and night:*

"He took not away the pillar of the cloud by day, nor the pillar of the fire by night, from before the people."

Concerning this, Mackintosh said: *"The Lord not only conducted them safely outside the bounds of Egypt, but He also came down, as it were, in His traveling chariot, to be their Companion through all the vicissitudes of their wilderness journey. This was Divine Grace. They were not merely delivered out of the furnace of Egypt and then allowed to make the best of their way to Canaan — such was not God's manner toward them."*

He went on to say, *"He went before them. He was 'a guide, a glory, a defense, to save them from every fear.'"*

If the Lord went into the wilderness with them, and it is plainly clear here that He did, then it is for certain that He would see them through the wilderness, and, thereby, bring them out of the wilderness.

We see in all of this a perfect portrayal of the *"Trinity."*

It was God the Father, as we would refer to Him now, Who heard the groanings of Israel, and Who raised up a deliverer for them.

The lamb without spot or blemish that was slain, with its blood applied, which secured protection and deliverance, typifies God the Son. Understanding that, we must come to the conclusion as well that the Pillar of Cloud given to Israel for their guidance, speaks to us of *"God the Holy Spirit."* In fact, at every point in all of this, we anticipate the teaching of the New Testament; in other words, the fulfillment of all of these things in Christ, which were only anticipated in the Old Testament.

It would seem in Verses 21 and 22 that there were two distinct appearances; however, Exodus 14:24 proclaims *"the Pillar of fire and of the cloud,"* as just one Pillar. It was the visible sign of the Lord's Presence with Israel. It seems that its upper portion rose up to Heaven in the form of a column; its lower being spread out cloudwise over Israel's camp. It seemed to be a *"Pillar of Fire"* in its upper portion, and a *"Cloud"* below. As stated, the *"Cloud"* typified the Holy Spirit.

Let's look at this as it's carried out in the Word of God, and see how it speaks to us presently.

THE CROSS MUST BE FIRST

Israel was delivered, and done so by the death of the Paschal Lamb, with its blood being applied to the doorposts. Then the *"Cloud"* was given. This is the order of the New Testament.

Jesus died on the Cross in order for man to be redeemed, rose from the dead, ascended on high, and then the Holy Spirit was sent back on the Day of Pentecost. As well, this is the manner of the Christian experience.

The sinner comes to Christ, is redeemed by the Blood of the Lamb, and then the Holy Spirit comes to indwell the soul. But His coming is always on the ground of Christ's shed Blood, and the Believer's Faith in that Atoning Work. It is never because of any moral fitness or merit in us.

It is beautifully amazing that the great doctrinal treatment of the Redemption Plan in Romans follows this guideline minutely.

Concerning this, Pink said: *"It is not until after the believing sinner is 'justified' (Rom. 5:1) that we read of the Spirit of God. In 2:4-10 we get repentance; in 3:22-28, Faith; and then in 5:5 we read, 'The Love of God is shed abroad in our hearts by the Holy Spirit which is given unto us!'"*

A GIFT TO THE CHILDREN OF ISRAEL

As should be obvious, the Children of Israel had absolutely no idea as to the manifestation that the Lord would bring forth as it regards the Pillar of Fire and the Cloud. This was solely a Gift of God. But let the Reader understand this:

Israel was now delivered from Egyptian bondage, and as stated, delivered through and by the applied blood of the slain lamb. As a result of what has happened, the Gifts of God will start now flowing freely.

Peter said: *"Repent, and be baptized everyone of you in the Name of Jesus Christ for the remission of sins* (the Greek says, be baptized because your sins have already been remitted), *and you shall receive the Gift of the Holy Spirit"* (Acts 2:38).

Before His Crucifixion, Resurrection, and Ascension, Jesus told His Disciples that He would send them another Comforter. There is no hint that any of the Apostles requested such because at the time they had no knowledge of such, even as the Children of Israel had no knowledge of what God would do as it regards the *"Cloud."* This great Gift, as Promised by our Lord, was altogether on the part of Christ and the Father (Jn. 4:16).

THE CLOUD SERVED AS A GUIDE

Verse 21 says, *"The LORD went before them by day in a pillar of a cloud, to lead them the way; and by night in a pillar of fire."* The Holy Spirit is given to us, and as our Lord said, *"To guide us into all truth"* (Jn. 16:13). If we are truly Children of God, at the same time, we will be *"led by the Spirit of God"* (Rom. 8:14).

THE CLOUD WAS LIGHT

This speaks not only of visibility, but as well, of spiritual illumination. Many hundreds of years after this great episode of the deliverance of the Children of Israel, Nehemiah said: *"Thou leadest them in the day by a cloudy pillar and in the night by a pillar of fire, to give them light in the way wherein they should go"* (Neh. 9:12).

As Israel was led both day and night by this particular *"Cloud,"* likewise, the Holy Spirit is to the Believer *"The Spirit of wisdom and understanding, the Spirit of counsel and might, the Spirit of knowledge and of the fear of the LORD"* (Isa. 11:2).

THE CLOUD WAS A COVERING

The Psalmist said: *"He spread a cloud for a covering"* (Ps. 105:39).

The *"covering"* of which the Psalmist spoke had little to do with physical covering, as it did protection. Unfortunately, there are many in the modern Church who look to man for their covering instead of the Lord. Such a position is disastrous to say the least.

Paul said that we owe Civil authorities obedience, that is if what they demand does not violate the Word of God; however, when it comes to Christians, we do not owe them the same obedience as we do Civil authorities. In fact, as Paul laid down the guidelines by the Spirit, as it regards submission to Civil authority in Romans 13:1-7, he then said as it regards fellow Christians, *"Owe no man anything, but to love one another: for he who loves another has fulfilled the Law"* (Rom. 13:8).

While I love all Brothers and Sisters in the Lord, no man is my covering; that can only come from the Lord.

GOD SPOKE FROM THE CLOUD

The Psalmist also said: *"He spoke unto them in the cloudy pillar"* (Ps. 99:7).

Concerning this, the Psalmist was no doubt referring to the following Passage: *"And it came to pass, as Moses entered into the Tabernacle, the cloudy pillar descended, and stood at the door of the Tabernacle, and the Lord talked with Moses"* (Num. 12:5).

Presently, and in fact ever since the Day of Pentecost, the Holy Spirit has been, and is, the Spokesman for the Holy Trinity. Jesus said: *"He who has an ear, let him hear what the Spirit says unto the Churches"* (Rev., Chpts. 2-3).

To be sure, whatever the Holy Spirit speaks to us as Believers will always and without exception coincide with the Word of God. If it deviates from the Word in any capacity, then it's simply not the Spirit speaking.

Concerning the Cloud, Exodus 14:20 says: *"And it came between the camp of the Egyptians and the camp of Israel, and it was a Cloud and darkness to them."* In other words, what was a great blessing to Israel was a great hindrance to the Egyptians, and meant to be so.

Jesus said: *"I thank You, O Father, Lord of Heaven and Earth, because You have hid these things from the wise and prudent"* (Mat. 11:25). It is said of the Holy Spirit: *"The Spirit of Truth Whom the world cannot receive"* (Jn. 14:17).

THE CLOUD RESTED UPON THE TABERNACLE

When Moses finished the work of building the Tabernacle, the Scripture says: *"Then a Cloud covered the tent of the congregation, and the Glory of the LORD filled the Tabernacle, and Moses was not able to enter into the tent of the congregation because the Cloud abode thereon, and the Glory of the LORD filled the Tabernacle"* (Ex. 40:33-35).

The Tabernacle was a Type of Christ. In fact, everything in this structure pointed to Christ.

Jesus said: *"The Spirit of the Lord is upon Me, because He has anointed Me . . ."* (Lk. 4:18).

John said of Christ: *"I indeed baptize you with water unto repentance: but He Who comes after me is mightier than I, Whose shoes I am not worthy to bear: He shall baptize you with the Holy Spirit and with fire"* (Mat. 3:11).

Every single thing we receive from the Lord as Believers comes exclusively through Christ, and more particularly, what Christ did at the Cross. In fact, the Holy Spirit works exclusively within the parameters of the Finished Work of Christ (Jn. 14:17).

As well, Paul said concerning the Holy Spirit: *"For the Law of the Spirit of Life in Christ Jesus has made me free from the law of sin and death"* (Rom. 8:2). The Believer can have everything for which Christ paid such a price, but only if his Faith is exclusively in Christ, and what Christ has done at the Cross (Gal. 5:5-6).

IN THE WILDERNESS, THE CLOUD NEVER LEFT ISRAEL

Nehemiah said: *"Yet You in Your manifold mercies forsook them not in the wilderness: the pillar of the Cloud departed not from them"* (Neh. 9:19). Despite the many failures of Israel, the Lord never withdrew the cloudy pillar. It rested over the Tabernacle, and when the Temple was built, it rested in that holy place. The Scripture says:

"And it came to pass, when the Priests were come out of the holy place, that the Cloud filled the House of the LORD" (I Ki. 8:10).

The *"Cloud"* only left when Israel, in essence, by her evil conduct, bade Him go. Even then, it was like He was extremely reluctant to leave. The Scripture says: *"Then did the Cherubims lift up their wings, and the wheels beside them; and the Glory of the God of Israel was over them above.

"And the Glory of the LORD went up from the midst of the city, and stood upon the mountain which is on the east side of the city" (Ezek. 11:22-23).

But thankfully, the Prophet Ezekiel also saw the *"Cloud"* return. In fact, it has not happened yet, but most definitely it shall. The Prophet said:

"And, behold, the Glory of the God of Israel came from the way of the east: and his voice was like a noise of many waters: and the Earth shined with His Glory.

"And it was according to the appearance of the vision which I saw, even according to the Vision that I saw when I came to destroy the city" (Ezek. 43:2-3).

This will be when the Lord has revealed Himself to Israel as it regards the Second Coming, and they have accepted Him as Lord, Saviour, and Messiah. He will then resume His Covenant relationship with them, and then shall be fulfilled the ancient Promise: *"When the Lord shall have washed away the filth of the daughters of Zion, and shall have purged the blood of Jerusalem from the midst thereof by the Spirit of Judgment, and by the Spirit of burning.*

"And the LORD will create upon every dwelling place of Mount Zion, and upon her assemblies, a Cloud and smoke by day, and the shining of a flaming fire by night: for upon all the glory shall be a defense.

"And there shall be a Tabernacle for a shadow in the daytime from the heat, and for a place of refuge, and for a covert from storm and from rain" (Isa. 4:4-6).

"I look at the Cross upon Calvary,
"And O what a wonder Divine!
"To think of the wealth it holds for me,
"The riches of Heaven are mine."

"I find at the Cross blessed victory,
"And Grace for each step of the way;
"The fount of God's love is flowing free,
"And sweeter it grows day-by-day."

"The Cross is my hope for eternity,
"No merit have I of my own;
"The shed Blood of Christ my only plea,
"My trust is in Jesus Alone."

NOTES

CHAPTER 14

(1) "AND THE LORD SPOKE UNTO MOSES, SAYING,

(2) "SPEAK UNTO THE CHILDREN OF ISRAEL, THAT THEY TURN AND ENCAMP BEFORE PI-HAHIROTH, BETWEEN MIGDOL AND THE SEA, OVER AGAINST BAAL-ZEPHON: BEFORE IT SHALL YOU ENCAMP BY THE SEA.

(3) "FOR PHARAOH WILL SAY OF THE CHILDREN OF ISRAEL, THEY ARE ENTANGLED IN THE LAND, THE WILDERNESS HAS SHUT THEM IN.

(4) "AND I WILL HARDEN PHARAOH'S HEART, THAT HE SHALL FOLLOW AFTER THEM; AND I WILL BE HONORED UPON PHARAOH, AND UPON ALL HIS HOST; THAT THE EGYPTIANS MAY KNOW THAT I AM THE LORD. AND THEY DID SO.

(5) "AND IT WAS TOLD THE KING OF EGYPT THAT THE PEOPLE FLED: AND THE HEART OF PHARAOH AND OF HIS SERVANTS WAS TURNED AGAINST THE PEOPLE, AND THEY SAID, WHY HAVE WE DONE THIS, THAT WE HAVE LET ISRAEL GO FROM SERVING US?

(6) "AND HE MADE READY HIS CHARIOT, AND TOOK HIS PEOPLE WITH HIM:

(7) "AND HE TOOK SIX HUNDRED CHOSEN CHARIOTS, AND ALL THE CHARIOTS OF EGYPT, AND CAPTAINS OVER EVERY ONE OF THEM.

(8) "AND THE LORD HARDENED THE HEART OF PHARAOH KING OF EGYPT, AND HE PURSUED AFTER THE CHILDREN OF ISRAEL: AND THE CHILDREN OF ISRAEL WENT OUT WITH AN HIGH HAND.

(9) "BUT THE EGYPTIANS PURSUED AFTER THEM, ALL THE HORSES AND CHARIOTS OF PHARAOH, AND HIS HORSEMEN, AND HIS ARMY, AND OVERTOOK THEM ENCAMPING BY THE SEA, BESIDE PI-HAHIROTH, BEFORE BAAL-ZEPHON."

The overview is:

1. The fear, unbelief, and anger of the very people who had witnessed God's wonders in the land of Egypt would appear incredible but

that each Bible student finds these evils in his own heart, and learns, by sad experience, that great depression of mind usually follows exceptional spiritual triumphs (Williams).

2. God would perform His greatest miracle in the very shadow of one of Egypt's chief gods.

3. Pharaoh would still try to stop Israel, in effect, brandishing his fists in the face of God. This time he would go too far, bringing upon himself and his army swift destruction.

THE LEADING OF THE LORD

Verses 1 and 2 read: *"And the LORD spoke unto Moses, saying,*

"Speak unto the Children of Israel, that they turn and encamp before Pi-hahiroth, between Migdol and the sea, over against Baal-zephon: before it shall you encamp by the sea."

The Lord will now direct Israel as to exactly where they should go. Up till now it had been to the southeast. Another day's journey in this direction would have taken them beyond the limits of Egypt, into the desert region east of the Bitter Lakes, which was dry, treeless, and waterless.

In view of this, God changed the direction of their route from the southeast to due south, made them take a course by which they placed the Bitter Lakes on their left hand, and so remained within the limits of Egypt, in a district fairly well watered, but shut off from the wilderness by the Bitter Lakes and the northern prolongation of the Gulf of Suez, with which they were connected.

This route was more suitable for them, providing water and some sustenance for the herds; however, it had one great drawback:

The drawback consisted of shutting them in-between their assailants, should Egypt come after them, which they did, on the one hand, and the sea upon the other; and this circumstance seems to have led Pharaoh to make his pursuit (Pulpit).

From a military point of view, Israel had blundered badly. In effect, they were hemmed in. But the following must be remembered:

God was leading them; and as well, He had a great plan and purpose for taking them on this particular route. He would rid them of Pharaoh and the Egyptian army once and for all.

NOTES

In regard to this, we are to see one of the greatest miracles recorded in the Old Testament, and in fact in the entirety of history. Actually, it was this notable event which made such a great impression upon the enemies of the Lord.

Rahab said: *"For we have heard how the LORD dried up the water of the Red Sea for you, when you came out of Egypt . . . and as soon as we had heard these things, our hearts did melt, neither did there remain any more courage in any man because of you: for the LORD your God, He is God in Heaven above, and in Earth beneath"* (Josh. 2:10-11).

The miracle of the Red Sea occupies the same place and position in the Old Testament, as the Resurrection of our Lord does in the New. It is appealed to as a standard of measurement, as the supreme demonstration of God's Power (Eph. 1:19).

FAITH AND UNBELIEF

Each generation of infidels and agnostics has directed special attacks against this miracle of the Red Sea crossing. But to the Child of God, miracles occasion no difficulty. Pink said: *"The great difference between Faith and unbelief is that one brings in God, the other shuts Him out."*

I want it stated unequivocally, clearly, and plainly, I am a Believer. I believe in a God Who can perform miracles, and Who performs miracles presently, and in fact, has never stopped performing miracles, and greater still, will never stop performing miracles. Jesus said: *"If you have faith as a grain of mustard seed, you shall say unto this mountain, Remove hence to yonder place; and it shall remove; and nothing shall be impossible unto you"* (Mat. 17:20).

Our Lord also said: *"If you can believe, all things are possible to him who believes"* (Mk. 9:23).

BAAL

It is believed that Baal-zephon was a shrine dedicated to Baal worship, in this case, referred to as *"Typhon, the evil demon of Egyptian mythology."* It is also believed that human sacrifices may have been offered here at this particular place.

At any rate, God would perform His greatest miracle in the very shadow of one of

Egypt's chief gods. In fact, as should be overly obvious, all the things accomplished by the Lord would make the gods of Egypt look worthless by comparison, which they were.

The Lord had Israel to camp right in front of this worthless idol, as if to say, *"You claim to be so powerful; now is the time to show how powerful you really are!"*

IDOL GODS

Nations of the world at that time worshiped particular idols, claiming them to be God. This means they were *"polytheistic."* In fact, Israel was the only nation in the world at that time that was *"monotheistic,"* which means they worshiped only one God, that is, Jehovah.

We may think that the world presently has advanced far beyond such superstition, etc.; however, if, in essence, the Bible is not adhered to as it regards the worship of the Lord, which can only be done through His Son, the Lord Jesus Christ, in effect, men are then worshiping idols. These idols may go under the name of various religions, such as Hinduism, Buddhism, Shintoism, or Islam, etc., in fact, demon spirits are behind these religions, just as they were behind the idols of old.

Unredeemed man may advance a little bit intellectually, but he cannot advance spiritually. So even though he may have traded his idol, which he once fashioned with his hands, for that which seems to be more intellectual, the end result is the same — he is worshipping devils.

The same can be said even for parts of Christianity that have been perverted, which means it no longer adheres to the Word of God. Concerning this, Paul said:

"Now the Spirit (Holy Spirit) *speaks expressly, that in the latter times* (the times in which we now live) *some shall depart from the faith* (Jesus Christ and Him Crucified), *giving heed to seducing spirits, and doctrines of devils"* (I Tim. 4:1).

This plainly tells us that evil spirits are behind all false doctrine, referred to by Paul as *"doctrines of devils,"* and unequivocally stating that these doctrines are fostered by *"seducing spirits,"* which means that while it may sound like the Lord, may act like the Lord, and may even claim to be of the Lord, in fact, it is an *"angel of light"* producing these *"doctrines of devils"* (II Cor. 11:13-15).

Please allow me to make a couple of strong statements:

THE CROSS

Unless the Believer has a proper understanding of the Cross, he simply will not be able to understand the Gospel, or in effect, the Word of God. Listen to Paul:

"For Christ sent me not to baptize, but to preach the Gospel: not with wisdom of words, lest the Cross of Christ should be made of none effect" (I Cor. 1:17).

In effect, Paul says here that the Cross of Christ is the Gospel. This refers to what Jesus did for us at the Cross, thereby given to us by the Holy Spirit, that is, upon believing Faith (Gal. 5:5-6). That's why Paul also said: *"But we preach Christ Crucified"* (I Cor. 1:23). He actually said that he preached Christ Crucified, even though the Cross was a stumbling block to the Jews, and *"unto the Greeks foolishness."*

So if the Preacher is not preaching the Cross, he is not preaching the Gospel. And if a person doesn't properly understand the Cross, then he cannot understand the Gospel.

WHAT DOES IT MEAN TO PREACH THE CROSS?

Paul said: *"For the preaching of the Cross is to them who perish foolishness; but unto us which are saved it is the Power of God."*

He also said: *"For after that in the wisdom of God the world by wisdom knew not God, it pleased God by the foolishness of preaching* (the Cross) *to save them who believe"* (I Cor. 1:18, 21).

Day before yesterday (April 5, 2002), Frances handed me an advertisement of a book written by Kenneth Hagin, which someone had been kind enough to send to us. It was from his magazine, April issue, 2002. In his advertising the book, he plainly stated, and I quote him, *"Whoever preaches the Cross preaches death."* In other words, he was boldly repudiating the Cross, and doing so in every capacity.

Sadly and regrettably, the Cross of Christ has no place in the Word of Faith doctrine, which has been accepted by great parts of the Charismatic and Pentecostal worlds. I do not mean to be unkind, but the truth is, the Word of Faith doctrine, is a *"doctrine of devils,"* and is perpetrated by *"seducing spirits."* In fact, it just might be, and I personally believe is, the worst doctrine that Satan has ever perpetrated on the Church.

It is grossly evil, and has destroyed, and is destroying, and shall destroy many, many people, simply because it is carried out by those who claim to be Spirit-filled, and who claim to adhere to the Word of God.

The truth is, the main emphasis of this doctrine is not the Atonement, and that's the reason that most of its followers are little aware of what it actually teaches about this subject. The main emphasis is money. In fact, that's the reason it draws so many adherents, the promise to be rich, etc. The sadness is, the only ones getting rich in this particular doctrine are the Preachers.

The true, Biblical position of any doctrine must be the manner and the way in which it looks at the Atonement. The Atonement is the heart of the Gospel. It's that for which Jesus died on Calvary, which refers to the manner in which people are saved, etc.

For instance, Christian Science repudiates Biblical Atonement, and is, therefore, false. Jehovah's Witnesses do the same. Modernism falls into the same category. In fact, the entirety of the Catholic Church places the Atonement in the confines of the Church, instead of Christ. While Christ, in a sense, is proclaimed in that particular Church, it is in reality another Jesus, instead of the Christ of the Bible (II Cor. 11:4).

The *"Word of Faith"* doctrine falls into the category of the above, simply because it has changed the Atonement from the Cross of Christ, to the confines of Hell, of all places. In other words, it teaches that while Jesus died on the Cross, this, in the words of Kenneth Hagin, *"was a place of great defeat."* In other words, this man, plus all adherents of the Word of Faith doctrine, teaches that there was no victory in the Cross. All of this is very strange, considering that Paul said:

"For the preaching of the Cross is to them who perish foolishness; but unto us which are saved it is the Power of God" (I Cor. 1:18).

NOTES

Now the preaching of the Cross, and what Jesus did there, is either the *"Power of God,"* or else it is *"a place of defeat."* One cannot have it both ways. This means that you can believe what Kenneth Hagin said, or you can believe what Paul said. As for me and my house, we'll take what Paul said.

Paul would hardly have preached the Cross, had it been a place of defeat. No, it was the place of the greatest victory that mankind has ever known, and ever shall know. I'll tell you what it did, continuing to quote Paul:

"But now in Christ Jesus you who in time past were far off are made nigh by the Blood of Christ" (Eph. 2:13). This plainly tells us that our Salvation is in the Cross, where Jesus shed His Precious, Life's Blood.

The Word of Faith Teachers claim that while Jesus did die on the Cross, this had nothing to do with our Salvation and victory.

They claim that He became a sinner on the Cross, died as a sinner, and as a sinner went to Hell, and we speak of the burning side of Hell. They also claim that He burned in Hell for some three days and nights, suffered the agony of the damned, with Satan thinking that he had now defeated Christ. But at the end of the three days and nights, they claim, God said, *"It is enough,"* and then Jesus was *"born again"* as any sinner is born again, and raised from the dead.

Now the truth is, all of this is made up out of whole cloth. In other words, it is a fabrication pure and simple, with not one shred of it being found in the Word of God.

They derive their interpretation, or at least a part of it, from a false interpretation of the word *"firstborn."* It comes from the following Scripture:

Paul said: *"For whom He* (God) *did foreknow, He also did predestinate to be conformed to the Image of His Son, that He* (Jesus) *might be the firstborn among many brethren"* (Rom. 8:29).

The word *"firstborn"* is the translation from the Greek word *"prototokos."* The Greek Scholars tell us that there is no proper English word which suitably explains the word *"prototokos,"* with the word *"firstborn"* being the best that English does produce.

As it regards Paul's statement, it definitely

doesn't mean that Jesus was *"born again,"* but rather it means, He was the Founder of the great Salvation Plan.

Colossians 1:15 says concerning Christ: *"Who is the Image of the invisible God, the firstborn of every creature."*

This doesn't mean that Jesus, as God, was created in the distant past. It rather means that He was the Creator of all things (Jn. 1:1-3).

Likewise, it says of Christ: *"And He is the Head of the Body, the Church: Who is the beginning, the firstborn from the dead; that in all things He might have the preeminence"* (Col. 1:18).

The term *"firstborn from the dead,"* as it speaks here of Christ, refers to Him being the Resurrection. In other words, what He did at the Cross, and in His Resurrection, makes the Resurrection possible for all Believers, which will shortly come to pass.

So, the word *"firstborn"* doesn't mean that Jesus was *"born again"* as a sinner is born again, but rather that He is the Founder of the great Salvation Plan, which in effect was made possible by the Cross.

Getting back to our original thought, *"preaching the Cross,"* doesn't mean that the Preacher has to give the story of the Cross every time he preaches. It simply means that he understands and believes that the Cross of Christ is the Foundation of all Doctrine. It is there where Jesus effected our Atonement. That means that our Salvation was not effected or brought about by His Resurrection, Ascension, and Exaltation, as necessary and significant as were all of these events. In fact, these events were made possible by what Jesus did at the Cross. All sin was atoned at the Cross, and not in the Resurrection. In fact, if even one sin had been left unatoned, the Resurrection of Christ would have been impossible, simply because *"the wages of sin is death."* But with all sin atoned, Satan could not stop the Resurrection of Christ. In fact, it was never in doubt.

Again, notice Paul. He said: *"But God forbid that I should glory* (boast) *save in the Cross of our Lord Jesus Christ...."* He didn't say: *"But God forbid that I should glory, save in the Resurrection of our Lord Jesus Christ...."*

NOTES

It is definitely true that we are Resurrection people; however, it is true only in respect to our understanding of the Cross. Again Paul said:

"For if we have been planted together in the likeness of His death, we shall be also in the likeness of His Resurrection" (Rom. 6:5).

This means that we can have Resurrection Life, only to the extent that we understand the *"Likeness of His death."*

If the Preacher of the Gospel truly understands the Cross, and thereby truly believes the Cross, he will make it the foundation of all his preaching, in effect, making it the center of all things. That doesn't mean that he'll preach about the Cross every time he preaches, etc., but does definitely mean that everything he does preach will be based on that sure foundation.

THE WILDERNESS

Verse 3 reads: *"For Pharaoh will say of the Children of Israel, They are entangled in the land, the wilderness has shut them in."*

Through foreknowledge, the Lord knew what Pharaoh would reckon in his evil heart, when he saw the Children of Israel seemingly hemmed in.

God knows all things, past, present, and future, and if we follow Him, no mistakes will be made. In other words, while He might lead us purposely into the wilderness, He will go with us, and to be sure, and as stated, will stay with us, and will bring us out. And we must ever understand that every single thing He does with us, of us, for us, by us, and in us, is all according to design, meant to ever bring us nearer to Him, Who is the Source of all life.

It is not for us to understand all His ways; it is up to us to have Faith in all His ways, whether we understand them or not.

The problem with man, and even with Christian man is he thinks he knows more than God. Or at least he acts that way. To fully know the Lord is to fully love Him, and to fully trust Him. And when one is completely placed in the center of God's Will, one will find the greatest security, the greatest assurance, the greatest joy, and the greatest fulfillment of life there could ever be. That's why Jesus said: *"The thief* (Satan) *cometh not, but for to steal, and to kill, and to destroy: I am come that they might have life, and that they might have it more abundantly"* (Jn. 10:10).

THE HARDENED HEART

Verse 4 reads: *"And I will harden Pharaoh's heart, that he shall follow after them; and I will be honored upon Pharaoh, and upon all his host; that the Egyptians may know that I am the LORD. And they did so."*

The idea is, God would provide the means by which Pharaoh would harden his own heart. God is said to do many things, when in fact, He does not Personally do such, but does set the stage.

In fact, this situation, as it regards Pharaoh, is but an example of what is going on every hour of every day all over the world, and in fact, has always functioned in this capacity. Everything that God does brings about a response from the hearts of men. They can either accept or reject. As we previously said, the sun hardens clay and softens wax. The sun doesn't change, but the response of the particular materials is different.

At this very moment, God is doing things all over the world, which are having a tendency to either cause people to rebel against God, or to accept the Lord and His Ways.

The will of man is never violated by God. The Scripture emphatically states, *"Whosoever will"* (Jn. 3:16; 7:37-38; Rom. 10:13; Rev. 22:17).

THE WILL OF MAN

In fact, God guards the will of man as it respects acceptance or rejection of Him. But that is the only aspect of the will that is so guarded by God. It applies to both the Redeemed and the unredeemed. Let us look first at the unredeemed:

Show me an alcoholic who is in the last stages of that terrible bondage, who cannot, within his own strength and power, quit drinking. But yet, if that alcoholic, or whomever it might be, desires to accept Christ, as the Holy Spirit moves upon him, he can do exactly that, and Satan cannot stop it. And in the Born-Again experience, the Lord will set that captive free of all bondages.

Unfortunately, when it comes to the Redeemed, most Christians have an erroneous concept of the *"will."* In fact, most think now that they have become a Christian, they are perfectly free to say either *"yes"* or *"no"* to sin. Consequently, they are taught that if one sins, and of course we're speaking of Believers, then it's because they want to do that, whatever it might be. None of that is correct!

The Believer is perfectly free in his spirit and will to say *"yes"* to Jesus Christ and what Christ has done for him at the Cross, which means to obey the Word, and to be guided by the Holy Spirit (Jn. 16:13).

But if the Christian attempts to overcome sin by his *"willpower,"* he will fail every time, meaning that Satan will actually override his will. Let's say it in a different way, so there will be no misunderstanding.

Yes, if the Believer is not looking fully to Christ and the Cross, which is the only answer for sin, Satan can override the Believer's will, despite the fact that the Christian is trying to say *"no"* to sin. Trusting in one's own willpower means that one is trusting in self, and not Christ and the Cross. Listen to what Paul said:

"For I know that in me (that is, in my flesh) dwelleth no good thing: for to will (willpower) *is present with me; but how to perform that which is good I find not"* (Rom. 7:18).

Paul is plainly saying here that before he understood Christ and the Cross, he tried to live for God by his own strength and willpower. When he said, *"to will is present with me,"* he was actually saying that he was trying to say *"no"* to sin, but to no avail. By using the term, *"But how to perform that which is good I find not,"* he was saying that despite all of his strength, and trying to say *"no"* to sin, he found himself failing just the same (Rom. 7:15). And that, regrettably, is the condition of most Christians, simply because they do not know or understand God's prescribed order of victory. But unfortunately, due to a lack of proper teaching, this is where most Christians find themselves — trying to live for God by their willpower, which guarantees defeat.

GOD'S PRESCRIBED ORDER

As we've already stated any number of times in this Volume, if the Believer will understand that everything he receives from the Lord comes to him exclusively through Christ and what Christ did at the Cross, and there place his Faith, and there keep his Faith, he will then find the Holy Spirit grandly working on his behalf, bringing about victory within his life.

But the sadness is, and again as we have repeatedly stated, most Christians have been taught little or nothing about the Cross of Christ, and in fact, many at this present time have actually been taught against the Cross. As we've already explained, the Word of Faith doctrine is probably the greatest culprit as it regards this terrible error, which brings defeat to so many Christians. Let's look at it closer:

CONCUPISCENCE

Paul said: *"But sin* (the sin, referring to the sin nature), *taking occasion by the Commandment* (the Law of Moses, the moral part, the Ten Commandments), *wrought in me all manner of concupiscence* (evil desire). *For without the Law, sin was dead"* (Rom. 7:8).

Concupiscence, as stated above, means *"passionate or evil desire."* It can pertain to anything in the realm of evil. The sad thing is, not understanding the Cross of Christ, the majority of Christians are in the same proverbial boat as was the Apostle Paul, before he understood the Cross, as it regards *"concupiscence."* In fact, there are millions of Christians at this very moment who are struggling with evil desires, fighting with all of their strength and might, and sadly, they are losing that fight.

They don't understand why they are losing, considering that they are struggling against this thing, whatever it might be, with every ounce of strength they have. Some have even thought that they are demon possessed because of these *"terrible evil desires."*

No, you aren't demon possessed, and neither are you a unique case. Your problem is this:

The Cross is God's answer to sin, and in fact, His only answer. Most Christians understand the Cross, at least up to a point, as it regards Salvation; however, they understand it not at all, as it regards Sanctification. And whether the Christian understands it or not, it is Sanctification of which we speak here.

SPIRITUAL ADULTERY

Sadly and regrettably, even as we've already stated, as it regards Sanctification, the Cross is either totally ignored, or else it is repudiated as the answer, which latter falls into the Word of Faith camp. Either way, the Believer is in trouble, because if he tries to live a life of victory outside of Faith in the Cross, it presents itself as unfaithfulness to Christ, and in fact, in the Mind of God, such a person is looked as a *"spiritual adulterer"* (Rom. 7:1-4). In other words, any Christian that's trying to live a life of victory outside of Faith in the Cross is being unfaithful to Christ. He may not realize that, and in fact may not think of himself in that capacity, and would probably vigorously deny such; however, the truth is, even as Paul explained it, whether he realizes it or not, he is living a life of spiritual unfaithfulness, which translates into *"spiritual adultery."* He is looking to things other than Christ and Him Crucified as the answer.

In such an atmosphere, the Holy Spirit will not work. In other words, He will not help you to live a victorious life with you trying to rely upon your own strength and ability, etc. If He helped you in such a capacity, He would be helping you to commit spiritual adultery, which of course, He will never do.

As a Believer, you have the help of the Holy Spirit, as long as you work within the parameters of the Finished Work of Christ (Rom. 8:1-2, 11). If you try to work outside of those parameters, which most of the modern Church does, you will do so on your own, which means the Holy Spirit will have no part in such a situation, which leaves you helpless. That's the reason that millions of Christians are struggling with concupiscence (evil desires), and despite trying to stop this problem, they are not only not succeeding in getting victory, the situation is actually becoming worse.

THE WORKS OF THE FLESH

In Galatians, Chapter 5, Paul outlined the works of the flesh. They are:

"Adultery, fornication, uncleanness, lasciviousness,

"Idolatry, witchcraft, hatred, variance, emulations, wrath, strife, seditions, heresies,

"Envyings, murders, drunkenness, revellings, and such like: of the which I tell you before, as I have also told you in time past, that they which do such things shall not inherit the Kingdom of God" (Gal. 5:19-21).

If it is to be noticed, *"heresies"* fall under the category of *"works of the flesh."*

There are untold numbers of Preachers, and untold numbers of Believers, who are, in a sense, not guilty of the sin of concupiscence, but are guilty of *"works of the flesh"* in other capacities.

For instance, *"heresies"* are listed as a *"work of the flesh."* This means that any Preacher who preaches erroneous doctrine, and any Believer who believes such, are guilty of heresy.

Heresy is a truth enlarged all out of proportion to its original intent. For instance, Grace is certainly a Biblical Doctrine; however, if people take Grace into license, which many were doing in Paul's day, and continue to do unto this hour, they have taken that truth into heresy. Let me say it in another way:

If the Believer, Preacher or otherwise, doesn't understand the Cross, in some way, irrespective of his efforts otherwise, *"works of the flesh"* are going to dominate his life in some manner. And if it is to be noticed, these particular *"works"* cover the waterfront. In other words, just because a Christian is not committing the sins of adultery, fornication, or drunkenness, etc., doesn't necessarily mean that works of the flesh aren't being manifested. There are many categories as it regards this particular realm of sin.

FRUIT OF THE SPIRIT

In the same Chapter, Paul refers to the Fruit of the Spirit. It is: *"Love, joy, peace, longsuffering, gentleness, goodness, faith,*

"Meekness, temperance: against such there is no law" (Gal. 5:22-23). Now let me make another statement as it regards the Cross. As it's impossible to overcome *"works of the flesh"* without properly understanding the Cross, likewise, it is impossible for the *"Fruit of the Spirit"* to be developed in one's life, unless one understands the Cross. If it is to be noticed, it is *"Fruit of the Spirit,"* and not fruit of our own efforts, etc. In other words, the Holy Spirit Alone can develop such fruit. And how does He do this?

Everything that is done in our lives, as it regards the Lord, is all done through the principle of Faith. Paul also said: *"For we through the Spirit wait for the hope of Righteousness by Faith."*

He then said: *"For in Jesus Christ neither circumcision availeth anything, nor uncircumcision; but Faith which worketh by love"* (Gal. 5:5-6).

And what does he mean by the use of the term *"Faith"*?

Always and without exception, when Paul uses the term *"Faith,"* or the term *"in Christ,"* or one of its derivatives, without exception, he is speaking of the Work of Christ on the Cross. In other words, we are to have Faith in Christ and what Christ did for us at the Cross. This is the Faith alone which God will honor.

If the Believer properly understands the Cross, all the other attributes promised to the Believer will be made available. But without that proper understanding, the Christian is greatly hindered in his spiritual progress. In fact, there can be precious little progress at all. We must ever understand that the Message always has been, is, and ever shall be, *"Jesus Christ and Him Crucified"* (I Cor. 1:23).

PHARAOH'S LAST FLING

Verse 5 reads: *"And it was told the king of Egypt that the people fled: and the heart of Pharaoh and of his servants was turned against the people, and they said, Why have we done this, that we have let Israel go from serving us?"*

Now begins the record of the greatest miracle to date, with the exception of creation itself. This miracle would be the opening of the Red Sea, which would be life to the Israelites, and death the Egyptians.

Egypt was extremely reluctant to give up hundreds of thousands of craftsmen, Engineers, and laborers, which were such a boon to the Egyptian economy. Hence they said, *"Why have we done this, that we have let Israel go from serving us?"*

What a fool that man is!

Understanding that the Israelites were *"entangled in the land,"* and that they were *"shut in"* by the wilderness, and as well, that they were trapped before the Red Sea, did Pharaoh suppose that the God of miracles, Who had acted so powerfully on behalf of Israel up to now, would simply let the tyrant destroy His people? God had already shown Himself strong, exceedingly strong, on Israel's behalf. Would not He continue to do so?

As stated, what a fool man is! Pharaoh had disregarded every warning. In the very face of God, he now marches out against Jehovah's redeemed to consume them in the wilderness, or so he thought.

In all the miracles performed by God in the last few weeks or months, Egypt's army had not been touched. Her chariots were intact, with her army still the fighting force it had always been. So Pharaoh evidently thinks that his time of vengeance had now arrived.

Concerning this time, Mackintosh said: *"It is when the people of God are brought into the greatest straits and difficulties that they are favored with the finest displays of God's character and actings; and for this reason He oftimes leads us into a trying position, in order that He may the more markedly show Himself."*

THE PURSUIT

Verses 6 through 9 read: *"And he made ready his chariot, and he took his people with him:*

"And he took six hundred chosen chariots, and all the chariots of Egypt, and captains over every one of them.

"And the LORD hardened the heart of Pharaoh king of Egypt, and he pursued after the Children of Israel: and the Children of Israel went out with an high hand.

"But the Egyptians pursued after them, all the horses and chariots of Pharaoh, and his horsemen, and his army, and overtook them in camping by the sea, beside Pi-hahiroth, before Baal-zephon."

The 600 chosen chariots comprised the king's guard, the pride of Egypt. And as well, all the other chariots of Egypt as the main body of the army, including the chariot drivers and combatants in each chariot, joined in with the king's guard. Josephus records that Pharaoh had 50,000 horsemen and 200,000 footmen, as well as all the chariots.

It is uncertain as to how long the Israelites remained encamped at Pi-hahiroth. But to be sure, they would wait so long as the Pillar of Cloud did not move (Num. 9:18-20).

It would have taken Pharaoh at least a day to hear of their march from Etham, at least another day to collect his troops, or perhaps even more, and three or four days to affect the march from Tanis to Pi-hahiroth.

The Jewish tradition is that the Red Sea was crossed on the night of the twenty-first of Nisan (Abib), which corresponds somewhat with our April.

Verse 8 says, *"The Children of Israel went out with an high hand."* This refers to a certain degree of pride and confidence. Regrettably, the *"high hand"* would change when they faced the Red Sea.

THE MODERN CHURCH

Tragically, there are millions of Christians presently who unwillingly serve the Devil. It is a travesty, because it doesn't have to be this way. Whenever the believing sinner is Born-Again, every bondage of Satan is broken, and that person no longer serves the Evil One. So, that being the case, how is it that we can say there are millions of Christians who are, in fact, presently serving Satan?

As we've just stated, at the moment of conversion, every single sin is washed clean, with every bondage broken. In fact, God could not accept anyone on any other basis. Concerning conversion, Paul said: *"You are washed . . . you are sanctified . . . you are justified in the Name of the Lord Jesus, and by the Spirit of our God"* (I Cor. 6:11).

It is impossible for one to be *"justified"* without being made perfectly clean, which can only be done by the Blood of Jesus, and Faith in that Finished Work. In other words, there is no such thing as a partial Justification. One is either justified, which means total and complete, or else one is not justified, which means that one is still in one's sins.

So, as we've already asked, that being the case, how is it that millions of Christians are presently continuing to serve Satan?

Paul explained that to us in Romans, Chapters 6, 7, and 8.

In Romans, Chapter 6, he told us how that when Jesus was crucified, we were, in effect, *"baptized into His death"* (Rom. 6:3). We were then *"buried with Him by baptism into death,"* and then raised with Him *"in newness of life"* (Rom. 6:4).

This means that *"our old man was crucified with Him,"* which refers to all that we were before Salvation. In other words, we died with Christ, and thereby, died to all of the things which once ensnared us. That's the reason that Paul now speaks of Believers by saying: *"Therefore if any man be in Christ, he is a new creature: old things are passed away; behold, all things are become new"* (II Cor. 5:17). As a result, *"the body of sin ... is destroyed, that henceforth we should not serve sin"* (Rom. 6:6). This means that the effectiveness of the sin nature is destroyed, with all bondages broken, and guilt removed.

However, even though the Scripture plainly tells us that we are dead, having died in Christ, it doesn't say that the sin nature is dead, even though its power is broken. It does say:

"Likewise reckon you also yourselves to be dead indeed unto sin, but alive unto God through Jesus Christ our Lord" (Rom. 6:11).

Once again we emphasize, while we are dead to the sin nature, the sin nature itself, although dormant, at least that's the way it ought to be, is not dead.

The reason we refer to the word *"sin"* as the *"sin nature,"* is because in most of the places in Romans, Chapter 6, where the word *"sin"* is used, in the original Text, it has before that word what is referred to as the definite article. In other words, it actually says *"the sin."* This means that it's not referring to particular acts of sin, but rather to the *"sin nature,"* or *"evil nature."*

Paul then said: *"Let not sin* (the sin nature) *therefore reign in your mortal body, that you should obey it in the lusts thereof"* (Rom. 6:12).

Now if it wasn't possible for the sin nature to once again reign or rule within our lives, exactly as it did before conversion, which means that despite all of our efforts otherwise, we will then serve Satan, then Paul would not have broached the subject.

His teaching here tells us that it is quite possible for the sin nature to once again rule and reign within the heart and life of the Believer, and will, in fact, do so if the Believer doesn't understand his place and position in Christ.

And how does this happen?

IMPROPER UNDERSTANDING OF THE CROSS

I think by now, you surely know what we're going to say.

If the Believer doesn't understand the Cross, and I refer to understanding the Cross as it regards our Sanctification, exactly that which Paul is teaching in Romans, Chapter 6, he will then try to live for the Lord in all the wrong ways. In doing such a thing, which every Believer will do if the Cross is misunderstood, in some way, failure is going to be the result. When this happens, it's like throwing fuel on smoldering coals of fire. Whereas the sin nature was dormant, now it flames anew, and the Believer finds himself being ruled by the sin nature instead of the Divine nature (II Pet. 1:4). This is a miserable state for a Believer to be in, but unfortunately, it is the state of most Believers, and simply because of their lack of understanding as it regards God's prescribed order of victory, which is the Cross of Christ.

Let the Reader understand that there is only one remedy for sin, and that is the Cross of Christ. There is no other, as there needs to be no other. If we take advantage of that remedy, victory will be ours, and perpetual victory at that; however, if we do not understand that prescribed order, and try to live for God by means and ways other than the Cross, the end result every single time will be failure, with the sin nature ruling such a Believer.

The only remedy for that situation is for the Believer to understand that his victory, in totality, is found in what Jesus did at the Cross, and his Faith in that Finished Work. This is the manner in which the Holy Spirit works, and if our Faith is properly placed, the Holy Spirit will definitely work mightily upon our behalf (Rom. 8:1-2, 11). Then, as Paul also said:

"Sin shall not have dominion over you: for you are not under the law, but under Grace" (Rom. 6:14).

FAILURE

This is the reason, a failure to understand the Cross as it refers to Sanctification, which brings about failure in the life of Believers. Please understand, the Preacher is in the same category. He must have the same Faith in the Cross as the layman, or he will face the same difficulty, even if God is using him.

Now the Church has tried to face this problem in many and varied ways other than the Cross. It doesn't really matter which way the Church chooses, and irrespective as to how good it might look on the surface. If it's not the Way of the Cross, continued failure will be the result. Let us say it again:

God has only one remedy for sin, and that is the Cross of Christ. So the Church can try humanistic psychology, it can try self-efforts, or it can try law of every description, but the end result will always be the same — failure.

WHY WON'T THE CHURCH EMBRACE THE CROSS?

Some small part of the Church is embracing the Cross, and is seeing tremendous results, even as the Word of God guarantees. But the truth is, that's only a small percentage, with the far greater majority advocating other things.

Why?

The reason is either *"unbelief"* or *"ignorance."* We'll address the latter first.

Most Christians, and especially Preachers, are loath to admit that they don't understand the Cross. But the truth is, most don't! The problem is pride.

Most Christians erroneously think of the Cross as something very elementary, which means that it's basic, and it's something they already know. Like one man wrote me the other day and stated, *"Why do you keep talking about the Cross? All Christians understand everything about the Cross."* The truth is, most Christians understand hardly anything about the Cross.

What little understanding most Christians have about the Cross refers only to Salvation, and even that is sketchy to say the least.

NOTES

When it comes to Sanctification, which we are addressing here, most Christians understand hardly anything at all as it regards the Cross in this all-important work within our lives. So the results are failure on every hand, and despite the Believer doing everything within his power to do otherwise. In other words, any and every true Christian wants to live for God, and wants to live for the Lord in the right way. Due to the fact that the Divine nature now resides within our hearts and lives, we don't want to sin. And any Christian who would claim that Christians desire to sin simply don't know what they are talking about. While the flesh may want something, the spirit of the Child of God definitely doesn't. But still, that Christian will sin, if they do not deny themselves, which means to deny their own ability, and thereby take up the Cross daily in our following Christ (Lk. 9:23-24).

So millions fall into the category of Scriptural ignorance. If a subject is not preached and taught behind the pulpit, then it's impossible for the people to know and understand what the Word of God actually says. *"Faith comes by hearing, and hearing by the Word of God"* (Rom. 10:17).

The only way for the problem of Scriptural ignorance to be solved is for the Word of God to be correctly taught as it regards the Cross.

Unbelief is another matter altogether. The longer I live for God, and the more that the Lord has shown me about the Cross, the more that I believe that unbelief is the problem with many. In fact, ignorance certainly may contain a modicum of unbelief also, and probably does.

When we speak of *"unbelief,"* we're speaking of the fact that the Preacher and the Layman simply don't believe that the Cross of Christ is the answer for the dilemma of mankind. They may pay lip service to the Cross, but the truth is their actions prove that their Faith lies elsewhere. That's the reason the Church has gone pell-mell into humanistic psychology. That's the reason its basic cry is, *"You need professional help."*

The truth is, if we turn toward the direction of the world and worldly wisdom, this means that we have placed the Cross of Christ into default. We either believe that Jesus Christ faced every problem at the Cross, and I speak of every problem that besets humanity, or else He didn't. I happen to believe that He did. The Scripture says:

"Blotting out the handwriting of ordinances that was against us, which was contrary to us, and took it out of the way, nailing it to His Cross.

"And having spoiled principalities and powers, He made a show of them openly, triumphing over them in it" (Col. 2:14-15).

This tells us that the claims of the broken law against us were forever settled at the Cross. There Jesus atoned for all sin. In doing so, He totally and completely defeated every demon spirit and power of darkness. None were excluded, with all being included.

So this means that Jesus addressed every single problem of mankind at the Cross; therefore, the Cross is the answer to man's dilemma, and in fact, the only answer.

(10) "AND WHEN PHARAOH DREW NIGH, THE CHILDREN OF ISRAEL LIFTED UP THEIR EYES, AND, BEHOLD, THE EGYPTIANS MARCHED AFTER THEM; AND THEY WERE SORE AFRAID: AND THE CHILDREN OF ISRAEL CRIED OUT UNTO THE LORD.

(11) "AND THEY SAID UNTO MOSES, BECAUSE THERE WERE NO GRAVES IN EGYPT, HAVE YOU TAKEN US AWAY TO DIE IN THE WILDERNESS? WHEREFORE HAVE YOU DEALT THUS WITH US, TO CARRY US FORTH OUT OF EGYPT?

(12) "IS NOT THIS THE WORD THAT WE DID TELL YOU IN EGYPT, SAYING, LET US ALONE, THAT WE MAY SERVE THE EGYPTIANS? FOR IT HAD BEEN BETTER FOR US TO SERVE THE EGYPTIANS, THAN THAT WE SHOULD DIE IN THE WILDERNESS.

(13) "AND MOSES SAID UNTO THE PEOPLE, FEAR YE NOT, STAND STILL, AND SEE THE SALVATION OF THE LORD, WHICH HE WILL SHOW TO YOU TODAY: FOR THE EGYPTIANS WHOM YOU HAVE SEEN TODAY, YOU SHALL SEE THEM AGAIN NO MORE FOREVER.

(14) "THE LORD SHALL FIGHT FOR YOU, AND YOU SHALL HOLD YOUR PEACE."

The exegesis is:

NOTES

1. Verses 10 through 12 record the complaints of Israel. The fear, unbelief, and anger of the very people who had witnessed God's wonders in the land of Egypt would appear incredible, but that each Bible student finds these evils in his own heart, and learns by sad experience that great depression of mind usually follows exceptional spiritual triumphs.

2. Unbelief cried out: *"The wilderness will become our grave"*; but the result was that the sea became Pharaoh's grave.

3. The Message from the Lord is ever *"fear not."*

4. *"Stand still"* refers to a total lack of dependence on the flesh.

FEAR

Verse 10 reads: *"And when Pharaoh drew near, the Children of Israel lifted up their eyes, and, behold, the Egyptians marched after them; and they were sore afraid: and the Children of Israel cried out unto the LORD."*

This was a sore trial of Faith, and sadly Israel did fail in the hour of testing. However, this as well is so often the case with us.

No matter how many times the Lord has delivered us in the past, no matter how signally His Power has been exerted on our behalf, when some new trial comes, or even the old trial with a more fierce face, we tend to forget God's previous interventions, and are swallowed up by the greatness of our present emergency, and conduct ourselves not unlike Israel of old.

Verse 10 says, *"The Children of Israel lifted up their eyes,"* which means they observed the Egyptians coming after them. Their eyes were upon the Egyptians, and not on the Lord.

How so easy it is for us to look at circumstances, to look at events, to look to the prattle of the Devil, thereby taking our eyes off the Lord. Such always leads to disaster.

We should remember that the 12 spies sent into Canaan, with the exception of Joshua and Caleb, saw only the walled cities and the giants. Joshua and Caleb saw the Lord, and said: *"Only rebel not against the LORD, neither fear ye the people of the land; for they are bread for us: their defense is departed from them, and the LORD is with us: fear them not"* (Num. 14:9).

I think one can say without fear of exaggeration or contradiction that the hardest thing for the Child of God to do is to keep his eyes on the Lord, when circumstances are screaming very negative things. This is always the great trial of Faith. And as it has been well said, Faith must always be tested, and great Faith must be tested greatly.

Pharaoh has a design to ruin Israel; therefore, God has a design to ruin Pharaoh.

The Egyptians were angry with themselves for the best deed they ever did, which was to finally let Israel go, while the Israelites were angry with God for the greatest kindness that was ever done them, their deliverance from Egypt; thus gross are the absurdities of unbelief (Henry).

COMPLAINT

Verse 11 reads: *"And they said unto Moses, Because there were no graves in Egypt, have you taken us away to die in the wilderness? Wherefore have you dealt thus with us, to carry us forth out of Egypt?"*

When things do not go right, the normal reaction is for one to vent one's anger on someone else. So, the leaders in Israel would vent their anger on Moses. They are talking death, when the greatest miracle the world has ever seen is about to take place. Unbelief talks this way because it looks at circumstances instead of looking to the Lord. While it is true that they cried out unto the Lord, even as the previous Verse proclaims, it evidently was not a cry of Faith, but rather of unbelief.

How absurd are the reasonings of unbelief! If death at the hands of the Egyptians was to be their lot, why had Jehovah delivered them from the land of bondage? The fact that He had led them out of Egypt was evidence enough that He was not going to allow them to fall before their enemies. Besides this, the Lord had promised that they would worship Him in Mount Horeb (Ex. 3:12). That being the case, how, then, could they now perish in the wilderness? But where Faith is not in exercise, the Promises of God bring no comfort, and afford no stay to the heart (Pink).

THE PATH CHOSEN BY GOD

While they were criticizing Moses, in reality, they were criticizing God. And in reality, that is always the case with complaining and unbelief.

Israel had been brought to their present position by God Himself. It was the Pillar of Cloud that had led them to where they were now encamped. This should be an important truth for us:

We must not expect the path of Faith to be an easy or smooth one. As one Preacher has well said, *"If it was easy, anyone could do it"*; but inasmuch as it's not easy, Faith, so to speak, separates the men from the boys.

Faith must ever be tested, in order that we may learn the sufficiency of our God!

Three reasons:

1. That we may prove from experience that He is able to supply our every need (Phil. 4:19).

2. That He can make a way of escape from every temptation, which is the way of the Cross (I Cor. 10:13).

3. That we might be able to see that He can do for us exceedingly, abundantly above all that we ask or think (Eph. 3:20).

LET US ALONE

Verse 12 reads: *"Is not this the word that we did tell you in Egypt, saying, Let us alone, that we may serve the Egyptians? For it had been better for us to serve the Egyptians, than that we should die in the wilderness."*

Why is it that it's so hard for Believers to trust God?

By trusting Him, I'm speaking of the future and His care for us. There was ample proof, in fact abundant proof, as it regarded the great miracles that God performed in the sight of all of the Children of Israel, affecting the entire nation of Egypt. So there was no excuse for this unbelief and complaining. But yet we must ask ourselves, are we doing any better? I will use myself and this Ministry as an example:

Since October of 1991, we have had to trust God totally and completely for everything that we have. By that I mean that if God didn't provide it, it simply could not be obtained.

Our Ministry is a Media Ministry, which reaches tremendous numbers of people, but yet requires large sums of money. To be sure, the price per person reached is far less than the expenses of Churches, but the number of people reached, which is quite large, demands large sums of cash. We had no place to get that cash, except to totally and completely trust God. Regrettably, virtually every Preacher in the world was urging their people not to give to us in any capacity. So we were cut off from sustenance and support except for the Lord. In other words, He would have to furnish a table in the wilderness, that is, if we were to survive.

Not only was our financial survival at stake, but above all, even our spiritual survival was at stake. I can well empathize with the words of Paul when he said: *"O wretched man that I am! Who shall deliver me from the body of this death?"* (Rom. 7:24).

Sadly, no one in the Church, and I speak of the Church world as a whole, could give me the answer to this dilemma. Of course, I'm sure there were some Preachers somewhere who had the answer, but they were few and far between.

For five years, I sought the Lord, and I speak of the time between October 1991 until 1996. I wept before Him day and night, asking Him to show me the way of victory for the Child of God. I knew that the ways being promoted by the Church simply were not Scriptural. Not being Scriptural, they simply would not work.

And then in 1996, the Lord began to open up to me the Message of the Cross, emphatically stating to me, *"That for which you seek is found totally and completely in the Cross."* I will never forget that hour; and to be sure, the Lord has continued to enlarge this Revelation from that day until now, and I trust the enlargement will ever continue. To be frank, the Cross of Christ is inexhaustible, hence Paul referring to it as the *"Everlasting Covenant"* (Heb. 13:20). It is everlasting because it is Perfect. What Jesus did there cannot be improved upon, simply because it doesn't need to be improved upon.

THE EGYPTIANS, THE WILDERNESS, THE DELIVERANCE

All Israel could see at this time was either slavery to the Egyptians, or to die in the wilderness. Regrettably, that is the condition of many, if not most, Christians presently. They do not understand deliverance because they're looking for it in the wrong place. As we've already explained, evil passions grip most, simply because they do not know or understand God's prescribed order of victory. But in the Cross, and we speak of what Jesus did there, there is deliverance for every single sinner on the face of this Earth, and every single Believer.

But many Christians, after trying so very, very hard, are simply at the point of giving up. They don't know what to do. They see only Egypt, allegorically speaking, or spiritual death, i.e., *"the wilderness."* The Church has said, *"Try this,"* and *"Try that,"* all to no avail.

But exactly as the Lord had deliverance for the Children of Israel, He has deliverance for every single Believer presently, and irrespective as to what the problem might be.

FORGIVENESS AND DELIVERANCE

Many Christians mistake forgiveness for deliverance. As wonderful and necessary as forgiveness is, forgiveness is not deliverance. What do I mean by that?

Many Christians, after failing the Lord, will ask Him to forgive them, and to be sure, He always will. He plainly tells us in His Word: *"If we confess our sins, He is faithful and just to forgive us our sins, and to cleanse us from all unrighteousness"* (I Jn. 1:9).

He meant exactly what He said, and places no limitation on the number of times that He will forgive.

Whenever the Believer receives forgiveness, and experiences the returned peace, many mistake that for deliverance. As stated, it isn't!

The Believer being freshly forgiven, with the joy and peace of the Lord instantly restored, and rejoicing in the feeling that brings, sometimes mistakes this for deliverance. They then believe that the besetting sin, which has plagued them for so long, and for which they have asked and received forgiveness many times, will now be no more. But over and over again, they have found that to not be the case.

Why?

WHAT IS DELIVERANCE?

Many Christians are loath to admit that they need deliverance, and then others do admit it, but think that a Preacher can effect such by the laying on of hands, etc. Now, while laying on of hands is certainly Scriptural and helpful, this is not the answer to the sin problem. Were it the answer, Jesus would not have had to come down here and die on a Cross. That should be understood. Others have been beset by a certain problem so long that they have come to believe that they are demon possessed. They then seek for a Preacher who will either cast out the so-called demon, or effect their deliverance, once again, by the laying on of hands. That doesn't work, either.

In the first place, while demon spirits definitely are involved in all manner of sin, and especially bondages of sin, no Christian can actually be demon possessed. And there is a reason that demon spirits have the latitude they have as it regards many Christians, which cause untold problems and troubles.

The problem with such Christians is not these things we have mentioned, plus many we haven't mentioned, but rather their Faith is placed in the wrong things. Now let's say that again:

To properly walk in victory before the Lord and the world, in other words, to have and maintain victory over the world, the flesh, and the Devil, the object of our Faith must ever be the Cross of Christ. This is supremely important. If our Faith is in something else, and even as we've already said several times, in the eyes of the Lord, we are actually committing spiritual adultery. Understanding that, we should surely know that the Holy Spirit, Whom we must have, and have Him working within our hearts and lives mightily, that is if we are to walk in victory, simply will not function in that type of atmosphere (Rom. 7:1-4). While He certainly will remain with us, He will not exhibit His Power under such circumstances.

WALKING AFTER THE FLESH

Paul said: *"There is therefore now no condemnation to them which are in Christ Jesus, who walk not after the flesh, but after the Spirit"* (Rom. 8:1).

From this Passage, we know and realize that it's possible for a Christian to *"walk after the flesh."*

Exactly what is *"walking after the flesh"*?

It is the placing of our Faith in anything, and irrespective as to what it is, other than the Cross of Christ.

"Walking after the Spirit," which certainly refers to the Holy Spirit, is simply our Faith being placed in the correct object, which is the Finished Work of Christ (Rom. 8:2, 11).

The moment the Believer begins to walk after the Spirit, which means that he has ceased to walk after the flesh, which means that he has placed his Faith in the Cross of Christ, he will find that deliverance is instantly his. It will be his without fanfare, without embarrassment, etc. The Holy Spirit will simply begin to work within his heart and life, and due to the fact that the Holy Spirit is God, the things that are great problems to us, to be sure, are no problem at all to Him. This is God's prescribed order of victory, and His only prescribed order. Let us say it again: it is the Cross of Christ.

FEAR NOT

Verse 13 reads: *"And Moses said unto the people, Fear ye not, stand still, and see the Salvation of the LORD, which He will show to you today: for the Egyptians whom you have seen today, you shall see them again no more forever."*

Several wonderful things are said in this Passage, so wonderful in fact, they defy all description. In this Verse, we have a compendium of our present spiritual experience as well. We would do well to heed what is being said here, because it applies to us figuratively, just as it applied to Israel literally.

1. *"And Moses said unto the people"*: We learn here what the Preacher is supposed to preach. In essence, Moses, in shadow and type, preached the Cross (I Cor. 1:23). What Moses told the people is what we as Preachers of the Gospel are to tell the people as well. If we veer, or err from this Message, whatever it is we tell the people will not bring victory to their lives, but rather the very opposite. Tragically, there are precious few Preachers today preaching the Cross. But let the Preacher know and understand,

preaching the Cross is the only Message that will set the captive free, and then keep the person free. That's why Paul said: *"For I determined not to know anything among you, save Jesus Christ and Him Crucified"* (I Cor. 2:2).

For those Preachers who would preach other things as an answer to man's dilemma, they are blatantly, openly, and purposely ignoring the plain Word given here by the Holy Spirit to Paul.

If it is to be noticed, Paul didn't substitute the word *"Resurrection"* for the word *"Crucified."* While he certainly preached a resurrected Christ, it was not the Resurrection, as important and as necessary as that was, which delivered humanity from the powers of darkness, but rather the Cross of Christ (Gal. 1:4).

2. *"You fear not"*: If the Message is right, which means that the Faith of the individual hearing the Message is now right, the Believer has no cause to fear.

There was a great difference in the Children of Israel during their day, than our position presently. They were depending on a miracle that had not yet been brought about, while we are looking to a miracle that has already been brought about, and I speak of what Christ did for us at the Cross. If Moses would tell the Children of Israel to fear not, even though the miracle had not yet been brought to pass, how much more are we being told by the Holy Spirit presently to *"fear not"*! They were asked to trust in a work which had not yet been completed, while we now are told to trust in a work which has been gloriously and wondrously completed.

The point is, if they had no occasion to fear, how much more presently do we have no occasion to fear?

Fear what?

They were fearing that the Egyptians would overtake them, and slaughter them where they stood. Now read carefully what I have to say:

If you as a Believer are not trusting in Christ and His Cross, in other words, if the Cross of Christ is not the object of your Faith, I can assure you that you have every reason to fear. In fact, I have no doubt that some of you holding this book in your hands greet each morning with fear. You wonder if you will make it through another day? You are fighting and struggling, but yet you are losing. You fear that you will be found out, but above all, you fear that you might even lose your soul.

Regrettably, the majority of the modern Church falls into this latter category. They live a life of fear, and it's because they are trusting in something that is not Biblical. What do I mean by that?

To make it simple and easy to understand, it means that the Believer has placed his Faith in something other than Christ and Him Crucified, and it really doesn't matter what the other thing might be, or even how holy it might be in its own right. The Cross of Christ, and Faith in that Finished Work, are the only means of Salvation and victory that God has afforded. He has nothing else, because He needs nothing else. To be sure, if you place your Faith in that Finished Work, you need never fear, and to be sure, you won't fear because you're standing on the Rock. The storms may come and they may go, but you will be unmoved. That's why the Psalmist said:

"Blessed is the man who walks not in the counsel of the ungodly, nor stands in the way of sinners, nor sits in the seat of the scornful.

"But his delight is in the Law of the LORD: and in His Law does he meditate day and night.

"And he shall be like a tree planted by the rivers of water, that brings forth his fruit in his season: his leaf also shall not wither; and whatsoever he does shall prosper" (Ps. 1:1-3).

To be frank, this *"Man"* of Whom the Psalmist speaks is Christ. But inasmuch as we are *"in Christ,"* then it applies to us as well, but only as we are *"in Christ."* And to be sure, we are *"in Christ,"* by virtue of our Faith in Him, and what He has done for us regarding His Finished Work.

Paul said: *"But God forbid that I should glory, save in the Cross of our Lord Jesus Christ, by Whom the world is crucified unto me, and I unto the world"* (Gal. 6:14).

3. *"Stand still"*: This would seem to be the simplest thing to do, but yet it is actually the hardest thing to do. All attempts at

self-help must end. All activities of the flesh must cease. The workings of nature must be subdued. This is the right attitude, and in fact, the only attitude of Faith in the presence of a trial — *"Stand still."*

Now this is impossible to flesh and blood. All who know, in any measure, the restlessness of the human heart under anticipated trial and difficulty, will be able to form some conception of what is involved in standing still. By contrast, nature must be doing something. It will rush hither and thither. Somehow, in all the activity, it thinks there is safety, when in reality, the very opposite is true.

Unbelief creates or magnifies difficulties, and then sets us about removing them, or rather attempting to remove them, by our own bustling and fruitless actions, which in reality, do not remove anything.

The flesh must always *"do something,"* while Faith, by contrast, trusts in something that has already been done. Let us ask this question:

Do you think you can deliver yourself from the powers of darkness by your own strength and ability? Can the sinner save his own soul? Can the Christian formulate his own victory, which means to subdue the powers of darkness?

Concerning this, the Prophet Jeremiah said: *"Can the Ethiopian change his skin, or the leopard his spots? Then may you also do good, who are accustomed to do evil"* (Jer. 13:23).

SO WHAT DOES IT MEAN TO ACTUALLY STAND STILL?

This is what Jesus was speaking about when He said: *"If any man will come after Me, let him deny himself, and take up his cross daily, and follow Me"* (Lk. 9:23).

When He spoke of one denying one's self, He wasn't speaking of asceticism, which is a denial of all pleasure, etc., as many think, but rather the denying of our own strength and ability, etc. We are rather to look to the Cross, which refers to what Jesus did there, and actually to do so on a *"daily"* basis.

So *"standing still,"* simply means that we do not trust our own strength and ability, but rather Christ, and more particularly, what He did at the Cross on our behalf. In other words, we're trusting in a Work that's already been done.

When we try to bring something about by our activity, whatever it might be, we are in effect saying that which Christ did at the Cross was insufficient, and that we have to do something else. But what does the Scripture say about Christ?

Paul wrote: *"Who (Christ) being the brightness of His Glory (the Glory of the Father), and the express Image of His Person (the express Image of the Father), and upholding all things by the word of His Power, when He had by Himself purged our sins (which He did at the Cross), sat down on the right hand of the Majesty on High"* (Heb. 1:3).

Jesus has *"sat down on the right hand of the Majesty on high"* simply because what He did at the Cross, as Paul stated here, finished the task; hence it is referred to as a *"Finished Work."* In fact, Paul also referred to this New Covenant as an *"Everlasting Covenant,"* simply meaning that there will never be a need for another Covenant (Heb. 13:20).

So, *"standing still"* refers to total trust in a work that has already been completed, meaning that we do not have to do anything else.

4. *"And see the Salvation of the Lord"*: Please notice, it is the *"Salvation of the Lord,"* which refers to the victory of the Lord, which means that it is totally and completely of Him, and not at all of us. Thus it is with Salvation, and in fact, every single thing that we receive from the Lord. None of it is from us or of us, but rather from Him, and by virtue of His Sacrificial, Atoning Work at the Cross.

In fact, that's why we are to *"stand still."* It is simply because none of this is of us, and all of it is of Him. So when we involve ourselves in some type of spiritual activity, thinking that such will bring about victory, we find the very opposite to be the case. It is only Faith that will bring about victory, and more specifically, Faith in Christ and Him Crucified. Hence Paul saying:

"For we through the Spirit wait for the hope of Righteousness by Faith" (Gal. 5:5).

5. *"Which He will show to you today"*: As the Lord was going to deliver Israel that

very day, likewise, to modern Believers who place their Faith totally and completely in Christ and the Cross, victory will come that very day. There may or may not be a struggle in the flesh, but victory is theirs the moment that Faith is properly placed. As well, the struggle may continue for a period of time. In fact, it could continue even for several years in one way or the other; however, the Believer will sense in his spirit that he is gaining strength every day, and to be sure, the realization of victory will ultimately come in totality. The Scripture clearly and plainly states: *"For sin shall not have dominion over you: for you are not under the Law, but under Grace"* (Rom. 6:14).

6. *"For the Egyptians whom you have seen today, you shall see them again no more forever"*: A better translation would be: *"For, as you have seen the Egyptians today, you shall see them again no more forever."*

In other words, they had seen the Egyptians in a menacing, destructive manner, intent upon totally destroying the Children of Israel, which it looked like they would certainly do. It didn't mean that they would never again see any Egyptians, but it meant that they would never see them in this posture of what looked like victory for the Egyptians.

It is the same with the modern Believer who places his Faith exclusively in Christ and His great Sacrifice. While Satan has sought to destroy you in the past, and at times, it looked like he would succeed, you will see him no more in this posture. You will now see him as a defeated foe because you understand how he was defeated.

HOW WAS SATAN DEFEATED?

He was defeated exclusively by what Christ did at the Cross. Jesus never grappled or physically wrestled with Satan. To be frank, Satan doesn't want any part of Christ, and in any capacity.

When Jesus died on the Cross, He satisfied, through His death, which necessitated the shedding of His Blood, the terrible sin debt that was against us. The Scripture said that He nailed the requirements of the Law *"to His Cross."*

When He did this, this took away Satan's legal right to hold man in captivity because of man's sin. In other words, sin is the legal right that Satan has to place man in captivity. But with all sin atoned, which Jesus did at the Cross, this completely *"spoiled principalities and powers . . . making a show of them openly, triumphing over them in it"* (Col. 2:14-15).

As the Believer understands that, to be sure, he will never again see Satan in a posture of victory. In other words, Satan's victory over him in any capacity has now come to an end. Satan *"steals, kills, and destroys"* (Jn. 10:10). In that capacity, the Believer with his Faith properly placed, which refers to being placed entirely in the Cross, will see him no more.

In that regard, it is *"forever."*
Hallelujah!

THE LORD SHALL FIGHT FOR YOU

Verse 14 reads: *"The LORD shall fight for you, and you shall hold your peace."*

The Lord could fight for Israel, only as long as they *"stood still."* Had they turned and tried to fight the Egyptians themselves, and in any capacity, this would have hindered the Lord fighting for them, and they no doubt would have been defeated.

Someone has well said, *"In Justification the Lord fights for us, and in Sanctification, He fights in us."*

Verse 14 is very dear to me personally, and in two ways especially.

The first way involves a very trying time in my life and Ministry. I want to relate to you how the Lord used this very Verse to bring victory.

THE LORD WILL DEFEND YOU

While there are certainly some Godly Preachers and Laity in Pentecostal Denominations, if I understand the Word of God correctly, it is my belief that the majority of these Denominations are functioning under law instead of Grace. As well, their Government has long since, at least for most of them, ceased to be Scriptural.

If in fact that is true, Preachers would do well to get out of it, and as well, the Laity would do well to find another Church. As it regards the Laity, there certainly may be the case that some Churches in these respective

Denominations are led by a Godly Pastor. That being the case, they certainly should remain where they are, but with the understanding that the problems of which I have mentioned, as it regards these Denominations, could invade their own particular Church at any time.

Concerning my own personal situation, one particular Denomination set out to completely destroy any Ministry that I might have. They used any method at their disposal, with nothing being excluded. To be frank, I actually feared for my life.

This would even be wrong were a Preacher a member of such a Denomination, but considering that he's no longer a member of such a group, it becomes even worse. It's one thing to withdraw fellowship, but it's something else altogether to deny the Blood of Christ, which they did, and then to take it into their own hands to wreck any Ministry that one might have left.

Jesus said: *"The Kingdom of Heaven is like unto leaven, which a woman took, and hid in three measures of meal, till the whole was leavened"* (Mat. 13:33).

In effect, Christ is referring to the Church as a whole, and as to how it would be in the last days.

When a *"woman"* is used in this fashion, it is always in an evil sense. The *"meal"* is a symbol of the Word of God. The *"leaven"* is, of course, a type of sin.

The idea is, the Church in the last days, at least as a whole, will be completely *"leavened,"* which means that the Word of God will be so corrupted that it would no longer be of any use.

Sadly and regrettably, this of which Jesus said is the condition of the modern Church. In fact, the Church presently has never been in such a negative spiritual condition, as it is presently. It falls into the category of the Laodicean Church, which Jesus addressed.

He said: *"Because you say, I am rich, and increased with goods, and have need of nothing; and knowest not that you are wretched, and miserable, and poor, and blind, and naked.*

"I counsel you to buy of Me gold tried in the fire, that you may be rich; and white raiment, that you may be clothed, and that the shame of your nakedness do not appear; and anoint your eyes with eyesalve, that you may see" (Rev. 3:17-18).

The wounds of the enemy hurt; however, the wounds of those which are your own, hurt far more.

The year was 1988. The month was May, if I remember correctly. Information came to us as to certain things this Denomination had done, and were then beginning to do. These things, which I will leave nameless, were so insidious, so evil, and so wicked, that they defied description. As stated, I feared for my life.

On the particular afternoon that this information came to us, I will confess, I did not sleep at all that night. For some part of the night, I walked up and down on our driveway in front of our house, seeking the Lord, asking Him as to what I should do.

At that particular time, I really did not receive any answer from the Lord. A little bit after daylight, I made up my mind that I would take steps to defend myself. When our office opened, I called our Television Department, and told them to prepare everything for a special that we would tape that afternoon. I planned to lay everything out as to exactly what this Denomination was doing, and to air it over our Telecast, which covered almost all of this nation, and even other countries of the world.

For one to defend one's self, I suppose, is a basic instinct; however, when we do such, we are, in effect, taking ourselves out from under the hand of the Lord, thereby, hindering His defense on our behalf. Now there are certainly times when an answer should be given, but as I was to find out, the way I was going about this was wrong.

While I was waiting for everything to be prepared, our two grandsons, Gabriel and Matthew came over to the house. If I remember correctly, Gabriel, at the time, was six years old, and Matthew was five. They wanted to go swimming in our pool, and I walked outside with them to watch them while they played in the water, etc.

To be sure, my heart was very, very heavy. It seemed like the weight of the world was on my shoulders, and I had nowhere to turn as it regards others outside of my family, and our Church, Family Worship Center.

I can still see this scene in my mind, as to what happened, which was such a blessing to me.

Even though I had given instructions for the Television program to be made, which I would do shortly, in my spirit, I didn't feel right about the situation. And then it happened:

The Lord would now answer my prayer, which I had cried to Him most of the night.

Frances came out the door holding the Bible in her hands. If I remember, she was weeping. She said to me the following:

"I was reading the Fourteenth Chapter of Exodus, and when I came to this Fourteenth Verse, 'The LORD shall fight for you, and you shall hold your peace,' the Presence of the Lord came all over me." And then she said, *"Is the Lord telling us something in this?"*

I took her Bible, and looked at the Scripture, and when I did, the Spirit of God came on me as well. I, too, began to weep, for I knew that this was the Lord's answer to my dilemma.

After praising the Lord for a period of time, and feeling great peace within my soul, I called our office and told them to stop all preparation as it regarded the Television program that I had planned to make.

Frances and I agreed at that moment that we would put all of this in the hands of the Lord, would not try to defend ourselves, in effect, *"holding our peace,"* and let the *"Lord fight for us."*

I will confess that this was hard to do at times, because the onslaught didn't let up when we made this decision. But I had the Promise of God, and that's all that mattered.

WHAT HAPPENED?

As I dictate these notes, it is April 10, 2002. I've never been stronger in the Lord, of which I will relate more in a moment, and our Ministry is growing by leaps and bounds.

At this particular time, we have 57 Radio Stations on the air, meaning that the Ministry owns these Stations, and we are now purchasing one almost every four weeks. We believe the Lord has told us to do this, and in effect, cover the entirety of this nation, and even the world. In other words, He is blessing abundantly.

Had I tried to defend myself, thereby ignoring what the Lord told us, I do not personally think this Ministry would even be in existence today.

In fact, had I not sought His face earnestly, asking Him for leading and guidance, I'm not so sure that guidance would have been given. If in fact that had been the case, I don't think we would have survived. The Lord did fight for us, and He did so grandly and gloriously, and we give Him all the praise and all the glory.

SPIRITUAL VICTORY

Now I want to deal with the second way that this Passage is so dear to me, and in reality, should be dear to every single Believer.

At this juncture, when Israel was about to cross the Red Sea, in which God would perform one of His greatest miracles, what the Lord was to do for them, was that which would happen very shortly. In other words, even though it would shortly come to pass, it had not then happened. But most definitely it would, and most definitely it did.

The *"fight"* of which I now speak has already been accomplished, and I refer to what Jesus did at the Cross. There He overcame every single power of darkness, excluding nothing of Satan, and including Satan himself.

Until 1996, while I understood the Cross as it regarded Salvation, preached it strongly, and saw the world touched by the power of the Gospel, the facts were, I did not understand the Cross as it regarded Sanctification. And to be factual, there aren't but a handful of Christians in the world presently, that is, when we consider the whole, who understand the Cross as it refers to Sanctification. And to not understand it in this fashion guarantees a life of spiritual defeat.

And yet, Paul dealt more with this subject than he did anything else. In fact, the entirety of his 14 Epistles are either taken up totally with this teaching, or else allude to it strongly. That being the case, why is it that most Christians, and even most Preachers, little understand that of which the great Apostle taught?

I think Satan fights the Message of the Cross as he fights nothing else. If he can keep the Gospel of the Cross of Christ from being preached as it regards Salvation, he can stop sinners from being saved. Regrettably, he has succeeded tremendously so in most Churches. And as well, if he can stop the Preacher from understanding and teaching the Cross as it regards Sanctification, he can rob the Christian of victory. And he has succeeded tremendously so in this capacity also.

When we read the Seventh Chapter of Romans, we are reading Paul's personal experience of trying to live for God after he was saved and baptized with the Holy Spirit, but yet not knowing and understanding the Message of the Cross, which the Lord would later give to him. He failed miserably, and if Paul failed miserably, where do you think that leaves us!

At any rate, if fighting the Devil will bring one victory, then to be sure, I would have had victory as no other human being. I put up one great fight, but as all who engage in such a conflict, I was the loser, as all are the loser.

This is a fight in which we must not engage, and simply because Jesus has already defeated Satan, even as we've already addressed.

Our major problem is, we simply do not properly understand the Word of God in many capacities. We think we do, but the truth is, we don't. And to not understand the Word is to not understand the instructions, which, as should be obvious, leaves us in a predicament.

We misinterpret the Word, and I think I know the reason why.

The foundation of all that God does for us and with us is the Cross of Christ. That means the foundation of the Word of God is the Cross. Actually, an understanding of the Cross was given, which in effect was the Word of God, even before the Word came to the world in written form. We find it in the Fourth Chapter of Genesis.

The Lord had told the first family, and evidently did so immediately after the Fall, how they were to have communion with Him, and experience forgiveness for sin, etc. It would be by the slain lamb, an innocent victim, which would be a Type of the coming Redeemer, namely Christ. Of course, that instruction was the Word of the Lord, but it is noteworthy to understand that the very first Word given pertained to the Cross.

So the main reason, I think, why people misinterpret the Word of God is simply because their Faith is not anchored in the Cross, but rather in other things. And if our Faith is anchored in other things, and no matter how good those things might be in their own right, this means that in some way we are depending on self. And for certain, we will go wrong, because outside of Christ and Him Crucified, our knowledge of God is very skewed.

To say it another way, if we have a proper knowledge of Christ and the Cross, we will have a proper knowledge of the Word of God. Otherwise, our interpretation will be skewed in some manner.

SALVATION

The moment the believing sinner comes to Christ, at that moment, he is free from all sin and every bondage. If at that moment he is taught the Message of the Cross, and taught it correctly, he will then understand the Word of God, and avoid many pitfalls, which could not be avoided otherwise.

As I have said elsewhere in this Volume, in October of 1991, I laid my Bible on the table in front of me. I made the statement to the people sitting there that day, *"I don't know the answer, but I know the answer to living a victorious, overcoming, Christian life is found in this Book. And by the Grace of God, I'm going to find that answer."*

Almost immediately, the Lord gave me instructions to begin Prayer Meetings, which we did. Those Prayer Meetings continue unto this hour. Over and over again, the Lord would speak to my heart while in prayer, and would give me strength, and encouragement, but it was not until 1996, in fact, when I began to study the Book of Romans, as it regards writing that Commentary, that the Holy Spirit began to open up to me what Paul was actually saying.

Even though I don't remember the exact date, or the day, I definitely do remember what took place in my soul. The moment the Holy Spirit revealed to me the Truth, at that moment, I knew it was the answer for which I had so long sought. In fact, a few days later, in one of the morning Prayer Meetings, the Spirit of the Lord clearly said to my heart, *"The answer for which you seek is found in the Cross, and in the Cross alone!"* I will never forget that moment either! I sat there on the floor for a period of time, weeping as I realized the great Truth, as simple as it was, that was being revealed to me.

A few days later, over our morning Radio program, 90 minutes in length each day, *"A Study In The Word"*, while teaching, the Spirit of God opened it up a little further, and told me the manner and the way in which He works within our hearts and lives. He told me that He functions entirely within the parameters of the Cross of Christ, in other words, the Cross gives Him the legal right, one might say, to function as He does. He then took me to Romans 8:2: *"For the Law of the Spirit of Life in Christ Jesus has made me free from the law of sin and death,"* which portrayed to me from the Scripture exactly what He had spoken to my heart.

It is all *"in Christ Jesus,"* which always and without exception refers to Christ and what He did at the Cross.

I then learned who I was in Christ, and the victory that He afforded me, and every Believer for that matter, by His Sacrificial, Atoning Work.

AN OVERCOMER

Millions of Christians read the statements given by Christ in Revelation, Chapters 2 and 3, about being an overcomer, and immediately realize the great significance of these statements, and thereby, set out to be an overcomer. By that manner, that is a position to which you will never attain. The truth is, every single Believer in the world is already an overcomer. We are that not according to the things we have done or not done, but rather because of what Christ did at the Cross. In other words, He has made me an overcomer by His Finished Work. That is so with every Believer. So how do I function accordingly?

I am what He has done for me, by Faith in His Sacrificial Work. Always and without exception it's by Faith (Eph. 2:8-9; Gal. 5:5-6).

At this moment, millions of Christians are trying to do things, thinking that the doing of these things, whatever they might be, will make them an overcomer. Regrettably, the only thing that it will do is to develop self-righteousness, which is, one might say, a stage of spiritual cancer. It doesn't really matter what one might do, and I speak of engaging in spiritual activity, and whatever it might be, one simply cannot work one's self into the position of *"overcomer."* Listen to what Paul said:

"I am crucified with Christ (this takes us back to Romans 6:3-5)*: nevertheless I live; yet not I, but Christ lives in me: and the life which I now live in the flesh* (our daily walk before God) *I live by the Faith of the Son of God* (*'the Faith'* being Christ and His Finished Work) *Who loved me, and gave Himself for me"* (Gal. 2:20).

If the Believer attempts to live for Christ in any other manner, the Believer is going to find himself in deep trouble. Notice what the Apostle said:

He didn't say, *"I am resurrected with Christ,"* even though that definitely was true, and is definitely very important. He rather said, and as the Holy Spirit guided him, *"I am crucified with Christ."*

Let the Reader understand that your Salvation hasn't come to you, and neither has your victory come to you, by the Resurrection of Christ, but rather by the Crucifixion of Christ.

The Word of Faith people claim that if one preaches the Cross, one is preaching death. In other words, they are telling the people to forsake the Cross, ignore the Cross, with them even repudiating the Cross. So you can accept that erroneous, fallacious doctrine, or you can accept what Paul said, *"I am crucified with Christ."* You can't have it both ways. It's either Paul, or else it's the leaven of the Word of Faith heresy, and heresy it is!

The day that I learned that the Lord has already fought for me, and did so at the Cross, and that my life and victory are in what He did, and not what I have done, that is the day that I learned to live.

(15) "AND THE LORD SAID UNTO MOSES, WHEREFORE DO YOU CRY UNTO ME? SPEAK UNTO THE CHILDREN OF ISRAEL, THAT THEY GO FORWARD.

(16) "BUT LIFT UP YOUR ROD, AND STRETCH OUT YOUR HAND OVER THE SEA, AND DIVIDE IT: AND THE CHILDREN OF ISRAEL SHALL GO ON DRY GROUND THROUGH THE MIDST OF THE SEA.

(17) "AND I, BEHOLD, I WILL HARDEN THE HEARTS OF THE EGYPTIANS, AND THEY SHALL FOLLOW THEM: AND I WILL GET ME HONOR UPON PHARAOH, AND UPON ALL HIS HOST, UPON HIS CHARIOTS, AND UPON HIS HORSEMEN.

(18) "AND THE EGYPTIANS SHALL KNOW THAT I AM THE LORD, WHEN I HAVE GOTTEN ME HONOR UPON PHARAOH, UPON HIS CHARIOTS, AND UPON HIS HORSEMEN.

(19) "AND THE ANGEL OF GOD, WHICH WENT BEFORE THE CAMP OF ISRAEL, REMOVED AND WENT BEHIND THEM; AND THE PILLAR OF THE CLOUD WENT FROM BEFORE THEIR FACE, AND STOOD BEHIND THEM:

(20) "AND IT CAME BETWEEN THE CAMP OF THE EGYPTIANS AND THE CAMP OF ISRAEL: AND IT WAS A CLOUD AND DARKNESS TO THEM, BUT IT GAVE LIGHT BY NIGHT TO THESE: SO THAT THE ONE CAME NOT NEAR THE OTHER ALL THE NIGHT."

The diagram is:

1. In Verse 15, God demands that Israel cease their complaining to Him.
2. The Lord said, *"Go forward."* Faith is ever forward.
3. The *"Stand still"* is strictly a command to the efforts of the flesh that Faith alone may *"go forward."*

GO FORWARD

Verse 15 reads: *"And the LORD said unto Moses, Why do you cry unto Me? Speak unto the Children of Israel, that they go forward."*

The time has now come. Everything previous to this was, in essence, a dress rehearsal, one might say.

The Children of Israel were crying unto the Lord, but their cry was not of Faith, but rather of defeat. They complained, and accused Moses, which was the same as accusing God. Let us address ourselves to such a situation:

The Lord, as should be understood, hears every single thing that we say. So, what are we saying?

Are we mouthing words of defeat, complaint, indecision, unbelief, etc.? Every time we do this, and to be sure, all of us have, we are insulting God. We are, in effect, saying that He cannot handle the situation, cannot see us through, cannot give us victory, and despite all that He has done in the past.

Every time we open our mouths, that which comes out of them should be words of Faith, trust, confidence, and power. The Lord is grossly displeased with our unbelief, and that's exactly what our complaining amounts to.

At the same time, He is greatly pleased with our words of Faith and confidence, irrespective as to what the circumstances might be. Whenever we praise the Lord, and do so in any fashion, we are in effect, saying, *"God can!"* We are saying the same thing that God said to Israel of old, *"Go forward."* There is no retreat as it regards the life and the living of the Child of God. If we go backwards, the Old Testament term of *"backsliding,"* comes into play. It's always *"go forward!"* It doesn't matter what the situation might be, what the circumstances are, how things look, the word still is, *"go forward!"* If we don't go forward, we will quickly find ourselves residing in a place that God has already left.

DIFFICULTIES

As is obvious here, going forward was not exactly a simple task. The Red Sea lay in front of them, so how could they go forward?

This tells us that obstacles and difficulties, while they may be such to us, aren't such to God. They matter little to Him. He has said, *"Go forward,"* and that doesn't mean that we are to do so, providing the way is clear. In fact, Faith always goes forward, and it doesn't really matter, as stated, what the obstacles might be. The Lord has already formed a plan to take care of those obstacles, whatever they might be. Faith has no reverse, and unbelief has no forward.

Some have stated that if they hear the command, *"go forward,"* that's what they will do; however, their thinking is wrong.

In the first place, the command to *"go forward"* has already been given. The Word of God is full of that of which we speak. In fact, the very foundation of all that we are in Christ, which is by Faith, screams, *"go forward."* As stated, that's what Faith is, so quit waiting on something that in fact, has already come.

DIVIDE THE SEA

Verse 16 reads: *"But lift up your rod, stretch out your hand over the sea, and divide it: and the Children of Israel shall go on dry ground through the midst of the sea."*

With the command to go forward came the provision of Grace. Now will begin one of the greatest miracles ever performed.

Hebrews 11:29 says: *"By Faith they passed through the Red Sea as by dry land."* From this it is very clear that the waters of the Red Sea did not begin to divide until the feet of the Israelites came to their very brink, otherwise they would have crossed by sight, and not *"by Faith."*

As well, it seems that the Sea did not open completely at once, but only the part that was next to those in the lead of the Children of Israel.

As someone has said, *"It does not require Faith to begin a journey when I can see all the way through; but to begin when I can merely see the first step, this is Faith."*

Unbelievers claim that this portion of the Red Sea was only a few inches deep. Of course, that is foolishness; however, the Scripture says that they walked across on *"dry ground,"* and again, the entirety of the army of Egypt drowned in these waters, as the Sea closed on them. I hardly think that an entire army of Egyptians would have drowned in just a few inches of water.

It seems that men are desperate to disprove God. Why?

Unbelief has an evil heart, and that's about the only reason that can be given.

HONOR

Verses 17 and 18 read: *"And I, behold, I will harden the hearts of the Egyptians, and they shall follow them: and I will get Me honor upon Pharaoh, and upon all his host, upon his chariots, and upon his horsemen.*

"And the Egyptians shall know that I am the LORD, when I have gotten Me honor upon Pharaoh, upon his chariots, and upon his horsemen."

We should realize from these two Verses that the honor of the Lord was at stake as it regards His people, and His dealing with the Egyptians. The idea is, He could deliver them, or He couldn't deliver them. Therefore, the Egyptians, by their stubbornness, had placed themselves in a position to where the Lord was left with no choice, but to bring destruction upon them. His honor must not be impugned. All of us should take a lesson from this.

On the part of the Egyptians, especially after the Lord had revealed Himself in performing miracle after miracle, they would obey, as it regards letting Israel go, or else they would suffer the consequences. As stated, the honor of the Lord was at stake.

As it regarded the Children of Israel, it didn't matter what it took to deliver them, or how difficult the miracle might be; the honor of the Lord was at stake, and to be sure, the miracle would be performed, irrespective as to its degree. In fact, it would seem that the Lord made the situation about as hard as it could be made in order that He might be honored.

As it regards each Believer, the honor of the Lord is always at stake. And there is only one thing that will satisfy His honor, and that is the Believer evidencing Faith in the Word of God.

Each Believer must understand that he is a part of the greatest thing this side of Heaven. It is a way, or rather a plan, that was formulated even before the foundation of the world (I Pet. 1:18-20).

In this great Plan of God, as stated, the honor of the Lord is at stake. The only way that honor can be properly satisfied is for the Believer to ever evidence Faith in Christ, and what Christ has done at the Cross.

THE PILLAR OF THE CLOUD

Verses 19 and 20 read: *"And the Angel of God, which went before the camp of Israel, removed and went behind them; and the Pillar of the Cloud went from before their face, and stood behind them:*

"And it came between the camp of the Egyptians and the camp of Israel: and it was a cloud and darkness to them, but it gave light by night to these: so that the one came not near the other all the night."

The *"Angel of God"* spoken of in Verse 19 is actually a preincarnate appearance of the Lord Jesus Christ. The Lord Jesus is Jehovah, and one might say, the Jehovah of the

Old Testament. He placed Himself between Israel and the enemy: this was protection indeed. Before Egypt could touch one single Israelite, they would have to come through the Almighty, and I think we all know how impossible that would be. Thus it is that God ever places Himself between His people and every enemy, so that *"no weapon formed against us can prosper."*

And even above our protection, He has placed Himself, through what He did at the Cross, between us and our sins. What a privilege! What a wonder! What glory!

Concerning this, Mackintosh said: *"In the same manner, the Believer may look for his difficulties, and not find them, because God is between him and them."*

There was a double aspect to this *"Pillar of the Cloud"* which stood between the Egyptians and the Israelites. While it *"gave light by night"* to the Children of Israel, it was *"a cloud and darkness"* to the Egyptians. Concerning this, Mackintosh also said: *"How like the Cross of our Lord Jesus Christ!"*

"Truly, that Cross has a double aspect likewise. It forms the foundation of the Believer's peace, and, at the same time, seals the condemnation of a guilty world. The self-same Blood which purges the Believer's conscience and gives him perfect peace, stains this Earth and consummates its guilt. The very mission of the Son of God which strips the world of its cloak, and leaves it wholly without excuse, clothes the Church with a fair mantle of Righteousness, and fills her mouth with ceaseless praise."

He then said: *"The very same Lamb Who will terrify, by His unmitigated wrath, all tribes and classes of Earth, will lead, by His gentle Hand, His Blood-bought flock through the green pastures and beside the still waters forever!"* (Rev. 6:15-17; 7:13-17).

(21) "AND MOSES STRETCHED OUT HIS HAND OVER THE SEA; AND THE LORD CAUSED THE SEA TO GO BACK BY A STRONG EAST WIND ALL THAT NIGHT, AND MADE THE SEA DRY LAND, AND THE WATERS WERE DIVIDED.

(22) "AND THE CHILDREN OF ISRAEL WENT INTO THE MIDST OF THE SEA UPON THE DRY GROUND: AND THE WATERS WERE A WALL UNTO THEM ON THEIR RIGHT HAND, AND ON THEIR LEFT.

(23) "AND THE EGYPTIANS PURSUED, AND WENT IN AFTER THEM TO THE MIDST OF THE SEA, EVEN ALL PHARAOH'S HORSES, HIS CHARIOTS, AND HIS HORSEMEN.

(24) "AND IT CAME TO PASS, THAT IN THE MORNING WATCH, THE LORD LOOKED UNTO THE HOST OF THE EGYPTIANS THROUGH THE PILLAR OF FIRE AND OF THE CLOUD, AND TROUBLED THE HOST OF THE EGYPTIANS,

(25) "AND TOOK OFF THEIR CHARIOT WHEELS, THAT THEY DROVE THEM HEAVILY: SO THAT THE EGYPTIANS SAID, LET US FLEE FROM THE FACE OF ISRAEL; FOR THE LORD FIGHTS FOR THEM AGAINST THE EGYPTIANS."

The overview is:

1. The *"strong east wind"* that God used to push back a path through the Sea was a Divine miracle, not something accomplished by the mere forces of nature itself.

2. Not only was this done suddenly by a Divine power, but it was likewise undone suddenly by the same power.

3. A wind blowing strong enough to make a path through the Sea, which was approximately 12 miles across, and hold the waters up like a wall some 75 to 100 feet high, would have been strong enough to blow all the Israelites and Egyptians away as well, had God not directed it.

4. Hebrews, Chapter 11 suggests that Israel had to keep believing while passing through the Sea that the waters would not overwhelm them. The Egyptians did not have to exercise any Faith at all, for they saw the open road before them, yet they were drowned. The way of Faith is life to the redeemed, but death to the rebellious.

THE MIRACLE

Verse 21 reads: *"And Moses stretched out his hand over the Sea; and the LORD caused the Sea to go back by a strong east wind all that night, and made the Sea dry land, and the waters were divided."*

The indication is, the Children of Israel began to walk out into the Sea, with God opening it before them. In other words, it seems that the entirety of the Sea was not opened all at one time, but did so at about the pace that a person could slowly walk. As to exactly how wide this path through the Red Sea was, we aren't told; however, it may have been at least a mile wide, which would have enabled the greater part of the entirety of the body of the Children of Israel to walk across at the same time, with at least the ones in the rear not being too very far back from those in the lead.

It seems that the *"Pillar of Cloud"* brought up the rear-guard, which would have posed itself between the Children of Israel and the Egyptians. This was the Presence of God. The Presence of the Lord, which had been leading them, now removes, and goes behind them. In effect, this means that while they had been led by the Presence of God heretofore, that Presence is no longer leading them, but is standing guard at the rear.

We should take a lesson from this. Sometimes the Lord withdraws Himself in grief, or even in anger; but more often He does so in Mercy. This is something that He desires to teach us.

More than likely, the Children of Israel little understood as to why the Lord had shifted from the front to the back. Whether it caused them consternation or not, we aren't told. They just knew that Moses had stated, *"go forward"*; therefore, they would obey, which the Lord requires of us.

However, even though the Presence of the Lord had shifted His position, He was doing so for the benefit of His people. They were in more danger from the Egyptians than they were the water. God can control the elements, and He can also control man; nevertheless, the control of man is a different aspect altogether. The elements do not have a will of their own, while man definitely does. So the Lord would position Himself between the Children of Israel and their greatest danger, the Egyptians.

GEOGRAPHY

The area where the Children of Israel are believed to have crossed is now dry land, made that way through the many centuries of gradual change, which happens all over the world for that matter. It has passed into permanent dry land.

NOTES

The location was probably in the vicinity of the modern Suez, between the Bitter Lakes. These lakes were then a part of the Gulf.

The width is anyone's guess, estimated to be anywhere from one mile across to as much as 12 to 15 miles. Considering the location, it was probably closer to 10 to 12 miles wide. Its depth was probably, and it's only a guess, at anywhere between 20 and 40 feet.

The *"strong east wind"* which the Lord caused, had to be directed by Jehovah, or else it would have blown the Children of Israel away, as well as the Egyptians. In fact, it was directed at a particular part of the Sea, and held to that particular point.

DRY GROUND

Verse 22 reads: *"And the Children of Israel went into the midst of the Sea upon the dry ground: and the waters were a wall unto them on their right hand, and on their left."*

As the Scripture plainly states here, where God opened a path through the Red Sea, the ground was dry. And above that, the water stood like a wall on either side of them, which had to be one of the most astounding sights that man has ever witnessed.

This miracle, which is at least one of the greatest performed in Old Testament Times, if not the greatest, is astounding in every respect. It defies several laws, as would be overly obvious. But of course, God, Who originally made the laws of creation, can override them with even greater laws, simply because He is the Source of all things.

Exodus 15:8 says, *"The flood stood upright as an heap."* In Psalms 78:13, it is also said: *"He made the waters to stand as an heap."*

THE MIRACLE-WORKING POWER OF GOD

Every True Believer knows and understands that God is a miracle-working God. He created this world by and through the performing of miracles, He sustains the world in the same manner, and He continues to perform miracles even unto this very hour, and in fact, will ever continue to do so. As stated, He was, is, and ever shall be a miracle-working God.

Sometime ago, in writing these Commentaries, I was studying the word *"miracles."*

God spoke to my heart that day, telling me that He not only continues to perform miracles, but actually, is doing so on a continuing basis, and even to a far greater degree than we could ever grasp or understand. Let me explain:

Any time the Lord does something for us, and to be sure, whether we are spiritual enough to understand it or not, He is constantly working on our behalf. Whatever He does, whether we understand it or not, or see it or not, He is performing miracles. In other words, He has to move people, places, things, and events, into a certain way, in order to bring things to pass, and at the same time, not violate the free moral agency of any individual. All of this can be constituted as none other than *"miracles."*

The sin of man, even the Church, is definitely not in overstating the case, but rather understating the case. In fact, I think it's impossible for one to overstate God. As Stuart Hamblin wrote sometime ago, *"It is no secret, what God can do."*

The Believer should expect miracles! Should anticipate miracles! Should, in fact, think of them as an everyday occurrence!

While some miracles are certainly more astounding than others, even as we are studying here about the opening of the Red Sea; nevertheless, anything and everything that God does, I think can be constituted as a *"miracle."* He Alone devised the laws of nature, which operates this universe, and He at His Own discretion, can circumvent those laws, or even override them.

Now that's not at all unusual! In fact, as God gives man the knowledge and the ability to understand His laws, man is constantly overriding one law with a greater law. For instance, the law of gravity is obvious to all; however, the Lord has given man the intelligence to also understand and to put into motion the laws of aerodynamics. How in the world can an airplane, some of them weighing many tons, fly through the air, when in fact, it is far heavier than the air? It does so by the operation of a law that's even greater than the law of gravity. In fact, these things are done constantly, so it should not be any surprise to anyone, that God, Who devised all these laws, can, at any time, according to His Own discretion, put into effect a law that will supercede or override other laws He has made. That's what He did at the Red Sea.

He simply used the law of aerodynamics as it regards the *"strong east wind,"* which overcame the law of gravity, both laws which He had created. In fact, that's the very same way that airplanes fly. A jet engine or a propeller instigates a strong wind, which pushes the airplane, and holds it up, and overrides the law of gravity, which would bring it down, were it able to do so.

So why do we doubt God, when His miracles are explainable, at least to a certain degree, meaning that in a sense, man does the same thing constantly.

We don't think of the flying of an airplane as a miracle, just the matter of the law of aerodynamics being applied, which overrides the law of gravity. But again, that's the way that God performs His miracles. However, He has total knowledge of all laws, for the simple reason that He devised them, while man only has a limited amount of knowledge. In fact, most of the knowledge of which I speak did not even begin until the beginning of the Twentieth Century. That is in keeping with Daniel's prophecy, given about 2,600 years ago, which said, *"Shut up the words, and seal the book, even to the time of the end: many shall run to and fro, and knowledge shall be increased"* (Dan. 12:4).

This plainly tells us that knowledge would be increased in the last days, which we have seen come to pass before our very eyes.

Unbelievers scoff at God, and scoff at miracles, not realizing how silly are their objections.

UNBELIEF

Sometime ago, I happened to see a Television program, where three *"unbelievers"* were going to debate three *"Believers."* I was to find out that the unbelief of the Believers was about as bad as the unbelief of the unbelievers.

The unbelievers scoffed at any of the miracles recorded in the Old Testament. Three of the miracles — the opening of the Red Sea, the walls of Jericho falling down, and the burn taken out of the fire for the Hebrew Children — were to be inspected closely.

Of course the unbelievers denied the actual happenings of these events. But as stated, the so-called Believers were not so far behind the rank unbelievers.

They tried to explain these miracles by natural phenomenon. In other words, they said that an earthquake opened the Red Sea, and as well, it was an earthquake that destroyed the walls of Jericho. To explain the fiery furnace, they claim that there is a *"cool spot"* in the midst of every fire, and the three Hebrew Children found this cool spot, and that's the way they survived.

As I listened to this foolishness, and foolishness it is, I wondered as to why the Preachers who claim to believe in God, couldn't just simply say that God did it, and inasmuch as God did it, He was not limited as to the ways that He could do it.

The Bible doesn't say there was an earthquake at the time of the opening of the Red Sea. It does say that God *"caused the Sea to go back by a strong east wind all that night, and made the Sea dry land, and the waters were divided."* So let's quit trying to explain away the miracles of God, and just simply understand that God is able to do all things, and in fact, will do all things for those who will believe Him. In other words, I believe in miracles. I think the Preachers of my illustration little believe in miracles, if at all. They claimed to believe the Bible, but if the truth be known, the Bible that they claimed to believe is a very abbreviated Bible. For if you take the miracles out of the Bible, there isn't a whole lot left.

THE EGYPTIANS

Verse 23 reads: *"And the Egyptians pursued, and went in after them to the midst of the Sea, even all Pharaoh's horses, his chariots, and his horsemen."*

Whether Pharaoh actually went in himself, the Scripture doesn't say. Some Scholars believe that he did, and some believe that he didn't. Exodus 14:10 does say, *"And when Pharaoh drew near . . ."* insinuating somewhat that Pharaoh may definitely have been with this pursuing army. Due to all the things that had happened in the intervening months, I choose to believe that the pride of Pharaoh demanded that he lead this charge and this attack, but whether he did or not is not really the point.

WHAT THE RED SEA CROSSING ACTUALLY MEANT

Typically (the type), the crossing of the Red Sea speaks of Christ, making a way of Redemption, by and through the death that He died on the Cross, which He did for all who will believe. The Red Sea is the figure of death, actually the boundary line of Satan's power.

Note the words of God to Moses: *"Lift thou up the rod, and stretch out your hand over the Sea, and divide it; and the Children of Israel shall go on dry ground through the midst of the Red Sea"* (Vs. 16).

Moses is plainly a Type of Christ, the *"rod"* a symbol of His power and authority. The Red Sea completely destroyed the power of Pharaoh (Satan) over God's people. Hebrews 2:14 gives us the antitype, or how the Lord did this: *"That through death He (Jesus) might destroy him that had the power of death, that is, the Devil."*

Some have tried to portray the crossing of the Red Sea as a type of physical death, but it having no power over the Child of God, with him going to be with Christ. But that's not what this is speaking about.

The opening of the Red Sea, and the crossing by the Children of Israel, and the defeat of Pharaoh, as the waters closed over his army, is a picture of what Jesus did for us at the Cross, and our death that we died in Him, which Paul explained by saying that we *"were baptized into His death"* (Rom. 6:3). The Children of Israel died to the old life, which was symbolized by the crossing of the Red Sea, and they gained newness of life by being released from the clutches of Pharaoh, who was a type of the Devil. So the Believer can look at this account given in the Bible, and can get a picture of the Born-Again experience, which brings one from spiritual death to spiritual life. It was the Cross Alone where Satan was totally and completely defeated, even as Pharaoh was completely defeated by the Passover, which typified the Death of Christ, and the Red Sea, which typified our part in that death.

THE PILLAR OF FIRE AND OF THE CLOUD

Verse 24 reads: *"And it came to pass, that in the morning watch the LORD looked unto the host of the Egyptians through the pillar of fire and of the cloud, and troubled the host of the Egyptians."*

I think the words *"the morning watch,"* portray to us the fact that the Children of Israel began to go onto the path formed in the Red Sea, immediately that night whenever it began to open. The *"morning watch"* of the Hebrews at this period of history lasted from 2 a.m. until sunrise. Sunrise in Egypt, which would have been early in April, would take place at about 6 a.m.

So the Children of Israel were probably about halfway cross this body of water, actually walking on dry ground, with a wall of water on either side, when the Egyptians started down after them.

When the Scripture says that the Lord *"troubled the host of the Egyptians,"* as they pursued the Children of Israel, Josephus further says: *"Showers of rain came down from the sky, and dreadful thunders and lightning, with flashes of fire; thunderbolts also were darted upon them; nor was there anything, which could be sent by God upon man as indications of His wrath, which did not happen upon this occasion."*

The words *"troubled the host,"* in the Hebrew, actually mean *"threw it into confusion."*

THE DOCTRINE

Continuing to look at this crossing as it regards it being a type of our Salvation in Christ, doctrinally the passage through the Red Sea sets forth the Believers union with Christ in His Death and Resurrection. As we've already stated, the *"Passover"* proclaimed what Christ did for us, while the Red Sea Crossing portrayed our union with Christ, as it regards being baptized into His death.

Paul said, *"I am crucified with Christ"* (Gal. 2:20). This refers to our judicial identification with our Substitute. That Israel passed through the Red Sea, and emerged safely on the far side, as stated, tells of our union with Christ in His death, and as well tells of the Resurrection, our being raised with Him *"in newness of life."* Paul said:

NOTES

"If we have been planted together in the likeness of His death, we shall be also in the likeness of His Resurrection" (Rom. 6:5). And again: *"When we were dead in sins, has quickened us* (made us spiritually alive) *together with Christ . . . and raised us up together"* (Eph. 2:5-6).

THE LORD FIGHTS FOR US

Verse 25 reads: *"And took off their chariot wheels, that they drove them heavily: so that the Egyptians said, Let us flee from the face of Israel; for the LORD fights for them against the Egyptians."*

The idea of this Passage is, the Lord made the chariots of the Egyptians, on which they were so heavily depending, useless.

The Lord evidently so situated the passage that sink holes appeared, with the chariot wheels bogging up the axles in those holes, which, in effect, stopped them.

Joining that with lightning bolts darting among them, with slashing rain, and perhaps other phenomenon as well, if in fact those things actually happened, and which they no doubt did, caused the Egyptians to realize, they had just raced into a trap. They saw that the Lord was not only fighting for the Children of Israel, but was at the same time, fighting against the Egyptians.

Let the modern Believer understand that we serve the same God, served by the Children of Israel. As well, He will do the same for us that He did for them. We must understand that, believe that, even as we know that.

(26) "AND THE LORD SAID UNTO MOSES, STRETCH OUT YOUR HAND OVER THE SEA, THAT THE WATERS MAY COME AGAIN UPON THE EGYPTIANS, UPON THEIR CHARIOTS, AND UPON THEIR HORSEMEN.

(27) "AND MOSES STRETCHED FORTH HIS HAND OVER THE SEA, AND THE SEA RETURNED TO HIS STRENGTH WHEN THE MORNING APPEARED; AND THE EGYPTIANS FLED AGAINST IT; AND THE LORD OVERTHREW THE EGYPTIANS IN THE MIDST OF THE SEA.

(28) "AND THE WATERS RETURNED, AND COVERED THE CHARIOTS, AND THE HORSEMEN, AND ALL THE HOST OF PHARAOH THAT CAME INTO THE SEA

AFTER THEM; THERE REMAINED NOT SO MUCH AS ONE OF THEM.

(29) "BUT THE CHILDREN OF ISRAEL WALKED UPON DRY LAND IN THE MIDST OF THE SEA; AND THE WATERS WERE A WALL UNTO THEM ON THEIR RIGHT HAND, AND ON THEIR LEFT.

(30) "THUS THE LORD SAVED ISRAEL THAT DAY OUT OF THE HAND OF THE EGYPTIANS; AND ISRAEL SAW THE EGYPTIANS DEAD UPON THE SEASHORE.

(31) "AND ISRAEL SAW THAT GREAT WORK WHICH THE LORD DID UPON THE EGYPTIANS: AND THE PEOPLE FEARED THE LORD, AND BELIEVED THE LORD, AND HIS SERVANT MOSES."

The structure is:

1. The Lord not only delivered Israel, but as well, defeated the Egyptians. At Calvary, the Lord not only delivered us, but He also defeated Satan (Col. 2:14-15).

2. As every Egyptian was totally and completely defeated, Satan was totally and completely defeated as well at the Cross. Not one single bondage of darkness was excluded, but rather, Jesus addressed them all.

3. Verse 30 says: *"Thus the LORD saved Israel that day out of the hand of the Egyptians."* Also, it is the Lord Alone Who can do these things, and not we ourselves. He did it all at the Cross, and our Faith in that Finished Work guarantees us all of His victory.

THE LORD OVERTHREW THE EGYPTIANS

Verses 26 and 27 read: *"And the LORD said unto Moses, Stretch out your hand over the sea, that the waters may come again upon the Egyptians, upon their chariots, and upon their horsemen.*

"And Moses stretched forth his hand over the sea, and the sea returned to his strength when the morning appeared; and the Egyptians fled against it; and the LORD overthrew the Egyptians in the midst of the sea."

The Children of Israel have all safely crossed as a result of the great miracle carried out by the Lord. With all safely on the other side, and the mighty army of Egypt bogged down in the very midst of the sea, and now even trying to turn and escape the dark waters, *"The LORD said unto Moses, Stretch out your hand over the sea, that the waters may come again upon the Egyptians,"* which he did, and it did.

A wall of water on both sides came crashing down upon this mighty army, and they were as helpless as helplessness could ever be. Exactly as the Lord had said, Israel would see those Egyptians no more.

It should be noticed that God used Moses to open the Sea, and to close it. Moses was a Type of Christ, even as the Rod was a Type of the Word of God. The Psalmist said: *"Yea, though I walk through the valley of the shadow of death, I will fear no evil: for You are with me; Your rod and Your staff they comfort me"* (Ps. 23:4).

VICTORY

Verses 28 and 29 read: *"And the waters returned, and covered the chariots, and the horsemen, and all the host of Pharaoh that came into the sea after them; there remained not so much as one of them.*

"But the Children of Israel walked upon dry land in the midst of the sea; and the waters waters were a wall unto them on their right hand, and on their left."

We as human beings need many things; however, God needs nothing in order to carry out that which He so desires. The elements are at His beck and call. Along with that, if a heart is stubborn and obstinate towards Him, which that is certainly not the way that He would desire it to be; still, He can even use that for His glory, exactly as He used the stubborn, obstinate heart of Pharaoh.

Pharaoh wanted to do what he did, so the Lord allowed him free rein. It would result in God getting honor and glory, and Pharaoh being destroyed, exactly as such incidents have taken place countless times since.

At this very moment, Satan is preparing for the debut of the Antichrist, which will be his trump card of the ages. But the Lord will use all of this as an occasion to bring Israel back to Himself, which means that the Devil's plans will, in a sense, be made to work for the Lord, as everything sooner or later, is made to work for the Lord. And if we are in the center of God's Will, then *"we know that all things work together for good to them who love God, to them who are the called according to His purpose"* (Rom. 8:28).

Two things are predicated on *"all things working together for good to us"*:

1. We must *"love God."*
2. We must function *"according to His purpose,"* and not according to ours. That's what I meant by being in the center of God's Will.

It was the Will of God for Israel to be delivered, and it is the Will of God for you to be delivered. If you'll believe God, stand upon His Promises, and look to the Cross where the price was paid, and which the deliverance of the Children of Israel was but a type, as they were delivered, you will be delivered. And it doesn't matter as to what type of deliverance is needed, God is able!

THE GREAT WORK OF THE LORD

Verses 30 and 31 read: *"Thus the LORD saved Israel that day out of the hand of the Egyptians; and Israel saw the Egyptians dead upon the seashore.*

"And Israel saw that great work which the LORD did upon the Egyptians: and the people feared the LORD, and believed the LORD, and His servant Moses."

Evidently a west wind set in, which assisted by the current, drove the bodies of the drowned Egyptians to the eastern side of the Gulf, where many of them were cast up upon the shore. In this way, Moses, according to Josephus, obtained weapons and armor for a considerable number of Israelites. This means that the Egyptian dead were cast upon the same shore where Israel had come out. It would not have been possible for Israel to have looked over that expanse of water, and observe dead bodies on the other shore, which could have been at least 10 or 12 miles away.

The *"great work"* which the Lord performed that day, was the destruction of the entire chariot force of Egypt, plus, no doubt, many of her footmen. In fact, the Egyptians kings mainly relied on their chariot force in times of war.

A GREAT WORK

God always performs a *"great work."* He is still performing great works, and He shall ever continue to perform great works. I think it can be said without fear of exaggeration or contradiction that any and every work performed by the Lord, while some may be grander than others, all could certainly be classed as a *"great work."* We serve a great God! Therefore, He does *"great works."*

THE RED SEA AND THE JORDAN RIVER

As we close this Chapter, which portrays one of the greatest miracles ever performed by God, I want us to try to understand the difference between the Red Sea crossing and the Jordan River crossing. They both have their antitype in the Death of Christ; but in the former we see separation from Egypt; and the latter, introduction into the land of Canaan. The idea is this:

The Red Sea Crossing, as stated, is pictured as our Born-Again experience, as we die to the old life, and are made alive to the other. The Passover typified what Christ has done for us, while the Red Sea Crossing typifies us being baptized into the Death of Christ, which alone guarantees us deliverance from this present evil world, and as well, guarantees us *"newness of life."* As well, what delivered Israel destroyed the Egyptians, i.e., *"the Devil."*

The Jordan River Crossing was very similar, but yet somewhat different.

If it matters, the Jordan River, at the time of the Crossing, was at flood tide, which means it was about a mile and a half wide, and about 40 feet deep. Normally, it's only about 30 to 100 feet in width.

If it is to be noticed, Joshua had Israel to keep the Passover, which evidently had not been kept in quite some time, after they had crossed the Jordan. This states that the crossing of the Jordan did not specify Salvation, as the Red Sea crossing did, with Israel, in fact, already saved. However, they were commanded to eat the Passover again, even as they were supposed to do on a continuing basis year by year, signifying that their Sanctification depended on what Christ did at the Cross, just as it had their Salvation. The crossing of the Jordan and the occupation of Canaan, did not typify Heaven as some think, but rather our spiritual experience in Christ in the gaining of our inheritance.

So we find from this, as there had to be a death to Egypt, which typified the world, and which was typified by the Red Sea Crossing, likewise, after conversion, there has to be a death to self, typified by the Jordan River Crossing, both Crossings being miracles from God. As the sinner cannot save himself, the Christian cannot sanctify himself. Both must be done by the Power of the Holy Spirit.

"Why did they nail Him to Calvary's tree?
"Why? Tell me, why was He there?
"Jesus the Helper, the Healer, the Friend,
"Why? Tell me, why was He there?"

"Why should He love me, a sinner undone?
"Why? Tell me, why should He care?
"I do not merit the love He has shown.
"Why? Tell me, why should He care?"

"Why should I linger afar from His love?
"Why? Tell me, why should I fear?
"Somehow I know I should venture and prove.
"Why? Tell me, why should I fear?"

CHORUS:

"All my iniquities on Him were laid,
"He nailed them all to the Tree.
"Jesus the debt of my sin fully paid,
"He paid the ransom for me."

CHAPTER 15

(1) "THEN SANG MOSES AND THE CHILDREN OF ISRAEL THIS SONG UNTO THE LORD, AND SPAKE, SAYING, I WILL SING UNTO THE LORD, FOR HE HAS TRIUMPHED GLORIOUSLY: THE HORSE AND HIS RIDER HAS HE THROWN INTO THE SEA.

(2) "THE LORD IS MY STRENGTH AND SONG, AND HE HAS BECOME MY SALVATION: HE IS MY GOD, AND I WILL PREPARE HIM AN HABITATION; MY FATHER'S GOD, AND I WILL EXALT HIM.

(3) "THE LORD IS A MAN OF WAR: THE LORD IS HIS NAME.

NOTES

(4) "PHARAOH'S CHARIOTS AND HIS HOST HAS HE CAST INTO THE SEA: HIS CHOSEN CAPTAINS ALSO ARE DROWNED IN THE RED SEA.

(5) "THE DEPTHS HAVE COVERED THEM: THEY SANK INTO THE BOTTOM AS A STONE.

(6) "YOUR RIGHT HAND, O LORD, IS BECOME GLORIOUS IN POWER: YOUR RIGHT HAND, O LORD, HAS DASHED IN PIECES THE ENEMY.

(7) "AND IN THE GREATNESS OF YOUR EXCELLENCY YOU HAVE OVERTHROWN THEM WHO ROSE UP AGAINST YOU: YOU SENT FORTH YOUR WRATH, WHICH CONSUMED THEM AS STUBBLE.

(8) "AND WITH THE BLAST OF YOUR NOSTRILS THE WATERS WERE GATHERED TOGETHER, THE FLOOD STOOD UPRIGHT AS AN HEAP, AND THE DEPTHS WERE CONGEALED IN THE HEART OF THE SEA,

(9) "THE ENEMY SAID, I WILL PURSUE, I WILL OVERTAKE, I WILL DIVIDE THE SPOIL; MY LUST SHALL BE SATISFIED UPON THEM; I WILL DRAW MY SWORD, MY HAND SHALL DESTROY THEM.

(10) "YOU DID BLOW WITH YOUR WIND, THE SEA COVERED THEM: THEY SANK AS LEAD IN THE MIGHTY WATERS.

(11) "WHO IS LIKE UNTO YOU, O LORD, AMONG THE GODS? WHO IS LIKE YOU, GLORIOUS IN HOLINESS, FEARFUL IN PRAISES, DOING WONDERS?

(12) "YOU STRETCHED OUT YOUR RIGHT HAND, THE EARTH SWALLOWED THEM.

(13) "YOU IN YOUR MERCY HAVE LED FORTH THE PEOPLE WHICH YOU HAVE REDEEMED: YOU HAVE GUIDED THEM IN YOUR STRENGTH UNTO YOUR HOLY HABITATION.

(14) "THE PEOPLE SHALL HEAR, AND BE AFRAID: SORROW SHALL TAKE HOLD ON THE INHABITANTS OF PALESTINA.

(15) "THEN THE DUKES OF EDOM SHALL BE AMAZED; THE MIGHTY MEN OF MOAB, TREMBLING SHALL TAKE HOLD UPON THEM; ALL THE INHABITANTS OF CANAAN SHALL MELT AWAY.

(16) "FEAR AND DREAD SHALL FALL UPON THEM; BY THE GREATNESS OF

YOUR ARM THEY SHALL BE AS STILL AS A STONE; TILL YOUR PEOPLE PASS OVER, O LORD, TILL THE PEOPLE PASS OVER, WHICH YOU HAVE PURCHASED.

(17) "YOU SHALL BRING THEM IN, AND PLANT THEM IN THE MOUNTAIN OF YOUR INHERITANCE, IN THE PLACE, O LORD, WHICH YOU HAVE MADE FOR YOU TO DWELL IN, IN THE SANCTUARY, O LORD, WHICH YOUR HANDS HAVE ESTABLISHED.

(18) "THE LORD SHALL REIGN FOREVER AND EVER.

The composition is:

1. Moses began and ended his wilderness life with a song. That of Deuteronomy, Chapter 32 is the one referred to in Revelation 15:3.

2. There was no singing in Egypt; there was groaning. Singing only follows Redemption.

3. The song portrayed in this Fifteenth Chapter is the oldest song of praise in existence. The greatest poets unite in admiration of its surpassing beauty and sublimity. It is a song of praise; its theme is Jehovah Jesus; it praises Him for His destruction of the enemy. It begins with Redemption and ends with Glory.

4. There were two companies of singers — one formed of men, led by Moses; the other of women, led by Miriam. She and her choir *"answered the men."*

5. This is the first of the ten songs of praise recorded in the Bible; the last is Revelation 14:3.

6. *"Self"* is absent from this song; it is all about Jehovah, and His Power to save.

THE FIRST SONG

Verse 1 reads: *"Then sang Moses and the Children of Israel this song unto the LORD, and spake, saying, I will sing unto the LORD, for He has triumphed gloriously: the horse and his rider has He thrown into the sea."*

The first song recorded in the Bible is that of Lamech, but it certainly is not of the Lord, being a song that glorifies man's inhumanity to his fellow man (Gen. 4:23-24).

This song recorded in Exodus, Chapter 15, which celebrates the deliverance of the Children of Israel from Egyptian bondage, glorifying the Lord Who has done the delivering, is the first song of Praise and Redemption,

NOTES

simply because Redemption has been carried out in type. The song was accompanied by tens of thousands of tambourines, i.e., *"timbrels,"* which were no doubt of every size and description. As well, tens of thousands of Israelite women, seemingly both young and old, dance before the Lord, to the accompaniment of the musical instruments, and the singing, as they gave praise to the Lord. Consequently, as it is recorded in the Word of God, Moses wrote the very first Gospel song, so to speak. He also wrote the very first Psalm (Ps. 90). More than likely, he also wrote Psalm 91.

So the very first thing we find after the Salvation of the Children of Israel is rejoicing.

REJOICING

When a person comes to Christ, any person, joy fills their heart, simply because the enmity between them and God, caused by sin, has now been removed, due to the shed Blood of Christ being applied to the heart and life, which is all done by Faith (Jn. 3:16; Eph. 2:8-9). So this which the Children of Israel did on the far shore of the Red Sea portrays the joy of the heart and the joy of the soul, as to what the Lord has done. It is the only true joy there is, the only true rejoicing there is.

This doesn't mean that every new convert, or every Christian for that matter, has to sing and dance before the Lord; but it definitely does mean that there will be a rejoicing heart. That goes with Salvation, and I really cannot see how in the world that anyone could come to Christ, which means to be *"born again,"* which means that they are now a new creature in Christ Jesus, and not have that rejoicing heart.

As well, there are, we are told, seven major religions in the world. Christianity, although not a religion, but rather a relationship, and that with Christ, still is put in that category. And Christianity is the only one of the seven which has a songbook because it's the only one of the seven that has anything to sing about.

To show the Reader how important music and singing are as it regards the worship of the Lord, that is, the right kind of music and singing, we need only look at the Book of Psalms, which is the largest Book in the Bible. This tells us what the Holy Spirit thinks of worship, and it tells us how that the greatest degree of worship is found in music and singing. There are certainly other ways to worship God, but I think that the greatest way of all, or possibly that which the Holy Spirit uses more than all, is music and singing.

MUSIC

Music, as devised by the Lord, is made up of *"rhythm,"* *"melody,"* and *"harmony."* If any one of those three is hindered, continuity is destroyed, and it becomes virtually impossible to worship the Lord by such music. Modern Christian Rock falls into that category. It may be referred to as *"Christian,"* but it is not Christian. While the flesh may respond to such music, it is impossible for the spirit of the individual to do so.

Most of these so-called Christian Rock entertainers, and that's what they are, look to the mainstream Rockers as their examples, which to be frank, is an abomination. The tragedy is, Pastors will shepherd their young people into these so-called concerts, which have absolutely no spirituality, at least as it regards the Lord. In fact, to be blunt, clear, and plain, this particular type of music is of Satan. It's not of God, it has never been of God, and it is abominable to even claim that it is. Pastors who promote such stuff are going to answer to God for the souls of the young people under their charge.

To be frank, the name of that game is money. And so-called Christian Rock is to the secular Rock Music scene as methadone is to the drug scene.

Radio Stations that refer to themselves as *"Christian,"* and play that type of music, are actually promoting the Devil. Christian Television shows that feature such fall into the same category. And to be sure, the owners of such Stations, the D.J.'s, the Pastors of Churches who promote this stuff, or even who place their seal of approval on it, once again, are going to answer to God, and the answer is not going to be very favorable.

Exactly as secular Rock Music, for all of its promotion of drugs, illicit sex, alcohol, murder, etc., contains a spirit of darkness that joins with the spirit of those who listen to such so-called music, it is the same identical thing with the so-called Christian Rock. There is a bondage to such music, exactly as there is to alcohol, drugs, gambling, nicotine, etc.

WIN THE YOUTH?

Ten years ago, it was claimed that such music would win young people to Christ. What a ridiculous statement that is! People are brought to Christ not by using the raw ways of the world, or any ways of the world, for that matter, but rather by the Holy Spirit. And to be sure, He not only doesn't need the ways of the world, He absolutely rejects the ways of the world. So anyone who would claim such a thing simply doesn't know the Bible, and has no knowledge of the Lord per se.

However, most now are not even claiming that such is winning youth to Christ, but rather, that it's *"good clean entertainment."* While it might be entertainment, it's definitely not good, and it's definitely not clean. And to be frank, there are almost as many drugs sold or used at these Christian Rock concerts, as in the secular concerts.

That particular type of music, if it can be called music, certainly doesn't glorify God. To be frank, to even insinuate that it does is an insult to the Lord.

Some years ago, Frances and I were in Budapest, Hungary, in a particular Church for a Service. Not being able to speak or understand Hungarian, I had no idea as to the words they were saying as it regards the songs they were singing; however, I did recognize the melodies, and you could sense the Presence of the Lord, as the people were worshipping. While they sang in Hungarian, I sang the same song in English.

Just before the Service was turned to me, they had a young man sing who had just come from the United States. He got up and sang a particular song he had learned in the States, which he had translated into Hungarian, which was one of the Christian Rock songs, etc. As stated, that particular music has no melody or harmony. As a result, the people just sat there and stared, because there was nothing else they could do. As stated, it is impossible to worship with that type of music, and to be frank, who would want to try to worship with that type of music!

The people in the Church little knew me, and I did not know them at all. So what I was seeing was not staged, but yet, was a perfect example of this of which I speak. As they sang the old songs of glory, they could worship the Lord, simply because the songs were of the Lord. When the young man sang, presenting the garbage, and that's exactly what it was that he had learned in the States, they could not worship, simply because worship to such is impossible. And those who claim they can worship the Lord according to such simply do not know what worship actually is.

One can pretty well judge the spiritual barometer of a Church by the type of music that it promotes. The Spirit of the Lord will portray Himself in this particular category of worship, as He does nothing else. As stated, the Book of Psalms is the largest Book in the Bible, telling us what the Holy Spirit thinks of worship according to music and singing. If in fact I am correct about music being a spiritual barometer, then the Churches in the United States are in sad shape indeed! There are exceptions, and thank God for those exceptions, but they are few and far between.

UNTO THE LORD

The song that Moses sang, along with the Children of Israel, was evidently given to him by the Lord. Immediately, it glorifies the Lord, speaking of the great victory that He had brought about for the Children of Israel. It begins that way, and it ends that way.

A PERSONAL EXPERIENCE

I was either eight or nine years of age; the exact year slips my mind. At any rate, I had just been saved and baptized with the Holy Spirit a short time earlier. On a particular night in question, while in Church, and observing the Evangelist as he played the piano, the Lord put it into my heart to seek Him as it regards the talent to play that particular instrument. I can remember sitting beside my Dad, and all through the Service asking the Lord for this particular talent. I remember very vividly some of the things I said to Him.

Being just a child, I knew very little about sin, but I remember promising Him that if He would give me this talent, I would forever use it for His glory. And I also remember saying that I would never play in a nightclub. That is about the limit that I had of things of the world at that particular time.

I can still see myself sitting beside my Dad, I can see myself praying, and once or twice, my whispering to the Lord must have become obvious, because my Dad looked at me and shook his head, as if to say, *"Be quiet."*

At any rate, I could hardly wait for the Service to conclude. I had asked the Lord for this talent, and I believed in my heart with simple childlike Faith, that the Lord had heard me, and He would give me that for which I had asked.

When the Service ended, I very hesitantly walked up onto the small platform. Our Church was very small, and the musical complement consisted only of the old upright piano.

To my recollection, I had never sat down on a piano stool in my life. So for the first time I sat down and put my fingers on the keys. Immediately, I began to make chords. I did not know what chords they were, but I do know the finger positions were right, because it sounded right to my ear.

After the Service, my Dad asked me as to where I had learned those chords, for evidently he had heard me. I shook my head in the negative, and replied that I have not learned them anywhere. Ignoring what I had said, he asked me if I had been up to my Aunt's house, who incidentally had a piano, and had been playing the instrument. *"No"* I replied! He then asked, *"Has Sister Culbreth* (our Pastor's wife, and who was an excellent pianist) *been showing you some chords?"* I again replied in the negative. He then asked, *"Well, have you been going to the Church to practice?"* Once again, I replied *"No!"*

"Well, where did you learn those chords?" he asked. I remember my reply, as though this happened yesterday.

"I asked the Lord to give me the talent to play the piano, and I guess He has already started," I answered!

I don't recall what he said then, but I do remember that he very much approved of my request.

Some may remonstrate by saying that musical talent runs in my family, and the Lord had nothing to do with what talent I do have. While it is certainly true that musical talent definitely runs in my family, with two of my cousins being quite prominent in the musical field, and I speak of Jerry Lee Lewis and Mickey Gilley; however, I believe that the Lord gave me the talent that I have. Along with the talent to play the piano, He also gave me an understanding, I believe, of music which glorifies His Name. Whatever style I have was not copied from anyone. The Lord gave it to me, exactly as it is. With our music, we have seen literally millions of people blessed, stirred, encouraged, and strengthened in the Lord. Of course, I give Him all the praise and all the glory.

In respect to what I've just said about the Lord giving me a knowledge of music which glorifies Him, that doesn't mean that for music to glorify the Lord, it has to be identical to the music that I play. That would be facetious to say the least! But I definitely do believe that it will be somewhat similar.

Music is not neutral. It was originated by God. The Word of God tells us that when God created the Earth, *"The morning stars (Angels) sang together, and all the sons of God shouted for joy"* (Job 38:4-7). Once again, going back to the Book of Psalms, and realizing that every one of the Psalms are songs, for that's what the word *"Psalms"* actually means, and realizing that the Holy Spirit even gave instructions to the writers of some of the Psalms as to what type of musical instrumentation should accompany the Psalm, we should then understand just how important music and singing actually are as it regards the worship of the Lord.

Over the SonLife Radio Network, we play only music that originates at Family Worship Center. Concerning this, a man wrote me the other day and stated, *"Brother Swaggart, thank you so much for putting the Station in our city. You are teaching us how to worship."*

I will confess that when I read his note, I was somewhat taken aback. But yet, after a moment, I realized that most Churches have been so off track regarding the worship of the Lord for such a long time that they hardly know what true worship actually is any more. I'm certainly not meaning that this applies to all Churches, for it doesn't; however, I definitely believe that it does apply to most. And as we've already stated, music is a barometer, I think, of the spirituality of the Church. When the spirituality starts to go wrong, which means the Pastor and people are veering away from the Word of God, it will tell first of all in the music that they produce.

So when I make statements about music, I am at least to a certain extent, making statements in the realm of Revelation from the Lord. In other words, I know somewhat of that of which I speak. That's at least one of the reasons I cannot stand to listen to modern so-called Christian Rock, which is nothing but a product of the flesh, and which only appeals to the flesh. Then I hear the voice of the Holy Spirit saying: *"So then they who are in the flesh cannot please God"* (Rom. 8:8).

That which we do as it regards anything done for the Lord, and especially our worship as it regards music and singing, must glorify His Name. As is portrayed to us here very clearly this great song as it was sung by Moses and the Children of Israel, I think we should conclude that the Holy Spirit would desire that we use this presentation as a foundation for our musical efforts. As we will see, the Lord is glorified throughout, with man glorified not at all.

THE LORD

Verse 2 reads: *"The LORD is my strength and song, and He is become my Salvation: He is my God, and I will prepare Him an habitation: my father's God, and I will exalt Him."*

The first phrase actually says in the Hebrew, *"My strength and song is Jah."* In fact, the name *"Jah"* had not previously been used. It is commonly regarded as an abbreviated form of Jehovah. It takes the place of *"Jehovah"* here, probably because of the rhythm of the song.

The *"Salvation"* addressed here refers to being delivered out of the hand of Pharaoh and his host; consequently, the Children of Israel were saved from destruction.

We certainly should get an idea from this as to what the word *"Salvation"* actually means. Without exception, it refers to what Jesus did for us in the giving of Himself on the Cross as a Sacrifice, which satisfied the demands of a thrice-Holy God, and thereby delivers the sinner from the clutches of Satan because all sin has been atoned. Sin being the legal right that Satan has to hold man in bondage, with all sin atoned, Satan has lost his authority. So any authority he presently exerts is a pseudo-authority. In other words, every sinner can turn to Christ if he so desires, and every bondage of sin will then be broken. Every Christian can look to Christ and the Cross, and as well, whatever authority that Satan has exerted over him will quickly fade. It is all in the Word, as given by Paul: *"Jesus Christ and Him Crucified"* (I Cor. 1:23).

"I will prepare Him an habitation," probably means in the Hebrew, *"I will glorify Him."* This is agreed upon by most of the Hebrew Scholars.

Moses is remonstrating by using the phrase, *"My father's God,"* that the Lord had given promises to Abraham, Isaac, and Jacob. Those promises had been kept in totality. Not one had fallen to the ground. As a result, Moses says, *"I will exalt Him."*

The pronouns, as it refers to the Lord, *"He,"* *"Him,"* *"Thy,"* *"Thou,"* and *"Thee"* are found 33 times in this Psalm! How significant and how searching is this! How entirely different from most modern hymnology! So many hymns today (if they deserve to be called *"hymns"*) are full of maudlin sentimentality, instead of Divine adoration. They announce our love to God, instead of His for us. They recount our experiences, instead of His mercies. They tell more of human attainments, instead of Christ's Atonement. As stated, sad index of our low state of spirituality! Different far was this Song of Moses and Israel: *"I will exalt Him,"* sums it all up (Pink).

REDEMPTION

This first Song of Scripture has been rightly designated the Song of Redemption, for it proceeded from the hearts of a redeemed people. From all of this, we find there are two parts to Redemption. They are:

1. Redemption is by *"purchase,"* which speaks of what Christ did at the Cross.
2. Redemption is by *"power,"* which speaks of the Power of the Holy Spirit, and which is made possible by the Cross of Christ.

Some Believers get *"Redemption"* and *"Ransom"* confused. Ransoming is but a part of Redemption. The two are clearly distinguished in Scripture.

It is said of Christ in Hosea 13:14: *"I will 'ransom' them from the power of the grave; I will 'redeem' them from death."* And again we read: *"For the LORD has 'redeemed' Jacob and 'ransomed' him from the hand of him who was stronger than he"* (Jer. 31:11).

Ransoming is the payment of the price, which Jesus did at the Cross; Redemption in the full sense, of which ransom is but a part, is the deliverance of the persons for whom the price was paid. It is the latter which is obviously the all-important item. Of what use is the ransom if the captive be not released? Without actual emancipation there will be no song of praise. Who would ever thank a ransomer who left him in bondage?

The Greek word for *"Redemption"* is rendered *"deliverance"* in Hebrews 11:35.

In the Book of Revelation, Jesus is pictured both as a *"Lamb,"* which refers to the Purchaser, and as a *"Lion,"* which refers to the powerful Emancipator.

On the Passover-night, Israel was secured from the *"doom"* of the Egyptians; at the Red Sea, they were delivered from the *"power"* of the Egyptians. Thus delivered — *"redeemed"* — they sang. It is only a ransomed and redeemed people, conscious of their deliverance, who can really praise the Lord, the Deliverer.

Not only is worship impossible for those yet dead in trespasses and sins, but also intelligent worship cannot be rendered by professing Christians who are in doubt as to their standing before God. And necessarily so. Praise and joy are essential elements of worship; but how can those who question their experience in the Beloved, who are not certain whether they would go to Heaven or Hell should they die this moment — how could such be joyful and thankful? Impossible!

Uncertainty and doubt beget fear and distrust, and not gladness and adoration.

(The author is indebted to Arthur W. Pink for the above material on *"Ransom"* and *"Redemption."*)

A MAN OF WAR

Verse 3 reads: *"The LORD is a man of war: the LORD is His Name."*

The Lord is a Man of war, and in every capacity. He had just defeated the mightiest field army on the face of the Earth, and did so without using a single human soldier. But to be frank, His capacity in the realm of spiritual warfare is of even greater magnitude.

At the Cross of Calvary, the Lord Jesus, even as we've already explained in this Volume, totally and completely defeated Satan. He did it not through mortal combat, as would be obvious, but rather by taking away Satan's authority. Sin gives him the authority to do what he does, but with all sin atoned, as it was at the Cross, his authority has been removed. If it seems as if he presently has authority, we must remember also as stated, that it is a pseudo-authority. This refers to authority which Christians allow Satan to have, simply because they do not know their place and position in Christ. The reason they don't know that place and position is simply because they do not understand the Cross. While most Christians do understand the Cross as it refers to Salvation, they have little knowledge at all as it refers to Sanctification. And this is the tragedy!

The Lord is the Man of war, not we ourselves. When we try to place ourselves in that position, we get defeated every time. In fact, the only fight that we are called upon to fight is *"the good fight of Faith"* (I Tim. 6:12).

"The Lord is His Name," could be translated, *"Jehovah, the Alone-existing One."* Before Him all other existence fades and falls into nothingness.

Let us say it again, in looking through the various notes of this song, we do not find a single note about *"self,"* its doings, its sayings, its feelings, or its fruits; it is all about Jehovah, from beginning to end.

NOTES

PHARAOH

Verse 4 reads: *"Pharaoh's chariots and his host has He cast into the sea: his chosen captains also are drowned in the Red Sea."*

It is not known as to exactly what percentage of Pharaoh's army is included here. Irrespective, the ones who did come after Israel seemingly were the chosen and the best. For sure, his finest charioteers were lost, as well as his *"chosen captains."*

Another thing is for sure: it would be some time before Egypt's army was back up to full potential.

THEY SANK

Verse 5 reads: *"The depths have covered them: they sank into the bottom as a stone."*

The warriors who fought in chariots commonly wore coats of mail, composed of bronze plates sewn onto a linen base, and overlapping one another. These coats covered the arms to the elbow, and descended nearly to the knee; consequently, being as heavy as they were, these warriors would have sunk at once, even without a struggle, like a stone or a lump of lead, as the waters cascaded down upon them (Pulpit).

THE RIGHT HAND OF THE LORD

Verse 6 reads: *"Your right hand, O LORD, is become glorious in power: your right hand, O LORD, has dashed in pieces the enemy."*

The *"right hand"* as it refers to the Lord is used as a figure of speech. It signifies power. Consequently, when it is said that Christ is now seated *"on the right hand of the Majesty on high,"* while that is literally true, it also signifies power.

That *"right hand of power,"* as it refers to the Lord, can and will be used on our behalf as well, providing our Faith is placed 100 percent in Christ and what Christ has done for us at the Cross. Then the Holy Spirit, Who is God, and Who can do all things, will saturate the Believer with power.

What kind of power?

This is not power or authority over other people, but rather over the spirits of darkness (Lk. 10:19; Eph. 6:11-18).

While of course, all Christians fight the Devil, we must understand that it's always indirectly. Christ has already defeated him, and we fight him simply by fighting the good fight of Faith, which refers to Faith in Christ and His Cross.

THE WRATH OF GOD

Verse 7 reads: *"And in the greatness of Your excellency You have overthrown them who rose up against You: You sent forth Your wrath, which consumed them as stubble."*

The verbs in this Verse are future. Consequently, it should read, *"You will overthrow them who rise up against You."* And then, *"You will send forth Your wrath."*

The last phrase, *"Which consumed them as stubble,"* is present tense, and concerns the victory over the Egyptians.

So in this Verse, we have an account not only of what the Lord has done regarding the Egyptians, but the Promise that He will fight thusly for us as well!

This first Song in the Bible was sung on a shore heaped with dead men — an appalling scene of Divine wrath — and the last Song in the Bible will be sung in a scene of yet greater wrath and destruction (Rev., Chpt. 19). These inspired records of God's Ways on Earth, and of His action towards sin, anger the self-righteous heart, but thrill the soul of the one dependent on the Righteousness of Christ.

GOD'S USE OF THE ELEMENTS

Verse 8 reads: *"And with the blast of Your nostrils the waters were gathered together, the floods stood upright as an heap, and the depths were congealed in the heart of the sea."*

Moses describes the east wind which God set in motion as *"the blast"* or *"breath of His nostrils."* He then represents the waters as *"standing in a heap"* on either side, and the depths as *"congealed."*

Some have taken this phrase concerning the word *"congealed,"* and taken it to mean that the waters froze; however, considering the climate of Egypt, that is unlikely, although it definitely could have happened.

Still others have asked the question, *"Are we justified in taking literally the strong expressions of a highly wrought poetical description?"*

We definitely are justified. It is the Holy Spirit Who gave Moses these very words, and to be sure, as highly poetical as they might be, still, the description in no way stretches the truth as it regards what God has done, and above all, what He can do. In fact, with Him, all things are possible!

THE ENEMY SAID

Verse 9 reads: *"The enemy said, I will pursue, I will overtake, I will divide the spoil; my lust shall be satisfied upon them; I will draw my sword, my hand shall destroy them."*

This Verse is very important, simply because it shows the thoughts of the soldiers who flocked to Pharaoh's standard, in regard to the pursuit of the Children of Israel.

The words, *"I will divide the spoil,"* proclaim the fact that Israel had gone out of Egypt laden with ornaments of silver and of gold, and as well, accompanied by flocks and herds of great value. Pharaoh probably told these soldiers that this plunder would be theirs, and they intended to appropriate it. They then boast, *"My hand shall destroy them."*

There is much to be learned from this statement.

The enemy declared fully as to what they intended to do, and full well meant every word; however, they were not able to do anything, and in fact, even as the next Verse proclaims, were destroyed themselves. Here's the point I wish to make:

Countless times, the Devil has told you that he is going to destroy you, or else, your children are going to be eternally lost, or else you're going to die from some terrible disease, or you will go bankrupt, etc. But have you ever stopped to think that none of that has ever come to pass?

To be sure, if Satan could do all of these things, or any part of these things, he would have done them a long time ago. But he hasn't done them, simply because he can't do them. He doesn't have the power! The truth is: *"You are of God, little children, and have overcome them: because greater is He* (the Holy Spirit) *Who is in you, than he* (Satan) *who is in the world"* (I Jn. 4:4).

CAMPMEETING

I was preaching a particular Service in one of our Campmeetings, when I began to bring out this thought. The Power of God swept that congregation, as every single Christian in the place understood what was being said, and even though my Message was not yet concluded, they could not contain themselves and, therefore, began to praise God, with the entire Service erupting in praise.

I want you the Reader to understand fully what is being said. The enemy has said much to you. He hopes to strike fear into your heart; however, never forget, if he could do all the things that he claims he's going to do, he would have done them a long time ago. And he hasn't done them, because he can't do them because the power that's in you is greater than that which is in him.

So the next time he tries to feed you his negative line, just shout the praises of God, because whatever he says, you know better.

THE LORD'S ANSWER

Verse 10 reads: *"You did blow with Your wind, the sea covered them: they sank as lead in the mighty waters."*

Here we have another fact that is not mentioned in the account, but yet which is implied. The immediate cause of the return of the waters was a wind. As a *"strong east wind"* had caused the waters to part, now this new wind, and that which had been devised by the Lord, must have arisen contrary to the former one, blowing from the northwest or the north, which would have driven the water of the Bitter Lakes southward, and thus produce the effect spoken of (Pulpit).

WHO IS LIKE UNTO YOU?

Verse 11 reads: *"Who is like unto You, O LORD, among the gods? Who is like You, glorious in Holiness, fearful in praises, doing wonders?"*

The *"gods"* mentioned in the previous Verse pertain to the gods worshipped by the Egyptians. They were pitiful up beside Jehovah. In fact, they were no gods at all, but rather figments of the imagination of evil men. If there was any power there at all, and to be sure there was some power, it would have been in the realm of demon spirits.

In this setting of all the gods of Egypt, and the Egyptians worshipped many gods, we find the whole series of miraculous visitations, which proclaim the fact that the True God, Jehovah, should be exalted far above all the gods of the heathen.

Moses makes all of this the foundation of his praise. He points to three attributes of God, which cannot be equaled elsewhere:

1. Holiness: In fact, God is thrice-Holy, hence the Cherubim saying, *"Holy, Holy, Holy, LORD God Almighty, which was, and is, and is to come"* (Rev. 4:8).

2. Fearful: The word in the Hebrew is *"yare,"* and means, *"to revere, dreadful, reverence, terrible."* The Lord is *"fearful"* because of His Holiness. He deserves praise, and in fact, all the praise that humanity can give Him, because He is our Creator, and as well, has delivered us from the powers of darkness.

3. Miraculous Power: He is to be viewed with awe even when we praise Him (Pulpit).

How entirely different is *"the Lord"* — Omnipotent, Immutable, Sovereign, Triumphant — from the feeble, changeable, disappointed, and defeated *"god"* which is the object of *"worship"* in thousands of Churches! How few today *"glory"* in God's *"Holiness!"* How few *"praise"* Him for His *"fearfulness!"* How few are acquainted with His *"wonders!"*

THE LORD'S RIGHT HAND

Verse 12 reads: *"You stretched out Your right hand, the Earth swallowed them."*

The idea is, all the Lord had to do to defeat the Egyptians, even though this was one of the mightiest armies in the world, was to simply stretch out His right hand, which means exert His Power, which was done at His Word. As a result, the *"Earth swallowed them,"* which refers to the Sea, which of course is a part of the Earth.

THE STRENGTH OF THE LORD

Verse 13 reads: *"You in Your Mercy have led forth the people which You have redeemed: You have guided them in Your strength unto Your holy habitation."*

Several things are said in this Verse:

1. Six times the pronoun *"Thou,"* or *"Thy,"* are used, which we have translated into the words *"You"* or *"Your,"* signifying that Salvation, and everything which pertains to that word, is found totally in God, and not at all in man. As the Holy Spirit gives this song

to Moses, and the Holy Spirit is most definitely the Author, He emphasizes the fact that the Lord has done all of this, which means that man cannot receive any credit, simply because man is not due any credit.

This of which I speak is probably the greatest bone of contention between God and man, which one could name. God gives His Way, and man attempts to change it to something else. God has one Way for the sinner to be saved, and that is by simple Faith and trust in Christ and what Christ has done for us at the Cross (Jn. 3:16). He also has one Way of Sanctification, and that is by simple Faith and trust in Christ and what Christ has done for us at the Cross (Rom. 6:3-14; 8:1-2, 11; I Cor. 1:17-18, 21, 23; 2:2, 5; Eph. 2:13-18; Col. 2:14-15). Regrettably, most in the world try to change God's Way of Salvation, and sadder still, most Christians attempt to change His Way of Sanctification. Both parties, the unredeemed and the Redeemed, revert to *"works."* It's ironical that the Redeemed will shake their heads sadly at the world and plainly tell them that they cannot earn their Salvation, which is certainly correct, but then turn right around and try to earn their Sanctification by the same method they have told the world cannot be done.

REDEEMED

2. The word *"redeemed"* in Hebrew is *"gaal,"* and means *"to deliver, to purchase, to ransom."* It also means to *"set free,"* which is the same meaning as its Greek derivative, *"to purchase the slave out of the marketplace."* God's Redeemed are a people whom He has purchased for Himself, to be with Himself forever — *"That where I am, there you may be also."* We are redeemed to be placed into His *"holy habitation,"* which we will address momentarily.

STRENGTH

3. The Unredeemed never think of themselves as being a slave, much less a slave to Satan, but that's exactly what they are. As such, only the strength of the Lord can extricate that person from this terrible bondage of darkness. Man is only fooling himself if he thinks otherwise.

NOTES

Most, if not all, Believers would agree with what I've just stated, but then seem to think, because they are saved, thereby a new creature in Christ Jesus (II Cor. 5:17), that they have the strength to sanctify themselves, i.e., *"to live a Godly life."* While they claim to *"trust God,"* or to *"stand upon the Word,"* or to *"trust Christ,"* most Christians are trying to do this outside of the Cross. In other words, they do not understand the part the Cross of Christ plays in their Sanctification experience, which has to do with their everyday life and living before God.

The truth is, the Christian has no more personal strength after Salvation than he does before Salvation. While it is certainly true that we have strength, even great strength, it is all in the Holy Spirit, and not at all in us. And the Holy Spirit, Who lives and resides within our hearts and lives (I Cor. 3:16), works and functions in one way, and one way only. That one way is the Cross of Christ. In other words, everything the Spirit does is within the parameters of the Finished Work of Christ, which has given Him the legal right to do what He does (Rom. 8:1-2, 11). This means, as we have repeatedly stated already in this Volume, that the Believer must anchor his Faith at all times in the great Sacrifice of Christ. Listen again to Paul:

"But God forbid that I should glory (boast), *save in the Cross of our Lord Jesus Christ, by whom the world is crucified unto me, and I unto the world"* (Gal. 6:14). To be frank, our Salvation and our victory depend upon three things:

1. The Cross,
2. Our Faith in the Cross,
3. Which gives the Holy Spirit latitude to work.

HOLY HABITATION

4. It is clear here that Moses, through Divine Revelation, knew there would be a place in the land of Canaan where God would *"put His Name"* (Deut. 12:5, 11, 14; 14:23-24; 16:6, 11; 26:2). It seems also that he knew where that place would be — Jerusalem.

But as most, if not all, the Old Testament prophecies, it has even a greater reference than the Temple in Jerusalem, in fact, referring in its conclusion, to the Holy

Spirit ultimately dwelling within the Child of God. Jesus told His Disciples: *"And I will pray the Father, and He shall give you another Comforter* (Helper), *that He may abide with you forever:*

"Even the Spirit of Truth; Whom the world cannot receive, because it sees Him not, neither knows Him: but you know Him; for He dwells with you, and shall be in you" (Jn. 14:16-17).

Then Paul said: *"Do you not know that you are the Temple of God, and that the Spirit of God dwells in you?"* (I Cor. 3:16).

All of this came by stages. First of all, God dwelt between the Mercy Seat and the Cherubim in the Tabernacle. He then dwelt in the Temple in the same manner. But His ultimate dwelling place, which was brought about by what Jesus did at the Cross, is the human heart. Before the Cross, He could not make the human heart and life His habitation, simply because the blood of bulls and goats couldn't take away sins (Heb. 10:4). But when Jesus came, and died on the Cross, He took away all sin (Jn. 1:29).

By simple Faith in Christ, one becomes *"His holy habitation."* This is a *"new standing,"* which means that we are literally placed in Christ, which is made possible by the Cross, and our Faith in that Finished Work. This is the *"position"* of all Believers in the Lord Jesus Christ. *"For Christ also has once suffered for sins* (the Cross), *the just for the unjust, that He might bring us to God"* (I Pet. 3:18). This is our place as His Redeemed.

God's whole moral nature, having been satisfied in the Death of Christ, He can now rest in us in perfect complacency. Jesus said:

"At that day (after Christ had gone to the Cross) *you shall know that I am in My Father, and you in Me, and I in you"* (Jn. 14:20).

The old hymn says:

"So near, so very near to God,
"I nearer cannot be,
"For in the Person of His Son,
"I am as near as He."

This place, all made possible by the Cross, and our Faith in that great Sacrifice, is indeed accorded to us in Grace, but nonetheless in Righteousness; so that not only are all the attributes of God's Character concerned in bringing us there, but He Himself is also glorified by it. It is an immense thought, and one which, when held in power, imparts both strength and energy to our souls — that we are even now brought to God.

The whole distance — measured by the Death of Christ on the Cross, when He was made sin for us, which means that He took upon Himself the total and complete sin penalty — has been bridged over, and our position of nearness is marked by the place He now occupies as Glorified by the right hand of God (Heb. 1:3).

In fact, even when we are transported to Heaven itself, we shall not be nearer, as it regards our *"position,"* than we are now, because it is *"in Christ."*

And because we are *"in Christ,"* and have that *"standing"* as the result of the Cross, God looks for a *"state"* corresponding with our *"standing."* Pink says, *"State and walk must ever flow from a known relationship. Unless therefore we are taught the truth of our standing before God, we shall never answer to it in our souls, or in our walk before God."*

This is the great Truth, the manner of Sanctification for the Saint, that I am continuously trying to bring out in this Volume. I am doing so, addressing it from every angle that I know, even in the fear of being overly repetitious. But I do so because I realize how hard Satan fights this Truth of truths, and how difficult it is, due to the flesh, for the Believer to grasp what is being said.

The Lord has given me the Revelation of how to live for God, which is not new, but actually that which He gave to Paul, and if I said otherwise, I would not be telling the truth. But yet, it is so difficult to get Christians out of the spiritual lethargy in which they sleep. That's why Paul said: *"Therefore let us not sleep, as do others; but let us watch and be sober"* (I Thess. 5:6).

THE VICTORY OF THE SAINTS

Verses 14 through 16 read: *"The people shall hear, and be afraid: sorrow shall take hold on the inhabitants of Palestina.*

"Then the dukes of Edom shall be amazed; the mighty men of Moab, trembling shall take hold upon them; all the inhabitants of Canaan shall melt away.

"Fear and dread shall fall upon them; by the greatness of Your arm they shall be as still as a stone; till Your people pass over, O LORD, till the people pass over, which You have purchased."

How so very much this portrays the fact that the doubt and unbelief of 10 of the 12 spies sent into Canaan, which brought untold sorrow and heartache, even the death of that generation in the wilderness, was so unnecessary (Num., Chpt. 13).

And why not! The inhabitants of Canaan had all heard of the great miracles performed by the Lord in Egypt, and especially the miracle of the Red Sea. This is evidenced by what Rahab said: *"I know that the LORD has given you the land, and that your terror is fallen upon us, and that all the inhabitants of the land faint because of you.*

"For we have heard how the LORD dried up the water of the Red Sea for you, when you came out of Egypt: and what you did unto the two kings of the Amorites, that were on the other side of Jordan, Sihon and Og, whom you utterly destroyed.

"And as soon as we had heard these things, our hearts did melt, and neither did there remain any more courage in any man, because of you: for the LORD your God, He is God in Heaven above, and in Earth beneath" (Josh. 2:9-11).

WHAT JESUS HAS DONE

All of this portrays in type what Christ accomplished at the Cross, when He *"spoiled principalities and powers* (fallen angels and demon spirits), (where) *He made a show of them openly, triumphing over them in it"* (Col. 2:14-15). Just as these enemy nations feared Israel, likewise, all fallen angels and demon spirits, even Satan himself, fear the Child of God, who understands and knows that he has *"passed over"* into our inheritance, purchased for us by the Lord Jesus Christ. In fact, the Scripture portrays Satan as a coward. James said:

"Submit yourselves therefore to God. Resist the Devil, and he will flee from you" (James 4:7).

HOW DO WE RESIST THE DEVIL?

We resist him in one way, and one way only, and that one way is the way of *"Faith"* (Heb., Chpt. 11). This means that we aren't to try to use our own strength and ability, but rather Faith.

What do we mean, resist him by Faith?

Whenever Faith is addressed in the Bible, either directly or indirectly, it speaks of Christ and what Christ did at the Cross. In other words, the Cross of Christ is to ever be the object of our Faith.

Satan will do everything within his power to move our Faith from the Cross to other things. And to be sure, he doesn't care too very much what those other things are, or even how holy they might be in their own right. Most of the time, he will use Preachers preaching false messages, in order to carry out this task. And tragically and sadly, most of the preaching done presently as it regards living for God is leading people's Faith away from the Cross, instead of to the Cross. This is the sure road of disaster.

While it is certainly true that most of this preaching of which I speak is done through ignorance; still, much of it is also in the realm of unbelief.

For instance, the doctrine of the Word of Faith Preachers is a doctrine that is totally opposed to the Cross. In fact, they are *"enemies of the Cross,"* even as Paul described (Phil. 3:18-19).

And even in the Denominations that claim to believe in the Cross, they little preach the Cross, but rather humanistic psychology.

So the Believer resists the Devil by making certain that his Faith is anchored in the Cross of Christ, and that it remains in the Cross. This is the *"good fight of Faith"* which he is called upon to fight constantly (I Tim. 6:12).

Now what I've given you is a tremendous truth. It really doesn't matter which way that Satan comes against you; whether it's in the realm of temptation to commit immorality, or to succumb to depression, or any one of a thousand other things which we could name, your defense is Christ, and more particularly, what He did for you in His Finished Work. That's why Paul said to the Corinthians: *"I determined not to know anything among you, save Jesus Christ, and Him Crucified"* (I Cor. 2:2).

I remind our Word of Faith friends that the Holy Spirit through Paul <u>didn't</u> say: *"For I determined not to know anything among you, save Jesus Christ, and Him Resurrected,"* which is what they teach, but rather, *"Crucified."*

THE INHERITANCE

Verses 17 and 18 read: *"You shall bring them in, and plant them in the mountain of Your inheritance, in the place, O LORD, which You have made for You to dwell in, in the Sanctuary, O LORD, which Your hands have established.*

"The LORD shall reign forever and ever."

This great Song proclaims Who God is, What He did, and How He did it.

It also proclaims, as given in Verse 17, that all of this was done for a purpose. It was to bring the Children of Israel to the place of the *"Lord's inheritance,"* which He had made for them to *"dwell in."* As stated, for the Children of Israel, it referred to Canaanland; however, its total meaning has to do with the Believer's position in Christ, for Biblical history has always strained toward this conclusion.

The phrase, *"Which Your hands have established,"* speaks of something already done, in other words, *"past tense."*

This means that even before the Children of Israel reached Canaanland, God had already ordained that the land would be theirs, and that despite the enemies which inhabited it; likewise, He has established the fact that we as Believers should be totally and completely victorious, all in Christ, which means that *"sin shall not have dominion over us"* (Rom. 6:14).

Now regrettably, many Israelites died lost, even before getting to the land, and even after being in the land because of a lack of Faith. It is the same with the modern Believer.

Despite the fact that God has already ordained our victory, if we as Believers harden our hearts against the Way of the Lord, which is Christ and Him Crucified, we too can lose our way (Heb. 6:4-6; 10:26-29).

The Apostle said: *"For we are made partakers of Christ, if we hold the beginning of our confidence* (continue to exhibit Faith in Christ and the Cross) *steadfast unto the end;*

"While it is said, today if you will hear His voice, harden not your hearts, as in the provocation (as did Israel).

"For some, when they had heard, did provoke: howbeit not all who came out of Egypt by Moses (it seems that some repented and continued to believe).

"But with whom was He grieved forty years? Was it not with them who had sinned (who lost Faith), *whose carcasses fell in the wilderness?*

"And to whom swear He that they should not enter into His rest, but to them who believed not?

"So we see that they could not enter in because of unbelief" (failure to trust Christ and His Finished Work) (Heb. 3:14-19).

SIN AND THE BELIEVER

God will never overthrow the Believer because of sin, even as vile as that sin might be, if the Believer faithfully repents, and continues to trust Christ, at least as best as he knows how. But of course, the bondage of sin is present in a Believer's life, simply because they do not understand their place and position in Christ, which was and is afforded by the Cross. Not understanding that it is the Cross which has guaranteed us all things, and that we must thereby keep our Faith in the Cross of Christ, most Christians, sadly and regrettably, place their faith in other things, which guarantees that sin will, in some way, dominate their heart and life.

As stated, God will not overthrow the Believer for sins within his heart and life, with the exception of the one sin of unbelief. That speaks of the Believer losing Faith in Christ and what Christ has done at the Cross, rather advocating other things. For this sin of unbelief, because the Cross is the great Foundation Truth of the Atonement, an individual who was once saved, can thereby pull themselves out of the Salvation of the Lord, and thereby be lost. Faith is what gets us in, and Faith is what keeps us in. And we speak of Faith in Christ and His Cross. If we lose such Faith, we have lost Salvation (Heb. 6:4-6; 10:26-29).

If the Lord threw Believers over because of sins of the flesh, etc., to be quite frank, there wouldn't be any Believers left. But let it be ever understood that any type of sin registered in the heart and life of the Believer is an occasion for misery. This is not the normal Christian experience. In fact, such a position pictures the Believer as living in a state of *"spiritual adultery"* (Rom. 7:1-4). This simply means that the Believer is married to Christ, but is being unfaithful to Christ, by placing his faith in things other than Christ and what Christ has done for us at the Cross. Paul, as stated, classifies such action as *"spiritual adultery."* There is no joy or peace of mind in such a life, even though the Believer is saved. Joy and peace can be found only in total and complete victory, which is what God intends for us to have, and which we can most certainly have, if we will simply follow God's prescribed order of victory.

OUR GOD REIGNS

The Eighteenth Verse, *"The LORD shall reign forever and forever,"* closes this great and beautiful Song. The Song ends as it began — with *"The LORD."* Faith views the eternal future without a tremor.

Let us never forget that we are able by Faith to enter this eternal future all because of the following:

"Having therefore, Brethren boldness to enter into the Holiest by the Blood of Jesus . . . Let us draw near with a true heart in full assurance of Faith . . . Let us hold fast the profession of our Faith without wavering" (Heb. 10:19-23).

Once again, let the Believer understand that it is all by Faith, and more particularly, it speaks of Faith in Christ, and more particular still, Faith in what He did for us in the shedding of His Precious Blood, which He did at the Cross.

And once again, I remind our Word of Faith friends that we *"enter into the Holiest,"* not by the Resurrection of Jesus, but rather *"the Blood of Jesus,"* which speaks of Him shedding such at the Cross.

(19) "FOR THE HORSE OF PHARAOH WENT IN WITH HIS CHARIOTS AND WITH HIS HORSEMEN INTO THE SEA, AND THE LORD BROUGHT AGAIN THE WATERS OF THE SEA UPON THEM; BUT THE CHILDREN OF ISRAEL WENT ON DRY LAND IN THE MIDST OF THE SEA.

(20) "AND MIRIAM THE PROPHETESS, THE SISTER OF AARON, TOOK A TIMBREL IN HER HAND; AND ALL THE WOMEN WENT OUT AFTER HER WITH TIMBRELS AND WITH DANCES.

(21) "AND MIRIAM ANSWERED THEM, SING YE TO THE LORD, FOR HE HATH TRIUMPHED GLORIOUSLY; THE HORSE AND HIS RIDER HAS HE THROWN INTO THE SEA."

The construction is:

1. Miriam, it seems, led Israel in worship.

2. When it says, *"And Miriam answered them,"* it is speaking of the men singing, and the women answering them, under the leadership of Miriam. Incidentally, Miriam was Moses' sister.

3. The *"timbrels"* suggest the pleasure of the Holy Spirit in using such to accompany the singing, which speaks of musical instruments.

4. There was great rejoicing, and rightly so, with even the women of Israel, which could have numbered a half million or more, leading Israel in *"dancing before the Lord,"* with worship and praise.

5. We are commanded here to *"Sing ye to the Lord, for He has triumphed gloriously."* This refers not only to Israel of old, but to all modern Believers as well, and in fact, every Believer who has ever lived.

VICTORY

Verse 19 reads: *"For the horse of Pharaoh went in with his chariots and with his horsemen into the sea, and the LORD brought again the waters of the sea upon them; but the Children of Israel went on dry land in the midst of the sea."*

In fact, a part of the song sung by Miriam and the women of Israel is given in this Verse. In other words, it is a compendium of what they sang.

We as Believers are to ever tell what the Lord has done for us, and most important of all, we are to proclaim the Salvation which He has given us, how He saved us, and by what means, which is *"Jesus Christ and Him Crucified"* (I Cor. 1:23).

In fact, after the time of the Great Tribulation foretold by Jesus (Mat. 24:21), those who come out of the Great Tribulation, both Jews and Gentiles, having gained victory over the beast, will sing this song again in Heaven. It is called *"the song of Moses the servant of God, and the song of the Lamb"* (Rev. 15:1-4).

MIRIAM THE PROPHETESS

Verse 20 reads: *"And Miriam the Prophetess, the sister of Aaron, took a timbrel in her hand; and all the women went out after her with timbrels and with dances."*

Miriam was the sister of both Moses and Aaron. She is the first woman whom the Bible honors with the title of *"Prophetess."*

Pulpit says of her: *"Miriam is regarded by the Prophet Micah (Mic. 6:4), as having had a share in the deliverance of Israel, and claims the prophetic gift in Numbers 12:2. Her claim appears to be allowed both in the present Passage, and in Numbers 12:6-8, where the degree of her inspiration, however, is placed below that of Moses."*

We find throughout Israel, and as well in the New Testament, that women often played a major role in the Work of God. As they were participants of the *"Callings,"* as is here made evident, Deborah was also selected by the Lord to be the Judge of Israel, during the particular time of the Judges. She was the fourth person to occupy that position. Along with her military commander, Barak, she won a great victory over the Canaanites (Judg. 4:1-5:31).

On the inaugural day of the Church, so to speak, Peter quoted the Prophet Joel: *"And it shall come to pass in the last days, saith God, I will pour out of My Spirit upon all flesh: and your sons and your daughters shall prophesy...."* And to emphasize the point, the Holy Spirit had him say it again: *"And on My servants and on My handmaidens I will pour out in those days of My Spirit; and they shall prophesy"* (Acts 2:17-18).

The Greek word for *"prophesy"* is *"propheteuo,"* and means, *"to foretell events, or to speak under inspiration."*

So this tells us that women are called to preach the same as men.

Paul said: *"But I suffer not a woman to teach, nor to usurp authority over the man, but to be in silence"* (I Tim. 2:12).

NOTES

First of all, the order that God has set up is that man is in authority. The Apostle also said: *"For Adam was first formed, then Eve"* (I Tim. 2:13).

The word *"authority"* proclaims the rule, that if a man is available who has the calling of Pastor, he should pastor the Church, and not a woman, even though she might have the calling as well of Pastor (Eph. 4:11). If no man is available, she could feel free to serve in that capacity.

"Silence" in the Greek is *"hesuchia,"* and means, *"desistance from bustle or language, quietness, silence."* The word goes back to *"authority,"* referring to the fact that while a woman is certainly allowed, and even encouraged to speak her mind, and that her wisdom is equal to that of the man, still, she is not to push forward, but rather to remember her place. If everything is done in God's order, the ability of any and every individual is given opportunity.

Other than the order which the Holy Spirit has set up, and which is obvious, Paul said: *"For you are all the children of God by Faith in Christ Jesus . . . there is neither male nor female: for you are all one in Christ Jesus"* (Gal. 3:26, 28).

GREAT REJOICING

The inspired scene that unfolds before us is a wonder to behold, to say the least. There could have been as many as 500,000 women playing tambourines and dancing before the Lord, or even more. As we've stated, the first reaction to the great deliverance was great rejoicing, as will always be the case in one way or the other, when a person comes to Christ, and is, therefore, delivered from the clutches of the Evil One. Concerning the women, sin had come into the human race through the woman, but now her heart is lifted up in praise, which testifies in itself of victory over it.

It seems like this great celebration was part rehearsed and part spontaneous.

We have some reason to believe that Moses may have also been an accomplished singer. He not only sang this song, but as well, the Lord gave him Psalm 90, and more than likely, even Psalm 91, both which are songs. Most of the time, when people write songs, they also have the ability to sing those songs.

The Scripture says that Moses and the Children of Israel sang this song, as given to us in this Fifteenth Chapter. Consequently, it would seem that the Lord first gave the song to Moses, with him having any number of Scribes to hurriedly make copies, which could have numbered into many hundreds.

He could have pulled together any number of people, both men and women, for the Scripture says *"the Children of Israel,"* which includes both, and then taught them this song. And quite possibly, as the Holy Spirit inspired Moses to write this song, He could very well have inspired the people to learn the song and to sing it.

At any rate, as many thousands began to sing because of the great joy that filled their hearts, spontaneously, it seems that Miriam took a timbrel in her hand, and playing the instrument, which refers to keeping rhythm, she began to dance before the Lord, and then with many thousands of women joining her. As stated, that must have been quite a sight.

I cannot recall any Campmeeting we've ever had where the people were that demonstrative. But we certainly ought to be!

Let it be understood as well that the dancing here was definitely not orchestrated or choreographed. As stated, it was all spontaneous. In fact, this method of dancing became quite common in Jewish history. It consisted of the women, usually playing tambourines as Miriam did here, and whirling about in joy before the Lord. The modern method of some Churches of hiring Choreographers can be constituted as nothing but the flesh. When the joy of the Lord fills the heart to such an extent that the women cannot keep still, but must dance before the Lord, which will always be in a fashion that glorifies God, and not the flesh, this should ever be desired.

We have two problems in the modern Church:

1. The first problem is spiritual deadness. In other words, there is absolutely no emotion whatsoever. Such an attitude and direction are not at all Scriptural, as should be obvious.

2. The second problem is that there is all type of emotion, but generated by the flesh.

NOTES

Both are equally bad. If the Spirit of God has His Way, there definitely will be emotion, but it will be the joy of the Lord, and not an operation of the flesh. In fact, both, spiritual deadness and mere emotionalism, are both of the flesh, although in opposite directions.

SING TO THE LORD

Verse 21 reads: *"And Miriam answered them, Sing ye to the LORD, for He has triumphed gloriously; the horse and his rider has He thrown into the sea."*

The phrase, *"And Miriam answered them,"* seems to imply that the men would sing a refrain, and then the women would answer by singing the refrain again. Whether they did this while dancing, or whether some danced and some sang, we aren't told.

At any rate, their worship and praise proclaimed the Lord as the triumphant One, and in every capacity.

The writer of Psalm 149 said:

"Praise ye the LORD. Sing unto the LORD a new song, and His praise in the congregation of Saints.

"Let Israel rejoice in Him Who made him: let the children of Zion be joyful in their King.

"Let them praise His Name in the dance: let them sing praises unto Him with the timbrel and harp.

"For the LORD takes pleasure in His people: He will beautify the meek with Salvation.

"Let the Saints be joyful in glory: let them sing aloud upon their beds.

"Let the high praises of God be in their mouth . . ." (Ps. 149:1-6).

(22) "SO MOSES BROUGHT ISRAEL FROM THE RED SEA, AND THEY WENT OUT INTO THE WILDERNESS OF SHUR; AND THEY WENT THREE DAYS IN THE WILDERNESS, AND FOUND NO WATER.

(23) "AND WHEN THEY CAME TO MARAH, THEY COULD NOT DRINK OF THE WATERS OF MARAH, FOR THEY WERE BITTER: THEREFORE THE NAME OF IT WAS CALLED MARAH.

(24) "AND THE PEOPLE MURMURED AGAINST MOSES, SAYING, WHAT SHALL WE DRINK?

(25) "AND HE CRIED UNTO THE LORD;

AND THE LORD SHOWED HIM A TREE, WHICH WHEN HE HAD CAST INTO THE WATERS, THE WATERS WERE MADE SWEET: THERE HE MADE FOR THEM A STATUTE AND AN ORDINANCE, AND THERE HE PROVED THEM,

(26) "AND SAID, IF YOU WILL DILIGENTLY HEARKEN TO THE VOICE OF THE LORD YOUR GOD, AND WILL DO THAT WHICH IS RIGHT IN HIS SIGHT, AND WILL GIVE EAR TO HIS COMMANDMENTS, AND KEEP ALL HIS STATUTES, I WILL PUT NONE OF THESE DISEASES UPON YOU, WHICH I HAVE BROUGHT UPON THE EGYPTIANS: FOR I AM THE LORD WHO HEALS YOU.

(27) "AND THEY CAME TO ELIM, WHERE WERE TWELVE WELLS OF WATER, AND THREESCORE AND TEN PALM TREES: AND THEY ENCAMPED THERE BY THE WATERS."

The overview is:

1. God tests Faith in order to strengthen and enrich it.

2. Israel journeys three days in the wilderness and finds no water. When water is found there is an added trial — the water is bitter, which is a type of this world, and what it has to offer.

3. Not to be thankful (Rom. 1:21), and to murmur lead to greater sins. Israel murmured, and their unbelief deepened as they murmured.

4. The smitten tree was cast into the waters, and the waters became sweet, which is a type of the Cross of Christ being placed into the bitterness of our souls. Thus life may be sweetened, if, in the energy of Faith, a Crucified Saviour is introduced into it.

5. The healing mentioned here refers not only to the physical healing of the body, but as well, the spiritual healing of the soul.

6. The refreshment enjoyed at Elim suggests that which would come with the Advent of Christ. The Lord sent out 12 Apostles and 70 others to revive His weary inheritance with the tidings that the Kingdom of Heaven was at hand (Williams).

THE WILDERNESS

Verse 22 reads: *"So Moses brought Israel from the Red Sea, and they went out into the wilderness of Shur; and they went three days in the wilderness, and found no water."*

We must understand, and as previously stated, that the Lord led the Children of Israel into the wilderness. And to be sure, this particular wilderness was about as inhospitable as anything could ever be.

Regrettably, the wilderness experience seemingly is needed by all Christians. First, the trials and testings of the wilderness make manifest the evil of our hearts, and the incurable corruption of the flesh, and this in order that we may be humbled.

Second, the entrance into the inheritance itself is also and solely a matter of sovereign Grace, seeing that there is no worthiness, no *"good thing"* in us.

While the wilderness may and will make manifest the weakness of God's Saints, and, as well, our failures, this is only to magnify the Power and Mercy of Him Who brought us into the place of testing. Further, and we must understand, God always has in view our ultimate good (Pink).

So we find that the *"wilderness"* gives us not only a Revelation of ourselves, but it also makes manifest the Ways of God.

The Children of Israel went *"three days into the wilderness,"* which speaks of Resurrection, for Christ was raised from the dead three days after His burial (I Cor. 15:4).

And yet, despite the Resurrection type, we find that almost immediately, they met with testing — no water, at least that which was useable.

While the world may look very attractive to the unbeliever, to the man of Faith, it is simply a *"wilderness,"* — barren and desolate. No one thinks of making their home in such a place, and neither should the Believer become too attached to this world. It is merely the place through which man journeys from time to eternity. And *"Faith"* it is which makes the difference between the way in which men regard this world.

The wilderness having no water is the first lesson that our experience is designed to teach us. There is nothing down here which can in any wise minister to that life which we have received from Christ. The pleasures of sin, the attractions of the world, no longer satisfy. These things, quite the contrary, which formerly charmed, now repel us. The companionships we use to find so pleasing have become distasteful. The things which delight the ungodly only cause us to groan. In fact, the Christian who is in communion with his Lord finds absolutely nothing around him that will or can refresh his thirsty soul. For him the shallow cisterns of this world have run dry. His cry will be that of the Psalmist: *"O God, You are my God; early will I seek You; my soul thirsts for You, my flesh longs for You in a dry and thirsty land, where no water is"* (Ps. 63:1).

God Alone can satisfy the longings of the heart. That's why Jesus said: *"If any man thirst, let him come unto Me, and drink"* (Jn. 7:37), so must he continue to go to Him Who Alone has the Water of Life (Pink).

We are going to find that the first lesson the Lord teaches the Children of Israel is the lesson of the Cross, just as He taught this lesson to the first family (Gen., Chpt. 4).

BITTER WATERS

Verse 23 reads: *"And when they came to Marah, they could not drink of the waters of Marah, for they were bitter: therefore the name of it was called Marah."*

The word *"Marah"* actually means, *"bitter."* Whether Israel gave it this name, or whether it had already been given this name, we aren't told; however, the likelihood is that it had borne this name for some time.

This is a test of Faith, and as we shall see, Israel didn't meet this test too very well.

In a sense, every single thing that comes the way of the Child of God is a test of sorts. Of course, some of these *"tests"* are of far greater magnitude than others; nevertheless, everything is a test, and we must look at every situation in this light.

How will we react? Will we trust God or murmur and complain?

Great blessings tell us Who God is; adversity tells us what we are!

MURMURING

Verse 24 reads: *"And the people murmured against Moses, saying, What shall we drink?"*

Three days before, the Children of Israel were rejoicing on the shores of the Red Sea. Now, some 72 hours later, they are *"murmuring against Moses,"* which speaks of complaining, and which was to very soon cause them tremendous problems.

Murmuring and complaining present a lack of Faith. But the problem is not so easily recognizable.

Probably one could say without fear of exaggeration, the Children of Israel had Faith, but it was in the wrong object. It seemed to have been in Moses. When everything is going well, he is their hero. At the slightest adversity, the tables turn.

As we shall see, and as the Lord will teach them, their Faith must be in the Cross of Christ. Lacking that, their problems will multiply, and fast. There is only one way to live this life, to walk in victory, to be what God wants us to be, and to have the joy of the Lord, which is the more abundant life promised by Christ, and that is to understand that everything that comes to us as Believers comes totally and completely by and through the Cross of Christ. As we've already said innumerable times, and will continue to say so, the Believer must anchor his Faith in that great Sacrifice. Then the Holy Spirit will work mightily with him, and the Holy Spirit being God, there is nothing He cannot do. The Believer is then guaranteed of success; otherwise, the Believer is guaranteed of failure (Rom. 6:3-14; 8:1-2, 11; I Cor. 1:23; 2:2; Col. 2:14-15).

THE BITTERNESS OF SOUL

The bitterness portrayed here proclaims not only the condition of this present world, but also what it produces. There are untold millions of people who have suffered bitter experiences in life. Many of these have suffered sexual or mental abuse as a child, which has left them emotionally disturbed. As a result, there is bitterness of soul, which without the help of the Lord, that person cannot shake off.

Or, life has dealt the person a bitter blow, with the individual harboring unforgiveness, etc., which occasions bitterness.

To be frank, these are not isolated situations. The problem is actually pandemic. In much of this, many actually hold a grudge against God. They feel that He could have prevented whatever it was that happened, and in their heart of hearts, they harbor resentment against Him.

When we get to Verse 25 of this Fifteenth Chapter of Exodus, I'm going to tell you how to have total and complete victory over this terrible problem. In fact, that which we will relate to you is the only manner of victory, there being no other. But first I want to deal with the manner in which the world attempts to address this problem, which sounds good to the carnal ear, but which in reality is no help at all.

INNER HEALING

From the world of humanistic psychology has come the phrase, *"inner healing,"* which, as stated, sounds good to the carnal mind and ear. And to be frank, there definitely is such a thing as inner healing, but not in the way that humanistic psychology proposes.

While all Psychologists, I suppose, will use the term *"inner healing,"* mostly, each of them has a different interpretation as to how the problem is to be addressed — all of it wrong, and simply because what they are proposing is not the Word of God.

Sadder still, many of those who refer to themselves as Christian Psychologists, actually propose for this malady that the individual in question forgive God.

Whatever nuance or direction the Psychologist might take, almost all of them will seek to delve into the past, as it regards the individual whom they are trying to help. As it should be understood, psychological teaching, which actually had its beginnings in Sigmund Freud, who was inspired by Satan, has no miracle drug, etc., that can be prescribed for the individual. They have only one thing, and that is *"talk."* And if *"talk"* can set the captive free, then Jesus came down to this sinful world, and died in vain (Gal. 2:21).

So they get the individual to regurgitate all of the happenings of the past, which is totally unscriptural. Concerning the past, Paul said: *"Forgetting those things which are behind, and reaching forth unto those things which are before,*

"I press toward the mark for the prize of the High Calling of God in Christ Jesus" (Phil. 3:13-14).

"Talk" has never healed anyone, as ought to be obvious.

NOTES

And then we have, as stated, so-called Christian Psychologists telling people to *"forgive God."* In the first place, God has never done anything untoward toward anyone, so to tell people to forgive Him only exacerbates the problem, putting the person on the road of falsehood and wrong thinking.

One Christian Psychologist uses as his therapeutic tool the practice of *"visualization."* What is that?

VISUALIZATION

The patient (victim, in these circumstances) is urged to visualize certain things. They are to lie quietly with their eyes closed, and visualize themselves standing by a babbling brook, in a beautiful meadow, with tall, stately trees around them. The scene is beautiful and peaceful. They are then to visualize Christ walking toward them, and then speaking softly to them, and putting His arms around them, and thereby, healing them of all of their problems.

Once again, there is nothing of this nature in the Bible. In fact, this is bordering on witchcraft. In some circles, it's called *"white magic."*

The Scripture plainly tells us: *"For whatsoever is not of Faith is sin"* (Rom. 14:23).

So, what is the answer to the terrible problem of bitterness of soul?

THE CROSS

Verse 25 reads: *"And he cried unto the LORD; and the LORD showed him a tree, which when he had cast into the waters, the waters were made sweet: there He made for them a Statute and an Ordinance, and there He proved them."*

For the answer to this dilemma in which Israel now found herself, i.e., *"bitter waters,"* Moses *"cried unto the Lord."*

Let me first of all say, and do so strongly, that there is no help outside of the Lord. And as well, he doesn't need the advice or the counsel of Freud, or any worldly wisdom for that matter. In fact, the Holy Spirit through James plainly said: *"This wisdom descendeth not from above, but is earthly, sensual, Devilish."*

He then said: *"But the wisdom that is from above is first pure, then peaceable, gentle,* and easy to be entreated, full of mercy and good fruits, without partiality, and without hypocrisy" (James 3:15, 17).

Peter said: "According as His Divine Power has given unto us *all* things that pertain unto life and Godliness, through the knowledge of Him Who has called us to glory and virtue:

"Whereby are given unto us exceeding great and precious Promises, that by these you might be partakers of the Divine Nature, having escaped the corruption that is in the world through lust" (II Pet. 1:3-4).

So the Lord has the answer to whatever problems we might have, whatever dilemmas in which we find ourselves, etc.

THE LORD SHOWED HIM A TREE

You don't have to be a Bible Scholar to figure this out. The Lord was showing Moses that the answer to his dilemma was the *"tree."* In fact, the Lord was using the *"tree"* as a type of the Cross.

I remember years ago mentioning this subject, and some Brother after Service tried to tell me how that the chemistry was changed in the water by this particular tree, etc.

The truth is, the Lord by His miracle-working Power, turned the bitter waters sweet. The tree, as far as its chemistry was concerned, had nothing to do with it. The Lord was using that to show Moses that the answer was found in the Cross. Now listen to this:

The Lord had showed Israel that the *"Passover"* delivered them out of Egypt, when nothing else could. It was a Type of Christ and what He would do for us as our Substitute on the Cross. The Red Sea crossing portrays the Believer entering into the great Sacrifice of Christ, as described in Romans 6:3-5). All of this constituted the Salvation process, one might say.

And now that they are delivered from Egypt, no longer under the slave master's whip, and no longer slaves to that despot, the Lord would show them, as the Cross was the answer to their Salvation, as well it is the answer to their Sanctification.

So the first thing that the Lord portrays to Israel through Moses is the Cross of Christ, implying strongly that this is their answer

NOTES

through the wilderness and into the Promised Land.

He's saying the same thing today to the modern Believer. It was the Cross that got them into Salvation, or rather their Faith in that Finished Work, and it is the Cross that will effect their Sanctification, and the Cross Alone.

Peter said: *"The God of our fathers raised up Jesus, Whom you slew and hanged on a tree"* (Acts 5:30).

Paul said: *"And when they had fulfilled all that was written of Him, they took Him down from the tree, and laid Him in a sepulcher"* (Acts 13:29).

The Apostle also said: *"Christ has redeemed us from the curse of the Law, being made a curse for us: for it is written, Cursed is every one who hangs on a tree"* (Gal. 3:13).

Peter also said: *"Who His Own Self bear our sins in His Own Body on the tree, that we, being dead to sins, should live unto Righteousness: by Whose stripes you were healed"* (I Pet. 2:24).

So the Holy Spirit through Moses, referring to the *"tree,"* is picked up by both Peter and Paul, using the same terminology, which applies to the Cross.

THE TREE WAS PUT INTO THE BITTER WATERS

The Believer is to appropriate the benefits of the Cross, which the Lord intends, and to do so on a continuing basis, even day-to-day. I'll tell you how to do that in a moment.

Jesus said: *"If any man will come after Me, let him deny himself* (deny his own ability and strength, etc.) *and take up his cross daily, and follow Me"* (Lk. 9:23).

When He spoke of *"denying oneself,"* He wasn't speaking of asceticism, which is a denial of all things that are pleasurable, etc. Unfortunately, many Christians have come to the conclusion that if it's something enjoyable, then it's sin. No, that has no bearing on what Jesus is saying here. That's what Satan would like to get people to believe, but it simply isn't true.

Living for God is the most exciting, thrilling, wonderful, and glorious life that one could ever live. And we're not under law, but under Grace (Rom. 6:14).

Now notice that He said we must take up our Cross, and even do so on a daily basis. Let's look at the first part of this statement.

"Taking up the Cross," simply means that we understand that everything we need, and in fact, everything that we receive from the Lord, all and without exception comes to us through the Cross of our Lord Jesus Christ.

The word "daily," means that we are to appropriate these blessings afresh and anew every single morning. The Prophet Jeremiah said: "This I recall to my mind, therefore have I hope.

"It is of the LORD's mercies that we are not consumed, because His compassions fail not.

"They are new every morning: great is Thy Faithfulness" (Lam. 3:21-23).

Now the manner in which this is done, or the "how" that we appropriate these benefits, are all by "Faith." Now what do we mean by that?

None of this is a physical or material thing. It is all in the realm of the spiritual, and it is all acquired strictly by Faith.

Now when we say "Faith," always, and without exception, we are speaking of the Believer having Faith in Christ and what Christ has done at the Cross. Paul said:

"Likewise reckon ye also yourselves to be dead indeed unto sin, but alive unto God through Jesus Christ our Lord" (Rom. 6:11).

This is the Believer evidencing Faith in Christ and what Christ has done for us in the Sacrifice of Himself.

Every Believer talks about Faith; however, most Believers do not understand that for our Faith to be recognized by God, its object must always be the Finished Work of Christ. Let me say that again:

It's the object of our Faith that is so very important. In fact, every human being on the face of the Earth has Faith, but it's not faith that God will recognize. The only Faith that He recognizes is Faith in His Son, and our Saviour, the Lord Jesus Christ, and what Christ has done.

ANOTHER JESUS

Almost every Christian will talk about having Faith in Christ. But let the Reader understand that we must comprehend the fact that it is always "Jesus Christ and Him Crucified" (I Cor. 1:23). In other words, if we try to divorce Christ from the Cross, we are in effect, according to the words of Paul, preaching "another Jesus," which the Lord, of course, cannot honor (II Cor. 11:4).

Millions profess to believe in Christ, and the truth is, they aren't properly aligning Christ with the Cross. No, Christ certainly is not still on the Cross, but rather, seated by the Right Hand of the Father in Heaven (Heb. 1:3). And in fact, we are seated with Him in Heavenly Places (Eph. 2:6).

What Paul is talking about, and what Jesus was talking about as it regards taking up the Cross daily, are the benefits of what Christ did on the Cross. I am saved because of what He did at the Cross. I am baptized with the Holy Spirit, because of what He did at the Cross. I am healed, because of what He did at the Cross. I am victorious, because of what He did at the Cross. In fact, everything I receive from the Lord is all made possible, and without exception, through what Jesus did at the Cross. So He must never be separated from the Cross, and if in fact He is separated accordingly, which regrettably many if not most Churches do, then pure and simple, we have accepted "another Jesus, which is put forth by another spirit, which projects another Gospel" (II Cor. 11:4).

If it's not "Jesus Christ and Him Crucified," then it's not the Gospel!

So by Faith, we put the Cross into the bitter waters of our life.

THE HEALING

The Scripture then says, "The waters were made sweet." This means that the Lord can turn the bitterness in your heart and life into that which is sweet. And in fact, He Alone can do this.

As you read these words, you may think that such is beyond reach. Well, it is beyond our reach as it regards our own personal strength; however, it's definitely not beyond the reach of our Lord. In fact, this is not something that He has to do in the future; He has already healed the bitterness in your heart, and all you have to do is simply appropriate it by Faith, in the manner in which we have described to you.

Some may ask the question, *"Will everything change immediately?"*

There will definitely be a change immediately in your heart and life, as you begin to realize, as the Spirit bears witness with your spirit, that you are now on the right track. However, it may take some time for the healing to be complete. Actually, the very word *"healing,"* refers to a process. But the truth is:

You are now on the right road, and while everything may not change immediately as it regards the situation, it will definitely change, even though it possibly will do so little by little. And then again, with some, the change regarding *"bitterness,"* may happen immediately. It has with untold thousands, and it may very well happen with you.

But that's not the point. The point is, Jesus has already healed these bitter waters, and once your Faith is anchored firmly in Him and what He did at the Cross, ever making that the object of your Faith, you are guaranteed of victory (Rom. 8:1-2, 11).

THE STATUTE AND THE ORDINANCE

The phrase, *"There He made for them a Statute and an Ordinance, and there He proved them,"* refers to the Promise of the next Verse.

The word *"proved them,"* refers to the testing of their Faith. Regrettably, they didn't come out too well, but rather murmured and complained against Moses; however, God is merciful and gracious, and didn't overthrow them, just as He is merciful and gracious to us. Thank God He is, or we wouldn't be here.

HEALING

Verse 26 reads: *"And said, If you will diligently hearken to the voice of the LORD your God, and will do that which is right in His sight, and will give ear to His Commandments, and keep all His Statutes, I will put none of these diseases upon you, which I have brought upon the Egyptians: for I am the LORD Who heals you."*

We learn several things from this Verse of Scripture.

The Lord tells Israel, and all of us as well, that we must keep *"all His Commandments and Statutes."* He didn't say *"some,"* but rather *"all."*

Now the truth is, no human being has ever done this, other than Christ. So this means that in the sight of God, we are shot down, so to speak, before we ever begin.

To receive the benefits of the Cross, I am obligated to do this which He commands. These are the conditions, and they will not be altered. So what am I to do?

I am to understand that my Salvation and my Victory don't lie within my own perfection, or the lack thereof. So if all of this is not in me, where is it?

All that I need is in Christ. Our Lord has kept every single Commandment and Statute, and has done so impeccably, and has done so all of the time. He is my Substitute and my Representative Man (I Cor. 15:45-50). My trust and Faith in Him grants to me, and does so automatically and immediately, all of His victory. Let's say it another way:

GOD DOESN'T GIVE VICTORY TO MEN, ONLY TO CHRIST

This is where we make our mistake. We think, in essence, that He is giving victory to us. While we certainly are recipients of victory, it is not actually to us that all of this is given. It is to Christ. God blesses Christ, and our Faith in Him grants us all the blessings that He has been given. All the victory is in Christ, and my Faith in Him, and my Faith in Him Alone, grants me His victory. In fact, this is the idea of the entire Salvation process. It is all in Christ, or it is nothing at all!

Therefore, I can stand before the Lord and honestly say that through Christ and in Christ, I have kept every single Commandment and Statute. I sense greatly the Presence of the Lord, even as I dictate these words. Listen again to Paul:

"And you are complete in Him, which is the Head of all principality and power" (Col. 2:10).

And then again: *"That ye may stand perfect and complete in all the Will of God"* (Col. 4:12).

DISEASES

The phrase, *"I will put none of these diseases*

upon you, which I have brought upon the Egyptians," proclaims the fact that the Lord is in charge of all things.

While sickness and disease originated with the Fall in the Garden of Eden, and has come upon the human race because of sin, this is all because of a decree from the Lord.

Some Christians act like the Lord answers to the Devil. It's the other way around. Satan answers to God! In other words, whatever it is that Satan wants to do, he can do only as the Lord gives him permission to do so. To be sure, he is not running loose, but is rather subject to the Lord at all times (Job, Chpts. 1-2).

Because of the idol worship of the Egyptians, the Lord caused certain diseases to come upon them. It is no different presently!

When men ignore God, they reap the results of their actions. While the Lord may use Satan as an instrument, which He often does, still, it is the Lord Who does the directing in all things.

The Lord can withhold blessings, and He can bestow blessings. It is all predicated on the individual, and whether our Faith is properly in Christ or otherwise! Even then, our Faith must be tested, and great Faith must be tested greatly.

THE HEALING POWER OF GOD

The phrase, *"For I am the LORD Who heals you,"* proclaims the fact that He is the Healer, and He Alone is the Healer. The name *"Lord"* in the Hebrew, as used here, is actually *"Jehovah-Ropheka,"* which means, *"Jehovah, the Healer."* So, the Lord revealed Himself here to Moses, and to the Children of Israel, in a more graphic way. He is telling them that He is now their Healer. What a comfort that must have been!

And let the Reader understand that while in fact they were in a wilderness, and that it was unpleasant to say the least, this is where God would reveal Himself to His people, even in a more advanced way. They had known Him as the Deliverer; now they know Him as the Healer as well!

Let the Reader also understand that as this Promise was given to Moses and the Children of Israel some 3,600 years ago, it is still just as appropriate now, as it was then. God does

NOTES

not change, simply because He cannot change, and we refer to His attributes. Whatever blessing He promised then, He promises now, and in fact, will ever do so.

A PERSONAL HEALING

The Promise of Healing is very real to me on a personal basis. If I remember correctly, the year was 1945, which means that I was 10 years old.

I had some type of physical problem, which the doctors did not seem to be able to find. My parents, in fact, took me to several doctors, but all to no avail. They ruled out malaria, plus other things, and seemed to be able to come to no satisfactory diagnosis.

I stayed nauseous constantly, and would at times go unconscious. Actually, I *"passed out"* several times at school. The last time it happened, the Principal told my parents, when they were called to come get me, *"Something is going to have to be done for Jimmy. And if something is not done, you're going to have to take him out of school."* The Principal then said, *"We don't want him dying on our hands."*

That's how critical that it was, and regrettably, the doctors, as stated, did not seem to be able to help.

PRAYER

I had been anointed with oil and prayed for any number of times by our Pastor, and others in the Church, but seemingly to no avail. But of the following, I am very thankful.

I'm so glad that we attended a Church where the Pastor believed that Jesus Christ still healed the sick. Had I not been a part of such a Church, I probably would not be alive today, for I believe that Satan was trying to kill me.

On the particular day in question, the day of my healing, Service had ended, and my parents were taking the Pastor and his wife out to lunch. Of course, my baby sister and myself were among the group.

But before going to lunch, they were to go by the home of one of the members of the Church, who had been ill, and had not been able to be in Service that morning. They lived in a very humble dwelling, and I remember us going to the bedroom, which was at the back, and the Pastor laying hands on the dear Brother, and praying for him.

As everyone walked back toward the front of the house, all of us stopped in the front room, in fact bidding the lady of the house goodbye, and saying something encouraging to her about her husband who was ill.

I was standing near the door, with the Pastor standing behind me, and my Dad to his left. This scene is forever freeze-framed in my mind.

Dad said to the Pastor, *"Brother Culbreth, anoint Jimmy with oil, and pray for him."* He further added, *"If the Lord doesn't do something for him, we're going to have to take him out of school."*

Brother Culbreth was standing there with the little bottle of oil in his hand, with which he had just anointed the Brother for whom he had come to pray.

He smiled and walked toward me. He turned the bottle of oil upside-down, whereas a small amount was released onto his finger, and he anointed my head and began to pray.

Now as stated, he had done this any number of times. So the question could be asked, why didn't the Lord heal me the other times?

I really don't have the answer to that, and I don't think anyone else does. We could say that He was testing our Faith, and possibly that is so. But as a 10 year old child, I didn't know that much about Faith, but I did know that the Lord was the Healer.

I think there are many questions which we have as it regards the Lord and the *"how"* of His doing of things. The Lord's Ways are not our ways, but this I do know of which the Bible teaches:

It teaches that Jesus Christ is still the Healer (I Pet. 2:24). And as well, the Lord taught us that if we don't get the answer at first, to keep knocking (Lk. 11:5-13).

THE HEALING

The moment the Pastor anointed me with oil, he at the same time began to pray, along with all others in the room. And then it happened!

I felt something like a hot ball of fire start at the top of my head, and then slowly go down through the entirety of my body, even down to my feet. I knew beyond the shadow of a doubt that I was healed. I knew that I would never have that sickness again, and that's exactly what happened. I've never had that problem again, not in any capacity.

Does this mean that everyone who truly receives healing from the Lord will experience a heat-like feeling go through their physical body? No, it doesn't, but some do! We could also ask the question, does God always heal according to our Faith? In other words, is the amount of Faith we have always the barometer?

No, it isn't! While Faith is certainly required, to be sure, the Lord is not sitting up in Heaven, refusing to heal us because we need five percent more Faith. Such thinking is silly! But unfortunately, many Preachers teach such error.

I cannot honestly answer as to why the Lord sometimes heals, and sometimes doesn't. I cannot answer as to why we are prayed for several times for the same problem, and receive no healing, and then seemingly out of the blue, just as the Lord did with me, prayer is answered, and we are healed.

All I know is this: the Lord is still in the healing business. In fact, He is still in the miracle-working business as well! While He doesn't always heal, I thank God for the times He does heal.

While I'm on the subject, I think it might be proper to make a few statements regarding some of the modern claims that are made as it respects healing and miracles.

The Lord, as should be obvious, receives no glory out of false claims. As well, the Preacher pronouncing people as healed, when there is no physical evidence that such has occurred, once again, doesn't bring Glory to God. The problem is, almost all of these people treated thusly are, in fact, not healed.

It hurts the cause of Christ, for a Preacher before thousands of people, to announce to that congregation that the dear soul standing before him, who incidentally is dying with cancer, is healed, when there is, in fact, no physical proof. Almost every time, those people, at least those of my acquaintance, have died. And yet it seems that the Church asks few questions, because they have been taught that to question such a Preacher about such practices, constitutes rebellion. In fact, it is actually taught that such individuals are above question.

When Preachers put themselves in such a position, and it is for certain that they have put themselves there, because the Lord surely hasn't, such is a sure sign that what they are doing is not of God. Any and every Believer, providing they are in a right spirit, has the Scriptural right to question what is done, that is, if it doesn't seem to be proper. And any true Preacher of the Gospel will welcome such scrutiny.

In fact, it is my belief that being prayed for by such Preachers, whomever they might be, not only doesn't help the individual in question, but in fact, can cause greater sickness. Listen to what Paul said:

"Wherefore whosoever shall eat this bread, and drink this cup of the Lord (the Lord's Supper), *unworthily, shall be guilty of the Body and Blood of the Lord.*

"But let a man examine himself, and so let him eat of that bread, and drink of that cup.

"For he who eats and drinks unworthily, eats and drinks damnation to himself, not discerning the Lord's Body.

"For this cause many are weak and sickly among you, and many sleep" (I Cor. 11:27-30).

Paul has made some serious charges here. He has said that if we do not properly discern the Lord's Body, sickness can be the result, and even premature death. Even though the person will not lose their soul, they will definitely have their life shortened. In fact, he used the term *"many sleep,"* which means that many were subject to this situation, which should give us pause for thought.

When he spoke of Believers being *"guilty of the Body and Blood of the Lord,"* he was meaning that such a Believer was not properly *"discerning the Lord's Body."*

For the Believer to properly discern the Lord's Body is to understand that everything he has from the Lord has come to him solely and completely through the Cross of Christ, on which Jesus died.

How does all this translate?

It means if the Preacher who prays for you isn't basing all that he does on the Sacrifice of Christ, he very well could be functioning with *"another spirit,"* and in fact, it is just about guaranteed that he is functioning accordingly (II Cor. 11:4). While thousands in the Church are clamoring for some particular Preacher to lay hands on them, the truth is, oftentimes, instead of bringing healing, it brings the very opposite.

But despite all of this, and we speak of the false claims, etc., the Lord is still the Healer, and the Believer is encouraged by the Word of God to ardently seek the Lord as it regards our needs, irrespective as to what they might be, and He has promised, in His Own Way, to answer (Lk. 11:5-13).

TWELVE WELLS OF WATER AND SEVENTY PALM TREES

Verse 27 reads: *"And they came to Elim, where were twelve wells of water, and threescore and ten palm trees: and they encamped there by the waters."*

This Passage carries a spiritual significance of what was to come in the future. Even though Israel would not have seen it then, looking back, we can see it now.

First of all, the *"twelve wells of water"* speak of the twelve Apostles who would be chosen by Christ, and on which, in a sense, the New Covenant would be built. The Scripture says: *"Now therefore you are no more strangers and foreigners, but fellow-citizens with the Saints, and of the Household of God;*

"And are built upon the foundation of the Apostles and Prophets, Jesus Christ Himself being the Chief Cornerstone;

"In Whom all the building fitly framed together groweth unto an Holy Temple in the Lord:

"In Whom you also are built together for an habitation of God through the Spirit" (Eph. 2:19-22).

The *"twelve wells of waters,"* symbolizing the *"Twelve Apostles,"* also symbolize the Government of God, for the number of government is *"twelve."* There were Twelve Tribes of Israel, Twelve Apostles, and the City, New Jerusalem, is twelve thousand furlongs square. As well, it has a wall with twelve foundations, on which are written the names of the Twelve Apostles of the Lamb. The wall is pierced by twelve gates, with twelve Angels standing at the twelve gates. As stated, *"Twelve"* portrays the Government of God. That Government is based on *"Apostles,"* and *"Prophets,"* which callings continue unto this hour.

The seventy Palm Trees are symbolic of Ministry, which must be built on the foundation of the Apostles and Prophets, Jesus Christ Himself, being the Chief Cornerstone.

The Scripture tells us that Jesus *"appointed other seventy also, and sent them two and two before His face into every city and place, whither He Himself would come"* (Lk. 10:1).

Luke added to that by saying: *"And the seventy returned again with joy, saying, Lord, even the Devils are subject unto us through Thy Name"* (Lk. 10:17).

THE ENCAMPMENT

The phrase, *"And they encamped there by the waters,"* signals the place in which the Believer is to rest. If we pitch our tent *"there"* so to speak, this will be according to the Word of God, and in the midst of this weary world, we will find relaxation, joy, peace, and serenity. This is what Jesus was speaking of when He said: *"Come unto Me, all who labor and are heavy laden, and I will give you rest"* (Mat. 11:28).

As long as the Doctrine is *"Jesus Christ and Him Crucified,"* which speaks of the foundation, typed by the *"twelve wells of water,"* and the Ministry, typed by the *"threescore and ten Palm Trees,"* Christ will be found in all His Glory, and will be to the Believer what He desires to be.

"O listen to our wondrous story,
"Counted once among the lost;
"Yes, One came down from Heaven's glory,
"Saving us at awful cost!"

"No Angel could His place have taken,
"Highest of the high though He;
"The loved One on the Cross forsaken
"Was one of the Godhead three!"

"Will you surrender to this Saviour?
"To His scepter humbly bow?
"You, too, shall come to know His favor,
"He will save you, save you now."

NOTES

CHAPTER 16

(1) "AND THEY TOOK THEIR JOURNEY FROM ELIM, AND ALL THE CONGREGATION OF THE CHILDREN OF ISRAEL CAME INTO THE WILDERNESS OF SIN, WHICH IS BETWEEN ELIM AND SINAI, ON THE FIFTEENTH DAY OF THE SECOND MONTH AFTER THEIR DEPARTING OUT OF THE LAND OF EGYPT."

(2) "AND THE WHOLE CONGREGATION OF THE CHILDREN OF ISRAEL MURMURED AGAINST MOSES AND AARON IN THE WILDERNESS:"

(3) "AND THE CHILDREN OF ISRAEL SAID UNTO THEM, WOULD TO GOD WE HAD DIED BY THE HAND OF THE LORD IN THE LAND OF EGYPT, WHEN WE SAT BY THE FLESH POTS, AND WHEN WE DID EAT BREAD TO THE FULL: FOR YOU HAVE BROUGHT US FORTH INTO THIS WILDERNESS, TO KILL THIS WHOLE ASSEMBLY WITH HUNGER."

The composition is:

1. The First Verse tells us that the Children of Israel had been on the road exactly one month, having left Egypt the fifteenth of the first month. This indicates that they moved slowly, and stopped perhaps several days at a time. About ten or more days would bring them to Sinai.

2. Verses 2 and 3 once again proclaim that the *"Children of Israel murmured."* It does not take very much to cause the average person or congregation to murmur. The slightest temporary lack of water, food, clothing, money, or convenience will test the mettle of every man. Regrettably, the best will finally complain if the pressure increases beyond normal.

3. The *"wilderness of Sin,"* which is between Elim, the place of the *"waters,"* and *"Sinai,"* the place of the *"Law,"* proves a very marked and interesting position — a position of failure no less, visited by Grace.

4. In Grace, there is no hindrance. The streams of blessing that emanate from the Lord flow onward without interruption. It is only when man puts himself under law that he forfeits everything; for then God

must allow him to prove how much he can claim on the ground of his own works.

THE WILDERNESS OF SIN

Verse 1 reads: *"And they took their journey from Elim, and all the congregation of the Children of Israel came unto the wilderness of Sin, which is between Elim and Sinai, on the fifteenth day of the second month after their departing out of the land of Egypt."*

It must be remembered that *"the Pillar of the Cloud"* led them in this direction. It was a direction that seemed to be most inhospitable.

The statement, *"came unto the wilderness of Sin,"* implies that they were not quite yet in this wilderness, but near.

Concerning this position that Israel now finds herself, which is a position of difficulty, it is all a test, just as it is a test with us presently. What would Israel do? How would Israel act?

Here, for the first time, the full privation of the desert stared the people fully in the face. Every step they took was now leading them farther away from the inhabited countries, and conducting them deeper into the land of desolation, and even seeing death.

The isolation of the wilderness presents the courage and Faith of Moses in bringing a multitude of at least three million people into such a howling waste. It demonstrates his firm confidence in the Lord God; and yet, some of the times would prove to even being trying for him.

Moses was not ignorant of the desert and its demands. He had lived for 40 years in its immediate vicinity (Ex. 3:1), and, therefore, he knew full well that only a miracle, even a series of miracles, could meet the vast needs of such a multitude. In this his Faith was superior to that of Abraham (Gen. 12:10).

THE FIFTEENTH DAY OF THE SECOND MONTH

Why did the Holy Spirit through Moses think it significant to record the exact date as given here? As a matter of history, it seems of little interest or importance. What difference does it make to us today which month and what day of the month it was when Israel entered the wilderness of Sin?

However, the very fact that the Holy Spirit has recorded this detail is sufficient proof it is not meaningless. In fact, there is nothing trivial in the Word of God. Every single word contains Divine purpose and significance.

It was on the *"second month"* that they went out. In Scripture *"two"* speaks of *"witness"* or *"testimony"* (Rev. 11:3). As well, it was the *"fifteenth day"* of the month. The factors of fifteen are *"five"* and *"three."* In Scripture, *"five"* signifies *"Grace or favor"* (Gen. 43:34), and *"three"* is the number of *"manifestations"* — hence the number of *"Resurrection,"* when life is fully manifested. By combining these definitions, we learn that God was now to give unto Israel a witness and manifestation of His Grace.

In order for Grace to shine forth, there must first be the dark background of sin. Grace is unmerited favor, and to enhance its glory the demerits of man must be exhibited. *"It is where sin abounded that Grace did much more abound"* (Rom. 5:20). Very shortly we will have an exhibition, regrettably so, of their sin; but overriding this, the Lord, through Grace, will do great and mighty things.

MURMURING

Verse 2 reads: *"And the whole congregation of the Children of Israel murmured against Moses and Aaron in the wilderness."*

Despite the fact of the Lord sweetening the bitter waters of Marah, pressure is now applied, and Israel responds very negatively. They *"murmur against Moses and Aaron"*; but it should be understood, if we murmur against God's man or woman, we have, in effect, murmured against God. And that's exactly the way the Lord looks at the situation. We as Believers must be very careful how we speak of any Believer; however, we must be especially careful as to how we speak of those on whom God has truly laid His Hand.

Concerning this situation, Pink said: *"Here was the selfsame people who had been Divinely spared from the ten plagues on Egypt, who had been brought forth from the land of bondage, miraculously delivered at the Red Sea, Divinely guided by a Pillar of Cloud and Fire, day and night —*

now *'murmuring,' complaining, rebelling!"*

More than likely, a few began murmuring, with others picking it up, until the Scripture says that the *"whole congregation"* was murmuring against Moses and Aaron.

How different the scene would have been, had the people begun praising God! Let the Reader understand that whatever it is we do, in one way or the other, will be contagious. If we murmur and complain, some around us will do the same. If we speak positive, some will do that as well.

While praise is contagious, I'm concerned that murmuring is even far more contagious. It is somewhat like a small fire kindling a bonfire.

James said: *"And the tongue is a fire, a world of iniquity, so is the tongue among our members, that it defileth the whole body, and sets on fire the course of nature; and it is set on fire of Hell.*

"But the tongue can no man tame; it is an unruly evil, full of deadly poison.

"Therewith bless we God, even the Father; and therewith curse we men, which are made after the similitude of God.

"Out of the same mouth proceeds blessing and cursing. My Brethren, these things ought not so to be.

"Does a fountain send forth at the same place sweet water and bitter?" (James 3:6, 8-11).

Even though man cannot tame the tongue, which refers to such being brought to pass by one's own strength and ability, the Lord definitely can accomplish this task — but He is the only One Who can!

THE CROSS

This problem is to be addressed, and it is a very serious problem, exactly as every other problem is to be addressed, by understanding that our victory comes solely through the Cross, i.e., *"what Jesus did there!"* It is the Holy Spirit Who Alone can develop proper fruit within our lives (Gal. 5:22-23).

The Holy Spirit functions within the parameters, and those parameters exclusively, of the Finished Work of Christ. It is all *"in Christ"* (Rom. 8:1-2).

We are obligated to do one thing, and one thing only, and that is to ever exhibit Faith in Christ and His great Sacrifice of Himself (Rom. 6:3-5; 8:1-2, 11; Gal. 5:5-6).

It is ever by Faith, which refers to Faith in Christ and His Sacrifice.

Following this prescribed order, the Holy Spirit can then work grandly within our lives, bringing about the Fruit of the Spirit, and, thereby, making us what we ought to be in Christ. We are then the overcomer, our *"condition"* being brought up to our *"position."* In other words, our *"state"* now comes up to our *"standing."*

THE OATH

Verse 3 reads: *"And the Children of Israel said unto them, Would to God we had died by the Hand of the LORD in the land of Egypt, when we sat by the flesh pots, and when we did eat bread to the full; for you have brought us forth into this wilderness, to kill this whole assembly with hunger."*

As we read these words, we are reading an *"oath."* This means that their sin was aggravated by an oath; they took the Divine Name *"in vain,"* when they said that they *"would to God we had died by the Hand of the LORD in the land of Egypt."*

As well, every evidence is they lied also. As slaves of the merciless Egyptians, there is no ground whatsoever for us to suppose that they *"sat by the fleshpots"* or *"ate bread to the full."*

To accuse Moses and Aaron of bringing them into the wilderness that they might die with hunger was, in effect, as stated, accusing God. It was *"Jehovah,"* not simply Moses and Aaron, Who had brought them forth; and He had promised that they should worship Him at Sinai (Ex. 3:12); consequently, it was not possible then, for them to die with hunger in the wilderness.

(4) "THEN SAID THE LORD UNTO MOSES, BEHOLD, I WILL RAIN BREAD FROM HEAVEN FOR YOU; AND THE PEOPLE SHALL GO OUT AND GATHER A CERTAIN RATE EVERY DAY, THAT I MAY PROVE THEM, WHETHER THEY WILL WALK IN MY LAW, OR NO.

(5) "AND IT SHALL COME TO PASS, THAT ON THE SIXTH DAY THEY SHALL PREPARE THAT WHICH THEY BRING IN; AND IT SHALL BE TWICE AS MUCH AS THEY GATHER DAILY.

(6) "AND MOSES AND AARON SAID UNTO ALL THE CHILDREN OF ISRAEL, AT EVENING, THEN YOU SHALL KNOW THAT THE LORD HAS BROUGHT YOU OUT FROM THE LAND OF EGYPT:

(7) "AND IN THE MORNING, THEN YOU SHALL SEE THE GLORY OF THE LORD; FOR THAT HE HEARS YOUR MURMURINGS AGAINST THE LORD: AND WHAT ARE WE, THAT YOU MURMUR AGAINST US?

(8) "AND MOSES SAID, THIS SHALL BE, WHEN THE LORD SHALL GIVE YOU IN THE EVENING FLESH TO EAT, AND IN THE MORNING BREAD TO THE FULL; FOR THAT THE LORD HEARS YOUR MURMURINGS WHICH YOU MURMUR AGAINST HIM: AND WHAT ARE WE? YOUR MURMURINGS ARE NOT AGAINST US, BUT AGAINST THE LORD.

(9) "AND MOSES SPOKE UNTO AARON, SAY UNTO ALL THE CONGREGATION OF THE CHILDREN OF ISRAEL, COME NEAR BEFORE THE LORD: FOR HE HAS HEARD YOUR MURMURINGS.

(10) "AND IT CAME TO PASS, AS AARON SPOKE UNTO THE WHOLE CONGREGATION OF THE CHILDREN OF ISRAEL, THAT THEY LOOKED TOWARD THE WILDERNESS, AND, BEHOLD, THE GLORY OF THE LORD APPEARED IN THE CLOUD."

The composition is:

1. The murmurings of Verses 6 through 8 proclaim that God hears and sees all the acts of man and will hold each person responsible as to *"right"* and *"wrong"* in every detail (I Cor. 3:11-15).

2. The Manna prefigured the descent of the True Bread, of which if a man eat he shall live forever (Jn. 6:51).

3. All of this was a test of appetite and of obedience. In Egypt, Israel had slave food; in the desert, Angels' food; and the test quickly revealed that the natural man has no appetite for heavenly things.

BREAD FROM HEAVEN

Verse 4 reads: *"Then said the LORD unto Moses, Behold, I will rain bread from Heaven for you; and the people shall go out and gather a certain rate every day, that I may prove them, whether they will walk in My Law, or no."*

The Holy Spirit referred to the sustenance as *"Bread from Heaven."* As stated, it was a Type of Christ, and the instructions given will portray how we are to address Christ.

As the Manna came from Heaven, likewise, Christ, of Whom it is a Type, came from Heaven also. As *"bread"* satisfies the hunger, likewise, Christ does the same. And in fact, Christ Alone can satisfy the hunger of the soul.

Exactly as to what type of nutriments this *"Bread from Heaven"* contained, we aren't told; nevertheless, it provided everything the human body needs, exactly as Christ provides everything the soul needs.

The people had to gather *"a certain rate every day,"* proclaiming the fact to us that we are to partake of Christ every day. He is there for the taking, so to speak, and He will satisfy the longing of the soul.

Unfortunately, some people go through a *"ceremony,"* or a *"ritual,"* thinking that constitutes the acceptance of Christ. It doesn't! Accepting Christ is done by Faith, meaning that we accept Him as Lord and Saviour, realizing that He Alone can meet our need, and as we believe in what He has done for us at the Cross, He, through the Power and Person of the Holy Spirit, comes into our hearts and lives to abide, and to abide forever (Jn. 14:16-20).

Also, the people had to go out and gather the Manna, proclaiming the fact that Faith must be exercised in order for Christ to be real within our lives.

PROVE THEM?

As we've already stated, everything the Lord does with us is to *"prove us."* How will we act? How will we react?

Israel should have understood that it was infinitely better to be in the desert with God than in the brickkilns with Pharaoh. But no; the human heart finds it immensely difficult to give God credit for pure and perfect love. It has, regrettably, far more confidence in Satan than God.

Look, for a moment, at all the sorrow and suffering, the misery and degradation, which man has endured by reason of his having hearkened to the voice of Satan; and yet he never gives utterance to a word of complaint of his service, or of desire to escape from under his hand. He is not discontented with Satan, or weary of serving him. Again and again he reaps bitter fruit in those fields that Satan has thrown open to him, and yet again and again he may be seen sowing the selfsame seed, and undergoing the selfsame labors.

But how different it is in reference to God! Ten thousand mercies are forgotten in the presence of a single trifling privation. He has done so much for us, which should cause us to praise Him forever, beginning right now; however, as stated, the slightest problem arises, which may in fact turn out to be a great blessing to us, but instead, we murmur and complain.

Nothing is more dishonoring to God than the manifestation of a complaining spirit on the part of those who belong to Him. The Apostle gives it as a special mark of Gentile corruption that: *"When they knew God, they glorified Him not as God, neither were thankful."* Then follows the practical result of this unthankful spirit — *"They became vain in their imaginations, and their foolish heart was darkened"* (Rom. 1:21).

This means that the heart that ceases to retain a thankful sense of God's goodness will speedily become *"dark."*

For Israel to know and understand the meaning and supply of this Heavenly Food, they needed a heart that was weaned from Egypt's influences. This had to be, for them to be satisfied with or enjoy *"Bread from Heaven."*

MODERN BELIEVERS

While the Believer must be in the world, we are definitely not to be of the world.

John plainly told us that the world is our enemy. He said: *"Love not the world, neither the things that are in the world. If any man love the world, the love of the Father is not in him.*

"For all that is in the world, the lust of the flesh, and the lust of the eyes, and the pride of life, is not of the Father, but is of the world."

And then: *"And the world passes away, and the lusts thereof: but he who does the Will of God abideth forever"* (I Jn. 2:15-17).

At least one of the greatest sins of the Church is the use of the world in order to attract people. What they seemingly fail to realize is, it doesn't matter how many are attracted in this fashion, none will be drawn to the Lord. The Holy Spirit, as should be obvious, doesn't use the world, or anything in the world, as far as its spirit is concerned, to draw men to Christ. In fact, and as stated, the moment the spirit of the world is engaged, the Holy Spirit will close the door.

THE TWO METHODS OF DESTRUCTION REGARDING THE CHURCH

The first method that Satan uses is to stop the Preacher from preaching the Cross. That done, he knows that the Christian is, for all practical purposes, defenseless. And regrettably, Satan has been successful in virtually closing down the preaching of the Cross. As a result, the Church doesn't know where it's been, where it is, or where it's going. In fact, it's never been in worse condition than it is now.

Second, the Spirit of the world, in the form of the music being presented by many, if not most, Churches, is completely destroying the young people, which are supposed to be the Church of tomorrow.

What type of spiritual climate is it whenever scores of Church busses line up in front of a night club, in order for the kids to hear some so-called Christian Rock group, when in reality, they are Christian just about as much as I'm President of the United States.

It's hard to blame the kids for this abomination, and an abomination it is. The Preachers are to be blamed. In fact, the modern Church is exactly like Israel of old, *"sheep without a shepherd."*

For Preachers to expose their kids to such demon-inspired direction is the same as feeding poison to an individual. In fact, it's worse, because it will not only cause physical wreckage, but the loss of the soul as well.

Jesus called such spiritual leaders, *"snakes."* He said: *"You serpents, you generation of vipers, how can you escape the damnation of Hell?"* (Mat. 23:33).

So the Devil has succeeded in pulling the

Church away from the Cross, which makes it very easy to introduce the spirit of the world, which he has very successfully done.

To mix the world with Christ will not work, as mixing Egypt with Israel would not work. In fact, the Lord purposely took them into the wilderness, in order that all remnants of Egypt would be purged from them. Even then, the problem persisted of the Children of Israel desiring to go back to Egypt, which seemed to be their response to most problems.

Can you imagine, desiring to go back to slavery! But that continues to be the problem of the human race.

The Lord must *"prove them,"* in order to see as to whether they will walk in His Law, or not. Regrettably they didn't, and that generation perished in the wilderness.

THE SIXTH DAY

Verse 5 reads: *"And it shall come to pass, that on the sixth day they shall prepare that which they bring in; and it shall be twice as much as they gather daily."*

The period of seven days was known to the Children of Israel as a week, and which appeared in the story of Jacob and Laban (Gen. 29:27).

There is little or no record that they called their days by specific names as we do presently, but rather by numbers. So it seems that the week actually began with the first day that the Manna was given. On the seventh day, the Lord instituted the Sabbath, which we will find later in this Chapter.

It seems they were to gather twice as much on the sixth day, as they had done on the previous days, but which the Lord would miraculously multiply, in order that they may have sustenance the next day, on which they would not be allowed to do any work.

This tells us that Christ, the True Bread of Life, will be enough for us, not only during the normal times, but as well, during times when it seems as though He has sent no provision. He has in fact sent provision, and enough for all, irrespective of the need.

As the Manna also had some type of miracle quality, as stated, which could cause it to multiply or diminish, irrespective as to what was gathered, likewise, Christ is to the person exactly as He ought to be. He is the giver of miracles, and will perform graciously and constantly for all Believers, at least those who will stand upon His Promises, or else He can withhold Blessings.

THE GLORY OF THE LORD

Verses 6 and 7 read: *"And Moses and Aaron said unto all the Children of Israel, At evening, then you shall know that the LORD has brought you out from the land of Egypt:*

"And in the morning, then you shall see the Glory of the LORD; for that He hears your murmurings against the LORD: and what are we, that you murmur against us?"

The *"evening"* of which Moses speaks here, when he said, *"Then you shall know,"* probably refers to the descent of the quails. Moses must have received a distinct intimation of the coming arrival of the quails, though he has not recorded it. In fact, it seems that he seldom recorded both the Divine Message and his delivery of it. In general, he places upon record either the Message only, or its delivery only.

While they would see the arrival of the quails in the evening, the next morning, they would see the Manna. All of this is referred to as the *"Glory of the Lord."*

In fact, Israel in Bible times, counted their day as beginning at about 6 p.m., with the *"evening"* being the beginning, and the morning, beginning at about 6 a.m., being the ending, the very opposite of our present view. It would conclude about 6 p.m. when the new day began. In fact, that's the way the Lord described it in the Genesis, Chapter 1 account, *"And the evening and the morning were the first day,"* etc. (Gen. 1:5).

Moses attempts to impress upon the people that their murmurings against he and Aaron were actually against the Lord. They asked the question, *"What are we, that you murmur against us?"*

In essence, he was saying, *"What power have we of our own? We have no hereditary rank, no fixed definite position. We are simply the leaders whom you have chosen to follow, because you believed us to have a commission from God. Apart from this, we are nobodies. But, if our commission is conceded, we are to you in the place of God;*

and to murmur against us is to murmur against Jehovah."

MURMURINGS

Verses 8 and 9 read: *"And Moses said, This shall be, when the LORD shall give you in the evening flesh to eat, and in the morning bread to the full; for that the LORD hears your murmurings which you murmur against Him: and what are we? Your murmurings are not against us, but against the LORD.*

"And Moses spoke unto Aaron, Say unto all the congregation of the Children of Israel, Come near before the LORD: for He has heard your murmurings."

Verse 8 is basically a repetition of Verse 7; but it emphasizes the statements of that Verse, and prepares the way for what follows (Pulpit).

When looking back toward Egypt, Israel murmured; when looking forward toward the wilderness, they saw the Glory of the Lord.

Discontent magnifies what is past, and vilifies what is present, without regard to truth or reason. The absurd then murmurs!

The Lord takes notice of the people's complaints. As a God of pity, He took cognizance of their necessity, which was the occasion of their murmuring; as a Just and Holy God, He took cognizance of their base and unworthy reflections upon His servant Moses, and was much displeased with them. When we begin to fret and to be uneasy, we ought to consider that God hears all our murmurings, though silent, or only the murmurings of the heart.

Those in positions of leadership do not hear all the murmurs of those whom they are attempting to lead. It is well that we do not, perhaps because we could not bear it: but God hears, and yet bears.

We must not think, because God does not immediately take vengeance on men for their sins that, therefore, He does not notice them. He hears the murmurings of Israel, and is grieved with this generation, and yet continues His care of them, as the tender parent of a froward child (Henry).

THE CLOUD

Verse 10 reads: *"And it came to pass, as Aaron spoke unto the whole congregation of the Children of Israel, that they looked toward the wilderness, and, behold, the Glory of the LORD appeared in the cloud."*

The Tenth Verse seems to indicate that the Lord had commanded Moses that the entirety of the Children of Israel should present themselves as a *"whole congregation"* to the Lord, hence the appearance of the Lord to the congregation in the cloud.

The Scripture says that *"they looked toward the wilderness,"* which means they were on the edge of that vast wasteland. But yet, the wilderness is where the *"Lord appeared in the cloud."*

Wherever the Lord is, that's where I want to be. Of course, we now realize that due to the Cross, the Lord, through the Person of the Holy Spirit, is with us constantly. In fact, Jesus said of Him: *"And I will pray the Father, and He shall give you another Comforter* (Helper), *that He may abide with you forever"* (Jn. 14:16).

However, I'm not speaking here of His abiding, but rather His Work, that is, what He is doing in this world, and especially, His Plan for me. God has a special plan for every single Believer, a special place, a special work, cut out for that particular individual. Accordingly, His Presence will lead me.

The Lord has led me in this capacity all of my life and Ministry. In 1969, He told me to go on Radio with a daily Program, 15 minutes in length, which we called *"The Campmeeting Hour"*. We were soon on some 600 Stations, with the largest daily audience in the nation as it refers to Gospel. In 1975, He told me to go on Television, and even told me how the Program was to be structured. About three or four years after making our debut on Television, which was not easy to say the least, the Lord told me to begin translating the Program from English into various languages, which we did, ultimately airing the Gospel through Television in many countries of the world.

The Lord told me, even as He led me, to take our Meetings from the Churches into large Auditoriums and Coliseums, which we did. He also instructed me regarding citywide and even nationwide Meetings in foreign countries, which we also carried out. We saw literally hundreds of thousands brought to a saving knowledge of Jesus Christ.

He led me, as well, to begin SonLife Radio in the first part of 1999, acquiring Stations all over this nation, which we have done, and continue to do even unto this hour. Someone asked me the other day as to why we didn't do the same thing with Television Stations. My answer was immediate, *"The Lord hasn't told me to do that!"*

As it regards SonLife Radio, the Lord told me exactly how to structure the programming and how to acquire Stations, even though we had no money.

In 1996, in answer to soul-searching prayer, which in fact, had lasted on a daily basis for the previous five years, the Lord began to open up to me the Message of the Cross. To be sure, it was not new, actually that which He had given to the Apostle Paul so long ago; but yet, this Message has been all but lost to the modern Church. That is beyond tragedy, if such a thing could be, considering that this Message is the very Foundation of the Gospel (Rom. 6:3-14; 8:1-2, 11; I Cor. 1:17-18, 21, 23; 2:2; Eph. 2:13-18; Col. 2:14-15). So what am I trying to say?

I'm saying that if we are to have the Presence of the Lord in our lives and Ministry, we must be where He wants us to be, even if it looks like a wilderness. Where the Presence of the Lord actually is has nothing to do with my likes or dislikes. In other words, I only want and desire to be where He is, and to be in the midst of what He is doing, wherever that location might be.

(11) "AND THE LORD SPOKE UNTO MOSES, SAYING,

(12) "I HAVE HEARD THE MURMURINGS OF THE CHILDREN OF ISRAEL: SPEAK UNTO THEM, SAYING, AT EVENING YOU SHALL EAT FLESH, AND IN THE MORNING YOU SHALL BE FILLED WITH BREAD; AND YOU SHALL KNOW THAT I AM THE LORD YOUR GOD.

(13) "AND IT CAME TO PASS, THAT AT EVENING THE QUAILS CAME UP, AND COVERED THE CAMP: AND IN THE MORNING THE DEW LAY ROUND ABOUT THE HOST.

(14) "AND WHEN THE DEW THAT LAY WAS GONE UP, BEHOLD, UPON THE FACE OF THE WILDERNESS THERE LAY A SMALL ROUND THING, AS SMALL AS THE HOAR FROST ON THE GROUND.

(15) "AND WHEN THE CHILDREN OF ISRAEL SAW IT, THEY SAID ONE TO ANOTHER, IT IS MANNA: FOR THEY DID NOT KNOW WHAT IT WAS. AND MOSES SAID UNTO THEM, THIS IS THE BREAD WHICH THE LORD HAS GIVEN YOU TO EAT.

(16) "THIS IS THE THING WHICH THE LORD HAS COMMANDED, GATHER OF IT EVERY MAN ACCORDING TO HIS EATING, AN OMER FOR EVERY MAN, ACCORDING TO THE NUMBER OF YOUR PERSONS; TAKE YOU EVERY MAN FOR THEM WHICH ARE IN HIS TENTS.

(17) "AND THE CHILDREN OF ISRAEL DID SO, AND GATHERED, SOME MORE, SOME LESS.

(18) "AND WHEN THEY DID METE IT WITH AN OMER, HE WHO GATHERED MUCH HAD NOTHING OVER, AND HE WHO GATHERED LITTLE HAD NO LACK; THEY GATHERED EVERY MAN ACCORDING TO HIS EATING.

(19) "AND MOSES SAID, LET NO MAN LEAVE OF IT TILL THE MORNING.

(20) "NOTWITHSTANDING THEY HEARKENED NOT UNTO MOSES; BUT SOME OF THEM LEFT OF IT UNTIL THE MORNING, AND IT BRED WORMS, AND STANK: AND MOSES WAS ANGRY WITH THEM.

(21) "AND THEY GATHERED IT EVERY MORNING, EVERY MAN ACCORDING TO HIS EATING: AND WHEN THE SUN WAXED HOT, IT MELTED.

(22) "AND IT CAME TO PASS, THAT ON THE SIXTH DAY THEY GATHERED TWICE AS MUCH BREAD, TWO OMERS FOR ONE MAN: AND ALL THE RULERS OF THE CONGREGATION CAME AND TOLD MOSES."

The construction is:

1. Past miracles are convincing. But unless there are fresh evidences of God, the natural man will soon forget and lapse into unbelief again.

2. Verses 13 through 20 record the miracle of the quails and the Manna. The Manna prefigured the descent of the True Bread of which, if a man eat, he shall live forever (Jn. 6:51).

3. In Egypt, Israel had slave food; in the desert, Angels' food. The test quickly revealed

that the natural man had little appetite for heavenly things, for the people soon called it *"light food."*

4. The Manna was so precious that it could not bear contact with the Earth. It fell upon the dew and had to be gathered before the sun came up. This teaches us that yesterday's Blessing will not do for today, nor today's for tomorrow. Thus, must the Christian feed upon Christ as He reveals Himself in the Scriptures.

5. Israel in the desert presented a striking picture! Egypt was behind them, Canaan was before them, the wilderness was around them, and the Manna was above them.

6. Every time they looked back toward Egypt they murmured; when looking forward toward the wilderness, they saw the Glory of the Lord. The Manna was a Type of Christ as well as the Word of God.

THE LORD SPOKE

Verse 11 reads: *"And the LORD spoke unto Moses, saying,"*

A Preacher told me the other day, considering one of the largest religious Denominations in the world, of which he was actually a part, that they did not believe that the Lord spoke to people in this day and age. In other words, they do not believe in any leading or guidance from the Lord, relying instead on common sense, etc. They claimed that the Word of God is the only instruction we need, and that when the Word was complete with the Book of Revelation, the Lord ceased to speak to anyone.

While it is certainly true that the Lord will not take away or add to His Word, and everything He says will definitely coincide with the Word, still, every indication is given in the Word of God that the Lord continues to lead His people, even with personal direction. As I gave regarding commentary on the previous Verse, the Lord has led me all of my life, and He has done so by speaking to my heart.

In fact, He speaks to me through His Word, through Songs, which always coincide with His Word, through dreams and visions, and through impressions upon my spirit, as well as Gifts of the Spirit (I Cor. 12:8-10).

No! The Lord didn't quit speaking to His people in the giving of direction when the Canon of Scripture was completed as it regards the Book of Revelation. Such a thought, to be frank, is absurd!

A PERSONAL EXPERIENCE

The following is typical of what I speak, of which I could give many instances.

If I remember correctly, the year was 1953. Frances and I were married in 1952, and Donnie was born in 1954. We then lived in northeast Louisiana.

We had gone to Baton Rouge, Louisiana, where we now reside, incidentally, and have for a goodly number of years, to hear Evangelist David Nunn.

The crowd that night was not overly large, and I remember Frances and myself, along with others with us, sitting on the second row of seats.

Along with being an excellent Preacher, Brother Nunn is also an excellent singer. And that night, as he stepped to the pulpit, accompanied by nothing but a piano, he began to sing a song that I had not heard at that time. The name of it was *"Job's God Is True"*.

As he began to sing, the Spirit of God began to move upon me, even to a degree, I think I can say, that I had never sensed before. I began to weep, in fact, actually weeping uncontrollably. The words of the song greatly ministered to me, and yet, I did not know exactly how, at least at the time. The words are:

"I can feel the hand of Satan,
"As the tempter press me sore,
"And he's been before the Father,
"Asking leave to tempt me more."

CHORUS:

"Though God slay me, yet I'll trust Him.
"For I'll then come forth as gold.
"For I know my Redeemer liveth,
"For I feel Him in my soul."

That night I knew that the Lord was saying something to me, but I did not know exactly what. In living for the Lord these many years, I have found that the Lord has spoken to my heart in that manner a number of times. In other words, many years before a certain situation would come to pass, in some way, He would reveal the future, but yet give me very little information, but in another sense of the word, would give much information as it regards victory.

A few days ago, the Lord brought the occasion of that happening back to my mind. To be frank, I don't remember having thought of it in several years. Actually, at the time of this dictation, it was 49 years ago that the Lord spoke to my heart concerning this of which I speak.

As the Lord brought it back to me, I relived the scene all over again in my mind. And then the Lord spoke to my heart, relating to me that on the particular night in question so long ago, He was telling me that I would be sorely tried by Satan, and even that He (the Lord) would give Satan permission to increase the degree of temptation. But then He reminded me of the Chorus of that song.

If I would trust Him, I would come forth as pure as gold. And then the Holy Spirit spoke this to my heart:

"You have trusted Me, and I have kept My Word. By the Grace of God, you have come forth as pure as gold. It was made possible by the Cross."

Oh yes, the Lord spoke to Moses, but He will speak to every one of His children, and often, if we will only draw near to Him.

I HAVE HEARD

Verse 12 reads: *"I have heard the murmurings of the Children of Israel: speak unto them, saying, At evening you shall eat flesh, and in the morning you shall be filled with bread; and you shall know that I am the LORD your God."*

The Lord pointedly tells Israel that He has heard their murmurings. And let it be understood that this is the first sin that was committed by Israel after being delivered from Egyptian bondage. We should take a lesson from this:

More than likely, that is the besetting sin of most Christians presently. To *"murmur"* in any capacity, which refers to complaining and finding fault, is in essence a complaint against God. In effect, we are telling Him that we can do the job better than He is doing it, which shows gross spiritual ignorance, and at the same time, portrays the fact that

NOTES

we aren't very thankful for all the wonderful things the Lord has in fact done for us. And to be sure, He has done much!

As we've already stated, you very seldom hear the children of the Devil complaining about the Devil. If they complain at all, it's that they are not able to serve him more, and better, whether they understand such or not. But we Christians are very quick to complain about God. The truth is, most Christians don't realize that what they are saying is actually against God. But to be sure, that's exactly what it is.

GRACE

Despite their *"murmurings,"* Grace overruled, exactly as Grace many times overrules our actions, and presented the Children of Israel with a miracle of tremendous proportions — Manna from Heaven in the mornings, and quails at night.

But let it ever be understood that despite the factor of Grace, if the murmuring continues, even as it did with Israel, ultimately, the Lord will take a hand, and chastisement will be the result.

We are seeing here the unbelief of Israel, which would ultimately result in the adult generation dying in the wilderness, being refused admittance into the land of Canaan. It all began with *"murmuring."* As stated, let that be a lesson to us.

THE QUAILS

Verse 13 reads: *"And it came to pass, that at evening the quails came up, and covered the camp: and in the morning the dew lay round about the host."*

It seems that the quails, as appears by the subsequent narrative, were supplied, not regularly, but only on rare occasions; in fact (so far as appears), only here in the wilderness of Sin, and at Kibroth Hattaavah in the wilderness of Paran (Num. 11:31-34). One might say that they were not a necessity, but rather an indulgence.

The mention of the *"dew"* in this manner implies that which looked like dew, and was, in part, dew, but not wholly so. The next Verse explains it to a greater degree.

Concerning the quails, they regularly migrated from Syria and Arabia in the autumn, and wintered in the interior of Africa, when they then returned northwards in immense masses in the spring. When these birds approach the coast after a long flight over the Red Sea, they are often so exhausted that they rather fall to the ground then settle, and are then easily taken by the hand or killed with sticks. Their flesh is regarded by the natives as a delicacy.

At any rate, the Lord would have had to perform a miracle to bring this about, in that the quail had to land at exactly the place where the Children of Israel were encamped. As well, there must have been at least 10 million to 20 million quails, to satisfy the hunger of some three million Israelites.

MANNA

Verses 14 and 15 read: *"And when the dew that lay was gone up, behold, upon the face of the wilderness there lay a small round thing, as small as the hoar frost on the ground.*

"And when the Children of Israel saw it, they said one to another, It is Manna: for they didn't know what it was. And Moses said unto them, This is the bread which the LORD has given you to eat."

It is only as we feed upon Christ Himself that we truly feed upon the written Word. And no one can properly understand Christ, unless one properly understands His Mission, which was the Cross. If we do not understand Christ in this fashion, hence Paul saying, *"We preach Christ Crucified"* (I Cor. 1:23), then in effect, we will be attending *"another Jesus"* (II Cor. 11:4). Let me make the statement simpler:

To properly understand the Word of God, we must, at the same time, properly understand the Cross. While everything He did was of immense significance, as should be overly obvious, it is always the Cross which must be the chief emphasis. That's why the Apostle said:

"For Christ sent me not to baptize, but to preach the Gospel: not with wisdom of words, lest the Cross of Christ should be made of none effect" (I Cor. 1:17).

Concerning this, Pink says: *"Beneath many a figure and behind innumerable shadows and symbols the anointed eye may discern the glories of our Blessed Lord. It should be our chief delight as we read the Old Testament Scriptures to prayerfully search for that which foreshadows Him of Whom 'Moses and the Prophets' did write. All doubt is removed as to whether or not the Manna pointed to the Incarnate Son by His Own Words in John 6:32-33. There we find the Saviour saying:*

'Verily, verily, I say unto you, Moses gave you not that bread from Heaven; but My Father gives you the True Bread from Heaven. For the Bread of God is He which cometh down from Heaven and gives life unto the world.'"

So we will take this occasion as it regards the Manna, to portray Christ in this sign and symbol of so long ago.

(The headings are derived from the material of Arthur Pink. The material is mine.)

THE OCCASION OF THE GIVING OF THE MANNA

The Manna was given to Israel, because of great need; likewise, Jesus came to this world simply because it was lost, in great need, and in fact, other than His Coming, would have been eternally lost.

Did man deserve this? The answer can be easily ascertained by asking the question as well of Israel. No, Israel didn't deserve the Manna, as the world didn't deserve Christ, as we don't deserve anything that's good. But what does the Scripture say?

"But God, Who is rich in mercy, for His great love wherewith He loved us,

"Even when we were dead in sins, has quickened us together (made us spiritually alive) *with Christ, (by Grace you are saved);*

"And has raised us up together, and made us sit together in Heavenly Places in Christ Jesus:

"That in the ages to come He might show the exceeding riches of His Grace in His kindness toward us through Christ Jesus" (Eph. 2:4-7).

I get amazed at times at Christians who have been taught wrong, who claim that a person forfeits Grace if they do something wrong, etc. If that is in fact the case, then no one can be saved. The truth is, the person who has done wrong, which includes every human being who has ever lived, is the one who desperately needs Grace, and the one to whom Grace is given.

For a Believer to fall from Grace, which Paul mentions in Galatians 5:4, that Christian has to trust in things other than the Cross. All Grace comes exclusively through the Finished Work of Christ, and our Faith in that Finished Work, which enables the Holy Spirit to carry out His work within our lives. If our faith is transferred from the Cross to other things, and irrespective as to what those other things are, we fall from Grace, as should be obvious (Gal. 2:21; 5:4).

No, it was the Grace of God that occasioned the Manna for Israel, and certainly not their good works. It is the same for us presently.

THE PLACE WHERE THE MANNA FELL

The Manna fell in the wilderness; likewise, this world is a wilderness. In fact, the place where the Manna fell was actually called *"the Wilderness of Sin"* (Ex. 16:1).

Likewise, to this *"Wilderness of Sin,"* which we refer to as the world, did Jesus come.

When He came, He exposed the hidden things of darkness! The response of both Jews and Gentiles to His *"Light,"* was to murder Him. Darkness, in fact, hates light.

THE GLORY OF THE LORD WAS LINKED WITH THE GIVING OF THE MANNA

In Verse 10, it tells us that *"the Glory of the Lord appeared in the cloud,"* as it concerned Israel. This is the first time we read of the appearing of that *"Glory."* Then the Manna was given.

Not until the Son of God became Incarnate was *"the Glory of the Lord"* fully revealed. But then, when the Eternal Word became flesh and lived among men, then, as the beloved Apostle declares: *"We beheld His Glory, the Glory as of the only-Begotten of the Father"* (Jn. 1:14). In fact, the *"Glory of God"* is seen *"in the Face of Jesus Christ"* (II Cor. 4:6).

THE MANNA CAME DOWN FROM HEAVEN

The Manna was not a product of the Earth nor anything that man could do. It was exclusively a product of Heaven.

In fact, God said to Moses: *"Behold I will rain bread from Heaven for you."*

This Manna had nothing to do with human ability or human skill. It descended strictly from God. It was a gift from Heaven to this sinful world, this *"Wilderness of Sin."*

As well, our Lord wasn't a product of this Earth, even though He was Incarnate — God became man by being born of a woman.

The Scripture says, *"The first man (Adam) was of the Earth, earthy; but the Second Man (Jesus Christ) was 'the Lord from Heaven'"* (I Cor. 15:47).

THE MANNA WAS A FREE GIFT FROM GOD

Israel did not earn this Manna, and in fact, could not earn the Manna. It was solely and completely a free gift from God. In fact, God has nothing for sale. And even if He did, there would be no way that you and I could come by the purchase price. But Jesus totally and completely paid the price for us.

I suppose the most oft quoted Scripture from the Bible amply explains this of what I say: *"For God so loved the world that He gave His only Begotten Son, that whosoever believeth in Him should not perish, but have everlasting life"* (Jn. 3:16).

Paul referred to the giving of Christ as *"God's unspeakable Gift"* (II Cor. 9:15).

THE MANNA WAS SENT TO ISRAEL ONLY

The Manna was God's provision for His elect people, and for none others. We do not read of the Lord raining Manna upon the Egyptians or the Canaanites, or anyone else for that matter. It was given to Israel in the wilderness, and to them alone.

Likewise, Christ is God's provision for Believers only. The unredeemed cannot have Christ, cannot know Christ, cannot experience Christ, and, therefore, cannot have His Blessings. That is for the Redeemed only.

Second, this Manna was sent to a needy people, as should be obvious. Likewise, Christ is sent to a needy world, and for those who accept Him, He will be all that we need.

In fact, the man cannot be complete, until

he knows The Man, the Lord Jesus Christ. Let's say it another way:

A person cannot even remotely be a whole person, until they know the Lord. Only then can that person begin to come up to the level of what God intended for a human being to be.

THE MANNA CAME RIGHT DOWN TO WHERE THE ISRAELITES WERE

We talk about people finding the Lord. The truth is, the Lord found the people. In fact, man being spiritually dead cannot in any way find the Lord or anything of the Lord, unless the Lord purposely reveals Himself to such a person, which He definitely did to all who are presently saved.

God does not tamper with the will. It is still *"whosoever will,"* and that will never change (Rev. 22:17; Jn. 3:16).

As the Gospel is preached, and the Holy Spirit anoints that Word, He at the same time strikes conviction to the heart of the unbeliever. This is when their will is brought into play. They can either accept or reject. Sadly, most, it seems, reject the Lord.

But if they accept the Lord, which all do by their *"free will,"* to be sure, the Lord will accept them. The Scripture says:

"All who the Father gives Me shall come to Me; and him who comes to Me I will in no wise cast out" (Jn. 6:37).

THE MANNA HAD TO BE GATHERED BY EACH INDIVIDUAL

The Lord said: *"Gather of it every man according to his eating"* (Vs. 16).

Receiving Christ is always a personal matter. No one can receive Christ for someone else; the individual in question must make the decision himself. There is no such thing as Salvation by proxy.

So this means that the Mormons cannot transfer someone to Heaven who has already died, but did not know the Lord. In fact, the Mormon doctrine being totally unbiblical, there is no Mormon who is saved.

Likewise, it is not possible for Catholics to get a person out of Purgatory, which place, incidentally, doesn't even exist.

All Salvation is on this side of the grave. There are no more opportunities after death.

NOTES

The Scripture says the Gospel of Christ is, *"The Power of God unto Salvation to every one who believes"* (Rom. 1:16), and the Scripture further says, *"He who believes not shall be damned"* (Mk. 16:16).

So, Salvation is strictly a personal matter, and a personal matter alone. Each individual has to have his own experience with Christ. Paul said: *"Who* (Christ) *loved me and gave Himself for me"* (Gal. 2:20).

THE MANNA MET A DAILY NEED

The Manna gathered today would not suffice for tomorrow. They needed to obtain a fresh supply each day.

This is where many Believers miss the mark. They do not understand that it is imperative that we feast on Christ each and every day.

Christ Himself said: *"Give us this day our daily bread."* While such *"daily bread"* can be looked at as a daily sustenance regarding our physical and material needs, it also speaks of Christ, Who is the Bread of Life.

THE APPETITE DETERMINED THE AMOUNT GATHERED

How true this is of the Believer, as it regards Christ. We all have as much of Christ as we desire, no more, no less. If our desires are large, if we open our mouth wide, He will fill it.

The Scripture says that the Children of Israel gathered the Manna, *"some more, some less"* (Vss. 16-17). So the appetite governed the amount gathered.

THE MANNA WAS DESPISED BY THOSE WHO WERE NOT THE LORD'S PEOPLE

The Scripture points out the mixed multitude who was among the Children of Israel, which consisted of Egyptians who had come out with them. Some of the Children of Israel joined with the Egyptians, criticizing the Manna (Num. 11:4-6).

The person who is losing his way with God is primarily losing his way simply because he doesn't understand his need for Christ.

Mostly, the reason for that pertains to the Believer trusting things other than Christ and Him Crucified. As a result, he is committing *"spiritual adultery"* (Rom. 7:1-4), which, as would be understood, cools one's love for Christ. This is the *"lukewarm"* situation of which Jesus mentioned in one of His Messages to the seven Churches of Asia (Rev. 3:15-16).

I am persuaded that a failure of the Believer to understand the Cross, and how it refers and plays into one's Sanctification, is the crowning sin of the Church. It is the cause of all problems, and I mean all problems.

THE MANNA FELL UPON THE DEW, NOT UPON THE DUST OF THE GROUND

"Dust" speaks of fallen man, and calls attention to the corruption which sin has worked in him (Gen. 3:19). So the Manna, typifying Christ, fell not upon *"the dust,"* but rather upon *"the dew."* The *"dew"* is a type of the Holy Spirit, which characterized Christ. *"He was anointed with the oil of gladness above all His fellows"* (Ps. 45:7). He said of Himself: *"The Spirit of the Lord is upon Me, because He has anointed Me . . ."* (Lk. 4:18).

He did not come down here to share our corrupt nature, for that would have done no good. He came to get us out from under the dominance of this corrupt nature, and did so by His Finished Work at the Cross (Col. 2:14-15).

He took upon Him the form of a servant, but the body which was prepared for Him (Heb. 10:5) belonged not to the *"dust"* of this Earth, but was rather a product of the Holy Spirit (Lk. 1:35). Let's say it another way:

He was not the product of Joseph's sperm or Mary's egg. Mary merely furnished a house for the gestation period before the birth of Christ. In fact, Jesus did not carry Joseph's features or those of Mary.

THE MANNA WAS WHITE IN COLOR

As we will later study, the Scripture says: *"And the House of Israel called the name thereof Manna; and it was like coriander seed, white"* (Ex. 16:31).

As should be obvious, this speaks of the spotless purity of our Lord, not only in His Person, but as well, as it was manifested outwardly in His daily walk. He *"knew no sin"* (II Cor. 5:21). *"He was without sin"* (Heb. 4:15). *"He did no sin"* (I Pet. 2:22). He was *"Holy, harmless, undefiled, separate from sinners"* (Heb. 7:26).

In I Peter, we are told that He was a Lamb *"without spot and without blemish"* (I Pet. 1:19). The former expression refers to the absence of outward pollution, while the latter refers to the absence of inward defect.

Pink says: *"In His walk through this scene of corruption He contracted no defilement. He alone could touch the leper without becoming contaminated. He was 'without spot', pure, white."*

As well, this completely lays aside the teaching that Christ became a sinner on the Cross, and died as a sinner, and thereby went to the burning side of Hell, where He was *"born again"* three days later, and then resurrected. There's nothing in the Bible as it concerns such teaching. In fact, this teaching, *"the Jesus died spiritually doctrine,"* shifts Redemption from the Cross to Hell itself, which of course is preposterous. Jesus died physically, which was the penalty for our sin; He did not die spiritually (I Pet. 3:18).

THE MANNA WAS SWEET TO THE TASTE

"The taste of it was like wafers of honey" (Vs. 31).

Christ is sweet to the taste. The Scripture says: *"As the apple tree among the trees of the wood, so is my Beloved among the sons. I sat down under His shadow with great delight, and His fruit was sweet to my taste"* (Song of Sol. 2:3).

The word *"sweet,"* which the Manna typified, is a beautiful description of Christ. David said: *"O taste and see that the LORD is good"* (Ps. 34:8).

Living for Christ, which refers to association and relationship with Christ, is the most wonderful, the most glorious, the most fulfilled life that one could ever know. In fact, there is no way for life to be what it ought to be, not even remotely so, without Christ.

Unfortunately, the unredeemed world, being spiritually dead, doesn't know this. In fact, they have no conception of what it is to live for God, and cannot have, until they are *"born again."*

But truly, the Manna, which is a Type of

Christ, being sweet, is a beautiful and apt description.

THE MANNA WAS GROUND AND BAKED

The Scripture says concerning the Manna, *"And they ground it in mills, or beat it in a mortar, and baked it in pans, and made cakes of it"* (Num. 11:8).

This speaks of the sufferings of our blessed Lord!

We sometimes erroneously think of Christ that He was never tempted. In fact, He was tempted to a far greater degree by Satan than we would ever be tempted. The Scripture actually says: *"He was in all points tempted like as we are, yet without sin"* (Heb. 4:15).

Others claim that while He may have been tempted, He, in fact, could not have succumbed to the temptation. They based their conclusion on the fact that Jesus was God, and God cannot sin.

Jesus was God. In fact, He never ceased to be God, even when He became man. But as one Greek Scholar put it, and rightly so, *"In the Incarnation, He laid aside His expression of Deity, while never losing the possession of Deity."* And yes, in this particular capacity, He could have failed. Otherwise, the temptations would have made no sense, and even more so, to be the Last Adam, which He was, He had to be subject to failure, exactly as was the first Adam, or else He would not have fulfilled the type (I Cor. 15:45-50).

The argument of His Deity is easily proven. Even though Jesus definitely was God, He also grew hungry and tired, etc., just like any other human being. And we know that God cannot be hungry or tired. But, as stated, He laid aside the expression of His Deity, although never losing its possession.

The Scripture says of Him: *"He is despised and rejected of men; a man of sorrows, and acquainted with grief: and we hid as it were our faces from Him; He was despised, and we esteemed Him not"* (Isa. 53:3).

As the Last Adam and the Second Man, He suffered all things that we should have suffered, and yet never failed in even the slightest degree. As our Representative Man (the Second Man), He did what we could not do for ourselves. As our Substitute, He did bear the penalty, which we should have borne, but couldn't.

THE MANNA WAS PRESERVED ON THE SABBATH

The Sabbath is a type of the *"rest"* we have in Christ. It was not a day of worship, but rather a day of *"rest."* It was meant to typify what Christ would do for us when He came. That's why Jesus said: *"Come unto Me all you who labor and are heavy laden, and I will give you rest"* (Mat. 11:28).

If the Manna was kept over till the next day, normally it would breed worms and stink. This was done so by the Lord, because He didn't want Israel gathering the Manna, except for the needs of that particular day; however, on the Sabbath, this did not happen. Whatever Manna was left over would be perfectly fresh on the Sabbath morning, even though that was not the case on the other mornings of the week.

The idea is, as stated, Christ is our *"rest."* But what does that mean?

It means the struggle is over. Normal Christianity is for us to place our Faith exclusively in Christ, and what He has done for us at the Cross, which will then give latitude to the Holy Spirit to work mightily within our lives. And then without fight or struggle, the Fruit of the Spirit will be developed within us, and victory on a perpetual basis will be ours (Rom. 8:1-2).

I know what it is to not understand the Cross as it refers to Sanctification, and to thereby try to make myself holy or righteous, etc. My labors were all in vain. It's like a man in quicksand. The more he struggles, the deeper he gets.

But when I learned through Revelation what Christ had done for me at the Cross, and how it effects my Sanctification, i.e., *"my everyday life and living before God,"* I then learned what *"more abundant life"* actually means (Jn. 10:10). Without strife, without struggle, I found victory to be mine, and due totally and completely to my Faith in Christ, and what He has done for me regarding His Finished Work. That's why Paul bluntly said: *"For in Jesus Christ *neither circumcision availeth anything, nor uncircumcision; but Faith which worketh by love"* (Gal. 5:6).

THE MANNA WAS LAID UP BEFORE THE LORD

The High Priest of the old Judiastic economy entered into the Holy of Holies once a year, and there offered up blood on the Mercy Seat, which was to atone for himself and Israel. It was all a type of what Christ would do when He, in fact, did come.

Well, Christ has come, has gone to the Cross, and has shed His Precious Blood. However, He did not enter into the Holy of Holies as the Aaronic High Priest, but rather *"into Heaven itself, now to appear in the Presence of God for us"* (Heb. 9:24).

There is no record that He offered up Blood on the Mercy Seat of Heaven, because had He done that, it would mean that the Cross of Calvary did not produce a Finished Work; however, we know that it did produce a Finished Work, simply because Jesus said, *"It is finished"* (Jn. 19:30).

His Presence before God means that God has accepted fully His Sacrifice, and His appearance at the very Presence of God guarantees that Work (Heb. 1:3).

The golden pot in which the Manna was preserved tells of how God is glorified in Him Whom it foreshadowed.

THE MANNA IS CALLED ANGELS' FOOD

The Psalmist said: *"Man did eat Angels' food: He sent them meat to the full"* (Ps. 78:25).

Christ not only feeds the souls of those of His people who are upon Earth, but He also satisfies the hearts of celestial beings. The unfallen Angels find their chief delight in feeding upon Christ. They worship Him, they serve Him, and they tell forth His praises. There are several Passages in the Book of Revelation that proclaim this fact (Rev. 6:11-14).

THE MANNA WAS GIVEN IN THE NIGHT

During the hours of darkness, the Manna fell. This is typical of the darkness of spiritual night, which had settled over the Earth when Jesus came. As well, it has settled over every unbeliever, and only by the Light being shown, which Light is Christ, can that person be brought from darkness to light.

In fact, the worst night of all is just ahead, when the Antichrist will make his debut for world leadership, and for a while, it will look like he will succeed. But at the darkest time, when Israel is pressed, and it looks like she will be totally destroyed, even with the Antichrist having taken half of Jerusalem, then the Lord of Glory will come back, and will do so with healing in His wings. He will come back crowned *"King of kings and Lord of lords."* Then for the first time in human history, the Light of Jesus Christ, and all of His Glory will fill the Earth.

THE MANNA IS NOW HIDDEN

In Revelation 2:17, we read, *"To him who overcomes will I give to eat of the hidden Manna."* This speaks of Christ.

Unseen by the eye of sense, He remains in Heaven till that day when He shall be manifested before the entire world. He is coming back!

The Scripture says: *"And when He had spoken these things, while they beheld, He was taken up; and the cloud received Him out of their sight.*

"And while they looked steadfastly toward Heaven as He went up, behold, two men stood by them in white apparel;

"Which also said, You men of Galilee, why stand ye gazing up into Heaven? This same Jesus, which is taken up from you into Heaven, shall so come in like manner as you have seen Him go into Heaven" (Acts 1:9-11).

Due to the fact that He is now *"hidden,"* the world scoffs at His return; but irrespective of that, the Lord of Glory is going to come back to this world, then and only then will it know peace.

What we've tried to say as it regards the Manna being a Type of Christ, we realize is woefully inadequate. But again, who can do justice to our Lord? But perhaps, we've said some things that will be a blessing to you.

THE COMMAND OF THE LORD

Verses 16 through 18 read: *"This is the

thing which the LORD has commanded, Gather it every man according to his eating, an omer for every man, according to the number of your persons; take ye every man for them which are in his tents.

"And the Children of Israel did so, and gathered, some more, some less.

"And when they did mete it with an omer, he who gathered much had nothing over, and he who gathered little had no lack; they gathered every man according to his eating."

As should be understood from the Text, all of this was very personal. First of all, as Verse 16 proclaims, this given is a Command of the Lord.

It says, *"An omer for every man."*

An *"omer"* is the equivalent of six pints. Considering there were approximately three million people, this would play out to some 18 million pints, or about 13 and one-half million pounds gathered daily. To help us understand it even more, it would take a train pulling 45 cars, each car having in it 15 tons, to take care of one day's supply. This means that approximately one and one-half million tons of Manna were gathered annually by Israel. And let it be remembered that this continued for nearly 40 years!

Verses 19 through 22 read: *"And Moses said, Let no man leave of it till the morning.*

"Notwithstanding they hearkened not unto Moses; but some of them left of it until the morning, and it bred worms, and stank: and Moses was angry with them.

"And they gathered it every morning, every man according to his eating: and when the sun waxed hot, it melted.

"And it came to pass, that on the sixth day they gathered twice as much bread, two omers for one man, and all the rulers of the congregation came and told Moses."

The Command was emphatic. They must not think they could gather a great deal of Manna, and that it would do for several days. The Lord told them specifically that they were to gather the Manna each morning, with the exception of the Sabbath. And if, in fact, they tried to leave it till the next morning in order for it to be used the next day, it would *"breed worms and stink."*

Now what spiritual meaning does this have?

As we have stated, the Manna was a Type of Christ. Basically, this is what Christ was referring to when He told us: *"If any man will come after Me, let him deny himself, and take up his Cross daily, and follow Me"* (Lk. 9:23).

"Denying oneself," as used here by Christ, is not speaking of asceticism, which refers to the denial of all things that are pleasurable, etc. It is rather speaking of the Believer not trusting in himself, but rather trusting totally in Christ.

When he spoke of taking up the Cross, he said that it must be done *"daily,"* which in essence, refers back to the Manna.

This simply means that we are to understand that everything we have from the Lord is made possible to us by what Jesus did at the Cross. As well, we must renew our Faith daily, so to speak, in the Cross, not depending on that which we had yesterday, etc.

The Manna as a Type of Christ, and the gathering of it each day, was meant to proclaim the fact that we must feed upon Christ each and every day. We must not try to live on yesterday's Faith. All of this has to do with our Spiritual Growth, and if not adhered to as Christ commanded, will result in spiritual declension.

On the sixth day, which would be Friday, they were to gather twice as much Manna, which they were not allowed to do on all the other days, with the extra Manna being preserved for the Sabbath. On that particular day, it would not breed worms and stink. So we see here that God was performing all type of miracles as it regards this wonderful supply.

(23) "AND HE SAID UNTO THEM, THIS IS THAT WHICH THE LORD HAS SAID, TOMORROW IS THE REST OF THE HOLY SABBATH UNTO THE LORD: BAKE THAT WHICH YOU WILL BAKE TODAY, AND SEETHE THAT YOU WILL SEETHE; AND THAT WHICH REMAINS OVER LAY UP FOR YOU TO BE KEPT UNTIL THE MORNING.

(24) "AND THEY LAID IT UP TILL THE MORNING, AS MOSES BADE: AND IT DID NOT STINK, NEITHER WAS THERE ANY WORM THEREIN.

(25) "AND MOSES SAID, EAT THAT TODAY: FOR TODAY IS A SABBATH UNTO THE LORD: TODAY YOU SHALL NOT FIND IT IN THE FIELD.

(26) "SIX DAYS YOU SHALL GATHER IT; BUT ON THE SEVENTH DAY, WHICH IS THE SABBATH, IN IT THERE SHALL BE NONE.

(27) "AND IT CAME TO PASS, THAT THERE WENT OUT SOME OF THE PEOPLE ON THE SEVENTH DAY FOR TO GATHER, AND THEY FOUND NONE.

(28) "AND THE LORD SAID UNTO MOSES, HOW LONG REFUSE YOU TO KEEP MY COMMANDMENTS AND MY LAWS?

(29) "SEE, FOR THAT THE LORD HAS GIVEN YOU THE SABBATH, THEREFORE HE GIVES YOU ON THE SIXTH DAY THE BREAD OF TWO DAYS; ABIDE YOU EVERY MAN IN HIS PLACE, LET NO MAN GO OUT OF HIS PLACE ON THE SEVENTH DAY.

(30) "SO THE PEOPLE RESTED ON THE SEVENTH DAY."

The overview is:

1. Verse 23 proclaims the *"Holy Sabbath,"* which was *"the rest."* The day of rest suddenly reappears after a silence of about 2,500 years.

2. Redemption being accomplished (deliverance) from Egypt, the Sabbath is given to Israel. But, sadly, man has little heart for God's rest, because man's nature is bad. He can neither rest with, nor work for, God.

3. If God makes a rest for him, he will not keep it, and if God tells him to work, he will not do it.

THE SABBATH

Verse 23 reads: *"And he said unto them, This is that which the LORD has said, Tomorrow is the rest of the Holy Sabbath unto the LORD: bake that which you will bake today, and seethe that you will seethe; and that which remains over lay up for you to be kept until the morning."*

Several things are said here:

1. The Sabbath, which is the seventh day, which is Saturday, is now introduced, and that, as stated, after a lapse of about 2,500 years (Gen. 2:1-3).

2. It was to be a day of *"rest,"* which means that no work was to be done on this day.

3. The *"rest"* typified Christ, and the spiritual rest that He would bring, as it regards what He would do at the Cross. Salvation can be explained as a *"rest in Christ."* Unfortunately, with millions trying to earn their Salvation in one way or the other, we seem not to have learned this lesson very well (Mat. 11:28-30).

4. This Ordinance of the Sabbath was given to Israel only, and was not meant to be carried over into the Church. In fact, the Sacrifices, Circumcision, and a host of other things were given to Israel only, and were not carried over into the Church.

5. All of this was a Type of Christ and what He would do for the human race, at least for those who would believe Him (Jn. 3:16). When He came, He fulfilled all of these types and in every capacity.

6. The Manna was not given by the Lord on the Sabbath, simply because to have done so would have violated the type. But He made provision for Israel, as stated, by giving twice as much on the sixth day, which means they were to gather twice as much, but on this day only.

UNBELIEF

Verses 24 through 30 read: *"And they laid it up till the morning, as Moses bade: and it did not stink, neither was there any worm therein.*

"And Moses said, Eat that today: for today is a Sabbath unto the LORD: today you shall not find it in the field.

"Six days you shall gather it; but on the seventh day, which is the Sabbath, in it there shall be none.

"And it came to pass, that there went out some of the people on the seventh day for to gather, and they found none.

"And the LORD said unto Moses, How long refuse you to keep My Commandments and My Laws?

"See, for that the LORD has given you the Sabbath, therefore He gives you on the sixth day the bread of two days; abide you every man in his place, let no man go out of his place on the seventh day.

"So the people rested on the seventh day."

Despite the Commands given, some it seems, persuaded themselves that they *"knew better."* Consequently, they went out on the seventh day to gather Manna, but *"found none."* From the terminology given in Verse 28, it seems like the Lord was somewhat put out with this refusal to obey Him.

This is a perfect example of the following problem, and in effect, the greatest problem, I think, in the modern Church, and in fact, always has been.

Our victory as a Child of God comes to us exclusively by and through Christ, and what He has done for us at the Cross. We obtain all of these benefits by simply believing in Him, and, thereby, trusting in what He did for us in His great Sacrifice. That's the reason I keep explaining the Cross over and over. If the Believer doesn't understand it, he will not enter into God's *"rest,"* but will instead, attempt to *"earn"* his Salvation, in one way or the other.

The Lord had told Israel that on the Sabbath day, they were to do nothing but *"rest."* As stated, this typified Christ, and what He would do for the human race, and by that we speak of the Cross. This means that it's not something I do, but rather trusting in something that is already done.

The sad fact is, much of the modern Church understands the Cross as it refers to Salvation, but understands the Cross not at all as it refers to Sanctification.

SANCTIFICATION

Unfortunately, one of the single most important principals in the Bible, the principal of Sanctification, is all but presently ignored. In fact, most Christians don't have the slightest idea as to what Sanctification actually is.

In the Greek, the word as a noun is *"Hagiasmos,"* and means, *"separation to God"* (I Cor. 1:30; II Thess. 2:13; I Pet. 1:2). Sanctification is that relationship with God into which men enter by Faith in Christ (Acts 26:18; I Cor. 6:11), and to which our sole title is the death of Christ, i.e., *"the death of Christ on the Cross"* (Eph. 5:25-26; Col. 1:22; Heb. 10:10, 29; 13:12).

Sanctification is also used in the New Testament of the separation of the Believer from evil things and ways. This Sanctification is God's Will for the Believer (I Thess. 4:3), and His purpose in calling us by the Gospel, as the Holy Spirit teaches it by God's Word (Jn. 17:17, 19; Ps. 17:4; 119:9).

Sanctification is not vicarious, meaning that it cannot be transferred or imputed. It is an individual possession, built up, little by little, as the result of obedience to the Word of God, and of following the example of Christ, with our Faith ever in the Finished Work of Christ (Mat. 11:29; Jn. 13:15; Eph. 4:20; Phil. 2:5).

The Holy Spirit is the Agent in Sanctification (Rom. 15:16; II Thess. 2:13; I Pet. 1:2; I Cor. 6:11). However, the Believer must know and understand how the Holy Spirit functions in order for the Sanctification process to take its rightful course.

In brief, Paul tells us how the Spirit works in the following Scripture:

"For the Law (the manner in which the Spirit works) *of the Spirit* (Holy Spirit) *of life* (the benefits of the Cross) *in Christ Jesus* (the Law of which is spoken here pertains to what Jesus did at the Cross, with the phrase *'in Christ Jesus'* always referring to the Sacrifice of Christ) *has made me free from the law of sin and death"* (Rom. 8:2).

While the Believer certainly must be willing, and in fact, ardently so, for the Fruit of the Spirit to be developed in his life, other than Faith, that is all that is required of the Believer. In other words, the Believer cannot sanctify himself by doing spiritual things, etc. As stated, we are sanctified solely by the Holy Spirit. The one thing that is required of us, and that which is so very, very important, is:

The Believer must evidence Faith in Christ and His great Sacrifice. He must understand that not only does Salvation come to him through what Jesus did at the Cross, but Sanctification as well. The foundation of this is given in Romans 6:3-14.

When the Believer evidences Faith in Christ and His Cross, the Holy Spirit, Who works within the legal boundaries of the Cross, will then function mightily in the heart and life of such a Believer, thereby developing the Fruit of the Spirit, and ever drawing the Believer closer to God. This is the only manner in which the *"law of sin and death"* can be defeated. In fact, that negative law is so strong that it is only *"The Law of the Spirit of Life in Christ Jesus"* that can overcome these evil passions.

This is actually what the Sabbath represented, *"rest"* in Christ! As stated, the Believer cannot sanctify himself, but the Holy Spirit definitely can, and will; however, He will do so only as we evidence Faith in Christ and

His Finished Work. As long as we make the Cross the object of our Faith, the Holy Spirit will then perform His Work. If our Faith is shifted to other things, and irrespective as to what those other things might be, the end result will be *"spiritual adultery"* (Rom. 7:1-4).

The Lord has one manner of Sanctification, exactly as He has one manner of Salvation. It is both, or one should say, all in Christ, and as Paul said, *"Christ and Him Crucified"* (I Cor. 1:23).

(31) "AND THE HOUSE OF ISRAEL CALLED THE NAME THEREOF MANNA: AND IT WAS LIKE CORIANDER SEED, WHITE; AND THE TASTE OF IT WAS LIKE WAFERS MADE WITH HONEY.

(32) "AND MOSES SAID, THIS IS THE THING WHICH THE LORD COMMANDS, FILL AN OMER OF IT TO BE KEPT FOR YOUR GENERATIONS; THAT THEY MAY SEE THE BREAD WHEREWITH I HAVE FED YOU IN THE WILDERNESS, WHEN I BROUGHT YOU FORTH FROM THE LAND OF EGYPT.

(33) "AND MOSES SAID UNTO AARON, TAKE A POT, AND PUT AN OMER FULL OF MANNA THEREIN, AND LAY IT UP BEFORE THE LORD, TO BE KEPT FOR YOUR GENERATIONS.

(34) "AS THE LORD COMMANDED MOSES, SO AARON LAID IT UP BEFORE THE TESTIMONY, TO BE KEPT.

(35) "AND THE CHILDREN OF ISRAEL DID EAT MANNA FORTY YEARS, UNTIL THEY CAME TO A LAND INHABITED; THEY DID EAT MANNA, UNTIL THEY CAME UNTO THE BORDERS OF THE LAND OF CANAAN.

(36) "NOW AN OMER IS THE TENTH PART OF AN EPHAH."

The exegesis is:

1. The Thirty-first Verse proclaims once again the name of the miracle bread from Heaven, *"Manna."* In the Hebrew, it means, *"What is it?"* They had no name for it because there had never been anything like it on Earth previously.

2. Actually, it was Angels' food, and was sent from Heaven (Ps. 78:25). As the people would reject the Manna, likewise, they would reject Christ.

3. The Lord would supply this Manna for some forty years, all the time the Children of Israel wandered in the wilderness, until they came to the land of Canaan.

MANNA

Verse 31 reads: *"And the House of Israel called the name thereof Manna: and it was like coriander seed, white; and the taste of it was like wafers made with honey."*

The Manna was a provision made for God's people. It was not a question of Redemption, that having been obtained in the Blood of the Cross, and there alone. The Manna was meant to proclaim Christ, and His sustenance for the Saints, and that on a daily basis. The wilderness afforded not one blade of grass, nor one drop of water for the Israel of God. In Jehovah Alone was their portion.

It is the same with Believers presently. This world is not our home! Truly we *"here have no continuing city, but we seek one to come"* (Heb. 13:14).

No wonder Paul wrote that we now have a much better Covenant based on better Promises (Heb. 8:6). Whereas Israel had only the Type of Christ, the Manna, we now feed upon a Risen and Glorified Christ, ascended up to Heaven in virtue of accomplished Redemption, which was carried out at the Cross, and done so by the shedding of His Own Precious Blood (Eph. 2:13-18).

As the Manna came everyday, with the exception of the Sabbath, this portrays the fact that it was Christ yesterday, and it must be Christ today, and Christ forever. Moreover, it will not do to feed partly on Christ and partly on other things. As in the matter of *"life"* it is Christ *"Alone,"* so in the matter of *"living"* it must be Christ *"Alone."* As we cannot mingle anything with that which *"imparts"* life, and I speak of the Cross, so neither can we mingle anything with that which *"sustains"* it, and I continue to speak of the Cross.

MEMORIAL

Verse 32 reads: *"And Moses said, This is the thing which the LORD commands, Fill an omer of it to be kept for your generations; that they may see the bread wherewith I fed you in the wilderness, when I brought you forth from the land of Egypt."*

A container of Manna was to be kept as a

most precious memorial of the Faithfulness of God. Once again, the Lord would perform a miracle.

Whereas the Manna held over would normally breed worms and stink, the Manna addressed here in this Verse would be sustained by the Power of God for many, many centuries.

The Manna was to ever be a testimony that God did not suffer them to die of hunger, as their foolish hearts had unbelievingly anticipated. He rained bread from Heaven for them, fed them with Angels' food, watched over them with all the tenderness of a nurse, did bear with them, carried them on eagles' wings, so to speak, and, had they only continued on the proper ground of Faith, He would have put them in eternal possession of all the Promises made to their Fathers.

While we do not live off of past Blessings, at the same time, we are to never forget the past Blessings, allowing them to be proof positive of what God can do, and in fact, has done. And this we must remember:

If God has done it in the past, He will definitely do it in the present and in the future. If He has ever opened a blinded eye, unstopped a deaf ear, unloosed a captive tongue, He most definitely will do it again. If He has ever set a captive free, loosed them from the chains that bind them, He will do it again! If He has ever answered prayer, opening the widows of Heaven, granting us that which He Alone can grant, He will do it again! If He has ever baptized one Believer with the Holy Spirit, and has done so with the evidence of speaking with other tongues, He will do it again! And if He came once, He most definitely will come again!

Furthermore, God never regresses, but ever goes forward. And as He goes forward, He always and without exception, enlarges the Revelation. So what He did yesterday, He will do today, but will do it even on a greater scale. That's why Jesus wondrously said: *"Verily, verily, I say unto you, he who believes on Me, the works that I do shall he do also; and greater works than these shall he do; because I go unto My Father"* (Jn. 14:12).

GREATER WORKS?

How in the world could Believers presently do greater works than Christ? And yet, this is exactly what He said would happen.

He was speaking of the expanded Revelation.

To make it very brief, up unto the Cross, men could only say that He will do this; after the Cross, we can now say, He has done it. To be sure, the possession is always greater than the Promise!

THE POT OF MANNA

Verses 33 and 34 read: *"And Moses said unto Aaron, Take a pot, and put an omer full of Manna therein, and lay it up before the LORD, to be kept for your generations.*

"As the LORD commanded Moses, so Aaron laid it up before the Testimony, to be kept."

The *"omer"* was a man's daily portion. Laid up before the Lord, it furnished a volume of truth. There was no worm therein, nor ought of taint. It was the record of Jehovah's Faithfulness in providing for those whom He had redeemed out of the hand of the enemy.

Not so, as stated, when man hoarded it up for himself. Then the symptoms of corruption soon made their appearance. We cannot, if entering into the truth and reality of our position in Christ, hoard up. It is our privilege, day-by-day, to enter into the preciousness of Christ, as the One Who came down from Heaven to give life unto the world.

But if any try to live off of past experiences, thereby failing to renew Christ afresh in their hearts daily, one will find spiritual declension setting in as it regards their experiences, and in the words of Scripture, *"breeding worms and stinking."*

The *"pot of Manna"* was laid up before the Lord with the *"Tables of the Covenant"* and *"Aaron's rod that budded."*

The *"Testimony"* was the Law of Moses, and more specifically, the moral Law, i.e., *"the Ten Commandments"* (Ex., Chpt. 20). This Law presents the Righteousness of God, and that which He demands of man.

The *"pot of Manna,"* as repeatedly stated, represented Christ, Who Alone *"kept the Testimony,"* and did it on our behalf, even as the Last Adam (I Cor. 15:45-50).

"Aaron's rod that budded," proclaims the *"life"* that comes exclusively from our High Priest, the Lord Jesus Christ, and our Faith

in Him, Who paid the price for our Redemption on the Cross of Calvary. As stated, it is all of Christ, in Christ, about Christ, with Christ, and Alone Christ!

FORTY YEARS

Verses 35 and 36 read: *"And the Children of Israel did eat Manna forty years, until they came to a land inhabited; they did eat Manna, until they came unto the borders of the Land of Canaan.*

"Now an omer is the tenth part of an ephah."

As the Lord continued the provision for the Children of Israel until they came *"unto the borders of the Land of Canaan,"* He does the same with Believers presently.

The wilderness was not exactly a place of victory for the Children of Israel. In fact, all of that generation died in the wilderness, with the exception of the children, Joshua, and Caleb. They died because of unbelief. But yet the Manna continued. It is the same with Believers presently.

When the new generation came to *"the borders of the Land of Canaan,"* the Manna ceased, and they were instructed by the Lord to eat the *"old corn of the land."*

The Scripture then said: *"And the Manna ceased on the morrow after they had eaten of the old corn of the land; neither had the Children of Israel Manna anymore; but they did eat of the fruit of the Land of Canaan that year"* (Josh. 5:11-12). Now what does that tell us?

As new Believers, the Lord, even for a long while, will bear with us, giving the Manna, that is, making Himself real to us, irrespective of our stumblings, etc. But there will come a time that He demands we *"grow up."* And how do we do that?

The Believer should be taught from the moment of conversion that his Spiritual Growth consists totally and completely in Christ, and what Christ did at the Cross on his behalf. The Cross of Christ must ever be the object of one's Faith.

While it is true that the Holy Spirit is the One Who performs the task in our lives, which in fact is unending, and I speak of Spiritual Growth, still, He carries out His great Work solely on the premise of the Sacrifice of Christ (Rom. 8:2). Paul said:

"But if the Spirit (Holy Spirit) *of Him* (God the Father) *Who raised up Jesus from the dead dwell in you, He* (God the Father) *Who raised up Christ from the dead shall also quicken your mortal bodies by His Spirit Who dwells in you"* (Rom. 8:11).

The *"quickening of our mortal bodies"* doesn't pertain to the coming Resurrection, but rather, to our everyday living for God. After a while, the Manna will stop, and you are now expected to eat the *"old corn of the land,"* i.e., *"abide strictly by the Word."*

*"Where He may lead me I will go,
"For I have learned to trust Him so,
"And I remember 'twas for me,
"That He was slain on Calvary."*

*"O I delight in His command,
"Love to be led by His dear hand;
"His Divine Will is sweet to me,
"Hallowed by Blood-stained Calvary."*

*"Onward I go, no doubt no fear,
"Happy with Christ my Saviour near,
"Trusting that I someday shall see
"Jesus my Friend of Calvary."*

CHAPTER 17

(1) "AND ALL THE CONGREGATION OF THE CHILDREN OF ISRAEL JOURNEYED FROM THE WILDERNESS OF SIN, AFTER THEIR JOURNEYS, ACCORDING TO THE COMMANDMENT OF THE LORD, AND PITCHED IN REPHIDIM: AND THERE WAS NO WATER FOR THE PEOPLE TO DRINK.

(2) "WHEREFORE THE PEOPLE DID CHIDE WITH MOSES, AND SAID, GIVE US WATER THAT WE MAY DRINK. AND MOSES SAID UNTO THEM, WHY CHIDE YOU WITH ME? WHEREFORE DO YOU TEMPT THE LORD?

(3) "AND THE PEOPLE THIRSTED THERE FOR WATER; AND THE PEOPLE MURMURED AGAINST MOSES, AND SAID, WHEREFORE IS THIS THAT YOU HAVE BROUGHT US UP OUT OF EGYPT, TO KILL US AND OUR CHILDREN AND OUR CATTLE WITH THIRST?

(4) "AND MOSES CRIED UNTO THE

LORD, SAYING, WHAT SHALL I DO UNTO THIS PEOPLE? THEY BE ALMOST READY TO STONE ME.

(5) "AND THE LORD SAID UNTO MOSES, GO ON BEFORE THE PEOPLE, AND TAKE WITH YOU OF THE ELDERS OF ISRAEL; AND YOUR ROD, WHEREWITH YOU SMOTE THE RIVER, TAKE IN YOUR HAND, AND GO.

(6) "BEHOLD, I WILL STAND BEFORE YOU THERE UPON THE ROCK IN HOREB; AND YOU SHALL SMITE THE ROCK, AND THERE SHALL COME WATER OUT OF IT, THAT THE PEOPLE MAY DRINK. AND MOSES DID SO IN THE SIGHT OF THE ELDERS OF ISRAEL.

(7) "AND HE CALLED THE NAME OF THE PLACE MASSAH, AND MERIBAH, BECAUSE OF THE CHIDING OF THE CHILDREN OF ISRAEL, AND BECAUSE THEY TEMPTED THE LORD, SAYING, IS THE LORD AMONG US, OR NOT?"

The diagram is:

1. Once again Faith must be tested. They are taken by the *"Commandment of the Lord"* to *"Rephidim."*
2. It would seem somewhat strange that God Who professed to love Israel should lead them into a desert both foodless, and waterless. However, it was love that led them there that they might learn the desperate unbelief of their own hearts.
3. The Child of God does not really know what he is until tested. And neither can the Child of God know Who God is until tested. In this situation Israel, without God would have nothing, but with God they would have everything.
4. Verses 5 through 7 record one of the greatest miracles yet, plus one of the greatest *"types"* found in the entire Word of God.

REPHIDIM

Verse 1 reads: *"And all the congregation of the Children of Israel journeyed from the Wilderness of Sin, after their journeys, according to the Commandment of the LORD, and pitched in Rephidim: and there was no water for the people to drink."*

The phrase, *"The Command of the Lord,"* means that their journey was being led by the Lord. In other words, the Cloud moved, giving them direction.

As we stated, it was love that led them to this waterless place. In fact, every single thing that the Lord does for us or to us as His children is motivated 100 percent by love.

Everything the Lord leads us into is always done for our good. Here they would learn the desperate unbelief of their own hearts, and the unfailing faithfulness of God's heart. Only in a desert could God reveal what He can be to those who trust Him: for only there was Israel dependent upon Him for everything. Without God — nothing; with God — everything.

"Rephidim" means, *"resting place."* This is an oasis, but at certain times of the year, the copious stream dries up, and this evidently was one of those times.

THE PATH OF FAITH

How so much all of this illustrates the fact that the path of Faith is a path of trial. Those who are led by God must expect to encounter that which is displeasing to the flesh, and also a constant and real testing of Faith itself. God's design is to wean us from everything down here, to bring us to the place where we have no reliance upon material and human resources, to cast us completely upon Himself.

Oh how slow, how painfully slow, we are to learn this lesson! How miserably and how repeatedly we fail! How longsuffering the Lord is with us! It is this which the introductory *"and"* is designed to point (Pink).

The Scripture says, *"There was no water for the people to drink."*

Did they remember that a few days before, God had sweetened the bitter waters of Marah? Did they remember that God had opened a path through the Red Sea?

In fact, the Lord certainly knew there was no water there, and yet, He directed them to this very place. Their reaction, as we will see momentarily, was again to *"murmur and complain."*

HOW DOES IT FIT US PERSONALLY?

Before we criticize Israel too strongly, and, thereby, be quick to point out their faults and failures, I think we ought to take a look at ourselves. Are we doing any better? Do we rejoice when the Blessings come, and find fault and complain when the tests and the trials come our way?

You see, anybody can praise God when the windows of Heaven are open; however, when those windows close, it's not so easy to praise God then. But let us say it again:

Every single thing that happens to us is designed by the Lord. We're not our own; we are bought with a price. That price is the shed Blood of the Lord Jesus Christ. As well, the Lord is training us for something. And we must realize that He is not only the One Who leads us into Blessing, which He definitely does, but as well, He is the One Who leads us to the place of testing. He is the same God on both counts. And as we have also stated, it is love that leads us to both places, and it is to show us our needs.

As we said some pages back, we learn a lot about God during the times of Blessings, but we don't learn very much about ourselves. We can only learn about ourselves during times of testing.

MURMURING

Verses 2 and 3 read: *"Wherefore the people did chide with Moses, and said, Give us water that we may drink. And Moses said unto them, Why chide you with me? Wherefore do you tempt the LORD?*

"And the people thirsted there for water; and the people murmured against Moses, and said, Wherefore is this that you have brought us up out of Egypt, to kill us and our children and our cattle with thirst?"

The questions of the wilderness are: *"What?" "Where?" "How?"* Faith has a brief but comprehensive answer to all three, namely, *"God!"* (Mackintosh).

There are several things here that must be noted:

First of all, we see that the people complained to Moses, in a form of astute criticism. But let the Reader understand that when we criticize God's man, we are in essence criticizing God. Hence, Moses would ask, *"Wherefore do you tempt the LORD?"*

To *"tempt the LORD"* is to exhibit a want of Faith, which arouses His anger, which provokes Him. It was the special sin of the Israelites during the whole period of their sojourn in the wilderness. They *"tempted and provoked the Most High God"* (Ps. 78:56). They *"provoked Him to anger with their inventions"* (Ps. 106:29). They *"murmured in their tents"* (Ps. 106:25). They *"provoked Him at the sea"* (Ps. 106:7). They *"tempted Him in the desert"* (Ps. 106:14). Considering all of this, God's longsuffering can only be looked at as amazing.

Next, we find the people *"murmuring,"* and doing so against Moses, which as stated, is the same as murmuring against God. And yet, the Lord will take Israel to a higher height of spiritual revelation, than they have yet seen. But let it be understood that He does this, which we shall momentarily see, despite their murmuring and complaining, and certainly not because of it. As we've just quoted from the Psalms, the Holy Spirit noted all the murmurings and complainings, and recorded it for posterity. So this tells us how displeased the Lord was with the actions of the Children of Israel.

At the same time, the phrase *"the people thirsted there for water,"* signifies intense thirst.

It is said that there is probably no physical affliction comparable to intense thirst. His thirst was the only agony which drew from the Son of Man an acknowledgment of physical suffering, and did so in the words *"I thirst."*

So their thirst was real, very real! And of course, the Lord knew this, and as well, knew exactly what He was going to do.

THE TEST!

Unfortunately, in the last few decades, a great part of the modern Church, in its embracing of the Word of Faith doctrine, has tried to eliminate all testing, etc. A proper confession, they teach, will rid one of such activity. Why would one need testing, when one is already perfectly Righteous, and in fact, a little god?

However, erroneous teaching regarding this subject, or even denying the validity of testing, in no way exempts the Believer, that is the true Believer, from God's Way. And to be sure, His Way is the way of testing, which He does constantly.

Considering the fact that a great percentage of people adhering to this doctrine are not really even Born-Again, there is no testing, of course, for such individuals. They don't belong to the Lord, and in fact, have nothing to test. But considering those who are truly Born-Again, irrespective of what they have been taught, the testing will come. As someone has well said, Faith must always be tested, and great Faith must be tested greatly.

But the problem is, such individuals, having believed that which is error, and I continue to speak of the Word of Faith doctrine, testing leaves them bewildered and confused, because it's against everything which they have been taught. Many at this stage, although truly Born-Again, simply lose Faith. They have been taught that none of these things will happen if they have the proper confession, but Jesus said that irrespective as to what we have been taught, *"The rain descendeth, and the floods came, and the winds blew, and beat upon that house."* If the house is built on the rock of true Faith, and we speak of Faith in Christ and what He has done for us at the Cross, it will not fall because it is *"founded upon a rock."* But otherwise, it will fall, *"and great will be the fall of it"* (Mat. 7:25-27).

The idea is not whether the rain and the floods will come, and the winds will blow; that is a given. The idea is, do you have proper Faith?

PROPER FAITH

What is proper Faith?

It is obvious that the Children of Israel had their faith placed in other things. Their faith should have been in the slain Lamb, inasmuch as they surely realized that this is what caused Pharaoh to buckle. But instead, their faith was in something else, whether themselves, or whatever; it made no difference. Unless it's Faith in Christ and Him Crucified, then it's not Faith that God will honor. Now let the Reader read these words very carefully.

The sadness is, the Word of Faith doctrine has talked about faith for the last several decades, as it has talked about nothing else, but with the truth being that there is less true Faith in the Church presently, than ever before in its history. Faith, yes! But not the kind that God will recognize.

Paul held up Faith as no other Apostle, and rightly so. He understood Faith as no one else in the world of his day. For it to be true Faith, the type of Faith that God will always recognize, it had to be Faith in Christ and the Cross. That's why he said: *"For in Jesus Christ neither circumcision availeth anything, nor uncircumcision; but Faith which works by love"* (Gal. 5:6).

John said: *"This is the victory that overcometh the world, even our Faith"* (I Jn. 5:4).

When false teachers came into the Churches in Galatia, and were teaching *"another gospel,"* which would pull them away from true Faith, Paul said very testily: *"But though we, or an Angel from Heaven, preach any other gospel unto you than that which we have preached unto you, let him be accursed"* (Gal. 1:8).

The Cross of Christ must ever be the object of our Faith. When it is the object of our Faith, we will begin to see the Bible in an entirely different light, actually understanding it to a far greater degree than ever before. In fact, the story of the Bible is the story of the Cross.

MOSES

Verse 4 reads: *"And Moses cried unto the LORD, saying, What shall I do unto this people? They be almost ready to stone me."*

Concerning this moment, Pulpit Commentary says: *"It is one of the most prominent traits of the character of Moses, that, at the occurrence of a difficulty, he always carries it straight to God"* (Ex. 15:25; 24:15; 32:30; 33:8; Num. 11:2, 11; 12:11; 14:13-19).

The fact that we are told that Moses *"cried unto the Lord"* indicates the earnestness and vehemence of his prayer. *"What shall I do?"* expressed a consciousness of his own inability to cope with the situation, and also showed his confidence that the Lord would come to his and their relief.

Every Believer, when facing problems and difficulties which we cannot solve, and in fact, even if we think we can solve them, should always go to the Lord, whether the situation is large or small, and say, *"What shall I do?"* Down through life, I have learned that the Holy Spirit, Who is God, that as such, He is an Architect, a Builder, a Plumber, a Truck Driver, a Pilot, a Teacher, a Fundraiser, in fact, anything that we need.

As Believers, let us never think that it is men who do the doing. While God might use men, and often does, it is still the Lord Who has maneuvered events, places, things, and people. We should look to Him for everything.

I get amused at times, regarding some young people who are considering our Bible College. Some will ask the question, *"After I graduate, who will get me a Church?"*, implying that Denominational heads can provide such, and we can't, etc. They are missing the point altogether. Their very question says that their faith is in man and not God. As such, irrespective as to where they go, they will serve no purpose for the Lord. In fact, they are a waste of time!

To be sure, if they come to this school, they will be taught to look to the Lord for leading, guidance, in fact, for everything. Even if man wants to help, he can only work within the limitation of man. God has no limitations, and can do all things. So it would make much better sense to look to God.

Moses cried unto the Lord, and we must do the same. We must not grow weary in doing this, and above all, we must not be faithless. If the answer doesn't come immediately, we are to continue. Our Lord said as much: *"I say unto you, though he will not rise and give him, because he is his friend, yet because of his importunity* (overly persistent in demand or request) *he will rise and give him as many as he needs.*

"And I say unto you, ask, and it shall be given you; seek, and you shall find; knock, and it shall be opened unto you." The Lord then promised this:

"For every one who asks receives; and he who seeks finds; and to him who knocks it shall be opened."

And then: *"If a son shall ask bread of any of you who is a father, will he give him a stone? Or if he asks a fish, will he for a fish give him a serpent?*

"Or if he shall ask an egg, will he offer him a scorpion (an egg containing a scorpion)*?"*

And finally: *"If you then, being evil, know how to give good gifts unto your children: how much more shall your Heavenly Father give the Holy Spirit* (Who makes possible all of these things) *to them who ask Him?"* (Lk. 11:8-13).

PRAYER

Why is it that prayer is almost a lost art in the modern Church? Why is it that most Christians, in fact almost none, take advantage of the great privilege to take our needs to our Heavenly Father? In fact, there are several reasons.

First of all, there is a higher percentage presently of unredeemed people in the Church than there has been in the last 200-300 years. Even in Churches which claim to be Fundamental, which means they claim to believe all the Bible, I think I can say without fear of exaggeration that most of the people in these Churches aren't Born-Again. A percentage is, but I fear that percentage is small.

Second, even among those who are truly Born-Again, unbelief regarding prayer is rampant, which is obvious, because we see so few Christians who have any prayer life at all. However, it's the type of unbelief that is enmeshed in false doctrine, and not so much a rank disavowal of the Word of God.

The reason for this, I think, can be laid at the doorstep of the Word of Faith doctrine, which in reality is no faith at all. In fact, this doctrine teaches that if a person seeks the Lord on a regular basis, this shows that something is wrong, and there can be nothing wrong, they say, with a new creation man, etc. They do not teach their adherence to seek the Lord, but rather to *"confess"* their way to riches, etc. So prayer is out, and confession is in. As stated, this has had a greater effect on the Church than any other false doctrine, or even a culmination of false doctrines.

As well, the Word of Faith doctrine pulls Believers from the Cross, actually repudiating the Cross. They claim that the Cross is little more than *"past miseries."* It is referred to by their chief teachers as *"the greatest defeat in human history."* They claim that if the Preacher preaches the Cross he is preaching death, etc. (from Kenneth Hagin's monthly magazine, April, 2002). That is strange, especially considering that Paul said: *"For the preaching of the Cross is to them* who perish foolishness; but unto us which are saved it is the Power of God" (I Cor. 1:18).

I think as well that a proper understanding of the Cross, with one's Faith anchored firmly in that Finished Work, and refusing to allow it to be moved, is the criteria for both understanding the Word of God, and to having a successful, consistent prayer life. Israel's safety, protection, leading, guidance, prosperity, and in fact, everything she received from the Lord, was predicated solely on the slain Lamb. The sacrificial system, which symbolized the coming Christ and what He would do to redeem humanity, which refers to going to the Cross, presented itself as the very center of the Old Testament economy. As well, the Cross of Christ functions in the same manner for the New Testament economy. To fail to understand the Cross is, in some way, to fail to understand the entirety of the Word of God. In other words, the Cross is the key to the Word, while Faith is the key to the Cross (Rom. 6:3-14; Gal. 2:20; 5:6; Eph. 2:13-18; Col. 2:14-15).

THE ROD

Verse 5 reads: *"And the LORD said unto Moses, Go on before the people, and take with you of the Elders of Israel; and your rod, wherewith you smote the river, take in your hand, and go."*

The Elders of Israel going with Moses, thereby being a witness of what was to transpire, and who served as representatives of the people, in effect, made them a part of the miracle which was to transpire. By doing this, the Lord was informing Israel that each and every person must call upon the Lord. In other words, quit murmuring, and start praying and praising. We serve a miracle-working God. If it's food we need, He will give food! If it's water we need, He will give water! If it's money we need, He will give money! If it's victory we need, He will give victory!

While Moses under God was definitely their leader, and they were always to look to him as such, the idea is, every single individual in Israel, be it man, woman, boy, or girl, was to be a person of Faith. I quite often tell our Church (Family Worship Center) that I want them to be people of Faith. I want them to believe in what we are doing, in what God has called us to do.

A PART OF THE VISION

The Lord guided and directed Israel through Prophets. He guides and directs the Church through Apostles. Emphasis and direction are given to Apostles, which are borne out in the Book of Acts, and the Epistles. As the Lord gives Revelation to Apostles, whomever they might be, which incidentally, will always coincide perfectly with the Word, He also calls a great number of people to support that Apostle and stand with him. Even though this which the Lord gives him affects the entirety of the Body of Christ all over the world, the Lord will always make certain that enough helping hands are given to ensure the propagation of the Revelation or Vision. So in essence, these particular people, whomever they might be privileged to be, actually become a part of the Revelation. It's almost like the Lord is giving them the Revelation as well, which in a sense, He does.

In 1996, the Lord began to give me the Revelation of the Cross, which has gloriously changed my life. As I continue to say, it's not anything new, actually that which was given to the Apostle Paul. But the Church has had so little preaching and teaching on the Cross in the last several decades that by and large, it is presently illiterate as it regards the very foundation of the Gospel; consequently, the modern Church little knows where it's been, where it is, or where it's going. So this Vision of the Cross, as should be overly obvious, is vitally significant.

In the latter part of 1998, if I remember the date correctly, the Lord began to give me a Vision also of the way and manner in which this great Revelation of the Cross can be taken to the world. I speak of Radio, but in a different way than we have known in the past.

While Television will always remain prominent, due to our limited time (one hour a week), the Message of the Cross cannot be properly explained and propagated. The Lord instructed me that instead of purchasing time on Radio Stations, we were to acquire the Stations themselves, which would give us ample time, actually 24 hours a day, seven days a week. This we immediately began to do, and will continue until we have covered the entirety of this nation, plus the world, which latter is covered by the Internet.

All who believe in what we are doing, and thereby support what we are doing, both prayerfully and financially, literally become a part of the Vision. In a sense, as stated, God is giving them the Revelation, as He has given it to me.

In fact, the entirety of Israel, in a sense, was to conduct themselves exactly as Moses. Regrettably, they didn't, and regrettably, that generation perished in the wilderness.

The *"Rod"* of which this Fifth Verse speaks, was a symbol of judgment. The first reference to it definitely determines that. When Moses in front of Pharaoh placed it on the floor, it became a *"serpent"* (Ex. 4:3) — a reminder of the curse. With this Rod, the waters of the Nile were smitten and turned into blood (Ex. 7:17). This proclaims the fact that the only answer to this *"curse,"* is the shed Blood of the Lord Jesus Christ.

So now, the *"Rod"* will smite the Rock, symbolic of Christ being smitten by God on the Cross, from which will come the life-giving rivers of water. And I remind the Reader that it wasn't the Resurrection which produced this, but rather the Cross.

THE ROCK

Verse 6 reads: *"Behold, I will stand before you there upon the rock in Horeb; and you shall smite the rock, and there shall come water out of it, that the people may drink. And Moses did so in the sight of the Elders of Israel."*

We are now about to witness one of the many Old Testament Types of the Lord Jesus, in fact, one of the most graphic of all. Concerning this *"Type"* Paul said:

"Moreover, Brethren, I would not that you should be ignorant, how that all our fathers were under the Cloud (the cloud of the Presence of the Lord which led Israel in the Wilderness), *and all passed through the Sea* (the great Red Sea miracle); *and were all baptized under Moses in the Cloud and in the Sea* (meaning that it was Moses whom God used to bring about these miracles, which were *'Types'*); *and did all eat the same spiritual meat; and did all drink the same spiritual drink; for they drank of that spiritual Rock that followed them: and that Rock was Christ"* (I Cor. 10:1-4).

In fact, Christ Personally affirmed that by saying *"Upon this Rock* (pointing to Himself, not referring to Peter's confession) *I will build My Church"* (Mat. 16:18).

This *"Rock"* was to be smitten. This, of course, speaks of the death of the Lord Jesus. It is striking to note the *"order"* of the teaching as it regards the *"types"* given in Exodus, Chapters 16 and 17. In the former, we have that which speaks of the Incarnation of Christ, and we speak of the giving of the Manna. In the Seventeenth Chapter, we see that which foreshadows the Crucifixion of Christ, and of course, we speak of the smitten Rock. Christ must descend from Heaven to Earth (as the Manna did) if He was to become the Bread of Life to His people; but He must be smitten by Divine Judgment if He was to be the Water of Life to them!

THE TIMING OF THE SMITTEN ROCK

Exodus, Chapter 17 opens not with praise and worship, as it should, but rather with murmuring and complaining. This was the occasion of the smitten Rock. But where sin abounded, Grace did much more abound (Rom. 5:20).

Jesus did not die on the Cross because the people were righteous and holy, but rather because they were the very opposite. He died on the Cross because of sin and shame, because of transgression and iniquity, because man desperately needed Christ and what Christ would do on the Cross, even though man was actually not aware of his terrible condition. That's why Jesus said: *"They who be whole need not a physician, but they who are sick.*

"But you go and learn what that means. I will have mercy, and not sacrifice: for I am not come to call the righteous, but sinners to repentance" (Mat. 9:12-13).

WATER OUT OF THE ROCK

The Rock mentioned here must have been of gigantic size. The water that would come out of it must slake the thirst not only for approximately three million Israelites, but as well, all their cattle and sheep. In fact, the Psalmist refers to this. He said:

"He (God) clave the rocks in the wilderness, and gave them drink as out of the great depths.

"He brought streams also out of the Rock, and caused waters to run down like rivers" (Ps. 78:15-16).

The Psalmist also said: *"Which turned the rock into a standing water, the flint into a fountain of waters"* (Ps. 114:8).

So what we're speaking of here was not a mere stream, but rather a river of water, which of course was needed.

This is what Jesus was speaking about when He said: *"If any man thirst, let him come unto Me, and drink.*

"He who believes on Me, as the Scripture has said, Out of his belly shall flow rivers of living water" (Jn. 7:37-38).

THE HOLY SPIRIT

In essence, this Living Water represents the *"Holy Spirit."* The smiting of the Rock by Moses, which symbolizes God smiting Christ (instead of us), which refers to the Cross, made it possible for the advent of the Holy Spirit in the hearts and lives of all Believers. Before the Cross, the Holy Spirit was very limited as to what He could do regarding Believers. That's why Jesus said: *"Even the Spirit of Truth; whom the world cannot receive, because it sees Him not, neither knows Him: but you know Him; for He dwells with you, and shall be in you"* (Jn. 14:17).

The Disciples, of course, knew exactly what Christ was talking about. This means that the Holy Spirit, before the Cross, could dwell with Believers, which He definitely did, but could not abide in them permanently. In truth, He did come into some Believers to help them perform certain tasks, but only for a period of time. But after the Cross, Jesus said: *"I will pray the Father, and He shall give you another Comforter* (Helper), *that He may abide with you forever"* (Jn. 14:16).

The Holy Spirit is the Member of the Godhead through Whom everything works on this Earth. In other words, whatever is done on this Earth by God is done by and through the Holy Spirit. The only thing, in fact, that the Holy Spirit didn't do, was that which Christ carried out by coming from Heaven, being born of a Virgin, and then going to the Cross to satisfy the terrible sin debt. Even then, the Holy Spirit attended Christ every step of the way, and throughout every moment of time (Ps. 45:7; Lk. 4:18-19).

Due to the Cross, which is beautifully symbolized by the smitten Rock, the Holy Spirit now has far greater latitude to work, than He did before the Cross. But again let us emphasize that it was the Cross which made all of this possible, and not the Resurrection of Christ, as important as that was.

WHY WAS THE CROSS SUCH A NECESSITY?

To show the Reader how much of a necessity it was, all the Old Testament Saints, upon death, were actually taken captive by Satan down into Paradise (Eph. 4:8-10). While the Evil One could not put them into the burning side of Hell, even with a great gulf which separated that part from Paradise (Lk. 16:26), still, all the Old Testament Saints were his captives.

Why was that the case?

Paul said it very clearly: *"For it is not possible that the blood of bulls and goats should take away sins"* (Heb. 10:4).

In other words, the sin debt, which hung heavily over man, could not be assuaged by animal blood. So in effect, the sin debt remained, which means that Satan, at least after a fashion, still had a claim on these individuals, even the greatest of the ones of the Old Testament. But when Jesus went to the Cross, as Peter said, *"We were not redeemed with corruptible things, as silver and gold . . . but with the Precious Blood of Christ, as of a Lamb without blemish and without spot:*

"Who verily was foreordained before the foundation of the world, but was manifest in these last times for you" (I Pet. 1:18-20).

After the Death of Christ, even as we've previously stated in this Volume, Christ went down into Paradise and *"led captivity captive,"* which means that all these who had been captives of Satan, were now a captive of the Lord Jesus Christ, because Christ is the strongest of the strong. He said: *"How can one enter into a strongman's house, and spoil his goods, except he first bind the strongman? And then he will spoil his house"* (Mat. 12:29).

While Satan was strong, Jesus, as would be obvious, was and is much stronger; consequently, He did spoil Satan's house, and there was nothing the Evil One could do about it.

I want to remind the Reader that Jesus set these people free, before the Resurrection because the debt was paid at the Cross. Now when a Believer dies, he immediately goes to be with Christ, for Satan has no claim on him whatsoever (Phil. 1:23).

When the people drank of that water, even though it slaked their physical thirst, even as it was meant to do, it was a type of the Living Water afforded by Christ, and brought to us by the Holy Spirit, which was paid for at Calvary's Cross. There may be other types in the Old Testament as potent as it regards the Cross of Christ, but I think there is none more potent. And let the following ever be understood:

As Israel then drank to their full, that River, so to speak, is still flowing, and all who come may drink to their fill.

The water from the smitten Rock foretold the Living Water, the Holy Spirit, to be sent forth by the smitten Saviour. The Holy Spirit was the fruit of Christ's Sacrifice (I Cor. 10:4). As we have stated, the Rock was smitten by the very same rod of judgment that smote the land of Egypt.

THE TEMPTING OF THE LORD

Verse 7 reads: *"And he called the name of the place Massah, and Meribah, because of the chiding of the Children of Israel, and because they tempted the LORD, saying, Is the LORD among us, or not?"*

"Massah" means, *"trial or temptation."*

"Meribah" means, *"chiding or quarrel."* To show how displeased the Lord was with the action of the Children of Israel, He did not tell Moses to refer to the great miracle of the smitten Rock, but rather, to place the name of *"temptation"* and *"quarreling,"* on the place. What an indictment!

NOTES

One should notice that the temptation, which refers to the name *"Massah,"* was the fact that they tempted God. What does that mean?

It means that they tried Him to such an extent, and did so by quarreling, murmuring, and complaining, that He was sorely tried as it regards eliminating the entirety of this people. This shows us exactly how contemptible in the Eyes of God is the act of faithlessness. The Lord can take many things which are negative, and bear with them far longer than we could ever think of doing so, but He angers quickly as it regards a lack of Faith. And of course, I'm speaking of Faith as it regards His Children.

The Lord wants us to believe Him, and He wants us to believe Him with praises, with victory, even with shouts of joy. To be frank, the Psalms are full of examples.

Now it's easy to do that when all things are going well, but something else again when nothing, seemingly, is going well. But we must remember this:

Irrespective of circumstances, difficulties, events, problems, trouble, etc., God does not change. He's the same when blessing us, as when putting us to the test. The idea is that we be brought to the place to where we do not change either, irrespective of the circumstances.

We must remember that God cannot fail. Our Word of Faith friends claim that God was the biggest failure ever, then listing Adam's circumstances, along with many others. They cap it all off by the Crucifixion, calling that *"the greatest defeat in human history."*

The problem is, they are reading in the middle of the Book. If they'll read the last two Chapters, they will plainly see, *"We win,"* which means that God wins, and does so gloriously. No, God has never been defeated, will never be defeated, and in fact, cannot be defeated!

And we cannot be defeated either, if we will hold our heads high, and *"look unto Jesus, the Author and Finisher of our Faith"* (Heb. 12:2). This Hebrew Text plainly tells us that what the Lord starts, He finishes. Let every Believer, to whom the Devil has lied, telling them that they won't make it, understand that whatever the Lord has begun, the Lord will finish!

Irrespective of circumstances, we must believe Him. And that means, in time of trouble and difficulties, our demeanor should be the same because the Lord won't fail us.

THE CROSS

There's one other thing I must say in regard to this.

Proper Faith is required if one is to be what one ought to be. And by proper Faith, we're speaking of the correct object of Faith, which must always be the Cross of Christ. I want the Reader to understand just how important all of this is. As we've previously stated, Paul used the term *"in Christ,"* or one of its derivatives, some 170 times in his 14 Epistles. In fact, those two words *"in Christ,"* explain Biblical Christianity as nothing else.

But without exception, those two words refer to what Jesus did at the Cross, and our Faith in that Finished Work (Rom. 6:3-14). Everyone talks about Faith, but most of the time it's misplaced Faith. God loves Faith, but it has to be Faith in the Finished Work of Christ, which means that we understand that all things come to us exclusively through what Jesus did at the Cross. This is the means and the manner in which the Holy Spirit works, and of course, anything which enables Him to do His work in a greater way is the greatest thing that could ever happen to us. And to be sure, the Cross provides that latitude.

(8) "THEN CAME AMALEK, AND FOUGHT WITH ISRAEL IN REPHIDIM.

(9) "AND MOSES SAID UNTO JOSHUA, CHOOSE US OUT MEN, AND GO OUT, FIGHT WITH AMALEK: TOMORROW I WILL STAND ON THE TOP OF A HILL WITH THE ROD OF GOD IN MY HAND.

(10) "SO JOSHUA DID AS MOSES HAD SAID TO HIM, AND FOUGHT WITH AMALEK: AND MOSES, AARON, AND HUR WENT UP TO THE TOP OF THE HILL.

(11) "AND IT CAME TO PASS, WHEN MOSES HELD UP HIS HAND, THAT ISRAEL PREVAILED: AND WHEN HE LET DOWN HIS HAND, AMALEK PREVAILED.

(12) "BUT MOSES' HANDS WERE HEAVY; AND THEY TOOK A STONE, AND PUT IT UNDER HIM, AND HE SAT THEREON; AND AARON AND HUR STAYED UP HIS HANDS, THE ONE ON THE ONE SIDE, AND THE OTHER ON THE OTHER SIDE; AND HIS HANDS WERE STEADY UNTIL THE GOING DOWN OF THE SUN.

(13) "AND JOSHUA DISCOMFITED AMALEK AND HIS PEOPLE WITH THE EDGE OF THE SWORD.

(14) "AND THE LORD SAID UNTO MOSES, WRITE THIS FOR A MEMORIAL IN A BOOK, AND REHEARSE IT IN THE EARS OF JOSHUA: FOR I WILL UTTERLY PUT OUT THE REMEMBRANCE OF AMALEK FROM UNDER HEAVEN.

(15) "AND MOSES BUILT AN ALTAR, AND CALLED THE NAME OF IT JEHOVAH-NISSI:

(16) "FOR HE SAID, BECAUSE THE LORD HATH SWORN THAT THE LORD WILL HAVE WAR WITH AMALEK FROM GENERATION TO GENERATION."

The structure is:

1. The reception of the Holy Spirit immediately causes war, and we speak of spiritual warfare.

2. There is an immense difference between Justification and Sanctification. The one is Christ fighting *for* us; the other, the Holy Spirit fighting *in* us.

3. The entrance of the new nature is the beginning of warfare with the old. Amalek pictures the old carnal nature.

4. This carnal nature wars against the Spirit, *"It is not subject to the Law of God neither indeed can be."* God has decreed war against it forever.

5. God did not destroy Amalek, but determined to have war with him from generation to generation. He was to dwell in the land, but not to reign in it. Romans, Chapter 6 says, *"Let not sin therefore reign in your mortal bodies."*

6. This command would be unmeaning if sin, i.e., *"the sin nature,"* were not existing in the Christian. Sin dwells in the Believer, but dwells and reigns in an unbeliever.

7. Verse 14 is the birth of the Bible as a written Book. It is remarkable that the first mention of the Bible should be in connection with the hostility of the natural man (Amalek) to the spiritual man (Israel).

8. As it regards the Bible, no Book has been so hated, and so loved.

AMALEK

Verse 8 reads: *"Then came Amalek, and fought with Israel in Rephidim."*

Beginning with the Twelfth Chapter of Exodus, and concluding with the Seventeenth Chapter, we have a beautiful description of the Plan of Redemption, and how it functions within our hearts and lives. It is as follows:

1. Chapter 12 proclaims the Passover, which typifies the great price paid for our Redemption in the Death of Christ on the Cross.

2. The Red Sea Crossing, typified in Exodus, Chapter 14, the Believer's entrance into Christ, and what His Crucifixion means to us.

3. Chapter 15 proclaims the great rejoicing of the Children of Israel on yonder shore, which typifies the joy of Salvation which comes to the believing sinner.

4. The latter portion of the Fifteenth Chapter also proclaims the Cross as the answer for life's problems, typified by the bitter waters of Marah, and the tree placed in those waters, which made them sweet.

5. Chapter 16 proclaims the Manna, which was a Type of Christ, and His blessing to the Believer.

6. The Sixteenth Chapter also proclaims the Sabbath, which is a type of the *"rest"* which one experiences after coming to Christ.

7. The smitten Rock of Chapter 17 portrays the Crucifixion of Christ, and the Living Water which flowed from that Rock, which typifies the Holy Spirit.

8. Last of all, upon the reception of the Holy Spirit, the latter portion of the Seventeenth Chapter proclaims the coming of Amalek, a type of the flesh. Satan little opposes the Believer who is not Spirit-filled. But once that Believer is baptized with the Holy Spirit, which we teach, is always accompanied by the speaking with other tongues (Acts 2:4), Satan knows that such a Believer can cause him much trouble. So now we have the struggle between the flesh and the Spirit.

THE FLESH AND THE SPIRIT

The Amalekites seem to have been descendants of Amalek, the grandson of Esau (Gen. 36:12).

NOTES

Esau had no time for God, and is a representative of the spirit of the world, and as it regards the Believer, that which we refer to as *"the flesh."* In other words, there is an unending war with the *"flesh,"*

WHAT DO WE MEAN BY *"FLESH"*?

Paul used this term more than anyone else. And it is extremely important to note that his use of the term was far more prominent in the Eighth Chapter of Romans and throughout the entirety of the Epistle to the Galatians.

Romans, Chapter 8 is the Holy Spirit Chapter. As someone has said, Romans, Chapter 6 portrays to us the *"mechanics"* of the Holy Spirit, in other words, *"how"* He does things, or more particularly, the manner in which He does them, which is by the Cross, while the Eighth Chapter of Romans proclaims to us the *"dynamics"* of the Holy Spirit, which proclaims *"what"* He does in our hearts and lives, once we understand the manner in which He works.

Galatians is the great Epistle which explains to us the doctrine of *"Galatianism."* This is according to the following:

The Galatians were brought to Christ under Paul's Ministry, or at least, one of his Associates. This means they were brought in right, given a firm foundation, which was the Foundation of the Cross. But after Paul left and went on to other endeavors, leaving others in charge, who incidentally had very little experience, false teachers came in from Judea, who were attempting to propagate the Law. In other words, they believed in Christ, but they gave little significance, if any, to the Cross, in effect, telling the Believers that to be the type of Christian they ought to be, they had to add the Law to their acceptance of Christ. In other words, all the men had to be circumcised, with the little boy babies circumcised at eight days old after they were born, along with Sabbath-keeping, etc. That's why Paul bluntly said to them: *"For in Jesus Christ neither circumcision availeth anything, nor uncircumcision; but faith which works by love"* (Gal. 5:6).

In fact, as the problem of *"the flesh,"* was the predominant problem with the Galatians, and all others in the Early Church we might quickly add, it has always been the predominant problem in the Church from then until now, and continues to be unto this hour. In fact, I personally believe that it is worse today than ever. So what did Paul mean by using the term *"flesh"*?

When Paul used the term *"flesh,"* which is what the Holy Spirit desired that he use, he was speaking either of the human being who lives in a body of flesh (Gal. 2:20), or our own personal efforts to live for God, which is by far, the most predominant way he used this particular word.

The word *"flesh"* in the Greek is *"sarx,"* and can refer to the *"meat on the bones of a physical body, or the frailties of human nature,"* which latter is the manner in which Paul uses it mostly. As stated, it is simply the Believer attempting to live for God, by his own sense knowledge, personal strength, or human ability, which means that the Holy Spirit is not helping him. Such a person is doomed to failure.

THE HOLY SPIRIT AND THE FLESH

Now here is where the great problem ensues:

Most Christians don't have the slightest idea as to how the Holy Spirit works. Our Denominational friends, who do not believe in the Baptism with the Holy Spirit, with the evidence of speaking with other tongues, just sort of take the Holy Spirit for granted. In fact, they know almost nothing about the Spirit.

Our Pentecostal friends, and I am Pentecostal, are a little more advanced as it regards the Spirit, but not much.

They think that if one is baptized with the Holy Spirit, that is, if they think about it at all, this automatically guarantees the fact that the Holy Spirit will do great and mighty things for them, etc. But yet, we have almost as much moral failure in the ranks of the Pentecostals, as we do in the other ranks. So what is happening here?

While it is certainly true that the Holy Spirit comes into the heart and life of the Believer at conversion, which is always without exception; however, there is a vast difference in being *"born of the Spirit,"* than being *"baptized with the Spirit."* If one reads the Book of Acts, and the Epistles for that matter, it becomes crystal clear that we are expected to go on and be baptized with the Holy Spirit after conversion, which will always be accompanied by speaking with other tongues (Acts 2:4; 10:44-46; 19:1-7). So having Scripturally settled that, let's go on to the Pentecostals who have been baptized with the Holy Spirit, but are still experiencing failure, as are almost all.

Why?

As stated, the Spirit-filled person, for the most part, not understanding anything about the Cross as it refers to Sanctification, which is the manner in which the Holy Spirit works, simply takes the Holy Spirit for granted. In fact, there is nothing else they can do, not knowing God's prescribed order of victory.

You should notice that in Romans, Chapters 6, 7, and 8, the word *"know,"* or *"knowing,"* or *"known,"* is used some 11 times. It refers to something, as should be obvious, that we ought to know. And in these three Chapters, it is referring to what the Believer ought to know as it regards the Cross of Christ as it refers to Sanctification, and how the Holy Spirit works. This is of vital significance, as should be understood.

HOW DOES THE HOLY SPIRIT WORK?

He works strictly from the realm of Faith (Gal. 5:6), but with its object ever being the Cross of Christ. In other words, the Cross plays just as much a part in one's Sanctification as it does one's Salvation. But most Christians don't know that; therefore, they live a defeated life. Let me say it again:

God has only one prescribed order of victory, not ten, not five, not even two, just one. And this means, if you do not know that prescribed way, then you are doomed to spiritual failure, no matter how hard you might try otherwise. And as stated, due to this gross Scriptural ignorance, virtually all of the modern Church walks in failure.

As we've already said any number of times in this Volume, the Holy Spirit works within our hearts and lives through the legal means of what Jesus did at the Cross. That's what the phrase *"in Christ"* means, which Paul used some 170 times in his 14 Epistles. It means we are in Christ by virtue of what Christ did at the Cross, and our Faith in that

Finished Work. We simply believe in what He did there, and in the mind of God, we are literally placed into Christ. That's why Jesus said: *"At that day* (after the Cross, and the Advent of the Holy Spirit) *you shall know* (there's the word *'know'* again) *that I am in My Father, and you in Me, and I in you"* (Jn. 14:20). But we are in Christ, only by virtue of the Cross, and our Faith in that Finished Work. Of course, the Holy Spirit is the One Who places us in Christ, keeps us in Christ, where we shall ever remain in Christ; however, He does so by virtue of our Faith, and more particularly, our Faith in that Finished Work (Rom. 6:3-14; 8:1-2, 11; Eph. 2:13-18; Gal. 6:14; Col. 2:14-15).

THE RENEWED MIND

Paul said: *"And be not conformed to this world: but be ye transformed by the renewing of your mind, that you may do what is that good, and acceptable, and perfect Will of God"* (Rom. 12:2).

Being *"conformed to this world,"* refers to the Christian trying to live for God by the same means that the world lives, and we're speaking of one's own personal efforts and strength, etc.

When the mind is transformed, which it must be done by being *"renewed,"* the Believer no longer leans on his own strength and ability, but leans totally upon Christ and what Christ has done at the Cross, which enables the Holy Spirit to work mightily within our lives (Rom. 8:13).

Now most Christians, and especially Pentecostals, think they are living by the Power of the Holy Spirit, simply because they are doing spiritual things. In other words, they heap Scriptures on the flesh, which incidentally are wrongly applied, and they think that is *"walking after the Spirit,"* when in reality, they are *"walking after the flesh"* (Rom. 8:1).

A PERSONAL EXPERIENCE

The year was 1989, if I remember correctly. I had been invited to preach in a particular Church in Florida. Frances and I, along with Donnie and one of my Associates, arrived a day early, in order to be in the service that particular night. I was to minister the next night.

The Preacher that night preached on *"spiritual warfare."*

Incidentally, we've had much preaching on that subject in the last two or three decades, but regrettably, with most of the Preachers not having the slightest idea as to what spiritual warfare is all about.

But at any rate, that was his subject that night. His theme was, *"Being militant in Christ."* After he preached his message, he then demonstrated what being militant actually meant.

At that particular time, while I had excellent knowledge as it regards the Cross concerning Salvation, I really did not understand the Cross at all as it regards Sanctification. But I did know that what most of the Church was doing wasn't right, and I speak of victory over the flesh, etc.

His idea of militancy was according to the following:

He asked how many people in the building needed help for problems of some particular time. A goodly number of people stepped forward and came to the Altar. He, along with other chosen Saints, gathered around these people, and began to vigorously stomp their feet, make faces, and scream at the Devil as loud as they could. This was supposed to scare the Devil I suppose, with him then leaving.

I looked at this debacle, and in no way do I intend to demean the motives of the young Preacher, but I knew this was foolishness.

After a period of time, Frances and I left. Donnie and my Associate informed me the next morning that they really rolled into high gear after we left. I suppose our presence hindered them in some manner.

First of all, is there anything in the Bible which substantiates such action? Of course, the answer is *"no!"* So where does the Church come up with all of this foolishness, which runs the gamut from the proverbial *"A"* to *"Z"*?

It comes up with all of these things simply because it doesn't know God's prescribed order of victory. In other words, it doesn't understand the Cross as the Cross refers to our Sanctification, and our Faith in what Christ did there, which gives the Holy Spirit latitude. In fact, what our dear Brother was doing was totally and completely, *"of the flesh."* And let me say this:

Anything that we do which is not Faith in Christ and what Christ has done at the Cross is in fact, *"the flesh."*

Actually, the term *"walking after the flesh"* (Rom. 8:1), simply means to trust in one's own strength and ability, versus *"walking after the Spirit,"* which of course, refers to the Holy Spirit, and refers to one's Faith being placed in Christ and the Cross, which of course, refers to His Finished Work. It's never in things that *"we do,"* but rather trust and Faith in that which *"He has already done."*

How many Preachers presently know this? Almost none!

Consequently, they may preach excellent things *"about the Gospel,"* but they will not be truly *"preaching the Gospel."*

Paul said:

"For Christ sent me not to baptize, but to preach the Gospel: not with wisdom of words, lest the Cross of Christ should be made of none effect" (I Cor. 1:17).

This is the reason that I plead with people to get these Commentaries, and as well, if possible, to get one or more Volumes for Preacher friends, or anyone else for that matter. The Lord in 1996, after some five years of daily seeking His Face, and with tears, opened up to me the Message of the Cross. In fact, He began to open it up at that particular time, with that Revelation continuing even unto this hour, and which I feel will ever continue, simply because it's impossible to exhaust the Finished Work of Christ. That's why Paul referred to it as *"the Everlasting Covenant"* (Heb. 13:20).

What the Lord gave me is not new, not by any means. It is actually what He had already given to Paul, which Paul gave to us. So what I'm teaching is what Paul taught. But sadly and regrettably, much of the modern Church has no idea as to what Paul taught; consequently they are doomed to spiritual failure.

THE REVELATION WHICH WAS GIVEN TO ME

I know what it is to try to live for the Lord, and to try with all of my might, but yet fail, simply because I was functioning *"in the flesh,"* but did not know that I was functioning in the flesh. That's the tragedy! And looking back, I did not know a single Preacher who knew any more then than I did. In other words, they did not understand God's prescribed order of victory, any more than I did. As stated, I understood the Cross as it refers to Salvation, but I had no knowledge whatsoever as it refers to Sanctification; consequently, I tried to live this life at that time, as most other Christians do, but which is guaranteed to bring on failure.

We do all type of spiritual things, and we think because these things are spiritual, that's *"walking after the Spirit."*

Satan comes against every Believer with the intention of destroying that Believer. The Believer need not worry or fret, and in fact, can walk in perpetual victory, providing the Believer understands what the Lord gave to Paul, as it refers to Sanctification. But regrettably, as repeatedly stated, most Believers don't know that. So despite their best efforts, they fail. The failure may come in many and varied ways, but whatever way it comes, it is always constituted as a *"work of the flesh"* (Gal. 5:19-21). Now let me say that again:

It is impossible for the Christian to live above *"works of the flesh,"* if that Christian doesn't know and understand the Cross as it refers to Sanctification. Paul said:

"But God forbid that I should glory, save in the Cross of our Lord Jesus Christ, by Whom the world is crucified unto me, and I unto the world" (Gal. 6:14).

Paul plainly says here that it is the *"Cross"* which gives us victory over the world. And remember, he is speaking to Believers and not unbelievers.

He also said: *"I am crucified with Christ* (taking us to the Cross)*: nevertheless I live; yet not I, but Christ lives in me: and the life which I now live in the flesh I live by the Faith of the Son of God, Who loved me, and gave Himself for me"* (Gal. 2:20).

To live a sanctified life, in other words, victory over the world, the flesh, and the Devil, Paul takes us immediately to the Cross, by saying, *"I am crucified with Christ."* He is referring to Romans 6:3-5. But if the Believer doesn't understand this, he will try to live this life by his own strength and machinations. Due to the fact, as stated, that he covers up these machinations with Scriptures, he thinks that he is functioning properly, when all the time, he is going in the wrong direction, which will guarantee defeat. He is then left very confused. And let's explain that:

Paul also said: *"For that which I do I allow not: for what I would, that do I not; but what I hate, that do I"* (Rom. 7:15).

Romans, Chapter 7 is the story of Paul's life immediately after he was saved and baptized with the Holy Spirit, and before the Lord gave him understanding as it regards personal victory.

The Apostle tells us that he struggled mightily to live a holy life, but found himself failing, despite the fact that he was a new creature in Christ Jesus, despite the fact that he was baptized with the Holy Spirit, and even despite the fact that he was a God-called Apostle. So what is wrong here?

That's what the Apostle in effect was asking. When he said: *"For that which I do I allow not,"* the word *"allow"* should actually have been translated *"understand,"* for that's what it actually means. He actually said: *"For that which I do I understand not."*

He was trying so hard, and despite his best efforts, he was failing the Lord in some way, which means that at that time, *"lusts of the flesh"* were manifesting themselves in and through him. Sadly, that is the lot presently of almost all Christians.

They struggle, they fight, they labor, they try, and they do so with all their strength, but they find themselves still failing, and in fact, with the problem getting worse instead of better, and that despite all their efforts. Paul described it perfectly; they simply don't understand.

I very well know the feeling, for I've been there. Only the Lord knows the number of times that I have shed hot tears, asking the Lord *"Why?"* The answer all the time was in the Word of God, and I refer to the Sixth Chapter of Romans. I thought I understood that Chapter, but the truth is, I didn't. And regrettably, there was no one to explain it to me, for the circle in which I traveled, did not have understanding as well. And after the

NOTES

Lord has given me this Revelation, and looking back, I now know that almost no one in the modern Church had proper understanding. Of course, I'm certain there were some who did, but they were few and far between.

And then when I failed, to have the entirety of the Church laughing at me, or worse yet, to exhibit pity, presents itself as about the worst thing that can happen to an individual. Had I not had a firm hold on Christ, I simply could not have survived. Tragically, I had both the News Media and the Church joining forces attempting to finish the task of destroying me completely.

I'll never forget the day that I sat with Frances and a group of friends, and laid my Bible on the table in front of me, and stated, *"I don't know the answer, but I know the answer's found in this Book, and by the Grace of God, I'm going to find that answer."*

And by the Grace of God, I did!

THE BELIEVER'S FUNCTION AND THE BELIEVER'S VICTORY

What I'm about to say, hopefully, will clear up some misunderstanding as it regards the function or calling of a Believer, and their personal victory. Most Christians don't understand this. They think if God is truly using a person, then this guarantees that such a person has victory in his personal life. It guarantees no such thing!

If God waited until people were perfect before He called them, He simply wouldn't call anyone. In fact, the Call of God on a person's life is there from the moment they give their heart to Christ. It may not materialize for some time, but to be sure, it is there.

All *"Callings"* are in effect *"gifts,"* which means they are not earned, or merited, but simply *"gifts from God"* (Eph. 4:11-12). In that *"gift"* or *"function"* the Lord will use that individual, and sometimes, use that person mightily.

But if the individual doesn't go God's Way as it regards personal victory, which refers to the Cross, even though the Lord will have patience for a long while, ultimately and eventually, the function will be hindered by the lack of personal victory. But that in no way means that the good work accomplished by this individual, whomever he or she might be, is bogus. In fact, at this very moment, there are tens of thousands of Preachers all over the world, who are being used of God, with some of them being used mightily, but yet are failing in some way, in their personal lives. Despite their Calling, and despite the Holy Spirit helping them greatly to carry out that Calling, if they do not know God's prescribed order of victory, on a personal basis, they will be living a defeated life. And tragically, if the failure is of the type that is scandalous, and please understand that they don't have any choice as to how Satan attacks them, most of the time, the Church will claim that their work is bogus also. Nothing could be further from the Truth!

This is what Paul was talking about when he said: *"Brethren, if a man be overtaken in a fault* (a severe moral fault, for this is what the word means), *you which are spiritual, restore such an one in the spirit of meekness; considering yourself, lest you also be tempted"* (Gal. 6:1). But regrettably, there aren't many *"spiritual"* people around.

The word *"spiritual"* here simply means that the person is functioning in the realm of the Holy Spirit. And what is that realm?

The Believer, who knows and understands God's prescribed order, is to then inform such a Believer who has failed, as to the reason why they failed. And what is that reason?

The person has failed, irrespective as to whom the individual might be, simply because they have relied on *"the flesh,"* instead of *"the Spirit."* This means that they didn't know God's Way, and attempted to live this life by their own strength, which guarantees failure, and that despite whatever Calling one might have.

The spiritual Believer is to lead that person to the Cross, tell them that this is where their Faith must be anchored, and where it must remain, which will then give the Holy Spirit latitude to work within their lives, which means that they will now be an overcomer, instead of one defeated. In other words, they will *"be"* what they already *"are"* in Christ.

REJECTION OF THE CROSS IS NEVER THEOLOGICAL BUT RATHER MORAL

But what if that individual will not accept the Message of the Cross?

Sadly and regrettably, this is the state of many Christians, even Preachers.

Sometime back, I had the occasion to invite a particular Preacher to be on our daily Telecast, *"A Study In The Word."* We were teaching exclusively on the Cross. He was present for several programs; however, I could tell that even though he was very readily hearing what was being said, that he really was not accepting it. I made mention of this fact to one of my Associates after the taping was concluded.

A short time later, my Associate was talking with the dear Brother, discussing the Cross, when he said, *"This teaching is necessary for some, but not for all."* In other words, he was saying, *"I don't need that particular teaching. I'm doing fine like I am."*

The truth was, and is it is with all such Believers, that even though he pastored a good Church, and in fact was doing an excellent work for the Lord, he wasn't doing fine. It came out just a little later that he was struggling with a severe problem within his life, which had been there ever since he was converted. As all such problems, and despite his best efforts otherwise, and despite the fact that God was using him, the problem was getting worse and worse. It was finally found out, which hurt his Church greatly, hurt him greatly, along with his family, and all who loved him.

But despite all of this, our dear Brother is still rejecting the Message of the Cross. He has chosen to address his problem in another manner, which will do no more good than the young Preacher who was stomping his feet and screaming at the Devil, to which we alluded some pages back.

What will happen to this man?

Now that he has been exposed to what Paul taught about the Cross, and has rejected it, his situation, and despite his best efforts otherwise, will continue to deteriorate unless he repents. If light is rejected, not only do we lose that which we could have had, but we lose what little light we presently have (Mat. 25:28-30).

What do we mean by the statement, *"No one rejects the Cross on theological grounds, but rather grounds which are moral"*?

To reject something on theological grounds

simply means that one doesn't understand the Word, or else misunderstands the Word. In other words, they think they understand it, when they in reality don't.

The Message of the Cross is about the simplest Message there is. It is so simple that anyone can understand its Message. How difficult is the following?

"For God so loved the world, that He gave His Only Begotten Son, that whosoever believes in Him, should not perish but have everlasting life" (Jn. 3:16). Anyone can understand that!

So the problem is not theological, but rather moral. And what do we mean by *"moral"*?

We mean that the Cross is rejected because of pride, stubbornness, envy, jealousy, or because of some pet sin we don't want to give up. In other words, there is something morally wrong. And the word *"moral"* refers to anything that is unrighteous.

IGNORANCE OR UNBELIEF?

When the Lord first began to give me the Revelation of the Cross, my thoughts in those days concerning the majority of the Church were that the lack of understanding in this area was the cause of Scriptural ignorance. After several years of surveying the situation, I have changed my mind.

While this is certainly true with some, and I speak of Scriptural ignorance, in other words, they simply don't know, I have found to my dismay that the major problem is *"unbelief."* And perhaps, there is some unbelief even in Scriptural ignorance.

Irrespective, the question is put before the Church, *"Do you believe that what Jesus did at the Cross answers every single problem that humanity might have?"*

I was reading a book the other day written by a so-called Christian Psychologist. He stated in his book that modern man is facing problems that those in the Bible didn't have to face; consequently, the Bible doesn't hold all the answers for modern man, and must have the help of humanistic psychology, or words to that effect.

What a travesty! What poppycock! But regrettably, many Christians are following these wolves in sheep's clothing into spiritual oblivion.

Concerning the problems that face man, modern or otherwise, what does the Bible say?

Peter said: *"According as His Divine Power has given unto us <u>all things</u> that pertain unto life and Godliness, through the knowledge of Him Who has called us to glory and virtue:*

"Whereby are given unto us exceeding great and Precious Promises, that by these you might be partakers of the Divine Nature, having escaped the corruption that is in the world through lust" (II Pet. 1:3-4).

Now either the Lord did give us through Christ *"all things that pertain unto Life and Godliness,"* or else the Holy Spirit through Peter didn't tell the truth. I happen to believe that the Holy Spirit through the Apostle definitely did tell the truth. You can't have it both ways, He either did or didn't!

PSYCHOLOGY

It is impossible to believe in and promote humanistic psychology, while at the same time believing in the Cross. One cancels out the other. Humanistic psychology comes purely from the wisdom of man, and not at all from God, as should be obvious. What Jesus did at the Cross pertains not at all to man, but solely of God. That's the reason I grieve when I see the leading Pentecostal Denominations, such as the Assemblies of God and the Church of God, plus others, at least in the United States and Canada, accept this nefarious system of the world, actually promoting it as the answer to the ills of man. I think we should look at the Catholic situation.

The Roman Catholic Church is a haven for homosexuals, admitted even by many of its leaders here in the United States. As such, and as we have seen in the news constantly, pedophilia is at pandemic levels.

The Catholics have some of the best Psychologists in the world. If this system is plausible, then why hasn't it had more effect in that particular situation? The truth is, it has had no positive effect at all, even as it can have no positive effect at all.

Every soul that's ever been set free, every sin that's ever been washed away, every bondage of sin that's ever been broken, and it numbers into the hundreds of millions, when we look down through the many centuries, all and without exception have been because of the Cross of Jesus Christ. So I have to come to the conclusion, especially as it regards so-called Spiritual Leaders, that if psychology is promoted, this either shows a gross ignorance of the Word, which should not be the case with so-called leaders, or else it shows rank unbelief. As I've repeatedly stated, one cannot have it both ways. I have to conclude that the problem is unbelief.

I thank God that in the last two or three years, some strong Evangelicals, men with a voice, have started speaking out against this nefarious system of humanistic psychology. But regrettably, at least as far as I know, none of these include Pentecostal Leaders. So the adage is true, that which once burned the brightest can dim the lowest. And such are, sadly and regrettably, the Pentecostal Denominations.

There would be hope, if the Leaders of these Denominations would admit that what I'm saying is correct, but sadly, every time in the past, when reading such statements that I've just made, or hearing me state them publicly, only grow more and more incensed. But that is my calling.

In fact, as it regards any true Preacher of the Gospel, Paul said: *"Preach the Word; be instant in season, out of season; reprove, rebuke* (and this is what I'm doing), *exhort with all longsuffering and doctrine.*

"For the time will come when they will not endure sound doctrine; but after their own lusts shall they heap to themselves teachers, having itching ears;

"And they shall turn away their ears from the Truth, and shall be turned unto fables" (II Tim. 4:2-4).

Humanistic psychology falls into the category of *"fables."*

CONFLICT

Verse 9 reads: *"And Moses said unto Joshua, Choose us out men, and go out, fight with Amalek: tomorrow I will stand on the top of the hill with the Rod of God in my hand."*

At the New Birth, the Divine Nature is imparted to the believing sinner (II Pet. 1:4). This new nature is created by the Holy Spirit; the *"seed"* (I Jn. 3:9) used is the Word of God.

When the new nature is communicated by God to the one Born-Again, the old sinful nature remains, and in effect, remains unchanged as far as its character is concerned, and will be unchanged accordingly till death or the coming of Christ, when it will be destroyed. The Scripture says that at this particular time *"this corruptible* (the sinful nature) *shall put on incorruption"* (nothing left but the Divine Nature) (I Cor. 15:53).

However, the power of the sin nature presently is definitely broken, with the guilt removed (Rom. 6:6-7).

In the Christian, and in fact, in every Christian, there are two conflicting natures: one sinful, the other sinless; one born of the flesh, the other born of God. These two natures differ from each other in origin, in character, in disposition, and in the activities they produce. They have nothing in common. In fact, they are bitterly opposed to each other. This is what is in view, typically in the second half of Exodus, Chapter 17, the Chapter of our study.

However, there is a way provided by the Lord, which we will address momentarily, which will give us continuous victory over the sin nature, with it, in effect, causing us no problem. Actually, even though it still remains in the Christian, it is supposed to be dormant, and in fact, will be dormant, if it is addressed after the Spirit (Rom. 6:11, 14).

JACOB

There are many types respecting this in the Old Testament. But one of the most illustrative is Jacob. In effect, he had two names: one which he received from his earthly parents, and one which he received from God. At the great wrestling match with God (Gen. 32:28), the Lord gave him the new name of *"Israel,"* which means, *"Prince of God,"* or *"soldier of God."* From that point onwards, the history of Jacob presents a series of strange paradoxes. His life exhibited a duel personality, which is characteristic of every Believer.

At one moment we see him trusting God with implicit confidence, at another we behold him giving way to an evil heart of unbelief — and it is unbelief which seems to characterize the major problem.

If the Bible student will read carefully Chapters 33 through 49 of Genesis, he will notice how that sometimes the Holy Spirit refers to the Patriarch as *"Jacob,"* and at other times as *"Israel."* When *"Jacob"* is referred to, it is the activities of the *"old nature"* which are in view, when *"Israel"* is mentioned it is the fruits of the *"new nature"* which are evidenced.

For example: when Joseph's Brethren returned to their father from Egypt and told him that his favorite son was yet alive and was now Governor over all the land of Egypt, we are told and *"Jacob's heart fainted for he believed them not"* (Gen. 45:26). But when *"they told him all the words of Joseph, which he had said unto them; and when he saw the wagons which Joseph had sent to carry him, the spirit of Jacob their father revived: and 'Israel' said, It is enough; Joseph my son is yet alive"* (Gen. 45:27-28)!

It is also very interesting to note the closing words concerning the Patriarch. It is as follows: *"When 'Jacob' had made an end of commanding his sons, he gathered up his feet into the bed, and yielded up the spirit . . . and the physicians embalmed 'Israel'"* (Gen. 49:33; 50:2)! *"Jacob"* died; *"Israel"* was embalmed. This means that at death only the *"new nature"* will be preserved.

But that which we wish to emphasize is that during the Christian's life on Earth there is a *"conflict"* between the two natures. Paul said:

"The flesh lusteth against the Spirit, and the Spirit against the flesh; and these are contrary the one to the other; so that you cannot do the things that you would" (Gal. 5:17).

HOW THEN CAN THE OLD NATURE BE TOTALLY SUBDUED?

What we are addressing here, we have already answered in detail, even several times in this Volume; however, due to the fact that it seems to be so difficult for many Believers to understand, and I continue to speak of this dual between the two natures, and how victory is obtained, it is incumbent upon me to state the same Truth over and over if I have to, in order that all may understand. As we shall see, this is the area that Satan fights the Christian the hardest, and regrettably, it is the area that most Christians understand the least. That is tragic because it leads to tragic consequences.

Considering that this is the single-most important thing for the Believer to learn, and considering that so few modern Believers have any understanding at all of this of which we speak, we then learn the reason for defeated lives. And it doesn't matter who the person is, as we've already said any number of times in this Volume, if the Believer doesn't know and understand God's prescribed order of victory, and we speak of victory over the *"sin nature,"* then such a person is doomed to spiritual failure, and spiritual failure which will continue to get worse and worse.

The following is God's Way, and in fact, His only Way:

THE CROSS

The Believer must ever understand that every single thing he receives from the Lord, and without exception, has all been made possible by the Cross of Christ. The Cross is where Satan was totally defeated, where all sin was atoned, all of this making it possible for the Believer to receive Eternal Life (Eph. 2:13-18; Col. 2:14-15; Jn. 3:16).

On one of our call-in Programs over SonLife Radio, a dear lady made a statement which is ever so true.

She basically said, *"If the Believer doesn't understand the Cross, then he will be subject to much false doctrine. If he understands the Cross, false doctrine will be quickly exposed."* How right she is! But sadly, the majority of the modern Church understands the Cross of Christ, at least as far as it pertains to the Sanctification process, not at all. As a result, false doctrine is rampant!

FAITH

Once the Believer understands that everything comes to him through what Christ has done at the Cross, which actually refers to what Paul is talking about, when he constantly used the phrase *"in Christ,"* he is then to anchor his Faith exclusively in the Sacrifice of Christ. To say it another way, the Cross of Christ must ever be the object of the Believer's Faith. He must not allow it to be moved elsewhere. That's one of the reasons that Paul said:

"For Christ sent me not to baptize, but to preach the Gospel: not with wisdom of words, lest the Cross of Christ should be made of none effect" (I Cor. 1:17). So in effect, he is telling us here that our Faith must be ever in the Cross, and not in other things, as important as those other things might be in their own right.

He also said: *"For I determined not to know anything among you, save Jesus Christ, and Him Crucified"* (I Cor. 2:2). This again tells us where our Faith must be anchored.

This is so very, very important! If Satan can get the Believer's faith anchored in things other than the Cross, he knows, despite how important those other things might be, he has then consigned such a Believer to constant, spiritual failure.

This which we are giving you is God's prescribed order of perpetual and constant victory. To ignore this is to ignore *"more abundant life"* (Jn. 10:10).

If the Believer thinks he can do it another way, he has just thrown in his lot with Cain, who determined to do things his way, instead of God's Way. And let the Reader understand the following:

If the Sacrifice is rejected, the one offering the Sacrifice is rejected as well. If the Sacrifice is accepted, then the one offering the Sacrifice is accepted. God doesn't so much look at the one submitting the Sacrifice, as He does the Sacrifice being submitted. Everything is in the Sacrifice, that is, the correct Sacrifice, which is the Sacrifice of Christ.

HOLY SPIRIT

Paul also said: *"For the preaching of the Cross is to them who perish foolishness; but unto us which are saved it is the Power of God"* (I Cor. 1:18).

The Power of God is not in the Cross itself, and it's certainly not in the Death which Jesus died, but in reality, it's in what that Death provided.

The Death of Christ, which was a Sacrifice, which means that He freely offered up His Own Life, was accepted by God as payment for all sin, past, present, and future. The terrible sin debt being lifted, and done so by the *"last Adam"* (I Cor. 15:45-50), the way was then cleared for the Holy Spirit, Who is God, to take up abode in the heart and life of all Believers, and to do so, on a permanent basis (Jn. 14:16-17; I Cor. 3:16). The power is in the Holy Spirit (Acts 1:8). And this is the key to everything. However, He works exclusively within the boundaries, as we've already stated, of the Finished Work of Christ. In other words, the Sacrifice of Christ made possible all which the Holy Spirit does. In fact, there is every Scriptural evidence that the Holy Spirit actually superintended the Death of Christ. The Scripture says:

"How much more shall the Blood of Christ, Who through the Eternal Spirit offered Himself without spot to God, purge your conscience from the dead works to serve the Living God?" (Heb. 9:14).

In this one Verse of Scripture, we are told how the flesh may be subdued.

As the Spirit of God superintended the Death of Christ, He did so, that every single thing may be done perfectly, which it was. Through that Sacrifice, and that Sacrifice alone, can we purge our conscience from dead works, to serve the Living God.

As well, the phrase, *"Who through the Eternal Spirit offered Himself without spot to God,"* completely refutes the Jesus died spiritually doctrine.

How could Christ die spiritually, which means that He died as a lost sinner, and at the same time, *"offer Himself without spot to God"*?

Then Paul said: *"And for this cause He* (Christ) *is the Mediator of the New Testament* (New Covenant) *that by means of death* (the death of the Cross), *for the Redemption of the transgressions that were under the First Testament* (Old Covenant), *they which are called might receive the promise of Eternal Inheritance"* (Heb. 9:15).

This Passage tells us that the Death of Christ not only addressed itself to all who lived then and forward, but as well, to all the Old Testament Saints. That's why Jesus could liberate all of these Saints from Paradise, where they had been held captive by Satan, and then take them with Him to Glory, where they are presently (Eph. 4:8-10).

Now when Believers die, which time frame spans everything from the Cross unto the present, and will definitely continue, they instantly go to be with Christ (Phil. 1:23).

THE TIME OF THE ATTACK BY THE AMALEKITES

Considering how precious water was and is, as it regards the desert, and considering that a veritable river was gushing out of the Rock, the Amalekites attacked Israel, thinking to take possession of this tremendous river. The Scripture says, *"Then came Amalek and fought with Israel."* The Holy Spirit has called our attention to the time when this occurred. It was when Moses smote the Rock and the waters gushed out.

Then, for the first time, Israel was called upon to do some fighting. They had done no fighting in the house of bondage, nor had the Lord called upon them to fight the Egyptians at the Red Sea. But now that this which typified the Holy Spirit had been given, their warfare commenced; it was that which typified the Holy Spirit, which caused the Amalekites to attack Israel! Wonderfully accurate is the type (Pink).

All of this corresponds with the Believer's struggle, and how it is to be carried out, even as we shall see in the following Verses.

The reception of the Holy Spirit immediately causes war. Up to this point God had fought for them; but the command now is to go out and fight.

As we've already stated, there is an immense difference between Justification and Sanctification. The one is Christ fighting *"for"* us; the other, the Holy Spirit fighting *"in"* us. The entrance of the New Nature is the beginning of warfare with the Old.

JUSTIFICATION BY FAITH

Paul plainly said: *"Therefore being justified by Faith, we have peace with God through our Lord Jesus Christ"* (Rom. 5:1).

Justification in the Greek, as a noun, is *"Dikaiosis,"* or *"Dikaioma."* As a Verb it is *"Dikaioo."*

Basically, all three words denote the act of pronouncing righteous, because of acquittal from guilt. All that was necessary on God's part for our Justification has been effected in the Death of Christ. On this account as well, He was raised from the dead. That God justifies the believing sinner on the ground of Christ's Death, involves His free gift of life.

To make it simple to understand, Righteousness is *"what God has declared to be right."*

The manner in which one is declared righteous by God is by and through Faith evidenced on the Part of the believing sinner toward Christ, and what Christ has done for us at the Cross. There is nothing that the believing sinner can do to justify himself, no price that he can pay, no merit of which we can come by, all being strictly by Faith. This is exactly what the Lord was speaking of when He said:

"For God so loved the world, that He gave His Only Begotten Son, that whosoever believeth in Him should not perish, but have everlasting life" (Jn. 3:16).

Whenever the believing sinner comes to Christ, and is Born-Again, God in effect declares such a person to be totally and completely righteous. No fault is found with that person, and irrespective as to what their past life has been, simply because their Righteousness is based solely on Christ, and what Christ has done at the Cross. And when the Lord justifies one, as He does every single person who comes to Him, He justifies totally and completely. There is no such thing as a partial Justification. One is either completely justified, or not justified at all!

To be brief, anyone can come to the Lord if they so desire. And all who come will be washed and cleansed, and declared perfectly righteous. The Scripture plainly says, *"For whosoever shall call upon the Name of the Lord shall be saved"* (justified) (Rom. 10:13).

SANCTIFICATION BY FAITH

Justification is one's *"standing,"* and Sanctification is one's *"state."*

In essence, one is perfectly sanctified the moment one comes to Christ. Paul said: *"And such were some of you: but you are washed, but you are sanctified, but you are justified in the Name of the Lord Jesus, and by the Spirit of God"* (I Cor. 6:11).

In fact, one must be washed clean, which

means to *"be made righteous,"* before one can be justified, which means, *"to be declared righteous."*

However, the Sanctification to which we have addressed ourselves to here, has to do with the Justification process, and as well, falls into the category of our *"standing."* In other words, God can accept nothing except perfection. This means that we are Sanctified and Justified on the premise of the Perfection of Christ, which refers to what He did for us at the Cross, as a Perfect Sacrifice.

However, there is a part to our Sanctification, which refers to our *"state."* Our *"standing"* never wavers, while our *"state"* is somewhat up and down. Paul addressed this particular aspect of Sanctification in this manner. He said:

"And the very God of peace sanctify you wholly; and I pray God your whole spirit and soul and body be preserved blameless unto the Coming of our Lord Jesus Christ" (I Thess. 5:23).

In essence, Paul is saying that the Holy Spirit wants to bring our *"state"* up to our *"standing."* In other words, He wants us to *"be"* what we actually *"are."*

This is where the struggle comes in. This is what the Holy Spirit is proclaiming to us in this latter portion of the Seventeenth Chapter, using Amalek as an example. This is where the Christian has his greatest problem. This is what I'm talking about when I say that the modern Church understands the Cross somewhat as it refers to Salvation, but almost none at all as it refers to Sanctification. The Believer, as we've already explained, must understand that his Faith had to be *"placed"* in the Cross in order to be saved, and that it must *"remain"* in the Cross, in order to be Sanctified.

While Sanctification, as it regards Justification, is a once-for-all work, as it regards our everyday living, it is, however, a progressive work. As stated, the Holy Spirit, Who is the Sanctifying Agent, is constantly attempting to bring our *"state"* up to our *"standing."* This is where Satan fights us the hardest, and this is where the Holy Spirit fights for us the hardest. But He can fight for us, only on the grounds of our Faith being properly placed, which always refers to the Cross of Christ.

JOSHUA

Verse 10 reads: *"So Joshua did as Moses had said to him, and fought with Amalek: and Moses, Aaron, and Hur went up to the top of the hill."*

The person who isn't Born-Again knows absolutely nothing of the conflict between the two natures nor of the abiding sense of inward corruption which this experience conveys. The unregenerate man is entirely under the dominion of the flesh; he serves its lusts; he does its will. In fact, the *"flesh"* doesn't fight its subjects; it rules over them. But as soon as we receive the New Nature the conflict begins.

It should be understood that Israel did not attack Amalek, but rather, Amalek attacked Israel. To correspond with this, note how that in Galatians 5:17 it is first said that *"The flesh lusteth against the Spirit,"* and not vice versa.

Some pages back, we explained to you what the *"flesh"* actually is, and what it means to be *"in the flesh,"* etc. So now, let us note carefully as to how Israel actually engaged Amalek as it regards this conflict.

As the water out of the Rock was a great Type, likewise, Amalek and how he was opposed presents another great type. In fact, the Seventeenth Chapter of Exodus portrays the entirety of the Plan of God.

Israel was without water, signifying the lost condition of mankind, and the inability of this world to change that condition.

The smitten Rock portrays Calvary, which is God's solution for sin and sinners. And now we have His prescription for victory.

Joshua now makes his entrance, who will prove to be one of the greatest men of God who ever lived. In the correct pronunciation he is *"Joshua ben Nun,"* which means, *"Joshua son of Nun."* His name means, *"Salvation,"* and in fact he is a Type of Christ. As well, the Name *"Jesus"* as it refers to our Saviour, which is the Greek derivative, is actually *"Joshua"* in Hebrew. So, Jesus was known by the name of *"Joshua."*

Moses chose him as a personal assistant, and gave him command of a detachment from the as yet unorganized Tribes to repel the raiding Amalekites.

We will find that Joshua was a man of great Faith. As the Ephraimite representative on the reconnaissance from Kadesh (Num., Chpts. 13-14), he backed Caleb's recommendation to go ahead with the invasion. As a result, he, along with Caleb, escaped the curse leveled by God on the unbelieving people, who at that time, refused to go in.

In the plains by the Jordan, he was formally consecrated as Moses' successor as it regards the leadership of the Children of Israel.

JOSHUA AS A TYPE OF CHRIST

Joshua was a conqueror. He was selected here by Moses to fight the Amalekites, just as he would fight Israel's enemies in the Promised Land, some 40 years later. As he conquered Israel's foes, Christ has conquered our foes. As should be obvious, Joshua in this capacity, as a *"type,"* is very, very important. In fact, this is where the Believer has his greatest problem. If he doesn't understand Christ, and what Christ has done for us, then he will try all over again to do the work that Christ has already done, and in fact, which he cannot do anyway. In other words, such a direction is guaranteed of defeat. But regrettably, that's where most Christians presently are.

To address an extremely complicated subject, and do so briefly, is not a simple task; however, that's what we will attempt to do here.

The following must be understood:

VICTORY IS ONLY IN CHRIST

Let's say it another way.

God does not give victory to fallen man; He gives victory alone to His Son, and our Saviour, the Lord Jesus Christ. To obtain the victory, we must enter into Christ, which is done by Faith (Rom. 6:3-5, 11, 14). But this is Christian man's greatest problem:

Man attempts to gain the victory in all type of ways, all without success.

WHAT DO WE MEAN BY *"VICTORY"*?

Pure and simple, we are referring to victory over sin. Satan tries to pull the Believer into sin in some fashion. It may be sins of the spirit, or sins of the flesh; nevertheless, it is sin, and all sin is terribly destructive, and that which God cannot abide.

The Church faces this problem in all types of ways. Our Word of Faith friends claim that sin is no longer a problem for the Believer, simply because he is a new creation in Christ, in effect, the Righteousness of God; therefore, sin is no longer a problem. He is instructed never to mention sin, for in so doing, they claim, such will develop a sin consciousness, which is detrimental to the new creation man.

Of course, there is some truth in what they say, even as all lies contain some truth. We are a new creation and, therefore, the Righteousness of God (II Cor. 5:17, 21). But if sin is no longer a problem, then the Holy Spirit wasted an awful lot of space instructing Believers through Paul, how to have victory over sin.

No! Sin is definitely the problem, in fact, the main problem by far. Ignoring sin or claiming it doesn't exist, does not change its status or effect.

It is certainly true that the Believer should dwell on Christ and certainly not on sin; however, Paul also said: *"Lest Satan should get an advantage of us: for we are not ignorant of his devices"* (II Cor. 2:11). Regrettably, because of false teaching, many, if not most, Christians are ignorant of Satan's devices.

So, when we speak of *"victory,"* we're speaking of victory over the world, the flesh, and the Devil. John the Beloved said: *"This is the victory that overcometh the world, even our Faith"* (I Jn. 5:4).

IN CHRIST

There was no way that man could extricate himself from his terrible dilemma, brought upon him by the Fall in the Garden of Eden. Cut off from God, He was spiritually dead, and dead means dead. This means he had no concept of God, didn't understand God, and in no way could have any feelings toward God, at least while in this terrible state.

So if man was to be delivered from this dilemma, God would have to take the initiative, which He did, and at a fearsome price. God would become man, which is referred to as the *"Incarnation."* However, just to become man was not enough; He had to be a Perfect Man; consequently, He would have to be born of a Virgin, for to be born otherwise would place Him in the position of all other men, for in Adam all died (I Cor. 15:22).

So, Christ was born of the Virgin Mary, which means He was born without the taint of original sin, which means that He didn't have a sin nature.

In His earthly life, He walked perfect in every capacity, neither sinning in word, thought, or deed. He had to do this, in order to be our Substitute Man. That's why Paul referred to Him as the *"Second Man"* (I Cor. 15:47). The first man, Adam, failed; the Second Man, Christ, succeeded on every count.

He was born under the Law (Gal. 4:4), for the Law, and we speak of the Law of Moses, was the Righteousness demanded by God of man. Man could not attain to this Righteousness, simply because of his fallen state, but Jesus would attain to this Righteousness, by keeping the Law perfectly in every respect, and do so as our Representative Man, all on our behalf. In other words, every single thing He did, and I mean in every capacity, was done exclusively for us, and not at all for Himself.

Even though He kept the Law perfectly, there still remained the most critical aspect, which was the Law that had been broken by all of humanity. This had to be addressed, and in fact, was the very purpose and reason for which Christ came. While everything that Christ did was of utmost significance, the main purpose of His coming was to serve as a Sacrifice (I Pet. 1:18-20).

So, Christ has already done every single thing for us, which we couldn't do for ourselves, and we obtained His victory, which He desires to give us, and for which He died, by evidencing Faith in Him, and what He did for us at the Cross. We are not to try to fight these battles all over again, but rather to trust in the battles He has already fought, and won.

OBEYING THE WORD

Every Christian is to obey the Word of God. In effect, that's not a question, in fact that which is obvious. But it's the manner in which we go about obeying the Word, that is brought into view.

So, how does one obey the Word?

Most Christians would retort by simply saying, *"Just simply do what it says to do!"*

Well that is correct, but it leaves much to be desired. We come back to our original question, *"How do we do what we're supposed to do as it regards the Word of God?"*

If the Christian sets out by his own efforts, intuition, ability, strength, and machinations to obey the Word, no matter how sincere he might be, no matter how studious he might be, no matter how zealous he might be, the end result will never be victory, but always failure. In other words, he will do the very thing that he's trying not to do, which is to disobey the Word. Paul brought this out very succinctly in the Seventh Chapter of Romans. He said:

"For that which I do I understand not: for what I would (desire to do), *that do I not; but what I hate* (fail the Lord) *that do I"* (Rom. 7:15).

So we learn from this Seventh Chapter that one cannot obey the Word by simply desiring to do so. In fact, it is impossible to obey in that manner.

We obey the Word by doing the very same thing that I've been telling you to do throughout the entirety of this Volume. We are to understand that Christ has already done all of this for us. He Alone has perfectly obeyed the Word. It is said of Christ: *"I have not departed from Your judgments: for You have taught Me"* (Ps. 119:102).

When we evidence simple Faith in Him, which refers to what He did for us at the Cross, the Holy Spirit then works strongly and mightily through us, Who always works within the parameters of the Finished Work of Christ, and then we become a *"doer of the Word,"* and not merely a *"hearer of the Word"* (James 1:22).

So our Heavenly Joshua has already fought all the battles, and won all the battles, and we enter into His victory by simply having Faith in Him and what He did, in order to win this victory, which refers to the Cross (Rom. 6:3-14; 8:1-2, 11; I Cor. 1:17-18, 21, 23; 2:2, 5; Gal. 6:14; Eph. 2:13-18; Col. 2:14-15; I Pet. 1:18-20).

We are never told in the Bible to fight the Devil, at least not in the sense of which most people think. We are told rather to *"fight the good fight of Faith"* (I Tim. 6:12).

While we do wrestle with the cohorts of Satan, and we of course speak of spiritual conflict, it is the manner that we address this, which decides the difference (Eph. 3:10-18). We do it by simple Faith in Christ and the Finished Work of the Cross.

MOSES

In this scenario, Moses is a type of the Body of Christ. The *"Rod of God"* which he held in his hand, is a type of victory over the serpent. Remember the rod turning into a serpent (Ex. 4:2-4)? This is the Believer's problem, not a lack of education, of finances, of social graces, etc., but rather sin and its destructive power caused by Satan, and that world of spiritual darkness. (Aaron was the head of Israel's Priesthood, and so speaks plainly of our great High Priest, the Lord Jesus Christ.

"Hur" (Vs. 10) means *"light"* — the emblem of Divine Holiness, and so points to the Holy Spirit of God. Thus God in His Grace has fully provided for us.

"Likewise the Spirit also helps our infirmities. For we know not what we should pray for as we ought; but the Spirit Himself makes intercession for us with groanings which cannot be uttered" (Rom. 8:26). This is the Earthly side, represented by Hur.

The heavenly side, represented by Aaron, speaks of Christ as the Messenger of the Covenant, coming and standing at the Altar having a golden censor; *"And there was given unto Him much incense, that He should offer it with the prayers of all Saints upon the Golden Altar which was before the Throne"* (Rev. 8:3). The *"hill"* represents Calvary, where all of this was accomplished.

So Joshua, who represents Christ, is fighting the Amalekites, who represents the world, the flesh, and the Devil. Moses represents all Believers, with Aaron representing Christ and His position as Great High Priest, with Hur representing the Holy Spirit. As stated, the *"hill"* represents the Cross.

PREVAILED

Verse 11 reads: *"And it came to pass, when Moses held up his hand, that Israel prevailed: and when he let down his hand, Amalek prevailed."*

Moses holding up his hands toward Heaven, with probably the Rod of God in one of them, or maybe in both of them, signified that all help comes from above. We need to take very seriously this *"type"* set before us, because it is a perfect example of our means of victory presently.

If it is to be noticed, when he let down his hands, *"Amalek prevailed."* Hands upraised signified that Israel was then prevailing.

This tells us that at no time are we to trust in anything other than the Lord Who Alone can give total and complete victory. Looking to Him brings victory, while looking to other things always brings defeat. And we look to Him by exhibiting Faith in Christ, and His Finished Work.

THE CONFLICT WITH THE FLESH

This of which we are discussing, and I speak of victory over the flesh, is, as we have stated, the single most important factor in the life of the Believer; but yet, as important as this is, the understanding of this particular aspect of the Believer's life, is a blank to most Christians. That's tragic, because this particular lack of knowledge can bring about all type of problems.

Many Christians look upon regeneration, or rather their Born-Again experience, as a total change or renewal of the old nature. Or else they think the old nature is completely eradicated. Of course, that's like trying to overlook an elephant in your living room. Perhaps one could attempt to do such a thing, but one will not be very successful, as would be obvious.

If in fact the old nature is eradicated, it would necessarily follow that the Believer has nothing to struggle with. If my old nature is taken away, and I have nothing left but the new nature, what have I to contend with? Nothing.

To all who maintain such a theory, it may be said that they seem to forget the place which Amalek occupies as it regards this *"type,"* in the history of the people of God. Had Israel conceived the idea that when Pharaoh's hosts were gone their conflict was at an end, they would have been sadly put about when Amalek, in fact, came upon them. The fact is, the conflict begins after the person comes to God, just as it began for Israel after they had been delivered from Egyptian bondage. And please note the following:

Thus it is with the Believer, for *"All these things happened unto Israel for examples, and they are written for our admonition"* (I Cor. 10:11).

But there could be no *"type,"* no *"example,"* no *"admonition,"* in *"these things"* for one whose old nature is made new or eradicated. Indeed, such a one can have but little need of any of those gracious provisions which God has made in His Kingdom for those who are the subjects thereof (Mackintosh).

THE OLD MAN

But irrespective of the false assumptions of many, we are distinctly taught in the Word that the Believer carries with him that which answers to Amalek, that is, *"the flesh"* — *"the old man"* — *"the carnal mind"* (Rom. 6:6; 8:7; Gal. 5:17).

If the Believer doesn't understand this, when the problems come, and they definitely will come, if we do not know how to face them, we are left defenseless. In other words, we will have no vantage-ground against the enemy.

The truth is, the flesh exists in the Believer, and will be there until the Trump sounds, or death claims us. The Holy Spirit fully recognizes this as existing, as we may easily see from various parts of the New Testament. In Romans, Chapter 6, we read, *"Let not* (the) *sin therefore 'reign' in your mortal bodies."* Such a precept would be entirely uncalled for if the flesh were not existing in the Believer. It would be out of character to tell us not to let (the) sin reign, if it were not actually dwelling in us. There is a great difference between *"dwelling"* and *"reigning."* Sin dwells in a Believer, but it reigns and rules in an unbeliever.

THE PRINCIPLE OF POWER

Although sin dwells in us, we have, thank God, a principle of power over it. Paul said: *"Sin shall not have dominion over you, for you are not under the Law, but under Grace"* (Rom. 6:14). The Grace which, by the Blood of the Cross, has put away sin, ensures us the victory, and gives us present power over its indwelling principle (Eph. 2:13-18).

We have Prayer Meeting every morning at 10 a.m. And I will be frank, most of my praying consists of thanking God for what He has done for me, as it regards the great Revelation of the Cross which He has graciously afforded me, which has given me victory over the world, the flesh, and the Devil. I find myself thanking Him over and over, never dreaming that what I now have would be this wonderful.

At the very lowest time of my life, when it looked like my Ministry was totally wrecked, and I was the laughingstock of the world, even as I was facing powers of darkness, which I could not seem to overcome, the Spirit of the Lord spoke to me. It was a Sunday Morning, and I was sitting on the platform at Family Worship Center. If I remember correctly, service had ended, and the people were praying around the Altar.

All of a sudden it happened: The Spirit of God spoke to my heart and said, *"This sickness is not unto death, but for the Glory of God, that the Son of God might be glorified thereby"* (Jn. 11:4).

To be frank with you, that Sunday Morning of 1991, I didn't know the Bible nearly as well as I do now; and even though I knew that this Word recently given to me by the Lord was in the Bible, I did not know exactly where it was to be found.

As the Lord spoke that to me, the Spirit of God covered me like a glove, and I knew exactly what the Lord was saying. Even though things looked black and dim, He was telling me that the end result would not be spiritual death, but rather victory, and for the Glory of God. Don't misunderstand, God never gets glory out of sin, but He definitely gets glory out of victory over sin.

And as I dictate these notes on the last day of April, 2002, what the Lord gave to me is coming to pass. And it definitely will bring glory, even great glory, to God!

Beautifully and wondrously, He has shown me the answer to the dilemma, not only mine, but for every Believer who names the

Name of Christ. That answer is, *"Jesus Christ and Him Crucified"* (I Cor. 1:23).

Little by little, the Lord opened up to me this great path of victory. I realize that I've already related this in this Volume, but I've found out the following through experience:

The Message of the Cross is the simplest Message there is; however, due to the fact that Satan fights this Message as he fights nothing else, it is very difficult for some Believers, as simple as it might be, to grasp what is being said. So it has to be approached from every angle, and said over and over again, before it finally becomes clear and plain to some Believers. That's the reason we have four Gospels, and fourteen Epistles as it regards Paul.

If one inspects the four Gospels, and all of the Epistles, even those other than Paul's, we will find that, for the most part, the Holy Spirit is saying the same thing over and over, even though it's said in a little different way each time. In fact, there is a reason for all of this, but I won't take the time now to go into detail.

TRUTH

Nevertheless, irrespective as to whom the person might be, their education, or the lack thereof; if such a person, any person, will earnestly ask the Lord to reveal the Truth unto them, to be sure, that person will be led to the Truth. I know that for a fact.

It was 1996 that the Lord began to open up to me this great Truth of the Cross. A few days later, after the initial inspiration, while in prayer one particular morning, the Spirit of God spoke to my heart again, and said: *"The answer for which you seek is in the Cross."* I don't guess I will ever forget that moment. It was so simple, as the Holy Spirit revealed it to me. I knew within my spirit that the Lord was giving me the answer for which I had so long sought. Then a few days later, He revealed to me as to how the Holy Spirit works, which is through the Faith that we have in Christ and what Christ has done for us at the Cross. To show me that, He took me to Romans 8:2.

However, this Revelation just keeps expanding, and that which I believe will ever continue. When I think I've seen every room in the house, so to speak, the Lord will gently say, *"Try that door,"* and as I walk through, things are opened up, which makes this Revelation even clearer. And always, everything the Lord gives me always coincides with the Scripture.

Since the Revelation of the Cross, prayer has taken on a brand-new meaning. My study of the Word of God falls into the same category. The Name of Jesus means far more than it ever did, with now a true understanding of that Name being prevalent. It's not so much that I have learned new things, but rather that the knowledge of the Cross has put a brand-new perspective of everything, and I mean everything!

Whenever the Believer is looking to Heaven for leading, guidance, and sustenance, symbolized by the hands of Moses being held high, the Believer walks in victory. Whenever he starts looking to man, and in any capacity, symbolized by Moses letting down his hands, the enemy prevails. Our help comes from above.

LOOKING SOLELY TO THE LORD

Paul said the examples given in the Old Testament were given for our benefit (I Cor. 10:11).

The way and the manner that we look solely to the Lord is by knowing, understanding, and following the Word of God. The Word holds the answer for everything that we need which *"pertains unto Life and Godliness"* (II Pet. 1:3).

Now please understand, the Bible tells us how to live. It's not a Book of engineering, mathematics, etc.; however, what little it has to say on those subjects, to be sure, is perfectly accurate. But the Bible is definitely a Book of social studies; it is definitely a Book regarding character; it is definitely a Book regarding human interaction; in fact, it is *the* Book of wisdom because it is the Word of God.

Some are fond of claiming that *"all Truth is God's Truth."* However, I remind those who claim such that Truth is not a philosophy, but rather a Person, in fact, the Lord Jesus Christ (Jn. 14:6).

We have what is referred to in the world of unregenerate men, *"subjective truth,"* and *"objective truth."* Subjective truth is that which is subject to whatever culture there is, or whatever someone wants it to be. In fact, subjective truth is no Truth at all, for the simple matter that Truth cannot change.

Objective Truth is that which is ordained by God, and is the same the world over, irrespective of culture, climate, nationality, or whatever. When nations abandon objective Truth, and replace it with subjective truth, they are soon destroyed. Jesus Christ, as the Living Word, is Truth, which refers to the Bible as well. Jesus said: *"Your Word is Truth,"* as He prayed to God the Father (Jn. 17:17). When society veers from the Truth of Jesus Christ, the Living Word, it has then embarked upon a *"lie."* In fact, every single religion in the world, which refers to that which is devised by man, is pure and simple, a *"lie."* They contain no Truth; consequently, they not only offer no help for their beleaguered followers, but rather harm.

CULTURE

Two members of the Board of Directors for Jimmy Swaggart Ministries are Roy Chacon and his wife, Beulah.

Roy is Native American and is, therefore, very familiar with that particular culture, having been raised accordingly. But when he gave his heart and life to the Lord Jesus Christ, he left that culture, and came into a brand-new culture, the culture of the Word of God.

He was relating to me how he had observed some fellow Native Americans, who incidentally claim Christ, and who appeared on a particular so-called Christian Television Network. They were advocating, he said, that particular aspects of their Native American culture be brought over into Christianity.

Roy went on to relate to me as to how this which they were advocating actually pertained to witchcraft, etc. The tragedy about it all, he went on to say, the host of that particular program, who was supposed to be a spiritual leader, applauded loudly such a suggestion, along with the audience roaring their approval.

Whoever these Native Americans were, they were wrong. But even more wrong were the host and people in the audience, all who claimed to be Christians, and who sanctioned such erroneous direction. And those more wrong than all were the leaders of this particular Network which promoted such.

All culture outside of the culture of the Bible is wrong. It holds no place in the Word of God and in the lives of Believers. When a person comes to Christ, irrespective as to who that person might be, or the color of their skin, or their nationality, they are to leave all of that which they have previously known, and abide strictly by the Word of God. The Word Alone is Truth. To try to mix the Word of God with superstition and foolishness is an abomination!

The following is an article written by an African American by the name of Thomas Sowell. Even though it has nothing to do with the Word of God, at least outwardly, actually in a sense, it does. Written by a black man, it ties in with what I've just said concerning culture. The title, which I will now give, is his, and the headings which follow will be mine.

SUCCESS OF *"ROOTS"* REALLY WAS TRAGEDY

"Roots" was the only book I knew my teenage son to read, aside from assigned school books, computer manuals, and chess books. He was thrilled to receive a copy autographed by Alex Haley, courtesy of George Haley, his brother, whom I had met (Alex Haley wrote *"Roots"*.)

ALEX HALEY

I never really met Alex Haley, though I saw him once because we went to the same barber in Los Angeles. Then and in his television appearances, Haley seemed like a very decent man. That is why it is especially painful to have to recognize, now that the Television Series based on *"Roots"* is being re-run on its Twenty-fifth Anniversary, that its enormous success a quarter of a century ago was a tragedy for black people and for American society in general.

TRAGEDY?

Why a tragedy? The short answer is what Winston Churchill said during Word War II: *"If the past sits in judgment on the present, the future will be lost."* Some disastrous policies had been followed in the years leading to

World War II, and Churchill sharply criticized those policies at the time, but now that the war was on, looking back could only interfere with his life-and-death job at hand.

There are some very big jobs at hand for black America — and looking back at centuries past is a costly distraction from the work that needs to be done. The past that people are looking back at in *"Roots"* is not a wholly real past. When challenged by professional historians, Haley called his work *"faction"* — part fact, and part fiction. He said he had tried to give his people some myths to live by.

It was not that *"Roots"* merely got some details wrong. It presented some crucially false pictures that continue to dominate thinking today.

SUBJECTIVE TRUTH

"Roots" has a white man leading a slave raid in West Africa, where the hero Kunta Kinte was captured, looking bewildered at the chains put on him as he was led away in bondage. The village Elders likewise were bewildered as to what these white men were doing, carrying their people away. In reality, West Africa was a center of slave trading before the first white man arrived there — and slavery continues in parts of it to this very moment.

Africans sold vast numbers of other Africans to Europeans. But they hardly let Europeans run around in their territory, catching people willy-nilly.

Because of the false picture of history presented by *"Roots"* and other sources, last year we had the farce of the President of Nigeria making demands on the United States because of the enslavement of people whom his own countrymen had enslaved, and on behalf of a country where slavery still persists, more than a century after emancipation occurred throughout the Western World.

SLAVERY

"Roots" also feeds the gross misconception that slavery was about white people enslaving black people. The tragedy of slavery was of a far greater magnitude than that. People of every race and color were both slaves and enslavers, for thousands of years, all around the world. Europeans enslaved other Europeans for centuries before the first African was brought across the Atlantic. Asians enslaved other Asians, as well as whatever Europeans they could seize. Slavery existed in the Western Hemisphere before Columbus got here.

Slavery, like cancer, was not limited to a particular country or race. To talk about cancer as if it were an American disease, or a white or black disease, would be absurd. If reparations were to be paid for slavery, everybody would owe everybody.

There is no danger of that happening. The danger is that too many black people, especially among the young and the ill-educated, will back into the third millennium still looking back at centuries past — or at fictions about centuries past — when opportunities are all around.

The ancestors of black Americans were not taken from some Eden, and there is no Eden for black Americans to return to today. If compensation were to be paid for the difference between where they are and where their ancestors came from, they would owe money, and not receive money. But it would be ridiculous to lose the future because of the past.

THE STONE

Verse 12 reads: *"But Moses' hands were heavy; and they took a stone, and put it under him, and he sat thereon; and Aaron and Hur stayed up his hands, the one on the one side, and the other on the other side; and his hands were steady until the going down of the sun."*

One writer suggested that Moses was holding the Rod of God up high with one hand, when it grew tired, he would transfer it to the other hand. Or perhaps, he was holding up the rod with both hands, spreading it out above his head. At any rate, he soon learned that his personal endurance was limited, and so the following was done:

They gave him a stone to sit on, which as well, was symbolic of Christ.

Moses sitting on the stone portrays the fact that our own efforts soon result in spiritual exhaustion. But once we are in God's glorious Way, the victory is ours.

With Aaron on one side of Moses holding up his hand, who as well was a Type of Christ as our Great High Priest, and Hur on the other side doing the same thing, with his name meaning *"light,"* which speaks to us of the Holy Spirit, the Scripture says, *"And his hands were steady until the going down of the sun."*

God has a way, and if we subscribe to something else as Believers, other than that *"way,"* to be sure, we will bring upon ourselves much difficulty. This is the most serious business in the world. It is so serious that God had to send His Only Begotten Son down to this world, and die on a Cross, in order for this problem to be properly addressed, to put it lightly.

It's about the same as an individual walking among high-powered, electrical lines that if touched, will bring death, or at least, very serious injury. If we walk strictly on the path laid out between these high-voltage lines, and not veer from the protected way, everything will be fine; otherwise, the end result, as would be obvious, won't be good.

It is the same with living this life, and trying to do so without God.

But the tragedy is, millions know the Lord, have accepted Him as Saviour, and are truly Born-Again; however, even though they have trusted Christ properly for Salvation, they are not at all properly trusting Him for Sanctification, i.e., *"the manner in which we are to live this life."*

That's the major problem for many Christians. They simply don't know how to live for God.

And just because they are Believers doesn't make them immune to the results of a wrong direction.

DECEPTION

When I speak of deception, perhaps it would be better to label it as *"self-deception."* In other words, the individual deceives himself. Why? How?

The reasons are probably as varied as the individuals involved. The most hurtful thing of all is to see Christians be presented with the Message of the Cross, for that alone is the answer, and for them to show no interest, or else, even outright reject that which they hear. I know the end result is not going to be pleasant. In other words, they have just bought for themselves untold sorrow, heartache, and difficulties. And in fact, they could lose their soul, and in reality, some will lose their soul.

THE WORD OF GOD

Verse 13 reads: *"And Joshua discomfited Amalek and his people with the edge of the sword."*

The *"sword"* here is a type of the Word of God (Eph. 6:17).

The Word of God holds the answer to every single problem we might have, at least that which pertains to *"Life and Godliness"* (II Pet. 1:3-4). It's when we step outside of the Word, trying to find help, that we run into grievous problems. And if problems which pertain to living seem to be persistent, we must come to the conclusion that our understanding of the Word is deficient in some manner. If we understand the Word, and abide by the Word, which we can only do by having a proper understanding of the Cross, we will then reap the results of the Word, which is the victory it promises, and the victory it delivers. Millions are trying to use the Word, without a proper understanding of the Cross; in some way, their understanding is going to be skewed, which will bring upon them tremendous difficulties (I Cor. 1:17; Gal. 6:14).

THE BIBLE

Verse 14 reads: *"And the LORD said unto Moses, Write this for a memorial in a book, and rehearse it in the ears of Joshua: for I will utterly put out the remembrance of Amalek from under Heaven."*

The original has, *"Write this in the Book."* It is clear that a Book already existed, in which Moses evidently entered events of interest, and that now he was Divinely commanded to record in it the great victory over Amalek, and the threat uttered against them.

This was the Book given to Joshua; to Solomon (I Ki. 2:1-4); to Joash (II Chron. 23:11); it was the Book found by Hilkiah (II Ki. 22); later on obeyed by Nehemiah (Chpts. 8, 13); declared by Malachi (Chpt. 4) to have been given to Moses; used by the Lord in preaching and teaching (Lk. 24:27-44); and declared by Him to be God's Word (Mk. 7:10, 13).

It is remarkable that the first mention of the Bible should be in connection with the hostility of the natural man (Amalek) to the spiritual man (Israel). War has ever since accompanied the Book. The Pagans, the Papists, the Skeptics, and the Critics have all warred against it. No Book has been so hated, and so loved (Williams).

As a nation, *"Amalek"* was ultimately blotted out, just as the Lord said they would be. In Hezekiah's day, the sons of Simeon attacked *"the remnant of the Amalekites that had escaped,"* taking their stronghold in Mount Seir (I Chron. 4:43). Thus, these people came to an end, exactly as predicted by the Lord!

THE SPIRITUAL VICTORY

The Lord promises here total and complete victory over the flesh, of which Amalek was a type, that is, if the Believer will follow the pattern of the Cross.

Even as I dictate these notes, there are untold numbers of Christians who do not understand or know the pattern of victory laid out for them by the Lord. Consequently, despite all of their best efforts otherwise, they are living a life of spiritual failure in some manner. Untold numbers of times they have wondered, *"Does it have to be this way?!"*

No, it doesn't have to be that way. There is victory for every Believer, if they will only follow God's pattern of the Finished Work of Christ.

THE ALTAR

Verse 15 reads: *"And Moses built an Altar, and called the name of it Jehovah-nissi."*

The *"Altar"* symbolizes the fact that the entire legacy of Israel is built upon the Cross of Calvary. *"Jehovah-nissi"* means, *"the Lord is my banner."*

This *"banner"* was most certainly a victory banner. In fact, there is some small evidence that on this *"flag"* or *"banner,"* was inscribed the posture of a rampant lion, in other words, a lion ready to pounce.

Concerning Christ, the Scripture says that *"He shall set an ensign for the nations, and shall assemble the outcasts of Israel, and gather together the dispersed of Judah from the four corners of the Earth"* (Isa. 11:12). This could very well be the same type of banner raised by Moses, and referred to as *"Jehovah-nissi."* Also, Christ is called, *"The Lion of the Tribe of Judah"* (Rev. 5:5).

NOTES

This we do know, whatever was inscribed on this banner, it was a war banner. It signified the first victory over the flesh, with Amalek serving as the type, and it will perhaps serve as the last banner that will fly, which will take place in the coming Kingdom Age, when Christ rules and reigns.

WAR

Verse 16 reads: *"For he said, Because the LORD has sworn that the LORD will have war with Amalek from generation to generation."*

The problem of the flesh is incumbent upon every generation. The victory that I have now, while sufficient for me, will not be sufficient for my son, or his son, etc. Every Believer must take to himself by Faith, that which has been done by Christ for us, and in effect, have his own experience with the Lord in this regard.

While this conflict has been fought and won, it still must be addressed not only by every generation, but as well by every individual in each particular generation, at least those who call upon the Name of Christ. Victory is found in Christ, and victory is found alone in Christ! (Rom. 6:3-14; 8:1-2, 11).

"Behold the Man of Galilee,
"Thorn-crown'd He hangs upon the tree;
"Knowing the depths of agony
"To save me from my sins."

"See how His flesh by nails is torn,
"Each wound the mark of hate and scorn;
"Yet freely shame and debt is borne
"To save me from my sins."

"The veil is rent, dark grows the skies,
"'Tis finished!' Loud the Saviour cries;
"And Heaven itself weeps as He dies,
"To save me from my sins."

"O Saviour, when I view Your Cross,
"All earthly gain I count but loss;
"Take Thou my heart, purge out the dross,
"And save me from my sins."

CHAPTER 18

(1) "WHEN JETHRO, THE PRIEST OF

MIDIAN, MOSES' FATHER-IN-LAW, HEARD OF ALL THAT GOD HAD DONE FOR MOSES, AND FOR ISRAEL HIS PEOPLE, AND THAT THE LORD HAD BROUGHT ISRAEL OUT OF EGYPT;

(2) "THEN JETHRO, MOSES' FATHER-IN-LAW, TOOK ZIPPORAH, MOSES' WIFE, AFTER HE HAD SENT HER BACK,

(3) "AND HER TWO SONS; OF WHICH THE NAME OF THE ONE WAS GERSHOM; FOR HE SAID, I HAVE BEEN AN ALIEN IN A STRANGE LAND:

(4) "AND THE NAME OF THE OTHER WAS ELIEZER; FOR THE GOD OF MY FATHER, SAID HE, WAS MY HELP, AND DELIVERED ME FROM THE SWORD OF PHARAOH:

(5) "AND JETHRO, MOSES' FATHER-IN-LAW, CAME WITH HIS SONS AND HIS WIFE UNTO MOSES INTO THE WILDERNESS, WHERE HE ENCAMPED AT THE MOUNT OF GOD:

(6) "AND HE SAID UNTO MOSES, I YOUR FATHER-IN-LAW JETHRO AM COME UNTO YOU, AND YOUR WIFE, AND HER TWO SONS WITH HER.

(7) "AND MOSES WENT OUT TO MEET HIS FATHER-IN-LAW, AND DID OBEISANCE, AND KISSED HIM; AND THEY ASKED EACH OTHER OF THEIR WELFARE; AND THEY CAME INTO THE TENT.

(8) "AND MOSES TOLD HIS FATHER-IN-LAW ALL THAT THE LORD HAD DONE UNTO PHARAOH AND TO THE EGYPTIANS FOR ISRAEL'S SAKE, AND ALL THE TRAVAIL THAT HAD COME UPON THEM BY THE WAY, AND HOW THE LORD DELIVERED THEM.

(9) "AND JETHRO REJOICED FOR ALL THE GOODNESS WHICH THE LORD HAD DONE TO ISRAEL, WHOM HE HAD DELIVERED OUT OF THE HAND OF THE EGYPTIANS.

(10) "AND JETHRO SAID, BLESSED BE THE LORD, WHO HAS DELIVERED YOU OUT OF THE HAND OF THE EGYPTIANS, AND OUT OF THE HAND OF PHARAOH, WHO HAS DELIVERED THE PEOPLE FROM UNDER THE HAND OF THE EGYPTIANS.

(11) "NOW I KNOW THAT THE LORD IS GREATER THAN ALL GODS: FOR IN THE THING WHEREIN THEY DEALT PROUDLY HE WAS ABOVE THEM.

(12) "AND JETHRO, MOSES' FATHER-IN-LAW, TOOK A BURNT OFFERING AND SACRIFICES FOR GOD: AND AARON CAME, AND ALL THE ELDERS OF ISRAEL, TO EAT BREAD WITH MOSES' FATHER-IN-LAW BEFORE GOD."

The construction is:

1. In some ways the events narrated in Chapter 18 give a prophetic picture of the coming Millennial Kingdom.

2. Verses 9 through 12 portray Jethro, a Gentile, united with Israel, even as the Gentiles, and we speak of Believers, will be united with a restored Israel in the coming Kingdom Age.

3. Some regard Zipporah and her children as representing the Church; however, the *"type"* breaks down in that capacity. Instead, Zipporah symbolizes a restored Israel coming to Christ, of whom Moses is a Type.

JETHRO

Verses 1 through 6 read: *"When Jethro, the Priest of Midian, Moses' father-in-law, heard of all that God had done for Moses, and for Israel His people, and the LORD had brought Israel out of Egypt;*

"Then Jethro, Moses' father-in-law, took Zipporah, Moses' wife, after he had sent her back,

"And her two sons; of which the name of the one was Gershom; for he said, I have been an alien in a strange land:

"And the name of the other was Eliezer; for the God of my father, said he, was my help, and delivered me from the sword of Pharaoh:

"And Jethro, Moses' father-in-law, came with his sons and his wife unto Moses into the wilderness, where he encamped at the Mount of God:

"And he said unto Moses, I your father-in-law Jethro am come unto you, and your wife, and her two sons with her."

It is obvious from the account given in Chapter 4 that Moses sent his wife, Zipporah, along with their two sons, Eliezer and Gershom, back to her own kinfolk, the Midianites, before he went to Egypt.

Reuel, Zipporah's father, was then dead,

and had been succeeded in his priesthood and headship of the Tribe by Jethro, probably his son and, therefore, the brother-in-law, and not the father-in-law, of Moses. In fact, the Hebrew word as used, has both meanings of brother-in-law and father-in-law; consequently, the first part of Verse 1 should read, *"When Jethro, the Priest of Midian, Moses' brother-in-law. . . ."*

It seems that Jethro gave protection to his sister and her children until he heard of the Passage of the Red Sea, when he then set forth to meet and congratulate Moses, and to convey back to him his wife and his sons. This meeting took place *"at the Mount of God,"* i.e., *"Sinai"* (Pulpit).

As it regards Zipporah, Verse 2 says, *"After he had sent her back,"* refers probably to Chapter 4, and while not previously mentioned, yet is assumed here as known.

We are given the account of the birth of Gershom, the son of Moses and Zipporah, in Exodus 2:22. Eliezer had not been previously mentioned by name; but he was probably the son circumcised by Zipporah, as related in Exodus 4:25.

We learn from I Chronicles 23:15-17 that Gershom had several sons, and Eliezer had only one son, *"Rehabiah,"* but that *"the sons of Rehabiah were very many,"* which means that Eliezer had quite a number of grandsons.

Concerning the time factor of this visit by Jethro, Pink says that Exodus, Chapter 18 is a parenthesis, interrupting the chronological order of the Book, which the Holy Spirit intended to do.

He went on to say that Exodus, Chapter 17 portrays Israel at Rephidim, and then in Chapter 19 they are viewed at Sinai. So the incident recorded in Exodus 18 occurred just as Israel was about to leave Sinai and enter the wilderness of Paran. It was in the third month after leaving Egypt that Israel reached the Mount of the Law; it was 11 months later that Jethro came to Moses bringing his wife and children.

In Numbers 10:11-12 we read, *"And it came to pass on the twentieth day of the second month, in the second year, that the cloud was taken up from off the Tabernacle of the Testimony. And the Children of Israel took their journey out of the wilderness of Sinai, and the Cloud rested in the wilderness of Paran."*

Following this, in Numbers 10:29-30 we are told, *"And Moses said unto Hobab, the son of Raguel, the Midianite, Moses' father-in-law, We are journeying unto the place of which the LORD said, I will give it you; come thou with us, and we will do you good; for the LORD has spoken good concerning Israel. And he said unto him, I will not go; but I will depart to my own land, and to my kindred"* — compare with this the last Verse of Exodus, Chapter 18.

In Exodus, Chapter 18, we find evidences that the Lord had already given Israel the Law when Jethro came to Moses, even though the account is given in the Bible before the Law was given. As stated, it is not in chronological order, and was not meant by the Holy Spirit to be in chronological order. It is placed here in order to teach a moral lesson.

Moses' statement that the people now came unto him to *"inquire of God"* (Vs. 15); his declaration that he *"made them know the Statutes of God and His Laws"* (Vs. 16), proclaim to us that the Law had already been given.

HUMILITY

Verses 7 through 12 read: *"And Moses went out to meet his father-in-law, and did obeisance, and kissed him; and they asked each other of their welfare; and they came into the tent.*

"And Moses told his father-in-law all that the LORD had done unto Pharaoh and to the Egyptians for Israel's sake, and all the travail that had come upon them by the way, and how the LORD delivered them.

"And Jethro rejoiced for all the goodness which the LORD had done to Israel, whom He had delivered out of the hand of the Egyptians.

"And Jethro said, Blessed be the LORD, Who has delivered you out of the hand of the Egyptians, and out of the hand of Pharaoh, and Who has delivered the people from under the hand of the Egyptians.

"Now I know that the LORD is greater than all gods: for in the thing wherein they

dealt proudly He was above them.

"And Jethro, Moses' father-in-law, took a Burnt Offering and Sacrifices for God: and Aaron came, and all the Elders of Israel, to eat bread with Moses' father-in-law before God."

We see here the humility of Moses as it regards the treatment of his brother-in-law. Here is a man who has seen the greatest miracles that history has ever known, at least to date, has seen the mightiest nation of the world humbled, and has just been given the Law of God, which is the foundation for all law in this world, at least that which attempts to have at least a semblance of Righteousness, who treats his brother-in-law as a superior. We could take a lesson from this.

He then relates to Jethro all of the mighty miracles that God had performed, which was the most astounding account that had ever come from the lips of any man, or had been heard by any man, as it was by Jethro.

When this great account was given, the Scripture says, *"Jethro rejoiced for all the goodness which the Lord had done to Israel . . ."* and no wonder!

In answer to this, Jethro *"blessed the Lord,"* and stated, *"Now I know that the Lord is greater than all gods."*

From this statement, it seems that Jethro, like most of the heathen, believed in a plurality of gods, and, therefore, had regarded the God of the Israelites as merely one among many equals. *"Now"* he renounces this creed, and emphatically declares his belief that Jehovah is above all other gods, greater, higher, more powerful. Compare the confessions of Nebuchadnezzar (Dan. 2:47; 3:26-27) and Darius the Mede (Dan. 6:26) (Pulpit).

At a coming glad day, that will happen, of which this is a type, of Gentiles coming to Christ from all over the world, which will be the time of the Kingdom Age. They will proclaim, even as Jethro before them, as to the veracity of the Lord Jesus Christ, which pertains to all His might, glory, and wonder!

THE SACRIFICE

Verse 12 proclaims the fact that Moses knew and understood, as well as all the Elders of Israel, which he now relates to Jethro, that Israel's might and power were all in the Blood of the Lamb. Jethro is now very much aware of the Passover, which is what really set the Children of Israel free. So he desires to offer a *"Burnt Offering and Sacrifices for God."*

As well, this foreshadows the coming Kingdom Age, when *"it shall come to pass in the last days, that the mountain of the LORD's house shall be established in the top of the mountains, and shall be exalted above the hills; and all nations shall flow into it. And many people shall go and say, Come ye, and let us go up to the Mountain of the LORD, to the house of the God of Jacob"* (Isa. 2:2-3).

(13) "AND IT CAME TO PASS ON THE MORROW, THAT MOSES SAT TO JUDGE THE PEOPLE: AND THE PEOPLE STOOD BY MOSES FROM THE MORNING UNTO THE EVENING.

(14) "AND WHEN MOSES' FATHER-IN-LAW SAW ALL THAT HE DID TO THE PEOPLE, HE SAID, WHAT IS THIS THING THAT YOU DO TO THE PEOPLE? WHY SIT YOU YOURSELF ALONE, AND ALL THE PEOPLE STAND BY YOU FROM MORNING UNTO EVENING?

(15) "AND MOSES SAID UNTO HIS FATHER-IN-LAW, BECAUSE THE PEOPLE COME UNTO ME TO INQUIRE OF GOD:

(16) "WHEN THEY HAVE A MATTER, THEY COME UNTO ME; AND I JUDGE BETWEEN ONE AND ANOTHER, AND I DO MAKE THEM KNOW THE STATUTES OF GOD, AND HIS LAWS.

(17) "AND MOSES' FATHER-IN-LAW SAID UNTO HIM, THE THING THAT YOU DO IS NOT GOOD.

(18) "YOU WILL SURELY WEAR AWAY, BOTH YOU, AND THIS PEOPLE WHO ARE WITH YOU: FOR THIS THING IS TOO HEAVY FOR YOU; YOU ARE NOT ABLE TO PERFORM IT YOURSELF ALONE.

(19) "HEARKEN NOW UNTO MY VOICE, I WILL GIVE YOU COUNSEL, AND GOD SHALL BE WITH YOU: BE YOU FOR THE PEOPLE TO GODWARD, THAT YOU MAY BRING THE CAUSES UNTO GOD:

(20) "AND YOU SHALL TEACH THEM ORDINANCES AND LAWS, AND SHALL SHOW THEM THE WAY WHEREIN THEY MUST WALK, AND THE WORK THAT THEY MUST DO.

(21) "MOREOVER YOU SHALL PROVIDE OUT OF ALL THE PEOPLE ABLE MEN, SUCH AS FEAR GOD, MEN OF TRUTH, HATING COVETOUSNESS; AND PLACE SUCH OVER THEM, TO BE RULERS OF THOUSANDS, AND RULERS OF HUNDREDS, RULERS OF FIFTIES, AND RULERS OF TENS:

(22) "AND LET THEM JUDGE THE PEOPLE AT ALL SEASONS: AND IT SHALL BE, THAT EVERY GREAT MATTER THEY SHALL BRING UNTO YOU, BUT EVERY SMALL MATTER THEY SHALL JUDGE: SO SHALL IT BE EASIER FOR YOURSELF, AND THEY SHALL BEAR THE BURDEN WITH YOU.

(23) "IF YOU SHALL DO THIS THING, AND GOD COMMAND YOU SO, THEN YOU SHALL BE ABLE TO ENDURE, AND ALL THIS PEOPLE SHALL ALSO GO TO THEIR PLACE IN PEACE."

The composition is:

1. Moses, for this particular time, succumbed to the temptation of the flesh, to rely on the weak arm of flesh. He listened to man instead of God. That problem persists with us even unto this hour.

2. While the responsibility of Moses was immense, he was not asked to bear this people alone, for God was with him.

3. It was God Who actually was bearing them; Moses was but the instrument. He might just as well have spoken of his rod as bearing the people.

4. He was merely an instrument in God's hand, as the rod was in his.

5. It is here the servants of Christ constantly fail; and the failure is all the more dangerous because it wears the appearance of humility.

6. If God has imposed the responsibility, He will surely do with the person in sustaining it.

7. With Him, the weight of a mountain is nothing; without Him, the weight of a feather is overwhelming.

8. It is never the fruit of humility to depart from a Divinely-appointed post. On the contrary, the deepest humility will express itself by remaining there, which is simple dependence upon God.

9. It is a sure evidence of being occupied with self when we shrink from service on the ground of inability. God does not call us unto service on the ground of our ability, but of His Own.

10. All power belongs to God, and it is quite the same whether that power acts through one agent or through 70 — the power is still the same.

11. God will not force people to abide in a place of honor if they cannot trust Him to sustain them there.

MOSES THE JUDGE

Verses 13 and 14 read: *"And it came to pass on the morrow, that Moses sat to judge the people; and the people stood by Moses from the morning unto the evening.*

"And when Moses' father-in-law (brother-in-law) *saw all that he did to the people, he said, What is this thing that you do to the people? Why sit you yourself alone, and all the people stand by you from morning unto evening?"*

As we've already stated, this account, even though given before the account of the Law in Chapter 20, actually falls into place after the Law was given; hence, Moses in effect, is attempting to teach the people the *"Statutes of God and His Laws."* He did it, it seems, by applying the Law to their various problems, which they brought to him for settlement.

We now have the entrance of Jethro as it regards what Moses was doing. He will offer his advice, as we shall see, as to how Moses should handle this.

The question is not of the advice offered by Jethro, whether good or bad, but rather that it came from the heart of man, and not from God. That's where the problem was. Moses was to look to the Lord for everything, which the Lord demands that we do presently.

The Lord never makes a mistake, and to be sure, He will definitely lead and guide all Believers, who will steadfastly look to Him. Jesus said of the Holy Spirit: *"He will guide you into all truth: for He shall not speak of Himself; but whatsoever He shall hear, that shall He speak: and He will show you things to come"* (Jn. 16:13).

But how hard it is for us to learn to look

exclusively to the Lord. I am persuaded that the greatest sin of the Church, perhaps all of us, is that we look to man instead of God. And let me emphasize this truth again: it is not whether the advice given by man is good or bad, but rather that it did not come directly from the Lord. The Lord desires, and strongly so, to be minutely involved in all of our proceedings, and that means *"all."* If He numbers the very hairs of our heads, and notes each sparrow's fall, and He certainly does, then we should certainly know that He desires the leadership of our lives, especially considering the price that He has paid (Mat. 10:29-30; I Cor. 6:20; 7:23).

THE STATUTES AND LAWS

Verses 15 and 16 read: *"And Moses said unto his father-in-law, Because the people come unto me to inquire of God:*

"When they have a matter, they come unto me; and I judge between one and another, and I do make them know the Statutes of God and His Laws."

In the initial stages, it was the business of Moses, delegated to him by God, that he teach the people what God had given to him as it regarded *"the Law."* In fact, until he was able to teach these Laws to his Elders, whomever they may have been, he was the only one, in fact, who could righteously judge.

God had anointed Moses to carry out this task, and not anyone else. If he wanted him to select others, He would tell him to do so, which information must not come from a man, much less a Gentile.

In the second place, Moses was not asked to bear this burden alone, for God was with him. As we've already stated, with the Lord, the weight of a mountain is nothing; without Him, the weight of a feather is overwhelming. It's not the task, irrespective as to how large it might be, but rather, whether God is with us or not.

It is a totally different thing if a man, in the vanity of his mind, thrust himself forward and take a burden upon his shoulder which God never intended him to bear and, therefore, never fitted him to bear it; we may then surely expect to see him crushed beneath the weight: but if God lays it upon him, He will qualify and strengthen him to carry it (Mackintosh).

As so many, Moses had treated Jethro royally, and evidently, he now thinks that he can counsel the Lawgiver. He was very foolish in his assumptions, but Moses was more foolish in hearing his prattle.

GOOD?

Verses 17 and 18 read: *"And Moses' father-in-law said unto him, The thing that you do is not good.*

"You will surely wear away, both you, and this people who are with you: for this thing is too heavy for you; you are not able to perform it yourself alone."

I want the Reader to look at the irony of this:

In the first place, what did Jethro know about the situation? Why would he propose to give advice and counsel to a man who, under God, had just delivered some three million people from Egyptian bondage? As someone has well said, *"Fools tread where Angels fear to walk."*

He proposes that what Moses is doing *"is not good."* He then states that the Lawgiver will break under the load.

One might well say that this is the first foray of the Church into humanistic psychology, which, any way you look at it, boils down to advice from men.

If God has told someone to do something, He will most definitely give that individual the power, strength, and Grace to carry it out. As we've also stated, Moses was a mere instrument in the hands of God, just as the Rod was an instrument in his hands. This rod had no power within itself, but with God directing the action, powerful things took place when this Rod was used in a certain way. Moses and every other human being are the same. As instruments, we can do very little within ourselves. But with God, all things are possible!

COUNSEL?

Verses 19 and 20 read: *"Hearken now unto my voice, I will give you counsel, and God shall be with you: be thou for the people to Godward, that you may bring the causes unto God:*

"And you shall teach them Ordinances

and Laws, and shall show them the way wherein they must walk, and the work that they must do."

Counsel?

Because it's so very important, I want to say it again:

It is not whether the counsel is good or bad; the problem is, man is very limited, and irrespective as to whom he might be, even if of God, he is still a man. And because he is a man, he can make mistakes. God is not a man and, therefore, will not, and cannot make mistakes. So if He is available, and to be sure, the Lord is always available, why not take our needs to Him directly! His counsel is perfect.

TELEVISION

We first went on Television in 1975. To be sure, our beginnings were not very noticeable. In fact, I had put it off as long as I could. For about a year, I had felt led of the Lord to take this step, but to be frank, I allowed fear to hinder me.

I knew nothing about Television, and I had no way to get the task accomplished, and I was thinking, how in the world can I produce a television program that is worthy of any note, up beside men who have been on Television for years as it regards the Gospel?

Once again, I was figuring all of this without the Lord.

At any rate, God blessed our beginnings, as humble as they were. People began to watch the program, and people began to be saved.

In those days, the program was only 30 minutes in length. As the Lord began to bless, and as I began to seek His Face as to how to carry out this task, He told me several things to do. The first thing He related to me was that I should include the Altar Call. As well, I was to extend the program from 30 minutes to an hour.

Seeking the Lord in prayer, I felt strongly in my spirit about these things, feeling that the Lord had given me direction, and thereby set the wheels in motion that this could be done.

I remember receiving word from one of the foremost Television Preachers of that particular time, advising me that I should not do this, because one hour religious programs, as he put it, were not in vogue.

Now here was a man who had several years of experience in Television broadcasting, and in fact, was one of the authorities on the subject. However, I knew I had heard from the Lord, and even though I appreciated his interest, I ignored what he said.

The consequences were, we quickly gained the largest audience in the world as it regards religious programming. As well, the Lord used the program to touch untold millions of people, for which we give Him all the glory.

I believe in seeking God about every single thing I do. I want His leading and direction in all things. And when I say *"all things,"* I'm speaking of both the large things, and that which we might deem to be small and insignificant. The Lord has the capabilities of addressing Himself to every single thing, so why not avail ourselves of such wisdom and counsel? In fact, if we are always led by the Lord, we will never go wrong, despite what it may look like at the beginning.

SPIRITUAL ADVICE!

Verses 21 through 23 read: *"Moreover you shall provide out of all the people able men, such as fear God, men of truth, hating covetousness; and place such over them, to be rulers of thousands, and rulers of hundreds, rulers of fifties, and rulers of tens:*

"And let them judge the people at all seasons: and it shall be, that every great matter they shall bring unto you, but every small matter they shall judge: so shall it be easier for yourself, and they shall bear the burden with you.

"If you shall do this thing, and God command you so, then you shall be able to endure, and all this people shall also go to their place in peace."

If it is to be noticed, the advice as given by Jethro was very spiritual; and many are deceived by this very method. There is no doubt that Jethro thought he was doing Moses a service. He meant well! In fact, his motives were good. That's not the question here, however!

Irrespective as to how good the advice seems

on the surface, it was not God Who gave the advice, but man. But oftentimes, we are deceived, because it does seem to be good!

Now some may ask, *"Could not God use one such as Jethro to give advice and counsel?"*

God can use anything; however, had He been using Jethro, He would first of all have related this to Moses. While the Lord may definitely give a Word to somebody else regarding me, He will first of all reveal to me what He wants and desires. In this case, the Word given to somebody else is merely a confirmation. Direction is never instigated outside of the Word of God, and His dealings with the individual on a personal basis. I've had many people to give me a Word, and rightly so, but I had already been given that Word by the Lord previously. As such, the confirmation has always been a tremendous blessing, which it is intended to be; but a *"Word"* that comes out of the blue for an individual, so to speak, is never from God. It must not be heeded!

(24) "SO MOSES HEARKENED TO THE VOICE OF HIS FATHER-IN-LAW, AND DID ALL THAT HE HAD SAID.

(25) "AND MOSES CHOSE ABLE MEN OUT OF ALL ISRAEL, AND MADE THEM HEADS OVER THE PEOPLE, RULERS OF THOUSANDS, RULERS OF HUNDREDS, RULERS OF FIFTIES, AND RULERS OF TENS.

(26) "AND THEY JUDGED THE PEOPLE AT ALL SEASONS: THE HARD CAUSES THEY BROUGHT UNTO MOSES, BUT EVERY SMALL MATTER THEY JUDGED THEMSELVES.

(27) "AND MOSES LET HIS FATHER-IN-LAW DEPART; AND HE WENT HIS WAY INTO HIS OWN LAND."

The overview is:

1. Moses complained of the burden, and the burden was speedily removed; but with it the high honor of being allowed to carry it.

2. There was no fresh power introduced. It was the same Spirit, whether in one or in 70. There was no more value or virtue in the flesh of 70 men than in the flesh of one man.

3. *"It is the Spirit Who quickeneth; the flesh profiteth nothing"* (Jn. 6:63). There was nothing in the way of power gained, but

NOTES

a great deal in the way of dignity lost, by this movement on the part of Moses, as he listened to Jethro.

4. If God honors a man by giving him a great deal of work to do, let him rejoice therein and not murmur; for if he murmurs, he can very speedily lose his honor. God is at no loss for instruments. He could from the stones raise up children unto Abraham, and He can raise up from the same the needed agents to carry on His glorious work.

HEARKEN TO THE WRONG VOICE?

Verse 24 reads: *"So Moses hearkened to the voice of his father-in-law, and did all that he had said."*

It is here that the servants of Christ constantly fail; and the failure is all the more dangerous because it wears the appearance of humility. It seems like distrust of one's self, and deep lowliness of spirit, to shrink from heavy responsibility; but all we need to inquire is, has God imposed that responsibility? If so, He will assuredly be with me in sustaining it; and having Him with me, I can sustain anything (Mackintosh).

Mackintosh went on to say: *"It is never the fruit of humility to depart from a Divinely-appointed post. On the contrary, the deepest humility will express itself by remaining there in simple dependence upon God. It is a sure evidence of being occupied about 'self' when we shrink from service on the ground of inability. God does not call us into service on the ground of our ability, but of His Own; hence, unless I am filled with thoughts about myself, or with positive distrust of Him, I need not relinquish any position of service or testimony because of the heavy responsibilities attaching thereto."*

ABLE MEN?

Verse 25 reads: *"And Moses chose able men out of all Israel, and made them heads over the people, rulers of thousands, rulers of hundreds, rulers of fifties, and rulers of tens."*

Whenever Moses chose these particular men, whomever they might have been, there was no fresh power introduced. It was the same Spirit, whether in one or in many.

The fact that these individuals were *"able*

men," is not in dispute. The problem is, as stated, God is not the One Who told him to do this. So we have a departure from the leading of the Spirit.

Whenever the Church begins to be operated by men, and the operation is of men, that's when the Government of God has been abandoned, and in its place, we have the government of man, which is tantamount to spiritual disaster. But regrettably, that's where most of the modern Church finds itself. Whatever it does is instituted by man, governed by man, led by man, and the Lord is outside knocking on the door, trying to get in (Rev. 3:20).

MOSES AND HIS BROTHER-IN-LAW

Verses 26 and 27 read: *"And they judged the people at all seasons: the hard causes they brought unto Moses, but every small matter they judged themselves.*

"And Moses let his father-in-law depart; and he went his way into his own land."

In this account could very well have begun the rebellion of Korah (Num., Chpt. 16). When the Lord chooses men, the rate of defection is much lower. When men choose men, the rate of defection is much higher. When God chooses men, normally they will not think of themselves more highly than they ought to think. As well, they will have no personal agenda, but would seek only to carry out the mission at hand.

When men choose men, no matter how much they may attempt to qualify the individuals involved, all of the above are missing.

So Moses chose these men, or else had Israel to vote on them in one way or the other. At any rate, there is no Scriptural clue that God ordained this; consequently, He cannot give the increase. While it's perfectly permissible for some to plant and some to water, they must do so under the leading and guidance of the Holy Spirit. Only then will God give the increase (I Cor. 3:6-7).

Paul said: *"Let no man beguile you of your reward in a voluntary humility . . . And not holding the Head* (Christ), *from which all the body* (the Church) *by joints and bands having nourishment ministered, and knit together, increases with the increase of God"* (Col. 2:18-19).

NOTES

*"At the Cross I was kneeling,
"When the Lord Himself revealing,
"Gave me peace in believing,
"When I sought His Mercy there."*

*"In the Cross I will glory,
"And to all proclaim the story,
"How I found my Redeemer,
"And He heard my humble prayer."*

*"To the Cross I am clinging,
"And my Faith and Hope are singing,
"Songs of praise to my Saviour,
"For His kind and gentle care."*

*"I was lost but He found me,
"With His love Divine He bound me,
"O my full heart adores Him,
"For He heard my humble prayer."*

CHAPTER 19

(1) "IN THE THIRD MONTH, WHEN THE CHILDREN OF ISRAEL WERE GONE FORTH OUT OF THE LAND OF EGYPT, THE SAME DAY CAME THEY INTO THE WILDERNESS OF SINAI.

(2) "FOR THEY WERE DEPARTED FROM REPHIDIM, AND WERE COME TO THE DESERT OF SINAI, AND HAD PITCHED IN THE WILDERNESS; AND THERE ISRAEL CAMPED BEFORE THE MOUNT.

(3) "AND MOSES WENT UP UNTO GOD, AND THE LORD CALLED UNTO HIM OUT OF THE MOUNTAIN, SAYING, THUS SHALL YOU SAY TO THE HOUSE OF JACOB, AND TELL THE CHILDREN OF ISRAEL;

(4) "YOU HAVE SEEN WHAT I DID UNTO THE EGYPTIANS, AND HOW I BEAR YOU ON EAGLES' WINGS, AND BROUGHT YOU UNTO MYSELF.

(5) "NOW THEREFORE, IF YOU WILL OBEY MY VOICE INDEED, AND KEEP MY COVENANT, THEN YOU SHALL BE A PECULIAR TREASURE UNTO ME ABOVE ALL PEOPLE: FOR ALL THE EARTH IS MINE:

(6) "AND YOU SHALL BE UNTO ME A KINGDOM OF PRIESTS, AND AN HOLY NATION. THESE ARE THE WORDS WHICH YOU SHALL SPEAK UNTO THE CHILDREN OF ISRAEL."

The exegesis is:

1. The Feast of the Passover witnessed Israel's departure from Egypt, and now they are soon to some to the Feast of Pentecost, which would occasion the giving of the Law, 50 days after the Passover. Actually, the word *"Pentecost"* in Hebrew means, *"fifty"*, or *"fiftieth."*

2. They evidently arrived at Sinai some 45 days after quitting Egypt (after the Passover), which would have been on a Wednesday. Five days later would commence the Day of Pentecost, which would occasion the giving of the Law, which incidentally, would be on a Sunday. (They had left out of Egypt on the fifteenth day of the first month, and now it was the first day of the third month, totaling 45 days.)

3. The Day of Pentecost was after seven Sabbaths (49 days) were completed after Passover. On the fiftieth day, which would be Sunday, would be the Day of Pentecost.

4. The Fourth Verse described Israel's Salvation as *"on eagles' wings."* The Lord then used the term *"brought you unto Myself,"* speaking of a Salvation wholly of God.

5. Verse 5 proclaims Israel being called *"a peculiar treasure,"* and then more specifically, *"unto Me."* Now, in Christ, spiritual Israel, which is the Church, is a part of this *"peculiar treasure."*

6. The *"kingdom of Priests and an holy nation"* of Verse 6 were to serve as a light of Salvation to a lost world.

MOUNT SINAI

Verses 1 and 2 read: *"In the third month, when the Children of Israel were gone forth out of the land of Egypt, the same day came they into the wilderness of Sinai.*

"For they were departed from Rephidim, and were come to the desert of Sinai, and had pitched in the wilderness; and there Israel camped before the Mount."

"The Desert of Sinai," which is said to be immediately before Mount Sinai, is approximately two miles long, and a half mile wide. It is nearly flat, and could easily accommodate the nearly three million Israelites, who would gather here.

It is also said that a line of hills encloses the near-vertical cliff, which answers to the *"bounds"* which were to keep the people from *"touching the Mount."*

The cliff from which God spoke rises like a huge Altar in front of the desert of Sinai, where the whole congregation would stand.

One engineer remarked, *"No spot in the world can be pointed out which combines in a more remarkable manner the conditions of a commanding height and of a plain in every part of which the sights and sounds described in Exodus would reach an assembled multitude of more than three million souls."*

Here was the scene of the giving of the Law.

This was the place which would constitute the great turning point in the moral history of man. The Covenant at Sinai placed Israel in a totally new relation to Jehovah. It conferred on that people an honor the lack of which no nation on Earth ever had, or ever has since, enjoyed. It gave rise to an economy, the express design of which was to prepare the way for Christ — to shut men up under a conviction of the hopelessness of attaining Righteousness by the Law, to the Faith that should afterwards be revealed (Gal. 3:23). This Covenant, as befitted the majesty of God, dealing with a sinful people, was to be ordained *"in the hand of a mediator"* (Gal. 3:19). Moses served as that mediator. The Law was as follows:

1. First of all, it was the Law of God, and totally of God, which means it was not at all of man. It is often referred to as the *"Law of Moses"*; however, the term merely refers to Moses being the instrument through which God gave the Law.

2. Inasmuch as the Law was wholly of God, it was perfect in every respect. It was actually given in three capacities — Civil, Ceremonial, and Moral. The first five Commandments of the Moral part of the Law dealt with the manner in which man should act toward God. The last five dealt with the manner in which man should act toward his fellow man.

3. The Law was the Righteousness of God. It was that which God demanded. In other words, it was that which was *"right."*

4. The Law, as would be obvious, would identify sin, portraying to man his awful, fallen condition.

5. The Law revealing man's fallen condition portrayed man's inability to keep its precepts, and despite how hard he might try.

6. Man seeing his inability, the Law was meant to point man to One Who, as man's Substitute, could keep the Law, and in fact, did keep the Law, namely Christ.

7. The law could not save man, as it had no power to do such. It could only point out man's futile condition.

8. There was a Righteousness to the Law, as would be obvious, but it was a Righteousness which could not be obtained by man and, therefore, was beyond his reach.

9. The Law showed Israel how to live, and as stated, how to relate to God and man, which placed Israel far above all other nations, regarding every way of life.

10. The Law was only meant to be temporary, in effect, serving as a schoolmaster, always pointing to Christ, Who Alone could meet its demands, and Who, in fact, did meet its demands.

11. While Christ fulfilled all of the Law, and I refer to the Civil, the Ceremonial, and the Moral (Col. 2:14-15), the Moral part of the Law is still incumbent upon mankind, simply because that which is Moral cannot change. However, man can successfully address the Moral part of the Law only in Christ. Otherwise, his attempt will be as futile as Israel of old.

12. Every just law in the world presently, and we speak of both Civil and Criminal, is based squarely on that which we refer to as the Ten Commandments, that given by God to Moses on Mount Sinai. The farther a nation strays from these laws, the less justice, freedom, and prosperity it has. The closer its laws are to the Law of God, the greater its Blessing.

THE UNITED STATES

It is a shame that many of the leaders of this nation little understand that Bible Christianity is the Foundation of our freedoms and prosperity. These men attribute it to other things.

Sometime back, the Post Office Department issued a stamp, commemorating Islam. My secretary wrote one of the United States Senators from our fair State, as to why this was done. He referred her letter to the Postal Authorities. Their answer was as follows:

"Thank you for sharing your comments. On September 1, 2001, as part of our Holiday Celebrations series, the Postal Service issued a new stamp for the Muslim holiday of Eid. Our Eid stamp features the Arabic phrase, 'Eid mubarak' in gold calligraphy on a blue background. English text on the stamps read 'EID GREETINGS.' This stamp highlights the business, educational, and social contributions of the estimated six to seven million Muslim citizens of this country whose cultural heritage has become an integral part of the diverse fabric of our great nation and who are patriotic Americans."

There are several things that should be said regarding this:

First of all, why is it against the law of the land for a stamp to be issued commemorating the contribution of Christianity to this nation, and it's not against the law as it regards the Muslim religion? Does the separation of Church and State refer only to Christianity, and not to other religions?

I'm all for the separation of Church and State, believing this to be one of the great foundations of our principles of freedom; however, let's be fair, and include all religions.

Second, of what contributions would Faith Beamon of the Postal Department be speaking, in her answer? Is she speaking of the nearly 5,000 people who had their lives snuffed out on September 11, 2001, of which many of the some seven million Muslims in this nation favored?

If you want to know what the Muslim religion actually is like, and the contributions that it makes to the world, all one has to do is to take a look at the countries of the world which favor the Muslim religion. All of them portray a failed culture, and failed in every respect. It has failed educationally, socially, economically, and above all, spiritually. For the most part, these countries are the most poverty stricken in the world. In fact, for the most part, they make up the nations of the world, which are still controlled by dictators, which means that there is no Democracy in most of these Muslim countries. Actually, if the sparkplugs of Islam had their way, they would usher the world back into the Dark Ages. There is a reason for this.

Out of all the religions of the world, Islam is the most violent, in fact, the source of 99 percent of the terrorism on planet Earth. It is a blood-thirsty religion, with the foundation of its principles being that of murder. And if one looks at the present happenings of terrorism in the world, and one cannot see that, then one is blind.

The reason?

Islam is not of God, and as well, *"Allah"* is not God, nor is it another name for God. It was the name chosen by Mohammad, from the over 300 idols worshipped then by the Arabs. In fact, this particular idol has its beginnings in Baal worship of ancient history, originating with the moon god, Ur, actually worshipped by Abraham, before his conversion to Jehovah. This means that the religion of Islam, which includes the Koran, is demon-instituted, demon-inspired, and demon-led. It began early in the Fifth Century, at about the same time incidentally that Christianity was losing its way, actually at about the time the Church first referred to the Bishop of Rome, as *"Pope."* So in a sense, both religions, that of Catholicism and Islam came into being at about the same time. (If the Bible is to be the criteria, Catholicism, by no stretch of the imagination, can be referred to as Christian.)

Even though Islam began so long ago, it was raised up by Satan primarily to rear its ugly head in the last of the last days, actually, the days in which we now live.

If it is to be noticed, Islam hates the United States and Israel above all other nations. The United States is referred to as the *"great Satan,"* with Israel referred to as the *"little Satan."* And to be sure, the hatred of Islam for the United States is not merely because of our support of Israel, but because of the Lord Jesus Christ.

ISLAM AND PEACE

President Bush declared that the Koran was a book of *"love and peace."* Our President could not be more wrong!

In fact, the word *"love"* is not mentioned in the Koran, even one time. And by no stretch of the imagination can the Koran be proclaimed as a book of peace. In fact, it is the very opposite. As stated, the religion of Islam is the thirstiest religion on the face of the Earth, thirsty for blood, with murder as the foundation of its principles, all inspired by the Koran. The idea that the terrible atrocities of September 11, 2001 were merely the efforts of a few misguided fanatics presents a refusal to see the obvious, which will soon come back to haunt this nation. Basing a policy on a lie cannot come out to a good conclusion, and that's exactly what we are presently doing. It is the religion of Islam that is the cause of the terrorism, and not a few misguided fools, as we would like to believe. The quicker we recognize the truth, the better off our nation will be.

SALVATION

Verses 3 and 4 read: *"And Moses went up unto God, and the LORD called unto him out of the mountain, saying, thus shall you say to the House of Jacob, and tell the Children of Israel:*

"You have seen what I did unto the Egyptians, and how I bear you on eagles' wings, and brought you unto Myself."

Despite every power of darkness which came against them, the Children of Israel, through a series of miracles performed by the Lord, had now come to this mountain. The Lord had told them, *"You shall serve God upon this mountain"* (Ex. 3:12), and this they did! No Word of God can fail. No matter how the enemy may rage, *"The counsel of the LORD shall stand"* (Prov. 19:21).

The sadness is, most Christians, and I think I exaggerate not by using the word *"most,"* don't walk close enough to the Lord, to hear His Voice. This means they do not study the Word of God as they should, and neither do they have much of a prayer life. In fact, most Christians have no prayer life at all.

Sometime back, in one of the Services of Family Worship Center, and it was a Wednesday night, if I remember correctly, I asked the people as to how many of them had not read the Bible completely through. I was shocked at the number of hands that went up, and that despite our constant admonishments that they study the Word of God.

I remember one Brother saying to me

after the Service that he was trying to read the Bible through for the first time. I looked at him in astonishment, knowing that he had been saved about 30 years.

In fact, every Believer should read the Bible completely through every year. And while it is being read, you should ask the Lord to reveal its contents to you. This He most definitely will do. And as well, I might quickly add, it is impossible to exhaust the knowledge of the Word. Inasmuch as it is God inspired, i.e., *"God-breathed,"* even down to its very words, its potential can never be exhausted. It tells where man came from, where man is, and where man is going. In fact, the Bible is the only revealed Truth in the world today, and is the only revealed Truth that ever has been. Jesus said: *"Thy Word is Truth"* (Jn. 17:17).

Those of you who are reading this Commentary show that you have a love for the Word of God. To be sure, that love will definitely be rewarded, by a leading of the Spirit, exactly as Israel of old was led. As the Lord had a plan for Israel, likewise, He has a plan for you.

THE LORD SPEAKS

Moses had known all along that Mount Sinai would be the place of something special from the Lord. At times, it seems that he had wavered in his Faith that they would ever arrive there, but now, and exactly as the Lord had said, they were at the Mount. Consequently, he climbs up the Mountain, or at least part way, no doubt led by the Holy Spirit. And then the Lord begins to speak to him:

He first of all reminds Moses of what He had done, in order to deliver the Children of Israel from Egyptian bondage. He uses a metaphor, *"I bear you on eagles' wings,"* which referred to the fact that they were not subject to the ordinary situations and problems, as would be all other human beings. The army of Pharaoh had no effect on them, the Red Sea didn't stop them, and the bitter waters of Marah were made sweet; likewise, the place of no water was suddenly turned into a verdant spring, as Moses smote the Rock, with water gushing out, even a veritable river. And then they fought the Amalekites, and won the victory. Notice the miracles!

Is it any less for the modern Believer? In fact, we have more, much more! Paul said: *"But now* (under the New Covenant) *has He* (Christ) *obtained a more excellent Ministry, by how much also He is the Mediator of a Better Covenant* (all brought about by the Cross), *which was established upon better promises.*

"For if that First Covenant (the Old Covenant under Moses) *had been faultless, then should no place have been sought for the second.*

"For finding fault with them (with the First Covenant), *He said, 'Behold, the days come, saith the Lord, when I will make a New Covenant with the House of Israel and with the House of Judah* (the New Covenant was made at the Cross, which made possible the Advent of the Holy Spirit in a new dimension)*"* (Heb. 8:6-8).

As Israel was a miracle people under the Old Covenant, how can we be less under the New Covenant! Their Covenant was meant only to be temporary, while our Covenant is *"Everlasting"* (Heb. 13:20). So what am I saying?

I'm saying that we should expect great things from God, simply because He is a great God. There is none other like unto Him, and in fact, there is no other God. There are those who claim to be God, but in reality, it is only demon spirits.

The phrase, *"And brought you unto Myself,"* refers to that which the Lord is ever doing. Throughout the entirety of the Word of God, the Lord is ever bringing His people ever closer.

First He was in the cloud, then between the Mercy Seat and the Cherubim in the Tabernacle and Temple. And now, due to the Cross, He abides within our hearts, and does so constantly (I Cor. 3:16). In the very near future, we will abide with Him in the New Jerusalem, and will do so forever (Rev. 21:3). So He's ever bringing us to Himself.

OBEDIENCE

Verses 5 and 6 read: *"Now therefore, if you will obey My Voice indeed, and keep My Covenant, then you will be a peculiar treasure unto Me above all people: for all the Earth is Mine:*

"And you shall be unto Me a kingdom of Priests and an holy nation. These are the words which you shall speak unto the Children of Israel."

Great Promises are given here to the Children of Israel. Those Promises are:

1. They were to be a peculiar treasure unto the Lord above all people.
2. They were to be unto Him a kingdom of Priests.
3. They were to be an holy nation.

They were God's people, in fact, the only people on the face of the Earth who fell into this category. While all the Earth was His because He Alone was and is the Creator, unfortunately, due to the Fall, all the people on the Earth didn't belong to Him, as all the people on the Earth don't belong to Him presently. But some do, and to that special group, then Israel, and now the True Church, all fall under these great Promises. As Israel was His Own *"peculiar treasure, even above all people,"* the Church is likewise. Peter said:

"But you (the Church) *are a chosen generation, a royal priesthood, an holy nation, a peculiar people; that you should show forth the praises of Him Who has called you out of darkness into His marvelous light:*

"Which in time past were not a people, but are now the people of God: which had not obtained mercy, but now have obtained mercy" (I Pet. 2:9-10).

So if God did great things for Israel, and He most definitely did, He will do even greater for us because we have a New Covenant, a Better Covenant, an Everlasting Covenant. The Church is now spiritual Israel, so to speak.

In fact, Paul said: *"And if some of the branches be broken off* (the Fall of Israel), *and you* (the Gentiles, i.e., 'the Church'), *being a wild olive tree, were grafted in among them* (grafted into the original Promises), *and with them partakers of the root and fatness of the olive tree;*

"Boast not against the branches (do not think yourself better than Israel), *but if you boast* (remember this), *you bear not the root, but the root you"* (Rom. 11:17-18).

THE LORD DEMANDS OBEDIENCE

On this one word *"obedience"* rests the entirety of the Promises of God, not only for Israel, but as well for the Church. So the great question is not the *"fact"* of obedience, but the *"how"* of obedience!

God demands obedience, and for all the obvious reasons. He, as our Creator, knows what we need, as should be obvious. So the things that He demands we do are always for our own good. In fact, God has nothing but good for us. And He knows the way for that good to be obtained, and in fact, He Alone knows the way.

He knows if we veer from this Word, which means we ignore the Word, or we disbelieve the Word, or we misinterpret the Word, whichever it may be, the results will be very negative. So it's incumbent upon us to know fully what He wants of us, and how we are to carry out His Word. That has ever been the problem, at least the area where Satan hits us the hardest.

The Lord gave the First Family the way and the means of restored fellowship, which was the slain lamb, which represented the coming Redeemer. Abel heeded, but his brother Cain didn't! Cain disobeyed the Word of the Lord, and substituted something else in place of the slain Lamb (Gen., Chpt. 4).

Cain did not refuse to offer up a sacrifice; in fact, he offered up a beautiful sacrifice, the labor of his own hands, whatever that was. But the Lord wasn't asking merely for a sacrifice, but for a certain type of sacrifice. The sacrifice was not to be that of the individual, but was to be that which represented something else. The lamb represented Christ. It was the lamb that would suffer, and not Abel.

In the sacrifice offered by Cain, he is the one who suffered labor in order for that particular sacrifice to be brought forth, which God couldn't accept, and for all the obvious reasons. But that is where humanity is presently, and, regrettably, most of the modern Church. Man keeps trying to atone for his sins, even those who claim Christ. It is a task that no human being can perform, hence the reason that God became man, in order to offer up Himself in Sacrifice, which He did (Gal. 1:4).

So in the next few Verses, we're going to look at the *"how"* of obedience. As stated, it is no less a problem now than it was then. If we misunderstand this, we misunderstand the entirety of Sanctification, which, without doubt, will bring untold problems and troubles on the one who registers unbelief or misunderstands it. So it's incumbent upon us that we know exactly *"how"* to render obedience to the Lord. To merely seek to obey is one thing, but it is *"how"* we obey that decides our destiny.

(7) "AND MOSES CAME AND CALLED FOR THE ELDERS OF THE PEOPLE, AND LAID BEFORE THEIR FACES ALL THESE WORDS WHICH THE LORD COMMANDED HIM.

(8) "AND ALL THE PEOPLE ANSWERED TOGETHER, AND SAID, ALL THAT THE LORD HAS SPOKEN WE WILL DO. AND MOSES RETURNED THE WORDS OF THE PEOPLE UNTO THE LORD.

(9) "AND THE LORD SAID UNTO MOSES, LO, I COME UNTO YOU IN A THICK CLOUD, THAT THE PEOPLE MAY HEAR WHEN I SPEAK WITH YOU, AND BELIEVE YOU FOREVER. AND MOSES TOLD THE WORDS OF THE PEOPLE UNTO THE LORD.

(10) "AND THE LORD SAID UNTO MOSES, GO UNTO THE PEOPLE, AND SANCTIFY THEM TODAY AND TOMORROW, AND LET THEM WASH THEIR CLOTHES,

(11) "AND BE READY AGAINST THE THIRD DAY: FOR THE THIRD DAY THE LORD WILL COME DOWN IN THE SIGHT OF ALL THE PEOPLE UPON MOUNT SINAI.

(12) "AND YOU SHALL SET BOUNDS UNTO THE PEOPLE ROUND ABOUT, SAYING, TAKE HEED TO YOURSELVES, THAT YOU GO NOT UP INTO THE MOUNT, OR TOUCH THE BORDER OF IT: WHOSOEVER TOUCHES THE MOUNT SHALL BE SURELY PUT TO DEATH:

(13) "THERE SHALL NOT AN HAND TOUCH IT, BUT HE SHALL SURELY BE STONED, OR SHOT THROUGH; WHETHER IT BE BEAST OR MAN, IT SHALL NOT LIVE: WHEN THE TRUMPET SOUNDS LONG, THEY SHALL COME UP TO THE MOUNT.

(14) "AND MOSES WENT DOWN FROM THE MOUNT UNTO THE PEOPLE, AND SANCTIFIED THE PEOPLE; AND THEY WASHED THEIR CLOTHES.

(15) "AND HE SAID UNTO THE PEOPLE, BE READY AGAINST THE THIRD DAY: COME NOT AT YOUR WIVES."

The diagram is:

1. Man has ever proclaimed his ability to obey God, and has ever portrayed his constant failure.

2. This was the Day of Pentecost, 50 days after the Passover, which had been eaten in Egypt. It was the day the Moral Law was to be given, which was by far the most important of all, and which would be followed on other days by the Civil and the Ceremonial.

3. Verses 7 through 15 proclaim the preparation of the people, which was commanded by God, in order that they may stand before the Lord. This foreshadowed another coming on another Day of Pentecost some 1,600 years later. The preparations to meet God by Israel of old are the same preparations to be enacted as it refers to being baptized with the Holy Spirit, with one exception: the preparations then were mostly physical, while now they are spiritual.

THE MANNER OF OBEDIENCE

Verses 7 and 8 read: *"And Moses came and called for the Elders of the people, and laid before their faces all these words which the LORD commanded him.*

"And all the people answered together, and said, All that the LORD has spoken we will do. And Moses returned the words of the people unto the LORD."

The Lord told Moses what must be done, and he told the Elders of Israel. They in turn told the people, and the response was, *"All that the Lord has spoken we will do."*

Many have criticized Israel for saying this, claiming they should have said, *"Lord, we cannot do this thing which is required, unless You help us."*

That certainly would have been the better response, with the response they did give showing their lack of knowledge concerning who they were, and Who God was.

Some claim that their response took them out from under Grace and put them under Law. That's not quite right.

In the first place, God intended for them to go under Law, and for specific reasons, which should be obvious. But yet, every good thing that the Lord had ever done for them was done exclusively by and through the Grace of God, and it would continue to be this way. Once again, the reasons should be obvious: we certainly do not merit anything that God gives us, so anything that comes, whether it was under the Old Covenant, or under the New, is all by the Grace of God.

Before the Cross, God was limited as to the degree of Grace that could be given, with the Cross opening up that avenue to a far greater extent. However, the Grace of God coming now to us in an unlimited manner, still, can do so only by a certain way. And it is that *"way"* that we wish to discuss.

HOW DOES ONE OBEY GOD?

Whether it was under the Old Covenant, or whether it is under the New Covenant, the manner doesn't change. We can only obey Him by following this prescribed pattern:

THE CROSS

1. As we have repeatedly stated in this Volume, everything that comes to the Child of God from the Lord comes exclusively through the Cross of Christ. That means that the Cross is the vehicle by and through which the Grace of God comes to us. We must understand that! We must believe that! We must rest upon that! That's why Paul said:

"For Christ sent me not to baptize, but to preach the Gospel: not with wisdom of words, lest the Cross of Christ should be made of none effect."

He then said: *"For the preaching* (Message or Word) *of the Cross is to them who perish foolishness; but unto us which are saved it is the Power of God."*

And then: *"But we preach Christ Crucified."*

And finally: *"For I determined not to know anything among you, save Jesus Christ, and Him Crucified"* (I Cor. 1:17-18, 23; 2:2).

OUR FAITH

2. The Cross of Christ is to ever be the object of our Faith. This is absolutely imperative! Everyone has Faith, even the unsaved, but for the far greater majority, it's not faith that God will honor. He honors only the Faith that's in the Cross (Rom. 6:3-14; I Cor. 2:5; Gal. 2:20).

THE HOLY SPIRIT

3. The Holy Spirit, Who Alone can help us to obey God, which can only be done by this method, works exclusively within the parameters of the Finished Work of Christ. In other words, what Christ did at the Cross gives Him the legal right to work within our lives. That's why Paul also said:

"For the Law of the Spirit of Life in Christ Jesus has made me free from the law of sin and death" (Rom. 8:2).

In fact, the manner in which the Holy Spirit works is so rigid that it is referred to as a *"Law."* This means that He will not deviate from this set principle. He demands that we understand that all comes to us by and through the Cross, and that our Faith ever be in that Finished Work. That being done, He can work mightily in our lives, and can help us, and in fact, will help us, to obey the Lord. In this manner, and this manner alone, can we obey.

If we set about to obey by rules and regulations, in other words by laws that we fabricate ourselves, we will simply fail. That is a given!

THE STATE OF THE MODERN CHURCH

Regrettably, Israel tried to obey in all the wrong ways. Paul said of them: *"For they being ignorant of God's Righteousness, and going about to establish their own righteousness, have not submitted themselves unto the Righteousness of God"* (Rom. 10:3).

Regrettably, much of the modern Church is attempting to do the same thing. And let me say this:

If the Believer doesn't understand the Cross, and this goes for entire Denominations as well, then without fail, they will go about trying to establish their own righteousness, and try to do so in many and varied ways, all of them wrong.

Now when we say, *"Understand the Cross,"* exactly what are we talking about?

In fact, most Christians automatically think that they understand all about the Cross. As one Brother wrote me sometime back, *"Why do you keep talking about the Cross? Christians already understand everything about the Cross."* Regrettably, that's the idea held by most Believers presently. The truth is, and as stated, most Christians understand almost nothing about the Cross, simply because there has been almost no teaching on the Cross in the last several decades. In fact, the *"Word of Faith"* people openly repudiate the Cross, calling it *"past miseries,"* and the *"greatest defeat in human history,"* etc. To be sure, this thinking has greatly influenced the modern Church, until presently, the Church, I believe, has never been in worse shape, at least since the Reformation.

While it's true that some few Christians understand the Cross as it refers to Salvation, virtually none understand it as it refers to Sanctification. As a result, *"works of the flesh"* will manifest themselves some way in such lives.

WORKS OF THE FLESH

Paul said: *"Now the works of the flesh are manifest, which are these; adultery, fornication, uncleanness, lasciviousness,*

"Idolatry, witchcraft, hatred, variance, emulations, wrath, strife, seditions, heresies,

"Envyings, murders, drunkenness, revelings, and such like: of the which I tell you before, as I have also told you in time past, that they which do such things shall not inherit the Kingdom of God" (Gal. 5:19-21).

So as to be crystal clear, let me make the statement in this fashion:

If the Believer doesn't understand the Cross, and I'm speaking of understanding the Cross as it refers to Sanctification, then the Believer is going to have *"works of the flesh"* manifested in his life in some manner. That's not *"maybe so,"* or *"possibly so,"* but guaranteed. To be sure, such a lifestyle presents nothing but misery. And the sadness is, many of these people are good Christians. In other words, they love the Lord. They're trying their best to serve Him, but they're doing so in the wrong way.

I realize that it may sound peculiar me calling these folk, *"good Christians,"* whenever *"works of the flesh"* are manifesting themselves in their lives, which could cause them to lose their souls. Well, I'll ask this question!

When one reads the Seventh Chapter of Romans, one is reading the personal experience of the Apostle Paul. And this experience pertains to the time after he was saved and baptized with the Holy Spirit, and even called to be an Apostle. In fact, he was an Apostle while all of this was taking place (Acts 9:15).

The account is such that it speaks of nothing but defeat. Are we going to say that Paul didn't love the Lord?

I am positive that we would understand that he loved the Lord very much, even during these most trying times.

I read the other day that one man said that whatever it was that Paul was doing, it must have been very minor, etc. Well, I don't know how minor it was; I just know two things:

1. Any sin is awful, even with the Apostle himself saying, *"A little leaven leaveneth the whole lump"* (Gal. 5:9). In other words, little sins quickly grow into big sins.

2. Whatever it was, it was bad enough that the Apostle said, *"O wretched man that I am! Who shall deliver me from the body of this death?"* (Rom. 7:24).

Most Christians completely misunderstand sin. They look at the act instead of what is causing the act. That's why the Holy Spirit through Paul referred to these particular sins as *"works of the flesh."*

Trying to stop these particular problems, whatever they might be, is really not the answer. If one does this, and that's what most Christians do, one is only addressing symptoms and not the real cause.

THE ERROR OF THE CHURCH!

The modern Church, little knowing the cause of these problems, attempts to address the problem, and mostly does so through punishment. The entire system is wrong.

In the first place, there is no Christian qualified to punish another. James addressed this by saying: *"There is one Lawgiver, Who is able to save and to destroy: who are you who judges another?"* (James 4:12).

He is bluntly saying here, or at least the Holy Spirit through him is saying, that no

Believer is given the latitude to punish another Believer. That lies strictly in the domain of God.

Furthermore, Jesus suffered all the punishment on the Cross. And for us to attempt to add to that is a great insult to Christ.

But the Church, not knowing what to do, uses the methods of the world, and simply because it is functioning in the realm of *"law,"* trying to establish its own righteousness.

The reason the Believer is failing, and in whatever way the works of the flesh may manifest themselves, is because the Believer doesn't understand the Cross as it refers to Sanctification. And what do we mean by that?

1. As we've already stated any number of times in this Volume, the Believer must understand that everything he receives from the Lord, everything he needs is found exclusively in Christ and what Christ has done for him at the Cross. It is a *"must"* that he understands that.

2. The Cross must ever be the object of his Faith. He must not allow his Faith to be moved to other things, irrespective as to how good those other things might be in their own right.

3. Understanding that Christ and His Cross is the means by which God gives us all things, and that the Cross must ever be the object of our Faith, the Holy Spirit, Who works exclusively within the parameters of the Sacrifice of Christ, will then mightily work within our lives, developing the *"Fruit of the Spirit"* (Gal. 5:22-23). Only then can we have victory over the flesh! Only then can we walk victorious in every capacity! Only then can we enjoy the *"more abundant life,"* promised by Christ! (Jn. 10:10).

HOW HARD IS IT TO DO WHAT I HAVE JUST STATED?

At first glance, it seems to be a very simple thing, so to speak; however, once we look at the Cross of Christ, and begin to inspect it closely, understanding that our Faith must be there and there alone, then all of a sudden, we start to see problems.

There cannot be any double-minded means and ways in our actions and attitudes. In other words, we cannot trust Christ and what He has done at the Cross, and trust other things as well. What do we mean by *"trusting other things"*?

For instance, most of the modern Church, the Pentecostals included, have opted for humanistic psychology as the answer for the ills and aberrations of the human race. As a result, the so-called Christian Bookstores are filled with this type of material. In fact, there are fewer Books on the Bible presently than ever before. To my knowledge, this Commentary that I am now writing is one of the few that's been written in the last 50 years. Satan has been very successful in turning people away from the Bible to other things.

And then we have the *"Word of Faith"* doctrine, which I believe is even worse than the Judaism that plagued the Churches during the time of Paul. It has led Believers away from the Cross, even repudiating the Cross, as previously stated. This false doctrine fits Paul's statement perfectly. The Apostle said:

"Now the Spirit speaks expressly (pointedly), *that in the latter times* (the times in which we now live) *some shall depart from the Faith* (the Faith refers to Christ and Him Crucified), *giving heed to seducing spirits, and doctrines of devils"* (I Tim. 4:1).

Most Christians completely misunderstand this, not really realizing what the Apostle is saying.

In the first place, Satan, as it regards his *"seducing spirits,"* doesn't look like Satan. In fact, he looks like the Lord. That is the very meaning of the word *"seduction."* These spirits seduce people, by making them think that what is being offered is of God. That's what Paul also referred to as *"Satan transforming himself into an angel of light"* (II Cor. 11:14).

He also referred to those who propagated such false doctrine as *"Satan's ministers"* (II Cor. 11:15).

There is no way that any Bible student who studies Paul to any degree, but that it is understood that Paul *"preached the Cross."* He *"preached the Cross"* not only as it regards Salvation, but also as it regards Sanctification. In fact, he preached the Cross far more as it regards Sanctification, than any other way. If you will notice, the entirety of the Bible, and Paul's writings as well, deal very little with the Salvation process. To be sure, it definitely does give the manner in which people are saved, and does so over and over; however, the far greater bulk of the Word of God is made up of telling people how to live for God, after they get saved, so to speak.

Paul was the founder of the Church, and the entirety of his 14 Epistles deal almost exclusively with the manner and the means by which the Believer should live for God. So his preaching of the Cross dealt far more with Sanctification than anything else.

A PERSONAL EXPERIENCE

After seeking the Lord for some five years, and doing so with tears, almost daily, the Lord began to open up to me this great Message of the Cross. The year was 1996. The moment the Holy Spirit began to open up to me this great Truth, I knew that at long last I had found that for which I had so long sought. To be sure, it wasn't new, actually what He had already given to Paul. He just helped me to understand what the great Apostle had said, in other words, what the Spirit of God had given to him.

You see, Paul's great cry, *"O wretched man that I am . . ."* was finally answered by the Lord giving him the meaning of the New Covenant, which, in essence, is the meaning of the Cross.

So the modern Believer is going to have to come down to the place that you choose what Paul taught, or else you choose what some of the modern teachers are proclaiming, which is the opposite of what Paul taught.

Now when you do that, and I speak of choosing that which Paul taught, you may have to leave your Church; you may have to change friends; even your own family may turn against you. In fact, that's the very price that Jesus said we would have to pay.

You see, when it comes down to the bottom line, irrespective as to whether we are speaking of the world without God, or the Church; it all refers to *"Jesus Christ and Him Crucified"* (I Cor. 1:17-18, 21, 23; 2:2, 5).

HOW DO THE WORKS OF THE FLESH MANIFEST THEMSELVES?

Many Christians look at the first four or five *"works of the flesh,"* and dismiss the others, or else they pay little attention to what Paul said.

In the first place, *"works of the flesh"* are ugly indeed; however, some of them do not appear that way, but rather come under the heading of the doctrine of *"angels of light"* (II Cor. 11:13-14). Let me deal with the second part first:

To use just one as an example, the teaching and believing of *"heresies"* constitute a *"work of the flesh."* But most people would not think of such in that capacity.

This means that all the Preachers who are teaching the *"Word of Faith"* doctrine, to use that as an example, are manifesting the *"works of the flesh."* But most Christians wouldn't think of such in that capacity. But the Holy Spirit through Paul proclaims that as a fact.

During Paul's day, the great error projected by Satan in the Church was the problem of *"Judaism."* It was the problem of trying to add Law to Grace, which in essence said that Christ didn't finish the work at the Cross, or else it gave the Cross of Christ no place at all, which is usually the case. Pure and simple, that was *"heresy."* And to be sure, it is no less presently!

As well, if a Christian, Preachers included, are trying to function outside of the Cross, which sadly most are, immorality in one way or the other will rear its ugly head. That's the reason that we presently see so many Christians, Preachers included, who are failing.

Many of these people are trying with all their strength not to fail. But they are trying in the wrong way because they do not know the Message of the Cross; consequently, their faith is placed in something else, which the Holy Spirit cannot honor, which makes them a perfect target for the Devil. And to be sure, he takes advantage of all of these opportunities. And again, to be sure, anything and everything that he does is always very, very ugly. He has no mercy, as should be understandable. Now we've come to the subject of willpower:

WILLPOWER!

The Church, not knowing and understanding the Message of the Cross as it refers to

Sanctification, mostly relies on *"willpower."* For the most part, the Church teaches that if a Believer sins, it's simply because he wants to sin. Let me ask this question!

When Paul said: *"For that which I do I allow* (understand) *not: for what I would, that do I not; but what I hate, that do I,"* what did he mean?

The Apostle is plainly saying that he finds himself doing the very thing he doesn't want to do, and in fact, is fighting with all of his strength not to do. Listen to what he said:

"For what I would," in essence says, *"that which I will,"* or *"that which I want to do,"* I cannot do.

He also said, *"To will is present with me; but how to perform that which is good I find not"* (Rom. 7:18).

He plainly tells us here that he is using his *"will,"* which refers to *"willpower,"* but that it simply wasn't enough. Despite exerting all of his willpower, he found himself doing the very thing he didn't want to do. Now let me make this statement:

If the Believer, even as Paul was before he understood the Message of the Cross, is trying to live for the Lord by the means of his *"willpower,"* which most are doing, Satan can literally override that person's will, and force them to do things they don't want to do. That is very obvious in this Seventh Chapter of Romans.

Now we can try to pass this off, even as do many Preachers, by saying this referred to Paul before his Salvation; however, such thinking is foolish, to say the least!

In the first place, no sinner is trying to quit sinning. In fact, they love sin.

No, the Seventh Chapter of Romans proclaims Paul's account after he was saved. And as well, what I'm about to say is very, very important! Paul is also saying that if the Believer, even himself, reverts back to means other than Faith in the Cross of Christ, irrespective as to who that Believer might be, spiritual failure will be the result.

Now when it comes to the *"will,"* naturally, such is very important. The Christian has to *"will"* to live for God, as the first prerogative of his experience with the Lord. The Scripture plainly says: *"And whosoever will, let him take the water of life freely"* (Rev. 22:17).

NOTES

So that being the case, how does the will come into play?

The Believer has to *"will"* to trust Christ and what Christ has done at the Cross, and that is the avenue and direction that the *"will"* must play. If the Believer attempts to live for God in any other way, it doesn't matter how much willpower he uses; he will fail.

The Church erroneously teaches that the Believer sins simply because he *"wills to do so."* To be frank, I don't think that's true of any. Admittedly, there are millions of people, who go under the guise of *"Christian,"* who in fact, aren't even saved. To be sure, those people will definitely want to do things which are wrong.

Now even in a good Christian, the flesh may desire something that's not right, and Paul also dealt with that by saying: *"Now then it is no more I that do it, but sin* (the sin, the sin nature) *that dwelleth in me"* (Rom. 7:17).

But even though it's only the flesh which desires such things, whatever those things might be, the Believer is still responsible, and what he does is still looked at by God as *"sin."*

The Believer has within himself three natures. They are:

1. Human nature: Christ even had a human nature, as should be obvious.

2. The Divine Nature: (II Pet. 1:4).

3. The sin nature: This nature, while dwelling in the Christian, must not rule and reign in the Christian (Rom. 6:12). In other words, the sin nature in the heart and life of the Believer is to be dormant. In fact, its power was broken at the Cross, and its guilt taken away (Rom. 6:6). But if the Believer doesn't function through Christ and Him Crucified, the sin nature will come to life, and will definitely rule and reign in one's life. Paul said: *"Let not sin* (the sin nature) *therefore reign in your mortal body, that you should obey it in the lust thereof"* (Rom. 6:12). It would have made no sense for him to have said that, if such were not possible, as many teach!

No, no true Christian wants to sin. The Divine Nature is in him, and sin has now become abhorrent to him. But yet millions are sinning, and why?

They are sinning, because they are trying to address themselves to these things with only their *"willpower,"* which is woefully insufficient, and in fact, will never work. As stated, you are to *"will"* to live according to Christ and Him Crucified, and that is as far as the will is to go. The Holy Spirit will do the rest (Rom. 8:1-2, 11).

When we say that Satan can override a Believer's will, it scares most Christians exceedingly, and rightly so! But that is the truth. However, he cannot override your will if your will is properly placed in Christ and what Christ has done for you at the Cross.

So when the Christian says, *"I will obey,"* we must understand that we can do so only in the capacity of the Holy Spirit working through us, which He does according to our Faith in Christ and His great Sacrifice.

THAT THE PEOPLE MAY BELIEVE

Verse 9 reads: *"And the LORD said unto Moses, Lo, I come unto you in a thick cloud, that the people may hear when I speak with you, and believe you forever. And Moses told the words of the people unto the LORD."*

God is *"thrice-Holy."* As such, He has to veil Himself when He speaks to sinful man, or else, man would not be able to stand the *"brightness of His Presence."* Pulpit says, *"If He takes a human form, that form is a veil; if He appears in a burning bush, the very fire is a shroud."*

The *"Cloud"* which would cover Him, was, no doubt, the same Cloud that accompanied Israel out of Egypt.

That which He would speak to Moses would be the *"Law."* His statement: *"And believe you forever,"* refers to the fact that in some sense, the Law is an eternal obligation of all men (Mat. 5:18). As we have previously stated, that which is moral cannot change. What was wrong thousands of years ago is wrong presently. Civil and ceremonial laws might change, and in fact do. But that which is moral presents itself as an abiding rule.

The moral part of the Law of Moses, which portrays the Ten Commandments, is not incumbent upon Believers, providing they understand that Christ, as our Substitute, has kept the Law perfectly in every respect, and as well, has suffered its penalty, which He did at the Cross. Paul said: *"Blotting out the handwriting of Ordinances that was against us, which was contrary to us, and took it out of the way, nailing it to His Cross"* (Col. 2:14).

As long as we trust Christ and the Cross, we need not worry about the Law, for it will definitely be kept in our hearts and lives, simply because Christ lives in us (Gal. 2:20). But the moment the Christian moves his Faith from the Cross to other things, he will find the Holy Spirit refusing to participate in such action, which means that he will then try to live for God, that is, to keep the Moral Law, by his own stratagems. As we have repeatedly stated, such are always doomed to failure.

The phrase, *"And Moses told the words of the people unto the Lord,"* is basically the same as that given in the latter portion of the previous Verse. The repetition is intentional!

The Holy Spirit is very desirous that we know that God hears what we say, etc.

SANCTIFY

Verse 10 reads: *"And the LORD said unto Moses, Go unto the people, and sanctify them today and tomorrow, and let them wash their clothes."*

The word *"sanctify"* actually means, *"to set apart,"* and in this case, *"to be set apart exclusively to the Lord."* These people belong to God, and their lives were to be dedicated to Him.

We find here that the Lord was very concerned about their outward appearance, which in some way mirrored their inward state. While Believers in those days, and we speak of the time before the Cross, didn't have the Holy Spirit abiding within them permanently, the sanctifying process was not nearly as it is now. It could only be, as we see here, in a ritualistic manner. They were to stand in the Presence of God, so the Lord demanded that they have clean clothing, with no doubt their bodies being washed as well, and also, even as Verse 15 proclaims, the husbands during this three-day period, were not to have any conjugal relationship with their wives.

WHY COULDN'T THE HOLY SPIRIT ABIDE PERMANENTLY WITHIN BELIEVERS BEFORE THE CROSS?

Hours before the Crucifixion, Jesus told His Disciples: *"And I will pray the Father, and He shall give you another Comforter* (Helper), *that He may abide with you forever:*

"Even the Spirit of Truth (Holy Spirit); *Whom the world cannot receive, because it sees Him not, neither knows Him: but you know Him; for He dwells with you, and shall be in you"* (Jn. 14:16-17).

So we know from this Text that the Holy Spirit had definitely been with all Believers, up unto the Cross, and as well, He did come into some to help them perform their task, whatever that calling may have been, but even that was temporary.

The reason for His limited help at that time was because of the sin debt owed by all, which the blood of bulls and goats could not satisfy (Heb. 10:4).

When Jesus died on the Cross, He atoned for all sin, satisfying every demand of the broken law, which then, in effect, *"took away all sin"* (Jn. 1:29; Col. 2:14-15).

As should be obvious, animal blood could not even remotely compare with the precious Blood of our Lord and Saviour, Jesus Christ (I Pet. 1:18-20).

So inasmuch as the Holy Spirit could not abide permanently in Believers before the Cross, the Sanctifying process was, of necessity, very limited. But now, the Holy Spirit, Who abides permanently within the heart and life of every Believer, can make us what we ought to be in Christ.

IS HIS WORK AUTOMATIC?

No, it isn't!

He functions exclusively within the parameters of the Finished Work of Christ, which gives Him the legal right to do whatever is needed. Consequently, He doesn't require much of us, but He does require that we evidence Faith exclusively in Christ and Him Crucified. That's why Paul said: *"For in Jesus Christ* (those who trust in Christ and what He has done for us at the Cross) *neither circumcision availeth anything, nor uncircumcision; but Faith* (Faith in Christ and His Sacrifice) *which works by love"* (Gal. 5:6).

There is no way that the Believer can effect Sanctification within his life by his own efforts and strength. It simply cannot be done. The Holy Spirit Alone can sanctify the Believer, and help him to grow in Grace and the knowledge of the Lord, but He does so strictly on the basis of our Faith in the Finished Work of Christ. This is absolutely essential!

Non-Pentecostals tend to give the Holy Spirit little thought. So whatever it is He is supposed to do, they would put it in the *"automatic"* section.

Regrettably, most Pentecostals and Charismatics are, for all practical purposes, in the same category. After being baptized with the Holy Spirit and speaking with other tongues, they tend to think that everything else thereafter is automatic. In other words, the Holy Spirit just does what He is going to do, etc. That is basely incorrect as well.

As I've already stated, the Holy Spirit doesn't require much of us, but He definitely does require that we exhibit Faith in Christ and His Cross. If we don't do that, this means that our Faith is placed in other things, which means, at least in the mind of the Holy Spirit, that we are committing spiritual adultery (Rom. 7:1-4). As should be obvious, if that indeed is correct, then He certainly is not going to have anything to do with such action — and please believe me, it is correct! But regrettably, that's where most Believers are.

If the Believer rejects the Cross, thereby placing his faith elsewhere, while the Holy Spirit will remain with such a Believer for a great period of time, if He cannot get such a Believer to function correctly, and that is by Faith, and I'm speaking of Faith in the correct object, which is the Cross, then to be sure, such a person is placing themselves in terrible, spiritual jeopardy.

The Lord has a way of doing things, and that way is the Cross. That rejected, He doesn't have a fall-back position. It's the Cross or nothing!

PARAMETERS

Verses 11 through 15 read: *"And be ready against the third day: for the third day the LORD will come down in the sight of all the people upon Mount Sinai.*

"And you shall set bounds unto the people round about, saying, Take heed to yourselves, that you go not up into the Mount, or touch the border of it: whosoever touches the Mount shall be surely put to death:

"There shall not an hand touch it, but he shall surely be stoned, or shot through; whether it be beast or man, it shall not live; when the trumpet sounds long, they shall come up to the Mount.

"And Moses went down from the Mount unto the people, and sanctified the people; and they washed their clothes.

"And he said unto the people, Be ready against the third day: come not at your wives."

If it is possible for anyone to properly imagine in one's mind as to exactly what happened on this particular day, it would have been something so awesome as to defy all description. While God could not be seen, His awful Presence could definitely be felt as He descended in the Cloud, which seemed to be wreathed in fire.

Moses was given instructions that a fence or barrier of some type would ring the particular side of the mountain where the people were. They were instructed to come no closer than that barrier, not even their cattle. If they touched anything on the other side of the barrier, they were to be immediately stoned to death.

This may seem to be harsh, but it was done for the protection of the people.

In all of this, we should learn something about the Holiness of God, and as well, what the Cross did for the human race. This is a perfect example!

The Cross took away the barriers, opening up the very Throne of God to any and every Believer — at least those who place their Faith and Trust in Christ, and what Christ has done for the human race, regarding the Sacrifice of Himself. In fact, the entirety of the Book of Hebrews deals with this very subject, how that Christ opened up the way.

Before the Cross, man was very limited as to how he could approach God. Without going into detail, however He was approached, it had to be by virtue of the sacrifice of a clean animal, which spoke of Christ, Who would ultimately come.

Surely the Reader can see from all of these examples the significance of the Cross. But regrettably, Satan has used all of his seductive spirits to cloud the issue, until most Christians hardly understand the Foundation of their Salvation. And to be sure, the lack of such knowledge can cause untold problems and difficulties.

(16) "AND IT CAME TO PASS ON THE THIRD DAY IN THE MORNING, THAT THERE WERE THUNDERS AND LIGHTNINGS, AND A THICK CLOUD UPON THE MOUNT, AND THE VOICE OF THE TRUMPET EXCEEDING LOUD; SO THAT ALL THE PEOPLE WHO WERE IN THE CAMP TREMBLED.

(17) "AND MOSES BROUGHT FORTH THE PEOPLE OUT OF THE CAMP TO MEET WITH GOD; AND THEY STOOD AT THE NETHER PART OF THE MOUNT.

(18) "AND MOUNT SINAI WAS ALTOGETHER ON A SMOKE, BECAUSE THE LORD DESCENDED UPON IT IN FIRE: AND THE SMOKE THEREOF ASCENDED AS THE SMOKE OF A FURNACE, AND THE WHOLE MOUNT QUAKED GREATLY.

(19) "AND WHEN THE VOICE OF THE TRUMPET SOUNDED LONG, AND WAXED LOUDER AND LOUDER, MOSES SPOKE, AND GOD ANSWERED HIM BY A VOICE.

(20) "AND THE LORD CAME DOWN UPON MOUNT SINAI, ON THE TOP OF THE MOUNT: AND THE LORD CALLED MOSES UP TO THE TOP OF THE MOUNT; AND MOSES WENT UP.

(21) "AND THE LORD SAID UNTO MOSES, GO DOWN, CHARGE THE PEOPLE, LEST THEY BREAK THROUGH UNTO THE LORD TO GAZE, AND MANY OF THEM PERISH.

(22) "AND LET THE PRIESTS ALSO, WHICH COME NEAR TO THE LORD, SANCTIFY THEMSELVES, LEST THE LORD BREAK FORTH UPON THEM.

(23) "AND MOSES SAID UNTO THE LORD, THE PEOPLE CANNOT COME UP TO MOUNT SINAI: FOR YOU CHARGED US, SAYING, SET BOUNDS ABOUT THE MOUNT, AND SANCTIFY IT.

(24) "AND THE LORD SAID UNTO HIM, AWAY, YOU GET DOWN, AND YOU SHALL

COME UP, YOU, AND AARON WITH YOU: BUT LET NOT THE PRIESTS AND THE PEOPLE BREAK THROUGH TO COME UP UNTO THE LORD, LEST HE BREAK FORTH UPON THEM.

(25) "SO MOSES WENT DOWN UNTO THE PEOPLE, AND SPOKE UNTO THEM."

The diagram is:

1. The words *"And God answered him,"* may be translated *"And God kept answering him by a voice"* (Vs. 19). This explains how the following Chapters were given to Moses (Williams).

2. The *"fire"* of Verse 18 was symbolic of the *"fire"* that would set upon the heads of those baptized with the Holy Spirit in Acts, Chapter 2.

3. The *"voice of the trumpet sounded long"* in Verse 19 was symbolic, in some way, of *"the sound of the mighty rushing wind"* in Acts, Chapter 2, which signaled the coming of the Holy Spirit on the Day of Pentecost.

4. Verse 20 says, *"And the Lord came down."* Acts, Chapter 2 portrays the Holy Spirit coming down.

5. Verse 25 says, *"So Moses went down unto the people, and spoke unto them"*; likewise, Peter, on the Day of Pentecost, said, *"Hearken to my words."*

(As we've already stated, the Law was given on the fiftieth day after the Passover, i.e., *"the Day of Pentecost."* The Holy Spirit came on the same day, some 1,500 plus years later.)

THE APPEARANCE OF THE LORD

Verse 16 reads: *"And it came to pass on the third day in the morning, that there were thunders and lightnings, and a thick cloud upon the Mount, and the voice of the trumpet exceeding loud; so that all the people who were in the camp trembled."*

The description given here represents a thrice-Holy God. In fact, His Holiness is to such an extent, to such degree, as to defy all description, except that given here. This means the Cross was an absolute necessity. As stated, sinful man could in no way approach a thrice-Holy God. But the Cross opened up the way because God, Who had become man, would atone for all sin, past, present, and future (Eph. 2:13-18).

The Cross, even as Paul described it over and over, is the center point of everything. It is not merely a doctrine, but rather the Foundation of all Doctrine. I am positive that Jesus looked at the sacrificial Sacrifice of Himself, His vicarious, efficacious Work, as more than a mere doctrine. In fact, there is no way that a Believer can properly understand the Word of God, unless he properly understands the Cross.

We find that the very first Word given by God to Satan through the serpent, after the Fall, addressed the Cross. The Lord said:

"And I will put enmity (hatred) *between you* (Satan) *and the woman* (women in general), *and between your seed* (mankind as a whole) *and her Seed* (the Lord Jesus Christ); *it* (He, namely Christ) *shall bruise your head* (that which Christ did at the Cross) *and you shall bruise His heel* (the sufferings of the Cross)" (Gen. 3:15).

WHY IS THE CROSS SO MISUNDERSTOOD?

Perhaps the following will shed some light on this all-important question.

In observing the record of the Sacrifice of our Saviour, a careful Reader will notice the varied mental and spiritual attitudes of the several types of people who stood before the Cross. There are at least five classes of people whose attitudes were fundamentally the same:

1. The common crowd, that *"passed by wagging their heads."*

2. The Jewish rulers who had connived the Crucifixion.

3. The railing malefactor who rejected Christ.

4. The Roman soldiers, who knew no king but Caesar.

5. The half-superstitious beholders, who in the cry of *"Eli, Eli,"* supposed Jesus to be calling for Elijah. Each of these five classes appealed alike to Christ to demonstrate that He was really the Messiah, by coming down from the Cross, and thereby, saving His life.

The crowd said, *"Ha, You Who claimed that You can destroy the temple and build it back in three days, save Yourself, and come down from the Cross"* (Mk. 15:29-30). The rulers said, *"He saved others, Himself He cannot save; let the Christ, the King of Israel, now come down from the Cross, that we may see and* believe" (Mk. 15:31-32). The malefactor said, *"Are You not the Christ? Save Yourself and us"* (Lk. 23:39). The soldiers said, *"If You are the King of the Jews, save Yourself"* (Lk. 23:37). The superstitious said, *"Let it be; let us see whether Elijah comes to take Him down"* (Mk. 15:36). Each of these observed, in effect, said to Jesus, *"Save Yourself."*

ONE SHINING EXCEPTION

These we have mentioned all saw chiefly the tragedy of the Crucifixion; they supposed the Cross in that sense to be a finality in the Life of Jesus. Unless our Saviour should use His miraculous Power to take Himself off the scaffold — supernaturally keep Himself alive — they would have no Faith in Him; the demonstration, to their minds, would be complete, that He was not what He claimed to be, the Son of God, the Messiah of Israel, the Saviour of the world.

Now, over against these five classes, there is a single shining exception, of one whose position radically differed from that of these types just noted, and He expresses himself differently: the dying penitent was the first and only one among all who spoke out at the Crucifixion of Jesus, who did not say, *"Save Yourself."* He did cry, *"Save me." "And he said of the Lord,"* (Lk. 23:42); that is, he used the saving name, one might say, and as well referred to Christ as God, which shows discernment of Who and What He really was. He and he alone, it seems, saw there was something deeper transpiring than the crucifiers recognized; that Jesus really was allowing the sanctuary of His Body to be taken down, in order that it might be rebuilt. He discerned that if Jesus would save others from their sins, that He, in fact, could not *"save Himself"*; He must endure what sin would impose upon Saviourhood; he saw that Jesus really was *"the King of Israel," "the Chosen of God," "the Good Shepherd,"* laying down His life for the sheep, so laying it down that He *"might take it again."*

THE ONLY ONE

This penitent was the first and only one at the Crucifixion who saw a whole new Kingdom lying beyond the impending Death of Jesus, of which he might become a member.

NOTES

That Kingdom, however, was to be built upon the Divine side of what was going on. In other words, it was all of God and none at all of man. He saw at least in principle the coming Resurrection, and the glorious possibilities in it; it was *"the hope of Israel,"* and as well, the hope of all mankind. Doubtless, he was spiritually, preternaturally endued with the insight of one on the borderland of the celestial world; and thus saw both sides of the Crucifixion event, the basely human, and the nobly Divine.

But he especially saw with great vividness the reality of the reconciliation, saw it from the Heaven-side, as God sees it — as we all should learn to see it — and he exclaimed in that model prayer, marked with its peculiar illumination, *"Lord, remember me when You come into Your Kingdom"* (Lk. 23:42) — a Kingdom conditioned on what was now being borne by Christ.

This man and this one only, so far as we know, of all who stood about Christ at Calvary, apprehended the reconciliation, God's act — an act as both deliberate and permissive — the reconciliation as distinguished from man's criminality in the Crucifixion. There was probably not a Disciple who stood there, not one of the women, not even the Saviour's Own Mother, Mary, who would not, if possible, in their sheer inability to perceive what God was achieving, have prevented the completion of Christ's purpose on the Cross, that is, if they'd had the power to have done so. As yet, none of these Disciples understood as they did afterwards in the light of Pentecost — the Cross of the Redemption.

This dying man, so unfortunately stigmatized in the common epithet, as *"the dying thief,"* is really the ideal penitent. He and he only had the vision of the Cross of reconciliation. He alone looked beyond the tragic horrors of the crucifying deed. He was absorbed with the larger reality that Christ, despite man's treatment of Him, was really bearing away the sin of the world, preparatory to a spiritual kingdom which lay beyond the moment of His dying hour. The penitent sought membership in that Kingdom, a privilege of Grace instantly assured by the reply of Christ, *"Verily I say unto you, today you shall be with Me in Paradise"* (Lk. 23:43).

One Theologian said, and rightly so: *"For the modern mind, as for the ancient, the attraction and the repulsion of Christianity are concentrated at the same point; the Cross of Christ is man's only glory, or it is his final stumbling block."*

God help us that the Cross never be a *"stumbling block,"* but rather a *"glory."* The chief of the Apostles said: *"God forbid that I should glory, save in the Cross of our Lord Jesus Christ, by whom the World is crucified unto me, and I unto the world"* (Gal. 6:14).

YOUR RESPONSE TO THE CROSS

The Cross is God's only way, as it regards Salvation and Sanctification. He has no other method, no other remedy, no other solution because no other is needed. So if the center of your vision is not *"Jesus Christ and Him Crucified,"* then your believing is wrong, and the consequences will not be pleasant. Now let the following be clearly and plainly understood:

There is no such thing, as one might say, as a *"closet Cross Christian."* In other words, if you're trying to believe in the Cross, but at the same time attending a Church which doesn't preach the Cross, which means that you have to keep your Faith quiet, the Lord will not allow such. It is one or the other!

One of the great problems with those who hear the Message of the Cross is, if they accept the Message, some may even have to leave their respective Churches. Many will have their friends and even their family to turn against them. In fact, this is what Jesus was speaking of when He said: *"If any man come to Me, and hate* (prefer) *not his father, and mother, and wife, and children, and brethren, and sister, yes, and even his own life also, he cannot be My Disciple."*

And then He said: *"And whosoever does not bear his cross, and come after Me, cannot be My Disciple"* (Lk. 14:26-27).

He then said: *"For which of you, intending to build a tower, sits not down first, and counts the cost, whether he have sufficient to finish it?"* (Lk. 14:28).

The idea is, when you set out to follow Christ, which one can do only by *"bearing his Cross,"* which refers to living by the benefits of the Cross, he should first count the cost. Christ and His Sacrifice must be first, irrespective of the cost. The question is:

Are you willing to do that? Are you willing to put Christ and the Cross first, forsaking all else? Regrettably, many aren't!

But for those who are exposed to the Light, and then reject that Light, they must understand the following:

Light offered, and then rejected, is Light withdrawn. To be sure, the end result of such a direction will not be pleasant. All victory, all life, all peace, all Grace, all love, are, without exception, found in the Sacrifice of Christ.

THE LORD DESCENDED

Verses 17 and 18 read: *"And Moses brought forth the people out of the camp to meet with God; and they stood at the nether part of the Mount.*

"And Mount Sinai was altogether on a smoke, because the LORD descended upon it in fire: and the smoke thereof ascended as the smoke of a furnace, and the whole Mount quaked greatly."

As stated, Moses had erected a fence or barrier, which extended on that side of the mountain, which undoubtedly was a mile or more long. The first tents were evidently erected several hundreds of yards back from this barrier. Moses then called the people, or at least their leaders, to come stand in this vacant space between the tents and the fence, in order to get as close to the Lord as they could. And as previously stated, all had been given strict instructions that they were not to touch anything beyond the fence, and if they did, death could quickly ensue.

When the people came close to the Mount, even as they were instructed to do, the scene was awful, one might say. The Scripture says, *"The whole Mount quaked greatly,"* signifying an earthquake, but an earthquake which centered up on the Mountain, and did not involve the area where the people were.

It seems that the entirety of the Mountain was aflame, with smoke ascending up from the fire. The Scripture says that it was as *"the smoke of a furnace."*

Coming to the foot of the Mountain, as God descended, was as close as sinful man could come. Had he come any further, he would have died.

It is not that God is unapproachable. In fact, He wanted man to approach, but due to the sinfulness of man, this at the time was the best that could be done.

As we've already stated, the Cross, thank God, changed all of that! And let the Reader be reminded that it was the Cross alone which changed all of that.

BOUNDS ABOUT THE MOUNT

Verses 19 through 25 read: *"And when the voice of the trumpet sounded long, and waxed louder and louder, Moses spoke, and God answered him by a voice.*

"And the LORD came down upon Mount Sinai, on the top of the Mount: and the LORD called Moses up to the top of the Mount; and Moses went up.

"And the LORD said unto Moses, Go down, charge the people, lest they break through unto the LORD to gaze, and many of them perish.

"And let the Priests also, which come near to the LORD, sanctify themselves, lest the LORD break forth upon them.

"And Moses said unto the LORD, the people cannot come up to Mount Sinai: for You charged us, saying, Set bounds about the Mount, and sanctify it.

"And the LORD said unto him, Away, get you down, and you shall come up, you, and Aaron with you: but let not the Priests and the people break through to come up unto the LORD, lest He break forth upon them.

"So Moses went down unto the people, and spoke unto them."

As the Lord descended down on Mount Sinai, with all of the attendant accompaniment of the fire, etc., the Scripture says that *"Moses spoke,"* which means that He spoke to God. Exactly what he said, we aren't told.

At any rate, *"God answered him by a voice,"* in other words, a voice that could be heard (Vs. 19).

The Lord told Moses to come to the top of the Mount, and there is a good possibility that Aaron was with him.

It seems that Moses had no sooner come up to the appointed place, that the Lord told him to go back down and *"charge the people,"* that they not break through the barrier.

There is a curiosity about all things pertaining to God, and to be sure, this particular manifestation of the Lord was the greatest that humanity had ever known. So the danger was very real that some would break through the barrier, even though Moses had strictly warned them of the penalty of doing so. For sure, the fence or barrier was not placed there to protect God, but rather the people.

Even though the Cross has changed all of this, we must not allow the lesson to be lost on us. The problem that persisted then persists now as well.

Far too often, the things of God are treated in a cavalier fashion. We must ever know that God is not merely *"the Man upstairs."* He should always be addressed or spoken of in reverential tones. We must not take His Name in vain, which can be done in more ways than one.

One of my dear friends was in a particular meeting sometime back, and the Evangelist, who would have done much better selling cars than trying to preach the Gospel, called himself praying for the sick. Some of his terminology was, *"Alright big guy, come on down here and get the job done,"* or words to that effect! Pure and simple, that is blasphemy!

However, I'm afraid that so much done by the modern Church could be included in that description. For instance, modern rock music in the Church can be labeled as none other than blasphemy! The same would go for the preaching of anything other than the Cross! Much of that which we label as *"worship,"* falls into the same category. It is *"will worship,"* which means that it originates in the hearts of men, and is not, therefore, Holy Spirit inspired. And let the following be known:

Just as breaking through the barriers would have caused death among the Israelites of so long ago, it is still causing death presently, i.e., *"spiritual death."* And as well, it even causes premature physical death.

Paul told us that if we *"eat this bread, and drink this cup of the Lord, unworthily,* (we) *shall be guilty of the Body and Blood of the Lord.*

"But let a man examine himself, and so let him eat of that bread, and drink of that cup.

"For he who eats and drinks unworthily, eats and drinks damnation to himself, not discerning the Lord's Body.

"For this cause many are weak and sickly among you, and many sleep" (I Cor. 11:27-30).

To *"eat and drink unworthily"* points to Faith that's in something other than the Cross. The Believer, when taking the Lord's Supper, must ever understand that all he has from the Lord has come about through what Christ did at the Cross. Our Faith is to be exclusively in His Finished Work. If that is not the case, we are not properly discerning the Lord's Body. In such a case, many Christians will be weak and sickly, and many will even die prematurely. While they won't lose their souls, they will definitely lose years of life they could have had.

I am persuaded that much of the sickness, and much of the premature deaths (not all), among Christians presently, are because of this very thing.

Some object to the word *"Priests"* as used in Verse 22, claiming that the Priestly order had not yet been set in motion, simply because the Law had not yet been given. However, Aaron had already been chosen to function as the High Priest, and his sons naturally fell into that order, plus others, who were of the Tribe of Levi. Even though they did not function at this particular time in the manner in which they would later function, they were still looked at by the Lord in the capacity of *"Priests."*

Let the Reader understand that under the New Covenant, there is no such thing now as a Priest. The very word *"Priest"* signifies one who serves as a mediator between God and men, which the Levitical Priests did! However, when Jesus came, and paid the supreme price on the Cross of Calvary, He fulfilled all the types and shadows of the Old Testament, thereby making that ancient order a closed case. In other words, the Priests could hang up their robes. Due to the Cross, Jesus now serves as the Mediator between God and men, and Christ Alone! (I Tim. 2:5; Heb. 8:6; 9:15; 12:24).

So the so-called Catholic Priesthood is completely unscriptural, and in effect, is an insult to Christ. The very fact that a man calls himself a *"Priest,"* says that Christ didn't complete the task at the Cross, and needs the help of mere mortals. This has always been man's problem.

He desires to subtract from the Word of God, or add to the Word of God. He is not content, it seems, to function as the Lord has demanded. And please understand, the direction given by the Lord is not that done on the mere fact of whim, but is rather the way of safety, security, protection, fulfillment, and blessings. Every other way is, in some way, a *"way of death"* (Prov. 14:12).

THE COMMAND OF THE LORD

No sooner had Moses climbed the Mountain, and that according to the command of the Lord, that he was told to immediately go back and warn the people not to break through the barrier that had been set up. Moses, it seems, felt this was not necessary, and was severely rebuked by the Lord. He said to Moses, *"Away, get you down."* This means that God wholly rejected the plea of Moses, that there was no need to give an additional warning. He knew best, and would not have issued the order to *"go down and charge the people,"* unless there had been a need for it.

Unfortunately, *"warnings"* have to be repeatedly given to the people as it regards their living for God.

We find in all of this that at first, the people stood afar off, but, later, began to press too near. This illustrates man's fallen nature; he stands afar off when he should draw nigh, and he presses to the front when he should keep back (Williams).

THE LAW

Some Commentators have claimed that Israel illegitimately placed themselves under *"Law."* In other words, they could have functioned in Grace, so they say, had they only desired to do so. That is incorrect!

In the first place, even though God definitely dealt with people then through and by Grace, for that's the only manner in which He can deal with people, still, Grace was limited before the Cross, due to the fact that animal blood could not take away sin. Since the Cross, which portrays the Precious shed

Blood of the Lord Jesus Christ, all sin has been atoned, which makes it possible for God to extend more Grace. Let the Reader understand that all Grace is predicated on the Cross of Christ.

So the Law was imperative. Some claim that the *"thunders and lightnings and the thick cloud which settled upon the Mount, and the voice of the trumpet exceeding loud,"* portrayed the response of the Lord to the choice of the people. But I remind those who would say that, the people really did not have a choice. The Law was imperative, even as we've already stated, that it may portray the Righteousness of God, and as well, to portray man's inability to live up to its demands, no matter how hard he tried.

As well, let it not be forgotten that in Heaven itself, the Apostle John is given to behold a Throne, out of which *"proceeded lightnings and thunderings and voices"* (Rev. 4:5) — the identical things witnessed on Sinai!

Concerning this, Pink says, and rightly so: *"There is a Passage in Deuteronomy which should forever settle the question as to whether or not Israel acted wisely in entering into the Siniatic Covenant, as to whether they did right or wrong in promising to do all that the Lord had said, and as to whether God was pleased or displeased with them. This Passage is found in the Fifth Chapter of that Book, and can be read by the Bible student, which I think will explain that Israel was definitely right in what they did, and in fact, if they were to please God, they had no choice."*

Before Grace could properly be revealed, which it would be revealed by and through the Cross, the Law was an absolute necessity, even as we've already stated, and for many and varied reasons.

"Years I spent in vanity and pride,
"Caring not my Lord was crucified,
"Knowing not it was for me He died,
"On Calvary."

"By God's Word at last my sin I learned;
"Then I trembled at the Law I'd spurned;
"Till my guilty soul imploring turned
"To Calvary."

"Now I've given to Jesus everything;
"Now I gladly own Him as my King;

"Now my raptured soul can only sing
"Of Calvary."

"Oh, the love that drew Salvation's plan!
"Oh, the Grace that brought it down to man!
"Oh, the mighty gulf that God did span
"At Calvary!"

CHAPTER 20

(1) "AND GOD SPOKE ALL THESE WORDS, SAYING,

(2) "I AM THE LORD YOUR GOD, WHICH HAVE BROUGHT YOU OUT OF THE LAND OF EGYPT, OUT OF THE HOUSE OF BONDAGE.

(3) "YOU SHALL HAVE NO OTHER GODS BEFORE ME.

(4) "YOU SHALL NOT MAKE UNTO YOURSELF ANY GRAVEN IMAGE, OR ANY LIKENESS OF ANYTHING THAT IS IN HEAVEN ABOVE, OR THAT IS IN THE EARTH BENEATH, OR THAT IS IN THE WATER UNDER THE EARTH.

(5) "YOU SHALL NOT BOW DOWN YOURSELF TO THEM, NOR SERVE THEM: FOR I THE LORD YOUR GOD AM A JEALOUS GOD, VISITING THE INIQUITY OF THE FATHERS UPON THE CHILDREN UNTO THE THIRD AND FOURTH GENERATION OF THEM WHO HATE ME;

(6) "AND SHOWING MERCY UNTO THOUSANDS OF THEM WHO LOVE ME, AND KEEP MY COMMANDMENTS.

(7) "YOU SHALL NOT TAKE THE NAME OF THE LORD YOUR GOD IN VAIN; FOR THE LORD WILL NOT HOLD HIM GUILTLESS WHO TAKES HIS NAME IN VAIN.

(8) "REMEMBER THE SABBATH DAY, TO KEEP IT HOLY.

(9) "SIX DAYS SHALL YOU LABOR, AND DO ALL YOUR WORK:

(10) "BUT THE SEVENTH DAY IS THE SABBATH OF THE LORD YOUR GOD: IN IT YOU SHALL NOT DO ANY WORK, YOU, NOR YOUR SON, NOR YOUR DAUGHTER, YOUR MANSERVANT, NOR YOUR MAIDSERVANT, NOR YOUR CATTLE, NOR YOUR STRANGER THAT IS WITHIN YOUR GATES:

(11) "FOR IN SIX DAYS THE LORD MADE HEAVEN AND EARTH, THE SEA, AND ALL THAT IN THEM IS, AND RESTED THE SEVENTH DAY: WHEREFORE THE LORD BLESSED THE SABBATH DAY, AND HALLOWED IT.

(12) "HONOR YOUR FATHER AND YOUR MOTHER: THAT YOUR DAYS MAY BE LONG UPON THE LAND WHICH THE LORD YOUR GOD GIVES YOU.

(13) "YOU SHALL NOT KILL.

(14) "YOU SHALL NOT COMMIT ADULTERY.

(15) "YOU SHALL NOT STEAL.

(16) "YOU SHALL NOT BEAR FALSE WITNESS AGAINST YOUR NEIGHBOR.

(17) "YOU SHALL NOT COVET YOUR NEIGHBOR'S HOUSE, YOU SHALL NOT COVET YOUR NEIGHBOR'S WIFE, NOR HIS MANSERVANT, NOR HIS MAIDSERVANT, NOR HIS OX, NOR HIS ASS, NOR ANYTHING THAT IS YOUR NEIGHBOR'S."

The structure is:

1. The Ten Commandments given by God to Moses on Mount Sinai are the Foundation of all Law, at least the Law that is righteous, for the entire world.

2. Every system of law, of righteous law, in every nation of the world, irrespective of religious preference, has at least in part the *"Ten Commandments"* as its basis of foundation.

3. Jesus, in Matthew, Chapter 22, divided the Ten Commandments into two groups. The first five direct our attention toward God and our responsibility to Him. The second five enjoin us to love others as the first five commanded that we love God.

4. The Lord encapsuled all ten in the words, *"Love the Lord Your God with all your heart . . . and your neighbor as yourself."*

5. Moses wrote the Ten Commandments and many others in a Book which he ratified by the blood of animals (Ex. 24:3-8).

6. Verse 5 says: *"The iniquity of the fathers."* Never does it say the iniquity of the mothers, and for the following reason: Adam, not Eve, was the fountainhead, the source, the moral, spiritual, and legal head, and representative of the whole race.

7. The First Commandment requires the worship of one God Alone, Jehovah.

8. The Second Commandment is a protest against idolatry and materialism.

9. The Third Commandment is against perjury, which is one of the greatest both of moral and of social offences.

10. The Fourth Commandment concerns the keeping of the Sabbath Day. It was to be a day of rest, and not necessarily that of worship.

11. The Fifth Commandment concerning the honoring of father and mother, in essence, teaches that if such is not done, men as well, will not honor God.

12. The Sixth Commandment, *"Thou shalt not kill,"* presents our first duty toward our neighbor, which is to respect his life.

13. The Seventh Commandment, *"Thou shalt not commit adultery,"* is our second duty toward our neighbor, which is to respect the bond on which the family is based.

14. The Eighth Commandment, *"You shall not steal,"* presents the right of property, and that such is honored by God.

15. The Ninth Commandment, *"You shall not bear false witness against your neighbor,"* refers to false witness of two kinds, public and private.

16. The Tenth Commandment, *"Thou shalt not covet,"* concerns the thoughts of man toward his fellow man.

I AM THE LORD YOUR GOD

Verses 1 and 2 read: *"And God spoke all these words, saying,*

"I am the LORD your God, which have brought you out of the land of Egypt, out of the house of bondage."

Anything that God says must be addressed in all seriousness, all responsibility, and all obedience. As well, anything that God says is not only of signal significance, but as well, is meant for our good. Even at the time it may seem to be negative, still, it is meant for our good, or else for the good of mankind in general. When men rebel against God constantly and unendingly, spurning all pleas of reconciliation, and as well, set themselves against God, determining to hinder and hurt His Work, at times, God has to visit such with judgment, and at times, even with death. But to be sure, such visitation is for the good of mankind in general, as should be obvious.

Kalisch said, referring to the giving of the Law, that it *"formed a decisive epoch in the history of the human race, and was even perhaps the greatest and most important event in human history, up to the time of its occurrence."*

And I will add to that, the Code or Law given by God was far and away a marked improvement upon anything that man had attempted to address out of his own ingenuity and ability. Sinful man cannot produce anything that is good, hence him being unable to produce an equitable law. Only God could do that, which He did.

Some have claimed that Moses derived the Law from Egypt; however, the Second, Fourth, and Tenth Commandments were totally foreign to Egyptian thinking. As well, even the Commandments which they had formulated regarding their Sages, which seemed to be similar to those given by God, if inspected closely, proved to have very little similarity.

DELIVERANCE

The Lord doesn't appeal to the Israelites as Creator, even though He definitely was that. He appealed to them as their Deliverer, *"Who has brought you out of the land of Egypt, out of the house of bondage."* As a result, he was to be obeyed by His people from a sentiment of love, not by fear (Pulpit).

The basis for communion with the Lord, for fellowship with Him presently, falls into the same category. He appeals to us on the basis of the Finished Work of Christ (Eph. 2:13-18; I Pet. 1:18-20). In fact, to attempt to give Scriptures to back up this statement is somewhat pointless, in that the entirety of the Bible speaks to this issue. Paul said:

"Grace be to you and peace from God the Father, and from our Lord Jesus Christ,

"Who gave Himself for our sins, that He might deliver us from this present evil world, according to the Will of God and our Father" (Gal. 1:3-4).

NO OTHER GODS

Verse 3 reads: *"You shall have no other gods before Me."*

The manner in which this First Commandment is given indicates that each individual of the nation is addressed severally, and is required personally to obey the Law, a mere general national obedience being insufficient.

This Commandment, as stated, requires the worship of one God Alone, Jehovah — the God Who had in so many ways manifested Himself to the Israelites, and implies that there is, in point of fact, no other God (Pulpit).

In fact, the Israelites were the only people in the world who worshipped only one God, i.e., *"Jehovah!"* All the other people of the nations of the world worshiped many gods.

Much could be said on this subject, as should be obvious; however, I think that which applies presently will be of greater help.

The only way that one can worship and know God is through Jesus Christ and what He has done for us at the Cross.

As we keep saying repeatedly, and will continue to say, Christ and what He has done for us in the giving of Himself as the Sacrifice, which atoned for all sin, is ever meant to be the standard.

In fact, when John had the great vision of the Throne of God, and saw Christ, he said: *"And in the midst of the Elders, stood a Lamb as it had been slain, having seven horns and seven eyes, which are the seven Spirits of God sent forth into all the Earth"* (Rev. 5:6).

This portrays the fact, among other things, that no one is going to get to the Throne of God, unless they go through the slain Lamb, i.e., *"the Crucified Christ."* As well, this portrays the fact that the Holy Spirit works exclusively within the parameters of the Finished Work of Christ, symbolized by the fact that Christ and the Spirit of God are so closely connected that they appear actually as One.

I remind the Reader that Christ was not portrayed here as on the Throne, which many modern Preachers proclaim, but rather as the way or the access to the Throne. Paul said:

"But now in Christ Jesus you who sometimes were far off are made nigh (brought near) *by the Blood of Christ."*

He then said: *"For through Him* (through Christ and what He did at the Cross) *we both* (Jews and Gentiles) *have access by one Spirit unto the Father"* (Eph. 2:13, 18).

In fact, this Eighteenth Verse tells us that if we try to come to the Father any other way than by Christ and His Sacrifice, the Holy Spirit will deny access. We should take that very seriously, as it is meant to be taken very seriously!

UNDERSTANDING THE CROSS

Once one begins to understand the Cross, one soon comes to the realization that this understanding affects every aspect of life and living. Then one begins to see the wrong of any direction other than the way of the Cross. In fact, a failure to understand the Cross, and especially as it refers to Sanctification, is the reason that Believers fall so easily for false doctrine. In fact, I think one can say without fear of exaggeration or contradiction that all who attempt to live by Law, whether they realize they are doing such or not, are, to some degree, deceived. In reality, this is what Paul said:

"Now the Spirit (Holy Spirit) *speaks expressly* (pointedly), *that in the latter times* (the times in which we now live) *some shall depart from the Faith* (Jesus Christ and Him Crucified) *giving heed to seducing spirits, and doctrines of devils"* (I Tim. 4:1).

As it should be understood, Satan dresses up his false doctrine in order that it might look very much like that which is true. That's why Jesus said, *"Beware of false prophets, which come to you in sheep's clothing, but inwardly they are ravening wolves.*

"You shall know them by their fruits" (Mat. 7:15-16).

NO IDOL WORSHIP

Verses 4 through 6 read: *"You shall not make unto you any graven image, or any likeness of anything that is in Heaven above, or that is in the Earth beneath, or that is in the water under the Earth.*

"You shall not bow down yourself to them, nor serve them: for I the LORD your God am a Jealous God, visiting the iniquity of the fathers upon the children unto the third and fourth generation of them who hate Me;

"And showing mercy unto thousands of them who love Me, and keep My Commandments."

The prohibition intended here does not forbid the arts of sculptor, painting, photography, etc., or even to condemn the use of them, but to disallow the worship of God under material forms (Pulpit).

Regardless of many commands in both Testaments against idolatry, the love of images and their worship are indulged in by millions today, even in so-called Christian lands. Idolatry was one of God's big problems with Israel, and it is still a problem with the world, and even with the Church.

It is believed that there were some pictures made by artists of the Apostles and Christ, but none have survived. I am positive that the Holy Spirit was instrumental in doing away with these things because of the urge of man to worship something he can see. And pictures of Christ and the Apostles, even poor reproductions as done by an artist, would have been prime efforts of Satan.

In 769, the Lateran Synod of the Catholic Church sanctioned images.

Tarasius, who advocated the worship of images, was made Patriarch of the East in 784, and in 787 the Synod of Nicea ascribed reverence to images and worship of God through them.

Sometime after A.D. 850, image worship in Churches began to grow, due to the idea that miracles, it is claimed, were performed through them, etc. The twenty-fifth session of the Council of Trent (1551) of the Catholic Church justified the worship of images, with many consequently thinking that such worship had been authorized by God.

As should be overly obvious here, the Scripture plainly condemns any image worship whatsoever, irrespective as to whom they are supposed to represent.

The term *"graven image,"* would probably have been better translated, *"any image,"* for the Hebrew term used (pesel) is applied, not only to *"graven,"* but also to *"molten images"* (Isa. 40:19; 44:10; Jer. 10:14).

The mention of all things as it regards *"Heaven and Earth, and the sea,"* is intended to embrace the whole material universe. In fact, much of the Egyptian religion, as well as others, consisted in the worship of animals and their images.

A JEALOUS GOD

The term *"jealous"* is not meant to address

success, or greatness, but that God is very jealous of His Own honor, and will not have the respect and reverence, which is His due, bestowed on other beings or on inanimate objects (Pulpit).

Some have objected to the Fifth Verse, claiming that it shows God as being mean and spiteful; however, to think such only portrays the fact that the Text is not properly interpreted.

The Lord promises to visit the iniquity of the fathers upon the children, as it regards those who continue to hate Him, and, thereby, spurn His Word. The very moment that individual, whomever they may be, turns to the Lord in humble contrition, the Sixth Verse plainly says that the Lord will *"show mercy unto thousands of them who love Me, and keep My Commandments."*

THE FAMILY CURSE?

In the last few years, a particular doctrine has grown out of this particular Passage, and others similar, referred to in some circles as *"the family curse."*

In brief, this teaching claims that certain Christians suffer problems and difficulties, because their father, grandfather, great-grandfather, etc., did something ungodly, which is now visited upon them. They were then encouraged to find a Preacher who understands these things, and will thereby lay hands on them, and rebuke the family curse, which will then guarantee victory for the present and the future. None of that is Biblical, and for two reasons:

1. The Scripture plainly says, as stated, that this curse comes upon *"children unto the third and fourth generation of them who hate Me."* In fact, there are all types of curses on those who do not know God, and we speak of family curses, generational curses, etc. These things do exist, but not for those who have come to the Lord.

2. The moment that a person comes to Christ, the Scripture plainly tells us: *"Therefore if any man* (and it means any person) *be in Christ, he is a new creature: old things are passed away; behold, all things are become new"* (II Cor. 5:17).

Now either *"old things are passed away,"* or else the Holy Spirit through Paul didn't

NOTES

tell the truth. I happen to believe that He told the truth. So this eliminates any family curse, or any other curses for that matter.

SO WHAT IS THE CAUSE OF PROBLEMS IN THE LIVES OF CHRISTIANS?

We do not deny that many Christians have problems, some of them very severe, and while many things could be said, I think the following will sum up the real cause, and will, as well, give the cure.

Whatever the reason on the surface might be, whether it's chastisement or whatever, the real cause is that the Believer has his faith improperly placed. Functioning in this capacity, he has cut off most of the help the Holy Spirit can give him, which brings about all type of problems.

The answer, and to whatever the difficulty or problem might be, is for the Believer to once again make the Cross of Christ the focus of his Faith. When this is done, the Holy Spirit becomes his power source, and the results, without exception, are always in the realm of victory.

So, Preachers telling people that their problem is a family curse, and all they need to do is have him lay his hands on them, and their problem will be solved, is not drawing people to Christ, but rather to *"self,"* which, within itself, is a grievous sin. The solution for the ills of the world, be it the unredeemed or the Redeemed, is the Cross of Christ. There is no other solution! That's why Paul said:

"For the preaching of the Cross is to them who perish foolishness; but unto us which are saved it is the Power of God" (I Cor. 1:18).

So if you want victory in your life, ask the Lord to reveal to you the great Truth of the Cross, which He most definitely shall, and you will find yourself beginning to grow in Grace and the knowledge of the Lord. Denying oneself, and taking up the Cross daily to follow Christ, plays out to the most fulfilled life that one could ever know or enjoy.

THE LORD'S NAME

Verse 7 reads: *"You shall not take the Name of the LORD your God in vain; for the LORD will not hold him guiltless who takes His Name in vain."*

Taking the Name of the Lord in vain pertains to all blasphemy, all swearing, all perjury, and in fact, all irreverent use of God's Name in ordinary life.

This Commandment also prohibits the use of God's Name in any type of witchcraft, black or white magic, in fact, any abuse of the sacred Name whatsoever.

Included in this sin is that of perjury. Pulpit says: *"Perjury has always been felt to be one of the greatest both of moral and social offences. It implies an absolute want of any reverence at all for God; and it destroys civil society by rendering the administration of justice impossible."*

The phrase rendered here, *"The Lord will not hold him guiltless who takes His Name in vain,"* proclaims the fact that judgment, in some way, will come upon such an individual. This being the case, the unredeemed heap upon themselves great judgment from God, which is the cause of many problems and difficulties, which in fact, are attributed to other things. But if the truth be known, it's the Judgment of God meted out for this particular sin, as well as others.

THE SABBATH

Verses 8 through 11 read: *"Remember the Sabbath Day, to keep it holy.*

"Six days shall you labor, and do all your work:

"But the seventh day is the Sabbath of the LORD your God: in it you shall not do any work, you, nor your son, nor your daughter, your manservant, nor your maidservant, nor your cattle, nor the stranger that is within your gates:

"For in six days the LORD made Heaven and Earth, the sea, and all that in them is, and rested the seventh day: wherefore the LORD blessed the Sabbath Day, and hallowed it."

The seventh day, i.e., *"the Sabbath,"* was not so much to be a day of worship, as we think of such now, but rather a day of *"rest."* Even the very beasts, pressed into man's service since the fall, shall rest. All were to observe this day, men, women, boys, and girls.

Animal suffering was generally regarded as a small account in the ancient world; and the idea of protecting animals from ill-usage was wholly unknown; however, as is obvious here, animals under the Mosaic Covenant were to be treated with kindness. This means that domestic animals were to be well-fed on the Sabbath, that they may as well enjoy its *"rest."*

Regrettably, the Jews, by Jesus' time, had taken this Commandment into extreme formality and literalism. For instance, a woman was not allowed to even brush her hair on the Sabbath, because there might be a speck of dust in her hair, and that could be looked at as *"plowing."* To pull a chair across the floor might upset some dust, and would be looked at in the same capacity.

All of these particular laws, which had no basis in the Word of God, were what was referred to as *"fence laws."* The general idea was, if they made enough fence laws around the original law, then they wouldn't break the Law. Jesus shot all of this down, by stating that it was not so much the act performed, but what was in the heart that really counted (Mat. 5:8, 28; 6:21; 12:34; 15:8, 18-19).

The Pharisees were incensed with Christ, because He healed on the Sabbath Day. Jesus' answer to them was: *"The Sabbath was made for man, and not man for the Sabbath;*

"Therefore the Son of Man is Lord also of the Sabbath" (Mk. 2:27-28).

THE EARLY CHURCH

Even though there was no written command by the Holy Spirit to do so, gradually, we find Believers, during the time of the Early Church, making Sunday, the first day of the week, the day of our Lord's Resurrection, their day of worship, etc. However, once again, we point out the fact that there was a difference in the Jewish Sabbath, and the Christian day of worship, in that the former was a day of rest, while the latter is a day of worship.

Paul explicitly stated that under the New Covenant, none of this is to be a hidebound rule. He said: *"Let no man therefore judge you in meat, or in drink, or in respect of an holy day, or of the new moon, or of the Sabbath days:*

"Which are (were) *a shadow of things to come; but the body* (all Believers) *is of Christ"* (Col. 2:16-17).

As stated, we find in the Early Church

that the first day of the week became the day that they dedicated to the Lord, which commemorated the Resurrection (Acts 20:7; I Cor. 16:2; Rev. 1:10).

REST IN CHRIST

Everything pertaining to the Law of Moses, in some way, spoke of Christ. The *"Sabbath"* was no exception. It was meant to portray the fact that there is *"rest"* in Christ, and in fact, there is rest *"only in Christ."* That's what Jesus was addressing when He said: *"Come unto Me, all you who labor and are heavy laden, and I will give you rest"* (Mat. 11:28).

He was speaking of the heavy burden of ritualistic religion, which the Jews had devised from the Law of Moses. As stated, they made all type of fence laws, actually over 600, with many of them claiming that the fence laws were more important than the original Law given by God. At any rate, they had become so legalistic that living for God was a heavy burden, hence the Master also saying: *"Take My yoke upon you, and learn of Me; for I am meek and lowly in heart: and you shall find rest unto your souls.*

"For My yoke is easy, and My burden is light" (Mat. 11:29-30).

In fact, the old Jewish Sabbath, at least that which was originally given by God, was the most beautiful description of the *"in Christ"* experience, given in the entirety of the Old Testament. It pictured and proclaimed that which the individual under the New Covenant could have in Christ.

The new way, and I speak of the New Covenant, is all by Faith. That's the reason Paul also said: *"For in Jesus Christ neither circumcision availeth anything . . . but Faith which worketh by love"* (Gal. 5:6).

THE SABBATH AND SANCTIFICATION

Sanctification does not come by doing, but by believing! But yet, virtually all of the Church tries to bring about this process, all by *"doing."* Of course, failure is always the result of such an effort; consequently, most in the modern Church little give Sanctification any thought whatsoever. In fact, it is hardly ever mentioned in modern pulpits.

And this is a tragedy, because most of the Word of God is actually given over to this process, and especially the writings of the Apostle Paul.

Sanctification is *"resting"* in what Christ has already done, which means that we place our Faith in the Finished Work of Christ, and refuse to allow it to be moved to other things. Then, the Holy Spirit, Who is the One Who must do this work within our lives, can function, thereby, bringing about the victory for which we seek (Rom. 8:1-2, 11).

So, this *"rest"* in Christ symbolizes, I think, the Sanctification process, more than anything else.

THE HONORING OF PARENTS

Verse 12 reads: *"Honor your father and your mother: that your days may be long upon the land which the LORD your God gives you."*

It is believed that the first five Commandments have to do with man's obligation toward God, while the last five have to do with his obligation toward his fellow man. Some object to this, claiming the Fifth Commandment deals with the human side only. That is incorrect!

Honoring the father and the mother is a requirement in order that we may honor God. In other words, man being taught to honor his parents is, at the same time, being taught that he must honor God. One prepares the way for the other.

Whenever we see society begin to break down because of sin, and sin is the only thing that can really break it down, we see respect, love, and devotion for parents being laid aside. This is the surest sign that reverence toward God is being laid aside as well!

As well, there is a promise of longevity that goes along with the keeping of this Commandment, which holds true even unto this hour.

Some may object to that, claiming that they are acquainted with families where proper devotion was extended to parents, but yet those engaging in such devotion contracted a disease and died, prematurely it seems.

Regarding any type of Promise of this nature given by God, we must understand that He governs the universe by general, not by universal laws. In other words, these laws are personal; due to the fact that they are personal, oftentimes other things are brought to bear which impacts the individual.

God upholds everything by a system of laws which He has Himself devised and instituted.

For instance, if a son or daughter seems to show devotion and love to parents, but at the same time is living a very ungodly life, which will seldom be the case, at any rate, the *"law of sin and death"* must be brought to bear on this situation, which very well could supercede the Promise of God, which regrettably, it often does. God cannot condone sin. So whatever Promises that God has given as it regards life and blessing, etc., can be canceled by disobedience on the part of the individual, which kicks in *"the law of sin and death"* (Rom. 8:2). In Galatians, Chapter 5, Paul gave a long list of sins of the flesh, and then said: *"Of the which I tell you before, as I have also told you in time past, that they which do such things shall not inherit the Kingdom of God"* (Gal. 5:21).

THE WANTON TAKING OF HUMAN LIFE

Verse 13 reads: *"You shall not kill."*

Our first duty toward our neighbor is to respect his life. When Cain slew Abel, he could scarcely have known what he was doing, at least as it regards murder, for the Commandment had not yet been given; yet a terrible punishment was awarded him for his transgression (Gen. 4:11-14) (Pulpit).

After the flood, which was about 1,600 years after the beginning of creation, the Lord instituted capital punishment for cold-blooded murder. He said, *"Whoso sheds man's blood, by man shall his blood be shed: for in the Image of God made He man"* (Gen. 9:6).

Some claim that capital punishment does not deter crime; they are right! It's not meant to deter crime, but rather to put a high value on human life, because man is made *"in the Image of God."* To kill a man in cold blood is to insult God, for the murder of the human being is a termination of God's highest creation, human life.

Capital punishment is carried over into the New Testament (Rom. 13:1-7).

This means that human government has the right to take the life of one who has murdered someone in cold-blood. It also means that government has the right to use force to put down criminal activity, and the right to use its army to put down criminal activity by bandit nations, which regrettably have always existed.

AN EXAMPLE

The September 11, 2001 horror is a perfect example. The United States was attacked both in New York City and Washington, D.C., by Muslims, resulting in the deaths of nearly 5,000 people. Under God, our government not only has a right, but a moral obligation, to put down any and all bandit nations which would join in such activity. President Bush was Scripturally correct when he declared war on terrorism. To not do so will invite much more bloodshed later on. The Scripture says regarding these type of things:

"Because sentence against an evil work is not executed speedily, therefore the heart of the sons of men is fully set in them to do evil" (Eccl. 8:11).

The only thing that concerns me is that President Bush will not follow through with his statement, and put the terrorism States out of business. I speak of Iraq, Iran, Syria, and as well, those among the Palestinians which fall into this category. And to be frank, the situation in Saudi Arabia and Egypt isn't much better. In fact, most of the homicide bombers on the planes that crashed into the buildings in both New York and Washington were Saudis and Egyptians.

Reaching further back, America's war against Germany and Japan falls into the same category. Where would the world be presently had America not taken the stand she did? The awfulness of such a contemplation defies all description!

While it's certainly wrong for any soldier to kill wantonly, it is not wrong for a soldier to kill in the realm of battle.

THE COURTS

I suppose we would like to think that the legal system in the United States is one of the best. Possibly that is so; however, even at its best, it falls woefully short. I speak of a Judge and jury passing the sentence of death on the condemned. While I definitely believe that capital punishment should stand for cold-blooded murder, I also feel that if there is the slightest doubt, the death penalty should not be given. Too many men and women have been sentenced to die, who in reality were innocent. Thank God for DNA testing, which has come into vogue in the last few years. It has set a number free, in other words, proven their innocence.

The ideal is that all get a fair hearing, in other words, equal protection under the law. But regrettably, it hardly falls out that way.

The poorest of the poor definitely do not get excellent representation, as should be obvious. The rich who can afford the best lawyers, as again should be obvious, have things weighted in their favor.

What is the answer?

Well of course, the answer to all of the inequalities and problems in the world is the Coming of the Lord; however, until that time, I personally feel that the jury system in our nation is woefully inadequate. It is regrettable when the defense tries with all their power to load the jury with the less competent. How in the world can a trial be fair with such foolishness? The O.J. Simpson fiasco should be an excellent case in point.

Let it also be stated, in the nations of the world where Christianity has little sway, human life is cheap. Man's problem is, he thinks he knows more than God. To be frank, that is our biggest problem even here in the United States!

THE EXTENSION OF THIS COMMANDMENT

The Commandment, *"Thou shalt not kill,"* not only addresses itself to the wanton taking of human life, but as well, it refers to the killing of one's reputation by the use of gossip, etc. Influence and reputation can definitely be killed in this manner, and often are. Consequently, the person doing such is guilty of breaking this Commandment. This should give us pause for thought!

As well, our Lord intimated *"That whosoever is angry with his brother without a cause shall be in danger of the judgment"* (Mat. 5:21-22). This means that hatred and undue anger expressed towards someone, when there is no cause for such, once again places such an individual in the position of committing this sin of *"murder."* While they may not actually do such a thing as the taking of a human life, still, in their heart, they wish such a person dead, and that means that God holds them guilty of the breaking of this Commandment, *"Thou shalt not kill."*

ADULTERY

Verse 14 reads: *"You shall not commit adultery."*

Regarding this sin, the Decalogue puts both man and woman in the same category.

Our second duty towards our neighbor is to respect the bond on which the family is based, and that conjugal honor, which to the true man is dearer than life. Marriage, according to the original institution, makes the husband and wife *"one flesh"* (Gen. 2:24); and to break in upon this sacramental union was at once a crime and a profanity. It is a sin against God, Who has made man, for it shows a lack of respect for God's creation, and it is a sin against one's fellow man, by taking and violating that which belongs to another.

Jesus also showed that adultery may be committed in the heart, without the act itself actually being committed. He said:

"You have heard that it was said by them of old time, You shall not commit adultery:

"But I say unto you, that whosoever looks on a woman to lust after her has committed adultery with her already in his heart" (Mat. 5:27-28).

STEALING

Verse 15 reads: *"You shall not steal."*

As it regards our neighbor, we are to respect his property. We simply don't take that which doesn't belong to us.

Matthew Henry says: *"Human laws punish various transgressions of this command; but disobedience to the Law of God will be punished whether human justice reach it or not. Imposing upon the ignorance, credulity, or necessity of others; abuse of confidence, extortion, and many other things, are transgressions of God's Law, though scarcely censured in society."*

He went on to say, *"Plunderers of kingdoms, and oppressors of millions, who consider themselves to be above human justice, will* be included in this sentence. *Defrauding the public, whether by oppressive rulers, or by evading payments lawfully required, contracting debts without prospect of paying them, or evading payment of just debts when enabled to do so, all extravagance, unnecessary subsistence upon charity, squeezing the poor in their wages, so as scarcely to allow them to subsist — all these, and many such like things, violate the spiritual meaning of this command."*

To Touch upon one of the ways this sin is oft committed is the failure to pay income taxes, or to defraud insurance companies, etc.

Jesus said: *"Render therefore unto Caesar the things which are Caesar's; and unto God the things that are God's"* (Mat. 22:21). To steal from the government, in a sense, is to steal from fellow Americans, who, in effect, are paying their fair share.

While we may try to excuse ourselves, by claiming that many *"fat cats,"* don't have to pay any taxes at all, etc., irrespective as to what that might be, that does not absolve us of honesty on our part. It's perfectly legitimate, Scriptural and otherwise, to avoid taxes in any way that is legal; however, to evade them is something else again. It is *"stealing!"*

And as well, it is just as wrong to steal from God, or even more so.

The Lord through the Prophet Malachi said: *"Will a man rob* (steal from) *God? Yet you have robbed Me. But you say, Wherein have we robbed You? In tithes and offerings.*

"You are cursed with a curse: for you have robbed Me, even this whole nation.

"You bring all the tithes into the storehouse, that there may be meat in My house, and prove Me now herewith, saith the LORD of hosts, if I will not open you the windows of Heaven, and pour you out a blessing, that there shall not be room enough to receive it" (Mal. 3:8-10).

And let the Reader understand that tithing was begun long before the Law, in fact, beginning with Abraham, at least as far as we know (Gen. 14:20).

Tithing is carried over under the New Covenant as well, with Abraham having laid down the principle.

Melchizedek was a type of Christ. Abraham paid tithes to him, and we the children of Abraham, spiritually speaking, are to continue to pay tithes to the Work of the Lord, which is of Christ (II Cor., Chpts. 8-9).

FALSE WITNESS

Verse 16 reads: *"You shall not bear false witness against your neighbor."*

According to Pulpit, *"False witness is of two kinds, public and private. We may either seek to damage our neighbor by giving false evidence against him in a court of justice, or simply culminate him to others in our social intercourse with them."*

Man has always realized the terrible crime of false witness. Going back into ancient history, at Athens the false witness was liable to a heavy fine, and if thrice convicted, lost all his civil rights. At Rome, by a law of the Twelve Tables, he was hurled headlong from the Tarpeian Rock. In Egypt, false witness was punished by amputation of the nose and ears.

However, all of this had to do with a recognized court of law. The Mosaic legislation was probably the first wherein it was positively forbidden to circulate reports to the prejudice of another, i.e., *"to lie about our fellow man."*

Someone said, and which is probably right, that the hardest thing for a Believer to do after he is converted is to quit lying. Perhaps that's one of the reasons that Jesus said: *"But let your communication be, yea, yea; nay, nay: for whatsoever is more than these cometh of evil"* (Mat. 5:37). In other words, let *"yes"* mean yes, and *"no"* mean no!

COVETOUSNESS

Verse 17 reads: *"You shall not covet your neighbor's house, you shall not covet your neighbor's wife, nor his manservant, nor his maidservant, nor his ox, nor his ass, nor anything that is your neighbor's."*

To be sure, when the Ten Commandments were given to Moses and the Children of Israel by Jehovah, there were many other laws in the world at that time; however, all of those particular laws, and wherever they may have been, were devised by man, and always stopped short at the deed. In other words, what was causing the deed was not addressed, simply because it was not possible for man to address such.

"Thou shalt not covet," teaches men that there is One Who sees the heart; to Whose eyes *"all things are naked and open"*; and Who cares far less for the outward act than the inward thought or motive from which the act proceeds (Pulpit).

Paul addressed this one Commandment when he said: *"For I had not known lust, except the law had said, You shall not covet"* (Rom. 7:7).

In essence, he is saying that the mere fact of not carrying out the deed, while certainly good as far as it goes, in the eyes of God, it's not good enough. The desire for that which is wrong must be eradicated as well. While he may not have taken the forbidden thing, there was *"lust"* in his heart, which deals with motive.

Some claim that this Commandment proves the point that man is not a slave to his natural desires and passions, but rather has a controlling power implanted within him, by means of which he can keep down ungodly passion, check desire, and resist evil impulse. That same idea claims that man is lord of himself, capable, by the exercise of his free-will, of molding his feelings, weakening, or intensifying his passions, shaping his character.

I maintain that the Seventh Chapter of Romans, plus other Passages in the Word of God, completely abrogates this thinking. The truth is, man is a slave of his natural desires and evil passions; and irrespective as to how hard he may fight with his *"will"* in order to check such desire. Within himself, he is unable to do so! Paul addresses this again by telling us how much we must have the Grace of God in order to live right, and to prove that point, he says: *"For if righteousness come by the law, then Christ is dead in vain"* (Gal. 2:21).

No, the very fact of the Cross is because of man's inability to save himself, or to better his condition. There is no way he can control evil impulses by what is referred to as *"self-control."* He may succeed some of the time, and in fact, may succeed all of the time with some particulars, but there will always be evil passions, over which he has no control, and which will tend to pull him downward.

NOTES

THE OBVIOUS

Concerning the terrible problem now prevalent in the Catholic Church as it regards pedophilia (child-molestation), the question is asked by many newsmen, *"Can this problem be cured?"*

Of course, if they'll stop and think a moment, the answer to that question has already been given. If it could be cured, at least by man's efforts and ability, and we speak of humanistic psychology, then there would be some evidence of such cures. But there is no evidence of such, because these evil passions cannot be checked by willpower, or any other effort devised by man. That goes not only for child-molestation, but for alcohol, for drugs, for gambling, for all stripes of immorality, etc. Again I emphasize, while it certainly may be possible for man to control some of these passions, he will not be able to control all the passions; and evil passions uncontrolled is like one weak link in a chain. While other parts of the chain may be perfectly sound, the one weak link will cause the chain to break.

Man has faced this problem from day one. He has not yet found a solution, because no solution lies with man. It is a part of the terrible consequences of the Fall.

THERE IS A SOLUTION

The solution, and in fact the only solution, is the Lord Jesus Christ, and more particularly yet, what He did for us at the Cross.

Whenever the Believer places his Faith totally in Christ and what Christ has done for us at the Cross, the Holy Spirit, Who is God and, therefore, can do anything, is able to rid us of these evil passions, to where the desire for them is completely gone. All the psychological therapy in the world cannot do that, as ought to be obvious (Rom. 8:1-2, 11).

THE LAW OF GOD

In the Law, God sets forth His Standard of Righteousness, in other words, what a man ought to be. He then pronounces a curse on him if he doesn't measure up. But irrespective as to how much man may claim that he is what he ought to be, he finds that when he looks at himself in the light of the Law of

God, he actually is the very thing which the Law condemns.

Paul tells us that *"the law entered that the offence might abound,"* showing us the very real object of the Law (Rom. 5:20).

The Law is like a mirror which is let down from Heaven, which shows man what he is, which to say the least, is not good at all, but gives man no means to rectify the situation. It reveals the crookedness, but does not remove it. Furthermore, the mirror did not create the evil it severely points out, but simply reveals what's already there. Thus it is with the Law; it does not create the evil in man's heart, and neither does it remove it; but, with unerring accuracy, it reveals it.

THE NATURE OF THE LAW

If it is to be noticed, the Law constantly tells us not to do certain things. It is fashioned in this manner, simply because it is in our fallen nature to, in fact, do these things. But because our nature is fallen, we cannot rectify the situation, even if we know what is wrong. And that's man's basic problem:

He knows there is something wrong. At times he will refuse to admit it, but his actions portray the fact that he knows there is a severe difficulty in his nature. He claims that it can be rectified with this or that method, but he always fails, as he has been failing now for nearly 6,000 years of recorded history.

One of the reasons that the Law does not address itself to the Believer and the Believer is not to address himself to the Law, which we will say more about momentarily, is simply because the Divine Nature now rests within the heart and life of the one who has accepted Christ (II Pet. 1:4).

If it is to be noticed, a child does not have to be taught to lie; they just do it naturally. It has to be taught to tell the truth. A child doesn't have to be taught to steal; it will just do it on its own initiative. It has to be taught not to steal. Now why is this so?

It is so simply because of the fallen nature of every human being, all due to the Fall. To claim that man has not suffered a Fall is to deny the obvious, and to accept the ridiculous!

THE CHRISTIAN AND THE LAW

Due to the fact that Paul dealt more with the Law than anything else, even though he was dealing primarily with Gentiles, who in fact, didn't know very much about the Law, if anything at all, tells us of the severity of this problem.

There is something about the Law of God, which is God's Standard of Righteousness, which challenges man, which perhaps it is intended to do. Of course, I'm speaking of Believers.

The Believer is so easily enticed, not by the Law, it merely being the vehicle which serves as the means. The enticement is a leftover from the Fall, despite the fact that we're speaking here of redeemed men. In other words, Believers tend to think that because they are new creations in Christ Jesus, they can do all things. Whereas they were not able to keep the Law of God, when in an unredeemed state, they seem to think that now it can be done.

All of this comes from an improper understanding of the Cross, to which we will address ourselves to a greater extent momentarily.

However, we must understand that the Christian is not to expose himself to the Law in any fashion. Jesus has already served as our Substitute as it regards the Law. On our behalf, and totally on our behalf, He kept it perfectly and in every respect. As well, He suffered its penalty on the Cross, which relieved us of that terrible judgment, which was due us.

The Believer must understand that if regeneration does not take us off the ground of Law, it cannot take us beyond the range of the curse of the Law. If the Christian is under the former, that is, under Law, he is, of necessity, exposed to the latter as well!

The Believer has perfection in Christ. But he must ever understand that it is not by Law, but rather by Grace. We cannot, and in fact we must not even try to confound the two economies. Scripture largely and distinctly declares that we are not justified by the Law; nor is the Law our rule of life. That which can only curse can never justify, and that which can only kill can never be a rule of life (Rom. 6:14; Gal. 2:21).

LEGALISM

Mackintosh says: *"There is no evil or error*

more abominable in the sight of the Lord than legalism."

We should hearken to the strong language, the accents of righteous indignation, which fell from the Holy Spirit, in reference to those Teachers of the Law — *"I would they were even cut off which trouble you"* (Gal. 5:12).

Thus, it is obvious that the Law is neither the ground of life to the sinner nor the rule of life to the Christian: Christ is both the one and the other — He is our life and He is our rule of life.

Let me ask a question!

Will the Commandment, *"Thou shalt not steal"* stop the thief from stealing? The same can be asked of all the other Commandments.

While the Law might make the thief realize that there are consequences, it can do nothing to check his evil nature that desires to take that which belongs to someone else. There has to be a new heart to address that problem, which can only be given by Christ.

We might ask the question, *"Is not the Law perfect? And if perfect, what more would you have?"*

To be sure, the Law is Divinely perfect. But, it is the very perfection of the Law which causes it to curse and slay those who are not perfect, if they attempt to stand before it. The Scripture comes screaming at us, *"The Law is spiritual, but I am carnal"* (Rom., Chpt. 7).

When this perfect Law comes in contact with fallen humanity, even redeemed humanity, and we try to meet it head on, in effect trying to do what Jesus Alone could do, we find that it only *"works wrath,"* in our lives (Rom. 4:15; 8:7).

THE CROSS AND THE LAW

The Believer is to ignore the Law. As stated, it has been satisfied in Christ. If he places his Faith totally in Christ, and the Finished Work of Christ, the Holy Spirit will work grandly within his life, and do so on a perpetual, continuous basis, and the demands of the Law will then be met because it was all met in Christ.

However, these demands will be met without the Believer having to address himself to the subject whatsoever. The Believer's life is to be a life of Faith, and I speak of Faith in Christ, and Faith in Christ exclusively, which refers to what Christ did at the Cross. That alone is our victory! That alone is our power! (I Cor. 1:18).

Then the Law is kept, and kept perfectly, without us even having to think about it. But unfortunately, much, if not most, of the Church world opts for law, rather than the Cross. Such a path is a path of destruction! There is nothing in the Law but wrath, whereas there is nothing in the Cross but victory!

(18) "AND ALL THE PEOPLE SAW THE THUNDERINGS, AND THE LIGHTNINGS, AND THE NOISE OF THE TRUMPET, AND THE MOUNTAIN SMOKING: AND WHEN THE PEOPLE SAW IT, THEY REMOVED, AND STOOD AFAR OFF.

(19) "AND THEY SAID UNTO MOSES, YOU SPEAK WITH US, AND WE WILL HEAR: BUT LET NOT GOD SPEAK WITH US, LEST WE DIE.

(20) "AND MOSES SAID UNTO THE PEOPLE, FEAR NOT: FOR GOD IS COME TO PROVE YOU, AND THAT HIS FEAR MAY BE BEFORE YOUR FACES, THAT YOU SIN NOT.

(21) "AND THE PEOPLE STOOD AFAR OFF, AND MOSES DREW NEAR UNTO THE THICK DARKNESS WHERE GOD WAS.

(22) "AND THE LORD SAID UNTO MOSES, THUS YOU SHALL SAY UNTO THE CHILDREN OF ISRAEL, YOU HAVE SEEN THAT I HAVE TALKED WITH YOU FROM HEAVEN.

(23) "YOU SHALL NOT MAKE WITH ME GODS OF SILVER, NEITHER SHALL YOU MAKE UNTO GODS OF GOLD.

(24) "AN ALTAR OF EARTH YOU SHALL MAKE UNTO ME, AND SHALL SACRIFICE THEREON YOUR BURNT OFFERINGS, AND YOUR PEACE OFFERINGS, YOUR SHEEP, AND YOUR OXEN: IN ALL PLACES WHERE I RECORD MY NAME I WILL COME UNTO YOU, AND I WILL BLESS YOU.

(25) "AND IF YOU WILL MAKE ME AN ALTAR OF STONE, YOU SHALL NOT BUILD IT OF HEWN STONE: FOR IF YOU LIFT UP YOUR TOOL UPON IT YOU HAVE POLLUTED IT.

(26) "NEITHER SHALL YOU GO UP BY STEPS UNTO MY ALTAR, THAT YOUR NAKEDNESS BE NOT DISCOVERED THEREON."

The construction is:

1. The word *"saw"* in Verse 18 is a particular type of Hebrew verb, which means, *"perceive, witness."* In other words, no one of the hundreds of thousands of the Children of Israel had any doubt as to what they had witnessed and experienced.

2. It seems from the last Verse of the Chapter that Moses, having been sent by the Lord back down the mountain to warn the people not to break through the barrier, was still with them when the Commandments were given. Elders of the Children of Israel requested of Moses that the Lord would speak through Moses to them, instead of speaking directly, which it seems they were not able to bear. In other words, the power of God's Voice was too much for them.

3. Moses now goes back up the mountain and evidently related this request to God, to which God, it seems, readily acquiesced.

4. Through Moses, the Lord again warns the people of idol worship. He then relates to them the manner of worship in which they should engage, which would be by and through the *"Altar,"* which was a type of the Cross.

THE POWER OF GOD

Verses 18 through 21 read: *"And all the people saw the thunderings, and the lightnings, and the noise of the trumpet, and the mountain smoking: and when the people saw it, they removed, and stood afar off.*

"And the said unto Moses, You speak with us, and we will hear: but let not God speak with us, lest we die.

"And Moses said unto the people, Fear not: for God is come to prove you, and that His fear may be before your faces, that you sin not.

"And the people stood afar off, and Moses drew near unto the thick darkness where God was."

Men have a great tendency to make God too little and themselves too big.

No doubt, when God opened the Red Sea, which was the greatest recorded miracle to date, other than creation itself, the people, no doubt, thought they had seen all of the Power of God, or rather His Power to its utmost. But after the giving of the Ten Commandments, which were done directly by God, in other words, with Him speaking out these Commandments, even though He was enveloped in darkness, the display of power, which manifested itself in thunderings, lightnings, and the noise of the trumpet, even with the mountain smoking, the people now witnessed a display beyond all comprehension. His voice was accompanied by such power that the people felt they were in mortal danger of dying. In fact, that was not the case, but yet the danger was real.

God's Power was, in fact, of such a nature, that He had sent Moses back down the mountain to warn the people that they must not break through the barrier and touch the mountain from which He spoke, lest they die.

But when God began to speak, there seemed to be little danger of them coming closer to the mountain, but rather removing far from it out of fear.

And yet what the people saw here, while representing both His Power and Love, was still not the highest manifestation. The highest manifestation of Who and What God really is would not be manifested until some 1,500 years later, with the birth of Christ.

Through the Incarnation, God becoming man, and dwelling with man, His mighty Power would be shown in the healing of the sick, the performing of miracles, in fact, miracles so astounding as to defy description, and then manifesting His Love by giving Himself in Sacrifice on the Cross of Calvary. In fact, whenever Philip said to Christ, *"Lord, show us the Father, and it sufficeth us,"* Jesus said to him, *"Have I been so long with you, and yet have you not known Me, Philip? He who has seen Me has seen the Father; and how sayest you then, Show us the Father?"* (Jn. 14:8-9).

Then Jesus clarified it by saying, *"Do you not believe that I am in the Father, and the Father in Me?"* He then said: *"At that day* (after the Cross) *you shall know that I am in My Father, and you in Me, and I in you"* (Jn. 14:10, 20).

The idea is, we are to be like the Father, which we can only do through Christ, and Christ Alone!

FEAR NOT

The *"fear"* spoken of in Verse 20 came for two reasons:

1. It was because of the Power of God, which was abundantly evident.
2. It came because of their sinfulness. They were no doubt afraid that this judgment would be leveled at them.

Moses explains to them that God has exhibited Himself in this fashion, that in fact, they might fear Him and, therefore, fear to sin.

Even though this type of fear is absolutely necessary, even now, fear within itself, even of the great Power of God will not stop the sin problem of the life of the sinner or the Saint. Now let us say this again, because it's so very important.

Every Believer must fear God; however, this is not the fear of a slave for a stern taskmaster, but rather fear that comes out of respect and love. The truth is, *"God is love"*; however, most people misunderstand that.

True love must hate sin, even though it loves the sinner. Any true parent, who truly loves his or her children, will most definitely hate the things that can destroy that child, as should be obvious. And it is because they love the child that they do hate these things, and will do everything within their power to stop destructive forces. It is because the parent loves the child.

God loves us! And He loves us supremely! Therefore, anything which He knows, and He knows all things, that will hurt us, He is bitterly opposed to that thing, and the category of harm is always in the realm of *"sin."*

We as Believers must have a fear of sin. We must realize its awfulness. We must know that sin is so strong, so powerful, that it has killed every single person on this Earth who has ever lived, with the exception of Enoch and Elijah. And they will come back during the coming Great Tribulation, and will themselves be killed in Jerusalem. Sin has filled the Earth with blood, with sorrow, with heartache, with pain and suffering, that knows no bounds. We as Believers must fear the consequences of sin, the terrible destructive force of sin; however, as already stated, that fear alone, even though proper fear, will not stop the Believer from sinning because of the following reasons:

THE LAW OF SIN AND DEATH

The Holy Spirit through the Apostle Paul spoke of this of which we addressed as *"the law of sin and death"* (Rom. 8:2). It is the strongest and most powerful force in the world, in fact, stronger than anything else, with the exception of *"The Law of the Spirit* (Holy Spirit) *of Life in Christ Jesus"* (Rom. 8:2).

When it comes to this *"law of sin and death,"* willpower cannot overcome it, fear cannot overcome it, nor any method devised by man. This is where the world runs aground, and even the Church. Regrettably, the Church attempts to face this monster in much the same way the world does, by humanistic psychology, which affords no help at all. And let me say that again:

I'm not meaning that humanistic psychology affords a little help; I am saying that it affords no help at all. In fact, it only does harm for the person, simply because it pulls them away from the true help they can get in Christ Jesus. And to be sure, the two, the Cross and psychology, cannot be mixed. God needs no help, and the truth is, man has no help to give Him. Anything that man produces is labeled by God as *"earthly, sensual, devilish wisdom"* (James 3:15).

Man desperately needs *"The wisdom that is from above"* (James 3:17).

WHAT IS THE LAW OF THE SPIRIT OF LIFE IN CHRIST JESUS?

It pertains to the manner and the way the Holy Spirit works. He is God; therefore, He can do anything.

As well, the Holy Spirit abides, and does so permanently, in the heart and life of every Believer (Jn. 14:16-17).

We should understand that everything carried out on this Earth by the Godhead is carried out exclusively through the Person of the Holy Spirit. Even though the Holy Spirit is God, and as such is everywhere, still, His sphere of operation is this Earth, and more particularly, in the hearts and lives of God's people. So it should be understood that the Holy Spirit definitely has more power than Satan, and can, therefore, put down *"the law of sin and death."* But it's the way that He does it, which is of critical significance.

If it is to be noticed, the manner in which the Holy Spirit works is referred to as a *"law."* Now this means that it is inviolate, which means that it cannot be broken. In other words, the Holy Spirit has one way in which He works, and He will not deviate from that way.

What is that way?

It is found in the words *"in Christ Jesus."* In other words, this great *"Law"* is found in Christ and what Christ has done for us at the Cross. Every time Paul uses the term, *"in Christ Jesus,"* or one of its derivatives, such as *"in the Lord,"* without exception, he is always speaking of what Christ did at the Cross on our behalf.

To be brief, it means that the Holy Spirit works within the confines of the Finished Work of Christ, which refers to the Cross.

But yet, He doesn't do all of this automatically. He requires Faith on our part, and when I say Faith, I'm speaking of Faith in Christ and what Christ did at the Cross (Rom. 6:3-5, 11, 14; 8:1-2, 11; I Cor. 1:18).

FAITH IN CHRIST

Most every Christian uses the term, *"Faith in Christ,"* but that's about as far as they go. If you would ask them to explain what they mean by that statement, most would look somewhat blank, and they would probably answer by saying, *"I trust the Lord,"* etc. While such a statement is correct, it really doesn't say very much.

When we speak of trusting Christ, which means that we are placing our Faith in Christ, without exception, it must mean that we are placing our Faith in Him and what He did at the Cross. We must never separate Christ from the Cross.

Of course, and as should be obvious, Christ is no longer on a Cross, but is rather seated by the Right Hand of the Father (Heb. 1:3). In fact, every Believer is seated with Him in Heavenly Places (Eph. 2:6). However, all of these great things which Christ now does, and all of these great things we now are, are all and without exception given to us by and through what Jesus did at the Cross. In other words, even though the Cross is a Finished Work which was carried out thousands of years ago, it has continuing benefits, and in fact, benefits which will never be discontinued; hence, it is referred to by Paul as *"The Everlasting Covenant"* (Heb. 13:20). It's the *"benefits"* of which I speak.

I'm not trying to take the Christian back to a wooden beam, but rather, that the Christian know and understand what Christ did there for him, and how he can appropriate all that Christ did.

I think it should go without saying, considering the great price that Jesus paid, and that he did it all strictly for us, that He would certainly want us to have everything which He had gained for us at such cost.

The Lord will now show Moses and the Children of Israel the manner and way in which He is to be approached, and the means by which it is to be done.

THE ALTAR

Verses 22 through 26 read: *"And the LORD said unto Moses, Thus you shall say unto the Children of Israel, You have seen that I have talked with you from Heaven.*

"You shall not make with Me gods of silver, neither shall you make unto you gods of gold.

"An Altar of earth you shall make unto Me, and shall sacrifice thereon your Burnt Offerings, and your Peace Offerings, your sheep, and your oxen: in all places where I record My Name I will come unto you, and I will bless you.

"And if you will make Me an Altar of stone, you shall not build it of hewn stone: for if you lift up your tool upon it, you have polluted it.

"Neither shall you go up by steps unto My Altar, that your nakedness be not discovered thereon."

Concerning the Altar, Williams said: *"Man, conscious that he was a sinner, stood afar off, directly God manifested Himself. But God loved him and desired to be near him, and therefore instructed him as to the Altar of Verse 24, and said, 'I will come unto you and I will bless you.'"*

As should be overly obvious, the Altar pictures Christ and what He would do for us at the Cross. The earth pictured His humanity; the stone, His Deity; the shed blood of the animal sacrificed, His priceless Life sacrificed to put away sin and bring the sinner back to God (I Pet. 3:18).

No tool was to embellish the Altar; it was perfect in its beauty to the eye of God. And such was and is Jesus. As well, one might seek to paint the lily or adorn the rose, as for man to attempt to add to the beauty of Him Who is altogether lovely. The Altar was to stand on a level with the people. Such was Jesus. He was accessible to all; even little children could come to Him.

There were to be no steps up to the Altar. When man exalts himself above God, he only exposes his own moral nakedness (Williams).

If it is to be noticed, even though one of the greatest manifestations ever recorded was exhibited by God at Mount Sinai, we find that when God would meet with man, it would be at an Altar, an Altar without hewn stone or a step — a place of worship which requires no human workmanship to erect, or human effort to oppose.

The Altar, which represented Christ and what He would do on the Cross, proclaims the place where all claims of law, of justice, and of conscience are perfectly answered!

Unfortunately, man has repeatedly attempted to change the Altar by erecting new ones, which speaks of a way other than the Cross of Christ, or ignoring the Altar altogether. But let all understand, the only way that sinful man can meet God, and we mean the only way, is through Jesus Christ, and the only way that one can accept Christ is by accepting Christ and what He has done for us in the Sacrifice of Himself (Gal. 1:4). The Father is reached only through Christ, and Christ is reached only through the Cross. To be frank, the Holy Spirit is the One Who has designed this particular procedure (Eph. 2:16-18).

Immediately following the Fall, we find the Lord addressing the Cross to Satan through the serpent. The first instructions given to man regarding fellowship with God after the Fall are found in Genesis, Chapter 4, which portrays the Cross. We find the Patriarchs erecting Altars, which all spoke of Christ and His Finished Work. We find that when the Children of Israel were delivered out of Egyptian bondage, it was through the Passover, which again speaks of the Cross. And now the Law is given, and its giving is immediately followed by instructions regarding the *"Altar."*

In essence, the Lord is saying that man cannot reach God through Law; he can only reach God through Grace, and Grace comes through the Cross alone!

STEPS

The Altar, which represented Christ and what He would do in the giving of Himself in Sacrifice, was represented by God as being on a level with the people; therefore, it was not to have any steps.

"Steps" are the means by which we lessen the strain of rising from a lower level to a higher level. The idea is, man cannot climb up to God by steps of his own making, spiritually speaking. In fact, all religion is a contrivance of man in order to reach God, or to better oneself in some way. In other words, religion constitutes *"steps"* of man's making. True Christianity is not a religion, for it is all of God, and not at all of man. God cannot accept anything that is devised by man, or in fact, touched by man in any way, as it regards the great Salvation Plan.

What God requires from man is that he shall take his true place before Him in the dust. There and there only will God meet with him.

In the first place, man is so morally and, therefore, spiritually separated from God, with the distance being so great that man, by his own contrivance, cannot bridge that gap. But though man cannot climb up to God, God, in the Person of His Son, the Lord Jesus Christ, has come down all the way to this mortal coil, to the poor sinner. We couldn't go to Him, so He came to us!

Pink says this descent is described in the Second Chapter of Philippians. Five distinct *"steps,"* but steps built by God, so to speak, are marked there. Five is the number of Grace. He Who was in the form of God, and thought it not robbery to be equal with God:

1. *"Made Himself of no reputation,"*

2. *"Took upon Him the form of a servant,"*
3. *"And was made in the likeness of men."*
4. *"Being found in fashion as a man He humbled Himself,"*
5. *"And became obedient unto death, even the death of the Cross."*

Those are the only *"steps"* which God will recognize. And they are steps on which the Lord descended. There is not any way possible for man to climb those steps, except solely through Jesus Christ.

NAKEDNESS

When man devises his own steps to God, which approaches the Altar, i.e., *"Cross,"* in the wrong way, or else ignores it altogether, he only tends to expose his moral nakedness. While such may not be so obvious to his fellow man, it is certainly obvious to God.

As well, if it is to be noticed, whether the Altar was made of *"earth"* or uncut *"stone,"* both pointed to Christ.

The *"earth,"* as should be obvious, pointed to His Incarnation. This is what the Second Chapter of Philippians brings out concerning the self-emptying of Christ.

"Stone" points to His Deity. While God became man, and fully man, which means He wasn't half man and half God, still, while becoming man, He never for a moment ceased to be God. As one Greek Scholar said, *"While Jesus laid aside the expression of His Deity, He never for a moment laid aside the possession of His Deity. He retained its possession at all times."*

But if it is to be noticed, if an Altar was to be made of stone, it was not to be made of *"hewn stone,"* but rather stone that was uncut. The Lord plainly said, *"For if you lift up your tool upon it, you have polluted it."*

Paul addressed this very succinctly. In all of his proclamation of Christ, the emphasis was always totally upon His Finished Work, which of course, speaks of the Cross. If men try to picture or present Christ in another fashion, Paul referred to such as *"another Jesus"* (II Cor. 11:4). In other words, they were lifting up their tool upon the stone, desiring to make it into their own likes or dislikes, and thereby, polluting the Message. God help us, this is the great sin of the modern Church.

ALL OF THIS SPEAKS OF THE CROSS

When the Lord announced the Cross (the *"Altar"* on which the great Sacrifice was to be offered), Peter said, *"Spare Yourself"*: in effect, even though this was Peter, it was really Satan through him, attempting to *"hew"* the *"stone"*; but the Lord suffered it not.

The modern Church basically is saying the same thing today. Thankfully, Peter repented of this direction, and God used him mightily as one of the greatest men of God who has ever lived; however, it remains yet for the modern Church to repent.

Presently, Jesus is mostly being presented in every way except the way of the Cross. He is being presented as the *"Healer,"* the *"Miracle Worker,"* the *"Prosperity Giver,"* the *"Great Philosopher,"* the *"Great Prophet,"* but precious little as the *"Saviour."* I remind the Reader that man's problem is *"sin."* That means that his problem is not social, agricultural, technological, educational, intellectual, mechanical, or medical. His problem is *"sin."* There is only one remedy for sin, and that is a *"Saviour."* And there is only one way that Christ can be a Saviour, and that is by and through the *"Cross,"* i.e., *"Altar."*

As we said at the beginning of our commentary regarding these last few Verses of the Twentieth Chapter of Exodus, immediately after God gave the great Ten Commandments, He then led man to the *"Altar,"* i.e., *"Cross."* Of course, He knew that man was woefully inadequate to keep the Commandments, so his only recourse was the *"Altar."*

It hasn't changed from then until now. Man's only hope presently, as it always has been, is the *"Cross."* The Cross alone stands between man and eternal Hell. The Cross alone, which represents what Jesus did there, can afford Salvation for man. The Cross alone can bring the Believer to Sanctification!

"I stand all amazed at the love Jesus offers me,
"Confused at the Grace that so fully He proffers me;
"I tremble to know that for me He was crucified
"That for me, a sinner, He suffered, He bled, and died."

"I marvel that He would descend from
His Throne Divine,
"To rescue a soul so rebellious and
proud as mine;
"That He should extend His great love
unto such as I;
"Sufficient to own, to redeem, and to
justify."

"I think of His Hands pierced and bleeding to pay the debt!
"Such Mercy, such love, and devotion
can I forget?
"No, no! I will praise and adore at the
Mercy-Seat,
"Until at the glorified Throne I kneel
at His Feet."

CHAPTER 21

(1) "NOW THESE ARE THE JUDGMENTS WHICH YOU SHALL SET BEFORE THEM.

(2) "IF YOU BUY AN HEBREW SERVANT, SIX YEARS HE SHALL SERVE: AND IN THE SEVENTH HE SHALL GO OUT FREE FOR NOTHING.

(3) "IF HE CAME IN BY HIMSELF, HE SHALL GO OUT BY HIMSELF: IF HE WERE MARRIED, THEN HIS WIFE SHALL GO OUT WITH HIM.

(4) "IF HIS MASTER HAVE GIVEN HIM A WIFE, AND SHE HAVE BORN HIM SONS OR DAUGHTERS; THE WIFE AND HER CHILDREN SHALL BE HER MASTER'S, AND HE SHALL GO OUT BY HIMSELF.

(5) "AND IF THE SERVANT SHALL PLAINLY SAY, I LOVE MY MASTER, MY WIFE, AND MY CHILDREN; I WILL NOT GO OUT FREE:

(6) "THEN HIS MASTER SHALL BRING HIM UNTO THE JUDGES; HE SHALL ALSO BRING HIM TO THE DOOR, OR UNTO THE DOORPOST; AND HIS MASTER SHALL BORE HIS EAR THROUGH WITH AN AUL; AND HE SHALL SERVE HIM FOREVER.

(7) "AND IF A MAN SELL HIS DAUGHTER TO BE A MAIDSERVANT, SHE SHALL NOT GO OUT AS THE MENSERVANTS DO.

NOTES

(8) "IF SHE PLEASED NOT HER MASTER, WHO HAS BETROTHED HER TO HIMSELF, THEN SHALL HE LET HER BE REDEEMED: TO SELL HER UNTO A STRANGE NATION HE SHALL HAVE NO POWER, SEEING HE HAS DEALT DECEITFULLY WITH HER.

(9) "AND IF HE HAVE BETROTHED HER UNTO HIS SON, HE SHALL DEAL WITH HER AFTER THE MANNER OF DAUGHTERS.

(10) "IF HE TAKE HIM ANOTHER WIFE; HER FOOD, HER RAIMENT, AND HER DUTY OF MARRIAGE, SHALL HE NOT DIMINISH.

(11) "AND IF HE DID NOT THESE THREE UNTO HER, THEN SHALL SHE GO OUT FREE WITHOUT MONEY."

The composition is:

1. The legislation involving this Chapter and the following two, points to a loving God charting a moral course for a corrupt people.

2. This legislation was called *"judgments."* Almost every conduct concerning life and limb was given by God to these former slaves.

3. There were laws in the world governing these things, hundreds of years before the giving of this sacred Law by God to Moses, but they were all man-made. These Laws were God-made. Some were ceremonial; some were civil; some were moral; all were from God.

JUDGMENTS

Verse 1 reads: *"Now these are the judgments which you shall set before them."*

The Law of Moses, to which we have already alluded, was in three parts: the Moral, the Civil, and the Ceremonial. The Ten Commandments dealt with the moral; the next three Chapters dealt with the Civil; the Book of Leviticus dealt with the Ceremonial.

The first defined man's obligation to God; the second defined man's conduct toward his fellow man; the third respected Israel's Spiritual Life, which was largely ceremonial, due to the fact that the Holy Spirit before the Cross was limited regarding that which He could do in hearts and lives.

At the first we see God the Father; in the second, we see the activities of God the Holy

Spirit; in the third we see a series of types concerning God the Son.

Verse 1 of Chapter 21 begins the series of *"Judgments"* or *"Statutes"* which God gave unto Israel for the regulation of their social and civil life. We see how God regulated every aspect of their life and living, as they dealt with their fellow man. And we must remember, all of these Laws were God's Laws, meaning that they were perfect.

The problem with the Laws lay not in God or the Laws themselves, but in the fact that sinful man was to abide by the regulations given to him.

In these Laws and Regulations, we will see a foreshadowing of the Lord Jesus Christ, in His most beautiful and blessed Person and Work.

In all of this, we see God's unsearchable wisdom and infinite goodness. We are able to form some type of idea of the character of a kingdom governed by laws of Divine appointment. But yet we are forever coming back to the realization that while the Laws were perfect, man wasn't and isn't.

It is humiliating to learn that such Laws had to be made to protect men from the appalling evil which prompted them to oppress one another. On the other hand, the tender Love of God shines forth like the sun in this legislation. That mighty Love required that a little slave girl should be set free if even her tooth were so slightly injured.

THE SERVING OF THE MASTER

Verses 2 through 6 read: *"If you buy an Hebrew servant, six years he shall serve: and in the seventh he shall go out free for nothing.*

"If he came in by himself, he shall go out by himself: if he were married, then his wife shall go out with him.

"If his master have given him a wife, and she have born him sons or daughters; the wife and her children shall be her master's, and he shall go out by himself.

"And if the servant shall plainly say, I love my master, my wife, and my children; I will not go out free:

"Then his master shall bring him unto the judges; he shall also bring him to the door, or unto the doorpost; and his master shall bore his ear through with an aul; and he shall serve him forever."

All of this proclaims the Servanthood of Christ, and thereby, the manner in which we are to serve the Lord.

Paul told us in Philippians, Chapter 2, which carries with it the spirit of this Text in Exodus, *"Let this mind be in you which was also in Christ Jesus"* (Phil. 2:5). He then went on to say, *"Who, being in the form of God thought it not robbery to be equal with God: but made Himself of no reputation, and took upon Him the form of a Servant, and was made in the likeness of man: and being found in fashion as a man, He humbled Himself, and became obedient unto death, even the death of the Cross"* (Phil. 2:6-8).

We find in this the self-emptying of Christ, which is to be our example. And yet, we can only go so far in our understanding of what Christ did.

To think of Him, the Mighty Maker, the Creator of all things, the King of kings, and the Lord of lords, taking upon Himself the form of a servant, is plainly beyond our comprehension.

In fact, Jesus as a servant is beautifully shown in Mark's Gospel. It portrays the motives and principles which regulated Him, the excellency of all that He did (Pink).

SERVANTS

This legislation concerning servants tells us several things:

First of all, the servants in the economy of Israel, as designed by God, had no kindred spirit whatsoever with that which we think today as slavery. It was the same as an individual hiring himself to a particular master or family, to serve for a period of time, which payment would include certain things.

It seems that the time set for this servitude was six years. The agreement called for a defined claim upon the individual for that period of time.

"Six" is the number of man (Rev. 13:18). Therefore, the picture is presented here of the measure of human responsibility as it regards what man owes to God. What do we owe to God?

We owe Him unqualified submission,

complete subjection, implicit obedience to His known Will.

Regrettably, man has woefully failed in this which he is supposed to do. Every descendent, not just some, but all, of fallen Adam must be placed in this category. The Law has proven all the world guilty before God (Rom. 3:19).

THE LORD JESUS CHRIST

Christ, as our Substitute, and meant to be our Substitute, is the only Man Who ever fully discharged human responsibility toward God and toward man.

When Jesus was born, the Scripture plainly says that He was *"made under the Law"* (Gal. 4:4). That's the reason He said: *"Think not that I am come to destroy the Law, or the Prophets: I am not come to destroy but to fulfill"* (Mat. 5:17). God's Law was in His heart (Ps. 40:8). In it He meditated day and night (Ps. 1:2).

In every capacity, in thought, in word, and in deed, He kept the Law, therefore, doing for us what we could not do for ourselves.

So Jesus was the perfect Law-Keeper, and we can only become such by understanding that it can be done only in Him. And it can be done only in Him through the Cross of Calvary, with us understanding that we died with Him, literally baptized into His Death, were buried with Him, and were raised with Him in newness of life (Rom. 6:3-5).

We obtained this marvelous work strictly by Faith, and by Faith alone! In other words, our Faith must ever have as its object Christ and Him Crucified. As repeatedly stated in this Volume, we must never divorce Christ from the Cross, or the Cross from Christ. While of course, He is no longer on the Cross, but rather seated at the Right Hand of the Father; still, all that He now is and all that we now are, comes to us exclusively through what Christ did at the Cross.

THE SEVENTH YEAR

After the servant had served for six years, on the seventh year, he was to go out completely free. Concerning this, Henry says: *"As the servant, in the state of servitude, was an emblem of that state of bondage to sin, Satan, and the Law, which man is brought into by his theft, the robbing God of His glory by the transgression of His precepts; so likewise in being made free, he was an emblem of that liberty wherewith Christ, the Son of God, makes free from bondage His people, who are free indeed; and made so, freely, without money and without price, pure free Grace, without any merit or desert of theirs; which freedom is attended with many bountiful blessings of Grace."*

All of this was also true of the Lord Jesus, the Antitype. With Him, the number *"seven,"* referred to perfection, and not to a number of years. In fact, He *"served"* for 33 and one-half years. His service was perfect in every capacity, therefore, completely fulfilling God's number of perfection, which is *"seven."* He perfectly fulfilled every righteous claim that God had upon man: He had loved His Father with all His heart, and did so as a Man, and His neighbor as Himself.

RELATIONSHIP

Verses 3 through 5 proclaim another aspect of the Master.

The Text says, if the man sold himself as a servant, and he was married when this took place, then his wife was to go free with him. If he married a wife while serving as a servant, the wife and children then belonged to his Master, and not to himself. This perfectly fit Christ as the great Antitype.

One might say that the Lord Jesus had no wife when He entered upon *"His service."* For Israel had been divorced from Him, and done so by their own volition (Isa. 50:1). So in effect, He served Alone.

Also, in His earthly sojourn, of which all of this is a type, there was no union possible with Him because of His perfection. The very perfections of this Servant of God only served to emphasize the more the distinction between Him and sinful man. It is only in the Cross which prefigures the Resurrection, that union with Christ is possible (Rom. 6:3-5).

It was only on the Resurrection morning, which shows the Cross to be complete, that He, for the first time, called His Disciples *"Brethren."*

THE PIERCED EAR

If the servant had married a wife and by

this union had children during the six years of servitude, he might say, if he so desired, *"I love my wife and my children, and I love my Master, and I do not desire to go free, but rather to remain as a servant of my Master forever."*

He was then to be taken to the door of his house, and was to stand with his ear pressed on the doorpost, with the lobe of his ear then pierced, thereby as well, making an indentation in the doorpost. This was to be the sign that he had given himself to his Master forever.

This perfectly types our Lord Jesus Christ. He indentured Himself to this human race, and served perfectly. During this time, He gained a wife, i.e., *"the Church"* (Rom. 7:4). The union of Himself with this corporate body has brought forth *"children"* (Eph. 2:13-18).

Furthermore, He was *"pierced"* on the Cross for you and me, thereby guaranteeing His position as *"Intercessor"* on our behalf, forever. He did this because He loves the Father, and He loves us. He said of Himself: *"I am the Good Shepherd: the Good Shepherd gives His life for the sheep"* (Jn. 10:11).

All of this applies to us, as well as to Christ. As He gave His Life for us, we are to give our lives to Him.

The *"ear"* further signifies that the servant would from henceforth *"hear"* only that which his Master would direct. As well, it is said of Christ: *"He* (Christ) *wakens morning by morning, He* (God the Father) *wakens My ear to hear as the learned.*

"The Lord GOD has opened My ear, and I was not rebellious, neither turned away back" (Isa. 50:4-5).

As well, we are to *"Hear what the Spirit says unto the Churches"* (Rev. 2:7, 11, 17, 29; 3:6, 13, 22).

A DAUGHTER

Verses 7 through 11 read: *"And if a man sell his daughter to be a maidservant, she shall not go out as the menservants do.*

"If she pleased not her master, who has betrothed her to himself, then shall he let her be redeemed: to sell her unto a strange nation he shall have no power, seeing he has dealt deceitfully with her.

"And if he have betrothed her unto his son, he shall deal with her after the manner of daughters.

"If he take him another wife; her food, her raiment, and her duty of marriage, shall he not diminish.

"And if he do not these three unto her, then shall she go out free without money."

Verses 7 through 11 deal with a father hiring out his daughter to another family as a *"maidservant."* If the man who had hired her be so minded, he could take her as his wife, or it would be permissible for his son, that is if he had a son, to take her for his wife.

If she didn't prove to be satisfactory, he could not sell her to a foreign nation, but only to other Hebrews. As well, if he took another wife, the *"maidservant"* was to continue to be cared for in every respect. If he didn't want to do any of this, the Law stated that such a woman was free to do whatever she liked, and no money had to be returned. In other words, her father was not to be called upon to refund any portion of the sum for which he had hired her out.

How does this picture Christ?

It does so in the fact that He has bought us (I Cor. 6:20; 7:23).

"The maidservant" refers to Israel. Israel desired to remain under the Law; therefore, she chose a secondary position.

"Another wife" refers to the Church. But yet Israel is to continue to be supported, which the Lord has done with this people in a distant way.

Not desiring to remain at all, she has been allowed to go her own way. But that way has proven to be most unsatisfactory. But even as Hosea predicted, and showed by his own personal experiences, Israel will return.

(12) "HE WHO SMITES A MAN, SO THAT HE DIE, SHALL BE SURELY PUT TO DEATH.

(13) "AND IF A MAN LIE NOT IN WAIT, BUT GOD DELIVERED HIM INTO HIS HAND; THEN I WILL APPOINT YOU A PLACE WHERE HE SHALL FLEE.

(14) "BUT IF A MAN COME PRESUMPTUOUSLY UPON HIS NEIGHBOR, TO KILL HIM WITH GUILE; YOU SHALL TAKE HIM FROM MY ALTAR, THAT HE MAY DIE.

(15) "AND HE WHO SMITES HIS FATHER, OR HIS MOTHER, SHALL BE SURELY PUT TO DEATH.

(16) "AND HE WHO STEALS A MAN, AND SELLS HIM, OR IF HE BE FOUND IN HIS HAND, HE SHALL SURELY BE PUT TO DEATH.

(17) "AND HE WHO CURSES HIS FATHER, OR HIS MOTHER, SHALL SURELY BE PUT TO DEATH.

(18) "AND IF MEN STRIVE TOGETHER, AND ONE SMITE ANOTHER WITH A STONE, OR WITH HIS FIST, AND HE DIE NOT, BUT KEEPS HIS BED:

(19) "IF HE RISE AGAIN, AND WALK ABROAD UPON HIS STAFF, THEN SHALL HE THAT SMOTE HIM BE QUIT: ONLY HE SHALL PAY FOR THE LOSS OF HIS TIME, AND SHALL CAUSE HIM TO BE THOROUGHLY HEALED.

(20) "AND IF A MAN SMITE HIS SERVANT, OR HIS MAID, WITH A ROD, AND HE DIE UNDER HIS HAND; HE SHALL BE SURELY PUNISHED.

(21) "NOTWITHSTANDING, IF HE CONTINUE A DAY OR TWO, HE SHALL NOT BE PUNISHED: FOR HE IS HIS MONEY.

(22) "IF MEN STRIVE, AND HURT A WOMAN WITH CHILD, SO THAT HER FRUIT DEPART FROM HER, AND YET NO MISCHIEF FOLLOW: HE SHALL BE SURELY PUNISHED, ACCORDING AS THE WOMAN'S HUSBAND WILL LAY UPON HIM; HE SHALL PAY AS THE JUDGES DETERMINE.

(23) "AND IF ANY MISCHIEF FOLLOW, THEN YOU SHALL GIVE LIFE FOR LIFE.

(24) "EYE FOR EYE, TOOTH FOR TOOTH, HAND FOR HAND, FOOT FOR FOOT,

(25) "BURNING FOR BURNING, WOUND FOR WOUND, STRIPE FOR STRIPE.

(26) "AND IF A MAN SMITE THE EYE OF HIS SERVANT, OR THE EYE OF HIS MAID, THAT IT PERISH; HE SHALL LET HIM GO FREE FOR HIS EYE'S SAKE.

(27) "AND IF HE SMITE OUT HIS MANSERVANT'S TOOTH, OR HIS MAIDSERVANT'S TOOTH; HE SHALL LET HIM GO FREE FOR HIS TOOTH'S SAKE."

An overview is:

1. All of these were the Laws of God, which in some way, fell under the Ten Commandments.

2. These Laws, as is obvious, dealt with every contingency of life.

3. And yet in these Laws, we constantly find and see mercy.

MURDER

Verse 12 reads: *"He who smites a man, so that he die, shall be surely put to death."*

This Law had actually already been given to Noah some 800-plus years earlier. This is speaking of what we refer to now as, *"cold-blooded murder."*

The death penalty for capital crimes was enacted because of the value of human life because man has been made in the Image of God. But yet, God held life so sacred that one witness to a murder would not be satisfactory for the one who commits the crime to be put to death. There must be more than one witness for the death penalty to be enacted (Num. 35:30).

In today's modern law, individuals are often sentenced to death, that is if the crime is cold-blooded murder, with only one witness, and sometimes with none.

When most think of these ancient Laws given by God, most think of them in severe terms. But yet, when inspected closely, we see that they were not severe, except in certain cases. As we proceed forward, it will quickly become clear as to why the severity was enacted as it was. The great crime of man is that he thinks he knows more than God.

CITIES OF REFUGE

Verse 13 reads: *"And if a man lie not in wait, but God deliver him into his hand; then I will appoint you a place where he shall flee."*

These statements involve aggravated assault, or even second-degree murder. Six cities of refuge were to be designated, where the shedder of blood might flee, and where he might be safe from relatives of the deceased, until his cause was tried before the men of his own city (Num. 35:22-25).

THE ALTAR

Verse 14 reads: *"But if a man come presumptuously upon his neighbor, to slay him with guile; you shall take him from My Altar, that he may die."*

Joab is a perfect example of this (I Ki. 2:28-34).

The idea is, in some cases, the condemned could grab hold of the horns of the Altar, and be spared. However, this was only in cases where his action had seemed justified. If he did this presumptuously, he could be taken from the Altar. Bringing it up to our present time, the idea is this:

The Holy Spirit is telling us here that one cannot claim to trust Christ and what Christ did at the Cross, and at the same time, continue presumptuously in sin. Many have the erroneous idea that if they claim to have Faith in Christ, this covers their wayward direction. It doesn't!

Jesus saves us from sin, not in sin!

Now this is not speaking of those who are struggling with a problem in their life, trying to overcome it, even though they may be trying in all the wrong ways. It speaks of the individual who wants to keep on sinning, plans to keep on sinning, has no thought of stopping his sinning, but thinks that a supposed trust in Christ gives him license to do such.

The very purpose of Faith in the Cross, at least as it regards the Child of God, is to give the Holy Spirit latitude, in order to root all sin out of our lives. The Holy Spirit cannot abide any sin, but seeks ardently to rid the Believer of all things that displease God. And if the Believer will register Faith in the Cross of Christ, to be sure, the Scripture emphatically states, *"Sin shall not have dominion over you"* (Rom. 6:14). In fact, this is the only way of victory, there being no need for any other way.

THE DEATH PENALTY

Verses 15 through 17 read: *"And he who smites his father, or his mother, shall be surely put to death.*

"And he who steals a man (kidnapping), *and sells him, or if he be found in his hand, he shall surely be put to death.*

"And he who curses his father, or his mother, shall surely be put to death."

Concerning these Laws, Pulpit Commentary says: *"The unsystematic character of the arrangement in this Chapter is remarkably shown by this interruption of the consideration of different sorts of homicide, in order to introduce offences of quite a different character, and those not very closely allied to each other."* Three capital crimes requiring capital punishment are noted here:

1. A son or a daughter who would strike their parents with their fist or with an instrument, etc. It doesn't refer to killing, that crime already addressed in Verse 12. The idea is: for a child to strike his parents, he is insulting God, Who has set up the family unit. In fact, this ties back to the Fifth Commandment, *"Honor your father and your mother."*

2. Kidnapping is as well punishable by death. The idea holds, whether for ransom, or to be sold into slavery.

During the Civil War, the Lord enacted this punishment upon the United States, for its terrible crime of *"kidnapping"* Africans, in order to sell them as slaves in this country, or other parts of the world. The Civil War, which was fought to put down this monstrosity, was the bloodiest war in which our nation has ever engaged. There was hardly a home that wasn't touched by its carnage. So we find here that God meant exactly what He said.

3. The cursing by a child of a father or mother was punishable by death. Blasphemy against God, and implications upon parents, were the only two sins of the tongue which the Law expressly required to be punished with death (Lev. 24:16). The severity of the sentence indicates that in God's sight, such sins are of the deepest dye (Pulpit).

Once again, such a sin dishonors God, Who has set up the family unit, which if destroyed, will destroy any nation.

Let the Reader understand that even though man may not fully obey the carrying out of these Laws, nevertheless, God definitely does! While He may not exact this penalty on all concerned all of the time, and for reasons known only to Himself, to be sure, in general, all of these Laws definitely are carried out by God, exacting the punishment required.

Some may argue that this is Old Testament Doctrine, and does not apply presently;

however, these things constitute the Moral Law of God, which cannot change, irrespective of the time frame. In fact, the Law of God is always carried out in one of two ways. They are:

THE LAW

1. The penalty of the broken Law was carried out on Christ, when He suffered its curse upon the Cross, and did so by the giving of His Perfect Life in Sacrifice (Gal. 3:13). This means that every single Believer who has trusted Christ, and continues to trust Christ, will never have the answer to the Law, that having been satisfied in Christ.

2. Every person who doesn't know Christ, and irrespective as to whom they might be, or where they live, or their nationality, will answer, and in fact, is answering to the great Law of God. That's the reason that if a person doesn't accept Christ, that person is lost. One way or the other, the penalty must be exacted, and one way or the other, the penalty is exacted.

GOD'S WAY OF LIVING

Verses 18 through 27 read: *"And if men strive together, and one smite another with a stone, or with his fist, and he die not, but keeps his bed:*

"If he rise again, and walk abroad upon his staff, then shall he who smote him be quit: only he shall pay for the loss of his time, and shall cause him to be thoroughly healed.

"And if a man smite his servant, or his maid, with a rod, and he die under his hand; he shall be surely punished.

"Notwithstanding, if he continue a day or two, he shall not be punished, for he is his money.

"If men strive, and hurt a woman with child, so that her fruit depart from her, and yet no mischief follow: he shall be surely punished, according as the woman's husband will lay upon him; and he shall pay as the judges determine.

"And if any mischief follow, then you shall give life for life,

"Eye for eye, tooth for tooth, hand for hand, foot for foot,

"Burning for burning, wound for wound, stripe for stripe.

NOTES

"And if a man smite the eye of his servant, or the eye of his maid, that it perish; he shall let him go free for his eye's sake.

"And if he smite out his man-servant's tooth, or his maid-servant's tooth; he shall let him go free for his tooth's sake."

We find here that legislation was given by God as it regards one's treatment of his fellow man. As should be understood, this was and is very important.

These Laws were to govern Israel, and all the conduct of its population. In fact, most of the laws of all nations, at least those which are included in what we refer to as *"Western Civilization,"* are based, in some way, on the Law of Moses.

For instance, in modern Civil cases, we have first-degree murder, second-degree murder, and manslaughter. All of these have a different sentence imposed, with the second not being as severe as the first, or the third as severe as the others.

The order of retaliation as it referred to *"an eye for an eye,"* etc., was seldom carried out under Jewish Law, but was rather settled by the giving of money, or labor, etc. But yet the Reader must understand that even though, in many cases, while the authorities may not function as they should, with the law even being abrogated at certain times, or perhaps applied unjustly, in the eyes of God, in some way, the rightful sentence will always be brought about. God is the One Who gave the Law, and to be sure, in one way or the other, He will see to it that these Laws are kept. The Scripture says, *"Vengeance is Mine; I will repay, saith the Lord"* (Lev. 19:18; Deut. 32:35).

As well, we see in Verses 26 and 27 that the rights of even slaves were to be protected, even down to the tooth of a little slave girl.

While this was meant for the Jewish people, it also included the whole of mankind. But of course, nations of the world which did not serve God, and none of them did in those days except Israel, would have little regard or concern for the Laws of God. But as Christianity came into vogue, and the Gospel of Christ, which in effect is the fulfillment of the Law, began to be ministered all over the world, nations began to attempt to formulate their laws after the Word of God, whether they do it consciously or unconsciously. Nations which do not adhere to the Word of God have the most unfair laws, which rob the people of their freedoms, etc. To be frank, man is not capable of governing himself without the help of God. But unfortunately, he thinks he is capable!

Using the United States as an example, regarding laws which are just and right, we will find that in some way, they have their basis in the Word of God, i.e., *"the Law of Moses."* The laws which are unjust in this nation, such as abortion, and certain laws concerning homosexuality, we find, if inspected closely, to be a detriment to the public. Whenever man thinks he knows more than God, that's when he's on the road down.

(28) "IF AN OX GORE A MAN OR A WOMAN, THAT THEY DIE: THEN THE OX SHALL BE SURELY STONED, AND HIS FLESH SHALL NOT BE EATEN; BUT THE OWNER OF THE OX SHALL BE QUIT.

(29) "BUT IF THE OX WERE WONT TO PUSH WITH HIS HORN IN TIME PAST, AND IT HAS BEEN TESTIFIED TO HIS OWNER, AND HE HAS NOT KEPT HIM IN, BUT THAT HE HAS KILLED A MAN OR A WOMAN; THE OX SHALL BE STONED, AND HIS OWNER ALSO SHALL BE PUT TO DEATH.

(30) "IF THERE BE LAID ON HIM A SUM OF MONEY, THEN HE SHALL GIVE FOR THE RANSOM OF HIS LIFE WHATSOEVER IS LAID UPON HIM.

(31) "WHETHER HE HATH GORED A SON, OR HAVE GORED A DAUGHTER, ACCORDING TO THIS JUDGMENT SHALL IT BE DONE UNTO HIM.

(32) "IF THE OX SHALL PUSH A MANSERVANT OR A MAIDSERVANT; HE SHALL GIVE UNTO THEIR MASTER THIRTY SHEKELS OF SILVER, AND THE OX SHALL BE STONED.

(33) "AND IF A MAN SHALL OPEN A PIT, OR IF A MAN SHALL DIG A PIT, AND NOT COVER IT, AND AN OX OR AN ASS FALL THEREIN;

(34) "THE OWNER OF THE PIT SHALL MAKE IT GOOD, AND GIVE MONEY UNTO THE OWNER OF THEM; AND THE DEAD BEAST SHALL BE HIS.

(35) "AND IF ONE MAN'S OX HURT ANOTHER'S, THAT HE DIE; THEN THEY SHALL SELL THE LIVE OX, AND DIVIDE THE MONEY OF IT, AND THE DEAD OX ALSO THEY SHALL DIVIDE.

(36) "OR IF IT BE KNOWN THAT THE OX HAS USED TO PUSH IN TIME PAST, AND HIS OWNER HAS NOT KEPT HIM IN; HE SHALL SURELY PAY OX FOR OX; AND THE DEAD SHALL BE HIS OWN."

The exegesis is:

1. As we can see, the legislation given by God covered just about every aspect of human life and living.

2. We see in these Laws fairness, equity, and with no partiality.

3. We also see in all of this that God is no respecter of persons. What was applicable to the poorest of the poor was just as applicable to the rich and the powerful. That's the way that law must be, that is, if it is to be just.

THE SANCTITY OF HUMAN LIFE

Verses 28 through 32 read: *"If an ox gore a man or a woman, that they die: then the ox shall be surely stoned, and his flesh shall not be eaten; but the owner of the ox shall be quit* (shall not be punished).

"But if the ox were wont to push with his horn in time past, and it has been testified to his owner, and he has not kept him in, but that he has killed a man or a woman; the ox shall be stoned, and his owner also shall be put to death.

"If there be laid on him a sum of money, then he shall give for the ransom of his life whatsoever is laid upon him.

"Whether he have gored a son, or have gored a daughter, according to this judgment shall it be done unto him.

"If the ox shall push a manservant or a maidservant; he shall give unto their master thirty shekels of silver, and the ox shall be stoned."

Concerning this, Pulpit says: *"For the purpose of inculcating as strongly as possible the principle of the sanctity of human life, the legislator notices the case where mortal injury is done to a person by a domesticated animal.*

"The ox is taken as the example, being the animal most likely to inflict such an injury. In accordance with the declaration already made to Noah (Gen. 9:6), it is laid down that the destructive beast must be killed.

"Further, to mark the abhorrence in which murder ought to be held, the provision is made, that none of the creature's flesh must be eaten. The question then arises, is the owner to suffer any punishment?

"This is answered in the way that natural equity points out — 'If he had reason to know the savage temper of the animal, he is to be held responsible; if otherwise, he is to go free.'

"In the former case, the Hebrew Law assigned a higher degree of responsibility than accords with modern notions; but practically the result was not very different.

"The neglectful Hebrew owner was held to have been guilty of a capital offence, but was allowed to 'redeem his life' by a fine. His modern counterpart would be held to have been guilty simply of neglect of duty, and would be punished by fine or imprisonment."

THE RIGHTS OF OTHERS

Verses 33 through 36 read: *"And if a man shall open a pit, or if a man shall dig a pit, and not cover it, and an ox or an ass fall therein;*

"The owner of the pit shall make it good, and give money unto the owner of him; and the dead beast shall be his.

"And if one man's ox hurt another's, that he die; then they shall sell the live ox, and divide the money of it, and the dead ox also they shall divide.

"Or if it be known that the ox has been accustomed to push in time past, and his owner has not kept him in; he shall surely pay ox for ox; and the dead shall be his own."

In this Text, we have compensation being provided for a man's ox being killed by falling into a pit, or well, of a neighbor. We also have provision made for one man's ox killing an animal which belonged to someone else.

Beyond the pure Text itself, we see the legislation provided to treat injuries done to property, etc.

In this we see the sins of omission, which are thought lightly of by most men, but God holds us answerable for them, as much as for sins of commission.

Orr says: *"The Psalmist defines the wicked man as one who neglects to 'set himself in any good way.'"*

NOTES

But once again, the Law, as explicit as it might be, and even though it comes from God, while showing the right way, doesn't give anyone any power in order for one to do that which ought to be done. Man, in his fallen nature, simply cannot obey God. Even the Believer cannot obey God, unless the Believer knows and understands God's prescribed order of victory. Now let us say that again, because it is so very, very important!

Many Christians have the idea that simply because they are Born-Again, with some even baptized with the Holy Spirit, surely they can now live for God. So they set out to do so, almost all of the time in the wrong way, and the end result is the Seventh Chapter of Romans being repeated all over again. In other words, the sin nature not only dwells in them, but rather rules them, exactly as it did before conversion. In fact, due to the paucity of knowledge as it regards the Cross of Christ, and especially as the Cross addresses Sanctification, most Believers, sadly and regrettably, are ruled by the sin nature. That makes for a tragic lifestyle. And to be sure, it is not the norm for Biblical Christianity.

For the Believer to live right, to do right, to be as he ought to be, to be Christlike, for the Fruit of the Spirit to be developed in his life, there is only one way it can be done. And please forgive my repetition, but I repeat it often because I feel it is absolutely necessary that it be repeated:

THE CROSS

The solution for all problems is found in the Cross, and found alone in the Cross.

FAITH

Inasmuch as everything comes to us from God, by the means of the Cross of Christ, the Sacrifice of our Lord must ever be the object of our Faith. This is critically important! The problem is not so much Faith, but rather Faith in the correct object, and the correct object always is the Cross of Christ (Eph. 2:13-18; Col. 2:14-15; Gal. 6:14).

THE HOLY SPIRIT

With our Faith properly placed, the Holy Spirit, Who works exclusively within the parameters of the Finished Work of Christ, will then work grandly within our hearts and lives, developing the Fruit of the Spirit, which gives us Christlikeness (Rom. 8:1-2, 11).

"There was One Who was willing to die in my stead,
"That a soul so unworthy might live;
"And the path to the Cross He was willing to tread,
"All the sins of my life to forgive."

"He is tender and loving and patient with me,
"While He cleanses my heart of the dross;
"But 'There's no condemnation' — I know I am free,
"For my sins are all nailed to the Cross."

"I will cling to my Saviour and never depart;
"I will joyfully journey each day.
"With a song on my lips and a song in my heart,
"That my sins have been taken away."

CHAPTER 22

(1) "IF A MAN SHALL STEAL AN OX, OR A SHEEP, AND KILL IT, OR SELL IT; HE SHALL RESTORE FIVE OXEN FOR AN OX, AND FOUR SHEEP FOR A SHEEP.

(2) "IF A THIEF BE FOUND BREAKING UP, AND BE SMITTEN THAT HE DIE, THERE SHALL NO BLOOD BE SHED FOR HIM.

(3) "IF THE SUN BE RISEN UPON HIM, THERE SHALL BE BLOODSHED FOR HIM; FOR HE SHOULD MAKE FULL RESTITUTION; IF HE HAVE NOTHING, THEN HE SHALL BE SOLD FOR HIS THEFT.

(4) "IF THE THEFT BE CERTAINLY FOUND IN HIS HAND ALIVE, WHETHER IT BE OX, OR ASS, OR SHEEP, HE SHALL RESTORE DOUBLE."

The diagram is:

1. We have here more information and legislation regarding property values.

2. If a man steals an animal such as an oxen or a sheep, and he kill it or sell it, when it is found out, he is to restore five oxen for each one he took and four sheep for each one he took.

3. If a thief breaks into the house at night, it is assumed that he will also do bodily harm to its occupants, and if he is killed in the process, the owner is not liable.

4. If a thief breaks into a house during daylight hours, and is caught in the act, the owner of the house is to assume that the thief doesn't have bodily harm in mind; therefore, the owner of the house is instructed not to hurt him bodily, that is, if he can avoid such. The thief is then to restore double what he has taken, or proposed to take.

If the owner of the house would kill him, and we continue to speak of daylight hours, then the slayer shall be liable to be put to death by the next of kin.

DEALING WITH THIEVES

Verses 1 through 4 read: *"If a man shall steal an ox, or a sheep, and kill it, or sell it; he shall restore five oxen for an ox, and four sheep for a sheep.*

"If a thief be found breaking up, and be smitten that he die, there shall no blood be shed for him.

"If the sun be risen upon him, there shall be blood shed for him; for he should make full restitution; if he have nothing, then he shall be sold for his theft.

"If the theft be certainly found in his hand alive, whether it be ox, or ass, or sheep; he shall restore double."

We find in these Passages that the Mercy of God extends even to thieves. They were to be treated a certain way if they had a murderous intent in their hearts, and another way, if they were bent only on theft.

As should be obvious, sometimes these laws would be difficult to carry out to the letter. If a thief broke into a house during daylight hours, and during the process was found out, and then pulled a knife on the owner of the house, the owner might be left with no alternative but to defend himself to the fullest degree, which might require the man being killed. Then the *"judges"* of Verse 8 were to be brought to bear.

As I'm certain is obvious by now, property rights were held sacred. These *"rights"* were not to be treated contemptuously, nor taken lightly. Strict laws were laid down as to how thieves should be treated. While the thieves had some rights as well, which means that the owner of the house or farm was not allowed to wantonly kill such individuals; at the same time, it is impossible, I think, to overlook the protection of property rights, as laid down in this legislation.

(5) "IF A MAN SHALL CAUSE A FIELD OR VINEYARD TO BE EATEN, AND SHALL PUT IN HIS BEAST, AND SHALL FEED IN ANOTHER MAN'S FIELD; OF THE BEST OF HIS OWN FIELD, AND OF THE BEST OF HIS OWN VINEYARD, SHALL HE MAKE RESTITUTION.

(6) "IF FIRE BREAK OUT, AND CATCH IN THORNS, SO THAT THE STACKS OF CORN, OR THE STANDING CORN, OR THE FIELD, BE CONSUMED THEREWITH; HE WHO KINDLES THE FIRE SHALL SURELY MAKE RESTITUTION.

(7) "IF A MAN SHALL DELIVER UNTO HIS NEIGHBOR MONEY OR STUFF TO KEEP, AND IT BE STOLEN OUT OF THE MAN'S HOUSE; IF THE THIEF BE FOUND, LET HIM PAY DOUBLE.

(8) "IF THE THIEF BE NOT FOUND, THEN THE MASTER OF THE HOUSE SHALL BE BROUGHT UNTO THE JUDGES, TO SEE WHETHER HE HAVE PUT HIS HAND UNTO HIS NEIGHBOR'S GOODS."

The structure is:

1. Next to theft, and not much behind it, is the wanton damage of what belongs to another — and the penalty demanded.

2. This particular legislation portrays the responsibility of each individual. Whatever it is that we do, we are responsible, if such an act injure our neighbors property, etc.

3. The Law given here, and considering that it was the Law of God, put Israel ahead of any other nation by far.

RESTITUTION

Verses 5 through 8 read: *"If a man shall cause a field or vineyard to be eaten, and shall put in his beast, and shall feed in another man's field; of the best of his own field, and of the best of his own vineyard, shall he make restitution.*

"If fire break out, and catch in thorns, so that the stacks of corn, or the standing corn, or the field, be consumed therewith; he who kindled the fire shall surely make restitution.

NOTES

"If a man shall deliver unto his neighbor money or stuff to keep, and it be stolen out of the man's house; if the thief be found, let him pay double.

"If the thief be not found, then the master of the house shall be brought unto the judges, to see whether he have put his hand unto his neighbor's goods."

To whomever the blame is allotted, and for whatever the amount of damage, restitution must be made according to the Law of God, as it regards the harm of someone else's property.

The Law of Moses, which in reality is the Law of God, taught Israel many things. First of all, it taught them how they should conduct themselves toward God, and went into minute detail as to how they should conduct themselves toward their fellow man. Nothing was left out, with every single thing covered, and Israel was expected to abide by this legislation.

Of all the legislation in the world, this was the fairest and the most equitable. It was totally of God, so how could it be otherwise!

Jesus summed all of this up by saying:

"You shall love the Lord your God with all your heart, and with all your soul, and with all your mind.

"This is the first and great Commandment.

"And the second is like unto it, You shall love your neighbor as yourself.

"On these two Commandments hang all the Law and the Prophets" (Mat. 22:37-40).

(9) "FOR ALL MANNER OF TRESPASS, WHETHER IT BE FOR OX, FOR ASS, FOR SHEEP, FOR RAIMENT, OR FOR ANY MANNER OF LOST THING WHICH ANOTHER CHALLENGES TO BE HIS, THE CAUSE OF BOTH PARTIES SHALL COME BEFORE THE JUDGES; AND WHOM THE JUDGES SHALL CONDEMN, HE SHALL PAY DOUBLE UNTO HIS NEIGHBOR.

(10) "IF A MAN DELIVER UNTO HIS NEIGHBOR AN ASS, OR AN OX, OR A SHEEP, OR ANY BEAST, TO KEEP; AND IT DIE, OR BE HURT, OR DRIVEN AWAY, NO MAN SEEING IT:

(11) "THEN SHALL AN OATH OF THE LORD BE BETWEEN THEM BOTH, THAT HE HAS NOT PUT HIS HAND UNTO HIS NEIGHBOR'S GOODS; AND THE OWNER

OF IT SHALL ACCEPT THEREOF, AND HE SHALL NOT MAKE IT GOOD.

(12) "AND IF IT BE STOLEN FROM HIM, HE SHALL MAKE RESTITUTION UNTO THE OWNER THEREOF.

(13) "IF IT BE TORN IN PIECES, THEN LET HIM BRING IT FOR WITNESS, AND HE SHALL NOT MAKE GOOD THAT WHICH WAS TORN.

(14) "AND IF A MAN BORROW OUGHT OF HIS NEIGHBOR, AND IT BE HURT, OR DIE, THE OWNER THEREOF BEING NOT WITH IT, HE SHALL SURELY MAKE IT GOOD.

(15) "AND IF THE OWNER THEREOF BE WITH IT, HE SHALL NOT MAKE IT GOOD: IF IT BE AN HIRED THING, IT CAME FOR HIS HIRE."

The diagram is:

1. There is a Bible way to do all things, and the Bible way is, of course, God's Way.

2. All wisdom other than the wisdom which comes from above is *"earthly, sensual, devilish"* (James 3:15).

3. While the Law was definitely fulfilled in Christ, and fulfilled in totality, which means that it is not now incumbent upon Believers, still, the principle of the Law will always, and without exception, be carried out in Christ, that is, if Christ is properly addressed.

JUDGES

Verse 9 reads: *"For all manner of trespass, whether it be for ox, for ass, for sheep, for raiment, or for any manner of lost thing which another challenges to be his, the cause of both parties shall come before the judges; and whom the judges shall condemn, he shall pay double unto his neighbor."*

The *"judges"* were obviously the Elders of Israel, appointed for the purpose of settling disputes.

The idea was, the parties in question were to make every effort to settle the dispute between themselves; however, if a settlement could not be reached, at least what was satisfactory to both parties, then they had to take the case before the judges.

Trusts are among the most important of the contracts and obligations, whereby human society is carried forth. Strict honesty and much thought and care are requisite on the one hand; confidence, gratitude, and tender consideration on the other.

There is always a right way to do everything, and if the Believer will earnestly seek the Lord, direction will always be given (Jn. 16:13).

THE OATH OF THE LORD

Verses 10 through 15 read: *"If a man deliver unto his neighbor an ass, or an ox, or a sheep, or any beast, to keep; and it die, or be hurt, or driven away, no man seeing it:*

"Then shall an oath of the LORD be between them both, that he has not put his hand unto his neighbor's goods; and the owner of it shall accept thereof, and he shall not make it good.

"And if it be stolen from him, he shall make restitution unto the owner thereof.

"If it be torn in pieces, then let him bring it for witness, and he shall not make good that which was torn.

"And if a man borrow ought of his neighbor, and it be hurt, or die, the owner thereof being not with it, he shall surely make it good.

"But if the owner thereof be with it, he shall not make it good: if it be an hired thing, it came for his hire."

The *"oath of the Lord"* simply meant that both individuals, or however many there were, claimed that what they were telling was the absolute truth, and they called on the Lord to witness their statement.

The Lord then gave instructions as to how events and circumstances should be handled, going into some detail as it regards particular happenings.

I think it is obvious here that the Law of Moses addressed itself to every aspect of human life and living. It called attention to one's duty to God, and it also called attention to one's duty to one's fellow man.

In all of these Laws, we see the principal of restitution put forward constantly. For instance, theft is dealt with on the principle of restitution; yet it calls for more than simple restitution. At the least, the restitution of the simple equivalent brings matters back to the position in which they were before the criminal act was committed. That position ought never to have been disturbed; and punishment is still due to the wrongdoer for having disturbed it. Hence the law that if the stolen animal is found in the thief's hand alive, he shall restore double; if he has gone the length of killing or selling it, he shall restore five oxen for an ox, and four sheep for a sheep.

We find that penalty is proportioned to the offence. If direct restitution was impossible, the thief would be compelled to make restitution by his labor — *"He shall be sold for his theft"* (Vs. 3). It would be an improvement, I think, in the administration of justice presently, if this principle were more frequently acted on.

(16) "AND IF A MAN ENTICE A MAID THAT IS NOT BETROTHED, AND LIE WITH HER, HE SHALL SURELY ENDOW HER TO BE HIS WIFE.

(17) "IF HER FATHER UTTERLY REFUSE TO GIVE HER UNTO HIM, HE SHALL PAY MONEY ACCORDING TO THE DOWRY OF VIRGINS.

(18) "YOU SHALL NOT SUFFER A WITCH TO LIVE.

(19) "WHOSOEVER LIES WITH A BEAST SHALL SURELY BE PUT TO DEATH.

(20) "HE WHO SACRIFICES UNTO ANY GOD, SAVE UNTO THE LORD ONLY, HE SHALL BE UTTERLY DESTROYED.

(21) "YOU SHALL NEITHER VEX A STRANGER, NOR OPPRESS HIM: FOR YOU WERE STRANGERS IN THE LAND OF EGYPT.

(22) "YOU SHALL NOT AFFLICT ANY WIDOW, OR FATHERLESS CHILD.

(23) "IF YOU AFFLICT THEM IN ANY WISE, AND THEY CRY AT ALL UNTO ME, I WILL SURELY HEAR THEIR CRY;

(24) "AND MY WRATH SHALL WAX HOT, AND I WILL KILL YOU WITH THE SWORD; AND YOUR WIVES SHALL BE WIDOWS, AND YOUR CHILDREN FATHERLESS.

(25) "IF YOU LEND MONEY TO ANY OF MY PEOPLE WHO ARE POOR BY YOU, YOU SHALL NOT BE TO HIM AS AN USURER, NEITHER SHALL YOU LAY UPON HIM USURY.

(26) "IF YOU AT ALL TAKE YOUR NEIGHBOR'S RAIMENT TO PLEDGE, YOU SHALL DELIVER IT UNTO HIM BY THAT THE SUN GOES DOWN:

(27) "FOR THAT IS HIS COVERING ONLY, AND IT IS HIS RAIMENT FOR HIS SKIN: WHEREIN SHALL HE SLEEP? AND IT SHALL COME TO PASS, WHEN HE CRIES UNTO ME, THAT I WILL HEAR; FOR I AM GRACIOUS.

(28) "YOU SHALL NOT REVILE THE GODS, NOR CURSE THE RULER OF YOUR PEOPLE.

(29) "YOU SHALL NOT DELAY TO OFFER THE FIRST OF YOUR RIPE FRUITS, AND OF YOUR LIQUORS: THE FIRSTBORN OF YOUR SONS SHALL YOU GIVE UNTO ME.

(30) "LIKEWISE SHALL YOU DO WITH YOUR OXEN, AND WITH YOUR SHEEP: SEVEN DAYS IT SHALL BE WITH HIS DAM; ON THE EIGHTH DAY YOU SHALL GIVE IT ME.

(31) "AND YOU SHALL BE HOLY MEN UNTO ME: NEITHER SHALL YOU EAT ANY FLESH THAT IS TORN OF BEASTS IN THE FIELD; YOU SHALL CAST IT TO THE DOGS.

The structure is:

1. Even though these Laws were perfect in every respect, due to the fallen nature of the Israelites, they fell far short in obeying their precepts.

2. More death penalty sins are addressed in these Passages.

3. All of these Laws have a spiritual meaning, which we will attempt to address.

IMMORALITY

Verses 16 and 17 read: *"And if a man entice a maid who is not betrothed, and lie with her, he shall surely endow her to be his wife.*

"If her father utterly refuse to give her unto him, he shall pay money according to the dowry of virgins."

If it is to be noticed here, the penalty for this act, adultery, falls with most weight on the man, who must either marry the young lady whom he has seduced, or provide her with a dowry, or, if she is a betrothed maiden (engaged to another man), suffer with her the penalty of death (Deut. 22:23-24) (Pulpit).

The latter part of this Law, the part found in Deuteronomy, pertains to the experience of John, Chapter 8.

The Scripture says that the Scribes and Pharisees *"brought unto Him a woman taken in adultery"* (Jn. 8:3).

They then said to Him: *"Now Moses in the Law commanded us, that such should be stoned: but what do You say?"* (Jn. 8:5).

Evidently this young lady was engaged to a young man to be married, but had been unfaithful to her betrothed. It was true, the Law did say that she should be stoned for such an act, but it also stated that the man was to be stoned as well! But if it is to be noticed, they did not bring the man to Christ, only the woman.

Jesus countered their demands by saying to them: *"He who is without sin among you, let him first cast a stone at her"* (Jn. 8:7).

When He made this statement, they were *"convicted by their own conscience* (and), *went out one by one, beginning at the eldest, even unto the last"* (Jn. 8:9).

Jesus then told the woman: *"Neither do I condemn you: go, and sin no more"* (Jn. 8:11).

WHAT DID JESUS DO WITH THE LAW?

First of all, He didn't condemn her, simply because she was already condemned. Of her guilt, there was no doubt. He simply told her, *"Go, and sin no more."*

But that left the matter of the Law to be satisfied. The Law did say that she should be stoned, along with the man. We know that Jesus came to fulfill the Law (Mat. 5:17). So how could He let the woman go, and at the same time satisfy the Law?

He did it the same way He does it with me and you. The Law condemned us, just as it condemned her. The penalty was the same — death. But yet that penalty has been removed.

It was removed at the Cross. In just a few days He would go to the Cross, and would satisfy the demands of the broken Law, redeeming us from its curse, *"being made a curse for us"* (Gal. 3:13).

Giving His Life, He satisfied all of its demands because He took the full penalty Himself. That allowed that young lady to go free, as well as every other person who has ever been saved, and irrespective as to whom they may have been.

The tragedy of all of this was, the men who were condemning her were even guiltier than she was. While adultery is a terrible sin, there are other sins just as bad, and even worse. These religious leaders were hypocrites, and as well, exactly as the near future would show, murderers also!

ACTUAL COMPLIANCE
WITH THE LAW

There is very little evidence in Jewish history that they adhered to these Laws. According as to who was High Priest, accordingly the Laws were addressed.

Even though the death penalty was demanded in certain cases, irrespective of the crime, before the penalty could be carried out, there had to be two witnesses, which we have previously addressed, who had personally observed the particular crime in question. I suspect that in most cases, two witnesses were hard to come by, which is exactly what the Holy Spirit intended.

Some may ask as to why the Lord demanded the death penalty for particular sins? For instance, let's go to the next Verse.

WITCHCRAFT

Verse 18 reads: *"You shall not suffer a witch to live."*

Witchcraft is the solicitation of the help of demon spirits, all which are diametrically opposed to God. It's one thing not to live for God, but it's something else altogether to personally and publicly forge a liaison with demon spirits and the world of spiritual darkness in general. If too much of that exists, demon spirits will literally take over a nation, bringing untold suffering.

AN EXAMPLE

Haiti was established as a government even before the United States. Under the rulership of France, it is said that one of their notorious witch doctors promised Satan that this island nation would be given to the Evil One, if Satan would help them achieve their freedom from France.

They did achieve their freedom, at least from that particular government, but they enslaved themselves to a tyrant a million times worse than what they had previously known.

Presently, there are probably more witch doctors in Haiti per capita, than any other nation in the world. The entire country, at least for all practical aspects, has been taken over by the powers of darkness. It has brought an untold misery of suffering to the people.

Our organization (Jimmy Swaggart Ministries) built some 32 schools on that particular island, educating approximately 20,000 children. We also have built a number of Churches. The only hope for those people, as it is really for any people or any nation, is the Gospel of Christ.

Unfortunately, the United States has gone a long way down the road of demon activity, respecting its government and all aspects of life. Whenever the Lord is pushed out, Satan always fills the vacuum. Of that one can be certain!

Other crimes that called for the death penalty, even as we are studying here in this Chapter, carry such a penalty for a reason. Every Law is given by God for a purpose. Every penalty is given for the same reason. As should be obvious, the Lord knows the end result of all sins; therefore, He exacts certain penalties because of what each sin will do in society. Consequently, due to results, certain penalties have to be attached in order to hold such sins and crimes in check.

BESTIALITY

Verse 19 reads: *"Whosoever lies with a beast shall surely be put to death."*

As should be obvious, this sin is grossly unnatural, in that it insults God as it regards His role as Creator. Any such act always pulls one down to the level of a beast, thereby, insulting God's highest form of creation, which is man.

As well, terrible physical results accrue from such a union.

It is said that syphilis came about as the result of men cohabiting with sheep. This disease can have a terrible, debilitating effect, if left untreated. It is said that nearly half of the population of Egypt is presently infected with this venereal disease, which takes its deadly toll on a daily basis.

If in fact these numbers are correct, this greatly weakens the ability of the nation of Egypt, and any other nation of similar comport, to function as they should, hence the terrible poverty and ignorance.

NOTES

IDOL WORSHIP

Verse 20 reads: *"He who sacrifices unto any god, save unto the LORD only, he shall be utterly destroyed."*

Pulpit says: *"Sacrifice was the chief act of worship; and to sacrifice to a false god was to renounce the True God. Under a theocracy this was rebellion, and rightly punished with death. In States which were not a theocracy (God-ruled), such would not be a civil offence, and would be left to the final judgment of the Almighty."*

Every unsaved person in the world lives in a spiritual death, which means separation from God. This means they have no spirituality whatsoever, no understanding of the Lord or His Ways, no understanding of His Word. In fact, they are dead to anything that is of God, which actually took place at the Fall in the Garden of Eden, and was passed down to all humanity. Men are born that way, due to all having been in Adam. And to be sure, dead is dead!

However, added penalties are placed upon individuals who do certain things, the worship of false gods being one of those things.

I would greatly suspect that even under the New Covenant, and especially under the New Covenant, many so-called *"accidents"* and premature deaths, if the truth be known, could be attributed to God in many cases. On the unsaved, these Laws of God, even though fulfilled by Christ at the Cross, are still incumbent upon the human race. In other words, it's to these Laws, these moral Laws, that men will answer, when they stand at the Great White Throne Judgment (Rev. 20:11-15). Paul said:

"And the times of this ignorance (Old Testament Times) *God winked at; but now commands all men everywhere to repent"* (Acts 17:30).

The only way that the Judgment of the Law can be escaped is for one to accept the Lord Jesus Christ as one's personal Saviour, which then satisfies the claims of the Law, which He took upon Himself, and did so by the Sacrificial Offering of His Own Life on Calvary's Cross (Gal. 3:13).

THE STRANGER

Verses 21 through 24 read: *"You shall

neither vex a stranger, nor oppress him: for you were strangers in the land of Egypt.

"You shall not afflict any widow, or fatherless child.

"If you afflict them in any wise, and they cry at all unto Me, I will surely hear their cry;

"And My wrath shall wax hot, and I will kill you with a sword; and your wives shall be widows, and your children fatherless."

We find here that the stranger, the widow, and the fatherless child are also protected. So when the State makes provisions in this respect, and we speak especially of the widow and the fatherless child, it is carrying out that which the Lord long ago commanded.

Concerning *"foreigners,"* Pulpit says: *"It may be doubted whether such a law as this was ever made in any other country. Foreigners are generally looked upon as 'fair game,' whom the natives of a country may ridicule and annoy at their pleasure. The Mosaic legislation protested strongly against this practice (Ex. 23:9; Lev. 19:33), and even required the Israelites to 'love the stranger who dwelt with them as themselves.'"*

The people of Israel were to remember that they once were *"strangers in the land of Egypt."*

The stranger is likewise placed with the widow and the orphan, and made the special objects of God's care. And if the Lord makes something His special object of care and concern, we must do the same!

Pulpit further says that it was in large measure, on account of the neglect of this precept that the capture of Jerusalem by Nebuchadnezzar, and the destruction of its inhabitants, was allowed to take place (Jer. 22:3-5).

The Lord plainly says here that if the widow or fatherless child cries unto Him, He will definitely hear their cry. And to be sure, the threatened judgment must not be taken lightly.

THE POOR

Verses 25 through 27 read: *"If you lend money to any of My people who are poor by you, you shall not be to him as an usurer, neither shall you lay upon him usury.*

"If you at all take your neighbor's raiment to pledge, you shall deliver it unto him by that the sun goes down:

NOTES

"For that is his covering only, it is his raiment for his skin: wherein shall he sleep? And it shall come to pass, when he cries unto Me, that I will hear; for I am gracious."

It may seem as though only the *"poor"* are included in this command; however, the Jews took these Passages to mean that it was forbidden to lend money at interest to a fellow Jew, irrespective of his financial status. On the other hand, it was distinctly declared that interest might be taken from strangers (Deut. 23:20).

If the poorest of the poor borrowed money, and gave his garment as a pledge, and we speak of the garment which was used at night, it was to be returned to him before the sun went down. This garment doubled as a sleeping gown as well.

The Lord plainly says that if such people are taken advantage of, and if they cry to the Lord, He will definitely hear. In such a case, He will have vengeance.

RULERS

Verse 28 reads: *"You shall not revile the gods, nor curse the ruler of your people."*

It is argued by almost all that the word *"gods"* refers here to God Himself! However, considering the latter phrase, I think the Hebrew word *"Elohim,"* as given here, should have been translated *"judges."*

In the first place, I would think that the Children of Israel knew not to revile the Lord. Second, I cannot remember anywhere in the Bible that the word *"Elohim"* as it refers to the Lord God, being translated in the plural such as this. As well, the word is used in Psalms 82:6, and there refers to *"judges"* or *"magistrates."* The idea is this:

Irrespective as to whether the one in authority was personable or not, he was not to be reviled. In today's terminology, that would go for the President, Congress, Governors, Mayors, Sheriffs, and even the cop walking the beat.

While these individuals may or may not be the type of individual they ought to be, they hold a place of authority as it regards government, and as such, they are not to be reviled. That doesn't mean we have to like them, or even vote for them. But it does mean that we are to respect them.

Actually, the Holy Spirit through Paul said, *"That, first of all, supplications, prayers, intercessions, and giving of thanks, be made for all men; for kings, and all who are in authority; that we may lead a quiet and peaceable life in all Godliness and honesty"* (I Tim. 2:1-2).

FIRSTFRUITS

Verses 29 and 30 read: *"You shall not delay to offer the first of your ripe fruits, and of your liquors: the firstborn of your sons shall you give unto Me.*

"Likewise shall you do with your oxen, and with your sheep: seven days it shall be with his dam; on the eighth day you shall give it Me."

The firstfruits and the firstborn of both man and beast were to be given to God in Sacrifice. Of course, we're speaking here of the beasts which were domestic animals.

As well, even though the firstborn of the sons were to be given to God, they were to be redeemed by a money payment (Ex. 13:13; Num. 3:46-48). Human sacrifice was absolutely forbidden!

"You shall not delay," implies that there would be reluctance to comply with this obligation, and that the offering could be continually put off. This was not to be done!

As it regarded the animals, such as oxen and sheep, they were not to be offered in sacrifice until the eighth day.

Due to the Fall, birth was viewed as an unclean process, which it was and is, and, therefore, nothing was fit for presentation to God excepting after a particular interval, here, seven days.

The *"firstborn"* stood for Christ, and His Incarnation, which He must do in order to redeem the human race, while *"firstfruits"* pointed to His Resurrection, which guarantees victory for the Child of God, *"raised with Him in newness of life"* (Rom. 6:3-5), and of the Resurrection which will take place when all the Sainted dead will come forth, as well, with all Believers who are alive, being instantly changed (I Cor. 15:45-58).

HOLY

Verse 31 reads: *"And you shall be holy men unto Me: neither shall you eat any flesh that is torn of beasts in the field: you shall cast it to the dogs."*

The word *"holy"* actually means, *"to be set apart exclusively unto God."* So the entirety of Israel was to be holy unto the Lord. That's the reason for so many regulations, etc.

The reason they were not to eat the flesh of an animal that had been killed by beasts, etc., is because the blood of such an animal would not be properly drained from it. Some would remain in the tissues, and thence the animal would be unclean.

The flesh of such an animal that had accordingly died was to be given to the dogs.

Dogs were looked at by the Jews as extremely unclean, inasmuch as they would eat almost anything.

"I met Jesus at the foot of the Cross
"When I was bound by sin;
"Jesus met me, cleansed my heart of its dross,
"He gave sweet peace within."

"I found pardon at the foot of the Cross,
"Forgiveness full and free;
"Now I love Him only, all else is loss,
"His Grace availed for me."

"I met Jesus when I needed Him most,
"Despair possessed my soul;
"I was under condemnation and lost,
"When Jesus made me whole."

CHAPTER 23

(1) "YOU SHALL NOT RAISE A FALSE REPORT: PUT NOT YOUR HAND WITH THE WICKED TO BE AN UNRIGHTEOUS WITNESS.

(2) "YOU SHALL NOT FOLLOW A MULTITUDE TO DO EVIL; NEITHER SHALL YOU SPEAK IN A CAUSE TO DECLINE AFTER MANY TO WREST JUDGMENT:

(3) "NEITHER SHALL YOU COUNTENANCE A POOR MAN IN HIS CAUSE.

(4) "IF YOU MEET YOUR ENEMY'S OX OR HIS ASS GOING ASTRAY, YOU SHALL SURELY BRING IT BACK TO HIM AGAIN.

(5) "IF YOU SEE THE ASS OF HIM WHO HATES YOU LYING UNDER HIS

BURDEN, AND WOULD FOREBEAR TO HELP HIM, YOU SHALL SURELY HELP WITH HIM.

(6) "YOU SHALL NOT WREST THE JUDGMENT OF YOUR POOR IN HIS CAUSE.

(7) "YOU KEEP FAR FROM A FALSE MATTER: AND THE INNOCENT AND RIGHTEOUS YOU MUST NOT KILL: FOR I WILL NOT JUSTIFY THE WICKED.

(8) "AND YOU SHALL TAKE NO GIFT: FOR THE GIFT BLINDS THE WISE, AND PERVERTS THE WORDS OF THE RIGHTEOUS.

(9) "ALSO YOU SHALL NOT OPPRESS A STRANGER: FOR YOU KNOW THE HEART OF A STRANGER, SEEING YOU WERE STRANGERS IN THE LAND OF EGYPT.

(10) "AND SIX YEARS YOU SHALL SOW YOUR LAND, AND SHALL GATHER IN THE FRUITS THEREOF:

(11) "BUT THE SEVENTH YEAR YOU SHALL LET IT REST AND LIE STILL; THAT THE POOR OF YOUR PEOPLE MAY EAT: AND WHAT THEY LEAVE THE BEASTS OF THE FIELD SHALL EAT. IN LIKE MANNER YOU SHALL DEAL WITH YOUR VINEYARD, AND WITH YOUR OLIVE YARD.

(12) "SIX DAYS YOU SHALL DO YOUR WORK, AND ON THE SEVENTH DAY YOU SHALL REST: THAT YOUR OX AND YOUR ASS MAY REST, AND THE SON OF YOUR HANDMAID, AND THE STRANGER, MAY BE REFRESHED.

(13) "AND IN ALL THINGS THAT I HAVE SAID UNTO YOU BE CIRCUMSPECT: AND MAKE NO MENTION OF THE NAME OF OTHER GODS, NEITHER LET IT BE HEARD OUT OF YOUR MOUTH."

The composition is:

1. Kindness, wherever possible, is to be shown even to our enemy.

2. A poor man is not to be allowed to break the Law, just because he is poor.

3. Bribery is a sin, both in its presentation, and in its acceptance.

4. The land was to be worked for six years, but on the seventh year, it was to remain idle.

5. The people were to learn the Law in totality. They were to be careful that it was obeyed in all things, at least to the best of their ability.

6. As well, they were not to mention the names of other gods, which would be giving the Devil too much due.

FALSE REPORTS

Verse 1 reads: *"You shall not raise a false report: put not your hand with the wicked to be an unrighteous witness."*

This deals with the Ninth Commandment, in that we must not bear false witness.

The idea as given here presents the fact that no false report must begin with God's people, and as well, no false report must be spread to others.

This is one of the most wicked sins that a person can commit, and regrettably, it's one of the most oft committed sins in the Church presently. I never cease to be amazed at people who will so quickly assume something, without any investigation, and then proceed to tell it as *"true,"* when in reality, it's the very opposite.

Why do modern Believers do such a thing?

Such people have very little relationship with Christ, if any at all, which means that their faith is not in the Cross, but something else altogether.

This is a problem of the tongue, which James said *"can no man tame; it is an unruly evil, full of deadly poison"* (James 3:8).

While it's certainly true that no man, even Believer's, can tame the tongue, at least by their own machinations, ability, and strength; the tongue can, however, definitely be tamed by the Holy Spirit, and by the Holy Spirit Alone! And how does He do that?

THE CROSS AND THE HOLY SPIRIT

By now I certainly believe that you know what I'm going to say:

Regrettably, most Christians do not have understanding as it regards the manner in which the Holy Spirit works. They either know absolutely nothing about Him, and simply because they're taught nothing from behind their pulpits, or else they know just enough to take Him for granted, which is almost as bad as knowing nothing.

To be sure, the Holy Spirit desires strongly to work within our hearts and lives, and actually, that's the very reason He has taken up residence in our hearts. Listen to what

Paul said:

"But if the Spirit (Holy Spirit) *of Him* (God the Father) *Who raised up Jesus from the dead dwell in you, He Who raised up Christ from the dead shall also quicken your mortal bodies by His Spirit Who dwells in you"* (Rom. 8:11).

We are told several things in this particular Verse:

We are told that it is the Holy Spirit Who raised Christ from the dead. This speaks of Almighty Power, and rightly so, because the Holy Spirit, as the Father and the Son, is God. This means He can do anything.

So whatever is needed in one's heart and life, to be sure, the Holy Spirit can do it.

As well, we are told here that this power, the power that raised Christ from the dead, is available to us. Now reading these words, many Believers would believe what is being said, because they respect and honor the Holy Spirit, but they are not seeing victory within their lives.

Why?

I can certainly remember my own experience in this arena. This was back in the 1980's. The Lord was using me mightily to reach millions of souls for Christ, and I exaggerate not! At that time, we had the largest audience in the world regarding Gospel Television, actually airing the program all over the world, translated into many languages. We were drawing the largest crowds in the world, in giant Crusades in the major cities of many countries. Tens of thousands of people were coming to Christ, and again, I exaggerate not! As well, thousands were being baptized with the Holy Spirit.

This was my calling as an Evangelist, and God was using me mightily in this respect, for which we give Him all the glory. But in my own personal life, I didn't have victory. I was struggling and fighting with all the strength that was within me, but seemingly to no avail. All I knew to do was to increase what I was doing, and surely, I thought, this would bring victory.

I would seek the Lord at least an hour a day, making certain that I didn't miss that hour of prayer. I would then get up at one o'clock or two o'clock in the morning, and pray another hour. To be sure, I was fighting for my life!

In those days, I understood the Cross as it regards Salvation, and preached it strongly all over the world, resulting in tens of thousands being brought to a saving knowledge of Jesus Christ. But I didn't know anything about the Cross as it regards Sanctification. In fact, I have never heard one single Message in this regard, nor had I read a Message in the hundreds of books that were in my library. And looking back now, I did not know a single Preacher who understood then these things of which I now speak.

The things I was doing were very good things, such as prayer and Bible study, etc. And to be sure, the Lord blessed me greatly in these endeavors. But the victory which I so earnestly sought constantly eluded me. And let the Reader understand the following:

SATAN AND SIN

The Devil hates every Child of God, which should be obvious! And when he strikes, it's never done in a pretty way. In fact, it's always very, very ugly! In fact, works of the flesh are never very pretty, but always very ugly (Gal. 5:19-21). And as well, the Believer doesn't have the luxury of choosing the manner in which Satan attacks him. And oftentimes, if not most of the time, he will be attacked in the manner that has absolutely no relationship to his personality. That's why people scratch their head and wonder, *"What went wrong?"*

If the Believer doesn't understand the Cross as it regards Sanctification, for all practical purposes, that Believer, irrespective as to whom he might be, Preacher or otherwise, is defenseless. Now most Christians would think that if anyone was praying two hours a day or more, and studying the Bible incessantly, and trying with all their strength to live as they should, certainly this would be the answer.

While all of these things are very, very good, and actually, things which any good Christian will do, if we try to make these particular disciplines work for us in the realm of victory, we turn them into *"works,"* which God can never honor.

Time and time again, in fact, countless times, I would ask the Lord through bitter tears why He wasn't helping me. He was anointing me greatly to preach His Word, and to see tens of thousands brought to Christ, but why wouldn't He help me in the realm of personal victory?

The truth was and is, He was helping me, exactly as He is helping all Christians. The answer is found in the Word of God. In other words, there doesn't have to be a new Revelation; the Word is replete with the solution to the problem, whatever the problem might be. Peter said, and rightly so:

"According as His Divine power has given unto us all things that pertain unto life and Godliness, through the knowledge of Him Who has called us to glory and virtue:

"Whereby are given unto us exceeding great and precious Promises, that by these you might be partakers of the Divine Nature, having escaped the corruption that is in the world through lust" (II Pet. 1:3-4).

Also, Paul said: *"For sin shall not have dominion over you: for you are not under the law, but under Grace"* (Rom. 6:14). The great Apostle also said:

"For the preaching of the Cross is to them who perish foolishness; but unto us which are saved it is the Power of God" (I Cor. 1:18).

And then: *"I am crucified with Christ* (Rom. 6:3-5)*: nevertheless I live; yet not I, but Christ lives in me: and the life which I now live in the flesh* (this daily walk) *I live by the Faith* (what Jesus did at the Cross) *of the Son of God, Who loved me, and gave Himself for me* (once again, the Cross)*"* (Gal. 2:20).

So the Word was there all the time, containing the answer for which I sought, but I simply didn't understand it. I thought I did, but I didn't! And as stated, looking back, I did not know then anyone who had understanding either. I'm sure there were some in the world, but the truth is, there were not very many. In fact, the Church has had so little teaching on the Cross in the last few decades, until presently it is Cross-illiterate, which means, it is all but defenseless. That's the reason for failures on every hand.

A VISION

If I remember the year correctly, it was the latter part of 1988. We were in Oklahoma City with a Crusade. The Churches there, and I especially speak of the Pentecostal Churches, fought us incessantly, trying to stop the Meeting. It hurt more deeply that I even begin to have words to express. The Lord had told me in 1982 that my own would turn against me; however, I did not really know or understand at the time to the extent of what the Lord was actually saying to me. I saw it come to pass before my very eyes, and in ugly, hurtful detail.

The Friday afternoon before the Crusade was to begin that night, I was studying and praying. It must have been about 3 o'clock that Friday afternoon. At a particular point in time, I believe the Lord gave me a Vision.

I saw men falling from the sky to the ground. All of them were very dignified, and very stylishly dressed. Some of them had gray hair, and as I stated, the very epitome of dignity and aplomb.

I recall looking at their faces after they had hit the ground, faces which mirrored such confusion and lack of understanding. They were saying, in essence, even by their very appearance, *"What has happened?" "Why has this happened to me?" "How could this happen to me?"*

In other words, how had they fallen? Why had they fallen? They were doing all the things they thought would bring life and victory, but now this terrible thing has happened to them!

The vision ended, with me not really knowing or understanding what the Lord had then showed me. I pondered what I had seen, and I suppose at the time, I thought I understood what I had witnessed.

In fact, I did understand it to a degree. But only now do I fully understand what the Lord was saying.

At that time in 1988, I didn't understand the Cross as it regards Sanctification, so I was, in effect, as puzzled as were these men whom I had seen in the vision.

When you've done everything you know to do, and have failed anyway, you are left very perplexed, very confused. That's why Paul said:

"For that which I do I allow not: for what I would, that do I not; but what I hate, that do I" (Rom. 7:15).

Now please understand, Paul experienced these things not long after his conversion and baptism with the Holy Spirit, and before he understood the Message of the Cross.

The word *"allow"* should have been translated *"understand,"* because that's what it means. He actually said: *"For that which I do I understand not."*

At that time, I didn't understand; the men I saw in the vision didn't understand. And the fact is, there are untold millions presently who do not understand. They're trying with all their strength to live for God, to be what they ought to be, but failing miserably, and they don't know why!

WHY THE FAILURE?

The reason for the failure, and in whatever capacity it might be, is because the Believer doesn't understand the Cross as it regards Sanctification. The tragedy is, there isn't one Preacher out of ten thousand who understands what Paul taught in his Epistles, and especially in Romans, Chapters 6, 7, and 8. And to be sure, Satan takes full advantage of such Scriptural ignorance.

What most Believers do not understand is the very thing they are doing, which they think will bring them victory, which in fact may be very good in its own right, still, throws them into the category of committing *"spiritual adultery."*

SPIRITUAL ADULTERY

I realize that most Christians have never even heard the term *"spiritual adultery,"* when the truth is, most are committing this terrible sin, and terrible it is!

Paul explained this in Romans 7:1-4.

He gave the example of a woman who was being unfaithful to her husband, and then he said, *"She shall be called an adulteress."*

Most Believers dismiss these first four Verses in Romans, Chapter 7, thinking that Paul is speaking of marriage and divorce, etc. No! The Apostle is dealing with Believers, and the reason for failure in their lives.

The example he gives was given to him by the Holy Spirit.

He then went on to say that we as Believers are married to Christ. That means that we are dead to the Law. However, if we try to function in the Law, while married to Christ, this constitutes us being unfaithful to Christ, thereby committing the sin of *"spiritual adultery."* Let's explain it further:

For instance, if a man is unfaithful to his wife, or a wife to her husband, this refers to them committing adultery, which is a grievous sin, as should be obvious.

As stated, Believers are married to Christ. This means that every single thing that we as Believers receive from God, we do so through Christ, and more particularly, what Christ did for us at the Cross. Our trust must be in Him exclusively. Our dependence must be in His Finished Work. That is the story of the Bible, and the story of Redemption.

All of this simply means that our Faith must be anchored squarely in Christ and His Finished Work. The secret to all of this is *"Faith,"* but Faith properly placed, which refers to the Cross. Now this is where we have our problem.

UNBELIEF

Many Christians do not accept the Scriptural truth that everything comes to us exclusively through the Cross. They want to hold up *"works,"* and refer to these works as Faith, which God will never honor. Concerning this, Paul said:

"For in Jesus Christ neither circumcision availeth anything, nor uncircumcision (works); but Faith which works by love" (Gal. 5:6).

So when we talk about *"Faith,"* we must always understand that for our Faith to be real, at least the kind that God will recognize, it must be exclusively in Christ and the Cross. That's why Paul said, *"We preach Christ Crucified"* (I Cor. 1:23).

RELATIONSHIP TO ONE'S FELLOW MAN

Verses 2 through 7 read: *"You shall not follow a multitude to do evil; neither shall you speak in a cause to decline after many to wrest judgment:*

"Neither shall you countenance a poor man in his cause.

"If you meet your enemy's ox or his ass going astray, you shall surely bring it back to him again.

"If you see the animal which belongs to him who hates you lying under his burden, and would forebear to help him, you shall surely help with him.

"You shall not wrest the judgment of the poor in his cause.

"Keep you far from a false matter: and the innocent and righteous you shall not kill: for I will not justify the wicked."

Just because a multitude of people may champion a particular cause doesn't necessarily mean that it's right. The idea is, a position must not be accepted simply because many favor that particular position. The Believer should investigate the matter fully, that is, if it definitely does require his attention, and then make a judgment on the facts. Many times the multitude isn't right!

Pulpit says: *"It is extraordinary that so many, even of professing Christians, are content to go with the many, notwithstanding the warnings against so doing, because of the law and of the Gospel."*

Regarding Verse 3, in courts of justice, strict justice is to be rendered, without any leaning either towards the rich, or towards the poor. To lean either way is to pervert judgment (Pulpit).

Regarding Verse 4, it is remarkable as to how close this particular law comes to New Testament Christianity. While it's true that Rabbinical teachers had come up with the conclusion that enemies were to be hated, the Law, in fact, said no such thing (Mat. 5:43). But in Truth, Christianity goes beyond the Mosaic injunctions, with Christ saying, *"love your enemies"* (Mat. 5:44).

However, the Law within itself, due to its very nature, cannot love. It can only state what should be done. Only Christ in the heart can produce the desired effect. While Verse 3 warned that the poor were not to be favored simply because they were poor, the Sixth Verse gives the very opposite, in effect stating that the poor must not be maltreated, simply because he is poor. Regrettably, that is not the case in most of the countries of the world.

Perhaps Western Civilization would come closer to obeying this injunction than most countries. And this can be said only because of the influence of New Testament Christianity.

NOTES

Concerning Verse 7, how so much strife would be avoided, if Christians didn't gossip and, thereby, peddle false matters.

In effect, the Holy Spirit through Moses is saying here that the innocent and the righteous can be seriously hurt by the spreading of *"false matters."* The Lord, in effect, says that those who spread such are *"wicked,"* and that He will not justify such, meaning that Judgment will come upon such perpetrators.

OBEDIENCE

Verses 8 through 13 read: *"And you shall take no gift: for the gift blinds the wise, and perverts the words of the righteous.*

"Also you shall not oppress a stranger: for you know the heart of a stranger, seeing you were strangers in the land of Egypt.

"And six years you shall sow your land, and shall gather in the fruits thereof:

"But the seventh year you shall let it rest and lie still; that the poor of your people may eat: and what they leave the beasts of the field shall eat. In like manner you shall deal with your vineyard, and with your olive yard.

"Six days you shall do your work, and on the seventh day you shall rest: that your ox and your animal may rest, and the son of your handmaid, and your stranger may be refreshed.

"And in all things that I have said unto you be circumspect: and make no mention of the name of other gods, neither let it be heard out of your mouth."

Verse 8 condemns all bribery. The worst thing that can be done is for a Judge or one in authority to take a bribe, and thereby render a decision accordingly. Regrettably, in one way or the other, this is done all too often. Justice and right doing can never be served if money is involved as a payoff of any kind. So the Word of God says, and understandably, *"Don't do it!"*

A REPETITION

Once again, the Ninth Verse warns Israel about oppressing strangers, virtually using the same words as Exodus 22:21.

When this is done, and I speak of the repetition, it is not done without purpose. The Holy Spirit desires that the stipulation in question would be understood as to its seriousness.

At times, the Holy Spirit will have the writer to repeat something, and at times, to do so almost verbatim. We are never to observe such, thinking that someone has made a mistake, but rather that the Spirit desires that we understand the importance of such a command or truth that is being given.

THE SABBATICAL YEAR

Verses 10 and 11 portray the seventh year as being a year of rest for the land. In other words, on this seventh year, no crops were to be planted, and whatever grew on its own accord was to be given to the poor and to the animals, etc.

In essence, the Lord promised that the harvest for the six years, and especially the sixth year, would be abundant, therefore, making up for the seventh year.

Regrettably, Israel little observed this command. Therefore, it is believed that the *"seventy years"* of captivity by the Babylonians, were intended to make up for the failure of this observance of the sabbatical year.

This being the case, we must understand that God says what He means, and means what He says! Failure to obey this which He has commanded will guarantee judgment. Obviously, the greed of the people caused them to ignore the sabbatical year, at least more often than not, which, as stated, ultimately brought judgment.

As well, they were to remember the Sabbath, which speaks of the seventh day.

All of this was given for several purposes, but the development of Faith was certainly not the least of one of those purposes. The people were to learn to trust God. To leave the land idle for an entire year seemed to be foolish; but to be sure, God knew exactly what He was doing. The land needed the rest, in order to replenish itself with the proper nutriments, which would guarantee better crops the other six years. Even now, and I speak of the present time, farmers have to add nutriments to the land, or else it simply will not produce. Farming it every single year, without adding those nutriments, would soon wear the land out. So the year of rest was as much for the people as it was for the Lord. The day of rest followed suit.

OTHER GODS

Verse 13 warns Israel that these Laws must not be taken lightly. Israel must be very careful that they understand what is being said, which, as is obvious, seems to be very simple as it regards comprehension. In other words, there should be no excuse.

Also, an Israelite was not to mention the name of the heathen gods, with the Lord adding the emphasis that such should not even come out of the mouth of His people.

Why?

I'm sure the Lord had many reasons; however, I'm afraid that all of us are too prone to talk of the Devil too much, thereby giving him undue recognition.

Every Believer should talk about the Lord, and do so constantly!

(14) "THREE TIMES YOU SHALL KEEP A FEAST UNTO ME IN THE YEAR.

(15) "YOU SHALL KEEP THE FEAST OF UNLEAVENED BREAD: (YOU SHALL EAT UNLEAVENED BREAD SEVEN DAYS, AS I COMMANDED YOU, IN THE TIME APPOINTED OF THE MONTH ABIB; FOR IN IT YOU CAME OUT FROM EGYPT: AND NONE SHALL APPEAR BEFORE ME EMPTY:)

(16) "AND THE FEAST OF HARVEST, THE FIRSTFRUITS OF OUR LABORS, WHICH YOU HAVE SOWN IN THE FIELD: AND THE FEAST OF INGATHERING, WHICH IS IN THE END OF THE YEAR, WHEN YOU HAVE GATHERED IN YOUR LABORS OUT OF THE FIELD.

(17) "THREE TIMES IN THE YEAR ALL THE MALES SHALL APPEAR BEFORE THE LORD GOD.

(18) "YOU SHALL NOT OFFER THE BLOOD OF MY SACRIFICE WITH LEAVENED BREAD; NEITHER SHALL THE FAT OF MY SACRIFICE REMAIN UNTIL THE MORNING.

(19) "THE FIRST OF THE FIRSTFRUITS OF YOUR LAND YOU SHALL BRING INTO THE HOUSE OF THE LORD YOUR GOD. YOU SHALL NOT SEETHE A KID IN HIS MOTHER'S MILK."

The diagram is:

1. Man's corrupt doctrine is never to be added to the fact of Atonement. Hence the importance and sweetness of the expressions *"My Sacrifice"* and *"Feast unto Me."*

2. Heathen Atonement conceives man propitiating an angry God. Biblical Atonement,

the God of Love making a propitiation on behalf of sinful man.

3. The Eighteenth Verse tells us that no interval is to be permitted between the death of the lamb and the eating of its fat. The joys of Salvation are not to be dissevered from their Author and His atoning death. That death is the one and only source of all spiritual blessing (Williams).

PASSOVER, UNLEAVENED BREAD, FIRSTFRUITS

Verses 14 through 17 read: *"Three times you shall keep a feast unto Me in the year.*

"You shall keep the Feast of Unleavened Bread: (you shall eat unleavened bread seven days, as I commanded you, in the time appointed of the month Abib; for in it you came out from Egypt: and none shall appear before Me empty:)

"And the Feast of Harvest, the firstfruits of your labors, which you have sown in the field: and the feast of ingathering, which is in the end of the year, when you have gathered in your labors out of the field.

"Three times in the year all the males shall appear before the LORD God."

All of this is broken down as follows:

There were to be three times a year that Feasts were to be kept. During these three times, seven Feasts were to be observed.

The first gathering was to be during the time of the barley harvest, which was the month of Abib, corresponding with our April. During this seven day period, three Feasts were observed.

1. The Passover: This was perhaps the greatest Feast of all, actually being the first Feast. During this Feast, the Children of Israel were to eat the Passover Lamb, as described in Exodus, Chapter 12. It commemorated the deliverance of the Children of Israel from Egyptian bondage. More particularly, it was a Type of the coming Redeemer, the Lord Jesus Christ, Who would be the Lamb of God, Who would take away the sin of the world by the atoning offering of Himself on the Cross of Calvary (Jn. 1:29).

2. The Feast of Unleavened Bread: This commenced with the Passover, and continued for seven days following, with a *"holy convocation"* on the first of the seven and

NOTES

on the last (Lev. 23:5-8). This Feast typified the sinless Christ, portrayed by the bread containing no leaven. He would live sinless, would die sinless, and would be buried sinless, would be raised from the dead sinless, would ascend sinless, and is seated now at the Right Hand of the Father, ever sinless. Of Him the Scripture says: *"For such an High Priest became us, Who is holy, harmless, undefiled, separate from sinners, and made higher than the heavens"* (Heb. 7:26).

3. Firstfruits: This commemorated two particular things, first of all the Resurrection of Christ, Who in effect was the Firstfruits of the great Resurrection which is yet to come. As well, it spoke of the *"firstfruits of the Spirit,"* which Paul addressed in Romans 8:23. While we now have the Holy Spirit abiding within us (Jn. 14:17), this is only the Firstfruits of that which is to come, which will be fulfilled in the coming Resurrection (I Cor. 15:45-58).

PENTECOST

The word, *"Pentecost"* actually means, *"fifty,"* or *"fiftieth,"* which speaks of 50 days after the Passover, held in our month of May. This was the day, as well, that the Law was given on Mount Sinai — 50 days after the Passover in Egypt. It is the day, as well, on which the Holy Spirit came in a new dimension, signifying that the great Sacrifice had been accepted, and that Christ had been received at the Throne of God. He had said: *"It is expedient for you that I go away: for if I go not away, the Comforter will not come unto you; but if I depart, I will send Him unto you"* (Jn. 16:7). The Scripture says: *"And when the Day of Pentecost was fully come . . ."* (Acts 2:1). This was the day, as stated, that the Holy Spirit came in a completely new dimension, due to the fact that Jesus had paid the price for man's sins at Calvary's Cross.

This was the time of the wheat harvest, and a time of great rejoicing in Israel. It was a Sunday, the first day of the week.

FULLY COME

Exactly what Luke meant in Acts 2:1 by the statement *"fully come,"* we aren't exactly told. The Jewish Sabbath, which was on a Saturday, ended at 6 p.m. Saturday evening, with the beginning of the new day of Sunday commencing at that time. So it could mean that the Holy Spirit came at that particular time, or the words *"fully come,"* could refer to the next morning.

At any rate, after the Sabbath ended, sometime between 6 p.m. and daylight the next morning, Priests would go out into a wheat field, and gather some sheaves, which were referred to as the Firstfruits of the wheat harvest. They would then come back into the Temple with these Firstfruits, when they would then separate the grain from the stalks. They would then make the grain into two loaves of bread, which was made as well of *"flour mingled with oil"* (Num. 28:26-28). The *"flour"* spoke of the purity of Christ, while the *"oil"* spoke of the Holy Spirit Who filled Him (Lk. 4:18-19). The two loaves, I believe, typified Jews and Gentiles (Eph. 2:13-18).

When the two loaves were finished, the Priests would go out and wave these loaves before the Lord, called a *"Wave-Offering."* So it is quite possible that at the very time the Priests were engaged in the Wave-Offering before the Lord, the Holy Spirit began to manifest Himself in a completely new dimension. The recipients, however many there were, began to speak with other tongues, as they were filled with the Spirit (Acts 2:4).

TRUMPETS, ATONEMENT, AND TABERNACLES

The third gathering of the year was to take place in our October, which was the time of the fruit harvest. These three Feasts occupied some 21 days.

On the first day was the *"Feast of Trumpets"* (Num. 29:1; Lev. 23:24). It was the beginning of the civil year. This particular day was also to be *"a day of solemn rest,"* in which *"no laborious work"* was to be done.

Tradition is not quite clear as to what precisely was meant by the trumpet-blowing, which was accompanied by reading relevant Passages of Scripture. Spiritually, it could well type the Rapture of the Church, with Jesus gathering His Own to the accompaniment of the *"Trump of God"* (I Thess. 4:17-18).

Some would object to this, claiming that all of these Feasts were strictly Jewish. While they certainly were Jewish, we also find that each Feast portrayed Christ in some manner, as it regards His Redemptive Work. The Scripture still says that *"God so loved the world . . ."* not just the Jewish people (Jn. 3:16).

The *"Great Day of Atonement"* took place 10 days after the blowing of the trumpets. In fact, it was not a Feast Day, but rather the only *"fast"* day given under the Old Covenant (Lev. 23:26-31; Ex. 30:10).

This was the day that the High Priest went into the Holy of Holies, there to offer up blood on the Mercy Seat for both himself and for Israel. It types Christ in His High Priestly Work, which He in fact has been carrying forth since the Ascension (Heb. 7:25-26). His intercessory work, as would be obvious, is a continuing work, and in fact will ever continue, bringing Israel into its accomplished fact, at the Second Coming (Zech. 13:1, 6; 14:9).

"The Feast of Tabernacles" begins on the fifteenth of the month and continues through the twenty-first. It is also called *"The Feast of Booths,"* or *"The Feast of Ingathering"* (Ex. 23:16; 34:22; Lev. 23:34; Deut. 16:13). As is obvious, it lasted seven days, the first and last days being holy convocations. The people dwelt in booths made of branches and boughs of trees (Lev. 23:39-43; Num. 29:12-38).

It typifies the coming Kingdom Age, when Jesus will rule supremely from Jerusalem, and Israel will, at long last, be at rest.

The *"type"* respecting the last three Feasts has yet to be fulfilled.

All of these Feasts had an agricultural setting, with the first three taking place, as stated, during the barley harvest, the fourth taking place during the time of the wheat harvest, with the last three taking place during the time of the fruit harvest. A representative male from every household was supposed to be at these Feasts, which, no doubt, as well included many of their wives and children.

RELATIONSHIP OF THESE FEASTS TO MODERN CHRISTENDOM

As such, there is no relationship; however, as a symbol, Williams portrays them according to the following:

1. First Feast: Passover, i.e., *"Forgiveness."*
2. Second Feast: Pentecost, i.e., *"Righteousness."*
3. Third Feast: Tabernacles, i.e., *"Glory."*

These three Feasts are fulfilled in Christ. They foreshadowed His Crucifixion, His Resurrection, and His Coronation.

The foundation of all blessing is Grace (Passover), and its completion is Glory (Tabernacles): its maintenance is Power, i.e., *"Pentecost — the Holy Spirit."*

SACRIFICE

Verses 18 and 19 read: *"You shall not offer the blood of My Sacrifice with leavened bread: neither shall the fat of My Sacrifice remain until the morning.*

"The first of the firstfruits of the land you shall bring into the House of the LORD your God. You shall not seethe a kid in his mother's milk."

Verse 18 portrays the fact that man's corrupt doctrine is not to be added to the fact of Atonement. Hence the importance and sweetness of the expressions *"My Sacrifice"* and *"Feasts unto Me."*

If the Church has a besetting sin, this is it. It seeks to take from the Cross, or add to the Cross, which the Sacrifice represents. To do so is looked at by God as *"corruption,"* i.e., *"leaven."* That's why Paul said, and speaking of false doctrine, *"A little leaven leaveneth the whole lump"* (Gal. 5:9). As the Cross is the answer to the sinner, and the only answer, likewise, it is the answer to the Believer. But yet the sinner will not believe what Jesus did there as it regards Salvation, and the Church will not believe what Jesus did there, as it regards Sanctification. Therefore, they ignore the Cross, add to the Cross, or reject the Cross altogether!

The following is a statement regarding the Cross, made by Oswald Chambers. We used it in our Revelation Commentary (Rev. 15:4), but I feel that it would be very proper to use it again in Exodus.

THE COLLISION OF GOD AND SIN

"The Cross of Christ is the revealed truth of God's judgment on sin. Never associate the idea of martyrdom with the Cross of Christ. It was the supreme triumph, and it shook the very foundations of Hell. There is nothing in time or eternity more certain and irrefutable than what Jesus Christ accomplished on the Cross — He made it possible for the entire human race to be brought back into a right-standing relationship with God. He made Redemption the foundation of human life; that is, He made a way for every person to have fellowship with God.

"The Cross was not something that happened to Jesus — He came to die; the Cross was His purpose in coming. He is 'the Lamb slain from the foundation of the world' (Rev. 13:8). The Incarnation of Christ would have no meaning without the Cross. Beware of separating 'God was manifested in the flesh . . .' from '. . . He made Him . . . to be sin for us . . .' (I Tim. 3:16; II Cor. 5:21). The purpose of the Incarnation was Redemption. God came in the flesh to take sin away, not to accomplish something for Himself. The Cross is the central event in time and eternity, and the answer to all the problems of both.

"The Cross is not the cross of a man, but the Cross of God, and it can never be fully comprehended through human experience. The Cross is God exhibiting His nature. It is the gate through which any and every individual can enter into oneness with God. But it is not a gate we pass right through; it is one where we abide in the life that is found there.

"The heart of Salvation is the Cross of Christ. The reason Salvation is so easy to obtain is that it cost God so much. The Cross was the place where God and sinful man merged with a tremendous collision where the way to life was opened. But all the cost and pain of the collision was absorbed by the heart of God."

THE GATE

I want you to notice the statement made, *"But it is not a gate we pass right through; it is one where we abide in the life that is found there."* Unfortunately, much of the Church has, in fact, passed right through this gate, which means they have left the life that is in the Cross, and now they meander and wander aimlessly, as it regards their spiritual experience. Outside of the Cross, there is no life; outside of the Cross, there is no true way; outside of the Cross, there is no channel of blessing. In fact, every single thing that we have from the Lord comes to us totally and completely by and through what Jesus did at the Cross.

It is not that we are trying to put Christ back on the Cross. In fact, Christ is now seated at the Right Hand of the Father, with every Believer, spiritually speaking, seated with Him (Eph. 2:6). It is the benefits of the Cross which we teach and preach. As stated, *"We abide in the life that is found there."* And if we seek to abide by any other manner, or in any other manner, whatever it is in which we are abiding, is not Christ. Jesus said: *"Abide in Me, and I in you. As the branch cannot bear fruit of itself, except it abide in the vine; no more can you, except you abide in Me"* (Jn. 15:4).

We abide in Him by *"eating His flesh and drinking His Blood"* (Jn. 6:53-56).

And we *"eat His flesh, and drink His Blood,"* by exhibiting Faith in what He did at the Cross (Jn. 3:16; Rom. 6:3-5; I Cor. 1:17-18, 21, 23; 2:2; Eph. 2:13-18; Gal. 6:14; Col. 2:14-15).

THE EATING OF THE FAT

Concerning the statement of Verse 18, *"Neither shall the fat of My Sacrifice remain until the morning,"* proclaims the fact that no interval is to be permitted between the death of the Lamb and the eating of its fat. This means that the joys of Salvation are not to be dissevered from their Author and His atoning death. That death is the one and only source of all spiritual blessing (Williams).

The *"fat"* represented the prosperity that is in the Lord. However, that prosperity comes to us through the Cross, and only the Cross, hence the fat being eaten immediately upon the sacrifice of the animal. Of course, it was to be cooked, as would be obvious. But it was to always be connected with the Sacrifice.

I think it should be obvious that the types and foreshadowings of the Old Testament bring out the fact of the Cross, and that everything comes through that great Sacrifice. To not see that is to completely ignore the obvious, and to ignore the obvious is to rebel against God's Way, which in effect is *"the way of Cain"* (Jude, Vs. 11).

FIRST OF THE FIRSTFRUITS AND THE LAMB

The first of the firstfruits could be considered as an Offering to the Lord, which it was, proclaiming thanksgiving, with the understanding that it was the Lord Who had brought about he harvest. He was to ever be given glory, and offering the very first of the harvest, whatever it may have been, portrayed the fact that the individual knew and understood the Blessings of the Lord.

Regrettably, many modern Christians do not really understand the source of their blessings. They think it's their own ability strength, or acumen. Or they give credit to other people.

The truth is, *"Every good gift and every perfect gift is from above, and comes down from the Father of Lights, with Whom is no variableness, neither shadow of turning"* (James 1:17). While the Lord might use other people, or even our own ability, to be sure, He is the One Who charts the course, thereby, making all things possible. Accordingly, we must understand this, and never fail to give Him glory.

The phrase, *"You shall not seethe a kid in his mother's milk,"* is important. In fact, it is repeated three times in the Law of Moses (Ex. 23:19; 34:16; Deut. 14:21).

Commentators are divided as it regards its meaning. Some refer to it as a superstition garnered from surrounding areas, while others saw a prohibition of cruelty.

Because this is the Word of the Lord, it definitely isn't a superstition; as well, while the Lord is definitely opposed to cruelty of any kind, I do not think this was the actual reason for this prohibition.

I personally think this prohibition had to do with the lamb being a symbol or even a Type of the coming Son of God, Who would give Himself for our sins on the Cross of Calvary. In fact, John the Baptist would introduce Him as *"The Lamb of God, which taketh away the sin of the world"* (Jn. 1:29). The little lamb recently born, or the unborn lamb, were definitely a delicacy, and especially if it was baked or boiled, or even roasted in the mother's milk. While lambs certainly were to be eaten, and in fact were a staple as far as meat was concerned, concerning the Jews of that day, preparing a baby lamb in this fashion was evidently held by God as an insult to Christ, of Whom the Lamb represented.

Christ did not die in the womb, and as well, even though Satan tried his hardest, He obviously was not killed as a baby. So it was prohibited that a baby lamb would be used in this fashion.

(20) "BEHOLD, I SEND AN ANGEL BEFORE YOU, TO KEEP YOU IN THE WAY, AND TO BRING YOU INTO THE PLACE WHICH I HAVE PREPARED.

(21) "BEWARE OF HIM, AND OBEY HIS VOICE, PROVOKE HIM NOT; FOR HE WILL NOT PARDON YOUR TRANSGRESSIONS: FOR MY NAME IS IN HIM.

(22) "BUT IF YOU SHALL INDEED OBEY HIS VOICE, AND DO ALL THAT I SPEAK; THEN I WILL BE AN ENEMY UNTO YOUR ENEMIES, AND AN ADVERSARY UNTO YOUR ADVERSARIES.

(23) "FOR MY ANGEL SHALL GO BEFORE YOU, AND BRING YOU IN UNTO THE AMORITES, AND THE HITTITES, AND THE PERIZZITES, AND THE CANAANITES, THE HIVITES, AND THE JEBUSITES: I WILL CUT THEM OFF.

(24) "YOU SHALL NOT BOW DOWN TO THEIR GODS, NOR SERVE THEM, NOR DO AFTER THEIR WORKS: BUT YOU SHALL UTTERLY OVERTHROW THEM, AND QUITE BREAK DOWN THEIR IMAGES.

(25) "AND YOU SHALL SERVE THE LORD YOUR GOD, AND HE SHALL BLESS YOUR BREAD, AND YOUR WATER; AND I WILL TAKE SICKNESS AWAY FROM THE MIDST OF YOU.

(26) "THERE SHALL NOTHING CAST THEIR YOUNG, NOR BE BARREN, IN YOUR LAND: THE NUMBER OF YOUR DAYS I WILL FULFILL."

The construction is:

1. The One Promised: *"He shall keep you,"* embraces all the exceeding great and precious promises, and assures a happy issue to the pilgrim life.

2. The legislation of these Chapters proves how incompetent is the conscience as a monitor and guide to man.

3. Conscience is a moral agent on which the Word of God acts — without that Word, it is likened to a lantern without any fuel in it.

THE ANGEL

Verses 20 through 23 read: *"Behold, I send an Angel before you, to keep you in the way, and to bring you into the place which I have prepared.*

"Beware of Him, and obey His voice, provoke Him not: for He will not pardon your transgressions: for My Name is in Him.

"But if you shall indeed obey His voice, and do all that I speak; then I will be an enemy unto your enemies, and an adversary unto your adversaries.

"For My Angel shall go before you, and bring you in unto the Amorites, and the Hittites, and the Perizzites, and the Canaanites, the Hivites, and the Jebusites: and I will cut them off."

The *"Angel"* mentioned here is the *"Son of God."*

Jewish Commentators claim the Angel to be Moses; however, the expressions *"He will not pardon your transgressions,"* and *"My Name is in Him,"* are too high for Moses, or any man for that matter. No, this is a pre-Incarnate appearance of our Lord, the same One Who died on the Cross for wayward mankind.

"To keep you in the way," means far more than simply being a guide through the wilderness, but rather refers to keeping Israel on the right path of Righteousness and Holiness.

However, Israel, without the help of the Holy Spirit, which speaks to their fallen state, simply could not obey, and obedience was definitely required. It was definitely not that the Lord lacked power, but rather that Israel lacked what it took to do what was demanded.

THE DIFFERENCE NOW IS THE CROSS

Due to the Cross, the Holy Spirit can now abide permanently within the hearts and lives of Believers, in fact, serving as our *"Helper"* in all things, at least all things that pertain to the Will of God (Jn. 14:16-17; Rom. 8:27).

However, there is one requirement of us as it regards the Holy Spirit doing His Work within our hearts and lives. He demands that we exhibit Faith in Christ and the Cross at all times. The Cross being the sphere of His operation, in other words, that which gives Him the legal right to function as He does, He demands our Faith in that Finished Work.

This is proven to us by Paul's statement: *"For the Law of the Spirit of Life in Christ Jesus has made me free from the law of sin and death"* (Rom. 8:2).

The word *"Law"* is used here by the Spirit of God, portraying to us the fact that He will not deviate from this Word, but will obey it to the full, so much in fact, that it is referred to as a *"Law."*

And what is this Law? It is *"The Spirit of Life in Christ Jesus,"* which refers to what He did for us at the Cross. Any time Paul uses the term *"in Christ Jesus,"* or one of its many derivatives, such as *"In Him,"* without exception, he is always speaking of what Christ did at the Cross. It is all in Him and His Sacrificial Work.

IN CHRIST JESUS

Some 170 times in his 14 Epistles, Paul uses the term *"in Christ,"* etc. Knowing that the Holy Spirit instructed him even to the very words that he used, we certainly should understand that the Spirit had a reason for this short phrase being used with such frequency.

Everything is *"in Christ."* This means that the entirety of our Salvation, which includes our Sanctification, is entirely in Him. What He did was done entirely by Himself, and accomplished as He was reduced to the far lower level of man. While He never ceased to be God, He definitely did lay aside His expression of Deity, while not losing its possession. He had only the Holy Spirit to help Him (Lk. 4:18-19).

In this capacity, He defeated Satan, every fallen angel, and every demon spirit.

HOW DID JESUS DEFEAT THE ENEMY OF OUR SOULS?

He did it by the giving of Himself on the Cross.

However, we must understand the type of victory that He actually won, which was all for us. In the first place, defeating Satan and all his cohorts, as we think of such, was no problem whatsoever. All the Lord had to do was simply speak the Word, and whatever it is that He desired would instantly be done. So the question was not really one of victory or defeat, for that was a settled fact. There was no question of Christ being victorious in any capacity.

However, the type of victory that Christ purchased for us was and is beyond our total comprehension. Due to the Fall, Satan had a legal right to hold sinful man in bondage. Sinful disobedience gave him that right!

This terrible crime could not be addressed by mere fiat. The Righteousness of God demanded that payment be made. And the payment was so high that man could not hope to satisfy the debt.

The Righteousness of God demanded payment, and the Love of God decreed that the payment be made by God paying it Himself. And how would He do that?

THE PAYMENT

God would have to become man, be born under the Law, and keep it in every respect (Gal. 4:4-5). He came down here to redeem us, which Redemption price was His very Life.

When He died on the Cross, actually being *"made sin, that we might be made the Righteousness of God in Him,"* the sin debt, past, present, and future was fully paid. This took away Satan's legal right to hold man in captivity. Consequently, Paul wrote:

"Blotting out the handwriting of Ordinances that was against us, which was contrary to us, and took it out of the way, nailing it to His Cross." This spoke of Him satisfying the Law, which condemned us.

"And having spoiled principalities and powers, He made a show of them openly, triumphing over them in it" (Col. 2:14-15).

In fact, Jesus never lifted a hand against Satan, any demon spirit, or any fallen angel. There was no mortal combat. He defeated him, and did so completely, by satisfying the claims of Heavenly Justice, which robbed the Evil One of his legal claim upon man. Consequently, he now has no legal claim on humanity, and if in fact, he now holds man captive, it is by consent of the governed. And what do we mean by that?

It means simply that if we will trust Christ

and what Christ has done for us at the Cross, Satan has no claim on us whatsoever. And if he does lay hold to us, it's because our trust and Faith are in something else instead of the Cross, which in effect, gives him consent to place us in bondage. That's why Paul said:

"Stand fast therefore in the liberty wherewith Christ has made you free, and be not entangled again with the yoke of bondage" (Gal. 5:1).

He then said, *"If you be circumcised, Christ shall profit you nothing"* (Gal. 5:2).

This means that if the Galatians, or any other Believer, even at the present, places one's Faith in anything other than the Cross, all that Christ did on the Cross will *"profit you nothing."* Now that's a startling statement!

ONE CANNOT HAVE IT BOTH WAYS . . .

One cannot place one's Faith in Christ and the Cross, and Christ and the Law, or works, at the same time. The Cross ever demands that the Believer makes a clean break with the flesh, i.e., *"works."*

So if the Believer claims to make the Cross the object of his Faith, but at the same time, feels that a certain Church or Denomination is a part of that Faith, or his own good works, he has just nullified the Faith that he has in the Cross. The Holy Spirit cannot allow such, because it constitutes *"spiritual adultery,"* i.e., *"unfaithfulness to Christ."*

As we've already stated several times, Paul, in the first four Verses of Romans, Chapter 7, tells us that we are married to Christ; consequently, He has all that we need, and in whatever specifics or capacity. We are to look solely to Him, which means to look to what He did for us at the Cross, and that exclusively. If we place our Faith in other things, and irrespective as to what those other things might be, or how good they might be in their own right, we are being unfaithful to Christ, which constitutes *"spiritual adultery,"* with which the Holy Spirit can have no part, as should be obvious!

Faith in every single thing other than the Cross must go. That doesn't mean that you cannot love your Church or the Denomination in question. It certainly doesn't mean that we are to stop the disciplines of our life, such as Bible study, prayer, etc. However, those things are now the *"result"* of our Faith, and never the *"cause"* of our Faith.

Faith in two or more things creates a double-mindedness, which makes one *"unstable in all his ways"* (James 1:6-8).

WHY DO WE TEACH SO MUCH ON THE CROSS?

We do so simply because the Lord has instructed us to do so; however, the reasons are obvious.

This is what Satan fights the most. He does all within his power to hinder our understanding of the Cross, because he knows that our Faith exclusively in Christ and the Cross is the key to all victory.

As we study Paul's Epistles, for Paul is the one to whom the Message of the Cross was given, which is the explanation of the New Covenant, we find that proper Faith in the Cross, and continued Faith in the Cross, was the greatest problem in the Early Church.

The major reason is man himself. Due to the Fall, the problem of so-called self-sufficiency hangs over the human race like a funeral shroud. This is true about Believers as well. In fact, one of the greatest problems that the Believer has after coming to Christ is that he thinks that because he is now a Christian, which means that he is a new creature in Christ Jesus, and the Holy Spirit now lives within him, he can do all type of things. In fact, one of the most oft quoted Scriptures is: *"I can do all things through Christ which strengtheneth me"* (Phil. 4:13).

Most of the time, this particular Passage is pulled completely out of context. Paul is actually saying, *"If I have to go hungry for Christ, I can do that; if I have to suffer need for Christ, I can do that; if I am to abound in Christ, I can do that as well!"* But we too often invert this Passage, making it mean what Paul never intended.

The truth is, we cannot live for God, at least do so properly, we cannot be victorious, we cannot overcome the powers of darkness, we cannot live the life of an overcomer, unless we place our Faith exclusively in Christ and not at all in ourselves, trusting completely in what He did for us in His great Sacrifice. That's why Paul said: *"We preach Christ Crucified"* (I Cor. 1:23).

TRANSGRESSIONS

Concerning the Angel described here, Who incidentally is Christ, which we will prove from the Word of God momentarily, Moses said of Him, *"Beware of Him, and obey His voice, provoke Him not; for He will not pardon your transgressions."*

What did Moses mean by these statements?

We know that this is Christ in a pre-Incarnate appearance, because the Scripture says of Him: *"For My Name is in Him."*

The Jews spoke of this Angel under a name, Metatron, which they have devised. They identify Him with the Messiah, and lightly ascribe to Him all the characteristics of the Divine Nature. They represent Him as performing the functions of a Mediator, saying that by Him Alone we have access to God. Some of their notions respecting Him are evidently derived from the prophecy of Isaiah 9:6, and they represent Him as making expiation for sin when in the wilderness, in a Tabernacle distinct from the Levitical Tabernacle — by the terms they use evidently pointing out the human body, in which the Angel of the presence was wont to appear, and in which He was at length to be born as an infant.

Concerning all of this, Matthew Henry stated: *"The views of the Jewish doctors are so remarkably clear on this point, that while we admire the good providence of God in having so amply prepared for the reception of the Messiah by the predictions and phraseology of the Old Testament, which were the only sources from which the Rabbins could derive their knowledge, we cannot but wonder at the blindness of the chosen people, in not perceiving that Christ is the end of the Law for Righteousness to everyone who believes."*

Henry went on to say, *"Christ is the Angel of Jehovah; this is explicitly taught by Paul. Speaking of the Israelites in the wilderness, he says, 'Neither let us tempt Christ, as some of them also tempted, and were destroyed of serpents' (I Cor. 10:9)."*

HE WILL NOT PARDON YOUR TRANSGRESSIONS?

What did Moses mean by that statement?

He meant that the Angel, i.e., *"the Lord,"* would not overlook their transgressions. God cannot condone sin in any capacity, and this we must ever understand. He could not condone it then, and He cannot condone it now. Sin will wreck the individual, as it has wrecked billions. It is the destroyer of all that is good. It is the opposite of God, Who is total Righteousness.

In fact, the very generation to whom Moses spoke these words perished in the wilderness because they functioned in an arena of unbelief. Paul addressed this very thing in the Fourth and Fifth Chapters of Hebrews. In fact, even after possessing the land of Canaan, Israel was finally led away into captivity by the Babylonians because of sin. Ultimately because of continued sin, this time the greatest sin of all, the rejection of Jesus Christ, the Lord allowed Rome to completely destroy the nation of Israel, with the Jews being scattered all over the world, where they wandered as vagabonds for nearly 2,000 years. All of this because of sin!

Let not the Church think that it fares much better, if any better at all! Unbelief is presently rampant in the modern Church. False doctrine abounds!

THE ONLY ANSWER FOR SIN IS THE CROSS

If I bore you with my continued expression of the Cross, then that's a sure sign that you do not know or understand what the Cross is all about. It means you do not properly understand yourself, and you certainly do not understand the Lord.

Man has ever tried to present another answer for sin, and man has ever failed. He has put forth his own efforts in every capacity, first labeling this and then labeling that, but always without success. Unfortunately, the Church does little better!

The only answer for sin is the Cross of Christ. The only way that God can look at poor, fallen, sin-benighted humanity is by and through Jesus Christ, and more particularly, through what Jesus did at the Cross. Man has no other access to God, no other way to approach God. It is by the Cross, or it is not at all!

And as the sinner comes to God through Christ and the Cross, likewise, the Believer remains in Christ by and through the Cross, and no other means or ways. As Chambers said, *"The Cross is the central event in time and eternity, and the answer to all the problems of both."* He also said, and that which we gave you some pages back: *"It is the gate through which any and every individual can enter into oneness with God. But it is not a gate we pass right through; it is one where we abide in the life that is found there."*

In the past several decades, the Church has been pushed from the Cross by Satan using several means. He has used humanistic psychology, and he has used the Word of Faith doctrine, which is perhaps the most lethal of all.

Both of these erroneous directions deny that the Cross is the answer for sin. The first claims that man holds the answer, and the second claims the same thing, but in another way. The Word of Faith doctrine, which has erroneously affected the Church, perhaps more than any other error, and I'm going all the way back to the days of the Early Church, and due to modern mass communication, basically ignores sin. In essence, it claims that man's *"Faith level"* is his greatest problem. They claim the way to overcome sin is to ignore it. If sin is mentioned or preached about, they say, it will create a sin consciousness in the person, which will cause them to sin. So the way not to sin is just simply not mention it, which, of course, is ridiculous!

It's somewhat like saying that a rattlesnake won't bite you if you ignore him, irrespective of the fact that he's in your house. I'm afraid that won't work!

No, sin is the problem for the unbeliever, and sin is the problem for the Believer! That's why the Holy Spirit through Paul went to such pains to explain to Believers how to have victory over sin (Rom., Chpts. 6-8; Gal., Chpt. 5).

If the modern Believer thinks that just because he is now a Believer and, therefore, a new creation, God will overlook sin in his life, he could not be more wrong. God cannot overlook sin anywhere, and again, the only answer for sin is the Cross of Christ.

AN ENEMY TO YOUR ADVERSARIES

Verse 22 says that if Israel would obey the Lord, and do all that He spoke to them, He would be *"An enemy unto their enemies, and an adversary unto their adversaries."* That holds true for us presently as well!

We're speaking here of the mightiest force in Heaven or on Earth. We're speaking of Almighty Power, which speaks of power without limitations. In other words, there is nothing that God cannot do.

But yet for us to have the availability of this power, we must obey Him. So this means that obedience is the key; however, the great question is, how do we obey?

That question not only loomed large for Israel, but it looms large in the vocabulary of modern Christendom as well. What God demanded of Israel, He certainly demands no less of us, and in fact, He demands even more.

Pulling all of this to modern times, many Christians think they can obey simply because they are now a Christian.

I had a dear Brother to tell me not long ago, *"Before I gave my heart to the Lord, I couldn't say 'no' to sin. But now that I'm a Believer, I can say 'no!'"*

He couldn't be more wrong, at least in the manner in which he was thinking.

It is definitely demanded of us that we obey the Lord, which refers to obeying His Word. That's a settled fact. But it's the manner in which we attempt to obey that desperately needs to be addressed.

HOW TO OBEY THE LORD

You must understand that even though you are now a Believer, within your own strength and ability, despite the fact that you are now a Believer, you cannot obey the Lord.

But of course, the instant retort to that is, *"I'm not doing this through my own strength; the Lord is helping me."*

But the truth is, most Christians are attempting to live for God, which means to obey Him, from the position of their own strength. They do not think of it in those terms, but that's exactly what is happening, and that's the reason for so much failure.

The truth is, we are equipped with everything we need to live a victorious life. The Divine Nature now resides within us (II Pet. 1:4). Also, the Holy Spirit abides within us, and does so on a permanent basis

(Jn. 14:16-17). But to activate all of this, one thing is required, and that is Faith; however, the type of Faith of which we speak is that which is anchored firmly in Christ and what He has done for us at the Cross.

In other words, Jesus has to live this life through you. Paul said: *"I am crucified with Christ* (Rom. 6:3-5)*: nevertheless I live; yet not I, but Christ lives in me: and the life which I now live in the flesh I live by the Faith of the Son of God, Who loved me, and gave Himself for me"* (Gal. 2:20).

Paul told us in this Passage that the way we obey God, which means to properly live for Him, is to do so *"by the Faith of the Son of God, Who loved me, and gave Himself for me."* This speaks entirely of what Jesus did at the Cross. It is actually referred to as *"the Faith."*

This means that our Faith must be exclusively in Christ and His Finished Work. With this accomplished, and our Faith remaining in the Finished Work of Christ, the Holy Spirit will then use His Almighty Power on our behalf, and it will be possible to obey God in every respect, and possible only through that means (Rom. 8:2, 11).

One can only *"mortify the deeds of the body, through the Spirit"* (Rom. 8:13). The Holy Spirit works exclusively within *"The Law of the Spirit of Life in Christ Jesus"* (Rom. 8:2). This refers to what Jesus did at the Cross, which means that these are the parameters within which the Holy Spirit works. You are to ever exhibit Faith in Christ and His Sacrifice. That will guarantee you the help of the Spirit, which will guarantee victory, which means that you will then be able to obey God. If you try to obey the Lord by any other method, no matter how good it may seem to be on the surface, you will ingloriously fail! If your Faith is properly placed, and that is the key, then you will gloriously succeed.

"Then the Lord will be an enemy unto your enemies, and an adversary unto your adversaries." This speaks of natural adversaries and supernatural adversaries. It speaks of men and demons.

VICTORY

In Verse 23, it tells us that the Lord would give Israel victory over the *"Amorites, Hittites, Perizzites, Canaanites, Hivites, and Jebusites."* He said, *"I will cut them off."* And that He did!

As we come to the Book of Joshua, which catalogs the history of Israel's victories in the land of Canaan, and their taking that country according to the Promises of God, we find that under Joshua, all of these enemies were defeated, exactly as the Lord said they would be defeated.

Sometimes we modern Christians put ourselves in the position of attempting to overcome spiritual Jebusites, Canaanites, etc. That is correct, but only if we understand it correctly.

At the Cross of Calvary, the Lord defeated every enemy, and that includes Satan, all fallen angels, and all demon spirits (Col. 2:14-15). Now perhaps some Christians may wonder that if the Lord has totally defeated these enemies, then why are they giving us so much trouble?

Let us understand that we're not speaking of outward opposition, but rather of inward opposition, and I'm referring to victory over the world, the flesh, and the Devil.

While the Lord has definitely defeated all of these enemies, and has done so completely, He has allowed them to remain active to a certain degree, and even to oppose us. I speak of lust, jealousy, envy, malice, in fact, all *"lusts of the flesh."* Paul said of this:

"Walk in the Spirit, and you shall not fulfill the lusts of the flesh.

"For the flesh lusteth against the Spirit (Holy Spirit), *and the Spirit against the flesh: and these are contrary the one to the other: so that you cannot do the things that you would"* (Gal. 5:16-17).

Of course, *"lusts of the flesh,"* if not handled properly, will lead to *"works of the flesh"* (Gal. 5:19-21).

For one to claim that there is no such thing as *"lusts of the flesh"* in the life of the Believer is obviously not correctly reading the Text. This is a problem that the Believer will have with him until the Trump sounds, or he dies.

The way to victory, and the only way to victory, is through the Holy Spirit. However, as we've been saying over and over, the manner in which the Believer can have the help of the Holy Spirit, Who Alone can overcome these *"lusts,"* is by the Believer evidencing Faith in the Cross of Christ. That's why Paul also said:

"But God forbid that I should glory, save in the Cross of our Lord Jesus Christ, by Whom the world is crucified unto me, and I unto the world" (Gal. 6:14). So once again, as we do every time, we come back to the Cross.

While these forces are allowed to be arrayed against us, we can have total victory, that is if we will function according to Christ and His Finished Work. But if you try to fight these things in the wrong way, you will be in essence saying that what Jesus did at the Cross was not enough, and now needs your help. I trust that one can see how this is an insult to Christ.

No, Christ doesn't need any help. But the truth is, we need a lot of help, and that help comes to us exclusively through Christ, and His great Sacrifice.

THE PROMISES OF GOD

Verses 24 through 26 read: *"You shall not bow down to their gods, nor serve them, nor do after their works: but you shall utterly overthrow them, and quite break down their images.*

"And you shall serve the LORD your God, and He shall bless your bread, and your water; and I will take sickness away from the midst of you.

"There shall nothing cast their young, nor be barren, in your land: the number of your days I will fulfill."

The Twenty-fourth Verse proclaims undeniably, even dogmatically, that the *"gods"* of the heathen were not to be yielded to in any manner. Of course, Israel was not to serve them in any manner, but even above that, they were to *"utterly overthrow them,"* even to the extent of breaking them into pieces.

If one knows the history, even in part, as it regards these so-called heathen deities, one would then understand the reason for the anger of God against these *"works of darkness."*

Two factors were involved in that type of worship:

1. The first consisted of gross immorality, both homosexual and heterosexual, and in the basest way. Men and women prostituted themselves to these temples, with every type of immorality carried out, all meant to glorify these *"gods."*

2. Then there was the matter of *"human sacrifices,"* which were so awful as to be beyond contemplation.

These idols were nothing; however, the demon spirits behind them are what promoted all of these abominable practices. Of course the people being used little understood the demon activity, and if they did, they thought to appease the demons by engaging in these shameful acts.

IDOLS

Sometime back, while conducting a Crusade in a Central American country, a couple of days before the Meetings were to begin, we went to a particular place in that country, which had once been a thriving city, but where now there was nothing left but ruins. Beautiful pyramids and temples had been built, all of this done approximately 1,000 or more years ago, with no idea held by the Archeologists as to what happened to that particular civilization. It has been ventured that quite possibly, these people literally sacrificed themselves to death.

We saw the Temple where it is believed that human sacrifices were carried out. And to appease these so-called *"gods,"* it is believed that not only did this particular civilization sacrifice so many of their young men and young ladies that the race was ultimately decimated, but other civilizations did the same thing. Jesus said of Satan, *"The thief cometh not, but for to steal, to kill, and to destroy"* (Jn. 10:10).

CHRISTIANITY

Christianity has brought the world a greater degree of light, despite the fact that the greater majority of the world still lives in unbelief. As such, most, but not all, idol worship, as we think of such, has been cast aside. But yet, John the Beloved said: *"Little children, keep yourselves from idols"* (I Jn. 5:21).

Why would he have made such a statement, considering that he was speaking to Believers?

An *"idol"* is anything that comes between the person and God. It may not be a material figure such as the heathen of old worshiped, but nevertheless, in the mind of God, if anything is placed before Him, it is constituted as an *"idol."*

Unfortunately, I think one can say without fear of exaggeration that the greatest idol of all is *"religion."* The Catholic Church, for instance, worships idols constantly, whether of the Virgin Mary, or so-called Saints! While the Protestant world is not so blatant, the truth is, many Protestants worship their particular Church or Denomination, actually placing it on the same level as Christ, or even above Christ. And how do they do that?

When we as Believers begin to think that our Salvation or victory have to do with us belonging to a certain Church or Denomination, we have just made an idol out of that particular Church, etc. It's certainly not wrong for one to love their Church, but one must understand that the Church, and we speak of the True Church, is an outgrowth of what Christ has done for us, and certainly not the cause of what we have in Christ. The Believer must look to Christ Alone, which means to look to what He did at the Cross on our behalf.

PROMISES

Verses 25 and 26 portray the Promises of God to Israel, providing they rendered obedience in that which He demanded. And let it ever be understood, what God demands of us is always for our good, and it's never difficult. Jesus said: *"Take My yoke upon you, and learn of Me; for I am meek and lowly in heart: and you shall find rest unto your souls.*

"For My yoke is easy, and My burden is light" (Mat. 11:29-30). The following is what He said He would do:

1. He would provide food for Israel, meaning that He would bless their crops, etc.

2. He would see to it that they always had an abundant supply of water. Water is not as plentiful in the Middle East as it is in other parts of the world.

3. He would take sickness away from their people.

4. The women would be fruitful in bringing forth children.

5. They would live to a ripe, old age.

Now all of this must be understood in the capacity of individuality as well as a national policy. While the Lord will definitely do exactly what He has said, any particular individuals, of which there always will be some, who do not render obedience, will not be a beneficiary of these Promises.

And then there are times when it seems as though the individual has rendered obedience to the Lord, when in fact they have, but they still suffer situations which seem to be the opposite of the Promises of God. The point I'm trying to make is this:

The manner of God's dealings with people must always be judged on the basis of God's sovereignty. By that we mean that at times, even though a person has rendered excellent obedience, and has evidenced Faith as they should, even then, at times, sickness invades that person, or even their life might be cut short. That being the case, which it often is, we have to understand that God does such because He knows that it will be good for the individual in the long run.

You must understand that God sees the picture from beginning to end, and everything in between. He knows all things, and acts accordingly.

The Believer must always allow God to be Sovereign. We must ever realize that He knows best for us. To be sure, as Believers, we must oppose every negative thing that comes our way. I'm sure that Paul did not want to spend time in prison. And I'm sure he asked the Lord repeatedly to ameliorate the situation; however, at the same time, the Apostle acquiesced to the Lord, that whatever the Lord wanted, that's what he as well wanted. This must be our attitude also.

The idea of us reaching a particular Faith level, which will abrogate all problems, is not taught in the Word of God. But to be sure, we can eliminate many of these problems, and all of us can experience the great Blessings of God. But we must never forget that the Lord is dealing with us individually, and that He knows us, and works with us accordingly. This means that at times, He will allow negative things, but it is only to strengthen our Faith.

(27) "I WILL SEND MY FEAR BEFORE YOU, AND WILL DESTROY ALL THE PEOPLE TO WHOM YOU SHALL COME, AND I WILL MAKE ALL YOUR ENEMIES TURN THEIR BACKS UNTO YOU.

(28) "AND I WILL SEND HORNETS BEFORE YOU, WHICH SHALL DRIVE OUT THE HIVITE, THE CANAANITE, AND THE HITITE, FROM BEFORE YOU.

(29) "I WILL NOT DRIVE THEM OUT FROM BEFORE YOU IN ONE YEAR; LEST THE LAND BECOME DESOLATE, AND THE BEAST OF THE FIELD MULTIPLY AGAINST YOU.

(30) "BY LITTLE AND LITTLE I WILL DRIVE THEM OUT FROM BEFORE YOU, UNTIL YOU BE INCREASED, AND INHERIT THE LAND.

(31) "AND I WILL SET YOUR BOUNDS FROM THE RED SEA EVEN UNTO THE SEA OF THE PHILISTINES, AND FROM THE DESERT UNTO THE RIVER: AND I WILL DELIVER THE INHABITANTS OF THE LAND INTO YOUR HAND; AND YOU SHALL DRIVE THEM OUT BEFORE YOU.

(32) "YOU SHALL MAKE NO COVENANT WITH THEM, NOR WITH THEIR GODS.

(33) "THEY SHALL NOT DWELL IN YOUR LAND, LEST THEY MAKE YOU SIN AGAINST ME: FOR IF YOU SERVE THEIR GODS, IT WILL SURELY BE A SNARE UNTO YOU."

The overview is:
1. Proper obedience causes the Lord to send His fear into the hearts of all adversaries.
2. We are living as Believers in a fallen world. It is ruled by the prince of darkness; consequently, the Lord sets boundaries as it regards His Children, with guaranteed victories within those boundaries, that is, if we properly follow the Lord.
3. God gives great Promises, as is obvious here; however, each and every one of these Promises, which again should be obvious, is conditional.

THE FEAR OF THE LORD

Verse 27 reads: *"I will send My fear before you, and will destroy all the people to whom you shall come, and I will make all your enemies turn their backs unto you."*

Pulpit says: *"Had their obedience been more complete, the power of the Canaanitish nations would have been more thoroughly broken, and the sufferings and servitudes related in the Book of Judges would not have had to be endured."*

Obedience can be rendered, but it can be rendered only in the capacity of the Believer understanding the Cross of Christ, and what it all means. The problem is, even as we have said repeatedly, most Christians understand the Cross as it regards Salvation, but little or none at all as it regards Sanctification. That being the case, despite how hard they may try otherwise, that particular Christian cannot walk in victory. But if the Believer renders proper obedience, and does so by the means of the Finished Work of Christ, which then guarantees the help of the Holy Spirit, I believe this Promise given to Israel so long ago will certainly extend to modern Believers. The Lord will place His fear in the hearts of our adversaries. That doesn't mean that all problems will be curtailed, but it definitely does mean that most will be handled before they even begin.

THE MEANS OF GOD

Verse 28 reads: *"And I will send hornets before you, which shall drive out the Hivite, the Canaanite, and the Hittite, from before you."*

Man is very limited as to what he can do; however, God is unlimited, having everything, all of His creation at His disposal. He uses the elements to carry out His Will, and as stated here, He also uses even such a lowly thing as the *"hornet."*

Even though we aren't given the actual account, the Lord said through Joshua, *"And I sent the hornet before you, which drove them out from before you, even the two kings of the Amorites; but not with your sword, nor with your bow"* (Josh. 24:12).

In other words, the army of Israel under Joshua, did not have to use their weaponry against the two kings of the Amorites because the Lord dispatched them by sending swarms of hornets.

Of course, this took a miracle for such to be brought to pass:
1. The Lord had to gather enough hornets together in order for such an expedition

to be carried out.

2. He had to guide the hornets as it regarded what they were to do.

While such, of course, is impossible with man, it is a very simple thing for the Creator to have His creatures do whatever He desires.

The point is, the Lord can do anything, and do it by any means which He so desires. He is not dependent on anything or anyone. The only thing that can limit Him is unbelief on our part. In fact, He told Israel, *"Yes, they* (the Israelites) *turned back and tempted God, and limited the Holy One of Israel"* (Ps. 78:41).

However, when it comes to *"Faith,"* we must make certain that what is being evidenced is actually Faith, and not presumption! Many are presently told that if they can get their *"Faith level"* high enough, they can get anything, and the *"anything"* is almost always centered up in *"things."* In other words, Righteousness, Holiness, and Christlikeness are little desired. In the first place, that's not Faith, but rather presumption. As well, God doesn't lead us according to so-called *"Faith levels."* That which is all-important is that we make certain that the *"object"* of our Faith is correct. That object must ever be the Cross.

The idea that the Lord will withhold things from us, simply because our *"Faith level"* is not high enough is ridiculous! However, this is not a new problem:

PROPER FAITH

The Apostles of the Lord said to Him once, *"Increase our Faith"* (Lk. 5:17).

Jesus answered them in effect by saying that it was not the quantity of Faith that counted, but rather the quality of Faith. He said:

"If you have Faith as a grain of mustard seed (one of the smallest seeds)*, you might say unto this sycamore tree, Be thou plucked up by the root, and be thou planted in the sea; and it should obey you"* (Lk. 17:6).

As is obvious, Jesus was speaking of quality Faith. So what is quality Faith?

It is Faith that is held in the correct object, i.e., *"the Cross."* The Believer must always understand that everything he receives from the Lord, and irrespective as to what it is, comes to him totally and completely through what Christ did at the Cross. In other words, the Believer never leaves the benefits of the Cross. In fact, there are no benefits outside of the Cross. That's why Paul said:

"For Christ sent me not to baptize, but to preach the Gospel: not with wisdom of words, lest the Cross of Christ should be made of none effect" (I Cor. 1:17).

Everyone in the world has Faith, but it's not the type of Faith that God will recognize. So the question actually isn't Faith, but rather the correct object of Faith, which always must be the Cross. Then, if it's the Will of the Lord, we can move mountains or trees, whichever might be the case.

REASONS

Verses 29 and 30 read: *"I will not drive them out from before you in one year; lest the land become desolate, and the beast of the field multiply against you.*

"By little and little I will drive them out from before you, until you be increased, and inherit the land."

In these two Verses, we find the reason for which the Lord does things.

He could easily have driven all the enemies of Israel out of the land of Canaan, and done so immediately. However, He didn't do that, simply because of the reasons stated.

We must commit our way unto the Lord, trust also in Him, and He will bring it to pass. But He will do it all in His good time, and in His Way. As already stated, we must learn to acquiesce to that time and that way.

He explained here as to why He would help Israel in this particular manner. But oftentimes He doesn't explain. He just simply tells us to trust Him. As someone has well said, *"I don't know what is in the future, but I know Who holds the future,"* or *"I don't know what tomorrow holds, but I know Who holds tomorrow."*

THE BOUNDS

Verse 31 reads: *"And I will set your bounds from the Red Sea even unto the Sea of the Philistines, and from the desert unto the River: for I will deliver the inhabitants of the land into your hand; and you shall drive them out before you."*

We have here the boundaries given to us by the Holy Spirit, as it regards the land area promised to Israel. It was realized only under David, who of course, was a Type of Christ.

The Red Sea marks the southern boundary promised to Israel, which takes in all of the Sinai, the exact area occupied by Israel some years back, when they defeated the Egyptians, but given back to Egypt in the Camp David Accords.

The *"Sea of the Philistines"* marked the western boundary, which of course is the Mediterranean Sea.

The *"desert"* marks the eastern boundary, which probably included some of modern day Saudi Arabia.

The *"river"* in the Pentateuch is always the *"Euphrates,"* which marked the northern boundary. So we can see from all of this that Israel was promised much more than what they actually attained, except under David.

The Lord, even as He did with Israel, has staked out boundaries for every Believer. Of course, we're speaking of spiritual boundaries. Exactly as Israel could have had all of this promised to them, even as they did under David, we as well can have all that the Lord has promised us. And to be sure, He has promised much. Our problem is, we fall far short of what we can have in Christ.

THE CROSS

Unless the Believer properly understands the Cross, even as we've already repeatedly stated, it is not possible for the Believer to properly grow in Grace and the knowledge of the Lord. While the Believer will certainly make Heaven, that is, if he maintains his Faith, the truth is, without a proper understanding of the Finished Work of Christ, it is impossible for the Believer to live a victorious life.

Please bear with my repetition; however, this is so important that I must take every opportunity to express the great truth of the Cross.

The Believer must understand that everything he is in the Lord, everything he wants to do, everything he hopes to do, and everything he can do, are all found exclusively in what Christ did at the Cross. In other words, it is not possible for the Believer to go beyond the benefits of the Cross, simply because there are no other benefits because there is no need for anything other than the Cross.

FAITH

Understanding that the Cross is the means by which everything comes to us from the Lord, our Faith must be ever anchored in the great Sacrifice of Christ. Again, as we've already stated, this is of vital significance. The object of our Faith must ever be the Cross, and in fact, that's what the Lord demands (I Cor. 1:17-18, 21, 23; 2:2, 5; Eph. 2:13-18; Gal. 6:14; Col. 2:14-15).

The Devil will fight the Believer harder here than any other place. He will do everything within his power to cause us to shift our Faith from the Cross to other things. And it doesn't matter what those other things might be, or how good they may be, or even Scriptural in their own right; if it's not the Cross, Satan knows that there is no help forthcoming from any other place. In fact, to do such a thing, and I speak of shifting our Faith from the Cross to other things, constitutes one living in *"spiritual adultery"* (Rom. 7:1-4).

THE HOLY SPIRIT

Once again, as we have already addressed, and even several times, the Holy Spirit works within the boundaries of the Finished Work of Christ. These parameters give Him the legal means to do the things He does in our hearts and lives. In other words, unless one's Faith is properly placed, and I speak of Faith in the Cross, the Holy Spirit is very limited in what He can do for us. For one to have their Faith properly placed guarantees His work, which guarantees victory (Rom. 8:1-2, 11, 13).

THE SNARE

Verses 32 and 33 read: *"You shall make no covenant with them, nor with their gods.*

"They shall not dwell in your land, lest they make you sin against Me: for if you serve their gods, it will surely be a snare unto you."

Every enemy must be rooted out of the land, just as every enemy must be rooted out of our own lives. Total trust in the Lord was and is the only way this can be done. Anything we leave in our lives that is a reproach to the Lord, bringing it all up to the present, will ultimately be a *"snare unto us."* Everything that is un-Christlike must be rooted out!

Once again, the only way this can be done is by proper Faith in the Cross.

"Must Jesus bear the Cross alone,
"And all the world go free?
"No; there's a Cross for everyone,
"And there is a Cross for me."

"The consecrated Cross I'll bear,
"Till death shall set me free,
"And then go home my crown to wear,
"For there's a crown for me."

"Upon the crystal pavement,
"Down at Jesus' pierced feet,
"Joyful, I'll cast my golden crown,
"And His dear Name repeat."

"O precious Cross! O glorious crown!
"O Resurrection day!
"Ye Angels, from the stars come down,
"And bear my soul away."

CHAPTER 24

(1) "AND HE SAID UNTO MOSES, COME UP UNTO THE LORD, YOU AND AARON, NADAB AND ABIHU, AND SEVENTY OF THE ELDERS OF ISRAEL: AND WORSHIP YE AFAR OFF.

(2) "AND MOSES ALONE SHALL COME NEAR THE LORD: BUT THEY SHALL NOT COME NEAR; NEITHER SHALL THE PEOPLE GO UP WITH THEM.

(3) "AND MOSES CAME AND TOLD THE PEOPLE ALL THE WORDS OF THE LORD, AND ALL THE JUDGMENTS: AND ALL THE PEOPLE ANSWERED WITH ONE VOICE, AND SAID, ALL THE WORDS WHICH THE LORD HAD SAID WILL WE DO.

(4) "AND MOSES WROTE ALL THE WORDS OF THE LORD, AND ROSE UP EARLY IN THE MORNING, AND BUILT AN ALTAR UNDER THE HILL, AND TWELVE PILLARS, ACCORDING TO THE TWELVE TRIBES OF ISRAEL.

NOTES

(5) "AND HE SENT YOUNG MEN OF THE CHILDREN OF ISRAEL, WHICH OFFERED BURNT OFFERINGS, AND SACRIFICED PEACE OFFERINGS OF OXEN UNTO THE LORD.

(6) "AND MOSES TOOK HALF OF THE BLOOD, PUT IT IN BASINS; AND HALF OF THE BLOOD HE SPRINKLED ON THE ALTAR.

(7) "AND HE TOOK THE BOOK OF THE COVENANT, AND READ IN THE AUDIENCE OF THE PEOPLE: AND THEY SAID, ALL THAT THE LORD HAS SAID WILL WE DO, AND BE OBEDIENT.

(8) "AND MOSES TOOK THE BLOOD, AND SPRINKLED IT ON THE PEOPLE, AND SAID, BEHOLD THE BLOOD OF THE COVENANT, WHICH THE LORD HAS MADE WITH YOU CONCERNING ALL THESE WORDS."

The exegesis is:

1. The short phrase *"afar off,"* proclaims the best that the Law can do.

2. One can search out the Law, and not be able to find the two words, *"Draw nigh."*

3. The Blood of Jesus Alone made it possible for believing sinners to *"draw nigh,"* and that alone!

4. The *"First Covenant,"* as we find here, is dedicated with blood, but it was the blood of animals, which was woefully insufficient.

AFAR OFF

Verses 1 and 2 read: *"And He said unto Moses, Come up unto the LORD, you, and Aaron, Nadab, and Abihu, and seventy of the Elders of Israel; and worship you afar off.*

"And Moses alone shall come near the LORD: but they shall not come nigh; neither shall the people go up with him."

Counting Moses, some 74 men are called to come into the very Presence of the Lord, which was one of the most astounding happenings of the entirety of the Old Testament economy.

Nadab and Abihu were sons of Aaron. Aaron also had two other sons, *"Eleazar and Ithamar."*

Strangely enough, the two sons which accompanied their father Aaron along with Moses into the very Presence of God, and who were Priests, according to Leviticus,

Chapter 10, would lose their way. Actually, they would be smitten by God in a most horrifying fashion because they disdained the Cross. In essence, they did *"trod under foot the Son of God, and counted the Blood of the Covenant, wherewith they had been sanctified, as an unholy thing, and did despite unto the Spirit of Grace"* (Heb. 10:29).

Concerning this, Pink said, *"There is one thing here that is very solemn, namely, the repeated mention of Nadab and Abihu; (Vss. 1, 9). They were both sons of Aaron, and with their father were selected for this singular privilege. But neither light nor privilege can insure Salvation, nor, if Believers, a holy and obedient walk."*

He went on to say, *"Both afterwards met with a terrible end. They 'offered strange fire before the LORD, which He commanded them not. And there went out fire from the LORD, and devoured them; and they died before the LORD' (Lev. 10:1-2)."*

Immediately after their meeting with the Lord, they were consecrated to the Priesthood, and it was while in the performance of their duty in this office, or rather because of their failure in it, that they fell under the Judgment of God.

Above all things, we should let this be a warning to us, power and privilege, which both of these men had, offer no Salvation. If that in fact is true, and it most definitely is, then that condemns the far greater majority of those in the world presently, who occupy high religious office, and who think that such a position saves them. It doesn't!

THE INABILITY OF THE LAW

The words given here by the Holy Spirit through Moses, *"Worship ye afar off,"* and *"They shall not come nigh,"* and *"Neither shall the people go up with him,"* must not be taken lightly. This portrays the very best that the Law could do. Even though the Law was the Righteousness of God, i.e., *"God's Standard of Righteousness,"* that within itself did not, and in fact, could not make man righteous. As we have previously stated, the Law was like a mirror, which showed man what he actually was, but had no power to change him.

Even though the sacrificial system would be instituted as the very centrality of the Levitical Law, still, it was woefully insufficient to take away sins because it was animal blood (Heb. 10:4).

Let all ponder these words very carefully, who are attempting to find their way with the Lord by the means of works. Such a venture is impossible! But yet the world understands that not at all, and sadder still, the Church, at least for the most part, seems to little understand it as well!

Concerning all of this, the great Apostle said: *"But now in Christ Jesus you who sometimes were far off are made nigh by the Blood of Christ.*

"For He is our peace, Who has made both one, and has broken down the middle wall of partition between us;

"Having abolished in His flesh the enmity, even the Law of Commandments contained in Ordinances; for to make in Himself of twain one new man, so making peace;

"And that He might reconcile both (Jews and Gentiles) *unto God in one body* (one Church) *by the Cross, having slain the enmity thereby"* (Eph. 2:13-16).

Notice the terms in Paul's statements, *"far off,"* and *"made nigh."*

All *"law"* and all *"works"* push man *"far off"* from God. Only the Blood, the Precious Blood, of our Lord and Saviour, Jesus Christ, can *"make nigh."*

THE MODERN CHURCH

Just this morning I read a little booklet written by a particular Bible Teacher who is prominent over Christian Television. Most of what he said concerning the Righteousness of God was correct. He even mentioned the Cross; however, the emphasis was by no means on the Cross, but rather on other things. He was, in a sense, telling Believers that which was right as it regards who they are in Christ, and even how their Righteousness was obtained. But when it came to maintaining such Righteousness, the emphasis was on the individual and their *"works,"* instead of the Cross of Christ.

Regrettably, this is where much of the Protestant world stands presently. It tells Believers who they are, and what they must do. But it seldom tells them correctly how to do what is demanded. They fail to tell them, simply because of a lack of Biblical knowledge, or else because of unbelief.

I happen to know that the Brother in question little believes in the Cross, referring to it as *"past miseries."* I also know that he says that *"The Cross of Christ was the greatest defeat in human history."* I know he also teaches that if one *"preaches the Cross, he is preaching death!"*

I know that he believes and teaches that a person is saved by trusting in Christ, Who he claims died spiritually on the Cross, which means that He died as a sinner, and went to the burning side of Hell, where He agonized for some three days and nights. At the end of that three days and nights, he claims that God said, *"It is enough,"* with Jesus then being *"born again,"* exactly as any sinner is Born-Again. He was then resurrected from the dead. In fact, far more emphasis is placed on the Resurrection in the teaching of our dear Brother, than is the Cross.

In one breath he says, *"The Blood atones,"* but then he says the Blood alone could not atone, but must be connected with Jesus going down into the burning side of Hell.

But yet, most Christians reading his little booklet would not see the subtle manner in which a false way of Sanctification is approached.

THE SIMPLE GOSPEL

Paul said: *"But I fear, lest by any means, as the serpent beguiled Eve through his subtilty, so your minds should be corrupted from the simplicity that is in Christ"* (II Cor. 11:3).

As stated, this is a simple Gospel. Jesus died for us, and our Faith in Him gives us the benefits for which He died, which is the Righteousness of God (II Cor. 5:21). Continued Faith in His Atoning Work helps us to maintain that Righteousness, and that alone will help us maintain that Righteousness.

SEVENTY ELDERS OF ISRAEL

Who these seventy were, we aren't told. As well, we aren't even told as to how they were selected. We do know that it was upon this inner circle of seventy that the Lord poured out the Spirit in order that they should share the government of the people with Moses (Num. 11:25).

As well, let it be understood that these seventy had nothing to do with those chosen upon the advice of Jethro, and recorded in Chapter 18. Those were the selection of men by men, while these seventy are the selection of men by God. There is a vast difference!

As well, the number *"seventy"* has a greater spiritual meaning than numerical. If six had been chosen from each Tribe, this would have amounted to 72 Elders. So we know they were not chosen in that manner. We do not even know or understand if in fact they were meant to represent the Tribes, or were rather chosen by the Lord at random, irrespective of their particular Tribes. This was probably the case!

Beside the 12 Disciples chosen by Christ, the Scripture says, *"The Lord appointed other seventy also, and sent them two and two before His Face into every city and place, whether He Himself would come."*

And it also says: *"And the seventy returned again with joy, saying, Lord, even the devils are subject unto us through Your Name"* (Lk. 10:1, 17).

Considering the *"seventy"* chosen by the Lord to represent Israel, and the *"seventy"* chosen as well, to represent the Master, we must come to the conclusion that they represent the Body of Christ, one might say. Even though the term *"Body of Christ"* would not have been used in Old Testament times, still, in reality, that's what it was.

THE PEOPLE ANSWERED

Verse 3 reads: *"And Moses came and told the people all the words of the LORD, and all the judgments: and all the people answered with one voice, and said, All the words which the LORD has said will we do."*

That which Moses told the people as he came down from the mountain pertains to the legislation given us in Chapters 21, 22, and 23.

As the people heard the *"words of the Lord, and all the judgments,"* they readily *"answered with one voice,"* that they would carry out this which the Lord commanded.

Incidentally, the *"Words of the LORD,"*

refer to the Ten Commandments, i.e., *"the Ten Words."* They are somewhat distinguished from the legislation in the previous Chapters, referred to as *"judgments."*

Most Commentators criticize Israel for promising to obey. They state that they should have answered Moses in the fashion of their inability. In other words, they should have said, *"We are a weak and flawed people, and cannot keep these Judgments, unless You help us greatly."*

Yes, that's exactly what they should have said; however, these people did not have the spiritual depth to answer in that capacity. As well, their response mirrors the response of most of us in the Church, and we have far less excuse than they.

Due to the Fall, there is something in man, with even a residue continuing to be in Believers, which makes us believe that we can live this life, and be what we ought to be. The unredeemed man thinks that his good works, whatever they might be, qualifies him for whatever there is after death. Most Believers have the idea that since they are Believers, with many being Spirit-filled, most certainly they can now live for God. In other words, they can say either *"no"* to sin or *"yes"* to sin.

While Believers dress up their boasts with Scriptures, still, it is ugly flesh speaking, which God cannot tolerate, and which the Holy Spirit cannot sanction. But regrettably, that's where most of the modern Church is.

DEPENDENCE

A total dependence on Christ is claimed, but almost all of the time, the Cross is ignored. So the concluding result of that is, whether the Believer understands it or not, they are, in effect, serving *"another Jesus"* (II Cor. 11:4). Please read the following very carefully:

It is impossible to place total dependence in Christ, unless our dependence is in *"Christ Crucified"* (I Cor. 1:17-18, 23; 2:2). But most of the modern Church ignores the Cross, with most little understanding, if they in fact have any understanding at all, of the Cross as it regards Sanctification. Consequently, the Church is left with a hodgepodge of efforts of the flesh, in their attempt to live for God.

THE HOLY SPIRIT

The only way the Holy Spirit is going to work in the Believer's life, without Whom we can do nothing, is that the Believer registers a continuous faith in the Cross of Christ. But unfortunately, in the last several decades, the Church has mostly been taught everything but the right thing. Most Christians simply do not know how to live for God, and that despite all the instructions given by the Holy Spirit through Paul, and other writers of the New Testament.

Please notice Israel's response, as they say, *"All the words which the Lord has said will we do,"* and then listen to the words of most modern Christians, as they say, *"I can do all things through Christ which strengtheneth me"* (Phil. 4:13).

We've already addressed this, so we'll not go into more detail; however, they are saying these words, totally different than the manner in which Paul said them. When Paul made this statement, the emphasis was on Christ; regrettably, when most modern Christians use the term presently, the emphasis is on *"self."* It's on the pronoun *"I."* In other words, the modern Church is, for all practical purposes, saying the same thing that Israel said so long ago, and is failing just as miserably. We seem to have learned much of nothing in the last 3,500 years.

The following Verses will tell us what the Lord told Moses to do, as it regards Israel, and which it regards us as well, at least in type.

THE ALTAR

Verses 4 and 5 read: *"And Moses wrote all the Words of the LORD, and rose up early in the morning, and built an Altar under the hill, and twelve pillars, according to the twelve Tribes of Israel.*

"And he sent young men of the Children of Israel, which offered Burnt Offerings, and sacrificed Peace Offerings of oxen unto the LORD."

Moses wrote in a Book all the legislation which the Lord had given to him, and which we now have in Chapters 20 through 23, which have been supernaturally preserved. Evidently, the Holy Spirit gave Moses the capacity to remember exactly what the Lord had said, and to do so even down to the very Words (II Pet. 1:21; Jn. 14:26).

This which we are now studying is the Old Covenant, which was meant to be temporary, and in fact was temporary, awaiting the coming of Christ, Who would fulfill this Covenant in totality. It would now be ratified by blood, without which no Covenant could be binding.

The Scripture says that Moses *"Built an Altar . . . and twelve pillars, according to the twelve Tribes of Israel."*

The *"Altar"* as is obvious, represents Christ and what He would do in order to redeem lost humanity. The *"twelve pillars"* represent the Government of God, with the number *"twelve"* in the Bible always standing for that principle. So we see here that the Government of God is built on the Foundation of the Cross, which in effect, was in the Mind of God from before the foundation of the world (I Pet. 1:18-20). If we attempt to build a government outside of the Cross, or to tamper in any way with the Cross, as it regards the changing of its meaning, we have just instituted that which God can never accept. Other than through the Cross, God cannot even look at sinful man, much less have fellowship with Him. It is the Cross alone which makes everything possible as it relates to God.

BURNT OFFERINGS AND PEACE OFFERINGS

The *"Burnt Offerings"* of Verse 5 were, in effect, *"Whole Burnt Offerings."* They signified that God would give His all as it refers to the Redemption of man, and that man must give God his all! They signified, as well, that man was a sinner, wholly deserving of eternal punishment, but that instead, Christ, Who the Offerings represented, would give Himself as a Sacrifice, in order that sinful man might be saved. Christ would give His all, drinking that bitter cup down to the very dregs (Lk. 22:42).

"Peace Offerings" signified that the *"Whole Burnt Offering"* was accepted by God, and peace is now restored. Normally, the Peace Offering would be eaten by the offerer and his friends, actually in a spirit of celebration because peace had been restored between God and man, except for the part given to the Priests.

With this legislation not yet given, as far as we know, it is not known if the Peace Offering was handled presently in this manner or not; nevertheless, the principle was being enjoined, as is obvious. There are several things that we see in this which is done.

First of all, and as stated, the *"Altar"* represents Christ and what He would do for us in the Sacrifice of Himself on the Cross. As well, we are made here to see, exactly as we did in Exodus, Chapter 20, that fellowship with God could not be obtained on the basis of law-keeping, and simply because man couldn't keep the Law. So there had to be a means for man to approach God, and the only way that could be done is through a Mediator, Who is Christ. But it must be Christ having paid the price in the giving of Himself in Sacrifice, of which all of this was a type. In fact, none of this is new, actually having been given at the very dawn of time, immediately upon the Fall of man, when the Lord told Satan through the serpent that *"the Seed of the woman would bruise the head of the serpent"* (Gen. 3:15). And then we have it laid out in graphic detail in Genesis, Chapter 4, with the episode concerning the sacrifices of Cain and Abel.

Also, the *"twelve pillars,"* which the Lord instructed Moses to build, while representing the twelve Tribes of Israel, in essence represented the great Government of God. This refers to the way that God does things. And please understand, this is very, very important:

God's Government, at least as it concerns man, is built 100 percent on the Cross of Christ. Now this is important, so important in fact that if we do not understand it properly, we can cause ourselves tremendous problems. And regrettably, that's where the modern Church, at least for the most part, is presently.

Having left the Cross, the Church devises its own government, which God can never accept, and which does tremendous harm to the Work of God all over the world.

We have stated it over and over again that the Cross of Christ is more than a mere doctrine. In fact, it is the foundation of all doctrine. I'm absolutely positive that Christ would have considered the Sacrifice of Himself on the Cross as more than a doctrine. In fact, the Cross was the destination, even planned from before the foundation of the world (I Pet. 1:18-20). Everything must be built on the Cross. In fact, one cannot really understand the Word of God, at least as one should, without a proper understanding of the Cross. The Word of God is the story of the Cross, as the Cross is the Word of God, i.e., *"Jesus Christ and Him Crucified"* (I Cor. 1:23).

And lastly, all of this was merely a symbol, a shadow, a Type, if you will, of the One Who was to come, namely Christ, Who would fulfill all of the Levitical Law, which He Alone could do, which means that the First Covenant was temporary, and in fact, was meant to be temporary.

THE BLOOD

Verse 6 reads: *"And Moses took half of the blood, and put it in basins; and half of the blood he sprinkled on the Altar."*

The Altar, of course, was for sacrifice, with the blood being poured out, as the result of that sacrifice.

Pulpit says: *"The blood, which symbolized the life of the victim, was the essential part of every Sacrifice, and was usually poured over the Altar, or at any rate, sprinkled upon it, as the very crowning act of offering"* (Lev. 1:5; 3:8).

We find here that the Covenant was established in the blood of the slain lamb. Half of the blood was sprinkled on the Altar, thus pledging God to His engagement; the other half, as we shall see, was sprinkled upon the people, so pledging them (Williams). All of this, as should be obvious, typified the Blood of Christ, which would be shed when He would die on the Cross, which alone could make Atonement, and which in fact, did make Atonement.

THE BIBLE

Verse 7 reads: *"And he took the Book of the Covenant, and read in the audience of the people; and they said, All that the LORD has said will we do, and be obedient."*

The first mention of the Bible, at least in its beginning form, is given in Exodus 17:14. It is interesting that the very first mention would be in connection with the hostility of the natural man, symbolized by Amalek, to the spiritual man, symbolized by Israel. And now the Bible is mentioned again in connection with the giving of the Law.

This tells us that man, even believing man, cannot keep the Law of God within his own strength and ability. He must, and without fail, place his dependence totally in Christ, and what Christ has done for him at the Cross. In this manner, and in this manner alone, can he successfully live for God.

As Moses read from the Bible, actually reading that which is given unto us in Exodus, Chapters 20 through 23, the people answered by saying, *"We will be obedient."*

Once again, they quite possibly desired to be obedient, but there was no way they could be because the obedience that God demands is a perfect obedience, which man is incapable of rendering. So as much as they desired to do that which was right, the only recourse was the *"Altar,"* i.e., *"the Cross."*

THE SPRINKLING OF THE BLOOD

Verse 8 reads: *"And Moses took the blood, and sprinkled it on the people, and said, Behold the Blood of the Covenant, which the LORD has made with you concerning all these words."*

We know that half of the Blood was sprinkled on the Altar, and half of it was sprinkled on the people, which probably pertained to their leaders and representatives. It could hardly have referred to being sprinkled on nearly three million people, as would be obvious. As well, Paul said in Hebrews: *"For when Moses had spoken every precept to all the people according to the Law, he took the blood of calves and of goats, with water, and scarlet wool, and hyssop, and sprinkled both the Book, and all the people"* (Heb. 9:19).

Once again, *"all the people"* probably were represented by the 70 Elders (Ex. 24:1).

So we have the *"blood"* being sprinkled on the Altar, the people, and the Book. This once again tells us that the foundation of all that we have, all that we are, is based strictly upon the Cross of Christ. While animal blood could not take away sins, that awaiting the coming of Christ (Jn. 1:29), it could cover the sins, at least for a period of time. Other animals would have to be offered, and in fact, there was a constant stream of sacrifices from then unto the time of Christ. His death on the Cross, which necessitated the shedding of His Own Precious Blood, would forever put an end to animal sacrifices.

Why do men desire to continue to try to offer up some type of sacrifice, other than the Precious Blood of Christ, thinking that such will atone for their sins? When I speak of *"sacrifice,"* I'm not speaking now of animal sacrifices, but rather *"works"* which we attempt to offer God. Let the Reader know and understand that the only sacrifice accepted by God is the Sacrifice of His Son, Jesus Christ. And it is Faith alone in that Sacrifice that God will honor. Anything else, He constitutes as *"flesh,"* which can never please Him (Rom. 8:8).

(9) "THEN WENT UP MOSES, AND AARON, NADAB, AND ABIHU, AND SEVENTY OF THE ELDERS OF ISRAEL:

(10) "AND THEY SAW THE GOD OF ISRAEL: AND THERE WAS UNDER HIS FEET AS IT WERE A PAVED WORK OF A SAPPHIRE STONE, AND AS IT WERE THE BODY OF HEAVEN IN HIS CLEARNESS.

(11) "AND UPON THE NOBLES OF THE CHILDREN OF ISRAEL HE LAID NOT HIS HAND: ALSO THEY SAW GOD, AND DID EAT AND DRINK.

(12) "AND THE LORD SAID UNTO MOSES, COME UP TO ME INTO THE MOUNT, AND BE THERE: I WILL GIVE YOU TABLES OF STONE, AND A LAW, AND COMMANDMENTS WHICH I HAVE WRITTEN; THAT YOU MAY TEACH THEM.

(13) "AND MOSES ROSE UP, AND HIS MINISTER JOSHUA: AND MOSES WENT UP INTO THE MOUNT OF GOD.

(14) "AND HE SAID UNTO THE ELDERS, TARRY YOU HERE FOR US, UNTIL WE COME AGAIN UNTO YOU: AND, BEHOLD, AARON AND HUR ARE WITH YOU: IF ANY MAN HAVE ANY MATTERS TO DO, LET HIM COME UNTO THEM.

(15) "AND MOSES WENT UP INTO THE MOUNT, AND A CLOUD COVERED THE MOUNT.

NOTES

(16) "AND THE GLORY OF THE LORD ABODE UPON MOUNT SINAI, AND THE CLOUD COVERED IT SIX DAYS: AND THE SEVENTH DAY HE CALLED UNTO MOSES OUT OF THE MIDST OF THE CLOUD.

(17) "AND THE SIGHT OF THE GLORY OF THE LORD WAS LIKE DEVOURING FIRE ON THE TOP OF THE MOUNT IN THE EYES OF THE CHILDREN OF ISRAEL.

(18) "AND MOSES WENT INTO THE MIDST OF THE CLOUD, AND GOT HIM UP INTO THE MOUNT: AND MOSES WAS IN THE MOUNT FORTY DAYS AND FORTY NIGHTS."

The diagram is:

1. Before the invitation of Verse 1 could be accepted, the blood of the Burnt and Peace Offerings must be shed.

2. Men, even though they may be as distinguished as these princes, cannot approach God in their own persons; they can only draw near through the Blood of Jesus.

3. The men who in Verse 1 are styled *"Elders,"* are named *"Nobles"* in Verse 11. Why? Because in Verse 10 they saw the God of Israel. To have fellowship with God ennobles men (Williams).

4. John 1:18 says, *"No man has seen God at any time."* The statement given to us in Verse 10 does not contradict that statement. For the word *"seen"* in John 1:18 refers to *"comprehend,"* or to *"fully comprehend."* In other words, *"No man has fully comprehended God at any time."*

5. The sapphire stone expressed the purity of God.

6. Verse 11 records the first *"Breaking of Bread"* as a religious feast in the Bible. It was the Fellowship of Access; Acts 10:41 was the Fellowship of Testimony; and in Luke 22:30, the Fellowship of Glory. The other communal meals recorded in the Scriptures under this title were rather social actions (Lk. 24:30; Acts 2:42; 20:7; I Cor., Chpts. 10-11).

7. Moses would need 40 days to write *"in the Book,"* from the Mouth of God all that appears in the following directions respecting the Tabernacle and its Ministry (Williams).

THE SAPPHIRE STONE

Verses 9 and 10 read: *"Then went up Moses, and Aaron, Nadab, and Abihu, and* seventy of the Elders of Israel:

"And they saw the God of Israel: and there was under His feet as it were a paved work of a sapphire stone, and as it were the body of Heaven in His clearness."

This event as recorded here has to be a happening of unique proportions. There is nothing else like it recorded in the Old Testament. These men would sit in the very Presence of God, would actually behold Him, would describe what they saw, and would eat a meal, evidently prepared by Angels, or possibly the Lord Himself.

In fact, this was a pre-Incarnate appearance of Christ, which means that the appearance here, at least in a sense, is very similar to the Transfiguration (Mat. 17:1-8).

And yet, Jesus Himself said, *"Notwithstanding, he who is least in the Kingdom of Heaven is greater . . ."* (Mat. 11:11).

This doesn't mean that we are now greater in character than John the Baptist, whom Jesus was addressing then, or Moses, etc., as should be obvious; it does mean that due to the Cross, and what Jesus accomplished there, our privileges now are so much greater than those under the Old Covenant.

While this event we are presently describing as it refers to Moses and the others actually seeing God, being in His Presence, and even eating before Him, was certainly great as would be obvious, still, it only lasted a short time, while we have presently, under the New Covenant, the Holy Spirit literally living in us, and on a permanent basis. The problem we have presently is, we do not really understand the magnitude of what we have, do not appreciate it as greatly as we should, and conduct ourselves accordingly, which is a shame!

But once again, we really cannot fully appreciate what we presently have, until we fully appreciate the Cross as we should. Then and only then does everything begin to come into proper focus.

DID THEY REALLY SEE GOD?

Concerning this, Pulpit Commentary says: *"These words can scarcely mean less than that they saw with their bodily eyes an appearance of the Divine Being Who had summoned them to His Presence for that very purpose. The Scripture further says, Moses saw a 'similitude of God' (Num. 12:8). Isaiah 'saw the Lord sitting upon His Throne' (Isa. 6:1). Ezekiel saw upon the Throne 'the appearance of a Man' (Ezek. 1:26)."*

Exactly what did Moses and the others see?

The Scripture plainly says, *"They saw the God of Israel."* It describes Him as having *"feet,"* and standing on a *"paved work of sapphire stone."* In essence, the phrase, *"And as it were the body of Heaven in His clearness,"* says that they saw Him clearly.

How does this compare with John 1:18 where it says, *"No man has seen God at any time; the only Begotten Son, which is in the Bosom of the Father, He has declared Him"*?

The Greek word for *"seen"* is *"horao,"* and means, *"to discern clearly, to experience, to fully comprehend."* While the word *"seen"* can certainly refer to a visible appearance, it also refers to a mental and spiritual understanding. No man has fully comprehended God. But as we've stated, every appearance of God in the Old Testament was a pre-Incarnate appearance of the Lord Jesus Christ. It is the Son Alone Who has declared the Father, even as Jesus mentioned in John 1:18.

While there is only one God, He is manifested in three Persons, *"God the Father, God the Son, and God the Holy Spirit."* Each is Omniscient, Omnipresent, and Omnipotent. But yet, the Ministry, one might say, of each Member of the Godhead is somewhat different. For instance, God the Son is the One Who came to this Earth and died on Calvary, in order to redeem mankind. The Holy Spirit superintended His Birth, Life, Death, Resurrection, Ascension, and Exaltation (Mat. 1:18; Lk. 4:18-19; Heb. 9:14; Rom. 8:11). But yet it was not the Holy Spirit Who died on the Cross. God the Father is the One to Whom Jesus prayed (Mat. 6:9; 5:19-23; Lk. 22:42). There is no record of the Father praying to the Son. As well, it is to the Father that the Kingdom will be delivered up by the Son, *"When He shall have put down all rule and all authority and power"* (I Cor. 15:24).

THE NOBLES

Verse 11 reads: *"And upon the nobles of*

the Children of Israel, He laid not His hand: also they saw God, and did eat and drink."

As we have stated, these *"Nobles"* are called *"Elders"* in Verse 1.

The phrase, *"He (God) laid not His hand,"* refers to the fact that even though these *"Nobles"* were in the very Presence of God, were actually looking upon Him, even eating and drinking in His Presence, they did not suffer any ill effect, even though this was the same God Who had spoken from the Mountain, and had done so with such force and power that the people trembled. As well, they were warned that if they broke through the barriers and touched the mountain where God was, they would die. So how do we explain here the difference?

God does not change, so we must assume that it was the *"Altar"* which made the difference. Blood had been shed, a Covenant had been made, and as the song says, *"Through the Blood into His Presence."* Even though His appearance was limited to those present, still, the Sacrificial Offerings had made it all possible, exactly as the Cross makes everything possible now.

COME UP TO ME

Verses 12 and 13 read: *"And the LORD said unto Moses, Come up to Me into the mount, and be there: and I will give you tables of stone, and a Law, and Commandments which I have written; that you may teach them.*

"And Moses rose up, and his minister Joshua: and Moses went up into the Mount of God."

After the events of the fellowship, Moses was instructed by the Lord to *"Come up to Me into the Mount."* He was evidently told by the Lord to take Joshua with him. Already, the Lord was anticipating the time when Moses would be taken, which would be nearly 40 years from this day, and Joshua would take his place.

It is doubtful that Joshua was able to go into the very Presence of God as did Moses; nevertheless, he at least went part way, and evidently stayed the entirety of the time, because we find him coming down with Moses, when some 40 days later, Moses descended from the mountain (Ex. 32:17).

NOTES

We find here that the Lord will Personally inscribe on the tables of stone the Ten Commandments.

Before the Cross, no one was allowed into the Presence of God, except selected individuals such as Moses and the High Priest, etc. Man couldn't come up to God because of his sinful condition, so God ultimately came down to man, in the form of the Lord Jesus Christ. And due to what Christ did on the Cross, it was made possible for man to come into the very Presence of God, and to do so boldly (Heb. 4:16).

THE ELDERS

Verse 14 reads: *"And he (Moses) said unto the Elders, Tarry ye here for us, until we come again unto you: and, behold, Aaron and Hur are with you: if any man have any matters to do, let him come unto them."*

As Moses prepares to go back up the mountain because it is demanded by the Lord, taking Joshua with him, he tells the Elders that Aaron, his brother, and Hur, who some believe was his brother-in-law, are in charge.

We will find that this scenario doesn't turn out very well. Aaron, who was no doubt the eldest, although he knew what was right, as we shall see, wouldn't take a stand, and the golden calf was the result. There has to be Preachers who will stand up and emphatically state what is right and what is wrong. That's our problem today! We have too many Preachers who won't take a stand on anything. If they oppose anything at all, it's always something that's popular to oppose. God forbid that they would oppose anything that might draw the anger of people toward them. So in essence, we have men who are more Politicians than Preachers.

As it was said by one great Preacher, a man can be a Prophet, or he can be a spiritual leader; he can't be both! So-called spiritual leaders, far too often, try to please the people. Prophets proclaim, *"Thus saith the Lord,"* with only one thought, and that is to please God. So if the man aspires to be a spiritual leader, he is aspiring, I suspect, to please men. Only Prophets aspire to please God! (I'm using the term *"Prophet"* in a loose sense; it could apply to any of the five-fold Callings.)

One thing is certain:

If men of God do not stand up and point out the right and point out the wrong, which means to squarely oppose false doctrine and false ways, and do so irrespective of the costs, the Church will be lost. And regrettably and sadly, at this present time (2002), it is almost lost.

A PERSONAL EXPERIENCE

In early 2000, I believe it was, the Lord began to lay it on my heart, as well as others in our Organization, that the modern Word of Faith doctrine, which had become so popular and so strong, must be opposed. It is not Scriptural, with its greatest fault being in its opposition to the Cross. It is most dangerous, because its adherents claim to be following the Word, and claim to be led by the Holy Spirit. Consequently, it has made inroads into the Charismatic world to such an extent that its influence is almost total. As well, the Pentecostal world has been greatly influenced by this false message.

Looking at our own situation, and I speak of Jimmy Swaggart Ministries, in that we are already fighting an uphill battle, literally fighting on a day-by-day basis to stay afloat financially, it makes no sense at all to come out over our network of Radio Stations and in our publications, to oppose one of the most popular doctrines in the Charismatic and Pentecostal worlds. Considering the popularity of this *"greed gospel,"* even those who know that what you are saying is the truth, will little stand with you, knowing the opposition that such a stand will draw.

But if God says to do something, it doesn't really matter what the circumstances are, nor does it matter what people think. As a Minister of the Gospel, and if I am to be true to my Calling, I must obey the Lord irrespective of the consequences. He'll have to take care of our situation, be it financial, or political, or any other way.

The crunch comes when strong supporters tell you that they will not support you any longer, especially considering the dire need. However, in all of this, we must ask ourselves the question, what is our purpose and mission? Are we here to please God or to please man? Are we here to be popular, or are we here to obey the Lord?

When I stand at the Judgment Seat of Christ, I will answer only to one Person, and that one Person is the Lord Jesus Christ. So it's Him and Him Alone Whom I must please!

As the Lord laid this burden on my heart, and I continue to speak of our speaking out against false doctrine, which includes the so-called Christian music scene as well, He was also moving on Donnie's heart and Loren Larson as well!

Donnie preached a series of Messages in our Campmeetings, as it regards the particular Word of Faith doctrine, which were aired over our Television Network, as well as the SonLife Radio Network. To say it drew fire is an understatement!

But the Lord mightily anointed Donnie to preach these Messages, as anyone would have to admit who heard them, that is if they were to be honest, and in the final analysis, that's all that counts. If the Anointing of the Holy Spirit is on something, that is the highest approval of all. That means that what is being said or done is that which the Lord wants said and done, and for the simple reason that He will never anoint error, etc.

WHAT DIFFERENCE WILL IT MAKE?

The full question should be, what difference will it make regarding the stand that we have taken?

That's not our business! Our business is to hear from Heaven, and then to deliver that which we have heard, changing it not at all! The Scripture says, however: *"So shall My Word be that goes forth out of My mouth: it shall not return unto Me void, but it shall accomplish that which I please, and it shall prosper in the thing whereto I sent it"* (Isa. 55:11).

The truth is, if the God-called Preacher doesn't take a stand, without fail, a golden calf will be the result! And the sickening truth is, the Church presently has built not only one golden calf, but many! And it's the Preachers who are conducting themselves as Aaron, which makes this travesty possible!

THE CLOUD

Verses 15 and 16 read: *"And Moses went up into the mount, and a cloud covered the mount.*

"And the Glory of the LORD abode upon Mount Sinai, and the Cloud covered it six days, and the seventh day He called unto Moses out of the midst of the cloud."

Evidently, Moses, along with Joshua, went a little distance up the Mountain, but went no farther. The *"cloud"* covered the Mountain, and he probably went to the edge of the cloud and stopped.

He waited there for six days, for the Lord to tell him what to do. However, during this time, he was not told how long he would have to wait. Concerning this, Pulpit says: *"God thus taught Moses, and through him the world, that mere approach to Him requires long and careful preparation."*

Unfortunately, we don't have much *"waiting on the Lord"* presently! The modern Word of Faith doctrine has so decimated the true Faith of the people that they have been led to believe that if they have to wait any time at all for anything, then their confession must be wrong. In fact, this doctrine teaches that God has already done everything He is going to do, and now, we who are the Righteousness of God have a franchise, so to speak, on what we will do for the Lord. Whatever decision the adherents to this doctrine make, whatever direction they take, with them deciding the issue completely, they claim is their prerogative. Consequently one would have to come to the conclusion that the Lord is not in any of these particular efforts. He does not follow man; man must follow Him!

I realize that even most of the adherents to this doctrine do not understand what I have said, so please let me make it a little clearer.

We teach and believe from the Bible that we must seek the Will of God in all things. John said: *"And this is the confidence that we have in Him, that, if we ask any thing according to His Will, He hears us"* (I Jn. 5:14).

As well, John also said concerning the Holy Spirit: *"He will guide you into all Truth"* (Jn. 16:13). Therefore, the idea that Christians now have some sort of spiritual franchise, which enables them to do whatever they want to do, with the Lord having no say in the matter, could not be more wrong. But yet in essence, that's what the Word of Faith doctrine teaches.

On the *"seventh day,"* the Lord called to Moses, *"out of the midst of the cloud,"* and then Moses went into the cloud, which in essence, was into the Presence of the Lord, where he would receive the two tablets of stone containing the Ten Commandments, actually written by the finger of God, along with plans for the Tabernacle and other legislation.

THE GLORY

Verses 17 and 18 read: *"And the sight of the Glory of the LORD was like devouring fire on the top of the Mount in the eyes of the Children of Israel.*

"And Moses went into the midst of the cloud, and went up into the Mount: and Moses was in the Mount forty days and forty nights."

Moses spent six days at the edge of the cloud, and then 34 days in the cloud, in the very Presence of God, and was without food or water for the entire length of time (Deut. 9:9). There is no evidence that Joshua went any further with him than the edge of the cloud.

What the Children of Israel saw from below was a sight that must have been spectacular to say the least! The Scripture says, *"The sight of the Glory of the Lord was like devouring fire."* So it looked like the entirety of the top of the mountain was on fire.

The Glory of God speaks of grandeur, splendor, greatness, power, etc. As I should think would be obvious, what little glory man has is nothing by comparison to the Glory of God. When men serve God, they are serving the Omnipotent One. When they serve anything else, it's not even a close second!

"Lift up, lift up your voices now!
"The whole wide world rejoices now;
"The Lord has triumphed gloriously;
"The Lord shall reign victoriously."

"In vain with stone the cave they barred;
"In vain the watch kept ward and guard;
"Majestic from the spoiled tomb,
"In pomp of triumph Christ is come."

"And all He did, and all He bear,
"He gives us as our own to share;
"And hope and joy and peace begin,
"For Christ has won, and man shall win."

"O Victory, aid us in the fight,
"And lead through death to realms of light;
"We safely pass where You have trod;
"In You we die to rise to God."

CHAPTER 25

(1) "AND THE LORD SPOKE UNTO MOSES, SAYING,

(2) "SPEAK UNTO THE CHILDREN OF ISRAEL, THAT THEY BRING ME AN OFFERING: OF EVERY MAN WHO GIVES IT WILLINGLY WITH HIS HEART YOU SHALL TAKE MY OFFERING.

(3) "AND THIS IS THE OFFERING WHICH YOU SHALL TAKE OF THEM; GOLD, AND SILVER, AND BRASS,

(4) "AND BLUE, AND PURPLE, AND SCARLET, AND FINE LINEN, AND GOATS' HAIR,

(5) "AND RAMS' SKINS DYED RED, AND BADGERS' SKINS, AND SHITTIM WOOD,

(6) "OIL FOR THE LIGHT, SPICES FOR ANOINTING OIL, AND FOR SWEET INCENSE,

(7) "ONYX STONES, AND STONES TO BE SET IN THE EPHOD, AND IN THE BREASTPLATE.

(8) "AND LET THEM MAKE ME A SANCTUARY; THAT I MAY DWELL AMONG THEM.

(9) "ACCORDING TO ALL THAT I SHOW YOU, AFTER THE PATTERN OF THE TABERNACLE, AND THE PATTERN OF ALL THE INSTRUMENTS THEREOF, EVEN SO SHALL YOU MAKE IT."

The structure is:

1. The materials, the furniture, the vessels, and everything within and without the Tabernacle symbolized the Person, the Atoning Work, the Ministries, the Glories, and the Perfections of Christ as Jehovah's Perfect Servant, and as the Saviour and High Priest of His people (Williams).

2. The number five, as we shall see, is prominent in the Tabernacle, which speaks of the Grace of God.

3. Everything about the Tabernacle was designed by the Lord, with nothing left to man. As such, it is a type of Salvation, of which God is solely the Author.

INSTRUCTIONS

Verse 1 reads: *"And the LORD spoke unto Moses, saying,"*

As we shall see, all the specifications for the Tabernacle and its furniture were given by God to Moses. Moses was not given just a plan, but, in fact, a literal model to go by. So, it was all of God and none of man, as Salvation is all of God, and none of man.

Every design of the Tabernacle, the furniture and all that pertained to it, were actually representations of the Heavenly. All were symbolic, but pointed to the real in Heaven.

As well, and even more important as it regards mankind, everything within and without the Tabernacle symbolized the Person of the Lord Jesus Christ, Who He was, and What He did, in order to redeem mankind.

Access to God is the lesson the Tabernacle and its furniture teaches. The Tabernacle, therefore, is a manifestation of the Glory of the Grace of our Lord Jesus Christ, and of His relationship with sinners who draw nigh unto Him.

Concerning the study of the Tabernacle, which we are about to enter into, Pink says: *"We have now arrived at the longest, and most blessed, but least read and understood section of this precious Book of Exodus. From the beginning of Chapter 25 to the end of 40 — excepting the important parenthesis in 32 to 34 — the Holy Spirit has given us a detailed description of the Tabernacle, its structure, furniture, and Priesthood."*

When we consider, and understand, that more space is devoted to the account of the Tabernacle than to any other single object or subject treated in Holy Writ, we then begin to understand its vast significance.

It took but two Chapters to portray the record of God's work in creating this Earth, and fitting it for human habitation. By comparison, some 12 Chapters are needed to tell us about the Tabernacle.

We make a vast mistake if we relegate the Tabernacle to ancient history, giving us only a record of Jewish manners and customs which have long since passed away, and which, we think, have no meaning for or value to us. But yet the Word of God says: *"All Scripture is given by inspiration of God and is profitable"* (II Tim. 3:16). Pink says, and rightly so, *"The Christian cannot neglect any portion of the Word without suffering loss."*

Again and again in the New Testament, the Holy Spirit through the various writers makes figurative reference to the Tabernacle and its furniture. Pink also says, *"And much in the Epistle to the Hebrews cannot be understood without reference to the contents of Exodus and Leviticus."*

THE LORD JESUS CHRIST

While the Tabernacle is actually a copy, one might say, of the original regarding that Heavenly Place in which God has His dwelling, but yet in another sense, greatly different as it regards its simple form given on Earth. To properly visualize the Throne of God, we must inspect Revelation, Chapters 4 and 5. Only then can we catch a glimpse, only a glimpse, of the glory and grandeur of the dwelling place of our Creator.

But that which brings the Tabernacle home to the Believer is the fact that its structure, its sacred furniture, its utensils, in fact, every single part of the Tabernacle, down to the lowliest pin which held the ropes in place, all and without exception portray Christ in His atoning, intercessory, High Priestly work. Actually, to fail to understand the Tabernacle is to fail to understand Christ. In beautiful type, symbolic and picture form, we see Christ represented in this structure, which helps us to understand Who He is, and What He is.

It is unfortunate that many in the ranks of the Charismatics little understand the Old Testament, and especially the section of our present study; hence, we find the reason for so much false doctrine in those ranks.

THE CROSS

As we study this Structure as it presupposes Christ, we will find that the central theme is the Brazen Altar, which symbolizes the Cross of Christ, where He paid the price for man's Redemption, taking the Judgment of God upon Himself, all in our stead. Of course, in trying to evaluate the various pieces of sacred furniture, most would probably first of all go to the Holy of Holies, which housed the Ark of the Covenant, covered by the Mercy Seat, where God Personally dwelt. But yet, let the Reader understand that this glorious destination of the Holy of Holies can never be reached, unless one first of all goes by the way of the Brazen Altar. Today I sit here behind my desk, holding this Dictaphone in my hand, knowing that my every sin has been washed away, and my name is written down in the Lamb's Book of Life. My heart swells with joy, knowing that I have Eternal Life. But yet, I also realize that it has come at such a price — not a price that I paid, but a price that He paid!

So, what the Lord spoke to Moses some 3,500 years ago, we would do well to study, for the glories contained in that which the Lord gave to the great Lawgiver can never be exhausted. I only pray that in some small way, we can hopefully do a modicum of justice to the subject matter at hand. If so, as the Lord helps us, and if He reveals to you the significance of all of this which will be addressed, and I certainly believe He will to every searching heart, when your study is complete, closing out this great Book of Exodus, I think you will have a greater picture of Christ than ever before, which the Tabernacle, in fact, is meant to portray.

THE OFFERING

Verse 2 reads: *"Speak unto the Children of Israel, that they bring Me an Offering: of every man who gives it willingly with his heart you shall take My Offering."*

We find from this that God will have no gifts but such as are freely offered. He *"loves a cheerful giver."* If a man gives *"grudgingly or of necessity,"* God rejects the gift. Of that, we will have more to say momentarily!

It would have been a very easy thing for God to have furnished all the materials Himself, which He could have readily done. But instead, He allowed the Children of Israel to have a part in this great work which would be carried out. It is the same way presently.

The Lord needs nothing! He is dependent on no one or no thing. He is Self-sufficient in all things. As well, He is Omnipotent (all-powerful), Omniscient (all-knowing), and

Omnipresent (everywhere). So He certainly needs no help from us, or anything else for that matter.

But yet, He allows us to have a part in His great work, just as He allowed the Children of Israel to have a part in what was to be done, by the giving of their means.

He has done all of this in a very remarkable way. He wants us to freely give to Him of the labor of our hands, and then He will freely bless us for our giving. In fact, He said to Israel, and it can be no less to us presently, and even greater: *"Prove Me now herewith, saith the LORD of hosts, if I will not open you the windows of Heaven, and pour you out a blessing, that there shall not be room enough to receive it"* (Mal. 3:10).

A PERSONAL EXPERIENCE

When the Lord laid it on my heart to begin the *"SonLife Radio Network,"* to be frank, I didn't know how in the world we could do such. We had no money, and yet what the Lord was telling me to do, in the final analysis, would cost hundreds of millions of dollars, if not more.

When we began this effort, the Lord told me to appeal to the people for help, which we did. But in reality, the help we received basically only covered the maintenance of the small Network, which then had a few translators, fed by our mother Station in Baton Rouge. Considering the way we were attempting to move forward, we could not add to the Network, so there had to be a change of some nature.

Of course, I took it to the Lord in prayer. And through many years of serving Him, I've learned a few of His Ways. At times, He will answer prayer the moment we begin to seek His Face, and then at other times, it will be months down the road before He answers. And then at other times, He will not answer us while we are praying, but will wait until later when we're doing other things.

This particular day, I was sitting behind my desk, contemplating what we had to do, and yet wondering how in the world we could get it done, considering that we had no money whatsoever. And all of a sudden, the Lord spoke to me:

He told me to use every other Friday over the Network to raise funds, which we immediately began to do. And the people began to respond.

I also knew that we had to reach the major cities in the nation, but knowing the tremendous cost of Stations in these cities, I didn't see how in the world it could be done. So again, as I do everything, I took it to the Lord in prayer. The Holy Spirit, Who *"guides us into all truth,"* as should be obvious, knows all things. And then he told me what to do, and how to do it, which immediately we set out to do.

We simply ask the people for offerings, exactly as Moses portrayed the need to the Children of Israel.

Unfortunately, far too many modern Christians are not as generous and liberal as were the Children of Israel, at that particular time of so long ago. I've noticed this in my many years of preaching the Gospel.

When the Faith of the people is right, and the Holy Spirit is moving in their midst, they, without reservation, will give, and will give liberally and abundantly. Otherwise, they won't!

THE TYPE OF OFFERING

Verses 3 through 7 read: *"And this is the offering which you shall take of them; gold, and silver, and brass,*

"And blue, and purple, and scarlet, and fine linen, and goats' hair,

"And rams' skins dyed red, and badgers' skins, and shittim wood,

"Oil for the light, spices for anointing oil, and for sweet incense,

"Onyx stones, and stones to be set in the Ephod and in the Breastplate."

To understand how the Israelites could supply all that was wanted and needed, we must remember that they had received large presents of gold and silver from the Egyptians, plus many other things, just before their departure (Ex. 12:35).

So in fact, they had an abundance of all that was needed. We need to briefly address that:

As is obvious in the First Verse, the Lord had supplied all of these riches to the Children of Israel, who had been slaves up unto a few days before. So everything they had was given to them by the Lord. So what He was asking of them was that which He had so freely given to them in the first place. It is no different presently!

Whenever the Lord blesses us, and He will definitely do so if we will walk in obedience to His Word, He, even as here, expects us to then help finance His Work. But sadly and regrettably, all too often, this isn't done, or else it isn't done to the degree it ought to be done.

Wealth had been given unto the Children of Israel for several reasons; however, the main reason was that they would be able to finance the building of the Tabernacle, and its furnishings, much of which were made out of gold. In fact, everything that went into the Tabernacle was of the finest of materials. Considering the amount of gold used, coupled with everything else, and especially considering the manner in which some items were made, the Tabernacle could easily have cost one hundred million dollars in 2002 money. Let me say something about that also:

THE WORK OF GOD

I personally feel that ostentatiousness is not required as it regards Church structures. But of course, all of that, as one would understand, is relative. But when it comes to the Work of God, no expense must be spared. And what do I mean by that?

We should give and give freely, to help take the Gospel to others — whether around the corner, or whether around the world. For instance, at this very moment, we are stretching every financial muscle, attempting to be led by the Holy Spirit in all that we do, in the purchase of Radio Stations, which will help us to present the Gospel 24 hours a day, seven days a week, and will do so until Jesus comes.

I personally feel that we have a Message, the Message of the Cross, which the Church must hear. I personally feel that the Church has been so far removed from the Cross, that anymore, it little knows its foundation; therefore, it little knows where it has been, where it is, or where it is going. In other words, it is like a rudderless ship. All of this aimless direction is because it has lost it moorings, and we continue to speak of the Cross.

When we purchase Radio Stations, which we cannot do without the help of the people, the first thing we look at, irrespective as to where the Station might be, is the number of people the Station covers. Just today, after some three months of negotiations, we are set to close on a particular Station which will reach nearly one and one-half million people. These people desperately need the Message of the Cross, as well as every other person in the entirety of the world. But I can obtain this Station only with the help of the people, exactly as the people helped to finance the Tabernacle during the time of Moses. It has not changed; the Message is the same, and that Message is *"Jesus Christ and Him Crucified"* (I Cor. 1:23).

SANCTUARY

Verse 8 reads: *"And let them make Me a Sanctuary; that I may dwell among them."*

As far as is known, the Ark of Noah, the Tabernacle of Moses, and the Temple of Solomon, with the plans actually given to David, are the only buildings ever erected from plans furnished by direct Revelation from God (Gen. 6:14-16; I Chron. 28:11-12, 19).

Since the Fall of man in the Garden of Eden, the Lord has been working steadily to bring man back to Himself. He longs to dwell with us.

In the Tabernacle and Temple, He dwelt between the Mercy Seat and the Cherubim, which was located in the Holy of Holies of both the Tabernacle and the Temple. Before the Cross, even as Paul explained graphically so in the Book of Hebrews, this was as close as God could dwell with man. The reason was the insufficiency of animal blood. Paul also said: *"For it is not possible that the blood of bulls and goats should take away sins"* (Heb. 10:4).

But since the Cross, and as should be obvious, the Cross is the centrality of the Gospel, the Holy Spirit can now dwell permanently in the hearts and lives of all Believers (Jn. 14:17). The reason is simple: the Blood of Jesus Christ atoned for all sin, thereby taking sin away (Eph. 2:13-18). Paul said: *"Know ye not that you are the Temple of God, and that the Spirit of God dwells in you?"* (I Cor. 3:16).

Everything of which Verses 3 through 8 mention portrays Christ in some manner, whether His atoning work, mediatorial work, or intercessory work.

The Third Verse speaks of *"gold, silver, and brass"* (copper). Gold was symbolic of His Deity, silver of the Redemption that He would afford for us by His Death on the Cross of Calvary, and the copper spoke of the Judgment He would suffer on our behalf.

Verse 4 speaks of *"blue,"* which speaks of the fact that He came from Heaven, *"purple,"* represents His Kingship, and *"scarlet"* represents the Blood that He would shed for the Salvation of humanity. The *"fine linen"* stands for His Righteousness. The *"goats' hair"* came from the beautiful Asian goats which had long beautiful hair almost as fine as silk and valued as much as wool from the sheep. It represents His *"Prophetic Office."*

In the Fifth Verse, the *"rams' skins"* represented His becoming a Sacrificial Offering, but yet as a King. They were *"dyed red,"* representing His shed Blood. The *"badgers' skins"* were the last covering on the Tabernacle. It is that, looking from the outside, which the world saw. It was not very attractive. Likewise, Christ's life as a peasant was not very attractive. Also, as the unbeliever looks at Christianity, there is nothing outwardly that looks attractive. But as the Tabernacle, if one comes inside, the beauty then is overwhelming. The Badger skins represent Christ as our Great High Priest.

The *"shittim wood"* came from the acacia tree, which produced a beautiful and durable wood, sometimes called indestructible wood; in other words, it would not rot. It was representative of His Perfect, sinless, spotless Body.

The Sixth Verse speaks of *"oil for the light."* This was representative of the Holy Spirit, Who rested on Christ above and beyond measure. The *"spices for sweet incense"* spoke of His prayerful and constant intercession on behalf of the Child of God.

The *"precious stones"* of the Seventh Verse that would ultimately go in the Ephod and the Breastplate were all symbolic of God's Grace and Glory toward the Children of Israel, which Grace and Glory can now be made more abundant and more evident to the Believer, and all because of Calvary.

Every part of the Tabernacle was typical of the nature of God: the coming Redemption, the sinfulness of man, the means of pardon through Grace, and the full reconciliation of man to God. God has always wanted to *"dwell"* with man. And thankfully, a million times over I might say, He dwells within my heart, as He does the hearts and lives of untold millions.

THE PATTERN

Verse 9 reads: *"According to all that I show you, after the Pattern of the Tabernacle, and the Pattern of all the instruments thereof, even so shall you make it."*

The *"Pattern"* was all of God, and none at all of man. This means that everything about the Tabernacle, down to the finest detail, were designed by God and God Alone!

This is symbolic of Salvation. It is all of God and none of man, and anything that man attempts to introduce into Salvation, other than that which God has already designed, only tends to corrupt the perfection of the Plan of God, which means that such Salvation is void. God will never accept any of man's patterns; He will only accept His Own *"Pattern,"* Who is Jesus Christ, and more particularly, *"Jesus Christ and Him Crucified"* (I Cor. 1:23).

We Christians are very quick to speak of God blessing us, and well we should; however, in truth, God does not really bless us, but actually Christ within us. Everything is in Christ, of Christ, by Christ, with Christ, through Christ, and in fact, is Christ Alone! It is only of Christ and never of man that God has said, *"This is My Beloved Son, in Whom I am well pleased"* (Mat. 3:17; 17:5; Mk. 1:11; Lk. 3:22).

The closest the Scripture comes to saying that God is pleased with man is found in the realm of Faith. It is said: *"By Faith Enoch was translated that he should not see death; and was not found, because God had translated him: for before his translation he had this testimony, that he pleased God.*

"But without Faith it is impossible to please Him: for he who comes to God must believe that He is, and that He is a rewarder of them who diligently seek Him" (Heb. 11:5-6).

But the actual meaning of what is stated here pertains to Faith in Christ, and what Christ would do at the Cross in order to redeem lost humanity. Such Faith pleases God, and such Faith alone pleases God.

So we can see that it is all in Christ, and without Christ it is impossible to please the Lord, but with Christ, and more particularly, Faith in Him, we can please God.

THE BIGGEST SIN

The greatest sin of all is man tampering with the *"Pattern"* (Rom. 1:18; Heb. 6:4-6; 10:26-29).

A few days ago, to which I have already alluded, a lady sent me a little booklet written by one of the leading Teachers of the Word of Faith doctrine. Most of what was said in this booklet, and I speak of the Believer's position in Christ, was said very similar to the way that I would say it, or anyone else, who places total and complete trust in Christ and what He has done for us at the Cross. While the Cross was mentioned in our Brother's booklet, it was only mentioned in passing. In other words, the Cross definitely was not the emphasis. And the following is what deceives most people:

The terminology is basically the same, as it regards those who would follow the Word of Faith doctrine, and those of us who proclaim the Biblical doctrine of Redemption. The catch is, they don't mean the same thing that we mean by these particular statements. In other words, they are tampering with the *"Pattern."*

To state it briefly, we teach that the entire Plan of Redemption was consummated at the Cross (Rom. 6:3-14; 8:1-2, 11; I Cor. 1:17-18, 21, 23; 2:2, 5; Gal. 6:14; Eph. 2:13-18; Col. 2:14-15; I Pet. 1:18-20).

Whatever terminology the Word of Faith people use, they are actually teaching that the Cross did not atone for sin, but was only a part of the process. They teach that Jesus died as a sinner on the Cross, went to the burning side of Hell, suffered there in the burning side of Hell for three days and three nights, tormented by demon spirits, with God then saying, *"It is enough,"* when at that time, the Son of God was born again, just like any sinner is born again, and then raised from the dead. That's what they actually believe! No, there's not a shred of that in the Word of God. As one of their teachers said, *"You won't find this in the Bible; it has to be given to you by Revelation."*

The dear lady who said that is exactly right! You can't find it in the Bible, because it's not in the Bible, and it's not in the Bible, because it's not Gospel. Pure and simple, it is a fabrication, instituted by Satan himself as *"an angel of light"* (II Cor. 11:13-15). Consequently, I have no choice but to make the statement that those who proclaim such a travesty, calling it the Gospel, can only be labeled as *"Satan's ministers"* (II Cor. 11:15).

Lest the Reader think that I'm being too harsh, I remind all concerned that we're speaking here of the single most important thing known to humanity, the Salvation of the soul. As well, if we tamper with the Pattern, which Pattern is the Cross of Christ, we have then presented a false way of Salvation. And there is nothing worse than a false way of Salvation!

(10) "AND THEY SHALL MAKE AN ARK OF SHITTIM WOOD: TWO CUBITS AND A HALF SHALL BE THE LENGTH THEREOF, AND A CUBIT AND A HALF THE BREADTH THEREOF, AND A CUBIT AND A HALF THE HEIGHT THEREOF.

(11) "AND YOU SHALL OVERLAY IT WITH PURE GOLD, WITHIN AND WITHOUT SHALL YOU OVERLAY IT, AND SHALL MAKE UPON IT A CROWN OF GOLD ROUND ABOUT.

(12) "AND YOU SHALL CAST FOUR RINGS OF GOLD FOR IT, AND PUT THEM IN THE FOUR CORNERS THEREOF; AND TWO RINGS SHALL BE IN THE ONE SIDE OF IT, AND TWO RINGS IN THE OTHER SIDE OF IT.

(13) "AND YOU SHALL MAKE STAVES OF SHITTIM WOOD, AND OVERLAY THEM WITH GOLD.

(14) "AND YOU SHALL PUT THE STAVES INTO THE RINGS BY THE SIDES OF THE ARK, THAT THE ARK MAY BE BORNE WITH THEM.

(15) "THE STAVES SHALL BE IN THE RINGS OF THE ARK: THEY SHALL NOT BE TAKEN FROM IT.

(16) "AND YOU SHALL PUT INTO THE

ARK THE TESTIMONY WHICH I SHALL GIVE YOU."

The composition is:

1. Verses 10 through 16 give the directions and description of the *"Ark of the Covenant."*

2. The *"Ark"* represents the Throne of God; likewise, Salvation begins with God and not man.

3. According to our study, we believe the cubit represents 18 inches.

4. The *"pure gold"* of Verse 11 was symbolic of the Deity of Christ. The *"Crown"* is symbolic of Christ the King. The *"shittim wood"* was symbolic of His perfect humanity.

5. The *"Staves"* of Verse 13 represent the fact that the Ark was constantly on the move because God's dwelling place was only symbolic. Even though redeemed man in Christianity enjoys the privilege of Christ dwelling within us by the power and the agency of the Holy Spirit, still, this present Tabernacle groans for Redemption and the Coming of the Lord.

6. *"The Testimony"* of Verse 16 was the Ten Commandments.

THE ARK OF THE COVENANT

Verse 10 reads: *"And they shall make an Ark of shittim wood: two cubits and a half shall be the length thereof, and a cubit and a half the breadth thereof, and a cubit and a half the height thereof."*

The *"Ark of the Covenant"* occupies a leading place in the Divine communications to Moses. Its position, too, in the Tabernacle was most marked. Shut in within the Veil, in the Holiest of all, it formed the base of Jehovah's Throne, so to speak. An Ark, so far as the Word instructs us, is designed to preserve intact whatever is put therein. When, therefore, we read of *"The Ark of the Covenant,"* we are led to believe that it was designed of God to preserve His Covenant unbroken in the midst of an erring people (Mackintosh).

But yet as far as man was concerned, the Brazen Altar was the most important vessel given to Moses in the Pattern. As we shall later study, it alone, which represented Christ and His Atoning Work, could get man to the Holiest of Holies.

Counting 18 inches to the cubit, the Ark was about three feet nine inches long, two feet three inches wide, and two feet three inches high.

The Ark was made at Sinai by Bezaleel as we shall see, to the Pattern given to Moses. It was used as a depository for the written Law (Deut. 31:9; Josh. 24:26) and played a significant part at the crossing of Jordan (Josh., Chpts. 3-4), the fall of Jericho (Josh., Chpt. 6) and the ceremony of remembering the Covenant at Mount Ebal (Josh. 8:30).

From Gilgal the Ark was moved to Bethel (Judg. 2:1; 20:27), but was taken to Shiloh in the time of the Judges (I Sam. 1:3; 3:3), remaining there until captured by the Philistines on the battlefield at Ebenezer (I Sam., Chpt. 4). Because its presence caused seven months of plagues, the Philistines returned it to Kirjath-jearim, where it remained at least for 20 years, and possibly much longer (II Sam. 5:1-7:2).

DAVID

David installed the Ark in a tent at Jerusalem (II Sam., Chpt. 6), and would not remove it during Absalom's rebellion (II Sam. 15:24-29). It was placed in the Temple with great ceremony in the reign of Solomon (I Ki. 8:1), and remained in the Sanctuary up unto, and through, Josiah's reforms (II Chron. 35:3), when Jeremiah anticipated an age without its presence (Jer. 3:16).

It is believed by the Jews that immediately before the invasion by the Babylonians, Jeremiah took the Ark out of the Holy of Holies in the Temple, and hid it in a cave. This was in 587 B.C. However, it has never been found from then until now. There was no Ark in the second Temple, and neither was there an Ark in the Temple built by Herod, in which Jesus ministered.

ISRAEL

Israel was chosen by God to be the leading nation in the world, in fact, the nation that would lead all other nations to Righteousness, i.e., *"to God."* Regrettably, Israel failed terribly, with the scepter of power being taken from her and given to the Gentiles. The first Gentile power was Babylon. That scepter of power now rests with the United States.

After the Rapture of the Church, it will pass to the Antichrist. Jesus said, and concerning the Jewish people: *"And they shall fall by the edge of the sword, and shall be led away captive into all nations* (this took place in A.D. 70, and continued for many, many centuries)*: and Jerusalem shall be trodden down of the Gentiles* (in a sense that continues to remain so, and will have its climax during the time of the Antichrist)*, until the times of the Gentiles be fulfilled"* (Lk. 21:24).

The *"times of the Gentiles"* will come to an end at the Second Coming of Christ, with Israel then accepting Him as Lord, Messiah, and Saviour, in which she will then be restored, and once again given her place as the leader of nations (Ezek., Chpts. 40-48; Rev., Chpt. 19).

SHITTIM WOOD

As we said in one of the headings, this was at times referred to as *"indestructible wood."* It was a type of wood that insects would not invade, and it would not rot. It came from the acacia tree.

It represented the perfect, pure, unsullied, physical body of our Lord Jesus Christ.

THE GOLD AND THE CROWN

Verse 11 reads: *"And you shall overlay it with pure gold, within and without shall you overlay it, and shall make upon it a crown of gold round about."*

The core of the making of the Tabernacle is found in Chapters 25 through 30. This section, as we shall see, contains two parts.

If it is to be noticed, the description begins with the Ark, which represents the Throne of God. We see Christ descending from that Throne, pictured in Chapters 25 through 27, to the Brazen Altar, that is, Calvary. This proclaims the gracious outcoming of God to meet the sinner.

Chapters 28 through 30 present man, in symbol, drawing near to God in the person of the Great High Priest. Thus the first half of this section of Exodus begins with the Ark and moves outward to the Brazen Altar; the second, begins with the Brazen Altar and moves inward to the Ark (Williams).

The Ark was overlaid with pure gold, both within and without. This represented the fact that Christ was God. It covered the shittim wood, which represented His humanity. Thus He was the God-Man, Jesus Christ.

This doesn't mean that He was half man and half God, for that is basely incorrect. He was fully God, and fully man. As one Greek Scholar said, *"When our Lord became man, He laid aside the expression of His Deity, while never losing the possession of His Deity."* While He was fully man, at the same time, He was fully God!

The *"Crown of Gold"* round about the Ark, represents His status as King.

As we have stated, and will continue to state, everything about the Tabernacle, its materials, its furniture, its vessels, everything within and everything without, symbolized the Person, the Atoning Work, the Ministries, the Glories, and the Perfections of Christ as Jehovah's Perfect Servant, and as the Saviour and High Priest of His people (Williams).

THE STAVES

Verses 12 through 15 read: *"And you shall cast four rings of gold for it, and put them in the four corners thereof; and two rings shall be in the one side of it, and two rings in the other side of it.*

"And you shall make staves of shittim wood, and overlay them with gold.

"And you shall put the staves into the rings by the sides of the Ark, that the Ark may be borne with them.

"The staves shall be in the rings of the Ark: they shall not be taken from it."

The four golden rings, two on each side, were placed there for staves to be inserted, so the Ark could be transported. This represented the fact that the Ark of the Covenant was to accompany the people in all their wanderings in the wilderness, which typified the world.

As well, it typified the fact that God desired to be with His people, despite the fact that they were an erring people.

However, the Ark was not always to be moved from place to place, hence the staves would ultimately be drawn out, and we speak of the coming time when the Temple would be built.

"The afflictions of David," as well as the wars of Israel, were to ultimately have an end. The prayer was yet to be breathed and answered, *"Arise, O LORD, into Your rest. You and the Ark of Your Strength"* (Ps. 132:8).

This petition would have its partial accomplishment in the days of Solomon, when the Priests would bring the Ark of the Covenant into the House of the Lord, place it under the giant Cherubim, and then would *"draw out the staves"* (I Ki. 8:6-8). But this would be approximately 600 years in coming.

Solomon's Temple, incidentally, and the situation of Israel at that time, foreshadowed the coming Kingdom Age, when all will be at rest.

The fact that the *"staves"* were not to be taken from the Ark, at least at the time of its wanderings, suggests the fact that there be no need of touching even the rings, much less the Ark, when it was set down or taken up. The bearers were to take hold of the staves only, which were actually no part of the Ark. We can see from II Samuel 6:6-7 the danger of touching the Ark.

Thank God that danger has been removed, symbolically speaking, by what Jesus did at the Cross, thereby, opening up the way that all may come, *"without money and without price"* (Isa. 55:1).

Since the Cross, we now enjoy the privilege of Christ dwelling within us by and through the Power, Agency, Ministry, and Person of the Holy Spirit; still, this Tabernacle of the Believer groans for Redemption and the Coming of the Lord, which will then place us literally with Christ, and will do so forever (Rom. 8:23).

THE TESTIMONY

Verse 16 reads: *"And you shall put into the Ark the Testimony which I shall give you."*

This is undoubtedly the two tables of stone, written with the finger of God, and forming His Testimony against sin (Deut. 31:26-27).

This seemed to be the main purpose of the Ark, the containing of the Testimony. Of course, it pictures Christ fully and totally keeping the Law in every respect, and in fact, the only One Who was able to accomplish this great task. However, it must always be remembered that He did all of this as our Representative Man, i.e., *"the Second Man"* (I Cor. 15:47). Simple Faith in what He did for us at the Cross gives us His perfection, i.e., *"perfect Law-keeping,"* thereby, making us, in the eyes of God, and all because of Christ, perfect Law-keepers. The Believer must ever understand that all of this represented Christ, what He would do in His Redemptive Work, in actuality, what He would do for us. Let us never forget that everything He did was all done, in its entirety, for sinners, i.e., *"for us."* So doesn't it make sense, especially considering the great price that He paid, that we should have all that He has done for us? And to be sure, we can have it all, but only in one way:

FAITH

All of these wonderful things which He has done for us can be obtained in only one way, and that is by *"Faith"* (Eph. 2:8-9; Heb. 11:5-6). However, when we use the word *"Faith,"* always and without exception, we are referring to Faith in Christ and what He did for us at the Cross. As we repeatedly state, if we separate Christ from His Cross, where the great price was paid, the faith we then exhibit, God cannot honor. The Faith He honors, and the only Faith He honors, is found in the words of Paul, *"We preach Christ Crucified"* (I Cor. 1:23). If we attempt to separate Christ from the Cross, which means to abandon the Cross, or even to minimize it in any way, we then do violence to the Word of God, which finds us then worshipping and serving *"another Jesus"* (II Cor. 11:4).

ANOTHER JESUS?

What in the world did Paul mean by statements such as *"another Jesus,"* and *"another spirit,"* and *"another gospel"*? As stated, we find this in II Corinthians 11:4.

He was speaking of preaching Jesus without emphasizing the Cross (I Cor. 1:17-18, 21, 23; 2:2). And regrettably, that's the sin of the modern Church. It lauds Jesus, but it's Jesus without the Cross.

Let all and sundry know and understand that if we preach *"Jesus Christ and Him Crucified,"* we will at the same time have Jesus as the Healer, Jesus as the Provider, Jesus as the Baptizer with the Holy Spirit, etc. But if we preach Jesus without the Cross, we will not only lose Salvation, but we will lose all the other as well!

If *"Jesus and Him Crucified"* is properly preached, not only will people be saved, but healing will occur, financial provision will be made, Believers will be baptized with the Holy Spirit with the evidence of speaking with other tongues. As well, we will have Peace and Grace, as well as the Fruit and Gifts of the Spirit. But take a look at the modern Church!

Christ and the Cross are not being preached, and as well, people aren't being saved, people aren't being healed, people aren't being delivered, the *"Fruit"* and the *"Gifts"* are but a distant memory, all because the Cross is being denied or ignored.

Oh yes, all type of miracles are being claimed, etc. But if close inspection is made, we find that most of the claims are empty and hollow!

THE VALUE OF THE STUDY OF THE TABERNACLE

One cannot make a serious study of the Tabernacle without coming away with a full understanding of Who Christ is and What Christ has done for us. It pictures His Work gloriously and completely.

But yet, far too many Christians spend their time studying foolishness, which has no bearing on anything. The pyramids of Egypt are studied minutely. Other places and points of historical interest are held up as great intellectual wonders, with this of which we speak, which is the only reality there is, receiving little study at all.

Of course, it's understandable as to the action and attitude of the world as it regards the things of God, but not so understandable as it regards the Church. I would daresay that at this present time, there aren't enough Preachers seriously studying the Tabernacle to even count. The Church has been so shot through with humanistic psychology that the Work of Christ, as it regards Redemption, which is the only answer, is all but being ignored. Oh yes, Jesus is held up as the great example, and even the provider of money, but with most, that's about as far as it goes. In many Charismatic circles, it is even stated that the Old Testament has no value for present-day study. The absurdity of such thinking beggars description! In fact, if one doesn't understand the Old Testament, then it's impossible for one to understand the New.

Needham says: *"The typical portions of Scripture are supremely important and as a study vastly interesting. Types are shadows. Shadows imply substance. A type has its lessons. It was the design of Jehovah to express His great thought of Redemption to His people Israel in a typical or symbolic manner.*

"By Laws, Ceremonies, Institutions, persons, and incidents, He sought to keep alive in Israel's hearts the hope of a coming Redeemer. Christ is therefore the key to Moses' Gospel. This then is our advantage, that we can minutely compare type and antitype, and learn thereby the lessons of Grace which brings Salvation."

Pink said: *"By means of the Tabernacle Jehovah revealed His Character and made known His purpose of Redemption. There, devouring Holiness and righteous indignation against sin, declared the fact that God was just even while He justified.*

"The Tabernacle was the place of Sacrifice; its most vivid spectacle was the flowing and sprinkling of blood, pointing forward to the sufferings and death of Christ.

"It was also the place of cleansing; there was the Blood for Atonement and also the water for washing away the stains of defilement. So Christ 'loved the Church and gave Himself for it, that He might sanctify and cleanse it, with the washing of water by the Word; that He might present it to Himself a glorious Church, not having spot or wrinkle, or any such thing, but that it should be holy and without blemish' (Eph. 5:25-27)."

THE GREATEST LESSON

The Tabernacle presents the way in which the sinner might approach God, and in that, is its most outstanding lesson. We are reminded here that sin has separated man from God, and as well, that there is only one way that God can be approached, and that is by the blood of the slain lamb, which typified the Cross of Christ, which would be taken into the Holy of Holies once a year, by the High Priest, who as well, typified Christ.

Paul's writings so much proclaimed the fact of Christ and His Work. For instance, he said, *"I determined not to know anything among you save Jesus Christ* (His Person) *and Him Crucified* (His Work)*"* (I Cor. 2:2). And then in John's visions, he said, *"I beheld . . . and in the midst of the Elders, stood a Lamb* (His Person) *as it had been slain* (His Work)*"* (Rev. 5:6).

Thus it was in this order of the Tabernacle furniture: first the Ark which tells of Christ's Person, then the Mercy Seat, which we will study momentarily, which points to His Work, with the Brazen Altar coming later, which will tell how He performed His Work, which speaks of the Cross.

(17) "AND YOU SHALL MAKE A MERCY SEAT OF PURE GOLD: TWO CUBITS AND A HALF SHALL BE THE LENGTH THEREOF, AND A CUBIT AND A HALF THE BREADTH THEREOF.

(18) "AND YOU SHALL MAKE TWO CHERUBIM OF GOLD, OF BEATEN WORK SHALL YOU MAKE THEM, IN THE TWO ENDS OF THE MERCY SEAT.

(19) "AND MAKE ONE CHERUB ON THE ONE END, AND THE OTHER CHERUB ON THE OTHER END: EVEN OF THE MERCY SEAT SHALL YOU MAKE THE CHERUBIM ON THE TWO ENDS THEREOF.

(20) "AND THE CHERUBIM SHALL STRETCH FORTH THEIR WINGS ON HIGH, COVERING THE MERCY SEAT WITH THEIR WINGS, AND THEIR FACES SHALL LOOK ONE TO ANOTHER; TOWARD THE MERCY SEAT SHALL THE FACES OF THE CHERUBIM BE.

(21) "AND YOU SHALL PUT THE MERCY SEAT ABOVE UPON THE ARK; AND IN THE ARK YOU SHALL PUT THE TESTIMONY THAT I SHALL GIVE YOU.

(22) "AND THERE I WILL MEET WITH YOU, AND WILL COMMUNE WITH YOU FROM ABOVE THE MERCY SEAT, FROM BETWEEN THE TWO CHERUBIM WHICH ARE UPON THE ARK OF THE TESTIMONY, OF ALL THINGS WHICH I WILL GIVE YOU IN COMMANDMENT UNTO THE CHILDREN OF ISRAEL."

The construction is:

NOTES

1. Verses 17 through 23 speak of the *"Mercy Seat."* It was *"pure gold."* This signified that Mercy and Grace overshadowed the Law, that judgment and death were the penalty for sin, and that justice and mercy could be reconciled through Grace and Faith in the Blood.

2. The *"two Cherubim of gold"* represent the Holiness of God. They are symbols of the Living Creatures of the Fourth Chapter of Revelation. These on the Mercy Seat were a symbol of the Divine Presence.

3. The Cherubim look down upon the Mercy Seat, beneath which was the Law, the Law, we might add that was broken.

So, blood applied to the Mercy Seat would shield the gaze of the Cherubim on the broken Law.

THE MERCY SEAT

Verse 17 reads: *"And you shall make a Mercy Seat of pure gold, two cubits and a half shall be the length thereof, and a cubit and a half the breadth thereof."*

The Mercy Seat formed the covering for the Ark. On it was sprinkled the atoning blood, which the High Priest did once a year, on the Great Day of Atonement. It was of this blood-sprinkled Mercy Seat that God spoke when He said: *"There will I meet with you."* Here, in type, was the only meeting place between God and the sinner. Here, Righteousness and Peace kissed each other. God demands, and the sinner needs, a spotless Righteousness. This is found only in the Cross of Christ. At this blood-sprinkled Mercy Seat God is perfectly glorified, and the Believer eternally saved (Williams).

The dimensions of the Mercy Seat were the same as the Ark, regarding length and width. It is believed to have been about an inch thick, or possibly more. It was made out of *"pure gold,"* typifying that Mercy and Grace are all of God, and none of man.

Gold is very heavy, and it is believed that such a slab would be about 750 pounds. If that were in fact the case, the Mercy Seat, made of pure gold, would have been worth about four million dollars in 2002 money.

The Mercy Seat differed from the Ark, as is obvious, in that no wood entered into its composition. There was only one other piece of furniture in the Tabernacle made solely of gold, namely the candlestick, which was smaller in size and weight; therefore, the Mercy Seat, according to its intrinsic worth, was the most valuable of all the Holy Vessels. This speaks to us of the preciousness in the sight of God of that which the Mercy Seat foreshadowed.

PROPITIATION

The Mercy Seat derived its name, as stated, from the Blood of Propitiation, which was sprinkled on it.

The word *"Propitiation"* means, *"that which atones,"* in this case, the Blood.

"Atone" or *"Atonement"* means, *"to supply satisfaction, to expiate, to make amends, to reconcile, to pay the price."*

Paul explains this in New Testament terms, by saying: *"Even the Righteousness of God* (the Law of God) *which is by Faith of Jesus Christ* (the Perfect Righteousness of God gained by anyone who expresses Faith in Christ) *unto all and upon all of them who believe* (excluding none): *for there is no difference:*

"For all have sinned, and come short of the Glory of God (meaning that none can have this Righteousness, without Faith in Christ);

"Being justified freely by His Grace through the Redemption that is in Christ Jesus (having Faith in Christ and what He did for us at the Cross):

"Whom God has set forth to be a propitiation (Atonement) *through Faith in His Blood* (we can only have this Righteousness by exhibiting Faith in Christ and what He did for us at the Cross), *to declare His Righteousness* (the Perfect Righteousness of Christ) *for the remission of sins that are past* (past, present, and future), *through the forbearance of God* (leniency);

"To declare, I say, at this time His Righteousness: that He might be just (demanding justice, which was rendered by Christ), *and the Justifier of him who believes in Jesus* (which God can do, because His Holiness and Righteousness have been satisfied in Christ)" (Rom. 3:22-26).

In this statement, the Holy Spirit through Paul bears testimony to the fact that God's Blessed Son is the One by Whom He was propitiated, the One by Whom His holy wrath against the sins of His people was pacified, the One by Whom the righteous demands of His Law were satisfied, the One by Whom every attribute of Deity was glorified.

The *"Type"* of Christ as *"the propitiation* (satisfaction) *for our sins"* is the bleeding victim on the Altar; the *"Type"* of Christ as God's resting place or propitiatory (God's demands are satisfied) is the Mercy Seat within the Veil. Christ has become God's rest, in Whom He can now meet poor sinners in all the fullness of His Grace because of the propitiation made by Him on the Cross.

In effect, Christ *is* the *"Mercy Seat."* But He is so by virtue of the propitiation (satisfaction) which He offered to God.

To make it easier to understand, Jesus Christ died on the Cross, thereby paying the price for all sin, past, present, and future, at least for all who will believe (Jn. 3:16), thereby satisfying the demands of a thrice-Holy God, Who had demanded satisfaction, and Who received satisfaction in what Christ did at the Cross. Consequently, for all who place their Faith and trust in Christ and what He did at the Cross, thereby believing that His precious shed Blood at the Cross atoned for all sin, deliverance from all sin will be granted, and eternal life will be given (Jn. 3:16; Gal. 1:4).

Thank God it is a *"Mercy Seat,"* and not a *"Judgment Seat!"*

THE IMPORTANCE OF THE MERCY SEAT

In our understanding of Salvation, and especially our understanding of Christ, we must realize that it is impossible to overestimate the importance of God's satisfaction in Christ. In other words, the price that Christ paid, the Work that He accomplished, the great Plan of Redemption, even planned before the foundation of the world, all have been completely brought about and in totality, due to what Christ did at the Cross. The Blood was applied to the Mercy Seat, typifying the Blood that would be shed by Christ, which would appease the Wrath of God against sin, and forever portrayed the debt as having been paid. In other words, all the sinner has to do in order to be saved is to simply place his Faith and trust exclusively in Christ, and what Christ did for him at the Cross, and Salvation will be instant (Jn. 3:16; Eph. 2:8-9; Rev. 22:17).

This means that the believing sinner must understand that his good works merit him nothing! His religiosity merits him nothing! In fact, there is nothing that God will accept other than our Faith in Christ, and His Atoning Work.

As it regards our Sanctification, and I speak of the Believer's growth in Christ, the Mercy Seat also is linked closely to the Altar of Incense; perhaps it would be better to say that the Altar of Incense, which we will study a little later, is linked very closely to the Mercy Seat.

THE DIMENSIONS OF THE MERCY SEAT

The Mercy Seat fit exactly on the top of the Ark of the Covenant. It was not smaller, and it was not wider. If it is to be noticed, the Mercy Seat was two cubits and a half long, exactly as the Ark of the Covenant. As well, it was a cubit and a half in width, exactly as the Ark.

There was a reason for this, as should be obvious. Some attempt to make the Mercy Seat wider than the Ark. But this is a vain delusion. And what do we mean by that?

In other words, they are claiming things other than the Blood of Christ. But let all and sundry understand that no Grace can be shown to any sinner apart from the Redemptive Blood of the Lord Jesus. Saving Mercy is extended to none except those who accept Christ; Who Alone met the demands of Divine Justice.

Let it be understood that Christ died not only to make possible the Salvation of the whole human race, even though most will not accept, but to make certain the Salvation of those who come to Him. The Scripture says:

"All who the Father gives Me, shall come to Me (shall come by Me, for that's the only way anyone can come)*; and him who comes to Me I will in no wise cast out"* (Jn. 6:37).

There are some who claim, perhaps many, that the Love of God will save them, despite the fact that they have rejected Christ. Such hope can only be classified as a fool's hope. There is no Salvation outside of Christ, as there can be no Salvation outside of Christ.

THE LAW

The primary reason that Christ came to this world is that the Law of God, which was God's Standard of Righteousness, and which Standard He must uphold, might be met in totality, and kept faithfully, which it was by Christ. As well, He not only kept the Law perfectly, but He also satisfied the demands of the broken Law, which included every human being who had ever lived, and who would live in the future, and did so by the Sacrificial Offering of Himself on the Cross of Calvary, which paid it all.

That is the connection by the Mercy Seat with the Ark of the Covenant. In that Ark was kept the two stones which contained the Ten Commandments, which incidentally had been broken by man. So the Mercy Seat fitting exactly the Ark of the Covenant stated unequivocally, and especially the blood applied to the Mercy Seat, that the Law had been satisfied. When God would look at the Mercy Seat, instead of seeing the broken Law, He would see the Blood. Hence Him saying, as it regards the Children of Israel being delivered from Egyptian bondage, *"When I see the blood, I will pass over you"* (Ex. 12:13). This was the criteria even before the Law was given, or instructions regarding the Tabernacle, even beginning with the First Family (Gen., Chpt. 4). It hasn't changed from then until now. The Mercy Seat with the applied Blood, the Blood of Christ, still says to all of mankind, *"When I see the blood, I will pass over you."* This means that the Judgment of God will pass you by because you are safely protected by the Blood of the Lamb.

CHERUBIM

Verses 18 through 20 read: *"And you shall make two Cherubim of gold, of beaten work shall you make them, in the two ends of the Mercy Seat.*

"And make one Cherub on the one end, and the other Cherub on the other end: even of the Mercy Seat shall you make the Cherubim on the two ends thereof.

"And the Cherubim shall stretch forth their

wings on high, covering the Mercy Seat with their wings, and their faces shall look one to another; toward the Mercy Seat shall the faces of the Cherubim be."

The phrase, *"Of beaten work shall you make them,"* records the fact that these strange creatures, made of gold, were not attached to the ends of the Mercy Seat, but were actually a part of the Mercy Seat. In other words, the Mercy Seat and the two Cherubs were all one piece of gold. And it was not merely gold plating, but rather, pure gold. So if one would attempt to estimate the cost presently, regarding the gold and the craftsmanship, this one item could easily have costs some ten million dollars, or more! But it's hardly worthwhile to mention money in connection with this.

The two Cherubs looked down on the Mercy Seat, in effect, on the Law which had been grossly broken by man. Of course, and as stated, when the blood was applied by the High priest once a year, then the blood would be seen, instead of the broken Law, which was the idea!

What these particular Cherubs looked like, we have no way of knowing.

Cherubim are mentioned for the first time in Scripture in Genesis 3:24. They are seen there as guarding the way to the Tree of Life, and doing so with a *"flaming sword."* This seems to suggest that they have to do with God's Judicial authority.

In Revelation 4:6-8, we find them related to the Throne of God; and quite possibly, they might be the highest among the Angelic order, or at least, in the capacity in which they function.

While the ones described by John in the Book of Revelation are not referred to as *"Cherubim,"* but rather as *"Living Creatures,"* it is almost certain that Cherubim are meant. And yet, in Isaiah, Chapter 6, we have Angelic beings referred to as *"Seraphim,"* which are very similar to the description given to those in John's vision. Both say, *"Holy, holy, holy"* (Isa. 6:2-3; Rev. 4:8). It seems that each have *"six wings"*; and they both are at the Throne of God.

In John's Vision, these Living Creatures had each a different face, that of a man, a flying eagle, a lion, and a calf. Isaiah doesn't say what the face of the Seraphim looked like.

We do know that these strange creatures do not add to the Holiness of God, but that they rather proclaim His Holiness. By crying *"Holy, holy, holy,"* they proclaim the fact that the Creator is a *"thrice-Holy God."* This is the reason that sinful man cannot approach Him, except in one capacity. And that is by and through Christ, and especially, His shed Blood.

Oh dear Reader, do you not sense the Presence of God, even as we attempt to lift up Christ and the great price that He paid?! Do you not realize how sinful it is, how wicked it is, to deny His Cross, or to ignore His Cross, or even to minimize the significance of His Cross?! Even if we pay lip service to the Cross, but register unbelief by our actions, that can be construed as none other than hypocrisy. What do I mean by that?

MAN'S SUBSTITUTE FOR THE CROSS

A little over 100 years ago, Sigmund Freud, a man who didn't know God, and in fact, who was bound by vices of immorality, instituted what is referred to now as humanistic psychology. It is the attempt of the world, nurtured and fostered by the Evil One himself, to meet the needs of man, other than by Christ and what Christ did at the Cross. Actually, one might refer to humanistic psychology as the religion of humanism.

Regrettably, about 30 to 40 years after Freud made his debut, during which time this philosophy girdled the globe, many in the Church who had strayed and drifted from the Biblical way, began to embrace this evil, and evil it is!

By the 1940's, most in the Denominational world had embraced this means and method almost completely. By the 1950's, sadly and regrettably, the Pentecostal Denominations, already beginning to lose their way, began to accept this vain philosophy a nibble at a time.

At the present time, the acceptance of humanistic psychology is almost total as it regards the Church, irrespective of its stripe. For instance, the Assemblies of God advocates that if a person has a problem, they should seek out a good 12-step program, which of course, as all know, at least who know anything at all about psychology, is the method of claimed help. The Church of God (Cleveland, Tennessee), the second largest Pentecostal Denomination at the time of this writing (2002), has a practicing Psychologist as its General Overseer. In fact, the example being set with almost all Church of God Preachers, in attempting to attain to higher education, major in psychology.

If anyone knows anything at all about psychology, know that this humanistic way is the total opposite of the Way of the Cross. Despite the fact that the practitioners of this shamanism, and a shamanism it is, try to meld the two, the two ways are poles apart. Either Jesus addressed at the Cross every problem which grips humanity, or else He didn't. I happen to believe He did, because the Bible says He did (Col. 2:14-15), and I know from personal experience that He did.

Humanistic psychology has never set one single captive free. Every single soul in this world who has ever been set free from the bondages of sin has been set free by Christ and what Christ has done for us at the Cross. And to be sure, Christ needs no help! As we have stated, the Mercy Seat fits exactly the top of the Ark of the Covenant. It is not too little or too big.

Some pages back, we mentioned the present problem that is now taking place as it regards the Catholic Church. Sadly, the Priesthood of the Catholic Church is a haven for homosexuals. The homosexual by Satanic nature is a predator. And to be sure, young boys are the highest victims on their list. And regrettably, once molested, many of these young boys turn out to be homosexuals themselves. I said all of that to say this:

The Catholic Church has long since majored in humanistic psychology; in fact, not knowing the Lord at all, humanistic psychology is their mainstay; consequently, they have some of the best Psychologists in the world.

If psychology is the answer, then why isn't it helping these Catholic Priests, many of them who have gone through every type of psychological therapy available?

It hasn't helped them, simply because there is no help from that source. So what am I saying in all of this?

NOTES

I'm saying that the Pentecostal Denominations, who once knew the Power of the Holy Spirit, have now, and for all practical purposes, abandoned the Cross of Christ. While they may continue to pay lip service to this vain philosophy, their actions speak louder than their words.

And to be sure, the statements I've just made are at least one of the reasons that these Denominations strongly detest Jimmy Swaggart. I regret that! However, as much as I regret that, I will not cease to tell the truth. My Ministry is not for sale, and in fact, it has never been for sale. Pure and simple, these particular Denominations, for all practical purposes, have ceased to be of any use to God. While there may be an exception here and there, as a whole, what I'm saying is true. The reason can be boiled down to the fact that they have abandoned the Cross of Christ. And until they come back to the Cross, their spiritual deterioration will only tend to accelerate. Those Cherubs are still looking down upon the Mercy Seat, and they are still saying, *"Holy, holy, holy."* And the only way that mankind can escape the *"flaming sword,"* is by full and total acceptance of the Blood that was placed on the Mercy Seat. It is still, *"When I see the Blood, I will pass over you."* That has not changed, and that never will change!

COMMUNICATION

Verses 21 and 22 read: *"And you shall put the Mercy Seat above the Ark; and in the Ark you shall put the Testimony that I shall give you.*

"And there I will meet with you, and I will commune with you from above the Mercy Seat, from between the two Cherubim which are upon the Ark of the Testimony, of all things which I will give you in Commandment unto the Children of Israel."

Thank God the Mercy Seat is above the Ark of the Covenant, which contains the Law, with the demands that it be kept by me, and every other human being, but which we are woefully inadequate to comply. I don't care how great others may think your faith might be, I don't care how many Gifts of the Spirit which may function through you; if your Faith is not properly placed in the Cross, typified by the blood on the Mercy Seat, the Blood shed by Christ at Calvary, you simply cannot live an overcoming, victorious, Christian life, irrespective as to whom you might be.

Point out to me the Preacher over Television whom the Church thinks is mightily used of God, and irrespective of the fact that they may be drawing gigantic crowds, and claiming all type of miracles, if that Brother or Sister doesn't understand the manner in which the Holy Spirit works, which refers to the Believer anchoring his Faith in the Finished Work of Christ, which gives the Holy Spirit latitude to work, then that particular Preacher, whomever he or she might be, is living a life of spiritual failure. It cannot be otherwise! God has only one remedy for sin, not ten, not five, not two, just one, and that is the Cross of Christ.

If you the Reader are wearied by my constant repetition regarding the Cross, approaching this subject in every way that I can, then this proves that you do not properly understand the Cross as you should, and I would advise you to earnestly seek the Lord, that He reveal to you this foundational Truth. If you will be honest and earnest before Him, I will assure you that this is a prayer He will answer.

The latter portion of Verse 21 about putting the Testimony (Ten Commandments) into the Ark is virtually the same as Verse 16, with the repetition intended by the Holy Spirit.

Any time there is a repetition of this nature, and the Bible occasionally registers such, it is always done for purpose and reason. The Holy Spirit is endeavoring to draw our attention to something which is very important. So what is important about this particular statement?

The Lord is telling us here that the Ten Commandments, referred to as the *"Testimony,"* is the moral Law of God. It is God's Standard of Righteousness, that to which He demands that man keep, and must do so without breaking them even one time.

Some have claimed in these last few years that God has set the Standard too high. No, the Standard is not too high. The problem is, man's moral strength is too low. Lowering the Standard will not help; in fact, it will only exacerbate the matter. A thrice-Holy God, symbolized by the Cherubim, cannot accept less than total and complete perfection. And when we say *"perfection,"* we're not speaking of perfection for a short period of time, but perfection constantly.

Sadly, this shoots man down before he even begins, for the simple reason that man is conceived in sin, and born in sin, and we're speaking of original sin, which is the state of the human race because of Adam's Fall. Paul explained to us how this happened:

He said: *"For since by man* (Adam) *came death* (the Fall) *by Man* (Christ Jesus) *came also the resurrection of the dead.*

"For as in Adam all died (died spiritually and physically), *even so in Christ shall all be made alive"* (I Cor. 15:21-22).

So due to the Fall, man in his weakened moral condition simply cannot attain to the level which God demands — and demand it He does! But there is a way out of this dilemma, portrayed to us by the *"Mercy Seat."*

God would become Man, the Man, Christ Jesus, and as our Substitute, would do for man what man could not do for himself. He would be born under the Law (Gal. 4:4), but without original sin, because He wasn't conceived by man, and was born of the Virgin Mary. He kept the Law perfectly in every respect, all on our behalf as our Substitute, but not only did He do that, He as well suffered the curse and penalty of the broken Law, which condemned every human being, thereby redeeming us from that curse, *"being made a curse for us"* (Gal. 3:13).

So, the Holy Spirit telling Moses that the Testimony must be placed in the Ark, is in fact telling us that these Commandments are the moral Laws of God, and must be kept, and in fact, were kept by Christ Jesus, and Christ Jesus Alone!

COMMUNION

Verse 22 tells us:

1. It is only above the bloodstained Mercy Seat that God will meet with sinful human beings, because that's the only place that He can meet with sinful human beings, and not malign His Righteousness and Holiness. Now let the Reader understand that:

When John in His great vision given in Revelation, Chapters 4 and 5, saw the Throne of God, the Scripture says: *"And I beheld, and, lo, in the midst of the Throne and of the four Living Creatures, and in the midst of the Elders, stood a Lamb as it had been slain, having seven horns and seven eyes, which are the seven Spirits of God sent forth into all the Earth"* (Rev. 5:6).

The Elders whom John saw, which represent all the Redeemed of the Earth, are able to stand at the Throne of God, all because of the *"slain Lamb."*

The Cross is the meeting place between God and man. It is the point where Grace and Righteousness meet and perfectly harmonize. Nothing but Perfect Righteousness could suit God, and nothing but Perfect Grace could suit the sinner. But where could these attributes meet in one point? Only in the Cross. There it is that *"Mercy and Truth are met together; Righteousness and Peace have kissed each other"* (Ps. 85:10).

Concerning this, Mackintosh said: *"Thus it is that the soul of the believing sinner finds peace. He sees that God's Righteousness and His Justification rest upon precisely the same basis, namely Christ's accomplished Work. When man, under the powerful action of the Truth of God, takes his place as a sinner, God can, in the exercise of Grace, take His place as a Saviour, and then every question is settled, for the Cross having answered all the claims of Divine justice, Mercy's copious streams can flow unhindered. When a Righteous God and a ruined sinner meet on a blood-sprinkled platform, all is settled forever — settled in such a way as perfectly glorifies God, and eternally saves the sinner."*

He then said, *"When man is so thoroughly brought down to the lowest point of his own moral condition before God as to be willing to take the place which God's Truth assigns him, he then learns that God has revealed Himself as the Righteous Justifier of such an one."*

2. It is through the Finished Work of Christ on the Cross, typified by the Mercy Seat, that not only will the Lord meet with fallen man, and in fact, the only place where God will meet with fallen man, it is as well, where He will fellowship with man, and there alone.

This tells us that if man attempts to come to God any way other than the Bloodstained Cross, he will be frozen out, and in fact, the Holy Spirit forever stands guard to keep out those who would attempt to reach God in any manner other than the Cross. Listen to what Paul said:

"But now in Christ Jesus you who sometimes were far off are made near by the Blood of Christ . . . For through Him we both (Jews and Gentiles) *have access by one Spirit* (the Holy Spirit) *unto the Father"* (Eph. 2:13, 18).

This tells us that *"access"* to the Throne of God, to the Grace of God, in fact, to all that God is, is gained only by one way, and that is by the Cross of Christ, and our Faith in that Finished Work. The Holy Spirit guarantees access for all who come by that route, but at the same time, guarantees that the door will be closed to all who attempt to come another way. When Jesus said, *"I am the Door,"* He was speaking of a Blood-splattered door, typified by the houses in Egypt where the blood was applied (Jn. 10:9; Ex. 12:13).

All of this typifies the Throne of God, and the way, the only way, that man can approach Him, which is by and through the Cross of Christ. That's the reason I'm so insistent upon the Cross! That's the reason I approach this subject from every angle which the Lord gives me! That's the reason I address it in every fashion which I know how, even to the place of being overly repetitive. I do so because man can meet God in no other manner, than by the Cross.

The two Cherubim speak of the Holiness of God, and the *"Testimony,"* as we have stated, speaks of the Standard of God, which is the Ten Commandments.

THE TESTIMONY

Because of man's inability to keep the Commandments, which means that he broke them, which means that he didn't obey God, which incurred upon him a terrible penalty, Paul said, and rightly so, that these things were against us. He said:

"Blotting out the handwriting of Ordinances that was against us, which was contrary to us, and took it out of the way, nailing it to His Cross" (Col. 2:14).

Jesus satisfied the curse and the penalty

of the broken Law, which was death, and did so by the giving of Himself in Sacrifice (Gal. 1:4).

To be sure, He Alone could pay this price because He Alone was Perfect, consequently, the only Sacrifice which God would accept.

Under the old Jewish Law, which we are now studying, the man bringing the animal for sacrifice was accepted by God on the basis of the Sacrifice being accepted. In other words, if the Sacrifice was approved, then the one offering the sacrifice was approved. It is no different now.

Our Faith in Christ and what Christ has done for us at the Cross guarantees our acceptance, simply because God has accepted Christ. Unfortunately, we get it backwards many times, thinking that something we do makes us accepted. It doesn't! We are accepted only on the basis of our Faith in Christ, and what He did for us at the Cross because Christ has been accepted by God (Eph. 2:13-18).

(23) "YOU SHALL ALSO MAKE A TABLE OF SHITTIM WOOD: TWO CUBITS SHALL BE THE LENGTH THEREOF, AND A CUBIT THE BREADTH THEREOF, AND A CUBIT AND A HALF THE HEIGHT THEREOF.

(24) "AND YOU SHALL OVERLAY IT WITH PURE GOLD, AND MAKE THERETO A CROWN OF GOLD ROUND ABOUT.

(25) "AND YOU SHALL MAKE UNTO IT A BORDER OF AN HAND BREADTH ROUND ABOUT, AND YOU SHALL MAKE A GOLDEN CROWN FOR THE BORDER THEREOF ROUND ABOUT.

(26) "AND YOU SHALL MAKE FOR IT FOUR RINGS OF GOLD, AND PUT THE RINGS IN THE FOUR CORNERS THAT ARE ON THE FOUR FEET THEREOF.

(27) "OVER AGAINST THE BORDER SHALL THE RINGS BE FOR PLACES OF THE STAVES TO BEAR THE TABLE.

(28) "AND YOU SHALL MAKE THE STAVES OF SHITTIM WOOD, AND OVERLAY THEM WITH GOLD, THAT THE TABLE MAY BE BORNE WITH THEM.

(29) "AND YOU SHALL MAKE THE DISHES THEREOF, AND SPOONS THEREOF, AND COVERS THEREOF, AND BOWLS THEREOF, TO COVER WITHAL: OF PURE GOLD SHALL YOU MAKE THEM.

(30) "AND YOU SHALL SET UPON THE TABLE SHEWBREAD BEFORE ME ALWAYS."

The exegesis is:

1. Verses 23 through 30 portray the instructions given for the making of the *"Table of Shewbread."*

2. This piece of sacred furniture was made of *"shittim wood,"* which was often called *"indestructible wood,"* which spoke of the perfect humanity of Christ. It was covered with gold, which spoke of His Deity.

3. Verse 25 speaks of *"a golden crown to the border."* Three items of furniture had crowns, which typify the Kingly Glory of the Lord Jesus Christ: *"The Ark," "The Table of Shewbread,"* and *"The Altar of Incense."*

4. Verse 30 says: *"The Table of Shewbread,"* meaning *"Bread of Face"* because it was before the Face of God always, and told of its acceptableness to Him, and foreshadowed the Person of Christ as the One in Whom the Father has ever found His delight. Jesus and Jesus Alone is the Bread of Life.

THE TABLE OF SHEWBREAD

Verse 23 reads: *"You shall also make a table of shittim wood: two cubits shall be the length thereof, and a cubit the breadth thereof, and a cubit and a half the height thereof."*

This Table was made of indestructible wood, which as stated, pictured and proclaimed the perfect humanity of Christ. The Table was 36 inches long, 18 inches wide, and 27 inches high.

We have had described for us the contents of the Holy of Holies, into which the High Priest could alone go, and only once a year, and then with blood. The Holy Spirit through Moses now takes us into the Holy Place, separated from the Holy of Holies by a Veil, which we will later study.

In the Holy of Holies, the High Priest ministered only one day a year, the Great Day of Atonement. In the Holy Place, the regular Priests, one might say, ministered daily. In the Holy Place stood three pieces of sacred furniture. If you were walking through the front door, to your left would be the Golden Lampstand, to the right would be the Table of Shewbread, which we are now studying, and immediately in front of the Veil in the center would be the *"Altar of Incense."*

Considering that the Altar of Incense is the first piece of Sacred Furniture that one would see upon coming out of the Holy of Holies, one would think that this would be the next one named; however, the Holy Spirit, as is obvious here, rather deals first with the Table of Shewbread. When we see the meaning of the Table, we shall then see why the Holy Spirit has pointed it out first.

No regular Israelite could enter into the Holy Place or the Holy of Holies. None but the Priestly family ever penetrated this sacred precinct. Under the old economy, all Priests were Types of Christ, with the High Priest of Israel being the greatest Type of all.

But presently, through what Jesus has done for us at the Cross, every Saint of God, no matter who the person might be, or where the person might be, is now a member of the *"chosen generation, a royal Priesthood"* (I Pet. 2:5, 9).

THE PURPOSE OF THE TABLE

The Shewbread consisted of 12 loaves, made of fine flour, baked, and placed in two rows upon the Table. Those loaves were to remain there for seven days, and then they were to be eaten by the Priests.

This is typical of Jesus as the Bread of Life. Thus the Holy Spirit reveals the sufficiency of Christ as the Bread of His people day-by-day, and always fresh.

As the number *"seven"* speaks of the perfection of Christ, which as well speaks of the perfection of His Work, the number *"twelve"* speaks of His perfect government.

Under the Law, the perfection of Christ could not be totally revealed, while under Grace, it is most definitely revealed in totality. The Priests of old could only eat the bread on the seventh day, while we partake of Christ presently on a daily basis.

In effect, this is what Christ was speaking about when He said: *"As the Living Father has sent Me, and I live by the Father, so he who eats Me, even he shall live by Me"* (Jn. 6:57).

The way that we *"eat Christ,"* and do so on a daily basis, is by trusting Him, which refers to trusting what He did at the Cross on our behalf.

To explain it even further, Jesus also said: *"If any man will come after Me, let him deny himself, and take up his Cross daily, and follow Me"* (Lk. 9:23).

As stated, the twelve loaves signify the Government of God, as the number twelve always signifies such as it relates to the Lord. As should be understood, there is nothing more important for the Believer than an understanding of God's Government, which means to understand His Ways. In this way alone can we have life and victory.

And to understand His Government, one must first understand the Cross. Without properly understanding the Cross, and what it actually means, it is impossible to understand God's Government.

COMMUNION

In Verse 22, the Lord mentioned *"Communion,"* and the Table, which He addresses next, speaks of Communion as well. In I Corinthians, Chapter 10, Paul taught us that the *"Table"* is inseparably connected with Communion. He refers to it as *"the Lord's Table,"* which is always symbolic of fellowship with Christ. Pink said: *"We learn that the blood-sprinkled Mercy-Seat speaks of Christ as the 'basis' of our fellowship with God, while the Table points to Christ as the 'substance' of that fellowship."* He then went on to say: *"The Table sets forth Jehovah's feast of love for His Saints and for Himself in fellowship with them."*

THE DIMENSIONS OF THE TABLE

We find that the Table, although the same height as the Ark, yet fell short of its length and width.

This tells us that it is impossible to exhaust Christ. No matter how much we partake of Him, we always fall short of exhausting His potential.

We can say the same thing as it regards the Cross. Whatever the Lord shows us about the Cross, however deep it might be, we will shortly find that we have not exhausted its potential. That's why Paul referred to the Cross as *"The Everlasting Covenant"* (Heb. 13:20).

When the Lord in 1996 first began to show me the meaning of the Cross as it refers to the Believer's Sanctification, I sensed in my spirit that as grand and as glorious as those beginning days were, still, I knew I had only scratched the surface. And in seeking the Lord, and sensing in my spirit as the Holy Spirit revealed it to me, that it was impossible to exhaust this potential, I implored the Lord that He would continue to open the door ever wider, which He most definitely has!

What I have learned has gloriously changed my life, and done so in such a remarkable way as to defy description. The victory that I now have in Christ is that for which I had so long sought, and it is all because of the Cross. As well, the Lord has opened up to me the joy of *"more abundant life"* (Jn. 10:10). In fact, every Believer has more abundant life, but regrettably, most Believers aren't enjoying it because they little understand the reason for its source.

GOLD

Verses 24 and 25 read: *"And you shall overlay it with pure gold, and make thereto a crown of gold round about.*

"And you shall make unto it a border of an hand breadth round about, and you shall make a golden crown to the border thereof round about."

The *"crown"* speaks of the Kingly position of Christ, and with the crown covered in gold, along with the entirety of the Table, speaks of His Deity.

The crown would tend to keep the Bread in place, so that it would not slip off the Table, especially during times when Israel was instructed by the Lord to move. This speaks of the security of the Believer, all in Christ.

It is interesting that the width of the crown is described as a *"hand breadth,"* which is approximately three to four inches high. All the dimensions of the Tabernacle otherwise are in cubits or half cubits.

This corresponds with the Words of Christ: *"Neither shall any pluck them out of My hand"* (Jn. 10:28).

There seems to have been a difference in the *"crown"* and the *"border."*

The *"border"* was as well to be the width of a hand, and seems to have been a broad flat bar, placed about halfway down the legs, uniting them and holding them together. At the top of the bar, there was also to be a crown of gold.

THE RINGS AND THE STAVES

Verses 26 through 28 read: *"And you shall make for it four rings of gold, and put the rings in the four corners that are on the four feet thereof.*

"Over against the border shall the rings be for places of the staves to bear the Table.

"And you shall make the staves of shittim wood, and overlay them with gold, that the table may be borne with them."

Wherever the Lord led Israel, even though it was in the wilderness, His Table accompanied them! So wherever the Christian's lot may be cast, even though it may be in a prison such as Paul, the Believer can continue to feed on Christ, for Christ is ever with him.

It seems that the gold rings were placed at either end of the Table, instead of the sides as the Ark.

The staves for carrying the Table were made of indestructible wood and overlaid with gold. This refers to the fact that anywhere is home, if Christ my Lord is there.

THE DISHES

Verse 29 reads: *"And you shall make the dishes thereof, and spoons thereof, and covers thereof, and bowls thereof, to cover withal: of pure gold shall you make them."*

The utensils and vessels were to be made of gold also.

The *"dishes"* were no doubt used by the Priests when they ate the Bread on the seventh day. The *"spoons"* and the *"cover"* were more than likely used in connection with the Frankincense, which was to be poured over the Bread, symbolizing the fragrance and purity of Christ.

The *"bowls"* were probably cups, and were used in connection with the *"Drink Offerings,"* which were poured out before the Lord *"in the Holy Place"* (Num. 28:7). Pink said: *"The fact that the 'cups,' used in connection with the 'Drink-Offerings,' were placed upon the Table, tells us that Communion is the basis of thanksgiving!"

PERPETUAL SHEWBREAD

Verse 30 reads: *"And you shall set upon the Table Shewbread before Me always."*

As previously stated, the Covenant of the Cross is referred to as *"The Blood of the Everlasting Covenant"* (Heb. 13:20). This means that the Way has been Christ, even from the very beginning, the Way presently is Christ, and the Way will always be Christ, i.e., *"always."* And more particularly, it is what Christ did, and I refer to the Cross.

In Chapters 21 and 22 of Revelation, which proclaim the Perfect Age to come, when Satan, fallen angels, and demons are forever locked away in the Lake of Fire, and when no more sin is present in this world, and in fact, the world and the universe have been cleansed from all sin, with at long last, the Son having delivered the Kingdom up to the Father (I Cor. 15:24), even then, Christ is referred to seven times in these last two Chapters as *"the Lamb"* (Rev. 21:9, 14, 22, 23, 27; 22:1, 3). This appellative is used of Christ in order that we may know and realize that the glorious Perfect Age, which will most assuredly come, and will last forever and forever, was in fact, made possible by what Jesus did at the Cross. We are to never forget it, i.e., *"always."*

(31) "AND YOU SHALL MAKE A CANDLESTICK OF PURE GOLD: OF BEATEN WORK SHALL THE CANDLESTICK BE MADE: HIS SHAFT, AND HIS BRANCHES, HIS BOWLS, HIS KNOPS, AND HIS FLOWERS, SHALL BE OF THE SAME.

(32) "AND SIX BRANCHES SHALL COME OUT OF THE SIDES OF IT; THREE BRANCHES OF THE CANDLESTICK OUT OF THE ONE SIDE, AND THREE BRANCHES OF THE CANDLESTICK OUT OF THE OTHER SIDE:

(33) "THREE BOWLS MADE LIKE UNTO ALMONDS, WITH A KNOP AND A FLOWER IN ONE BRANCH: AND THREE BOWLS MADE LIKE ALMONDS IN OTHER BRANCH, WITH A KNOP AND A FLOWER: SO IN THE SIX BRANCHES THAT COME OUT OF THE CANDLESTICK.

(34) "AND IN THE CANDLESTICK SHALL BE FOUR BOWLS MADE LIKE UNTO ALMONDS, WITH THEIR KNOPS AND THEIR FLOWERS.

(35) "AND THERE SHALL BE A KNOP UNDER TWO BRANCHES OF THE SAME, AND A KNOP UNDER TWO BRANCHES OF THE SAME, AND A KNOP UNDER TWO BRANCHES OF THE SAME, ACCORDING TO THE SIX BRANCHES THAT PROCEED OUT OF THE CANDLESTICK.

(36) "THEIR KNOPS AND THEIR BRANCHES SHALL BE OF THE SAME: ALL IT SHALL BE ONE BEATEN WORK OF PURE GOLD.

(37) "AND YOU SHALL MAKE THE SEVEN LAMPS THEREOF: AND THEY SHALL LIGHT THE LAMPS THEREOF, THAT THEY MAY GIVE LIGHT OVER AGAINST IT.

(38) "AND THE TONGS THEREOF, AND THE SNUFF DISHES THEREOF, SHALL BE OF PURE GOLD.

(39) "OF A TALENT OF PURE GOLD SHALL HE MAKE IT, WITH ALL THESE VESSELS.

(40) "AND LOOK THAT YOU MAKE THEM AFTER THEIR PATTERN, WHICH WAS SHOWED YOU IN THE MOUNT."

The diagram is:

1. The Candlestick did not begin with indestructible wood, but was made entirely out of *"pure gold."*

2. The six branches, three coming out from each side, symbolized the Church. The number six is the number of man, and which speaks of imperfection; however, Christ is the main stem in the middle, and makes up the seventh branch, thereby denoting perfection, as the Church is joined to Christ.

3. The branches were not welded or fastened to the main branch, but were actually a part of the branch, showing the oneness of the Child of God with the Lord Jesus Christ.

4. The four bowls were made like almonds, and the almond is the emblem of Resurrection.

5. The *"knop"* portrays *"pomegranates,"* which speaks of fruit.

6. The *"flowers"* speak of *"lilies,"* which speak of purity.

7. At the end of each stem was a *"Lamp,"* totaling seven in all, which speaks of perfect illumination, i.e., *"Jesus, as the Light*

of the world."

8. Moses was to be careful that he fashioned these items according to the directions which God gave him, taking nothing away, nor adding anything.

THE CANDLESTICK

Verse 31 reads: *"And you shall make a Candlestick of pure gold: of beaten work shall the Candlestick be made: his shaft, and his branches, his bowls, his knops, and his flowers, shall be of the same."*

The Lampstand, unlike many of the other vessels, was made of *"pure gold."* It contained no indestructible wood, which served as a type of the humanity of Christ; and yet, the next phrase does, in a sense, speak of His humanity.

Incidentally, the Hebrew word *"M'nourah"* means, *"lightbearer,"* and should have been translated *"lampstand,"* instead of candlestick. A candlestick holds candles, and there were no candles on this particular Sacred Vessel.

If you had come through the front door of the Tabernacle, the Lampstand would have sat to your left, which would have been the south side, for the Tabernacle always faced the east.

None but Priests could enter the Holy Place, so in essence, the people of Israel did not actually ever see the Golden Lampstand.

The Lampstand was the only source of light in the entirety of the Holy Place; consequently, the Priests could see to eat the Shewbread, and offer up Incense on the Golden Altar, only by the light of the Lampstand.

The Lampstand is a Type of Christ as the Light of the world, whether in His earthly Ministry, pertaining to His first Advent, or through His Church. While Believers are the light of the world presently, we are such light only as a reflection of Christ (Mat. 5:14).

The Lampstand as well portrays the Holy Spirit, typified by the oil, in his work within and upon Christ (Lk. 4:18-19).

The phrase, *"Of beaten work shall the Lampstand be made,"* portrays the second time the word *"beaten"* is used, the first being the Cherubim (Ex. 25:18).

In the literal sense, the word *"beaten"* refers to the fact that the Lampstand was not cast in a mold, but was rather fashioned by hand. This means the entire Lampstand was fashioned and made out of one piece of Gold, which some say no craftsman in the world presently could do such a thing.

In the spiritual sense, it refers to the humanity of Christ, God becoming man, which in actuality, is beyond our comprehension. The Creator becoming a creature is beyond our pale of understanding. But that's what happened!

"Beaten" speaks of the suffering of Christ, and by that we refer to the Cross, Who now is glorified, and done so as the reward of His perfect but painful Work.

Due to His Finished Work, Christ now occupies an even greater position than before His Incarnation. The Scripture says of Him: *"And being found in fashion as a man, He humbled Himself, and became obedient unto death, even the death of the Cross."*

"Wherefore God also has highly exalted Him, and given Him a Name which is above every name" (Phil. 2:8-9).

Considering that Christ is God, and that He has always been perfect, how can perfection become greater?

In fact, perfection cannot be made greater; however, one can definitely add to perfection, and this is exactly what happened with Christ.

He is Creator, but due to His Atoning Work on the Cross of Calvary, He is also now Saviour, which makes Him more exalted than ever before (Heb. 1:3-4).

THE BOWLS, THE KNOPS, AND THE FLOWERS

The three items of the heading could be translated *"cups, pomegranates, and lilies."*

The *"bowls"* or *"cups"* form the first ornament on each branch, and are likened to almonds, which signify the Resurrection (Num. 17:1-8).

The *"knops"* could have been translated *"pomegranates,"* which speak of fruit.

The *"flowers"* could have been translated *"lilies,"* and speak of purity. The lily blossoms supported the lamps, which were separate.

So the Lampstand, in its portrayal of light, first of all speaks of *"Resurrection,"* which pertains to the believing sinner being baptized into the death of Christ, buried with Him by baptism into death, and then raised with Him in *"newness of life,"* which speaks of Resurrection (Rom. 6:3-4).

Paul also said: *"For if we have been planted together in the likeness of His death, we shall be also in the likeness of His Resurrection"* (Rom. 6:5).

This particular Passage doesn't speak of the coming Resurrection, but rather, the Resurrection of a new life as it regards the Born-Again experience.

The Believer, as Christ now lives through him, and thereby aided by the Holy Spirit, even as he maintains his Faith in the Finished Work of Christ, now begins to bring forth *"fruit."*

Jesus said: *"I am the Vine, you are the branches: he who abides in Me, and I in him* (Rom. 6:3-5; Jn. 14:20), *the same brings forth much fruit: for without Me you can do nothing"* (Jn. 15:5).

The *"lily"* speaks of *"purity,"* and which one can have only as one looks totally to Christ, and what Christ has done at the Cross. The individual cannot make himself pure, that being a work entirely of the Holy Spirit. He functions entirely upon the basis of the Finished Work of Christ, thereby, demanding that we always have and maintain Faith in that great Sacrifice.

THE BRANCHES

Verse 32 reads: *"And six branches shall come out of the sides of it; three branches of the Candlestick out of the one side, and three branches of the Candlestick out of the other side."*

There is tremendous spiritual meaning in the design of the Lampstand. It had three branches to the side totaling six, which is the number of man, and which is the Body of Christ, whether Israel or the Church. Actually, in Christ we have been *"both made one"* (Eph. 2:14).

Verse 36 tells us that the entirety of the Lampstand was *"one beaten work of pure gold,"* meaning that these branches were not welded or fastened to the side of the main stem, but were rather a part of the main stem. This speaks of our being *"in Christ."*

Paul used the term *"in Christ,"* or one of its derivatives such as, *"in Him,"* some 170 times in his 14 Epistles. We are *"in Christ,"* as stated, by virtue of being baptized into His death, and buried with Him by baptism into death, and then raised with Him in newness of life (Rom. 6:3-4).

This tells us how significant the Cross is to the Believer. It is the manner by which we were able to be grafted into Christ. This makes us one with Christ, which in effect, is intended. Without proper Faith in the Cross, there is no union with Christ, as should be obvious!

THE APPEARANCE OF THE BRANCHES

Verse 33 reads: *"Three bowls made like unto almonds, with a knop and a flower in one branch; and three bowls made like almonds in the other branch, with a knop and a flower: so in the six branches that come out of the Candlestick."*

The ornamentation of these branches seem to be as follows:

There were three *"bowls"* shaped like almond blossoms, with each branch having the same number. The three were then followed by a pomegranate and a lily-flower.

We might ask the question as to why there were three bowls (almond blossoms) on each stem, and only one pomegranate and only one lily?

This tells us that the almond blossom, which represents Resurrection, which speaks of the Cross, is the foundation on which everything is based. This is where the emphasis must always be. This is why Paul said:

"For Christ sent me not to baptize, but to preach the Gospel: not with wisdom of words, lest the Cross of Christ should be made of none effect" (I Cor. 1:17).

As well, we must ever understand that we have Resurrection Life only as we understand the Crucifixion, and what it means to us. Paul also said:

"For if we have been planted together in the likeness of His death, we shall be also in the likeness of His Resurrection" (Rom. 6:5).

Many Christians are fond of saying that they are *"Resurrection people."* While that is certainly true, it is only true, in other words we can enjoy Resurrection Life, only as we understand that *"we have been planted together in the likeness of His death."* The victory was won at the Cross, with the Resurrection being one of the results and benefits of that victory.

There was never any doubt that Jesus was going to be raised from the dead. The only thing that could have stopped Him would be that He didn't atone for all sin, for the wages of sin is death; however, by the very fact of His Resurrection, we know that He atoned for all sin, past, present, and future, at least for those who will believe (Jn. 3:16). Always remember this:

Paul said as well: *"But God forbid that I should glory, save in the Cross of our Lord Jesus Christ, by Whom the world is crucified unto me, and I unto the world"* (Gal. 6:14).

I remind the Reader that Paul didn't say, *"But God forbid that I should glory, save in the Resurrection of our Lord Jesus Christ...."* No, in no way was he minimizing the Resurrection, and in no way are we minimizing the Resurrection. We are merely stating, as he merely stated, that the Cross is the Foundation of all that we have in Christ, and the Cross alone, which of course produced the Resurrection.

If we properly understand the Cross, we will have Resurrection Life, and the *"Fruit of the Spirit,"* typified by the pomegranates, will be developed in our lives, which will always result in *"purity,"* represented by the lily, i.e., *"flower."*

THE CENTRAL SHAFT

Verse 34 reads: *"And in the Lampstand shall be four bowls made like unto almonds, with their knops and their flowers."*

By the short phrase, *"And in the Lampstand,"* we know that Moses is speaking of the central shaft or stem. Where the branches had three *"bowls"* with one *"knop"* and one *"flower,"* the middle stem had *"four bowls,"* along with *"four knops"* and *"four flowers."* This made 12 ornaments, which spoke of the Government of Christ.

This tells us that His Government has as its Foundation the Cross, which will produce much fruit and much purity.

There were five ornaments on each stem, *"three bowls,"* with *"one knop"* and *"one flower."* Five is the number of Grace, and means that we as Believers have these great qualities, not at all because of our merit, but strictly because of the Grace of God (Eph. 2:8-9).

THE BRANCHES

Verses 35 and 36 read: *"And there shall be a knop under two branches of the same, and a knop under two branches of the same, and a knop under two branches of the same, according to the six branches that proceed out of the Lampstand.*

"Their knops and their branches shall be of the same: all it shall be one beaten work of pure gold."

Two things are said here:

1. Addressing the latter first, even as we've already stated, the entirety of the Lampstand was of one piece of gold, crafted according to the design given by the Holy Spirit, and exactly according to the design given by the Holy Spirit.

2. Even though the branches came out even at the top, even with the main shaft, as would be obvious, the outward branch would be the longest of all, with the middle branch next to the longest, with the branch closest to the stem being the shortest. But yet, all of them had the same number of ornamentation.

This tells us that all Believers can enjoy Resurrection Life, bear fruit, and develop purity. Of course, all of this is a work of the Holy Spirit, which we shall see.

THE SEVEN LAMPS

Verses 37 through 40 read: *"And you shall make the seven lamps thereof: and they shall light the lamps thereof, that they may give light over against it.*

"And the tongs thereof, and the snuff dishes thereof, shall be of pure gold.

"Of a talent of pure gold shall he make it, with all these vessels.

"And look that you make them after their pattern, which was showed you in the Mount."

1. The *"Lamps"* were at the top of each branch and the main stem. They were separate from the ornamentation.

2. There were *"seven"* of these Lamps, which speaks of perfect illumination, which

only the Holy Spirit can do. If we follow Him, we will have a perfect leading.

3. It seems as if the Lamps were cleaned and lit twice a day, at sunset and at sunrise (Ex. 27:21; 30:8; Lev. 24:3), or possibly it could have been at the time of the morning (9:00) and evening (3:00) Sacrifices.

4. They gave light over against the Table of Shewbread and the Altar of Incense. In fact, and as stated, this was the only light provided in the Holy Place.

5. The *"tongs"* and the *"snuff dishes"* had to do with the cleaning of the wick, or replacing the wick, in order that the light might burn clean and bright.

6. A talent of pure gold weighed about 120 pounds. At 16 ounces to the pound, we come up with 1,920 ounces. At $300 per ounce, we have a total of about $576,000, which would have been the present cost of the gold, as it regards the Lampstand. This would not have included the craftsmanship that it took to make the Sacred Vessel.

7. Moses was instructed to follow the Pattern exactly, which means it was not to be deviated from in any capacity.

This tells us that the Work of the Spirit in our hearts and lives must be carried out strictly on God's terms, and His terms alone. The moment we begin to tamper with this which the Lord has done, in other words, to tamper with His Plan, at that moment, we destroy the Work of God in our lives. And regrettably, this is the great sin of the Church.

His *"Pattern"* is the Cross, and our Faith in that Finished Work. We must understand that the moment we attempt to put our own strength and ability into the mix, we have wrecked the victory that we could have. The Holy Spirit will not function in that capacity whatsoever. He demands that we exhibit Faith exclusively in Christ and the Cross, which gives Him the ability to work within our lives, and which guarantees victory in every capacity. In this manner, and this manner alone, can we have what we should have in the Lord as Believers, which refers to victory over the world, the flesh, and the Devil (Rom. 6:3-14; 8:1-2, 11; I Cor. 1:17-18, 21, 23; 2:2; Eph. 2:13-18; Col. 2:14-15).

NOTES

"There is a Fountain open for my cleansing,
"Where sin's Atonement by my Lord was made;
"He was the Lamb Who was led to the slaughter,
"His Blood the fountain where my debt was paid."

"There is a Rock that stands, by storms unshaken,
"Redemption's Author the foundation laid;
"By Faith my stand on His Righteousness I've taken,
"He will not fail, I shall not be dismayed."

"There is a Book that points the path to Glory,
"Eternal guidepost for the wayward soul;
"On its fair pages is told the wondrous story
"Of life in Christ, the everlasting goal."

"There is a Hope, a wondrous consolation,
"In a benighted world a constant star;
"These eyes now dulled by the shadows that surround me
"My Saviour shall behold in realms afar."

"There is a Home my Saviour is preparing
"I may not need to cross death's sullen vale;
"Soon from Earth's bondage His Coming will release me
"To live where joys eternal shall prevail."

CHAPTER 26

(1) "MOREOVER YOU SHALL MAKE THE TABERNACLE WITH TEN CURTAINS OF FINE TWINED LINEN, AND BLUE, AND PURPLE, AND SCARLET: WITH CHERUBIM OF CUNNING WORK SHALL YOU MAKE THEM.

(2) "THE LENGTH OF ONE CURTAIN SHALL BE EIGHT AND TWENTY CUBITS, AND THE WIDTH OF ONE CURTAIN FOUR CUBITS: AND EVERY ONE OF THE

(3) "THE FIVE CURTAINS SHALL BE COUPLED TOGETHER ONE TO ANOTHER; AND OTHER FIVE CURTAINS SHALL BE COUPLED ONE TO ANOTHER.

(4) "AND YOU SHALL MAKE LOOPS OF BLUE UPON THE EDGE OF THE ONE CURTAIN FROM THE SELVEDGE IN THE COUPLING; AND LIKEWISE SHALL YOU MAKE IN THE UTTERMOST EDGE OF ANOTHER CURTAIN, IN THE COUPLING OF THE SECOND.

(5) "FIFTY LOOPS SHALL YOU MAKE IN THE ONE CURTAIN, AND FIFTY LOOPS SHALL YOU MAKE IN THE EDGE OF THE CURTAIN THAT IS IN THE COUPLING OF THE SECOND; THAT THE LOOPS MAY TAKE HOLD ONE OF ANOTHER.

(6) "AND YOU SHALL MAKE FIFTY TACHES OF GOLD, AND COUPLE THE CURTAINS TOGETHER WITH THE TACHES: AND IT SHALL BE ONE TABERNACLE."

The overview is:

1. The Tabernacle was one, as it regarded its purpose. It pictured the Person and Work of Christ.

2. Grace was its keynote. This was expressed by the number *"five"* and its multiples.

3. These *"ten curtains"* constituted the ceiling or inner covering of the Tabernacle.

4. The *"fine twined linen,"* portrayed the perfection of Christ.

5. Figures of Cherubs were to be woven into the hangings in the loom itself, not embroidered upon them afterwards.

TEN CURTAINS

Verses 1 through 3 read: *"Moreover you shall make the Tabernacle with ten curtains of fine twined linen, and blue, and purple, and scarlet: with Cherubim of cunning work shall you make them.*

"The length of one curtain shall be eight and twenty cubits, and the width of one curtain four cubits: and every one of the curtains shall have one measure.

"The five curtains shall be coupled together one to another; and other five curtains shall be coupled one to another."

While the Scripture is not perfectly clear on the subject, it seems that these *"ten curtains"* had to do with the inner covering of the Tabernacle. They were elaborately embroidered, and joined together.

It would seem like the next description after the Lampstand would be the walls of the Tabernacle, but the Lord's Ways are not our ways. Everything He does is perfect, and He has a reason for doing it in the manner in which it is done, whatever it might be.

It is the business and obligation of the Believer to allow the Holy Spirit to work in our lives to such an extent that we begin to see things as the Lord sees them, and in effect, to think like Him, at least as far as is possible to do so.

Each of these curtains was 42 feet long, and six feet wide.

They were coupled together in fives, thus giving a total length of 42 feet, and width of 60 feet, which would not only reach across the Tabernacle, which was 15 feet wide, but would overlap its sides, which they were intended to do.

The two sets of five white curtains were linked together by 50 loops of blue in each, which were fastened with 50 taches or clasps of gold, thus firmly uniting the whole together in one solid piece (Pink).

FINE TWINED LINEN

This *"linen"* was not linen merely, but rather *"fine linen,"* linen of peculiar excellency.

This linen was perfectly white, and typified the Perfect Righteousness of Christ, which as well typifies the Righteousness of the Saints, that is if their Faith is totally in Christ and what He has done at the Cross (Rev. 19:8).

Cherubim were to be woven into the material, using the colors of *"blue, and purple, and scarlet."* The *"blue"* represented the fact that all of Salvation comes from Heaven, and not at all from this Earth, meaning that Christ was all of Heaven.

"Purple" speaks of royalty, meaning that Jesus Christ was a King as well, in effect, *"the King."*

The *"Scarlet"* speaks of blood, and thereby, the sufferings of Christ. Of course, the Cherubim denote His Holiness.

So in these curtains, we have Righteousness, Holiness, the Heavenly, the Kingly, and as well, the Cross.

As the Golden Lampstand illuminated the Holy Place, the white would have been brilliant, with the colors standing out in bold relief, all typifying Christ, and portraying the beauty which would not be seen from the outside. In fact, there was nothing beautiful about the Tabernacle on the outside, all beauty reserved for the interior.

So, the world looks at Christ, *"and there is no beauty that they should desire Him,"* at least outwardly. But the Tabernacle tells us differently. It tells us that He is beautiful beyond compare. But one has to come inside the Tabernacle, i.e., *"into Christ,"* which can only be done in the Born-Again experience, before one can fully know What and Who Christ actually is.

Without this Revelation, Christ is just another figure in history, and a peasant at that! But to those who have accepted Him as Lord and Saviour, we know Him to be of such beautiful composure as to defy all description.

When He came the first time, He came as the outward appearance of the Tabernacle. There was little attraction there. But when He comes the second time, which Revelation, Chapter 19 describes, He will come as *"King of kings and Lord of lords,"* which refers to a power, glory, and beauty beyond compare.

THE LENGTH AND WIDTH OF THE CURTAINS

The length of one curtain was 28 cubits, and its width was four cubits.

"Seven" the perfect number, God's number, goes four times into the length, with the curtains as well, being four cubits wide. This speaks of the perfection of *"seven,"* and the completeness of *"four."*

Dennett said concerning this: *"The curtains of the Tabernacle, consequently, speak of the complete unfolding perfections of Christ as Man when passing through this scene."*

THE REASON

I personally believe that the reason the Lord gave the dimensions of the curtains first, before He went to the walls, is because the curtains formed the ceiling of the Tabernacle. This suggests that the curtains set before us the One Who humbled Himself, and became obedient unto death, but Who is now exalted and glorified on High.

In John's Visions, we have an idea of what all of this means:

1. John saw Christ in His Glory (Rev. 1:12-17).

2. He saw Him as *"a Lamb as it had been slain . . ."* (Rev. 5:6).

This tells us that the Glory and Beauty of Christ cannot be properly seen except through His Cross. As beautiful as it is, the white linen, which spoke of His Righteousness, typifies His perfection in every capacity, but especially as it regards the Sacrifice. The *"blue"* tells us that there was none on Earth worthy to offer Himself in Sacrifice, so One would have to come from Heaven, Who is the Lord Jesus Christ. The *"purple"* speaks of His Kingship, but yet, He could not have been King, unless He had gone to the Cross. The *"Scarlet"* speaks of the price that He paid, leading us directly to the Cross.

So even though the ceiling was beautiful beyond compare, and which pictures Christ, as it could only picture Christ, it all portrays His Atoning Work on the Cross, which the Cherubim addressed by constantly saying, *"Holy, holy, holy."*

THE LOOPS

Verses 4 through 6 read: *"And you shall make loops of blue upon the edge of the one curtain from the selvedge in the coupling; and likewise shall you make in the uttermost edge of another curtain, in the coupling of the second.*

"Fifty loops shall you make in the one curtain, and fifty loops shall you make in the edge of the curtain that is in the coupling of the second; that the loops may take hold one of another.

"And you shall make fifty taches of gold, and couple the curtains together with the taches: and it shall be one Tabernacle."

As would be obvious, the loops were appointed for the joining of the curtains together.

The *"ten curtains,"* arranged in two sets of five each, point out something to us.

First of all, the meaning of the number *"ten"* is that of human responsibility.

As an example, we see that there were ten plagues upon Egypt, with Pharaoh continuing to rebel, which demonstrated the failure of his responsibility. He and his hosts were destroyed at the Red Sea.

In these last days, the Scripture tells us that Gentile domination will consist of *"ten kingdoms,"* and then will be fully manifested in the breakdown of its responsibility.

God gave Ten Commandments to the human race. The first five pertain to man's responsibility to God, with the second five pertaining to our responsibility to our fellow man.

Consequently, the *"ten curtains"* speak of Christ, as the Representative of His people, meeting the whole of our obligations both Godwards and manwards. He loved God with all His heart, and His neighbor as Himself. He was the only One by Whom these responsibilities were fully and perfectly met (Pink).

The loops were blue, the color of Heaven, again signifying that everything we have from the Lord came entirely from Heaven, and none at all from Earth, even though its consummation was on Earth, and I speak of the Cross.

The word *"taches"* means *"couplings."* They were made of gold, and they united the curtains together, as they were passed through the loops of blue.

All of this may seem insignificant; however, without these loops and couplings, the beautiful curtains would have hung apart one from another, and thus the one main feature of their manifestation would have been lost.

These *"couplings"* fastened the whole of the ten curtains together so that they were *"one Tabernacle."* Thus they pointed to the blessed unity and uniformity of the character and life of Christ (Pink).

The 50 loops were expressed by the number *"five"* and its multiples. As we shall see, there were 50 boards, 15 bars, and 100 sockets. There were 50 loops and 50 taches of gold, and 50 taches of brass. As we have stated, five is the number of Grace, which denotes this Tabernacle, and is the attribute of Christ (Jn. 1:17).

(7) "AND YOU SHALL MAKE CURTAINS OF GOATS' HAIR TO BE A COVERING UPON THE TABERNACLE: ELEVEN CURTAINS SHALL YOU MAKE.

(8) "THE LENGTH OF ONE CURTAIN SHALL BE THIRTY CUBITS, AND THE WIDTH OF ONE CURTAIN FOUR CUBITS: AND THE ELEVEN CURTAINS SHALL BE ALL OF ONE MEASURE.

(9) "AND YOU SHALL COUPLE FIVE CURTAINS BY THEMSELVES, AND SIX CURTAINS BY THEMSELVES, AND SHALL DOUBLE THE SIXTH CURTAIN IN THE FOREFRONT OF THE TABERNACLE.

(10) "AND YOU SHALL MAKE FIFTY LOOPS IN THE EDGE OF THE ONE CURTAIN THAT IS OUTMOST IN THE COUPLING, AND FIFTY LOOPS IN THE EDGE OF THE CURTAIN WHICH COUPLES THE SECOND.

(11) "AND YOU SHALL MAKE FIFTY TACHES OF BRASS, AND PUT THE TACHES INTO THE LOOPS, AND COUPLE THE TENT TOGETHER, THAT IT MAY BE ONE.

(12) "AND THE REMNANT THAT REMAINS OF THE CURTAINS OF THE TENT, THE HALF CURTAIN THAT REMAINS, SHALL HANG OVER THE BACKSIDE OF THE TABERNACLE.

(13) "AND A CUBIT ON THE ONE SIDE, AND A CUBIT ON THE OTHER SIDE OF THAT WHICH REMAINS IN THE LENGTH OF THE CURTAINS OF THE TENT, IT SHALL HANG OVER THE SIDES OF THE TABERNACLE ON THIS SIDE AND ON THAT SIDE, TO COVER IT.

(14) "AND YOU SHALL MAKE A COVERING FOR THE TENT OF RAMS' SKINS DYED RED, AND A COVERING ABOVE OF BADGERS' SKINS."

The diagram is:

1. There were four coverings to the top of the Tabernacle. The second covering immediately above the fine twined linen, which was the part that could be seen, was a covering of *"Goats' hair,"* which could not be seen.

2. As the white linen symbolized the Righteousness of Christ, the *"Goats' hair,"* which provided the second covering, symbolized His Prophetic Office.

3. Whereas the first covering of linen contained ten curtains, the covering of Goats' hair contained 11 curtains. This was done for purpose, as everything God does is for purpose.

The Lord knowing that we would not quite understand why He would desire 11 curtains for this covering, solved the mystery for us, at least as to how these curtains are to be interpreted, by dividing them into two sections. One section had five curtains, and the other section had six curtains.

In order to discover the spiritual significance of this number 11, we are thus shown that we are not to consider it by itself as a whole, but as made up of five and six. This simplifies things very much.

"Five" stands for Grace, while *"six"* is the number of man.

GOATS' HAIR

Verse 7 reads: *"And you shall make curtains of Goats' hair to be a covering upon the Tabernacle: eleven curtains shall you make."*

The *"Goats' hair"* covering was totally hidden from view. It signified Christ's Prophetic Office. But even though He definitely was a Prophet, and in fact, the greatest Prophet of all, as would be obvious, He was not recognized or *"seen"* as such! Israel rejected Him, and would not own Him at all. When He predicted that He would be killed in Jerusalem, and then would rise from the dead on the third day, His Own Disciples rebuked Him (Mat. 16:21-23).

It was at this time that Jesus said: *"If any man will come after Me, let him deny himself, and take up his cross, and follow Me"* (Mat. 16:24).

In effect, He was telling His Disciples not only that He would be killed, but that the Cross would be used to bring about this terrible crime.

However, we must quickly say that while murder was in the heart of the Jews, they in effect did not take His life from Him; He purposely laid it down (Jn. 10:17-18). So, as the *"Goats' hair"* covering was hidden from view, likewise, the Prophetic Office of Christ was hidden from view as well!

Whereas 10 curtains had been joined together to make the ceiling of fine twined linen, 11 curtains were to be used as it regards the Goats' hair covering.

Why 11 curtains? The next two Verses provide some small clue.

DOUBLED

Verses 8 and 9 read: *"The length of one curtain shall be thirty cubits, and the width of one curtain four cubits: and the eleven curtains shall be all of one measure.*

"And you shall couple five curtains by themselves, and six curtains by themselves, and shall double the sixth curtain in the forefront of the Tabernacle."

The idea of the eleventh curtain seems to be twofold.

First of all, these coverings, or curtains, seem to have been laid crossways over the Tabernacle, with the ends hanging down on both sides. In other words, there was no hip roof on the Tabernacle, the top being flat, which top was actually the coverings.

The adding of the eleventh curtain created enough extra width that it could be doubled at the forefront, which referred to it being pulled under the linen covering, which would provide greater protection from the elements.

The width of the Goats' hair curtains was the same as the linen curtains, but the Goats' hair curtains were two cubits longer.

The Tabernacle itself was 30 cubits long (45 feet), ten cubits broad (15 feet), and ten cubits high (15 feet).

Due to being 28 cubits, the linen curtain would not come down all the way to the ground on either side of the Tabernacle. But the Goats' hair covering being 30 cubits, which is 45 feet, would cover the Tabernacle and the sides completely, actually reaching to the ground on either side, thereby giving it proper protection.

The prophetic Ministry of Christ was perfect in every respect, and in fact, the only perfect prophetic Ministry which has ever existed. The Earthly Ministry of Christ, as it refers to prophecy, dealt with every single aspect of the human condition, what was to come, and as well, the complexities of the State of Israel (Mat., Chpt. 24). So, as the Goats' hair covering was total, likewise, the prophetic Ministry of Christ!

THE LOOPS AND THE TACHES

Verses 10 through 13 read: *"And you shall make fifty loops in the edge of the one curtain that is outmost in the coupling, and fifty loops in the edge of the curtain which couples the second.*

"And you shall make fifty taches of brass, and put the taches into the loops, and couple the tent together, that it may be one.

"And the remnant that remains of the curtain of the tent, the half curtain that remains, shall hang over the backside of the Tabernacle.

"And a cubit on the one side, and a cubit on the other side of that which remains in the length of the curtains of the tent, it shall hang over the sides of the Tabernacle on this side and on that side, to cover it."

The *"fifty loops"* joined the portions together, which means that the two portions of the Goats' hair covering were to be united in exactly the same way as those of the inner awning of linen.

In the linen covering, the *"taches"* were of gold, while the taches here are of copper.

While *"copper"* can speak of judgment, it also can speak of humanity. And that is the meaning I believe is given here. Deity does not function in the realm of prophecy. Deity is Omniscient, meaning that it knows everything, past, present, and future. The Prophetic Office could only be held by a man or woman, and in this case, the Lord Jesus Christ.

RAMS' SKINS AND BADGERS' SKINS

Verse 14 reads: *"And you shall make a covering for the tent of Rams' skins dyed red, and a covering above of Badgers' skins."*

If it is to be noticed, while dimensions were given as it regarded the linen and the Goats' hair coverings, no dimensions are given regarding the Rams' and Badgers' skin coverings. More than likely, they were the same size as the Goats' hair coverings. But yet, the dimensions were left off for a purpose and reason.

Could this not intimate that which these coverings foreshadowed was beyond our power to measure! There was a depth and a height in our Saviour's devotion to God and in His humiliation before men, which it is utterly impossible for us to gauge (Pink).

The Rams' skins dyed red typified Christ as King. Due to the fact they were dyed red, this tells us that it was a King Who died on the Cross for lost humanity. And yet, Israel laughed at His Kingship, but had they checked the genealogies in the Temple, they would have known that had the Davidic dynasty continued, Joseph would have been king, and Jesus as the eldest Son would have followed suit. In fact, the Holy Spirit referred to Him as the *"Son of David"* (Mat. 1:1).

JESUS

Jesus was not popular! The multitude might follow Him for a short time, because His Ministry stood connected, in their judgment, with *"the loaves and fishes"* which met their needs; but another crowd would shortly say, *"Away with Him!"*

But none of this moved Him, and simply because He was on this Earth to carry out the Will of the Father. He was the only Perfect Servant Who ever stood in God's vineyard. He had one object, which He pursued with an undeviating course from the manger to the Cross, and that was to glorify the Father, and to finish His Work (Mackintosh).

BADGERS' SKINS

The Badgers' skins were no doubt the same size as the Rams' skins, and were the last covering to go over the Tabernacle. So in effect, there were four coverings which made up the top of the Tabernacle. The fine twined linen, the Goats' hair, the Rams' and now the Badgers'. If in fact, the Goats' hair covering typified the Prophetic Office of Christ, and the Rams' skins that of the Office of King, then the Badgers' skins had to denote the Office of High Priest. These were the three roles filled by Christ, in His Atoning Work.

Admittedly, and considering that Christ came from the Tribe of Judah and not from the Priestly Tribe of Levi, He did not look like a High Priest, or in reality, a Priest of any kind. But neither did He fit the mold of a King or a Prophet. While He was all of this, His demeanor was different in every aspect. In fact, His Office as King, even though as real then as it will be in the future, still will not come to fruition until the coming Kingdom Age. And as well, His role as High Priest did not begin until after His Ascension, with the Scripture saying: *"But this man* (Jesus), *because He continues ever, has an unchangeable Priesthood* (He will always be High Priest).

"Wherefore He is able also to save them

to the uttermost who come unto God by Him, seeing He ever lives to make intercession for them.

"For such an High Priest became us, Who is holy, harmless, undefiled, separate from sinners, and made higher than the Heavens;

"Who needeth not daily, as those High Priests (those of Israel) *to offer up Sacrifice, first for His Own sins, and then for the people's: for this He did once, when He offered up Himself"* (Heb. 7:24-27).

The last covering, which was of Badgers' skins, was appropriate for three reasons:

1. Of all the coverings over the Tabernacle, this particular covering was the least of all as it regards ostentatiousness and beauty. In fact, the Goats' hair covering was beautiful, which looked almost like silk. As well, the Rams' skin covering had a regal beauty, especially considering that they were dyed red. But the Badgers' skins pointed to no beauty whatsoever. This means that the great Offices of Prophet, King, and High Priest, while definitely present, were not obvious at all.

The Badgers' skins covering also points to the fact, *"There was no beauty that we should desire Him"* (Isa. 53:2). So, when the passerby looked at the Tabernacle, there would have been nothing there that had attraction. If anything at all, the Badgers' skins definitely had no attraction.

WHAT DOES THIS TELL US?

While outwardly the Tabernacle had no attraction, to be sure, the interior was beautiful beyond compare. Such is Christianity!

When the unredeemed look at Christianity from the outside, for that's the only way it can be observed from that point, they see absolutely nothing that sparks their interest; however, once they come to Christ, the beauty and the glory of this Christian experience then becomes very obvious, and the only regret they have is that they didn't come to Christ sooner!

2. The Badgers' skins tell us that this Christian experience, even though it is wonderful and glorious, in fact the greatest thing on Earth; still, it is nothing by comparison to what will be given to us at the coming Resurrection. That's why Paul said: *"But*

NOTES

ourselves also, which have the firstfruits of the Spirit, even we ourselves groan within ourselves, waiting for the adoption, to wit, the Redemption of our body" (Rom. 8:23).

3. The Badgers' skins spoke of humility, as should be obvious. This was the only thing that the Master ever said of Himself: *"For I am meek and lowly in heart"* (Mat. 11:29).

The world looks at the outside of everything, because that's all it has. But Christ directs us to the miracle of transformation, typified by the interior of the Tabernacle.

(15) "AND YOU SHALL MAKE BOARDS FOR THE TABERNACLE OF SHITTIM WOOD STANDING UP.

(16) "TEN CUBITS SHALL BE THE LENGTH OF A BOARD, AND A CUBIT AND A HALF SHALL BE THE WIDTH OF ONE BOARD.

(17) "TWO TENONS SHALL THERE BE IN ONE BOARD, SET IN ORDER ONE AGAINST ANOTHER: THUS SHALL YOU MAKE FOR ALL THE BOARDS OF THE TABERNACLE.

(18) "AND YOU SHALL MAKE THE BOARDS FOR THE TABERNACLE, TWENTY BOARDS ON THE SOUTH SIDE SOUTHWARD.

(19) "AND YOU SHALL MAKE FORTY SOCKETS OF SILVER UNDER THE TWENTY BOARDS; TWO SOCKETS UNDER ONE BOARD FOR HIS TWO TENONS, AND TWO SOCKETS UNDER ANOTHER BOARD FOR HIS TWO TENONS.

(20) "AND FOR THE SECOND SIDE OF THE TABERNACLE ON THE NORTH SIDE THERE SHALL BE TWENTY BOARDS:

(21) "AND THEIR FORTY SOCKETS OF SILVER; TWO SOCKETS UNDER ONE BOARD, AND TWO SOCKETS UNDER ANOTHER BOARD.

(22) "AND FOR THE SIDES OF THE TABERNACLE WESTWARD YOU SHALL MAKE SIX BOARDS.

(23) "AND THE TWO BOARDS SHALL YOU MAKE FOR THE CORNERS OF THE TABERNACLE IN THE TWO SIDES.

(24) "AND THEY SHALL BE COUPLED TOGETHER BENEATH, AND THEY SHALL BE COUPLED TOGETHER ABOVE THE HEAD OF IT UNTO ONE RING: THUS SHALL IT BE FOR THEM BOTH; THEY

SHALL BE FOR THE TWO CORNERS.

(25) "AND THEY SHALL BE EIGHT BOARDS, AND THEIR SOCKETS OF SILVER, SIXTEEN SOCKETS; TWO SOCKETS UNDER ONE BOARD, AND TWO SOCKETS UNDER ANOTHER BOARD."

The structure is:

1. The fifty boards were of indestructible wood overlaid with gold, as was also the Ark, i.e., *"the Humanity and Deity of Christ."*

2. The boards were based on Redemption silver and crowned with the same. The crown was visible, the foundation not. The Redemption Work of Christ reaches from the depths of the sinner's need to the heights of God's Throne.

3. Every board set out some moral glory in the nature and life of Christ.

THE BOARDS

Verses 15 through 19 read: *"And you shall make boards for the Tabernacle of Shittim Wood standing up.*

"Ten cubits shall be the length of a board, and a cubit and a half shall be the width of one board.

"Two tenons shall there be in one board, set in order one against another: thus shall you make for all the boards of the Tabernacle.

"And you shall make the boards for the Tabernacle, twenty boards on the south side southward.

"And you shall make forty sockets of silver under the twenty boards; two sockets under one board for his two tenons, and two sockets under another board for his two tenons."

We now come to the framework and foundation of the Tabernacle proper. In fact, it was a simple arrangement. There were 50 boards in all, 20 on the south side, 20 on the north side, six on the west end, with two boards on each corner at the back, making 50 in all.

The boards were 15 feet high, and about 27 inches wide. We aren't told how thick they were.

The boards were of indestructible wood, which came from the acacia tree. They were overlaid with gold (Vs. 29), thereby portraying the Manhood of Christ, typified by the wood, and the Deity of Christ, typified by the gold.

NOTES

THE HAND

The Hebrew word for *"tenon"* is *"yad,"* and means *"an open hand."* There were two of them under each board, making a total of 100 tenons. The Scripture doesn't say of what type of metal they were made; however, they were probably made of silver.

Each board overlaid with gold, with the *"tenons"* under each corner, were set into two sockets of silver.

It is believed that each socket of silver weighed about a talent, which is about 120 pounds. This would have provided a tremendous foundation, which was intended!

SILVER

If there were 50 boards, and two *"sockets"* of silver for each board, this would have made 100 sockets, which formed the foundation, and upon them rested the whole fabric of the Tabernacle.

Silver was meant to represent Redemption, which is evidenced more clearly in Exodus, Chapter 30, as it regards the *"shekel of the Sanctuary,"* which was the ransom money for each person. The idea, as we will explain more fully upon arriving at that Chapter, was not that Redemption could be purchased by man, but in fact that it was purchased, and by the Lord Jesus Christ, Who at that time, of course, had not yet come.

All of this tells us that Redemption is the basis on which Christ has become the meeting-place between the thrice-Holy God and His inherently unholy people. It is only through Redemption that the Perfect Humanity and Divine Glory of Christ could bring us to Himself. John 12:24 tells us that Christ could multiply Himself only by dying, which He did, which *"brought forth much fruit."*

"Redemption" and the *"Crucifixion"* are intertwined, so to speak. Paul, and angry at the Galatians for turning away from the Truth of the Cross to other things, said:

"O foolish Galatians, who has bewitched you, that you should not obey the Truth, before whose eyes Jesus Christ has been evidently set forth, crucified among you?" (Gal. 3:1).

If you will notice, Paul didn't say, *"Jesus Christ has been evidently set forth, resurrected among you."* I say that because the Word of Faith doctrine, which has ensnared so many, in essence, preaches that Salvation is in the Resurrection.

Of course, the Resurrection is of supreme significance. That should go without stating; however, I remind the Reader that Paul says here, and many places elsewhere, that the Cross must be set before us, and not the suffering in the Garden, the Resurrection, as wonderful as that was, the Ascension, or the Exaltation. While all of these things were absolutely necessary, and of course, are supremely important, it was the Crucified Christ which purchased our Redemption, and nothing else. That's why the Apostle also said:

"But God forbid that I should glory, save in the Cross of our Lord Jesus Christ, by Whom the world is crucified unto me, and I unto the world" (Gal. 6:14).

It is my feeling that the Word of Faith doctrine is the doctrine of the last days, set forth by Satan, to pull the Church away from the Cross. Paul said:

"Now the Spirit (Holy Spirit) *speaks expressly* (pointedly), *that in the latter times* (the times in which we now live) *some shall depart from the Faith* (Jesus Christ and Him Crucified), *giving heed to seducing spirits, and doctrines of devils"* (I Tim. 4:1).

"Seducing spirits" are successful, simply because they appear as *"angels of light"* (II Cor. 11:13-15).

Regrettably, this erroneous doctrine, which is causing so many to be lost, has millions of followers, pouring hundreds of millions of dollars into its coffers. Its vehicle for giving it mass appeal is T.B.N. (Trinity Broadcasting Network), although there are others as well! This Network, coupled with this false doctrine, has helped pull the Church down to an abysmal low, spiritually speaking.

The only Salvation for the Church is to come back to the Cross. And to be sure, the Cross is not one of several ways; it is the only way!

The *"Atonement-money"* in Exodus, Chapter 30, does not imply that Salvation can be purchased. The Scripture plainly tells us: *"You were not redeemed with corruptible things as silver and gold . . . but with the Precious Blood of Christ, as of a Lamb without blemish and without spot"* (I Pet. 1:18-19). The old Law also said: *For it is the blood that makes an Atonement for the soul"* (Lev. 17:11).

So why did the Holy Spirit use shekels of silver, as a form of Atonement?

It was done for two reasons:

1. It proclaimed the *"preciousness"* of Christ's Atonement.

2. While silver and gold couldn't purchase Redemption, as stated, most definitely it was purchased, but by the Precious Blood of Christ. So the silver here represents Redemption, even as in a sense, the entirety of the Tabernacle represents Christ and Redemption. And let it be understood, the Tabernacle didn't merely represent Christ, but Christ and the manner in which He would redeem fallen humanity.

COUPLINGS

Verses 20 through 25 read: *"And for the second side of the Tabernacle on the north side there shall be twenty boards:*

"And their forty sockets of silver; two sockets under one board, and two sockets under another board.

"And for the sides of the Tabernacle westward you shall make six boards.

"And two boards shall you make for the corners of the Tabernacle in the two sides.

"And they shall be coupled together beneath, and they shall be coupled together above the head of it unto one ring: thus shall it be for them both; they shall be for the two corners.

"And they shall be eight boards, and their sockets of silver, sixteen sockets; two sockets under one board, and two sockets under another board."

If it is to be noticed, there were no boards on the eastern end of the Tabernacle. In fact, there were five pillars there, with the entire front covered by a curtain, which we will look into momentarily. The Tabernacle was to always face the east; therefore, this was the entrance as well.

Also, if it is to be noticed, we have given the *"cubit"* a measurement of 18 inches, which of course, is a foot and a half. It is doubtful that it was exactly that, but more than likely, that's about as close as we can come in today's modern measurements.

The *"couplings,"* as would be obvious, held all the boards together. This had to do with the *"tenons"* or *"hands,"* as well as the sockets of silver, at least on the bottom. At the top, one of the *"bars"* which we will study momentarily, held everything in place.

All of this proclaims and prefigures the God-Man, the Lord Jesus Christ, Who, in His voluntary humiliation, would be dependent upon, and in subjection to, the Father. As the Perfect Servant He was upheld and sustained by the hands of God the Father from above, the Spirit below ministering to Him. Of old the Spirit of Prophecy cried, *"Let Your hand be upon the Man of Your right hand, upon the Son of Man Whom You made strong for Yourself"* (Ps. 80:17). As well, our Lord said: *"My times are in Your hand"* (Ps. 31:15). And then from the Cross: *"Father, into Your hands I commend My spirit"* (Lk. 23:46). And now, He is seated on *"the Right Hand of the Majesty on high"* (Heb. 1:3)! (Pink).

As we've already stated, the Tabernacle not only in its entirety represented Christ, but more than all, presented Christ in His Atoning, Mediatorial, Intercessory Work. In other words, it represented Him in what He would do in order to redeem fallen humanity. The entirety for the reason of His Coming to this Earth, thereby becoming Man, was in order to redeem fallen humanity. To be sure, none of this was done for Himself, for Heaven, for Angels, etc. It was all done for sinners. This tells us that man's problem is sin, and the solution alone is the Saviour, the Lord Jesus Christ.

So in essence, all of these boards proclaim the various aspects of the Ministry of Christ in some way, and one could say, I think, the benefits of the Cross. Those benefits are literally inexhaustible!

THE BENEFITS OF THE CROSS

One of the ways that is noticeable as it regards the spiritual declension of the Church is the ways and means by which it addresses the human problem. We speak of sin! The Church has seminars or particular gatherings, as it regards various, different problems. For instance, there are Marriage Seminars, which, as should be understood, are conducted for those who are having marriage problems. As well, the Church has adopted a form of Alcoholics Anonymous, or else recommends that particular scenario, which of course, is for those who are bound by the bondage of alcohol. There are groups for immorality, for gambling, etc. Almost all of these fly in the face of what Christianity claims to propose, so mostly the Church recommends various 12-step programs, which of course, are all psychological. The point I'm making is this:

The Cross of Christ takes care of every single problem in the human heart and mind, irrespective as to what it might be. The Holy Spirit through Peter said: *"According as His Divine Power has given unto us all things that pertain unto Life and Godliness, through the knowledge of Him Who has called us to glory and virtue:*

"Whereby are given unto us exceeding great and precious Promises, that by these you might be partakers of the Divine Nature, having escaped the corruption that is in the world through lust" (II Pet. 1:3-4).

So what am I saying?

I'm saying, if the Believer can be correctly taught the Word of God, victory in every capacity can be had.

As we've already said any number of times in this Volume, when Jesus died on the Cross, He atoned for all sin. Now that statement is very simple, but its worth and value are beyond compare.

To atone for all sin, past, present, and future, which Jesus did by the giving of Himself in Sacrifice, means that Satan now has no more legal hold on any person, who will place his faith and trust in Christ, and what Christ has done at the Cross. Sin is the legal right which Satan has to hold man in captivity (Rom. 6:23), and with that right removed, he is now helpless (Col. 2:14-15). This is the manner in which Christ *"spoiled principalities and powers, making a show of them openly, triumphing over them in it"* (Col. 2:15).

This means that every single problem that man has had due to the Fall, every bondage of darkness, every sinful aberration, sin and all of its forms, not merely the acts, but as well the cause of sin, were totally and completely addressed at the Cross. Nothing was left unattended or unaddressed. In fact, had there been one single sin left unatoned, Christ could not have risen from the dead. The very fact that He rose from the dead tells us that He atoned for all sin, *"taking away the sin of the world"* (Jn. 1:29).

CONSENT

This means that no Believer should ever be overcome by sin in any fashion. I speak of spiritual bondage, of being ruled by the sin nature (Rom. 6:12-13). So if all of this is true, some may ask, how is it that many Christians, if not most, are in fact, ruled by the sin nature, which means they are terribly failing in some way?

Any Christian who fails the Lord in any capacity, irrespective as to what it might be, fails because he doesn't understand the Cross of Christ. That's a simple statement, but oh so true!

In 1996, the Lord began to open up to me the Revelation of the Cross. To be sure, it was not new, actually that which had been given to the Apostle Paul, and which he grandly gave to us in his 14 Epistles; however, the Church has been so moved away from the Cross, especially in these last several decades, that any more, most of the modern Church little understands this foundational truth. And to be sure, if the foundation is wrong, everything else in some way is going to be wrong as well. The Cross of Christ is not a mere doctrine, but rather the Foundation of all Doctrine. That's the reason that Paul said: *"We preach Christ Crucified"* (I Cor. 1:23). And: *"I determined not to know anything among you, save Jesus Christ, and Him Crucified"* (I Cor. 2:2). That's the reason the Apostle said:

"According to the Grace of God which is given unto me, as a wise masterbuilder, I have laid the foundation, and another builds thereon. But let every man take heed how he builds thereupon.

"For other foundation can no man lay than that is laid, which is Jesus Christ" (I Cor. 3:10-11). The *"foundation"* of which he speaks is the Cross, which he has amply proclaimed (I Cor. 1:17-18, 21, 23; 2:2, 5).

So, if the Believer is being overcome by the powers of darkness in any capacity, whether he realizes it or not, he is, in effect, giving consent to Satan to rule him, i.e., *"the sin nature"* (Rom. 6:12).

THE CROSS AND SANCTIFICATION

We teach the Cross approximately six hours a day, seven days a week, over the SonLife Radio Network, as well as over our Telecast. The testimonies we are receiving from Christians who have been set free by this Message are astounding to say the least! Jesus said: *"You shall know the Truth, and the Truth shall make you free"* (Jn. 8:32).

The freedom of which we speak runs the proverbial gamut from *"A"* to *"Z"*. It includes all types of *"works of the flesh"* (Rom. 7:8; Gal. 5:19-21). And to be sure, if the Believer doesn't understand the Cross as it regards Sanctification, in some way, *"works of the flesh"* are definitely going to rule that person's life. And we're speaking here of a most miserable existence! Yes, the individual is still saved, but the truth is, millions have lost their souls, simply because they ultimately gave up and quit. In fact, the entirety of the Book of Hebrews as written by Paul examines this terrible problem. (Please see our Commentary on that particular Epistle.)

Tragically, the modern Church understands almost nothing as it regards the Cross and Sanctification. Most have never even heard one Message on this all-important subject, which means they are consigned to spiritual defeat in some way. It doesn't matter how hard they struggle, how hard they fight, how much effort they put forth, victory will not be their lot, but rather failure, and with the failure steadily getting worse. That's why Paul also said: *"A little leaven leaveneth the whole lump"* (Gal. 5:9). Sin never evaporates of its own accord, but rather gets worse and worse! There is only one answer for sin, not ten, not five, not two, only one, and that is *"Jesus Christ and Him Crucified."*

SANCTIFICATION?

For the heading, I have placed the word *"Sanctification,"* and put a question mark behind it. I've done that because most modern Believers don't have the foggiest idea as to what Sanctification actually is.

In its most simplistic form, it means simply, *"to be set apart exclusively for the Lord."* It basically has the same meaning as *"Holiness."* Sanctification is what *"makes one clean,"* while Justification *"declares one clean."* Both are legal works, which Jesus made possible at the Cross.

As the Cross is the foundation of Salvation, it is also the foundation of Sanctification. What does that mean?

In some way, even as we've already explained some pages back, for the sinner to be saved, he must believe in Christ, and whether he understands it very much or not, what Jesus did for him at the Cross. *"Jesus died for me,"* is about the limit of what the unsaved person can know and understand. But that is most definitely required.

But once the person comes to Christ, that's another story indeed! The Divine Nature now resides within the Believer's life, and does so from the moment of conversion (II Pet. 1:4). While the old sin nature remains in the life of the Believer, it is now dormant, with the Believer ruled by the Divine Nature, or at least that's the way it should be!

In fact, that's the way it will be, if the Believer doesn't get his eyes on himself, but rather keeps his eyes on Christ and the Cross. While it's very difficult for the unsaved person to throw himself entirely on Christ, unfortunately, that seems to be the problem for the Believer as well. And what do we mean by that?

The Believer far too often tries to sanctify himself. In other words, it's Salvation by Grace, and Sanctification by self. That is the problem, and will cause nothing but ruin! As the unsaved cannot save himself, neither can the Believer sanctify himself. It doesn't matter how faithful one is to Church, how many Chapters a day one reads in the Bible, how much one prays each day, how many souls he wins to the Lord, or how much money he gives; while all of these things are definitely good, and definitely that which any good Christian will do, they do not add one single thing to one's Holiness or Sanctification. That's why Paul bluntly said: *"Behold, I Paul say unto you, that if you be circumcised* (depend on works) *Christ shall profit you nothing"* (Gal. 5:2).

He then said: *"For in Jesus Christ neither circumcision availeth anything, nor uncircumcision* (works); *but Faith which works by love"* (Gal. 5:6).

So he plainly tells us here that our Sanctification comes exclusively by *"Faith."* What did he mean by that?

FAITH

He was speaking of having Faith in Christ, and what Christ did for us at the Cross. That must ever be the object of our Faith, *"Jesus Christ, and Him Crucified."* The Apostle had already said:

"I am crucified with Christ (back to Romans 6:3-5): *nevertheless I live* (raised with Him in newness of life); *yet not I, but Christ lives in me: and the life which I now live in the flesh* (my daily walk) *I live by the Faith of the Son of God* (Jesus Christ and Him Crucified), *Who loved me, and gave Himself for me"* (Gal. 2:20).

Everything the Believer needs comes to him through the Cross. In other words, it was at the Cross where Jesus addressed every single problem, and our Faith in that Finished Work guarantees us the help of the Holy Spirit, Who can bring about all things within our lives (Rom. 8:1-2, 11).

So when we speak of *"Faith,"* it must always be Faith in Christ and what Christ has done for us at the Cross. That is the same as saying *"Faith in the Word,"* that is, if one understands that the Word is the story of the Cross. Such Faith will guarantee victory, because it then gives the Holy Spirit latitude to work. And to be sure, the work of Sanctification can only be brought about by the Holy Spirit. The Believer cannot sanctify himself, irrespective of what he might do or not do. It is the Holy Spirit Alone Who can perform this task. He requires very little of us, but He definitely does require that we have Faith in Christ, and what Christ has accomplished in the giving of Himself in Sacrifice (Gal. 1:4).

(26) "AND YOU SHALL MAKE BARS OF SHITTIM WOOD; FIVE FOR THE BOARDS OF THE ONE SIDE OF THE TABERNACLE,

(27) "AND FIVE BARS FOR THE BOARDS OF THE OTHER SIDE OF THE

TABERNACLE, AND FIVE BARS FOR THE BOARDS OF THE SIDE OF THE TABERNACLE, FOR THE TWO SIDES WESTWARD.

(28) "AND THE MIDDLE BAR IN THE MIDST OF THE BOARDS SHALL REACH FROM END TO END.

(29) "AND YOU SHALL OVERLAY THE BOARDS WITH GOLD, AND MAKE THEIR RINGS OF GOLD FOR PLACES FOR THE BARS: AND YOU SHALL OVERLAY THE BARS WITH GOLD.

(30) "AND YOU SHALL REAR UP THE TABERNACLE ACCORDING TO THE FASHION THEREOF WHICH WAS SHOWED YOU IN THE MOUNT."

The composition is:

1. The bars were of indestructible wood, which speaks of the perfect humanity of Christ, and were overlaid with gold, which speaks of His Deity.

2. There were five boards each on the south side, north side, and west end. Five speaks of Grace, which characterized Christ (Jn. 1:17).

3. *"According to the fashion"* of Verse 30, pertains to the fact that Moses was not to deviate at all from the pattern given to him *"in the Mount."*

THE FIVE BARS

Verses 26 through 28 read: *"And you shall make bars of Shittim Wood; five for the boards of the one side of the Tabernacle,*

"And five bars for the boards of the other side of the Tabernacle, and five bars for the boards of the side of the Tabernacle, for the two sides westward.

"And the middle bar in the midst of the boards shall reach from end to end."

The order of these bars seems to be as follows:

First of all, the *"middle bar"* of the five, which would run horizontal in the middle from end to end, would be approximately 45 feet long. This united and held all the 20 boards together, at least on the south and north sides. It would be the same with the west end, although a much shorter distance of only 15 feet.

The other four bars, two below and two above, are not described as running all the length, but perhaps only extended half the distance, in other words, being in two pieces, although extending the entire length of the Tabernacle.

The five bars symbolize the Grace of God, with Grace made possible to us through Christ by what He did for us at the Cross. In other words, the Cross, of which the Tabernacle is a type, opened up the way for Grace to be given in an unlimited way to the Believer. God has always had Grace, and in fact, every single thing He has ever given man has come through Grace; however, before the Cross, due to the sin debt remaining, Grace could not be extended as abundantly as it does now, since the Cross.

The five bars could also represent the fivefold Callings, *"Apostles, Prophets, Evangelists, Pastors, and Teachers"* (Eph. 4:11).

These are referred to as *"Gifts"* (Eph. 4:8), which of course, speaks of Grace.

In other words, as individuals are called by God to one of these Offices, which is supposed to be: *"For the perfecting of the Saints, for the work of the Ministry, for the edifying of the Body of Christ,"* we must conclude this to be Grace (Eph. 4:12).

And if these Offices function as they should function, they will proclaim Christ in every capacity, and above all, His Finished Work at the Cross. In fact, that is their very purpose.

RINGS OF GOLD

Verse 29 reads: *"And you shall overlay the boards with gold, and make their rings of gold for places for the bars: and you shall overlay the bars with gold."*

The *"rings of gold"* were evidently attached to the boards, through which the bars passed. As to how many rings there were to each link, we aren't told. As everything about the Tabernacle pertained to Christ in His Atoning, Mediatorial, Work, we know that these *"rings of gold"* had a spiritual meaning as well.

More than likely, they pertained to the Work of the Spirit in connecting all the Ministries of Christ. Even though our Saviour had different Ministries, all ultimately played out to Christ as Saviour. The *"bars,"* which held all of this together, were themselves held in place by *"rings of gold."*

The ultimate Work of Christ was Salvation for lost humanity. He would accomplish this task by and through the Cross, even though every aspect of His multifaceted Ministry contributed to the ultimate goal.

We must allow this to be a lesson to us as well, that these *"rings of gold"* still apply spiritually, hence Paul saying: *"For Christ sent me not to baptize, but to preach the Gospel: not with wisdom of words, lest the Cross of Christ should be made of none effect"* (I Cor. 1:17).

THE FASHION

Verse 30 reads: *"And you shall rear up the Tabernacle according to the fashion thereof which was showed you in the Mount."*

This is basically the same statement as was given in Exodus 25:40. As stated, the repetition is for purpose, and is, therefore, brought forth by design.

As in the previous Verse, the Holy Spirit is saying that all of the instructions given here to Moses by God were to be held to exactly. In other words, Moses must not add anything to the design, nor take something from the design. It was all of God and none of man.

As well, Moses was to minutely inspect each thing done by the craftsmen, that they not deviate from the pattern at all.

This beautifully symbolizes Salvation, and as well, points to the great problem of the Church, and mankind in general.

As Cain of old, man is not satisfied with the Plan of Salvation brought forth by God, but feels that he must complement that pattern in some way, or ignore it altogether. And to be sure, when men attempt to add to or take away, soon there is nothing left that originally was given by God.

This has always been a problem for the Church, but I suspect it is more of a problem now than ever before. As a case in point, we will look at humanistic psychology.

Even as we've already quoted several times, Peter said: *"According as His Divine Power has given unto us all things that pertain unto life and Godliness, through the knowledge of Him Who has called us to glory and virtue:*

"Whereby are given unto us exceeding great and precious Promises, that by these you might be partakers of the Divine Nature, having escaped the corruption that is in the world through lust" (II Pet. 1:3-4). In essence, this means that Jesus addressed at the Cross every single problem that besets fallen humanity (Col. 2:14-15). But several decades ago, the Church, losing Faith in the Cross because it was not faithfully preach, began to turn to humanistic psychology. Today, that particular direction is almost complete, which means that the entirety of the Church has gone in that direction. Of course, there is an exception here and there, but those exceptions are few and far between.

Using Preachers as an example, if the Preacher, through lack of knowledge of the Cross, is overcome by the powers of darkness, instead of that Preacher being directed to the Cross, he will be directed toward humanistic psychology. And here is the clincher:

If he doesn't go that route, the Church, for all practical purposes, will write him off, in effect, blackballing him, in effect, doing everything within their power to destroy whatever vestige of Ministry which might remain.

This erroneous direction is not content to merely proclaim their false way, thereby deceiving the people, but they are also intent upon destroying anything that opposes that false way. All of this goes back to the saga of Cain and Abel (Gen., Chpt. 4).

According to the directions of the Lord, both offered a sacrifice. But Cain departed from the type of sacrifice demanded by God. He instead produced the fruit of his own hands, which God could not accept. And if the sacrifice was rejected, which it was, then the one offering the sacrifice was rejected as well, which standard holds to this very hour.

But Cain wasn't satisfied with his position of holding up a sacrifice of his own making, but rather felt that he had to destroy Abel, who in fact, had offered the correct sacrifice. Consequently, he murdered his own brother. That spirit continues in the Church, and in fact, has been the overriding spirit from then until now.

If men reject the Cross, and I continue to speak of the Church, they attempt to destroy those who are preaching the Cross, and will use any means at their disposal to carry out their wicked task. As stated, the murderous intent of Cain continues to abide in the hearts of all who oppose the Cross.

UNBELIEF

In 1996, the Lord began to open up to me the Message of the Cross, in essence, explaining to me what Paul had already taught. At first, I thought that the great problem of the Church was that of ignorance. And to be sure, that definitely is the problem with some. In other words, they have not rejected the Cross in their hearts; they just simply don't know anything about the Cross, at least as it refers to Sanctification.

But since that time, I have been forced to come to the conclusion that the greater majority of rejection does not center up in ignorance, but rather unbelief. In other words, as a whole, the modern Church simply doesn't believe that the Cross is the *"Power of God."* Paul said:

"For the preaching of the Cross is to them who perish foolishness; but unto us which are saved it is the Power of God" (I Cor. 1:18).

The Greek word translated here *"preaching,"* is *"logos."* It is not normally translated *"preaching,"* and it should not have been translated *"preaching"* in this Verse as well. It should have been translated, *"The Message of the Cross . . ."* or *"The Word of the Cross. . . ."* Preaching is the act of proclaiming that which is already given, hence the *"Message"* or the *"Word."*

As I've also repeated several times, I personally believe that the Holy Spirit is presently bringing forth the Message of the Cross to such an extent, and doing so boldly, that it will either have to be accepted or rejected. The Cross of Christ, I believe, is the dividing line between the True Church and the apostate church. That means the dividing line is not Denominations, or particular doctrines, etc., but rather, *"the Cross"* (I Cor. 1:23; 2:2).

One might say that the Cross is the *"pattern"* or *"fashion,"* and it must ever be held up accordingly. To deviate any way from the Cross is to deviate from the plain Word of God, and will always, and without exception, invite disaster.

(31) "AND YOU SHALL MAKE A VEIL OF BLUE, AND PURPLE, AND SCARLET, AND FINE TWINED LINEN OF CUNNING WORK: WITH CHERUBIM SHALL IT BE MADE:

(32) "AND YOU SHALL HANG IT UPON FOUR PILLARS OF SHITTIM WOOD OVERLAID WITH GOLD: THEIR HOOKS SHALL BE OF GOLD, UPON THE FOUR SOCKETS OF SILVER.

(33) "AND YOU SHALL HANG UP THE VEIL UNDER THE TACHES, THAT YOU MAY BRING IN THITHER WITHIN THE VEIL THE ARK OF THE TESTIMONY: AND THE VEIL SHALL DIVIDE UNTO YOU BETWEEN THE HOLY PLACE AND THE MOST HOLY.

(34) "AND YOU SHALL PUT THE MERCY SEAT UPON THE ARK OF THE TESTIMONY IN THE MOST HOLY PLACE.

(35) "AND YOU SHALL SET THE TABLE WITHOUT THE VEIL, AND THE LAMPSTAND OVER AGAINST THE TABLE ON THE SIDE OF THE TABERNACLE TOWARD THE SOUTH: AND YOU SHALL PUT THE TABLE ON THE NORTH SIDE.

(36) "AND YOU SHALL MAKE AN HANGING FOR THE DOOR OF THE TENT, OF BLUE, AND PURPLE, AND SCARLET, AND FINE TWINED LINEN, WROUGHT WITH NEEDLEWORK.

(37) "AND YOU SHALL MAKE FOR THE HANGING FIVE PILLARS OF SHITTIM WOOD, AND OVERLAY THEM WITH GOLD, AND THEIR HOOKS SHALL BE OF GOLD: AND YOU SHALL CAST FIVE SOCKETS OF BRASS FOR THEM."

The structure is:

1. Many Christians have an erroneous interpretation of the Tabernacle, thinking it represents Israel, or the House of God, or the Church as a whole, etc. They conclude as well that the boards represent the individual members of the Church, and the central bar the Divine life that makes them one. But the Holy Spirit's statement in Psalms 29:9, that every whit of this building uttered Christ's praise, militates against that interpretation (Williams).

2. The Tabernacle contained two rooms, the Holy Place and the Holy of Holies, with the latter containing the Ark of the Covenant.

3. The Tabernacle always faced the east, the rising of the sun. So this meant that Israel worshipped with their backs to the sun.

4. There were two Veils, the first hung

upon five pillars; these stood on sockets of brass and were overlaid with gold. This hanging with its pillars pictured Christ; the five pillars, His Grace; the Shittim Wood, His humanity; the gold, His Deity; the brass, His faithfulness; the hanging itself, the glorious mystery of His Being in His Incarnation (Williams).

5. Inside the first Veil, which was the Holy Place, were placed the Lampstand to the left, the golden Table to the right, and the Altar of Incense immediately in front of the second Veil.

6. The inner Veil was ornamented with Cherubim, the outward not. Hebrews, Chapter 9 states that this Veil pictured Christ's flesh rent in expiation.

THE VEIL

Verse 31 reads: *"And you shall make a Veil of blue, and purple, and scarlet, and fine twined linen of cunning work: with Cherubim shall it be made."*

This was the inner Veil which separated the Holy Place from the Holy of Holies.

This *"Veil"* in effect announced to all that the way of approach to God was not then made known. But inasmuch as it was a curtain and not a wall of stone or metal, there was more than a hint given of its temporary nature, and that ultimately a way of access would be revealed. And to be sure, it was, and that way was made possible by what Jesus did on the Cross.

This speaks of the Veil that was in the Temple at the time of Christ, which it is believed was approximately 30 feet high, and 30 feet wide (I Ki. 6:20). Concerning the death of Christ on the Cross, the Scripture says: *"Jesus, when He had cried again with a loud voice, yielded up the ghost."*

It then said: *"And, behold, the Veil of the Temple was rent in twain from the top to the bottom; and the Earth did quake, and the rocks rent"* (Mat. 27:50-51).

It was the death of Christ on the Cross alone that could open up the way to the very Presence of God, as it regards sinful man. By the giving of Himself in Sacrifice, He atoned for all sin, which then made it possible for man to enter into the very Presence of God, which heretofore was impossible!

The giving here of the colors is identical to that of Exodus 26:1 concerning the curtains, but with one exception. In connection with the curtains, the *"fine twined linen"* was mentioned first; here it is mentioned last.

Concerning this, Pink says, *"This seems to intimate that our attention now is to be concentrated more on what was prefigured by the blue and purple and scarlet, rather than on what was foreshadowed by the linen itself. The colors told of Heaven, the Cross, and the Throne. Probably the colors were used so freely that little of the white linen would be visible."*

The *"blue"* signified that this great Plan of Redemption was all of Heaven and none of Earth. The *"purple"* signified the royalty of Christ, as King. The *"Scarlet"* signified the price that He would pay by the shedding of His Blood on the Cross of Calvary.

The *"fine twined linen"* spoke of the humanity of Christ in its perfection. The whiteness of the pure linen used in the Veil pointed to the sinless purity of *"the Man Christ Jesus"* both in His inward thoughts and desires and in His outward ways and works.

Jesus was what man ought to be, what God intended! The Veil, therefore, was a fitting type that Christ Incarnate was Perfect God and Perfect Man.

The object of a *"Veil"* is to hide. *"Come not"* (Lev. 16:2) was the warning which it consistently gave forth. Thus the Veil foreshadowed the moral glories of the Saviour, but at the same time showed, by the very display of such heavenliness of character, how far fallen man was away from God (Pink).

The Perfect Manhood of Christ exhibited the only humanity which can approach unto God, which can live in His Presence, which can dwell in the blazing light of His manifested glory. So the perfections of the God/Man only served to emphasize the imperfections of fallen man (Pink).

THE CROSS

As should be obvious, the Veil was never meant to give access to God; actually, it was that which prevented it.

This proclaims to us that the perfection of the Life of Christ on Earth, as beautiful and wonderful as that was, and as necessary as it was, could never bring us into the Presence of God.

The only way that one could pass by this Veil, and which pertained to the High Priest only, was by the blood of sacrifice (Lev. 16:19). And yet, all of this gave testimony to the temporary nature of that dispensation. The very fact of the blood of the sacrifice, at the same time, stated that a Perfect Sacrifice was to come, which would open up the way to all. That Perfect Sacrifice, of course, was Christ on the Cross.

So we might say, if the unrent Veil signified that the true way was not yet make known, it also implied it would be made known.

All of this tells us that the Sacrifice of Christ is the true ground of approach to God, and the true ground alone. His death, His Blood, has opened up the way to His Presence.

CUNNING WORK

The phrase, *"And fine twined linen of cunning work,"* tells us that this fabric was skillfully wrought. Literally, the Hebrew is: *"The work of a devisor."* This means that Divine wisdom was given for its manufacture and it was copied from a heavenly pattern: its equal never again being found on Earth. It foreshadowed the humanity of our Lord, but yet, a humanity which was without sin.

But again I emphasize because it's so very, very important, that His perfect humanity, and even His miracles, could not save anyone. That remained to be brought about by the Cross. But yet this perfection was necessary, and absolutely so, or else the Sacrifice could not be accepted. And when we speak of *"perfection,"* we're speaking of sinless perfection. While there was no physical blemish on His body, there was no moral blemish as well, on His soul. No other human being could say such a thing.

His Divine birth, and it was Divine, demanded that He be born of a Virgin, i.e., *"the Virgin Mary."* Otherwise, He would have been born after Adam's fallen race, therefore, born into original sin, as are all other human beings. But Jesus was not born by the means of natural procreation, but rather by the decree of the Holy Spirit, which overshadowed Mary, and brought about this miracle — and a miracle it was!

This means that Jesus did not carry any of the personality or physical traits of His foster father, or even his mother. In other words, Jesus was not the product of Joseph's seed or Mary's egg. In fact, she only provided a house for Him for the nine months of His gestation.

CHERUBIM

The colors of *"blue, purple, and scarlet"* probably were incorporated in the embroidered Cherubim. The Cherubim emphasized the Holiness of Christ, and the fact that He was no less holy in His Incarnate form, than He had been in His form of Deity. While He laid aside the expression of Deity, He never for a moment lost possession of Deity, hence the Holiness. Let's say it another way:

As the Cherubim cry, *"Holy, holy, holy, Lord God Almighty,"* to God the Father, they say the same identical thing to *"God the Son,"* even though He was in Incarnate form. The absolute Holiness of His person diminished not at all!

THE SEDUCTION OF THE CHURCH

As the Scripture amply provides, and which quickly becomes obvious, it is the Cross alone, as stated, which opened up the *"Veil"* (Mat. 27:51). Consequently, if the Preacher is preaching the Gospel, He is preaching the Cross (I Cor. 1:18, 21, 23; 2:2; Col. 2:14-15; Gal. 6:14). If he's not preaching the Cross, while he may be preaching about the Gospel, he actually is not preaching the Gospel. Consequently, very few lives will be changed because the *"Power of God"* is in the preaching of the Cross (I Cor. 1:17-18).

The Cross itself contains no power, as would be obvious, and in fact, the death of Christ contains no power as well. Actually, the Scripture says, *"For though He was crucified through weakness, yet He lives by the Power of God. For we also are weak in Him, but we shall live with Him by the Power of God toward you."*

Paul said, *"Examine yourselves, whether you be in the Faith; prove your own selves. Know ye not your own selves, how that Jesus Christ is in you, except you be reprobates?"* (II Cor. 13:4-5).

The power is in the Holy Spirit, as would be obvious! However, the Holy Spirit will not exhibit His Power on our behalf, which is the source of all overcoming Grace, except by and through the Finished Work of Christ. In fact, He cannot exhibit His Power by any other means.

So if the Believer wants the power of the Holy Spirit, and I'm speaking of that power made real within our lives on a daily basis, even a constant basis, he can only have such by ever making the Cross of Christ the object of His Faith (Rom. 8:2). In fact, the Lord Jesus Christ as the slain Lamb is forever intertwined, one might say, with the Holy Spirit, and the Holy Spirit with Christ in this manner (Rev. 5:6).

But the Church has been moved away from the Cross. Many forces have contributed to this present dilemma, but irrespective of the cause or the reason, the dirty deed has been done!

In the Early Church, and we specifically speak of the times of Paul, Satan used the Law/Grace issue to hinder the preaching of the Cross; hence, almost all of Paul's 14 Epistles were directed toward this difficulty, and in fact, were largely corrective.

Teachers whom Paul referred to as *"Satan's ministers"* (II Cor. 11:15), came into the Churches built by the Apostle, and attempted to pull the people away from Faith in the Cross, toward the Mosaic Law. To this effort, an effort engineered by Satan, we might quickly add, the Apostle strongly stated: *"But though we, or an Angel from Heaven preach any other Gospel unto you than that which we have preached unto you, let him be accursed"* (Gal. 1:8-9).

In effect, the Apostle is saying, if the Preacher is not preaching the Cross, then he's not preaching the Gospel, and in fact, is cursed by God, and as well, all who listen to such prattle are cursed by God. As I would hope is obvious, Paul's Message was not a compromised Message. In other words, it could not be compromised, and if it had been, you and I would not have the privilege of Salvation at this present time.

In fact, God-called Preachers aren't diplomats. They are supposed to be Prophets, and they (we) are to deliver no less than *"Thus saith the Lord!"*

The problem presently is not so much Law versus Grace; although anything proposed other than the Cross must, of necessity, fall into the category of *"works"* in some way or fashion. The modern Word of Faith doctrine falls into that category, and takes up where the Law/Grace issue left off. In fact, in my personal opinion, it is far more lethal than the Law/Grace problem because it's not as clear cut. In fact, millions follow this doctrine, and really do not know what it teaches. One thing is for certain, it doesn't teach the Cross!

I've already addressed this form of belief several times in this Volume, in one way or the other, so there's no need covering that ground again. Suffice to say, it is not possible for one to embrace the Word of Faith doctrine, and at the same time, proclaim the True Gospel. The Gospel of Jesus Christ is the Cross of Jesus Christ. One cannot read the writings of Paul, to whom was given the meaning of the New Covenant, which in effect, is the meaning of the Cross, without coming to that conclusion.

So the Church, in one way or the other, has been pulled away from the Cross, and is, therefore, powerless, simply because the Holy Spirit will not function in that particular climate.

Charles Solomon said, *"Since the vast majority of Christians do not understand the Cross experientially, the only other foundation on which to build their lives is the flesh, which is an inadequate undergirding for life and a Spirit-filled witness (I Cor. 3:11)."*

FOUR PILLARS

Verse 32 reads: *"And you shall hang it upon four pillars of Shittim Wood overlaid with gold: their hooks shall be of gold, upon the four sockets of silver."*

As we shall see, five pillars stood at the front of the Tabernacle, while four pillars stood between the Holy Place and the Holy of Holies. The Veil was to be hung over these four pillars. The pillars were made of indestructible wood, *"overlaid with gold,"* once again, proclaiming the humanity of Christ as well as His Deity.

The *"hooks"* were of pure gold, and were evidently attached to the pillars. Considering that the *"Veil"* was attached to these hooks, and covered the pillars, this tells us that the humanity and Deity of Christ were but for one purpose, and that was to die on the Cross.

Inasmuch as there were four Pillars, we have to assume that this represents the four-fold Gospel, i.e., *"Salvation by the Blood of Jesus; the Baptism with the Holy Spirit, with the evidence of speaking with other tongues; Divine Healing; and the imminent return of our Lord to take away the True Church in that which we refer to as the Rapture, and as well, the fact of Christ coming back to this Earth to stay, i.e., 'the Second Coming.'"*

The fact that the four Pillars were seated *"upon four sockets of silver,"* speaks of Redemption, which was the purpose of the Cross.

THE HOLY PLACE AND THE MOST HOLY

Verse 33 reads: *"And you shall hang up the Veil under the taches, that you may bring in thither within the Veil the Ark of the Testimony: and the Veil shall divide unto you between the Holy Place and the Most Holy."*

Once again we remind the Reader that the Veil was placed between the Holy Place and the Most Holy, in order that entrance to the Most Holy would be barred. In fact, the whole ritual of Israel's worship emphasized the distance between God and fallen man. Bounds were set about Sinai, so that not even a beast must touch it. One Tribe alone was permitted to encamp immediately around the Tabernacle; that Tribe was that of Levi. One family alone of that Tribe was singled out and allowed to enter the Holy Place: and one man alone of that family had access into the Holiest, and that, only once a year, and with such awe-inspiring preparation and ceremonies as must have filled him with fear lest he should incur the judgment of the Most High (Pink).

As beautiful as was the Veil, it was not that beauty which made entrance possible, but rather, the sprinkling of atoning blood before it! That beauty might be admired by the worshipper: he might sing hymns in its praise, and give all sorts of sentimental and endearing names to it. He might use all kinds of poetical language in describing it; he might even copy it, and produce similar patterns of embroidery, or schemes of colors; but there was only one way of passing to the other side of it, and of standing alive in the Presence of God's Glory; and that was by sprinkling the blood before it, and taking the blood of the victim beyond it. This blood told of Substitution, and acknowledged that he who entered did so as a sinner. By no other means could he stand on the other side of that Veil and live. He still says, *"When I see the Blood, I will pass over you"* (Ex. 12:13).

THE FURNITURE OF THE HOLY PLACE

Verses 34 and 35 read: *"And you shall put the Mercy Seat upon the Ark of the Testimony in the Most Holy Place.*

"And you shall set the Table without the Veil, and the Lampstand over against the Table on the side of the Tabernacle toward the south: and you shall put the Table on the north side."

In the Holy Place, we have the Lampstand on the south side, that is the left side, if one is standing facing the Tabernacle, with the Table of Shewbread on the opposite side, which would have been the north. Even though it's not mentioned here, the Altar of Incense would have sat immediately in front of the Veil in the Holy Place.

In effect, the Tabernacle was divided into three distinct parts, namely, *"The Holy of Holies,"* where were the Ark of the Covenant and the Mercy Seat, *"The Holy Place,"* just described, and *"the Court of the Tabernacle."* The entrances into each of these were of the same materials — *"blue, purple, scarlet, and fine twined linen."*

THE DOOR AND THE FIVE PILLARS

Verses 36 and 37 read: *"And you shall make an hanging for the door of the tent, of blue, and purple, and scarlet, and fine twined linen, wrought with needlework.*

"And you shall make for the hanging five pillars of Shittim Wood, and overlay them with gold, and their hooks shall be of gold: and you shall cast five sockets of brass for them."

The *"door of the tent,"* led from the outside into the Holy Place. As well, there were several major differences:

The Veil had *"Cherubim"* embroidered upon it, while the Door had none. The Veil was suspended from four Pillars, while the Door was suspended from five. The four Pillars had no *"Chapiters,"* on them, while the five Pillars did. The sockets of the four were made of silver, while the sockets of the five were made of brass. But the outstanding difference between them was this:

The Veil was to shut out, where as the Door was to give admittance: the Veil barred the way into the Holiest, the *"Door"* was for the constant entrance of the Priests into the Holy Place.

As stated, the *"Door"* was at the eastern end of the Tabernacle, which was the front, and faced the east. The Door or *"Hanging"* was not narrow, but rather stretched across the whole of its width, which was some 15 feet. It was also 15 feet high.

The fact that the Tabernacle faced the east carried with it a spiritual meaning as well.

In Genesis 3:24, we read that the Lord God *"drove out the man, and He placed at the east of the Garden of Eden Cherubim, and a flaming sword which turned every way, to keep the way of the Tree of Life."* We find from this that because of his sin, man was banished into darkness; and at the *"east"* was stationed a flaming barrier. But here, there was a door on the eastern side of the Tabernacle, which admitted men, after a fashion, into Jehovah's dwelling place!

THE NEEDLEWORK

Of the *"Veil"* it is said that it was made *"of cunning work."* Of the *"Door"* the term is used, *"wrought with needlework."*

We must ever understand that there is nothing meaningless in Scripture. This means that there is a profound spiritual significance in everything that is stated. It's up to us to find out what it is.

"Needlework" is mentioned only in the description of the Gate in the Outer Court (Ex. 27:16) and the Girdle of the High Priest (Ex. 28:39).

Looking at the Hebrew word rendered here *"needlework,"* which is also rendered *"the work of the embroiderer"* (I Chron. 29:2), *"divers colors"* (Ezek. 17:3), and in Psalm 139:15, it is translated *"curiously wrought."*

Combining these slightly varied meanings, the term would denote *"minutely variegated."* Thus it appears that the Holy Spirit here intimates that attention should be fixed upon the manner in which the different colors were wrought into and interwoven with the fine linen (Pink).

THE COLORS

Once again we have the colors, *"blue, and purple, and scarlet."* No less than 24 times is this combination repeated, yet never once is the order varied. This tells us something!

We know that everything in the Tabernacle pictures Christ in some manner, as it regards His Atoning, Mediatorial, Intercessory Work.

It is said that if the blue and the scarlet were placed side-by-side, without the intervention of some other color, the eye would be offended with the violent contrast; for, though each is beautiful in itself, and suitable to its own sphere, yet there is such a distinction, we might almost say opposition, in their hues, as to render them inharmonious if seen in immediate contrast. But the *"purple"* placed between the blue and the scarlet, softens this impact. In fact, the *"purple"* is a mingling of both blue and scarlet.

So we find that the *"scarlet"* and the *"blue"* are never placed in juxtaposition throughout the fabrics of the Tabernacle. Understanding that the Spirit of God is the One Who has arranged this order, and seeing as to how He so minutely adhered to this order, we will now learn something about Christ, which the Divine Spirit intends to teach.

The *"blue"* tells us from whence Christ has come, and we speak of Heaven. The *"purple"* tells us of His royalty as King. The *"scarlet"* proclaims to us the price that He paid in order that fallen man might be saved. So we learn that the One Who died for us is a *"King,"* but not just any king, but rather a King from Glory, hence, the *"King of kings"* (Rev. 19:16).

Consequently, and inasmuch as Christ is the *"King of kings,"* this speaks not only of His Deity, but as well of His *"Finished Work."* In other words, even though the plans for the Tabernacle were given some 1,500 years before Christ would come, in the Mind of God, there was no doubt that He would come, and that He would accomplish the task at hand. He would go to the Cross, shed His Life's Blood, atone for all sin, and thereby effect Redemption for all who will believe (Jn. 3:16).

The term *"King"* is applied to Christ only as it regards His humanity, and speaks of an accomplished work.

David is the man whom I personally believe was intended by God to be the first king of Israel. Saul was an aberration, the desire of the people, and not the Will of God; hence, his reign was anything but successful! He won some victories, even as the flesh will do, but couldn't win complete victory, even as the flesh cannot do. That remained for David to accomplish, which he did!

David was placed on the throne by God, hence God's choice. He would be the earthly type of the coming King, Who in fact, would be called *"the Son of David"* (Mat. 1:1).

So this one color *"purple"* placed between the *"blue"* and the *"scarlet,"* tells us that the work for which Christ came from Heaven to accomplish would in fact be accomplished, and without fail!

FIVE PILLARS

There were *"five Pillars"* at the front of the Tabernacle, whereas there were four, as stated, between the Holy Place and the Holy of Holies. They were made of indestructible wood, typifying, as also stated, the perfect humanity of Christ, and overlaid with gold, typifying His Deity.

"Hooks" were placed on these five Pillars, also of gold, in order to hold the *"door of the tent."*

The number *"five"* speaks of Grace. For instance, Jesus had five names (Isa. 9:6); He suffered five wounds at His Crucifixion, the nails in His hands, the nails in His feet, the spear in His side, the thorns on His brow, and the whip across His back. As well, David *"chose him five smooth stones out of the brook,"* when he fought and defeated Goliath (I Sam. 17:40).

Whereas the *"sockets"* under the four Pillars were of silver, signifying Redemption, these sockets under the five Pillars at the front of the Tabernacle, are of *"brass,"* i.e., *"copper."*

NOTES

"Brass" when used symbolically, prefigures Judgment, which Jesus would endure at the Cross, all in our stead. Thus is the worshipper reminded once more that Christ is the Door by reason of His sufferings in death. Pink said, and rightly so: *"May the Spirit of God ever keep before us the tremendous price which was paid to enable the Redeemed to come before God by sacrifices of Praise and Thanksgiving."*

> *"Would you be free from the burden of sin?*
> *"There's power in the Blood, power in the Blood;*
> *"Would you o'er evil a victory to win?*
> *"There's wonderful power in the Blood."*

> *"Would you be free from your passion and pride?*
> *"There's power in the Blood, power in the Blood;*
> *"Come for a cleansing to Calvary's tide;*
> *"There's wonderful power in the Blood."*

> *"Would you be whiter, much whiter than snow?*
> *"There's power in the Blood, power in the Blood;*
> *"Sin stains are lost in its life-giving flow;*
> *"There's wonderful power in the Blood."*

> *"Would you do service for Jesus, your King?*
> *"There's power in the Blood, power in the Blood;*
> *"Would you live daily His praises to sing?*
> *"There's wonderful power in the Blood."*

CHAPTER 27

(1) "AND YOU SHALL MAKE AN ALTAR OF SHITTIM WOOD, FIVE CUBITS LONG, AND FIVE CUBITS BROAD; THE ALTAR SHALL BE FOURSQUARE: AND THE HEIGHT THEREOF SHALL BE THREE CUBITS.

(2) "AND YOU SHALL MAKE THE HORNS OF IT UPON THE FOUR CORNERS THEREOF: HIS HORNS SHALL BE OF THE SAME: AND YOU SHALL OVERLAY IT WITH COPPER.

(3) "AND YOU SHALL MAKE HIS PANS TO RECEIVE HIS ASHES, AND HIS SHOVELS, AND IIIS BASINS, AND HIS FLESHHOOKS, AND HIS FIREPANS: ALL THE VESSELS THEREOF YOU SHALL MAKE OF COPPER.

(4) "AND YOU SHALL MAKE FOR IT A GRATE OF NETWORK OF COPPER; AND UPON THE NET SHALL YOU MAKE FOUR COPPER RINGS IN THE FOUR CORNERS THEREOF.

(5) "AND YOU SHALL PUT IT UNDER THE COMPASS OF THE ALTAR BENEATH, THAT THE NET MAY BE EVEN TO THE MIDST OF THE ALTAR.

(6) "AND YOU SHALL MAKE STAVES FOR THE ALTAR, STAVES OF SHITTIM WOOD, AND OVERLAY THEM WITH COPPER.

(7) "AND THE STAVES SHALL BE PUT INTO THE RINGS, AND THE STAVES SHALL BE UPON THE TWO SIDES OF THE ALTAR, TO BEAR IT.

(8) "HOLLOW WITH BOARDS SHALL YOU MAKE IT: AS IT WAS SHOWED YOU IN THE MOUNT, SO SHALL YOU MAKE IT."

The diagram is:

1. The great Brazen Altar represented Jesus and Calvary.

2. The copper pictured judgment, which He took in our place.

3. Its polished surface pictures His sinlessness.

4. Its measurements, three by five, His Deity and His Grace.

5. Its shape, foursquare, expressed its provision and sufficiency for the four quarters of the Earth.

6. Its position, in front of the entrance to the Tabernacle, pictures the fact that the Crucified Lamb of Calvary is the one and only way to God.

7. It was carried by staves, thereby accompanying the people in their pilgrim way to Canaan, so teaching the lesson that there never comes a period in the Christian life where the Atoning Blood of Christ can be dispensed with.

THE BRAZEN ALTAR

Verse 1 reads: *"And you shall make an Altar of Shittim Wood, five cubits long, and five cubits broad; the Altar shall be foursquare: and the height thereof shall be three cubits."*

The Brazen Altar was the largest Sacred Vessel in the entirety of the seven Vessels of the Tabernacle. It was seven and one-half feet long, and seven and one-half feet wide. It was four and one-half feet high.

Going back to the *"cubits,"* the number *"five"* portrays the Grace of God, in sending His Son, the Lord Jesus Christ, Who would suffer on our behalf. The number *"three"* again respecting cubits, but spoke of the height, refers to the Deity of Christ.

Inasmuch as the Altar was *"foursquare,"* this tells us that it is the same Gospel for all of mankind, whether north, south, east, or west. The problem is sin, and the solution is the Saviour. It doesn't matter what nationality the person might be, what race they might be, or whatever their status in society; the need is the same!

The Church makes a terrible mistake when it tries to address the Gospel in a particular way to fit a particular people. When we read the Book of Acts, which proclaims the manner in which the Holy Spirit carried out the Work of God on Earth, through the Apostles, and others, we find that the same Message was preached everywhere, irrespective as to whom the people may have been. The Message didn't change, simply because the Message didn't need to change. As stated, the problem is sin, and the solution is the Saviour, and we might well say that the Saviour Alone is the solution.

Inasmuch as the Brazen Altar was the largest of all the Sacred Vessels, its size indicated its importance. As well, it was placed *"before the Door"* (Ex. 40:6), just inside the Outer Court (Ex. 40:33), and would thus be the first object to meet the eye of the worshipper as he entered the fenced enclosure. It is designated *"The Brazen Altar"* (Ex. 38:30), to distinguish it from the *"Golden Altar."* It is also called *"The Altar of Burnt Offering"* (Ex. 30:28).

ITS SIGNIFICANCE

The Altar typified Christ, and it typified what He would do in order to redeem humanity. Irrespective as to how one might try to dress it up, the Brazen Altar was a gruesome sight. The greasy smoke from the burning sacrifices, constantly typifying the Judgment of God upon sin, and more specifically, upon an innocent victim, which was the lamb, which represented Christ and was not, to say the least, a pleasant sight to behold. There it stood: ever smoking, ever bloodstained, ever opened to any guilty Hebrew who might wish to approach it. The sinner, having forfeited his life by sin, another life — one that was innocent — must be given in his stead (Pink).

In many ways, the Brazen Altar must be construed as the most important vessel designed by the Holy Spirit. Could it be more important than the Ark of the Covenant, over which sat the Mercy Seat? This represented the very Holy of Holies, the very Throne of God! However, no one could reach that place and position, except for the Brazen Altar, which typified Calvary. I would have to say that the Cross of Christ stands supreme at the very intersection of humanity, and as well, of Heaven itself. Concerning this, Paul said: *"That in the dispensation of the fullness of times He* (God the Father) *might gather together in one all things in Christ, both which are in Heaven and which are on the Earth; even in Him"* (Eph. 1:10).

The phrase, *"In Christ,"* speaks entirely of the Cross, and as well, this Verse tells us that the Cross addressed itself not only to fallen man, but to the revolution led by Satan in eternity past. This is proven by the word *"Heaven."* So if we want to try to put a label on these all-important things, I think we can safely say that the Cross stands at the intersection of both Heaven and Earth. It is impossible, I think, to overemphasize the Cross, while very much possible to minimize its significance.

THE HORNS

Verse 2 reads: *"And you shall make the horns of it upon the four corners thereof: his horns shall be of the same, and you shall overlay it with copper."*

This Altar of indestructible wood was to be *"overlaid with copper."*

Until the metallurgy of the not-too-distant past, copper had a greater resistance to fire even than gold or silver. It would consequently protect the wood, that it would not catch fire and be consumed. Pink says, *"As the copper plates on the Altar protected it from the fervent heat and prevented it from being burned up, so, Christ passed through the fires of God's wrath without being consumed. He is mighty to save, because He was mighty to endure."*

"Copper" in Scripture symbolizes judgment. This is the reason that Moses was instructed to make *"a serpent of copper"* and place it on a pole. The Children of Israel, who had been bitten by serpents, were instructed to look at this copper serpent, and upon looking, they would be healed (Num. 21:8).

The serpent on the pole symbolized Christ on the Cross; consequently, many have wondered, why would the Holy Spirit have used a serpent made of copper as a symbol of the perfect, untainted, unsullied, Son of God? A dove, yes! But a serpent? Surely this would be the last of all objects suited to portray Him Who is fairer than the children of men!

No, it wasn't a mistake. The *"serpent"* was the only symbol which could properly portray what would be carried out on the Cross. The *"serpent"* was the reminder of the *"curse"* (Gen., Chpt. 3), and in Galatians 3:13, we are expressly told that Christ was *"made a curse"* for His people.

As well, the serpent which Moses was instructed to make at that particular time, was to be of *"copper"* and not of silver or of gold, because it was to represent Jesus suffering the Judgment of God on the Cross.

THE AWFULNESS OF SIN

In both the Brazen Altar and the Brazen Serpent, we see the awfulness of sin. We see that it is so horrible, so deadly, so degrading, so destructive, that even though God could speak worlds into existence, He could not speak Redemption into existence. Sin and all of its effects had to be addressed, and the only way it could be addressed was for the price to be paid regarding Atonement. No man could pay that price, so God Himself would have to pay that which was owed.

This means that man has absolutely no argument left. If God had demanded that man pay the price, perhaps man might have an argument; however, if God would pay the price, which He did, and at frightful cost, then we have no argument as to how steep that price actually was. In fact, we learn how bad sin is by the price that was paid in order for sin to be assuaged.

What Jesus did on the Cross must not only address the effects of sin, which it did, which means to atone for the terrible ravages of sin, which Jesus did by the shedding of His Precious Blood, but He must also address the cause of sin. The cause is twofold:

All sin stems from Satan himself, the archenemy of God. It has as its receptacle the evil hearts of men. That's the reason that it's impossible to address sin by addressing the environment, education, economic structure, or social rehabilitation. Those things only address symptoms, and not at all the cause. The cause, as far as man is concerned, is the evil heart. In other words, sin comes from within, which means that man has no solution for this terrible problem.

But when Jesus died on the Cross, He atoned for all sin, which totally and completely defeated Satan and all his evil cohorts, and did so by removing the legal right that the Evil One had to hold man in bondage. And that's why Paul said:

"And having spoiled principalities and powers (Satan and his minions), *He made a show of them openly, triumphing over them in it."* He did this by and through what He did at the Cross (Col. 2:14-15).

THE CONQUERING OF SIN

My next statement will be somewhat shocking because it flies in the face of the thinking of most Christians. Let us proceed:

There is nothing in the Bible that even remotely mentions that fact that Believers must conquer sin! The truth is, sin has already been conquered by Jesus Christ, as it could only be conquered by Jesus Christ. And when we try to conquer it ourselves, we are in effect saying that what Christ did at the Cross was insufficient, and must have our contribution in order for His Work to be complete.

Such an idea borders on blasphemy! But this is where most modern Christians are, albeit ignorantly!

NOTES

Most Christians do not understand the cause of sin in their lives, and please remember, we're speaking of true Christians. So when they fail the Lord, almost invariably, the Christian addresses the symptom instead of the real cause. Let us state it again:

Most of the time one doesn't address the cause, simply because one doesn't know or understand the cause; consequently, the lives of most Christians play out to a constant struggle, with most of the time, them losing this struggle. In other words, Satan is overcoming them, and they are perpetually failing the Lord in some way.

Why?

The Christian fails the Lord, in other words, he sins in some way, because he is rebelling against God's prescribed order of victory. With some it is a deliberate rebellion, while with others, it is rebellion because of ignorance of this prescribed order. Either way though, hurt and harm will be the result.

God's prescribed order of victory is the Cross of Christ, through and by which the Holy Spirit works (Rom. 8:1-2, 11).

The Christian is to understand that Jesus won a complete victory at the Cross, atoning for all sin, thereby defeating the powers of darkness in their totality. His work was a *"Finished Work."*

This means that whatever sin, iniquity, or transgression with which Satan would approach the Child of God, it has already been addressed at the Cross. And Satan is able to peddle his wares, only because the Christian doesn't understand who he really is in Christ.

THE CROSS

The Christian must, without fail, understand that his victory is totally and completely in the Cross. It was there that the price was paid, there that victory was won, and there that all sin was atoned. When we sing the song, *"Jesus Paid It All,"* it means exactly what it says!

It would seem, would it not, that what we've just said is very, very simple, and not hard at all to understand. In fact it is simple! And in fact, it is not hard to understand! So the problem is not theological, but rather moral. And what do I mean by that?

In order for the Christian to put his Faith totally and completely in Christ and what Christ had done for him at the Cross, he has to overcome two obstacles:

1. He will soon find out that most of the Church world, and it probably includes where he presently attends Church, while they pay lip service to the Cross, in effect, place little confidence in the Cross. This is proven by the crises that arise in the Church. In other words, if failure is enjoined, it is seldom that the Cross is recommended as the solution, but rather the psychological way. In fact, the far greater majority of the modern Church will not even accept the victory and deliverance that comes through the Cross. They demand a sign-off by a Psychologist. So the whole tenor of the Church militates against the Cross. In fact, and as previously stated, the Cross of Christ is the dividing line between the True Church and the apostate church.

So the Believer, and especially the Preacher, is going to have to understand that when he places his Faith and trust exclusively in Christ and what He did at the Cross, he will probably be ostracized by the far greater majority of the Church. Most, regrettably, aren't willing to pay that price.

Never mind that there is no victory whatsoever in the direction of the apostate Church, most Christians simply cannot buck the tide.

2. There is something in us, even the most consecrated, that wants to try to believe that whatever it is we are facing, we can handle it ourselves. In other words, even though everybody else has failed, *"I can do it,"* seems to be the attitude of most all of us.

But the truth is, you can't do it. And I'm speaking of living a righteous, holy life, other than by fully trusting Christ and His Sacrifice.

You would be surprised how hard it is for most Christians to admit this. We are loath to give up our little pet stratagems, in favor of living a life totally dependent on Christ and what He did for us at the Cross. However, there is victory in no other means or methods, than the Cross. The Cross alone provides what we must have, and of course we speak of the benefits of the Cross, and that Scriptural Truth will never change (Rom. 6:3-14; 8:1-2, 11; I Cor. 1:17-18, 21, 23; 2:2; Gal. 6:14; Eph. 2:13-18; Col. 2:14-15).

THE BINDING OF THE SACRIFICE

The horns, which were on each corner, and pointing outward, were for the binding of the sacrifice to the Altar (Ps. 118:27). In Scripture, the *"horn"* stands for power and strength (Hab. 3:4).

One might say that it was not the nails which held Christ to the Cross, but rather the unfaltering purpose of the Saviour, and the strength of His Love.

While on the Cross, His enemies challenged Him to come down; His refusal to do so evidenced the cords which bound Him to its *"horns"* (Pink).

THE ASHES

Verse 3 reads: *"And you shall make his pans to receive his ashes, and his shovels, and his basins, and his fleshhooks, and his firepans: all the vessels thereof you shall make of copper."*

Pink said, *"Ashes testified to the thoroughness of the fire's work in having wholly consumed the offering. They also witnessed to the acceptance of the sacrifice on behalf of the offerer, and so they were to him a token that his sins were gone. The Words of Christ from the Cross express the fulfillment of this detail of our type: 'It is finished' announced that the Sacrifice had been offered, accepted, and gone up to God as a sweet savor."*

As it regards the various utensils, all designed by the Holy Spirit, we might quickly add, all played their part as it regards the sacrifice being offered up properly.

When it comes to the Crucifixion of Christ, the Scripture says: *"How much more shall the Blood of Christ, Who through the Eternal Spirit offered Himself without spot to God"* (Heb. 9:14).

This means that the Holy Spirit planned every detail of the death of the Son of God, even down to the moment which He would tell Him that He could die. Ever let it be understood that Jesus was not executed. Even though such was in the murderous hearts of those who demanded His Crucifixion, He in fact, laid down His life freely. In other words, no one took it from Him (Jn. 10:17-18).

That all were made of *"copper"* emphasizes, again, the prominent and dominant truth associated with this Altar — the unsparing judgment of God upon the believing sinner's Substitute (Pink).

THE GRATE

Verses 4 and 5 read: *"And you shall make for it a grate of network of copper; and upon the net shall you make four copper rings in the four corners thereof.*

"And you shall put it under the compass of the Altar beneath, that the net may be even to the midst of the Altar."

The Altar was hollow; although, after the Temple was built, and it became a fixed object, more than likely it was filled up with earth, with the *"grate"* over the top. But during the wilderness experience, it is almost certain that it remained hollow, to make it easier to move, which it often was.

The *"grate of network of copper"* provided a top for the Altar, on which the parts of the animals were laid. The *"network"* was held up by *"four copper rings in the four corners."*

Somewhere alongside the middle of the Altar, there seemed to be a protrusion all the way around, on which the Priests could stand, in order to properly attend to the sacrifices.

THE STAVES

Verses 6 through 8 read: *"And you shall make staves for the Altar, staves of Shittim Wood, and overlay them with copper.*

"And the staves shall be put into the rings, and the staves shall be upon the two sides of the Altar, to bear it.

"Hollow with boards shall you make it: as it was showed you in the Mount, so shall they make it."

The entire camp of Israel often moved while in the wilderness; consequently, everything had to be moved, as would be obvious. The Brazen Altar was carried by staves, so teaching the lesson that there never comes a period in the Christian life where the Atoning Blood of Christ can be dispensed with. But yet, and tragically so, this is exactly what most modern Christians do. After the initial Salvation experience, they leave the Cross for other things, thereby placing their faith in other things, which is the cause of all spiritual tragedy.

THE CROSS AND SANCTIFICATION

As the believing sinner must look to Christ and the Cross as it regards the initial Salvation experience, likewise, the Believer must continue to look to the Cross as it regards Sanctification. In other words, the Cross of Christ plays the signal part in every aspect of the Believer's experience, irrespective as to what it might be. But tragically, most Christians don't know this.

Having so little teaching on the subject, after conversion, many, if not most, Christians attempt to live for God in all the wrong ways. While there are any number of wrong ways, there's only one right way, and that is for the Believer to continue to look to Christ and the Cross for all things, irrespective as to what they might be, ever placing his Faith in the Finished Work of Christ, never allowing it to be moved to other things, which then gives the Holy Spirit the latitude to work as only the Holy Spirit can work (Rom. 8:1-2, 11).

When the Priests burned incense on the Golden Altar, which they did twice a day, morning, and evening, coals of fire were taken from the Brazen Altar each time, and placed on the Golden Altar, with incense poured over these coals. This signified that all intercession by Christ, along with the presentation of our praises, is made possible by what Christ did at the Cross. In other words, Christ is making intercession for us in Heaven at this very moment, due to the fact of what He did at the Cross on our behalf. So unless one understands the Cross, one cannot understand much of anything carried out by Christ.

(9) "AND YOU SHALL MAKE THE COURT OF THE TABERNACLE: FOR THE SOUTHSIDE SOUTHWARD THERE SHALL BE HANGINGS FOR THE COURT OF FINE TWINED LINEN OF AN HUNDRED CUBITS LONG FOR ONE SIDE:

(10) "AND THE TWENTY PILLARS THEREOF AND THEIR TWENTY SOCKETS SHALL BE OF COPPER; THE HOOKS OF THE PILLARS AND THEIR FILLETS

SHALL BE OF SILVER.

(11) "AND LIKEWISE FOR THE NORTH SIDE IN LENGTH, THERE SHALL BE HANGINGS OF AN HUNDRED CUBITS LONG, AND HIS TWENTY PILLARS, AND THEIR TWENTY SOCKETS OF COPPER; THE HOOKS OF THE PILLARS AND THE FILLETS OF SILVER.

(12) "AND FOR THE BREADTH OF THE COURT ON THE WEST SIDE SHALL BE HANGINGS OF FIFTY CUBITS: THEIR PILLARS TEN, AND THEIR SOCKETS TEN.

(13) "AND THE BREADTH OF THE COURT ON THE EAST SIDE EASTWARD SHALL BE FIFTY CUBITS.

(14) "THE HANGINGS OF ONE SIDE OF THE GATE SHALL BE FIFTEEN CUBITS: THEIR PILLARS THREE, AND THEIR SOCKETS THREE.

(15) "AND ON THE OTHER SIDE SHALL BE HANGINGS FIFTEEN CUBITS: THEIR PILLARS THREE, AND THEIR SOCKETS THREE."

The composition is:

1. Verses 9 through 15 portray the *"Outer Court."* Using 18 inches to the cubit, it was 150 feet long and 75 feet wide.

2. The curtain was of *"fine twined linen,"* and surrounded the enclosure, which typified the Perfect Righteousness of Christ.

3. The Pillars holding the curtain were socketed in *"copper."* Copper stakes were driven in the ground close by the Pillars with silver rods running between the Pillars and the brass stakes to hold up the posts and the curtains.

4. The worshipper would approach the Tabernacle and see the beautiful white curtains of the Court enriched with brass and silver. This again was a portrayal of the Lord Jesus Christ Whose Life was sinless, but yet Who suffered the Judgment of God, all on our behalf, typified by the *"copper"* which purchased for us our Redemption, typified by the *"silver."*

THE COURT

Verse 9 reads: *"And you shall make the Court of the Tabernacle: for the south side southward there shall be hangings for the Court of fine twined linen of an hundred cubits long for one side."*

NOTES

The Tabernacle stood in the Court. The Court consisted of a fence which was 150 feet long, and 75 feet wide, measuring 18 inches to the cubit. The height of the fence was seven and one-half feet (Vs. 18).

The fence was made of *"fine twined linen,"* which meant that it was snow white, and which typified, as previously stated, the perfect Righteousness and Life of our Lord and Saviour, Jesus Christ.

In effect, the Tabernacle was situated in the very midst of the encampment of Israel, at least where the terrain allowed such.

Immediately around the Court of the Tabernacle were the tents of the Levites; beyond, but encircling them, were grouped the 12 Tribes, three on either side; thus forming a square of vast extent. The Tabernacle, therefore, formed the center of Israel's camp.

The Court foreshadowed Christ on Earth tabernacling among men, accessible to all who sought Him, but His glory beheld only by those who drew near in Faith (Jn. 1:14).

As everything centered around the Tabernacle, everything must center around Christ, of which the Tabernacle is a Type.

But yet, the smallness of the Court stands in contrast to the vastness of the Camp, which numbered upwards of three million people. This contains more than a hint of the fewness of those, from among the crowds of professing Christians, who really enter into God's Presence! God's *"flock"* is only a *"little one"* (Lk. 12:32); only the *"few"* are in the *"Narrow Way"* (Mat. 7:14). And yet, the clarion call still is, *"Whosoever will!"* (Rev. 22:17).

THE PILLARS

Verses 10 through 15 read: *"And the twenty Pillars thereof and their twenty sockets shall be of copper; the hooks of the Pillars and their fillets shall be of silver.*

"And likewise for the north side in length there shall be hangings of an hundred cubits long, and his twenty Pillars and their twenty sockets of copper; the hooks of the Pillars and their fillets of silver.

"And for the breadth of the Court on the west side shall be hangings of fifty cubits: their Pillars ten, and their sockets ten.

"And the breadth of the Court on the east

side eastward shall be fifty cubits.

"The hangings of one side of the Gate shall be fifteen cubits: their Pillars three, and their sockets three.

"And on the other side shall be hangings fifteen cubits: their Pillars three, and their sockets three."

There were 60 Pillars, placed at intervals of five cubits all around the Court. This, as well, and I speak of one being placed every five cubits, speaks of the Grace of God. Considering the number of Pillars, it speaks of unlimited Grace.

The Grace of God is simply the Goodness of God extended to undeserving man. That is about the simplest explanation, I think, which can be given.

God has always dealt with man by Grace, because that's the only way He can deal with man; however, the Cross made it possible for Grace to be extended to undeserving man in a much more abundant manner. It's not that God now has more Grace than He once had, for that's incorrect. The Cross has made it possible for God to dispense Grace in a more abundant way.

So the 60 Pillars, situated five cubits apart from each other, signified not only that God dealt with man through the medium of Grace, but as well, that abundant Grace was coming, of which all of this was but a type.

THE MATERIAL OF WHICH THE PILLARS WERE MADE

It would seem from Verse 10 that the Pillars were made of copper; however, in the original Hebrew, in which this was written, there is indication that the modifying clause *"of copper"* refers only to the *"sockets,"* and not to the Pillars.

Even though the Scripture doesn't say, more than likely, the *"Pillars"* were made of *"Shittim Wood."* The other *"Pillars,"* and I speak of those used for the Door and for the support of the Veil, were all of wood; therefore, in the absence of any word to the contrary, we naturally conclude that these also were made of the same material.

As well, as it regards the amount of copper used (Ex. 38:25, 27), seemingly, there would not have been enough copper to have cast the Pillars of that metal.

If in fact the Pillars were made of indestructible wood, this would have fit perfectly with the *"fine twined linen,"* signifying the Righteousness of Christ, as it regards His humanity.

(16) "AND FOR THE GATE OF THE COURT SHALL BE AN HANGING OF TWENTY CUBITS, OF BLUE, AND PURPLE, AND SCARLET, AND FINE TWINED LINEN, WROUGHT WITH NEEDLEWORK: AND THEIR PILLARS SHALL BE FOUR, AND THEIR SOCKETS FOUR.

(17) "ALL THE PILLARS ROUND ABOUT THE COURT SHALL BE FILLETED WITH SILVER; THEIR HOOKS SHALL BE OF SILVER, AND THEIR SOCKETS OF COPPER.

(18) "THE LENGTH OF THE COURT SHALL BE AN HUNDRED CUBITS, AND THE BREADTH FIFTY EVERYWHERE, AND THE HEIGHT FIVE CUBITS OF FINE TWINED LINEN, AND THEIR SOCKETS OF COPPER.

(19) "ALL THE VESSELS OF THE TABERNACLE AND ALL THE SERVICE THEREOF, AND ALL THE PINS THEREOF, AND ALL THE PINS OF THE COURT, SHALL BE OF COPPER.

(20) "AND YOU SHALL COMMAND THE CHILDREN OF ISRAEL, THAT THEY BRING TO YOU PURE OIL OLIVE BEATEN FOR THE LIGHT, TO CAUSE THE LAMP TO BURN ALWAYS.

(21) "IN THE TABERNACLE OF THE CONGREGATION WITHOUT THE VEIL, WHICH IS BEFORE THE TESTIMONY, AARON AND HIS SONS SHALL ORDER IT FROM EVENING TO MORNING BEFORE THE LORD: IT SHALL BE A STATUTE FOREVER UNTO THEIR GENERATIONS ON THE BEHALF OF THE CHILDREN OF ISRAEL."

The construction is:

1. The Gate which led into the Outer Court was 30 feet wide.

2. It is interesting as to how wide the Gate was. It took almost half of the entire front and was symbolic of the great invitation, *"Whosoever will, let him come."*

3. Verse 18 says that the fence of the Outer Court was seven and one-half feet high. It was tall enough that the inquisitive need not approach.

4. The one Gate at the front symbolized the One Redeemer, the Lord Jesus Christ.

5. Verses 20 and 21 portray the *"pure oil olive,"* which is a Type of the Holy Spirit.

6. It was made by olives being bruised in a mortar or mill without the application of heat, *"beaten for the light."* Likewise, He was *"bruised for our iniquities."*

7. It was to *"burn always"*; as well, the Child of God is to let his light shine constantly, which can only be done by the Power of the Holy Spirit.

THE GATE OF THE COURT

Verse 16 reads: *"And for the Gate of the Court shall be an hanging of twenty cubits, of blue, and purple, and scarlet, and fine twined linen, wrought with needlework: and their Pillars shall be four, and their sockets four."*

The *"Gate"* to the Outer Court is very similar to the Gate which opened into the Tabernacle, and the Veil, which hid the Holy of Holies. Each of them served as a door, hiding the interior from one approaching from the outside.

All were made of the same materials, and the colors are mentioned in the same order.

The Gate that led into the Court was 30 feet wide. The total width of the enclosure on the east, as well as the west, was 75 feet. So the Gate in the front took up nearly half of the space.

Its colors of *"blue, purple, scarlet, and fine twined linen,"* portrayed Christ in every capacity. He Alone is *"the Door!"*

So, the Israelite who came to the Brazen Altar with his offering must pass through this Gate of the Court; the Priest who placed incense on the Golden Altar must enter by the Door of the Tabernacle; the High Priest who entered the Holy of Holies on the Day of Atonement must do so through the Veil, thus realizing the thrice-repeated proof of the only way of access to God.

However, a *"Gate"* or *"Door,"* must be understood in the following fashion:

It's not enough to have access to the Gate or Door; it's not even enough to recognize that it is the Gate or Door. The Gate or Door must be entered, before one can reap the benefits therein. The very specific demands that it be entered, or else it is of no value.

As well, when the Israelite came through the *"Gate,"* the first thing he would see would be the *"Brazen Altar."* In effect, the presence of the Altar stated that sinful man could go no further. And the only way he could come at all was to offer up sacrifice on the Altar, which would typify the One Who was to come, and would give His Life for lost humanity.

THE COURT AND THE HOLY PLACE

Verses 17 through 21 read: *"All the Pillars round about the Court shall be filleted with silver: their hooks shall be of silver, and their sockets of copper.*

"The length of the Court shall be an hundred cubits, and the breadth fifty cubits everywhere, and the height five cubits of fine twined linen, and their sockets of copper.

"All the vessels of the Tabernacle, and all the service thereof, and all the pins thereof, and all the pins of the Court, shall be of copper.

"And you shall command the Children of Israel, that they bring you pure oil olive beaten for the light, to cause the Lamp to burn always.

"In the Tabernacle of the congregation without the Veil, which is before the Testimony, Aaron and his sons shall order it from evening to morning before the LORD: it shall be a statute forever unto their generations on the behalf of the Children of Israel."

The Court was as far as the Israelite, other than the Priests, could come, at least as it regards the Tabernacle, and then only so far as the Brazen Altar. But everything about the Outer Court, as well as the Tabernacle, spoke of Christ in either His Atoning, Mediatorial, or Intercessory Work, even down to the small pins, which were of brass (copper). As always, this spoke of the Judgment that He would undergo on our behalf.

THE LAMPSTAND

The olive oil was to be pure, which was obtained by olives being beaten or crushed. There was to ever be a ready supply, in order that the Lamp not go out. There was no source of light in the Tabernacle, with the exception of the Golden Lampstand.

Of course, this portrays Christ as the Light

of the world, but as well, it portrays the Work of the Holy Spirit within his heart and life, which was to a degree not known by anyone else.

The word *"beaten"* emphasizes the fact that this particular oil did not come easily. The crushing of the olives was typical of the price paid by Christ for our Redemption. The Scripture says of Him:

"He was wounded for our transgressions, He was bruised for our iniquities: the chastisement of our peace was upon Him; and with His stripes we are healed . . . He was oppressed, and He was afflicted, yet He opened not His mouth . . . yet it pleased the LORD to bruise Him" (Isa. 53:5, 7, 10).

Twice a day Aaron and his sons, and those who would follow him in that order, would replenish the oil in the Golden Lampstand, and trim the wicks. It was commanded by God that this be done into infinity.

While it was true that Jesus was coming, Who would fulfill the Law in every respect, thereby making these things unnecessary, the fact is, even after Israel accepts Christ as Lord and Saviour, as a memorial of what Christ has done, the Temple practices will again be instituted. More than likely, in the Millennial Temple, described in Ezekiel, Chapters 40 through 48, there could very well be 10 Golden Lampstands, five on one side and five on the other, as they were in Solomon's Temple (I Ki. 7:49).

Some have questioned as to whether the light burned during the daytime. The Scripture says, *"to burn always,"* and I would think it meant 24 hours a day. There was really very little way that light could come into the Holy Place, unless the front Door was left open. Even then, it would be very sparse, it seems to me, continuing to need the glow of the Lampstand.

Inasmuch as it typified the Life and Ministry of Christ, it would stand to reason that the Lamp was to burn without fail.

"Blessed be the Fountain of Blood, to a world of sinners revealed;
"Blessed be the dear Son of God: only by His stripes we're healed.
"Tho' I've wandered far from His fold, bringing to my heart pain and woe,
"Wash me in the Blood of the Lamb, and I shall be whiter than snow."

"Thorny was the crown that He wore, and the Cross His body overcame;
"Grievous were the sorrows He bore, but He suffered thus not in vain.
"May I to that Fountain be led, made to cleanse my sins here below;
"Wash me in the Blood that He shed, and I shall be whiter than snow."

"Father, I have wandered from Thee, often has my heart gone astray;
"Crimson do my sins seem to me, water cannot wash them away.
"Jesus, to that Fountain of Thine, leaning on Thy Promise, I go;
"Cleanse me by Thy washing Divine, and I shall be whiter than snow."

CHAPTER 28

(1) "AND YOU TAKE UNTO YOU AARON YOUR BROTHER, AND HIS SONS WITH HIM, FROM AMONG THE CHILDREN OF ISRAEL, THAT HE MAY MINISTER UNTO ME IN THE PRIEST'S OFFICE, EVEN AARON, NADAB, AND ABIHU, ELEAZAR AND ITHAMAR, AARON'S SONS.

(2) "AND YOU SHALL MAKE HOLY GARMENTS FOR AARON YOUR BROTHER FOR GLORY AND FOR BEAUTY.

(3) "AND YOU SHALL SPEAK UNTO ALL WHO ARE WISE HEARTED, WHOM I HAVE FILLED WITH THE SPIRIT OF WISDOM, THAT THEY MAY MAKE AARON'S GARMENTS TO CONSECRATE HIM, THAT HE MAY MINISTER UNTO ME IN THE PRIEST'S OFFICE.

(4) "AND THESE ARE THE GARMENTS WHICH THEY SHALL MAKE; A BREASTPLATE, AND AN EPHOD, AND A ROBE, AND A BROIDERED COAT, A MITRE, AND A GIRDLE: AND THEY SHALL MAKE HOLY GARMENTS FOR AARON YOUR BROTHER, AND HIS SONS, THAT HE MAY MINISTER UNTO ME IN THE PRIEST'S OFFICE.

(5) "AND THEY SHALL TAKE GOLD, AND BLUE, AND PURPLE, AND SCARLET,

AND FINE LINEN.

(6) "AND THEY SHALL MAKE THE EPHOD OF GOLD, OF BLUE, AND OF PURPLE, OF SCARLET, AND FINE TWINED LINEN, WITH CUNNING WORK.

(7) "IT SHALL HAVE THE TWO SHOULDER PIECES THEREOF JOINED AT THE TWO EDGES THEREOF; AND SO IT SHALL BE JOINED TOGETHER.

(8) "AND THE CURIOUS GIRDLE OF THE EPHOD, WHICH IS UPON IT, SHALL BE OF THE SAME, ACCORDING TO THE WORK THEREOF; EVEN OF GOLD, OF BLUE, AND PURPLE, AND SCARLET, AND FINE TWINED LINEN.

(9) "AND YOU SHALL TAKE TWO ONYX STONES, AND GRAVE ON THEM THE NAMES OF THE CHILDREN OF ISRAEL:

(10) "SIX OF THEIR NAMES ON ONE STONE, AND THE OTHER SIX NAMES OF THE REST ON THE OTHER STONE, ACCORDING TO THEIR BIRTH.

(11) "WITH THE WORK OF AN ENGRAVER IN STONE, LIKE THE ENGRAVINGS OF A SIGNET, YOU SHALL ENGRAVE THE TWO STONES WITH THE NAMES OF THE CHILDREN OF ISRAEL: YOU SHALL MAKE THEM TO BE SET IN OUCHES OF GOLD.

(12) "AND YOU SHALL PUT THE TWO STONES UPON THE SHOULDERS OF THE EPHOD FOR STONES OF MEMORIAL UNTO THE CHILDREN OF ISRAEL: AND AARON SHALL BEAR THEIR NAMES BEFORE THE LORD UPON HIS TWO SHOULDERS FOR A MEMORIAL.

(13) "AND YOU SHALL MAKE OUCHES OF GOLD;

(14) "AND TWO CHAINS OF PURE GOLD AT THE ENDS; OF WREATHEN WORK SHALL YOU MAKE THEM, AND FASTEN THE WREATHEN CHAINS TO THE OUCHES."

The overview is:

1. Verse 1 portrays Aaron being chosen by God as the Great High Priest, with his four sons chosen to the Priesthood as well.

2. The garments worn by Aaron were beautiful beyond compare. They were designed solely by the Lord, and were designed to portray Christ.

3. The Holy Spirit is shown in Verse 3 as giving wisdom to those who would make the garments, that they might be made exactly as designed. The Holy Spirit will likewise help us!

4. Verse 5 tells us that *"gold"* was added to the colors, and was actually a fine wire which could be woven with the linen threads, etc. Along with the other colors symbolizing Christ, the gold thread was added to symbolize His Deity.

5. The Ephod was essentially the Priestly garment. It was worn by Aaron the Priest, Samuel the Prophet, and David the King. Christ combined all three Offices.

6. The Ephod was made of the same materials as the Veil, but with threads of gold and no Cherubim.

7. The golden thread in the Ephod declared the Divine Righteousness of the Priest; the Cherubim on the Veil, the judicial authority of the Son of Man. Christ, as Priest, is the Divine Righteousness; Christ, as Man, the Divine Judgment (Williams).

THE OFFICE OF THE PRIEST

Verse 1 reads: *"And you take unto you Aaron your brother, and his sons with him, from among the Children of Israel, that he may minister unto Me in the Priest's Office, even Aaron, Nadab, and Abihu, Eleazar, and Ithamar, Aaron's sons."*

Aaron and the beautiful garments to which we will momentarily address ourselves, present, as everything else in the Tabernacle, a beautiful picture of Christ, our Great High Priest, Who has now passed into the Heavens. But yet our study of Aaron, his sons, and all that pertained to their Priestly duties, will help us to understand Christ even more. That's the reason these Old Testament Books are of such significance. And the Reader should understand that when we speak of understanding Christ, we're speaking of understanding His Atoning, Mediatorial, Intercessory Work, all on our behalf. The Tabernacle, its furnishings, and its attendance by the Priests, all portrayed what Christ would do to redeem humanity, in effect, telling us Who He was, and What He did!

THE PRIESTHOOD

Under the Levitical Law, the Priesthood,

which was of the Tribe of Levi, was a privileged class, at least as it regards special privileges before the Lord. For instance, they were privileged to enter the Holy Place, and to partake of the bread from the Table, which was done every Sabbath. They were also privileged to attend the Lampstand, as well as pour Incense over the burning coals on the Golden Altar. In fact, they were only feet away from the Ark of the Covenant. In other words, no Israelite outside of the Priesthood could enter into the Holy Place, except some of the Levites of special orders, who helped to move the Tabernacle and its furnishings, at particular times.

But the Cross changed all of that! What Jesus did there wrote *"Finished,"* to all of the ancient Levitical order, and did so in totality, with Judaism ceasing, and Christianity taking its place.

Two symbolic actions gave plain intimation of this:

1. In Matthew 26:65, we are told, *"The High Priest rent his clothes,"* which was expressly forbidden by the Law (Lev. 21:10). But God permitted this to show that Israel's Priesthood was ending — clothes are only torn to pieces when there is no further use for them.

2. The rending of the Veil (Mat. 27:51): the barrier into God's Presence no longer existed for His people.

In Hebrews, Chapters 5 and 7, the Holy Spirit carefully calls attention to a number of contrasts between the Priesthood of Aaron and that of Christ.

In the first place, all of the Priests of Israel, even the High Priest, were sinful men; consequently, even though they were types of Christ, they had to offer up sacrifice for their own sins, as well as the sins of the people. But with Christ, our Great High Priest, it was and is totally different. He needed not at all to offer sacrifice for Himself, because He *"knew no sin."*

As well, the Priests of Israel were mere mortals, who consequently died, with others taking their place. But with Christ He is *"a Priest forever after the order of Melchisedec"* (Heb. 7:21). Christ was *"after the power of an endless life"* (Heb. 7:16). In other words, He will be our Great High Priest forever!

THE MODERN PRIESTHOOD

In fact, other than the fact that all Believers are now *"Priests,"* and that all of God's people alike enjoy liberty of access into the Holiest (I Pet. 2:5, 9; Heb. 10:19, 22), there is no such thing, Biblically, as a modern Priesthood. To even insinuate such is an insult to Christ. In essence, it says that what He did on the Cross was not sufficient, meaning that He Alone cannot be our Mediator, but needs help from earthly mortals. Such can only be constituted as blasphemy!

This means that the Roman Catholic Priesthood, and as well others which fall into the same category, are grossly unscriptural. In fact, Rome attempts to perpetuate the Levitical Order, claiming that her Priests, like Aaron and his sons, are especially authorized and qualified to go to God on behalf of their fellowmen. But this is something made up out of whole cloth, so to speak, having no Biblical foundation whatsoever. As stated, such a position as the modern Priesthood is a gross insult to Christ. In fact, the entire Catholic system is a wicked denial of the perpetual efficacy (effectiveness) of the one Offering of the Lord Jesus Christ.

Before the Cross, a Priesthood was necessary in order that there be mediators between God and man. Consequently, that Priesthood was ordained by God, and in fact, originated by God. But even this Priesthood was meant only to be temporary, which it was, ultimately fulfilled by what Christ did at the Cross.

In other words, when Jesus died on the Cross, saying *"It is finished,"* in the Mind of God, there was no more need for any earthly mediators, and the entire Jewish system was now of no further use.

Regrettably, Israel did not see this, nor accept this. In fact, it was even very difficult for the Jewish segment of the Early Church to understand what Christ had actually done at the Cross. The answer to all of this was given to the Apostle Paul, and more than likely, a man of lesser stature, of lesser courage and fortitude, would not have been able to have held their ground, as did the great Paul. In fact, the meaning of the New Covenant, which Christ gave to Paul, is in actuality, the meaning of the Cross.

The Lord suffered the impertinence of Israel in their continuing the Levitical Order, for about 37 years. He then used an unwitting subject, the Roman General Titus, the son of Vespasian the Roman Caesar, to completely destroy the Temple, as well as Jerusalem. This made it impossible for Israel to continue their erroneous direction, at least as it regarded Temple worship. In fact, the entirety of the Book of Hebrews was written by Paul in order to point out to Christian Jews the terrible sin they were committing by forsaking the Cross, and going back into Judaism, which some of them were doing.

Aaron was chosen by God originally to minister *"unto Me* (God) *in the Priest's Office,"* along with his four sons. The Aaronic order was to continue until Christ, which more or less, it did! But the Lord doesn't need such now, in that Christ, *"Ever liveth to make intercession for them . . . But this Man* (Christ), *because He continues ever, has an unchangeable Priesthood"* (Heb. 7:24-25).

UNCONDITIONAL ETERNAL SECURITY?

All four sons of Aaron were chosen by God to be a part of the Levitical Order, a privileged position to say the least! Even though the account is not given here, sadly and regrettably, of the four sons of Aaron, *"Nadab and Abihu,"* because of their sinfulness, were judged by God, and died, and we might say, most tragically (Lev. 10:1-2). In a sense, the terrible sin committed by Nadab and Abihu is exactly that which some of the Christian Jews of Paul's day were committing, which we have just addressed, as it regards the writing of the Book of Hebrews by the great Apostle.

Part of the tasks of these Priests was to take coals of fire from the Brazen Altar, put those coals on the Golden Altar in the Holy Place, pour incense over them, which would fill the Holy Place, typifying the Intercession of Christ. Instead, they took coals of fire from some other ignition, and attempted to use that, which in effect, was an end run around the Cross, so to speak, which God could never accept. As we've already stated, the Brazen Altar was a Type of Christ and what He would do at the Cross, in regard to the giving of Himself in Sacrifice, thereby suffering the Judgment of God on our behalf. That is the only Sacrifice that God will accept. This means that no one can bypass the Cross, but which in effect, millions are

NOTES

presently attempting to do. There are two things here that must be noticed:

1. These two Priests were definitely in the Covenant, which means they were saved. But they transgressed the Law of God, and did so with impunity, which destroyed them, which as well destroys the myth of unconditional eternal security.

2. It was the type of sin they committed, which is the sin that will destroy the soul, irrespective as to whom the individual might be. That is the sin of unbelief, as it regards the Cross of Christ. The only way anyone can be saved and the only way anyone can maintain one's Salvation is to understand that it is all in Christ and what He did at the Cross. In other words, our Faith must be exclusively in Him and in His great Sacrifice. We must never separate Christ from the Cross, for the Cross is the very reason for which He came to this Earth. But regrettably and sadly, this is exactly what many in the modern Church are presently doing. They are separating Christ from the Cross, which in effect, places them in a position of serving *"another Jesus"* (II Cor. 11:4).

THE PSYCHOLOGICAL WAY AND THE WAY OF THE CROSS

Even though we have already addressed ourselves to this particular subject, due to its vast significance, I feel we must take every opportunity given to us to point out the terrible dangers which the Church is now facing.

As a whole, the modern Church has opted for the psychological way. While some have totally abandoned the Cross, thereby registering total unbelief as it regards the Finished Work of Christ, others pay lip service to the Cross, but embrace, as well, the psychological way, and do so wholeheartedly. One cannot have it both ways. It is either the Cross, or it is something else! It cannot be the Cross and something else! The Lord simply will not tolerate such.

The Word of God emphatically states: *"But this Man* (Christ), *after He had offered one Sacrifice for sins forever, sat down on the right hand of God"* (Heb. 10:12).

This tells us that there is only one Sacrifice for sins, and that is the Cross, and it will stand that way *"forever."* Jesus now sitting down *"on the right hand of God,"* tells us that this one Sacrifice has been accepted, and it is the only Sacrifice which God has accepted, or will ever accept. So when we try to replace the Cross with other things, we, in effect, are committing the same sin which Nadab and Abihu committed. In other words, we are offering *"strange fire"* on the Altar, which God can never accept, and which He must judge with death, i.e., *"spiritual death"* (Lev. 10:1-2).

THE CROSS AND THE MODERN CHURCH

I realize that the far greater majority of the modern Laity will not understand what I am about to say, but it is true nevertheless.

As a whole, the modern Church will not accept deliverance by the Cross, which in effect, is the only true deliverance there is. Let's use Preachers for an example:

Biblical restoration is graphically pointed out to us in the Word of God. Paul wrote:

"Brethren, if a man be overtaken in a fault (this refers to a serious, moral fault), *you which are spiritual, restore such an one in the spirit of meekness; considering yourself, lest you also be tempted"* (Gal. 6:1).

So how is restoration to be carried out?

In essence, the great Apostle says that all the *"works"* we may prescribe can never bring about restoration. He wrote:

"As many as desire to make a fair show in the flesh, they constrain you to be circumcised; only lest they should suffer persecution for the Cross of Christ" (Gal. 6:12).

Even then, and I speak of the Early Church, many were saying that certain works such as *"circumcision,"* were the answer. Promoting these things, they would suffer no *"persecution for the Cross of Christ."* It has not changed presently; in fact, it is the same!

The Apostle then said: *"But God forbid that I should glory, save in the Cross of our Lord Jesus Christ, by Whom the world is crucified unto me, and I unto the world"* (Gal. 6:14).

In other words, He plainly, even bluntly, tells us here that the Cross of Christ is the only answer for the sins, aberrations, and perversions of mankind. So the battle presently is not new, but actually ancient, in fact, going all the way back to Genesis, Chapter 4, as it regards the saga of Cain and Abel.

The modern Church little recommends the Cross presently, but rather *"circumcision,"* i.e., *"the psychological way."* And if the Preacher whom we have previously mentioned, who got himself into trouble, doesn't accept the psychological way, rather placing his Faith in the Cross of Christ, and that exclusively, he will not at all be accepted by most modern Church Denominations. Not only will they not accept him, but at the same time, they will do all within their power to attempt to destroy his Ministry, and will use any tactic at their disposal. So when I tell you that the Cross of Christ is the dividing line between the True Church and the apostate church, I'm not joking!

As stated, most of the Laity do not understand what I've just said, because most of the time, these situations little affect them, at least at the beginning. But it will definitely affect them spiritually, as the Spirit of God, at a point in time, leaves, simply because He cannot abide where the Cross of Christ is rejected.

HOLY GARMENTS

Verse 2 reads: *"And you shall make holy garments for Aaron your brother for glory and for beauty."*

The garments mentioned here are for Aaron the High Priest, which were designed by the Lord, and which were *"for glory and for beauty."* Aaron was a Type of Christ, in fact, the greatest type at that particular time.

It is interesting to note that there were seven garments so desired, once again speaking of perfection.

They were:

1. The Breastplate;
2. The Ephod;
3. The Robe;
4. The Coat;
5. The Mitre;
6. The Girdle;
7. The *"Plate of pure gold"* which was fastened to the front of the Mitre, which would have been positioned on his forehead, and on which was engraved the words *"Holiness to the Lord."*

FOR GLORY AND FOR BEAUTY

The time of Alexander the Great was approximately 300 years before the time of Christ. It would have been approximately 1,200 years after the time of Moses.

He formed the mighty Grecian Empire, laying mighty cities waste in the process.

In his conquest of all of these cities, he now came to Jerusalem. He would do the same with it as he had done with the others, which was to issue a cryptic ultimatum, *"Surrender and live; rebel and die!"*

But the night before the siege was to begin the next morning, he had a dream. He dreamed that he approached the city, and a man came out of the gates dressed in the most beautiful garments he had ever seen, pleading that the city be spared. The dream troubled him greatly, so much so, that he accompanied his generals the next morning when they made their approach to Jerusalem.

Exactly as in his dream, the gate of the city opened, and a man came out dressed in garments that were beyond anything he had ever seen. It was the Great High Priest of Israel. He pleaded for the city, and as he pleaded, the dream which Alexander had, stood constantly before him. Fearful that he was insulting the *"gods"* as he put it, he acceded to the request, and turned his army away from Jerusalem, thus sparing the city.

But the main point of these garments is, they represented Christ, even as we shall see.

THE SPIRIT OF WISDOM

Verse 3 reads: *"And you shall speak unto all who are wise hearted, whom I have filled with the Spirit of wisdom, that they may make Aaron's garments to consecrate him, that he may minister unto Me in the Priest's Office."*

The *"Spirit of Wisdom"* had to do with the Holy Spirit, Who would enable the workers to properly make these garments which the Lord had designed. They must have been out of the ordinary, for the *"Spirit of Wisdom"* to be needed.

As well, we must remember that this design was all of the Lord, and none of Moses, or any other man; consequently, it must be adhered to minutely. Aaron could minister unto the Lord in the Priest's Office, only as he followed the directions totally.

NOTES

As we've already stated, our great problems in the Church are that we seek to deviate from that which the Lord has given, desiring to institute our own design, etc. Of course, the Lord will have none of that.

GOD'S PRESCRIBED ORDER OF VICTORY

For instance, the Lord has only one prescribed order of victory for the Child of God, and we speak of the way that one is to live for the Lord. That way is very simple, and that which we've already given several times. But due to the difficulty that man seems to have in following these simple directions, allow me, please, to once again describe this order:

THE CROSS

1. I'll be brief, the Believer must understand that all of his victory, and in every capacity, is totally and completely wrapped up in Christ, and what Christ has done for him at the Cross. The Cross is the key, hence Paul saying: *"But God forbid that I should glory, save in the Cross of our Lord Jesus Christ, by Whom the world is crucified unto me, and I unto the world"* (Gal. 6:14).

Someone asked me once, where should the emphasis be, on Christ or on the Cross?

It's a wrong question, inasmuch as Christ is the only One Who could have carried out this task. He Alone was perfect, and He Alone could provide the Perfect Sacrifice (Rom. 6:3-14; I Cor. 1:17-18, 21, 23; 2:2).

However, we must remember that Jesus as God has always existed. As God He had no beginning, and as such, was not formed or created in any manner. He has always been. But at the same time, we must also understand that as God, as important as that was and is, He did not redeem anyone. It remained unto the Cross, before Redemption could be given.

THE OBJECT OF FAITH

2. Understanding that the Cross is the key, it must ever be the object of our Faith, and this is critically important. Understanding that the Cross is the means of all blessings, we must, without fail, ever make it the emphasis of our Faith (Eph. 2:13-18; Col. 2:14, 18).

HOLY SPIRIT

3. When this is done, the Holy Spirit will function mightily on our behalf, helping us to live the life we ought to live. But He will not work outside of the legal confines of the Cross, and this we must ever understand (Rom. 8:1-2, 11).

If we try to place our Faith in things other than the Cross, the Lord calls it *"spiritual adultery"* (Rom. 7:1-4). Of course, the Holy Spirit will have no part in our unfaithfulness to Christ, and that's what spiritual adultery is!

But if we follow God's prescribed order, victory will be ours, and irrespective as to what the problems have been. And I might quickly add, that is a guarantee!

THE EPHOD

Verses 4 through 7 read: *"And these are the garments which they shall make; a Breastplate, and an Ephod, and a Robe, and a broidered Coat, a Mitre, and a Girdle: and they shall make holy garments for Aaron your brother, and his sons, that he may minister unto Me in the Priest's Office.*

"And they shall take gold, and blue, and purple, and scarlet, and fine linen.

"And they shall make the Ephod of gold, of blue, and purple, of scarlet, and fine twined linen, with cunning work.

"It shall have two shoulder pieces thereof joined at the two edges thereof; and so it shall be joined together."

The *"Ephod"* is the first garment described in detail. It was the outer Robe worn by the High Priest. It was made of two parts, one covering the back, and the other the front, these being joined together at the shoulders by golden clasps, which formed the setting for the onyx stones. The Ephod also contained the *"Breastplate,"* which we will study momentarily.

The colors were to be *"gold, blue, purple, scarlet, and fine linen."* The *"gold"* was probably gold thread, or even very thin wire, and spoke of the Deity of Christ. The *"blue"* spoke of His Heavenly origin, and specified that Salvation was designed totally by God, and not at all by man. The *"purple"* pertained to the fact that Christ was the King. The *"scarlet"* portrayed the price that He would pay, as it regards the shedding of His Blood on the Cross. The *"fine twined linen"* was white, and signified His perfect Righteousness. It was a *"cunning work,"* of which all of this was done, describing as well, in type, the Work which Christ would perfect on the Cross, in order that dying men could be redeemed.

The back and the front would be joined together by shoulder straps, where would be placed the *"onyx stones,"* to which we will address ourselves shortly.

As should be noted from Verse 4, these garments were labeled as *"holy"* because they were totally designed by the Lord.

THE CURIOUS GIRDLE

Verse 8 reads: *"And the Curious Girdle of the Ephod, which is upon it, shall be of the same, according to the work thereof: even of gold, of blue, and purple, and scarlet, and fine twined linen."*

The *"Curious Girdle"* was a sash of sorts, tied around the waist. It was made of the same materials as was the Ephod. It speaks of preparation for service. This is brought out by Luke.

"Blessed are those servants, whom the Lord, when He comes, shall find watching: verily I say unto you, that He shall 'gird Himself,' and make them sit down to meat, and will come forth and 'serve' them" (Lk. 12:37).

And then John said, in the days of His flesh: *"He took a towel and girded Himself, and then He washed the Disciples' feet"* (Jn. 13:4-5).

And then John also said: *"In the midst of the seven candlesticks One like unto the Son of Man, clothed with a garment down to the foot, and girt about the paps with a golden girdle"* (Rev. 1:13).

All of this tells us that the present gracious activities of Christ's Priestly service on our behalf are according to the perfections of His Own Person and Character as the God-Man! (Pink). Though glorified, He is a Servant still; He is gone into Heaven to appear in the Presence of God for us (Heb. 9:24), and there He *"ever liveth to make intercession for us"* (Heb. 7:25).

ONYX STONES

Verses 9 through 14 read: *"And you shall*

take two onyx stones, and grave on them the names of the Children of Israel:

"Six of their names on one stone, and the other six names of the rest on the other stone, according to their birth.

"With the work of an engraver in stone, like the engravings of a signet, you shall engrave the two stones with the names of the Children of Israel: you shall make them to be set in ouches of gold.

"And you shall put the two stones upon the shoulders of the Ephod for stones of memorial unto the Children of Israel: and Aaron shall bear their names before the LORD upon His two shoulders for a memorial.

"And you shall make ouches of gold;

"And two chains of pure gold at the ends; of wreathen work shall you make them, and fasten the wreathen chains to the ouches."

These two onyx stones were a part of the Ephod, and were actually designed to join the back and the front of the Ephod together at the shoulders. But they were designed for more than merely holding the garment together.

First of all, these stones referred to as *"onyx"* were very different from the onyx of our times. Presently, it signifies a very ordinary stone. But the Hebrew word translated *"onyx"* here, means, *"to shine with the luster of fire."* Some argue that it was the *"beryl,"* with others claiming that it was the *"sardonyx."* More than likely it is the latter, being very expensive if large, and these definitely were.

As stated, these two stones were on the shoulders of the High Priest, with the front and the back of the Ephod joined to them. On the stones were inscribed the names of the Twelve Tribes of the Children of Israel, six on one side, and six on the other. They were to be inscribed according to the order of their birth.

The two large stones on the shoulders were set in plates of gold, held together by chains of gold.

Twice it states that this is done *"for a memorial."*

Concerning the Lord's Supper, twice He also said, *"This do in remembrance of Me"* (I Cor. 11:24-25).

While that which pertained to the High Priest was before the fact, and that of the Lord's Supper after the fact, both speak of the Cross.

The shoulder speaks of security and strength, meaning that the Lord did carry Israel on His shoulders. He was able to do that because of the price that He would pay, guaranteeing Redemption. Spiritually speaking, this holds true for us presently, and even more so than ever before.

Concerning the lost sheep that was found, as Christ related the parable, He said: *"And when he had found it, He laid it on His shoulders, rejoicing"* (Lk. 15:5).

All of this signifies the strength of Christ, and not at all our own personal strength. We are *"kept by the Power of God"* (I Pet. 1:5). It is not our perseverance, but His: *"He is able to keep that which I have committed unto Him"* (II Tim. 1:12).

In the words of Pink, he said: *"The shoulder which sustains the universe (Heb. 1:3), upholds the feeblest and most obscure member of the Blood-bought congregation."*

Spiritually speaking, we are carried on the shoulders of Christ, and not on the shoulders of anything else. Consequently, all Believers who have separated their Faith, partially believing in Christ, and partially in something else, are in trouble, as would be obvious. Every other shoulder is feeble and unable to bear the load. Christ Alone can take us through. And when we say *"Christ Alone,"* we're speaking of what He did for us at the Cross. In that and that alone our Faith must rest!

(15) "AND YOU SHALL MAKE THE BREASTPLATE OF JUDGMENT WITH CUNNING WORK; AFTER THE WORK OF THE EPHOD YOU SHALL MAKE IT; OF GOLD, OF BLUE, AND OF PURPLE, AND OF SCARLET, AND OF FINE TWINED LINEN, SHALL YOU MAKE IT.

(16) "FOURSQUARE IT SHALL BE BEING DOUBLED; A SPAN SHALL BE THE LENGTH THEREOF, AND A SPAN SHALL BE THE BREADTH THEREOF.

(17) "AND YOU SHALL SET IN IT SETTINGS OF STONES, EVEN FOUR ROWS OF STONES: THE FIRST ROW SHALL BE A SARDIUS, A TOPAZ, AND A CARBUNCLE: THIS SHALL BE THE FIRST ROW.

(18) "AND THE SECOND ROW SHALL BE AN EMERALD, A SAPPHIRE, AND A DIAMOND.

(19) "AND THE THIRD ROW A LIGURE, AN AGATE, AND AN AMETHYST.

(20) "AND THE FOURTH ROW A BERYL, AND AN ONYX, AND A JASPER: THEY SHALL BE SET IN GOLD IN THEIR INCLOSINGS.

(21) "AND THE STONES SHALL BE WITH THE NAMES OF THE CHILDREN OF ISRAEL, TWELVE, ACCORDING TO THEIR NAMES, LIKE THE ENGRAVINGS OF A SIGNET; EVERY ONE WITH HIS NAME SHALL THEY BE ACCORDING TO THE TWELVE TRIBES.

(22) "AND YOU SHALL MAKE UPON THE BREASTPLATE CHAINS AT THE ENDS OF WREATHEN WORK OF PURE GOLD.

(23) "AND YOU SHALL MAKE UPON THE BREASTPLATE TWO RINGS OF GOLD, AND SHALL PUT THE TWO RINGS ON THE TWO ENDS OF THE BREASTPLATE.

(24) "AND YOU SHALL PUT THE TWO WREATHEN CHAINS OF GOLD INTO TWO RINGS WHICH ARE ON THE ENDS OF THE BREASTPLATE.

(25) "AND THE OTHER TWO ENDS OF THE TWO WREATHEN CHAINS YOU SHALL FASTEN IN THE TWO OUCHES, AND PUT THEM ON THE SHOULDER PIECES OF THE EPHOD BEFORE IT.

(26) "AND YOU SHALL MAKE TWO RINGS OF GOLD, AND YOU SHALL PUT THEM UPON THE TWO ENDS OF THE BREASTPLATE IN THE BORDER THEREOF, WHICH IS IN THE SIDE OF THE EPHOD INWARD.

(27) "AND TWO OTHER RINGS OF GOLD YOU SHALL MAKE, AND SHALL PUT THEM ON THE TWO SIDES OF THE EPHOD UNDERNEATH, TOWARD THE FOREPART THEREOF, OVER AGAINST THE OTHER COUPLING THEREOF, ABOVE THE CURIOUS GIRDLE OF THE EPHOD.

(28) "AND THEY SHALL BIND THE BREASTPLATE BY THE RINGS THEREOF UNTO THE RINGS OF THE EPHOD WITH A LACE OF BLUE, THAT IT MAY BE ABOVE THE CURIOUS GIRDLE OF THE EPHOD, AND THAT THE BREASTPLATE BE NOT LOOSED FROM THE EPHOD.

(29) "AND AARON SHALL BEAR THE NAMES OF THE CHILDREN OF ISRAEL IN THE BREASTPLATE OF JUDGMENT UPON HIS HEART, WHEN HE GOES IN UNTO THE HOLY PLACE, FOR A MEMORIAL BEFORE THE LORD CONTINUALLY.

(30) "AND YOU SHALL PUT IN THE BREASTPLATE OF JUDGMENT THE URIM AND THE THUMMIM: AND THEY SHALL BE UPON AARON'S HEART, WHEN HE GOES IN BEFORE THE LORD: AND AARON SHALL BEAR THE JUDGMENT OF THE CHILDREN OF ISRAEL UPON HIS HEART BEFORE THE LORD CONTINUALLY."

The overview is:

1. Verses 15 through 30 speak of the *"Breastplate of Judgment."*

2. As the names of the Tribes of the Children of Israel were to be inscribed on the shoulders of the High Priest, likewise, these same names were to be engraved in precious stones, worn on the Breastplate. In effect, this would be over his heart.

3. In the Breastplate, which seemed to be a bag of sorts, the *"Urim"* and the *"Thummim"* were to be placed. The first word means *"Lights,"* while the second means *"Perfections."*

THE BREASTPLATE OF JUDGMENT

Verses 15 and 16 read: *"And you shall make the Breastplate of Judgment with cunning work; after the work of the Ephod you shall make it; of gold, of blue, and of purple, and of scarlet, and of fine twined linen, shall you make it.*

"Foursquare it shall be being doubled; a span shall be the length thereof, and a span shall be the breadth thereof."

The *"Breastplate"* was designed of the same colors as the Ephod and the Curious Girdle. Incidentally, the word *"curious"* simply means *"cunning,"* signifying that its design was extraordinary.

Even though the Scripture doesn't relate to us specifically as to how these colors were to be enjoined, it is believed that the garments themselves, unless specified otherwise, were all of white, for that's the color of *"fine twined linen."* But around the borders, first of all there was a gold thread or wire, with the latter probably being the case, followed with another of blue, and then of purple, and then of scarlet.

THE JEWELS

Verses 17 through 21 read: *"And you shall set in it settings of stones, even four rows of stones: the first row shall be a sardius, a topaz, and a carbuncle: this shall be the first row.*

"And the second row shall be an emerald, a sapphire, and a diamond.

"And the third row a ligure, an agate, and an amethyst.

"And the fourth row a beryl, and an onyx, and a jasper: they shall be set in gold in their inclosings.

"And the stones shall be with the names of the Children of Israel, twelve, according to their names, like the engravings of a signet: every one with his name shall they be according to the twelve Tribes."

There were twelve jewels in number, one for each Tribe, set in four rows of three each. As the names of the Tribes of the Children of Israel were inscribed on the onyx stones on the shoulders of the High Priest, signifying strength, likewise the names were to be inscribed on the twelve stones worn over the heart of the High Priest, signifying the Love of God. So this means that every single Believer, for we are spiritual Israel, is secured by both *"strength"* and *"love."* This *"strength"* and *"love"* are anchored in the Cross (Jn. 3:16).

Incidentally, it is virtually certain that all of these stones were the same size, which would have required an extraordinary skill of cutting, as well as of engraving, as it regards the names being placed on each stone. As an aside, perhaps one could say without fear of contradiction that the greatest diamond cutters in the world presently, as well as other precious stones, are the Jews. Without a doubt, the great ability for this art began with the making of the Breastplate.

THE RINGS OF GOLD AND THE CHAINS OF GOLD

Verses 22 through 29 read: *"And you shall make upon the Breastplate chains at the ends of wreathen work of pure gold.*

"And you shall make upon the Breastplate two rings of gold, and shall put the two rings on the two ends of the Breastplate.

"And you shall put the two wreathen chains of gold in the two rings which are on the ends of the Breastplate.

"And the other two ends of the two wreathen chains you shall fasten in the two ouches, and put them on the shoulder pieces of the Ephod before it.

"And you shall make two rings of gold, and shall put them upon the two ends of the Breastplate in the border thereof, which is in the side of the Ephod inward.

"And two other rings of gold you shall make, and shall put them on the two sides of the Ephod underneath, toward the forepart thereof, over against the other coupling thereof, above the Curious Girdle of the Ephod.

"And they shall bind the Breastplate by the rings thereof unto the rings of the Ephod with a lace of blue, that it may be above the Curious Girdle of the Ephod, and that the Breastplate be not loose from the Ephod.

"And Aaron shall bear the names of the Children of Israel in the Breastplate of Judgment upon his heart, when he goes in unto the Holy Place, for a memorial before the LORD continually."

We find here that the *"Breastplate"* was fastened by *"chains at the ends of wreathen work of pure gold,"* and these were passed through *"two rings of gold on the ends of the Breastplate."* Thus the people of God, as represented by their names, were chained to the High Priest!

One could translate the beautiful artwork given here as it relates to its spiritual meaning, to the Words of Christ, when He said: *"Take My yoke upon you, and learn of Me; for I am meek and lowly in heart: and you shall find rest unto your souls.*

"For My yoke is easy, and My burden is light" (Mat. 11:29-30).

The *"yoke"* in a sense, is a harness or chain, binding two or more objects together. We are *"bound"* to Christ, so much so in fact, that He said of His Own: *"I am the Vine, you are the branches: he who abides in Me, and I in him, the same brings forth much fruit: for without Me you can do nothing"* (Jn. 15:5).

Once again, let us emphasize the fact that

these precious stones were worn over the heart of the High Priest, signifying the Love of God for His people.

As a parent or even a grandparent, we know somewhat, at least as far as a human being can know, of the Love that God has for us. For our children we want the best, and they are continually on our heart. As well, we are continually on the heart of God, as He loves us with an undying love.

THE URIM AND THE THUMMIM

Verse 30 reads: *"And you shall put in the Breastplate of Judgment the Urim and the Thummim; and they shall be upon Aaron's heart, when he goes in before the LORD: and Aaron shall bear the judgment of the Children of Israel upon his heart before the LORD continually."*

It seems that in the back of the Breastplate there was a pocket of sorts, right next to Aaron's heart, where was kept that referred to as the *"Urim and the Thummim."* The first word means *"Lights,"* while the second means *"Perfections."* So we must conclude that the judgment rendered would be *"perfect."*

The Bible doesn't say exactly what these things were, but some believe they must have been material objects of some kind, possibly one stone with the word *"yes"* inscribed on it, and the second stone with the word *"no"* inscribed on it.

It seems that when a decision was to be made, the king, or whomever, would inquire of the High Priest, who would give an answer by the *"Urim and the Thummim."* The answer would be *"yes"* or *"no,"* according to the question asked.

As an example, it is said of David that he *"Inquired of the LORD, saying, Shall I go and smite these Philistines? And the LORD said unto David, Go, and smite the Philistines, and save Keilah"* (I Sam. 23:2).

It seemed at this time that Abiathar had the Ephod which contained the Breastplate and, therefore, the *"Urim and the Thummim,"* to which David inquired (I Sam. 22:20-23).

THE HOLY SPIRIT

Some may read these words and think as to how wonderful it would presently be to have something similar. Well, the truth is, what we have is a thousand times better. Due to the Cross, we now have the Holy Spirit, of which these *"Lights and Perfections"* were but symbolic, in our hearts and lives. Jesus said of the Divine Spirit: *"He will guide you into all truth: for He shall not speak of Himself; but whatsoever He shall hear, that shall He speak: and He will show you things to come"* (Jn. 16:13).

During the time of Israel, only a few had access to the High Priest and, therefore, the Urim and the Thummim, but now the most recently Born-Again Saint has total, full, and complete access to the leading and guidance of the Holy Spirit, and on a continuing basis (Jn. 14:16). Our problem is, we take so little advantage of Who the Holy Spirit is and What He can do for us. If anything at all, we mostly take Him for granted, meaning, that we know so little about Him and how He works.

THE WILL OF GOD

The first problem we have is that we do not know the Will of God for our lives. And it's because we have not ardently sought the Will of God for our lives. The Holy Spirit works entirely within the parameters of the Will of God. He will not deviate from that one iota. And far too often, we are setting about in other directions, which are not according to the Will of God, which means that the Holy Spirit, although continuing to abide within our hearts and lives, simply will not help us. In other words, He won't help us to do wrong, or to go wrong.

As stated, if the Believer, and whomever he might be, will simply seek the Face of the Lord as it regards the Will of God, it will most definitely be shown and given (Rom. 12:1-2).

WALKING AFTER THE SPIRIT

Paul said: *"There is therefore now no condemnation to them which are in Christ Jesus, who walk not after the flesh, but after the Spirit"* (Rom. 8:1).

What did Paul mean by *"walking after the Spirit"*?

If most Christians were asked this question, they would say that it refers to being faithful to Church, reading one's Bible each day, witnessing to souls, having a set prayer time each day, etc.

Now all of these things are very good, and actually what any good Christian will do; however, they have nothing to do with walking after the Spirit.

Walking after the Spirit refers to the Believer placing his Faith exclusively in Christ and what Christ has done at the Cross, understanding that everything he receives from the Lord comes exclusively from that Source. That is walking after the Spirit (Rom. 8:1-2, 11, 13).

"Walking after the flesh" is the Believer trusting in self. And what exactly does that mean?

Let's use the disciplines we have just mentioned, such as Bible study, etc., all which are very good things, and as stated, which any and every good Christian will most definitely do. But yet, if the Believer thinks that doing these things, as good as they are, will guarantee him victory, this means that his faith is placed in *"self,"* and not in Christ and what Christ has done at the Cross. All of this is very subtle, simply because the things we have mentioned are very good things, actually very right things, so we think because that is the case, doing such will guarantee victory. It won't! Concerning such things, Paul said: *"For in Jesus Christ neither circumcision availeth anything, nor uncircumcision; but Faith which worketh by love"* (Gal. 5:6).

The idea is, if our Faith is not placed properly in Christ and the Cross, we will turn good things into *"works,"* which God can never accept. As stated, these things deceive us, simply because they are good things. But the Believer must understand, Holiness and Righteousness, and being led by the Spirit, all come by *"Faith,"* which refers to Faith in Christ, and what Christ has done as it regards His Finished Work.

FAITH

Now when we speak of Faith, most Christians will agree that this is the ingredient by which all things come to us from the Lord. But what most Christians don't know is that it's the object of Faith that is so very, very important! Actually, all-important! (I Cor. 1:17-18, 23; 2:2).

Everyone in the world has faith. Even the Atheist who claims he doesn't have faith, in fact does, simply because he has faith in the very fact that he doesn't have faith. The Scientist who claims that he cannot accept faith, only fact, in fact, engages every experiment on the basis of faith. In other words, he believes that he's going to find the solution to the problem which he is addressing.

So it's not really a question of faith, but rather the object of one's faith. That object must be *"Christ and Him Crucified"* (I Cor. 1:23).

Christians talk about faith constantly, but in reality, at least for the most part, their faith is in *"self."* They think they receive from the Lord by *"doing,"* when in reality, it is by *"believing,"* but it is believing the right thing. And what is the right thing?

Once again, we say what we've already said innumerable times. It is *"Jesus Christ and Him Crucified."* Now let me ask this question!

Do you the Reader have doubts about the Cross? Do you think that Faith in Christ and what He has done at the Cross is enough, or do you think something should be added? Let me warn you that if you try to add anything, you've just nullified your Faith. James said: *"A double minded man is unstable in all his ways."* He also said: *"For he who wavereth is like a wave of the sea driven with the wind and tossed.*

"For let not that man think that he shall receive anything of the Lord" (James 1:8, 6-7).

Put your Faith exclusively in Christ and the Cross, and do not allow it to be moved, *"Lay hold on eternal life,"* and you will find, *"This is the victory that overcometh the world, even our Faith"* (I Tim. 6:12; I Jn. 5:4).

(31) "AND YOU SHALL MAKE THE ROBE OF THE EPHOD ALL OF BLUE.

(32) "AND THERE SHALL BE AN HOLE IN THE TOP OF IT, IN THE MIDST THEREOF: IT SHALL HAVE A BINDING OF WOVEN WORK ROUND ABOUT THE HOLE OF IT, AS IT WERE THE HOLE OF A HABERGEON, THAT IT BE NOT RENT.

(33) "AND BENEATH UPON THE HEM OF IT YOU SHALL MAKE POMEGRANATES OF BLUE, AND OF PURPLE, AND OF SCARLET, ROUND ABOUT THE HEM THEREOF; AND BELLS OF GOLD BETWEEN THEM

(34) "A GOLDEN BELL AND A POMEGRANATE, A GOLDEN BELL AND A POMEGRANATE, UPON THE HEM OF THE ROBE ROUND ABOUT.

(35) "AND IT SHALL BE UPON AARON TO MINISTER: AND HIS SOUND SHALL BE HEARD WHEN HE GOES IN UNTO THE HOLY PLACE BEFORE THE LORD, AND WHEN HE COMES OUT, THAT HE DIE NOT."

The exegesis is:

1. Verses 31 through 35 speak of the *"Robe of the Ephod."* This symbolizes Christ as our Great High Priest in Heaven (Heb. 8:4).

2. This *"Robe"* was all of *"blue,"* signifying that the Intercession would be carried forth in Heaven.

3. When the High priest went into the Holy of Holies on the Great Day of Atonement, this beautiful *"coat of blue,"* had to be laid aside, but would play a very important part when he came out of the Holy of Holies. He was to go in wearing only the *"holy linen coat,"* the *"linen breeches,"* and *"girded with a linen girdle,"* and *"with the linen Mitre on his head"* (Lev. 16:4).

4. When the High Priest came out of the Holy of Holies, he was to once again put on the *"blue robe,"* which at the hem hung pomegranates and bells. As he put on the blue robe, the bells would ring, signifying that the Sacrifice had been accepted by God.

THE ROBE

Verses 31 and 32 read: *"And you shall make the Robe of the Ephod all of blue.*

"And there shall be an hole in the top of it, in the midst thereof: it shall have a binding of woven work round about the hole of it, as it were the hole of a habergeon, that it be not rent."

Underneath the *"Ephod"* and *"Breastplate"* the High Priest was to wear a robe, or frock, wholly of blue. This robe was to have a hole for the head at the top, and was to be woven without seam (Ex. 39:22). It was put on over the head, like a coat of mail, and probably reached below the knee.

The fact that it was *"all of blue,"* offered a strong contrast to the other colors of the *"Breastplate"* and *"Ephod."* It threw the portions of that attire into greater prominence.

The fact that it was all of blue tells us that it represents the Ministry of Christ in Heaven, where He makes Intercession for us, and does so by His very Presence (Heb. 7:25-26).

INTERCESSION

Exactly what does it mean that Christ *"makes intercession for us"*?

Let's look at *"why"* first, and then let's look at *"how."*

If any Believer thinks that they do not need the Intercession of Christ, this means they have a convoluted impression of themselves, which desperately needs to be corrected.

No matter how close to God we are, we still aren't perfect. In fact, Paul plainly says: *"For all have sinned, and come short of the Glory of God"* (Rom. 3:23).

Most Christians read this Passage and conclude it as to something having taken place in the past. While it definitely includes that, the actual Greek says that now, at this present time, we, even the best of us, whomever that might be, are continually *"coming short of the Glory of God."* Consequently, and as stated, even the best of us need Intercession on our behalf.

And then of course, as all of us know, there are many Christians, regrettably, even most, who do not walk very close to the Lord. It should be obvious that these individuals desperately need the Intercession of Christ.

And to be factual, and as I trust we have made abundantly clear, all of us desperately need such Intercession. And we will need such Intercession, until the Trump sounds, and *"this corruptible puts on incorruption, and this mortal puts on immortality"* (I Cor. 15:53). That's why the Apostle said:

"Wherefore He (Christ) *is able also to save them to the uttermost who come unto God by Him, seeing He ever liveth to make Intercession for them.*

"For such an High Priest became us, Who is holy, harmless, undefiled, separate from sinners, and made higher than the heavens" (Heb. 7:25-26).

Now let's look at *"how"* He makes this Intercession!

To answer the question immediately, His very Presence makes the Intercession, and in fact, guarantees the Intercession. Some Christians have in their mind that the Lord seeks forgiveness on our part from the Father, by stating to the Father that He died for us, etc. That may sound romantic, but that's not what happens.

If He had to do these things, this would state that what He did at the Cross was insufficient, and needs this added work. But we know that everything was finished at the Cross, with nothing needed to be added. Paul further said:

"For Christ is not entered into the holy places made with hands, which are the figures of the True (speaking of the Tabernacle and Temple of Old); *but into Heaven itself, now to appear in the Presence of God for us"* (Heb. 9:24).

As stated, His very Presence at the Throne of God automatically makes Intercession for us, meaning that God has accepted the Sacrifice, and that all who exhibit Faith in Christ and what He has done for us at the Cross, is guaranteed Salvation, and continued Intercession.

THE GREAT DAY OF ATONEMENT

Verses 33 through 35 read: *"And beneath upon the hem of it you shall make pomegranates of blue, and of purple, and of scarlet, round about the hem thereof; and bells of gold between them round about:*

"A golden bell and a pomegranate, a golden bell and a pomegranate, upon the hem of the robe round about.

"And it shall be upon Aaron to Minister: and his sound shall be heard when he goes into the Holy Place before the LORD, and when he comes out, that he die not."

These Passages speak of the High Priest going into the Holy of Holies once a year, on the Great Day of Atonement, actually going in twice, once for himself, and once for Israel. Both times, he would sprinkle blood on the Mercy Seat, which made Atonement.

When he went into the Holy of Holies, he would divest himself of all the outer garments, including the robe of blue, leaving only the linen undergarments, signifying that Christ redeemed us, not with *"glory and beauty,"* but rather with His spotless Righteousness, signified by His shed Blood, symbolized by the white linen.

He would offer up blood on the Mercy Seat, and then come back into the Holy Place, where he would then put on the blue robe.

THE POMEGRANATES AND THE BELLS

The pomegranates were probably made like tassels, and had the colors of blue, purple, and scarlet. These colors signified the same as on the Ephod, etc. These tassels went all the way around the robe of blue, but were interspersed with *"bells of gold."* These were real bells, as would be obvious, and would ring whenever the Priest walked or moved. Of how many these were, the Scriptures are silent.

However, when the High Priest came out of the Holy of Holies, once again putting on the blue robe, the bells, as would be obvious, would begin to ring, which signified that he, of course, was alive, and that the blood of the sacrifice had been accepted.

As should be obvious, the pomegranates signified fruit. The Lord addressed this when He said: *"I am the Vine, you are the branches: he who abides in Me, and I in him, the same brings forth much fruit: for without Me you can do nothing"* (Jn. 15:5). So the pomegranates represent the *"Fruit of the Spirit"* (Gal. 5:22-23).

The *"bells of gold"* represent the *"Gifts of the Spirit"* (I Cor. 12:7-10).

All of this signifies that our Great High Priest, the Lord Jesus Christ, has shed His Life's Blood, thereby making Atonement, a Sacrifice which will never again have to be repeated. We know His Sacrifice of Himself has been accepted by God, because He has sent back the Holy Spirit with the *"Fruit of the Spirit"* (Pomegranates) and as well the *"Gifts of the Spirit"* (the ringing of the bells). So every time one begins to speak with other tongues, or else Gifts of the Spirit are manifested, one might say that this is the *"ringing of the bells."*

Israel knew that when the bells began to ring, the Great High Priest was soon to come out of the Holy Place. Likewise, we know now that the manifestation of the Holy Spirit proclaims the fact that our Great High Priest, the Lord Jesus Christ, is about to come back.

(36) "AND YOU SHALL MAKE A PLATE OF PURE GOLD, AND GRAVE UPON IT, LIKE THE ENGRAVINGS OF A SIGNET, HOLINESS TO THE LORD.

(37) "AND YOU SHALL PUT IT ON A BLUE LACE, THAT IT MAY BE UPON THE MITRE; UPON THE FOREFRONT OF THE MITRE IT SHALL BE.

(38) "AND IT SHALL BE UPON AARON'S FOREHEAD, THAT AARON MAY BEAR THE INIQUITY OF THE HOLY THINGS, WHICH THE CHILDREN OF ISRAEL SHALL HALLOW IN ALL THEIR HOLY GIFTS; AND IT SHALL BE ALWAYS UPON HIS FOREHEAD, THAT THEY MAY BE ACCEPTED BEFORE THE LORD."

The diagram is:

1. Aaron's hat, worn only by the High Priest, and shaped like a crown, was to carry on its front a golden plate, bearing the words, *"HOLINESS TO THE LORD."*

2. In the Millennium, this engraving will appear on the bells of the horses (Zech., Chpt. 14).

3. This Golden Plate and its engraving pictured Israel as perfect before the Lord. As imperfect as Israel actually was within herself, as thus represented by Aaron and his crown, a Type of Christ, she was Holiness itself. The same is said for modern Believers.

HOLINESS TO THE LORD

Verse 36 reads: *"And you shall make a plate of pure gold, and grave upon it, like the engravings of a signet, HOLINESS TO THE LORD."*

This Golden Plate was the symbol of the essential Holiness of the Lord Jesus. The Saints are represented by Him and accepted in Him. Because of our legal and vital union with Him, His Holiness is ours. So what am I saying?

I am saying that you as a Believer must look away from yourself, with your ten thousand failures, and put your eye on that Golden Plate. You can behold in the perfections of your Great High Priest the measure of your eternal acceptance with God. Christ is our Sanctification as well as our Righteousness!

THINGS THE BELIEVER MUST KNOW

Every true Believer in the Lord is looked at by God as perfectly Righteous, perfectly Holy, perfectly pure, and perfectly Christlike! In fact, God can accept no less. However, we are all of this, not because of anything we have done, but simply and purely because of Christ. He is the altogether Perfect One. Our Salvation is in Him, just as our Sanctification is in Him.

We are *"in Him,"* by virtue of being *"baptized into His death,"* and *"buried with Him by Baptism into death."* We were then raised with Him *"in newness of life"* (Rom. 6:3-4).

This is not speaking of Water Baptism, but rather of the Crucifixion of Christ, His Burial and Resurrection, and our part in that threefold Work.

Whenever you as a believing sinner registered Faith in Christ, in the Mind of God, you were literally *"in Christ,"* when He died, was buried, and raised from the dead. As stated, your Faith put you there!

And it's your Faith which keeps you there, which refers to your Sanctification. You were saved by *"Faith,"* and you must understand that you are sanctified by *"Faith"* as well! So whatever you do, don't fall into the trap of being saved by Faith, and then trying to be sanctified by *"self."*

Now this means that every single Believer on the face of the Earth, in fact all who have ever lived, and naturally we're speaking of true Believers, are all looked at identically by the Lord. I speak of perfection, for God can accept no less!

Therefore, understanding that all are perfect in His sight because of Christ, what is the difference in the consecrated Christian and the unconsecrated Christian?

The difference is twofold:

1. The consecrated enjoys the Blessings of the Lord, and in many and varied ways. The unconsecrated Christian is under chastisement more often than not, which means that he is deprived of much of what the Lord would like to do for him, but simply cannot do, because of obvious reasons. The one who walks close to the Lord enjoys benefits which are absolutely phenomenal to say the least! He has the leading of the Spirit, the Power of the Spirit, and in fact, the help of the Spirit in every capacity. The unconsecrated Christian enjoys precious little of this.

Now please understand, we're speaking here of true Believers, and not of the millions who profess Salvation, but actually have never been Born-Again.

2. When we all stand at the Judgment Seat of Christ, where eternal rewards will be given, it should be obvious that the consecrated Believer will receive eternal rewards far greater than the unconsecrated counterparts.

Paul said, *"There is one glory of the sun, and another glory of the moon, and another glory of the stars: for one star differs from another star in glory."*

He then said: *"So also is the Resurrection of the dead"* (I Cor. 15:41-42).

This tells us that the *"glory"* which speaks of rewards, and of every description, will be different with Believers. Considering that we're speaking of eternal consequences, we should understand as to how important all of this actually is.

Many Christians flippantly state that they will be happy just making Heaven, meaning that they couldn't care less about the rewards. Such thinking is foolish to say the least!

WHAT IS HOLINESS?

Once again, Holiness is not what we necessarily do, but it's what we believe. And if we believe right, we will do right!

There is no way that a Believer, irrespective as to what he might do, can make himself holy. It is not within our power to do such!

All of our Holiness is 100 percent in Christ. If it is to be noticed, this Golden Plate engraved with the words *"HOLINESS TO THE LORD,"* was on the forehead of the High Priest, and not on anyone else. This signified that the Holiness is 100 percent in Christ.

Whenever the Believer places his Faith exclusively in Christ, and what Christ has done for us at the Cross, that is Holiness. The Holy Spirit can then work within our hearts and lives, making us what we ought to be. But regrettably, far too many Believers count themselves as holy, or others, if they do certain things. Let us state it again: Holiness is not attained by doing, but rather by believing, and more particularly, believing in the right thing, which is Christ and Him Crucified. All Holiness is in Christ.

And that means all of our Holiness is because of Christ, and solely because of Christ.

THE BLUE LACE

Verse 37 reads: *"And you shall put it on a blue lace, that it may be upon the Mitre; upon the forefront of the Mitre it shall be."*

The *"blue lace"* once again, signifies Heaven. As we have stated, every single thing about the Tabernacle and its furnishings, as well as the attire of the Priests, all and without exception had reference to Christ, as it regarded His Atoning, Mediatorial, and Intercessory Work. That's the reason that we constantly say that Believers ought to understand the Old Testament, and unless they understand it, they cannot really understand the New.

In fact, the entirety of the Bible portrays Christ. But more particularly, it portrays Christ as it regards His Sacrificial Work. It is impossible to separate the Word of God from the Cross of Christ, or the Cross of Christ from the Word of God. If you study the Bible at all, you will quickly come to see that everything in it, in one way or the other, portrays Christ and His Cross.

When I speak of the Cross, I'm speaking of something that took place some 2,000 years ago, but which has continued benefits, and in fact, benefits which will never be discontinued. It's the benefits of which we speak and certainly not a wooden beam!

The Golden Plate was to occupy a place of prominence on the front of the Mitre or hat. This certainly should signify the importance of the emphasis which God places on Holiness.

THE FOREHEAD

Verse 38 reads: *"And it shall be upon Aaron's forehead, that Aaron may bear the iniquity of the holy things, which the Children of Israel shall hallow in all their holy gifts; and it shall be always upon his forehead, that they may be accepted before the LORD."*

"Upon his heart before the Lord . . . continually" (Vs. 29) and *"upon his forehead before the Lord continually"* proclaim the fact that these statements united together reveal the untiring activity of the heart and mind of the Greater than Aaron on behalf of

His people.

What does it mean, *"That Aaron may bear the iniquity of the holy things . . ."*?

Imperfection attaches to everything that man does; and even the Sacrifices that the people offered to God required to be atoned for and purified. It was granted to the High Priest in his official capacity to make the necessary Atonement, and so render the people's gifts acceptable (Pulpit).

Christ is now the Mediator between God and men, and He Alone is the Mediator! (I Tim. 2:5; Heb. 8:6; 9:15; 12:24). As stated, God can accept nothing but that it is perfectly Holy. Christ is perfectly Holy, and our Faith in Him grants us His perfect Holiness as well. Then whatever we do, and I speak of our efforts to live for the Lord, are *"accepted before the Lord."*

(39) "AND YOU SHALL EMBROIDER THE COAT OF FINE LINEN, AND YOU SHALL MAKE THE MITRE OF FINE LINEN, AND YOU SHALL MAKE THE GIRDLE OF NEEDLEWORK.

(40) "AND FOR AARON'S SONS YOU SHALL MAKE COATS, AND YOU SHALL MAKE FOR THEM GIRDLES, AND BONNETS SHALL YOU MAKE FOR THEM, FOR GLORY AND FOR BEAUTY.

(41) "AND YOU SHALL PUT THEM UPON AARON YOUR BROTHER, AND HIS SONS WITH HIM; AND SHALL ANOINT THEM, AND CONSECRATE THEM, AND SANCTIFY THEM, THAT THEY MAY MINISTER UNTO ME IN THE PRIEST'S OFFICE.

(42) "AND YOU SHALL MAKE THEM LINEN BREECHES TO COVER THEIR NAKEDNESS; FROM THE LOINS EVEN UNTO THE THIGHS THEY SHALL REACH:

(43) "AND THEY SHALL BE UPON AARON, AND UPON HIS SONS, WHEN THEY COME IN UNTO THE TABERNACLE OF THE CONGREGATION, OR WHEN THEY COME NEAR UNTO THE ALTAR TO MINISTER IN THE HOLY PLACE; THAT THEY BEAR NOT INIQUITY, AND DIE: IT SHALL BE A STATUTE FOREVER UNTO HIM AND HIS SEED AFTER HIM."

The structure is:

1. The linen vest and breeches symbolized the inward personal purity of our Great High Priest.

2. Aaron's sons were to wear similar undergarments; but Aaron's vest was to be embroidered. No one saw this embroidered linen vest but God. His eye Alone could estimate and enjoy its beauty. Such was Jesus. None but God sees the exquisite perfections of His hidden, sinless Manhood, and the absolutely pure affections which energize Him as the Heavenly Priest (Williams).

3. As symbolized by the pure linen, Aaron and his sons stood and ministered in the one Righteousness.

THE COAT, THE MITRE, AND THE GIRDLE

Verse 39 reads: *"And you shall embroider the coat of fine linen, and you shall make the Mitre of fine linen, and you shall make the girdle of needlework."*

Both Aaron's sons and himself were to wear similar undergarments; but Aaron's vest was to be embroidered. We aren't told if the embroidery had colors or not, but probably not! The embroidery on Aaron's undergarment alone signified the following:

The very fact of embroidery speaks of a Finished Work. The fact that the garments of Aaron's sons contain no embroidery tells us that their work was never finished, which in fact, it wasn't. They were continually offering up sacrifices, simply because the blood of bulls and goats could not really take away sins. But Aaron being the more particular Type of Christ specified what the Work of Christ would be, which would be one Sacrifice, once and for all, the Sacrifice of Himself. The *"embroidery"* specified this.

As well, the *"fine linen"* of both the undergarment and the Mitre, which was the hat or crown worn by Aaron, signified also the Perfect Righteousness of Christ.

The *"girdle of needlework"* spoke of Service, and various different types of service, symbolized by the *"needlework."*

FOR GLORY AND FOR BEAUTY

Verse 40 reads: *"And for Aaron's sons you shall make coats, and you shall make for them girdles, and bonnets shall you make for them, for glory and for beauty."*

The mention of *"Aaron's sons"* referred to his actual sons at the time, and his descendants afterwards, to whom the Priesthood was rigidly confined.

It seems to imply that the attire of the Priests, other than the High Priest, was a dress of pure white, without anything ornamental, such as the colors on Aaron's garments. Still, these snow white garments, which signified, as stated, the Righteousness of Christ, were still looked at as garments *"for glory and for beauty."* In fact, white robes have certainly a vast amount of Scriptural testimony in their favor (Lev. 16:4; Mk. 9:3; Jn. 20:12; Acts 1:10; Rev. 4:4; 6:11; 7:9, 14, etc.) (Pulpit).

As well, all of the Priests, with the exception of Aaron the High Priest, wore *"bonnets,"* which seem to be close fitting caps. These were not *"bonnets"* in the modern sense. They were probably shaped like a cup, and did fit snugly on the head. They were totally different than the *"Mitre"* worn by Aaron.

THE ANOINTING

Verse 41 reads: *"And you shall put them upon Aaron your brother, and his sons with him; and shall anoint them, and consecrate them, and sanctify them, that they may minister unto Me in the Priest's Office."*

We are told here that they were to be anointed, consecrated, and set apart for the Work of God exclusively; however, it remains unto Chapter 29 for us to be told how all of this took place. It was, as we shall see, a very involved process.

But yet, everything that was done, the entirety of the ceremony was only a representation in symbolic form, of what Christ would do in reality. That's the reason that Paul said: *"But now (since the Cross) has He obtained a more excellent Ministry, by how much also He is the Mediator of a Better Covenant, which was established upon Better Promises.*

"For if that first Covenant had been faultless, then should no place have been sought for the second" (Heb. 8:6-7).

A COVERING

Verse 42 reads: *"And you shall make them linen breeches to cover their nakedness; from the loins even unto the thighs they shall reach."*

The clothing covering the *"nakedness"* had as much, or more, to do with the Judgment of God than it did modesty. While it

NOTES

certainly included the latter, the greater meaning has to do with Judgment upon sin.

When Adam fell, he told the Lord, *"I was afraid, because I was naked; and I hid myself"* (Gen. 3:10).

It is believed that Adam and Eve were covered by light before the Fall. Because of the Fall, the light was now gone, and they were very much aware now of their *"nakedness."*

However, they were much more naked to the Judgment of God than anything else. In a sense, clothing symbolizes the covering for sin, but we must remember it is only a symbol. The immodesty in much of the modern dress, especially as it regards the female gender, in essence is saying that they deny that they have sin, and, consequently, do not need a covering. But that's been man's problem all along!

He doesn't like to admit that he's a sinner, and even above that, he doesn't want to admit that it is only the shed Blood of Jesus Christ, which can cleanse from all sin (I Jn. 1:9).

DEATH

Verse 43 reads: *"And they shall be upon Aaron, and upon his sons, when they come in unto the Tabernacle of the congregation, or when they come near unto the Altar to minister in the Holy Place; that they bear not iniquity and die: it shall be a Statute forever unto him and his seed after him."*

The Lord took this so seriously that the Priests were warned, if they ignored any part of their garments, even those which were covered, such as the undergarments, they could be stricken that they die. In fact, two of Aaron's sons were stricken by God, but it was because of offering up *"strange fire"* (Lev. 10:1-2). Then the Lord added this further warning: *"It shall be a Statute forever unto him and his seed after him."*

Many would claim that this no longer holds, simply because it was all fulfilled in Christ.

In a sense, that is true; however, spiritually speaking, it continues to hold true, and in fact, must hold true. What do we mean by that?

All of these rules and ceremonies were given by the Lord for a particular purpose and reason. To be sure, He was dead serious about what He was doing. It involved the Salvation of souls, and was meant to portray Christ and His Atoning Work. So this question may be asked:

If death visited those who took lightly the symbol, how much more, spiritually speaking, will it visit those who insult the reality?

To ignore, add to, or take from the Finished Work of Christ in any way demands the Judgment of God. It cannot be otherwise! It even pertains to Believers.

This is why Paul said, and concerning the Lord's Supper, *"Wherefore whosoever shall eat this bread, and drink this cup of the Lord, unworthily, shall be guilty of the Body and Blood of the Lord."*

He then said: *"For he who eats and drinks unworthily, eats and drinks damnation to himself, not discerning the Lord's Body."*

"For this cause many are weak and sickly among you, and many sleep" (I Cor. 11:27, 29-30).

What did Paul mean by *"eating and drinking unworthily"*?

He was speaking of not properly *"discerning the Lord's Body"* (I Cor. 11:29).

All of this refers to the fact that we as Believers, when we take the Lord's Supper, must understand, and without fail, that all the blessings from the Lord, which come to us, are all made possible by the Cross, symbolized by the broken bread, which spoke of His broken body, and the grape juice, which spoke of His shed Blood.

The Lord doesn't require perfection, but He definitely does require Faith, but Faith in the proper object, and we continue to speak of Christ and Him Crucified.

> *"When they crucified my Saviour on the Cross of Calvary,*
> *"There a blessed Fount was opened for my cleansing full and free,*
> *"And my sins were all forgiven just by Faith in His shed Blood;*
> *"They are washed away forever by the crimson flood!"*
>
> *"Now I plead the Blood of Jesus, and He's with me all the way;*
> *"I am happy and rejoicing in His favor everyday;*
> *"In the burden and the trial there is none so kind as He;*
> *"My Redeemer is my kinsman, and His Blood saves me!"*

NOTES

> *"He will robe me with white raiment when my pilgrimage is past,*
> *"And present me pure and spotless with the Sanctified at last;*
> *"I will sing His praise and glory unto all eternity,*
> *"Telling evermore the story how His Blood saves me!"*

CHAPTER 29

(1) "AND THIS IS THE THING THAT YOU SHALL DO UNTO THEM TO HALLOW THEM, TO MINISTER UNTO ME IN THE PRIEST'S OFFICE: TAKE ONE YOUNG BULLOCK, AND TWO RAMS WITHOUT BLEMISH,

(2) "AND UNLEAVENED BREAD, AND CAKES UNLEAVENED TEMPERED WITH OIL, AND WAFERS UNLEAVENED ANOINTED WITH OIL: OF WHEATEN FLOUR SHALL YOU MAKE THEM.

(3) "AND YOU SHALL PUT THEM INTO ONE BASKET, AND BRING THEM IN THE BASKET, WITH THE BULLOCK AND THE TWO RAMS.

(4) "AND AARON AND HIS SONS YOU SHALL BRING UNTO THE DOOR OF THE TABERNACLE OF THE CONGREGATION, AND SHALL WASH THEM WITH WATER.

(5) "AND YOU SHALL TAKE THE GARMENTS, AND PUT UPON AARON THE COAT, AND THE ROBE OF THE EPHOD, AND THE EPHOD, AND THE BREASTPLATE, AND GIRD HIM WITH THE CURIOUS GIRDLE OF THE EPHOD:

(6) "AND YOU SHALL PUT THE MITRE UPON HIS HEAD, AND PUT THE HOLY CROWN UPON THE MITRE.

(7) "THEN SHALL YOU TAKE THE ANOINTING OIL, AND POUR IT UPON HIS HEAD, AND ANOINT HIM."

The composition is:

1. The Twenty-ninth Chapter of Exodus pertains to the consecration of the Priests.

2. Their consecration would begin with sacrifice, *"One young bullock, two rams without blemish."*

3. The very life of Jesus Christ was a Sacrifice; consequently, the Priests, who were

types of Christ, would begin their consecration with Sacrifice.

4. The second Verse speaks of *"unleavened bread,"* which pertains to the sinless life of Christ, which, as well, was *"tempered with oil,"* which symbolizes the Holy Spirit upon Christ.

5. The Fourth Verse says: *"Shall wash them with water."* The washing portrayed a death of sin and self, as it pertained to the Priests; however, Christ had no sin, and needed no death of self. So the water here pertained to His Water Baptism, which Baptism symbolized His death, burial, and Resurrection, as it regards the Redemption of the human race.

THE SACRIFICES

Verse 1 reads: *"And this is the thing that you shall do unto them to hallow them, to minister unto Me in the Priest's Office: take one young bullock, and two rams without blemish."*

All of this was meant to be a Type of Christ, and what He would do to redeem lost humanity. Inasmuch as the very Life of Christ was meant to be a Sacrifice, and in fact was, as stated, a Sacrifice, the consecration of the Priests would begin accordingly!

The *"young bullock"* symbolized the Manhood of Christ, while the two rams symbolized His Kingly nature.

Today, and due to the Cross, all Believers, and we mean all, are now kings and priests unto the Lord. Understanding this, we should take all of this symbolic ceremony to heart, apply it to ourselves spiritually, and register our Faith accordingly.

First of all, our Faith must rest exclusively in Christ and His Sacrificial Work, symbolized by the *"one young bullock, and the two rams without blemish."* Christ was without blemish, and He desires us to be so accordingly.

THE UNLEAVENED BREAD AND THE OIL

Verse 2 reads: *"And unleavened bread, and cakes unleavened tempered with oil, and wafers unleavened anointed with oil: of wheaten flour shall you make them."*

The *"unleavened bread"* signified the perfect life of Christ, and the *"oil"* typified the Holy Spirit, which was upon Him without measure (Jn. 3:34).

The flour which went into the unleavened bread was to be made of *"wheat,"* which was the finest of the grains. It symbolized the purity and glory of Christ.

THE BASKET

Verse 3 reads: *"And you shall put them into one basket, and bring them in the basket, with the bullock and the two rams."*

The unleavened bread and the wafers were put into one basket, because all pertains to Christ.

Williams says: *"The consecration of Aaron and his sons furnishes 'shadows of good things to come' — but only shadows. But yet, we can learn more about Christ by learning about these 'shadows,' which makes them very important!"*

THE WASHING WITH WATER

Verse 4 reads: *"And Aaron and his sons you shall bring unto the door of the Tabernacle of the congregation, and shall wash them with water."*

Even though it's not mentioned here, it was probably to the great Laver, which sat immediately in front of the Tabernacle, to which they were to be brought. Its main purpose was to be a vessel, placed ready for the various ablutions which the Law required. Water, blood, and oil in this Chapter symbolize cleansing, Atonement, and the Holy Spirit. Shed blood, which pertains to the sacrifice of the young bullock and the two rams, was the foundation of all. There was the bullock for the Sin-Offering, the ram for the Burnt-Offering, and a second ram for the Peace-Offering. Everything is Jesus; He is all of the Offerings.

The washing with water pertained to Aaron and his sons. This speaks of the Word of God which proclaims Salvation.

When the believing sinner comes to Christ, he is *"washed, sanctified, and justified* (all) *in the Name of the Lord Jesus, and by the Spirit of our God"* (I Cor. 6:11).

The *"washing"* here, as it regards Aaron and his sons, is symbolic of the Believer now being washed in the Blood of the Lamb.

THE GARMENTS

Verses 5 and 6 read: *"And you shall take the garments, and put upon Aaron the Coat, and the Robe of the Ephod, and the Ephod, and the Breastplate, and gird him with the Curious Girdle of the Ephod:*

"And you shall put the Mitre upon his head, and put the Holy Crown upon the Mitre."

All of the fittings of Aaron with these special garments, garments incidentally designed by the Lord, were topped off by the placing of the *"Holy Crown"* upon his head. It marked the royal character of the High Priest, who, as the main Type of Christ in the Mosaic Law, was bound to be *"Prophet, Priest, and King."* Everything here, as previously stated, presents Christ in some fashion, as it regards His Atoning Work.

But yet, all of these things were but types, and carried no reality, except by Faith. Everything looked forward to the One Who was to come, Who would redeem humanity, and do so by going to the Cross.

THE ANOINTING OIL

Verse 7 reads: *"Then shall you take the anointing oil, and pour it upon his head, and anoint him."*

The *"anointing oil"* signified, as would be obvious, the Holy Spirit. It was poured upon his head, signifying that he must understand that he is to do everything under the guidance of the Holy Spirit, not deviating at all from the direction laid down by Moses, as it was given to him by God, actively seeking the help of the Divine Spirit. Once again, this points to Christ.

Immediately after Christ's Baptism in the Jordan, He was anointed with the Holy Spirit. He needed no Atonement Personally, as should be obvious. As He began His earthly Ministry, He would say, *"The Spirit of the Lord is upon Me, and He has anointed Me . . ."* (Lk. 4:18-19).

(8) "AND YOU SHALL BRING HIS SONS, AND PUT COATS UPON THEM.

(9) "AND YOU SHALL GIRD THEM WITH GIRDLES, AARON AND HIS SONS, AND PUT THE BONNETS ON THEM: AND THE PRIEST'S OFFICE SHALL BE THEIRS FOR A PERPETUAL STATUTE: AND YOU SHALL CONSECRATE AARON AND HIS SONS.

(10) "AND YOU SHALL CAUSE A BULLOCK TO BE BROUGHT BEFORE THE TABERNACLE OF THE CONGREGATION: AND AARON AND HIS SONS SHALL PUT THEIR HANDS UPON THE HEAD OF THE BULLOCK.

(11) "AND YOU SHALL KILL THE BULLOCK BEFORE THE LORD, BY THE DOOR OF THE TABERNACLE OF THE CONGREGATION.

(12) "AND YOU SHALL TAKE OF THE BLOOD OF THE BULLOCK, AND PUT IT UPON THE HORNS OF THE ALTAR WITH YOUR FINGER, AND POUR ALL THE BLOOD BESIDE THE BOTTOM OF THE ALTAR.

(13) "AND YOU SHALL TAKE ALL THE FAT THAT COVERS THE INWARDS, AND THE CAUL THAT IS ABOVE THE LIVER, AND THE TWO KIDNEYS, AND THE FAT THAT IS UPON THEM, AND BURN THEM UPON THE ALTAR.

(14) "BUT THE FLESH OF THE BULLOCK AND HIS SKIN, AND HIS DUNG, SHALL YOU BURN WITH FIRE WITHOUT THE CAMP: IT IS A SIN OFFERING."

The construction is:

1. The Office of the High Priest was to remain in the family of Aaron, until the Great High Priest, the Lord Jesus Christ, would come.

2. Verses 10 through 14 portrayed the *"Sin Offering."* Even though Aaron was a Type of Christ, still, he was a sinner, and had to offer sacrifice for his own sins. Christ offered Himself for the world's sins.

3. In Verse 12, they took the *"blood of the bullock, and put it upon the horns of the Altar."* The horns pointing in all directions of the compass signified that all men everywhere must come by the shed Blood of the Lamb.

4. Then they did *"pour all the blood beside the bottom of the Altar."* This spoke of Jesus shedding His Blood at Calvary.

5. Verse 13 speaks of the *"fat"* and the *"caul,"* as well as the *"two kidneys,"* and then it said, *"And burn them upon the Altar."* These items, plus *"the fat,"* spoke of the prosperity of Israel. They were to forever remember that it came through Calvary.

6. Verse 14 speaks of the *"flesh"* as well as the *"skin"* and *"dung."* Concerning these things, it says that Aaron was to *"burn with fire without the camp."* The flesh of the Sin-Offering was destroyed outside the camp as a Type of Christ paying the penalty for sin outside the camp (Heb. 13:11-13).

A PERPETUAL STATUTE

Verses 8 and 9 read: *"And you shall bring his sons, and put coats upon them.*

"And you shall gird them with girdles, Aaron and his sons, and put the bonnets on them: and the Priest's Office shall be theirs for a perpetual Statute: and you shall consecrate Aaron and his sons."

The consecration of the High Priest consisted of nine acts; that of the ordinary Priest of three only. They do not seem to have been anointed, as Aaron was, by having the Holy Oil poured upon their heads, but only by having some of it sprinkled upon their garments (Ex. 29:21; Lev. 8:30).

The Office of the High Priest was to remain in the family of Aaron, and do so until Christ, the Great High Priest, would come!

If it is to be noticed, Aaron was anointed before the blood was shed, as it respects the sacrifices being offered. This was done in this manner, because he stands before us as the Type of Christ, Who, in virtue of what He was in His Own Person, was anointed with the Holy Spirit, long before the work of the Cross was accomplished. The sons of Aaron, even as we shall see, on the other hand, were not anointed until after the blood was shed.

As it presently regards the Church, the Blood of the Cross lies at the foundation of everything. The Church could not be anointed with the Holy Spirit until a risen Head had gone into Heaven, and had stood before the Throne of the Divine Majesty, presenting Himself as the record of His accomplished Sacrifice.

From the days of Abel downward, souls have been regenerated, influenced, acted upon, and qualified for Office by the Holy Spirit; but the Church could not be anointed with the Holy Spirit until her victorious Lord had entered Heaven, and had been received by the Father there, which meant that the Sacrifice was fully accepted, and then, He could send back the *"Promise of the Father,"* i.e., *"the Holy Spirit,"* Who would now come in a brand-new Dispensation. The truth of this Doctrine is taught in the most direct and absolute manner, throughout the New Testament; and its strict integrity is maintained in the type before us, by the obvious fact that though Aaron was anointed before the blood was shed, yet his sons were not, and could not be anointed until after.

All of this proclaims to us, in no uncertain terms, the absolute veracity of the Cross, its significance, its foundational principles, and that the Church is built entirely upon that particular Rock (Mat. 16:13-19).

Regrettably and sadly, the Church is farther away today from this Truth, than possibly it has been since the Reformation.

THE CHURCH

Almost all the modern Church falls into the category of either an ignorance of the Cross, or outright denial! If the principle of the Cross is believed at all, it is only in passing. In other words, men pay lip service to the Cross, and quickly scurry on to other things. Regrettably, these *"other things"* have degenerated mostly to material things, with Righteousness and Holiness all but completely ignored. But there is a reason for that:

It is impossible to come by these great qualities of the Holy Spirit unless one's Faith is anchored supremely in the Finished Work of Christ. If it is to be remembered, for quite a number of recent decades, the Church has attempted to perfect Righteousness and Holiness by works of the Law, which will never suffice. It only succeeds in breeding self-righteousness. But now, even that is being quickly abandoned!

The truth is, man cannot accomplish anything of God within himself, by his own efforts, strength, and ability. All of it, and without exception, is a work of the Holy Spirit, Who carries out what He does, all within the framework of the Finished Work of Christ. The Holy Spirit demands of us that we exhibit Faith in that Finished Work, and that our Faith be maintained in that Finished Work. But that is where the great controversy commences!

THE SACRIFICE

Verses 10 and 11 read: *"And you shall cause a bullock to be brought before the Tabernacle of the congregation: and Aaron and his sons shall put their hands upon the head of the bullock.*

"And you shall kill the bullock before the LORD, by the door of the Tabernacle of the congregation."

In all of these things, the types stand out so dramatically, which prayerfully, the Lord will help us to enumerate:

1. *"A bullock was to be brought before the Tabernacle of the congregation,"* which typifies Christ giving His life, in order that humanity might be redeemed from the terrible ravages of sin. As repeatedly stated, all of this proclaims Christ in one way or the other.

2. *"Aaron and his sons shall put their hands upon the head of the bullock,"* in effect, transferring their sins to this innocent victim. This portrays Christ taking our sins upon Himself, and then paying the penalty for those sins, which we shall see momentarily.

Today, as is obvious, we do not personally lay our hands on Christ. The evidence of our Faith toward Him, in effect, serves the same purpose. It is Christ Alone Who can address sin, and He does so by what He did on the Cross, all on our behalf.

It should be noted that no psychological counseling entered into any of this, or anything else for that matter. It was strictly *"Christ and Him Crucified"* (I Cor. 1:23).

Some may argue that they did not have that great science then. My answer to that is threefold:

1. Psychology is not a science, irrespective as to how much some may claim it to be.

2. Psychology holds no answer for anyone. Pure and simple, it is a lie.

3. One cannot believe in the Cross and humanistic psychology at the same time. One cannot trust God and mammon.

THE GREAT QUESTION!

So the question must be asked, do you believe that Jesus answered everything at the Cross, and that what He did at the Cross is the cure for every bondage, irrespective as to how bad it might be, every sin, irrespective of its description, etc.?

If you do believe that, then there is no need for anything else, and to be frank and plain, there is no other answer or solution, irrespective of the claims of men. Now let's say that again:

There is only one solution for sin, and it doesn't really matter how bad it is, or what type it is; that solution is the Cross of Christ (Col. 2:14-15; Rom. 6:3-14; Gal. 6:14).

"They then killed the Bullock before the Lord" meaning that it was commanded by the Lord.

This tells us that Jesus had to die. In fact, His Crucifixion was not an execution, neither was it an assassination. It was a sacrifice. This had been planned by God from before the foundation of the world (I Pet. 1:18-20). It was the very purpose for why Christ came.

Had the Ministry of Christ stopped short of the Cross, even though it would have been wonderful and good, still, it would have redeemed no one. His Virgin Birth, although necessary, did not save anyone. His miracles and healings, although necessary, did not save anyone. The great Messages He preached, although necessary, did not save anyone. It was the Cross and the Cross alone which effected Redemption for mankind.

THE BLOOD

Verse 12 reads: *"And you shall take of the blood of the bullock, put it upon the horns of the Altar with your finger, and pour all the blood beside the bottom of the Altar."*

The *"blood"* of the slain bullock was to be smeared on the four horns of the Altar, and the balance of the blood poured out at the *"bottom of the Altar."* This signified two things, and we'll address the latter first.

The blood poured out at the bottom of the Altar specified what Christ would do in delivering humanity, which would be the shedding of His life's Blood. When He was crucified, as would be obvious, the Blood came from His many wounds, and fell to the ground beneath the Cross, i.e., *"the bottom of the Altar."*

"Horns" represent power. The blood applied to these horns, which protruded toward all four corners of the planet, signified

that the death of Christ would provide power in that Satan and all of his minions of darkness would be totally defeated, which they were (Col. 2:14-15). That's why Paul said:

"For the preaching of the Cross is to them who perish foolishness; but unto us which are saved it is the Power of God" (I Cor. 1:18).

So the poured out blood at the base of the Altar was a type of Atonement for all sin, with the blood on the horns, specifying the power that would be brought forth, as a result of the Atonement.

When we sing the song *"There is Power in the Blood,"* we're singing the Word of God. There is power in the Blood, and there is power only in the Blood, which signifies the Cross.

THE FAT

Verse 13 reads: *"And you shall take all the fat that covers the inwards, and the caul that is above the liver, and the two kidneys, and the fat that is upon them, and burn them upon the Altar."*

The *"fat"* along with certain organs of the animal were to be burned on the Altar. The *"fat"* signified the health and prosperity of the animal, and likewise the prosperity of Israel. This signified that Israel knew that the Lord was the secret of their blessing, and the Lord Alone, as the secret of their blessing.

SIN-OFFERING

Verse 14 reads: *"But the flesh of the bullock, and his skin, and his dung, shall you burn with fire without the camp: it is a Sin Offering."*

Such was the rule with Sin-Offerings generally (Lev. 4:11-12).

The curse of sin, which was on them, made them unfit for food, and even unworthy of burial within the camp. So the remains were to be taken outside the camp, and burned with fire (Pulpit).

Jesus was the Sin-Offering. He suffered *"without the camp,"* i.e., *"without the gate."*

(15) "YOU SHALL ALSO TAKE ONE RAM; AND AARON AND HIS SONS SHALL PUT THEIR HANDS UPON THE HEAD OF THE RAM.

(16) "AND YOU SHALL SLAY THE RAM, AND YOU SHALL TAKE HIS BLOOD, AND SPRINKLE IT ROUND ABOUT UPON THE ALTAR.

(17) "AND YOU SHALL CUT THE RAM IN PIECES, AND WASH THE INWARDS OF HIM, AND HIS LEGS, AND PUT THEM UNTO HIS PIECES, AND UNTO HIS HEAD.

(18) "AND YOU SHALL BURN THE WHOLE RAM UPON THE ALTAR: IT IS A BURNT OFFERING UNTO THE LORD: IT IS A SWEET SAVOUR, AN OFFERING MADE BY FIRE UNTO THE LORD.

(19) "AND YOU SHALL TAKE THE OTHER RAM; AND AARON AND HIS SONS SHALL PUT THEIR HANDS UPON THE HEAD OF THE RAM.

(20) "THEN SHALL YOU KILL THE RAM, AND TAKE OF HIS BLOOD, AND PUT IT UPON THE TIP OF THE RIGHT EAR OF AARON, AND UPON THE TIP OF THE RIGHT EAR OF HIS SONS, AND UPON THE THUMB OF THEIR RIGHT HAND, AND UPON THE GREAT TOE OF THEIR RIGHT FOOT, AND SPRINKLE THE BLOOD UPON THE ALTAR ROUND ABOUT.

(21) "AND YOU SHALL TAKE OF THE BLOOD THAT IS UPON THE ALTAR, AND OF THE ANOINTING OIL, AND SPRINKLE IT UPON AARON, AND UPON HIS GARMENTS, AND UPON HIS SONS, AND UPON THE GARMENTS OF HIS SONS WITH HIM: AND HE SHALL BE HALLOWED, AND HIS GARMENTS, AND HIS SONS, AND HIS SONS' GARMENTS WITH HIM."

The composition is:

1. Verses 15 through 18 portray the *"Whole Burnt Offering."* The Whole Burnt Offering signified that God would give His all for Israel, and Israel must give their all for God. Even in a more direct sense, Jesus Christ would give His all. This is the reason it was *"a sweet savour"* unto the Lord.

2. Verses 19 through 21 portray the consecration Offering of the Priests. Putting their hands upon the head of the ram signified that they were sinners, and that they were transferring their transgressions to this innocent victim. The portrayal in the Levitical Offerings of Substitution and Identification is the very heart of the Gospel. Jesus Christ became our Substitute, and we identify with Him, and are, thereby, saved.

3. Verse 20 proclaims that the blood must be applied to the *"tip of the right ear,"* and *"upon the thumb of their right hand,"* and *"upon the great toe of their right foot."* This spoke of three things:
   A. The ear: hear only that which is of God.
   B. The thumb: grasp only that which is of God.
   C. The toe: go only in God's direction.

4. The blood applied to their bodies and their garments served to make the awfulness of sin and its penalty more vivid. It was a visible evidence that life had been taken away and God's Law vindicated.

THE WHOLE BURNT OFFERING

Verses 15 through 18 read: *"You shall also take one ram; and Aaron and his sons shall put their hands upon the head of the ram.*

"And you shall slay the ram, and you shall take his blood, and sprinkle it round about upon the Altar.

"And you shall cut the ram in pieces, and wash the inwards of him, and his legs, and put them unto his pieces, and unto his head.

"And you shall burn the whole ram upon the Altar: it is a Burnt Offering unto the LORD: it is a sweet savour, an Offering made by fire unto the LORD."

As the *"young Bullock"* represented Christ at the height of His Manhood, giving Himself for the sin of the world, the *"Ram"* represented Christ in His position as King. The *"Ram"* signified that the death of Christ was not merely the death of just anyone. It was the death of the Son of God, the *"King of kings and Lord of lords."*

As on the bullock, they were likewise to put their hands upon the head of this animal, in effect, transferring their sins. An innocent victim must pay the price, typifying Christ.

They would then kill the ram, signifying the Crucifixion, and then they would take the blood of the animal and sprinkle it round about upon the Altar. This signified the death that Christ would die.

Now some may ask, why did this action have to be repeated, when to an extent, it had already been done with the previous animal?

In the first place, this was a *"Whole Burnt Offering,"* whereas the first Offering was a *"Sin Offering."* It all represented Christ, but pertained to a different principle. The Sin-Offering pertained to *"sin"* while the second Offering pertained to *"consecration."*

THE SWEET SAVOUR

The animal was to be cut in pieces, with the pieces then washed, and then placed upon the Altar, and then consumed with fire, all of it representing Christ. He was stricken, smitten, wounded, and bruised, all for our iniquities (Isa. 53:4-5).

That the animal was washed after it was cut in pieces, and then laid on the Altar portrays the purity of Christ.

As this animal was burned on the Altar, the Scripture said, *"It is a sweet savour."* How could this be?

It was a *"sweet savour"* unto the Lord simply because it represented what Christ would do on a coming glad day, which would redeem fallen humanity. In the natural, an animal burning on an Altar, sending a plume of greasy smoke toward the heavens, could hardly be construed as something desirable; however, it was desirable unto the Lord because of what it represented.

Most of the world presently understands the Cross not at all. Even the Church little understands the Cross. In fact, when Jesus first mentioned His death to His Disciples, they recoiled in distaste (Mat. 16:21-25).

MISUNDERSTANDING THE CROSS

In fact, most modern Christians totally misunderstand the Cross. To them it is not at all a *"sweet savour,"* but rather something else! While they know that Jesus said that we must *"deny ourselves, and take up our Cross daily"* (Lk. 9:23), they would rather not discuss it, as stated, completely misunderstanding what He said.

Most think that *"taking up the Cross,"* in their following of Christ, and especially having to do it *"daily,"* constitutes terrible suffering. Consequently, when something bad happens to a fellow Christian, the reaction most of the time is, *"I sure hope the Lord doesn't ask me to do that,"* or words to that effect! As stated, even though Christ commanded it, it is certainly not a *"sweet savour"* to most Believers.

The truth is, denying ourselves and taking up the Cross daily in our following of Christ is the single most wonderful thing that could ever happen to any Believer. In this is the secret of all life, all living, in fact, *"more abundant life"* (Jn. 10:10).

Yes the Cross represents suffering, but it's the suffering which Christ has already carried out, and did so once and for all, meaning that it will never have to be repeated. In truth, Christ is not going to get back on the Cross, and neither does He want us on the Cross. In fact, we are seated with Him in Heavenly Places (Eph. 2:6). It is the benefits of the Cross of which we speak, which is what makes this thing so wonderful.

"Denying ourselves," simply refers to denying our own strength and ability, rather trusting the strength and ability of Christ. Taking up the Cross and doing so on a daily basis, refers to looking to the benefits of the Cross, and doing so everyday. As stated, it's the most wonderful life there could ever be. It is truly a *"sweet savour!"*

THE BLOOD

Verses 19 and 20 read: *"And you shall take the other Ram; and Aaron and his sons shall put their hands upon the head of the Ram.*

"Then shall you kill the Ram, and take of his blood, and put it upon the tip of the right ear of Aaron, and upon the tip of the right ear of his sons, and upon the thumb of their right hand, and upon the great toe of their right foot, and sprinkle the blood upon the Altar round about."

A second Ram is now to be killed, with Aaron and his sons repeating the action of putting their hands upon its head. This action portrayed the fact that they were stating that they could not hear right, do right, or walk right, without the power of the Crucified Christ. This is a lesson that most of the modern Church has never learned.

The taking of the blood and putting it upon the *"tip of the right ear"* of Aaron, and his sons, specified that their ear would ever be opened to the Divine voice. Placed upon the *"thumb of their right hand,"* signified their *"doing right."* Upon the *"great toe of their right foot,"* it signified their whole walk in life, their *"going out"* and their *"coming in."*

The *"blood"* applied thereon proclaimed the fact that they could not live as they ought to live, do as they ought to do, be as they ought to be, without Faith in Christ and what He would do for us at the Cross.

What you are seeing here is exactly what Paul taught in Romans, Chapter 6. We were *"baptized into His death,"* then *"buried with Him by baptism into death,"* and then raised with Him in *"newness of life"* (Rom. 6:3-5). The Believer is then to *"reckon himself as dead unto sin, but alive unto God, through Jesus Christ our Lord"* (Rom. 6:11).

This very thing taught by the Apostle, which is God's prescribed order of victory, is given to us in type regarding the consecration ceremony of the Priests.

THE BLOOD AND THE OIL

Verse 21 reads: *"And you shall take of the blood that is upon the Altar, and of the anointing oil, and sprinkle it upon Aaron, and upon his garments, and upon his sons, and upon the garments of his sons with him: and he shall be hallowed, and his garments, and his sons, and his sons' garments with him."*

We have here a further type of the victory that is only in Christ.

It seems that the *"blood"* and the *"anointing oil,"* were mixed together, and then sprinkled upon Aaron, upon his garments, as well as upon his sons, etc.

This proclaims the way in which the Holy Spirit works. He works entirely within the parameters of the great Sacrifice of Christ, typified by the *"blood."* That's why Paul also said:

"For the Law of the Spirit of Life in Christ Jesus has made me free from the law of sin and death.

"For what the Law could not do, in that it was weak through the flesh, God sending His Own Son in the likeness of sinful flesh, and for sin, condemned sin in the flesh" (Rom. 8:2-3).

This proclaims the fact that Jesus died for our sin, thereby, condemning sin in the flesh. This was a legal work, in which the Holy Spirit functions. That's the reason he referred to this as *"the Law of the Spirit of Life in Christ Jesus."* Any time Paul used the statement, *"In Christ Jesus,"* or one of its derivatives such as *"in Him,"* He is referring to what was carried out at the Cross.

The Holy Spirit functions only within the parameters of the Finished Work of Christ, proven by the statement given in Romans 8:2. He will not deviate from that course, and actually refers to such deviation as *"spiritual adultery"* (Rom. 7:1-4).

Anything done in our hearts and lives, in the spiritual sense, is done without exception by the Holy Spirit. If we try to do it ourselves, He will not assist.

We are to understand that all things come from God through the Cross, and that the Cross must ever be the object of our Faith. This done, and continuing to be done, the Holy Spirit will function within His realm of power, and considering that He is God, this means there is nothing He cannot do. As repeatedly stated, this is *"God's prescribed order of victory."*

(22) "ALSO YOU SHALL TAKE OF THE RAM THE FAT AND THE RUMP, AND THE FAT THAT COVERS THE INWARDS, AND THE CAUL ABOVE THE LIVER, AND THE TWO KIDNEYS, AND THE FAT THAT IS UPON THEM, AND THE RIGHT SHOULDER; FOR IT IS A RAM OF CONSECRATION:

(23) "AND ONE LOAF OF BREAD, AND ONE CAKE OF OILED BREAD, AND ONE WAFER OUT OF THE BASKET OF THE UNLEAVENED BREAD THAT IS BEFORE THE LORD:

(24) "AND YOU SHALL PUT ALL IN THE HANDS OF AARON, AND IN THE HANDS OF HIS SONS; AND SHALL WAVE THEM FOR A WAVE OFFERING BEFORE THE LORD.

(25) "AND YOU SHALL RECEIVE THEM OF THEIR HANDS, AND BURN THEM UPON THE ALTAR FOR A BURNT OFFERING, FOR A SWEET SAVOUR BEFORE THE LORD: IT IS AN OFFERING MADE BY FIRE UNTO THE LORD.

(26) "AND YOU SHALL TAKE THE BREAST OF THE RAM OF AARON'S CONSECRATION, AND WAVE IT FOR A WAVE OFFERING BEFORE THE LORD: AND IT SHALL BE YOUR PART.

(27) "AND YOU SHALL SANCTIFY THE BREAST OF THE WAVE OFFERING, AND THE SHOULDER OF THE HEAVE OFFERING, WHICH IS WAVED, AND WHICH IS HEAVED UP OF THE RAM OF THE CONSECRATION, EVEN OF THAT WHICH IS FOR AARON, AND OF THAT WHICH IS FOR HIS SONS:

(28) "AND IT SHALL BE AARON'S AND HIS SONS' BY A STATUTE FOREVER FROM THE CHILDREN OF ISRAEL: FOR IT IS AN HEAVE OFFERING: IT SHALL BE AN HEAVE OFFERING FROM THE CHILDREN OF ISRAEL OF THE SACRIFICE OF THEIR PEACE OFFERINGS, EVEN THEIR HEAVE OFFERING UNTO THE LORD."

The overview is:

1. Verses 22 through 28 portray the Wave and Heave Offerings. The bread of different kinds was intended to show gratefulness for God's Blessings of abundant supply for daily needs.

2. All the parts of the Ram and the different breads were waved and heaved before God to acknowledge Him. This is the motive of all true worship.

3. *"Heaving"* being a single lifting up of the Offering toward Heaven, while *"Waving"* was a repeated movement in a horizontal direction. Such Offerings were always connected with the portions of the Priests, or with things dedicated to God's service (Ex. 25:2; 35:22, 24; 38:24, 29; Lev. 7:30-34; Num. 18:11, 19, 24).

THE WAVE-OFFERING

Verses 22 through 24 read: *"Also you shall take of the Ram the fat and the rump, and the fat that covers the inwards, and the caul above the liver, and the two kidneys, and the fat that is upon them, and the right shoulder; for it is a Ram of consecration:*

"And one loaf of bread, and one cake of oiled bread, and one wafer out of the basket of the unleavened bread that is before the LORD:

"And you shall put all in the hands of Aaron, and in the hands of his sons; and shall wave them for a Wave Offering before the LORD."

More than likely, different Priests took different parts of the animal and the bread, and then waved it before the Lord, acknowledging Him as the Giver of all good things.

We have in this now a thankfulness for material blessings.

In these Passages, the sins are addressed, typified by the Blood, the help of the Holy Spirit is addressed, typified by the oil, and now thankfulness for all of these things, plus material prosperity, is tendered by the *"Wave Offering."*

We must look to the Lord for all that we need, and then we must be careful to thank Him for Him meeting these needs. While it was done in Old Testament times with a *"Wave Offering,"* it is done now through the lifting of hands in praise, worship, and adoration of the Lord. In fact, how can one serve the Lord, and not do such?!

THE SWEET SAVOUR

Verse 25 reads: *"And you shall receive them of their hands, and burn them upon the Altar for a Burnt Offering, for a sweet savor before the LORD: it is an Offering made by fire unto the LORD."*

After the Wave-Offering is finished, they are to place these items on the Altar, and offer them for a *"Burnt Offering."* It, as well, is a *"sweet savour before the Lord."*

Among other things, it is a *"sweet savour"* because *"it is an Offering made by fire unto the LORD."*

"Fire" refers to judgment, but it refers to judgment that will come upon Christ, in order that the sin of the world may be expiated (Jn. 3:16; 1:29).

All of this proclaims the tremendous love that God has for the human race. That the suffering of His Own Son could be to Him a *"sweet savour"* because He loves humanity, who in fact hates Him, presents itself as beyond our comprehension. We cannot fathom the depths of such love; therefore, we only skirt the edges.

PEACE-OFFERINGS

Verses 26 through 28 read: *"And you shall take the breast of the Ram of Aaron's consecration, and wave it for a Wave Offering before the LORD: it shall be your part.*

"And you shall sanctify the breast of the Wave Offering, and the shoulder of the Heave Offering, which is waved, and which is heaved up of the Ram of the consecration, even of that which is for Aaron, and of that which is for his sons:

"And it shall be Aaron's and his sons' by a Statute forever from the Children of Israel: for it is an Heave Offering: and it shall be an Heave Offering from the Children of Israel of the Sacrifice of their Peace Offerings, even their Heave Offering unto the LORD."

From here on out, Aaron and his sons were to have the breast of all Wave-Offerings (Lev. 7:31-34).

In fact, on this one occasion, the breast of the Wave-Offering was to be given to Moses. But hereafter, it was to belong to the Priests. Actually, both the breast and the right shoulder were to belong to the Priests. The shoulder was to be *"heaved,"* while the breast was to be *"waved."* As to the reason one is *"heaved"* and one is *"waved"* we aren't told!

This would pertain, it seems, at least according to Verse 28, to the *"Peace Offerings."*

The Peace-Offerings were generally offered immediately after the offering of the Whole Burnt Offering, the Sin-Offering, or the Trespass-Offering. It signified that peace had now been restored, because the sin had been covered.

The *"Peace Offering"* was to be a time of rejoicing. The Priests, even as we've already stated, were to be given the breast and the shoulder, with the family which had brought the Offering in the first place, being given the rest, with which they could now have a feast. If they so desired, they could call in friends, etc.

In our Commentary on the Book of Leviticus, we go into much greater detail as it regards the Sacrifices, which I believe would be a great interest to the lover of the Word of God.

(29) "AND THE HOLY GARMENTS OF AARON SHALL BE HIS SONS' AFTER HIM, TO BE ANOINTED THEREIN, AND TO BE CONSECRATED IN THEM.

(30) "AND THAT SON WHO IS PRIEST IN HIS STEAD SHALL PUT THEM ON SEVEN DAYS, WHEN HE COMES INTO THE TABERNACLE OF THE CONGREGATION TO MINISTER IN THE HOLY PLACE.

(31) "AND YOU SHALL TAKE THE RAM OF THE CONSECRATION, AND SEETHE HIS FLESH IN THE HOLY PLACE.

(32) "AND AARON AND HIS SONS SHALL EAT THE FLESH OF THE RAM, AND THE BREAD THAT IS IN THE BASKET, BY THE DOOR OF THE TABERNACLE OF THE CONGREGATION.

(33) "AND THEY SHALL EAT THOSE THINGS WHEREWITH THE ATONEMENT WAS MADE, TO CONSECRATE AND TO SANCTIFY THEM: BUT A STRANGER SHALL NOT EAT THEREOF, BECAUSE THEY ARE HOLY.

(34) "AND IF OUGHT OF THE FLESH OF THE CONSECRATIONS, OR OF THE BREAD, REMAIN UNTO THE MORNING, THEN YOU SHALL BURN THE REMAINDER WITH FIRE: IT SHALL NOT BE EATEN, BECAUSE IT IS HOLY.

(35) "AND THUS SHALL YOU DO UNTO AARON, AND TO HIS SONS, ACCORDING TO ALL THINGS WHICH I HAVE COMMANDED YOU: SEVEN DAYS SHALL YOU CONSECRATE THEM.

(36) "AND YOU SHALL OFFER EVERY DAY A BULLOCK FOR A SIN OFFERING FOR ATONEMENT: AND YOU SHALL CLEANSE THE ALTAR, WHEN YOU HAVE MADE AN ATONEMENT FOR IT, AND YOU SHALL ANOINT IT, TO SANCTIFY IT.

(37) "SEVEN DAYS YOU SHALL MAKE AN ATONEMENT FOR THE ALTAR, AND SANCTIFY IT; IT SHALL BE AN ALTAR MOST HOLY: WHOSOEVER TOUCHES THE ALTAR SHALL BE HOLY."

The exegesis is:

1. The Priests were to eat the flesh of the Ram, which incidentally had been roasted, as well as the bread, which typified the eating of Christ, which Jesus addressed in John, Chapter 6, Verses 53 and 63.

2. A stranger could not partake of this repast, referring to the fact that the person who doesn't know Christ surely cannot partake of His Blessings.

3. The consecration process required seven days, with the number *"seven"* typifying perfect consecration, which characterized Christ.

4. The *"Altar"* itself had to be cleansed, which it was by the offering of a bullock each day, for seven days. Christ sanctified the Cross, but the Cross didn't sanctify Him because He didn't need such.

NOTES

THE HOLY GARMENTS

Verses 29 and 30 read: *"And the Holy Garments of Aaron shall be his sons' after him, to be anointed therein, to be consecrated in them.*

"And that son who is Priest in his stead shall put them on seven days, when he comes into the Tabernacle of the congregation to minister in the Holy Place."

When Aaron died, one of his sons took his place as High Priest, which was supposed to continue through the centuries, which it did. These are the *"garments"* outlined in Chapter 28. They were *"holy,"* because they were designed by the Lord, and furthermore, they were to be worn by the High Priest, who was a Type of Christ.

This consecration period of some seven days was for purpose and reason. Everything done was a figure of Christ in some manner, which we have endeavored to explain.

THE RAM OF THE CONSECRATION

Verses 31 through 35 read: *"And you shall take the Ram of the consecration, and seethe his flesh in the Holy Place.*

"And Aaron and his sons shall eat the flesh of the Ram, and the bread that is in the basket, by the door of the Tabernacle of the congregation.

"And they shall eat those things wherewith the Atonement was made, to consecrate and to sanctify them: but a stranger shall not eat thereof, because they are holy.

"And if ought of the flesh of the consecrations, or of the bread, remain unto the morning, then you shall burn the remainder with fire: it shall not be eaten, because it is holy.

"And thus shall you do unto Aaron, and to his sons, according to all things which I have commanded you: seven days shall you consecrate them."

All of this was for consecration, as I trust is obvious.

The eating of the Ram, which had been roasted (seethed), and the bread, pertained to the eating of Christ, which Jesus addressed in John, Chapter 6, Verses 53 through 63. It refers to believing Christ to the extent that one has accepted Him in totality; literally giving Him one's all.

The Priests were to eat the roasted flesh and the bread, *"by the door of the Tabernacle of the congregation"* (Vs. 32). This pertains to the fact that Jesus is the Door (Jn. 10:1, 9).

Following the directions which God had given to Moses as to the conduct of the Priests, it would *"consecrate and sanctify them."* In essence, this meant that they would be set apart unto God totally, with their lives lived completely in His Service and for His Work. Consequently, if attended to as it should have been, it would provide the most joyous experience in living that one could know. It is the same presently:

MADE POSSIBLE BY THE CROSS

Due to what Christ has done at the Cross, every Believer is now a king and a priest (Rev. 1:6). So the consecration demanded of these Priests of old is demanded of all Believers presently, at least in the spiritual sense.

All of this gives us the pattern as to how we presently should live for the Lord. As I trust is overly obvious, all is in Christ. What He did at the Cross made it possible for us to be saved. I would trust that every Christian knows that; however, most do not know or understand that what He did at the Cross also gives us the power to walk in victory before Him and before the world.

Even though I have given this elsewhere in this Volume, due to its vast significance, I feel that it is imperative that I take every opportunity to present this great truth to you. The following constitutes an abbreviated manner in which one must follow in order to properly live for the Lord. Now please understand, we're speaking now of living for the Lord, which means that one has already been saved. It is the Will of God that you walk in perpetual victory, with sin not having dominion over you whatsoever. There is only one way that can be done, and that is God's prescribed order. Even though what we will give is very simple, please study it very carefully:

1. Focus: The Cross of Christ must ever be the focus of the Child of God, realizing that all things come to us through the great Sacrifice of Christ.

2. Object of Faith: The Finished Work of Christ must ever be the object of Faith, in which it will never change. That's why Paul referred to the Finished Work as *"The Everlasting Covenant"* (Heb. 13:20). This *"Covenant"* referred to as the *"New Covenant,"* will never need to be replaced, or amended. That is because it is a Perfect Covenant, which means that what Jesus did at the Cross is totally and completely a Finished Work. Let me say it again: the Finished Work of Christ must ever be the object of your Faith. This is critical, so whatever you do, don't be deterred from this great principle (Rom. 6:3-14; I Cor. 1:17-18, 21, 23; 2:2).

3. Power Source: When one's focus is on the Cross, and the great Sacrifice of Christ is ever the object of one's Faith, one's power source will then be the Holy Spirit. He is God, so there is nothing that He cannot do. He resides within your heart and life in order to carry out a particular purpose and mission, and that is to make you Christlike, which refers to a development of the Fruit of the Spirit. The Holy Spirit Alone can bring about these things within one's life. It is impossible otherwise! (Rom. 8:1-2, 11).

4. Results: Following that which we have given in the above diagram, the results will be victory, and not only victory, but perpetual victory. In other words, sin will not have dominion over you, but you will rather walk in the Power of the Holy Spirit, with Christ living this life through you (Gal. 6:14; Eph. 2:13-18; Rom. 6:11, 14).

THE ALTAR

Verses 36 and 37 read: *"And you shall offer everyday a bullock for a Sin Offering for Atonement: and you shall cleanse the Altar, when you have made an Atonement for it, and you shall anoint it, to sanctify it.*

"Seven days you shall make an Atonement for the Altar, and sanctify it; and it shall be an Altar most holy: whatsoever touches the Altar shall be holy."

During this seven day period of consecration, a bullock was to be offered each day for a *"Sin Offering,"* with the blood applied to the horns of the Altar, with the remainder poured out at its base. Leviticus 8:15 goes into detail regarding this. Two things should be noted here as it regards the Altar:

1. The Altar, within itself, was not holy; however, when the blood was applied, it became holy. This speaks of the Cross of Christ. Within itself, it wasn't holy; but Christ on the Cross made it holy.

2. The blood that was applied to the horns of the Altar, and poured out at its base was typical of the shed Blood of Christ, which was yet in the future. But the point is well taken, that just any blood wouldn't do. It had to be the Blood of Christ, of which the bullocks were a type here.

Due the Altar now being sanctified, all who touched it would now be holy as well. But of course, only Priests could touch the Altar.

The Altar typified the Cross and Believers now are holy due to what Christ did for us at the Cross. That and that alone makes us holy.

Unfortunately, many in the Church have ever tried to make themselves holy, and to do so by various types of works, etc. Holiness is never achieved by works, but always by Faith, and when we speak of Faith, we're speaking of Faith in Christ and His Finished Work. Such Faith gives us the Holiness of Christ, which is the only way that Holiness can be obtained. But unfortunately, many think they are holy because they belong to a certain Church, or a certain Denomination, or they do certain things, or don't do certain things. Holiness is not in doing, but rather in *"believing,"* and of course believing the right thing, which is *"Jesus Christ and Him Crucified."*

Let the statement, *"Whatsoever touches the Altar shall be holy,"* ring out loud and true! The Altar is a type of the Cross. When we trust completely in Christ, and what Christ did at the Cross, all that Christ is becomes ours as well, which includes Holiness, and which Paul constantly mentioned by using the phrase, *"In Christ Jesus,"* or one of its derivatives.

(38) "NOW THIS IS THAT WHICH YOU SHALL OFFER UPON THE ALTAR; TWO LAMBS OF THE FIRST YEAR DAY BY DAY CONTINUALLY.

(39) "THE ONE LAMB YOU SHALL OFFER IN THE MORNING; AND THE OTHER LAMB YOU SHALL OFFER AT EVENING:

(40) "AND WITH THE ONE LAMB A TENTH DEAL OF FLOUR MINGLED WITH THE FOURTH PART OF AN HIN OF BEATEN OIL; AND THE FOURTH PART OF AN HIN OF WINE FOR A DRINK OFFERING.

(41) "AND THE OTHER LAMB YOU SHALL OFFER AT EVENING, AND SHALL DO THERETO ACCORDING TO THE MEAT OFFERING OF THE MORNING, AND ACCORDING TO THE DRINK OFFERING THEREOF, FOR A SWEET SAVOR, AN OFFERING MADE BY FIRE UNTO THE LORD.

(42) "THIS SHALL BE A CONTINUAL BURNT OFFERING THROUGHOUT YOUR GENERATIONS AT THE DOOR OF THE TABERNACLE OF THE CONGREGATION BEFORE THE LORD: WHERE I WILL MEET YOU, TO SPEAK THERE WITH YOU.

(43) "AND THERE I WILL MEET WITH THE CHILDREN OF ISRAEL, AND THE TABERNACLE SHALL BE SANCTIFIED BY MY GLORY.

(44) "AND I WILL SANCTIFY THE TABERNACLE OF THE CONGREGATION, AND THE ALTAR: I WILL SANCTIFY ALSO BOTH AARON AND HIS SONS, TO MINISTER TO ME IN THE PRIEST'S OFFICE.

(45) "AND I WILL DWELL AMONG THE CHILDREN OF ISRAEL, AND WILL BE THEIR GOD.

(46) "AND THEY SHALL KNOW THAT I AM THE LORD THEIR GOD, WHO BROUGHT THEM FORTH OUT OF THE LAND OF EGYPT, THAT I MAY DWELL AMONG THEM: I AM THE LORD THEIR GOD."

The composition is:

1. Verses 38 through 42 speak of the daily Burnt-Offerings. The time of the offering of the morning lamb was 9 a.m., and the evening lamb was at 3 p.m. Jesus was put on the Cross at the time of the morning sacrifice, 9 a.m., and died at the time of the evening sacrifice, 3 p.m. He fulfilled both Offerings.

2. Once again Verse 41 calls it *"a sweet savour,"* only because it typifies the death of Christ to redeem fallen humanity.

3. Verses 43 through 46 portray the promise of God's Glory and Presence among His people, providing the sacrifices and obligations were carried out exactly as commanded.

4. In Verse 45 He said, *"And I will dwell among the Children of Israel, and will be their God."* God will not meet with us or dwell with us unless we go by the route of

the slain Lamb.

THE DAILY SACRIFICES

Verses 38 and 39 read: *"Now this is that which you shall offer upon the Altar; two lambs of the first year day by day continually.*

"The one lamb you shall offer in the morning; and the other lamb you shall offer at evening."

These were to be *"Burnt Offerings,"* or as they were sometimes called, *"Whole Burnt Offerings"* (Vs. 42). In fact, the *"Burnt Offering"* is the highest type of Sacrifice in Scripture. The first reference to it in the Word is found in Genesis 22:2 where the Lord told Abraham: *"Take now your son, your only son, Isaac, whom you love, and go into the land of Moriah; and offer him there for a 'Burnt Offering' upon one of the mountains which I will tell thee of."* The Hebrew word for *"Burnt Offering"* literally means, *"that which goes up."* It might well be designated *"the ascending Offering."*

All of it was to be consumed upon the Altar, with the exception of the skin. Leviticus, Chapter 1 furnishes full details concerning the Burnt Offering.

As it regards the consecration of the Priests, a bullock was to be offered each day for seven days as a *"Sin Offering."* But the Offerings mentioned here, which are to take place everyday, actually twice a day, were to be *"lambs."* Both the bullock and the lamb speak of Christ; however, the *"Lamb"* speaks in a more distinct way, representing what He would do to redeem humanity, more than anything else. The Prophet Isaiah said: *"He is brought as a lamb to the slaughter, and as a sheep before her shearers is dumb, so He opened not His mouth"* (Isa. 53:7).

Two lambs were to be offered each day, with that doubled on the Sabbath. The morning sacrifice would be at 9 a.m., with the evening sacrifice at 3 p.m. As we stated in the headings, Jesus was placed on the Cross at 9 a.m., and He died at 3 p.m., fulfilling the types to the letter.

Verse 38 says that these lambs must be offered *"day by day continually."* This speaks to us that our dependence on Christ and the Cross is to be continuous, actually, never ending. This is what we have been saying to you over and over in this Volume, concerning your Sanctification. You are to continue to look to the Cross *"continually."*

Many Christians are taught that the Cross is necessary as it regards Salvation, but after one is saved, they should go on to other things, leaving the Cross. That is not only wrong Scripturally, but it will bring disaster to that Christian. The only way that we can walk victorious over the world, the flesh, and the Devil, is by a *"continuing Faith"* in Christ and what Christ did for us at the Cross. That's the reason that Paul said: *"I determined not to know anything among you, save Jesus Christ, and Him Crucified"* (I Cor. 2:2).

If it is to be noticed, he didn't say, *"And Him Resurrected,"* as important as that was! Neither did he say, *"And Him exalted. . . ."*

We definitely aren't minimizing the Resurrection or the Exaltation of Christ. In fact, anything and everything that Christ did was of utmost significance, and played its part in the Redemption process. But it's unmistakable in the manner in which the Holy Spirit spoke through Paul, as it regards the Cross. The victory was accomplished at the Cross, of which all of these sacrifices of the Old Testament proclaimed to us in type and shadow. There are very few *"types"* and *"shadows"* of the Resurrection, but there are untold numbers of the Cross.

CONTINUALLY

The natural mind would think that one sacrifice a week would be enough, or maybe even one a day, but we find here that the Holy Spirit said that two a day must be offered; and that without fail! This shows us to the degree that the great Covenant of Salvation with Israel depended totally and completely on the Cross of Christ. And please understand, these two lambs which were to be offered each day, with each of them being *"without blemish,"* and as well, no more than one year old, speaks loudly to us of our constant need of the benefits of the Cross. That's one of the reasons why Jesus said that we must *"deny ourselves, and take up the Cross daily"* (Lk. 9:23).

The benefits of the Cross are available to me 24 hours a day, seven days a week, in fact, unending into eternity (Heb. 13:20).

As the Priests were unfailingly to offer up the sacrifices each day, I am to unfailingly depend on the benefits of the Cross on a daily basis, and even every hour of every day. What Jesus did there, of which all of this is a type, provides not only my Salvation, but as well, my Sanctification.

THE COMPLETE SACRIFICE

Verses 40 and 41 read: *"And with the one lamb a tenth deal of flour mingled with the fourth part of an hin of beaten oil; and the fourth part of an hin of wine for a Drink Offering.*

"And the other lamb you shall offer at evening, and shall do thereto according to the Meat Offering of the morning, and according to the Drink Offering thereof, for a sweet savour, an Offering made by fire unto the LORD."

Along with the Lamb that was offered, about three pounds of flour, mixed with about one quart of oil, were to be offered as well. About one quart of wine, i.e., *"fruit juice,"* was to be used also. It was to be poured out at the base of the Altar.

The *"flour"* spoke of His Perfect Life, while the *"oil"* spoke of the Holy Spirit abiding in and upon Him. The *"Drink Offering"* spoke of *"joy."* It speaks of the Father's joy in Christ, *"This is My Beloved Son, in Whom I am well pleased."*

As well, it speaks of the joy that accompanies the heartfelt Salvation of the Child of God, typified by the *"Drink Offering."*

Gloominess in the Christian is not glorifying unto God. A long-faced Believer is no commendation of Christ to those who know Him not. God does not desire His people to be miserable. He moved upon John to say: *"These things write we unto you, that your joy may be full"* (I Jn. 1:4).

If the Christian is sad and miserable, the fault is entirely his own. Lack of joy is due to lack of fellowship with God.

Such a disposition or attitude shows that the Believer has moved his Faith from the Cross of Christ to something else. The way, and the only way, to regain that joy, *"the Joy of the Lord,"* is to once again make the Cross the object of your Faith.

It should be overly obvious that the *"Drink Offering,"* was connected with the offering of the Lamb, which was typical of Christ. In other words, the *"joy"* is connected to the *"Cross."* If we separate the *"Drink Offering"* from the Cross, it then becomes an offering which God will not accept. He accepts it, and rewards it with joy, as it is connected with the offering of the Lamb in Sacrifice, which typified Christ. All of this is a *"sweet savour"* unto Him.

THERE I WILL MEET WITH YOU

Verses 42 and 43 read: *"This shall be a continual Burnt Offering throughout your generations at the door of the Tabernacle of the congregation before the LORD: where I will meet you, to speak there unto you.*

"And there I will meet with the Children of Israel, and the Tabernacle shall be sanctified by My Glory."

Plain, pure, and simple, the Lord tells us here through Moses that He will meet with us in Christ, and more particularly, the Sacrifice of Christ. In other words, we come to Him, and in fact are able to come to Him, solely through Christ, and we can come to Him through Christ, only because of what Christ did at the Cross. Christ and the Cross are inseparable, as should be obvious. The sacrifices on the Brazen Altar proclaim to us how the way is opened, while the Tabernacle proclaims to us what the Sacrifices have made possible. Through the Cross, Jesus is made real in the Word, typified by the Brazen Laver. He is the Bread of Life, typified by the Table of Shewbread. He is the Light of the world, typified by the Golden Lampstand. He is our Intercessor, typified by the Golden Altar. Access into the very Holy of Holies is made possible to us by and through what He did at the Cross, and by that means alone! (Eph. 2:13-18).

THE GLORY

Verse 43 mentions the *"Glory of God."*

As the Cross makes it possible for the Lord to meet with us, and the Cross alone, likewise, the Cross makes it possible for the Glory of God to be lavished upon God's people. His glory is only upon that which is of Christ. Christ and what He would do at the Cross is the *"sweet savour."*

SANCTIFICATION

Verse 44 reads: *"And I will sanctify the Tabernacle of the congregation, and the Altar: I will sanctify also both Aaron and his sons, to minister to Me in the Priest's Office."*

The Lord sanctified the Tabernacle, because it was a Type of Christ. The Altar as well was sanctified, because it represented Christ and what He would do at the Cross. All the Priests were sanctified because they were types of Christ. It must be noticed that it is all in Christ.

"Sanctify" or *"Sanctification,"* in its literal sense, means *"to be set apart,"* and in actuality, *"to be set apart exclusively unto God."* Concerning Sanctification, Paul said: *"And the very God of peace sanctify you wholly; and I pray God your whole spirit and soul and body be preserved blameless unto the coming of our Lord Jesus Christ"* (I Thess. 5:23).

Sanctification is a work of the Holy Spirit, and the Holy Spirit Alone! This means that the Believer cannot sanctify himself, despite the fact that Christians have been trying to do so for ages upon end. To be sure, considering the total failure of such efforts, the human being simply cannot do such within himself, irrespective as to how close he might walk with the Lord. As stated, this is a work of the Spirit.

And how does He accomplish this task?

Paul also said: *"For the flesh lusteth against the Spirit, and the Spirit against the flesh: and these are contrary the one to the other: so that you cannot do the things that you would"* (Gal. 5:17).

This speaks of the continuous war between the *"flesh"* and the *"Spirit."* Of course, this is speaking of the Holy Spirit.

WHAT IS THE FLESH?

The *"flesh"* as Paul uses the term, pertains to human effort, ability, strength, and endeavor. It's what the human being does outside of the Holy Spirit. This means that the Christian who attempts to live for God in any manner outside of God's prescribed order, which is *"Christ and Him Crucified,"* will function in the flesh, which will then open the door for *"lusts of the flesh,"* which will translate ultimately into *"works of the flesh"* (Gal. 5:16, 19-21).

If a person is operating *"in the flesh,"* we automatically think of sin. Sin is not the flesh, but rather the *"works of the flesh."* In other words, it's what the flesh will ultimately translate into.

As we've already stated, the person who walks after the flesh (Rom. 8:1), is in effect, functioning outside of God's prescribed order. The prescribed order is *"walking after the Spirit!"*

WHAT IS WALKING AFTER THE SPIRIT?

Walking after the Spirit (Rom. 8:1) brings about Sanctification, which is Christlikeness. In the simplest explanation that I can give, it refers to the Believer looking exclusively to Christ, and what He did for us at the Cross, which then gives the Holy Spirit latitude to work (Rom. 8:2).

Most Christians think that walking after the Spirit constitutes the doing of spiritual things. That is not the case at all! It is not really *"doing"* anything; it is rather *"believing"* the right thing. That's why Paul said: *"For in Jesus Christ neither circumcision availeth anything, nor uncircumcision; but Faith which works by love"* (Gal. 5:6).

If you as a Believer will put your Faith exclusively in Christ, believing totally in what He did for us at the Cross, that is *"walking after the Spirit."* Then He will be able to sanctify you. Then you will walk in perpetual victory.

WHERE GOD DWELLS

Verses 45 and 46 read: *"And I will dwell among the Children of Israel, and will be their God.*

"And they shall know that I am the LORD their God, that brought them forth out of the land of Egypt, that I may dwell among them: I am the LORD their God."

As is obvious here, God loved Israel. And as should be obvious, He loves us as well! (Jn. 3:16).

God wanted to dwell with Israel, but inasmuch as God was thrice-Holy, and Israel was wicked and sinful, this created a terrible problem. So all of these rituals and ceremonies that we are reading about here were brought forth in order to typify Christ, and to make it possible for God to dwell in the midst of Israel, at least as much as He could before the Cross.

Due to the Cross, the Lord now lives within our hearts and lives, which is far greater than His dwelling among Israel of old. Paul said:

"Don't you know that you are the Temple of God, and that the Spirit of God dwells in you?" (I Cor. 3:16).

It was the Holy Spirit Who dwelt between the Mercy Seat and the Cherubim in the Tabernacle and Temple of old. It is the Holy Spirit Who dwells in our hearts and lives presently.

In Old Testament times, why did the Lord have to dwell in the Tabernacle, when now He can dwell within our hearts and lives?

Paul answered that very succinctly by informing us that animal blood was insufficient to take away sins (Heb. 10:4). Consequently, the sin debt remained.

But when Jesus went to the Cross, His shed Blood was definitely sufficient, and took away all sin (Jn. 1:29). That's why He can now dwell in the heart and life of the Believer, whereas in Old Testament Times, He couldn't. It is all because of Christ and the Cross.

"I know a Fount where sins are washed away,
"I know a place where night is turned to day;
"Burdens are lifted, blind eyes made to see,
"There's a wonder-working power, in the Blood of Calvary."

"I have a Saviour, He's a faithful Friend,
"One Who is with me, will be to the end.
"He's now in Glory, intercedes for me,
"'Twas His precious cleansing Blood, that once flowed on Calvary."

"I have a peace, this world can never give,
"Wonderful peace, for now in Christ I live.
"From condemnation He has made me free,
"What a wonder-working power, in the Blood of Calvary."

"I have a hope, my Lord will surely come,
"All His redeemed ones shall be gathered home.
"With Him in Glory evermore to be,
"Then we'll praise Him for the Blood, that was shed on Calvary."

CHAPTER 30

(1) "AND YOU SHALL MAKE AN ALTAR TO BURN INCENSE UPON: OF SHITTIM WOOD SHALL YOU MAKE IT.

(2) "A CUBIT SHALL BE THE LENGTH THEREOF, AND A CUBIT THE BREADTH THEREOF; FOURSQUARE SHALL IT BE: AND TWO CUBITS SHALL BE THE HEIGHT THEREOF: THE HORNS THEREOF SHALL BE OF THE SAME.

(3) "AND YOU SHALL OVERLAY IT WITH PURE GOLD, THE TOP THEREOF, AND THE SIDES THEREOF ROUND ABOUT, AND THE HORNS THEREOF; AND YOU SHALL MAKE UNTO IT A CROWN OF GOLD ROUND ABOUT.

(4) "AND TWO GOLDEN RINGS SHALL YOU MAKE TO IT UNDER THE CROWN OF IT, BY THE TWO CORNERS THEREOF, UPON THE TWO SIDES OF IT SHALL YOU MAKE IT; AND THEY SHALL BE FOR PLACES FOR THE STAVES TO BEAR IT WITHAL.

(5) "AND YOU SHALL MAKE THE STAVES OF SHITTIM WOOD, AND OVERLAY THEM WITH GOLD.

(6) "AND YOU SHALL PUT IT BEFORE THE VEIL THAT IS BY THE ARK OF THE TESTIMONY, BEFORE THE MERCY SEAT THAT IS OVER THE TESTIMONY, WHERE I WILL MEET WITH YOU.

(7) "AND AARON SHALL BURN THEREON SWEET INCENSE EVERY MORNING: WHEN HE DRESSES THE LAMPS, HE SHALL BURN INCENSE UPON IT.

(8) "AND WHEN AARON LIGHTS THE LAMPS AT EVENING, HE SHALL BURN INCENSE UPON IT, A PERPETUAL INCENSE BEFORE THE LORD THROUGHOUT YOUR GENERATIONS.

(9) "YOU SHALL OFFER NO STRANGE INCENSE THEREON, NOR BURNT SACRIFICE, NOR A MEAT OFFERING; NEITHER

SHALL YOU POUR DRINK OFFERING THEREON.

(10) "AND AARON SHALL MAKE AN ATONEMENT UPON THE HORNS OF IT ONCE IN A YEAR WITH THE BLOOD OF THE SIN OFFERING OF ATONEMENTS: ONCE IN THE YEAR SHALL HE MAKE ATONEMENT UPON IT THROUGHOUT YOUR GENERATIONS: IT IS MOST HOLY UNTO THE LORD."

The overview is:

1. Verses 1 through 10 proclaim the command to make the Altar of Incense.

2. The Priests were to *"burn sweet incense"* every morning and evening. Constantly the Lord is making intercession for us and constantly we should praise His Name, morning and evening.

3. Verse 9 speaks of *"strange incense."* This speaks of incense that was poured on coals of fire that didn't come from the Brazen Altar, or else, incense made of ingredients other than those given by the Lord. When we trust in anything other than Christ and Him Crucified, we are in essence offering *"strange incense,"* which God can never accept, and which will ultimately bring spiritual death.

THE ALTAR OF INCENSE

Verses 1 through 3 read: *"And you shall make an Altar to burn Incense upon: of Shittim Wood shall you make it.*

"A cubit shall be the length thereof, and a cubit the breadth thereof: foursquare shall it be: and two cubits shall be the height thereof: the horns thereof shall be of the same.

"And you shall overlay it with pure gold, the top thereof, and the sides thereof round about, and the horns thereof; and you shall make unto it a crown of gold round about."

Back in Chapter 25, instructions were given to Moses as it regards the Ark of the Covenant, the Table of Shewbread, and the Golden Lampstand. The latter two were in the Holy Place, and the Ark of the Covenant was in the Holy of Holies. It has been conjectured as to why the Holy Spirit didn't give the dimensions for the Altar of Incense when the instructions were given regarding the Table and the Lampstand.

As well, instructions for the Brazen Altar were given in Chapter 27, but no mention was made there of the Brazen Laver, which was the second Vessel outside of the Tabernacle, actually the one which sat immediately in front of the Door. It instead is detailed in this Thirtieth Chapter, along with the Altar of Incense.

We know that every single word in the Bible was given by the Holy Spirit, and of course we speak of the original Text. We know as well that the order of material given in each Book was superintended by the Holy Spirit also. All of this means that it is error free. Now when we use that term, *"error free,"* we're not speaking of the translation, or of the Chapter and Verse divisions. Those things were done by men, and are subject to mistakes. But we do claim the original Text to be perfect.

Unfortunately, there aren't any original Texts left, but there are thousands of copies of those Texts, some reaching back to the year A.D. 300. Scholarship says if there are as many as 10 copies of any proven work, it is looked at as authentic. The truth it, there are more copies of the Scriptures, both Old and New Testaments, than any other Work in existence. So the authenticity of the original Text is not in doubt.

I have read behind quite a number of authors. And to be frank, there are about as many reasons given for the manner in which the Holy Spirit presented the Text, as there are writers. We do know that the Holy Spirit saved the instructions for these two vessels for this particular Chapter, but no one really knows why. Any suggestion is speculation at best; considering that, I will remain silent as it regards this particular question.

INCENSE

The Golden Altar was designed by the Lord for the purpose of burning Incense. In the latter part of this Chapter, the various spices are given which make up the Incense, to which we will address ourselves at that time.

The purpose and reason for this Incense was to symbolize the Intercession made by our Lord on a continuing basis, for all Believers, and for all time, since the Cross. The Cross is what made the Intercessory Work of our Lord possible. Paul said: *"He* (Christ) *ever liveth to make Intercession for them"* (Heb. 7:25-26).

Even though I have already addressed the Intercession of Christ, due to its vast significance, please allow my repetition!

Just how does the Lord make intercession for Believers, of which the Golden Altar was a type?

Just this morning I was reading behind one of the great Theologians, who is now with the Lord. He was stating that Christ prays for us before the Throne of God, etc. In other words, this was the manner of His Intercession.

That is incorrect, and it is incorrect simply because the necessity of doing such would mean that the work carried out at the Cross was unfinished.

To properly understand the Intercession of Christ, we must first understand that His Work at the Cross was total and complete. It was a Finished Work, and that term means exactly what it says. When Jesus said, *"It is finished,"* this meant that the price had been fully and totally paid for the Redemption of humanity, at least for those who will believe (Jn. 19:30; 3:16).

Even though we have a perfect Redemption, we as the receptacles of this perfect Redemption aren't perfect within ourselves. In fact, all Believers still have a *"sin nature"* (Rom. 6:1-2, 6-7, 10-13, etc.).

In every Scripture we've given, where the word *"sin"* is used, in the original Text, it had in front of that particular word what is referred to as *"the definite article."* In other words, it said, *"the sin,"* which refers to the sin nature.

I realize that many Preachers claim that Believers no longer have a sin nature. If that is the case, then the Holy Spirit wasted a lot of time explaining to us through Paul as to how to have victory over this malady of darkness. Victory is achieved by the Believer, even as we've already stated innumerable times, understanding that all comes through the Cross, which must ever be the object of our Faith.

Understanding that we definitely do have a sin nature, the truth is, all Believers still fail the Lord, at one time or the other. The Bible doesn't teach sinless perfection.

NOTES

As it regards sin on the part of the Christian, John told us to *"sin not."* But then he said, *"If any man sin, we have an advocate with the Father, Jesus Christ the Righteous:*

"And He is the propitiation for our sins: and not for ours only, but also for the sins of the whole world" (I Jn. 2:1-2).

Christ is our Advocate, and our Mediator. As such, He is our High Priest. Paul said of Him: *"We have such an High priest, Who is set on the Right Hand of the Throne of the Majesty in the Heavens"* (Heb. 8:1). This High Priest is *"Holy, harmless, undefiled, separate from sinners, and made higher than the heavens"* (Heb. 7:26).

Understanding that as our High Priest, He intercedes for us, exactly how does He do such?

Paul also said: *"For Christ is not entered into the holy places made with hands, which are the figures of the true; but into Heaven itself, now to appear in the Presence of God for us"* (Heb. 9:24).

In this Twenty-fourth Verse, we are told how He makes intercession for us. *"Now to appear in the Presence of God for us,"* tells us that His appearance in the Presence of God, which refers to the Throne of God, guarantees intercession. He doesn't have to do anything. He doesn't have to pray, He doesn't have to ask, He has to perform no work. His appearance proclaims the fact that He has paid the price, and that God has accepted this price.

THE SIZE OF THE ALTAR

This Altar was 18 inches long and 18 inches wide. It was three feet high. As is obvious, it was foursquare.

In its application to Christ Himself, this tells us that His intercession embraces all His people.

It was made of *"Shittim Wood,"* i.e., *"indestructible wood,"* which, as we've already stated, portrayed the humanity of Christ in all its perfection.

This indestructible wood was overlaid with pure gold, which typified His Deity. This is the God-Man, Jesus Christ!

It had four horns protruding outward from all corners, once again portraying power. Our dominion is in Christ, and Christ Alone!

However, the dominion of which we speak, and which the Altar represents, is a total dominion, hence the horns on all four corners. This means that the Believer should be victorious in every capacity of his or her life. What Jesus did at the Cross was complete, and that means a complete victory.

We can have that complete victory if we look exclusively to Him, ever making the Cross the object of our Faith. That being the case, the Holy Spirit guarantees the victory (Rom. 8:11).

There was a *"crown of gold"* all the way around the Altar, which signified the Kingly Character of Christ.

THE STAVES

Verses 4 and 5 read: *"And two golden rings shall you make to it under the crown of it, by the two corners thereof, upon the two sides of it shall you make it; they shall be for places for the staves to bear it withal.*

"And you shall make the staves of Shittim Wood, and overlay them with gold."

There were to be two golden rings on the Altar, one on either side, through which staves could be placed in order for the Altar to be carried, when the camp was moved.

"Two" is the number of *"witness,"* and speaks of the Holy Spirit Who is here to testify of Christ (Jn. 15:26). The *"staves"* of wood, overlaid with gold, intimate that it is the God-Man Whom the Spirit is here to glorify.

These *"rings"* and *"staves"* are as well a proclamation of our pilgrim character, in other words, that this world is not our home, but that we are merely traveling through.

THE POSITION OF THE ARK

Verse 6 reads: *"And you shall put it before the Veil that is by the Ark of the Testimony, before the Mercy Seat that is over the Testimony, where I will meet with you."*

The *"Golden Ark"* was positioned in the Holy Place, immediately in front of the beautiful *"Veil,"* which hid the Holy of Holies, which contained the Ark of the Covenant. Consequently, only the Veil separated the Altar of Incense from the Ark of the Covenant, which meant they were only a very few feet apart.

NOTES

Even though the *"Veil"* separated these two Sacred Vessels, the very fact that they were this close tells us that the separation was only temporary. Upon the Cross being a fact, the Veil, spiritually speaking, was removed, and now Christ our Intercessor is in the very Presence of God, all on our behalf. In a sense of the word, and presently speaking, the Altar of Incense, signifying Intercession and worship, has now become one with the Ark of the Covenant, signifying the Throne of God (Heb. 1:3; 9:24).

(The *"Ark of the Testimony"* is the Ark of the Covenant, and the *"Testimony"* is the Ten Commandments.)

THE BURNING OF INCENSE

Verses 7 and 8 read: *"And Aaron shall burn thereon sweet incense every morning: when he dresses the lamps, he shall burn incense upon it.*

"And when Aaron lights the lamps at evening, he shall burn incense upon it, a perpetual incense before the LORD throughout your generations."

The incense was to be burned morning and evening, perhaps at about the time that the sacrifices were offered, which would have been 9 a.m. and 3 p.m. It was burned in the following manner:

The Priest who was officiating, would take one or more coals of fire from the Brazen Altar, place them on top of the Golden Altar, and then pour incense over the coals, with the resultant cloud and fragrance filling the Holy Place. As stated, it represented the intercession of the Lord Jesus Christ, our Great High Priest, on behalf of the Saints. Of course, this was only a symbol, and actually a symbol in two ways:

1. Jesus had not yet gone to the Cross; therefore, the representation was future.

2. And as would be obvious, this which the Priests did twice a day were only symbolic.

Also, we might quickly add, that the Intercession of Christ presently includes the making of our worship acceptable unto the Lord.

If it is to be noticed, before this worship could commence, the Sacrifices had to be offered, which meant in symbolic form, that His precious Blood had first to be poured out before the Spirit could be poured forth; and sinners must first be washed from their sins in that precious Blood before they can receive the Holy Spirit. Thus cleansed and sanctified, worship at the Golden Altar of Incense is possible; but not otherwise.

Concerning this, Williams said: *"God having brought His people out of Egypt established the Brazen Altar outside the Tabernacle and the Golden Altar inside; and appointed a Mediator to maintain relationship with Him* (the High Priest) *in order that He might dwell among them. The Brazen Altar symbolized the perfection of Christ's sacrifice for sin; the Golden Altar, the preciousness of His Person. The Altar itself spoke of Jesus, and what He would do on the Cross to redeem humanity. The wood and the gold prefigured His humanity and Deity; it was crowned; and it had staves to bear it so as to be the day and night companion of a pilgrim people. The Incense burned upon it spoke of Him. Aaron himself, in his robes of glory, pictured Him; and the light of the Golden Lampstand foretold Him, Who being the light of that world that needs no sun came into this world to be its Light."*

Williams went on to say: *"The fire of Verse 7 and the blood of Verse 10, teach that there can be no acceptable worship apart from Atonement."*

The word *"perpetual"* in Verse 8 doesn't mean for eternity, but rather as long as the First Covenant lasted. When Jesus came, He, being the Incense, fulfilled the symbol, with there being no more need for such presently because Christ is now in Heaven appearing in the Presence of God on our behalf (Heb. 9:24).

STRANGE INCENSE

Verse 9 reads: *"You shall offer no strange incense thereon, nor Burnt Sacrifice, nor Meat Offering; neither shall you pour Drink Offering thereon."*

We know from Leviticus 16:12-13 and Numbers 16:46 that the coals of fire placed on the Golden Altar were taken from off the Brazen Altar, where the Sin-Offering was consumed. There was, therefore, a very intimate connection between the two Altars: the activities of the latter based squarely upon those of the former; in other words, the Incense was kindled upon that fire which had first fed upon the sacrifice; thus identifying the Priest's service at both Altars.

Concerning this, Pink said: *"This, in figure, tells us that our Great High Priest expects no blessings which His Blood has not purchased, and expects pardon from Divine Justice for no sins for which Faith has not been evidenced. And incidentally, the measure of the blessings which are given is God's estimate of the life which He gave. In His Mediatorial Prayer in John, Chapter 17, before He presents a single petition concerning His people, Christ said, 'I have glorified You on the Earth; I have finished the work which You gave Me to do' (Jn. 17:4). That was the foundation on which all His pleas were based and urged."*

So it is imperative that three things be done here:

1. The coals of fire had to come from the Brazen Altar, which represented the Cross of Calvary. This tells us, and as stated, that all intercession and all worship, at least that which is recognized by the Lord, are based squarely on what Jesus did at the Cross. If any other type of fire would be used on that Golden Altar, the Priests would be stricken dead, just as in fact, Nadab and Abihu actually were (Lev. 10:1-2).

Unfortunately, untold thousands of Churches have abandoned the Cross, and are in fact, offering *"strange fire."* Spiritual death is the result!

2. The coals of fire had to be placed on the Golden Altar, which refers to a Faith and dependence placed in Christ, as it regards His Intercession, all on our behalf. And let it quickly be stated, such cannot be done, and in fact, such will not be done, unless there is Faith in what the Brazen Altar represents. As stated, the two, the Brazen Altar and its Finished Work, and the Golden Altar, and its intercessory work go hand-in-hand.

3. The Incense poured on the burning coals had to be that which the Lord had designed, and no other kind. Anything else would be called *"strange incense,"* and would be unacceptable! As we will later study, the

Incense was made of ingredients which pictured and portrayed Christ in His Atoning Work. That and that alone is what God will recognize. Once again, we speak exclusively of the Cross! Everything is based on the Cross! Everything stems from the Cross!

THE BLOOD

Verse 10 reads: *"And Aaron shall make an Atonement upon the horns of it once in the year with the blood of the Sin Offering of Atonements: once in the year shall he make Atonement upon it throughout your generations: it is most holy unto the LORD."*

This particular Verse speaks of the Great Day of Atonement, which took place once a year. On that day, the High Priest would sacrifice a clean animal, remove his garments of glory and beauty, and take the blood of that slain victim into the Holy of Holies, where it would be applied to the Mercy Seat on the Ark of the Covenant. Actually he would do this twice, once for himself because he was a sinful man, despite the fact that he was the High Priest, and once for the nation of Israel. Always, their Salvation, as well as our Salvation, was based on Blood Atonement.

As well, he would apply some of that *"blood"* on the *"horns"* of the Golden Altar. So in essence, we have two factors at work here:

1. The blood applied to the Mercy Seat speaks of our Salvation, in other words, what makes the Born-Again experience possible!

2. The blood applied to the horns of the Golden Altar at that particular time spoke of our Sanctification. To which we've already alluded, horns in the Bible represent dominion. The very fact that these horns are on the Golden Altar tells us that the Lord expects us to have dominion over every single sin, barring none! As well, this can be done only by one's Faith in Christ and what Christ did for him at the Cross, symbolized by the blood.

SACRIFICES AND THE ALTAR OF INCENSE

All of this which we've just said concerning the blood applied to the horns once a year harks back to Verse 9. The Lord through Moses informed the Priests that no *"Burnt Sacrifice, or Meat Offering, or Drink Offering,"* were to be used on the Altar of Incense. Why?

Sin in its totality is handled at the Brazen Altar, i.e., *"the Cross."* The Altar of Incense, which speaks of intercession and worship, is not meant to atone for sin. So when the Believer thinks that he can overcome sin by increasing his prayer life, by fasting more, by witnessing to souls, by giving more money, by experiencing manifestations of any kind, while all of these things may be good in their own right, he will find that his faith is wrong, and he will never find victory in that manner. His faith regarding overcoming strength must ever rest in the Cross of Christ; that alone will guarantee victory. But this is a lesson that the modern Church seems not to have learned. It keeps trying to gain victory in all the wrong ways. And because it's so important, let's say it again:

All victory is found at the Cross, and the Cross alone! The coals of fire taken from the Brazen Altar to the Altar of Incense speaks of a work already done and completed. For us to add to that, we are in essence saying that what was done at the Brazen Altar was not enough, in effect, that the Sacrifice was not enough, which as should be obvious, God can never honor. This comes back to what Paul said:

"That if you be circumcised, Christ shall profit you nothing" (Gal. 5:2).

It's not what one does, but rather what one believes. And if one believes right, then one will do right.

(11) "AND THE LORD SPOKE UNTO MOSES, SAYING,

(12) "WHEN YOU TAKE THE SUM OF THE CHILDREN OF ISRAEL AFTER THEIR NUMBER, THEN SHALL THEY GIVE EVERY MAN A RANSOM FOR HIS SOUL UNTO THE LORD, WHEN YOU NUMBER THEM; THAT THERE BE NO PLAGUE AMONG THEM, WHEN YOU NUMBER THEM.

(13) "THIS THEY SHALL GIVE, EVERY ONE WHO PASSES AMONG THEM WHO ARE NUMBERED, HALF A SHEKEL AFTER THE SHEKEL OF THE SANCTUARY: (A SHEKEL IS TWENTY GERAHS:) AN HALF SHEKEL SHALL BE THE OFFERING OF THE LORD.

(14) "EVERY ONE WHO PASSES AMONG THEM WHO ARE NUMBERED FROM TWENTY YEARS OLD AND ABOVE, SHALL GIVE AN OFFERING UNTO THE LORD.

(15) "THE RICH SHALL NOT GIVE MORE, AND THE POOR SHALL NOT GIVE LESS THAN HALF A SHEKEL, WHEN THEY GIVE AN OFFERING UNTO THE LORD, TO MAKE AN ATONEMENT FOR YOUR SOULS.

(16) "AND YOU SHALL TAKE THE ATONEMENT MONEY OF THE CHILDREN OF ISRAEL, AND SHALL APPOINT IT FOR THE SERVICE OF THE TABERNACLE OF THE CONGREGATION; THAT IT MAY BE A MEMORIAL UNTO THE CHILDREN OF ISRAEL BEFORE THE LORD, TO MAKE AN ATONEMENT FOR YOUR SOULS."

The diagram is:

1. Verses 11 through 16 portray the ransom or redemption money. The money was a special tax of registration in Israel as a memorial or reminder of God's provision of Redemption and of their obligation under the terms of the Mosaic Covenant.

2. Verse 13 says, *"Half a shekel."* It was no doubt silver. Hence, silver, and all of the Tabernacle furniture and fittings mean Redemption.

3. Verse 15 says, the *"rich"* and the *"poor"* would give the same. This placed every man in Israel on an equal footing in relation to God and obligation to the Law.

4. It should be noted that the money did not actually redeem the soul. Not even the blood of bulls and other animals did this (Heb. 10:4; I Pet. 1:18-23), but rather Faith in the Blood of the coming Redeemer of which the blood of sacrifices was a type.

A RANSOM FOR HIS SOUL

Verses 11 and 12 read: *"And the LORD spoke unto Moses, saying,*

"When you take the sum of the Children of Israel after their number, then shall they give every man a ransom for his soul unto the LORD, when you number them; that there be no plague among them, when you number them."

When a census was to be taken of the Children of Israel, a half shekel of silver was to be given to the Sanctuary by each person. It was referred to as *"a ransom for his soul."* And it was to be given *"unto the Lord."* If they refused, sickness could come upon them, etc. So what did all of this mean?

How do we correlate this command with Isaiah 55:1, *"without money and without price"*? As well, does this command given by the Lord to Moses in any way clash with I Peter 1:18, *"Forasmuch as you know that you were not redeemed with corruptible things as silver and gold"*?

1. The numbering of Israel was very important, because these were God's people. And they were His people by virtue of a tremendous price that would be paid. Admittedly, it wasn't paid yet, but it definitely would be paid, and by that we refer to Christ and His Atoning Death on the Cross of Calvary. So this tells us that each person who knows the Lord is very important in God's sight, and very important as well to this world. Jesus said: *"You are the light of the world. A city that is set on an hill cannot be hid"* (Mat. 5:14).

2. The half shekel as a ransom for the soul was of silver, and was probably just a small amount of silver, that came close to a certain weight. Coins were not minted at that particular time. Silver in the Old Testament is a type of Redemption, just as gold is a type of Deity. So the half shekel of silver was to be paid by each person every time a census was taken in the country, that they may remember that they have been bought with a price. The idea is not presented here that this half shekel of silver ransomed the soul, but rather it was meant to be a reminder or a symbol of what they already had in Christ. It wasn't meant to purchase their Salvation, for not even the blood of the animal sacrifices could do that. It was strictly to be a *"memorial"* even as Verse 16 proclaims.

SILVER AND THE CROSS

As silver pointed toward Redemption, it at the same time pointed to the Cross, because there is no Redemption outside of the Cross. So in essence, the ransom money was labeled that because they were to remember that they had been ransomed. They had been slaves in Egypt, but had been set free by the

Power of God. In fact, it was the Passover which effected their release, which was a Type of Christ and what He would do at the Cross.

In fact, almost everything they did as it pertains to the Lord reminded the Children of Israel of the Cross. Of course, they would not have thought of Redemption in that capacity, for the term *"Cross"* would have been an unknown factor to them. But the fact of Redemption, and the great price that would have to be paid for Redemption to be effected, were ever before them. I speak of the sacrifices that were an ongoing affair in their daily lives. Placing their hands on the head of the animal, and confessing their sins upon him, thereby transferring the guilt to an innocent victim, and then above all, killing the little animal, seeing its hot blood poured out, and then parts of its body placed on the Altar and being consumed by fire, presented itself as a vivid illustration, to say the least! So the ransom money played a part in this as well, even as in some sense, everything that was done pointed to the Redeemer, and the manner in which Redemption would be effected.

THE SHEKEL OF THE SANCTUARY

Verse 13 reads: *"This they shall give, every one who passes among them who are numbered, half a shekel after the shekel of the Sanctuary: (a shekel is twenty gerahs:) an half shekel shall be the offering of the LORD."*

The *"shekel of the Sanctuary"* referred to a standard weight. In other words, the measure was decided by the Sanctuary, meaning in essence, that it was decided by Christ. He set the price, which He would pay Himself, of which this shekel of the Sanctuary was a token. It was letting Israel know that a price had to be paid for the ransom of the soul, and what they were required to give, as little as it was, was to help them realize the great price that was to be paid.

In our money presently, it was probably worth about five dollars.

THE SAME PRICE

Verses 14 through 16 read: *"Every one who passes among them who are numbered, from twenty years old and above, shall give an offering unto the LORD.*

"The rich shall not give more, and the poor shall not give less than half a shekel, when they give an offering unto the LORD, to make an Atonement for your souls.

"And you shall take the Atonement money of the Children of Israel, and shall appoint it for the Service of the Tabernacle of the Congregation; that it may be a memorial unto the Children of Israel before the LORD, to make an Atonement for your souls."

As we've stated, the ransom money of a half shekel, referred to as *"Atonement money,"* was strictly for a *"memorial."* It certainly didn't mean that one could purchase Salvation, and especially considering the paltry amount.

One must understand that before the Cross, things were not so clear cut as they are presently. It would seem in some ways, especially considering the Sacrifices, that the Redemption Plan would have been even more obvious; however, as graphic as were those particular examples, the details of the Cross were still in shadow and type. The Cross, as an accomplished fact, speaks for itself, and needs no buttressing of any nature. But even now, it must be taught and preached constantly, or else the enemy of the souls of men will quickly snatch away this foundation truth of the entirety of the Bible.

(17) "AND THE LORD SPOKE UNTO MOSES, SAYING,

(18) "YOU SHALL ALSO MAKE A LAVER OF BRASS, AND HIS FOOT ALSO OF BRASS, TO WASH WITHAL: AND YOU SHALL PUT IT BETWEEN THE TABERNACLE OF THE CONGREGATION AND THE ALTAR, AND YOU SHALL PUT WATER THEREIN.

(19) "FOR AARON AND HIS SONS SHALL WASH THEIR HANDS AND THEIR FEET THEREAT:

(20) "WHEN THEY GO INTO THE TABERNACLE OF THE CONGREGATION, THEY SHALL WASH WITH WATER, THAT THEY DIE NOT; OR WHEN THEY COME NEAR TO THE ALTAR TO MINISTER, TO BURN OFFERING MADE BY FIRE UNTO THE LORD:

(21) "SO THEY SHALL WASH THEIR HANDS AND THEIR FEET, THAT THEY DIE NOT: AND IT SHALL BE A STATUTE

FOREVER TO THEM, EVEN TO HIM AND TO HIS SEED THROUGHOUT THEIR GENERATIONS."

The exegesis is:

1. Verses 17 through 21 speak of the *"Laver of brass."* It is a type of the Word of God.

2. Verses 19 through 21 say that the Priests, including the High Priest, must wash their *"hands"* as well as their *"feet"* before going into the *"Tabernacle of the Congregation,"* or to offer Burnt-Offerings on the Brazen Altar. This was mandatory, even with the penalty of death, if they ignored this command.

The *"hands"* spoke of *"doing,"* as the *"feet"* spoke of *"going."* We as Believers need the constant application of the Word.

3. The Laver was made solely of copper, with the exterior highly burnished. So the Priests saw their reflection in the water, as well as in the copper. Likewise, the Child of God sees himself in the Word of God, or at least he will, if he is honest with himself.

THE LAVER OF COPPER

Verses 17 and 18 read: *"And the LORD spoke unto Moses, saying,*

"You shall also make a Laver of copper, and his foot also of copper, to wash withal: and you shall put it between the Tabernacle of the Congregation and the Altar, and you shall put water therein."

Whereas the Brazen Altar was made of indestructible wood and overlaid with copper, the *"Laver"* was made of nothing but copper. (Even though the King James translators used the word *"brass,"* it should have been translated *"copper,"* simply because brass is a mixture of metals, of which such metallurgy was not known at that time. The original Text did not use the word *"brass."*)

Measurements for all of the vessels were given, with the exception of the Brazen Laver and the Golden Lampstand. The Brazen Altar had rings and staves for carrying it; the Laver had none. The Brazen Altar was to be covered when Israel journeyed, but nothing is said of this regarding the Laver. The Altar was for fire; the Laver for water.

It sat between the Brazen Altar and the Tabernacle, thereby stating by its very presence that cleansing from daily defilement must be engaged by the Priests before they entered the Tabernacle. The Laver alone, which was a type of the Word of God, was able to effect such cleansing. The idea is this, at least as it regards modern Believers:

It is the Word of God, of which the Laver was a type, which tells us what is right and what is wrong, and how we can be cleansed from all wrong. The Laver testifies that the Believer doesn't have to get saved over and over again, of which the Brazen Altar was a type, but that cleansing can be effected on a daily basis, even an hourly basis, by the Word of God. It tells us what to do, which the next few Verses proclaim, and which cleansing will be effected. One might say that the Brazen Altar was for the sinner; the Brazen Laver for the Saint. The former testified of the Blood of Christ; the latter, of the Word of God; the former cleansed the conscience; the latter, the conduct (Williams).

WATER AND NOT BLOOD

If it is to be noticed, water and not blood was to be the element appointed and used for the purification of the Priests. It was plainly a figure of the written Word of God. The Psalmist said: *"Wherewithal shall a young man cleanse his way? By taking heed thereto according to Thy Word"* (Ps. 119:9). Jesus said: *"Now you are clean through the Word which I have spoken unto you"* (Jn. 15:3). The Disciples didn't need to be saved, that having already been accomplished, but they definitely needed to be cleansed, and on a constant basis, as we shall shortly see.

THE WASHING

Verses 19 through 21 read: *"For Aaron and his sons shall wash their hands and their feet thereat:*

"When they go into the Tabernacle of the Congregation, they shall wash with water, that they die not; or when they come near to the Altar to minister, to burn offering made by fire unto the LORD:

"So they shall wash their hands and their feet, that they die not: and it shall be a Statute forever to them, even to him and to his seed throughout their generations."

The Brazen Altar and the Brazen Laver must not be confused; and yet, I'm concerned that they are repeatedly confused with many, if not most Christians.

Verse 19 tells us that Aaron and his sons had to wash their hands and their feet every time they went into the Tabernacle to perform their duties. However, they didn't have to offer up a lamb every time they did this. The Brazen Altar was a figure of Regeneration; the Brazen laver typified the Christian's need of daily cleansing.

We have a portrayal of this in John, Chapter 13. It is the example of Jesus washing the feet of the Disciples.

As Jesus began to wash the feet of the Disciples, Peter said to Him, *"You shall never wash my feet."* The answer of our Lord was very cryptic. He said: *"If I wash you not, you have no part with Me."*

Then Peter, in typical fashion, answered, *"Lord, not my feet only, but also my hands and my head.*

"Jesus said to him, 'He who is washed, needs only to wash his feet'" (Jn. 13:8-10).

THE FEET AND THE HANDS

The Exodus Text tells us that the Priests had to wash both their hands and their feet, but Jesus says here that it is only the feet that need to be washed. Why the difference?

Christ wasn't attempting to institute an Ordinance, which some have tried to claim. Some have thought that a foot-washing Service denoted humility, and should thereby be carried out on a regular basis. That's not what Jesus was teaching.

To institute such an Ordinance, which we do not find in the Book of Acts, which is an account of the Early Church, while Paul did mention the washing of the feet of the Saints by widows, he wasn't speaking of an Ordinance, but rather of service being rendered and performed (I Tim. 5:10). To make an Ordinance out of this takes us back to the Law, which Jesus has fulfilled, and which we must not do.

Jesus mentioned only the feet, while the Priests, as stated, had to wash both hands and feet. The reason is this:

The hands signify *"doing,"* and in Christ, relative to what He did at the Cross, all has been done. So, to wash the hands, symbolically speaking, would in effect state that Christ hadn't paid the price, etc.

As is obvious, the feet are symbolic of our daily walk before the Lord. It concerns our everyday living, in other words, how we order our behavior. Considering that we are living in a defiled world, mixing with unbelievers who are perpetually defiled, states that our *"walk,"* symbolized by the feet, must ever be corrected and cleansed. This is done by a constant application of the Word of God, which keeps us walking in a straight path, and as well, which cleanses our walk.

THE WORD OF GOD

The mere reading of the Word, although necessary, is not enough within itself. We must understand what it means, and then apply it to our hearts and lives, which the Holy Spirit will definitely do, if we are sincere before the Lord.

Just having the Brazen Laver there was not enough within itself. The Priests had to wash constantly, and this speaks of every time they went into the Tabernacle, showing the constant need. That's one of the reasons that Jesus said that we must *"take up our cross daily"* (Lk. 9:23).

A PERSONAL EXPERIENCE

In October 1991, broken of heart, not knowing what to do, I laid my Bible on the table in front of me, and said to a group of friends who were there that day, *"I don't know the answer to a victorious life, but I do know that the Bible contains that answer. And by the Grace of God, I'm going to find it."*

I was exactly right! The answer totally and completely was and is found in the Word of God, and is found only in the Word of God. And I never will forget that day, that the Holy Spirit began to open it up to me. I found it in the Sixth Chapter of Romans. To be sure, I had read that Chapter at least 50 times, but until the Holy Spirit began to reveal to me exactly what it meant, it had no affect on my life. But when He began to show me what it meant, which was the same as *"washing,"* then I found a victory that was so total and so complete, as to defy all description.

In effect, the Brazen Laver showed the Priests the effect that the Brazen Altar had on their lives. The Altar was a symbol of the Covenant, which was sealed in blood, typified by the slain lamb.

The Word (Brazen Laver) now tells me constantly what the great Sacrifice of Christ means to me, and means to me on a daily, even minute-by-minute basis. The understanding provided by the Word cleanses my walk and as well, keeps it straight. And unless that water (Word) is applied on a constant basis, the results will not be pleasant.

SPIRITUAL DEATH

Verse 20 says, *"They shall wash with water, that they die not."* I should think that we ought to understand that we're dealing with something here that is very serious.

Let us understand that no dimensions were given as it regards the size of the Laver. I'm sure the Lord gave a particular size to Moses, according to which the Laver would be constructed, but Moses didn't give it to us. Why?

The idea is twofold:

1. There was a constant need for the Laver, even as there is a constant need for the Word.

2. It doesn't really matter how dirty the feet and the hands of the Priests became; there was to be enough water to accomplish the task, which demanded that the Laver be constantly replenished, which is the reason no size or dimension are given to us.

If the Priests didn't follow this command concerning constant washings, as given by the Lord, they could be stricken dead. It is the same presently.

If the Believer ignores what the Word of God tells us as it regards cleansing respecting our daily walk, spiritual death can definitely be the result.

As I dictate these notes on June 16, 2002, the news is filled with reports concerning the Catholic dilemma regarding the terrible sin and crime of pedophilia. Unfortunately, this problem, and others similar, is not confined to the Catholic Church. It is pandemic in Protestant circles as well!

The following is what I believe the Lord has spoken to my heart.

NOTES

THE CROSS IS THE DIVIDING LINE

Through this Ministry and others, the Lord is making plain and clear the Message of the Cross (I Cor. 1:17-18, 21, 23; 2:2, 5). Constant Faith in the Cross, to which the Word clearly points us, is demanded, or else, as stated, spiritual death will be the result.

This means that the Church must heed what Paul taught, which is the meaning of the New Covenant, which is the meaning of the Cross, which is the Gospel (I Cor. 1:17).

Satan has been very successful in the last few decades at pushing the Church away from the Cross; consequently, and as previously stated, the modern Church little knows where it's been, where it is, or where it's going. False doctrine is rampant, and getting worse! The answer to all of this is the Cross and the Cross alone.

If this *"Light"* is rejected, spiritual death will be the result, which will play out to spiritual wreckage, which has already begun. Most modern Christians have little idea as to how to live a Godly life. In fact, the subject is rarely broached any more from behind modern pulpits; and if it is, the poor people are mostly given the wrong instructions. In other words, they are directed to *"law,"* which only tends to exacerbate the problem. Most Christians live a life of spiritual failure, with some of them trying very hard not to do so, but it seems the harder they try, the worse the situation becomes. Why?

Even though their motives and intentions are good, they are trying to do something which, in the first place, Christ has already done, and which they cannot do anyway. The Brazen Laver (the Word) alone holds the answer to their dilemma, but regrettably and sadly, they don't understand the Word.

The Cross of Christ, to which the Word directs us (Rom. 6:3-14; 8:1-2, 11; Eph. 2:13-18; Col. 2:14-15), is the dividing line between the True Church and the apostate church. Let us look at that a little closer.

INSTITUTIONALIZED RELIGION

I was asked the other day to define institutionalized religion. The explanation is this:

It is the part of the Church world, which incorporates almost all, which has as the object of its Faith something other than the

Cross. In other words, the people are directed toward the particular Denomination, or toward a doctrine which is unbiblical. That is the difference.

I certainly do not mean to say that every religious Denomination in the world presents as the object of Faith something other than the Cross. But I do know that most in the United States and Canada fall into that category. For the most part, the situation comes to the place of spiritual disaster very slowly; consequently, the people are somewhat like a frog placed in a pot of water, with the pot then placed over the fire. The water heats up slowly, so slowly in fact, that the frog little notices it, until it's too late. In other words, it acclimates itself to the changing temperature, until finally the water is boiling, and the frog dies. It is the same with Believers. Things change slowly, so slowly in fact, that the change is difficult to notice. But then spiritual death starts taking place all around them, and many wonder as to the cause.

The Believer had better inspect minutely as to what is the object of his Faith. Paul said: *"Examine yourselves, whether you be in the Faith; prove your own selves. Know ye not your own selves, how that Jesus Christ is in you, except you be reprobates?"* (II Cor. 13:5).

Each person claiming Christ had better take a minute inventory of the Church with which he is involved, irrespective as to what it is. Is the Cross of Christ being preached? That means the Cross of Christ must ever be the object of our Faith! If other things are being touted, such a Believer had best seek the Lord earnestly, about changing Churches. The Believer is by and large going to be what he hears preached from behind the pulpit, wherever that pulpit might be. That needs qualification!

If error is being preached, and the person continues to listen to such error, they will ultimately become that error. It is inevitable! However, if the Truth is being preached, and even if the person constantly hears the Truth, it doesn't necessarily hold that they will heed that Truth. The opportunity is present, but regrettably, all do not heed. That's why Jesus constantly said: *"He who has ears to hear, let him hear"* (Mat. 11:15; 13:9, 43; Mk. 4:9).

NOTES

Faith is the key (Gal. 5:6), but it must be Faith in the correct object, and that object must be the Cross of Christ, which in effect, is the story of the Word of God (I Cor. 1:17; Col. 2:14-15).

(22) "MOREOVER THE LORD SPOKE UNTO MOSES, SAYING,

(23) "TAKE YOU ALSO UNTO YOU PRINCIPAL SPICES, OF PURE MYRRH FIVE HUNDRED SHEKELS, AND OF SWEET CINNAMON HALF SO MUCH, EVEN TWO HUNDRED AND FIFTY SHEKELS, AND OF SWEET CALAMUS TWO HUNDRED AND FIFTY SHEKELS,

(24) "AND OF CASSIA FIVE HUNDRED SHEKELS, AFTER THE SHEKEL OF THE SANCTUARY, AND OF OIL OLIVE AN HIN:

(25) "AND YOU SHALL MAKE IT AN OIL OF HOLY OINTMENT, AN OINTMENT COMPOUND AFTER THE ART OF THE APOTHECARY: IT SHALL BE AN HOLY ANOINTING OIL.

(26) "AND YOU SHALL ANOINT THE TABERNACLE OF THE CONGREGATION THEREWITH, AND THE ARK OF THE TESTIMONY,

(27) "AND THE TABLE AND ALL HIS VESSELS, AND THE CANDLESTICK AND HIS VESSELS, AND THE ALTAR OF INCENSE,

(28) "AND THE ALTAR OF BURNT OFFERING WITH ALL HIS VESSELS, AND THE LAVER AND HIS FOOT.

(29) "AND YOU SHALL SANCTIFY THEM, THAT THEY MAY BE MOST HOLY: WHATSOEVER TOUCHES THEM SHALL BE HOLY.

(30) "AND YOU SHALL ANOINT AARON AND HIS SONS, AND CONSECRATE THEM, THAT THEY MAY MINISTER UNTO ME IN THE PRIEST'S OFFICE.

(31) "AND YOU SHALL SPEAK UNTO THE CHILDREN OF ISRAEL, SAYING, THIS SHALL BE AN HOLY ANOINTING OIL UNTO ME THROUGHOUT YOUR GENERATIONS.

(32) "UPON MAN'S FLESH SHALL IT NOT BE POURED, NEITHER SHALL YOU MAKE ANY OTHER LIKE IT, AFTER THE COMPOSITION OF IT: IT IS HOLY, AND IT SHALL BE HOLY UNTO YOU.

(33) "WHOSOEVER COMPOUNDS ANY

LIKE IT, OR WHOSOEVER PUTS ANY OF IT UPON A STRANGER, SHALL EVEN BE CUT OFF FROM HIS PEOPLE."

The structure is:

1. The ointment set out the spiritual and personal perfections of Christ.

2. The ointment was not to be imitated, nor poured upon man's flesh. Spiritual graces cannot be imitated, nor can they be given to men *"in the flesh."*

3. The *"principal spices"* were types of Christ, in His Mediatorial, Intercessory Work.

THE PRINCIPAL SPICES

Verses 22 through 24 read: *"Moreover the LORD spoke unto Moses, saying,*

"Take you also unto you principal spices, of pure myrrh five hundred shekels, and of sweet cinnamon half so much, even two hundred and fifty shekels, and of sweet calamus two hundred and fifty shekels,

"And of cassia five hundred shekels, after the shekel of the Sanctuary, and of oil olive an hin."

There were four principal spices selected by the Holy Spirit, which were to be mixed with olive oil. These spices all represented Christ, as it regards His Mediatorial, Intercessory Work. Of course, the olive oil represents the Holy Spirit, which was upon Christ without measure. The results of this mixture were that it was called *"an Holy Anointing Oil."* We will see momentarily that for which it was to be used.

The four principal spices are:

1. *"Pure myrrh"*: This came from a dwarf tree that grew in Arabia. The gum exudes from the trunk either spontaneously or through incisions made for the purpose. This typifies Christ Who was pierced for us, from Whose wounds there flowed a sweet smelling savour to God. Incidentally, these spices were probably given to the Children of Israel by the Egyptians, upon them leaving that particular land.

The amount to be used was *"five hundred shekels."* A shekel is thought of now as a coin, but during the time of Moses, it was looked at as a weight. Coinage was not adopted until about 400 B.C., approximately 1,000 years after Moses. In the terms of money, a gold shekel was worth about $325 in today's money (2002), and a silver shekel was worth about five dollars. However, as the *"shekel"* was used in Exodus, it pertained to weight only, and not value. So there must have been about 500 ounces used of *"pure myrrh."* How much it would have been worth in money, we have no way of knowing, but it must have been very valuable, probably worth as much as $50 an ounce. Considering the weight, quite a bit was produced.

2. *"Sweet cinnamon"*: Cinnamon was said, at least at that time, to be a far rarer spice than myrrh. It is the inner bark or rind of a tree allied to the laurel, which by and large grows in India, parts of China, and Ceylon.

3. *"Sweet calamus"*: This came from aromatic reeds, which grew in Mesopotamia, India, Arabia, and parts of the area which would shortly be known as *"Israel."*

4. *"Cassia"*: This comes from the inner bark of a tree distinct from the cinnamon tree, and is a native of India, Java, and the Malay Peninsula.

5. *"Olive Oil"*: The above spices mixed with olive oil would, no doubt, have given the mixture a particular aroma, etc. This was what the Holy Spirit desired because it was to represent Christ in His Atoning, Mediatorial, and Intercessory Work.

All of these spices were extracted from particular trees, and in one case, a particular reed. Without going into detail as to how the spice was brought about, suffice to say, there had to be a cutting or crushing, or both, in order to concoct this principal spice. Such proclaimed the fact that the great Work carried out by Christ on the Cross of Calvary was not done, even as it could not be done, by fiat. There had to be a price that was paid, and that price was the Cross. There *"He was wounded for our transgressions, He was bruised for our iniquities: the chastisement of our peace was upon Him; and with His stripes we are healed"* (Isa. 53:5).

And of course, the *"olive oil"* mixed with the spices typified the Holy Spirit, Who empowered Christ, and was actually the means by which He performed all of His miracles and healings, etc. (Lk. 4:18-19). In fact, the Holy Spirit led Him and guided Him to such an extent that He even told Christ the moment that He was to die (Heb. 9:14).

HOLY ANOINTING OIL

Verses 25 through 30 read: *"And you shall make it an oil of holy ointment, an ointment compound after the art of the apothecary: it shall be an holy anointing oil.

"And you shall anoint the Tabernacle of the congregation therewith, and the Ark of the Testimony,

"And the Table and all his Vessels, and the Lampstand and his Vessels, and the Altar of Incense,

"And the Altar of Burnt Offering with all his Vessels, and the Laver and his foot.

"And you shall sanctify them, that they may be most holy: whatsoever touches them shall be holy.

"And you shall anoint Aaron and his sons, and consecrate them, that they may minister unto Me in the Priest's Office."*

If it is to be noticed, every single thing about the Tabernacle, all its Vessels, and all the Priests, were to be anointed with this *"holy anointing oil."* All of this was typical of the Holy Spirit.

Before the Cross, due to the fact that the blood of bulls and goats could not take away sin, the sin debt still remained outstanding over every single individual, even the Godliest (Heb. 10:4). Consequently, the Holy Spirit could not come in and dwell permanently within the hearts and lives of Believers, even the Godliest, even though He was with them. This is why Jesus said to His Disciples shortly before His Crucifixion: *"And I will pray the Father, and He shall give you another Comforter, that He may abide with you forever:

"Even the Spirit of Truth; Whom the world cannot receive, because it sees Him not, neither knows Him: but you know Him; for He dwells with you, and shall be in you"* (Jn. 14:16-17).

If it is to be noticed, Jesus spoke of the Holy Spirit dwelling with the Saints, and of course this was before the Cross, but after the Cross, He said, *"He shall be in you."*

When Jesus died on the Cross, the sin debt was forever paid, hence John introducing Christ by saying, *"Behold the Lamb of God, which taketh away the sin of the world"* (Jn. 1:29).

NOTES

The blood of bulls and goats could not take away sin, but Jesus took it all away, meaning that there is no more claim that Satan has against the Child of God.

THE NECESSITY OF THE HOLY SPIRIT

As Believers, the Holy Spirit is to lead us and guide us in all things (Jn. 16:13-14). In fact, we are to so walk after the Spirit that every single thing we do is instigated by the Holy Spirit. If not, this means that it is of the flesh, which also means that it is not recognized by God. Without the leading, guidance, and empowerment of the Spirit, we can do nothing for the Lord. The quicker we learn this, the better everything will be.

If there is a sin of the Church, this is it! I'm speaking of Believers attempting to function without the leading and guidance of the Holy Spirit.

THE HOLY SPIRIT AT CONVERSION

As should be obvious, the moment the believing sinner comes to Christ, at that moment, the Holy Spirit comes into his heart and life, and comes in to dwell permanently (Jn. 3:5-8; 14:16). However, there is a vast difference in the Believer being *"born of the Spirit"* than *"baptized with the Spirit."* Without the Spirit Baptism, the Holy Spirit is severely limited as to what He can do in one's heart and life. In fact, the Baptism with the Holy Spirit is as revolutionary to the Believer as Salvation is to the sinner.

THE BAPTISM WITH THE HOLY SPIRIT, AN EXPERIENCE WHICH FOLLOWS SALVATION

We believe and teach, according to the Word of God, that the Baptism with the Holy Spirit is an experience distinct and separate from Salvation. It doesn't make one more saved, nor is it meant to do so. In fact, the Baptism with the Holy Spirit has nothing to do with one being saved. One is saved simply by trusting Christ, and what He has done for us at the Cross (Rom. 10:9-13; Eph. 2:8-9). In fact, the Baptism with the Spirit is given to us for power (Acts 1:8), in order to carry out the Work of the Lord.

To prove that the Baptism with the Spirit is an experience separate and apart from

Salvation, which in fact follows Salvation, please note the following Scriptures:

COMMANDED THEM

Just before His Ascension, Christ addressed His followers. He said:

"And, being assembled together with them, commanded them that they should not depart from Jerusalem, but wait for the Promise of the Father, which, saith He, you have heard of Me.

"For John truly baptized with water, but you shall be baptized with the Holy Spirit not many days hence" (Acts 1:4-5).

Now please note, the Master was talking to people who were already saved. And as well, please notice that He *"commanded them."* In other words, this was not a suggestion!

In effect, He was telling them, do not go and try to preach the Gospel, build Churches, or do anything for Me, until you are first *"baptized with the Holy Spirit."*

DAY OF PENTECOST

Acts, Chapter 2 tells us of the initial filling of the Believers on the Day of Pentecost. Now please understand, these individuals who were filled were already saved. Actually, it included all of the Disciples, with the exception of Judas, with Matthias having taken his place.

SAMARITANS

Acts, Chapter 8 gives us the account of Philip going down to the city of Samaria, and there *"preaching Christ unto them."* In essence, the Scripture tells us that many were saved. The Scripture says: *"The people with one accord gave heed unto those things which Philip spoke, hearing and seeing the miracles which he did"* (Acts 8:5-6).

But the Scripture also says that *"when the Apostles which were at Jerusalem heard that Samaria had received the Word of God, they sent unto them Peter and John:*

"Who, when they were come down, prayed for them, that they might receive the Holy Spirit."

It then said: *"For as yet He was fallen upon none of them: only they were baptized in the Name of the Lord Jesus.*

"Then laid they their hands on them, and they received the Holy Spirit" (Acts 8:14-17).

As is obvious, these individuals were not baptized with the Holy Spirit the moment they were saved, which holds true for all Believers, proving that this is an experience separate and distinct from Salvation.

PAUL

Acts, Chapter 9 tells of the Salvation and Holy Spirit Baptism of the Apostle Paul.

Paul was saved on the road to Damascus. This is proven by several things.

After he was saved and then went into the city, the Scripture says that the Lord spoke to a man by the name of Ananias, and told him to go and pray for Paul.

Obeying the Lord, the Scripture says: *"Ananias went his way, and entered into the house; and putting his hands on him said, Brother Saul* (proving he had already been saved), *the Lord, even Jesus, Who appeared unto you in the way as you came, has sent me, that you might receive your sight, and be filled with the Holy Spirit"* (Acts 9:17).

Once again, it is obvious here that the Holy Spirit was received by Paul after he was saved.

CORNELIUS AND HIS HOUSEHOLD

Acts, Chapter 10 records the conversion and Spirit Baptism of Cornelius and his household. The Chapter tells of Peter being led by the Lord to go to this particular house, and to preach to these Gentiles. Peter obeyed the Lord, and the Scripture says: *"While Peter yet spake these words, the Holy Spirit fell on all them which heard the word"* (Acts 10:44).

These Gentiles were saved, and then moments later were baptized with the Holy Spirit.

EPHESIANS

Acts, Chapter 19 records the Ephesians being baptized with the Spirit. Incidentally, this was about 20 years after the Day of Pentecost.

Paul was with these people, whomever they may have been. And the Scripture says: *"He said unto them, Have you received the Holy Spirit since you believed? And they said unto him, We have not so much as heard whether there be any Holy Spirit"* (Acts 19:1-2).

The Scripture says that he then explained to them what the Holy Spirit Baptism was, and then he *"laid his hands upon them, (and) the Holy Spirit came on them"* (Acts 19:6).

Some may argue that these individuals had never been saved; however, the Scripture refers to these 12 men as *"Disciples,"* which means, *"learners, and followers of Christ"* (Acts 19:1). Actually, every time in the Book of Acts the word *"Disciples"* is used, it always, and without exception, refers to followers of Christ, meaning that such individuals have been saved.

Yes, they had already been saved, but they had not heard anything about the Baptism with the Holy Spirit. And it should be noted that Paul, speaking with them, detected that they were bereft of this glorious gift. In other words, it was obvious, and in fact, it is always obvious as it regards those who have not been baptized with the Spirit.

So we find that after the Day of Pentecost, the converts of Philip were baptized with the Holy Spirit some days or weeks after their initial conversion. Paul was filled with the Spirit, some three days after his conversion. Cornelius was filled immediately after his conversion. The followers of John at Ephesus were filled some years after they had been Born-Again.

But all of this Scripturally proves that the Baptism with the Spirit is an experience distinct from Salvation, and in fact, which always follows Salvation. In fact, Jesus, in addressing this subject, said: *"Even the Spirit of Truth; Whom the world cannot receive, because it sees Him not, neither knows Him"* (Jn. 14:17). In other words, one has to first be Born-Again, before one can be baptized with the Holy Spirit.

THE INITIAL, PHYSICAL EVIDENCE THAT ONE HAS BEEN BAPTIZED WITH THE HOLY SPIRIT

We believe and teach, according to the Scriptures, that there is an initial evidence that one has been baptized with the Holy Spirit, and that it is physical, and that it is the same with all. We believe that evidence is speaking with other tongues as the Spirit of God gives the utterance.

There are five accounts given, to which we have actually already alluded, of Believers being baptized with the Spirit. These accounts are as follows:

1. We go again to the Day of Pentecost. The Scripture plainly says of these Believers: *"And they were all filled with the Holy Spirit, and began to speak with other tongues, as the Spirit gave them utterance"* (Acts 2:4).

As it was the Feast of Pentecost, Jews had come to Jerusalem from all over the Roman Empire, which they always did at these particular Feast times. All of these Jews, of course, spoke Hebrew, as well as Greek. As well, most of them spoke dialects of the particular part of the world in which they then lived. In other words, most of them, if not all, knew at least three languages.

Luke, in writing the account, listed many of these places (Acts 2:7-12), proclaiming as to how they had heard the individuals who had been baptized with the Spirit, speaking in all of these different languages. Yes, tongues are always a language. They are never incoherent babble, or mere gibberish, etc.

2. Chapter 8 of Acts, which was some months after the Day of Pentecost, records the second incident of Believers being baptized with the Spirit. The Scripture doesn't say anything about them speaking with other tongues, but it doesn't say that they didn't speak with tongues. In fact, it really didn't say anything about what happened when they received the Holy Spirit.

But we do know that something happened to these individuals, because the Bible says that a man by the name of *"Simon saw that through laying on of the Apostles' hands* (that) *the Holy Spirit was given"* (Acts 8:18).

The Scripture says that he offered them money, if they would bestow upon him the power to lay hands on people, with them receiving the Spirit.

The Scripture further says: *"Peter said unto him, Your money perish with you, because you have thought that the Gift of God may be purchased with money.*

"You have neither part nor lot in this matter" (Acts 8:19-21).

Two things here are brought to light: A. I hardly think that Simon the sorcerer would have tried to purchase a gift which manifested nothing; and, B. The phrase, *"You have neither part nor lot in this matter,"* actually says in the Greek, *"You have neither part nor lot in this utterance."*

Every evidence is the Samaritans spoke with other tongues when they were filled with the Spirit, exactly as the Believers did on the Day of Pentecost.

3. When Ananias laid hands on Paul, as recorded in Acts, Chapter 9, and he was baptized with the Spirit, the Scripture once again doesn't say anything about what happened. It just says that he was *"filled with the Holy Spirit"* (Acts 9:17).

Even though it doesn't say anything here about Paul speaking with tongues, or not speaking with tongues, the Apostle later said: *"I thank my God, I speak with tongues more than you all"* (I Cor. 14:18).

And as should be obvious, Paul wasn't speaking of a linguistic ability; he was speaking of the utterance of tongues, which accompanies every Spirit-baptized Believer.

4. Acts, Chapter 10, which we've already addressed, records Cornelius and those with him who were saved when Peter preached to them, and were also baptized with the Holy Spirit. The Scripture says: *"For they heard them speak with tongues, and magnify God"* (Acts 10:46).

When Peter was later explaining the conversion and Spirit Baptism of Cornelius and his household, he said: *"And as I began to speak, the Holy Spirit fell on them, as on us at the beginning . . . Forasmuch then as God gave them the like gift as He did unto us"* (Acts 11:15, 17).

5. Acts, Chapter 19 plainly says that when the 12 Ephesians were baptized with the Holy Spirit, when Paul prayed for them, that *"they spoke with tongues, and prophesied"* (Acts 19:6).

So of the five times where it is recorded that Believers were baptized with the Holy Spirit, three of those five times record that they spoke with tongues. And the other two strongly implied such. In fact, Paul devoted an entire Chapter as to how tongues were to be used (I Cor., Chpt. 14). As well, the Book of Acts proclaims the fact that the Early Church was a Pentecostal Church. They believed and taught that Jesus saves, Jesus baptizes with the Holy Spirit, Jesus heals, and Jesus is coming again.

WHAT GOOD ARE TONGUES?

1. In the first place, tongues were given by God. Anything He gives is of tremendous benefit and value to those who are privileged to receive. To be sure, He gives nothing that is useless.

2. The Scripture says: *"We do hear them speak in our tongues the wonderful Works of God"* (Acts 2:11). Anything that speaks the wonderful Works of God, which one does when worshipping in tongues, has to be labeled as good.

3. The Prophet Isaiah said: *"For with stammering lips and another tongue will He speak to this people.*

"To whom He said, This is the rest wherewith you may cause the weary to rest; and this is the refreshing: yet they would not hear" (Isa. 28:11-12).

Incidentally, Paul quoted this Verse in I Corinthians 14:21.

The Holy Spirit through the Prophet plainly tells us that speaking with other tongues brings about a *"rest,"* and brings about a *"refreshing."* If more Christians worshipped in tongues, and did so often, I think the Scripture plainly tells us here that there will be less stress, less emotional disturbances, less concern, less worry, and anxiety. The Lord said it, and I believe it, and in fact, I have proven it in my own life.

THE DIFFERENCE IN TONGUES AS THE INITIAL PHYSICAL EVIDENCE, AND TONGUES AS A GIFT

In essence, everything the Lord gives us is a *"gift."* But we will distinguish them, to make it easier to understand.

As stated, every Believer, upon being baptized with the Holy Spirit, speaks with other tongues as the Spirit of God gives the utterance. Consequently, the Believer should continue to worship the Lord in tongues the rest of his life. This can be done in prayer, and can even be done silently, as the Spirit of God moves upon the individual. In fact, the Spirit-filled Believer can utilize worship in tongues any time He so desires. However, this of which we now speak is not the *"Gift of Tongues,"* which Paul specified in

I Corinthians 12:8-10. The *"Gift of Tongues"* outlined in these Verses has to do with the nine Gifts of the Spirit. They are to be used in a certain way, and at a certain time. But that is different than one's prayer language of tongues, which we have previously been discussing. Many of our non-Pentecostal friends get the two confused. They think that every time tongues are uttered, there has to be an interpretation. That is incorrect.

An interpretation is expected, only when the Gift of Tongues is in operation, not in the worship that one does for their own edification (I Cor. 14:4). The two, prayer language, and the Gift of Tongues, should not be confused.

The Holy Spirit outpouring in these last days is a fulfillment of Bible Prophecy (Joel 2:23; Acts 2:16-21). There is no excuse for any Believer not to receive. In fact not to do so is to ignore the command given by Christ (Acts 1:4). Modern Believers not being baptized with the Spirit can only be because of lethargy or unbelief.

To be baptized with the Holy Spirit, thereby living the Spirit-filled life, i.e., *"walking after the Spirit,"* is the most wonderful experience that one could ever know.

THE FLESH

Verses 31 through 33 read: *"And you shall speak unto the Children of Israel, saying, This shall be an holy anointing oil unto Me throughout your generations.*

"Upon man's flesh shall it not be poured, neither shall you make any other like it, after the composition of it: it is holy, and it shall be holy unto you.

"Whosoever compounds any like it, or whosoever puts any of it upon a stranger, shall even be cut off from his people."

Under the Old Testament economy, only the Priests among the people were to be anointed with this *"holy anointing oil."* Typically, this means that only the people of God, those in Christ, can have the Holy Spirit.

The graces of the Spirit can never be connected with *"the flesh."* Now what do we mean by that?

It is Jesus Who baptizes with the Holy Spirit. One might say it this way:

At conversion, the Holy Spirit baptizes us into Christ (Rom. 6:3-5). After conversion, it is Christ Who baptizes us into the Spirit (Mat. 3:11).

In a sense, every single Spirit-filled Believer is *"anointed by the Spirit"* (I Jn. 2:27).

Also, the *"Anointing"* has to do with the Call of God upon a particular heart and life.

When David was called of God, the Scripture says that *"Samuel took the horn of oil, and anointed him in the midst of his brethren: and the Spirit of the LORD came upon David from that day forward"* (I Sam. 16:13).

In fact, every person in history, from day one, unto the present time, who has been called by the Lord for a particular task, is as well anointed by the Lord for that task. The degree of help given by the Holy Spirit as it regards the Anointing is predicated on the consecration or the lack thereof concerning the individual in question (Acts 13:1-4).

As well, no human being can transfer the Anointing from himself, that is if he has any, to someone else. This particular modern practice is facetious to say the least, and bordering on blasphemy at the most. One individual attempting to pass the Anointing to another is the same as the holy anointing oil being put on an individual's flesh, in Old Testament times. The Lord plainly stated that if such happened, the person attempting to do such a thing, *"shall even be cut off from his people,"* i.e., *"will lose his soul"* (Ex. 30:33). That Verse says as well that it must not be *"put upon a stranger,"* which refers to someone who doesn't know God.

(34) "AND THE LORD SAID UNTO MOSES, TAKE UNTO YOU SWEET SPICES, STACTE, AND ONYCHA, AND GALBANUM; THESE SWEET SPICES WITH PURE FRANKINCENSE: OF EACH SHALL THERE BE A LIKE WEIGHT:

(35) "AND YOU SHALL MAKE IT A PERFUME, A CONFECTION AFTER THE ART OF THE APOTHECARY, TEMPERED TOGETHER, PURE AND HOLY:

(36) "AND YOU SHALL BEAT SOME OF IT VERY SMALL, AND PUT OF IT BEFORE THE TESTIMONY IN THE TABERNACLE OF THE CONGREGATION, WHERE I WILL MEET WITH YOU: IT SHALL BE UNTO YOU MOST HOLY.

(37) "AND AS FOR THE PERFUME

WHICH YOU SHALL MAKE, YOU SHALL NOT MAKE TO YOURSELVES ACCORDING TO THE COMPOSITION THEREOF: IT SHALL BE UNTO YOU HOLY FOR THE LORD.

(38) "WHOSOEVER SHALL MAKE LIKE UNTO THAT, TO SMELL THERETO, SHALL EVEN BE CUT OFF FROM HIS PEOPLE."

The overview is:

1. The spices mentioned in Verse 34 are those which made up the Incense that was poured upon the coals of fire, which were brought from the Brazen Altar, and placed on the Altar of Incense.

2. There were four spices, *"Stacte, Onycha, Galbanum, and pure Frankincense."* These four typified the Intercessory Work of Christ, on our behalf.

3. Verse 36 says that it was *"beaten very small,"* referring to the fact that Intercession is needed in every capacity, even for small things that we would think little or nothing about. God can honor nothing but perfection, and perfection is found only in Christ. Faith in Him Alone guarantees us His perfection.

THE INCENSE

Verse 34 reads: *"And the LORD said unto Moses, take unto you sweet spices, Stacte, and Onycha, and Galbanum; these sweet spices with pure Frankincense: of each shall there be a like weight."*

These were the spices, properly mixed together, which made the Incense, that was to be poured over the coals of fire on the Altar of Incense, brought from the Brazen Altar. This was to be done twice a day, which would fill the Holy Place with a smoke of sorts, which had a very pleasant aroma. It was meant to typify the Intercession of our Lord, after His Work was complete on the Cross, and He had appeared in the Presence of God, all on our behalf, which has now been done, and is being done. In other words, His Intercession continues unto this hour, and will ever continue.

The particular spices were meant to typify His Work as it regards Intercession. But all of it was tied to the Cross, hence the coals of fire from the Brazen Altar, which Altar typified His Crucifixion.

Without going into detail as it regards the origin of these particular spices, suffice to say, they each typified Christ, and were, as the spices for the holy anointing oil, produced as a result of cutting, or crushing, or both.

It seems that of each of these spices, they were all to be used in the same amount.

A PERFUME

Verse 35 reads: *"And you shall make it a perfume, a confection after the art of the apothecary, tempered together, pure and holy."*

Pulpit says, *"Like the holy oil, the Incense was to be artistically compounded by one accustomed to deal with such ingredients."*

As is surely noticed, the directions for all of this were explicit. All of it represented Christ, and so nothing was to be done after human ingenuity.

The concoction was to be a *"perfume,"* which referred to the fact that the smoke from the Incense would have a very pleasant aroma, and would fill the Holy Place, typical of the Intercession of Christ before the Father, once again, all on our behalf. The very word *"perfume"* presents the fact that God the Son will always represent us in a very positive manner, as of course, should be obvious. Irrespective of our conduct on Earth, that which comes to the Father as it regards the Son, is always of a very pleasant aroma, one might say!

BEFORE THE TESTIMONY

Verse 36 reads: *"And you shall beat some of it very small, and put of it before the Testimony in the Tabernacle of the Congregation, where I will meet with you: it shall be unto you most holy."*

The idea seems to be that some was to be kept before the Altar of Incense constantly, so a supply would ever be available. As well, it presents the fact that Christ *"ever lives to make Intercession for us"* (Heb. 7:25).

Considering that the Incense was very near the vicinity of the Divine Presence rendered it *"most holy."*

Again we emphasize that our conduct may not at all times be *"most holy,"* but to be sure, His Intercession for us is always *"most holy."*

SENTENCE OF DEATH

Verses 37 and 38 read: *"And as for the*

perfume which you shall make, you shall not make to yourselves according to the composition thereof: it shall be unto you holy for the LORD.

"Whosoever shall make like unto that, the smell thereto, shall even be cut off from his people."

If this *"perfume"* was ever used to be placed on the physical bodies of individuals, those persons were to be executed by Civil authorities. It was *"most holy,"* and was to be used exclusively for its designed purpose.

Before the fact, and we speak of before the Cross, it is not certain as to exactly how much the Priests knew, as it regards the antitype. It is easy for us to look back now and discern, at least to a point, as to the meaning of these *"types."* But before the fact, it would not have been so simple. They were given the Word of the Lord, that it was *"most holy,"* and that it was never to be used other than for that which it had been designed. To ignore this command, to be sure, would ensure the Judgment of God.

PRESENT APPLICATION

How does the *"type"* hold as it regards present Believers?

I think it can be summed up in our taking of the Lord's Supper.

The Holy Spirit through Paul plainly tells us, *"Wherefore whosoever shall eat this bread, and drink this cup of the Lord, unworthily, shall be guilty of the Body and Blood of the Lord.*

"But let a man examine himself, and so let him eat of that bread, and drink of that cup.

"For he who eats and drinks unworthily, eats and drinks damnation to himself, not discerning the Lord's Body.

"For this cause many are weak and sickly among you, and many sleep" (I Cor. 11:27-30).

We must never forget that Intercession by Christ is made for us, and done so continuously, on the basis of the Sacrifice of Christ, typified by the coals of fire from the Brazen Altar. So what does all of this mean as it was given to Paul?

God doesn't demand perfection from us, although we are definitely to strive to walk as close to Him as is humanly possible. But He does demand one thing, and He demands that exclusively:

When we take the Lord's Supper, eating the bread, which typifies His broken Body, and drinking of the cup (grape juice), which typifies His shed Blood, we are to ever remember that everything we have from Him is because of what He did at the Cross. In fact, the Cross of Christ is to be the object of our Faith at all times.

If we partake of the Lord's Supper, and our Faith is in other things, and irrespective as to what those other things might be, the Holy Spirit through Paul plainly tells us that such an attitude will bring sickness on the individual, and could even result in premature death. While the person will not lose their soul, the results of such action are definitely not what one would desire.

We are no longer under *"law"*; consequently, the soul is not lost. But still, even under Grace, the results of disobeying the Lord, especially as it regards the single-most important thing of all, our Faith in His Finished Work, cannot be pleasant!

I grieve presently as I observe Christians who are in deep trouble, but yet continue to reject the Cross. If the coals of fire were not brought from the Brazen Altar, death as well would be the result. It is no less presently! When our Faith is placed in something other than the Cross, the Intercession that Christ died to give us is cut off. The latter portion of Verse 38 says, *"Shall even be cut off from his people."* It was speaking there of the individual, but I'm speaking of Christ. We cut Him off by our faith being wrongfully placed, and as a result, He is cut off from representing us.

We must never forget that everything hinges on the Cross. It is there the price was paid, the Sacrifice was offered. The whole of the Work of God, the great Plan of God, centers up in the Cross. The whole of history before the Cross flowed toward that coming Sacrifice. The whole of history now flows from that completed Sacrifice. It is the Foundation of all doctrine, the story of the Bible. To be frank, if one has a wrong conception of the Cross, one will have a wrong conception in some manner of the entirety of the Word of God. To be wrong about the Cross is plainly to be wrong!

"There is a Fountain filled with Blood
"Drawn from Immanuel's veins,
"And sinners plunged beneath that Flood
"Lose all their guilty stains."

"The dying thief rejoiced to see
"That Fountain in his day,
"And there may I, though vile as he,
"Wash all my sins away."

"Dear dying Lamb, Thy precious Blood
"Shall never lose its power,
"Till all the ransomed Church of God
"Be saved to sin no more."

"E'er since by Faith I saw the stream
"Thy flowing wound supply,
"Redeeming love has been my theme
"And shall be till I die."

"When this poor lisping, stamm'ring tongue
"Lies silent in the grave,
"Then in a nobler, sweeter song,
"I'll sing Thy power to save."

CHAPTER 31

(1) "AND THE LORD SPOKE UNTO MOSES, SAYING,

(2) "SEE, I HAVE CALLED BY NAME BEZALEEL THE SON OF URI, THE SON OF HUR, OF THE TRIBE OF JUDAH:

(3) "AND I HAVE FILLED HIM WITH THE SPIRIT OF GOD, IN WISDOM, AND IN UNDERSTANDING, AND IN KNOWLEDGE, AND IN ALL MANNER OF WORKMANSHIP,

(4) "TO DEVISE CUNNING WORKS, TO WORK IN GOLD, AND IN SILVER, AND IN BRASS,

(5) "AND IN CUTTING OF STONES, TO SET THEM, AND IN CARVING OF TIMBER, TO WORK IN ALL MANNER OF WORKMANSHIP.

(6) "AND I, BEHOLD, I HAVE GIVEN WITH HIM AHOLIAB, THE SON OF AHISAMACH, OF THE TRIBE OF DAN: AND IN THE HEARTS OF ALL WHO ARE WISE HEARTED I HAVE PUT WISDOM, THAT THEY MAY MAKE ALL THAT I HAVE COMMANDED YOU;"

The exegesis is:

1. God calls individuals for the task at hand, even as He has a particular person for each and every work.

2. He gave them the Spirit of God, Who would help them accomplish the task. In other words, they were helped by the Holy Spirit.

3. We find from this that the Holy Spirit will help us in every participation, irrespective as to what it is, that is, if it's for the Glory of God, which means that we're doing what God wants us to do.

THE CALLING

Verses 1 and 2 read: *"And the LORD spoke unto Moses, saying,*

"See, I have called by name Bezaleel the son of Uri, the son of Hur, of the Tribe of Judah."

The Lord had a particular person for this work, exactly as He has a particular person for every work of the Kingdom. The Work of God is definitely not a volunteer program. Irrespective as to what it is the Lord has a work for every single Believer, always and without exception, it is a *"Calling!"* The problem is, we have so many who attempt to do that which the Lord has never called them to do. The result is always confusion, hurt, and an increase of problems.

It seems that *"Bezaleel"* was the *"grandson"* of Hur, who it is believed was the brother-in-law of Moses, having married his sister, Miriam.

As should be obvious by now, the choice of these principal workmen was that of God's, and not Moses'. The *"pattern"* for the Tabernacle and all of its accessories was given to Moses, but the building of the apparatus was to be done by another, one chosen by the Lord.

Bezaleel was of the Tribe of Judah, which means, *"praise."* It was the Kingly Tribe, from which Christ would come.

In a sense, Moses is a Type of Christ, with Bezaleel being a type of the Holy Spirit. Christ was the *"Pattern,"* and it was the business of the Holy Spirit to make of Him what was intended, i.e., *"the Saviour."*

THE SPIRIT OF GOD

Verse 3 reads: *"And I have filled him with the Spirit of God, in wisdom, and in understanding, and in knowledge, and in all manner of workmanship."*

Bezaleel, within himself, could not have carried forth this work. He had to have the Spirit of God in order to accomplish the task. And it is the same now with every single Believer, who is to satisfy the Call of God on their lives.

Before the Cross, all true Believers were in the Covenant; however, due to the fact that the Holy Spirit was limited as to His involvement, all didn't have a specific call. But since the Cross, and due to the fact that the Holy Spirit lives within the hearts and lives of all Believers, every single Believer has a call of some kind from the Lord. That *"Call"* is definitely not of the fivefold Ministry in every case (Eph. 4:11), but it does pertain to a function of some nature.

But to carry out that function, whether it's one of the fivefold callings, or otherwise, the Believer must have the empowerment of the Holy Spirit. Many take the Holy Spirit for granted, thinking that because He is present, He will just automatically do things. He won't!

The infilling of the Spirit provides potential, but potential only. For us to have His Leading, Guidance, Power, and Anointing, we must earnestly seek the Face of the Lord, making ourselves available for that which He desires to do. Unfortunately, there isn't a whole lot of consecration among most Christians; consequently, there isn't a lot of leading of the Spirit. But one thing is certain:

If we are to carry out the Work of God, we must, and without fail, have the Operation of the Holy Spirit within our lives. He Alone can give the wisdom, the understanding, and the knowledge that we need to carry out the task, whatever that task might be.

IN ALL MANNER OF WORKMANSHIP

Verses 4 and 5 read: *"To devise cunning works, to work in gold, and in silver, and in brass,*

"And in cutting of stones, to set them, and in carving of timber, to work in all manner of workmanship."

In this, we are made to see that the Holy Spirit can help us in whatever task is assigned to us.

When most people think of working for the Lord, they generally think of one of the fivefold Ministry Gifts. Or at the least, they think of music and singing, etc. However, the truth is according to the following:

If as a Believer we will earnestly seek the Lord as to what He desires that we do, and that's a prayer that He will definitely answer, and then we actively seek the help of the Spirit, that help will be forthcoming. Not only will it be forthcoming for that particular *"Calling,"* but the Holy Spirit will also help us in every other aspect of our life and living. In other words, if one is a carpenter, a truck driver, a plumber, a teacher, an accountant, or whatever, the Holy Spirit desires to be involved in that, and will definitely help; however, I firmly believe that such help is forthcoming only if we carry out the Will of God for our lives.

The Lord wants to bless us, and to be sure, He knows how to do all things, as should be obvious. He only desires that we ardently seek His Will, and do so in all things.

We must remember that we are bought with a price, which means that we belong to the Lord. Our every thought, so to speak, is to be of Him. We make a great mistake when we think that such a life is only for Preachers. It is for every Believer. And to be sure, such a life is the most fulfilling, the most rewarding, the most joyful that a life could ever be. In fact, it is the only joyful life there is.

Many laymen, especially those in business, tend to put their business first, which can spell disaster. God should be first, second, third, fourth, etc.

WISE HEARTED

Verse 6 reads: *"And I, behold, I have given with him Aholiab, the son of Ahisamach, of the Tribe of Dan: and in the hearts of all who are wise hearted I have put wisdom, that they may make all that I have commanded you."*

If it is to be noticed, the Lord said here *"wise hearted,"* instead of *"wise headed."* This means that the Holy Spirit functioned in the hearts of these individuals, helping them to do all that they were called to do.

Aholiab was *"of the Tribe of Dan."* Judah was the first Tribe, while Dan brought up the rear; thus, the entirety of Israel was represented here.

There is no doubt that there were other workmen included, but it was Bezaleel who was in charge, with Aholiab assigned to help him. As well, the Lord promised here that all who helped them, however many there were, they would be helped as well!

(7) "THE TABERNACLE OF THE CONGREGATION, AND THE ARK OF THE TESTIMONY, AND THE MERCY SEAT THAT IS THEREUPON, AND ALL THE FURNITURE OF THE TABERNACLE,

(8) "AND THE TABLE AND HIS FURNITURE, AND THE PURE LAMPSTAND WITH ALL HIS FURNITURE, AND THE ALTAR OF INCENSE,

(9) "AND THE ALTAR OF BURNT OFFERING WITH ALL HIS FURNITURE, AND THE LAVER AND HIS FOOT,

(10) "AND THE CLOTHS OF SERVICE, AND THE HOLY GARMENTS FOR AARON THE PRIEST, AND THE GARMENTS OF HIS SONS, TO MINISTER IN THE PRIEST'S OFFICE,

(11) "AND THE ANOINTING OIL, AND SWEET INCENSE FOR THE HOLY PLACE: ACCORDING TO ALL THAT I HAVE COMMANDED YOU SHALL THEY DO."

The composition is:

1. In Verses 7 through 11, the Holy Spirit is explicit concerning the exact items. Likewise, the Holy Spirit is that explicit regarding the Call of God that is placed upon people's hearts and lives.

2. I think it would go without saying that Bezaleel and Aholiab were extremely proficient in that which God, by His Spirit, had called them to do; however, if they had gone into other areas of service, it would have been without the help of the Spirit of God.

3. What a blessing it is to know the Call of God on our lives, and to function therein. In effect, that is the whole duty of man (Eccl. 12:13-14).

THE TABERNACLE

Verse 7 reads: *"The Tabernacle of the Congregation, and the Ark of the Testimony, and the Mercy Seat that is thereupon, and all the furniture of the Tabernacle."*

The Tabernacle is mentioned first, and then the Ark of the Covenant, along with the Mercy Seat. All of it, in one way or the other, represented Christ, in His Atoning, Mediatorial, and Intercessory Work. Consequently, Moses was under great restraint that he order Bezaleel, along with Aholiab, to minutely follow the pattern that was given. These men, who were given the Holy Spirit to help them carry out this formidable task, must make certain that the items were constructed correctly, and above all, that the pattern was followed to the proverbial *"T."*

Whereas these two men, along with all of their helpers, were responsible for this construction, in a sense, every single Believer presently falls into the same category. As previously stated, we as Believers have the Holy Spirit, and as such, He resides within our hearts and lives in order to carry out a specific purpose, and that purpose is *"Christlikeness."* Just exactly as to how this is to be done only He knows, as He carries out the Will of God (Rom. 8:26-29).

ALL THE FURNITURE

Verses 8 through 11 read: *"And the Table and his furniture, and the pure Lampstand with all his furniture, and the Altar of Incense,*

"And the Altar of Burnt Offering with all his furniture, and the Laver and his foot,

"And the cloths of service, and the holy garments for Aaron the Priest, and the garments of his sons, to minister in the Priest's Office:

"And the Anointing Oil, and sweet Incense for the Holy Place: according to all that I have commanded you shall they do."

As stated, every iota of the Tabernacle, along with all of its Sacred Vessels, was designed in totality to prefigure Christ. As also stated, it had to do with the Work of Christ which He would carry out when He came, as it regards the Cross, and all that would be accomplished there. In some way, every work of our Lord, and irrespective of its description, is based upon the Finished Work of the Cross. So the idea is this:

All that which the Holy Spirit desires to carry out in our respective lives is based squarely on the Finished Work of Christ. We are washed and cleansed from all our sins, typified by the Brazen Altar, and the sacrifices offered thereon. We wash daily with the Word, or at least we certainly should, typified by the Brazen Laver. We partake of the Bread of Life, typified by the Table of Shewbread; likewise, we are able to ascertain and understand all of this by the light of the Golden Lampstand. Christ makes intercession for us on a constant basis, all typified by the Altar of Incense, which pleasant aroma fills the Holy Place, due to the coals of fire brought from the Brazen Altar, typical of the Crucifixion of Christ. Due to what Christ accomplished at the Cross, the beautiful Veil has been permanently pulled aside, that we may enter boldly into the very Holy of Holies, into the very Presence of God, and do so at any time (Heb. 4:16).

Aaron the High Priest of Israel, due to a Better Covenant, has been replaced by our Great High Priest, the Lord Jesus Christ. In fact, the Tabernacle is now no more because it has all been fulfilled in Christ, with the very Heaven of the Heavens itself, taking its place (Heb. 8:1-6).

(12) "AND THE LORD SPOKE UNTO MOSES, SAYING,

(13) "SPEAK YOU ALSO UNTO THE CHILDREN OF ISRAEL, SAYING, VERILY MY SABBATHS YOU SHALL KEEP: FOR IT IS A SIGN BETWEEN ME AND YOU THROUGHOUT YOUR GENERATIONS; THAT YOU MAY KNOW THAT I AM THE LORD WHO DOES SANCTIFY YOU.

(14) "YOU SHALL KEEP THE SABBATH THEREFORE; FOR IT IS HOLY UNTO YOU: EVERY ONE WHO DEFILES IT SHALL SURELY BE PUT TO DEATH: FOR WHOSOEVER DOES ANY WORK THEREIN, THAT SOUL SHALL BE CUT OFF FROM AMONG HIS PEOPLE.

(15) "SIX DAYS MAY WORK BE DONE; BUT IN THE SEVENTH IS THE SABBATH OF REST, HOLY TO THE LORD: WHOSOEVER DOES ANY WORK IN THE SABBATH DAY, HE SHALL SURELY BE PUT TO DEATH.

(16) "WHEREFORE THE CHILDREN OF ISRAEL SHALL KEEP THE SABBATH, TO OBSERVE THE SABBATH THROUGHOUT THEIR GENERATIONS, FOR A PERPETUAL COVENANT.

(17) "IT IS A SIGN BETWEEN ME AND THE CHILDREN OF ISRAEL FOREVER: FOR IN SIX DAYS THE LORD MADE HEAVEN AND EARTH, AND ON THE SEVENTH DAY HE RESTED, AND WAS REFRESHED.

(18) "AND HE GAVE UNTO MOSES, WHEN HE HAD MADE AN END OF COMMUNING WITH HIM UPON MOUNT SINAI, TWO TABLES OF TESTIMONY, TABLES OF STONE, WRITTEN WITH THE FINGER OF GOD."

The diagram is:

1. What distinguishes God's people is participation in God's rest. Christ is God's rest (Heb., Chpt. 4).

2. The honor, or dishonor, done to the Sabbath was the test under Law. The honor, or dishonor, done to Christ, the test under Grace.

3. Death was the penalty of dishonoring the Sabbath; a similar penalty attaches to dishonoring Christ (Williams).

THE SABBATH

Verses 12 and 13 read: *"And the LORD spoke unto Moses, saying,*

"Speak you also unto the Children of Israel, saying, Verily My Sabbaths you shall keep: for it is a sign between Me and you throughout your generations; that you may know that I am the LORD Who does sanctify you."

Several things are said here:

1. Israel, even under the pain of death, as we shall see, was admonished to keep the Sabbath.

2. The Sabbath was to be a sign between God and Israel, which did not include the Gentile world, so would not include the Church, which would come about many centuries later.

3. The Sabbath, again as we shall see, was a day of rest, and not a day of worship.

4. Jesus fulfilled all of the Law when He came, including Sabbath keeping, which is now no more incumbent upon Believers.

5. Finally, all of this was a part of Israel's Sanctification process.

DEATH

Verses 14 and 15 read: *"You shall keep the Sabbath therefore; for it is holy unto you:*

every one who defiles it shall surely be put to death: for whosoever does any work therein, that soul shall be cut off from among his people.

"Six days may work be done; but in the seventh is the Sabbath of rest, holy to the LORD: whosoever does any work in the Sabbath day, he shall surely be put to death."

Picking up on the headings, the honor, or dishonor, done to the Sabbath was the test under Law. Now it is the honor, or dishonor, done to Christ, which is the test under Grace. If the Sabbath was purposely violated, death was the penalty. To my knowledge, there is no record that Israel ever carried out this particular penalty, even though they very well may have done so. But bringing it over to modern times, Christ is the true Sabbath, which it was always meant to be, and to dishonor Him for certain, brings spiritual death.

THE DISHONORING OF CHRIST

Regrettably, the sin of dishonoring Christ is carried out by the Church almost constantly! And how is it done?

Proper Faith in Christ and what He did at the Cross all on our behalf is the manner in which Christ is properly honored. But whenever the Church advocates a way other than the Cross, such constitutes a gross dishonoring of Christ. In fact, to minimize what He did for us at the Cross, which means to add to it, or take from it, or to change it in any manner, constitutes the greatest dishonoring of all, as should be obvious!

Such a position brings spiritual death, as it can only bring spiritual death!

REST

Verses 16 and 17 read: *"Wherefore the Children of Israel shall keep the Sabbath, to observe the Sabbath throughout their generations, for a perpetual Covenant.*

"It is a sign between Me and the Children of Israel forever: for in six days the LORD made Heaven and Earth, and on the seventh day He rested, and was refreshed."

The *"rest"* in which the Lord engaged after the six days of creation, and the Sabbath rest under Israel, were always meant to typify the *"rest"* which would be provided by Christ, because of what He did at the Cross. That's what Jesus was speaking of when He said: *"Come unto Me, all you who labor and are heavy laden, and I will give you rest.*

"Take My yoke upon you, and learn of Me; for I am meek and lowly in heart: and you shall find rest unto your souls" (Mat. 11:28-29). As we have stated, the Sabbath was not for worship, but rather for *"rest."* Now that Christ has come, the symbol is no longer needed, as should be obvious.

But the sad fact is, the far greater majority of the modern Church little understands this *"rest,"* rather continuing to try to earn whatever it is that they have from the Lord. Sinners try to earn Salvation, and the Church tries to earn Sanctification. Neither can be gained by that method. It is all by *"Faith,"* which refers to Faith in Christ and what He did at the Cross. When we speak of *"Faith,"* always, and without exception, we must understand that the object of Faith, which is so very, very important, without fail, must be Christ and the Cross. To attempt to have Faith in Christ alone, which means to push the Cross aside, concludes by the individual worshipping *"another Jesus"* (II Cor. 11:4).

If a Christian attempts to find *"rest"* by Sabbath keeping presently, rest will not be found, and that goes for any other similar effort. *"Rest"* is found only in Christ, which always refers to His great Sacrifice on the Cross of Calvary.

THE FINGER OF GOD

Verse 18 reads: *"And He gave unto Moses, when He had made an end of communing with him upon Mount Sinai, two Tables of Testimony, tables of stone, written with the Finger of God."*

Five Commandments were on one tablet of stone, and five were on the other.

The phrase, *"Written with the Finger of God,"* means that the Lord burned the words into the stone with His Own finger. In other words, it was supernaturally done. For 40 days Moses had been on the Mount receiving instructions from God. That those instructions closed with the giving of these two tables of stone is most significant.

On this Law, referred to as the *"Ten Commandments,"* (Ex. 20:2-17), is the foundation of all Law in the world. Without this

Law being administered in some way, chaos is the result. The more that a nation allows this Law to form their thinking, freedom and prosperity become the order. The further away from this Law, the opposite takes effect.

However, when we speak of the Law in this manner, we aren't speaking of the Church. In Christ, the Church is supposed to already be lawful. So the Law is only for the unlawful (I Tim. 1:9-10).

"Low in the grave He lay
"Jesus, my Saviour!
"Waiting for the coming day,
"Jesus, my Lord!"

"Vainly they keep His bed
"Jesus, my Saviour!
"Vainly they seal the dead
"Jesus, my Lord!"

"Death cannot keep its prey
"Jesus, my Saviour!
"He tore the bars away
"Jesus, my Lord!"

CHAPTER 32

(1) "AND WHEN THE PEOPLE SAW THAT MOSES DELAYED TO COME DOWN OUT OF THE MOUNT, THE PEOPLE GATHERED THEMSELVES TOGETHER UNTO AARON, AND SAID UNTO HIM, UP, MAKE US GODS, WHICH SHALL GO BEFORE US; FOR AS FOR THIS MOSES, THE MAN WHO BROUGHT US UP OUT OF THE LAND OF EGYPT, WE DO NOT KNOW WHAT IS BECOME OF HIM.

(2) "AND AARON SAID UNTO THEM, BREAK OFF THE GOLDEN EARRINGS, WHICH ARE IN THE EARS OF YOUR WIVES, OF YOUR SONS, AND OF YOUR DAUGHTERS, AND BRING THEM UNTO ME.

(3) "AND ALL THE PEOPLE BROKE OFF THE GOLDEN EARRINGS WHICH WERE IN THEIR EARS, AND BROUGHT THEM UNTO AARON.

(4) "AND HE RECEIVED THEM AT THEIR HAND, AND FASHIONED WITH A GRAVING TOOL, AFTER HE HAD MADE IT A MOLTEN CALF: AND THEY SAID, THESE BE YOUR GODS, O ISRAEL, WHICH BROUGHT YOU UP OUT OF THE LAND OF EGYPT.

(5) "AND WHEN AARON SAW IT, HE BUILT AN ALTAR BEFORE IT; AND AARON MADE PROCLAMATION, AND SAID, TOMORROW IS A FEAST TO THE LORD.

(6) "AND THEY ROSE UP EARLY ON THE MORROW, AND OFFERED BURNT OFFERINGS, AND BROUGHT PEACE OFFERINGS; AND THE PEOPLE SAT DOWN TO EAT AND TO DRINK, AND ROSE UP TO PLAY."

The structure is:

1. Israel, as we shall see, could not go very long without strong spiritual leadership, and neither can the modern Church.

2. Without Moses being present, the people would cry, *"Make us gods."* It has little changed. Aaron will acquiesce to the demands of the people, as too much of the spiritual leadership does presently.

3. Verses 2 and 3 proclaim the giving of the *"golden earrings."* Strangely enough, the next time they would do such would be to make the Tabernacle. This is a perfect picture of religious man who is very quick to go from the ridiculous to the sublime and then back again. Tragically, unless we hover close to Christ, none of us are very far from the *"golden calf."*

4. Verse 4 says that Aaron *"made it a molten calf."* Everything was done by Aaron, under the cover of *"religion."* The design of Satan is not to abolish God, but to represent Him by something visible.

5. Aaron now builds an Altar, and offers sacrifices, but in reality it is *"another Jesus, another spirit, and another gospel"* (II Cor. 11:4).

MAKE US GODS

Verse 1 reads: *"And when the people saw that Moses delayed to come down out of the Mount, the people gathered themselves together unto Aaron, and said unto him, Up, make us gods, which shall go before us; for as for this Moses, the man who brought us up out of the land of Egypt, we do not know what is become of him."*

Without proper spiritual leadership, 99 percent of the people will go astray. That's a blunt statement, but I believe it to be true.

Without the strong leadership of Moses, the people would lose their way. It seemed to have been very easy for them to get Aaron to acquiesce to their demands. Likewise, there are plenty of Aaron's presently, who try to do what the people want, say what the people want said, proclaim what the people want proclaimed, instead of *"Thus saith the Lord!"*

At times, people get angry with us because we take a stand respecting doctrine and issues. We say, *"This is right and that is wrong,"* which is what God has called me to do, plus all who are associated with this Ministry. Far too many Preachers follow the example of opposing only that which is popular to oppose. They say nothing concerning anything else.

Pure and simple, such Preachers are hirelings. The people have itching ears, and they have no trouble finding a Preacher to accommodate those itching ears.

Let us say it again because it's so very, very important! The Church must have a strong voice, one that's not afraid to stand up for what is right, irrespective of the cost, that is, if it is to survive as a work for God.

AARON

Verses 2 and 3 read: *"And Aaron said unto them, Break off the golden earrings, which are in the ears of your wives, of your sons, and of your daughters, and bring them unto me.*

"And all the people broke off the golden earrings which were in their ears, and brought them unto Aaron."

At this time, Aaron should have taken a firm stand, and settled the issue then and there as it regards Moses. He knew where Moses was. Even though, at this time, he didn't know how long the Prophet would be there, but still he knew that he was with God. Also, Aaron had been left in charge (Ex. 24:14).

Why did he instead ask for golden earrings?

More than likely, the crowd was very restless. So instead of seeking the Lord, asking directions, he instead decided to make a golden calf. He decided such, because a golden calf was in his heart. As well, it was much easier to do this than to admonish the people.

NOTES

THE GOLDEN CALF

Verse 4 reads: *"And he received them at their hand, and fashioned it with a graving tool, after he had made it a molten calf: and they said, These be your gods, O Israel, which brought you up out of the land of Egypt."*

Williams said: *"The calf was the great god of the Egyptians. It was carried in the vanguard of their processions. Sacrifices were offered to it, and lascivious dances executed in its honor. It was worshipped as the generator of life."*

Some may wonder how could these people, who had seen the great miracles of God, actually greater than any generation had ever seen, had even felt the mountain tremble at His Presence, now stoop to the low level of fashioning a golden calf, and referring to it as *"god!"*

Those who know the human heart know that man is capable of any type of sin, irrespective of what the past may have been. Even the ardent Believer must watch, as well as pray, thereby keeping his Faith anchored solely in the Sacrifice of Christ, which tells the Lord that such an individual knows and understands that within himself, he is lacking in capability; therefore, he must have the help of the Holy Spirit, even on a continuing basis. Trust in Christ and His great Sacrifice, among other things is a statement which shows that the individual understands his weakness, and that Christ must live this life through him, or else it simply cannot be lived (Gal. 2:20).

THE SIN NATURE

Regrettably, much of the modern Church denies the existence of the sin nature in the heart and life of the Believer. While they may agree that such existed before conversion, they deny that it continues to reside in the heart after conversion.

While it is definitely true that the sin nature should be dormant after conversion, which means that it should cause no problems, the facts are, if we do not follow God's prescribed order of victory, we will definitely find the sin nature once again ruling in our lives, even as it did before coming to Christ.

In Romans, Chapter 6 alone, Paul uses the word *"sin"* some 17 times. In the original

Text, some 14 times he placed the definite article before the word sin, making it read *"the sin,"* which refers to *"the sin nature."* And the other three times implies the sin nature.

We must remember that Paul is writing to Believers, and if the sin nature doesn't exist in the heart and life of a Believer, even as many teach, then the Apostle wasted a lot of time explaining something that doesn't exist. But he didn't waste his time. There is a sin nature in the heart and life of every Believer, with the Apostle telling us how to have victory over this monster, which is through the Cross, and through the Cross solely!

Anyone who tries to have victory any other way, who tries to live for God by any other manner, is pure and simple, entertaining a fool's hope.

WHAT IS THE SIN NATURE?

First of all, the sin nature is the result of the Fall in the Garden of Eden. At that time, man lost God-consciousness, and fell to the far lower level of self-consciousness. As a result, he has a nature that is prone to do wrong. In fact, that's the cause for all the crime, war, jealousy, envy, pride, and man's inhumanity to man in the world today, and in fact, has ever been.

Every person has a human nature as well, which is totally corrupted by the sin nature. That's the reason the Believer cannot function on human nature alone, but must have the help of the Holy Spirit, in order to be what he ought to be in Christ.

When the believing sinner comes to Christ, he also takes unto himself the *"Divine Nature"* (II Pet. 1:4). The Divine Nature is stronger than the human nature or the sin nature; however, for its strength to be exercised, the Believer must function in the realm of Faith, and never by relying on his human nature. In other words, the Believer's Faith must ever rest in the Cross of Christ, where the price was paid in order that we might be saved, and might live victoriously (Rom. 6:3-14). Living by one's Faith in Christ and the Cross guarantees a constant flow of the Grace of God. If the Believer transfers his Faith from the Cross to something else, this frustrates the Grace of God, which leaves the Believer in a perilous situation. In fact, in such a state, the sin nature will once again begin to rule and reign (Gal. 2:21; Rom. 6:12).

So, without Faith properly placed, every time, a golden calf will be the result. Man has taken his *"graving tool,"* and has fashioned calf after calf, all in the name of the Lord, even referring to it as *"God,"* and giving it credit for his deliverance. Let's say it another way:

FRUSTRATING THE GRACE OF GOD

Paul said: *"I do not frustrate the Grace of God: for if Righteousness come by the Law, then Christ is dead in vain"* (Gal. 2:21).

This simply tells us that without the Grace of God the Believer simply cannot function in a victorious manner.

What is the Grace of God?

It is simply the Goodness of God extended to an undeserving person, and it comes by virtue of what Christ did at the Cross. In other words, the Cross of Christ made it possible for the Grace of God to come to a Believer in an uninterrupted flow.

Whenever we attempt, however, to live for God by any means other than Faith in the Cross, we stop that flow of Grace, thereby frustrating it, which means that what we have done, whatever in the world it might be, is pure and simple, another *"golden calf."*

As we shall see, golden calves are very religious. And due to the fact that they are very religious, we equate them with God. But the truth is, as it brought death then, it will bring death now!

Whenever a Believer sets out to live this Christian life, and to do so by any means other than simple Faith in Christ, and what Christ has done for him at the Cross, as already stated, he has just taken out his *"graving tool,"* and whether he realizes it or not, he is making another golden calf. To be frank, the Church is full of them! Many may deny that, but Paul did not share this incredulity, for he declared that these facts admonish the Christian Church (I Cor., Chpt. 10).

THE ALTAR

Verses 5 and 6 read: *"And when Aaron saw it, he built an Altar before it; and Aaron made proclamation, and said, Tomorrow is a feast to the LORD.*

"And they rose up early on the morrow, and offered burnt offerings, and brought peace offerings, and the people sat down to eat and to drink, and rose up to play."

We would sanctify our golden calves by building an altar before them and then offering up burnt offerings and peace offerings. The Church actually is full of such!

Moses had gone up to the Mountain and his return was delayed, at least as far as the people were concerned. So they proceeded to make a god that they could see. So is it today. Some in the Church, at least that which is referred to as the Church, prefer a human Priest, and a little piece of bread that may be seen and handled, to the Divine Priest Who is passed into the Heavens.

One of the great ploys of Satan is not to abolish God, but to represent Him by something visible (Williams). As well, Williams said: *"Also Satan can through a religious teacher like Aaron associate idolatry with Christ, recognize the good in all religions, and provide a worship that appeals to man's natural heart. In fact, everything was done by Aaron under the cover of 'religion.'"*

It is obvious as to what all of this produced.

The phrase, *"And rose up to play,"* refers to licentiousness and vulgarity of the worst order.

Actually, what Israel did at this particular time, more than likely reverting back to what they possibly had been doing in Egypt, was so bad that the Lord stood ready to destroy this generation, and in effect start all over.

As we shall see, Moses interceded on their behalf, and the people were spared, with the exception of some 3,000. But a short time later, that same generation was consigned to spiritual oblivion, in other words, to die in the wilderness, because of unbelief.

The truth was, Israel as a nation was only typically redeemed — the vast majority of them being children in whom was no faith (Deut. 32:20); therefore, we must allow these things to be examples to us, *"to the intent that we should not lust after evil things, as they also lusted"* (I Cor. 10:6).

MOSES

Moses was away for some 40 days and nights. In the Bible, *"forty"* is the number of probation.

We know that God could have handled the situation regarding the giving of the Law in a much shorter time. So, Moses being gone this long must have been in the Plan of God, which would put Israel to the test. The Lord never tempts man, but He definitely does test man. Israel miserably failed this test, as is overly obvious!

To which we have already briefly addressed, the failure of Israel could probably be said to be a failure of leadership, and we speak of Aaron more than anything else. Thus it has been in the history of Christendom: instead of the leaders refusing to follow the worldly wishes of their people, they have heeded, and oftentimes encouraged them. Unfortunately, this problem is rampant at present!

As Aaron built his *"altar,"* thus it has always been, and still is: man ever seeks to hide the shame of his idolatry by putting over it the name of Deity.

What is before us in Verses 5 and 6 presents a prototype of what is now going on almost everywhere in modern Christendom. Men have set up their idols and then sought to dignify and sanctify their inventions by worshipping them in the name of Christ. Ritualism, worldliness, fleshly indulgences, and erroneous doctrines are just a few. Aaron had no Scripture to justify his position, nor have the present day leaders any Word from God to warrant their doings (Pink).

(7) "AND THE LORD SAID UNTO MOSES, GO, GET YOU DOWN; FOR YOUR PEOPLE, WHICH YOU BROUGHT OUT OF THE LAND OF EGYPT, HAVE CORRUPTED THEMSELVES:

(8) "THEY HAVE TURNED ASIDE QUICKLY OUT OF THE WAY WHICH I COMMANDED THEM: THEY HAVE MADE THEM A MOLTEN CALF, AND HAVE WORSHIPPED IT, AND HAVE SACRIFICED THEREUNTO, AND SAID, THESE BE YOUR GODS, O ISRAEL, WHICH HAVE BROUGHT YOU UP OUT OF THE LAND OF EGYPT.

(9) "AND THE LORD SAID UNTO MOSES, I HAVE SEEN THIS PEOPLE, AND, BEHOLD, IT IS A STIFFNECKED PEOPLE:

(10) "NOW THEREFORE LET ME ALONE, THAT MY WRATH MAY WAX HOT

AGAINST THEM, AND THAT I MAY CONSUME THEM: AND I WILL MAKE OF YOU A GREAT NATION.

(11) "AND MOSES BESOUGHT THE LORD HIS GOD, AND SAID, LORD, WHY DOES YOUR WRATH WAX HOT AGAINST YOUR PEOPLE, WHICH YOU HAVE BROUGHT FORTH OUT OF THE LAND OF EGYPT WITH GREAT POWER, AND WITH A MIGHTY HAND?

(12) "WHEREFORE SHOULD THE EGYPTIANS SPEAK, AND SAY, FOR MISCHIEF DID HE BRING THEM OUT, TO SLAY THEM IN THE MOUNTAINS, AND TO CONSUME THEM FROM THE FACE OF THE EARTH? TURN FROM YOUR FIERCE WRATH, AND REPENT OF THIS EVIL AGAINST YOUR PEOPLE.

(13) "REMEMBER ABRAHAM, ISAAC, AND ISRAEL, YOUR SERVANTS, TO WHOM YOU SWEAR BY YOUR OWN SELF, AND SAID UNTO THEM, I WILL MULTIPLY YOUR SEED AS THE STARS OF HEAVEN, AND ALL THIS LAND THAT I HAVE SPOKEN OF WILL I GIVE UNTO YOUR SEED, AND THEY SHALL INHERIT IT FOREVER.

(14) "AND THE LORD REPENTED OF THE EVIL WHICH HE THOUGHT TO DO UNTO HIS PEOPLE."

The construction is:

1. It is interesting that Verse 7 proclaims the Lord disowning these people, by referring to them as *"your people,"* meaning that they belonged to Moses, and then in Verse 11, Moses disowns them himself, referring to them also as *"Your people,"* meaning that they belonged to God. In a sense, the entirety of the nation of Israel, at least as a whole, had made spiritual orphans of themselves.

2. They were a *"stiffnecked people"* because of a hardened heart.

3. The Lord heeded the appeal of Moses, at least for the time being. This same generation would perish in the wilderness, although over a period of time. Without a change of heart, it is not possible to change direction, spiritually speaking.

THE LORD

Verses 7 and 8 read: *"And the LORD said unto Moses, Go, get you down; for your people, which you brought out of the land of Egypt, have corrupted themselves:*

"They have turned aside quickly out of the way which I commanded them: they have made them a molten calf, have worshipped it, and have sacrificed thereunto, and said, These be your gods, O Israel, which have brought you up out of the land of Egypt."

By the Lord proclaiming Israel as belonging to Moses, hence the use of the term *"your people, which you brought . . .",* proclaims the fact that the Lord had, in essence, disowned Israel. As we shall see, Moses would intercede on behalf of these people, but the end result would ultimately be that all over 20 years of age, with the exception of Joshua and Caleb, would die in the wilderness. In other words, they would never reach the Promised Land. As we've already stated, they were a people *"in whom was no Faith"* (Deut. 32:20). The actual meaning of that statement is as follows:

In fact they did have faith, but it was faith in the wrong thing, as is the faith of many, if not most, Christians.

Faith within itself is never really the criteria. All have faith, even the atheist who claims he has no faith. The truth is, he has faith in the fact that he doesn't have any faith, etc.

The object of Faith is the crucial point. What is the object of our faith? When it comes to most Christians, I suppose that most would say, *"the object of my Faith is the Word of God, or Christ Himself, etc."* Those answers are correct, at least as far as they go. But the truth is, they really don't say that much.

One can claim to have Faith in Christ, and in fact actually have Faith in Christ, but not in the Cross, with the end result being that they will be serving *"another Jesus"* (II Cor. 11:4). Let's say it this way:

The only type of Faith that God will recognize is Faith which has as its object *"Jesus Christ and Him Crucified"* (I Cor. 1:23).

The Old Testament Saints would not have known anything about the Cross, or Jesus as well, for that matter. They knew, however, two things, or at least they were supposed to know two things:

1. It was prophesied over and over again,

even beginning in the Garden of Eden, that the Lord was going to send a Redeemer into this world (Gen. 3:15). So they were looking for this One to come. Isaiah even said that He would be born of a Virgin (Isa. 7:14). Jacob had prophesied: *"The Sceptre* (emblem of power) *shall not depart from Judah, nor a lawgiver from between his feet, until Shiloh come* (another name for the Redeemer); *and unto Him shall the gathering of the people be"* (Gen. 49:10). In fact, the prophecies were many.

2. They were made to understand, or should have been made to understand that the sacrifices represented this coming Redeemer, and what He would do in order to redeem fallen humanity.

So it was Faith in this coming One Who would suffer the penalty that mankind should have suffered, in order that we might be saved. Isaiah spelled it out in Chapter 53 of his Book.

In essence, the Faith of the Old Testament Saints was very similar to our Faith today. They looked forward to One Who was to come, and Who would pay the price, while we look backward to One Who has already come, and has already paid the price. Even though it may have been worded a little different, the reality is, the object of Faith was the same in both cases. It was *"Christ and Him Crucified."*

The object of Faith for the Israelites at this particular time was a *"molten calf."* And before we criticize them too heavily, we must understand that there are many *"molten calves"* presently in use as well!

A STIFFNECKED PEOPLE

Verses 9 and 10 read: *"And the LORD said unto Moses, I have seen this people, and, behold, it is a stiffnecked people:*

"Now therefore let Me alone, that My wrath may wax hot against them, and that I may consume them: and I will make of you a great nation."

"Stiffnecked" refers to the fact that the people were obstinate, refusing to listen. It means they did not take the Lord too seriously.

Now that's hard to understand, considering that they had witnessed and observed the greatest miracles that any generation had ever seen. They had witnessed the opening of the Red Sea, the bitter waters of Marah being made sweet, and then the water coming out of the rock like a veritable river. They had witnessed the mountain quake and shake, and had even heard the Voice of God, which was so powerful that they felt they would die if that Voice continued.

The observation of miracles, while a stimulation to Faith, does not really generate Faith itself. Faith itself must be born, at least the type that God will recognize, from, by, and through, the Word of God (Rom. 10:17). In fact, that's one of the great problems with the modern Pentecostal and Charismatic Churches, its faith in signs and wonders, instead of Faith in the Bible. While the signs and wonders definitely have their place, they are never to be the object of Faith, but rather the Word of God. It is *"Truth"* which makes people free, and not other things (Jn. 8:32).

We find here that God cannot condone sin, and especially idolatry. And we need to understand that idolatry comes in many packages. In fact, the greatest idolatry of all is religious idolatry. To be frank, the *"golden calf"* was religious idolatry, and as stated, there are still many golden calves rearing their ugly heads.

When one places their particular Church or Denomination in the wrong position, in other words, they think by belonging to such, it gives them a greater spirituality, etc., they have then made an idol out of that particular institution. Pure and simple, they are practicing idolatry. And to be sure, the Lord is no more pleased now than He was then; consequently, we must take a lesson from what we are reading here. As He grew very angry then, I can assure all and one that He grows no less angry now.

INTERCESSION

Verses 11 through 14 read: *"And Moses besought the LORD his God, and said, LORD, why does Your wrath wax hot against Your people, which You have brought forth out of the land of Egypt with great power, and with a mighty hand?*

"Wherefore should the Egyptians speak, and say, For mischief did He bring them out,

to slay them in the mountains, and to consume them from the face of the Earth? Turn from Your fierce wrath, and repent of this evil against Your people.

"Remember Abraham, Isaac, and Israel, Your servants, to whom You swore by Your Own Self, and said unto them, I will multiply your seed as the stars of Heaven, and all this land that I have spoken of will I give unto your seed, and they shall inherit it forever.

"And the LORD repented of the evil which He thought to do unto His people."

Much has been written on this episode as it regards Moses interceding on behalf of Israel in order that they may be spared. However, having studied this situation from the viewpoint of several Scholars, I'm not so sure that I agree with any of them, at least as it regards their final summation. To a person, I feel they have made Moses too big and God too little!

1. We must never limit God. Whatever it is that He says, and irrespective as to how impossible it may seem to us, we must always remember that it is not at all impossible to Him.

2. When it comes to the human race, even Moses, everything is a test with God. God is never in a dilemma as to what He will do. He knows the beginning from the end, and the end from the beginning, and everything in-between.

I personally feel that this entire episode, as sordid as it was, at least contained a degree of test as it regards Moses. When the Lord told Moses that He would consume Israel, and would make of him a great nation, I feel this was a test for Moses. How would he respond to such an offer?

Of course, God knew how Moses would respond; so the test was not given in order that God may know. God knows all things, past, present, and future. The test would have been given, in order that Moses might know!

A test that is passed must, of necessity, take the Believer to a higher level of Faith. In other words, the Faith needed for the journey, whatever that journey might be, is available, but only through testing. Moses had a lot of hard days ahead of him, which the Lord, of course, knew would come. He was going to need all the rock-solid foundation he could muster for those coming days. Faith must be tested, and great Faith must be tested greatly!

3. Moses, as stated, passed this test with flying colors. This particular generation did die because of unbelief. In other words, the unbelief that fostered the golden calf also balked at their going into the Promised Land, which is recorded in Numbers, Chapters 13 and 14. Their unbelief delayed Israel (the younger generation), some 38 years in taking the land. While Satan may delay whatever the Lord has ordained, if we continue to believe, he definitely cannot stop the plan from coming to fruition. We should never forget that.

THE REPENTANCE OF THE LORD?

Verse 14 talks about the Lord repenting of that which He had proposed to do regarding the destruction of Israel. The way the word *"repented"* is used here, and as it concerns the Lord, doesn't mean at all that He did something wrong, but rather, that He simply turned aside from the proposed direction. In fact, the word *"repentance"* means, *"to turn."* To turn this around, quite possibly we might consider the following:

If the Lord turned aside from this proposed negative action against Israel, as He definitely did, is it possible that the Lord, at times, is forced to repent or turn aside from doing good to those, to whom He desires to do good, because of unbelief on their part? I think that Israel proves that definitely to be the case. The very fact that He repented of the negative things which He had thought to do, at the same time, I think, demands that He repent of the good things He had planned to give, but couldn't. One demands the other.

As we look here at Intercession, at least on the part of Moses, we automatically think of him as interceding for Israel. The truth is, whether he understood it or not, I think that he very well could have been interceding for himself. While it is a moot point, had he agreed to accept the Lord's offer, it would have put everything in jeopardy.

The Lord had to have a man who put God first in all things, in other words, the Will of God. There must not be any hidden agenda, or exaltation of self. As stated, Moses passed this test with flying colors.

(15) "AND MOSES TURNED, AND WENT DOWN FROM THE MOUNT, AND THE TWO TABLES OF THE TESTIMONY WERE IN HIS HAND: THE TABLES WERE WRITTEN ON BOTH THEIR SIDES; ON THE ONE SIDE AND ON THE OTHER WERE THEY WRITTEN.

(16) "AND THE TABLES WERE THE WORK OF GOD, AND THE WRITING WAS THE WRITING OF GOD, GRAVEN UPON THE TABLES.

(17) "AND WHEN JOSHUA HEARD THE NOISE OF THE PEOPLE AS THEY SHOUTED, HE SAID UNTO MOSES, THERE IS A NOISE OF WAR IN THE CAMP.

(18) "AND HE SAID, IT IS NOT THE VOICE OF THEM WHO SHOUT FOR MASTERY, NEITHER IS IT THE VOICE OF THEM WHO CRY FOR BEING OVERCOME: BUT THE NOISE OF THEM WHO SING DO I HEAR.

(19) "AND IT CAME TO PASS, AS SOON AS HE CAME NEAR UNTO THE CAMP, THAT HE SAW THE CALF, AND THE DANCING: AND MOSES' ANGER WAXED HOT, AND HE CAST THE TABLES OUT OF HIS HANDS, AND BROKE THEM BENEATH THE MOUNT.

(20) "AND HE TOOK THE CALF WHICH THEY HAD MADE, AND BURNT IT IN THE FIRE, AND GROUND IT TO POWDER, AND STRAWED IT UPON THE WATER, AND MADE THE CHILDREN OF ISRAEL DRINK OF IT."

The overview is:

1. Verses 15 through 18 point out *"The two Tables of the Testimony."* This moment portrays at least one of the greatest hours to date in human history. God is ready, but the people are not.

2. They, instead, have forsaken *"the Writing of God,"* which was God's Word, for a work of their own hands. By and large, the Church has done the same thing.

3. Moses broke the Tablets, at least in part, because the people in spirit had already broken them.

THE TWO TABLES OF THE TESTIMONY

Verses 15 and 16 read: *"And Moses turned, and went down from the Mount, and the two Tables of the Testimony were in his hand: the Tables were written on both their sides; on the one side and on the other were they written.*

"And the Tables were the Work of God, and the writing was the Writing of God, graven upon the Tables."

We find here the difference in man and God, in which that difference is vast.

When Moses saw what Israel was doing, then he grew angry as well. God already knew what Israel was doing, and simply because He knows all things, at all times. That's at least one of the many reasons that we should seek His Face regarding all things. Our knowledge is so limited, while His is unlimited!

The *"Two Tables of the Testimony"* which Moses now had, were significant beyond all compare. They were the Ten Commandments, five on one Tablet, and five on the other. These Commandments portrayed God's Standard of Righteousness and, therefore, what was demanded of man. So as we shall see, the Law will begin with judgment, even as the Law must begin with judgment.

God had Personally written His Word, even with His Own finger, on these two Tablets.

However, those two stone Tablets that Moses carried with him were no more the Word of God, than the Bible we presently have.

It is regrettable that many, if not most, Christians little seek to properly understand the Word of God as they should. Actually, the Bible ought to be prayerfully read completely through each year. As well, aids such as this Commentary should be obtained, that will help us, prayerfully, to understand the Word of God even more. The Psalmist said, and concerning the Word: *"Your Word is a Lamp unto my feet, and a Light unto my path"* (Ps. 119:105).

Irrespective as to what many may claim, no individual can consider himself to be properly educated, unless they are first of all educated in the Word of God. As the Word of God, it is alive, which means that it literally cannot be exhausted. For every single problem that man might have as it regards life and living, the Bible contains the answer, and the Bible alone contains the answer. Peter said: *"According as His Divine* power has given unto us all things that pertain unto life and Godliness, through the knowledge of Him Who has called us to glory and virtue:

"Whereby are given unto us exceeding great and precious promises: that by these you might be partakers of the Divine Nature, having escaped the corruption that is in the world through lust" (II Pet. 1:3-4).

JOSHUA

Verses 17 and 18 read: *"And when Joshua heard the noise of the people as they shouted, he said unto Moses, There is a noise of war in the camp.*

"And he said, It is not the voice of them who shout for mastery, neither is it the voice of them who cry for being overcome: but the noise of them who sing do I hear."

Joshua hasn't been mentioned for quite some time now. It seems that he must have waited about halfway down the mountain for Moses, probably living off of Manna, until the great Lawgiver returned. He will now accompany Moses to the base of the Mountain.

Before they got within sighting distance of what was going on below, Joshua, and no doubt Moses as well, heard the din of activity which was taking place. It is said that the plain at the base of Sinai is shut out from sight, due to the topography of the Mountain, until one arrives almost at the bottom, which means that sound could be heard, before the source of the activity came into view.

It sounded like *"the noise of war,"* but they were to find that wasn't the case. In truth, it was a *"war,"* but rather a spiritual war, and a war incidentally which Israel lost!

The noise which Joshua and Moses heard was for the obvious sinful reasons; however, I'm afraid that much of the noise in most modern Churches is far too often generated by the flesh, and not at all by the Holy Spirit.

A short time back, I happened to go past a particular Church Service being aired over Television. I was not acquainted with the Church. As the choir sang, a young lady with a flowing white garment was dancing in front of the congregation. It was an orchestrated, choreographed dance, which she had been taught, which means that it was of the flesh, which also means that it definitely was not of the Holy Spirit.

Much of these efforts are taken from Psalms 150:4, which says: *"Praise Him with the timbrel and dance."*

It is true that the people of Israel did dance before the Lord on certain occasions. And it is true that many have danced before the Lord, which refers to being led by the Holy Spirit, many times since. But the idea, which has been adopted by many Churches, that a dance choreographer be hired to show the correct steps, etc., I hardly think is of the Holy Spirit, but is rather a borrowing of the ways of the world. Our Churches are not to be stages for Broadway productions. The Las Vegas stage show should have no place in the Church. It's quite alright for the world to borrow from the Church, but it's sad indeed when the Church borrows from the world!

THE BROKEN TABLES

Verse 19 reads: *"And it came to pass, as soon as he came near unto the camp, that he saw the calf, and the dancing: and Moses' anger waxed hot, and he cast the Tables out of his hands, and broke them beneath the Mount."*

I do not personally think that Moses broke the Tables in a fit of anger. While he definitely was angry, and rightly so, of which we will have more to say in a moment, I think he broke the Tables as a symbol of the anger of God. The people had broken every one of these Commandments, and were breaking them even as they were being brought down from the Mountain, fresh from the Finger of God. That being the case, Moses, as a symbol of God's displeasure, would shatter the stone Tablets, even as the people had spiritually shattered the Commandments.

There is one thing we do know: the Lord never reprimanded Moses for this act. And had he broken these Tablets in a fit of anger, I hardly think that the Lord would have allowed it to pass unaddressed.

Incidentally, the sort of dancing that was being carried out by the Children of Israel seemed to be of the lascivious kind.

THE ANGER OF MOSES

I think that one would have to conclude

that the anger of the great Lawgiver was that of righteous indignation. It was the same type of anger which Jesus manifested when He cleansed the Temple (Jn. 2:14-17).

One of the problems that seems to manifest itself in many modern Christians is that there is little or no righteous indignation as it regards sin, or false doctrine, etc. There should be a holy anger, and in fact there will be a holy anger, if the person is right with God.

THE CALF

Verse 20 reads: *"And he took the calf which they had made, and burnt it in the fire, and ground it to powder, and spread it upon the water, and made the Children of Israel drink of it."*

Why did Moses do this?

I think the Lord had him to do this. It's unlikely that he would have done it on his own.

I think the Lord wanted Moses to do what he did, in order to show the people the utter, absolute worthlessness of this idol they had made. So he would reduce it to dust, mix it with water, and force them to drink it.

(21) "AND MOSES SAID UNTO AARON, WHAT DID THIS PEOPLE UNTO YOU, THAT YOU HAVE BROUGHT SO GREAT A SIN UPON THEM?

(22) "AND AARON SAID, LET NOT THE ANGER OF MY LORD WAX HOT: YOU KNOW THE PEOPLE, THAT THEY ARE SET ON MISCHIEF.

(23) "FOR THEY SAID UNTO ME, MAKE US GODS, WHICH SHALL GO BEFORE US: FOR AS FOR THIS MOSES, THE MAN WHO BROUGHT US UP OUT OF THE LAND OF EGYPT, WE DO NOT KNOW WHAT IS BECOME OF HIM.

(24) "AND I SAID UNTO THEM, WHOSOEVER HAS ANY GOLD, LET THEM BREAK IT OFF. SO THEY GAVE IT TO ME: THEN I CAST IT INTO THE FIRE, AND THERE CAME OUT THIS CALF.

(25) "AND WHEN MOSES SAW THAT THE PEOPLE WERE NAKED; (FOR AARON HAD MADE THEM NAKED UNTO THEIR SHAME AMONG THEIR ENEMIES:)

(26) "THEN MOSES STOOD IN THE GATE OF THE CAMP, AND SAID, WHO IS ON THE LORD'S SIDE? LET HIM COME UNTO ME. AND ALL THE SONS OF LEVI GATHERED THEMSELVES TOGETHER UNTO HIM.

(27) "AND HE SAID UNTO THEM, THUS SAITH THE LORD GOD OF ISRAEL, PUT EVERY MAN HIS SWORD BY HIS SIDE, AND GO IN AND OUT FROM GATE TO GATE THROUGHOUT THE CAMP, AND SLAY EVERY MAN HIS BROTHER, AND EVERY MAN HIS COMPANION, AND EVERY MAN HIS NEIGHBOR.

(28) "AND THE CHILDREN OF LEVI DID ACCORDING TO THE WORD OF MOSES: AND THERE FELL OF THE PEOPLE THAT DAY ABOUT THREE THOUSAND MEN."

The composition is:

1. Verses 21 through 24 record Aaron's excuse. He blames his actions on the people. Bible repentance demands that God be justified and we be condemned. This means that God demands that we accept the blame for our failure. That is the only kind of repentance that He will honor.

2. Verse 25 says, *"The people were naked."* Quite possibly they had removed their clothing; however, the greater meaning has to do with Israel being exposed to the Judgments of God because of their sin, and the vengeance of their enemies without God's protection.

3. For those who refused to cease their sinning at this time, the command was *"Kill them."* This was the day of the giving of the Law, and on this day, 3,000 men died. If it is to be noted, on the Day of Pentecost, when the Holy Spirit came, 3,000 men were saved (Acts 2:41).

THE BLAME

Verse 21 reads: *"And Moses said unto Aaron, What did this people unto you, that you have brought so great a sin upon them?"*

Moses did not ask this question actually thinking that the people had threatened Aaron; he rather asked the question as a reproach. The idea is, they had done nothing to him, had in no way injured him, and yet, he easily allowed this thing to happen, which was a great sin, and which resulted in 3,000 men dying.

The sin is referred to as *"a great sin."*

The idea is, if Aaron had taken a stand, it is hardly likely that they would have committed this great sin. One can only say, and especially as we consider Aaron's answer, which we will address momentarily, that the fault belonged to the brother of Moses.

Once again we emphasize the fact that presently, we have far too few men like Moses, and far too many like Aaron, as it regards the Ministry.

THE EXCUSE

Verses 22 through 24 read: *"And Aaron said, Let not the anger of my lord wax hot: you know the people, that they are set on mischief.*

"For they said unto me, Make us gods, which shall go before us: for as for this Moses, the man who brought us up out of the land of Egypt, we do not know what is become of him.

"And I said unto them, Whosoever has any gold, let them break it off. So they gave it to me: and I cast it into the fire, and there came out this calf."

Aaron would have been far better off, had he answered Moses in the correct way.

"It is my fault, and I have no excuse!"

But instead, he blames the people, and then gives one of the most ridiculous excuses found anywhere in the Bible. He threw the gold in the fire, and out popped this calf!

If he was going to lie, it seems that surely he could have made up a better story than this!

But yet, at least as far as we know, the Lord did not direct Moses to punish Aaron in any way. Was it because he was Moses' brother? No! God is no respecter of persons.

The Scripture is silent on the subject, so all we can do is offer a suggestion. Quite possibly, the magnitude of what he had done, which directly caused the deaths of some 3,000 men, creating a terrible amount of suffering, was punishment enough. As the High Priest, he was to stand as a mediator between God and the people, thereby saving their lives. And for him to be the cause of their deaths had to weigh heavily upon him.

NAKED

Verse 25 reads: *"And when Moses saw that the people were naked; (for Aaron had made them naked unto their shame among their enemies:)"*

Several things are said here:

1. The Scripture proclaims the fact that Aaron was to blame for the predicament of Israel at this time.

2. The people *"were naked,"* which not only referred to licentiousness, but as well, refers to them being naked to the Judgment of God.

3. The Amalekites were probably still in the hills lurking about, and no doubt saw this spectacle. What they knew about Israel wasn't much, but they surely knew that all of this was amiss!

Sin takes a frightful toll! The price is always more than one can afford to pay. In fact, sin has such a power to it that it took the Cross to address this monster. And if man rejects the Cross, and that includes the Church, there is no other solution for sin. That's the reason I take every opportunity in this Commentary to address the Cross. I know the destructive power of sin! I know the sorrow and the heartache that sin brings! I also know there is only one solution for this terrible horror, and that is the Cross of Christ. If the Believer looks in any other direction, he will bring upon himself terrible difficulties and problems, which could even result in the loss of his soul.

THE CROSS, THE ONLY ANSWER!

I believe the Lord has impressed upon me something of extreme significance. As more and more the Light of the Message of the Cross is being spread abroad, the Holy Spirit is saying, if that Light is rejected, *"There remains no more sacrifice for sins"* (Heb. 10:26).

In other words, if the Message of the Cross is rejected, the result will be spiritual death. In effect, Galatians, Chapter 5 says so!

So the Message of the Cross, which we are preaching, is not optional. When the light was dim on this foundational Truth, the Lord has had great patience with all of us. But now that this great Truth is being revealed to the Church, the patience, so to speak, is no more.

And considering that this is certainly not a new Message, but rather the same Message preached by the Apostle Paul, makes it even more urgent.

FEAR

There is evidence in the above Text that Aaron did what he did because of *"fear."* In other words, he feared that if he didn't acquiesce to the people, they may turn on him, etc.

To be frank, *"fear"* is one of the greatest problems in the hearts and lives of Preachers. If they take a stand as it regards correct doctrine, or as it regards issues, they are afraid that they could lose their Church, or their strong Tithe payers will leave, or they will fall out of favor with their Denomination, etc. So as Aaron, they do nothing, they say nothing.

Just the other day I received a letter from a particular Pastor who mentioned this very thing. Knowing that the ways and means of a particular Evangelist were not Scriptural, he felt he should address the subject; however, he was quickly made to realize that if he did so, he stood to lose his Church. So the problem of man fear is one of the greatest problems of all as it regards our taking a stand as we know we should. This is why Jesus said: *"What I tell you in darkness, that speak you in light: and what you hear in the ear, that preach you upon the housetops.*

"And fear not them which kill the body, but are not able to kill the soul: but rather fear Him Who is able to destroy both soul and body in Hell" (Mat. 10:27-28).

WHO IS ON THE LORD'S SIDE?

Verse 26 reads: *"Then Moses stood in the gate of the camp, and said, Who is on the LORD's side? Let him come unto me. And all the sons of Levi gathered themselves together unto him."*

The Camp obviously had many gates, so it stands to reason that Moses was standing at the principal entrance to the Camp, wherever that was.

There, at this particular site, he asked the question, *"Who is on the LORD's side?"* The Hebrew actually says, *"Who for Jehovah?"* Pulpit said, and rightly so, *"It formed an excellent rallying cry."*

Considering that there were upwards of three million people in this encampment, Moses, even though the Scripture doesn't say, must have sent runners out among all the people. I think it is obvious that some of the drunken revelry was continuing even at this particular time.

For whatever reason, many of the sons of Levi gathered around Moses. According to the next Verse, it seems that even some of the Levites were among the idolaters. But the righteous ones among the Tribe of Levi stand out.

Why did this Tribe take this position, or at least many in the Tribe, with the other Tribes, it seems, holding back?

I personally think that the Lord had intended all along to use the Tribe of Levi for the Priesthood. So He placed a desire in the hearts of the Levites, or at least those among them who desired to do right, to take the stand they did. The Lord will never override a person's will. But He definitely will move favorably upon one who has a heart after Him, as undoubtedly, some of the Levites did! However, and even as we shall momentarily see, they were to be put to a very difficult test. All types of people claim to be on the Lord's side, but the great question is, how many actually are? Jesus Himself said: *"Not every one who says unto Me, Lord, Lord, shall enter into the Kingdom of Heaven; but he who does the will of My Father which is in Heaven"* (Mat. 7:21).

THE SWORD

Verse 27 reads: *"And he said unto them, Thus saith the LORD God of Israel, Put every man his sword by his side, and go in and out from gate to gate throughout the Camp, and slay every man his brother, and every man his companion, and every man his neighbor."*

This which was to be done, first of all, was instruction from the Lord. Moses put that in its proper perspective by saying, *"Thus saith the LORD God of Israel."*

The Levites were to go among the thousands of Israel, and they were to kill every single person who was still engaging in a form of worship regarding the golden calf.

Pink says: *"So in preaching to idolaters today it is the 'wrath' of a Holy God, and not His love (which is a truth for His Own people only), which needs pressing upon them."*

From the time that Moses arrived on the scene, until the judgment fell, seems to have been some hours, possibly even an entire day or more. During this time, the call had gone out over the Tribes of Israel, for all to rally to the Lord's side.

So it seems that a space was given for people to repent, which possibly some did. But yet, others, at least 3,000, continued on in their wicked revelry. It was these ones who spurned the Gospel call, who suffered the judgment.

There is no record that God has ever turned aside one who honestly came to Him seeking Mercy, Grace, and forgiveness. In fact, the entirety of the tenor of Scripture is that the Call of God is extended to sinners, and irrespective as to the degree of their sin; if they will honestly repent, Mercy and Grace will always be shown.

As well, if God had not exacted judgment upon these individuals, their rebellion could have turned the entirety of the nation of Israel toward even further ungodliness. These rebels must be dealt with and these rebels would be dealt with!

THREE THOUSAND MEN

Verse 28 reads: *"And the Children of Levi did according to the word of Moses: and there fell of the people that day about three thousand men."*

Evidently, these were the individuals who had mocked the call of Moses, and had continued on in their wicked ways. They were determined to worship the golden calf, irrespective as to what Moses said, or anyone else said for that matter. So one cannot fault the Lord for what was done. They had only themselves to blame. In fact, but for the Mercy of God, many more thousands would have died, and in fact, deserved to die. But it was only these *"three thousand"* rebels, who insisted upon their rebellious ways, and despite the clarion call to repentance, who would suffer the ultimate judgment.

(29) "FOR MOSES HAD SAID, CONSECRATE YOURSELVES TODAY TO THE LORD, EVEN EVERY MAN UPON HIS SON, AND UPON HIS BROTHER: THAT HE MAY BESTOW UPON YOU A BLESSING THIS DAY.

(30) "AND IT CAME TO PASS ON THE MORROW, THAT MOSES SAID UNTO THE PEOPLE, YOU HAVE SINNED A GREAT SIN: AND NOW I WILL GO UP UNTO THE LORD; PERADVENTURE I SHALL MAKE AN ATONEMENT FOR YOUR SIN.

(31) "AND MOSES RETURNED UNTO THE LORD, AND SAID, OH, THIS PEOPLE HAVE SINNED A GREAT SIN, AND HAVE MADE THEM GODS OF GOLD.

(32) "YET NOW, IF YOU WILL FORGIVE THEIR SIN — ; AND IF NOT, BLOT ME, I PRAY YOU, OUT OF YOUR BOOK WHICH YOU HAVE WRITTEN.

(33) "AND THE LORD SAID UNTO MOSES, WHOSOEVER HAS SINNED AGAINST ME, HIM WILL I BLOT OUT OF MY BOOK.

(34) "THEREFORE NOW GO, LEAD THE PEOPLE UNTO THE PLACE OF WHICH I HAVE SPOKEN UNTO YOU: BEHOLD, MY ANGEL SHALL GO BEFORE YOU: NEVERTHELESS IN THE DAY WHEN I VISIT I WILL VISIT THEIR SIN UPON THEM.

(35) "AND THE LORD PLAGUED THE PEOPLE, BECAUSE THEY MADE THE CALF, WHICH AARON MADE."

The exegesis is:

1. The words, *"Consecrate yourselves today to the LORD,"* referred to *"being installed as Priests to the Lord this day."*

2. The words, *"May bestow upon you a blessing this day,"* were the granting of the Priesthood to the Tribe of Levi.

3. Verse 30 says, *"Peradventure I shall make an Atonement for your sin,"* refers to that which Moses could not do, because no man can atone for sin. There is no Atonement without blood sacrifice, and the only blood sacrifice that God will accept is that of Christ Himself.

4. Moses even offered himself as an Atonement, portrayed in Verse 32. But Moses was a sinner and could not be accepted as such.

5. For the first time, *"The Book"* is mentioned in which all the names of the Righteous are written.

6. Scripture teaches plainly that God blots the names of the rebellious out of His Book.

CONSECRATION

Verse 29 reads: *"For Moses had said, Consecrate yourselves today to the LORD, even every man upon his son, and upon his brother; that he may bestow upon you a blessing this day."*

When those of the Tribe of Levi did as the Lord through Moses commanded, which meant that they had to personally kill every single person who was continuing in this orgy, even if it meant their own brother, etc., that day they won the *"blessing."* The blessing was that they would become the Priestly Tribe of Israel, which was the most coveted position.

From this episode, we should ascertain that a *"blessing"* awaits all who are obedient to the Lord. Sometimes that obedience involves things that are not very pleasant.

A PERSONAL EXPERIENCE

In the last 18 months (counting back from the year 2002), we have felt led of the Lord at this Ministry to address certain doctrines which we know to be false, and which are hurting many people. To oppose something that is unpopular with the people doesn't take much courage at all. Unfortunately, most Preachers stay on the safe side, so to speak, by doing exactly that.

But when the Lord lays it on your heart to oppose doctrines which are very popular with the people, even though they are very wrong, is another matter altogether. In such a situation, even the Preachers who know right and wrong will not stand with you. They simply don't want to take the heat. And the opposition, to be sure, will be fierce, as it has been!

Paul was hated by many during his day because of his stand on certain particulars. He minced no words, and pulled no punches. He even faced down Simon Peter, even though Peter was older than he was, and had been personally selected by the Lord. In fact, he was looked at in the Early Church, and rightly so, as the chief of the Apostles. But yet, when Peter vacillated as it regards the Law/Grace issue, which if left unchecked could have done serious damage to the Church, if not outright destroying it, Paul said: *"But when Peter was come to Antioch, I withstood him to the face, because he was to be blamed."*

The Apostle of Grace said to Peter: *"Knowing that a man is not justified by the works of the Law, but by the Faith of Jesus Christ, even we have believed in Jesus Christ, that we might be justified by the Faith of Christ, and not by the works of the Law: for by the works of the Law shall no flesh be justified"* (Gal. 2:11, 16).

It was not easy for Paul to do that, but to Peter's credit, the great Apostle took it with humility, and in fact, stood with Paul. But of course, there aren't many like Simon Peter!

But irrespective as to what people may say or think, the criteria must never be the popularity of the Preacher, but rather that which the Lord wants and desires.

ATONEMENT?

Verse 30 reads: *"And it came to pass on the morrow, that Moses said unto the people, You have sinned a great sin: and now I will go up unto the LORD; peradventure I shall make an Atonement for your sin."*

The people had sinned, and the only thing that could make Atonement for sin was the Cross of Christ, which was portrayed in symbolic form respecting the sacrifices. Moses could not atone for sin; the following terminology proves the point. For all practical purposes, the Lord ignored his statements.

How much the Lord had revealed to Moses at this time concerning Redemption we really have no way of knowing; however, as time went by, every evidence is the great Lawgiver became extremely knowledgeable, as the Lord revealed it to him, as to exactly how Redemption would be carried out.

On the Mount of Transfiguration where Moses and Elijah appeared and talked with Christ, the Scripture says that these two men *"appeared in glory, and spoke of His decease which He should accomplish at Jerusalem"* (Lk. 9:30-31). So Moses came to know, as possibly few men did know, as to the Redemption Plan which would be carried out in Christ, and which was symbolized by the many Sacrifices of Israel.

A GREAT SIN

Moses was quick to tell the people that they

had sinned a great sin. Speaking this bluntly about sin, I doubt that Moses would be too very well accepted in most modern Churches.

In fact, the Word of Faith doctrine teaches that the Preacher should never say anything about sin. To do so, they claim, develops a sin consciousness and will cause the person to sin.

Such thinking is amazing to say the least! The idea that merely not mentioning something will stifle its power, presents a gross misunderstanding as to what sin actually is. In fact, sin is so awful, so horrible, so powerful, that it took the Cross of Calvary to address this monster. Perhaps that's at least one of the reasons that the Word of Faith people demean the Cross as they do. They simply don't know or realize the power of sin, or the solution to the sin problem, which is the Cross. And it is the only solution to the sin problem!

FORGIVENESS

Verses 31 and 32 read: *"And Moses returned unto the LORD, and said, Oh, this people have sinned a great sin, and have made them gods of gold.*

"Yet now, if You will forgive their sin —; and if not, blot me, I pray You, out of Your Book which You have written."

In a sense, Moses was asking the Lord to forgive the nation of Israel, which in essence, had not asked His forgiveness. While individuals may certainly have sought such Mercy, every evidence is that the general population sought no forgiveness at all. And God will not, in fact, cannot forgive, those who are hell-bent toward their own destruction. As it was then, so it is now. God does not forgive people who do not seek forgiveness, and in fact do not want forgiveness, and in actuality, are opposed to God.

While it is true that we as Believers are importuned to forgive those who trespass against us, whether they seek such or not, that is done far more for our good than for the party who has wronged us.

God is merciful, and He is merciful all the time; however, while Mercy will always be extended to the seeking soul, and no matter the infraction, Mercy will not, and as stated, cannot be extended to those who do not seek such, and in fact, don't even want such.

THE BOOK OF LIFE

This is the first mention of such a Book in the Bible, and speaks of the *"Book of Life,"* where all the names of the Righteous are written. These Passages tell us two things:

1. It tells us that names can be added or removed.

2. It emphatically tells us that names, at times, are removed, completely refuting the unscriptural doctrine of *"unconditional eternal security."* Any person who claims security despite the fact that they are in rebellion against God, and are no longer exhibiting Faith in Christ, is entertaining a fool's hope!

Every evidence is that names were blotted out at this particular time, as should be obvious.

What did Moses mean in telling the Lord to blot him out of the Book of Life, if He (the Lord) wouldn't forgive Israel?

In the first place, I think it should be understood that this was just a gesture. As the Lord will answer, Atonement cannot be made by individuals, who in effect, need Atonement themselves, even as Moses did, and in fact, every human being has needed from the very beginning, with the exception of Christ.

I personally think that Moses was trying his best to intercede for Israel, especially knowing and considering how grievous their sin had been.

THE GUILTY PARTY

Verse 33 reads: *"And the LORD said unto Moses, Whosoever has sinned against Me, him will I blot out of My Book."*

Concerning one being punished for the sins of another, that is not taught in Scripture. The Scripture plainly says that, *"The son shall not bear the iniquity of the father, neither shall the father bear the iniquity of the son: the Righteousness of the Righteous shall be upon him, and the wickedness of the wicked shall be upon him"* (Ezek. 18:20).

There is, and in fact, there can <u>only</u> be one Atonement, which refers to one bearing the punishment or penalty of another, and that is the One Who is at the same time man and God — Who has, Himself, no sin — and can, therefore, take the punishment of others. This *is* the reason that the Cross is so very, very important, in fact, the single most important act that God has carried out on this Earth, and in fact, will ever carry out (Jn. 3:16; Heb. 13:20).

Actually, the great Sacrificial System, which was given in the Law of Moses, presented itself as a constant reminder of the Atonement which would be made, of which these Sacrifices were a symbol.

Williams said: *"Moses descended from on high with the Law. Confronted with man's sin, he broke both Tables, and then returned with a cheerless, 'peradventure' on his lips to seek an uncertain forgiveness. He failed!*

"Christ descended from on high, fulfilled the Law; and having, on behalf of sinners, suffered its full penalty, returned to Heaven having shed His precious Blood, the sign of His accomplished Atonement, to obtain an absolutely certain forgiveness."

THE ANGEL

Verse 34 reads: *"Therefore now go, lead the people unto the place of which I have spoken unto you: behold, My Angel shall go before you: nevertheless in the day when I visit I will visit their sin upon them."*

It has been argued, and even conjectured, that this *"Angel"* is different than the *"Angel"* of Exodus 23:20. It is my thought that this is the same Angel.

It seems as though the Lord had threatened to remove this Angel, Who in essence, was a pre-Incarnate appearance of Christ, but now consents that He may remain with Israel, thereby continuing to lead and to watch over them.

Concerning the unrepentant, of which there must have been many, the Lord tells Moses that just because judgment didn't come immediately, they are not to think that it's not coming at all. He said, *"In the day when I visit,"* referring to the fact that there is always a day of judgment. Through Paul, the Holy Spirit would say, some 1,600 years in the future, *"Vengeance is Mine; I will repay, saith the Lord"* (Rom. 12:19).

Judgment and vengeance can be stopped, but only by proper repentance!

NOTES

THE PLAGUE

Verse 35 reads: *"And the LORD plagued the people, because they made the calf, which Aaron made."*

The Hebrew word for *"plagued"* here means, *"to push, gorge, defeat, inflict disease, slay, smite, put to the worse."* Exactly what the Lord did, we aren't told.

While such may come upon those who are out of Covenant, and in fact, often does; still, this pertains more so to those who claim to know the Lord, than otherwise. It is a blessing of unprecedented proportions, for one to live for God. But when one begins to be unfaithful to one's Lord, and then refuses to repent of such a direction, judgment will come. It will come, despite the fact that we are living in the day and age of Grace!

As well, it should be noticed that the Holy Spirit plainly says concerning the making of the golden calf that both the *"people,"* and *"Aaron"* were responsible. This means that the people could not absolve themselves of responsibility, by laying the blame on Aaron, and neither could Aaron absolve himself of blame, by pointing to the people. But that is a favorite ploy of many, if not most! We should understand that none of that cuts any ice, proverbially speaking, with God!

"Welcome, happy morning! Age to age shall say;
"Hell today is vanquished! Heaven is won today!
"Lo! The dead is living, God forevermore,
"Him, their true Creator, all His works adore."

"Earth with joy confesses, clothing her for spring,
"All good gifts return with her returning King;
"Bloom in every meadow, leaves on every bough;
"Speak His sorrows ended, hail His triumph now."

"Maker and Redeemer, life and health of all,
"Thou from Heaven beholding human nature's fall,
"Of the eternal Father true and only Son,

"Manhood to deliver, manhood did put on."

"Thou, of life, the Author, death did undergo,
"Tread the path of darkness, saving strength to show;
"Come then, True and Faithful, now fulfill Thy Word;
"'Tis Thine Own third morning; rise, O buried Lord!"

CHAPTER 33

(1) "AND THE LORD SAID UNTO MOSES, DEPART, AND GO UP HENCE, YOU AND THE PEOPLE WHICH YOU HAVE BROUGHT UP OUT OF THE LAND OF EGYPT, UNTO THE LAND WHICH I SWEAR UNTO ABRAHAM, TO ISAAC, AND TO JACOB, SAYING, UNTO YOUR SEED WILL I GIVE IT:

(2) "AND I WILL SEND AN ANGEL BEFORE YOU; AND I WILL DRIVE OUT THE CANAANITE, THE AMORITE, AND THE HITTITE, AND THE PERIZZITE, THE HIVITE, AND THE JEBUSITE:

(3) "UNTO A LAND FLOWING WITH MILK AND HONEY: FOR I WILL NOT GO UP IN THE MIDST OF YOU; FOR YOU ARE A STIFFNECKED PEOPLE: LEST I CONSUME YOU IN THE WAY.

(4) "AND WHEN THE PEOPLE HEARD THESE EVIL TIDINGS, THEY MOURNED AND NO MAN DID PUT ON HIM HIS ORNAMENTS.

(5) "FOR THE LORD HAD SAID UNTO MOSES, SAY UNTO THE CHILDREN OF ISRAEL, YOU ARE A STIFFNECKED PEOPLE: I WILL COME UP INTO THE MIDST OF YOU IN A MOMENT, AND CONSUME YOU: THEREFORE NOW PUT OFF YOUR ORNAMENTS FROM YOU, THAT I MAY KNOW WHAT TO DO UNTO YOU.

(6) "AND THE CHILDREN OF ISRAEL STRIPPED THEMSELVES OF THEIR ORNAMENTS BY THE MOUNT HOREB."

The structure is:

1. As we shall see, Grace meets the cry of need, but judgment must deal with rebellion.

2. Grace clothes naked sinners; but a sinner decked in ornaments must be stripped.

3. The reason for Israel's problem was that they were *"stiffnecked,"* i.e., *"dense, tough, severe, cruel, grievous, hard."*

ABRAHAM, ISAAC, AND JACOB

Verse 1 reads: *"And the LORD said unto Moses, Depart, and go up hence, you and the people which you have brought up out of the land of Egypt, and to the land which I did swear unto Abraham, to Isaac, to Jacob, saying, Unto your seed will I give it."*

Many, if not most, Expositors claim that Moses gained many concessions from the Lord as it regards His treatment of Israel. I don't really think so.

As previously stated, I think the Lord's statement to Moses that He would destroy Israel because of what they had done, and make of Moses a great nation, was more of a test for Moses than anything else. As we also stated, the Lord already knew what was in the heart of Moses, but He wanted Moses to know as well! Thankfully, Moses would pass this test with flying colors.

But the claim that the Lord changed His Mind, of that I think there is little evidence. The adult generation, which committed this terrible sin, was ultimately destroyed in the wilderness. They were children in whom there was no Faith.

The Lord had made grand promises to Abraham, Isaac, and Jacob. And the Lord keeps His Promises. There would be a people who would occupy the land of Canaan, irrespective as to what the Lord would have to do for this thing to be accomplished. This was the Plan, and it was a Plan which would come to fruition.

It is the same presently with the Church. Even though the far greater majority have gone in wrong directions, with most having abandoned the Cross, which means they are no longer preaching or living the Gospel; nevertheless, there has always been a Remnant who gives the Lord their all, and there is a Remnant presently!

THE REVELATION OF THE CROSS

The Revelation which the Lord has given me as it regards the Cross, I personally feel, if heeded, will take the Church, or at least all who will believe, to a higher spiritual level than it has heretofore known. I have hesitated to say that; however, the Holy Spirit has been pressing me, I believe, that these things must be said.

What we're giving to the people isn't new, actually having been given to the Apostle Paul by Christ Himself (Gal. 1:12). But due to not having been taught, the great Truth of the Cross, as it regards our Sanctification, and as well, the means and the ways by which the Holy Spirit works, have all been lost to the modern Church. As a result, we have Christians who, despite their best efforts, simply cannot rise above a lifestyle of spiritual failure, and no matter how hard they try otherwise. The Church has addressed this with about every conceivable *"fad"* that one could contemplate; however, none have been successful, even as none can be successful. They may sound good, and even look good, but they simply will not work.

In the early 1970's, demons being cast out of Christians was all the rage. If a Christian had a problem with temper, immorality, lust, unforgiveness, jealousy, alcohol, nicotine, gambling, drugs, etc., the idea was, this person had a *"demon of lust,"* or a *"demon of gambling,"* etc., and so the answer was, at least according to some Preachers, this particular demon must be cast out.

Even though I was a young, rookie Preacher just getting started, I knew this was wrong. In the first place, Christians cannot be demon possessed. I didn't know the answer, but I knew what was being proposed was not the answer. Many Preachers grew very angry with me for my stand, but nevertheless, I felt my position was right, and in retrospect, it was right.

In the mid 1970's, *"confession"* became all the rage, and still continues to a certain degree unto this hour. If Christians were having problems, it was because their confession was wrong, at least that's what was taught. If they would select several good Scriptures to fit their problem, confess those Scriptures over and over, plus how strong they were in the Lord, etc., the problems would vanish. I bought into this for awhile, but soon came to realize that God cannot be manipulated.

In the 1980's, the *"buddy system"* came into vogue. Pastors, one in particular, of large Churches began to advocate that all Christians should get them a buddy in whom they could confide and that two would be far stronger than one, and all problems could be solved. I knew this was wrong, simply because it was just a take off on psychology.

And then in the early 1990's, the *"laughing phenomenon"* became the rage. Christians were taught that if they would go into a fit of giggles for a period of time, this would solve all of their problems. Once again, I knew this wasn't Scriptural. A little bit after that, the *"family curse"* craze took hold. Christians were taught that if they were having problems, it was because of something very evil that was done by their forefathers several generations back. They should go to the right Preacher, the Preacher, incidentally, who understood the family curse, who would rebuke this curse, and the person would then be free. In fact, this is still being taught in some circles.

Along with all of this, being *"slain in the Spirit,"* was always in vogue, and in fact, up to a certain point, is Scriptural and, therefore, real. But Christians were finding that despite the fact of this beautiful manifestation, their problem remained.

While all of these things may have some Scriptural validity, or none at all, still, they hold no answer to the dilemma of the Christian, as to how to live right. All of these things we have mentioned are spiritual; however, to those who were disillusioned with the spiritual way, they have long since turned to humanistic psychology.

In 1996, the Lord began to open up to me the great Message of the Cross. He began to show me that which, as stated, was given to the Apostle Paul nearly 2,000 years ago. And as also stated, He began to open it up to me in a fashion that I think had little been known, if in fact, known at all. Even though I'm being overly repetitive, I feel like I must say it again. What the Lord gave me was not new. It was just light shed on that which had already been given to Paul.

He took me to the Sixth Chapter of Romans. He first of all explained to me the "sin nature" as it was taught in that great Chapter. He then told me that the Cross was the only answer to this problem, which again is found in Romans 6:3-5. He then showed me that my Faith must ever remain in the Cross, and for that, took me to Romans 6:11.

Now what I have just stated has been taught by some Bible Scholars of the past. But what I'm about to mention now, I've never heard it taught anywhere, or even read anything said in the following respect.

THE HOLY SPIRIT

The Lord showed me the manner and the way in which the Holy Spirit works, which I had not previously heard. For that, He took me to Romans 8:2. But please allow me to relate again an experience which I had in 1988.

This particular time was a period of tremendous trouble as it regards this Ministry. Spiritual failure is an awful thing, but when you've tried with all the strength you have not to fail, and you've done everything you know to do, but failure still has occurred, it leaves one in a very confused state. Of course, all of this was my fault, but still, as I have related it, that's exactly what had happened and was happening.

On this particular day, which if I remember correctly was a Monday, I had stayed home in order to pray and seek the Lord the entirety of the day.

As I went to prayer that morning, for a particular period of time, Satan hindered greatly. I will not go into detail, but it was one of the most severe attacks I think I've ever experienced. It was so severe, in fact, that I can recall it in detail even unto this moment.

But at any rate, as quickly as this spirit of oppression had come upon me, as quickly it left. At that time, the Spirit of God came on me greatly and mightily. As severe had been the oppression, as glorious were the Moving and the Operation of the Holy Spirit.

And then the Lord spoke something to me. He said:

"I have taught you many things about the Holy Spirit, and He has helped you greatly in your Ministry; however, I'm going to teach you some things about the Spirit that you have not previously known." Even though there was nothing else spoken to my heart, the implication was that this which would be given to me would change my life. It would answer every question!

I pondered that which the Lord gave me, and did so for quite some period of time. I thought that I understood the Holy Spirit; at least as far as a poor human being can understand the Holy Spirit, especially considering that He is God. But yet I knew what the Lord had spoken to my heart.

Months and even years passed, and there was nothing given that I felt was an answer to that promise made in 1988.

In fact, some eight years passed before the Lord would fulfill in totality what He had told me in 1988. Even as I relate this account, I greatly sense the Presence of God!

When the Lord opened up to me in 1996 the manner in which the Holy Spirit works within our lives, as it regards Sanctification, I knew that this was the answer for which I had so long sought.

He told me that the Holy Spirit always, and without exception, worked within the parameters of the Finished Work of Christ. In other words, the Cross gave Him the legal right to do the things which only He can do. And to be sure, He Alone can give us the power that will help us to live the life we ought to live, and be the overcomer we must be. As stated, when He gave this to me, He took me to Romans 8:2. Paul said:

"For the Law of the Spirit of Life in Christ Jesus has made me free from the law of sin and death."

I will not again go through a dissertation regarding this Verse, having already done it several times in this one Volume; however, I will hurriedly say that despite the fact that the Holy Spirit resides in the hearts and lives of every true Believer, He cannot function as He desires to function, unless our Faith is properly placed in the Cross. The Cross, at all times, must ever be the object of our Faith! This being done, the Holy Spirit will then work grandly and glorious for us, but only in this respect. Listen again to Paul:

"But if the Spirit (Holy Spirit) *of Him* (God the Father) *Who raised up Jesus from*

the dead dwell in you, He Who raised up Christ from the dead shall also quicken your mortal bodies by His Spirit Who dwells in you" (Rom. 8:11).

Now most Christians mistake this Verse for the coming Resurrection; however, that's not what Paul is addressing here.

He is telling us that we have available to us, through the Holy Spirit, the same power that raised Jesus from the dead. And to be sure, we should understand that such power can do anything. This means that it's foolish for us to be overcome by any sin of the flesh or spirit.

If it is to be noticed, Paul said that the Spirit will *"quicken our mortal bodies."* The *"mortal body"* is the weak link as it regards the Child of God. The Apostle had already addressed that when he said: *"Let not sin (the sin nature) therefore reign (rule) in your mortal body, that you should obey it in the lust thereof"* (Rom. 6:12).

This tells us that the *"sin nature"* definitely does reside in the heart and life of the Believer; however, if we function as we should function, the sin nature will be dormant, causing no problem. And to function correctly, we must place our Faith exclusively in the great Sacrifice of Christ, which then gives the Holy Spirit latitude to work. Without fail, He will then bring our *"state"* up to our *"standing."* But unless we function as we should, the sin nature will *"rule"* within our lives, and will do so exactly as it did before we came to Christ.

BY FAITH

By now, we certainly should understand that all of this is by Faith, and not at all by works or performance. And when we say Faith, without fail, we are speaking of Faith in Christ and His great Sacrifice.

THE ANGEL

Verse 2 reads: *"And I will send an Angel before you: and I will drive out the Canaanite, the Amorite, and the Hittite, and the Perizzite, the Hivite, and the Jebusite."*

The heathen tribes mentioned here occupied the land that would later be called *"Israel."* They were extremely wicked, engaging in wholesale incest, pedophilia, homosexuality, and bestiality. In fact, one archeologist in his excavations of certain sites which these people had occupied made the statement, *"The God of the Old Testament Who gave instructions for these people to be eliminated totally did future generations an untold service."*

This man didn't make this statement out of religious feelings, but rather because he saw the evidence in his work, evidence of gross evil, incidentally, which would have been a terrible corruption on future generations, at least had these people been allowed to survive. At any rate, the Lord told Moses and the Children of Israel that He would drive out these enemies. Unfortunately, this particular generation to whom He made this statement were people of no Faith; consequently, they did not believe the Lord, and refused to go in. As a result, they had to remain in the wilderness for some 38 years, until this particular unbelieving generation died off.

GOD DOES NOT GIVE VICTORY TO FALLEN MAN

God gives victory only to His Son, and our Saviour, the Lord Jesus Christ. Consequently, we obtain victory only by being *"in Christ."*

Any serious Bible student knows and understands that the taking of Canaan presents itself as a type of our spiritual experience in Christ, more particularly, the Baptism with the Holy Spirit. Deliverance out of Egypt pictures Salvation, while possessing the land of Canaan pictures the Holy Spirit Baptism. The defeat of these enemies listed here picture the defeat of our enemies in the spiritual sense. Consequently, the two Books of Joshua and Judges portray to us the manner in which this ought to be done, and not to be done.

Joshua, who took the land, was a Type of Christ. But the mistake we make presently is that we think we have to take this land all over again, thereby, defeating these enemies all over again. It's difficult for us to understand that through the Cross, Jesus, as our Substitute, has already taken the land, and defeated all the enemies. As a result, the Holy Spirit will not help modern Believers fight a battle which has already been fought and won. And God knows how often we make the mistake of trying to do all over again, which we cannot do to begin with, and in fact, which Jesus has already done. As a result, we insult Him greatly!

Let me say again because it's so very, very important, what we said at the beginning of this particular segment:

God does not give victory to man per se. We constantly talk about having the victory, or obtaining the victory, or getting the victory, etc. Such terminology is not wrong, providing we know and understand what we are saying. But the trouble is, most of the time we don't! We keep trying to get the victory through our own machinations, ability, strength, and religiosity. While our effort may be noble, our defeat is certain. The Lord gives victory only to His Son, the Lord Jesus Christ. As our Substitute, Christ has already fought all of these battles (I said all), and has won them all, and His victory is our victory. The only way that we can have victory is by entering into His victory, which has already been accomplished. But for some reason, it's hard for us to do that. We keep wanting to try and gain victory through our own strength and ability, an effort which God will never sanction.

FIGHT THE GOOD FIGHT OF FAITH

To be sure, this Christian experience is a struggle! It is a fight! Paul said: *"For we wrestle not against flesh and blood, but against principalities, against powers, against the rulers of the darkness of this world, against spiritual wickedness in high places"* (Eph. 6:12).

Paul told Timothy, *"War a good warfare"* (I Tim. 1:18).

But the great question is, how do we engage this struggle? Now that's the problem. Not knowing and understanding God's prescribed order of victory, we engage this thing in the wrong way. As stated, any way, with the exception of God's Way, is doomed to failure. Listen again to Paul:

"For though we walk (live) *in the flesh, we do not war after the flesh:"*

He then went on to say, *"For the weapons of our warfare are not carnal, but mighty through God to the pulling down of strongholds"* (II Cor. 10:3-4).

Now what did he mean by not warring after the flesh? He answered that in another Epistle.

"I am crucified with Christ: nevertheless I live; yet not I, but Christ lives in me: and the life which I now live in the flesh I live by the Faith of the Son of God, Who loved me, and gave Himself for me" (Gal. 2:20).

The key is found in the statement, *"I am crucified with Christ."* In that particular statement, even as we've already stated in this Volume, Paul takes us back to Romans 6:3-5. He tells us there that the believing sinner is *"baptized into the death of Christ,"* also *"buried with Him by baptism into death,"* and then *"raised with Him in newness of life."*

Contrary to what most people think, Paul is not speaking here of Water Baptism. In fact, Water Baptism enters into this not at all! Paul is speaking of the Crucifixion of Christ, and our Faith in that Finished Work. When we exhibit Faith in Christ, in the Mind of God, He literally places us in Christ. And He places us into Christ, in the realm of the Crucifixion of our Saviour, His Burial, and His Resurrection. That's what Paul is talking about when he uses the term *"in Christ,"* or one of its derivatives, again and again. You are *"in Christ,"* by virtue of what He did at the Cross, all on our behalf. In other words, He was literally our Substitute and our Representative Man (I Cor. 15:45-50).

If you will notice, Paul kept pulling people back to the Cross (I Cor. 1:17-18, 21, 23; 2:2; Gal. 6:14; Eph. 2:13-18; Col. 2:14-15). He did this simply because the Holy Spirit wanted him to do this because it was at the Cross that all victory was won, and all victory is maintained.

In all of this, we do fight; however, it is the *"good fight of Faith,"* and that is the only fight we're called upon to engage (I Tim. 6:12).

WHAT DOES IT MEAN TO FIGHT THE GOOD FIGHT OF FAITH?

The *"Faith"* that's being spoken of here is Faith exclusively in Christ and what He accomplished at the Cross. That must ever be the object of our Faith, and that is the place where the fight commences.

Satan will do everything within his power to push our Faith away from the Cross of Christ, onto something else. He doesn't much care what the something else is, just as long as it's not in Christ and Him Crucified. It was at the Cross where Jesus atoned for all sin, and thereby it was at the Cross where Satan was totally defeated.

Satan's legal hold over humanity is the fact of sin. With sin being removed, which Jesus did by His atoning death, constituted by the shedding of His Precious Blood, this left Satan with no legal right to hold anyone in captivity, that is if they will only place their Faith and confidence solely in Christ. Understanding that, he will try to push the Believer's faith to another objective. If he can do that, irrespective as to how righteous the other objective may be in its own place and position, he knows that the Believer will be disobeying God in doing this, which will stop the help of the Holy Spirit, which means that such a Believer is going to fail. Satan can then get another hold onto the individual because the Faith of the individual is improperly placed.

Let all understand that all of this is in the realm of Faith. But more particularly, it's Faith in the correct object, which is Christ and Him Crucified. You as a Believer can have all the Faith in the world in anything else, but it won't do you any good. In fact, faith in other things translates into faith in self, which God can never recognize. We don't think of it as faith in self, simply because we load it up with Scriptures and good intentions; however, in the Mind of God, when we do these things, and I'm speaking of moving our Faith from Christ and the Cross, to something else, we are in effect, committing *"spiritual adultery"* (Rom. 7:1-4).

We are married to Christ, and this means that we are to look to Him for all of our needs, and more specifically what He did for us at the Cross. If we look elsewhere, we are being unfaithful to Him, and the Holy Spirit likens it to *"spiritual adultery,"* with which He will have no part.

SPIRITUAL ADULTERY

I suspect that most Believers have never heard the term *"spiritual adultery,"* in all of their lives. As we've just stated, Paul deals with this in the first four Verses of Romans, Chapter 7, as He begins to explain in that Chapter the efforts of the Believer in trying to live for God, and in all the wrong ways. In fact, in this particular Chapter, he was speaking of himself. And we should be given to understand that if Paul couldn't live for God outside of the Cross of Christ, at least successfully, how do you think you can?

Looking at the term *"adultery"* in the literal sense, all of us know what this means. The husband or the wife is unfaithful to their mate, which constitutes a serious crime against God and against the one to whom they have pledged their faithfulness. Consequently, this of which we speak as it regards *"spiritual adultery,"* is so serious that the Holy Spirit used the word *"adultery"* in this context. In the eyes of God, Whose eyes alone actually matter, if the Believer is not maintaining his Faith in Christ and what Christ did at the Cross, understanding that this is the means by which God gives all things to His people, the Believer is committing *"spiritual adultery."* Sadly and regrettably because the far greater majority of the modern Church understands little or nothing about the Cross, especially as it regards their Sanctification, this means that most Christians are in fact, committing *"spiritual adultery."* In that state, there can be no victory, no abundant life, no joy in the Lord, and in fact, no matter how hard we try, defeat will be the result.

All Salvation and all victory are found exclusively in Christ. And it's found in Christ due exclusively to what He did at the Cross. That's why the Apostle said:

"But God forbid that I should glory (boast) *save in the Cross of our Lord Jesus Christ, by Whom the world is crucified unto me, and I unto the world"* (Gal. 6:14).

HOW HARD IS THIS TO UNDERSTAND?

On the surface, as should be obvious, it's not difficult at all. But the major problem is, virtually all of our preaching and teaching in the last several decades have been in wrong directions, at least as it regards this all-important subject of the

Believer's Sanctification. *"Faith comes by hearing, and hearing by the Word of God"* (Rom. 10:17). If we do not hear something taught and preached, then it's virtually impossible for us to understand the Truth, which is being so woefully neglected.

And then again, due to the Fall, man has this ridiculous idea that he can save himself. A residue of this continues to hang even over Believers. We may not think of it in those terms, but in reality, this self-sufficiency problem lingers on. We call it *"faith,"* but in reality, it is *"self."* That's the reason that Jesus said that if we were going to follow Him, we would have to *"deny self, and take up our Cross daily"* (Lk. 9:23).

When He mentioned *"self"* in that statement, He wasn't speaking of asceticism, which is the denial of all things which are pleasurable, which most Christians think. He was rather speaking of us denying our own ability and strength, rather relying completely on Christ and what Christ did at the Cross. In fact, this is so very important that Jesus said that it must be done *"daily,"* which in effect is a renewing of our Faith in Him and the Cross, even on a daily basis.

THE UNDERSTANDING OF THE CROSS IS NOT THEOLOGICAL BUT RATHER MORAL

And what do we mean by that heading?

It means that if in fact we do lack understanding as it regards the Cross, that lack is not brought on by a theological problem, but rather a moral problem. The question at hand is not really difficult, so it's not theological. The question at hand regarding the Cross is *"moral,"* which means that if we reject the Cross, it's for moral reasons.

This means that it is pride, self-will, fear of man, or whatever, which keeps us from accepting God's Way. Let me give you an example:

As we've already stated several times in this Volume, most Denominations have long since abandoned the Cross, thereby opting for other things, mostly humanistic psychology. If a Preacher or even a layperson in one of these Denominations, whatever it might be, hears the Message of the Cross, determines in his heart and life that this is Scriptural and that he is going to allow his life to be guided by this principle from now on, he will find out soon enough that the direction which his Denomination is going is the total opposite. And to such a person, that dividing line will become wider and wider. So now the question must be asked, what is he going to do?

Does he say, I'm going to follow Christ no matter what, or does he make the decision in his heart to go along in order to get along? Now I think it is easier to see that this situation has become a moral choice. But this makes it all the worse. This means that this individual, whether he be Preacher or layperson, has in effect, chosen the way of Cain, and, thereby, rejected the way of Abel (Gen., Chpt. 4).

To properly follow Christ, we have to give up everything. That's the reason that Jesus said: *"If any man come to Me, and hate not his father, and mother, and wife, and children, and brethren, and sisters, yea, and his own life also, he cannot be My Disciple."*

He then said: *"And whosoever does not bear his Cross, and come after Me, cannot be My Disciple."*

And then bluntly, *"For which of you, intending to build a tower, sits not down first, and counts the cost, whether he have sufficient to finish it?"* (Lk. 14:26-28).

As should be obvious, Jesus pulled no punches. He didn't make it easy because it's not easy. He used those things which are dearest to the heart. Are you willing to give all of that up in order to follow Him? Now let me say this:

If you accept the way of the Cross, you will probably have to give up your Denomination, you may have to change Churches, you may have to change friends, and even your own family may turn against you. And why would this be so?

The entire religious bent of the religious world is in the opposite direction of the Cross. And if the Cross is accepted by enough people, those wrong ways will be exposed, because a correct view of the Cross does this. That's the reason the Psalmist said: *"Through Your precepts I get understanding: therefore I hate every false way"* (Ps. 119:104).

So, as stated, the Cross is a moral choice, and not a theological choice. It's not so much a question of understanding it, as a question of doing it.

A LAND FLOWING WITH MILK AND HONEY

Verse 3 reads: *"Unto a land flowing with milk and honey: for I will not go up in the midst of you; for you are a stiffnecked people: lest I consume you in the way."*

Several very important things are said in this Verse:

The Lord plainly tells the Children of Israel that the place He wishes to take them is a good place, in fact, *"a land flowing with milk and honey."* It is the same presently.

If we go God's Way, which is the Way of the Cross, one will find *"more abundant life"* (Jn. 10:10). Spiritually speaking, it is truly *"a land flowing with milk and honey."*

Now, were Christians asked if they were enjoying such an experience, most would unequivocally answer, *"yes!"* But the truth is, while all Believers definitely have more abundant life, all Believers aren't enjoying *"more abundant life."* In fact, with most Believers, living for the Lord is a constant struggle; and of course, I'm speaking of those who truly love the Lord, and are trying to do His Will. Is it supposed to be that way?

While there definitely is a *"fight,"* even as we've already stated, no, the type of fight in which most Christians are engaged brings nothing but misery.

In my own experience, and right in the midst of God using me to reach much of the world with the Gospel of Christ, and literally seeing hundreds of thousands of people brought to Christ, the truth was, I couldn't live a victorious life, despite the fact that I was trying so hard that it almost killed me. It was like Paul said: *"For that which I do I allow* (understand) *not: for what I would, that do I not; but what I hate, that do I"* (Rom. 7:15). In fact, the Scripture I've just quoted is the place and position, regrettably, of most Christians.

During that particular time, I would do my best to make certain that I prayed at least an hour each day. And then I would get up at 1:00 or 2:00 in the morning, and pray another hour. To be sure, the Lord blessed me greatly in my prayer times, as He always will; however, I found no source of victory in this manner because my faith was in my prayer life and not in the Cross of Christ. To be frank, during those times, I did not understand at all the means and manner of the Cross as it regards Sanctification, which was my problem all along. And as I've repeatedly stated, that's the condition of most Christians presently. They see that land flowing with milk and honey, they know this is what the Bible teaches, and they will even claim to have it. But the truth is, they don't have it. They know something is wrong, but they don't know exactly what. The *"sin nature"* is ruling these Christians, and in fact, has been ruling them for most of their Christian experience. Yes they are saved! And yes, many of them are even baptized with the Holy Spirit! And this makes it all the more confusing. They don't understand how they can be baptized with the Spirit, and even being blessed by the Lord in certain ways, and at the same time, failing!

Even though we've dealt with the sin nature at some length, please allow me to address it again, perhaps in a little different way.

THE SIN NATURE

As long as the sin nature rules in the heart and life of the Believer, such a Believer is not really going to enjoy his experience in Christ, to say the least! In fact, this thing is so serious that many have simply given up and quit, with some even committing suicide. And I exaggerate not! Let's look at five different ways that the sin nature is addressed, and perhaps it will shine some light on the subject and bring us to a place of victory:

IGNORANCE

1. The truth is, most Christians know little or nothing about the sin nature. If it's mentioned at all behind the pulpit where they attend Church, it's only mentioned in passing, if that. So the truth is, these people are ignorant of this all-important aspect of their Christian experience.

Now let's remember that the Holy Spirit, through Paul, addressed the sin nature in many and varied ways. He did that because it is a problem and in fact, a huge problem.

Some pages back, I went into detail as it

regards the Sixth Chapter of Romans, and how we are to understand how the sin nature is addressed in this particular Chapter, and other Chapters as well. So I won't cover that ground again. But let the Reader understand the following:

God places no premium on ignorance. In other words, ignorance does not keep us away from the danger. In fact, and it depends on that which we are addressing, ignorance can kill you.

Despite the fact that most Christians are totally ignorant of the sin nature, this in no way absolves them of its consequences. Such a Christian is doomed to living a life of spiritual failure, which brings nothing but misery.

DENIAL

2. Many Preachers deny the fact of the sin nature. They claim that such does not exist. While the Believer, they say, may have had a sin nature before conversion, at the moment they get saved, the sin nature is taken away.

The sin nature means what its name says. It means that it is the nature of an individual to sin or do wrong, providing that person doesn't function in God's prescribed order of victory. All of this is a result of the Fall. While it's certainly true that the believing sinner becomes a *"new creation"* at conversion, with old things having passed away, and all things becoming new (II Cor. 5:17), still, although dormant, the sin nature remains in the heart and life of every Believer. In fact, Paul said that we are to *"reckon ourselves as being dead to the sin nature, but alive unto God through Christ Jesus our Lord"* (Rom. 6:11). Now if no sin nature existed, why is Paul even addressing the subject?

No, denial does not change the facts.

LICENSE

3. On the other side of the coin, many Christians know they have a sin nature, or else they know that something is there driving them in the wrong direction, so their claim is, Grace is greater than sin, so I don't have to worry about the situation. Paul addressed this by saying: *"Shall we continue in sin, that Grace may abound?*

"God forbid. How shall we, who are dead to sin (the sin nature), *live any longer therein?"* (Rom. 6:1-2).

The Lord doesn't save us in sin, but rather from sin. In fact, even though the Lord will always forgive anyone who comes to Him in contrition and humility, it is not God's Will for us to live a sinning and repenting experience. But regrettably, that is the position of many Christians.

They claim they can't help but sin, so that's what they do.

This could hardly be construed as a life of victory, as I think should be obvious.

STRUGGLE

4. Most Christians have it in their minds that this Christian experience is just one great gigantic struggle. They feel they've got to struggle against sin constantly, and they chalk up their victories, but never mention the defeats. But the truth is, there are more defeats than victories.

Do you realize that the Bible doesn't teach a struggle against sin! How does a struggle against sin figure into the Words of Christ, when He said: *"Come unto Me, all you who labor and are heavy laden, and I will give you rest"* (Mat. 11:28)? No matter how hard we try, we simply cannot reconcile the two.

But regrettably, the *"struggle"* is the lifestyle of most good Christians. Notice I said *"good Christians!"* I do not say that sarcastically either. I'm speaking of people who truly love the Lord, and are doing their best to be a good Christian. And in fact, other than this terrible problem of which I speak, they are good Christians. So what's wrong?

They are addressing the sin nature in the wrong way. As a result, they are living a life of spiritual failure, which is definitely not the Will of God. Now let's look at the fifth and last manner in which this thing can be addressed, and which manner alone is the manner and way of victory.

GRACE

5. The Grace of God, which is simply the Goodness of God, flows to the Believer as a result of what Christ did at the Cross. Whenever the Believer understands this, thereby

looking to Christ for all things, and understanding that Christ gives him all things as a result of His Finished Work, the Grace of God will then flow to that Believer in an uninterrupted flow. He now has the help of the Holy Spirit, Who will use His Power in a mighty way, guaranteeing victory. Such a Believer has no fear of the sin nature, and no problem with the sin nature. He can rest on the Promise of the Lord as given to Paul, that, *"Sin shall not have dominion over you: for you are not under the Law, but under Grace"* (Rom. 6:14).

Even though the word *"sin"* in this Verse is not preceded by the definite article (the sin, or the sin nature), it is in fact used here as a noun instead of a verb; consequently, it is not really referring to acts of sin, but rather the sin nature.

As the Believer understands this, he will walk in victory, and enjoy the *"rest"* which Jesus promised, which is found only in Him. He will be dead to the sin nature, but alive unto God, all through Jesus Christ (Rom. 6:11).

This way and this way alone guarantees one, spiritually speaking, *"the land flowing with milk and honey."*

I'm certain that the Reader, going through this particular Volume, notices that there is much repetition. I do that for a purpose. Sometimes, something has to be said over and over, and especially spiritual things, before the individual finally understands what is being said. In fact, we are trying to break through many centuries of unbelief, and that's the reason it's very difficult to get the modern Church to see and understand this which the Lord gave to Paul nearly 2,000 years ago.

How many times have I had people say to me, even after hearing me teach this for several years, *"Brother Swaggart, I see it now!"* Why did it take so long? And why does it take so long?

Well of course, that answer is as varied as the number of people involved.

At any rate, if I continue to expound this Truth in every manner in which I know, if there is a believing heart, at some point in time, the Holy Spirit is going to be able to help them to grasp this which is so very, very important.

THE PRESENCE OF THE LORD

Of course it is understood that we're living under Grace and not under Law; however, to a certain degree, this great Truth, expounded in this Verse, holds true even now, as it regards the Presence of the Lord. In order to spare the people because of their wrong direction, the Lord will keep His distance, so to speak. As a result, such people are deprived of so much which they could have in the Lord, if they would only go His Way.

The Presence of the Lord cannot abide rebellion. And whenever Believers try to live this life in a manner other than Faith in Christ and His Cross, that is rebellion against God. It cannot be described in any other manner.

While the Lord is patient, loving, and kind, and as well, very longsuffering, and thank God He is, because if not, I don't know where I would be; however, I am persuaded that His Presence, and I speak of His Presence truly, simply cannot abide in the realm of unbelief. While He will continue to deal with such a person, in order to bring them to the right way, the truth is, they are going in the wrong direction; and as such, such a direction could ultimately lead to the loss of the soul, even as it often has (Heb. 6:4-6; 10:26-29).

STIFFNECKED

As it was said of Israel so long ago, probably the word *"stiffnecked"* would apply more than anything else as it regards the rejection of the Cross. In its common usage, the word refers to a neck that will not turn. It is looking in the wrong direction, but even though it hears a voice coming from another direction, it simply will not turn and listen; consequently, God labels such a person as *"stiffnecked,"* which refers to them being stubborn, obstinate, and unyielding.

Whenever we acquire Radio Stations in particular cities, which cover anywhere from 50 to 250 or more towns and cities being reached by that one Station, this means that the Message of the Cross has come to these communities. Many Christians will not even bother to listen to the programming, even though the Lord has sent it directly to them. Why?

The only answer is that which is given here, they are *"stiffnecked."*

But let me remind all and sundry, when one refuses the Cross, especially considering that the Lord has made it so available, one is tampering with their very soul. These individuals, whom the Lord referred to as *"stiffnecked,"* ultimately lost their way and, thereby, their souls. The Word of God describes them as *"children in whom there was no Faith"* (Deut. 32:20).

To reject the Cross is, in effect, to reject Christ; in reality, it's not possible to accept Christ without accepting the Cross. To do so constitutes one worshipping and serving *"another Jesus"* (II Cor. 11:4).

ORNAMENTS

Verses 4 through 6 read: *"And when the people heard these evil tidings, they mourned: and no man did put on his ornaments.*

"For the LORD had said unto Moses, Say unto the Children of Israel, You are a stiffnecked people: I will come up into the midst of you in a moment, and consume you: therefore now put off your ornaments from you, that I may know what to do with you.

"And the Children of Israel stripped themselves of their ornaments by the Mount Horeb."

The stripping of the ornaments, whatever they may have been, from themselves was demanded by God, for the following reason:

He wanted them to know that they were in serious difficulty because they had sinned, and sinned greatly; consequently, there was no time now for festivities, levity, or decorations. They were to be made to realize that they had sinned, and they had sinned greatly. The Scripture says that the people *"mourned,"* and that's exactly what they should have done.

A PERSONAL EXPERIENCE

If I remember correctly, it was the winter of 1992. The Lord had instructed me to begin two Prayer Meetings a day, one in the morning, and one at night, which we did. Actually, I kept up that regimen for some 10 years, and at the present time, still continuing with one Prayer Meeting a day. I don't want the Reader to think that doing such earned me anything with the Lord, for it didn't. Turning prayer into works can definitely be done, but I now certainly knew better than to even think of such a thing. In fact, the Lord had instructed me that I was to seek Him not so much for what He could do, but rather for Who He was. I will never forget that, as the Holy Spirit spoke to my heart. This is very similar to what Paul said:

"That I may know Him, and the power of His Resurrection, and the fellowship of His sufferings, being made conformable unto His death" (Phil. 3:10).

During one of the morning Prayer Meetings, early in 1992, there was a powerful moving of the Holy Spirit. I was earnestly seeking the Lord, feeling keenly my unworthiness, and that I desperately needed His Grace. At that time, I did not really know or understand the Message of the Cross, except in a fundamental way. What I did know, I preached strongly, as the hope of the world, and in fact, the only hope of the world. But as it regards the Sanctification of the Saint, I had no idea at that particular time as to the significance of the Cross, regarding our continued walk before God. That would come in 1996.

But that morning as I was earnestly seeking the Lord, and His Spirit was mightily upon me, even as I sought His Grace for my own person, the Lord spoke to my heart, saying:

"You are seeking My face for a move upon your own heart and life." He then said: *"The entirety of the Church world desperately needs such a move."* And then: *"I will begin a move in this place that will go all around the globe."*

I have hesitated to give the last part, because who am I that God would do anything as it regards this Ministry, especially to start a move here that would girdle the globe! But I now feel I should relate what the Spirit told me, and I trust I've handled it in such a way that attention will be totally drawn to Christ, and not poor, pitiful, human flesh.

Some 800 years before Christ, the Spirit of God spoke through the great Prophet Isaiah, saying: *"Ah sinful nation, a people laden with iniquity, a seed of evildoers, children who are corrupters: they have forsaken* the LORD, they have provoked the Holy One of Israel unto anger, they are gone away backward... the whole head is sick, and the whole heart faint.

"*From the sole of the foot even unto the head there is no soundness in it; but wounds, and bruises, and putrefying sores: they have not been closed, neither bound up, neither mollified with ointment*" (Isa. 1:4-6).

Even though those words were spoken of Israel so long, long ago, I'm afraid they also fit the modern Church, and that goes for all of us.

THE MESSAGE OF THE CROSS

It is my belief that the Message of the Cross, which has been given to this unworthy Evangelist, is the beginning of that Move of God. The Church must return to the Cross. It must know and understand that its only hope is the Cross; therefore, it must forsake all other proposed solutions in order that the Holy Spirit may profitably work within hearts and lives. He will not work otherwise! Any way proposed other than the Cross shuts out the Spirit and, therefore, spells doom for anyone who would walk such an erroneous path.

JUDGMENT

In Verses 4 through 6, the Lord through Moses warned the people that they were in serious danger of being literally consumed. What Pharaoh couldn't do, He could do in a moment.

Modern Believers may read these words and automatically dismiss themselves and the Church as a whole from such introspection, concluding that the dispensation of Grace, in which we now live, cancels out all such judgment.

While this is truly the Dispensation of Grace, the truth is, due to the Cross, which has made the spread of the Gospel possible all over the world, God expects far more of us now under Grace, than He did of Israel in Old Testament Times. Concerning this very thing, Paul said:

"*And the times of this ignorance* (Old Testament Times) *God winked at* (did not exact judgment); *but now* (this Day of Grace) *commands all men everywhere to repent*"

NOTES

(Acts 17:30).

The truth is, because of the Church rebelling against God, and I speak of forsaking the Cross, and, thereby, embracing the wisdom of the world, judgment is being poured out on the Church, in that the Holy Spirit has all but totally departed. And without the Holy Spirit, Who will work only within the parameters of the Cross, the Church is nothing! Far better for God to chastise His people than to forsake them. And I firmly believe that the Church is at the position presently, as was Israel during the time of our study.

(7) "AND MOSES TOOK THE TABERNACLE, AND PITCHED IT WITHOUT THE CAMP, AFAR OFF FROM THE CAMP, AND CALLED IT THE TABERNACLE OF THE CONGREGATION. AND IT CAME TO PASS, THAT EVERY ONE WHICH SOUGHT THE LORD WENT OUT UNTO THE TABERNACLE OF THE CONGREGATION, WHICH WAS WITHOUT THE CAMP.

(8) "AND IT CAME TO PASS, WHEN MOSES WENT OUT UNTO THE TABERNACLE, THAT ALL THE PEOPLE ROSE UP, AND STOOD EVERY MAN AT HIS TENT DOOR, AND LOOKED AFTER MOSES, UNTIL HE WAS GONE INTO THE TABERNACLE.

(9) "AND IT CAME TO PASS, AS MOSES ENTERED INTO THE TABERNACLE, THE CLOUDY PILLAR DESCENDED, AND STOOD AT THE DOOR OF THE TABERNACLE, AND THE LORD TALKED WITH MOSES.

(10) "AND ALL THE PEOPLE SAW THE CLOUDY PILLAR STAND AT THE TABERNACLE DOOR: AND ALL THE PEOPLE ROSE UP AND WORSHIPPED, EVERY MAN IN HIS TENT DOOR.

(11) "AND THE LORD SPOKE UNTO MOSES FACE TO FACE, AS A MAN SPEAKS UNTO HIS FRIEND. AND HE TURNED AGAIN INTO THE CAMP: BUT HIS SERVANT JOSHUA, THE SON OF NUN, A YOUNG MAN, DEPARTED NOT OUT OF THE TABERNACLE."

The construction is:

1. The word "*Tabernacle*" of Verse 7, should have been translated "*tent*," for it is the Hebrew word "*ohel*," which means,

"*tent.*" The Hebrew word for *"Tabernacle"* is *"mishkan."*

2. The *"cloudy pillar"* denoted the Presence of God.

3. While *"all the people rose up and worshipped,"* it seemed to have been more out of fear than anything else. In other words, it wasn't worship from a sincere, earnest heart.

4. The Lord spoke to Moses, *"face to face,"* thereby, giving him instructions.

5. Joshua was even now being groomed by the Holy Spirit to take the place of Moses, even though it would be some 40 years in the future before Joshua would assume the role of leadership.

THE TENT

Verse 7 reads: *"And Moses took the Tabernacle, and pitched it without the Camp, afar off from the Camp, and called it the Tabernacle of the Congregation. And it came to pass, that every one which sought the LORD went out unto the Tabernacle of the Congregation, which was without the Camp."*

As we've already stated, the word *"Tabernacle"* used here should have been translated *"tent."* In fact, the Tabernacle, even though its design had already been given to Moses, had not yet been constructed.

This particular *"tent,"* was probably an *"office"* of sorts, where Moses carried on daily business, etc.

The Lord instructed him to take this tent, and to pitch it without the Camp, probably about a mile distant from any of the congregation. In essence, by the Lord having the Lawgiver to do this, He was telling Israel that their sin had excluded Him from their midst. So two things are said here:

1. We must understand that God cannot abide sin presently, any more than He did then. In fact, due to the Cross now being a fact, His tolerance is even lower. Perhaps it would be better to say it in the following manner:

Sin is an awful business, so awful, in fact, that it defies description; however, God has made Atonement for sin, all sin, which He did at the Cross (I Jn. 2:1-2).

Man's great sin in this age is not taking his sin to the right place, which is the Cross. It is the problem of Cain all over again. He would rather submit to humanistic psychology, or try to apply some false doctrine to his need. So the real sin of the Church is not taking its sin to the Cross!

2. The Lord telling Moses to take his tent outside of the Camp was really an act of Grace. Had it remained in the Camp, Judgment may very well have fallen.

Let the Reader understand that Grace does not wink at sin. It is rather the solution for sin, which speaks of the Holy Spirit working in the heart and life of the Believer, and being able to do so as a result of the Cross (Rom. 8:1-2, 11; Gal. 2:20-21).

TO SEEK THE LORD

All the people who desire to truly worship the Lord were instructed to go to the tent which was stretched outside the Camp. More than likely, the people didn't go inside the tent, because it would not have held many, but rather must have stood outside. Their very act of going out to this particular place showed that they understood the terrible plight in which Israel now found herself, and that they didn't want to be a part of that rebellion. Instead, they desired to worship the Lord, and to do so in spirit and in truth.

It has reached the place in the modern Church, at least in many places, to where one cannot profitably worship the Lord in the midst of those who claim Christ, but in reality, do not really possess Christ. I do not speak here of failure, or sinless perfection, because the latter doesn't exist. I do speak of wrong direction! I do speak of those who repudiate the Cross! That being the case, and which it is in many circles, I cannot fellowship with such people. To do so would be to deny my Lord, and the great price that He paid in order that I might have Redemption.

THE CLOUDY PILLAR

Verses 8 through 10 read: *"And it came to pass, when Moses went out unto the Tabernacle, that all the people rose up, and stood every man at his tent door, and looked after Moses, until he was gone into the Tabernacle.*

"And it came to pass, as Moses entered into the Tabernacle, the cloudy pillar descended, and stood at the door of the Tabernacle, and

the Lord talked with Moses.

"And all the people saw the cloudy pillar stand at the Tabernacle door: and all the people rose up and worshipped, every man in his tent door."

The main theme of these Verses is the fact that the *"cloudy pillar,"* denoting the Presence of God, came and stood over the door of this particular tent. This tells us two things:

1. It tells us that the Presence of God was with Moses, and in fact, was not with the people.

2. The *"cloudy pillar"* standing over the door of this particular tent, specified that this was the correct door, which refers to all of its spiritual implications. Even though the Scripture is silent, there is a possibility that other similar tents had been stretched somewhere in the Camp, with claims being made of the Presence of God. But in unmistakable terms, the Lord will show the place upon which His approval rests.

It comes down to the Altar that represents the Cross, or the Altar that represents the golden calf!

As is obvious, the people here were watching Moses, as they should have been watching Moses. They surmised that the Lord was giving instructions to him, which He was.

If any desire to seek the Lord, and humble themselves before Him, they were required to show abhorrence of the idolatry of Israel, by separating from among them, and following the Tabernacle out of the Camp.

It seems that some of the people may have moved their tents close to the Tabernacle, which Verse 7 implies; consequently, they could then see what was happening at the Tabernacle, and could respond accordingly. How many did this, if in fact that is what was done, the Scripture is silent. But it does draw attention to the fact that some definitely did, meaning that despite the idolatry, some in Israel loved the Lord.

JOSHUA

Verse 11 reads: *"And the LORD spoke unto Moses face to face, as a man speaks unto his friend. And he turned again into the Camp: but his servant Joshua, the son of Nun, a young man, departed not out of the tent."*

Joshua would one day take the place of Moses, even though it would be about 40 years into the future. But the Holy Spirit had already begun his training, showing the preparation time that was needed.

Someone asked me the other day, and concerning a potential Move of God, *"Are you ready?"*

My answer was far different than it would have been 30 years ago, had I been asked the same question.

"No, I'm not ready, and I'm not certain that anyone can be ready. If we think we are ready, we're only deceiving ourselves." And then I added, *"The readiness that is required, the Lord will have to accomplish, that being beyond my strength and ability."*

The Lord, speaking to Moses *"face to face,"* portrays a relationship not equaled by many human beings, even from the very beginning. In fact, it possibly was never equaled, at least in Old Testament times.

But yet, when men looked upon Christ during His earthly sojourn, they were nearer the Father than even Moses had been. And due to the Cross, we now have the Holy Spirit, Who is God, abiding within us, which gives us a greater relationship even than Moses. That's what Jesus was speaking about when He said of John the Baptist: *"For I say unto you, among those who are born of women there is not a greater Prophet than John the Baptist: but he who is least in the Kingdom of God is greater than he"* (Lk. 7:28).

He wasn't meaning that we are greater in character than John, but rather our privileges in Christ are greater, due to what Christ has done for us at the Cross.

So let not the Reader wish for a relationship with God as had Moses, as great as that was, considering that what we now have is far, far greater. The Scripture says: *"For the Law was given by Moses, but Grace and Truth came by Jesus Christ"* (Jn. 1:17).

(12) "AND MOSES SAID UNTO THE LORD, SEE, YOU SAY UNTO ME, BRING UP THIS PEOPLE: AND YOU HAVE NOT LET ME KNOW WHOM YOU WILL SEND WITH ME. YET YOU HAVE SAID, I KNOW YOU BY NAME, AND YOU HAVE ALSO FOUND GRACE IN MY SIGHT.

(13) "NOW THEREFORE, TO YOU I PRAY, IF I HAVE FOUND GRACE IN YOUR

SIGHT, SHOW ME NOW YOUR WAY, THAT I MAY KNOW YOU, THAT I MAY FIND GRACE IN YOUR SIGHT: AND CONSIDER THAT THIS NATION IS YOUR PEOPLE.

(14) "AND HE SAID, MY PRESENCE SHALL GO WITH YOU, AND I WILL GIVE YOU REST.

(15) "AND HE SAID UNTO HIM, IF YOUR PRESENCE GO NOT WITH ME, CARRY US NOT UP HENCE.

(16) "FOR WHEREIN SHALL IT BE KNOWN HERE THAT I AND YOUR PEOPLE HAVE FOUND GRACE IN YOUR SIGHT? IS IT NOT IN THAT YOU GO WITH US? SO SHALL WE BE SEPARATED, I AND YOUR PEOPLE, FROM ALL THE PEOPLE WHO ARE UPON THE FACE OF THE EARTH.

(17) "AND THE LORD SAID UNTO MOSES, I WILL DO THIS THING ALSO THAT YOU HAVE SPOKEN: FOR YOU HAVE FOUND GRACE IN MY SIGHT, AND I KNOW YOU BY NAME."

The overview is:

1. Moses seizes upon the word *"Grace,"* and with wonderful spiritual intelligence, pleads that God should continue to accompany them, because they were a stiffnecked people! (Ex. 34:9).

2. The fact that they were a stiffnecked people is urged as an argument.

3. In a sense, Moses is appointed as Mediator.

4. He demands that the Presence of God accompany him, and that the enterprise was impossible without the companionship of the Lord.

5. It was that companionship, and nothing else, that separated Israel from the surrounding nations (Williams).

GRACE

Verse 12 reads: *"And Moses said unto the LORD, See, You say unto me, Bring up this people: and You have not let me know whom You will send with me. Yet You have said, I know you by name, and you have also found Grace in My sight."*

Knowing full well that the Lord has moved His Presence out of the Camp of Israel, and to the tent of Moses, which was stretched outside of the Camp, Moses now opens his argument.

First of all, he pleads Grace by saying, *"I have found Grace in Your sight."* He makes *"Grace"* the foundation of his petition, which foundation alone God will honor. If we come to Him on the basis of supposed merit, we will not be received. And we must always remember, Grace comes to the Believer strictly on the premise of the Finished Work of Christ. In fact, it can come no other way!

If we approach the Lord on this basis, the basis of Grace, and what we ask is in His Will, we can have the same relationship that Moses had, and in fact, at this present time, even greater. Moses took his needs to the Lord; we should do the same. In fact, there was no one else who could answer the questions which Moses proposed, or give him direction, which he desperately needed, other than the Lord. To be sure, it is the same with us presently.

We must seek the Face of the Lord, and do so constantly, and He, without fail, will give us Grace also, answer our questions, and meet our need.

PRAYER

When I was a child, my Grandmother taught me to pray. She taught me to believe God, and to believe Him for great and mighty things. I can see her even now, as she would begin to discuss what the Lord could do, and how that a faraway look would come into her eyes, and she would tell me, *"Jimmy, God is a big God, so ask big!"* I never forgot that. In fact, it has helped me to touch the world for Christ, literally to see hundreds of thousands brought to a saving knowledge of Jesus Christ. *"God is a big God, so ask big!"*

She taught me to be specific in my praying. To tell the Lord what I wanted and what I needed, but above all to seek His Will in all things. In effect, she was my Bible College, my Seminary, my training ground for this work which the Lord has called me to do.

When Frances and I first married, almost immediately upon getting off from work, I would go over to her house, most of the time with Frances accompanying me, and we would have a prayer meeting. It was in those prayer meetings where I really received my education, so to speak. But yet, I go back also to when I was eight, nine, and ten years old, and I remember those prayer meetings as well.

Before we went to prayer, and sometimes there would be five or six, or even eight or ten in the room, we would give prayer requests, and then each of us would draw a *"Promise Card."* I'm not sure if most reading this Volume would remember those little boxes of cards, which had Scriptures written on them?

We would all take one, and read it out loud. My Grandmother taught me that all of these things that I read in those days of so long ago could be mine. She drilled into me that this was God's Word to me. When I would read these cards, reading these great Promises, a thrill could come to my soul. God had said it, and I believed it, and I found out in coming times, my Grandmother was right. I could have those Promises, and by the Grace of God, I have had, and will have those Promises.

Oh, how I sense the Presence of God, even as I dictate these words. He is just as real today as He was with Moses, and as He was when I was a child. He changes not! What He did then, He'll do now!

THY WAY

Verse 13 reads: *"Now, I pray you, if I have found Grace in Your sight, show me now Your way, that I may know You, that I may find Grace in Your sight: and consider that this nation is Your people."*

Moses wanted to know God's Ways, and to be sure, the Lord wanted to show Moses His Ways. God has a way for everything. It's up to us to find out what that way is. I think one can say without fear of contradiction that it's always found somewhere in His Word. But yet, at times, personal direction is needed, of which the Word may not be specific. But if we will earnestly seek the Lord, even as Moses earnestly sought the Lord, the Lord will definitely show us His Way.

Despite the fact that Israel has sinned, and sinned greatly, Moses asked the Almighty to *"consider that this nation is Your people."* By the actions of the Lord, the sense was there that He had disowned them.

The idea is, if in fact Moses has found Grace in the sight of the Lord, then the Lord, at the same time, will not withhold from him the *"way"* in which He will lead the Children of Israel to Canaanland.

THE PRESENCE OF GOD

Verses 14 and 15 read: *"And He said, My Presence shall go with you, and I will give you rest.*

"And he said unto Him, If Your Presence go not with me, carry us not up hence."

If Moses was to succeed, he knew beyond the shadow of a doubt that he had to have the Presence of God with him. The Presence of God, as should be obvious, refers to the Person of God. In other words, He is there in Person.

That which Moses requested so long ago, in fact demanded, is that which we must have as well, that is if we are to get the Work of God accomplished. The *"Presence of the Lord,"* in essence, is the same thing as the Anointing.

In my Services, in fact wherever I may preach, I earnestly seek for the Presence of God. I know that without this *"Presence"* nothing will be accomplished in the hearts of the people. But with this *"Presence,"* beautiful and wonderful things will be carried out.

In fact, due to the Holy Spirit occupying our hearts and lives, and of course, I'm speaking of Born-Again, Spirit-filled Believers, we have the Presence of God with us constantly; however, that actually means that the potential of His Presence is with us, but it remains to be seen as to exactly what His Presence will do, that being dependent on several things. Some of those things are:

1. The Cross of Christ must ever be the object of our Faith (Rom. 6:3-5; Eph. 2:13-18; Col. 2:14-15).

2. That being the case, we must expect the Holy Spirit to work within our lives. We must let Him know that we want His leading, guidance, and above all, the Will of God (Jn. 16:13-15).

3. We must have a consecrated prayer life. This doesn't mean that we earn things by so much praying, but it does mean that this is

the manner, usually, where we find the Will of God, even as the Holy Spirit deals with our hearts (Rom. 8:26-32).

THE PEOPLE OF GOD

Verses 16 and 17 read: *"For wherein shall it be known here that I and Your people have found Grace in Your sight? Is it not in that You go with us? So shall we be separated, I and Your people, from all the people who are upon the face of the Earth.*

"And the LORD said unto Moses, I will do this thing also that you have spoken: for you have found Grace in My sight, and I know you by name."

Moses as the Mediator was able to obtain favor from God as it regarded the Children of Israel, even though they had sinned grievously. I think as well, a sufficient number, whatever that may have been, had repented, had earnestly sought Mercy and Grace from the Lord, which carried much weight.

If the Reader is to remember, as Abraham petitioned the Lord concerning the sparing of Sodom and Gomorrah, if even ten righteous had been found in these cities, they would have been spared (Gen. 18:32). For a city, a nation, or a people to be spared, the repentance of a few will serve, in a sense, as an Atonement for the many.

I am persuaded that even a few righteous people in any given town or city, guarantees withheld judgment, and even blessing upon that particular place. Of course, the unredeemed, who make up the far greater majority, do not at all know this of which I have said, and in fact, would vehemently deny such if the question was posed to them, claiming that the people of God have nothing to do with prosperity and blessing. But of course, we know better!

KNOWING BY NAME

That God knew Moses by name must not be taken as it appears on the surface. God knows everything, which refers to every single name in the universe. Not only does He know the name of each person and thing, but as well, He goes much further than that, and keeps an account on a constant basis, even of the *"very hairs of our head"* (Mat. 10:30). Such knowledge, we cannot even begin to fathom!

So, knowing Moses by name speaks of relationship. It speaks of intimacy, and to a far greater degree than we could imagine.

Does He know your name in this fashion? Does He know my name in this fashion?

(18) "AND HE SAID, I BESEECH YOU, SHOW ME YOUR GLORY.

(19) "AND HE SAID, I WILL MAKE ALL MY GOODNESS PASS BEFORE YOU, AND I WILL PROCLAIM THE NAME OF THE LORD BEFORE YOU; AND WILL BE GRACIOUS TO WHOM I WILL BE GRACIOUS, AND WILL SHOW MERCY ON WHOM I WILL SHOW MERCY.

(20) "AND HE SAID, YOU CANNOT SEE MY FACE: FOR THERE SHALL NO MAN SEE ME, AND LIVE.

(21) "AND THE LORD SAID, BEHOLD, THERE IS A PLACE BY ME, AND YOU SHALL STAND UPON A ROCK:

(22) "AND IT SHALL COME TO PASS, WHILE MY GLORY PASSES BY, THAT I WILL PUT YOU IN A CLIFT OF THE ROCK, AND WILL COVER YOU WITH MY HAND WHILE I PASS BY:

(23) "AND I WILL TAKE AWAY MY HAND, AND YOU SHALL SEE MY BACK PARTS: BUT MY FACE SHALL NOT BE SEEN."

The exegesis is:

1. Grace comes first, then glory.

2. Law blots out the sinner; Grace blots out the sin.

3. God would show Moses His *"goodness"* instead of His wrath.

4. God reserves the right to show Grace and Mercy to whom He desires. Even though He has acquiesced to Moses' requests, still, the recipients of Grace and Mercy are decided by God and not by others.

5. The *"Rock"* of Verse 21 was the Lord Jesus Christ.

6. The *"clift of the Rock"* is the precious shed Blood of Jesus Christ that *"will cover you."*

YOUR GLORY

Verse 18 reads: *"And he said, I beseech You, show me Your glory."*

In reply to this request, Henry says: *"God denied what was not fit to be granted, and which Moses could not bear. A full discovery* of the Glory of God would overpower the faculties of any mortal man in this present state, and overwhelm even Moses himself. Man is mean and unworthy of it, weak and could not bear it, guilty and could not but dread it. There is a knowledge and enjoyment of God, which must be waited for in another world, when we shall see Him as He is (I Jn. 3:2)."*

On the Mount of Transfiguration, God would ultimately answer that prayer. The Scripture says concerning Christ: *"And was transfigured before them: and His face did shine as the sun, and His raiment was white as the light.*

"And, behold, there appeared unto them Moses and Elijah talking with Him" (Mat. 17:2-3).

MERCY AND GRACE

Verse 19 reads: *"And He said, I will make all My goodness pass before you, and I will proclaim the Name of the LORD before you; and will be gracious to whom I will be gracious, and will show mercy on whom I will show mercy."*

One might say that the *"Goodness"* of God is, at the same time, the *"Glory"* of God.

The proclamation of *"the Name of the Lord,"* presents the fact that God is all of these things. The *"Name of the Lord"* is far more than mere identification. It is His Character and His Nature. His Name is what He is, translating into what He does!

The Lord expressing Himself to Moses in this manner is what we would refer to presently as *"putting our name on the dotted line."* In effect, Moses now has assurance from the Lord regarding most all which he has requested.

GRACE AND MERCY

Sometime in eternity past, long before it was created, the Lord made the decision that He would deal with the human race through the principle of Grace. Grace had to be a choice, or else it couldn't be Grace. (Grace is simply the Goodness of God extended to undeserving people.) But once Grace was decided upon by the Godhead, God literally had no choice but that *"Mercy"* be extended as well. Grace demands that Mercy follow.

However, the Grace and Mercy of God are not given by the Lord on an arbitrary whim. It is given strictly to those who place their Faith and trust in the Lord Jesus Christ, and what He did at the Cross, which of course, is not by works. In fact, works nullify Grace! The Goodness of God cannot be extended to anyone who nourishes the idea that he has earned such.

Christ and the Cross, as the means by which Grace is extended, are portrayed from the very beginning. I speak of Genesis, Chapter 4, which continues through the entirety of the Word of God.

TO SEE GOD!

Verse 20 reads: *"And He said, You cannot see My face: for there shall no man see Me, and live."*

We must remember that Moses was asking to see God in all His Glory, which we learn here, is impossible. Factually, God has been seen out of His Glory, one might say, a number of times (Gen. 32:30).

John said: *"No man has seen God at any time; the only Begotten Son, which is in the bosom of the Father, He has declared Him"* (Jn. 1:18).

The word *"seen"* would have probably been better translated *"fully comprehended,"* making it read, *"No man has fully comprehended God at any time."*

THE ROCK

Verse 21 reads: *"And the LORD said, Behold, there is a place by Me, and you shall stand upon a rock."*

Henry says: *"The 'Rock' in Horeb was typical of Christ the Rock; the Rock of Israel and the Rock of Ages, the Rock of refuge, Salvation, and strength; comparable to one for shelter, solidity, firmness, strength, and duration. Happy are they who stand upon this Rock. They are safe and secure, they stand on high, and have noble prospects of the perfections of God, and of the riches of His Grace and Goodness (Ps. 40:2; Isa. 33:16; Mat. 7:24)."*

THE CLIFT OF THE ROCK

Verses 22 and 23 read: *"And it shall come to pass, while My glory passes by, that I will put you in a clift of the Rock, and will cover* you with My hand while I pass by:

"And I will take away My hand, and you shall see My back parts: but My face shall not be seen."

The *"clift of the Rock"* could be likened to the precious shed Blood of Jesus Christ, which covers the individual whose Faith is placed therein.

It is believed that this particular *"clift"* is the same cave where Elijah would go, while in a very depressed state, some 800 years into the future (I Ki. 19:9).

ANTHROPOMORPHISM

Concerning certain statements made by God, such as Him referring to His *"hand,"* and His *"back,"* and as well, His *"face,"* many claim these are merely anthropomorphisms.

An anthropomorphism is human terms being ascribed to God, which claims that this is done in Scripture, that we might understand the Lord, etc.

Personally, I don't think that is correct. If God doesn't have a face, or hands, etc., I don't think He would have said that He had such. It is my belief that God has a spirit body, which is very similar to a human body, except it's not flesh, but rather *"spirit"* (Jn. 4:24).

The arguments over this have raged from the very beginning, I suppose; however, in studying the Word of God for over 50 years, I personally feel that the Holy Spirit, Who is the Author of the written Word (II Pet. 1:20-21), meant for us to take the Word of God literally, unless it is obvious that it should not be taken literally. Of course, when Jesus said *"You are the salt of the Earth,"* it should be understood that He was using a metaphor. Salt is a preservative, and He was merely saying that the Saints of God are, in effect, the preservative of this Earth. In other words, it's the Saints who hold back the Judgment of God, and the Saints alone! Otherwise, God would have been forced to have destroyed this planet a long time ago because without the Saints of God, civilization would have finally become so corrupt that it would, in effect, have destroyed itself.

No, I personally believe that God has hands, a back, a face, etc., in other words, *"a body,"* but not a body as we think of such, but rather a *"spirit body."* As such, it doesn't age, and is not subject to the laws to which physical bodies are subject.

"I know that my Redeemer lives
"And ever prays for me;
"A token of His love He gives,
"A pledge of liberty."

"I find Him lifting up my head;
"He brings Salvation near;
"His Presence makes me free indeed,
"And He will soon appear."

"He wills that I should holy be:
"What can withstand His Will?
"The counsel of His Grace in me
"He surely shall fulfill."

"Jesus, I hang upon Your Word:
"I steadfastly believe
"You will return and claim me, Lord,
"And to Yourself receive."

CHAPTER 34

(1) "AND THE LORD SAID UNTO MOSES, HEW THEE TWO TABLES OF STONE LIKE UNTO THE FIRST: AND I WILL WRITE UPON THESE TABLES THE WORDS THAT WERE IN THE FIRST TABLES, WHICH YOU BROKE.

(2) "AND BE READY IN THE MORNING, AND COME UP IN THE MORNING UNTO MOUNT SINAI, AND PRESENT YOURSELF THERE TO ME IN THE TOP OF THE MOUNT.

(3) "AND NO MAN SHALL COME UP WITH YOU, NEITHER LET ANY MAN BE SEEN THROUGHOUT ALL THE MOUNT; NEITHER LET THE FLOCKS NOR HERDS FEED BEFORE THAT MOUNT.

(4) "AND HE HEWED TWO TABLES OF STONE LIKE UNTO THE FIRST; AND MOSES ROSE UP EARLY IN THE MORNING, AND WENT UP UNTO MOUNT SINAI, AS THE LORD HAD COMMANDED HIM, AND TOOK IN HIS HAND THE TWO TABLES OF STONE.

(5) "AND THE LORD DESCENDED IN THE CLOUD, AND STOOD WITH HIM THERE, AND PROCLAIMED THE NAME OF THE LORD.

(6) "AND THE LORD PASSED BY BEFORE HIM, AND PROCLAIMED, THE LORD, THE LORD GOD, MERCIFUL AND GRACIOUS, LONGSUFFERING, AND ABUNDANT IN GOODNESS AND TRUTH,

(7) "KEEPING MERCY FOR THOUSANDS, FORGIVING INIQUITY AND TRANSGRESSION AND SIN, AND THAT WILL BY NO MEANS CLEAR THE GUILTY; VISITING THE INIQUITY OF THE FATHERS UPON THE CHILDREN, AND UPON THE CHILDREN'S CHILDREN, UNTO THE THIRD AND TO THE FOURTH GENERATION."

The diagram is:

1. *"Grace"* is the keynote of this Chapter.
2. Whenever man fails, God retires into Christ in Whom is no failure.
3. The Ten Commandments were given again, but they were to be committed to the Ark — the symbol of Him Who said, *"Thy Word have I hid in My heart"* (Williams).

THE TWO TABLES

Verses 1 through 4 read: *"And the LORD said unto Moses, Hew thee two tables of stone like unto the first: and I will write upon these tables the words that were in the first tables, which you broke.*

"And be ready in the morning, and come up in the morning unto Mount Sinai, and present yourself there to Me in the top of the Mount.

"And no man shall come up with you, neither let any man be seen throughout all the Mount; neither let the flocks nor herds feed before that Mount.

"And he hewed two tables of stone like unto the first; and Moses rose up early in the morning, and went up into Mount Sinai, as the LORD had commanded him, and took in his hand the two tables of stone."

While the Lord told Moses to hew the tables of stone all over again, because he (Moses) had broken the first two, there is no record that God reprimanded him. Perhaps we could say that the repetition of the giving of the Ten Commandments the second time underlines God's love and patience with us. Many times He has to do the work all over again within our lives.

The Ten Commandments constitute the moral Government of God on this Earth. One might say that when Jehovah issued the Ten Commandments, He took His rightful place as Lord of all the Earth. His Standard of Righteousness is now in the world, or at least it will be, just as soon as Moses completes the fashioning of the two tablets of stone, and God Personally writes the Ten Commandments all over again.

So Moses did what the Lord commanded, *"And took in his hand the two tables of stone,"* on which the Lord would once again inscribe the moral Law.

THE WORD OF THE LORD

Verses 5 through 7 read: *"And the LORD descended in the cloud, and stood with him there, and proclaimed the Name of the LORD.*

"And the LORD passed by before him, and proclaimed, The LORD, the LORD God, merciful and gracious, longsuffering, and abundant in goodness and truth,

"Keeping mercy for thousands, forgiving iniquity and transgression and sin, and that will by no means clear the guilty; visiting the iniquity of the fathers upon the children, and upon the children's children, unto the third and to the fourth generation."

Moses stands in the clift of the Rock, exactly as the Lord had told him to do. Then the cloud descended to where Moses was, and the Lord was *"in the cloud."* He not only revealed Himself to Moses, but as well, He *"proclaimed the Name of the Lord,"* which revealed God's Character and Nature.

1. The Lord proclaims Himself as *"merciful and gracious."* When we consider that we are serving One Who is all-powerful, meaning that He can do anything, how thrilled we are that His first attributes are *"Mercy"* and *"Grace."*

2. He is *"longsuffering,"* referring to infinite patience. The first thing that comes to mind is how patient the Lord has been with me. We humans will bear with someone for awhile, but very soon we lose patience. But God will deal with the human heart, even long after there seems to be any chance of that heart turning. He is *"longsuffering, not willing that any should perish, but that all should come to repentance."*

3. And then He is *"abundant in goodness*

and truth," specifying that there can be no *"goodness"* unless it is based on *"truth."* Unfortunately, the world most of the time bases its so-called goodness on a lie. As such, it will not recognize the Goodness of God.

"Keeping mercy for thousands" proclaims the fact that God continually shows mercy in all its various exercises to thousands of sinners, and has treasures for thousands more, which cannot be exhausted, even by increasing numbers, to the end of time.

The idea of the statement, *"Keeping mercy for thousands,"* refers to the Lord keeping the sinner from destruction until the time that he yields to the Lord, at which time all his iniquities, transgressions, and sins are forgiven.

I daresay that most holding this book in your hands, when contemplating your past, and I speak of the time before you came to the Lord, looking back, you can see how the Lord kept you until the time came when you gave your heart to Christ. That was the Lord *"keeping mercy for you."* When we think of such, we know that the Lord is *"merciful, gracious, longsuffering, and abundant in goodness and truth."*

THE GUILTY . . .

However, even though God is all of these things because that is His Character and Nature, at the same time, because that is His Character and Nature, He cannot overlook sin in anyone irrespective as to whom that person might be. He stands ready to forgive, cleanse, change, and perform a miracle of Redemption on all who would come to Him. But if the individual refuses to do so, their iniquity will be visited upon them in judgment, and if their lineage continues in iniquity and transgression, the sin will compound itself. In other words, the great grandchildren, etc., continuing in sin, will suffer judgment just as did their forefathers because the wages of sin is death in every generation.

These Passages completely debunk moral evolution. In other words, man doesn't get better and better, but rather worse and worse!

But let it be quickly stated that the moment anyone comes to Christ, at that moment they become a new creation, with old things passing away, and all things becoming new (II Cor. 5:17).

THE FAMILY CURSE

Even though we addressed this back in Exodus, Chapter 20, due to its significance, please allow me the latitude of touching the subject again.

There is a doctrine presently being proclaimed, referred to as the *"family curse."* The idea is, if a Christian is having problems, it is because his great, great grandfather, or someone in his family, who years past, committed some grievous sin, and judgment for that sin is now coming upon this particular individual, and despite the fact that they are now a Believer.

The solution to this dilemma, these people are told, is for them to go to a Preacher who understands these things, who will lay hands on them, rebuking the family curse, and their problem will be solved, etc.

There's nothing in the Word of God which even remotely lends credence to such an idea.

While it is true that there are all type of curses on unregenerate man, the moment a person comes to Christ, not only are their present circumstances addressed, but as well, their past and their future. In fact, that's what the word *"born again"* actually means, i.e., *"a complete break from the past, the present, and the future, as it has been, as it is, and as it shall be."* In other words, everything changes. In fact, there is a qualifier added in Chapter 20. The statement there closes with the words, *"of them who hate Me"* (Ex. 20:5).

The idea is, if succeeding generations continue to hate the Lord, the curse will definitely continue upon them, whatever that curse might be. But as stated, the moment the person turns to Christ, at that moment, everything changes.

THE REAL CAUSE OF THE PROBLEM

While it is certainly true that many Christians are having problems, while there may be many causes and reasons, the primary cause is a faulty understanding of their place and position in Christ. A Believer, although Born-Again, simply cannot live for God as he ought to live for God, unless he understands the

Cross as it refers to his Sanctification. In a sense, one might say that Redemption is a two part experience.

The believing sinner is granted Salvation, which, as stated, changes everything. But then the Holy Spirit sets about to make that person into the Image of Christ. It is called *"Sanctification."* The word means, *"to be set apart exclusively for the Lord."* If it is to be noticed, almost all of the Bible is given over to this particular aspect of the believing experience. In other words, there are salient Passages in the Word of God which tell us how to be saved, with all the balance of the Scripture, at least 99 percent or more, telling us then how to live for God, which refers to our Sanctification.

The Cross of Christ figures as the principal function in both Salvation and Sanctification. But the major problem with Believers, even New Testament Believers, is that they are saved by Faith, and then they try to sanctify themselves by the virtue of self. It translates into Salvation by Faith and Sanctification by self. Sanctification cannot be obtained in this manner. So the Church finds itself in the same condition as Israel of old. Paul said of Israel:

"For they being ignorant of God's Righteousness, and going about to establish their own righteousness, have not submitted themselves unto the Righteousness of God" (Rom. 10:3).

UNDERSTANDING THE BIBLE

The Bible is the story of Redemption, and the story of Redemption is the Cross. Of course, all of it is centered up in Christ, and what He would do to redeem fallen humanity.

If the Believer understands the Cross, then the Believer can understand the Bible. And to the degree that the Believer doesn't understand the Cross, to that degree will the Believer have a false interpretation of the Word of God.

When one begins to look at the Bible from the understanding of the Cross, it quickly becomes obvious as to what the Word of God is all about. In other words, it becomes much easier to understand. It is when we attempt to take it out of that realm that we run into difficulties. But if one sees the Bible for what it really is, which is the story of Redemption, which is the story of the Cross, then the Word of God will be easily understood.

JESUS AS OUR EXAMPLE, OR JESUS AS OUR SAVIOUR?

While Jesus, of course, is our example, still, if that is the way we look at Him, then we will miss the whole point of His coming to this world.

It's not an example that man actually needs, but rather a Saviour. Man's problem is not a poor example; man's problem is sin, and to rectify that situation, a Saviour is required, and that Saviour is the Lord Jesus Christ. And as well, the means and the way by which Salvation is effected is the Cross of Christ. The Scripture beautifully and bluntly says: *"And, having made peace through the blood of His Cross, by Him to reconcile all things unto Himself; by Him, I say, whether they be things in Earth, or things in Heaven"* (Col. 1:20). There *"Mercy and Truth have met together, Righteousness and Peace have kissed each other."* Sin is perfectly put away, and the believing sinner perfectly justified, *"by the Blood of His Cross."*

When we get a view of God as thus unfolded, we have only, like Moses, to *"bow our head toward the Earth and worship"* — suited attitude for a pardoned and accepted sinner in the Presence of God! (Mackintosh).

(8) "AND MOSES MADE HASTE, AND BOWED HIS HEAD TOWARD THE EARTH, AND WORSHIPPED.

(9) "AND HE SAID, IF NOW I HAVE FOUND GRACE IN YOUR SIGHT, O LORD, LET MY LORD, I PRAY YOU, GO AMONG US; FOR IT IS A STIFFNECKED PEOPLE; AND PARDON OUR INIQUITY AND OUR SIN, AND TAKE US FOR YOUR INHERITANCE.

(10) "AND HE SAID, BEHOLD, I MAKE A COVENANT: BEFORE ALL YOUR PEOPLE I WILL DO MARVELS, SUCH AS HAVE NOT BEEN DONE IN ALL THE EARTH, NOR IN ANY NATION: AND ALL THE PEOPLE AMONG WHICH YOU ARE SHALL SEE THE WORK OF THE LORD: FOR IT IS A TERRIBLE THING THAT I WILL DO WITH YOU.

(11) "YOU OBSERVE THAT WHICH I

COMMAND YOU THIS DAY: BEHOLD, I DRIVE OUT BEFORE YOU THE AMORITE, AND THE CANAANITE, AND THE HITTITE, AND THE PERIZZITE, AND THE HIVITE, AND THE JEBUSITE.

(12) "TAKE HEED TO YOURSELF, LEST YOU MAKE A COVENANT WITH THE INHABITANTS OF THE LAND WHERE YOU GO, LEST IT BE FOR A SNARE IN THE MIDST OF YOU:

(13) "BUT YOU SHALL DESTROY THEIR ALTARS, BREAK THEIR IMAGES, AND CUT DOWN THEIR GROVES:

(14) "FOR YOU SHALL WORSHIP NO OTHER GOD: FOR THE LORD, WHOSE NAME IS JEALOUS, IS A JEALOUS GOD:

(15) "LEST YOU MAKE A COVENANT WITH THE INHABITANTS OF THE LAND, AND THEY GO A WHORING AFTER THEIR GODS, AND DO SACRIFICE UNTO THE THEIR GODS, AND ONE CALL YOU, AND YOU EAT OF HIS SACRIFICE;

(16) "AND YOU TAKE OF THEIR DAUGHTERS UNTO YOUR SONS, AND THEIR DAUGHTERS GO A WHORING AFTER THEIR GODS, AND MAKE YOUR SONS GO A WHORING AFTER THEIR GODS."

The composition is:

1. The wondrous Revelation of God in this Chapter is declared in II Corinthians to have been the ministration of death; for as the people were still under Law, the more gracious God was, the more guilty they were.

2. In Verse 13 is found the first mention of Phallic worship in the Bible. For such was the object of worship described here as a *"grove"* or *"Ashera."* In blunt language, this is the male organ.

3. God's name is *"Jealous."* This corresponds with the statement given by James, *"The Spirit Who dwells in us lusts to envy"* (James 4:5), and Paul's statement, *"For the flesh lusteth against the Spirit, and the Spirit against the flesh: and these are contrary the one to the other: so that you cannot do the things that you would"* (Gal. 5:17).

THE BASIS OF THE APPEAL FOR GRACE

Verses 8 and 9 read: *"And Moses made haste, and bowed his head toward the earth, and worshipped.*

"And he said, If now I have found Grace in Your sight, O LORD, let my Lord, I pray You, go among us; for it is a stiffnecked people; and pardon our iniquity and our sin, and take us for Your inheritance."

It may seem strange for Moses to appeal to the Lord on the basis that Israel is a *"stiffnecked people"*; however, we should let this be a lesson to us. It was their need which Moses spread before Jehovah; it was His Grace to which he appealed. At the time of the golden calf, God had referred to these people as a *"stiffnecked people"* (Ex. 32:9-10). So Moses was only admitting what God had already said.

We make a grave mistake when we go before the Lord, telling Him how wonderful and how great we are. He will not respond favorably to a lie. He will respond favorably, if we admit to Him what we really are, which occasions our need. That type of need, based on the truth, will always be attended by the Lord, and Grace will be forthcoming. Otherwise, we close the door!

THE PHARISEE AND THE PUBLICAN

Jesus gave us an illustration that answers this perfectly.

He spoke of a Pharisee and a Publican, who went up to the Temple to pray. He told of the Pharisee who *"stood and prayed thus with himself, God, I thank You, that I am not as other men are, extortioners, unjust, adulterers, or even as this Publican."*

He then went on to exclaim his goodness by saying, *"I fast twice in the week, I give tithes of all that I possess."*

Jesus then told of the Publican who *"standing afar off, would not lift up so much as his eyes unto Heaven, but smote upon his breast, saying, God be merciful to me a sinner."*

Jesus then said, *"I tell you, this man went down to his house justified rather than the other: for everyone who exalts himself shall be abased; and he who humbles himself shall be exalted"* (Lk. 18:10-14).

Despite the fact that Israel was indeed a *"stiffnecked people,"* and despite the fact that they were full of iniquity and sin, Moses pleads with the Lord, saying, *"Take us for Your inheritance."*

And that He did!

And that He does with us as well!

COVENANTS WITH THE UNGODLY

Verses 10 through 13 read: *"And He said, Behold, I make a Covenant: before all your people I will do marvels, such as have not been done in all the Earth, nor in any nation: and all the people among which you are shall see the Work of the LORD: for it is a terrible thing that I will do with you.*

"You observe that which I command you this day: behold, I drive out before you the Amorite, and the Canaanite, and the Hittite, and the Perizzite, and the Hivite, and the Jebusite.

"Take heed to yourself, lest you make a covenant with the inhabitants of the land where you go, lest it be for a snare in the midst of you:

"But you shall destroy their altars, break their images, and cut down their groves."

The Children of Israel were raised up out the loins of Abraham and the womb of Sarah for three specific reasons:

1. To give the world the Word of God, which they did: It seems that every writer of the Old Testament and the New is Jewish, with possibly the exception of Luke, who wrote the Book of Acts and the Gospel which bears his name. And there are even some who claim that he was Jewish as well.

2. To serve as the womb, so to speak, of the Messiah: Even though they didn't accept Him when He came, nevertheless, He did come, and fulfilled that which had to be done in order to redeem lost humanity.

3. They were to evangelize the world, which they failed to do: But they will yet fulfill this task, which will be carried out in the coming Kingdom Age (Isa. 66:19).

The Lord predicts here that He will *"do marvels,"* even *"such as have not been done in all the Earth, nor in any nation,"* which He most definitely did. The Old Testament is replete with miracles.

Verse 11 proclaims the fact that He would go before them, and make the heathen nations in the land of Canaan subject to them. But He warned them:

They must not make a covenant with the inhabitants of the land. In fact, they were to destroy their altars, break their images, and cut down their groves. In other words, they were to do away with all idol worship of any and every nature. Regrettably, Israel did not obey in this respect, and suffered disastrous consequences.

God will do great and mighty things for all who will dare to believe Him; however, the same power that works for the Believer, can work against the Believer, if the individual turns his or her back on God.

The Believer has at his disposal the greatest power that man has ever known. God is an abundant Blesser. But if men forsake Him, if they take lightly His Word, if they begin to make up their own way, thereby disavowing the Way of the Cross, the same power that worked for them will now work against them. And that's a state in which no sane individual would desire to be.

The *"groves"* had to do with Phallic worship, which represented the god of reproduction, i.e., *"the male organ."* Unfortunately, Israel began to worship this abominable thing, which brought about their destruction by Nebuchadnezzar. The worship of these heathen gods was unspeakably abominable! It usually involved every type of immorality, from bestiality, to homosexuality, to incest, to pedophilia, all coming under the heading of fornication.

All religions of the world presently, in effect, come under the same heading, and the same condemnation. If it's not Bible Christianity, then in some way, it had its beginnings in the idol worship of ancient religions. I speak of Hinduism, Islam, Shintoism, Confucianism, Catholicism, Mormonism, Buddhism, etc.

A JEALOUS GOD

Verses 14 through 16 read: *"For you shall worship no other god: for the LORD, Whose name is Jealous, is a jealous God:*

"Lest you make a covenant with the inhabitants of the land, and they go a whoring after their gods, and do sacrifice unto their gods, and one call you, and you eat of his sacrifice;

"And you take of their daughters unto your sons, and their daughters go a whoring after their gods, and make your sons go a whoring after their gods."

Verse 14 is a reference to the Second Commandment.

Emphatically and even dogmatically, the Lord refers to Himself here as *"a jealous God,"* even going so far as to say that His Name is *"Jealous."*

In this sense, the jealousy of God is of the essence of His moral character, a major cause for worship and confidence on the part of His people, and a ground for fear on the part of His enemies.

As is obvious here, the Lord will not share His people with Satan, and it amounts to exactly that!

However, the jealousy of God is totally unlike the jealousy of individuals, for His jealousy is not selfish. He is jealous over us because He knows what sinful activity will do in our hearts and lives. In a sense, it's the same as a parent who is jealous over his or her child, exactly as they ought to be, as it regards outside forces which can destroy that child, such as drugs, alcohol, immorality, etc. The jealousy of such a parent is not selfishness, but rather for the good of the child in question.

As Israel was warned not to co-mingle with the heathen, and we speak of the sense of becoming a part of their doings, likewise, the Word of God teaches separation, and does so strongly, as it regards the Church. We're in the world, but we're never to be a part of the world. While the Bible does not teach isolation, it definitely does teach separation, and for the Church as well as it did for Israel of old. We as Believers are in the world, and as such, must let our light shine. In fact, the only curing effect in this world is that of the Child of God, whom Jesus likens as *"light"* and *"salt,"* i.e., *"illumination and preservation"* (Mat. 5:13-16).

(17) "YOU SHALL MAKE YOURSELF NO MOLTEN GODS.

(18) "THE FEAST OF UNLEAVENED BREAD SHALL YOU KEEP. SEVEN DAYS YOU SHALL EAT UNLEAVENED BREAD, AS I COMMANDED YOU, IN THE TIME OF THE MONTH ABIB: FOR IN THE MONTH ABIB YOU CAME OUT FROM EGYPT.

(19) "ALL WHO OPENS THE MATRIX IS MINE; AND EVERY FIRSTLING AMONG YOUR CATTLE, WHETHER OX OR SHEEP, THAT IS MALE.

(20) "BUT THE FIRSTLING OF AN ASS YOU SHALL REDEEM WITH A LAMB: AND IF YOU REDEEM HIM NOT, THEN SHALL YOU BREAK HIS NECK. ALL THE FIRSTBORN OF YOUR SONS YOU SHALL REDEEM. AND NONE SHALL APPEAR BEFORE ME EMPTY.

(21) "SIX DAYS YOU SHALL WORK, BUT ON THE SEVENTH DAY YOU SHALL REST: IN EARING TIME AND IN HARVEST YOU SHALL REST.

(22) "AND YOU SHALL OBSERVE THE FEAST OF WEEKS, OF THE FIRSTFRUITS OF WHEAT HARVEST, AND THE FEAST OF INGATHERING AT THE YEAR'S END.

(23) "THRICE IN THE YEAR SHALL ALL YOUR MENCHILDREN APPEAR BEFORE THE LORD GOD, THE GOD OF ISRAEL.

(24) "FOR I WILL CAST OUT THE NATIONS BEFORE YOU, AND ENLARGE YOUR BORDERS: NEITHER SHALL ANY MAN DESIRE YOUR LAND, WHEN YOU SHALL GO UP TO APPEAR BEFORE THE LORD YOUR GOD THRICE IN THE YEAR.

(25) "YOU SHALL NOT OFFER THE BLOOD OF MY SACRIFICE WITH LEAVEN; NEITHER SHALL THE SACRIFICE OF THE FEAST OF PASSOVER BE LEFT UNTIL THE MORNING.

(26) "THE FIRST OF THE FIRSTFRUITS OF YOUR LAND YOU SHALL BRING UNTO THE HOUSE OF THE LORD YOUR GOD. YOU SHALL NOT SEETHE A KID IN HIS MOTHER'S MILK."

The overview is:

1. It is touching to recognize the love which repeated the Ten Commandments and the Sacrifices and Feasts connected therewith. This was not mere repetition; it was loving instruction.

2. This repeated instruction taught Israel that although there was a change of relationship, there was no change of affection or of foundation truth.

3. Redemption by blood, surrender of self, Sabbath rest for the soul, enjoyment of the Feasts, and a compassion for all living things so great that it would not seethe a little lamb in its mother's milk — all this revealed how unchangeable and eternal are the foundations of Justification and Sanctification (Williams).

NO GRAVEN IMAGES

Verse 17 reads: *"You shall not make any molten gods."*

This pertained to the Second Commandment, and as well, alluded to the golden calf.

While the sin of man, even Believers, at the present time, little falls into the category of graven images, whenever we attempt to devise another way of Salvation, or another way of Sanctification, we are, in effect, spiritually speaking, taking a graving tool, and attempting to fashion another god. While we may not think of it as such, the truth is, if it's not *"Jesus Christ and Him Crucified,"* then pure and simple, we have fashioned another god.

THE FEAST OF UNLEAVENED BREAD

Verse 18 reads: *"The Feast of Unleavened Bread shall you keep. Seven days you shall eat unleavened bread, as I commanded you, in the time of the month Abib: for in the month Abib you came out from Egypt."*

This Passage has to do with both Salvation and Sanctification.

Sanctification is mentioned first, as it relates to the *"Feast of Unleavened Bread."* This particular Feast began with the Feast of the Passover, and would end with the Feast of Firstfruits. All three were conducted at one time, one might say, during the barley harvest, which would be in our April.

The *"unleavened bread"* spoke of the Perfect Body and Perfect Life of our Lord Jesus Christ, Who would offer Himself in Sacrifice. It being kept *"seven days"* refers to perfection. Christ was Perfect!

"Leaven" was a form of yeast, which brought about corruption in bread dough, or in a fruit drink, turning it alcoholic. There is to be nothing in the life of the Believer that is of sinful corruption, which life we can have (Rom. 6:14), if our Faith is anchored firmly in Christ and what He did for us at the Cross.

While Israel was commanded to keep the Feast of Unleavened Bread, and to do so for seven days, all as a symbol of Christ, spiritually speaking, under the New Covenant, we are to keep it perpetually.

It is sad that the modern Church knows almost nothing about Sanctification. It becomes sadder still when we realize that almost the entirety of the Bible is given over to this particular work (I Cor. 1:30; I Thess. 4:3-4; II Thess. 2:13; I Pet. 1:2; Jn. 10:36; 17:19; Acts 20:32; 26:18; Rom. 15:16; I Cor. 1:2; 6:11; 7:14; I Tim. 4:5; II Tim. 2:21; Heb. 2:11; 10:10, 14, 29; Jude, Vs. 1, etc.).

Salvation is mentioned in the latter part of Verse 18, speaking of the time that Israel was delivered out of Egyptian bondage. This was an exact time, the month of Abib, and, thereby, shows how important Salvation is in the eyes of God. There was a definite time that I was saved and you were saved, and that time should be very special to us, because that's when we really began to live.

THE FIRSTBORN

Verses 19 and 20 read: *"All that opens the matrix is Mine; and every firstling among your cattle, whether ox or sheep, that is male.*

"But the firstling of an ass you shall redeem with a lamb: and if you redeem him not, then shall you break his neck. All the firstborn of your sons you shall redeem. And none shall appear before Me empty."

This command was also given in Exodus 13:12-13, and is again given in Leviticus 27:26-27.

The *"firstborn"* not only of man, but even the male animals, were to be given to the Lord.

When a boy baby was born, a lamb was to be offered up in sacrifice, signifying that the child was given to the Lord. It also signified what Jesus would do to redeem fallen humanity, by the giving of Himself in Sacrifice. The firstborn of male animals was to be sacrificed, signifying what Jesus would do to redeem the whole of creation (Rom. 8:19-22).

None were to appear before the Lord *"empty,"* meaning that they must be faithful to obey this which the Lord has commanded.

REST

Verse 21 reads: *"Six days you shall work, but on the seventh day you shall rest: in earing time and in harvest you shall rest."*

"Earing" spoke of *"plowing,"* which referred to getting the land ready for planting. The Holy Spirit is saying here that irrespective as to how urgent it may seem to be to get the plowing done or the harvest in, the

Children of Israel were not to fail to keep the Sabbath.

As we said some pages back, what distinguishes God's people is participation in God's rest. Christ is God's rest (Heb., Chpt. 4). The honor, or dishonor, done to the Sabbath was the test under Law. The honor, or dishonor, done to Christ, the test under Grace. Death was the penalty of dishonoring the Sabbath; a similar penalty attaches to dishonoring Christ.

THE FEAST OF PENTECOST AND THE FEAST OF TABERNACLES

Verse 22 reads: *"And you shall observe the Feast of Weeks, of the firstfruits of wheat harvest, and the Feast of Ingathering at the year's end."*

The Feast of Pentecost is sometimes referred to as the *"Feast of Weeks,"* in that it was to be conducted on the day after seven weeks had ended, beginning with Passover. So, Pentecost actually means *"fifty,"* or *"fiftieth,"* which refers to this Feast being conducted 50 days after Passover. This was conducted during the time of the *"wheat harvest,"* which was to begin by the Priests waving the bread before God, made from *"the firstfruits of the wheat harvest."*

The *"Feast of Ingathering"* is another name for the *"Feast of Tabernacles,"* which as well lasted some seven days, and took place during the time of the fruit harvest, which would be in our October.

It would seem that Moses is mentioning three Feasts here, but actually, the *"Feast of Weeks,"* and the *"firstfruits of wheat harvest,"* both pertain to the one Feast of Pentecost. So only two Feasts are mentioned here, *"the Feast of Pentecost,"* and the *"Feast of Tabernacles"* (Ingathering).

THREE TIMES A YEAR

Verse 23 reads: *"Thrice in the year shall all your menchildren appear before the Lord GOD, the God of Israel."*

Seven Feasts were to be conducted each year in Israel. They were to be held during three different gatherings. Those gatherings are as follows:

1. Three Feasts were conducted at the first gathering. That of Passover, Unleavened Bread, and Firstfruits. These were conducted at the time of the barley harvest, which was in our April.

2. One Feast was conducted at the second gathering, the Feast of Pentecost, which took place 50 days after Passover. It was at the time of the wheat harvest, and took place during our month of May.

3. The third gathering took place at the time of the fruit harvest, which was in our October, and consisted of three Feasts. The Feast of Trumpets, of Atonement, and of Tabernacles.

A representative man from every household in Israel was to attend each of these Feasts. Of course, this would be done after they reached the Promised Land, and more specifically, when the Temple was constructed.

This was to keep the Word of the Lord fresh in their hearts and minds at all times.

In fact, every single Law, every single Commandment, every ceremony, was in some way to picture Christ. Unfortunately, it seems that most did not understand this too very well!

PROTECTION

Verse 24 reads: *"For I will cast out the nations before you, and enlarge your borders, neither shall any man desire your land, when you shall go up to appear before the LORD your GOD thrice in the year."*

The Lord promised Israel the land, which borders would go all the way from the Nile to the Euphrates. If that referred to the entirety of the Euphrates River, it would have included all of the Arabian Peninsula as well. It would also have included the Sinai, as stated, up to the Nile River (I Ki. 4:21, 24; II Chron. 9:26).

As well, the Lord promised that He would watch over the land while all the representative men went to these gatherings. The Lord would be their Protector, which He was.

THE SACRIFICE

Verse 25 reads: *"You shall not offer the blood of My Sacrifice with leaven; neither shall the sacrifice of the Feast of the Passover be left unto the morning."*

Many, if not most, Jewish Scholars, I believe, limit this prohibition to the Passover

Lamb. In fact, concerning the Feast of Pentecost, leaven is required (Lev. 23:17).

At the very beginning, when the ritual of the Passover Lamb was instituted, which was when the Children of Israel were in Egypt, all leaven was forbidden, even for a period of some seven days (Ex. 12:15).

While the modern Reader may wonder at all of these regulations, it must be understood that all of this represented Christ as it regards His Atoning, Mediatorial, Intercessory Work. *"Leaven"* represents corruption, and thereby, *"sin."* Christ as our Passover Lamb had no sin in His Life whatsoever. So all of this was meant to be a type.

Furthermore, on the Day of the Passover, all of the lamb was to be eaten on that particular day, with none left over until the morning. This represented the fact that one must partake of Christ in totality, and not partially.

TITHES

Verse 26 reads: *"The first of the firstfruits of your land you shall bring unto the House of the LORD your God. You shall not seethe a kid in his mother's milk."*

Even though the word *"tithe"* is not mentioned here, *"firstfruits"* are. Some have concluded that *"firstfruits"* as it regards the harvest, and especially an offering given the Lord, are the same as tithe. The *"first of the firstfruits"* were to be brought to the *"House of the Lord."* This referred to both the Tabernacle and especially the Temple. However, Israel in the wilderness would have had precious little harvest, if any at all. But all of that would change when they occupied the Promised Land.

The *"kid"* mentioned here was a baby lamb. *"Seethe"* refers to *"boiling."* The little baby lamb was not to be boiled in his mother's milk, signifying the fact that while lambs were definitely to be eaten as food, with their wool used as clothing, more than any other animal, the lamb was to be used in sacrifice, representing Christ. In a sense, killing the little animal at its birth, and cooking it in this manner, showed a disrespect for the coming Redeemer, Who the lamb represented.

(27) "AND THE LORD SAID UNTO MOSES, WRITE THOU THESE WORDS: FOR AFTER THE TENOR OF THESE WORDS I HAVE MADE A COVENANT WITH YOU AND WITH ISRAEL.

(28) "AND HE WAS THERE WITH THE LORD FORTY DAYS AND FORTY NIGHTS; HE DID NEITHER EAT BREAD, NOR DRINK WATER. AND HE WROTE UPON THE TABLES THE WORDS OF THE COVENANT, THE TEN COMMANDMENTS.

(29) "AND IT CAME TO PASS, WHEN MOSES CAME DOWN FROM MOUNT SINAI WITH THE TWO TABLES OF TESTIMONY IN MOSES' HAND, WHEN HE CAME DOWN FROM THE MOUNT, THAT MOSES DID NOT KNOW THAT THE SKIN OF HIS FACE DID SHINE WHILE HE TALKED WITH HIM.

(30) "AND WHEN AARON AND ALL THE CHILDREN OF ISRAEL SAW MOSES, BEHOLD, THE SKIN OF HIS FACE SHONE; AND THEY WERE AFRAID TO COME NEAR HIM.

(31) "AND MOSES CALLED UNTO THEM; AND AARON AND ALL THE RULERS OF THE CONGREGATION RETURNED UNTO HIM: AND MOSES TALKED WITH THEM.

(32) "AND AFTERWARD ALL THE CHILDREN OF ISRAEL CAME NEAR: AND HE GAVE THEM IN COMMANDMENT ALL THAT THE LORD HAD SPOKEN WITH HIM IN MOUNT SINAI.

(33) "AND TILL MOSES HAD DONE SPEAKING WITH THEM, HE PUT A VEIL ON HIS FACE.

(34) "BUT WHEN MOSES WENT IN BEFORE THE LORD TO SPEAK WITH HIM, HE TOOK THE VEIL OFF, UNTIL HE CAME OUT. AND HE CAME OUT, AND SPOKE UNTO THE CHILDREN OF ISRAEL THAT WHICH HE WAS COMMANDED.

(35) "AND THE CHILDREN OF ISRAEL SAW THE FACE OF MOSES, THAT THE SKIN OF MOSES' FACE SHONE: AND MOSES PUT THE VEIL UPON HIS FACE AGAIN, UNTIL HE WENT IN TO SPEAK WITH HIM."

The diagram is:

1. Moses being now Mediator, his face did shine because God had spoken with him. This was the Presence of God on Moses.

2. This shining indicated that the Glory

of God on Moses' face was like rays or darts of lightning shooting forth. Consequently, Aaron and others were afraid to come near Moses, and rightly so!

3. Due to the *"glory"* on Moses' face, the Lawgiver was forced to wear a veil when speaking with other individuals.

THE COVENANT

Verses 27 and 28 read: *"And the LORD said unto Moses, Write thou these words: for after the tenor of these words I have made a Covenant with you and with Israel.*

"And he was there with the LORD forty days and forty nights; he did neither eat bread, nor drink water. And he wrote upon the Tables the Words of the Covenant, the Ten Commandments."

The *"words"* which the Lord told Moses to write consist of that found in Verses 10 through 26. What Moses wrote these on we aren't told, but it was probably an animal skin.

The latter portion of Verse 28 seems to imply that Moses wrote the Ten Commandments on the two Tables of stone, which he had carved out; however, in Verse 1 we are told that *"God said, I will write upon these tables"*; and the same is repeated in Deuteronomy 10:2. Moreover in that Passage, it is distinctly declared, *"He"* (meaning God) *"wrote on the tables according to the first writing."* We must, therefore, regard *"He"* in Verse 28 as meaning *"the Lord,"* which is quite possible according to the Hebrew idiom (Pulpit).

While it's possible for a human being to go 40 days and 40 nights without food, that is if they are healthy, and Moses certainly was, it's not possible to go without water for that length of time, unless God would supernaturally make such possible, which He definitely did. Moses, Elijah (I Ki. 19:8), and our Lord have alone accomplished a fast of this duration.

FASTING

Some have thought that God can be moved to action by *"fasting"*; however, there is nothing in Scripture which validates such thinking. While fasting is definitely Scriptural, that is if done in the right way, and will definitely be blessed and honored by the Lord, the Lord, plus His Word, doesn't change, irrespective as to what we might do. Of course, the answer could quickly come back that fasting changes the person.

That's not exactly the case either. It is the Holy Spirit Alone Who can change an individual, and He does such according to our Faith in Christ and the Cross (Rom. 8:1-2, 11).

So what good is fasting?

The process of Sanctification, and that's actually what we are talking about, is carried out 100 percent, as stated, by the Holy Spirit, according to the Finished Work of Christ as it regards the Cross, and our Faith in that Sacrifice. Fasting definitely does aid and abet that process; but that is its limitation.

One young Preacher said to me a short time ago, as it regards sin, if he would fast three days, that would handle the problem. So every time he encountered temptation, and in whatever capacity, he went on to state how he would go on another three day fast.

It should have been obvious to him, but evidently wasn't, that he was having to repeat the process over and over, which states that something was amiss.

No, it's not any *"works"* which we carry out that will give us victory, but rather Faith in Christ and what Christ did at the Cross, and that alone! As stated, fasting will definitely aid us in this particular *"walk,"* but that is its limitation.

THE BRILLIANT LIGHT AND THE VEIL

Verses 29 through 35 read: *"And it came to pass, when Moses came down from Mount Sinai, with the two Tables of Testimony in Moses' hand, when he came down from the Mount, that Moses was not aware that the skin of his face did shine while he talked with him.*

"And when Aaron and all the Children of Israel saw Moses, behold, the skin of his face did shine; and they were afraid to come near him.

"And Moses called unto them; and Aaron and all the rulers of the congregation returned unto him: and Moses talked with them.

"And afterward all the Children of Israel came near: and he gave them in Commandment all that the LORD had spoken with him in Mount Sinai.

"And till Moses had done speaking with them, he put a veil on his face.

"But when Moses went in before the LORD to speak with Him, he took the veil off, until he came out. He came out, and spoke unto the Children of Israel that which he was commanded.

"And the Children of Israel saw the face of Moses, that the skin of Moses' face did shine: and Moses put the veil upon his face again, until he went in to speak with him."

When the Lord revealed Himself to Moses, as is recorded in Verses 5 through 7, because Moses had looked upon the Lord, at least that which the Lord allowed him to see, the Glory of God did shine on Moses' face, and in fact, the Hebrew implies that darts and small lightning bolts, so to speak, were constantly emitting from the countenance of Moses, making it well nigh impossible for others to look upon his countenance. Therefore, when the Lawgiver spoke with the Israelites, he covered his face with a veil. But *"whenever he entered the Lord's Presence,"* and referring to the Tabernacle, he removed the veil.

Paul addresses this incident in II Corinthians, Chapter 3. In a context that stresses the transforming Power of God in the life of the Believer, Paul first explores Moses' motive in using the veil. It was so that the Israelites might not gaze at his face *"while the radiance was fading away"* (II Cor. 3:13).

Paul's application of this incident seems to indicate the following:

1. Israel still cannot see God's Glory when they read the Scriptures (II Cor. 3:14-15).

2. The veil is removed from the heart and mind of anyone who accepts the Gospel of Jesus Christ (II Cor. 3:16).

3. The veil symbolizes hiding our real selves from one another and must be removed in our relationships with other Believers. Because Jesus is within Believers, effecting our inner transformation, we see His Face in one another's lives, for we *"are being transformed into His likeness"* by the Work of the Holy Spirit. This attitude of openness is in contrast to the position Moses took, but it is necessary within the Church (Richards).

"Christ the Lord is risen today, Hallelujah!

"Sons of men and Angels say, Hallelujah!
"Raise your joys and triumphs high, Hallelujah!
"Sing, you heavens and Earth reply, Hallelujah!"

"Lives again our glorious King, Hallelujah!
"Where, O death, is now your sting? Hallelujah!
"Once He died, our souls to save, Hallelujah!
"Where's your victory, boasting grave? Hallelujah!"

"Love's redeeming work is done, Hallelujah!
"Fought the fight, the battle won, Hallelujah!
"Death in vain forbids Him rise, Hallelujah!
"Christ has opened Paradise, Hallelujah!"

"Soar we now where Christ has led, Hallelujah!
"Following our exalted Head, Hallelujah!
"Made like Him, like Him we rise, Hallelujah!
"Ours the Cross, the grave, the skies, Hallelujah!"

CHAPTER 35

(1) "AND MOSES GATHERED ALL THE CONGREGATION OF THE CHILDREN OF ISRAEL TOGETHER, AND SAID UNTO THEM, THESE ARE THE WORDS WHICH THE LORD HAS COMMANDED, THAT YOU SHOULD DO THEM.

(2) "SIX DAYS SHALL WORK BE DONE, BUT ON THE SEVENTH DAY THERE SHALL BE TO YOU AN HOLY DAY, A SABBATH OF REST TO THE LORD: WHOSOEVER DOES WORK THEREIN SHALL BE PUT TO DEATH.

(3) "YOU SHALL KINDLE NO FIRE THROUGHOUT YOUR HABITATIONS UPON THE SABBATH DAY."

The structure is:

1. God's rest (the Sabbath) opens this section, and His resting place (the Tabernacle) closes it.

2. In the greatness of His love He invites man into His Own rest, and then comes and dwells with him (Heb., Chpt. 4).

3. Even when building the Tabernacle the Sabbath Rest was to be observed (Williams).

THE COMMAND OF THE LORD

Verse 1 reads: *"And Moses gathered all the Congregation of the Children of Israel together, and said unto them, These are the words which the LORD has commanded, that you should do them."*

Moses is quick to warn the people that what he is telling them are not fabrications made up out of his own mind, or other leaders in Israel, but rather the Word of the Lord; consequently, these instructions were not to be changed in any way. There must not be additions added to them, and there must be no subtraction of what has been said. All were to be followed minutely.

If it is to be noticed, Moses said, *"Which the LORD has commanded,"* not *"which the Lord has suggested."*

Many people act as if the Word of God is a mere suggestion. It isn't!

We should understand that the very *"words"* of the Bible are inspired, and not merely the thought. Jesus said: *"Man shall not live by bread alone, but by every word that proceedeth out of the Mouth of God"* (Mat. 4:4).

THE SABBATH

Verses 2 and 3 read: *"Six days shall work be done, but on the seventh day there shall be to you an holy day, a Sabbath of rest to the LORD: whosoever does work therein shall be put to death.*

"You shall kindle no fire throughout your habitations upon the Sabbath day."

I've already given the following a couple of times, but it is so good that I want its great Truth to sink deep into the hearts of our Readers. I can say this because the statements were not originated by this Evangelist, but rather by George Williams. He said: *"What distinguishes God's people is participation in God's rest. Christ is God's rest* (Heb., Chpt. 4). *The honor, or dishonor, done to the Sabbath was the test under Law. The honor, or dishonor, done to Christ, the test under Grace. Death was the penalty of dishonoring the Sabbath; a similar penalty attaches to dishonoring Christ."*

The Sabbath was associated with the Manna (Chpt. 16), with the giving of the Law (Chpt. 20), and with the making of the Tabernacle (Chpt. 31).

Williams went on to say, *"Zeal in building the Tabernacle, enthusiasm in observing the Law, and energy in gathering the Manna, were not permitted to disturb God's rest."*

Why was the instruction so minute, and even so commanding, as it regards the keeping of the Sabbath?

More than anything else, the Sabbath symbolized the *"rest"* which would be effected through Christ. And to be sure, this is no small matter. It looked forward to the day that the struggle to keep the Law would be ended because Jesus as our Substitute would keep it perfectly, all on our behalf. As well, He would not only keep the Law perfectly, but He also would suffer its dire penalty of death, thereby paying the debt that man owed, but could not pay. And then, what made all of this so wonderful, God had decreed that inasmuch as Jesus was our Substitute, and was meant to be our Substitute, hence Paul referring to Him as the *"Last Adam,"* and the *"Second Man"* (I Cor. 15:45-47), hence Faith in Him, and what He had done for us at the Cross, would guarantee us His Life and His Victory (Eph. 2:8-9, 13-18; Gal. 5:6). As we have already quoted several times, this is what Jesus was speaking about when He said: *"Come unto Me, all you who labor and are heavy laden, and I will give you rest"* (Mat. 11:28).

So the type must not be abrogated in any way, hence the stern and sharp commands concerning the Sabbath. And one more thing:

To those who presently think that Saturday keeping is still incumbent upon Believers, they are missing the point entirely. God Himself rested on the Sabbath (Gen. 2:2-3), and then the command in the Law regarding the Sabbath, was all meant to serve as a *"type,"* of the One Who was to come, Who would fulfill all of these things, and we as

Believers would find a great *"rest"* in Him. If we miss that, we miss the whole point. People presently who think that keeping the Jewish Saturday Sabbath adds something to them spiritually, should as well, begin observing the Jewish Feast days, etc. No, Jesus fulfilled all of that. In fact, the entirety of the Law was meant to be temporary, actually given for many reasons, but basically to serve as a Type of Christ Who would come, and fulfill all of its requirements, which God demanded, and which regrettably, man could not do.

(4) "AND MOSES SPOKE UNTO ALL THE CONGREGATION OF THE CHILDREN OF ISRAEL, SAYING, THIS IS THE THING WHICH THE LORD COMMANDED, SAYING,

(5) "TAKE FROM AMONG YOU AN OFFERING UNTO THE LORD: WHOSOEVER IS OF A WILLING HEART, LET HIM BRING IT, AN OFFERING OF THE LORD; GOLD, AND SILVER, AND BRASS,

(6) "AND BLUE, AND PURPLE, AND SCARLET, AND FINE LINEN, AND GOATS' HAIR,

(7) "AND RAMS' SKINS DYED RED, AND BADGERS' SKINS, AND SHITTIM WOOD.

(8) "AND OIL FOR THE LIGHT, AND SPICES FOR ANOINTING OIL, AND FOR THE SWEET INCENSE.

(9) "AND ONYX STONES, AND STONES TO BE SET FOR THE EPHOD, AND FOR THE BREASTPLATE.

(10) "AND EVERY WISE HEARTED AMONG YOU SHALL COME, AND MAKE ALL THAT THE LORD HAS COMMANDED;

(11) "THE TABERNACLE, HIS TENT, AND HIS COVERING, HIS TACHES, AND HIS BOARDS, HIS BARS, HIS PILLARS, AND HIS SOCKETS,

(12) "THE ARK, AND THE STAVES THEREOF, WITH THE MERCY SEAT, AND THE VEIL OF THE COVERING,

(13) "THE TABLE, AND HIS STAVES, AND ALL HIS VESSELS, AND THE SHEWBREAD.

(14) "THE LAMPSTAND ALSO FOR THE LIGHT, AND HIS FURNITURE, AND HIS LAMPS, WITH THE OIL FOR THE LIGHT,

(15) "AND THE INCENSE ALTAR, AND HIS STAVES, AND THE ANOINTING OIL, AND THE SWEET INCENSE, AND THE HANGING FOR THE DOOR AT THE ENTERING IN OF THE TABERNACLE,

(16) "THE ALTAR OF BURNT OFFERING WITH HIS BRAZEN GRATE, HIS STAVES, AND ALL HIS VESSELS, THE LAVER AND HIS FOOT,

(17) "THE HANGINGS OF THE COURT, HIS PILLARS, AND THEIR SOCKETS, AND THE HANGING FOR THE DOOR OF THE COURT,

(18) "THE PINS OF THE TABERNACLE, AND THE PINS OF THE COURT, AND THEIR CORDS,

(19) "THE CLOTHS OF SERVICE, TO DO SERVICE IN THE HOLY PLACE, THE HOLY GARMENTS FOR AARON THE PRIEST, AND THE GARMENTS OF HIS SONS TO MINISTER IN THE PRIEST'S OFFICE."

The composition is:

1. The minute repetition in these Chapters of the materials used in the construction of the Tabernacle, and of the vessels and furniture of that place of worship, is tiresome to a secular Reader, but precious to a spiritual eye.

2. Why this minute repetition? Because the Tabernacle, its curtains, its boards, its hooks, its sockets, its pins, its spoons — everything connected with it displayed to God's heart the infinite perfections and glories of His Dearly Beloved Son.

3. Consequently, the frequent repetition of all these words should be noted. Nothing was to be left to man's ingenuity or taste (Ex. 39:42-43).

THE OFFERING

Verses 4 and 5 read: *"And Moses spoke unto all the Congregation of the Children of Israel, saying, This is the thing which the LORD commanded, saying,*

"Take from among you an Offering unto the LORD: whosoever is of a willing heart, let him bring it, an Offering of the LORD; gold, and silver, and copper."

Several things are said here:

1. These commands were for the entirety of the people of Israel. None were to be excluded.

2. What was being said, as previously

stated, was a command from the Lord.

3. All the people were to give an Offering to the Lord, but it must be from a willing heart. In other words, this was not a tax, but an Offering.

Far too many modern Christians treat giving to the Lord as something they have to do. In other words, they're fearful not to do it, so it means they aren't giving with a *"willing heart."* Let us say it again:

If our Offerings to the Lord aren't given with a willing heart, then it's really not an Offering, but rather a tax. As such, we completely miss what the Lord is attempting to teach us. And what is He attempting to teach us, as it regards giving?

Among other things, He is teaching us trust in Him. We are, as Believers, to look solely to Him for all things. In fact, when a person comes to Christ, that individual enters into God's economy, which is the greatest economy in the world. It's the economy of Faith, and we must remember, proper Faith can move mountains (Mat. 17:20).

GOD'S ECONOMY

Concerning the economy of Heaven, which the Lord brings us into, Jesus said: *"Therefore I say unto you, take no thought for your life, what you shall eat, or what you shall drink; nor yet for your body, what you shall put on. Is not the life more than meat, and the body than raiment?*

"Behold the fowls of the air: for they sow not, neither do they reap, nor gather into barns; yet your Heavenly Father feedeth them. Are you not much better than they?"

And then He said: *"Which of you by taking thought can add one cubit unto his stature?*

"And why take you thought for raiment? Consider the lilies of the field how they grow; they toil not, neither do they spin:

"And yet I say unto you, that even Solomon in all his glory was not arrayed like one of these.

"Wherefore, if God so clothed the grass of the field, which today is, and tomorrow is cast into the oven, shall He not much more clothe you, O ye of little faith?" (Mat. 6:25-30).

That is God's economy! And it's the most exciting life that one could ever live.

NOTES

WISE HEARTED

Verses 6 through 10 read: *"And blue, and purple, and scarlet, and fine linen, and goats' hair,*

"And rams' skins dyed red, and badgers' skins, and shittim wood,

"And oil for the light, and spices for anointing oil, and for the sweet incense,

"And onyx stones, and stones to be set for the Ephod, and for the Breastplate.

"And every wise hearted among you shall come, and make all that the LORD has commanded."

These are the Offerings that would be needed, and these things would go into the making of the Tabernacle and all of the items that went with the Tabernacle, and especially the Sacred Vessels.

Everyone was to participate, as everyone now is to participate. Most would give, and some would also give of their time and labor, i.e., *"wise hearted."*

There were nearly three million Israelites in the congregation, so there should not be any problem acquiring all the things needed, whether gold, silver, precious stones, etc., or whether labor to actually construct these items. While Bezaleel was in charge, he, as would be obvious, would need many helpers.

All of this can be likened presently to the Preachers of the Gospel who take the Word to the people, with Bezaleel and his helpers serving as a type of this function, and the people with their gifts, serving as a type of the laity who would support the labor and work of the actual builders.

As should be obvious, if most of the people did nothing, it would make it very difficult to get the work done. But if everyone did what they could do, whatever that might be, there would be an ample supply to get the work done, and get it done speedily, and get it done right.

SONLIFE RADIO

We have been led by the Lord to carry out efforts of Evangelism in order to take the Gospel to the world, for many years. SonLife Radio is the latest effort in this lifelong pursuit. It is what the Lord has told us to do. In other words, the same Lord Who told

Moses to construct the Tabernacle, and told him how to construct it, is the same Lord Who spoke to my heart respecting SonLife Radio, and as well, all the other efforts of Evangelism in which we have been engaged. While I'm not saying that SonLife Radio is as important as the construction of the Tabernacle, I definitely am saying that because it comes from the Lord, it definitely is important, with its worth being measured only by the Lord.

Whenever the Lord told me to do this thing, at the same time, it also becomes the responsibility of every person which comes under its sound. In other words, wherever a SonLife Station is acquired, and however big its coverage area might be, to the number of Believers in that area, all are responsible to keep it on the air, and as well, to help acquire other Stations in other places.

But sadly, because of prejudice, apathy, denominationalism, or a hundred and one other things that could be named, most Believers will not participate, which then makes it very difficult to get the work done. Regrettably, this is not something new, but in fact, the way it's always been.

When Paul was attempting to take the Gospel to the Gentiles, and trying to establish Churches, there were some who helped him. But there were also many who opposed what he was doing, and even though they named the Name of Christ, they were a hindrance instead of a help. To help us explain all of this a little better, let's look at it from another side.

What if many of the Children of Israel, even the majority, had told Moses that they were not going to help, were not going to do their part, etc., what would have become of the Tabernacle? It would have been built, but it would have been much more difficult and would have taken far longer. Regrettably, Satan does his best work from inside the Church. Even more regrettable, most Christians little think for themselves. They automatically take the word of others, which means they are little led by the Lord, if at all! This is the cause of a great lack of Spiritual Growth, as should be obvious.

It's incumbent upon every Believer to find the Will of God, which can be easily found if the person will only seek, and then to function within that Will. Only then can that person grow in the Lord, and be what he ought to be as it regards the Fruit of the Spirit, etc.

THE TABERNACLE

Verses 11 through 19 read: *"The Tabernacle, his tent, and his covering, his taches, and his boards, his bars, his pillars, and his sockets,*

"The Ark, and the staves thereof with the Mercy Seat, and the Veil of the covering,

"The Table, and his staves, and all his vessels, and the Shewbread,

"The Lampstand also for the light, and his furniture, and his lamps, with the oil for the light,

"And the Incense Altar, and his staves, and the anointing oil, and the sweet Incense, and the hanging for the door of the entering in of the Tabernacle,

"The Altar of Burnt Offering, with his brazen grate, his staves, and all his vessels, the Laver and his foot,

"The hangings of the court, his pillars, and their sockets, and the hanging for the door of the court,

"The pins of the Tabernacle, and the pins of the court, and their cords,

"The cloths of service, to do service in the Holy Place, the holy garments for Aaron the Priest, and the garments of his sons, to minister in the Priest's Office."

I want the Reader to understand that the construction of this Tabernacle, as unimposing as it actually was, was the single most important thing, by far, going on in the world at that time. It was the place where God would dwell, which would be between the Mercy Seat and the Cherubim. And yet, other than a few people among the Children of Israel, no one else in the world would have given it a second thought. It has little changed at present.

The world understands not at all the things of the Lord because those who are of the world are spiritually dead. But regrettably, most in the modern Church little understand the things of the Lord, as well! Satan is a master at getting Believers to believe that what is of the Lord, isn't, and what isn't of the Lord, is!

The people had a part in this great thing that God would do, and they were blessed by the Lord for taking part. As a result, virtually everything needed for the construction of the Tabernacle, and the making of all the Sacred Vessels, were given by the people. The account of their faithfulness is recorded in the Sacred Text. To be sure, the account is recorded in Heaven concerning the participation of every Believer and for all time. Whenever they did wrong, that was recorded as well. Whenever they did right, the account of that was given also.

One day the Books will be opened, and the activity of every Child of God will be judged. It's called the *"Judgment Seat of Christ,"* in which every single Believer will participate. At that particular time, what we did, how we did it, when it was done, our motives for doing it, will all be judged by Christ, Who knows all things. Understanding that, we should do our very best to perform every act according to that coming time.

(20) "AND ALL THE CONGREGATION OF THE CHILDREN OF ISRAEL DEPARTED FROM THE PRESENCE OF MOSES.

(21) "AND THEY CAME, EVERY ONE WHOSE HEART STIRRED HIM UP, AND EVERY ONE WHOM HIS SPIRIT MADE WILLING, AND THEY BROUGHT THE LORD'S OFFERING TO THE WORK OF THE TABERNACLE OF THE CONGREGATION, AND FOR ALL HIS SERVICE, AND FOR ALL THE HOLY GARMENTS.

(22) "AND THEY CAME, BOTH MEN AND WOMEN, AS MANY AS WERE WILLING HEARTED, AND BROUGHT BRACELETS, AND EARRINGS, AND RINGS, AND TABLETS, ALL JEWELS OF GOLD: AND EVERY MAN WHO OFFERED OFFERED AN OFFERING OF GOLD UNTO THE LORD.

(23) "AND EVERY MAN, WITH WHOM WAS FOUND BLUE, AND PURPLE, AND SCARLET, AND FINE LINEN, AND GOATS' HAIR, AND RED SKINS OF RAMS, AND BADGERS' SKINS, BROUGHT THEM.

(24) "EVERY ONE WHO DID OFFER AN OFFERING OF SILVER AND COPPER BROUGHT THE LORD'S OFFERING: AND EVERY MAN, WITH WHOM WAS FOUND SHITTIM WOOD FOR ANY WORK OF THE SERVICE, BROUGHT IT.

(25) "AND ALL THE WOMEN WHO WERE WISE HEARTED DID SPIN WITH THEIR HANDS, AND BROUGHT THAT WHICH THEY HAD SPUN, BOTH OF BLUE, AND OF PURPLE, AND OF SCARLET, AND OF FINE LINEN.

(26) "AND ALL THE WOMEN WHOSE HEARTS STIRRED THEM UP IN WISDOM SPUN GOATS' HAIR.

(27) "AND THE RULERS BROUGHT ONYX STONES, AND STONES TO BE SET, FOR THE EPHOD, AND FOR THE BREASTPLATE;

(28) "AND SPICE, AND OIL FOR THE LIGHT, AND FOR THE ANOINTING OIL, AND FOR THE SWEET INCENSE.

(29) "THE CHILDREN OF ISRAEL BROUGHT A WILLING OFFERING UNTO THE LORD, EVERY MAN AND WOMAN, WHOSE HEART MADE THEM WILLING TO BRING FOR ALL MANNER OF WORK, WHICH THE LORD HAD COMMANDED TO BE MADE BY THE HAND OF MOSES."

The construction is:

1. The *"willing hearted,"* the *"wise hearted,"* and the *"stirred hearted"* offered themselves and their gifts to the Lord. Thus willingness and obedience characterized the people.

2. We learn from all of this that it seems no one objected. None asked why a Tabernacle was wanted, or was needed, or why the tent which Moses had made a place of worship of sorts, would not suffice.

3. All felt that what they brought was *"the Lord's Offering"* — a real gift to Jehovah, which it was.

WILLING HEARTED

Verses 20 through 22 read: *"And all the congregation of the Children of Israel departed from the Presence of Moses.*

"And they came, every one whose heart stirred him up, and every one whom his spirit made willing, and they brought the LORD's Offering to the Work of the Tabernacle of the Congregation, and for all his service, and for all the holy garments.

"And they came, both men and women, as many as were willing hearted, and brought bracelets, and earrings, and rings, and tablets, all jewels of gold: and every man who offered offered an Offering of gold

unto the LORD."

The Scripture plainly says that their *"hearts stirred them up,"* and their *"spirits made them willing"*; however, this was the case because they opened their hearts to the Lord. The Lord didn't arbitrarily force the issue, as He never forces the issue in such circumstances. A person has to be open to the Lord, before the Lord can successfully speak to such a heart. If a Believer is willing, the Lord will do the rest; however, it is shocking to know how many Believers aren't willing.

In other words, they desire their own way and they really want no part of the Way of God, whatever that Way might be!

I wish I could honestly say that the hearts of most Christians are open to the Lord. But regrettably, that isn't the case. A heart opened to the Lord will definitely be led by the Lord, will definitely have the Blessings of the Lord, and will definitely grow in Grace and the knowledge of the Lord. But a heart that is closed to God, and opened to self-will, simply cannot be led by the Lord.

The Holy Spirit moves on hearts which are open to Him, which means that He definitely will not move on hearts that are closed to Him. Of course, such individuals, who regrettably make up the far greater majority of the modern Church, are quickly heading toward spiritual oblivion.

THE LORD'S OFFERING

Verses 23 through 29 read: *"And every man, with whom is found blue, and purple, and scarlet, and fine linen, and goats' hair, and red skins of rams, and badgers' skins, brought them.*

"Every one who did offer an offering of silver and copper brought the LORD's Offering: and every man, with whom was found shittim wood for any work of the service, brought it.

"And all the women who were wise hearted did spin with their hands, and brought that which they had spun, both of blue, and of purple, and of scarlet, and of fine linen.

"And all the women whose hearts stirred them up in wisdom spun goats' hair.

"And the rulers brought onyx stones, and stones to be set, for the Ephod, and for the Breastplate;

"And spice, and oil for the light, and for the anointing oil, and for the Sweet Incense.

"The Children of Israel brought a willing Offering unto the LORD, every man and woman, whose heart made them willing to bring for all manner of work, which the LORD had commanded to be made by the hand of Moses."

As we read all of these minute instructions, and then understand the function of the Tabernacle after it was constructed, all of this should make us even more appreciative of what Jesus has done for us at the Cross, which in effect, fulfilled all of this, making it unnecessary anymore. And yet, to understand the Tabernacle is to understand Christ. It is to understand His function, and that for which He came. But we must never forget, all that He did, His entire purpose, was all for one reason, and that was the Cross. His Atoning Work took place at the Cross. His Mediatorial Work is because of what He did at the Cross. His work as an Intercessor, all on our behalf, is because of the price He paid at the Cross.

In many ways the Church seems to have forgotten the very reason for its being, or else, it simply little more believes.

In Verse 29, *"the Children of Israel brought a willing Offering unto the LORD."* At Calvary, Christ became a *"Willing Offering."*

(30) "AND MOSES SAID UNTO THE CHILDREN OF ISRAEL, SEE, THE LORD HAS CALLED BY NAME BEZALEEL THE SON OF URI, THE SON OF HUR, OF THE TRIBE OF JUDAH;

(31) "AND HE HAS FILLED HIM WITH THE SPIRIT OF GOD, IN WISDOM, IN UNDERSTANDING, AND IN KNOWLEDGE, AND IN ALL MANNER OF WORKMANSHIP;

(32) "AND TO DEVISE CURIOUS WORKS, TO WORK IN GOLD, AND IN SILVER, AND IN BRASS,

(33) "AND IN THE CUTTING OF STONES, TO SET THEM, AND IN CARVING OF WOOD, TO MAKE ANY MANNER OF CUNNING WORK.

(34) "AND HE HAS PUT IN HIS HEART THAT HE MAY TEACH, BOTH HE, AND AHOLIAB, THE SON OF AHISAMACH, OF THE TRIBE OF DAN.

(35) "THEM HAS HE FILLED WITH

WISDOM OF HEART, TO WORK ALL MANNER OF WORK, OF THE ENGRAVER, AND OF THE CUNNING WORKMAN, AND OF THE EMBROIDERER, IN BLUE, AND IN PURPLE, IN SCARLET, AND IN FINE LINEN, AND OF THE WEAVER, EVEN OF THEM WHO DO ANY WORK, AND OF THOSE WHO DEVISE CUNNING WORK."

The composition is:

1. The implication is, the Tabernacle with all of its holy vessels, could not have been fashioned and built, at least in the manner the Lord had designed them, without the help of *"the Spirit of God."*

2. A part of the Work of the Holy Spirit was to give to Bezaleel the gift of being able to teach others, and so enabled him to form a body of skilled workmen to carry out his conceptions.

3. We learn from all of this that the Holy Spirit can do anything; consequently, we as Believers should ardently seek the help of the Spirit in all things.

THE SPIRIT OF GOD

Verses 30 through 33 read: *"And Moses said unto the Children of Israel, See, the LORD has called by name Bezaleel the son of Uri, the son of Hur, of the Tribe of Judah;*

"And He has filled him with the Spirit of God, in wisdom, in understanding, and in knowledge, and in all manner of workmanship;

"And to devise curious works, to work in gold, and in silver, and in copper,

"And in the cutting of stones, to set them, and in carving of wood, to make any manner of cunning work."

From this we learn much about the activities of the Holy Spirit.

Presently, many Believers think of Him, that is if they think of Him at all, in a manner that is foreign to Who He actually is, and What He actually does.

The truth is, if you are a carpenter, He will help you to be a better carpenter. If you are a sales person, He will help you to be a better sales person. If you are a teacher, He will help you to be a better teacher. As long as the occupation is legitimate, He will help you to perform it, far beyond your natural ability, if we will only have Faith in Christ, as we should have, and want, seek, and desire the involvement of the Divine Spirit in all that we do.

In Old Testament Times, the Holy Spirit was very limited as to what He could do. Man had a terrible sin debt hanging over his head, and due to the fact that the blood of bulls and goats could not pay that debt, the Holy Spirit could not come into the hearts and lives of all Believers, but only a select few, those who had to carry out a special Divine task, such as Bezaleel. But due to the Cross, which paid the terrible debt, the Holy Spirit can now come into the hearts and lives of all Believers, and work and function in them, even as He did in the heart and life of Bezaleel, and even to a greater degree. Our trouble is, we do not understand this, and in fact, take Him for granted, that is if we take Him any way at all.

The point is, we as Believers only get a tiny fraction of the help from Him we could get because we do not function in God's prescribed order. That prescribed order is Faith in Christ and what Christ has done at the Cross. In this manner alone will the Holy Spirit work within our lives (Rom. 8:1-2, 11).

ANOINTED TO TEACH

Verses 34 and 35 read: *"And He has put in his heart that he may teach, both he, and Aholiab, the son of Ahisamach, of the Tribe of Dan.*

"Them has He filled with wisdom of heart, to work all manner of work, of the engraver, and of the cunning workman, and of the embroiderer, in blue, and in purple, in scarlet, and in fine linen, and of the weaver, even of them who do any work, and of those who devise cunning work."

Along with showing Bezaleel how to do the work, He gave this man the ability to teach others, in order to multiply himself, which he did!

Considering all of this, I think that one can say without any fear of contradiction that the Tabernacle, along with all of its holy vessels, presented craftsmanship unequaled anywhere in the world. As well, if the Holy Spirit has His Way within our hearts and lives, as He no doubt perfected a beautiful work of art as it regards the structure in question, at the same time, He will do the same thing for us in a spiritual and moral sense. He will truly *"devise cunning work!"*

"The day of Resurrection! Earth, tell it out abroad;
"The Passover of gladness, the Passover of God!
"From death to life eternal, from Earth unto the sky,
"Our Christ has brought us over with a victory battle cry."

"Our hearts be pure from evil, that we may see aright
"The Lord in rays eternal of Resurrection light,
"And, listening to His accents, may hear, so calm and plain,
"For own 'All Hail' and, hearing, may raise the victor strain."

"Now let the Heavens be joyful, let Earth her song begin;
"Let the round world keep triumph and all that is therein;
"Invisible and visible, their notes let all things blend,
"For Christ the Lord has risen, our joy then has no end."

CHAPTER 36

(1) "THEN WROUGHT BEZALEEL AND AHOLIAB, AND EVERY WISE HEARTED MAN, IN WHOM THE LORD PUT WISDOM AND UNDERSTANDING TO KNOW HOW TO WORK ALL MANNER OF WORK FOR THE SERVICE OF THE SANCTUARY, ACCORDING TO ALL THAT THE LORD HAD COMMANDED.

(2) "AND MOSES CALLED BEZALEEL AND AHOLIAB, AND EVERY WISE HEARTED MAN, IN WHOSE HEART THE LORD HAD PUT WISDOM, EVEN EVERY ONE WHOSE HEART STIRRED HIM UP TO COME UNTO THE WORK TO DO IT:

(3) "AND THEY RECEIVED OF MOSES ALL THE OFFERING, WHICH THE CHILDREN OF ISRAEL HAD BROUGHT FOR THE WORK OF THE SERVICE OF THE SANCTUARY, TO MAKE IT WITHAL. AND THEY BROUGHT YET UNTO HIM FREE OFFERINGS EVERY MORNING.

(4) "AND ALL THE WISE MEN, WHO WROUGHT ALL THE WORK OF THE SANCTUARY, CAME EVERY MAN FROM HIS WORK WHICH THEY MADE;

(5) "AND THEY SPOKE UNTO MOSES, SAYING, THE PEOPLE BRING MUCH MORE THAN ENOUGH FOR THE SERVICE OF THE WORK, WHICH THE LORD COMMANDED TO MAKE.

(6) "AND MOSES GAVE COMMANDMENT, AND THEY CAUSED IT TO BE PROCLAIMED THROUGHOUT THE CAMP, SAYING, LET NEITHER MAN NOR WOMAN MAKE ANY MORE WORK FOR THE OFFERING OF THE SANCTUARY. SO THE PEOPLE WERE RESTRAINED FROM BRINGING.

(7) "FOR THE STUFF THEY HAD WAS SUFFICIENT FOR ALL THE WORK TO MAKE IT, AND TOO MUCH."

The overview is:

1. There is a volume of instruction in all of this. We are too prone to regard the Word of God as insufficient for the minute details connected with His Worship and Service. This is a great mistake — a mistake which has proved the fruitful source of evils and errors in the professing Church.

2. The Word of God is amply sufficient for everything, whether it regards personal Salvation and walk, or the order and rule of the Assembly.

3. Paul said: *"All Scripture is given by inspiration of God, and is profitable for doctrine, for reproof, for correction, for instruction in Righteousness, that the man of God may be perfect, thoroughly furnished unto all good works"* (II Tim. 3:16-17).

This settles the question. If the Word of God furnishes a man thoroughly unto *"all good works,"* it follows, as a necessary consequence, that whatever I find not in its pages cannot possibly be a good work.

4. And, further, be it remembered that the Divine Glory cannot connect itself with anything that is not according to the Divine Pattern.

BEZALEEL

Verses 1 and 2 read: *"Then wrought Bezaleel*

and Aholiab, and every wise hearted man, in whom the LORD put wisdom and understanding to know how to work all manner of work for the service of the Sanctuary, according to all that the LORD had commanded.

"And Moses called Bezaleel and Aholiab, and every wise hearted man, in whose heart the LORD had put wisdom, even every one whose heart stirred him up to come unto the work to do it."

The repetition in these two Verses is for purpose and reason. In other words, the Holy Spirit had it said in this manner, and with the repetition, that all may know and understand that everything was done with the help of the Holy Spirit.

If we are *"wise hearted"* we will understand what is being done here, and will learn more and more to lean on the wisdom and understanding of the Divine Spirit.

I am persuaded that the Holy Spirit will do much more for us if we will only do our part. And what is that part?

1. We must never take the Holy Spirit for granted.

2. We must understand how He works. It is the Cross of Christ which gives Him the legal right to function as He does. We must understand that, and, thereby, ever place our Faith in the Finished Work of Christ (Rom. 6:3-5; 8:1-2, 11).

3. We must not limit Him in His activities. But all the time we must ever understand that His business is to ever glorify Christ (Jn. 16:13-14).

THE GIFTS OF THE PEOPLE

Verses 3 through 7 read: *"And they received of Moses all the offering, which the Children of Israel had brought for the work of the service of the Sanctuary, to make it withal. And they brought yet unto him free offerings every morning.*

"And all the wise men, who wrought all the work of the Sanctuary, came every man from his work which they made;

"And they spoke unto Moses, saying, The people bring much more than enough for the service of the work, which the LORD commanded to make.

"And Moses gave Commandment, and they caused it to be proclaimed throughout the camp, saying, Let neither man nor woman make any more work for the offering of the Sanctuary. So the people were restrained from bringing.

"For the stuff they had was sufficient for all the work to make it, and too much."

We find in these Passages a beautiful picture of the devotion that the people gave to the Work of the Lord, as it involved the Sanctuary. It needed no effort to move the hearts of the people to give, no earnest appeals, no impressive arguments. The Scripture says that their *"hearts stirred them up."* This was the true way, and it is still the true way. Consequently, the streams of voluntary devotion flowed from within. They all felt it was their sweet privilege to give to the Lord, not with a narrow heart, but after a princely fashion, until they had given *"enough, and too much."*

I've been in the Work of the Lord all of my life. I suppose I have preached in hundreds of Churches, all over the world. And I've noticed in these many years of Evangelistic Work that if the Church was free in their giving, they would, at the same time, be free in their worship, with a spirit of freedom paramount in the entirety of the Services.

I've also noticed the Churches which were stingy and tight in their giving were bound up every other way as well. God loves a cheerful giver, which says at the same time that He has a problem with one who does not fit that mold. The whole idea of giving to the Work of the Lord contains far more meaning than merely an exchange of funds.

The idea is, God has given so much to us, and continues to give to us even on a daily basis. In fact, every single thing we have that is good has been given by Him (James 1:17), so how can we refuse to give back to Him, when in fact, giving to Him is the source of all blessings? Actually, Paul said that we are to give to the Lord, *"to prove the sincerity of our love"* (II Cor. 8:8).

JOY AMONG THE PEOPLE

As is obvious in the Text, as the people began to give to the Lord, there was a joy among them, and despite the fact that they had failed miserably a short time before as it regards the golden calf. Had they remained in this state, a state of Faith, a state of believing, which is characterized by giving, they would not have wasted their lives in the wilderness.

I firmly believe that our giving, to a large degree, decides many things with God. It's not that one can purchase things from the Lord, for He has nothing for sale. Everything He has, He gives freely. But He expects us to do the same. So I think I can say without any fear of contradiction that our giving decides our Faith, our joy, our peace, in fact, every single thing that we receive from the Lord. Let's put it another way:

Our giving must be in proportion to His giving, at least as far as it is possible for us to do so. That's why Paul also said: *"He which soweth sparingly shall reap also sparingly; and he which soweth bountifully shall reap also bountifully"* (II Cor. 9:6).

Now this is so important that I feel I should say it again so you, the Reader, will not misunderstand:

The degree of our Faith, our joy, our peace, even the Grace of God extended to us is predicated to a great degree on our giving to the Work of the Lord. And I again want to emphasize it is not that we can earn or purchase something from Him, for that is not possible. The idea is, our giving shows that we understand what He has given to us. A lack of proper giving shows that we do not understand, or else we have little regard for what He has done for us.

BUT WHAT IF CHRISTIANS GIVE TO THAT WHICH IS ACTUALLY NOT OF GOD?

Unfortunately, that is the case with most giving. I think I can explain the answer to that question in the following fashion:

Paul was called of God to be the recipient of the great Gospel of Grace, which He was to give to the Church. In fact, he was the masterbuilder of the Church, doing all under the leading and guidance of the Holy Spirit (I Cor. 3:10).

During that time, false apostles came into the Churches which he had planted, seeking to undermine his Gospel of Grace, and doing so by inserting *"law."* This is the occasion of much of his writing. That's the reason that he said, *"But though we, or an Angel from Heaven, preach any other gospel unto you than that which we have preached unto you, let him be accursed"* (Gal. 1:8).

The tragedy is, there were Christians in these Churches who were giving money to these false apostles (II Cor., Chpt. 11). Now please allow me to ask this question:

Do you think the money that Christians gave to these false apostles (II Cor. 11:13-19), who in effect were sent by Satan, was counted by God as giving to His Work? I think not! In fact, what they were supporting was not the Gospel of Jesus Christ, thereby, could get no one saved, and no one delivered. In effect, they were supporting the work of Satan. Now that's a tragedy, but it was true!

I'm afraid that many fall into the same category presently. As it regards the Work of God, we need to know where our money goes! What it does! What kind of gospel it is supporting!

For instance, Christians who support the Word of Faith doctrine are not supporting the Work of God. This doctrine is not of God, is opposed to the Cross, and is thereby *"another gospel"* (II Cor. 11:4). And if it is *"another gospel,"* then it's not the Gospel of Jesus Christ, but something else entirely. To support it is to support the work of Satan.

Likewise, Christians who support Denominations, which espouse humanistic psychology as the answer to man's dilemma, instead of the Cross of Christ, pure and simple, are supporting the work of Satan. Christians who support doctrine which denies the Baptism with the Holy Spirit, which initial, physical evidence is speaking with other tongues, are supporting a powerless gospel.

Christians are fond of saying, *"I support my Church."* And that's exactly what you should do, that is if your Church is truly preaching the Gospel of Jesus Christ. Some few are, and definitely deserve support, but the far greater majority aren't preaching the Gospel, and deserve no support at all. It's bad enough for one to throw one's money away, but worse yet to support that which is actually the very opposite of the True Gospel of Jesus Christ, despite its claims on the surface.

(8) "AND EVERY WISE HEARTED MAN AMONG THEM WHO WROUGHT THE WORK OF THE TABERNACLE MADE TEN CURTAINS OF FINE TWINED LINEN, AND BLUE, AND PURPLE, AND SCARLET: WITH CHERUBIMS OF CUNNING WORK MADE HE THEM.

(9) "THE LENGTH OF ONE CURTAIN WAS TWENTY AND EIGHT CUBITS, AND THE BREADTH OF ONE CURTAIN FOUR CUBITS: THE CURTAINS WERE ALL OF ONE SIZE.

(10) "AND HE COUPLED THE FIVE CURTAINS ONE UNTO ANOTHER: AND THE OTHER FIVE CURTAINS HE COUPLED ONE UNTO ANOTHER.

(11) "AND HE MADE LOOPS OF BLUE ON THE EDGE OF ONE CURTAIN FROM THE SELVEDGE IN THE COUPLING: LIKEWISE HE MADE IN THE UTTERMOST SIDE OF ANOTHER CURTAIN, IN THE COUPLING OF THE SECOND.

(12) "FIFTY LOOPS MADE HE IN ONE CURTAIN, AND FIFTY LOOPS MADE HE IN THE EDGE OF THE CURTAIN WHICH WAS IN THE COUPLING OF THE SECOND: THE LOOPS HELD ONE CURTAIN TO ANOTHER.

(13) "AND HE MADE FIFTY TACHES OF GOLD, AND COUPLED THE CURTAINS ONE UNTO ANOTHER WITH THE TACHES: SO IT BECAME ONE TABERNACLE."

The structure is:

1. These detailed instructions regarding *"curtains"* would seem to be totally insignificant, and in fact, as far as the world was concerned, was totally insignificant; however, the truth was, this was the single most important thing on the face of the Earth at this particular time.

2. It was important, and vastly so, simply because these curtains had to do with the building of the Tabernacle, where God would dwell between the Mercy Seat and the Cherubim.

3. They were important also, because these things were types of Christ, as it regards His Righteousness and Holiness.

4. Everything of God, irrespective as to what it might be, as ought to be obvious, is of extreme significance, inasmuch as it has to do with our lives and living.

NOTES

5. If it is important, and it definitely is, and supremely so, every Believer ought to understand what it means.

THE CURTAINS

Verses 8 through 10 read: *"And every wise hearted man among them who wrought the work of the Tabernacle made ten curtains of fine twined linen, and blue, and purple, and scarlet: with Cherubims of cunning work made he them.*

"The length of one curtain was twenty and eight cubits, and the breadth of one curtain four cubits: the curtains were all of one size.

"And he coupled the five curtains one to another: and the other five curtains he coupled one unto another."

The *"fine twined linen"* would have been snow white, therefore, representative of the Perfect Righteousness of Christ.

Embroidered on the curtains, which was the innermost covering of the Tabernacle, the part that was observed by the Priests when they were in the Holy Place, were Cherubims of, *"white, blue, purple, and scarlet."* As stated, all of it symbolized Christ. The white His Righteousness, the blue His Heavenly origin, the purple His royal lineage, and the scarlet the price that would be paid on the Cross, by the shedding of His Blood.

ONE TABERNACLE

Verses 11 through 13 read: *"And he made loops of blue on the edge of one curtain from the selvedge in the coupling: likewise he made in the uttermost side of another curtain, in the coupling of the second.*

"Fifty loops made he in one curtain, and fifty loops made he in the edge of the curtain which was in the coupling of the second: the loops held one curtain to another.

"And he made fifty taches of gold, and coupled the curtains one unto another with the taches: so it became one Tabernacle."

The *"couplings,"* as would be obvious, tied everything together, so the covering became one.

The top of the Tabernacle was flat. It had four coverings, the last three we will study momentarily.

As stated, the innermost covering, the one

observed by the Priests when they were in the Tabernacle, was the innermost covering of linen. All of these curtains were laced together with gold taches or hooks, signifying that God had ordained everything as it pertained to Christ, with the curtains hanging over the sides of the Tabernacle, reaching almost to the ground on either side.

All of this signifies that the Body of Christ is *"one."* We are all saved by the Blood of Jesus. Our names are written down in the same Book of Life, and we're on our way by the Grace of God to the same Heaven. This is the reason, or at least the main reason, that Believers should place their Faith totally and completely in Christ and His Finished Work of the Cross. While we certainly should love the Church where we attend, and the Preachers whom the Lord has called; still, all of that must ever be secondary, with the understanding that our part, place, and position in the Body of Christ are all because of Christ.

Regrettably, millions of Christians have it in their minds that their particular Church or Denomination have something to do with their Salvation. It doesn't!

I was in a particular Denomination for well over 50 years. It was often said by Preachers in that particular Denomination, and concerning others, *"If they are right with God, they'll be with us. And if they aren't with us, that means that something is wrong with them."* They would also say, *"If God moves, He will move in this Denomination."*

All of this shows that these individuals, whomever they may have been, were accrediting that particular Denomination as to having a part in their Salvation. This being the case, that Denomination had become an idol unto them, which means their Faith is no longer in Christ and Him Crucified, although they may continue to pay lip service to this Foundational Truth, but rather in a human institution. One can lose one's soul by following that course. And the truth is, millions have lost their souls by following such a course.

(14) "AND HE MADE CURTAINS OF GOATS' HAIR FOR THE TENT OVER THE TABERNACLE: ELEVEN CURTAINS HE MADE THEM.

(15) "THE LENGTH OF ONE CURTAIN WAS THIRTY CUBITS, AND FOUR CUBITS WAS THE BREADTH OF ONE CURTAIN: THE ELEVEN CURTAINS WERE OF ONE SIZE.

(16) "AND HE COUPLED FIVE CURTAINS BY THEMSELVES, AND SIX CURTAINS BY THEMSELVES.

(17) "AND HE MADE FIFTY LOOPS UPON THE UTTERMOST EDGE OF THE CURTAIN IN THE COUPLING, AND FIFTY LOOPS MADE HE UPON THE EDGE OF THE CURTAIN WHICH COUPLED THE SECOND.

(18) "AND HE MADE FIFTY TACHES OF BRASS TO COUPLE THE TENT TOGETHER, THAT IT MIGHT BE ONE.

(19) "AND HE MADE A COVERING FOR THE TENT OF RAMS' SKINS DYED RED, AND A COVERING OF BADGERS' SKINS ABOVE THAT.

The composition is:

1. The covering of goats' hair laid over the linen covering, and represented Christ as *"Prophet."*

2. A covering of *"rams' skins dyed red,"* was laid over the covering of goats' hair, and represented Christ as *"King"* — a King Who would die for humanity, thereby the skins dyed *"red."*

3. The outer covering was of badgers' skins, which represented Christ as the *"High Priest"* of His people.

GOATS' HAIR

Verses 14 through 18 read: *"And he made curtains of goats' hair for the tent over the Tabernacle: eleven curtains he made them.*

"The length of one curtain was thirty cubits, and four cubits was the breadth of one curtain: the eleven curtains were of one size.

"And he coupled five curtains by themselves, and six curtains by themselves.

"And he made fifty loops upon the uttermost edge of the curtain in the coupling, and fifty loops made he upon the edge of the curtain which coupled the second.

"And he made fifty taches of brass to couple the tent together, that it might be one."

As we have stated, the first covering over the Tabernacle was that of linen, which was snow white, embroidered with Cherubims of blue, purple, and scarlet. It would have been beautiful to behold. That was the Righteousness and Holiness of Christ. This was what the Priests saw when they went into the Tabernacle.

The second covering was that of goats' hair, which represented Christ as Prophet. Christ, in fact, filled three roles, *"Prophet, King, and Priest."*

This meant that in a sense, all of the true Prophets of the Old Testament were types of Christ. In fact, Israel was guided by *"Thus saith the Lord,"* as it regarded the Prophets. (Apostles fill that role under the New Covenant.)

This means that every prophecy given by the Prophets of old was given to them by the Lord Jesus Christ, Who spoke through the Holy Spirit (Jn. 1:1).

RAMS' SKINS DYED RED, AND BADGERS' SKINS

Verse 19 reads: *"And he made a covering for the tent of rams' skins dyed red, and a covering of badgers' skins above that."*

Of the four coverings of the Tabernacle, the third covering was that of *"rams' skins dyed red,"* which represented the Kingly nature of Christ, and that He died on a Cross, thereby shedding His Life's Blood, i.e., *"dyed red."* In other words, Christ was a King, i.e., *"The King."* Consequently, when He comes back to this Earth the second time, it will be as *"King of kings and Lord of lords"* (Rev. 19:16). However, He was no less a King when He was on this Earth the first time, than He will be at the Second Coming.

"Badgers' skins" were the last covering, and that which was seen by the congregation of Israel. It represented Christ as High Priest of His people. So, Christ was Prophet, represented by goats' hair, and King, represented by the rams' skins, and High Priest, represented by badgers' skins.

The covering of badgers' skins was the covering observed by the congregation of Israel. As would be obvious, there was nothing attractive about this particular covering, as there was nothing attractive about Christ, at least as far as the outward was concerned. In fact, He was a peasant, which means that He did not at all belong to the aristocracy of Israel. He was raised in an obscure village, Nazareth, which in fact, was looked down upon by most of the Israel of that day. In fact, one of the favorite sayings in that particular time was, *"Can there any good thing come out of Nazareth?"* (Jn. 1:46).

He was a carpenter by trade, although certainly honorable regarding its profession, at the same time, however, meant that He was not of the elite of Israel. In fact, the Scripture plainly says: *"There is no beauty that we should desire Him"* (Isa. 53:2).

While on Earth He did not necessarily conduct Himself as the Prophets of old, and He certainly didn't look like a King, and not being from the Tribe of Levi, but rather of the Tribe of Judah, He was not thought of at all as being a Priest, much less the High Priest. But all of that He was, and more!

(20) "AND HE MADE BOARDS FOR THE TABERNACLE OF SHITTIM WOOD, STANDING UP."

(21) "THE LENGTH OF A BOARD WAS TEN CUBITS, AND THE BREADTH OF A BOARD ONE CUBIT AND A HALF.

(22) "ONE BOARD HAD TWO TENONS, EQUALLY DISTANT ONE FROM ANOTHER: THUS DID HE MAKE FOR ALL THE BOARDS OF THE TABERNACLE.

(23) "AND HE MADE BOARDS FOR THE TABERNACLE; TWENTY BOARDS FOR THE SOUTH SIDE SOUTHWARD:

(24) "AND FORTY SOCKETS OF SILVER HE MADE UNDER THE TWENTY BOARDS; TWO SOCKETS UNDER ONE BOARD FOR HIS TWO TENONS, AND TWO SOCKETS UNDER ANOTHER BOARD FOR HIS TWO TENONS.

(25) "AND FOR THE OTHER SIDE OF THE TABERNACLE, WHICH IS TOWARD THE NORTH CORNER, HE MADE TWENTY BOARDS,

(26) "AND THEIR FORTY SOCKETS OF SILVER; TWO SOCKETS UNDER ONE BOARD, AND TWO SOCKETS UNDER ANOTHER BOARD.

(27) "AND FOR THE SIDES OF THE TABERNACLE WESTWARD HE MADE SIX BOARDS.

(28) "AND TWO BOARDS MADE HE FOR THE CORNERS OF THE TABERNACLE

IN THE TWO SIDES.

(29) "AND THEY WERE COUPLED BENEATH, AND COUPLED TOGETHER AT THE HEAD THEREOF, TO ONE RING: THUS HE DID TO BOTH OF THEM IN BOTH THE CORNERS.

(30) "AND THERE WERE EIGHT BOARDS; AND THEIR SOCKETS WERE SIXTEEN SOCKETS OF SILVER, UNDER EVERY BOARD TWO SOCKETS.

(31) "AND HE MADE BARS OF SHITTIM WOOD; FIVE FOR THE BOARDS OF THE ONE SIDE OF THE TABERNACLE,

(32) "AND FIVE BARS FOR THE BOARDS OF THE OTHER SIDE OF THE TABERNACLE, AND FIVE BARS FOR THE BOARDS OF THE TABERNACLE FOR THE SIDES WESTWARD.

(33) "AND HE MADE THE MIDDLE BAR TO SHOOT THROUGH THE BOARDS FROM THE ONE END TO THE OTHER.

(34) "AND HE OVERLAID THE BOARDS WITH GOLD, AND MADE THEIR RINGS OF GOLD TO BE PLACES FOR THE BARS, AND OVERLAID THE BARS WITH GOLD."

The composition is:

1. We are taken from the exterior of the Tabernacle to the interior. While there was nothing attractive about the outside, inside all was gold, thereby representing the Deity of Christ.

2. The *"sockets of silver"* represented Redemption, which was the reason that God became Man, *"The Man, Christ Jesus."*

3. The boards were made of *"Shittim Wood,"* representing His humanity, but then overlaid with gold, representing His Deity.

THE BOARDS

Verses 20 through 25 read: *"And he made boards for the Tabernacle of Shittim Wood, standing up.*

"The length of a board was ten cubits, and the breadth of a board one cubit and a half.

"One board had two tenons, equally distant one from another: thus did he make for all the boards of the Tabernacle.

"And he made boards for the Tabernacle; twenty boards for the south side southward:

"And forty sockets of silver he made under the twenty boards; two sockets under one board for his two tenons, and two sockets under another board for his two tenons.

"And for the other side of the Tabernacle, which is toward the north corner, he made twenty boards."

As should be obvious, the Lord gave to Moses minute instructions concerning the design of the Tabernacle. Everything was planned by God, down to the minutest detail, and nothing at all planned by Moses. Likewise, and as previously stated as well, Bezaleel, who did the actual construction work on this project, along with those who helped him, was not allowed to deviate at all from the design that was given.

This should be of great significance to us, proclaiming the fact that Salvation is all of the Lord and none at all of man. This means that if man tampers with the design of Redemption, typified by the silver sockets on which the boards stood, man forfeits Redemption. And that is the greatest sin of the Church, adding to, or taking away.

THE SILVER AND THE GOLD

Verses 26 through 34 read: *"And their forty sockets of silver; two sockets under one board, and two sockets under another board.*

"And for the sides of the Tabernacle westward he made six boards.

"And two boards made he for the corners of the Tabernacle in the two sides.

"And they were coupled beneath, and coupled together at the head thereof, to one ring: thus he did to both of them in both the corners.

"And there were eight boards; and their sockets were sixteen sockets of silver, under every board two sockets.

"And he made bars of Shittim Wood; five for the boards of the one side of the Tabernacle,

"And five bars for the boards of the other side of the Tabernacle, and five bars for the boards of the Tabernacle for the sides westward.

"And he made the middle bar to shoot through the boards from the one end to the other.

"And he overlaid the boards with gold, and made their rings of gold to be places for the bars, and overlaid the bars with gold."

All of the boards were made of Shittim

Wood, i.e., *"indestructible wood,"* which, as stated, represented the humanity of Christ. They sat upon sockets of silver, which served as a foundation, and in fact, a very strong foundation, for each socket was quite large and very heavy. Silver, as it regards the Tabernacle, represents Redemption. So, God became man, in order to die on a Cross, thereby, to redeem humanity.

It would not have done mere mortals any good to have died on a Cross, attempting to serve as a sacrifice. Man, who is born in original sin, could not serve in that capacity. So if the price was to be paid, God would have to pay it Himself, for such a price lay completely outside of the ability of man to pay.

While the price was high, in fact, a human being who would be perfect, life forfeited, which it was at the Fall, could only be regained by life given, a perfect life, which God Alone could pay. Therefore, man has no complaint, as ought to be obvious!

The boards covered with gold represented Christ as not only human, but as well, as Deity. He was the God-Man, Jesus Christ. And that is the great argument in the world today!

Was He a mere peasant, or was He God manifest in the flesh? The evidence is overwhelming that He was exactly Who He said He was. He fulfilled every prophecy, fulfilled all Scripture, was of the Kingly line of David, hence called, *"the Son of David,"* so why wasn't He accepted by Israel?

As their Messiah, He did not fit their evil designs. They did not at all recognize their need for a Saviour, and He came as the Saviour. And regrettably, that's the problem with most of the Church presently. It doesn't recognize its need for a Saviour. Consequently, it looks at Jesus as the Miracle Worker, the great Provider, the Healer, even the great Example, but not as Saviour. However, I would remind all concerned that His very Name, *"Jesus,"* means *"Saviour"* (Mat. 1:21).

(35) "AND HE MADE A VEIL OF BLUE, AND PURPLE, AND SCARLET, AND FINE TWINED LINEN: WITH CHERUBIMS MADE HE IT OF CUNNING WORK.

(36) "AND HE MADE THEREUNTO FOUR PILLARS OF SHITTIM WOOD, AND OVERLAID THEM WITH GOLD: THEIR HOOKS WERE OF GOLD; AND HE CAST FOR THEM FOUR SOCKETS OF SILVER.

(37) "AND HE MADE AN HANGING FOR THE TABERNACLE DOOR OF BLUE, AND PURPLE, AND SCARLET, AND OF FINE TWINED LINEN, OF NEEDLEWORK;

(38) "AND THE FIVE PILLARS OF IT WITH THEIR HOOKS: AND HE OVERLAID THEIR CHAPITERS AND THEIR FILLETS WITH GOLD: BUT THEIR FIVE SOCKETS WERE OF BRONZE."

The construction is:

1. Verse 35 portrays the Veil, which separated the Holy Place and the Holy of Holies. Its manner of material specified that it was temporary; and, in fact, Christ by His atoning death on the Cross, opened up the way to the very Holy of Holies, for all who will believe (Eph. 2:13-18).

2. The Veil was hung on four pillars made of indestructible wood, which represents the fourfold Gospel, *"Jesus saves, Jesus baptizes with the Holy Spirit, Jesus heals, and Jesus is coming again."*

3. The door that went into the Holy Place, which in effect, was the entrance into the Tabernacle, was very similar to the Veil, with the exception that it did not contain Cherubims embroidered in its fabric. It was supported by five pillars, which represents the Grace of God, i.e., *"the fivefold Ministry of 'Apostles, Prophets, Evangelists, Pastors, and Teachers'"* (Eph. 4:11).

THE VEIL

Verse 35 reads: *"And he made a Veil of blue, and purple, and scarlet, and fine twined linen: with Cherubims made he it of cunning work."*

As we've already stated several times, every single thing in the Tabernacle represented Christ in some manner, as it regarded His Atoning, Mediatorial, and Intercessory Work; therefore, to understand the rudiments of the Tabernacle is to understand Christ, which it was meant to portray.

As we stated many pages back, many in the modern Church will lavish attention on the pyramids, or other such so-called wonders, and pay scant attention to the Tabernacle. But let the Reader understand that anything we learn which portrays Christ to us in a more expanded manner presents itself as incalculable as it regards its worth. In other words, to learn Christ is to learn everything!

The Tabernacle, as it regards its design, is very simple, and of course, was intended by the Holy Spirit to be that way. Once we understand that it represents Christ, and that it represents Christ in totality, then the understanding and comprehension of its design takes on new meaning altogether.

The Veil was beautiful, but yet by its very design, was intended to be temporary. If it had been intended to be permanent, the Lord would have designed it in a much different manner, for instance of wood or even precious metal. But this wall, so to speak, was made out of simple cloth, but yet with a beautiful design, noting the fact that it was not meant to be permanent. In fact, nothing about the Tabernacle was meant to be permanent because Christ would fulfill everything in detail, making its use of temporary nature only. But regrettably, this was something the Jews really could not grasp. After Christ came, paid the price on Calvary's Cross, thereby fulfilling all the prophecies, the types, and the shadows, even the Christian Jews had difficulty in laying aside the temporary. In fact, this was one of Paul's greatest problems in establishing the Church. Jewish Christians kept wanting to insert law on top of Grace, which of course, could never work.

By its colors, the Veil stated the mission of Christ, in that the *"blue"* represented His Heavenly origin, the *"purple"* His nature as King, and the *"scarlet"* His Blood shed on the Cross of Calvary for the Redemption of lost humanity. The *"fine twined linen"* represented His spotless Righteousness, which alone would suffice. The *"Cherubim"* represented not only the Holiness of the Holy of Holies, in effect, the very Throne of God, but as well, the Holiness of Christ.

FOUR PILLARS

Verse 36 reads: *"And he made thereunto four pillars of Shittim Wood, and overlaid them with gold: their hooks were of gold; and he cast for them four sockets of silver."*

The Veil was held up by four pillars, all of it separating the Holy Place from the Holy of Holies, where God dwelt between the Mercy Seat and the Cherubim.

The four Pillars represent the fourfold Gospel, typified by the Gospel of John, Jesus saves; the Gospel of Mark, Jesus Heals; the Gospel of Luke, Jesus Baptizes with the Holy Spirit; and the Gospel of Matthew, Jesus is coming again.

Although all four of the Gospels represent the totality of Christ, each Gospel emphasizes a particular work. In John, we have the great emphasis placed on being *"born again,"* i.e., *"saved"* (Jn., Chpt. 3). Luke characterizes the Holy Spirit, in that he wrote both the Gospel which carries his name, and as well the Book of Acts, which of course, is the Holy Spirit Book. The entirety of the Gospel of Mark proclaims the healing power of Christ, as does no other Gospel. Matthew, in his Twenty-fourth Chapter, proclaims in the Words of our Lord the greatest characterization of the Second Coming.

These four pillars were made of indestructible wood, typifying the humanity of Christ, and overlaid with *"gold,"* typifying His Deity. He was the God-Man, Jesus Christ. The four Pillars sat on *"four sockets of silver,"* which typifies Redemption, which was the purpose of Christ.

THE DOOR

Verse 37 reads: *"And he made an hanging for the Tabernacle door of blue, and purple, and scarlet, and fine twined linen, of needlework."*

As the Veil separated the Holy of Holies from the Holy Place, the Door was the entrance into the Tabernacle, i.e., *"the Holy Place,"* in which were situated the Golden Lampstand, the Table of Shewbread, and the Altar of Incense. The *"Door"* as well represents Christ, Who Alone could open up the way to God. In fact, He said of Himself: *"I am the Door: by Me if any man enter in, he shall be saved, and shall go in and out, and find pasture"* (Jn. 10:9).

But I remind the Reader that this *"Door"* is a bloody door, typified by the color of *"scarlet"* on the material. It goes all the way back to the land of Egypt and the deliverance of the Children of Israel. The lamb was to be killed, and its blood was to be applied to the doorposts and the header of the front door of each house, and the Lord said: *"When I see the Blood, I will pass over you, and the plague shall not be upon you to destroy you"* (Ex. 12:7, 13).

Once again, we see how the entirety of the Tabernacle proclaims not only the Person of Christ, but as well, His Mission, which was the Redemption of humanity, which was effected at the Cross.

The colors of the Door were the same as the colors of the Veil, but there was one exception; whereas the Veil had Cherubim embroidered in the material, the Door did not have such. The Veil led into the Holy of Holies, but the Door led into the Holy Place. The former was occupied by God, therefore, the Cherubim.

THE FIVE PILLARS

Verse 38 reads: *"And the five pillars of it with their hooks: and he overlaid their chapiters and their fillets with gold: but their five sockets were of bronze."*

Four pillars held up the Veil, typifying the fourfold Gospel, whereas *"five pillars"* held up the material of the Door. *"Five"* in Biblical numerology, specifies, *"Grace."* Jesus had five names, *"Wonderful, Counselor, The Mighty God, The Everlasting Father, The Prince of Peace"* (Isa. 9:6). The Ministry is made up of five Callings, *"Apostles, Prophets, Evangelists, Pastors, and Teachers"* (Eph. 4:11). As well, Jesus, in His Crucifixion, suffered five wounds, that is if we combine the hands and combine the feet. They are, *"the nails driven in His hands, the nails driven in His feet, the spear thrust in His side, the whip laid on His back, and the thorns in His brow."* John said, *"For the Law was given by Moses, but Grace and Truth came by Jesus Christ"* (Jn. 1:17).

As well, on top of the five Pillars there were *"Chapiters,"* which the four Pillars between the Holy Place and the Holy of Holies did not contain. The *"Chapiters"* represented the *"Finished Work of Christ."* We derive this from I Kings 7:15-20, on which we will not now elaborate. The Chapiters were overlaid with *"gold,"* proclaiming the Deity of Christ. It doesn't tell us here of what the pillars were made, but it does relate that information in Exodus 26:37. They were of *"Shittim Wood,"* the same as the four Pillars between the Holy Place and the Holy of Holies, as well, typifying the humanity of Christ.

However, these *"five Pillars"* were set in *"sockets of copper,"* whereas the others were in sockets of silver. The *"copper"* represents the Judgment of God, which Jesus would suffer on our behalf. It would result in Redemption, hence the *"silver sockets"* under the four Pillars. Once again, we not only see Christ, but we see as well, the Cross.

"Golden harps are sounding, Angel voices ring,
"Pearly gates are opened, opened for the King;
"Christ, the King of Glory, Jesus, King of Love,
"Is gone up in triumph to His Throne above."

"He Who came to save us, He Who bled and died,
"Now is crowned with glory at His Father's side:
"Never more to suffer, never more to die,
"Jesus, King of Glory, is gone up on high."

"Interceding for His children in that blessed place,
"Calling them to Glory, sending them His Grace;
"His bright home preparing, faithful ones, for you;
"Jesus ever liveth, ever loveth too."

CHAPTER 37

(1) "AND BEZALEEL MADE THE ARK OF SHITTIM WOOD: TWO CUBITS AND A HALF WAS THE LENGTH OF IT, AND A CUBIT AND A HALF THE BREADTH OF IT, AND A CUBIT AND A HALF THE HEIGHT OF IT:

(2) "AND HE OVERLAID IT WITH PURE GOLD WITHIN AND WITHOUT, AND MADE A CROWN OF GOLD TO IT ROUND ABOUT.

(3) "AND HE CAST FOR IT FOUR RINGS OF GOLD, TO BE SET BY THE FOUR CORNERS OF IT; EVEN TWO RINGS UPON THE ONE SIDE OF IT, AND TWO RINGS UPON THE OTHER SIDE OF IT.

(4) "AND HE MADE STAVES OF SHITTIM WOOD, AND OVERLAID THEM WITH GOLD.

(5) "AND HE PUT THE STAVES INTO THE RINGS BY THE SIDES OF THE ARK, TO BEAR THE ARK."

The overview is:

1. The Ark of the Covenant contained the Ten Commandments, placed on two tablets of stone. They represented the Righteousness of God.

2. The Ark was made of *"Shittim Wood,"* referred to as indestructible wood, typifying the humanity of Christ. It was overlaid with gold, typifying the Deity of our Lord.

3. It had a crown of gold around it, signifying Christ as King.

4. It had a ring of gold set on each corner, and two staves made of indestructible wood, overlaid with gold, to be inserted in the rings, when the Ark was to be moved. This signified that God would be with His people, wherever they were directed to go. He would not direct them to a place to where He wouldn't go, and they were not to go to a place without Him directing the way.

THE ARK OF THE COVENANT

Most everything that we will give here, and in the following Chapters as well, have already been given in previous Chapters.

But at the same time, we must understand, when the Holy Spirit repeats something, He always does it for purpose and design. In the first place, He is wanting us to know the significance of what is being addressed. And of course, anything about Christ is significant indeed!

In view of this, and especially considering the manner in which most Commentaries are studied, even though there will be some repetition, I feel it is incumbent upon us to address these Chapters, albeit somewhat abbreviated.

Verses 1 and 2 read: *"And Bezaleel made the Ark of Shittim Wood: two cubits and a half was the length of it, and a cubit and a half the breadth of it, and a cubit and a half the height of it:*

"And he overlaid it with pure gold within and without, and made a crown of gold to it round about."

Without going into detail regarding description which we've already given in previous Commentary, suffice to say that the Ark described here is a replica of the pattern or the real Ark in Heaven. In Revelation 11:19, it says: *"And there was seen in His Temple the Ark of His Testament."* Concerning this, Williams said: *"The Ark containing God's Covenant with His Anointed* (Christ) *is here disclosed as a demonstration not only of God's faithfulness to this Covenant made with Christ promising Him the ends of the Earth for His possession, as well as the House of Israel, but also as evidence that the sovereignty of the world is really His. This Ark in the Heavenly Temple is a pledge of God's Covenant with Christ, as the Ark in its earthly counterpart was a pledge of God's Covenant with Israel."*

The Ark of the Covenant remained with Israel for about 1,000 years. The Prophet Ezekiel saw the Holy Spirit leave the Temple (Ezek. 11:23), and not so long after that (about seven years), Nebuchadnezzar overran Jerusalem, and destroyed the Temple. Tradition says that the Prophet Jeremiah took the Ark of the Covenant out of the Temple before it was taken by the Babylonian Monarch, and hid it somewhere in a cave, with the location going with him to the grave. One thing is clear: when the soldiers of Nebuchadnezzar broke into the Holy of Holies, the room was empty. So when Israel forsook the Lord, which they did, the Ark was lost as well. When Herod built the beautiful Temple that graced this sight, in which Christ ministered, the Holy of Holies was empty. In fact, Israel will not be back in Covenant until she accepts Christ, which she will at the Second Coming (Zech., Chpts. 13-14).

THE MOBILITY OF THE ARK

Verses 3 through 5 read: *"And he cast for it four rings of gold, to be set by the four corners of it; even two rings upon the one side of it, and two rings upon the other side of it.*

"And he made staves of Shittim Wood, and overlaid them with gold.

"And he put the staves into the rings by the sides of the Ark, to bear the Ark."

The Lord guided Israel in all her wanderings in the wilderness, and of course, continued to do so, even minutely, when they entered the Promised Land. In fact, this was a great part of the Covenant.

Consequently, when Israel was given instructions to move, the Cloud would lift, thereby showing the way, and that being the case, the Tabernacle was to be taken down, along with all the Sacred Vessels, and transported unto the next camping place. The staves were to be inserted in the two rings on each side, with the Ark then being borne by the Priests. In fact, about 500 years later, David would get into serious trouble because he had the Ark transported by the means of a new cart. A man died as the result (II Sam. 6:3-7).

The Priests were types of Christ; therefore, they alone could carry the Ark because it was a Type of the Throne of God, in other words, where God dwelt.

This tells us that the only way to God is through Jesus Christ, and more particular yet, by believing in what He did at the Cross on our behalf. In fact, Jesus said of Himself: *"I am the Way, the Truth, and the Life: no man comes unto the Father, but by Me"* (Jn. 14:6).

(6) "AND HE MADE THE MERCY SEAT OF PURE GOLD: TWO CUBITS AND A HALF WAS THE LENGTH THEREOF, AND ONE CUBIT AND A HALF THE BREADTH THEREOF.

(7) "AND HE MADE TWO CHERUBIMS OF GOLD, BEATEN OUT OF ONE PIECE MADE HE THEM, ON THE TWO ENDS OF THE MERCY SEAT;

(8) "ONE CHERUB ON THE END ON THIS SIDE, AND ANOTHER CHERUB ON THE OTHER SIDE ON THAT SIDE: OUT OF THE MERCY SEAT MADE HE THE CHERUBIMS ON THE TWO ENDS THEREOF.

(9) "AND THE CHERUBIMS SPREAD OUT THEIR WINGS ON HIGH, AND COVERED WITH THEIR WINGS OVER THE MERCY SEAT, WITH THEIR FACES ONE TO ANOTHER; EVEN TO THE MERCY SEATWARD WERE THE FACES OF THE CHERUBIMS."

The exegesis is:

1. It seems that the Mercy Seat and the Cherubim were of one piece of gold. This signifies that the Mercy of God is based entirely upon His Holiness.

2. His Mercy, based on His Holiness, tells us that only Christ can come near. He Alone is Holy!

3. While the way has definitely been opened for unholy man to come into the very Presence of God, it is done only by Faith in Christ, and what Christ did at the Cross.

THE MERCY SEAT

Verse 6 reads: *"And he made the Mercy Seat of pure gold: two cubits and a half was the length thereof, and one cubit and a half the breadth thereof."*

Thank God that it is a Mercy Seat, and not a Judgment Seat. The very name signifies Who and What God actually is.

God functions entirely on the principle of Grace, and because He functions entirely on that principle, which is a position of choice, He then has no choice, but to show Mercy, that is, if men function properly in His Grace.

The great question is, how does man obtain this Mercy from God?

It is obtained in only one way, and that is through Jesus Christ. But as repeatedly stated, more particularly, it is obtained through what He did at the Cross, and our Faith in that Finished Work. Men cannot enjoy the Mercy of God, unless they come through Jesus Christ. And they cannot come through Jesus Christ, unless they come through *"Jesus Christ and Him Crucified"* (I Cor. 1:23; 2:2; Rom. 6:3-14; Eph. 2:13-18).

All the world wants mercy, that is, if they believe in God at all; however, the great problem pertains as to how we come by this Mercy.

Regarding those who claim to believe the Bible, almost all would pay lip service to the Cross. While some few definitely do believe what they are saying, the actions of most point to other directions. Even as we have stated several times in this Volume, the greater majority of the Church, in fact, almost all, have opted for humanistic psychology. While the Reader may tire of me constantly mentioning this problem, the Reader must remember that this is one of the great problems of this present age.

Humanistic psychology is not an ancient philosophy, although it has its roots in Greek myth. It was actually begun by Sigmund Freud, a little over 100 years ago, at least from the time of this writing. And anyone who has even a small amount of knowledge as it regards this philosophy knows that the two, the Cross of Christ and humanistic psychology, cannot mix. They are totally antagonistic to each other. In other words, if one trusts in the Cross, one is going to have to leave, and I mean leave totally, all rudiments of psychology. On the other side of the coin, if one accepts humanistic psychology, this means that one no longer believes in the Cross, irrespective as to what they might say.

The great sin of the modern Church is that it claims to believe both. It does this by claiming that humanistic psychology is a science. The truth is, it is not a science, has never been a science, and never will be a science. Its methods are as varied as the people who practice its philosophy.

CHRISTIANS

Now the tragedy is, most laypersons have no knowledge whatsoever of this evil philosophy, and evil it is! But to be sure, their leaders, at least for the most part, definitely do have knowledge of the psychological way, and have accepted it wholeheartedly. To be frank, this is at least one of the reasons, and in fact, the major reason, that the leaders of most of the Pentecostal Denominations in the United States and Canada dislike this Evangelist, and do so stringently. They do not at all like for anyone to draw attention to this fact, much less one who has a voice, as does this Ministry.

In fact, the Cross is quickly becoming the dividing line between the True Church and the apostate church. As we've repeatedly stated, this is not new, but in fact, has always been. But the Holy Spirit is going to make the Cross so pronounced, and in fact, has already begun to do so, that the Believer will either have to live up to his name and properly believe in Christ and what Christ has done, or else, opt for other things.

CHERUBIM

Verses 7 through 9 read: *"And he made two Cherubims of gold, beaten out of one piece made he them, on the two ends of the Mercy Seat;*

"One Cherub on the end on this side, and another Cherub on the other end on that side: out of the Mercy Seat made he the Cherubims on the two ends thereof.

"And the Cherubims spread out their wings on high, and covered with their wings over the Mercy Seat, with their faces one to another; even to the Mercy Seatward were the faces of the Cherubims."

As we have stated, it seems from the description of the Text that the Mercy Seat and the Cherubim were all one piece of gold. In other words, the Cherubim, were not made separately and then somehow attached to the ends, but in fact, were a part of the Mercy Seat.

These particular creatures, which John saw in his vision at the Throne of God (Rev. 4:6-9), were in a sense the real or the pattern after which these were made on the Mercy Seat. The Scripture says: *"And they rest not day and night, saying, Holy, holy, holy, LORD God Almighty, which was, and is, and is to come"* (Rev. 4:8). In the King James Version, they are translated *"Beasts,"* but should have been translated, *"Living Creatures."*

It seems their sole purpose is to exclaim the Holiness of God, in fact, to declare that God is a *"thrice-Holy God."* Now it should be noted that the Mercy Seat and these Cherubim are all one piece, signifying something very important.

As sinful men, we desperately want and need the Mercy of God, but at the same time, we have the principle of His Holiness. So how do we reconcile the two?

MERCY AND TRUTH ARE MET TOGETHER

God's Holiness must never be violated! And if He grants mercy to sinful men, without His Justice and Nature being satisfied, He definitely would be violating His Holiness.

So understanding the principle of His Holiness, how can He grant mercy to sinful men?

The Psalmist said: *"Mercy and Truth are met together; Righteousness and Peace have kissed each other"* (Ps. 85:10).

There is only one way that this could be done, and in fact was done, and that was by God becoming man, and going to the Cross, where there *"Mercy and Truth met together; Righteousness and Peace kissed each other."*

"Truth" and *"Righteousness"* had to be addressed. Jesus Christ was both. He is Truth (Jn. 14:6), and He is Perfect Righteousness. This doesn't mean that He merely <u>has</u> Righteousness, but rather that He <u>is</u> Righteousness (II Cor. 5:21). When Jesus went to the Cross, and did so as Truth and Righteousness, thereby shedding His Life's Blood, this made it possible for *"Mercy"* and *"Peace"* to be given to sinful men. But it is possible only on the foundation of sinful man exhibiting Faith in Christ and Him Crucified (Eph. 2:8-9, 13-18).

(10) "AND HE MADE THE TABLE OF SHITTIM WOOD: TWO CUBITS WAS THE LENGTH THEREOF, AND A CUBIT THE BREADTH THEREOF, AND A CUBIT AND A HALF THE HEIGHT THEREOF:

(11) "AND HE OVERLAID IT WITH PURE GOLD, AND MADE THEREUNTO A CROWN OF GOLD ROUND ABOUT.

(12) "ALSO HE MADE THEREUNTO A BORDER OF AN HANDBREADTH ROUND ABOUT; AND MADE A CROWN OF GOLD FOR THE BORDER THEREOF ROUND ABOUT.

(13) "AND HE CAST FOR IT FOUR RINGS OF GOLD, AND PUT THE RINGS UPON THE FOUR CORNERS THAT WERE IN THE FOUR FEET THEREOF.

(14) "OVER AGAINST THE BORDER WERE THE RINGS, THE PLACES FOR THE STAVES TO BEAR THE TABLE.

(15) "AND HE MADE THE STAVES OF SHITTIM WOOD, AND OVERLAID THEM WITH GOLD, TO BEAR THE TABLE.

(16) "AND HE MADE THE VESSELS WHICH WERE UPON THE TABLE, HIS DISHES, AND HIS SPOONS, AND HIS BOWLS, AND HIS COVERS TO COVER WITHAL, OF PURE GOLD."

The diagram is:

NOTES

1. The above Verses portray the Table of Shewbread, a Type of Christ as the Bread of Life.

2. The *"crown of gold"* around the top portrayed Him as a King.

3. The Table in the Tabernacle was built for transport, if need be. It portrayed Christ as ever being with His people.

THE TABLE OF SHEWBREAD

Verse 10 reads: *"And he made the Table of Shittim Wood: two cubits was the length thereof, and a cubit the breadth thereof, and a cubit and a half the height thereof."*

The Table of Shewbread represented Christ as the Bread of Life. This Table was made to hold 12 loaves of bread, placed in two rows upon the Table, on which was sprinkled pure frankincense for a memorial. Here they remained before the Lord for seven days, when they were removed and eaten by Aaron and his sons, in the Holy Place, with fresh loaves taking their place (Lev. 24:5-9).

The *"Bread"* represents Christ as the Sustainer of His people. As stated, He is the Bread of Life (Jn. 6:35). The very words *"Bread of Life"* speak of our life and living. There can be no true happiness, joy, peace of mind, or proper hope outside of Christ. He is all of these things, and more! If you have Him, you have everything; if you don't have Him, despite what you might have otherwise, still, you have nothing. So it must be settled that in Him Alone, we have life, and in Him, we can have it *"more abundantly"* (Jn. 10:10).

The idea that there were 12 loaves of bread on the Table represents the fact of the Government of God. In other words, we must do things His Way. The number *"twelve"* represented Government and, therefore, there were 12 Tribes of Israel, and 12 Apostles. The Government of God, signified by these 12 loaves, must be followed at all cost. Let me give you an example concerning the Ark of the Covenant.

As we mentioned above, David tried to bring the Ark of God into Jerusalem, but did so by placing it on a new cart. This was opposed to the Word of God, and a man died as the result.

When David finally inquired of the Word

of the Lord as to exactly how the Ark must be transported, he then prepared the Priests, who in fact, were to carry the Ark. He said to them: *"You are the chief of the fathers of the Levites: sanctify yourselves, both you and your brethren, that you may bring up the Ark of the LORD God of Israel unto the place that I have prepared for it.*

"For because you did it not at the first, the LORD our God made a breach upon us, for that we sought Him not after the due order" (I Chron. 15:12-13).

Please notice the words, *"For that we sought Him not after the due order."*

God's Government was that the Ark was to be transported in a certain way, and for very important reasons. In fact, every single thing as it pertains to the Lord has to it a *"due order."* That is the *"Government of God."* It must be properly followed, or else spiritual death will be the result.

GOD'S PRESCRIBED ORDER OF VICTORY

As we have already stated many times in this Volume, and as we state constantly over our Radio and Television broadcasts, God has a prescribed order of victory. If we follow that order, we will walk in victory, but if not, and irrespective as to whom we might be, disaster will be the results.

That prescribed order is Jesus Christ and Him Crucified. We are to place our Faith exclusively in Christ, which refers to placing our Faith in what He did at the Cross, and when that is done, and continues to be done, the Holy Spirit will grandly help us, thereby guaranteeing victory. That is God's prescribed order! (Rom. 6:3-14; 8:1-2, 11; I Cor. 1:17-18, 21, 23; 2:2).

No matter how sincere we might be, if we violate that order, which is God's Government, we will meet with very unhappy results.

FRANKINCENSE

Frankincense was to be poured over the bread, before it was eaten. This particular spice had a bitter taste, which was meant to portray the price that would be paid for man's Redemption, hence the Cross of Christ (Lev. 24:6-7).

In fact, I think it can be said without fear of contradiction that in some way, every part and particle of the Tabernacle, along with its Sacred Vessels, not only typified Christ, but typified, as well, His Cross. This is so, because the Cross, and the Cross alone, fulfilled all of the types and symbols of the Tabernacle, making its use unnecessary, and thereby, bringing it to an end. It was the Cross alone which did that!

THE EATING OF THE BREAD

It was commanded by the Lord that the bread be eaten every Sabbath, which was every seventh day. This, in fact, was what Jesus was addressing when He said: *"I am the Living Bread which came down from Heaven: if any man eat of this bread, he shall live forever: and the bread that I will give is My flesh, which I will give for the life of the world.*

"Verily, verily, I say unto you, except you eat the flesh of the Son of Man, and drink His Blood, you have no life in you.

"Whoso eats My flesh, and drinks My Blood, has eternal life; and I will raise him up at the last day.

"For My flesh is meat indeed, and My Blood is drink indeed.

"He who eats My flesh, and drinks My Blood, dwells in Me, and I in him" (Jn. 6:51, 53-56).

Jesus wasn't speaking here in the literal sense, but rather in the spiritual sense. He was speaking of one believing in Him and what He would do at the Cross by the giving of Himself in the shedding of His Blood. Simple Faith in that Finished Work obeys this injunction.

This was also typified by the demand that all of the Passover Lamb be eaten, with none remaining (Ex. 12:10-11).

THE SABBATH

As stated, the 12 loaves were to be eaten on the Sabbath, which was the seventh day, with new loaves then taking their place. *"Seven"* is God's perfect number, denoting totality, completion, and perfection.

The idea is, that which is of Christ is Perfect, which refers to a Perfect Salvation. It is a Salvation, that is, if received as it should be received, that answers every question, and solves every problem. Christ is surely all in all!

The *"Sabbath"* which speaks of *"rest,"* would come in Christ. In fact, the entirety of the Sabbath, which was entirely between the Lord and the Jews, and did not include the Gentiles, was meant to portray the *"rest"* which could be found only in Christ. In other words, when Christ came, He fulfilled the Sabbath, with it no more incumbent upon Believers.

There are only two Ordinances that are incumbent now upon Believers, and we speak of the time from the Cross forward, those are *"Water Baptism"* and the taking of the *"Lord's Supper,"* both representing Christ and His Finished Work. If we engage in anything else, and especially that of the old Law, we are in fact, entering into Law, in which Grace cannot function.

THE CROWNS

Verses 11 and 12 read: *"And he overlaid it with pure gold, and made thereunto a crown of gold round about.*

"Also he made thereunto a border of an handbreadth round about; and made a crown of gold for the border thereof round about."

In essence, there were two crowns on the Table. There was a border about the width of a hand, which extended the Table all around. There was a crown on that, which seemed to be at the edge. There was another crown that circled the Table on the inside of the border. All of this specified the fact that Christ was King, and not only King, but *"KING OF KINGS, AND LORD OF LORDS"* (Rev. 19:16).

The two crowns spoke of both of His Comings. He came the first time as a King, but was not recognized as such. When He comes back the Second Time, He definitely will be recognized as King, and as stated, *"King of kings, and Lord of lords."*

TO BEAR THE TABLE

Verses 13 through 16 read: *"And he cast for it four rings of gold, and put the rings upon the four corners that were in the four feet thereof.*

"Over against the border were the rings, the places for the staves to bear the Table.

"And he made the staves of Shittim Wood, and overlaid them with gold, to bear the Table.

"And he made the vessels which were upon the Table, his dishes, and his spoons, and his bowls, and his covers to cover withal, of pure gold."

There were rings of gold attached to the four corners of the Table, where staves could be inserted, and the Table could be carried, when it was moved to another place. In the wilderness, this happened at times, as the Lord would change locations. Unfortunately, because of unbelief, the Children of Israel had to remain in the wilderness for nearly 40 years. How many times the Tabernacle, with all of its furniture, was moved, we aren't told; but it definitely was moved some.

The idea is, Christ remained with them, even during their wanderings, despite their unbelief. Thank the Lord that He doesn't leave us when we fail. If He did, where would any of us be?!

(17) "AND HE MADE THE LAMPSTAND OF PURE GOLD: A BEATEN WORK MADE HE THE LAMPSTAND; HIS SHAFT, AND HIS BRANCH, HIS BOWLS, HIS KNOPS, AND HIS FLOWERS, WERE OF THE SAME:

(18) "AND SIX BRANCHES GOING OUT OF THE SIDES THEREOF; THREE BRANCHES OF THE LAMPSTAND OUT OF THE ONE SIDE THEREOF, AND THREE BRANCHES OF THE LAMPSTAND OUT OF THE OTHER SIDE THEREOF:

(19) "THREE BOWLS MADE AFTER THE FASHION OF ALMONDS IN ONE BRANCH, A KNOP AND A FLOWER; AND THREE BOWLS MADE LIKE ALMONDS IN ANOTHER BRANCH, A KNOP AND A FLOWER: SO THROUGHOUT THE SIX BRANCHES GOING OUT OF THE LAMPSTAND.

(20) "AND IN THE LAMPSTAND WERE FOUR BOWLS MADE LIKE ALMONDS, HIS KNOPS, AND HIS FLOWERS:

(21) "AND A KNOP UNDER TWO BRANCHES OF THE SAME, AND A KNOP UNDER TWO BRANCHES OF THE SAME, AND A KNOP UNDER TWO BRANCHES OF THE SAME, ACCORDING TO THE SIX BRANCHES GOING OUT OF IT.

(22) "THEIR KNOPS AND THEIR BRANCHES WERE OF THE SAME: ALL OF IT WAS ONE BEATEN WORK OF PURE GOLD.

(23) "AND HE MADE HIS SEVEN LAMPS, AND HIS SNUFFERS, AND HIS SNUFFDISHES, OF PURE GOLD.

(24) "OF A TALENT OF PURE GOLD MADE HE IT, AND ALL THE VESSELS THEREOF."

The structure is:

1. The Lampstand is a Type of Christ as the Light of the world. Incidentally, the Hebrew word should have been translated Lampstand, because it's not a candlestick. In fact, no candles were involved.

2. Six of the prongs represent the people of God, with six being the number of man. The middle prong represents Christ, totaling seven, which is God's perfect number. The idea is, the people of God cannot be complete, not at all, without Christ.

3. The Lampstand was made out of one piece of gold, signifying the fact that all are one in Christ.

THE LAMPSTAND

Verse 17 reads: *"And he made the Lampstand of pure gold: of beaten work made he the Lampstand; his shaft, and his branch, his bowls, his knops, and his flowers, were of the same."*

We have already looked at these various vessels in particular, so our comments now will be generalized.

As is obvious, the Lampstand is a Type of Christ as the Light of the world. Jesus said as much of Himself: *"I am the Light of the world: he who follows Me shall not walk in darkness, but shall have the light of life"* (Jn. 8:12).

If men do not know Christ, they are spiritually blind, because one cannot know the Father unless one first knows the Son (Jn. 14:6). And one cannot know Christ unless one understands the very purpose of Christ, which is the Cross, which was a necessity, that is if man was to be redeemed. Man's everlasting problem is trying to reach the Father outside of the Son, or trying to accept the Son, without accepting what the Son has done. God's Way is the way of the Cross, and there is no other way. When man knows that and believes that, he then has *"light"*; otherwise, there is no light. To try to understand Christ outside of the Cross is to invent *"another Jesus"* (II Cor. 11:4). The following we have already said several times, but because of this great significance, we'll continue to say it.

THE WORD AND THE CHURCH

If the Believer doesn't have proper light on the Cross, he cannot properly understand the Bible. To the degree that he misunderstands the Cross, to that degree he will misunderstand everything else in the Word of God. Now let me explain that:

He may get some things right, and no doubt will, but most will be wrong. And even that which he gets right will be colored by the wrong direction. In fact, it cannot be any other way.

As well, the Holy Spirit has made the Cross the dividing line between the True Church and the apostate church. In fact, that is not new, having always been the case. But the Holy Spirit is making this *"light of the Cross"* so very prominent that it cannot be ignored, at least through ignorance. To deny it, as many no doubt will, will place one on the side of the apostate church.

THE BRANCHES

Verse 18 reads: *"And six branches going out of the sides thereof; three branches of the Lampstand out of the one side thereof, and three branches of the Lampstand out of the other side thereof."*

The Lampstand, as is obvious, and as stated, represents Christ as the Light of the world; however, it also prefigures the Church. The prefiguring of the Church pertains to the six branches; three on each side of the main stem, with the main stem representing Christ. Six is the number of man, which always speaks of incompletion. But with the six branches being a part of the main stem, the Lampstand is then complete.

This tells us that man is complete only in Christ, which changes the number from *"six"* to *"seven,"* God's perfect number, which speaks of totality and completion.

As well, the Lampstand was made out of one piece of gold, which means that the six branches were not fashioned or welded into the main stem, but were rather a part of the main stem. Now how can this be?

THE CROSS

Jesus said of Himself, the Father, and Believers: *"At that day* (after the Cross and the sending of the Spirit) *you shall know that I am in My Father, and you in Me, and I in you"* (Jn. 14:20). Someone has rightly referred to this as the *"Divine entanglement."*

Christ being in the Father speaks of His Deity. The Believer being in Christ speaks of Redemption. Christ being in the Believer speaks of Sanctification, without which the Believer cannot live a holy life.

The Believer in Christ, and Christ in the Believer, is carried out by the work accomplished by Christ at the Cross, and the Faith of the Believer in that Finished Work. That's why Paul used the term, *"Know ye not, that so many of us as were baptized into Jesus Christ were baptized into His death?"* (Rom. 6:3).

When Paul used the word here *"baptized,"* he wasn't speaking of Water Baptism, but rather the Crucifixion of Christ. When the believing sinner expresses Faith in Christ, in the Mind of God, that believing sinner is placed into Christ, and actually becomes a part of His Death, His Burial, and His Resurrection (Rom. 6:3-5). As stated, all of this is accomplished by Faith. Christ becomes our Substitute, and our Faith in Him gives us all that He has accomplished, which in fact, was done on our behalf. Paul further addressed this by saying:

"I am crucified with Christ (this takes us back to Romans 6:3)*: nevertheless I live; yet not I, but Christ lives in me: and the life which I now live in the flesh I live by the Faith of the Son of God, Who loved me, and gave Himself for me"* (Gal. 2:20).

THE FRUIT OF THE SPIRIT

Verses 19 through 21 read: *"Three bowls made after the fashion of almonds in one branch, a knop and a flower; and three bowls made like almonds in another branch, a knop and a flower: so throughout the six branches going out of the Lampstand.*

"And in the Lampstand were four bowls made like almonds, his knops, and his flowers:

"And a knop under two branches of the same, and a knop under two branches of the same, and a knop under two branches of the same, according to the six branches going out of it."

The *"almonds"* represent Resurrection, while the *"knop"* represents pomegranates, i.e., *"fruit,"* and the *"flower"* was no doubt the lily, denoting *"purity."*

The Fruit of the Spirit listed in Galatians 5:22-23, portray Christlikeness. All of this is attached to the *"Lampstand,"* denoting *"light."* The idea is this:

I personally feel the *"Resurrection"* addressed here, while definitely addressing the coming Resurrection, with Christ being the Firstfruits, more than all, it represents *"Resurrection Life,"* which can only come about by the Believer properly understanding the Cross of Christ. Paul said this:

"For if we have been planted together in the likeness of His death, we shall be also in the likeness of His Resurrection" (Rom. 6:5).

This plainly tells us that we can enjoy Resurrection Life, but only if we properly understand the *"likeness of His Death,"* and our part in that death.

As well, Resurrection Life, symbolized by the *"almonds,"* is guaranteed to produce the *"Fruit of the Spirit,"* represented by the *"knops,"* which of course, demands *"purity,"* represented by the flowers. This is the illumination or light which the Holy Spirit desires for us to know and understand. That which was only in symbolism for so long is now a reality, all a work of the Spirit, due to what Christ did at the Cross. We must ever realize that all He has accomplished, all on our behalf, came at great price.

PURE GOLD

Verses 22 through 24 read: *"Their knops and their branches were of the same: all of it was one beaten work of pure gold.*

"And he made his seven lamps, and his snuffers, and his snuffdishes, of pure gold.

"Of a talent of pure gold made he it, and all the vessels thereof."

The phrase, *"One beaten work of pure gold,"* tells us that the Lampstand was all of one piece, which more than likely, could not be duplicated by modern craftsmen.

The *"gold"* represents the Deity of Christ, and proclaims the fact that the Believer, in a sense, can enter into that Deity. But let us never forget, we can do that only by and through what Jesus did for us at the Cross. The One Who hung on that Cross was the God-Man, Jesus Christ. While He died as a human being, at the same time, He was fully God, as He had always been God, and will always be God.

While believing man will never be Deity, for that's not the idea here at all, still, the Truth is, when we become a part of Christ, we in a sense are part and parcel of His Supreme Being (Jn. 14:20).

(25) "AND HE MADE THE INCENSE ALTAR OF SHITTIM WOOD: THE LENGTH OF IT WAS A CUBIT, AND THE BREADTH OF IT A CUBIT; IT WAS FOURSQUARE; AND TWO CUBITS WAS THE HEIGHT OF IT; THE HORNS THEREOF WERE OF THE SAME.

(26) "AND HE OVERLAID IT WITH PURE GOLD, BOTH THE TOP OF IT, AND THE SIDES THEREOF ROUND ABOUT, AND THE HORNS OF IT: ALSO HE MADE UNTO IT A CROWN OF GOLD ROUND ABOUT.

(27) "AND HE MADE TWO RINGS OF GOLD FOR IT UNDER THE CROWN THEREOF, BY THE TWO CORNERS OF IT, UPON THE TWO SIDES THEREOF, TO BE PLACES FOR THE STAVES TO BEAR IT WITHAL.

(28) "AND HE MADE THE STAVES OF SHITTIM WOOD, AND OVERLAID THEM WITH GOLD.

(29) "AND HE MADE THE HOLY ANOINTING OIL, AND THE PURE INCENSE OF SWEET SPICES, ACCORDING TO THE WORK OF THE APOTHECARY."

The composition is:

1. The Incense Altar was a type of the Intercessory Work of our Lord, as our Great High Priest.

2. It was *"foursquare,"* stipulating the fact that the Intercession is the same for all men everywhere, at least for those who believe.

3. It had *"horns"* on each corner, stipulating dominion, which was gained by Christ, and which can be ours, if our trust is in Him and His Cross.

4. There was *"a crown of gold about it,"* signifying that Christ is *"King."*

THE INCENSE ALTAR

Verse 25 reads: *"And he made the Incense Altar of Shittim Wood: the length of it was a cubit, and the breadth of it a cubit; it was foursquare; and two cubits was the height of it; the horns thereof were of the same."*

The Intercessory Work of Christ, symbolized by the Altar of Incense, is desperately needed by all Believers everywhere. Christ is Prophet and King, but in this role, He functions as our Great High Priest (Heb. 7:15-17, 24-28).

The Intercession made by Christ is that which pertains to sin, and of course, we're speaking of sin on the part of the Believer. No Believer has to sin (I Jn. 2:1-2), but the truth is, all Believers, none excepted, are continuously coming short of the Glory of God (Rom. 3:23). And that refers to even the best of Christians, whomever they may be. Consequently, all of us, as stated, need the Intercessory Work of Christ.

In fact, both Christ and the Holy Spirit intercede for the Saints; however, the Intercession of the Holy Spirit pertains to all things other than sin (Rom. 8:26). The Intercession of Christ, as stated, pertains to sin (Heb. 7:25-28).

THE HORNS

Verse 26 reads: *"And he overlaid it with pure gold, both the top of it, and the sides thereof round about, and the horns of it: also he made unto it a crown of gold round about."*

Even though we have dealt with the *"horns"* in previous commentary, because of the great significance in this symbolism, I feel we should state the case again.

In the Bible, horns symbolize power and dominion. The idea is:

What Jesus did at the Cross guarantees total and complete dominion by the Believer, over every sin or ungodly passion. The Lord saves us from sin, not in sin. So, if there are sins which are easily besetting us, then in some manner we are falling short of that which Jesus purchased for us by His death on the Cross of Calvary. Considering the price that He has paid, certainly we should understand that He wants us to have <u>all</u> for which He has paid such a price. In other words, the dominion is to be total (Col. 2:14-15).

To be brief, this total dominion, and we're

not referring to sinless perfection, for the Bible doesn't teach such, but rather that sin will not have dominion over us (Rom. 6:14), without fail, our Faith must rest in Christ and His great Sacrifice. We can have *"Resurrection Life,"* providing we understand that *"we have been planted together in the likeness of His death"* (Rom. 6:5). In other words, the Resurrection Life will take care of itself, which speaks of total dominion, providing we understand the Cross correctly, and that our emphasis ever be placed in the Cross. Unfortunately, some Preachers place the emphasis on the Resurrection. That must never be the case. While the Resurrection, of course, was of vast significance, as should be obvious, it was not the Resurrection which set us free, but rather what Jesus did at the Cross (Eph. 2:13-18). If it is to be noticed, Paul <u>didn't</u> say, *"If I glory, I will glory in the Resurrection of Jesus Christ,"* but rather, *"If I glory, I will glory in the Cross of Jesus Christ . . ."* (Gal. 6:14). So the Cross is to ever be our emphasis, which will guarantee Resurrection Life, which speaks of dominion over the world, the flesh, and the Devil.

THE STAVES

Verses 27 through 29 read: *"And he made two rings of gold for it under the crown thereof, by the two corners of it, upon the two sides thereof, to be places for the staves to bear it withal.*

"And he made the staves of Shittim Wood, and overlaid them with gold.

"And he made the holy Anointing oil, and the pure Incense of sweet spices, according to the work of the apothecary."

While in the wilderness, the Camp of Israel at times moved, and according to the leading of the Lord. When this happened, the entirety of the Tabernacle was moved, along with all the Sacred Vessels, which would be obvious. There was even a prescribed way in which everything was to be handled.

But the spiritual lesson we learn from this, and I speak of the staves that were inserted in the rings, by which the Altar of Incense could be handled when it was moved, speaks to us of the constant need of Intercession, irrespective as to where we might be.

Actually, this world is a wilderness. As Believers, our situation ebbs and flows. But whatever, Intercession by Christ on our part is always needed. For the composition of the oil, see Exodus 30:23-25.

The composition of the Incense is given in Exodus 30:34-35.

"Hail! Thou once despised Jesus! Hail, Thou Galilean King!
"You did suffer to release us; You did free Salvation bring.
"Hail, You agonizing Saviour, Bearer of our sin and shame!
"By Your merits we find favor; life is given through Your Name."

"Paschal Lamb, by God appointed, all our sins on You were laid:
"By almighty love anointed, You have full Atonement made.
"All Your people are forgiven, through the virtue of Your Blood;
"Opened is the gate of Heaven, Peace is made between man and God."

"Jesus, hail! Enthroned in glory, there forever to abide;
"All the heavenly hosts adore Thee, seated at Your Father's side.
"There for sinners You are pleading, there You do our place prepare,
"Ever for us interceding, till in Glory we appear."

"Worship, honor, power, and blessing, You are worthy to receive;
"Loudest praises, without ceasing, mete it is for us to give.
"Help, You bright angelic spirits, bring your sweetest, noblest ways;
"Help to sing our Saviour's merits, help to chant Immanuel's praise!"

CHAPTER 38

(1) "AND HE MADE THE ALTAR OF BURNT OFFERING OF SHITTIM WOOD: FIVE CUBITS WAS THE LENGTH THEREOF, AND FIVE CUBITS THE BREADTH THEREOF; IT WAS FOURSQUARE; AND THREE CUBITS THE HEIGHT THEREOF.

(2) "AND HE MADE THE HORNS THEREOF ON THE FOUR CORNERS OF IT; THE HORNS THEREOF WERE OF THE SAME: AND HE OVERLAID IT WITH BRASS.

(3) "AND HE MADE ALL THE VESSELS OF THE ALTAR, THE POTS, AND THE SHOVELS, AND THE BASINS, AND THE FLESHHOOKS, AND THE FIREPANS: ALL THE VESSELS THEREOF MADE HE OF BRASS.

(4) "AND HE MADE FOR THE ALTAR A BRAZEN GRATE OF NETWORK UNDER THE COMPASS THEREOF BENEATH UNTO THE MIDST OF IT.

(5) "AND HE CAST FOUR RINGS FOR THE FOUR ENDS OF THE GRATE OF BRASS, TO BE PLACES FOR THE STAVES.

(6) "AND HE MADE THE STAVES OF SHITTIM WOOD, AND OVERLAID THEM WITH BRASS.

(7) "AND HE PUT THE STAVES INTO THE RINGS ON THE SIDES OF THE ALTAR, TO BEAR IT WITHAL; HE MADE THE ALTAR HOLLOW WITH BOARDS."

The construction is:

1. The precious objects that mark this Passage are thus associated: the Golden Throne and the Golden Altar; the Lampstand and the Table; and the Altar of Brass and the Laver — all represent Christ as Prince and Priest; as Light and Life; and as Saviour and Sanctifier.

2. The Brazen Altar was the largest of the Vessels, and in a sense, signified its importance.

3. The *"copper,"* which characterizes this particular Vessel, speaks of Judgment, and Judgment which came upon Christ instead of upon us.

THE BRAZEN ALTAR

Verse 1 reads: *"And he made the Altar of Burnt Offering of Shittim Wood: five cubits was the length thereof, and five cubits the breadth thereof; it was foursquare; and three cubits the height thereof."*

It could be argued, I suppose, as to which Vessel was the most important, but considering that all played a very significant part, the argument would, more than likely, be fruitless. But for the sake of hopefully helping all of us to understand the great Plan of God just a little more, I think it would be correct to state that the Brazen Altar is the key to the whole of the entirety of the thought of the Tabernacle. While of course, our first thought would go to the Holy of Holies, which houses the Ark of the Covenant and the Mercy Seat, still, it is the Cross of which the Brazen Altar is a type, which opened up the way to the Holy of Holies. Without the Cross, there was no way that sinful man could have access to the Throne of God. The Cross made it all possible (Eph. 2:13-18). As we've stated repeatedly, the story of the Bible, in effect, is the story of the Cross. If one understands the Cross, or at least makes it the proper emphasis, everything else concerning the Word of God will fall into place. It is the misunderstanding of the Cross, which is a misunderstanding of the Plan of God for the human race, that brings about much error in the Church. This is not something new, having begun with Cain and Abel (Gen., Chpt. 4).

THE HORNS

Verse 2 reads: *"And he made the horns thereof on the four corners of it; the horns thereof were of the same: and he overlaid it with copper."*

In a sense, the *"horns"* on the Brazen Altar had the same meaning as the *"horns"* on the Altar of Incense.

Standing for power and dominion, the idea is that the Sacrifice of Christ would be a total and complete Sacrifice, answering every problem of the human race. What Jesus did there left nothing undone, therefore, every demon spirit, along with Satan, were defeated, and the great Sacrifice is referred to as a *Finished Work"* (Heb. 1:3; 4:3).

If Christ has won total dominion over the powers of darkness, and did so by atoning for all sin, which He most definitely did, we must understand that all of this was done totally and completely for you and me. He did nothing for Himself, not for Angels, not for the Godhead in any capacity, but strictly for sinners. Considering that He did all of this for us, and us alone (Jn. 3:16), then it should stand to reason that all that He did is available to us.

How is it available to us?

THE CROSS OF CHRIST

It is available to us 100 percent through and by what Christ did at the Cross, and the giving of Himself in Sacrifice. Paul said:

"Who gave Himself for our sins, that He might deliver us from this present evil world, according to the Will of God and our Father" (Gal. 1:4).

COPPER

Verses 3 and 4 read: *"And he made all the vessels of the Altar, the pots, and the shovels, and the basins, and the fleshhooks, and the firepans: all the vessels thereof made he of copper.*

"And he made for the Altar a copper grate of network under the compass thereof beneath unto the midst of it."

Even though the King James people translated the Hebrew word *"brass,"* it should have been translated *"copper"* or *"bronze."* Brass demands a metallurgy that was not available during the time of Moses, so the translation is not correct. It was copper, which in effect, served two purposes:

1. The copper, which sheathed the Shittim Wood, offered a great resistance to heat, more so than most other metals of that day.

2. Inasmuch as copper was used to cover the Brazen Altar, it stands for Judgment. Sin must be judged. Let every single person understand that; no one gets by with sin. Every single sin must be called to account, which it was at the Cross.

Had God demanded full payment from humanity, all of humanity would have been eternally lost. But the truth is, Jesus Christ paid the debt, which means that He took the Judgment of God that was due us, which necessitated the giving of Himself in Sacrifice. Eternal life was forfeited in the Garden of Eden with the Fall of man. For that life, which comes solely from God, to be regained, a perfect life had to be given, which alone could pay the price. No human being could fit that role, because the Fall doomed every human being, even all who would be born, referred to as *"original sin."* Angels could not pay the price, simply because they were of another creation. God as God couldn't pay it, simply because God cannot die, and death was demanded. So God would become Man, the Man Christ Jesus, and while never ceasing to be God, as Man, would die on the Cross, thereby satisfying the demands of a thrice-Holy God.

What was done was so perfect, so complete, so total, that it will never have to be done again. Its results will last forever, hence Paul referring to the Sacrifice of Christ as *"The Everlasting Covenant"* (Heb. 13:20).

UNDERSTANDING THE ATONEMENT

It is tragic that most Christians do not seem to properly understand the Atonement. They talk about *"Jesus having paid it all,"* but then they conduct themselves in the very opposite manner, trying to add to the Finished Work of Christ.

For instance, most Christians have the idea that if someone sins, they must be punished. To think in this manner, much less to promote such, shows a total ignorance of the Atonement, and does great injustice to the Grace of God. In effect, it says that what Jesus did at the Cross, despite all of His great suffering, simply was not enough, and something else needs to be added. When it's put that way, in a stark, cold, reality, we begin to see, I pray, just how awful it is to misinterpret the Atonement. As stated, we sing *"Jesus paid it all,"* and then we keep trying to pay, even though it's already paid. God help us!

That Brazen Altar glowing red hot, with the Sacrifice consumed, should portray to us the finality of the great Redemption Price.

THE STAVES

Verses 5 through 7 read: *"And he cast four rings for the four ends of the grate of copper, to be places for the staves.*

"And he made the staves of Shittim Wood, and overlaid them with copper.

"And he put the staves into the rings on the sides of the Altar, to bear it withal; he made the Altar hollow with boards."

As all the other Sacred Vessels had to be transported when the Camp of Israel moved, so did the great Brazen Altar. This tells us, among other things, that there is never a time, place, or situation in which we no longer need the Cross of Christ.

THE NEED OF THE CROSS WILL NEVER CEASE

II Corinthians 4:10 reads: *"Always bearing about in the body the dying of the Lord Jesus."* The word dying is *"nekrosis"* — a *"putting to death."*

The Greek Lexicon says it is *"expressive of the action being incomplete and in progress."*

The Greek Lexicon also says that this describes the cessation of life of any kind, i.e., *"the putting to death,"* of all activity of the old life of nature — the old nature. This is *"not once for all, but continuously."* This is what Jesus was addressing when He said: *"If any man will come after Me, let him deny himself, and take up his cross daily, and follow Me"* (Lk. 9:23).

So it means that from center to circumference, the identification of the Believer with Christ in His death is a necessity for the growth of the new life as it comes out from the center of our being, changed by the Power of God, into full maturity.

And to say it again, this means that there never comes a time that we do not need fully the benefits of the Cross. So this also means that the Believer makes a grand mistake when he listens to the false teaching that claims the Believer, after getting saved, must then leave the Cross, and go on to other things. The Bible no place teaches such an erroneous doctrine, and in fact, teaches the very opposite.

HEBREWS 6:1-2

Paul said: *"Therefore leaving the principles of the Doctrine of Christ, let us go on unto perfection; not laying again the foundation of Repentance from dead works, and of Faith toward God,*

"Of the Doctrine of Baptisms, and of laying on of hands, and of Resurrection of the dead, and of eternal judgment."

Many Christians misunderstand this statement, thinking that Paul is telling us to leave the principles of the Doctrine of Christ, which they interpret as the Cross.

But they never go on to realize that if that were correct, they would also be leaving the *"Doctrine of Baptisms,"* and of *"laying on of hands,"* and of *"Resurrection of the dead,"* and of *"eternal judgment."*

Paul is saying that the Saints must leave the first principles of the Doctrine of Christ, which refers to the Law of Moses. He was writing to Jewish Christians, who were contemplating going back to the old Jewish Law, thereby forsaking Christ.

In this Text, Paul tells us that Christ is the theme of the entirety of the Bible. But we must leave the *"first principles of the Doctrine of Christ,"* which is the Law, and go on to the perfection that is given to us through the Cross.

He told these Jewish Christians that if they forsook Christ and what He did at the Cross, thereby going back to Temple worship, they would be attempting to *"lay again the foundation of repentance from dead works,"* which characterizes the old Jewish Law. Christ had fulfilled it all, and now attempting to revive it, presented itself as a grievous sin against Christ.

He is telling these people, and us, that *"Faith toward God,"* cannot be founded on *"dead works,"* but only on Christ, and what He has done at the Cross, which alone God will recognize.

The *"Doctrine of Baptisms,"* should have been translated, *"the Doctrine of washings,"* because that's what it meant. The Jews had many washings associated with the Law of Moses, which had to do with the Sacrifices, and which the Priests had to do, as it regarded the Brazen Laver.

The *"laying on of hands,"* had nothing to do with laying on of hands as we think of such presently, but rather the sinner who brought his lamb to the sacrifice, and then would lay his hands on the head of the animal, confessing his sins, thereby transferring his sins from himself to the innocent victim, typical of Christ.

The *"Resurrection of the dead,"* if one went back to the old Law, consigned Believers to Paradise, simply because they couldn't be taken to Heaven, due to the fact that the blood of bulls and goats couldn't take away sins. So the Resurrection in Old Testament times was totally dependent in Jesus coming to this world and dying on the Cross, thereby paying the debt, which animal blood could not pay. Then and only then would the Resurrection be made possible, which it now is.

Before the Cross, *"eternal judgment"* stared every human being in the face. Once again, the blood of bulls and goats could not pay this debt, so if Jesus had not come and died on the Cross, judgment awaited all. Now that judgment has been effected in Christ, to which no true Believer will ever have to answer.

No, this Passage in no way refers to Believers leaving the Cross, and going on to other things. In fact, it says the very opposite!

(8) "AND HE MADE THE LAVER OF COPPER, AND THE FOOT OF IT OF COPPER, OF THE LOOKINGGLASSES OF THE WOMEN ASSEMBLING, WHICH ASSEMBLED AT THE DOOR OF THE TABERNACLE OF THE CONGREGATION.

(9) "AND HE MADE THE COURT: ON THE SOUTH SIDE SOUTHWARD THE HANGINGS OF THE COURT WERE OF FINE TWINED LINEN, AN HUNDRED CUBITS:

(10) "THEIR PILLARS WERE TWENTY, AND THEIR COPPER SOCKETS TWENTY; THE HOOKS OF THE PILLARS AND THEIR FILLETS WERE OF SILVER.

(11) "AND FOR THE NORTH SIDE THE HANGINGS WERE AN HUNDRED CUBITS, THEIR PILLARS WERE TWENTY, AND THEIR SOCKETS OF COPPER TWENTY; THE HOOKS OF THE PILLARS AND THEIR FILLETS OF SILVER.

(12) "AND FOR THE WEST SIDE WERE HANGINGS OF FIFTY CUBITS, THEIR PILLARS TEN, AND THEIR SOCKETS TEN; THE HOOKS OF THE PILLARS AND THEIR FILLETS OF SILVER.

(13) "AND FOR THE EAST SIDE EASTWARD FIFTY CUBITS.

(14) "THE HANGINGS OF THE ONE SIDE OF THE GATE WERE FIFTEEN CUBITS; THEIR PILLARS THREE, AND THEIR SOCKETS THREE.

(15) "AND FOR THE OTHER SIDE OF THE COURT GATE, ON THIS HAND AND THAT HAND, WERE HANGINGS OF FIFTEEN CUBITS; THEIR PILLARS THREE, AND THEIR SOCKETS THREE.

(16) "ALL THE HANGINGS OF THE COURT ROUND ABOUT WERE OF FINE TWINED LINEN.

(17) "AND THE SOCKETS FOR THE PILLARS WERE OF COPPER; THE HOOKS OF THE PILLARS AND THEIR FILLETS OF SILVER; AND THE OVERLAYING OF THEIR CHAPITERS OF SILVER; AND ALL THE PILLARS OF THE COURT WERE FILLETED WITH SILVER."

The overview is:

1. The copper Laver, filled with water, symbolized the Word of God.

2. This Vessel was all of copper, whereas the Brazen Altar was made of indestructible wood, covered with copper. This signifies Christ as the Living Word, which alone judges everything. *"To the Law and to the Testimony."* The Word of God is to be the criteria for all things.

3. The Court of the Tabernacle was enclosed by a fence of fine twined linen, which was snow white. This symbolized the Righteousness of Christ.

THE BRAZEN LAVER

Verse 8 reads: *"And he made the Laver of copper, and the foot of it of copper, of the lookingglasses of the women assembling, which assembled at the door of the Tabernacle of the Congregation."*

Concerning the *"lookingglasses of the women,"* Pulpit says: *"This interesting fact has not been previously mentioned. Bronze plates, circular or oval, emitting of a high polish, were used by the Egyptian women as mirrors from a very early date, and may be seen in the Egyptian collection of the British Museum.*

"They have handles like those of our fire screens, generally also of bronze. It was natural that the Hebrew women should possess similar articles, and should have taken care to bring them with them out of Egypt. The sacrifice of them for a sacred purpose is rather to be ascribed to their own self-denying piety, than to any command issued by Moses."

The Text proclaims the fact that women assembled themselves in numbers at the entrance of the *"tent of meeting,"* set up by Moses. The women who showed this zeal were those who made the sacrifice of their mirrors for God's service.

THE NORTH AND THE SOUTH

Verses 9 through 11 read: *"And he made*

the Court: on the south side southward the hangings of the Court were of fine twined linen, an hundred cubits:

"Their pillars were twenty, and their copper sockets twenty; the hooks of the pillars and their fillets were of silver.

"And for the north side of the hangings were an hundred cubits, their pillars were twenty, and their sockets of copper twenty: the hooks of the pillars and their fillets of silver."

The north and the south sides of the Court were each 150 feet long.

The material used to make the fence was *"of fine twined linen,"* which was snow white, and as stated, symbolized the Righteousness of Christ (Rev. 19:8). The spotless white walls that surrounded the Tabernacle on every side were a standing witness to the Holiness of Him Whose dwelling it was.

This was in striking contrast to the unholiness of those who inhabited the surrounding tents, which were made, most probably, from goats' hair, and of a very dark color. There would be, then, a most vivid contrast between the white linen surrounding Jehovah's dwelling place and the dark fabric of the Israelites' tents, and was meant to portray the unholiness of man, even the Israelites, and the Holiness of God. The stark contrast served that purpose!

Inside the sacred precincts stood the Atoning Altar and the Cleansing Laver, which moved David to sing, *"How amiable are Your Tabernacles, O LORD of Hosts! My soul longs, yes, even faints, for the Courts of the LORD"* (Ps. 84:1-2).

This snow white fence was hung, so to speak, on 60 pillars, 20 to each side, and ten at either end. The pillars were anchored in *"copper sockets."* This refers to the fact that the Righteousness of Christ can come to us only by the way of the Cross, where judgment, symbolized by the copper sockets, paid the price.

THE EAST AND THE WEST

Verses 12 and 13 read: *"And for the west side were hangings of fifty cubits, their pillars ten, and their sockets ten; the hooks of the pillars and their fillets of silver.*

"And for the east side eastward fifty cubits."

The ends of the Court were each 75 feet wide. These two ends faced the east and the west, with the front of the Tabernacle always facing the east. There were ten pillars on each end, and ten sockets. All the hooks and the connecting rods (fillets) were of silver, typifying Redemption, even as the sockets were of copper, typifying Judgment.

THE GATE AND THE DOOR

Verses 14 through 17 read: *"The hangings of the one side of the gate were fifteen cubits; their pillars three, and their sockets three.*

"And for the other side of the Court gate, on this hand and that hand, were hangings of fifteen cubits; their pillars three, and their sockets three.

"All the hangings of the Court round about were of fine twined linen.

"And the sockets for the pillars were of copper; the hooks of the pillars and their fillets of silver; and the overlaying of their chapiters of silver; and all the pillars of the Court were filleted with silver."

The *"gate"* or entrance into the Court was 20 cubits, or 30 feet wide (Ex. 27:16), which left 15 cubits, or 22-1/2 feet on each side, making up the total of 50 cubits or 75 feet for each end. As one can see, the gate or entrance to the Court was wide. The entrance was a Type of Christ, Who said, *"I am the Door: by Me if any man enter in, he shall be saved, and shall go in and out, and find pasture"* (Jn. 10:9).

There was a pillar every five cubits, set in sockets of copper. *"Five"* is God's number for Grace. So we find that Redemption is built upon the Doctrine of Grace.

(18) "AND THE HANGING FOR THE GATE OF THE COURT WAS NEEDLEWORK, OF BLUE, AND PURPLE, AND SCARLET, AND FINE TWINED LINEN: AND TWENTY CUBITS WAS THE LENGTH, AND THE HEIGHT AND THE BREADTH WAS FIVE CUBITS, ANSWERABLE TO THE HANGINGS OF THE COURT.

(19) "AND THEIR PILLARS WERE FOUR, AND THEIR SOCKETS OF COPPER FOUR; THEIR HOOKS OF SILVER, AND THE OVERLAYING OF THEIR CHAPITERS AND THEIR FILLETS OF SILVER.

(20) "AND ALL THE PINS OF THE TABERNACLE, AND OF THE COURT ROUND

ABOUT, WERE OF COPPER.

(21) "THIS IS THE SUM OF THE TABERNACLE, EVEN OF THE TABERNACLE OF TESTIMONY, AS IT WAS COUNTED, ACCORDING TO THE COMMANDMENT OF MOSES, FOR THE SERVICE OF THE LEVITES, BY THE HAND OF ITHAMAR, SON TO AARON THE PRIEST."

The exegesis is:

1. The gate is a Type of Christ, as stated, Who is the Door.

2. The blue stipulated that Salvation originated solely in Heaven, the purple, the Kingship of Christ, the scarlet, that He would shed His Blood, and the fine twined linen, a portrayal of His Righteousness.

3. The structure was referred to as the *"Tabernacle of Testimony"* because it was the Testimony solely of Christ.

THE GATE

Verse 18 reads: *"And the hanging for the gate of the Court was needlework, of blue, and purple, and scarlet, and fine twined linen: and twenty cubits was the length, and the height and the breadth was five cubits, answerable to the hangings of the Court."*

As we have stated, the gate at the front of the Court, the only entrance to the Court, was 30 feet (20 cubits). It was made of beautiful colors of *"blue, purple, and scarlet,"* on a background of *"fine twined linen,"* which of course was white. These colors were the same as the door that led into the Tabernacle proper, and as well, of the Veil which hung between the Holy Place and the Holy of Holies. As to exactly how the colors were used on the *"gate,"* we aren't told. They could have been in the form of Cherubim, or some other form; nevertheless, the colors represented Christ and His Work, as we've already explained.

To have a gate 30 feet wide at the front of the Court, which was typical of Christ, tells us many things.

The greatest lesson of all, I think, is the broadness of Christ, so to speak. Christ is not some mysterious figure Who has to be understood by great intellectualism, etc. He is perfectly obvious in all that He is, and all that He does. One either believes that He truly is the Son of God, or one doesn't believe. One must believe that in order to be saved, Jesus died on the Cross for sinners, and that Faith in Him will guarantee Redemption (Jn. 3:16). Or else one doesn't believe that! As stated, the matter of Salvation, and even the manner of Salvation, is very simple, hence the wideness of the gate.

THE PILLARS

Verses 19 and 20 read: *"And their pillars were four, and their sockets of copper four; their hooks of silver, and the overlaying of the chapiters and their fillets of silver.*

"And all the pins of the Tabernacle, and of the Court round about, were of copper."

There were four pillars in the gate, five cubits apart. The material hung on these pillars, with the pillars being anchored in the sockets of copper. But all the hooks that held the material onto the pillars were of silver, which represented Redemption, as the copper represented judgment. All pertained to Christ!

In actuality, this was not a *"gate"* as such, but rather a curtain, which was pulled back for entrance. All were welcomed to come, who desired to do so; likewise, all who desire to come to Christ may do so as well!

The entrance to the Tabernacle proper included five pillars, where the entrance to the Court included four. The *"four"* could speak of the four Gospels, and as well, the four corners of the compass, meaning that the Gospel is for all. The five pillars regarding the entrance to the Tabernacle proper speak of the fivefold Ministry of the Gospel, *"Apostles, Prophets, Evangelists, Pastors, and Teachers"* (Eph. 4:11), and of Grace.

THE TABERNACLE

Verse 21 reads: *"This is the sum of the Tabernacle, even of the Tabernacle of Testimony, as it was counted, according to the Commandment of Moses, for the service of the Levites, by the hand of Ithamar, son to Aaron the Priest."*

This structure, referred to as the *"Tabernacle of Testimony,"* pertained to the Ark of the Covenant, along with the Mercy Seat and the Cherubim, which it housed. Of course, all of this was a Type of Christ.

We see here that Ithamar, another son of

Aaron, is appointed to head up the Levites, which pertains to all the service of the Tabernacle, which involved many things. It is somewhat remarkable that this is assigned to him, rather than to Nadab or Abihu. Ithamar, in fact, was the youngest son of Aaron. Of course, the Holy Spirit knew that Nadab and Abihu would come to a disastrous end, hence the reason for the choosing of Ithamar (Lev. 10:1-2).

(22) "AND BEZALEEL THE SON OF URI, THE SON OF HUR, OF THE TRIBE OF JUDAH, MADE ALL THAT THE LORD COMMANDED MOSES.

(23) "AND WITH HIM WAS AHOLIAB, SON OF AHISAMACH, OF THE TRIBE OF DAN, AN ENGRAVER, AND A CUNNING WORKMAN, AND AN EMBROIDERER IN BLUE, AND IN PURPLE, AND IN SCARLET, AND FINE LINEN.

(24) "ALL THE GOLD THAT WAS OCCUPIED FOR THE WORK IN ALL THE WORK OF THE HOLY PLACE, EVEN THE GOLD OF THE OFFERING, WAS TWENTY AND NINE TALENTS, AND SEVEN HUNDRED AND THIRTY SHEKELS, AFTER THE SHEKEL OF THE SANCTUARY.

(25) "AND THE SILVER OF THEM THAT WERE NUMBERED OF THE CONGREGATION WAS AN HUNDRED TALENTS, AND A THOUSAND SEVEN HUNDRED AND THREESCORE AND FIFTEEN SHEKELS, AFTER THE SHEKEL OF THE SANCTUARY:

(26) "A BEKAH FOR EVERY MAN, THAT IS, HALF A SHEKEL, AFTER THE SHEKEL OF THE SANCTUARY, FOR EVERY ONE WHO WENT TO BE NUMBERED, FROM TWENTY YEARS OLD AND UPWARD, FOR SIX HUNDRED THOUSAND AND THREE THOUSAND AND FIVE HUNDRED AND FIFTY MEN.

(27) "AND OF THE HUNDRED TALENTS OF SILVER WERE CAST THE SOCKETS OF THE SANCTUARY, AND THE SOCKETS OF THE VEIL; AN HUNDRED SOCKETS OF THE HUNDRED TALENTS, A TALENT FOR EVERY SOCKET.

(28) "AND OF THE THOUSAND SEVEN HUNDRED SEVENTY AND FIVE SHEKELS HE MADE HOOKS FOR THE PILLARS, AND OVERLAID THEIR CHAPITERS, AND FILLETED THEM.

(29) "AND THE BRASS OF THE OFFERING WAS SEVENTY TALENTS, AND TWO THOUSAND AND FOUR HUNDRED SHEKELS.

(30) "AND THEREWITH HE MADE THE SOCKETS TO THE DOOR OF THE TABERNACLE OF THE CONGREGATION, AND THE BRAZEN ALTAR, AND THE BRAZEN GRATE FOR IT, AND ALL THE VESSELS OF THE ALTAR,

(31) "AND THE SOCKETS OF THE COURT ROUND ABOUT, AND THE SOCKETS OF THE COURT GATE, AND THE PINS OF THE TABERNACLE, AND ALL THE PINS OF THE COURT ROUND ABOUT."

The diagram is:

1. The Lord was the Owner and the Architect of the Tabernacle, and in totality, while Moses and Bezaleel, plus a host of other workmen, put it all together.

2. Everything was designed by the Lord, even down to the minute details. These designs were to be followed minutely and without fail.

3. All of this represented Christ, and His Atoning, Mediatorial, High Priestly Work, and the Godhead only understood these things. So the design must not be infringed upon by man.

THE WORKERS

Verses 22 and 23 read: *"And Bezaleel the son of Uri, the son of Hur, of the Tribe of Judah, made all that the LORD commanded Moses.*

"And with him was Aholiab, son of Ahisamach, of the Tribe of Dan, an engraver, and a cunning workman, and an embroiderer in blue, and in purple, and in scarlet, and fine linen."

The Lord called these men to perform these tasks, with the Holy Spirit actually helping them to do so.

Likewise, every single Believer presently has a job to do for the Lord. While all, as would be obvious, were not permitted to work on the Tabernacle, all now definitely are permitted to labor in the work of the Lord. Jesus said: *"The harvest truly is plenteous, but the laborers are few;*

"Pray ye therefore the Lord of the harvest, that He will send forth laborers into

His harvest" (Mat. 9:37-38).

Every Believer can do the following:

1. Pray: Prayer is the greatest thing that can be done, and can be engaged by every single Believer, irrespective as to whom the Believer might be. Unfortunately, Intercessors seem to be in short supply. That is so tragic when one realizes that all victories are won in some manner, in some way, in the prayer closet, so to speak.

It was through prayer and the Word of God that the Lord gave me the Revelation of the Cross. And in fact, it has been through prayer and the Word that every single blessing has come to me.

When I was but a child, my Grandmother taught me the value of prayer. I have made it a standard in my life from then until now. To be sure, she could not have taught me anything better.

I can still see the twinkle in her eye as she would begin to talk about the Lord. She told me over and over, *"Jimmy, God is a big God, so ask big."* I've never forgotten that. It has helped me to touch this world for Christ.

2. Give: As with prayer, every single Believer can give to the Work of God. This is very, very important! Tragically and sadly, much, if not most, of the giving as it regards Believers goes for that which has little to do with the Gospel. In other words, they think they are giving to the Gospel, but they really aren't.

You as a Believer need to know to what you are giving, and what it is doing. It's bad enough to give to that which is not of God, irrespective of its profession, but worse yet, to realize that we are going to answer to the Lord one day, as it regards our stewardship on this Earth. We should seek the Lord minutely as it regards our giving. To be sure, He will let us know where to give, and how much to give.

3. Witnessing: Every Believer can tell others about Christ. In fact, our lives are to be such that we will actually be a living Testimony. This pertains to Sanctification and Holiness, and which can become a part of us only by Faith — Faith in Christ and what Christ has done at the Cross (Rom. 6:3-14; 8:1-2, 11; Gal. 5:6; 6:14; Eph. 2:13-18; Col. 2:14-15).

NOTES

THE GOLD AND THE SILVER

Verses 24 and 25 read: *"All the gold that was occupied for the work in all the work of the Holy Place, even the gold of the Offering, was twenty and nine talents, and seven hundred and thirty shekels, after the shekel of the Sanctuary.*

"And the silver of them that were numbered of the congregation was an hundred talents, and a thousand seven hundred and threescore and fifteen shekels, after the shekel of the Sanctuary."

Twenty-nine talents of gold were used in the construction of the Tabernacle, which was the equivalent of 2,222 pounds. At 2002 prices for gold, that would equal approximately $11,000,000.

Of the silver, 100 talents were used, totaling about 7,500 pounds. At $5 an ounce, this would come out to about $600,000.

It has been argued by some that so large an amount of gold at this time by the Hebrew nation is inconceivable. But most critics are of a different opinion.

Gold was very abundant in Egypt at this period, being imported from Ethiopia, a rich gold-producing country. As well, tribute was taken from other nations of Asia. Actually, the wealth of Rameses III, a little later than the Exodus, was enormous.

It is quite possible that much of the wealth of Egypt, as it regarded gold and silver, as well as other things, was transferred to the Hebrews when they left the country.

POPULATION

Verse 26 reads: *"A bekah for every man, that is, half a shekel, after the shekel of the Sanctuary, for every one who went to be numbered, from twenty years old and upward, for six hundred thousand and three thousand and five hundred and fifty men."*

There were, as is obvious here, a little over 600,000 men in the camp of Israel at that time, counted from 20 years old, upward. This probably pertained to fighting men, and probably stopped at 50 or 60 years old. So that means there were that many women as well, which would push the population to about 1.2 million. Counting 19 years old and downward would probably add another million, making the population about 2.2 million. Counting those above 50 or 60 years old, the number would be approximately three million people, at least at this particular time.

All who were numbered, and of course we speak of fighting men from 20 years old and upward, were taxed at the rate of half a shekel, which pertains to silver, and was probably about one-third of an ounce, and worth presently about $1.50, or maybe a little more. Any time the fighting men were numbered they were to pay this tax or ransom of silver, which signified Redemption, and as well, that Israel's power and strength did not rest upon force of arms, but rather on the Power of God, and more particularly, the shed Blood of the Lamb, which Redemption portrayed.

THE SILVER AND THE COPPER

Verses 27 through 31 read: *"And of the hundred talents of silver were cast the sockets of the Sanctuary, and the sockets of the Veil; an hundred sockets of the hundred talents, a talent for a socket.*

"And of the thousand seven hundred seventy and five shekels he made hooks for the pillars, and overlaid their chapiters, and filleted them.

"And the copper of the Offering was seventy talents, and two thousand and four hundred shekels.

"And therewith he made the sockets to the door of the Tabernacle of the Congregation, and the Brazen Altar, and the Brazen grate for it, and all the vessels of the Altar.

"And the sockets of the Court round about, and the sockets of the Court Gate, and all the pins of the Tabernacle, and all the pins of the Court round about."

All of this explains, as is obvious, what was done with the silver and the copper, especially considering that so much silver was used. As stated, the silver represented Redemption as afforded by Christ, even as the gold represented His Deity, and the copper, the Judgment which He suffered on our behalf.

Everything, down to the small *"pins"* was designed totally and completely by the Lord, with nothing being left to the imagination of man. As such, it represented our Salvation, which as well, is all of the Lord and none of man.

> *"Rock of Ages, cleft for me, let me hide myself in Thee.*
> *"Let the water and the Blood, from Thy wounded side which flowed,*
> *"Be of sin the double cure, save from wrath and make me pure."*

> *"Could my tears forever flow, could my zeal no languor know?*
> *"These for sin could not atone — Thou must save, and Thou alone:*
> *"In my hand no price I bring, simply to Thy Cross I cling."*

> *"While I draw this fleeting breath, when my eyes shall close in death,*
> *"When I rise to worlds unknown, and behold Thee on Thy Throne,*
> *"Rock of Ages, cleft for me, let me hide myself in Thee."*

CHAPTER 39

(1) "AND OF THE BLUE, AND PURPLE, AND SCARLET, THEY MADE CLOTHS OF SERVICE, TO DO SERVICE IN THE HOLY PLACE, AND MADE THE HOLY GARMENTS FOR AARON; AS THE LORD COMMANDED MOSES.

(2) "AND HE MADE THE EPHOD OF GOLD, BLUE, AND PURPLE, AND SCARLET, AND FINE TWINED LINEN.

(3) "AND THEY DID BEAT THE GOLD INTO THIN PLATES, AND CUT IT INTO WIRES, TO WORK IT IN THE BLUE, AND IN THE PURPLE, AND IN THE SCARLET, AND IN THE FINE LINEN, WITH CUNNING WORK.

(4) "THEY MADE SHOULDERPIECES FOR IT, TO COUPLE IT TOGETHER: BY THE TWO EDGES WAS IT COUPLED TOGETHER.

(5) "AND THE CURIOUS GIRDLE OF HIS EPHOD, THAT WAS UPON IT, WAS OF THE SAME, ACCORDING TO THE WORK THEREOF; OF GOLD, BLUE, AND PURPLE, AND SCARLET, AND FINE TWINED LINEN; AS THE LORD COMMANDED MOSES.

(6) "AND THEY WROUGHT ONYX STONES ENCLOSED IN OUCHES OF GOLD, GRAVEN, AS SIGNETS ARE GRAVEN, WITH THE NAMES OF THE CHILDREN OF ISRAEL.

(7) "AND HE PUT THEM ON THE SHOULDERS OF THE EPHOD, THAT THEY SHOULD BE STONES FOR A MEMORIAL TO THE CHILDREN OF ISRAEL; AS THE LORD COMMANDED MOSES."

The structure is:

1. The reason the study of the Tabernacle is of such spiritual profit is simply because every part and parcel of this structure, plus all of its Sacred Vessels, symbolized Christ in some manner. Therefore, to learn the Tabernacle is to learn Christ.

2. As nothing else in the Bible, the Tabernacle proclaims the various Ministries of our Lord, whether Atonement, Mediatorial, or Intercessory.

3. Failure to learn these things is the failure to learn Christ. And the failure to learn Christ is failure indeed!

THE EPHOD

Verses 1 and 2 read: *"And of the blue, and purple, and scarlet, they made cloths of service, to do service in the Holy Place, and made the holy garments for Aaron; as the LORD commanded Moses.*

"And he made the Ephod of gold, blue, and purple, and scarlet, and fine twined linen."

The *"Holy Place"* presents the major service area of the Priests. In this place were the Table of Shewbread, the Lampstand, and the Altar of Incense. As one came into the Holy Place, the Table sat on the right, the Lampstand on the left, and the Altar immediately in front of the Veil, which hid the Holy of Holies.

In fact, if one had stood outside of the Tabernacle, immediately in front of the Brazen Altar, and the Tabernacle structure had been taken down, leaving the Sacred Vessels, they would have formed a perfect Cross. The Lampstand and the Table would have formed the Cross, with the Brazen Altar, the Brazen Laver, the Altar of Incense, and the Ark of the Covenant forming the upright posts, so to speak. The *"Ephod"* was the outer Robe worn by the High Priest. It was made of two parts, one covering the back, and the other the front, these being joined together at the shoulders by golden clasps, which formed the setting for the onyx stones.

It contained all the colors used by the other material, but with one addition, *"gold."* Actually this was more than a mere color, but rather gold wires, as portrayed in Verse 3, and were probably woven into the hem.

CUNNING WORK

Verses 3 and 4 read: *"And they did beat the gold into thin plates, and cut it into wires, to work it in the blue, and in the purple, and in the scarlet, and in the fine linen, with cunning work.*

"They made shoulderpieces for it, to couple it together: by the two edges was it coupled together."

This garment must have been strikingly beautiful! In fact, as far as we know, these are the only garments in the history of man that were designed by the Lord of Glory. Not only did He design these garments, but as well, He gave the workmen the cunning skill required to tailor each piece.

The colors in the garments represented not only Who Christ was — God and King (gold and purple) — but as well, the manner in which He would redeem humanity, i.e., *"the shedding of His Blood"* (scarlet). The linen (white) represented His Righteousness, while the *"blue"* emphasized the fact that all of this originated in Heaven.

THE CURIOUS GIRDLE

Verse 5 reads: *"And the Curious Girdle of His Ephod, that was upon it, was of the same, according to the work thereof; of gold, blue, and purple, and scarlet, and fine twined linen; as the LORD commanded Moses."*

The *"Curious Girdle,"* one might say, was a sash, tied around the waist. It was made of the same materials as was the Ephod. It speaks of preparation for service.

THE NAMES OF THE CHILDREN OF ISRAEL

Verses 6 and 7 read: *"And they wrought onyx stones enclosed in ouches of gold, graven, as signets are graven, with the names* of the Children of Israel.

"And he put them on the shoulders of the Ephod, that they should be stones for a memorial to the Children of Israel; as the LORD commanded Moses."

These were shoulder boards, one might say, made of gold, with two onyx stones, one on either side, with the names of the Children of Israel inscribed on these stones, six to each side.

Inasmuch as they were worn on the shoulders of the High Priest, it tells us that these 12 Tribes were, in effect, worn on the shoulders of Christ, with the shoulders denoting strength.

(8) "AND HE MADE THE BREASTPLATE OF CUNNING WORK, LIKE THE WORK OF THE EPHOD; OF GOLD, BLUE, AND PURPLE, AND SCARLET, AND FINE TWINED LINEN.

(9) "IT WAS FOURSQUARE; THEY MADE THE BREASTPLATE DOUBLE: A SPAN WAS THE LENGTH THEREOF, AND A SPAN THE BREADTH THEREOF, BEING DOUBLED.

(10) "AND THEY SET IT IN FOUR ROWS OF STONES: THE FIRST ROW WAS A SARDIUS, A TOPAZ, AND A CARBUNCLE: THIS WAS THE FIRST ROW.

(11) "AND THE SECOND ROW, AN EMERALD, A SAPPHIRE, AND A DIAMOND.

(12) "AND THE THIRD ROW, A LIGURE, AN AGATE, AND AN AMETHYST.

(13) "AND THE FOURTH ROW, A BERYL, AN ONYX, AND A JASPER: THEY WERE ENCLOSED IN OUCHES OF GOLD IN THEIR ENCLOSINGS.

(14) "AND THE STONES WERE ACCORDING TO THE NAMES OF THE CHILDREN OF ISRAEL, TWELVE, ACCORDING TO THEIR NAMES, LIKE THE ENGRAVINGS OF A SIGNET, EVERY ONE WITH HIS NAME, ACCORDING TO THE TWELVE TRIBES.

(15) "AND THEY MADE UPON THE BREASTPLATE CHAINS AT THE ENDS, OF WREATHEN WORK OF PURE GOLD.

(16) "AND THEY MADE TWO OUCHES OF GOLD, AND TWO GOLD RINGS; AND PUT THE TWO RINGS IN THE TWO ENDS OF THE BREASTPLATE.

(17) "AND THEY PUT THE TWO WREATHEN CHAINS OF GOLD IN THE TWO RINGS ON THE ENDS OF THE BREASTPLATE.

(18) "AND THE TWO ENDS OF THE TWO WREATHEN CHAINS THEY FASTENED IN THE TWO OUCHES, AND PUT THEM ON THE SHOULDERPIECES OF THE EPHOD, BEFORE IT.

(19) "AND THEY MADE TWO RINGS OF GOLD, PUT THEM ON THE TWO ENDS OF THE BREASTPLATE, UPON THE BORDER OF IT, WHICH WAS ON THE SIDE OF THE EPHOD INWARD.

(20) "AND THEY MADE TWO OTHER GOLDEN RINGS, AND PUT THEM ON THE TWO SIDES OF THE EPHOD UNDERNEATH, TOWARD THE FOREPART OF IT, OVER AGAINST THE OTHER COUPLING THEREOF, ABOVE THE CURIOUS GIRDLE OF THE EPHOD.

(21) "AND THEY DID BIND THE BREASTPLATE BY HIS RINGS UNTO THE RINGS OF THE EPHOD WITH A LACE OF BLUE, THAT IT MIGHT BE ABOVE THE CURIOUS GIRDLE OF THE EPHOD, AND THAT THE BREASTPLATE MIGHT NOT BE LOOSE FROM THE EPHOD; AS THE LORD COMMANDED MOSES."

The composition is:

1. The Breastplate carried the names of the 12 Tribes of Israel, inscribed on precious stones. Thus, Israel was carried not only on the shoulders of Christ, but as well, over His heart.

2. The fact that these stones were most precious signified the love that the Lord had for Israel.

3. All of this is what the Lord commanded Moses to do.

THE BREASTPLATE

Verses 8 and 9 read: *"And he made the Breastplate of cunning work, like the work of the Ephod; of gold, blue, and purple, and scarlet, and fine twined linen.*

"It was foursquare; they made the Breastplate doubled: a span was the length thereof, and a span the breadth thereof, being doubled."

The *"Breastplate"* as is obvious, had the same colors as the Ephod.

The Scripture doesn't tell us exactly how these colors were embroidered into these garments. Many Scholars believe that the garments were all of white, but around the borders there was first of all a gold thread or wire, followed with a colored band of blue, and then of purple, and then of scarlet.

The *"Breastplate"* being doubled, probably pertains to the pouch, which contained the Urim and the Thummim.

All of this is explained in greater detail, in Chapter 28.

THE PRECIOUS STONES

Verses 10 through 14 read: *"And they set in it four rows of stones: the first row was a sardius, a topaz, and a carbuncle: this was the first row.*

"And the second row, an emerald, a sapphire, and a diamond.

"And the third row, a ligure, an agate, and an amethyst.

"And the fourth row, a beryl, an onyx, and a jasper: they were enclosed in ouches of gold in their enclosings.

"And the stones were according to the names of the Children of Israel, twelve, according to their names, like the engravings of a signet, every one with his name, according to the twelve Tribes."

Several things could be said about these stones:

1. They were the most precious of precious stones, signifying the worth and value which God placed upon His people.

2. They were stones, signifying the solidity of His Covenant with Israel.

3. Each stone was no doubt the same in size, signifying that all were of equal value.

4. The name of each Tribe was inscribed upon the stone, signifying the worth of this Covenant.

5. They were 12 in number, signifying that Israel had the privilege of owning the Government of God, so to speak.

6. There were four rows, three to the row. This portrayed the fact that the Gospel was foursquare, with the three stones to each row signifying the Trinity.

7. The stones were worn over the heart, signifying the Love of God for His people.

THE CHAINS

Verses 15 through 18 read: *"And they made upon the Breastplate chains at the ends, of wreathen work of pure gold.*

"And they made two ouches of gold, and two gold rings; and put the two rings in the two ends of the Breastplate.

"And they put the two wreathen chains of gold in the two rings on the ends of the Breastplate.

"And the two ends of the two wreathen chains they fastened in the two ouches, and put them on the shoulderpieces of the Ephod, before it."

The chains fastened the Breastplate to the shoulderpieces of the Ephod.

The chains signify the binding of Christ to the Believer. In effect, this is what Jesus was addressing when He said: *"At that day, you shall know that I am in My Father, and you in Me, and I in you"* (Jn. 14:20).

THE RINGS

Verses 19 through 21 read: *"And they made two rings of gold, and put them on the two ends of the Breastplate, upon the border of it, which was on the side of the Ephod inward.*

"And they made two other golden rings, and put them on the two sides of the Ephod underneath, toward the forepart of it, over against the other coupling thereof, above the Curious Girdle of the Ephod.

"And they did bind the Breastplate by his rings unto the rings of the Ephod with a lace of blue, that it might be above the Curious Girdle of the Ephod, and that the Breastplate might not be loose from the Ephod; as the LORD commanded Moses."

All of the *"chains,"* *"rings,"* and tedious explanations as it regards the garment worn by the High priest might seem somewhat excessive to the unspiritual eye; however, the Holy Spirit has a reason for including all of this information.

Inasmuch as the High Priest was a Type of Christ, this helps us to learn more about His Person, as it regards His Atoning, Mediatorial, and High Priestly Work. As well, it shows our relationship with Him, inasmuch as we are tied to Him, even as portrayed by the *"chains,"* and forever fastened to Him, as portrayed by the *"rings."*

It is worthy of note that the garments of

Aaron, which were *"for glory and for beauty,"* were seven in number. The Breastplate, the Ephod, the Robe, the Broidered Coat, the Mitre (hat), and a Girdle. In addition to the six articles mentioned here is the *"plate of pure gold,"* which fastened to the front of the Mitre, on which was engraved the words *"Holiness to the Lord."* This, as Leviticus 8:9 tells us, was *"the Holy Crown."*

Of all of these garments, the *"Breastplate"* was the chief and most costly of the vestments, the other garments being, as it were, a foundation and background for it — this central article pointing to the very *"heart"* of Christ Himself (Pink).

The *"Curious Girdle,"* which we have already briefly addressed, tells us that the present gracious activities of Christ's Priestly service on our behalf are according to the perfections of His Own Person and Character as the God-Man! Though glorified, He is a Servant still; He is gone into Heaven to appear in the Presence of God (Heb. 9:24), and there He *"ever liveth to make intercession for us"* (Heb. 7:25).

(22) "AND HE MADE THE ROBE OF THE EPHOD OF WOVEN WORK, ALL OF BLUE.

(23) "AND THERE WAS AN HOLE IN THE MIDST OF THE ROBE, AS THE HOLE OF AN HABERGEON, WITH A BAND ROUND ABOUT THE HOLE, THAT IT SHOULD NOT REND.

(24) "AND THEY MADE UPON THE HEMS OF THE ROBE POMEGRANATES OF BLUE, AND PURPLE, AND SCARLET, AND TWINED LINEN.

(25) "AND THEY MADE BELLS OF PURE GOLD, AND PUT THE BELLS BETWEEN THE POMEGRANATES UPON THE HEM OF THE ROBE, ROUND ABOUT BETWEEN THE POMEGRANATES;

(26) "A BELL AND A POMEGRANATE, A BELL AND A POMEGRANATE, ROUND ABOUT THE HEM OF THE ROBE TO MINISTER IN; AS THE LORD COMMANDED MOSES.

The construction is:

1. In Chapter 28, as well as the Passage of our study, presents the first time the Robe is mentioned in Scripture. How striking that the *"Robe"* is never seen until the High Priest comes before us!

2. This Robe embodied the color of the heavens; it was all of blue, stipulating the Heavenly Character of our Great High Priest.

3. It also points to the place where He is now ministering on our behalf.

THE ROBE OF THE EPHOD

Verses 22 and 23 read: *"And he made the Robe of the Ephod of woven work, all of blue.*

"And there was a hole in the midst of the Robe, as the hole of an habergeon, with a band round about the hole, that it should not rend."

Even though this Robe was worn by the High Priest of Israel, the very embodiment of the Levitical Law, still, this is most important, for it defines the essential nature of Christianity as contradistinguished from Judaism. The whole system takes its character from the Priest. Because Christ is the Heavenly Priest, His people are partakers of a Heavenly Calling (Heb. 3:1), and our inheritance is there (I Pet., Chpt. 1).

Being worn beneath the Ephod itself, this *"Robe"* announces that the official Character of Christ is sustained by what He is Personally as the Heavenly One (I Cor. 15:47) (Pink).

THE FRUIT AND THE BELLS

Verses 24 through 26 read: *"And they made upon the hems of the Robe Pomegranates of blue, and purple, and scarlet, and twined linen.*

"And they made Bells of pure gold, and put the Bells between the Pomegranates upon the hem of the Robe, round about between the Pomegranates;

"A Bell and a Pomegranate, a Bell and a Pomegranate, round about the hem of the Robe to minister in; as the LORD commanded Moses."

The colored tassels in the form of *"Pomegranates"* on the hem of the Robe presents *"fruit,"* which seeds float in a crimson liquid.

This portrays the fact that the Ministry of Christ brings forth much *"fruit,"* and as well, we are to do the same (Jn., Chpt. 15).

Between each of these *"Pomegranates"* was a *"golden bell."* Whereas the *"Pomegranate"* was merely a form, and was actually a tassel, the *"golden bell"* was actually a real article, which rang every time the High Priest walked or moved.

The words *"His sound shall be heard when he goes into the Holy Place before the LORD, and when he comes out"* (Ex. 28:35) have a dispensational significance.

It was at His Ascension that our Great High Priest passed into the Heavenly Sanctuary, and consequent upon this, on the Day of Pentecost, His *"sound"* was heard in the outpouring of the Spirit, which was carried by the Apostles, ultimately to the ends of the Earth. The *"fruit"* is seen in the multitude who has been saved.

Even more glorious will be His sound and fruit when *"He comes out"* again, and returns to this Earth and redeems His people, Israel, and sets up His Kingdom.

(27) "AND THEY MADE COATS OF FINE LINEN OF WOVEN WORK FOR AARON, AND FOR HIS SONS,

(28) "AND A MITRE OF FINE LINEN, AND GOODLY BONNETS OF FINE LINEN, AND LINEN BREECHES OF FINE TWINED LINEN,

(29) "AND A GIRDLE OF FINE TWINED LINEN, AND BLUE, AND PURPLE, AND SCARLET, OF NEEDLEWORK; AS THE LORD COMMANDED MOSES.

(30) "AND THEY MADE THE PLATE OF THE HOLY CROWN OF PURE GOLD, AND WROTE UPON IT A WRITING, LIKE TO THE ENGRAVINGS OF A SIGNET, HOLINESS TO THE LORD.

(31) "AND THEY TIED UNTO IT A LACE OF BLUE, TO FASTEN IT ON HIGH UPON THE MITRE; AS THE LORD COMMANDED MOSES.

(32) "THUS WAS ALL THE WORK OF THE TABERNACLE OF THE TENT OF THE CONGREGATION FINISHED: AND THE CHILDREN OF ISRAEL DID ACCORDING TO ALL THAT THE LORD COMMANDED MOSES, SO DID THEY."

The overview is:

1. The golden plate was the symbol of the essential Holiness of the Lord.

2. The Saints are represented by Him and accepted in Him.

3. Because of our legal and vital union with Him, His Holiness is ours (Pink).

NOTES

THE TURBAN

Verses 27 through 29 read: *"And they made coats of fine linen of woven work for Aaron, and for his sons,*

"And a Mitre of fine linen, and goodly bonnets of fine linen, and linen breeches of fine twined linen,

"And a Girdle of fine twined linen, and blue, and purple, and scarlet, of needlework; as the LORD commanded Moses."

The word *"coats"* of Verse 27 is an unfortunate translation. Actually, these were underclothes, which consisted of a long white linen tunic or shirt, having tightfitting sleeves, and reaching nearly to the feet. The sleeves probably showed, as they were the only covering of the Priest's arms, and the lower part of the tunic probably showed below the *"Robe of the Ephod."*

The *"Girdle"* mentioned in Verse 29 was the Curious Girdle, described in Exodus 28:39, which was for Aaron. It is described much more fully here, than it was in Chapter 28.

HOLINESS TO THE LORD

Verses 30 through 32 read: *"And they made the plate of the Holy Crown of pure gold, and wrote upon it a writing, like to the engravings of a signet, HOLINESS TO THE LORD.*

"And they tied unto it a lace of blue, to fasten it on high upon the Mitre; as the LORD commanded Moses.

"Thus was all the work of the Tabernacle of the tent of the congregation finished: and the Children of Israel did according to all that the LORD commanded Moses, so did they."

The Golden Plate, inscribed with *"HOLINESS TO THE LORD,"* and attached to the Mitre by a lace or ribbon, resembles the *"diadems"* worn in the East by Monarchs, and regarded as the main emblem of their sovereignty. The assignment of a crown to the High Priest gave him that quasi-royal dignity which marked him as a type of our Lord in His threefold Office of Prophet, Priest, and King (Ellicott).

More than all, and as stated, this Golden Plate was a symbol of the essential Holiness of the Lord Jesus. The Saints are represented by Him and accepted in Him.

Pink says: *"Because of our legal and vital union with Him, His Holiness is ours."* Pink went on to say, *"O Christian Reader, look away from yourself, with your ten thousand failures, and fix your eyes on that Golden Plate. Behold in the perfections of your Great High Priest the measure of your eternal acceptance with God. Christ is our Sanctification as well as our Righteousness!"*

(33) "AND THEY BROUGHT THE TABERNACLE UNTO MOSES, THE TENT, AND ALL HIS FURNITURE, HIS TACHES, HIS BOARDS, HIS BARS, AND HIS PILLARS, AND HIS SOCKETS,

(34) "AND THE COVERING OF RAMS' SKINS DYED RED, AND THE COVERING OF BADGERS' SKINS, AND THE VEIL OF THE COVERING,

(35) "THE ARK OF THE TESTIMONY, AND THE STAVES THEREOF, AND THE MERCY SEAT,

(36) "THE TABLE, AND ALL THE VESSELS THEREOF, AND THE SHEWBREAD,

(37) "THE PURE CANDLESTICK, WITH THE LAMPS THEREOF, EVEN WITH THE LAMPS TO BE SET IN ORDER, AND ALL THE VESSELS THEREOF, AND THE OIL FOR LIGHT,

(38) "AND THE GOLDEN ALTAR, AND THE ANOINTING OIL, AND THE SWEET INCENSE, AND THE HANGING FOR THE TABERNACLE DOOR,

(39) "THE BRAZEN ALTAR, AND HIS GRATE OF COPPER, HIS STAVES, AND ALL HIS VESSELS, THE LAVER AND HIS FOOT,

(40) "THE HANGINGS OF THE COURT, HIS PILLARS, AND HIS SOCKETS, AND THE HANGING FOR THE COURT GATE, HIS CORDS, AND HIS PINS, AND ALL THE VESSELS OF THE SERVICE OF THE TABERNACLE, FOR THE TENT OF THE CONGREGATION,

(41) "THE CLOTHS OF SERVICE TO DO SERVICE IN THE HOLY PLACE, AND THE HOLY GARMENTS FOR AARON THE PRIEST, AND HIS SONS' GARMENTS, TO MINISTER IN THE PRIEST'S OFFICE.

(42) "ACCORDING TO ALL THAT THE LORD COMMANDED MOSES, SO THE CHILDREN OF ISRAEL MADE ALL THE WORK.

(43) "AND MOSES DID LOOK UPON ALL THE WORK, AND, BEHOLD, THEY HAD DONE IT AS THE LORD HAD COMMANDED, EVEN SO HAD THEY DONE IT: AND MOSES BLESSED THEM."

The diagram is:

1. All was accomplished *"as the Lord commanded Moses."* The frequent repetition of these words should be noted. Nothing was left to man's ingenuity or taste.

2. Everything was brought to Moses for his approval — not perhaps all things at once, but each as it was finished — and was judged by him *"according to the pattern which he had seen upon the Mount."*

3. Moses concluded all by *"blessing"* the workers, thereby signifying, not his own approval only, but the Divine approval of their diligence and obedience.

THE TABERNACLE

Verse 33 reads: *"And they brought the Tabernacle unto Moses, the tent, and all his furniture, his taches, his boards, his bars, and his pillars, and his sockets."*

As all the parts of the Tabernacle are brought to Moses, which he no doubt inspected carefully according to the pattern which he had been given by the Lord, the single most important work in the world of that day had now been completed. It was to be the *"House of the Lord."* And yet, other than the lavish amount of gold that was used on the interior of this structure, the world would not have given it a passing glance. There were, in fact, untold numbers of impressive structures in the world of that day, which would have carried great architectural and engineering design. In other words, those structures, wherever they may have been, would have put to shame the smallness of the Tabernacle, and especially its humble exterior. But there was a vast difference:

The Lord dwelt in this structure, and in fact, it was the only structure on the face of the Earth in which He did dwell. This made it 100 percent different than any other building of any kind in the world of that day. The Lord was there!

THE SACRED VESSELS

Verses 34 through 39 read: *"And the covering of rams' skins dyed red, and the covering of badgers' skins, and the Veil of the covering,*

"The Ark of the Testimony, and the staves thereof, and the Mercy Seat,

"The Table, and all the vessels thereof, and the Shewbread,

"The pure Lampstand, with the lamps thereof, even with the lamps to be set in order, and all the vessels thereof, and the oil for light,

"And the Golden Altar, and the anointing oil, and the sweet incense, and the hanging for the Tabernacle door,

"The Brazen Altar, and his grate of copper, his staves, and all his vessels, the Laver and his foot."

As all of these very important items were presented to Moses. There is no hint that any were rejected. We must remember, besides receiving instruction from Moses, the workmen were Divinely assisted in the production of their several works. So, more than likely, all that they did was right the first time.

In all of this, and as we have repeatedly stated, nothing is left to chance, no place allowed for scheming. All is of God.

Those skilled in all the wisdom of the Egyptians, the greatest builders in the world of that day, Moses was not left to draw the plans for Jehovah's dwelling place; instead, he was bidden to make all things after the pattern shown him in the Mount.

And as well, after the *"Pattern"* had been completely set before him, the Lord makes known who were to be the principal workmen. The choice of them was His, not Moses'; and this means that their equipment for the work was Divine and not human.

All of this pertains to the fact that Salvation is all of the Lord, and not at all of human participation.

ACCORDING TO ALL THAT THE LORD COMMANDED MOSES

Verses 40 through 43 read: *"The hangings of the Court, his pillars, and his sockets, and the hanging for the Court gate, his cords, and his pins, and all the vessels of the service of the Tabernacle, for the tent of the congregation.*

"The cloths of service to do service in the Holy Place, and the holy garments for Aaron the Priest, and his sons' garments, to minister in the Priest's Office.

NOTES

"According to all that the LORD commanded Moses, so the Children of Israel made all the work.

"And Moses did look upon all the work, and, behold, they had done it as the LORD had commanded, even so had they done it: and Moses blessed them."

As we know, Bezaleel was from the Tribe of Judah, while Aholiab was of the Tribe of Dan. As Judah took the lead when Israel was on the march, so Dan brought up the rear. Thus, the spiritual principle here exemplified was that, in the two men appointed, to be the chief artificers, all Israel were represented.

So the Lord Jesus, in the glorious Work that He accomplished, represented all God's people, the feeblest, as well as the strongest. The name *"Dan"* signifies *"Judge."* The Tabernacle of God is a place for worship and praise, because therein is revealed God's great act of judgment upon sin in the Sacrifice of the Lamb of God.

Coates said this: *"Such a selection speaks of Divine sovereignty. God has taken pains to show by many examples that He acts for Himself, and that He does not find His motive in the character, conduct, or genealogy of those whom He blesses. It is a comfort to see that a man from Dan comes in as well as from Judah. It shows the principle on which all really comes in; that is, as 'vessels of mercy.'"*

Pink said, *"Dan was the very last Tribe from which the natural understanding would expect to find a man selected to be one of the principal artificers of the Tabernacle. Yes, and fishermen and publicans are the last classes among whom one would look for the Apostles of the Lamb! But, God's thoughts and ways are ever different from man's."*

We must ever remember that these things which are *"highly esteemed among men are abomination in the sight of God"* (Lk. 16:15). *"For God has chosen the foolish things of the world to confound the wise; and God has chosen the weak things of the world to confound the things which are mighty; and base things of the world, and things which are despised, has God chosen, and things which are not, to bring to naught things that are"* (I Cor. 1:27-28).

Why?

Pink also said, *"That no flesh should glory in His Presence."* May the Lord bless His Own Truth to His poor and needy people.

"Man of Sorrows what a name
"For the Son of God, Who came
"Ruined sinners to reclaim!
"Hallelujah, what a Saviour!"

"Bearing shame and scoffing rude,
"In my place condemned He stood
"Sealed my pardon with His Blood:
"Hallelujah, what a Saviour!"

"Guilty, vile, and helpless we,
"Spotless Lamb of God was He;
"Full Atonement can it be?
"Hallelujah, what a Saviour!"

"Lifted up was He to die,
"'It is finished' was His cry;
"Now in Heaven exalted high:
"Hallelujah, what a Saviour!"

"When He comes, our glorious King,
"All His ransomed home to bring,
"Then anew this song we'll sing:
"Hallelujah, what a Saviour!"

CHAPTER 40

(1) "AND THE LORD SPOKE UNTO MOSES, SAYING,

(2) "ON THE FIRST DAY OF THE FIRST MONTH SHALL YOU SET UP THE TABERNACLE OF THE TENT OF THE CONGREGATION.

(3) "AND YOU SHALL PUT THEREIN THE ARK OF THE TESTIMONY, AND COVER THE ARK WITH A VEIL.

(4) "AND YOU SHALL BRING IN THE TABLE, AND SET IN ORDER THE THINGS THAT ARE TO BE SET IN ORDER UPON IT; AND YOU SHALL BRING IN THE LAMPSTAND, AND LIGHT THE LAMPS THEREOF.

(5) "AND YOU SHALL SET THE ALTAR OF GOLD FOR THE INCENSE BEFORE THE ARK OF THE TESTIMONY, AND PUT THE HANGING OF THE DOOR TO THE TABERNACLE.

(6) "AND YOU SHALL SET THE ALTAR OF THE BURNT OFFERING BEFORE THE DOOR OF THE TABERNACLE OF THE TENT OF THE CONGREGATION.

(7) "AND YOU SHALL SET THE LAVER BETWEEN THE TENT OF THE CONGREGATION AND THE ALTAR, AND SHALL PUT WATER THEREIN.

(8) "AND YOU SHALL SET UP THE COURT ROUND ABOUT, AND HANG UP THE HANGING AT THE COURT GATE."

The composition is:

1. The setting up of the Tabernacle, with the Sacred Vessels placed in order, that the proper worship of the Lord may begin, was the single most important thing on Earth at this particular time.

2. Only with these people did God dwell.

3. All the things done were instituted totally and completely by the Lord, and not at all by man.

THE COMMAND FROM THE LORD

Verses 1 and 2 read: *"And the LORD spoke unto Moses, saying,*

"On the first day of the first month shall you set up the Tabernacle of the tent of the congregation."

The work on the Tabernacle and all its Sacred Vessels was now completed. As well, Moses had inspected it, and had determined that it had been made correctly, exactly according to the pattern which had been given him by the Lord; however, he did not at once set it up, awaiting instructions from the Lord as when to begin. After a short interval, the command came.

One year had passed since they had left Egypt. So the Lord would begin the sacred worship on the first day of the Jewish year, which would have corresponded to our April.

They had reached the wilderness of Sinai in the third month, and had encamped in front of Sinai shortly after (Ex. 12:6; 19:1-2). The two periods of Moses on the Mountain had taken up approximately three months, and were probably separated by an interval of several days. Consequently, it would have been the sixth or seventh month before the work was commenced on the Tabernacle, and very late in the year, possibly even the twelfth month, before it was finished. Hence, the new year is now approaching, and the Lord would have Israel to wait until a few days had passed, and would begin the sacred worship on the first day of the new year.

It had been a year of miracles, of God manifesting Himself in mighty ways to His people. But yet, it had also been a time of great failure, and I speak of the golden calf. In fact, they had escaped total destruction from the Judgment of God by the proverbial hair's breadth.

By waiting to begin all of this on the first day of the new year, it was as if the Lord was telling Israel that they now had an opportunity for a new beginning. If they so desired, and would honestly seek the Lord, and determine to live for Him, and to do their very best to obey the Commandments which He had laid down, they could in fact, have a new beginning.

How many of them fully grasp what the Lord was doing is anyone's guess. From future actions, which consigned all of the adult population to die in the wilderness, with the exception of Joshua and Caleb, we must come to the conclusion that they little took advantage of this glorious opportunity, if at all!

Evidently, the entirety of the Tabernacle was set up in one day, with all the Sacred Vessels placed accordingly, which could have easily been done.

THE SACRED VESSELS

Verses 3 through 8 read: *"And you shall put therein the Ark of the Testimony, and cover the Ark with the Veil.*

"And you shall bring in the Table, and set in order the things that are to be set in order upon it; and you shall bring in the Lampstand, and light the Lamps thereof.

"And you shall set the Altar of gold for the Incense before the Ark of the Testimony, and put the hanging of the Door to the Tabernacle.

"And you shall set the Altar of the Burnt Offering before the Door of the Tabernacle of the Tent of the Congregation.

"And you shall set the Laver between the Tent of the Congregation and the Altar, and shall put water therein.

"And you shall set up the Court round about, and hang up the hanging at the Court Gate."

To which we have already alluded several times, the Lord had given the most direct instructions, even down to the finest detail, as it regarded the entire work of the Tabernacle. Every pin, every socket, every loop, and every tach was accurately set forth. There was no room left for man's efforts whatsoever. This means that the Lord did not give a great outline and leave man to fill it up. He left no margin whatever in which man might enter his personal ideas or regulations. In fact, He told Moses to *"make all things according to the pattern showed to you in the Mount"* (Ex. 25:40; 26:30; Heb. 8:5). This left no room for human device.

If man had been allowed to make a single, small pin, that was other than the directions given by the Lord, that pin would most assuredly would have been out of place in the Judgment of God. In fact, we can see what man's *"graving tool"* produces as it regards the golden calf (Ex., Chpt. 32).

The workmen were to do exactly as they were told, nothing more, and nothing less!

Paul said: *"Now these things* (the happenings of the Old Testament) *were our examples, to the intent we should not lust after evil things, as they also lusted. You must not be idolaters, as were some of them"* (I Cor. 10:6-7).

As the Lord gave every design as it regards the Tabernacle, and as well, helped the workmen to properly construct it, exactly as He had ordered, likewise, this should be, and is definitely meant to be, an example, of our present Salvation, which is all in Christ. The Word of God is replete. In fact, it is amply sufficient for everything, whether it regards personal Salvation and walk, or the order and rule of the Church. Paul said:

"All Scripture is given by Inspiration of God, and is profitable for doctrine, for reproof, for correction, for instruction in Righteousness, that the man of God may be perfect, thoroughly furnished unto all good works" (II Tim. 3:16-17). This settles the question.

If the Word of God furnishes a man thoroughly unto *"all good works,"* it follows, as a necessary consequence, that whatever I find not in its pages cannot possibly be a good work. And, further, be it remembered that the Divine Glory cannot connect itself with that which is not according to the Divine

Pattern (Mackintosh).

MODERN THOUGHT

Now let me ask this question . . .

Almost the entirety of the Church world has opted for humanistic psychology, as the answer to the perversions, aberrations, and sinfulness of man. My question is, *"Can we find anything in the Word of God that gives the Church latitude to adopt such humanistic wisdom?"*

The answer to that is overly obvious. Humanistic psychology is worldly wisdom, and as such, has no place in our lives or living. Peter said:

"According as His Divine Power has given unto us all things that pertain unto life and Godliness, through the knowledge of Him Who has called us to glory and virtue:

"Whereby are given unto us exceeding great and precious Promises: that by these you might be partakers of the Divine Nature, having escaped the corruption that is in the world through lust" (II Pet. 1:3-4).

Now as I've already said in this Volume, either the Holy Spirit through Peter told the truth, or else He didn't. I prefer to believe that He definitely did tell the truth.

That being the case, He has *"given unto us all things that pertain unto life and Godliness."*

This means that we do not need the help of the world, which in fact, provides no help at all. In other words, they have no solution whatsoever for the perversions, aberrations, wickedness, and sinfulness of man. The Catholic question is an excellent case in point.

The whole world has looked at the terrible problem of pedophilia among the Priests in the Catholic Church. Let me remind all and one that the Catholics have the best Psychologists in the world. Most of the Priests involved in this terrible sin and crime have had at least some, if not much, psychological therapy. It has all been to no avail, even as it must be to no avail!

So what is the answer?

THE ANSWER IS THE CROSS

I might quickly add that the answer is the Cross, and the Cross alone! There is no other panacea, solution, therapy, or answer for sin, other than the Cross (Heb. 7:25-26; 8:6; 9:14, 22).

NOTES

So why isn't the Church preaching the Cross (I Cor. 1:17-18, 21, 23; 2:2)?

That's a good question! The truth is, the Church, with some few exceptions, is not preaching the Cross. In fact, it is preaching humanistic psychology, or it is preaching its own personal fads, made up out of whole cloth.

There are many Preachers who preach about the Gospel, and many of the things they say are good; however, preaching about the Gospel is not the same things as preaching the Gospel. For one to preach the Gospel, in some way, one must preach the Cross (I Cor. 1:17-18; Gal. 6:14).

WHAT DOES IT MEAN TO PREACH THE CROSS?

It means that the Preacher must know and understand that every single thing we receive from the Lord comes to us exclusively by and through Christ, and what He did for us at the Cross (Gal. 5:1-6; Eph. 2:13-18; Col. 2:14-15).

This doesn't mean that he preaches about the Cross in every single Message, but it does mean that he understands that all things, at least all things from God, come to us due to what Christ did at the Cross.

Jesus must never be separated from the Cross. True, He is not still on a Cross, but is rather in Heaven, seated by the Right Hand of the Father (Heb. 1:3). And in fact, we are seated there with Him, spiritually speaking (Eph. 2:6); however, He is there, and we are with Him, solely because of the Cross.

If we separate Christ from the Cross, we are then left with *"another Jesus,"* which produces *"another spirit,"* and plays out to *"another gospel"* (II Cor. 11:4).

Jesus answered every question at the Cross, paid every debt, atoned for every sin, and defeated every power of darkness (Col. 2:14-15). That must be fully understandable by the Preacher of the Gospel. And if it is fully understandable, and believed exactly as the Word of God gives it to us, the Preacher will preach this great Gospel, which is the Gospel of deliverance, and he will see lives gloriously and wondrously changed. Otherwise, no lives will be changed (Lk. 4:18-19).

And if he preaches the Cross (I Cor. 1:21, 23; 2:2), he will be vehemently opposed to any intrusion of a supposed answer, other than the Cross. He will oppose humanistic psychology, and he will oppose any doctrine which belittles the Cross of Christ, such as the modern Word of Faith doctrine, which in reality, is no faith at all! In fact, the entirety of the Epistle to the Galatians was written by Paul to refute the Gospel of the Crossless Christ, which was prevalent in his day. We speak of the Judaizers and the Law/Grace issue. As well, much of his 14 Epistles were made up of correction. It is no less incumbent upon us presently to do the same thing, as it regards *"Earnestly contending for the Faith which was once delivered unto the Saints"* (Jude, Vs. 3).

The Message of the Cross must not suffer deletion or addition. In other words, the Work of Christ is a *"Finished Work,"* and, therefore, needs no help. In fact, if we add anything, or take away anything, it would have been the same as Moses, or anyone else for that matter, attempting to change the pattern of the Tabernacle. We can well imagine what the answer of the Lord would have been as it regards that.

The only answer for a hurting world, and in every capacity, whether Saint of sinner, is the preaching of the Cross. Is your Pastor preaching the Cross? Is the Evangelist to whom you listen quite often, whether over Radio or Television, preaching the Cross?

WHY WON'T ALL PREACHERS PREACH THE CROSS?

It is either because of ignorance or unbelief! In other words, they simply don't know the Scripture, or else they don't believe the Scripture. There could be no other reason.

Most Preachers know and understand the Cross as it regards Salvation. In other words, they will quickly say, that is if they believe the Bible at all, *"Jesus died for me,"* etc. And of course, that is correct, at least as far as it goes. But after that, and I speak of Sanctification, most Preachers don't have a clue as to the fact that Sanctification is predicated on the Cross of Christ, and the Cross of Christ exclusively. So we have the problem because of erroneous preaching, of Salvation by Faith, which is correct, and Sanctification by self, which is basely incorrect. In other words, the same Preacher who tells people that they cannot save themselves, but must trust exclusively in Christ, which is totally correct, at the same time, tells Believers that they must sanctify themselves, by many and various means, all other than the Cross, which are totally wrong.

If a Believer or Preacher knows and understands the Cross, false direction, as preached by most, will leap out at him immediately.

The other night I happened to listen to a Preacher for a few moments over Television. The crowd was immense! He was giving the people that which sounds good to the ear.

He was telling them that they should repeat after him, *"I am a conqueror,"* which they did! He went on to say that they must think constantly in their minds that they are victorious, and that Satan will never have any of that which belongs to them, etc.

All of that sounds good to the ear, but the truth is, this man wasn't preaching the Cross, doesn't know anything about the Cross, at least as it regards Sanctification, which leaves the people with the right way, but with no means to get there. The Cross of Christ is the means by which we obtain these things, and the means alone by which we obtain these things.

Yes, there is total victory in Christ! Yes, we are *"more than conquerors,"* etc., but we obtain these things strictly by our Faith in Christ, and what Christ has done for us at the Cross. But this dear Brother doesn't know this of which I speak; therefore, he shows people the way, and does so correctly, but does not tell them the means by which they are to get there. In fact, the pulpits of the land are full of that type of direction.

Consequently, the people are left with their own strength and ability, which are woefully inadequate for the task. In other words, we know what Jesus did for us, but we can obtain all of these things only by Faith in Him, and the price He paid at the Cross. If we eliminate the Cross, as I've already stated, we are preaching and teaching *"another Jesus,"* to which the Holy Spirit cannot subscribe.

In fact, it is the Holy Spirit Who makes possible all of these things of which we speak. But He makes them possible strictly through what Jesus did in His great Sacrifice. In other words, the Cross of Christ is the legal means by which the Holy Spirit is able to function (Eph. 2:13-18). Listen to Paul:

"Stand fast therefore in the liberty wherewith Christ has made us free, and be not entangled again with the yoke of bondage" (Gal. 5:1).

He was speaking here of the bondage of attempting to live for the Lord, by the means of law rather than Grace. And please understand, if the Believer doesn't understand the Cross, such a Believer will not understand Grace, and will at the same time, revert to law, because there's no place else to go. And when I say *"law,"* I'm not really referring to the Law of Moses, but rather to laws that we make up ourselves, or others make up, and we try to follow. In fact, the Church is full of such laws. And let us say it again:

If the Believer doesn't understand that every single thing He has from the Lord comes to him by and through the Cross, all made possible by the Holy Spirit, he will find himself functioning in law. He may not understand that it's a law, and may even vehemently deny that it is law, but if it's not the Cross, there is no other place to be, other than law.

THE CROSS IS EVER NEEDFUL

Paul said: *"Always bearing about in the body the dying of the Lord Jesus, that the life also of Jesus might be made manifest in our body"* (II Cor. 4:10).

The word *"dying"* in the Greek refers to an action that is never complete, but is always continuous, and in fact, is always in progress. It means that there will never come a time that the Believer can dispense with the Cross. What Jesus did there must function in our hearts and lives constantly, that is, on a continuing basis. And what do I mean by that?

When Jesus died on the Cross, it was a work that was finished once and for all. So we're not trying to put Him back on the Cross, and neither are we trying to get on the Cross ourselves. The idea is, the Cross has benefits that are continuing, and in fact, will never be discontinued. It is these benefits of which I speak.

What He did there made it possible for me to be saved, and as well, to live a righteous, holy life. I obtain all the things that He did for me by exhibiting Faith in Him, and His great Sacrifice (Gal. 1:4). That's why Paul also said: *"Behold, I Paul say unto you, that if you be circumcised, Christ shall profit you nothing"* (Gal. 5:2).

Once again, we come back to Law versus Grace. Paul is saying that if these people put their faith in law, and whatever that law might be, that *"Christ will profit them nothing."* In other words, what He did at the Cross will be to no avail. Listen again to the Apostle:

"For in Jesus Christ neither circumcision availeth anything, nor uncircumcision; but Faith which works by love" (Gal. 5:6).

All of these things that Christ did for us on the Cross are made available to us by Faith.

By that, I'm speaking of the fact that we must evidence Faith in Christ and His Cross, which is the means by which all of this is done. It is by Faith! This is the way the Holy Spirit works, and the only way that He works.

So our dear Brother, whom I mentioned some paragraphs back, was telling the people what they could be, but giving them an entirely erroneous means, by which to arrive at that place of victory. What he was telling them to do was strictly through *"Self,"* which Paul labeled as *"the flesh"* (Rom. 8:1-2, 8).

Now if this Preacher was questioned, or the people to whom He was ministering were question, they would all declare that they were depending on Christ. But let the Reader understand that it's impossible to depend on Christ if His Cross is misunderstood, or eliminated. Once again we come back to the statement of Paul that to do such finds us worshipping and serving *"another Jesus"* (II Cor. 11:4).

And that's the biggest problem in the modern Church; people simply do not know how to live for God. Because when one doesn't understand the Cross, and one cannot understand the Cross if the Cross is not properly preached from behind the pulpit, then one cannot understand Grace, or the Holy Spirit, which leaves such a person outside of the Word of God, no matter how much he quotes the Word. Accordingly, it is simply Impossible for such a person to walk in victory. Regrettably and sadly, this characterizes virtually all of the modern Church. They are Cross illiterate and, therefore, victory is denied!

(9) "AND YOU SHALL TAKE THE ANOINTING OIL, AND ANOINT THE TABERNACLE, AND ALL THAT IS THEREIN, AND SHALL HALLOW IT, AND ALL THE VESSELS THEREOF: AND IT SHALL BE HOLY.

(10) "AND YOU SHALL ANOINT THE ALTAR OF THE BURNT OFFERING, AND ALL HIS VESSELS, AND SANCTIFY THE ALTAR: IT SHALL BE AN ALTAR MOST HOLY.

(11) "AND YOU SHALL ANOINT THE LAVER AND HIS FOOT, AND SANCTIFY IT.

(12) "AND YOU SHALL BRING AARON AND HIS SONS UNTO THE DOOR OF THE TABERNACLE OF THE CONGREGATION, AND WASH THEM WITH WATER.

(13) "AND YOU SHALL PUT UPON AARON THE HOLY GARMENTS, AND ANOINT HIM, AND SANCTIFY HIM; THAT HE MAY MINISTER UNTO ME IN THE PRIEST'S OFFICE.

(14) "AND YOU SHALL BRING HIS SONS, AND CLOTHE THEM WITH COATS:

(15) "AND YOU SHALL ANOINT THEM, AS YOU DID ANOINT THEIR FATHER, THAT THEY MAY MINISTER UNTO ME IN THE PRIEST'S OFFICE: FOR THEIR ANOINTING SHALL SURELY BE AN EVERLASTING PRIESTHOOD THROUGHOUT THEIR GENERATIONS.

(16) "THUS DID MOSES: ACCORDING TO ALL THAT THE LORD COMMANDED HIM, SO DID HE."

The construction is:

1. The Tabernacle, having been made according to the Divine Pattern, was filled with Divine Glory.

2. It was filled with glory, only after it had been sprinkled with precious blood, and anointed with holy oil.

3. Only in a Crucified and Anointed Saviour can God dwell with man.

THE ANOINTING OIL

Verse 9 reads: *"And you shall take the Anointing Oil, and anoint the Tabernacle, and all that is therein, and shall hallow it, and all the Vessels thereof: and it shall be holy."*

The *"Anointing Oil"* was a Type of the Holy Spirit. As is declared in this Verse, everything about the Tabernacle, which included all of the Sacred Vessels, were anointed with this holy oil. This in effect states to us presently that the Holy Spirit must abide on all that we do, must instigate all that we do, must institute all that we do, and actually, must be upon all that we do. The Church without the Holy Spirit leaves it as no more than any other type of earthly club, etc. In fact, as it regards the action of the Church, this is what makes Christianity different than the religions of the world.

THE BAPTISM WITH
THE HOLY SPIRIT

It is my contention that the Scripture teaches that the Baptism with the Holy Spirit, which follows Salvation, is a definite work of Grace, and is commanded upon Believers, at least as far as it regards its reception. Jesus said concerning the infilling of the Holy Spirit: *"And, being assembled together with them, commanded them that they should not depart from Jerusalem, but wait for the Promise of the Father"* (Acts 1:4). As someone has well said, this was not a suggestion, but rather a command.

In other words, He was saying to His Disciples, as well as all of His followers, *"Don't go try to preach the Gospel, heal the sick, build Churches, witness for Me, or in fact, do anything for Me, until you are first baptized with the Holy Spirit."* He then said:

"But you shall receive power, after that the Holy Spirit has come upon you" (Acts 1:8). In other words, without the Baptism with the Holy Spirit, the Saint of God, although saved, simply has no power; consequently, whatever he does, at least as it purports to be for the Lord, will be on his own initiative, which in effect, will see nothing done for the Lord. There may be much religious machinery involved, but there will be nothing accomplished for Christ, simply because the Holy Spirit must be prevalent, pertinent, and present for anything to be accomplished for the Lord.

THE INITIAL PHYSICAL EVIDENCE
OF THE BAPTISM WITH
THE HOLY SPIRIT

To which we've already alluded, we believe

that the receiving of the Holy Spirit Baptism is an experience separate, different, and apart from Salvation. One is saved by simply trusting Christ, and one cannot be more saved thereafter, even though one should certainly grow in Grace and the knowledge of the Lord. So what we're speaking of here has nothing to do with one's Salvation, but rather has everything to do as it regards one's service to the Lord.

In another part of this Commentary, we've already given a Biblical dissertation as it regards the Baptism with the Holy Spirit as a Work of Grace, different and separate from Salvation. So we won't go through that again, but will simply say that the Bible teaches that the initial, physical evidence that one has been baptized with the Holy Spirit is that they will speak with other tongues, as the Spirit of God gives the utterance (Acts 2:4; 10:45-46; 19:1-7). There are no exceptions to this. In other words, the Lord doesn't fill some with tongues, and some without tongues, as some Preachers teach.

ANOINTING

The word *"Anointing"* in the Hebrew is *"Moshchah,"* and means, *"to consecrate."*

Every modern Believer, and we speak of all since the Cross, have the Holy Spirit, that is, if they are a true Believer. Now this doesn't mean that they have been baptized with the Holy Spirit as we have been discussing, but it does mean that they definitely have the Holy Spirit; actually, it's impossible to be saved without having the Holy Spirit (Jn. 3:5-8). To be *"born of the Spirit,"* which pertains to Salvation, is one thing, while to be *"baptized with the Spirit,"* is something else altogether, and pertains to an induement of power (Acts 1:8). As we've already stated, Jesus demanded that all Believers be baptized with the Holy Spirit (Acts 1:4). As we read the Book of Acts, we cannot help but come to the conclusion that the Church represented in this Book as written by Luke was a Church that believed in Salvation by the Blood, the Baptism with the Holy Spirit with the evidence of speaking with other tongues, Divine Healing, and the imminent return of the Lord Jesus Christ. In other words, if the modern Church doesn't ape, so to speak, the Book of Acts Church, then actually, at least in the eyes of God, it's not Church. And for the modern Church to be as the Book of Acts Church, the Holy Spirit must be pertinent and prevalent in all that is done. That is overly obvious in the Book of Acts.

So that means Churches that do not believe in the Baptism with the Holy Spirit, pure and simple, aren't going to see anything done for the Lord. As we've already stated, there may be a lot of religious activity, but there will be nothing carried out for Christ. The reason is simple:

For anything to be recognized by the Lord, it must be instituted by the Holy Spirit.

Now this doesn't mean that Churches which espouse the Holy Spirit Baptism are guaranteed of great spiritual success. In fact, the Holy Spirit Baptism functions at the beginning in the realm of potential only. In other words, the potential is there for all type of things, but if proper consecration is not enjoined, very little will actually be done. In truth, and sadly, this is the state of the modern Pentecostal Church, at least for the most part. Regrettably, most, it seems, have abandoned the Moving and the Operation of the Holy Spirit. Let me make a statement that I've made several times, but which I think is so very important:

The Denominational Church world has attempted to preach the Cross, at least to a certain degree, without the Holy Spirit. It has resulted in a fruitless effort. The Pentecostal Church, conversely, has tried to preach the Holy Spirit without the Cross. That always goes into fanaticism.

As we shall see in the Tabernacle, both the Holy Spirit and the Cross are vital to the Work of God (Vs. 29).

In fact, the Holy Spirit and the Cross are so intertwined, or else we should say that the Crucified Christ and the Holy Spirit are so intertwined, that they look to be one in the same.

In the Vision that John the Beloved had, as it regards the Throne of God, he said: *"And I beheld, and, lo, in the midst of the Throne and of the four Beasts* (Living Creatures), *and in the midst of the Elders, stood a Lamb as it had been slain, having seven horns and seven eyes, which are the seven*

Spirits of God sent forth into all the Earth" (Rev. 5:6).

As is obvious here, three things are represented, and represented so closely as to be almost indivisible.

Those three are, Jesus, His Crucifixion, and the Holy Spirit. This tells us that the Throne of God is accessible only by virtue of the slain Lamb, i.e., *"Christ and Him Crucified,"* by and through which the Holy Spirit works (Rom. 8:2).

As Moses dedicated the Tabernacle, the word used is *"Anointing Oil,"* and for a reason. All of this translates into what the Holy Spirit would do, when He was able to abide permanently within the Saint of God, which would take place after the Cross, which made it possible (Jn. 14:17).

But yet, a person can be baptized with the Holy Spirit, with the evidence of speaking with other tongues, and still not be anointed by the Lord, etc. Even though the Tabernacle was anointed with oil, along with all of the Sacred Vessels, still, if it was used improperly, none of that mattered. The Presence of the Lord simply would not function in the hearts and lives of those who addressed the Tabernacle and its work, improperly. It is likewise with the modern Church. Two things have to happen, in order for the Anointing to be prevalent in hearts and lives.

THE CROSS AND CONSECRATION

To the degree that one understands the Cross, to that degree will the Anointing of the Holy Spirit work within one's life, that is, if the consecration of the individual is as it ought to be. And the consecration cannot be as it ought to be without a proper understanding of the Cross. The only way that the Believer can walk in victory, and I mean the only way, is for the Believer to express proper Faith in Christ and His Cross, which then gives the Holy Spirit latitude to work (Rom. 8:1-2, 11).

The lack of understanding as it regards the Cross is the reason there is so little Anointing as it regards the preaching of the Gospel. If one understands the Anointing, one will look in vain, as it regards most Television and Radio Preachers. With some few exceptions, there is no Anointing. And what one sees over Television and hears over Radio is indicative of what is happening in the modern Church. To find the reason for the lack is to find a lack of Scriptural understanding as it regards the Cross.

THE SACRED VESSELS

Verses 10 and 11 read: *"And you shall anoint the Altar of the Burnt Offering, and all his vessels, and sanctify the Altar: and it shall be an Altar most holy.*

"And you shall anoint the Laver and his foot, and sanctify it."

Even though these vessels were representations of the Cross and the Word, for them to be effective, the Holy Spirit had to be a part of all that was happening, typified by the *"oil."*

There is every evidence that the Holy Spirit was present at the Crucifixion, actually relating to Christ when He could die (Heb. 9:14). And Christ as the Living Word (Jn. 1:1) was *"Anointed by the Holy Spirit, to preach the Gospel to the poor, heal the brokenhearted, to preach deliverance to the captives, and recovering of sight to the blind, to set at liberty them who are bruised, to preach the acceptable year of the Lord"* (Lk. 4:18-19).

THE ANOINTING OF THE PRIESTS

Verses 12 through 16 read: *"And you shall bring Aaron and his sons unto the door of the Tabernacle of the Congregation, and wash them with water.*

"And you shall put upon Aaron the holy garments, and anoint him, and sanctify him; that he may minister unto me in the Priest's Office.

"And you shall bring his sons, and clothe them with coats:

"And you shall anoint them, as you did anoint their father, that they may minister unto Me in the Priest's Office: for their Anointing shall surely be an everlasting Priesthood throughout their generations.

"Thus did Moses: according to all that the LORD commanded him, so did he."

Not only were the Tabernacle and Sacred Vessels anointed with oil, but as well, Aaron and his sons were anointed, typifying all the Priesthood.

In fact, the function of the Tabernacle, which typified the Finished Work of Christ, was predicated on the proper actions of the Priests, hence their anointing and consecration, being so very, very important. We need not concern ourselves about the function of the Plan of God, if we function correctly.

While there is no more Priesthood in the New Covenant because Christ has satisfied all the demands of Mediation, with Himself becoming the Mediator, the truth is, every Believer is now a *"king and priest unto God, Who is our Father"* (Rev. 1:6).

While the Priests under the Old Covenant mostly only had a symbolic operation of the Holy Spirit, represented by the Anointing Oil, we at present, and I speak of all times since the Cross, have the reality of the Spirit. The truth is, we should presently function in a much more consecrated way, than any of the Priests of old because of the perpetual indwelling of the Holy Spirit (Jn. 14:16).

(17) "AND IT CAME TO PASS IN THE FIRST MONTH IN THE SECOND YEAR, ON THE FIRST DAY OF THE MONTH, THAT THE TABERNACLE WAS REARED UP.

(18) "AND MOSES REARED UP THE TABERNACLE, AND FASTENED HIS SOCKETS, AND SET UP THE BOARDS THEREOF, AND PUT IN THE BARS THEREOF, AND REARED UP HIS PILLARS.

(19) "AND HE SPREAD ABROAD THE TENT OVER THE TABERNACLE, AND PUT THE COVERING OF THE TENT ABOVE UPON IT; AS THE LORD COMMANDED MOSES.

(20) "AND HE TOOK AND PUT THE TESTIMONY INTO THE ARK, AND SET THE STAVES ON THE ARK, AND PUT THE MERCY SEAT ABOVE UPON THE ARK:

(21) "AND HE BROUGHT THE ARK INTO THE TABERNACLE, AND SET UP THE VEIL OF THE COVERING, AND COVERED THE ARK OF THE TESTIMONY; AS THE LORD COMMANDED MOSES.

(22) "AND HE PUT THE TABLE IN THE TENT OF THE CONGREGATION, UPON THE SIDE OF THE TABERNACLE NORTHWARD, WITHOUT THE VEIL.

(23) "AND HE SET THE BREAD IN ORDER UPON IT BEFORE THE LORD; AS THE LORD HAD COMMANDED MOSES.

NOTES

(24) "AND HE PUT THE LAMPSTAND IN THE TENT OF THE CONGREGATION, OVER AGAINST THE TABLE, ON THE SIDE OF THE TABERNACLE SOUTHWARD.

(25) "AND HE LIGHTED THE LAMPS BEFORE THE LORD; AS THE LORD COMMANDED MOSES.

(26) "AND HE PUT THE GOLDEN ALTAR IN THE TENT OF THE CONGREGATION BEFORE THE VEIL:

(27) "AND HE BURNT SWEET INCENSE THEREON; AS THE LORD COMMANDED MOSES.

(28) "AND HE SET UP THE HANGING AT THE DOOR OF THE TABERNACLE.

(29) "AND HE PUT THE ALTAR OF BURNT OFFERING BY THE DOOR OF THE TABERNACLE OF THE TENT OF THE CONGREGATION, AND OFFERED UPON IT THE BURNT OFFERING AND THE MEAT OFFERING, AS THE LORD COMMANDED MOSES.

(30) "AND HE SET THE LAVER BETWEEN THE TENT OF THE CONGREGATION AND THE ALTAR, AND PUT WATER THERE, TO WASH WITHAL."

The overview is:

1. The first day of the month of the second year, in a sense, tells Israel that they now have a new beginning. They should be careful that they make the most of it.

2. Over and over again, the Scripture brings out the statement, *"As the Lord commanded Moses,"* signifying that everything was done at the command of the Lord, with nothing left to the ideas of man.

3. As we have repeatedly stated, all of these Sacred Vessels portrayed Christ in His Atoning, Mediatorial, or Intercessory Work.

THE FIRST DAY OF THE FIRST MONTH

Verse 17 reads: *"And it came to pass in the first month in the second year, on the first day of the month, that the Tabernacle was reared up."*

One year has passed since the Children of Israel have left Egyptian bondage. Despite the problems they have had, the Lord has made Himself very real in their midst. They have witnessed miracle after miracle; but the greatest miracle of all was the giving of the

Law on Mount Sinai. This one piece of legislation, which was all of God, and none of man, would take Israel, and in fact, the entirety of the human race, to a much higher level than it had heretofore known. The Law was God's Standard of Righteousness.

But yet, man was wholly incapable of keeping the Law because of the Fall in the Garden of Eden. So the Tabernacle system, with the Sacrificial System at its core, was set up in order that man could have forgiveness of sins, all typified by the Sacrifices. So in fact, while everything played its excellent part, the Sacrificial System was, in reality, the core of the Mosaic institution. Without the shedding of innocent blood, there was no remission of sins (Heb. 9:22). So, much more attention was given to the details of the Tabernacle, and all its function, than anything else, and rightly so!

THE TABERNACLE

Verses 18 and 19 read: *"And Moses reared up the Tabernacle, and fastened his sockets, and set up the boards thereof, and put in the bars thereof, and reared up his pillars.*

"And he spread abroad the tent over the Tabernacle, and put the covering of the tent above upon it; as the LORD commanded Moses."

Even as I copy these Scriptures, I sense the Presence of God. I think how far this great Revelation has come. Today, these things are but a memory, having all been satisfied by what Christ did at the Cross, which made them unnecessary. But until Christ came, the Tabernacle and the Temple were necessary, for God sought to dwell among His people.

It seems that the fence and the gate were reared up last, which means that thousands of the Children of Israel, no doubt, watched and observed, as Moses first of all erected the Tabernacle.

It says that Moses did it, but more than likely, he just superintended the work as it was carried out by Bezaleel and others.

As we've already stated, the structure, from all outward appearances, would not have been imposing at all. In fact, with its outer cover being badger skins, there was no attractiveness whatsoever. But inside the Tabernacle,

NOTES

which was altogether covered with gold, except the floor, the beauty would have been indescribable. It is the same with Christ and Christianity.

Outwardly, *"there is no beauty that we should desire Him,"* but once He is accepted, and comes to abide in our hearts and lives through the Person of the Holy Spirit, all is beauty, and all is light!

THE ARK OF THE COVENANT

Verses 20 and 21 read: *"And he took and put the Testimony into the Ark, and set the staves on the Ark, and put the Mercy Seat above upon the Ark:*

"And he brought the Ark into the Tabernacle, and set up the Veil of the covering, and covered the Ark of the Testimony; as the LORD commanded Moses."

It seems that the *"Brazen Altar"* was anointed first, and the *"Brazen Laver"* second (Vss. 10-11), which I think typifies more than the mere fact that they were the first Vessels, even located outside the Tabernacle. While we may think of the Ark of the Covenant as being the most important of all the Holy Vessels, in which in a sense it is; still, without the Brazen Altar, which typifies the Cross, it simply would be impossible for one to reach the Holy of Holies, which housed the Ark of the Covenant, which typified the Throne of God. We have access to the Throne only because of the Cross (Heb. 4:16).

The Ark of the Covenant was placed in the Holy of Holies, with the Mercy Seat being placed on the Ark, actually serving as a lid, which included the Cherubim protruding from either end, with their faces looking down toward the Mercy Seat; and then the Veil was hung between the Holy Place and the Holy of Holies, thereby, separating the two.

THE TABLE

Verses 22 and 23 read: *"And he put the Table in the tent of the congregation, upon the side of the Tabernacle northward, without the Veil.*

"And he set the bread in order upon it before the LORD; as the LORD had commanded Moses."

"The Veil" refers to the material that

separated the Holy Place from the Holy of Holies. The Ark of the Covenant, as stated, was placed in the Holy of Holies, and now all the balance of the Sacred Vessels will be placed in the Holy Place. The Table of Shewbread is mentioned first. It was situated, as one stands in the front door, on the right side of the Tabernacle, which was to the north, inasmuch as the Tabernacle faced the east. If one stood in the door of the Tabernacle, facing inward, his back would be to the east, therefore, to the right would be the north.

The bread, some 12 loaves, and freshly baked, would have been placed on the Table. This represented Christ as the *"Bread of Life."*

THE LAMPSTAND

Verses 24 and 25 read: *"And he put the Lampstand in the tent of the congregation, over against the Table, on the side of the Tabernacle southward.*

"And he lighted the Lamps before the LORD; as the LORD commanded Moses."

As one stood in the doorway, facing the interior of the Tabernacle, the Lampstand would have been to his left, therefore, southward.

Moses lit the Lamps *"before the Lord,"* which referred to the fact that the Lord was minutely inspecting everything that was done. Due to the fact that the Holy Spirit, Who is God, now abides within us permanently, His introspection is even far more minute presently, than it was with Moses. Concerning our everyday actions, and in fact, all that we do, we should not forget this. Everything that we do as Believers is *"before the Lord."* That's a sobering thought; as well it is intended to be!

THE ALTAR OF INCENSE

Verses 26 and 27 read: *"And he put the Golden Altar in the tent of the congregation before the Veil:*

"And he burnt sweet Incense thereon; as the LORD commanded Moses."

The Priests would have obtained coals of fire from the Brazen Altar, on which sacrifices were even now being offered, with these coals being placed on the Golden Altar, with Incense poured over them. The interior would have been filled with a very pleasant fragrance, with a smoke of sorts filling the Tabernacle, typifying the Intercession of Christ, all on our behalf.

As we read these words as written by Moses nearly 3,600 years ago, and realize that all of this was a type of what Christ has done, and is doing, we are sobered, to say the least! At this very moment, Christ, by His very Presence at the Throne of God, which proclaims a Finished Work, is making Intercession for us. How we thank God for our Great High Priest! Every Believer is today safe and secure, despite, as Pink said, our ten thousand failures, all because of what Jesus did at the Cross, which now makes possible His Intercession on our behalf.

THE DOOR

Verse 28 reads: *"And he set up the hanging at the Door of the Tabernacle."*

The *"Door"* was actually a curtain that hung over the entirety of the front of the Tabernacle, and was pulled aside when the Priests entered. It was snow white, with beautiful colors embroidered on it, even as was the Veil that hung between the Holy Place and the Holy of Holies. The *"hanging"* typifying that it was a curtain, but referred to as a *"Door,"* symbolizes Christ. He said of Himself: *"I am the Door: by Me if any man enter in, he shall be saved, and shall go in and out, and find pasture"* (Jn. 10:9).

THE SACRIFICES

Verse 29 reads: *"And he put the Altar of Burnt Offering by the Door of the Tabernacle of the tent of the congregation, and offered upon it the Burnt Offering and the Meat Offering; as the LORD commanded Moses."*

As we stated many paragraphs back, the Tabernacle, having been made according the Divine Pattern, even as we shall see, was filled with the Divine Glory; but, not until precious blood had been shed by the Sacrifices on the Brazen Altar, and withal anointed with holy oil. Only in a Crucified and Anointed Saviour can God dwell with man.

These Sacrifices were probably offered at 3 p.m. in the afternoon, which would be the time of the evening sacrifices, with 9 a.m. being the time of the morning sacrifices. This would be carried on everyday, with two lambs offered each time on the Sabbath. This would be besides the people constantly bringing lambs to offer in sacrifice, and for various different reasons. So, all of Israel was placed on the foundation of the shed blood of the Lamb. There was, and there is, nothing more important! This is the same thing that Paul was saying, when he penned the words: *"We preach Christ Crucified"* (I Cor. 1:23).

Perhaps one could say that the *"Burnt Offering,"* or at times referred to as the *"Whole Burnt Offering,"* was the most important of the five Levitical Offerings. The Lamb, minus his skin, would be wholly burnt upon the Altar, signifying that God would give His all for dying humanity, and that we, in turn, must give our all.

The *"Meat Offering,"* actually contained no meat as we think of such presently. It was made solely of fine flour, with oil poured upon it, along with frankincense. It was, in essence, a Thanksgiving Offering, with some portion burnt on the Altar, and the other portion given to the Priests (Lev. 2:1-11).

THE BRAZEN LAVER

Verse 30 reads: *"And he set the Laver between the tent of the congregation and the Altar, and put water there, to wash withal."*

The Brazen Laver stood between the Brazen Altar and the entrance to the Tabernacle. Every time any Priest went into the Tabernacle, he had to first wash his hands and his feet in the water, provided by the Brazen Laver. The Laver signified Christ as the Living Word, i.e., *"the Bible."*

(31) "AND MOSES AND AARON AND HIS SONS WASHED THEIR HANDS AND THEIR FEET THEREAT:

(32) "WHEN THEY WENT INTO THE TENT OF THE CONGREGATION, WHEN THEY CAME NEAR UNTO THE ALTAR, THEY WASHED; AS THE LORD COMMANDED MOSES.

(33) "AND HE REARED UP THE COURT ROUND ABOUT THE TABERNACLE AND THE ALTAR, AND SET UP THE HANGING OF THE COURT GATE. SO MOSES FINISHED THE WORK.

(34) "THEN A CLOUD COVERED THE TENT OF THE CONGREGATION, AND THE GLORY OF THE LORD FILLED THE TABERNACLE.

(35) "AND MOSES WAS NOT ABLE TO ENTER INTO THE TENT OF THE CONGREGATION, BECAUSE THE CLOUD ABODE THEREON, AND THE GLORY OF THE LORD FILLED THE TABERNACLE.

(36) "AND WHEN THE CLOUD WAS TAKEN UP FROM OVER THE TABERNACLE, THE CHILDREN OF ISRAEL WENT ONWARD IN ALL THEIR JOURNEYS:

(37) "BUT IF THE CLOUD WERE NOT TAKEN UP, THEN THEY JOURNEYED NOT TILL THE DAY THAT IT WAS TAKEN UP.

(38) "FOR THE CLOUD OF THE LORD WAS UPON THE TABERNACLE BY DAY, AND FIRE WAS ON IT BY NIGHT, IN THE SIGHT OF ALL THE HOUSE OF ISRAEL, THROUGHOUT ALL THEIR JOURNEYS."

The exegesis is:

1. As the Tabernacle is finished, and its procedures begin, the Plan of God for the Salvation of the human race is brought one giant step closer.

2. Even though the process was tedious and cumbersome, all of it was necessary because of the sinfulness of man.

3. The glory that filled the Tabernacle fills our hearts and lives presently in the Person of the Holy Spirit, and of course, we speak of Believers.

4. As the Cloud led Israel in their wilderness journeys, likewise, the Holy Spirit, of which the Cloud was a Type, leads us presently.

MOSES AND AARON

Verses 31 and 32 read: *"And Moses and Aaron and his sons washed their hands and their feet thereat:*

"When they went into the tent of the congregation, and when they came near unto the Altar, they washed; as the LORD commanded Moses."

Even Moses and Aaron, as is obvious here, had to wash their hands and their feet, before they went into the Tabernacle. As great as they were, and especially Moses, still, they were sinful men, and needed the cleansing provided by the Brazen Laver. The idea is this:

If these men needed these *"washings,"* then it should be understood that the need is incumbent upon us as well.

Even though there is no more Tabernacle or Brazen Laver, still, what they symbolized, Christ and the Word, are ever with us. Every time we read the Bible, and especially if we read it with the idea in mind that it searches our hearts, we are, in a sense, washing at the Brazen Laver.

This procedure would never stop, being required of all Priests every time they entered the Tabernacle, even upon pain of death if they omitted this procedure. Of course, it was done away, with Christ the Son of God having fulfilled it all.

But it seems that the Anointing of the Priests with oil, as we go back to Verse 15, was a one time Anointing. In other words, the Jewish Commentators maintain that the one Anointing of the sons of Aaron sufficed for all time, and was not repeated in the case of any subsequent Priests, who became fully possessed of the office without it. Each High Priest was, on the contrary, inducted into his Office by Anointing, whence the High Priest came to be spoken of as *"the anointed Priest"* (Lev. 4:3, 5, 16; 21:12).

THE COURT AND THE GATE

Verse 33 reads: *"And he reared up the Court round about the Tabernacle and the Altar, and set up the hanging of the Court Gate. So Moses finished the work."*

Last of all, the fence, which was snow white, was erected around the Tabernacle. The Gate was set up as well!

Most of the tents occupied by the Children of Israel, which would have numbered hundreds of thousands, were black on their tops and sides, or at least fairly dark. They used the skins or coats of lambs and goats for this purpose, and the darker colors didn't show wear and tear nearly as much as the lighter.

At any rate, this snow white fence, typifying the Righteousness of Christ, would have looked beautiful in the midst of these darkened tents, and especially considering that the outer covering of the Tabernacle, made of badgers' skins, was also dark.

THE CLOUD

Verse 34 reads: *"Then a Cloud covered the tent of the congregation, and the Glory of the LORD filled the Tabernacle."*

NOTES

This was the secret of Israel's power and strength. It is the secret of the strength of the Church as well, at least, if the Church has any strength.

Presently, our blessings are not in beautiful buildings, educated Preachers, or how much money is taken in on a weekly basis, but rather the *"Glory of the Lord."* But how many Churches presently can claim this of which Moses speaks?

In answer to that question, I suppose almost all would claim such, but the truth is, the Churches that really have such are few and far between. And how do I know that?

Many Charismatic and Pentecostal Churches have learned how to *"talk the talk,"* and as well, they specialize in racket and noise, but the truth is, *"talking the talk,"* doesn't necessarily mean that one is *"walking the walk."*

For instance, Churches cannot have the Spirit of God, and at the same time have the music of the world. While they might put in a Christian word here and there, the truth is, it's the spirit of the world, which characterizes such effort. In other words, what is carried on under the guise of worship and praise is in reality an abomination in the Eyes of God. There is no *"Glory of the Lord"* in such blasphemy, and blasphemy it is!

Also, one cannot have humanistic psychology and at the same time, have the *"Glory of the Lord."* To opt for this humanistic wisdom, which in reality is no wisdom at all, means that one has repudiated the Cross. And to repudiate the Cross is to repudiate the very basis of Christianity. The *"Glory of the Lord"* cannot abide in such an atmosphere.

The sordid truth is, we have abandoned the Brazen Altar, and substituted another Altar of our own choice. We've put Kool-Aid, so to speak, in the Brazen Laver, and we offer strange fire on the Altar of Incense. The bread we eat is of our own making, and the light that is shown is a false light. Consequently, there is no Ark of the Covenant, i.e., *"Throne of God,"* and because the Cross has been abandoned, and the only way to the Throne of God is by the Way of the Cross (I Cor. 1:17-18, 21, 23; 2:2, 5; Rom. 6:3-5, 11, 14; 8:1-2, 11; Gal. 5:1-6; 6:14; Eph. 2:13-18; Col. 2:14-15).

THE POWER

Verse 35 reads: *"And Moses was not able to enter into the tent of the congregation, because the Cloud abode thereon, and the Glory of the LORD filled the Tabernacle."*

The idea seems to be that Moses attempted to enter the Tabernacle, but the Glory of the Lord was occupying the Tabernacle, at least at this time, in such a powerful way that the Lawgiver was unable to do so. There is even a possibility that it knocked him off his feet.

Does the Lord manifest Himself in this fashion at the present time?

Most definitely He does at times! There have been untold cases where the Power of God has been so present in a particular Service, that people would be knocked off their feet, and actually unable to get off the floor for a period of time.

So, why doesn't the Lord do this all the time?

As wonderful as that is, and as much as we like to see such, and as helpful as it is in many ways, still, such demonstrations, as exciting as they are, really don't set the captive free. Let me explain.

Jesus said: *"You shall know the Truth, and the Truth shall make you free"* (Jn. 8:32). Unfortunately, far too much of the modern Church would rather have the demonstrations, than the Truth. But the question begs to be asked, *"Can we not have both?"*

Yes we can, and that's the ideal! But the major problem is, if men get their eyes on demonstrations, as wonderful as they are for the moment, much of the time, they have little desire for the Truth. In other words, they make the demonstration and the Truth one and the same, when they actually aren't.

Notice what Jesus said: *"The Spirit of the Lord is upon Me, because He has anointed Me . . . to preach deliverance to the captives"* (Lk. 4:18).

If it is to be noticed, He didn't say, *"To deliver the captives,"* which would have been by a demonstration, but rather, *"To preach deliverance to the captives."* That preached was to be the *"Truth,"* which will bring about deliverance for such an individual.

When I am proclaiming to you in this Commentary the Truth of the Cross, I am *"preaching the Truth,"* and if you believe this Truth, and apply it to your own heart and life, it will definitely *"set you free,"* and will do so, irrespective of the problem you may have had in the past. As one of my friends said, *"Believers need the 'Truth,' a whole lot more than they need a 'touch.'"*

I suspect that the Lord would give many more demonstrations of power, if Believers would keep the proper perspective. But we have such a tendency to get our eyes on the things that are exciting, etc. Listen again to Paul:

"For Christ sent me not to baptize, but to preach the Gospel: not with wisdom of words, lest the Cross of Christ should be made of none effect" (I Cor. 1:17).

Paul tells us here, or rather the Holy Spirit through him tells us, that the emphasis must always be on the Cross, and not on other things. He uses the Ordinance of Water Baptism as an example, but it could be anything.

As well, this tells us that the preaching of the Cross is, in actuality, the preaching of the Gospel. And if the Preacher preaches anything else other than the Cross, while what he is saying might very well be good, he's not preaching the Gospel, and will not see the results which only the Gospel can bring. As we've previously stated, if one doesn't preach the Cross, one is merely preaching about the Gospel. To preach the Gospel, in one way or the other, one must preach the Cross. This refers to the fact that the Preacher understands that every single Promise in the Word of God is granted to us solely on the basis of the Finished Work of Christ, i.e., *"the Cross."*

THE MOVING OF THE CLOUD

Verses 36 and 37 read: *"And when the Cloud was taken up from over the Tabernacle, the Children of Israel went onward in all their journeys:*

"But if the Cloud were not taken up, then they journeyed not till the day that it was taken up."

All of this simply means that Israel was led exclusively by the Spirit of God. They did not determine or decide where they would go, or how long they would stay where they were. Not even Moses decided this. It was all decided by the moving of the Cloud. This should be a lesson for every Believer.

Millions of Christians have settled into a particular place, spiritually speaking, and refuse to leave, even though the Cloud has long since moved. Such is the road to spiritual disaster!

There are Churches that once had the glory, even entire Denominations, but which no longer do. The people shouldn't remain where the Glory of God no longer abides. The criteria for where we go to Church ought to be two things:

1. Is the Word of God faithfully preached from behind the pulpit?
2. Is there a Moving and Operation of the Holy Spirit in the Church?

If the answer is *"yes"* to both counts, this means that the *"Cloud"* is in that place, and that's where the Believer ought to be as well. Otherwise, the Believer ought to search for such a place.

And that place might not be a particular Church or Denomination, but could very well be a Media program, such as Television or Radio. But the truth is, whatever is on Television and Radio mirrors the Church, which means that the *"Cloud"* is not easy to find.

THE CLOUD AND THE FIRE

Verse 38 reads: *"For the Cloud of the LORD was upon the Tabernacle by day, and fire was on it by night, in the sight of all the House of Israel, throughout all their journeys."*

This must have been quite a sight for the many thousands of Israelites.

Even though there were nearly three million people in this encampment, which means that some of the tents were located quite a distance away, the idea is the *"Cloud"* extended up high enough that it could be seen by all, without much trouble.

At night, it could probably be seen even in a greater way, as it looked as if a fire protruded up from the Tabernacle. As stated, this must have been quite a sight!

More than likely, this appearance hovered over the Holy of Holies, where the Lord resided between the Mercy Seat and the Cherubim.

More than likely, there were heathen Tribes somewhere close to some of the encampments of Israel, and I wonder what they thought, as they looked down from particular mountains, on this particular scene. Even though they would have understood it not at all, even to them, it must have been quite a sight.

So the great Book of Exodus closes out with the *"Glory of the Lord."* It began with the people of God serving as slaves in Egypt. It ends with them free from Egyptian bondage, and furthermore, the Glory of the Lord residing in their midst.

The great question should be asked, do we have that Glory presently?

If we do, we should be of all people most grateful and most thankful! If not, we should do whatever needs to be done in order that the Glory is in our midst.

"I hear the Saviour say,
"Your strength indeed is small!
"Child of weakness, watch and pray,
"Find in Me your all in all."

"Lord, now indeed I find
"Thy Power, and Thine alone,
"Can change the leopard's spots
"And melt the heart of stone."

"For nothing good have I
"Whereby Your Grace to claim
"I'll wash my garments white,
"In the Blood of Calvary's Lamb."

"And when before the Throne
"I stand in Him complete,
"Jesus died my soul to save,
"My lips shall still repeat."

CONCLUSION

It is July 15, 2002, as I finish work on the Book of Exodus. Even though, as the Introduction will show, I have only spent a short period of time on this effort, at least as far as the actual writing is concerned, the truth is, I've spent nearly 60 years in gathering the information given. If it provides any type of blessing, we'll give God all the glory.

A dear Brother wrote the other day, and said, *"Brother Swaggart, most Commentaries provide information only. Yours not only provide information, but as well, the truths given therein challenge my Faith."*

I don't think that our efforts could receive any greater compliment. Yes, we want information to be provided, because that's one of the reasons for the writing of these Commentaries; however, if, by the help of the Lord, the Truths we give you can indeed challenge your Faith, and fall out to your Spiritual Growth, then our efforts will have been well worthwhile.

One does not write merely what one knows. One writes mostly as to what one is!

THE CROSS

I have taken every opportunity in this Volume, even as I told you I would do in the Introduction, to place before you the great Truth of the Cross. How can I do less, when the Lord has been so gracious to me in the giving of this Revelation? As we've said repeatedly, what we give you is really not new, having first been given to the Apostle Paul. But I do believe that the Lord has shown us greater light as it regards this all-important subject. If in fact that is the case, then it should go without saying that what you will learn will be invaluable. Jesus said: *"You shall know the Truth, and the Truth shall make you free"* (Jn. 8:32).

In fact, the Book of Exodus, even as written by Moses nearly 3,600 years ago, is freighted with information about the Cross. The entire Levitical system, which was given to the great Lawgiver, has as its central core the great Sacrificial System, which is but a portrayal of the Cross.

Consequently, I will close this effort with the words of at least one of the greatest Hymns ever written. I speak of that great song written by John Newton so long ago.

> *"Amazing Grace, how sweet the sound*
> *"That saved a wretch like me!*
> *"I once was lost, but now am found*
> *"Was blind, but now I see."*
>
> *"'Twas Grace that taught my heart to fear,*
> *"And Grace my fears relieved;*
> *"How precious did that Grace appear*
> *"The hour I first believed!"*
>
> *"Through many dangers, toils, and snares,*
> *"I have already come;*
> *"'Tis Grace has brought me safe thus far,*
> *"And Grace will lead me home."*
>
> *"The Lord has promised good to me,*
> *"His Word my hope secures;*
> *"He will my shield and portion be*
> *"As long as life endures."*
>
> *"And when this flesh and heart shall fail,*
> *"And mortal life shall cease;*
> *"I shall possess within the Veil*
> *"A life of joy and peace."*
>
> *"When we've been there ten thousand years,*
> *"Bright shining as the sun,*
> *"We've no less days to sing God's praise,*
> *"Than when we first begun."*

BIBLIOGRAPHY

Ellicott's Commentary On The Whole Bible

The Student's Commentary On The Holy Scriptures, Williams

The Pulpit Commentary

Notes On The Pentateuch by C. H. Mackintosh

Matthew Henry Commentary On The Holy Bible

Strong's Exhaustive Concordance Of The Bible

Gleanings In Exodus, Arthur W. Pink

Wilson's Old Testament Word Studies

New Bible Dictionary

Josephus, The Essential Writings

Young's Literal Translation Of The Holy Bible

Vine's Expository Dictionary Of New Testament Words

The Zondervan Topical Bible

Richards Expository Dictionary Of Bible Words

Plain Talk On Exodus

The International Standard Bible Encyclopedia

Study Of The Types, Ada R. Habershon

Theological Wordbook Of The Old Testament

The Zondervan Pictorial Encyclopedia Of The Bible

Word Studies In The Greek New Testament, Kenneth S. Wuest

Living Hymns

INDEX

The index is listed according to subjects. The treatment may include a complete dissertation or no more than a paragraph. But hopefully it will provide some help.

As well, even though extended treatment of a subject may not be carried in this Commentary, one of the other Commentaries may well include the desired material.

AARON, 57, 63, 527
ABLE MEN, 326
ABRAHAM, ISAAC, AND JACOB, 542
ACTUAL COMPLIANCE WITH THE LAW, 378
ADULTERY, 355
ADVERSITY, 91
AFFLICTION, 28, 33
ALIVE WITH CHRIST, 203
ALL OF CHRIST IS TO BE ACCEPTED, 161
ALL OF THIS SPEAKS OF THE CROSS, 364
ALTAR, THE, 319, 362, 369, 406, 496, 528
ALTAR OF INCENSE, THE, 502, 625
AMALEK, 299
ANGEL, THE, 392, 541, 545
ANGER, 153
ANGER OF MOSES, THE, 534
ANGER OF THE LORD, THE, 56
ANOINTED TO TEACH, 578
ANOINTING, THE, 484, 621
ANOINTING OF THE PRIESTS, THE, 622
ANOINTING OIL, THE, 487, 620
ANOTHER JESUS, 190, 263, 422
ANSWER IS THE CROSS, THE, 617
ANTHROPOMORPHISM, 560
ANTINOMIANISM, 192
APPEARANCE OF THE BRANCHES, THE, 436
APPEARANCE OF THE LORD, THE, 342
APPETITE DETERMINED THE AMOUNT GATHERED, THE, 280
ARK, THE, 16, 420, 589, 624
ASHES, THE, 462
ASPECT OF DELIVERANCE, THE, 34
ATONEMENT?, 539
AWFULNESS OF SIN, THE, 460
BAAL, 213

BACKSIDE OF THE DESERT, THE, 23
BADGERS' SKINS, 443
BAPTISM WITH THE HOLY SPIRIT, THE, 514, 620
BASIS OF THE APPEAL FOR GRACE, THE, 564
BASKET, THE, 486
BATTLE IN THE SPIRIT WORLD, THE, 95
BEFORE THE TESTIMONY, 519
BEGINNING, THE, 155
BELIEVER AND THE CROSS, THE, 73
BELIEVER'S FUNCTION AND THE BELIEVER'S VICTORY, THE, 303
BENEFITS OF THE CROSS, THE, 447
BESTIALITY, 379
BIBLE, THE, 318, 408
BIBLICAL RESTORATION, 172
BIGGEST SIN, THE, 419
BINDING OF THE SACRIFICE, THE, 462
BITTER HERBS, 159, 161
BITTER WATERS, 260
BITTERNESS OF SOUL, THE, 260
BLAME, THE, 535
BLESSED, 4
BLOOD, THE, 54, 104, 158, 165, 178, 408, 489, 492, 506
BLUE LACE, THE, 482
BOARDS, THE, 445, 585
BOILS, 123
BOOK OF LIFE, THE, 540
BORROW, 150
BOUNDS, THE, 401
BOWLS, THE KNOPS, AND THE FLOWERS, THE, 435
BRANCHES, THE, 436, 437, 595
BRAZEN ALTAR, THE, 459, 599

BRAZEN LAVER, THE, 602, 626
BREAD FROM HEAVEN, 271
BREASTPLATE, THE, 609
BREASTPLATE OF JUDGMENT, THE, 475
BRILLIANT LIGHT AND THE VEIL, THE, 570
BROKEN TABLES, THE, 534
BURDENS, THE, 78
BURNING BUSH, THE, 25
BURNING OF INCENSE, THE, 504
BURNT OFFERINGS AND PEACE OFFERINGS, 407
BY FAITH, 545
CALF, THE, 535
CALLING, THE, 521
CAMPMEETING, 250
CANDLESTICK, THE, 435
CAUSE, THE, 39
CENTRAL SHAFT, THE, 437
CHAINS, THE, 610
CHARGE, A, 96
CHARGE TO PHARAOH, THE, 97
CHERUBIM, 426, 454, 591
CHILDREN OF ISRAEL AND LIGHT, THE, 142
CHILDREN OF ISRAEL, THE, 2, 4
CHRIST AND HIM CRUCIFIED, 33
CHRIST IN US, 199
CHRISTIAN AND THE LAW, THE, 358
CHRISTIANITY, 398
CHRISTIANS?, 182
CHURCH, THE, 39, 488
CIRCUMCISION, 189, 195
CITIES OF REFUGE, 369
CIVIL AUTHORITIES, 15
CLIFT OF THE ROCK, THE, 559
CLOUD, THE, 274, 412, 627
CLOUD AND THE FIRE, THE, 629
CLOUD RESTED UPON THE TABERNACLE, THE, 211
CLOUD SERVED AS A GUIDE, THE, 210
CLOUD WAS A COVERING, THE, 210
CLOUD WAS LIGHT, THE, 210
CLOUDY PILLAR, THE, 554
COAT, THE MITRE, AND THE GIRDLE, THE, 483
COLLISION OF GOD AND SIN, THE, 390
COLORS, THE, 457
COMMAND, THE, 100, 176
COMMAND FROM THE LORD, A, 100
COMMAND OF THE LORD, THE, 283, 346, 572, 615
COMMUNICATION, 428
COMMUNION, 429, 432
COMPARISON OF UNREDEEMED MAN AND THE DUMB ANIMAL, THE, 203

COMPLAINT, 224
COMPLAINT OF THE PEOPLE, THE, 88
COMPLETE SACRIFICE, THE, 499
COMPROMISE, 113, 135, 142
CONCLUSION OF THE DISPENSATION OF PROMISE, THE, 188
CONCUPISCENCE, 218
CONFESSION OF SCRIPTURE, 201
CONFLICT, 306
CONFLICT WITH THE FLESH, THE, 313
CONQUERING OF SIN, THE, 461
CONSECRATION, 539
CONSENT, 448
COPPER, 600
CORNELIUS AND HIS HOUSEHOLD, 515
COUNSEL?, 324
COUPLINGS, 446
COURT, THE, 354, 464
COURT AND THE GATE, THE, 627
COURT AND THE HOLY PLACE, THE, 466
COVENANT, THE, 22, 90, 570
COVENANTS WITH THE UNGODLY, 565
COVERING, A, 484
COVETOUSNESS, 356
CROSS, THE, 19, 23, 38, 52, 56, 60, 61, 73, 149, 178, 199, 214, 261, 270, 298, 307, 334, 373, 402, 415, 453, 461, 472, 596, 630
CROSS ALONE, THE, 123
CROSS AND CONSECRATION, THE, 622
CROSS AND SANCTIFICATION, THE, 448, 463
CROSS AND SATAN, THE, 163
CROSS AND THE HOLY SPIRIT, THE, 382
CROSS AND THE LAW, THE, 358
CROSS AND THE MODERN CHURCH, THE, 471
CROSS IS EVER NEEDFUL, THE, 619
CROSS IS THE DIVIDING LINE, THE, 511
CROSS MUST BE FIRST, THE, 210
CROSS OF CHRIST, THE, 600
CROSS OF CHRIST AND THE FLESH, THE, 18
CROSS, THE ONLY ANSWER! THE, 536
CROWNS, THE, 594
CRY OF THE CHILDREN OF ISRAEL, THE, 21
CULTURE, 316
CUNNING WORK, 454, 608
CURIOUS GIRDLE, THE, 473, 608
CURTAINS, THE, 582
DAILY SACRIFICES, THE, 498
DARKNESS, 139
DAUGHTER, A, 368
DAUGHTER OF PHARAOH, THE, 14
DAVID, 420
DAY OF PENTECOST, 515

DEAD FROGS, 110
DEALING WITH THIEVES, 374
DEATH, 484, 524
DEATH PENALTY, THE, 370
DECEPTION, 318
DELIVERANCE, 24, 34, 146, 180, 196, 197, 204, 349
DELIVERANCE PREACHER?, 36
DENIAL, 31, 550
DEPENDENCE, 406
DESIGN OF SATAN, THE, 11
DESTROYER, THE, 178
DIFFERENCE IN TONGUES AS THE INITIAL PHYSICAL EVIDENCE, AND TONGUES AS A GIFT, THE, 517
DIFFERENCE NOW IS THE CROSS, THE, 392
DIFFICULTIES, 234
DIMENSIONS OF THE MERCY SEAT, THE, 426
DIMENSIONS OF THE TABLE, THE, 32
DISEASES, 264
DISHES, THE, 433
DISHONORING OF CHRIST, THE, 525
DO YOU UNDERSTAND THE CROSS?, 160
DOCTRINE, THE, 240
DOES GOD SEND JUDGMENT UPON HIS CHILDREN?, 152
DOOR, THE, 587, 625
DOOR AND THE FIVE PILLARS, THE, 456
DRY GROUND, 237
EARLY CHURCH, THE, 352
EATING OF THE BREAD, THE, 593
EATING OF THE FAT, THE, 391
EDGE OF THE WILDERNESS, THE, 208
EGYPT, 41, 58, 64, 102, 135
EGYPTIAN RECORDS, THE, 3
EGYPTIANS, THE, 7, 239
EGYPTIANS, THE WILDERNESS, THE DELIVERANCE, THE, 225
ELDERS, THE, 411
ENCAMPMENT, THE, 268
ENCHANTMENTS, 106
ENEMIES IN THE LAND, 35
ENEMY TO YOUR ADVERSARIES, AN, 396
EPHESIANS, 515
EPHOD, THE, 473, 608
ERRONEOUS PRACTICES, 76
ERROR, 147
ERROR OF THE CHURCH, THE, 335
EVENING SACRIFICE, THE, 158
EXCEPT YOU REPENT, 183
EXCUSE, THE, 55, 536
EXODUS, THE, 187
FADS, 118

FAILURE, 222
FAILURE TO UNDERSTAND THE CROSS OF CHRIST, A, 10
FAITH, 15, 42, 64, 307, 373, 402, 422, 449, 478
FAITH AND UNBELIEF, 213
FAITH IN CHRIST, 362
FAITH IN THE SHED BLOOD OF THE LORD JESUS CHRIST, 165
FAITH OF JOCHEBED, THE, 12
FALSE REPORTS, 382
FALSE WITNESS, 356
FAMILY CURSE, THE, 10, 351, 562
FASHION, THE, 451
FASTING, 570
FAT, THE, 490
FEAR, 223, 537
FEAR NOT, 226, 361
FEAR OF THE LORD, THE, 400
FEAST OF PENTECOST AND THE FEAST OF TABERNACLES, THE, 568
FEAST OF UNLEAVENED BREAD, THE, 173, 567
FEAST TO THE LORD, A, 66, 171, 199
FEET AND THE HANDS, THE, 510
FINE TWINED LINEN, 439
FINGER OF GOD, THE, 525
FIRST OF THE FIRSTFRUITS AND THE LAMB, 391
FIRST PLAGUE, THE, 105
FIRST SONG, THE, 244
FIRSTBORN, THE, 59, 152, 197, 567
FIRSTFRUITS, 381
FIVE BARS, THE, 450
FIVE PILLARS, THE, 458, 588
FLESH, THE, 18, 518
FLESH AND THE SPIRIT, THE, 299
FOCUS, 133
FOR GLORY AND FOR BEAUTY, 472, 483
FOREHEAD, THE, 482
FOREKNOWLEDGE, 50
FOREVER, 171, 179
FORGIVE, 138
FORGIVENESS, 540
FORGIVENESS AND DELIVERANCE, 225
FORTY YEARS, 289
FOUR PILLARS, 455, 587
FRANKINCENSE, 593
FREE WILL, 79
FRUIT, 119
FRUIT AND THE BELLS, THE, 611
FRUIT OF THE SPIRIT, THE, 219, 596
FRUSTRATING THE GRACE OF GOD, 49, 118, 194, 528
FURNITURE OF THE HOLY PLACE, THE, 456

GALATIANISM, 193
GALATIANS, THE, 115
GATE, THE, 390, 604
GATE AND THE DOOR, THE, 603
GATE OF THE COURT, THE, 466
GEOGRAPHY, 237
GIFT TO THE CHILDREN OF ISRAEL, A, 210
GIFTS OF THE PEOPLE, THE, 580
GLORY, THE, 208, 413, 499
GLORY OF THE LORD WAS LINKED WITH THE GIVING OF THE MANNA, THE, 279
GLORY OF THE LORD, THE, 273
GOATS' HAIR, 442, 583
GOD DOES NOT GIVE VICTORY TO FALLEN MAN, 264, 545
GOD OF ABRAHAM, THE GOD OF ISAAC, AND THE GOD OF JACOB, THE, 28, 45
GOD'S ECONOMY, 574
GOD'S PRESCRIBED ORDER OF VICTORY, 29, 61, 217, 472, 593
GOD'S TIMING, 38
GOD'S USE OF THE ELEMENTS, 250
GOD'S WAY OF LIVING, 371
GOLD, 433
GOLD AND THE CROWN, THE, 421
GOLD AND THE SILVER, THE, 606
GOLDEN CALF, THE, 527
GOOD?, 324
GOSHEN, 112
GOSPEL, THE, 69
GOSPEL OF THE GRACE OF GOD, THE, 71
GOVERNMENT OF GRACE, THE, 49, 73, 117
GOVERNMENT OF LAW, THE, 74, 116
GRACE, 32, 127, 194, 202, 277, 550, 556
GRACE AND MERCY, 559
GRACE OF GOD, THE, 98
GRACE OR LAW, 81
GRATE, THE, 463
GREAT DAY OF ATONEMENT, THE, 480
GREAT REJOICING, 257
GREAT SIN, A, 539
GREAT WORK OF THE LORD, THE, 242
GREAT WORK, A, 242
GREATER WORKS, 288
GREATEST LESSON, THE, 423
GUILTY, THE, 562
GUILTY PARTY, THE, 540
HAIL, 126
HAND, THE, 445
HARDENED, 131
HARDENED HEART, THE, 59, 101, 114, 130, 144, 153, 217

HEALING, THE, 263, 264, 266
HEALING POWER OF GOD, THE, 265
HEARKEN TO THE WRONG VOICE, 326
HEART, THE, 124
HEAVEN, 141
HEBREWS 6:1-2, 37, 601
HOLINESS TO THE LORD, 481, 612
HOLY, 381
HOLY ANOINTING OIL, 514
HOLY GARMENTS, THE, 471, 495
HOLY GROUND, 27
HOLY HABITATION, 252
HOLY PLACE AND THE MOST HOLY, THE, 456
HOLY SPIRIT AND THE FLESH, THE, 300
HOLY SPIRIT AT CONVERSION, THE, 514
HOLY SPIRIT, THE, 19, 62, 65, 132, 296, 308, 334, 373, 402, 406, 473, 477, 544
HONOR, 235
HONORING OF PARENTS, THE, 353
HORNS, THE, 460, 597, 599
HOW DID JESUS DEFEAT THE ENEMY OF OUR SOULS?, 393
HOW DO THE WORKS OF THE FLESH MANIFEST THEMSELVES?, 337
HOW DO WE RESIST THE DEVIL?, 254
HOW DO WE STAY DEAD TO THE SIN NATURE?, 30
HOW DOES ONE OBEY GOD?, 334
HOW DOES THE HOLY SPIRIT WORK?, 300
HOW THE CHURCH ADDRESSES THE SIN NATURE, 30
HOW THEN CAN THE OLD NATURE BE TOTALLY SUBDUED?, 307
HOW TO LIVE FOR GOD, 159
HOW TO OBEY THE LORD, 396
HOW WAS SATAN DEFEATED?, 229
HUMANISTIC PSYCHOLOGY, 40
HUMBLE YOURSELF, 132
HUMILITY, 321
HYSSOP, 177
I AM THAT I AM, 43
I AM THE LORD, 132, 164
IDOL GODS, 214
IDOL WORSHIP, 379
IDOLS, 398
IGNORANCE, 31, 549
IGNORANCE OR UNBELIEF, 173, 305
IMMORALITY, 377
IMPORTANCE OF THE MERCY SEAT, THE, 425
IMPROPER UNDERSTANDING OF THE CROSS, 221
IN ALL MANNER OF WORKMANSHIP, 522

IN CHRIST JESUS, 311, 393
IN THE WILDERNESS, THE CLOUD NEVER LEFT ISRAEL, 211
INABILITY OF THE LAW, THE, 404
INCENSE, THE, 502, 519
INCREASED JUDGMENT, 108
INHERITANCE, THE, 255
INITIAL, PHYSICAL EVIDENCE THAT ONE HAS BEEN BAPTIZED WITH THE HOLY SPIRIT, THE, 516, 620
INNER HEALING, 261
INSINCERE REPENTANCE, 130
INSTITUTIONALIZED RELIGION, 511
INSTRUCTIONS, 414
INTENSIFIED OPPOSITION, 85
INTERCESSION, 479, 531
ISLAM AND PEACE, 330
ISRAEL, 420
JACOB, 306
JEALOUS GOD, A, 350, 565
JEHOVAH, 90
JESUS AS OUR EXAMPLE, OR JESUS AS OUR SAVIOUR?, 563
JESUS DIED SPIRITUALLY DOCTRINE, THE, 128
JETHRO, 58, 320
JEWELS, THE, 476
JOSEPH, 1, 3, 207
JOSHUA, 310, 534, 555
JOSHUA AS A TYPE OF CHRIST, 311
JOY AMONG THE PEOPLE, 580
JUDGES, 376
JUDGMENT, 70, 161, 182, 183, 365, 553
JUDGMENT OF GOD, THE, 66
JUSTIFICATION BY FAITH, 309
KING OF EGYPT, 8
LAMB FOR AN HOUSE, A, 156
LAMPSTAND, THE, 466, 595, 625
LAND FLOWING WITH MILK AND HONEY, A, 198, 549
LAST DAY PLOY OF SATAN, THE, 82
LAVER OF COPPER, THE, 509
LAW, THE, 346, 371, 426
LAW OF GOD, THE, 357
LAW OF SIN AND DEATH, THE, 361
LEADING OF THE LORD, THE, 205, 213
LEGALISM, ANTINOMIANISM, AND GALATIANISM, 191, 358
LENGTH AND WIDTH OF THE CURTAINS, THE, 440
LEPROSY, 53
LESSON THAT MOSES WAS TO LEARN, THE, 60
LET MY PEOPLE GO, 125, 132
LET US ALONE, 224
LICENSE, 31, 550
LIGHT, 140
LOCUSTS AND THE LAND OF EGYPT, THE, 134, 137
LOOKING SOLELY TO THE LORD, 315
LOOPS, THE, 440
LORD, THE, 88, 247
LORD DEMANDS OBEDIENCE, THE, 332
LORD DESCENDED, THE, 344
LORD FIGHTS FOR US, THE, 240
LORD JESUS CHRIST, THE, 127, 367, 415
LORD OVERTHREW THE EGYPTIANS, THE, 241
LORD SHALL FIGHT FOR YOU, THE, 229
LORD SHOWED HIM A TREE, THE, 262
LORD SPEAKS, THE, 276, 331
LORD WILL DEPEND ON YOU, THE, 229
LORD'S ANSWER, THE, 251
LORD'S NAME, THE, 351
LORD'S OFFERING, THE, 577
LORD'S PASSOVER, THE, 162
LORD'S RIGHT HAND, THE, 251
MADE POSSIBLE BY THE CROSS, 496
MAGICIANS, THE, 103, 108, 124
MAKE US GODS, 526
MAN OF WAR, A, 249
MAN'S SUBSTITUTE FOR THE CROSS, 427
MANNA CAME DOWN FROM HEAVEN, THE, 278, 279, 280, 281, 287
MANNER OF OBEDIENCE, THE, 333
MANNER OF THE CHARGE, THE, 97
MATERIAL OF WHICH THE PILLARS WERE MADE, THE, 465
MEANS OF GOD, THE, 400
MEMORIAL, A, 171, 287
MERCY AND GRACE, 559
MERCY AND TRUTH ARE MET TOGETHER, 591
MERCY SEAT, THE, 424, 590
MESSAGE, THE, 71
MESSAGE OF THE CROSS, THE, 77, 553
MIDIAN, 20
MIDNIGHT, 151, 182
MIDWIVES, 9
MIRACLE, THE, 102, 137, 236
MIRACLE-WORKING POWER OF GOD, THE, 237
MIRIAM THE PROPHETESS, 257
MISUNDERSTANDING THE CROSS, 491
MIXED MULTITUDE, A, 209
MOBILITY OF THE ARK, THE, 589
MODERN BELIEVERS, 272
MODERN CHURCH WORLD, THE, 128
MODERN CHURCH, THE, 69, 220, 404

MODERN PRACTICES, 75
MODERN PRIESTHOOD, THE, 469
MODERN THOUGHT, 617
MOSES, 16, 26, 130, 292, 313, 529
MOSES AND AARON, 626
MOSES AND HIS BROTHER-IN-LAW, 327
MOSES IN THE PALACE, 20
MOSES THE JUDGE, 323
MOUNT SINAI, 328
MOVING OF THE CLOUD, THE, 628
MURDER, 369
MURMURING, 260, 269, 274, 291
MUSIC, 245
NAILING IT TO HIS CROSS, 93
NAKED, 536
NAKEDNESS, 364
NAMES, THE, 1
NAMES OF THE CHILDREN OF ISRAEL, THE, 608
NATURE, 72
NATURE OF THE LAW, THE, 358
NECESSITY OF THE HOLY SPIRIT, THE, 514
NEED OF THE CROSS WILL NEVER CEASE, THE, 601
NEEDLEWORK, THE, 457
NEW COVENANT, THE, 91
NO BROKEN BONE, 190, 195
NO GRAVEN IMAGES, 567
NO IDOL WORSHIP, 350
NO OTHER GODS, 349
NO SUCH THING AS MORAL EVOLUTION, 72
NOBLES, THE, 410
NOT ONE HOOF WILL BE LEFT BEHIND, 144
NURSE, A, 15
OATH OF THE LORD, THE, 270, 376
OBEDIENCE, 181, 331, 386
OBEYING THE WORD, 312
OBJECT OF FAITH, THE, 26, 133, 472
OCCASION OF THE GIVING OF THE MANNA, THE, 278
OFFERING, THE, 415, 573
OFFICE OF THE PRIEST, THE, 468
OLD MAN, THE, 314
ONE LAW, 196
ONE OF THE GREAT KEYS TO VICTORY, 166
ONE TABERNACLE, 582
ONLY ANSWER FOR SIN IS THE CROSS, THE, 395
ONYX STONES, 473
OPPRESSION, 38
ORDER, THE, 143, 206
ORNAMENTS, 552
OTHER GODS, 387

OUR FAITH, 19, 334
OUR GOD REIGNS, 256
OVERCOMER, AN, 167, 233
PARAMETERS, 340
PARENTS OF MOSES, THE, 12
PART OF THE VISION, A, 294
PASSOVER, THE, 189
PASSOVER, UNLEAVENED BREAD, FIRSTFRUITS, 388
PATH CHOSEN BY GOD, THE, 224
PATH OF FAITH, THE, 290
PATTERN, THE, 418
PAUL, 515
PAYMENT, THE, 393
PEACE-OFFERINGS, 494
PENTECOST, 388
PERFUME, A, 519
PERPETUAL SHEWBREAD, 434
PERPETUAL STATUTE, A, 488
PERSONAL APPLICATION, 165
PHARAOH, 46, 65, 95, 249
PHARAOH AND MOSES, 19
PHARAOH, MOSES, AND AARON, 185
PHARAOH'S LAST FLING, 219
PHARISEE AND THE PUBLICAN, THE, 564
PHYLACTERIES, 200
PIERCED EAR, THE, 367
PILLAR, THE, 209, 464, 604
PILLAR OF FIRE AND OF THE CLOUD, THE, 240
PILLAR OF THE CLOUD, THE, 235
PLACE WHERE THE MANNA FELL, THE, 279
PLAGUE, THE, 169, 541
PLAGUE OF FLIES, THE, 112
PLAGUE OF FROGS, THE, 107
PLAGUE OF LICE, THE, 110
PLAGUE OF POSSESSIONS, THE, 120
PLAGUE OF SIN, THE, 170
PLAGUES, 125
PLANS OF PHARAOH, THE, 4
POMEGRANATES AND THE BELLS, THE, 480
POOR, THE, 380
POPULATION, 606
POSITION OF THE ARK, THE, 504
POT OF MANNA, THE, 288
POWER, THE, 628
POWER OF DEATH, THE, 13
POWER OF GOD, THE, 50, 55, 360
POWER SOURCE, 133
PRAYER, 265, 293, 556
PRECIOUS STONES, THE, 610
PREDICTION, A, 150
PREPARATION, 24, 150, 187

PRESENCE, THE, 68
PRESENCE OF GOD, THE, 551, 557
PRESENT CHARGE, THE, 96
PREVAILED, 313
PRIESTHOOD, THE, 468
PRINCIPAL SPICES, THE, 513
PRINCIPLE OF POWER, THE, 314
PROMISE, THE, 179
PROMISE OF GOD, THE, 92, 398
PROMISES, 399
PROPER FAITH, 292, 401
PROPITIATION, 425
PROTECTION, 568
PSYCHOLOGICAL WAY AND THE WAY OF THE CROSS, THE, 470
PSYCHOLOGY, 305
PURE GOLD, 596
PURPOSE OF GOD, THE, 67
PURPOSE OF THE TABLE, THE, 432
PURSUIT, THE, 220
PURTENANCE, THE, 161
QUAILS, THE, 277
QUITTING EGYPT, 186
RAM OF THE CONSECRATION, THE, 495
RAMS' SKINS AND BADGERS' SKINS, 443, 584
RANSOM FOR HIS SOUL, A, 507
REAPING OF JUDGMENT CAN'T BE STOPPED, THE, 9
REASONS, 401
RED SEA AND THE JORDAN RIVER, THE, 242
REDEEMED, 252
REDEMPTION, 202, 248
REJECTION OF THE CROSS IS NEVER THEOLOGICAL BUT RATHER MORAL, 304
REJOICING, 244
RELATIONSHIP, 94, 367
RELATIONSHIP OF THESE FEASTS TO MODERN CHRISTENDOM, 389
RELATIONSHIP TO ONE'S FELLOW MAN, 385
RENEWED MIND, THE, 301
REPENTANCE OF THE LORD?, 532
REPETITION, A, 386
REPHIDIM, 290
REST, 525, 567
REST IN CHRIST, 353
RESTITUTION, 375
RESULTS, 134
RESURRECTION, 208
RESURRECTION PEOPLE?, 184
REVELATION OF THE CROSS, THE, 542
REVELATION WHICH WAS GIVEN TO ME, THE, 302

RICHES, 51
RIGHT HAND OF THE LORD, THE, 249
RIGHTS OF OTHERS, THE, 373
RINGS, THE, 610
RINGS AND THE STAVES, THE, 433
RINGS OF GOLD, 450, 476
ROBE, THE, 479
ROBE OF THE EPHOD, THE, 611
ROCK, THE, 295, 559
ROD, THE, 52, 58, 294
RULERS, 380
SABBATH, THE, 285, 352, 524, 572, 593
SABBATICAL YEAR, THE, 387
SACRED VESSELS, THE, 613, 616, 622
SACRIFICE, THE, 48, 69, 84, 156, 322, 390, 486, 489, 568, 625
SACRIFICE OF CHRIST, THE, 179
SACRIFICE TO THE LORD, THE, 87
SACRIFICES AND THE ALTAR OF INCENSE, 506
SALVATION, 232, 330
SAMARITANS, 515
SANCTIFICATION, 286, 448, 500
SANCTIFICATION BY FAITH, 309
SANCTIFY, 339
SANCTITY OF HUMAN LIFE, THE, 372
SANCTUARY, 417
SAPPHIRE STONE, THE, 409
SATAN AND SIN, 383
SATAN AND THE CROSS, 185
SATAN'S METHODS, 111
SATAN'S PSEUDO-AUTHORITY, 168
SEDUCTION OF THE CHURCH, THE, 454
SELF, 166
SENTENCE OF DEATH, 519
SERPENT, THE, 53
SERVANTS, 366
SERVING OF THE MASTER, THE, 366
SET TIME, A, 121
SEVEN LAMPS, THE, 437
SEVENTY ELDERS OF ISRAEL, 405
SHEKEL OF THE SANCTUARY, THE, 508
SHITTIM WOOD, 421
SIGN, A, 200
SIGNS, THE, 64
SILVER, 445
SILVER AND THE COPPER, THE, 607
SILVER AND THE CROSS, 507
SILVER AND THE GOLD, THE, 585
SIMPLE GOSPEL, THE, 405
SIN AND THE BELIEVER, 80, 255
SIN NATURE, THE, 30, 527, 549
SING TO THE LORD, 258

SIN-OFFERING, 490
SIXTH DAY, THE, 273
SIXTH PLAGUE, THE, 122
SIZE OF THE ALTAR, THE, 503
SLAVERY, 317
SNARE, THE, 402
SO HOW DOES THE CHRISTIAN WALK IN VICTORY?, 80
SO WHAT DOES IT MEAN TO ACTUALLY STAND STILL?, 228
SO WHAT IS THE CAUSE OF PROBLEMS IN THE LIVES OF CHRISTIANS?, 351
SO WHAT SHOULD BE DONE TO THE CHRISTIAN WHO SINS?, 81
SONLIFE RADIO, 6, 206, 574
SORROW, 152
SOWING AND REAPING, 9
SPIRIT OF GOD, THE, 522, 578
SPIRIT OF WISDOM, THE, 472
SPIRITUAL ADULTERY, 148, 218, 385, 547
SPIRITUAL ADVICE, 325
SPIRITUAL BLINDNESS, 78
SPIRITUAL DEATH, 511
SPIRITUAL VICTORY, THE, 231, 319
SPRINKLING OF THE BLOOD, THE, 408
STATE OF THE MODERN CHURCH, THE, 334
STATUTE AND THE ORDINANCE, THE, 264
STATUTES AND LAWS, THE, 324
STAVES, THE, 421, 463, 504, 598, 600
STEALING, 355
STEPS, 363
STIFFNECKED, 531, 551
STONE, THE, 317
STRANGE INCENSE, 505
STRANGER, THE, 379
STRENGTH, 252
STRENGTH OF THE LORD, THE, 251
STRONG HAND, A, 90
STRUGGLE, 31, 550
SUBJECTIVE TRUTH, 317
SUBSTITUTE, A, 155
SUPERIORITY, 99
SWEET SAVOUR, THE, 491, 494
SWORD, THE, 537
TABERNACLE, THE, 523, 575, 604, 613, 624
TABLE OF SHEWBREAD, THE, 431, 592
TABLE, THE, 624
TASKMASTERS, THE, 86
TEARS, 14
TELEVISION, 325
TEMPORAL BLESSINGS, 188
TEMPTING OF THE LORD, THE, 297
TEN CURTAINS, 439
TENT, THE, 554
TEST, THE, 291
TESTIMONY, THE, 422, 430
THINGS THE BELIEVER MUST KNOW, 481
THREE DAYS, 70
THUNDER, HAIL, AND FIRE, 127
THY WAY, 557
TIME FRAME, THE, 130
TIME OF THE ATTACK BY THE AMALEKITES, THE, 309
TIMING OF THE SMITTEN ROCK, THE, 295
TITHES, 569
TITLE, THE, 44
TO BEAR THE TABLE, 594
TO SEEK THE LORD, 554
TODAY, 109
TOKEN, 168
TOTAL COMMITMENT, 86
TRAGEDY, 316
TRANSGRESSIONS, 395
TREASURE CITIES, 4
TREE WAS PUT INTO THE BITTER WATERS, THE, 262
TRUMPETS, ATONEMENT, AND TABERNACLES, 389
TRUTH, 36, 315
TURBAN, THE, 612
TWELVE WELLS OF WATER AND SEVENTY PALM TREES, 267
TWO METHODS OF DESTRUCTION REGARDING THE CHURCH, THE, 272
TWO TABLES, THE, 561
TWO TABLES OF THE TESTIMONY, THE, 533
TYPE OF CHRIST, A, 157
TYPE OF OFFERING, THE, 416
UNBELIEF, 52, 55, 95, 238, 285, 385, 452
UNCIRCUMCISED LIPS, 96
UNCONDITIONAL ETERNAL SECURITY, 470
UNDERSTANDING THE ATONEMENT, 600
UNDERSTANDING THE BIBLE, 563
UNDERSTANDING THE CROSS, 350
UNITED STATES, THE, 329
UNLEAVENED BREAD, 161, 198
UNLEAVENED BREAD AND THE OIL, THE, 486
UNTO THE LORD, 246
URIM AND THE THUMMIN, THE, 477
VALUE OF THE STUDY OF THE TABERNACLE, THE, 423
VEIL, THE, 453, 586
VERY HEART OF CHRISTIANITY, THE, 165
VERY NATURE OF THE UNREDEEMED, THE, 71
VICTORY, 241, 256, 397

VICTORY IS ONLY IN CHRIST, 311
VICTORY OF THE SAINTS, THE, 253
VISION, A, 384
VISUALIZATION, 261
WALKING AFTER THE FLESH, 226
WALKING AFTER THE SPIRIT, 25, 147, 477
WANTON TAKING OF HUMAN LIFE, THE, 354
WAR, 319
WASHING, THE, 509
WASHING WITH WATER, THE, 486
WATER AND NOT BLOOD, 509
WATER OUT OF THE ROCK, 295
WAVE-OFFERING, THE, 493
WEALTH AND HEALTH, 206
WESTERN CIVILIZATION, 142
WHAT DID JESUS DO WITH THE LAW?, 378
WHAT DIFFERENCE WILL IT MAKE?, 412
WHAT DO WE MEAN BY "FLESH"?, 18, 299
WHAT DO WE MEAN BY "VICTORY"?, 311
WHAT DO WE MEAN BY FAITH?, 47
WHAT DOES IT MEAN TO FIGHT THE GOOD FIGHT OF FAITH?, 546
WHAT DOES IT MEAN TO PREACH THE CROSS?, 214, 617
WHAT GOOD ARE TONGUES?, 517
WHAT IS DELIVERANCE, 226
WHAT IS HOLINESS?, 482
WHAT IS THE FLESH?, 500
WHAT IS THE LAW OF THE SPIRIT OF LIFE IN CHRIST JESUS?, 361
WHAT IS THE SIN NATURE?, 528
WHAT IS WALKING AFTER THE SPIRIT?, 500
WHAT JESUS HAD DONE, 254
WHAT THE RED SEA CROSSING ACTUALLY MEANT, 239
WHAT WE LEARN FROM THE WILDERNESS EXPERIENCE, 207
WHERE GOD DWELLS, 500
WHO IS ON THE LORD'S SIDE?, 537
WHO IS THE LORD?, 67
WHOLE BURNT OFFERING, THE, 491
WHY BLOOD?, 170
WHY COULDN'T THE HOLY SPIRIT ABIDE PERMANENTLY WITHIN BELIEVERS BEFORE THE CROSS?, 340
WHY DO WE TEACH SO MUCH ON THE CROSS?, 394
WHY IS THE CROSS SO MISUNDERSTOOD?, 342
WHY THE CROSS?, 170
WHY THE FAILURE?, 385
WHY WAS MOSES REQUIRED TO PULL OFF HIS SHOES?, 28
WHY WAS THE CROSS SUCH A NECESSITY?, 296
WHY WON'T ALL PREACHERS PREACH THE CROSS?, 618
WHY WON'T THE CHURCH EMBRACE THE CROSS?, 222
WILDERNESS, THE, 207, 216, 259
WILDERNESS OF SIN, THE, 269
WILL OF GOD, THE, 477
WILL OF MAN, THE, 217
WILLING HEARTED, 576
WILLPOWER, 337
WIN THE YOUTH?, 245
WISE HEARTED, 522, 574
WITCHCRAFT, 378
WITNESS, A, 46
WONDERS, 153
WORD AND THE CHURCH, THE, 595
WORD OF GOD, THE, 141, 318, 510
WORD OF GOD AND THE HOLY SPIRIT, THE, 79
WORD OF OUR TESTIMONY, THE, 168
WORD OF THE LORD, THE, 561
WORK OF GOD, THE, 417
WORKERS, THE, 605
WORKS OF THE FLESH, THE, 218, 335
WORLD AND GOD'S PEOPLE, THE, 116
WORLD OF THE LORD, THE, 104
WORSHIP, 181
WRATH OF GOD, THE, 250
WRONG WAY, 134
YOUR CHILDREN, 180
YOUR FAITH, 61
YOUR RESPONSE TO THE CROSS, 344

For information concerning the *Jimmy Swaggart Bible Commentary,* please request a Gift Catalog.

You may inquire by using Books of the Bible.

- Genesis (656 pages) (11-201)
- Exodus (656 pages) (11-202)
- Leviticus (448 pages) (11-203)
- Numbers
  Deuteronomy (512 pages) (11-204)
- Joshua
  Judges
  Ruth (336 pages) (11-205)
- I Samuel
  II Samuel (528 pages) (11-206)
- I Kings
  II Kings (560 pages) (11-207)
- I Chronicles
  II Chronicles (528 pages) (11-226)
- Ezra
  Nehemiah
  Esther (288 pages) (11-208)
- Job (320 pages) (11-225)
- Psalms (688 pages) (11-216)
- Proverbs (320 pages) (11-227)
- Ecclesiastes
  Song Of Solomon (288 pages) (11-228)
- Isaiah (688 pages) (11-220)
- Jeremiah
  Lamentations (688 pages) (11-070)
- Ezekiel (528 pages) (11-223)
- Daniel (416 pages) (11-224)
- Hosea
  Joel
  Amos (496 pages) (11-229)
- Obadiah
  Jonah
  Micah
  Nahum
  Habakkuk
  Zephaniah (544 pages) (11-230)
- Haggai
  Zechariah
  Malachi (448 pages) (11-231)

- Matthew (888 pages) (11-073)
- Mark (24 pages) (11-074)
- Luke (736 pages) (11-075)
- John (736 pages) (11-076)
- Acts (832 pages) (11-077)
- Romans (704 pages) (11-078)
- I Corinthians (656 pages) (11-079)
- II Corinthians (608 pages) (11-080)
- Galatians (496 pages) (11-081)
- Ephesians (576 pages) (11-082)
- Philippians (496 pages) (11-083)
- Colossians (384 pages) (11-084)
- I Thessalonians
  II Thessalonians (512 pages) (11-085)
- I Timothy
  II Timothy
  Titus
  Philemon (704 pages) (11-086)
- Hebrews (848 pages) (11-087)
- James
  I Peter
  II Peter (736 pages) (11-088)
- I John
  II John
  III John
  Jude (384 pages) (11-089)
- Revelation (592 pages) (11-090)

For telephone orders you may call 1-800-288-8350 with bankcard information. All Baton Rouge residents please use (225) 768-7000.

For mail orders send to:
Jimmy Swaggart Ministries
P.O. Box 262550
Baton Rouge, LA 70826-2550

Visit our website: www.jsm.org

NOTES

NOTES

NOTES

NOTES

NOTES

NOTES